CASES AND MATERIALS ON THE EUROPEAN CONVENTION ON HUMAN RIGHTS

To Tony,

With thanks for all your help over many years.

Alastair

Cases and Materials on the

EUROPEAN CONVENTION ON HUMAN RIGHTS

Alastair Mowbray LLB (Warw), PhD (Edin)
Professor of Public Law,
University of Nottingham

OXFORD
UNIVERSITY PRESS

OXFORD
UNIVERSITY PRESS

Great Clarendon Street, Oxford OX2 6DP

Oxford University Press is a department of the University of Oxford.
It furthers the University's objective of excellence in research, scholarship,
and education by publishing worldwide in

Oxford New York

Auckland Cape Town Dar es Salaam Hong Kong Karachi
Kuala Lumpur Madrid Melbourne Mexico City Nairobi
New Delhi Shanghai Taipei Toronto

With offices in

Argentina Austria Brazil Chile Czech Republic France Greece
Guatemala Hungary Italy Japan Poland Portugal Singapore
South Korea Switzerland Thailand Turkey Ukraine Vietnam

Oxford is a registered trade mark of Oxford University Press
in the UK and in certain other countries

Published in the United States
by Oxford University Press Inc., New York

British Library Cataloguing in Publication Data

Data available

Library of Congress Cataloging in Publication Data

Data available

Typeset by Newgen Imaging Systems (P) Ltd, Chennai, India
Printed in Great Britain
on acid-free paper by
Ashford Colour Press Ltd, Gosport, Hampshire

ISBN 978–0–19–920674–2

10 9 8 7 6 5 4 3 2 1

PREFACE

My observation in the preface to the first edition of this work that we were living in interesting times for the ECHR has continued to remain apposite throughout the ensuing years. These have witnessed the maturing in confidence of the full-time Court to build upon the jurisprudential foundations of the original Court (e.g. to elaborate the elements of effective investigations into killings in *Kelly v UK* (4/5/2001)) and to depart from earlier case law where contemporary circumstances mandate a higher level of protection for persons (e.g. to classify a wider range of welfare benefits as 'possessions' under Article 1 of Protocol No 1 in *Stec and Others v UK* (6/7/2005)). A fascinating feature of the Court's jurisprudence in recent years has been the numerous and diverse cases raising challenges to the aftermath of the collapse of the USSR and its satellite Communist States. The Court has had to deal with complaints concerning, *inter alia*, the convictions of the leaders of former East Germany for their policy of ordering the killing of persons seeking to escape to the West (*Streletz, Kessler and Krenz v Germany* (22/3/2001)), compensation claims in respect of property seized by Communist regimes (*Kopecky v Slovakia* (28/9/2004)) and the expulsion of persons linked to the military forces of the USSR (*Slivenko v Latvia* (9/10/2003)).

The Court has continued to adjudicate on the legal aspects of persistent problems such as the Turkish military occupation of northern Cyprus.(e.g in *Cyprus v Turkey* (10/5/2001) and *Xenides-Arestis v Turkey* (22/12/2005)), the Turkish authorities response to Kurdish terrorism (e.g in *Dogan and Others v Turkey* (29/6/2004) and *Ocalan v Turkey* (12/5/2005)), and the failure of some domestic legal systems to determine cases within a reasonable time (e.g. *Riccardi Pizzati v Italy* (29/3/2006)). Protocol 11's, positive, reform of enabling applicants to lodge complaints with the Court against the (now 46) member States, combined with increasing awareness of the rights guaranteed by the Convention has resulted in the Court facing a deluge of applications. Protocol 14 has been agreed to provide more efficient mechanisms for the processing of applications by the Court. However, the Committee of Ministers is already contemplating more far reaching long-term reforms of the Strasbourg control system to safeguard its effectiveness. Therefore, procedural and institutional reforms are likely to be of continuing importance in the coming years for both the Court and potential applicants.

I have taken the opportunity of this new edition not only to update the jurisprudence (with over 200 new judgments being included) but also to widen the scope of the book to include all the substantive rights of the Convention and its Protocols that have been subject to significant litigation. New chapters have also been added on the creation of the Convention and Articles 1 and 47. The chapter on the Strasbourg system has been completely re-written to examine the reforms noted above. I trust that undergraduate and postgraduate students will continue to find the work a helpful exposition of the extensive jurisprudence of this pioneering and successful human rights Convention.

I have sought to state the law as it stood at 1 September 2006.

A.R.M

CONTENTS

ACKNOWLEDGEMENTS

The author would like to thank the Registrar (Mr E. Fribergh) and Deputy Registrar (Mr M. O'Boyle) of the European Court of Human Rights and the Council of Europe for permitting the reproductions of extracts from the judgments of the Court and related materials.

Chapter 7 is the author's revision of a chapter originally written by his colleague Emeritus Professor D. J. Harris, CMG.

Grateful acknowledgement is made to all the authors and publishers of copyright material that appears in this book, and in particular to the following for permission to reprint material from the sources indicated:

Cambridge Law Journal and the author: extracts from Colin R. Munro, 'The Value of Commercial Speech' (2003), 62(1), *Cambridge Law Journal* 134.

N. P. Engel Verlag: extract from Peter Leuprecht in M. Nowak, D. Steurer, and H. Tretter (eds), *Progress in the Spirit of Human Rights* (Engle, 1988).

Koninklijke Brill NV: extracts from H. A. Robertson (ed.), *Collected Edition of the 'Travaux Preparatories'*, Vol. 1 (Martinus Nijhoff, The Hague, 1975).

Sweet & Maxwell Ltd: extracts from A. Mowbray, 'The Role of the European Court of Human Rights in the Promotion of Democracy' (1999), *Public Law* 703; and E. Wicks, 'The United Kingdom Government's Perceptions of the European Convention on Human Rights at the Time of Entry' (2000), *Public Law* 438.

Every effort has been made to trace and contact copyright holders prior to publication. If notified, the publisher will undertake to rectify any error or omissions at the earliest opportunity.

The author wishes to also thank Tom Young and Nicola Haisley, together with the other OUP staff involved with the production of this book.

TABLE OF STATUTES

United States

TABLE OF EUROPEAN LEGISLATION

TABLE OF CASES

1 THE CREATION OF THE CONVENTION

The idea of a regional system of human rights protection operating across European States preceded the formation of the Council of Europe in 1949. In the years following the ending of the Second World War (in 1945) a number of non-governmental groups were established in various Western European States to champion European unity. They combined together to form the International Committee of the Movements for European Unity. The Committee organized a major gathering, in the Hague, of politicians (including former leaders such as Winston Churchill (as he then was), current Ministers such as Françoise Mitterand and future leaders such as Konrad Adenauer) and representatives of civil society including academics, business leaders, trade unionists and religious leaders. The 'Congress of Europe' lasted from 7 to 10 May 1948 and was attended by about 1,000 persons, mainly drawn from Europe but also with representatives from the United States of America and the Commonwealth. At the end of the gathering the Congress issued the following declaration.

EUROPE IS THREATENED, EUROPE IS DIVIDED, AND THE GREATEST DANGER COMES FROM HER DIVISIONS

Impoverished, overladen with barriers that prevent the circulation of her goods but are no longer able to afford her protection, our disunited Europe marches towards her end. Alone, no one of our countries can hope seriously to defend its independence. Alone, no one of our countries can solve the economic problems of today. Without a freely agreed union our present anarchy will expose us tomorrow to forcible unification whether by the intervention of a foreign empire or usurpation by a political party.

The hour has come to take action commensurate with the danger.

Together with the overseas peoples associated with our destinies, we can tomorrow build the greatest political formation and the greatest economic unit our age has seen. Never will the history of the world have known so powerful a gathering of free men. Never will war, fear and misery have been checked by a more formidable foe.

Between this great peril and this great hope, Europe's mission is clear. It is to unite her peoples in accordance with their genius of diversity and with the conditions of modem community life, and so open the way towards organised freedom for which the world is seeking. It is to revive her inventive powers for the greater protection and respect of the rights and duties of the individual of which, in spite of all her mistakes, Europe is still the greatest exponent.

Human dignity is Europe's finest achievement, freedom her true strength. Both are at stake in our struggle. The union of our continent is now needed not only for the salvation of the liberties we have won, but also for the extension of their benefits to all mankind.

Upon this union depend Europe's destiny and the world's peace.

Let all therefore take note that we Europeans, assembled to express the will of all the peoples of Europe, solemnly declare our common aims in the following five articles, which summarise the resolutions adopted by the Congress:

PLEDGE

1. *We desire a United Europe, throughout whose area the free movement of persons, ideas and goods is restored;*

2. *We desire a Charter of Human Rights guaranteeing liberty of thought, assembly and expression as well as the right to form a political opposition;*
3. *We desire a Court of Justice with adequate sanctions for the implementation of this Charter;*
4. *We desire a European Assembly where the live forces of all our nations shall be represented;*
5. *And pledge ourselves in our homes and in public, in our political and religious life, in our professional and trade union circles, to give our fullest support to all persons and governments working for this lofty cause, which offers the last chance of peace and the one promise of a great future for this generation and those that will succeed it.*

Subsequently, the International Council of the European Movement sought to develop these Pledges by approving, in February 1949, a 'Declaration of Principles of European Union'. The latter provided, *inter alia*,

No State should be admitted into the European Union which does not accept the fundamental principles of a Charter of Human Rights, and which does not declare itself willing and bound to ensure their application. . . . the barrier which divides the Free States from the other European nations must not be accepted as permanent. Our aim is the union in freedom of all the peoples of Europe.

The European Movement also established an International Judicial Section chaired by M. Pierre-Henri Teitgen (a former senior French Resistance leader and Minister) together with Sir David Maxwell-Fyfe (a former British Conservative MP, Law Officer, and Deputy Chief Prosecutor at the Nuremberg war crimes trials) and Professor Fernand Dehousse (a Belgian politician and international lawyer) as *rapporteurs*. They produced a draft European Convention on Human Rights and Statute of the European Court of Human Rights. These documents were later given to the Committee of Ministers of the Council of Europe by the European Movement in July 1949.

On the governmental level ten States (Belgium, France, Luxembourg, The Netherlands, United Kingdom, Ireland, Italy, Denmark, Norway, and Sweden) signed the Statute of the Council of Europe creating the latter international organization during May 1949. The major aim of the Council of Europe was to achieve greater unity between the Member States. A basic condition of membership, elaborated in Article 3 of the Statute, was that: 'Every member of the Council of Europe must accept the principles of the rule of law and the enjoyment by all persons within its jurisdiction of human rights and fundamental freedoms . . .'

During the summer of 1949 the Committee of Ministers of the Council of Europe (the executive body of the organization, see further below p 13) authorized the Consultative Assembly (comprising of representatives of the national parliaments of Member States and now known as the Parliamentary Assembly) to include the topic of the maintenance and further realization of human rights on its agenda. In the ensuing discussions at the first session of the Consultative Assembly both M. Teitgen and Sir David Maxwell-Fyfe made passionate speeches arguing for the creation of an international Convention and Court to protect basic human rights in Member States of the Council of Europe.

FIRST SESSION OF THE CONSULTATIVE ASSEMBLY HELD AT STRASBOURG 10TH AUGUST TO 8TH SEPTEMBER 1949 SITTINGS HELD FROM 16TH AUGUST TO 8TH SEPTEMBER 1949

[Taken from: Collected Edition of the "Travaux Préparatoires" Volume I, Martinus, Nijhoff, The Hague, 1975]

M. Teitgen (France) (*Translation*).—Mr. President, in Article 1, and later in Article 3, our Statute runs as follows:

'The aim of the Council of Europe is to achieve a greater unity between its Members for the purpose of safeguarding and realising the ideals and principles which are their common heritage and facilitating their economic and social progress.

'Every Member of the Council of Europe must accept the principles of the rule of law and of the enjoyment by all persons within its jurisdiction of human rights and fundamental freedoms, and collaborate sincerely and effectively in the realisation of the aim of the Council as defined in Chapter I.'

This fundamental affirmation is thus inscribed at the very foundation of our union: every man, by reason of his origin, his nature and his destiny, has certain indefensible rights, against which no reason of State may prevail.

And so, Mr. President, at our first meeting, with the friendly agreement of the Committee of Ministers, we are opening a debate with the object of working out proposals which will enable Europe to fulfil its promise.

Europe should in fact be, first and foremost, the land of freedom. The history of our countries tells on every page the price she has had to pay for freedom in the past: nearly twenty centuries of suffering, of struggle, wars, revolutions; tears and bloodshed without end; and ever, above the weariness of its often exhausted peoples, the ceaseless call of the hero and the saint.

Finally, we won our freedom, and our countries became as used to it as to the air they breathed—with the result that they did not perhaps esteem it highly enough.

When the scourges of the modern world descended—Fascism, Hitlerism, Communism—they found us relaxed, sceptical and unarmed. We needed war, and for some of us, enemy occupation, to make us realise afresh the value of our humanism.

Does this mean, Mr. President, that to-day, after the victory, all danger is henceforth banished? Allow me to say that we do not think so. Three things still threaten our freedom. The first threat is the eternal reason of State.

Behind the State, whatever its form, were it even democratic, there ever lurks as a permanent temptation, this reason of State.

Montesquieu said: 'Whoever has power, is tempted to abuse it.' Even parliamentary majorities are in fact sometimes tempted to abuse their power. Even in our democratic countries we must be on guard against this temptation of succumbing to reasons of State.

Then there is the second threat: Fascism and Hitlerism have unfortunately tainted European public opinion. These doctrines of death have infiltrated into our countries. They have left their mark. They have poisoned certain sections of public opinion.

Racialism did not die out with Hitler. I will be even more specific, and say that a certain brand of anti-Communism, which claims to fight Communism not with democratic methods but with dictatorial methods, sometimes puts in jeopardy the very principles of democracy.

Finally, and above all, freedom is in danger in our countries—let us have the courage to admit it—because of the economic and social conditions of the modern world.

Mr. President, freedom, in its bold and conquering youth, meant freedom of the person, of work, and of conscience. It also meant political freedom; it meant economic liberalism, free enterprise, freedom of competition, of profit and of money.

What so often followed, as we must admit, was the formation of a huge proletariat, reduced to undeserved poverty, and for whom freedom and the freedoms had proved a disappointment.

Millions of men still lack the practical means of exercising these freedoms, and of benefiting from them, personally, in their daily lives.

It is true that the freedoms are written into the laws; they exist on paper for them as for the others, the privileged ones; but those poverty-stricken creatures lack the means to exercise them and to benefit by them day by day.

What indeed does freedom mean, what does the inviolability of the home mean for a man who has got no home ?

What is the value of sacred family rights and family liberties for the father who is permanently haunted by the spectre of unemployment?

Of what value is the principle of free access to public appointments, if, in practice, education, culture, and humanism are the privilege of inherited wealth?

We must have the courage to recognise that freedom of money, of competition and of profit has sometimes threatened to destroy the freedom of men. In such a case may I recall the saying of Lacordaire, that it is freedom which enslaves and law which liberates.

Communism was quick to take advantage of disorder. It came, and said to the oppressed that freedom and social justice cannot exist together. Freedom, because it implies liberalism, harsh competition and, sometimes, the crushing of the weak by the strong, does not and cannot provide social justice; you should therefore choose equality. And some poor creatures have yielded to this temptation. So they agreed to renounce their freedom in exchange for a little more bread, and that is a great misfortune for the modern world and for our European democracies. We must find some means of repelling this abominable temptation, by proposing to the world solutions which will enable the triumph of justice and the possession of freedom to be inseparably allied.

The doctrines of so-called directed economy arose as a reaction against liberalism. Men of standing, who had been champions of free enterprise, and politicians of various schools declared themselves in favour of a certain amount of direction in economic matters, and of a despotically controlled sharing of profits and consumer goods as a remedy for the excesses and injustices, of liberalism. They were actuated by a desire for justice, but they, too, were fully aware that the machinery they have set up could easily degenerate into a meddling administration, purposeless interference and sometimes unbearable tyrannies, and even into autarchy. I am sure that they too are concerned about the problem of freedom, and its safeguards in the world to-day, in a planned, concerted or directed economy; and so Mr. President, whatever may be our political colour, we must measure the difficulty of the task that faces us if we are all in earnest in desiring at the same time, both freedom and social justice.

Very fortunately, the concept of Europe was born before it was too late. Experience has proved to us all that the problem I have just stated is insoluble, on the national plane. It can only be solved by means of a collective effort. The debate now opening is evidence of our wish to make that effort. What is it that we can do?

The task with which we are faced could be undertaken in three stages. Our first decision must be the choice of the distant, near, or immediate objective at which we are going to aim. There is, of course a desirable maximum, a theoretical ideal. It would consist in drawing up for Europe a complete code of all the freedoms and fundamental rights; all the individual freedoms and rights, and all the so-called social freedoms and rights.

A full and complete realisation of this aim would, however, be something beyond our powers.

We should need years of mutual understanding, study, and collective experiments, even to attempt after many years, with any hope of success, to formulate a complete and general definition of all the freedoms and all the rights which Europe should confer on the Europeans. Let us therefore discard for the moment this desirable maximum. Failing this, however, let us be content with the minimum which we can achieve in a very short period, and which consists in defining the seven, eight or ten fundamental freedoms that are essential for a democratic way of life and which our countries should guarantee to all their people. It should be possible to achieve a common definition of these.

If we start to work now and if for example we instruct a Committee of this Assembly, with your permission Mr. President and with that of the Assembly, to prepare this common definition of the essential democratic freedoms, we shall be in a position to propose it to the various Governments in a very short time. The latter could sanction it, and the essential freedoms would thus be guaranteed in the same form by the laws of all our countries. They would be safeguarded by the Court of Justice to which I shall presently refer.

I shall shortly ask you to submit to the Assembly a Resolution, embodying this first decision, which will be prepared immediately, with the purpose of obtaining a definition, common to all the peoples of

Europe: namely, an examination of the fundamental freedoms, now in a position to be included in this collective definition.

But Mr. President, with your permission, we shall not stop there; we shall try, even during this Session, to bring before the peoples and before public opinion an immediate proposal, which we must adopt even before we have defined the essential freedoms for our countries.

The problem can be stated in very simple terms. All the States that have taken part in drawing up, signing and promulgating our Statute have bound themselves to respect the fundamental rights of the human individual. They have accepted the principle of a collective guarantee of fundamental freedoms.

We cannot propose that they should all immediately accept a common definition of these freedoms, but, we can ask them to agree forthwith to a collective guarantee, within the framework of the Council of Europe, of these fundamental freedoms, as they are at present defined in their own respective laws, until the time comes when they can guarantee them in the form of a general and collective definition.

If this principle is accepted by the Assembly, we can immediately make a practical and concrete proposal. We shall tell the Member States, who agreed to including this debate on the Agenda, that we should like them to negotiate forthwith a Convention, which they would all sign and which would be ratified by their Parliaments. It would contain, briefly, the following provisions: the principle of a collective guarantee of the fundamental rights and freedoms, within the framework of the Council of Europe, by all Member States belonging to the Council. For example—security of person; freedom from arbitrary arrest; freedom from slavery and servitude; freedom of speech and expression; freedom of religious belief, practice and teaching; freedom of association and assembly; the natural rights deriving from marriage and paternity and those pertaining to the family, the sanctity of the home, equality before the law, protection from discrimination on account of religion, race, national origin, political or philosophical opinion; freedom from arbitrary deprivation of property.

The foregoing could be taken as examples of the fundamental, undisputed freedoms. I grant you, it is far from complete; there are other freedoms. But we might be content with these to begin with. States would bind themselves by conventions to guarantee these freedoms collectively, within the framework of the Council, by a certain procedure and under the control of a European Court.

They would guarantee these fundamental freedoms in the very near future, in the form of a common definition of each of them, which we could then propose after a period of study.

They would, however, guarantee them immediately, without waiting for this common definition, to the extent that such rights are secured by the constitutions, laws or administrative practice of the respective countries.

They should guarantee these freedoms now, at once, and bind themselves to the observance of the guarantee by an international Convention, signed in the name of Europe.

The same Convention should then create a guaranteeing organ, namely a European Court of Human Rights and a European Commission of Human Rights, within the framework of the Council of Europe.

This Commission could form a kind of barrier—a practical necessity well known to all jurists—which would weed out frivolous or mischievous petitions.

Petitions would be addressed to the Commission which could 'screen' them, retaining only those worthy of serious consideration. These serious petitions would be investigated by the Court. The Court could be composed of nine eminent lawyers, appointed by the Committee of Ministers and by the Consultative Assembly. The Court would give its decision on these petitions. It could set aside governmental decisions, and legislative, administrative or legal measures which were clearly contrary to the principle of the guaranteed rights.

Member States of the Council of Europe, all corporate bodies and all individuals might petition the Court.

The Court would either find that rights and freedoms had been violated, and in that case it would annul the action taken, and, if necessary, prescribe measures for reparation; or it would decide that there had been no violation of the guaranteed rights and freedoms, and that in that case the petition would be dismissed.

Mr. President, while I was in the Gestapo prisons, while one of my brothers was at Dachau and one of my brothers-in-law was dying at Mauthausen, my father, who was also a member of our French Parliament, was interned at Buchenwald. He told me that on the monumental gate of the camp was this outrageous inscription: 'Just or unjust, the Fatherland.'

I think that from our first Session we can unanimously proclaim that in Europe there will henceforth only be *just* fatherlands.

Sir David MAXWELL-FYFE (United Kingdom).—In order to appreciate the significance of the proposal which has been put before us so well and so movingly by my friend and colleague in this field, M. Teitgen, it is necessary to envisage the suggestion for a Convention and a Court of Human Rights both in the light of the aims of the Council of Europe and the present position of Europe. This has been the basis of the work of the European Movement on this subject since our conference at The Hague.

With regard to the Council of Europe, three points must be in our minds: the first, as the Statute says, is the method of achieving the aims of the Council and the maintenance and further realisation of human rights and fundamental freedoms. The very word 'further' means that we cannot rest, that we must proceed with this task. Second, it is important to make clear the minimum standard consistent with membership of our body. This is the condition precedent to the general acceptance of the moral basis of our further activities.

Third, Sir, the creation and working of the machinery for the agreement and enforcement of human rights will be an effective method of promoting integration in Europe by means of functional co-operation, Especially will this be so if we accept a means of international assurance that these rights will continue.

From the world point of view we cannot let the matter rest at a declaration of moral principles and pious aspirations, excellent though the latter may be. There must be a binding convention, and we have given you a practical and workable method of bringing this about.

We must face the fact that many parts of the world, either because their political systems are totalitarian or because their civilisations are backward, have 'shown themselves to be unready in temperament and aspiration for the ideals and standards which the great democracies have set for themselves. In our gathering, on the other hand, as M. Lannung has said this morning, countries with a similar outlook upon problems of human rights and long experience in enforcing human rights are in the most favourable position to set an example to nations not yet Members, of their circle. This example is not limited to the enforcement of personal rights, but embraces the fundamental principles of Western democracies, namely, freedom to elect and to change government, and freedom to organise political oppositions, with the freedom to nominate opposition candidates.

Our European Convention is a practical proposition, and will not be faced with the same initial difficulties as a Convention on a world-wide scale. If it can come into existence reasonably soon, it will assist those who are trying to work out a world-wide Convention, by showing them how it will work in practice between States who are accustomed, by legal and political tradition, to enforcing the fundamental rights of man.

With that background in mind, Mr. President, let us consider the most important aspect of our proposals and the criticisms suggested.

In Article I of our project there is set out a short list of basic personal rights. Those rights are all understood, for we are dealing with domestic rights, and negative rights or freedoms which, in any system of law, will be found to be more fundamental than even positive rights. Our list, it is true, contains none of the so-called economic or social rights which appear in the U.N.O. Declaration. Such rights would, in my view, be too controversial and difficult of enforcement even in the changing state of social and international development in Europe, and their inclusion would jeopardise the acceptance of the Convention. Examples, on which I need not expatiate, are the right to free choice of employment, and the right, unknown to you, I am sure, Mr. President, of rest or leisure.

Our second Article sets out the fundamental principles of democracy which the contracting States must all respect. It includes, as I have said, the right to organise political opposition, with the implication of the right to nominate opposition candidates at elections.

I have stated that the list has been shortened, and I wish to say a word about the criticism adumbrated by Mr. Ungoed-Thomas that the rights have not been defined with sufficient precision for legal enforcement. I think that this is a highly disputable thesis. The old view that judges took no cognisance of the facts of life is, fortunately, becoming less and less tenable. With some experience in propounding judicial issues before international tribunals, and the experience which we have all had as legislators in clarifying such issues for our national courts, I take leave to doubt whether the task of enforcement would be insurmountable in respect of our draft.

I am entitled to crave in aid the Bill of Rights in the Constitution of the United States as a parallel and a very successful piece of experience. The Supreme Court of the United States of America has not found it difficult to administer and enforce the Bill of Rights in general terms.

. . .

I come now to the vexed question, which has been so often in our minds during the last few days, of the surrender of sovereignty. Of course this proposal is a new departure. It is an international assurance of what ordinary people want.

Like all treaties, the proposed Convention would involve some voluntary surrender of sovereignty: namely, the sovereign right to suppress liberty and democratic institutions. I cannot imagine that any Member State of the Council of Europe would wish to insist upon this power, or that their citizens would not be happier if it did not exist.

But that is not the only answer. The Governments of the peoples represented here have publicly proclaimed their earnest desire to create a supranational authority. All the Members of U.N.O. are morally bound by the Declaration of Human Rights and committed in principle to trying to make a binding treaty or covenant for the preservation of fundamental human liberties. I have already mentioned our own Statute. Therefore, it is crystal clear that the draft Convention before this Assembly proposes nothing for which the States concerned are not pledged to work, through both U.N.O. and the Council of Europe. The difference—and it is a great one—is that we ask our countries to face up to action at once, which is so simple and practical that it will take effect immediately.

Now let us look for a moment at the criticism from the other end of the scale—that because there is no international police force the Court will be impotent. I point out that under Article 14 the matter can be brought before the Council of Europe, which can take such action as it may consider appropriate. But before we consider such action, I ask my colleagues to estimate the effect of a judgment with the moral prestige of the Court behind it. All Governments are reluctant to be regarded and held up as violators of their people's liberty.

. . .

The Consultative Assembly established a Committee on Legal and Administrative Questions, chaired by Sir David Maxwell-Fyfe. That Committee produced a report, written by M. Teitgen, advocating the drafting of a Convention protecting ten basic human rights. The Consultative Assembly recommended that the Committee of Ministers should undertake such a process. In November 1949 the Committee of Ministers appointed a committee of government experts to draft a human rights Convention. The experts utilized the Teitgen report and agreed many of the elements of a draft Convention. On some issues (e.g. whether the Convention rights should be defined in detail or expressed in general terms) the experts were divided and in regard to others (such as whether a European Court should be created) the experts decided that they were political decisions that should be left to the Committee of Ministers. The latter body resolved, in April 1950, to hold a conference of senior officials to determine the unresolved issues. In June 1950 the senior officials agreed most of the text of a draft Convention. Some rights were elaborated whilst others were left in general terms. The proposed European Court was given an optional jurisdiction. Whether there should be a right of petition by individual complainants was referred back to the Committee of Ministers. In August 1950 the Committee of Ministers agreed a draft Convention incorporating a conditional right of individual petition and optional jurisdiction for the Court. This draft was weaker than the Consultative Assembly's proposals. Despite further criticisms of the Ministers' draft by the Assembly's Legal committee, the Committee of Ministers rejected most of them and approved the final text based upon the August draft. The Convention for the Protection of Human Rights and Fundamental Freedoms (subsequently generally referred to as the European Convention on Human Rights) was opened for signature at the Committee of Ministers' meeting in Rome on 4 November 1950.

The Legal committee's (of the Consultative Assembly) suggestion that three additional rights (encompassing the right to property, the right to education, and political liberties) should be included in the Convention was referred to the government experts by the Committee of Ministers. During 1951 they drafted a Protocol to the Convention, in dialogue with the Consultative Assembly's Legal committee, guaranteeing protection of property, the right to education and the right to free elections. The Protocol was opened for signature in May 1952.

From the above account (drawing heavily upon A. H. Robertson's introductory narrative to the *Travaux Preparatoires* of the Convention) we can discern the interaction between the different organs of the nascent Council of Europe during the creation of the Convention. The Governments of the Member States, acting through the Committee of Ministers, were the dominant actors as they had the final say over the text of the Convention. Nevertheless, the Consultative Assembly through the work of leading figures, including Teitgen and Maxwell-Fyfe, made a significant contribution to the substance of the Convention. From the extracts of the debates in the Consultative Assembly we also gain an understanding of some of the major forces shaping the arguments in favour of the Convention. They include the delegates' personal experiences of the atrocities committed by the Nazis and their allies in the recent past, the current threat to personal liberties posed by the communist regimes in central and eastern Europe, and the United Nation's initial steps towards the development of a global system of human rights.

Professor A. W. Brian Simpson in his major study of the British contribution to the creation of the Convention noted: '[t]he story, as I tell it, is that the European Convention and its First Protocol were the product of conflicts, compromise, and happenstance. There is no simple answer to the question why the members of the Council of Europe signed the Convention in November 1950 and its First Protocol in 1952', *Human Rights and the End of Empire* (Oxford University Press Oxford, 2001) p. vii] Regarding the conflicts and compromise between States during the creation of the Convention Dr Elizabeth Wicks has observed:

During the process of drafting the ECHR, two opposing schools of thought emerged from the participating states. One group of states approved the approach taken in the draft prepared by the Consultative Assembly of the Council of Europe by which rights were expressed in terms of general principles. Another group of states, including most vociferously the United Kingdom, argued for a more narrowly defined series of rights. The disagreement may be in part a legacy of the different approaches of the common law and civil law systems, although a few states with civil law systems did share the United Kingdom's view (the Netherlands, Norway, Denmark and Greece). The existence of these two schools of thought meant that a compromise was required, but the compromise draft did not seek to bridge the gap between the two opposing views. Instead, the United Kingdom was successful in promoting most of its favoured provisions into the draft with only a few concessions (albeit on matters of great significance, most noticeably individual petition and a permanent European Court of Human Rights).

Why was the United Kingdom so successful at winning concessions during the negotiation process? Although the representatives of the United Kingdom at no stage explicitly threatened to withdraw from the negotiating process, or to refuse to sign the final Convention, the other negotiators were in no doubt about the strength of feeling on the part of the United Kingdom. For example, the report to the Committee of Ministers submitted by the Committee of Experts (which outlined the views of the United Kingdom government in greater detail than that of other states) quoted the United Kingdom view that precise definitions were an 'essential prerequisite to any Convention' (*Travaux Preparatoires*, vol IV, p. 10) . . .

While the United Kingdom broadly achieved the definition of rights it sought, it was less successful with regard to implementation measures. The acceptance of optional clauses on an individual petitions system and a permanent European Court of Human Rights, both of which the United Kingdom was opposed to at the early stages of negotiations, were the price paid by the United Kingdom for its success on other issues. [E. Wicks 'The United Kingdom Government's Perceptions of the European Convention on Human Rights at the Time of Entry' [2000] *Public Law* 438 at 439–40.]

According to Dr Danny Nicol:

the negotiators were split into two camps with competing ideologies. One camp believed that the ECHR should indeed only serve to protect existing rights, the other camp pursued the more ambitious goal of a cross-frontier Bill of Rights. Some have sought to explain this gulf by reference to the distinction between common law and civil law systems. This may have played a part, but a more compelling explanation relates to constitutional culture. Countries with a strong faith in a written constitution enshrining supra-legislative rights were pitted against countries where the political culture did not favour review of parliamentary legislation. To be sure, there were Left–Right divisions on issues such as property ownership which split even representatives of the same state along party lines. When it came, however, to the overall aim of the ECHR, Assembly members tended to divide on national lines. This indicates the strength of the constitutional culture within each country. [D. Nicol 'Original Intent and the European Convention on Human Rights' [2005] *Public Law* 152 at pp. 170–1.]

The British (Labour) Government, under Prime Minister Harold Wilson, accepted the right of individuals to petition the European Commission of Human Rights in respect of alleged breaches of their Convention rights by the United Kingdom (but not in regard to matters occurring in dependent territories) from 1966. At the same time the British Government also accepted the jurisdiction of the European Court of Human Rights. Lord Lester QC has identified, *inter alios*, Lord McNair (the first President of the European Court of Human Rights) and the Lord Chancellor (Lord Gardiner) as significant figures supporting the taking of these steps by the Government (see Lord Lester, 'U.K. Acceptance of the Strasbourg Jurisdiction: What Really went on in Whitehall in 1965' [1998] *Public Law* 237.]

After the adoption of the ECHR and its First Protocol the Member States have undertaken a number of modifications to the institutional arrangements provided for in the original Convention (e.g. the creation of the full-time Court under Protocol 11, see below p 14). They have also extended the rights/freedoms that States will respect by creating additional Protocols that individual States can ratify (e.g. abolishing the use of the death penalty in peacetime under Protocol 6). The method of drafting these further Protocols has broadly followed the pattern established during the creation of the Convention. The Committee of Ministers has made the big decisions on matters of principle and policy (such as the decision to replace the European Commission of Human Rights and the part-time Court with a single full-time Court) and utilized a committee of government experts to produce detailed proposals for the draft text of the new Protocol. The Parliamentary Assembly (formerly the Consultative Assembly) has also been involved in these processes of reform (e.g. by agreeing formal Recommendations to the Committee of Ministers). Depending upon the complexity and political sensitivity of the reform proposals it can take many years for the recognition of the need for a new Protocol and the agreeing of its text (over ten years in respect of Protocol 11).

An American academic has concluded:

The Convention was founded by visionaries, and, to date, their vision is being carried out. So, whatever its problems (a charitable characterization might be that they are growing pains), the existence of the Convention and the Strasbourg Court is a major achievement for the entire world. Paul L. McKaskle, 'The European Court of Human Rights: What It Is, How It Works, and Its Future' (2005) 40(1) *University of San Francisco Law Review* 1 at pp. 72–3.

2 THE STRASBOURG SYSTEM FOR DETERMINING APPLICATIONS UNDER THE CONVENTION

Introduction

A new institutional system for determining applications brought under the Convention was created by Protocol 11 and it began to operate from November 1998. However, the Protocol 11 system built upon the institutional, procedural and jurisprudential heritage of the original system. Therefore, a brief overview of the original decision-making bodies and their processes will be given before the Protocol 11 system is examined. In May 2004 further reforms to the Protocol 11 system were agreed by Member States and Protocol 14 was opened for signature. Those changes will be considered in the final section of this chapter.

The original system

As the diagram overleaf reveals the determination of applications under the original system was the shared responsibility of three institutions: the European Commission of Human Rights, the European Court of Human Rights and the Committee of Ministers of the Council of Europe.

The European Commission of Human Rights came into existence in 1954 and, under Article 20 (of the pre-Protocol 11 text of the European Convention on Human Rights), it was composed of a number of members equal to the number of States that were parties to the Convention. Individual members of the Commission were elected by the Committee of Ministers from a list (normally of three persons in ranked order) submitted by the Parliamentary Assembly of the Council of Europe. No two members of the Commission could be nationals of the same State. Members were elected for six-year terms of office and could be re-elected. Under the former Article 23 of the Convention, members of the Commission were to sit as independent persons and not as representatives of the States in respect of which they were elected. In 1990 the Convention was amended, by Protocol 8, to formally strengthen the stature and independence of the Commission members by requiring

The original Strasbourg System for determining applications under the Convention

Application by a State   Application by an individual

European Commission of Human Rights

Is application admissible?

Yes   No ⟶ Case closed

Is a friendly settlement between the parties possible?

No   Yes ⟶ Case closed

Commmission finds facts

Does Commission think there is a violation of the Convention?

Yes   No

Is case referred to the Court by the Commission or an individual applicant under Protocol 9 or a concerned State?

Yes   No ⟶ **Commission reports to The Committee of Ministers of the Council of Europe**

European Court of Human Rights

Is Convention violated?

Is there a violation of the Convention?

Yes   No ⟶ Case closed

Yes   No ⟶ Case closed

Judgment of Court, which is binding on State. (May also afford just satisfaction to successful applicants)

Committee indicates what measures should be taken by the State

Does the State comply?

Committee of Ministers

No   Yes ⟶ Case closed

Supervises the execution of the judgment

Case closed

Committee decides what effect is to be given to its Report

that they be: '... of high moral character and must possess the qualifications required for appointment either to high judicial office or be persons of recognised competence in national or international law.... During their term of office they shall not hold any position which is incompatible with their independence and impartiality as members of the Commission or the demands of this office.' These requirements consolidated a well established trend in the nomination and election of members such that: 'in practice, the election of Government officials has generally not been regarded as appropriate and most members of the Commission, although nationals of the State in respect of which they were elected, hold independent judicial or academic legal appointments in their own countries.' FG Jacobs, *The European Convention on Human Rights* (1975), p 217. The Commission was a part-time body which during its final years met for about eight two-weekly sessions each year. The Commission was dissolved in October 1999.

The original Court came into existence in January 1959. It had a number of members equal to the number of States that were parties to the Council of Europe. Hence in the early decades of the Court it had judges drawn from States that had not yet ratified the Convention, but were members of the Council of Europe. However, from the late 1980s States were not allowed to join the Council unless they agreed to ratify the Convention (either at the time of joining the Council or soon afterwards). The judges were elected by the Parliamentary Assembly from a list of candidates nominated by each Member State. Candidates had to be, 'of high moral character and must either possess the qualifications required for appointment to high judicial office or be jurisconsults of recognised competence' (former Article 39). Once appointed they were to act independently and were forbidden from holding any position which was incompatible with their impartiality as members of the Court (former Article 40). Judges held office for nine years and were eligible for re-election. There was no formal age limit for judges, although the Parliamentary Assembly (unsuccessfully) requested its members not to vote for candidates who refused to give an undertaking that they would retire when they reached the age of 75. The Court was a part-time body which held sessions each month.

The Committee of Ministers is the executive body of the Council of Europe and, therefore, has its constitutional foundations in the Statute of the Council of Europe. The Committee is formally composed of the Foreign Ministers of Member States, but most of the work of the Committee is undertaken by the Ministers' Deputies (ambassadorial members of States' diplomatic services). Under the original Convention system the Committee had, *inter alia*, to determine applications which had been subject to a report by the Commission and had not been referred to the Court (former Article 32). In performing this quasi-judicial task the Committee sat *in camera* and did not allow the individual applicant (or his/her lawyer) to participate in the proceedings. The Committee had to decide, by a two-thirds majority of the members entitled to sit, whether there had been a breach of the Convention. In most cases the Committee followed the opinion of the Commission. However, in a few cases the Committee was unable to reach a decision. A critical analysis of the Committee's performance under the old system was provided by a former Secretary of the Committee.

The Ministers' Deputies are generally career diplomats, namely, the Permanent Representatives of Member States at the Council of Europe. They act, in human rights cases as in other matters, on instructions from their capitals. They usually have no special training or competence to deal with human rights issues. They are trained to defend State interests—or what their central authority regards as interests of their State—and, if necessary, to seek compromise solutions; they are not trained to make clear-cut legal pronouncements on human rights issues. When their own State is 'in the dock' they will have a natural inclination to defend it. When other States are concerned they may find it inopportune, embarrassing or even indecent to judge their human rights performance, unless it is considered as being in the interest of their own State to do so, which is not often the case within this group of, in principle, 'likeminded' States.

[Peter Leuprecht, 'The Protection of Human Rights By Political Bodies—The Example of the Committee of Ministers of the Council of Europe', at pp 98 and 106–107 in M Nowak & D Steurer (eds) *Progress in the Spirit of Human Rights* (1988).]

One of the fundamental improvements in the new system of determining applications introduced by Protocol 11 (examined below) was the abolition of the Committee of Ministers' original decision-making role in respect of applications described above. With the ending of the former USSR's domination of central and eastern Europe, and the subsequent emergence of many new democracies, the Committee of Ministers now contains representatives from forty-six States.

The Protocol 11 system

Background

In the early 1980s the idea began to develop at Strasbourg that it might be desirable for the Commission and the Court to merge into one institution, so as to facilitate greater efficiency in the determination of the increasing number of complaints being brought under the Convention. In 1985 the Swiss government supported this idea. Four years later a Committee of Experts, which was ultimately accountable to the Committee of Ministers, produced a report which summarised arguments for (e.g. simplifying the control system for applicants) and against (e.g. prejudicing the encouragement of friendly settlements by the Commission) the notion of merging the two bodies. The Committee of Experts concluded that in its view, 'no single and decisive argument for or against a merger has been found.' (Document H(89)2, para 57) Subsequently the Committee of Experts drew up an outline structure for a new single full-time Court (Document DH-PR(90)6). Because of political deadlock, amongst States over the benefits of creating such a court, the Dutch and Swedish governments suggested the creation of a two-tier judicial control system:

The central idea in both proposals is that the opinions of the Commission … would be transformed into legally binding decisions. In other words, there would be established a two-tier judicial system, i.e. the Commission would operate like a court of first instance from which individual applicants and States would be accorded the right of appeal to the Court against the Commission's decisions on the merits, subject to leave to appeal being granted by the Court … [*Report to the Steering Committee for Human Rights*, 23/3/ 1992, para 8]

The Committee of Experts was divided over the desirability of the Dutch–Swedish proposal. However, a majority of the Commission supported it. A minority of the Court favoured the creation of a new single court and this form of institutional reform was also backed by the Parliamentary Assembly of the Council of Europe which approved Recommendation 1194 (1992):

The Assembly therefore recommends that the Committee of Ministers … give clear preference to the proposal to create a single court as a full-time body in place of the existing Commission and Court;

refrain from opting for a temporary solution that would further delay the necessary reform. [See further, A. R. Mowbray, 'Reform of the Control System of the European Convention on Human Rights' [1993] *Public Law* 419.]

By May 1993 the Committee of Ministers had reached a political decision to approve the idea of creating a new single Court.

However, the price of States' acceptance of the single court was the demand that the new court provide a mechanism for the re-hearing of exceptional cases, with the national judge participating in that process. This unusual requirement, that a single court provide the possibility of a second judgment on the merits, is a contemporary political compromise analogous to the original Convention agreement concerning the various functions of the Commission, Court and Committee of Ministers. [A. R. Mowbray, 'A New European Court of Human Rights' [1994] *Public Law* 540.]

Some States (and some members of the British Cabinet) were reluctant to grant individual applicants the right of direct access to the new court, however this was included in Protocol 11 (... *Restructuring The Control Machinery Established Thereby*) when it was opened for signature in May 1994.

Protocol 11 created a new full-time European Court of Human Rights. Although the new Court has the same title as the original Court, it is an entirely different body with new functions, powers and composition. Judges are elected, by the Parliamentary Assembly, in respect of each State which is a party to the Convention. They are appointed for a six year term of office and can be re-elected. (Article 22) This reduction in the length of the term of office compared to their predecessors (which was unsuccessfully opposed by the Parliamentary Assembly) is another reflection of States' continuing cautious attitude towards the Strasbourg control system. Judges now have to retire when they reach the age of 70. (Article 23) The introduction of a compulsory age limit on judges was opposed by the old Court, but enshrined in Protocol 11 on the grounds that the workload faced by the judges of the new full-time Court would be much more demanding than that undertaken by the former part-time judges. The qualifications for office and the obligation to be independent from national States required of the judges were exactly the same as those demanded of the members of the old Court. (Article 21)

The old Court ceased to exist at the end of October 1998. Complex transition arrangements were contained in Protocol 11 for cases pending before the old Court and Commission. The latter body continued to function for one year after the creation of the new Court. Protocol 11 did not alter the definition of inter-State applications (new Article 33) or individual applications (new Article 34). Likewise, the former admissibility criteria applicable to both types of applications were retained (new Article 35). The new Court has assumed responsibility for seeking to secure friendly settlements of cases (new Article 38). When the new Court has found a violation of the Convention it can award 'just satisfaction' (see below, Ch 19). The Committee of Ministers retains responsibility for supervising the execution of the new Court's judgments (Article 46).

Composition of the Court

Under Article 22 of the Convention the appointment of judges to the Court is the shared responsibility of Member States and the Parliamentary Assembly of the Council of Europe (composed of members drawn from national legislatures). Each Member State must nominate a list of three candidates (who satisfy the criteria under Article 21: having 'high moral character' [e.g. not having engaged in acts contrary to the values of the Convention] and either possess the qualifications required for appointment to high judicial office or be 'jurisconsults' (e.g. academics) of recognized competence). The Parliamentary Assembly then elects one of the nominees by means of a majority vote. Significantly, the Convention does not specify how Member States should select their nominees. Professor Schermers, a member of the former Commission, was highly critical of the nominations made by some States to the new Court.

Some governments nominated candidates who were obviously not fully independent from their governments. Several of the candidates held posts as ambassador ... the nominations of several governments convey the impression that political arguments play too important a role in nominations. This harms the reputation of the Court. H. G. Schermers, Election of Judges to the European Court of Human Rights (1998) 23 *EL Rev* 568 at pp 574–5

He also considered that there had been problems in the Parliamentary Assembly's scrutiny of candidates. The Assembly asked candidates to submit a standard *curriculum vitae* and attend an interview before an *ad hoc* sub-committee of the Assembly:

Not all candidates sent their *curriculum vitae* in accordance with the standard formula. Some candidates thus managed to hide aspects and to underline others. Their *curricula vitae* were nonetheless accepted.

The interviewing of some 120 candidates proved to be difficult. It was hard to find qualified members for the *ad hoc* sub-committee charged with the interviewing. Some of the members finally chosen hardly knew the Convention, let alone the case law of the Commission and Court. The interviews were short, between 10 and 15 minutes each.

... The final report of the *ad hoc* sub-committee was not very satisfactory. Political nominations by some governments, former ambassadors and permanent representatives were accepted ... Schermers ibid. pp 676–7.

The candidates elected by the Assembly comprised ten members of the original Court, ten members from the 1997–8 membership of the Commission and twenty persons who had not previously served on those institutions (according to Schermers six were diplomats/officials, six were domestic judges, four were lawyers, and four were law professors). The influx of new judges created a comparatively young Court, with an average age of approximately 54 years: for greater detail see, A. R. Mowbray 'The Composition and Operation of the New European Court of Human Rights' [1999] *Public Law* 219.

Subsequently, the Parliamentary Assembly has sought to encourage Member States to adopt more open processes for selecting nominees and to enhance the rigour of it own scrutiny of candidates. For example, in 2004 the Assembly passed Recommendation 1649 (2004) Candidates for the European Court of Human Rights [Recommendations are addressed to the Committee of Ministers and their implementation is within the competence of member governments]. The Recommendation stated:

2. In order that the European Court of Human Rights continues to command public confidence, it is vital that the process by which judges are selected and appointed must also command confidence.

3. The Parliamentary Assembly insists that the process of appointment must echo the principles of the democratic method, the rule of law, non-discrimination, accountability and transparency.

...

17. ... recalling that the national procedures for selecting candidates are not always satisfactory, it urges Member States to publish their procedures for the selection of candidates.

19. In addition to the moral qualities and experience properly expected of candidates, laid down in Article 21(1) of the Convention, the Assembly recommends to the Committee of Ministers to invite the Governments of the Member States to met six other criteria before submitting lists of candidates for the office of judge in the European Court of Human Rights and explicitly to ensure:
  i.   that a call for candidates has been issued through the specialised press;
  ii. that the candidates have experience in the field of human rights;
  iii. that the list contains candidates of both sexes in every case;
  iv. that the candidates have a sufficient knowledge of at least one of the official languages;
  v.   that the names of the candidates are placed in alphabetical order;
  vi. that as far as possible no candidate should be submitted whose election might result in the necessity to appoint an *ad hoc*

The Assembly also passed Resolution 1366 (2004) Candidates for the European Court of Human Rights [Resolutions are decisions of the Assembly which it is empowers to implement]. The Resolution provided that:

3. The Assembly decides not to consider lists of candidates where:
  i.   the areas of competence from which the candidates have been selected appears to be unduly restricted;
  ii. the list does not include at least one male and at least one female candidate;
  iii. on examination of the candidates, (a) they do not appear to have sufficient knowledge of at least one of the official languages, or (b) they do not appear to be of the stature to meet the criteria in Article 21(1) of the Convention.
4. The Assembly continues to believe that the process of interviews provides additional insight into the qualities of the candidates and decides;

… that a fair and efficient interview process requires a continuous process of training and re-assessment for the members and staff involved in panels …

The Assembly demonstrated its commitment to the above requirements when, in April 2004, it decided not to proceed, at that time, with the election of judges in respect of Malta and Slovakia (because the lists of nominees did not include candidates of both genders and the procedures at national levels did not meet the Assembly's recommendations regarding publicity/transparency) and Portugal (because the national procedures were not sufficiently transparent and only one candidate met all the qualifications required by the Convention).

The new Court, sitting in plenary session (under Article 26), elected Luzius Wildhaber as it first President. He had been the Swiss judge on the original Court since 1991, prior to that he has been a Professor and (later) Rector of Basle University. The Court has re-elected him on two subsequent occasions. In November 2006, Jean-Paul Costa, the French judge and Vice-President of the Court since 2001, was elected President to replace the retiring Luzius Wildhaber.

Status of the Judges

Judges appointed to the Court sit in their individual capacity (Article 21(2)), which means that they are to exercise independent judgment when deciding cases. Their independence is emphasised by the requirement (in Article 21(3)) that during their period of office they must not engage in any activity which is incompatible with their independence (e.g. holding office in a national government). They are also prohibited from taking on any activity which is incompatible with the full-time responsibilities of their office (e.g. any other significant form of work, paid or unpaid). During their term of office judges can only be dismissed by a two thirds majority of the other judges concluding that a particular judge no longer fulfils the conditions of office (Article 24), this has never occurred.

President Wildhaber has sought to protect the independence of the judges from improper reselection pressures. In a speech, given at the Ministerial Conference on Human Rights (held in November 2000) to commemorate the fiftieth anniversary of the Convention, he warned that:

We should, however, remain vigilant, and this is particularly important in relation to procedures for the election of judges. Put crudely, sitting judges must not be under the impression that their reselection as a candidate will depend on their voting record. I am confident that the informal consultation process carried out by the Committee of Ministers and the controls exercised by the Parliamentary Assembly will ensure that the selection of candidates, *a fortiori* where the candidate is a sitting judge, is determined solely on the basis of experience, particularly judicial experience and ability.

In practice the overwhelming majority of serving judges who have been eligible for reselection (and wished to be serve another term) have been re-appointed (e.g. in 2001 fifteen serving judges were re-elected).

Organization of the Court

The Court is divided into five Sections. Each Section is balanced in terms of the gender of the judges and the geographical parts of Europe from where they have been nominated. Also, each Section has a membership which takes account of the different legal systems of Member States. Each Section is presided over by either a Vice-President of the Court or a Section President (both categories of presidents having been elected by the Court sitting in plenary session). The composition of each Section is fixed for three years. Chambers, composed of seven members, are created within each Section on a rotational basis (the Section President and judge elected in respect of the respondent State always being members of a particular Chamber). Other members of the relevant Section sit as substitute members of the Chamber. Committees, composed of three judges, are established by Chambers for periods of twelve months. The Grand Chamber, composed of seventeen members, includes the President, Vice-Presidents and Section Presidents plus twelve other judges (chosen on a rotational basis).

The Registry of the Court

This body of officials provides legal and administrative support to the Court. The constitutional foundation of the Registry is Article 25 of the Convention. The head of the Registry is the Registrar and he/she is appointed by the plenary Court (under Article 26(e)). The first Registrar of the full-time Court was Michele de Salvia (an Italian national) and in 2001 he was succeeded by Paul Mahoney (a British national). The current Registrar, appointed in November 2005, is Erik Fribergh (a Swedish national). Each Section of the Court has a Section Registrar. The Registry is composed of approximately 500 persons (roughly 200 lawyers, known as 'legal secretaries', and 300 support staff, such as administrators and translators). About half the Registry staff are permanent employees of the Council of Europe and the other half are fixed-term employees of the organization. All the staff are required to undertake their work on the basis of independence and impartiality (e.g. they must not seek to favour the interests of their national State). Members of the Registry do not decide cases. In the autumn of 2006 a specialist secretariat was established to focus on helping the Court reduce the backlog of pending cases. At the same time forty-six additional staff were recruited.

Cost of the Court

Under Article 50 the expenditure on the Court shall be borne by the Council of Europe. The budget of the Court is part of the Council of Europe's general budget which is agreed by the Committee of Ministers (Member States fund the Council of Europe according to a scheme which takes account of States' populations and Gross National Products). In 2005 the Court's budget amounted to 41,739,000 euros. This sum covered the remuneration of judges and staff plus general expenditure (including, information technology, translation services and official journeys), but not the costs of buildings and infrastructure (e.g. telecommunications). By Resolution, Res (2004) 50, the Committee of Ministers set the judges' annual salary at 198,349 euros (the President receives an additional allowance of 12,092 euros and the Vice-Presidents/Presidents of Sections an additional allowance of 6,046 euros). These salaries and allowances are paid tax free (Council of Europe, General Agreement on Privileges and Immunities (1949)). The above salaries are linked to a specified grade of Council of Europe staff and will rise as that grade's pay is increased (my thanks to Professor Paul McKaskle, University of San Francisco, for alerting me to the information regarding judicial salaries). In his speech to mark the opening of the judicial year 2006 (Strasbourg, 20 January 2006), President Wildhaber criticized:

... the total lack of a scheme of pensions and social security for judges [at the Court]. ... The present situation is incompatible with the notion of an independent judiciary under the rule of law, as well as being contrary to the Council of Europe's own Social Charter. It is high time for the Council of Europe to address the issue of principle at stake and assume the responsibilities flowing from it.

The determination of applications

The Convention provisions dealing with the procedure of the Court have been supplemented by detailed Rules of Court, issued by the Plenary Court (composed of all the judges) under Article 26(d). The Rules of Court are regularly revised to take account of changing methods of working by the Court. In 2003 the Court supplemented the Rules of Court by initiating the issuing of Practice Directions. The Registry explained that these Directions had two purposes; first, to provide guidance to parties on different facets of their dealings with the Court and secondly to introduce more standardised procedures thereby facilitating the Court's processing of cases. They deal with matters including: how requests for interim measures should be communicated to the Court (not by ordinary mail) and the structure of written pleadings (composed of sections replicating judgments of the Court—'facts', 'domestic law and practice' etc). The Practice Directions will be particularly useful for applicants' lawyers who are not experienced in bringing cases at Strasbourg.

(i) ADMISSIBILITY

Applications may be brought by Member States ('inter-State cases' under Article 33) or persons ('individual applications' under Article 34). Inter-State cases are very rare (only two have resulted in judgments of the Court: *Ireland v United Kingdom* A.25 (1978), below p 145 and *Cyprus v Turkey* ECHR 2001-IV, below p 64). This is because the political and economic ties between Member States discourage the initiation of 'hostile' applications against a fellow party to the Convention except in the most extreme circumstances (e.g. in *Ireland* where the applicant State alleged widespread violations of Convention rights by the authorities in

The Protocol 11 Strasbourg system for determining applications under the Convention

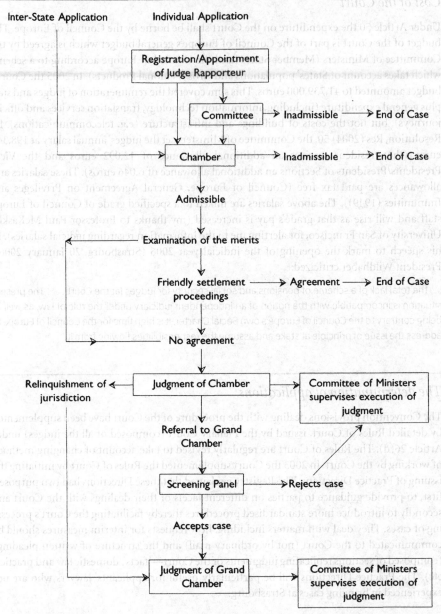

Northern Ireland and in *Cyprus* where the applicant State alleged that the military occupation of the northern part of Cyprus had resulted in numerous violations of many Convention Articles). The admissibility of inter-State cases is determined by a Chamber.

Individual applications are most commonly brought by persons who claim that they have suffered a violation of a right/freedom guaranteed by the Convention. Legal persons may also make an application (e.g. *Krone Verlag GmbH & Co KG v Austria (No 3)*, Judgment of 11 December 2003, below p 674) as can a non-governmental organization or group of individuals. An example of an applicant that fell within the concept of a non-governmental organization was the *Vereinigung Demokratischer Soldaten Österreichs* association which published 'The Hedgehog' journal for soldiers, see below p 703. Several journalists were considered to be a group of individuals in *Sunday Times v United Kingdom* A.30 (1979), below p 633. The full-time Court elaborated upon the scope of Article 34 applicants in *Danderyds Kommun v Sweden* (Application No 52559/99) Decision of 7 June 2001. The applicant was a Swedish municipality which sought to challenge the amount of municipal tax it was allocated by the Tax Authority of Stockholm. The Swedish courts refused to hear the challenge. Thereupon, the applicant complained to the Court alleging breaches of it rights under Article 1 of Protocol No 1 and Article 6.

... The Court considers that it should first examine whether, under Article 34 of the Convention, the applicant has *locus standi* to introduce an application. According to Article 34, the Court may receive applications from 'any person, non-governmental organisation or group of individuals'. The question therefore arises whether the applicant can be deemed to be a non-governmental organisation or a group of individuals within the meaning of that provision.

The applicant notes that previous Convention case-law has emphasised the fact that municipalities perform official duties on behalf of the State, assigned to them by the Constitution and other legislation. However, a Swedish municipality is an independent legal person, acting in its own capacity, which cannot be considered to be exercising its competence on behalf of the Government. Furthermore, in this case the municipalities act with the governmental authorities as their only counterpart. The municipality should therefore be entitled to make an application under Article 34 of the Convention.

The Court notes that the jurisprudence of the Court and the former Commission has already dealt with the question whether a municipality can be considered to be a non-governmental organisation or a group of individuals within the meaning of Article 34 (formerly Article 25) of the Convention (see, e.g. 16 *Austrian Communes and some of their Councillors v Austria*, Application Nos 5765/77 et al:, Commission decision of 31 May 1974, Collection 46, p 118; *Commune Rothenthurm v Switzerland*, No. 13252/87, Commission decision of 14 December 1988, *Decisions and Reports* (DR) 59, p. 251; *The Province of Bari, Sorrentino and Messeni Nemagna v Italy* (dec.), No 41877/98, 22 March 2001; *The Municipal Section of Antilly v France* (dec.), No 45129/98, ECHR 1999-VIII and *Ayuntamiento de Mula v Spain* (dec.), No 55346/00, to be published in ECHR 2001).

According to this jurisprudence it is not only the central organs of the State that are clearly governmental organisation, as opposed to non-governmental organizations, but also decentralised authorities that exercise public functions, notwithstanding the extent of their autonomy *vis-à-vis* the central organs. This is the case even if the municipality is claiming that in this particular situation it is acting as a private organ.

Moreover, to consider a Swedish municipality a non-governmental organisation is clearly contradicted by the fact that its acts can engage the responsibility of the Swedish State under the Convention. From the Court's perspective the hierarchy between different organs of the State is thus not relevant while examining an application before it. Furthermore, a conflict between a central State organ and a municipality is rather a conflict of jurisdiction which is not for the Court to solve.

Neither can a municipality be considered to be a group of individuals. Such an interpretation would not be compatible with the distinction made between groups of individuals on the one hand and non-governmental organisations on the other.

Turning to the present case, the Court finds that the applicant is clearly a public organ exercising public functions. It must therefore be considered to be a governmental organisation.

It follows that the application is incompatible with the provisions of the Convention within the meaning of Article 35 § 3. The Court must therefore reject the application as being inadmissible *ratione personae*.

Consequently, the unanimous Chamber determined that the application was inadmissible. Hence, it is clear that the Court will not allow disputes between public authorities at different levels of domestic governmental structures to be litigated at Strasbourg.

All applicants under Article 34 must be claiming that they were the victims of a violation of a right/freedom protected by the Convention (and relevant Protocols) by one (or more) of the Member States. The Court elaborated upon the concept of a 'victim' in *Klass v Germany*, A.28 (1978) (see also below, p 560) [note, in the pre-Protocol 11 text of the Convention the victim criterion was contained in Article 25]. The applicants were lawyers who complained about a German statute, the G10 Act, which allowed the Government to authorize the secret interception of designated persons' mail and telecommunications on national security grounds. According to the Court:

... Article 25 requires that an individual applicant should claim to have been actually affected by the violation he alleges ... Article 25 does not institute for individuals a kind of *actio popularis* for the interpretation of the Convention; it does not permit individuals to complain against a law in *abstracto* simply because they feel that it contravenes the Convention. In principle, it does not suffice for an individual applicant to claim that the mere existence of a law violates his rights under the Convention; it is necessary that the law should have been applied to his detriment. Nevertheless, as both the Government and the Commission pointed out, a law may by itself violate the rights of an individual if the individual is directly affected by the law in the absence of any specific measure of implementation.

Article 25, which governs the access by individuals to the Commission, is one of the keystones in the machinery for the enforcement of the rights and freedoms set forth in the Convention. ... The question arises in the present proceedings whether an individual is to be deprived of the opportunity of lodging an application with the Commission because, owing to the secrecy of the measures objected to, he cannot point to any concrete measure specifically affecting him. In the Court's view, the effectiveness (*l'effet utile*) of the Convention implies in such circumstances some possibility of having access to the Commission. If this were not so, the efficiency of the Convention's enforcement machinery would be materially weakened. The procedural provisions of the Convention must, in view of the fact that the Convention and its institutions were set up to protect the individual, be applied in a manner which serves to make the system of individual applications efficacious. The Court therefore accepts that an individual may, under certain conditions, claim to be the victim of a violation occasioned by the mere existence of secret measures or of legislation permitting secret measures, without having to allege that such measures were in fact applied to him. The relevant conditions are to be determined in each case according to the Convention right or rights alleged to have been infringed, the secret character of the measures objected to, and the connection between the applicant and those measures.

As to the facts of the particular case, the Court observes that the contested legislation institutes a system of surveillance under which all persons in the Federal Republic of Germany can potentially have their mail, post and telecommunications monitored, without their ever knowing this unless there has been either some indiscretion or subsequent notification in the circumstances laid down in the Federal Constitutional Court's judgment ... To that extent, the disputed legislation directly affects all users or potential users of the postal and telecommunication services in the Federal Republic of Germany. Furthermore, as the Delegates [of the Commission] rightly pointed out, this menace of surveillance can be claimed in itself to restrict free communication through the postal and telecommunication services, thereby constituting for all users or potential users a direct interference with the right guaranteed by Article 8. ...

Having regard to the specific circumstances of the present case, the Court concludes that each of the applicants is entitled to '(claim) to be the victim of a violation' of the Convention, even though he is not able to allege in support of his application that he has been subject to a concrete measure of surveillance. (paras 33, 34, 37, and 38)

Therefore, generally individual applicants have to show that they were directly affected by some form of State action/inaction if they are to be classified as a 'victim'. For a further examination of cases where the existence of legislation had a direct effect upon individuals enabling them to claim to be victims see below, p 487 [*Norris*]. Other examples of individuals complaining about secret surveillance are discussed below, p 556 [*Halford*].

The representatives (family members) of the estates of the deceased terrorists in *McCann v UK* (below, p 77) were able to lodge their applications against the UK. The full-time Court elaborated upon the circumstances where an application could be continued despite the death of the applicant in *Karner v Austria* (see below, p 822). The applicant lodged his application with the Commission in July 1997. The application was transferred to the Court in 1998. The applicant died in 2000. During September 2001 the Court declare the application partly admissible. Two months later the applicant's lawyer informed the Court of his client's death and that the applicant's mother had waived her right to succeed to the estate. In the light of the applicant's death and the absence of heirs wishing to continue the case, the Government requested the Court to strike out the application (under Article 37(1)). The applicant's lawyer sought the continued examination of the case as he asserted that it involved an important issue of Austrian law. The Chamber held:

22. The Court notes that in a number of cases in which an applicant died in the course of the proceedings it has taken into account the statements of the applicant's heirs or of close family members expressing the wish to pursue the proceedings before the Court (see, among other authorities, *Deweer v Belgium*, judgment of 27 February 1980, Series A No 35, pp 19–20, §§ 37–8; *X v the United Kingdom*, judgment of 5 November 1981, Series A No 46, p 15, § 32; *Vocaturo v Italy*, judgment of 24 May 1991, Series A No 206-C, p 29, § 2; *G. v Italy*, judgment of 27 February 1992, Series A No 228-F, p 65, § 2; *Pandolfelli and Palumbo v Italy*, judgment of 27 February 1992, Series A No 231-B, p 16, § 2; *X v France*, judgment of 31 March 1992, Series A No 234-C, p 89, § 26; and *Raimondo v Italy*, judgment of 22 February 1994, Series A No 281-A, p 8, § 2).

23. On the other hand, it has been the Court's practice to strike applications out of the list of cases in the absence of any heir or close relative who has expressed the wish to pursue an application (see *Scherer v Switzerland*, judgment of 25 March 1994, Series A No 287, pp 14–15, § 31; *Öhlinger v Austria*, No 21444/93, Commission's report of 14 January 1997, § 15, unreported; *Malhous v the Czech Republic* (dec.) [GC], No 33071/96, ECHR 2000-XII). Thus, the Court has to determine whether the application in the present case should also be struck out of the list. In formulating an appropriate answer to this question, the object and purpose of the Convention system as such must be taken into account.

24. The Court reiterates that, while Article 33 (former Article 24) of the Convention allows each Contracting State to refer to the Court (Commission) 'any alleged breach' of the Convention by another Contracting State, a person, non-governmental organisation or group of individuals must, in order to be able to lodge a petition in pursuance of Article 34 (former Article 25), claim 'to be the victim of a violation ... of the rights set forth in the Convention or the Protocols thereto'. Thus, in contrast to the position under Article 33—where, subject to the other conditions laid down, the general interest attaching to the observance of the Convention renders admissible an inter-State application—Article 34 requires that an individual applicant should claim to have been actually affected by the violation he alleges (see *Ireland v the United Kingdom*, judgment of 18 January 1978, Series A No 25, pp 90–1, §§ 239–40, and *Klass and Others v Germany*, judgment of 6 September 1978, Series A No 28, pp 17–18, § 33). Article 34 does not institute for individuals a kind of *actio popularis* for the interpretation of the Convention; it does not permit individuals to complain against a law *in abstracto* simply because they feel that it contravenes the Convention (see *Norris v Ireland*, judgment of 26 October 1988, Series A No 142, pp 15–16, § 31, and *Sanles Sanles v Spain* (dec.), No 48335/99, ECHR 2000-XI).

25. While under Article 34 of the Convention the existence of a 'victim of a violation', that is to say, an individual applicant who is personally affected by an alleged violation of a Convention right, is indispensable for putting the protection mechanism of the Convention into motion, this criterion cannot be

applied in a rigid, mechanical and inflexible way throughout the whole proceedings. As a rule, and in particular in cases which primarily involve pecuniary, and, for this reason, transferable claims, the existence of other persons to whom that claim is transferred is an important criterion, but cannot be the only one. As the Court pointed out in *Malhous* (decision cited above), human rights cases before the Court generally also have a moral dimension, which must be taken into account when considering whether the examination of an application after the applicant's death should be continued. All the more so if the main issue raised by the case transcends the person and the interests of the applicant.

26. The Court has repeatedly stated that its 'judgments in fact serve not only to decide those cases brought before the Court but, more generally, to elucidate, safeguard and develop the rules instituted by the Convention, thereby contributing to the observance by the States of the engagements undertaken by them as Contracting Parties' (see *Ireland v the United Kingdom*, cited above, p 62, § 154, and *Guzzardi v Italy*, judgment of 6 November 1980, Series A No 39, p 31, § 86). Although the primary purpose of the Convention system is to provide individual relief, its mission is also to determine issues on public-policy grounds in the common interest, thereby raising the general standards of protection of human rights and extending human rights jurisprudence throughout the community of Convention States.

27. The Court considers that the subject matter of the present application—the difference in treatment of homosexuals as regards succession to tenancies under Austrian law—involves an important question of general interest not only for Austria but also for other States Parties to the Convention. In this connection the Court refers to the submissions made by ILGA-Europe, Liberty and Stonewall, whose intervention in the proceedings as third parties was authorised as it highlights the general importance of the issue. Thus, the continued examination of the present application would contribute to elucidate, safeguard and develop the standards of protection under the Convention.

28. In these particular circumstances, the Court finds that respect for human rights as defined in the Convention and the Protocols thereto requires a continuation of the examination of the case (Article 37 § 1 *in fine* of the Convention) and accordingly rejects the Government's request for the application to be struck out of its list.

The Austrian *ad hoc* Judge dissented as he did not consider the case one of 'general importance'. The judgment in *Karner* is to be welcomed as the Court should be able to determine cases raising significant issues even if the applicant has died during the Strasbourg proceedings and there are no strong personal/family reasons why the case should be struck out.

Article 35(1) imposes two admissibility criteria in respect of both inter-State cases and individual applications. First, the Court can only examine the merits of applications where the applicant (person or State) has exhausted all domestic remedies in regard to the complaint. The Court has explained its approach to this requirement in *Isayeva, Yusupova, Bazayava v Russia*, 24 February 2005 (see below, p 97).

144. The Court recalls that the rule of exhaustion of domestic remedies referred to in Article 35 § 1 of the Convention obliges applicants first to use the remedies that are normally available and sufficient in the domestic legal system to enable them to obtain redress for the breaches alleged. The existence of the remedies must be sufficiently certain, in practice as well as in theory, failing which they will lack the requisite accessibility and effectiveness. Article 35 § 1 also requires that the complaints intended to be brought subsequently before the Court should have been made to the appropriate domestic body, at least in substance and in compliance with the formal requirements laid down in domestic law, but that no recourse should be had to remedies which are inadequate or ineffective (see the *Aksoy v Turkey* judgment of 18 December 1996, *Reports* 1996-VI, pp 2275–6, §§ 51–2, and the *Akdivar and Others v Turkey* [1996-IV] p. 1210, §§ 65–7).

145. The Court emphasises that the application of the rule of exhaustion of domestic remedies must make due allowance for the fact that it is being applied in the context of machinery for the protection of

human rights that the Contracting States have agreed to set up. Accordingly, it has recognised that Article 35 § 1 must be applied with some degree of flexibility and without excessive formalism. It has further recognised that the rule of exhaustion is neither absolute nor capable of being applied automatically; for the purposes of reviewing whether it has been observed, it is essential to have regard to the circumstances of the individual case. This means, in particular, that the Court must take realistic account not only of the existence of formal remedies in the legal system of the Contracting State concerned but also of the general context in which they operate, as well as the personal circumstances of the applicant. It must then examine whether, in all the circumstances of the case, the applicant did everything that could reasonably be expected of him or her to exhaust domestic remedies (see the *Akdivar and Others* judgment cited above, p 1211, § 69, and the *Aksoy* judgment cited above, p 2276, §§ 53 and 54).

146. The Court observes that Russian law provides, in principle, two avenues of recourse for the victims of illegal and criminal acts attributable to the State or its agents, namely civil procedure and criminal remedies.

147. As regards a civil action to obtain redress for damage sustained through alleged illegal acts or unlawful conduct on the part of State agents, the Court recalls that the Government have relied on two possibilities, namely to lodge a complaint with the Supreme Court or to lodge a complaint with other courts. The Court notes that at the date on which the present application was declared admissible, no decision had been produced to it in which the Supreme Court or other courts were able, in the absence of any results from the criminal investigation, to consider the merits of a claim relating to alleged serious criminal actions. In the instant case, however, the applicants are not aware of the identity of the potential defendant, and so, being dependent for such information on the outcome of the criminal investigation, did not bring such an action.

148. As regards the case of Mr Khashiyev, who had brought a complaint to the Court (No 57942/00), to which the Government refer, it is true that, after receiving the Government's claim that a civil remedy existed, he brought an action before the Nazran District Court in Ingushetia. That court was not able to, and did not, pursue any independent investigation as to the person or persons responsible for the fatal assaults, but it did make an award of damages to Mr Khashiyev on the basis of the common knowledge of the military superiority of the Russian federal forces in the district in question at the relevant time and the State's general liability for the actions by the military.

149. The Court does not consider that that decision affects the effectiveness of a civil action as regards exhaustion of domestic remedies. Despite a positive outcome for Mr Khashiyev in the form of a financial award, it confirms that a civil action is not capable, without the benefit of the conclusions of a criminal investigation, of making any findings as to the identity of the perpetrators of fatal assaults, and still less to establish their responsibility. Furthermore, a Contracting State's obligation under Articles 2 and 13 of the Convention to conduct an investigation capable of leading to the identification and punishment of those responsible in cases of fatal assault might be rendered illusory if, in respect of complaints under those Articles, an applicant would be required to exhaust an action leading only to an award of damages (see *Yaşa v Turkey*, judgment of 2 September 1998, *Reports* 1998-VI, p 2431, § 74).

150. The Court also notes the practical difficulties cited by the applicants and the fact that the law-enforcement bodies were not functioning properly in Chechnya at the time. In this respect the Court is of the opinion that there existed special circumstances which affected their obligation to exhaust remedies that would otherwise be available under Article 35 § 1 of the Convention.

151. In the light of the above the Court finds that the applicants were not obliged to pursue the civil remedies suggested by the Government in order to exhaust domestic remedies, and the preliminary objection is in this respect unfounded.

152. As regards criminal law remedies, the Court observes that a criminal investigation was instituted into the attack on the refugee convoy, albeit only after a considerable delay—in May 2000, despite the

fact that the authorities were aware of it immediately after the incident. The complaints to the authorities made by other victims of the attack, the Committee of the Red Cross and Ms Burdynyuk, in November and December 2000, did not lead to an investigation. The Court further notes that, at least for several years after the incident, the applicants were not questioned about the event, were not granted victim status, had no access to the investigation file and were never informed of its progress. No charges were brought against any individuals.

153. The Court considers that this limb of the Government's preliminary objection raises issues concerning the effectiveness of the criminal investigation in uncovering the facts and responsibility for the attack of which the applicants complain. These issues are closely linked to those raised in the applicant's complaints under Articles 2, 3 and 13 of the Convention. Thus, it considers that these matters fall to be examined under the substantive provisions of the Convention invoked by the applicants. In view of the above, it is not necessary for the Court to decide whether there was indeed a practice of non-investigation of crimes committed by police or military officials, as claimed by the applicants.

Therefore, the Court, unanimously, rejected the Government's claim that the applicants had not satisfied the admissibility criterion of exhausting domestic remedies.

Both the applicant and the respondent State face evidential burdens in seeking to demonstrate that domestic remedies have or have not been exhausted. These were outlined by the Grand Chamber in *Cyprus v Turkey* 2001-IV (see below, p 64):

116. The Court further recalls that, in the area of the exhaustion of domestic remedies, there is a distribution of the burden of proof. In the context of the instant case, it is incumbent on the respondent Government claiming non-exhaustion to satisfy the Court that the remedy was an effective one available in theory and in practice at the relevant time, that is to say, that it was accessible, was one which was capable of providing redress in respect of the aggrieved individuals' complaints and offered reasonable prospects of success. However, once this burden of proof has been satisfied it falls to the applicant Government to establish that the remedy advanced by the respondent Government was in fact exhausted or was for some reason inadequate and ineffective in the particular circumstances of the case, or that there existed special circumstances absolving the persons concerned from the requirement of exhausting that remedy. One such reason may be constituted by the national authorities remaining totally passive in the face of serious allegations of misconduct or infliction of harm by State agents, for example where they have failed to undertake investigations or offer assistance. In such circumstances it can be said that the burden of proof shifts once again, so that it becomes incumbent on the respondent Government to show what the authorities have done in response to the scale and seriousness of the matters complained of (see, *mutatis mutandis*, the above-mentioned *Akdivar and Others* judgment, p 1211, § 68).

This admissibility criterion emphasises the subsidiary nature of the Strasbourg system for enforcing Convention rights/freedoms. Member States have the primary responsibility for safeguarding those rights/freedoms within their own domestic legal systems and only where there has been a failure at the national level will the Strasbourg system become a final method of protection. States benefit by being given the opportunity to resolve alleged violations within their domestic institutions (prospective applicants must exhaust domestic remedies to the highest effective level possible within the relevant national legal system: e.g. in *Mogos and Krifka v Germany* (No 78084/01), decision of 27 March 2003, the applicants had not appealed to the German Federal Constitutional Court therefore the European Court determined their application inadmissible for failure to exhaust domestic remedies) and the Court is accorded a degree of shielding from applications which have not been properly pursued at the domestic level.

The Court has held that inter-State applicants are not bound to exhaust domestic remedies, in the respondent State, where the applicant State is alleging 'a practice' of widespread linked breaches of Convention rights/freedoms.

A practice incompatible with the Convention consists of an accumulation of identical or analogous breaches which are sufficiently numerous and inter-connected to amount not merely to isolated incidents or exceptions but to a pattern or system; a practice does not of itself constitute a violation separate from such breaches. It is inconceivable that the higher authorities of a State should be, or at least should be entitled to be, unaware of the existence of such a practice. Furthermore, under the Convention those authorities are strictly liable for the conduct of their subordinates; they are under a duty to impose their will on subordinates and cannot shelter behind their inability to ensure that it is respected.

The concept of practice is of particular importance for the operation of the rule of exhaustion of domestic remedies. This rules, as embodied in Article 26 of the Convention, applies to State applications (Article 24), in the same way as it does to 'individual' applications (Article 25), when the applicant State does no more than denounce a violation or violations allegedly suffered by 'individuals' whose place, as it were, is taken by the State. On the other hand and in principle, the rule does not apply where the applicant State complains of a practice as such, with the aim of preventing its continuation or recurrence, but does not ask the Commission or the Court to give a decision on each of the cases put forward as proof or illustrations of that practice. [(para 159) *Ireland v UK* A.25 (1978) and see below, p 145.]

In *Akdivar v Turkey* 1996-IV–1193 (1996) 1 BHRC 137 (see below, p 553), the Court also implied that the rule was inapplicable where individual applicants were able to establish the existence of an administrative practice incompatible with the Convention and 'of such a nature as to make [domestic] proceedings futile or ineffective'. (para 67) However, in that case the Court was not able to reach a conclusion regarding the applicants' allegation that there was an administrative practice involving the security forces burning homes in South East Turkey.

Later, in *Cyprus v Turkey* the Grand Chamber held that:

99. . . . The Court recalls in this latter respect that the exhaustion rule is inapplicable where an administrative practice, namely a repetition of acts incompatible with the Convention and official tolerance by the State authorities, has been shown to exist and is of such a nature as to make proceedings futile or ineffective (see, *mutatis mutandis*, the *Akdivar and Others v Turkey* judgment of 16 September 1996, *Reports* 1996-IV, p 1210, §§ 66–7).

More controversially, a majority of the Grand Chamber (ten votes to seven) ruled that remedies available in the 'Turkish Republic of Northern Cyprus' [the Turkish occupied area, which is not recognised by the international community as a State] could be classified as 'domestic remedies' of Turkey under Article 35. As to whether such remedies were to be considered effective that would depend upon the individual circumstances in which it was claimed that they had been available and were not used.

The second criterion within Article 35(1) is that applicants must lodge their applications with the Registry of the Court within six months from the date of the final decision by the highest national authority (usually the constitutional/supreme court) to have considered their complaints. What is necessary to satisfy this criterion was explained by the Court in *Allan v United Kingdom* (No 48539/99), decision of 28 August 2001.

The running of the six month time-limit imposed by Article 35(1) is, as a general rule, interrupted by the first letter from the applicant indicating an intention to lodge an application and giving some indication of the nature of the complaints made. As regards complaints not included in the initial application, the running of the six month time-limit is not interrupted until the date when the complaints are first submitted to the Court.

The Court ruled that the applicant's solicitors had not informed the Court of his complaint regarding an alleged violation of the right to silence until twenty months after the Court of Appeal had dismissed his appeal. Therefore, that complaint was made outside the six months' time limit. The former Commission noted that the justification for this time limit was '... the wish of the High Contracting Parties [Member States] to prevent their past judgments being constantly called into question' (*De Becker v Belgium* Yearbook of the European Convention on Human Rights 1958–9, p 244). The Court has, generally, taken a strict approach to this requirement. Hence, in *Walker v United Kingdom* (No 34979/97), decision of 25 January 2000, the Court ruled that it could apply this criterion of its own motion, even where the respondent Government had not raised it as a preliminary objection:

... it was recalled that this rule, in reflecting the wish of the Contracting Parties to prevent past decisions being called into question after an indefinite lapse of time, serves the interests not only of the respondent Government but also of legal certainty itself. It marks out the temporal limits of supervision carried out by the organs of the Convention and signals to both individuals and State authorities the period beyond which supervision is no longer possible.

Consequently, as the applicant had not applied to the Court within six months of the High Court's determination of his claim for judicial review (the highest domestic remedy available to him) his application was declared inadmissible. However, where there is a continuing violation of Convention rights this criterion does not apply. So, for example, in *Cyprus v Turkey* the Grand Chamber (sixteen votes to one) found a continuing violation of Turkey's procedural obligation under Article 2 to conduct an effective investigation into the fate of the many hundreds of missing Greek-Cypriots who disappeared in life threatening circumstances during the military occupation of 1974.

Individual applicants also have to satisfy six further criteria of admissibility specified under Article 35(2) and (3). (1) They must not be anonymous, though applicants can request the Court not to disclose their identity in public documentation (as is quite common in complaints invoking Article 8 rights, such as respect for private life: e.g. *K.A. and A.D. v Belgium*, 17 February 2005, below p 497). (2) Applications must not be 'substantially the same as a matter' that has already been examined by the Court. This criterion is designed to prevent an applicant making a second application on essentially the same grounds as a previous application. An example of an application being declared inadmissible on the basis of this criterion was *X v United Kingdom* 25 DR 147 (1981), where the same applicant had raised a similar complaint in an earlier application (*X v United Kingdom* 8 DR 212 (1976)). (3) Applications which have 'already been submitted to another procedure of international investigation or settlement and contain no relevant new information' are also inadmissible. Although the passage of time has witnessed the emergence of a few international procedures, such as the United Nations Human Rights Committee, these rarely offer a more advantageous form of redress for individuals complaining of serious human rights violations than the Convention. Furthermore, the Court has tended to be reluctant to find this condition satisfied in those rare applications where an applicant has previously invoked another international mechanism. For example, in *Smirnova v Russia* (No 46133/99) Decision of 3 October 2002, the respondent Government raised the preliminary objection that the first applicant's complaints to the Court should be declared inadmissible as the UN Human Rights Committee was also examining her alleged unlawful arrest. The Court rejected this objection as the applicant's complaints to the Court raised wider factual issues (including being forced to surrender her identity document to the district court) than her complaint to the UN. (4) Applications must not be 'incompatible with the provisions of the Convention'. This criterion includes applications which are determined to be inadmissible *ratione loci* (i.e. the alleged violations took place at a location outside the jurisdiction of the respondent State) by the Court. For example, in *Yonghong v Portugal* (No 50887/99) decision of 25 November 1999, the Macao Supreme

Court had ordered the applicant's extradition to China. From June 1999 the Macao courts had exclusive jurisdiction in the territory and Portuguese administration of the territory was to end in December 1999. Portugal had never made a declaration, under Article 56, extending the Convention to Macao. Therefore, the Court held that the application was inadmissible *ratione loci*. Applications which relate to events that took place before the respondent State had become bound by the Convention are determined to be inadmissible *ratione temporis*. In *Kozak v Ukraine* (No 21291/02) decision of 17 December 2002, the applicant complained about the withdrawal of her title to land in the 1980s. The Court declared her application inadmissible *ratione temporis* as the events had occurred over a decade before the Convention entered into force in regard to Ukraine. Where an applicant seeks to assert a right that is not enshrined within the Convention (or any Protocols binding upon the respondent State) the application will be determined to be inadmissible *ratione materiae*. For example, in *Frette v France* (No 36515/97) decision of June 2001, the applicant alleged, *inter alia*, a breach of Article 12 in conjunction with Article 14 in regard to the authorities refusal of leave for him to adopt a child. The Court determined that element of his complain was inadmissible *ratione materiae* as neither Article guaranteed a right to adopt. However, his complaint under Articles 8 and 14 was declared admissible, but he subsequently lost on the merits see below p 823. **(5)** Applications which are 'manifestly ill-founded' are inadmissible. This criterion is concerned with the extent of the evidence applicants have to back up their applications. In *Gongadze v Ukraine* (No 34056/02) decision of 22 March 2005, the applicant contended that the respondent State was responsible for the murder of her husband (a journalist). The respondent denied any involvement. The unanimous Chamber stated that:

The Court considers, in the light of the parties' submissions, that the complaint raises serious issues of fact and law under the Convention, the determination of which requires an examination of the merits. The Court concludes therefore that this complaint is not manifestly ill-founded within the meaning of Article 35 § 3 of the Convention.

So, applicants who cannot satisfy the Court to this standard will have their applications declared manifestly ill-founded. **(6)** Finally, applications which the Court considers to be 'an abuse of the right of application' will be declared inadmissible. This criterion covers applicants who make defamatory/abusive comments about members of the Court and its Registry. A dramatic example occurred in *Duringer and others v France* (No 61164/00) decision of 4 February 2003:

The applications of Messrs Duringer and 'Forest Grunge' were held inadmissible: those applicants had sent numerous communications containing serious accusations against judges of the Court and officials of the Registry and statements without any foundation which were extremely insulting and wild and repeatedly reiterated, and did not fall within the ambit of Article 34 of the Convention. The intolerable conduct of Mr Gérard Duringer and, assuming that he existed, 'Forest Grunge' was contrary to the aim of the right of individual application as provided for by Articles 34 and 35 of the Convention. It was an abuse of the right of application within the meaning of Article 35(3).

If an applicant submits false documentation to the Court that will also result in the application being declared inadmissible as an abuse of the right of application. For example, in *Jian v Romania* (No 46640/99) decision of 30 March 2004:

The Court noted that the applicant had, firstly, obscured part of a document in order to conceal the fact that he had decided not to lodge a criminal complaint and had foregone an expert medical report and, secondly, submitted a forged medical certificate in support of his allegations of ill-treatment. The Court stressed that the applicant had thus deliberately sought to mislead it by presenting a distorted view of the most serious part of his application. This was a flagrant and aggravated abuse of the right of application.

Therefore, his application was declared inadmissible.

The overwhelming majority of individual applications fail to satisfy all of the above admissibility criteria. In 2005 the Court determined that 26,852 applications were inadmissible whilst 1,000 were found to be admissible. Each individual applications is allocated to a Section of the Court and the President of that Section will appoint one of the member judges as the rapporteur for the application. After an examination of the application, the rapporteur will decide whether the application should be submitted to a Committee (of three judges) or a Chamber (of seven judges) to determine the admissibility of the application. Where it appears to the judge rapporteur that the application is inadmissible the application will be referred to a Committee. If the Committee, unanimously, determines that the application is inadmissible the application is rejected. If the Committee do not unanimously agree to reject the application it is referred to a Chamber. The Chamber will then determine the admissibility of the application, by a majority vote. In very rare cases (involving, *inter alia*, a serious question regarding the interpretation of the Convention) a Chamber may, provided neither the applicant or the respondent State objects, refer the application to Grand Chamber for it to determine (relinquishment under Article 30). The determination of admissibility by a Chamber is normally a written procedure, but the Chamber may decided to hold a public hearing to help resolve difficult issues. Where such a hearing is held the parties will normally be required to also address the merits of the case. Chambers may give separate decisions for the admissibility and merits of a case which is determined to be admissible or produce a combined decision.

(II) INTERIM MEASURES

The Court, following the practice of the former Commission, has adopted a rule empowering it to indicate interim measures (i.e. actions which should/should not be taken by a party to the proceedings whilst the latter are continuing). A large majority, fourteen votes to three, of a Grand Chamber espoused a radical new approach to the legal status of such measures in *Mamatkulov and Askarov v Turkey*, judgment of 4 February 2005. The applicants were Uzbek nationals who had been arrested in Turkey. The police detained Mamatkulov as he arrived at Istanbul airport under an international police warrant on suspicion of causing injuries by exploding a bomb in Uzbekistan and an attempted terrorist attack on the President of that State. Uzbekistan sought his extradition under a bi-lateral treaty. Two days after his arrest Mamatkulov was brought before a judge who remanded him in custody. A week later, on the 11 March 1999, Mamatkulov, accompanied by his lawyer, was again interviewed by the judge who ordered his extradition under an expedited procedure. On the same day Mamatkulov lodged an application against Turkey with the Court. On the 15 March, Marmatkulov appealed to the Bakirkoy Assize Court against the extradition order, but the Assize Court dismissed his appeal on the 19 March. Askarov entered Turkey, on a false passport, in December 1998. He was arrested by the police on the 5 March 1999 following an extradition request from Uzbekistan, where he was suspected of homicide, causing injuries by a bomb and an attempted terrorist attack on the President. Two days later a judge remanded Askarov in custody. On the 15 March after a hearing the Fatih Criminal Court made an order for the detention of Askarov pending his extradition. The Istanbul Assize Court dismissed his appeal on 26 March. Askarov lodged an application against Turkey with the Court on 22 March.

On the 18 March the President of the Chamber of the Court indicated to the Government of Turkey that it was desirable, in the interest of the parties and the smooth progress of the applications before the Court, that the applicants should not be extradited to Uzbekistan before the scheduled meeting of the Chamber (on the 23 March). The President acted under Rule 39 of the Rules of Court which provided that:

(1) The Chamber or, where appropriate, its President may, at the request of a party or of any other person concerned, or of its own motion, indicate to the parties any interim measure which it considers should be adopted in the interests of the parties or of the proper conduct of the proceedings before it.

(2) Notice of these measures shall be given to the Committee of Ministers.

(3) The Chamber may request information from the parties on any matter connected with the implementation of any interim measure it has indicated.

However, on the 19 March the Government of Turkey ordered the applicants' extradition. When the Chamber met it decided to extend the interim measures until further notice. The applicants were surrendered to the Uzbek authorities on the 27 March. The Turkish Government informed the Court, on 19 April, that it had received assurances from the Government of Uzbekistan (prior to the applicants' extradition) that they would not be tortured nor sentenced to capital punishment. During July 1999 the Turkish Government notified the Court that the Supreme Court of Uzbekistan had convicted the applicants of the offences for which they had been extradited. Mamatkulov had been sentenced to twenty years' imprisonment and Askarov to eleven years' imprisonment. The applicants' Turkish lawyers informed the Court, in September 1999, that they had not been able to communicate with the applicants, they had not had fair trials and conditions in Uzbek prisons were bad. During the following month officials from the Turkish embassy in Tashkent visited the applicants in prison and found them to be in good health and they did not complain about their conditions of detention. Whilst relatives of the applicants have been able to visit them during their imprisonment, the Turkish legal representatives of the applicants have been unable to contact them.

The Chamber of the Court determined (by six votes to one), *inter alia*, that the Turkish Government's extradition of the applicants contrary to the Court's indication of interim measures constituted a breach of Article 34 of the Convention. The relevant part of that Article states, '... the High Contracting Parties undertake not to hinder in any way the effective exercise of this right'. (judgment of 6 February 2003).

110. ... any State Party to the Convention to which interim measures have been indicated in order to avoid irreparable harm being caused to the victim of an alleged violation must comply with those measures and refrain from any act or omission that will undermine the authority and effectiveness of the final judgment.

111. Consequently, by failing to comply with the interim measures indicated by the Court under Rule 39 of the Rules of Court, Turkey is in breach of its obligations under Article 34 of the Convention.

Subsequently, the Turkish Government applied for the case to be referred to the Grand Chamber of the Court. The request was granted and the President of the Court granted leave for the International Commission of Jurists, Human Rights Watch and the AIRE Centre to submit written observations.

Before the Grand Chamber the applicants' lawyers claimed, *inter alia*, that the Turkish Government's extradition of their clients despite the Court's indication of interim measures constituted a breach of Article 34. This was because once the applicants had been extradited the lawyers were unable to communicate with them. Therefore, the lawyers had been denied the opportunity to obtain further evidence to support their assertions of breaches of the applicants' substantive Convention rights by the Turkish authorities (including a violation of

Article 3 by extraditing them to a State where they faced a real risk of ill-treatment contrary to that provision). Consequently, the extradition of the applicants had created an obstacle to the effective presentation of their application to the Court. In response, the Turkish Government argued that under the Convention Member States were not legally obliged to comply with indications of interim measures. This view was supported by the judgment of the original Court in *Cruz Varas v Sweden* A.201 (1991). Furthermore, international courts were governed by the treaties that established them and if a particular treaty did not empower a court to issue binding interim measures then relevant States were not legally bound to obey indications of such measures. The International Commission of Jurists contended that having regard to the general principles of international law, the law of treaties and international case-law interim measures indicated by the Court were legally binding upon Member States.

The Grand Chamber considered that previous jurisprudence, including *Kurt v Turkey* 1998-III 1192, established that Article 34 not only prevents States from applying pressure on applicants but also from doing any act which prevents the Court from considering the application. Regarding the indication of interim measures the Court follows the practice of the former Commission and does so only in restricted circumstances. The Court receives a number of requests for interim measures but will only issue them where there is '104. . . . an imminent risk of irreparable damage'. Requests are usually linked to applications concerning Article 2 and Article 3. Occasionally, other rights are invoked including Article 8. Where the Court has indicated interim measures the cases have mainly involved extradition or deportation proceedings. Interim measures have primarily been directed at governments but they can also be indicated to applicants (e.g. in *Ilascu and Others v Moldova and Russia*, judgment of 8 July 2004, where the President 'urged' one of the applicant/detainees to end his hunger strike; the applicant complied on the same day). It has been very rare for States to disregard interim measures indicated to them. From the late 1950s the former Commission began the practice of requesting States to stay extradition or deportation proceedings where their implementation would undermine pending applications. Then in 1974 the Commission adopted Rule 36 of its Rules of Procedure which provided that:

The Commission, or when it is not in session, the President may indicate to the parties any interim measure the adoption of which seems desirable in the interest of the parties or the proper conduct of the proceedings before it.

Nine years later the original Court issued a similar Rule:

36(1) Before the constitution of a Chamber, the President of the Court may, at the request of a Party, of the Commission, of the applicant or of any other person concerned, or *proprio motu*, indicate to any Party and, where appropriate, the applicant, any interim measure which it is advisable for them to adopt. The Chamber when constituted or, if the Chamber is not in session, its President shall have the same power.

The Grand Chamber noted that the original Court had held, in *Cruz Varas*, that the indication of interim measures by the Convention organs were not legally binding on parties. However, the Grand Chamber considered that judgment should be examined in the light of subsequent pronouncements on interim measures by other international bodies. These included the jurisprudence of the Human Rights Committee of the United Nations that a State's failure to comply with interim measures was a breach of its legal obligations under the International Covenant on Civil and Political Rights and the Optional Protocol. The Inter-American Court of Human Rights' rulings that States had to refrain from conduct that may irreversibly violate the rights of alleged victims. Also, the judgment of the International Court of Justice that its indications of provisional measures were legally binding (*LaGrand (Germany v United States of America)*, judgment of 27 June 2001). The Grand Chamber then sought to place *Cruz Varas* in the context of the historical institutional arrangements at Strasbourg:

118. ... The Court thus confined itself to examining the Commission's power to order interim measures, not its own. ...

119. The Court emphasises in that connection that, unlike the Court and the Committee of Ministers, the Commission had no power to issue a binding decision that a Contracting State had violated the Convention. The Commission's task with regard to the merits was of a preliminary nature and its opinion on whether or not there had been a violation of the Convention was not binding.

Regarding the decision of a Chamber of the full-time Court in *Conka and Others v Belgium* ((dec.) No 51564/99 of 13 March 2001), where the respondent Government expelled the Slovakian applicants contrary to the Court's indication of interim measures, the Grand Chamber observed that the Chamber had expressed the view that the Government's conduct was 'difficult to reconcile with good faith co-operation with the Court'. After repeating the orthodox principles that the Court should not, without good reason, depart from its own precedents and that the Convention is a living instrument which must be interpreted in the light of contemporary circumstances the Grand Chamber held that:

123. In this context, the Court notes that in the light of the general principles of international law, the law of treaties and international case-law, the interpretation of the scope of interim measures cannot be dissociated from the proceedings to which they relate or the decision on the merits they seek to protect. The Court reiterates in that connection that Article 31 § 1 of the Vienna Convention on the Law of Treaties provides that treaties must be interpreted in good faith in the light of their object and purpose ... and also in accordance with the principle of effectiveness.

124. The Court observes that the International Court of Justice, the Inter-American Court of Human Rights, the Human Rights Committee and the Committee against Torture of the United Nations, although operating under different treaty provisions to those of the Court, have confirmed in their reasoning in recent decisions that the preservation of the asserted rights of the parties in the face of the risk of irreparable damage represents an essential objective of interim measures in international law. Indeed it can be said that, whatever the legal system in question, the proper administration of justice requires that no irreparable action be taken while proceedings are pending ...

It has previously stressed the importance of having remedies with suspensive effect when ruling on the obligations of the State with regard to the right to an effective remedy in deportation or extradition proceedings. The notion of an effective remedy under Article 13 requires a remedy capable of preventing the execution of measures that are contrary to the Convention and whose effects are potentially irreversible. Consequently, it is inconsistent with Article 13 for such measures to be executed before the national authorities have examined whether they are compatible with the Convention (*Čonka v Belgium*, No 51564/99, § 79, ECHR 2002-I). It is hard to see why this principle of the effectiveness of remedies for the protection of an individual's human rights should not be an inherent Convention requirement in international proceedings before the Court, whereas it applies to proceedings in the domestic legal system.

125. Likewise, under the Convention system, interim measures, as they have consistently been applied in practice ... play a vital role in avoiding irreversible situations that would prevent the Court from properly examining the application and, where appropriate, securing to the applicant the practical and effective benefit of the Convention rights asserted. Accordingly, in these conditions a failure by a respondent State to comply with interim measures will undermine the effectiveness of the right of

individual application guaranteed by Article 34 and the State's formal undertaking in Article 1 to protect the rights and freedoms set forth in the Convention.

Indications of interim measures given by the Court, as in the present case, permit it not only to carry out an effective examination of the application but also to ensure that the protection afforded to the applicant by the Convention is effective; such indications also subsequently allow the Committee of Ministers to supervise execution of the final judgment. Such measures thus enable the State concerned to discharge its obligation to comply with the final judgment of the Court, which is legally binding by virtue of Article 46 of the Convention.

126. Consequently, the effects of the indication of an interim measure to a Contracting State—in this instance the respondent State—must be examined in the light of the obligations which are imposed on the Contracting States by Articles 1, 34 and 46 of the Convention.

127. The facts of the case, as set out above, clearly show that the Court was prevented by the applicants' extradition to Uzbekistan from conducting a proper examination of their complaints in accordance with its settled practice in similar cases and ultimately from protecting them, if need be, against potential violations of the Convention as alleged. As a result, the applicants were hindered in the effective exercise of their right of individual application guaranteed by Article 34 of the Convention, which the applicants' extradition rendered nugatory.

3. CONCLUSION

128. The Court reiterates that by virtue of Article 34 of the Convention Contracting States undertake to refrain from any act or omission that may hinder the effective exercise of an individual applicant's right of application. A failure by a Contracting State to comply with interim measures is to be regarded as preventing the Court from effectively examining the applicant's complaint and as hindering the effective exercise of his or her right and, accordingly, as a violation of Article 34 of the Convention.

129. Having regard to the material before it, the Court concludes that, by failing to comply with the interim measures indicated under Rule 39 of the Rules of Court, Turkey is in breach of its obligations under Article 34 of the Convention.

Judge Cabral Barreto issued a concurring opinion in which he expressed the view that the Grand Chamber's judgment represented a departure from *Cruz Varas*. Whilst he accepted that the actions of the Turkish authorities had in this case violated Article 34:

If I have correctly understood the reasoning of the majority, the mere fact that a Government have failed to comply with a request to take interim measures *per se* entails a violation of Article 34 of the Convention.

It is this 'mechanical' finding of a violation [of] Article 34 of the Convention which I am unable to agree with.

To my mind, the fact that States have always refused to accord binding force to interim measures prevents the Court from doing so and imposing on the States obligations which they have declined to accept.

He considered that there would only be a breach of Article 34 where a State's failure to comply with interim measures prevented the Court from undertaking an effective examination of the application.

Judges Caflisch, Turmen, and Klover issued a joint partly dissenting opinion in which they described the majority's judgment as being 'ambiguous'. The dissentients believed that the Court's stance regarding interim measures had been clearly elaborated in *Cruz Varas*. Furthermore, the full-time Court had affirmed that approach in *Conka*. Therefore, the dissentients considered that the majority's view that *Cruz Varas* merely related to the powers of the former European Commission of Human Rights regarding interim measures was 'not very persuasive' As to the International Court of Justice's ruling in *LaGrand* that could be distinguished as the International Court was interpreting its own constitutive treaty. However, the dissentients did not accept that there was a comparable Article of the Convention that provided for compulsory interim measures.

11. . . . To put it differently, there is a wide difference between the mere *interpretation* of a treaty and its *amendment*, between the exercise of judicial functions and international law-making.

12. What the Grand Chamber has done, and the Chamber before it, in their *Mamatkulov and Askarov* judgments is to exercise a *legislative function*, for the Convention as it stands nowhere prescribes that the States parties to it must recognise the binding force of provisional measures indicated by this Court. That is why, in our view, the Court cannot go down the path shown by the Hague Court and why there is no reason to depart from the existing case-law.

25. . . . To conclude that this Court is empowered, *de lege lata*, to issue binding provisional measures is *ultra vires*. Such a power may appear desirable; but it is up to the Contracting parties to supply it.

The judgment of the Grand Chamber in *Mamatkulov and Askarov* was a dramatic departure from the previous approach of the Court to the legal effects of indications of interim measures. Prior to this case both the original and full-time Court had not held such measures to be legally binding. The majority's use of Article 34 as the basis for turning interim measures into compulsory obligations was an ingenious route to circumvent the absence of an express power enshrined in the Convention. However, given the persistent refusal of States to add such a power (during the drafting of Protocol 11 both the Commission and the original Court had proposed that the power to order mandatory interim measures be included in the Convention), there is substance in the dissentients' opinion that the majority were legislating in defiance of the clear intention of Member States. Whilst the majority could assert that they were seeking to protect vulnerable applicants, it may be concluded that a very desirable procedural reform has been achieved by judicial creativity that extends beyond the permissible limits of Convention interpretation.

(III) EXAMINATION OF THE MERITS

Where an application has been declared admissible the Chamber (which will include the judge elected in respect of the respondent State: Article 27(2)) may invite the parties to submit additional evidence and written observations. A hearing may be held, but the Court has increasingly been seeking to determine applications purely on the basis of written submissions as a way of increasing its efficiency. In very exceptional cases, where complicated factual issues cannot be resolved on the basis of documentary evidence, the Court may appoint some of its members to undertake a fact-finding investigation (under Article 38(1)(a)) in the respondent State. For example, in *Ilascu and Others v Moldova and Russia*, judgment of 8 July 2004 (and see below p 61), the Grand Chamber appointed four of it members as delegates to visit 'Transdniestria' and discover the situation there. The delegates heard forty-three witnesses including the imprisoned applicants and members of the Russian Federation armed forces stationed in 'Transdniestria'.

Under Article 36(1) Member States (which are not the respondent State) have the right to submit written comments and take part in hearings where one of their nationals is an applicant. States do not often participate in individual applications brought by their nationals against other States (most likely for the same reasons that they do not bring inter-State cases). An example where a State asserted its right to submit third-party written comments was in *Demades v Turkey*, judgment of 31 July 2003 and see below, p 545). The President of the Chamber also has the power to invite/grant leave for any Member State (which is not a party to the proceedings) or any interested third-party to submit written comments and (exceptionally) take part in any hearings (Article 36(2)). Non-governmental organizations (such as human rights groups) seek permission to submit written briefs in some cases raising particularly important issues. For example, as we have seen above in *Mamatkulov and Askarov* the International Commission of Jurists, Human Rights Watch and the AIRE Centre were given permission to submit written comments on the legal significance of interim measures. Article 38(1)(a) provides that respondent States are required to 'furnish all necessary facilities' to enable the Court to undertake its examination of cases. Occasionally, the Court has been obliged to find a State in breach of this duty; e.g. in *Dizman v Turkey*, judgment of 20 September 2005, the Chamber found Turkey had violated this provision by repeatedly failing to respond to the Court's requests for documents and information concerning the applicant's complaints of serious ill-treatment by police officers.

A Chamber may, under Article 30, relinquish jurisdiction over a case to the Grand Chamber where it (a) raises a serious question affecting the interpretation of the Convention or (b) where resolution of the case might have a result inconsistent with a previous judgment. The Chamber cannot relinquish jurisdiction if one of the parties to the case objects. Relinquishment is not a common phenomenon. An example of a case where it did take place was *Vo v France*, judgment of 8 July 2004 and see below p 101, concerning the highly contentious issue of the scope of the right to life under Article 2 in respect of the unborn.

(IV) FRIENDLY SETTLEMENTS

Whilst the Chamber is examining the merits of a case the Registrar, on behalf of the Court, will see if a friendly settlement can be achieved by agreement between the parties (Article 38(1)(b)). These discussions are confidential (Article 38(2)). Friendly settlements can be of benefit to the parties as they resolve the dispute without the need for a formal judgment. Individual applicants may gain from a swifter and more comprehensive/generous settlement than would arise through a later judgment and States can benefit from avoiding the stigma of a later judgment which finds them to be in breach of the Convention. Friendly settlements also benefit the Court by reducing the number of cases which require a judgment (followed by a possible referral to the Grand Chamber). However, the Court must be satisfied that the proposed settlement between the parties meets the condition of 'respect for human rights' (Article 38(1)(b)). A rare example of the Court refusing to accept a proposed friendly settlement agreed between the parties occurred in *Ukrainian Media Group v Ukraine*, judgment of 29 March 2005. The applicant published a daily newspaper and had been ordered by the domestic courts to pay compensation to two politicians in respect of critical comments it had published about them. The applicant alleged that the Ukrainian courts had failed to apply Article 10 (especially the Strasbourg jurisprudence on the difference between factual and value comments). A few days before the Court was due to hold a hearing on the merits of the case the parties submitted a friendly settlement proposal to the Court. After examining the proposal the Court rejected it.

36. ... the Court took note of the of the serious nature of the complaints made in the case regarding the alleged interference with the applicant's freedom of expression. Because of this, the Court did not find it appropriate to strike the application out of the list of its cases. It considers that there are special

circumstances regarding respect for human rights as defined in the Convention and its Protocols which require the further examination of the application on its merits (Articles 37(1) *in fine* and 38(1)(b) of the Convention).

As the Court, unanimously, went on to find that '69. … the standards applied by the Ukrainian courts in the present case were not compatible with the principles embodied in Article 10 …', we can presume that the Court wished to make clear in a binding judgment how domestic law failed to safeguard the essential freedom of political expression. Where a friendly settlement is agreed by the parties and approved by the Court, the latter will strike the case out and provide a brief statement of the facts and the agreement reached (Article 39). A significant minority of admitted cases are resolved by this mechanism; e.g. in 2005 the Court endorsed thirty-seven friendly settlements.

A dramatic example of a friendly settlement in the context of a rare inter-state case occurred in *Denmark v Turkey* (application No 34382/97: judgment of 5 April 2000). Denmark had complained that one of its citizens had been subject to ill-treatment, violating Article 3, whilst detained by the authorities in the latter State during 1996. The Court declared the, rare, inter-State application admissible in June 1999. Subsequently, the parties engaged in consultations and proposed an agreed friendly settlement which provided:

1. In order to settle the first part of the application, the respondent Government has agreed to pay to the applicant Government an amount *ex gratia* of DKK 450,000 which includes legal expenses connected with the case.

2. The applicant Government notes with satisfaction the enclosed declaration of the respondent Government, which constitutes an integral part of the friendly settlement.

3. In the light of the first part of the case, the applicant Government appreciates the acknowledgement and regret expressed by the respondent Government concerning occasional and individual cases of torture and ill-treatment in Turkey.

4. The applicant Government welcomes the steps taken by Turkey in order to combat ill-treatment and torture since the filing of the application on 7 January 1997.

5. The applicant Government and the respondent Government agree that the use of inappropriate police interrogation techniques constitutes a violation of Article 3 of the Convention and that such techniques shall be prevented in the future. The two Governments recognise that this aim can best be attained through training. To this end the applicant Government and the respondent Government recall that the Council of Europe has launched a comprehensive project the objective of which is a re-organisation of the content of the basic, in-service and management training of the police in the member countries. The applicant Government notes with satisfaction the voluntary participation of the respondent Government in this open-ended project. One element of the project is training in police investigation. The project is dependent on funding from Turkey and other members of the Council of Europe. The applicant Government will make a significant financial contribution to this Council of Europe project. Furthermore, the applicant Government will finance a bilateral project. This project— subject to agreement between the two parties—will be aimed at the training of Turkish police officers, in order to achieve further knowledge and practical skills in the field of human rights.

6. On the basis of the Action Plan for the Development of the Bilateral Relations Between Turkey and Denmark which was agreed by the Minister for Foreign Affairs of Denmark and the Minister of Foreign Affairs of Turkey in Copenhagen on 26 November 1999, the Government of Denmark and the Government of Turkey have decided to establish a continuous bilateral Danish–Turkish political dia- logue. This dialogue will also focus on human rights issues with a view to improving the human rights situation in concrete fields. The parties have agreed that individual cases, including cases concerning

allegations of torture or ill-treatment, as well as general issues—such as the issues mentioned in the declaration by the Government of Turkey—may be raised by either party within the framework of this dialogue.

DECLARATION BY THE GOVERNMENT OF TURKEY

The Turkish Government regrets the occurrence of occasional and individual cases of torture and ill-treatment despite the resolute action of the Government and existing legislation as well as administrative regulations. New legal and administrative control and punishment regulations have been adopted as a consequence of which such individual acts substantially decreased. Within the last year, Articles 243, 245 and 354 of the Turkish Penal Code (TPC) were amended to redefine and prevent torture and ill-treatment in accordance with international conventions and the penalty for such criminal acts were increased. The amendment of Article 354 stipulates the prosecution of doctors and other medical personnel charged with drafting false reports regarding cases of torture or ill-treatment. 'The Regulation on Apprehension, Custody and Interrogation', which came into force on 1 October 1998, brought procedures in line with the standards of the Convention for the Prevention of Torture and Inhuman or Degrading Treatment or Punishment and the European Convention for the Prevention of Torture (CPT). A circular of the Prime Ministry concerning increased respect for human rights, issued on 25 June 1999, introduced measures to ensure the effective implementation of the above-mentioned regulation by all relevant public authorities and enhanced control of implementation. The circular stipulates that Governors, District Governors, Public Prosecutors, Public Inspectors, other officials entitled for inspection, Commanders of Gendarmerie and Police Directors are authorised to implement random controls and inspections. The circular also stipulates that necessary measures will be rapidly taken to remedy the deficiencies found during these inspections and necessary procedures will be initiated for faulty officials. In addition, the Ministries of Justice and the Interior will submit once in every three months from 1 January 2000 on, written information to the Prime Ministry's Human Rights Co-ordinating High Committee on the results of reports prepared with regard to these controls and inspections. Finally, the Law on the Prosecution of Civil Servants and Other Officials, which was approved by Parliament on 2 December 1999 and entered into force, facilitates the initiation of investigations and prosecution of public officials. In this context, the request for permission to initiate an investigation by public prosecutors of civil servants for crimes alleged to have been committed in connection to their duties has to be concluded within 4–5 months, the period for appeal included. The new law clarified many issues concerning the trial of public officials, determined the bodies authorised to allow an investigation and stipulated the authorities entitled to carry out preliminary examinations and preparatory investigations. Allegations of torture and ill-treatment have been greatly reduced during the past two years as a result of the measures which have been taken by Turkish authorities. This progress has also been acknowledged since 1997 by the CPT, operating within the framework of the Convention for the Prevention of Torture, to which Turkey is a party. In order to ensure the continuation of these reforms, our Government will undertake further improvements in the field of human rights, especially concerning the occurrence of incidents of torture and ill-treatment. Turkey will continue co-operation with international organs and mechanisms as contained in international human rights instruments to which Turkey is a party—in particular the CPT. Turkey will also continue to inform such organs and mechanisms on developments with regard to the implementation of the legal and administrative measures in this field in accordance with their relevant rules and procedures.

The terms of the above agreement reveal how both parties benefited from a friendly settlement. Denmark obtained compensation on behalf of its national, whilst Turkey avoided a potential Court judgment finding it in breach of one of the most important Articles of the Convention. Furthermore, the Danish government will provide funding for the improved training of Turkish police officers. The highly political context of inter-State cases was also illustrated by the meeting between the two States' Foreign Ministers which preceded the agreed friendly settlement of the complaint.

A friendly settlement can also be agreed in regard to the extent of just satisfaction to be paid (and any other necessary remedial measures) following a judgment on the merits. In *Broniowski v Poland*, judgment (Friendly Settlement) of 28 September 2005 (see below, p 925 for an examination of the substantive judgment), the Grand Chamber established the approach to evaluating the acceptability of a friendly settlement agreement subsequent to the delivery of a 'pilot-judgment' by the Court. A pilot-judgment is one given in relation to an individual application which revealed systemic or structural problem in the legal order of the respondent State. The substantive judgment in *Broniowski* was the first occasion that the Court had so designated one of its judgments. Following the enactment of new legislation providing for enhanced levels of compensation for all Bug River claimants (approximately 80,000 persons), the Government and the applicant agreed a friendly settlement in which the Government declared it would, *inter alia*, take practical measures to make the compensation scheme effective and pay 54,000 euros compensation for pecuniary and non-pecuniary damage to the applicant. The Grand Chamber, unanimously, held that:

37. .... it is appropriate for the Court to have regard not only to the applicant's individual situation but also to measures aimed at resolving the underlying general defect in the Polish legal order identified in the principal judgment as the source of the violation found.

Taking account of both the general and individual measures undertaken by the Government in the friendly settlement the Grand Chamber concluded that the agreement was based on 'respect for human rights' and therefore the case should be struck out.

The Committee of Ministers formally underlined the importance of 'giving further consideration in all cases to the possibilities of concluding friendly settlements' in Resolution Res (2002) 59. The Committee noted that friendly settlements could help alleviate the workload of the Court and provide 'a rapid and satisfactory solution for the parties'.

(v) STRIKING OUT

The Court has power, under Article 37(1), to strike out an application at any time where (a) the applicant does not intend to pursue his/her application or (b) the matter has been resolved or (c) for any other reason the Court considers that it is no longer justified to continue the examination of the application. We have already considered above (*Karner*) how Article 37(1) has been applied where the applicant has died during the Strasbourg proceedings. Another contentious application of this provision has been where a respondent State makes a unilateral declaration in respect of the application (e.g. apologising and offering to pay a sum of money *ex gratia* to the applicant) and then asks the Court to strike the case out, whilst the applicant refuses to accept the unilateral offer (which is not a 'friendly settlement') and wishes the Court to continue examining the case. A Grand Chamber articulated the principles to be applied to such a situation in *Tahsin Acar v Turkey*, judgment (Preliminary Issue) of 6 May 2003. The applicant made an application to the Commission alleging that his brother had forcibly disappeared at the hands of State agents. The Commission declare the application admissible and it was transferred to the Court when the former body was dissolved. The parties were not able to agree a friendly settlement. The Government then requested the Court to strike the case out on the basis of the following unilateral declaration:

I declare that the Government of the Republic of Turkey offer to pay *ex gratia* to the applicant, Mr Tahsin Acar, the amount of 70,000 pounds sterling [in respect of] the application registered under No 26307/95.

This sum, which covers any pecuniary and non-pecuniary damage as well as costs, shall be paid in pounds sterling, free of any taxes that may be applicable and to an account named by the applicant.

The sum shall be payable within three months from the date of delivery of the judgment by the Court ... This payment will constitute the final resolution of the case.

The Government regret the occurrence of the actions which have led to the bringing of the present application, in particular the disappearance of the applicant's brother Mr Mehmet Salim Acar and the anguish caused to his family.

It is accepted that unrecorded deprivations of liberty and insufficient investigations into allegations of disappearance constitute violations of Articles 2, 5 and 13 of the Convention. The Government undertake to issue appropriate instructions and adopt all necessary measures with a view to ensuring that all deprivations of liberty are fully and accurately recorded by the authorities and that effective investigations into alleged disappearances are carried out in accordance with their obligations under the Convention.

The Government consider that the supervision by the Committee of Ministers of the execution of Court judgments concerning Turkey in this and similar cases is an appropriate mechanism for ensuring that improvements will be made in this context. To this end, necessary cooperation in this process will continue to take place. ...

The applicant objected to the Government's request. Subsequently, the Chamber, by six votes to one, decided to strike the application out, under Article 37(1)(c):

64. The Court has examined carefully the terms of the respondent Government's declaration. Having regard to the nature of the admissions contained in the declaration as well as the scope and extent of the various undertakings referred to therein, together with the amount of compensation proposed, the Court considers that it is no longer justified to continue the examination of the application. [judgment of 9 April 2002]

The applicant applied to the Grand Chamber, under Article 43, for the case not to be struck out on the basis that there were substantial grounds for holding that "respect for human rights" required the Court to continue examining the merits of the case. The Grand Chamber, subject to the dissent of the Turkish *ad hoc* Judge, held that:

74. The Court observes at the outset that a distinction must be drawn between, on the one hand, declarations made in the context of strictly confidential friendly-settlement proceedings and, on the other, unilateral declarations—such as the one at issue—made by a respondent Government in public and adversarial proceedings before the Court. In accordance with Article 38 § 2 of the Convention and Rule 62 § 2 of the Rules of Court, the Court will proceed on the basis of the Government's unilateral declaration and the parties' observations submitted outside the framework of friendly-settlement negotiations, and will disregard the parties' statements made in the context of exploring the possibilities for a friendly settlement of the case and the reasons why the parties were unable to agree on the terms of a friendly settlement.

75. The Court considers that, under certain circumstances, it may be appropriate to strike out an application under Article 37 § 1 (c) of the Convention on the basis of a unilateral declaration by the respondent Government even if the applicant wishes the examination of the case to be continued. It will, however, depend on the particular circumstances whether the unilateral declaration offers a sufficient basis for finding that respect for human rights as defined in the Convention does not require the Court to continue its examination of the case (Article 37 § 1 *in fine*).

76. Relevant factors in this respect include the nature of the complaints made, whether the issues raised are comparable to issues already determined by the Court in previous cases, the nature and scope of any measures taken by the respondent Government in the context of the execution of judgments delivered by the Court in any such previous cases, and the impact of these measures on the case at issue. It may also be material whether the facts are in dispute between the parties, and, if so, to what extent, and what prima facie evidentiary value is to be attributed to the parties' submissions on the

facts. In that connection it will be of significance whether the Court itself has already taken evidence in the case for the purposes of establishing disputed facts. Other relevant factors may include the question of whether in their unilateral declaration the respondent Government have made any admission(s) in relation to the alleged violations of the Convention and, if so, the scope of such admissions and the manner in which they intend to provide redress to the applicant. As to the last-mentioned point, in cases in which it is possible to eliminate the effects of an alleged violation (as, for example, in some property cases) and the respondent Government declare their readiness to do so, the intended redress is more likely to be regarded as appropriate for the purposes of striking out the application, the Court, as always, retaining its power to restore the application to its list as provided in Article 37 § 2 of the Convention and Rule 44 § 5 of the Rules of Court.

77. The foregoing list is not intended to be exhaustive. Depending on the particulars of each case, it is conceivable that further considerations may come into play in the assessment of a unilateral declaration for the purposes of Article 37 § 1 (c) of the Convention.

78. As to whether it would be appropriate to strike out the present application on the basis of the unilateral declaration made by the Government, the Court notes in the first place that the facts are to a large extent in dispute between the parties. The applicant claimed that his brother had been abducted in 1994 by, or at least with the connivance of, State agents, that he had subsequently been detained at the hands of the State, and that no effective domestic investigation had been conducted into those claims or into the alleged sighting of his brother on television in 2000 by relatives. According to the Government, the abduction and disappearance of the applicant's brother—including the allegations made by relatives against two gendarmes and a village guard, and the subsequent alleged sighting of the applicant's brother on television—did indeed form the subject of effective and ongoing investigations by the competent authorities, albeit without any tangible results to date.

79. Secondly, although the Government on the one hand agreed to state, in their unilateral declaration, that unrecorded deprivations of liberty and insufficient investigations into allegations of disappearance, 'such as in the present case', constituted violations of Articles 2, 5 and 13 of the Convention, on the other hand they subsequently made firm submissions to the effect that their unilateral declaration could in no way be interpreted as entailing any admission of responsibility or liability for any violation of the Convention alleged by the present applicant, who made complaints under Articles 2, 3, 5, 6, 8, 13, 14, 18, 34 and 38 of the Convention. The Government thereby negated the admission of liability contained in their declaration.

80. Thirdly, the Court considers that *Akman* [v *Turkey* 2001-VI] and the unilateral declaration made in that case differ from the present case and the present unilateral declaration in a number of crucial respects.

81. To begin with, it was not disputed between the parties in *Akman* that the applicant's son had been killed by Turkish security forces. The parties only disagreed as to whether the security forces had acted in legitimate self-defence or whether the killing had resulted from the excessive use of force by the security forces.

Furthermore, in their unilateral declaration—submitted shortly before the Court was about to take evidence itself—the Government admitted a violation of Article 2 of the Convention by conceding that the applicant's son had died as a result of the use of excessive force notwithstanding domestic legislation.

In addition, the Government undertook to issue appropriate instructions and to adopt all necessary measures to ensure that the right to life (guaranteed by Article 2)—including the obligation to carry out effective investigations—would be respected in the future and, in this connection, referred to new legal and administrative measures adopted recently, which they said had already resulted in a reduction of deaths in circumstances similar to that of the applicant's son. The Government further undertook to cooperate with the Committee of Ministers in its supervision of the execution of the Court's judgments in this and similar cases in order to ensure that improvements would be made in this context, and to provide the applicant redress in the form of a payment of 85,000 pounds sterling.

Finally, as the Court had already specified the nature and extent of the obligations arising under the Convention for the respondent State in cases of alleged unlawful killings by security forces in various other applications it had previously decided, it could be satisfied that respect for human rights as defined in the Convention did not warrant a continuation of the examination of the application.

82. In the opinion of the Court, an undisputed killing by security forces where the respondent Government have admitted that this was the result of the use of excessive force in violation of Article 2 of the Convention cannot be compared to the unresolved disappearance of a person after an abduction allegedly by, or with the alleged connivance of, State agents. In *Akman*, cited above, further investigation of the facts either by domestic authorities or by the Court was less pressing as the respondent State had already assumed liability for the killing under Article 2 of the Convention. Moreover, in connection with the execution—supervised by the Committee of Ministers—of previous judgments of the Court in several similar cases where the Court had found Turkey to be in breach of its obligations under the Convention, the Government had already adopted or undertaken to adopt specific measures designed to prevent in future the shortcomings identified by the Court.

83. In the present case, however, the unilateral declaration made by the Government does not adequately address the applicant's grievances under the Convention. No reference is made to any measures to deal with his specific complaints, the Government merely undertaking a general obligation to pursue their efforts to prevent future disappearances, without regard to what pertinent and practicable measures might be called for in this particular case.

84. The Court accepts that a full admission of liability in respect of an applicant's allegations under the Convention cannot be regarded as a condition *sine qua non* for the Court's being prepared to strike an application out on the basis of a unilateral declaration by a respondent Government. However, in cases concerning persons who have disappeared or have been killed by unknown perpetrators and where there is prima facie evidence in the case-file supporting allegations that the domestic investigation fell short of what is necessary under the Convention, a unilateral declaration should at the very least contain an admission to that effect, combined with an undertaking by the respondent Government to conduct, under the supervision of the Committee of Ministers in the context of the latter's duties under Article 46 § 2 of the Convention, an investigation that is in full compliance with the requirements of the Convention as defined by the Court in previous similar cases (see, for example, *Kurt v Turkey*, judgment of 25 May 1998, *Reports of Judgments and Decisions* 1998-III; *Çakıcı v Turkey* [GC], No 23657/94, ECHR 1999-IV; *Ertak v Turkey*, No 20764/92, ECHR 2000-V; *Timurtaş v Turkey*, No 23531/94, ECHR 2000-VI; and *Taş v Turkey*, No 24396/94, 14 November 2000).

85. As the unilateral declaration made by the Government in the present case contains neither any such admission nor any such undertaking, respect for human rights requires that the examination of the case be pursued pursuant to the final sentence of Article 37 § 1 of the Convention. Accordingly, the application cannot be struck out under sub-paragraph (c) of Article 37 § 1 of the Convention since the declaration offers an insufficient basis for holding that it is no longer justified to continue the examination of the application.

86. In conclusion, the Court rejects the Government's request to strike the application out under Article 37 § 1 (c) of the Convention and will accordingly pursue its examination of the merits of the case.

The above judgment indicated that the Grand Chamber took a robust attitude towards whether a respondent State's unilateral declaration was sufficient comprehensive to justify the Court striking out the case. In the subsequent judgment on the merits in *Tahsin Acar* [judgment of 8 April 2004], the Grand Chamber, unanimously, found a breach of the procedural (investigation) duties required by Article 2.

An example of the Court accepting a respondent State's unilateral declaration as a basis for striking out a case against the wishes of the applicant occurred in *Meriakri v Moldova*, judgment of 1 March 2005. The applicant alleged that whilst he was in prison the authorities opened his correspondence with his lawyer and the Court in breach of Article 8. After the failure of the parties to agree a friendly settlement, the Government informed the Court that to settle the case they had made the following declaration:

— the payment to the applicant of the equivalent (at the exchange rate then applying) of 890 euros (EUR) (14,000 Moldovan Lei (MDL)), as compensation for any non-pecuniary damage caused to him by the interference with his correspondence with the Court and with his lawyer. The Government mentioned in this connection that the minimum monthly salary in Moldova was MDL 100;

— an official apology to the applicant for the fact that his correspondence was interfered with by the prison authorities;

— the harmonisation of national law with the requirements of the Convention as regards the rights of convicted prisoners to confidentiality for their correspondence with the Court and with other legal bodies.

The Chamber, unanimously, determined that having regard to the scope of the Government's undertakings, the amount of compensation to be paid and the Court's established case law on prisoners' right to respect for their correspondence it was no longer justified to continue the examination of the case.

(VI) JUDGMENT

Where a friendly settlement has not been agreed and the case has not been either relinquished to the Grand Chamber or struck out then the Chamber will deliver its judgment. Chambers determine cases by a majority vote amongst the participating judges. Any judge of the Chamber can issue a separate opinion (concurring or dissenting). The judgment will state the facts as established by the Chamber. The evidential standard applied by the Court is that of 'beyond reasonable doubt'. The full-time Court expressly endorsed this standard in its Grand Chamber judgment in *Cyprus v Turkey* ECHR 2001-IV.

112. The Court also observes that in its assessment of the evidence in relation to the various complaints declared admissible, the Commission applied the standard of proof 'beyond reasonable doubt' as enunciated by the Court in its *Ireland v the United Kingdom* judgment of 18 January 1978 (Series A No 25), it being noted that such proof may follow from the coexistence of sufficiently strong, clear and concordant inferences or of similar unrebutted presumptions of fact (ibid, pp 64–5, § 161).

113. The Court, for its part, endorses the application of this standard, all the more so since it was first articulated in the context of a previous inter-State case and has, since the date of the adoption of the judgment in that case, become part of the Court's established case-law (for a recent example, see *Salman v Turkey* [GC], No 21986/93, § 100, ECHR 2000-VII).

Some applicants and human rights groups have criticised this standard as imposing too high an evidential standard, which enables States to escape findings of liability under the Convention. For example, in *Nachova and Others v Bulgaria* judgment of 6 July 2005, Interights and the applicant families challenged the use of this standard in discrimination cases involving Article 14. The Grand Chamber upheld the continued use of this standard, but explained how it differed from the domestic criminal law standard in paragraph 147 of its judgment (below, p 823).

The Chamber will then apply the law of the Convention (i.e. the established legal principles of its jurisprudence regarding the relevant Convention Articles) to the established facts. Where a Chamber finds a breach of the Convention and the applicant has applied for just satisfaction (under Article 41) the Chamber will determine whether to make an award (see Ch. 19).

In 2004, following a submission by the Court, the Committee of Ministers issued a Resolution, Res (2004)3, inviting the Court to identify:

... in its judgments finding a violation of the Convention, what it considers to be an underlying systemic problem and the source of this problem, in particular when it is likely to give rise to numerous applications, so as to assist States in finding the appropriate solution and the Committee of Ministers in supervising the execution of judgments.

For the first time in *Broniowski v Poland* ECHR 2004-V (see above, p 39), the Court designated a judgment as a 'pilot judgment'. This was because the case disclosed a systemic/structural problem in the respondent State's legal order that affected many other persons. At the time of the judgment 167 other applications concerning the Bug River claimants were pending before the Court. In the Grand Chamber's later just satisfaction judgment in *Broniowski* it stated that

35. The object in designating the principal judgment as a 'pilot judgment' was to facilitate the most speedy and effective resolution of a dysfunction affecting the protection of the right of property in the national—Polish—legal order. One of the relevant factors considered by the Court was the growing threat to the Convention system and to the Court's ability to handle its ever increasing caseload that resulted from large numbers of repetitive cases deriving from, among other things, the same structural or systemic problem. Indeed, the pilot-judgment procedure is primarily designed to assist the Contracting States in fulfilling their role in the Convention system by resolving such problems at national level, thereby securing to the persons concerned the Convention rights and freedoms as required by Article 1 of the Convention, offering to them more rapid redress and, at the same time, easing the burden on the Court which would otherwise have to take to judgment large numbers of applications similar in substance. It will be recalled that in the pilot judgment in Mr Broniowski's application the Court, after finding a violation, also adjourned its consideration of applications deriving from the same general cause 'pending the implementation of the relevant general measures' (ibid, § 198).

Hence, this exceptional judicial response highlights violations of Convention rights which affect many persons and consequently need swift resolution by the respondent State in order to both safeguard the individuals concerned and to prevent the Court being inundated with applications based on similar breaches.

In the later case of *Xenides-Arestis v Turkey*, judgment of 22 December 2005, a Chamber gave a pilot judgment concerning the denial of access, by Turkish authorities, to a Greek Cypriot person's home and property located in northern Cyprus. The Chamber, subject to the dissent of the Turkish national judge, found breaches of Article 8 and Article 1 of Protocol No 1. After noting that there were approximately 1,400 similar property cases against Turkey pending before the Court, the Chamber (unanimously) held that under Article 46:

40. The Court considers that the respondent State must introduce a remedy, which secures genuinely effective redress for the Convention violations identified in the instant judgment in relation to the present applicant as well as in respect of all similar applications pending before the Court, in accordance with the principles for the protection of the rights laid down in Articles 8 of the Convention and 1 of Protocol No. 1 and in line with its admissibility decision of 14 March 2005. Such a remedy should be available within three months from the date on which the present judgment will be delivered and the redress should occur three months thereafter.

. . . .

50. ... Pending the implementation of the relevant general measures, which should be adopted as provided for in paragraph 40 above, the Court will adjourn its consideration of all applications deriving from the same general couse.

Note, the earlier difficulties faced by the Committee of Ministers in securing Turkish implementation of the judgment in *Loizidou v Turkey* (below, p 47) concerning property located in northern Cyprus.

The application of the pilot judgment procedure was challenged before the Grand Chamber by the Government in *Hutten-Czapska v Poland*, judgment of 19 June 2006 (see below, p 953). The Government, *inter alia*, contended that the applicant's circumstances were not those of a typical landlord. The Grand Camber, by sixteen votes to one, upheld the Chamber's invocation of this procedure:

236. ... While the number of similar applications pending before the Court currently stands at eighteen—a figure which, in comparison with the *Broniowski* case, may seem insignificant—one of those cases has been lodged by an association of some 200 landlords asserting a breach of their individual rights. At any rate, the identification of a 'systemic situation' justifying the application of the pilot-judgment procedure does not necessarily have to be linked to, or based on, a given number of similar applications already pending. In the context of systemic or structural violations the potential inflow of future cases is also an important consideration in terms of preventing the accumulation of repetitive cases on the Court's docket, which hinders the effective processing of other cases giving rise to violations, sometimes serious, of the rights it is responsible for safeguarding.

So, in determining whether to designate a case as a pilot judgment, the Court will have regard to both the existing number of pending applications concerning the same structural problem and the potential for future applications regarding the problem.

In his partly dissenting opinion Judge Zagrebelsky expressed concerns about the 'weakness of the legal basis of the pilot-judgment procedure'. He disagreed with the approach of the majority as he believed the Court's approach interfered with the competence of the Committee of Ministers to supervise the execution of judgments.

(VII) REFERRAL TO THE GRAND CHAMBER

Within three months of a judgment being delivered by a Chamber any party to the case may (exceptionally) apply, under Article 43, to the Grand Chamber for the case to be re-heard by the Grand Chamber. This unusual possibility, of a single court providing a second judgment on the merits, was a political comprise that was necessary to secure all the Member State's approval of the Protocol 11 reforms. A screening panel (composed of the President of the Court, two Presidents of Sections [designated by rotation] and two Judges [elected by the remaining Sections]: Rule 24(5), Rules of Court, July 2006) will only accept the case for re-hearing if it raises: a serious question affecting the interpretation or application of the Convention, or a serious issue of general importance (Article 43(2)). The Grand Chamber has been strict in the application of these criteria, for example the first acceptance of a request did not take place until October 2000 in *K. and T. v Finland*, judgment of 12 July 2001 (and see below, p 535 on the substance of the applicants' complaints under Article 8). In that case the Grand Chamber set out its approach to the scope of its jurisdiction under Article 43.

140. The Court would first note that all three paragraphs of Article 43 use the term 'the case' ('l'affaire') for describing the matter which is being brought before the Grand Chamber. In particular, paragraph 3 of Article 43 provides that the Grand Chamber is to 'decide *the case*'—that is the whole case and not simply 'the serious question' or 'serious issue' mentioned in paragraph 2—'by means of a judgment'.

The wording of Article 43 makes it clear that, whilst the existence of 'a serious question affecting the interpretation or application of the Convention or the protocols thereto, or a serious issue of general importance' (paragraph 2) is a prerequisite for acceptance of a party's request, the consequence of acceptance is that the whole 'case' is referred to the Grand Chamber to be decided afresh by means of a new judgment (paragraph 3). The same term 'the case' ('l'affaire') is also used in Article 44(2) which defines the conditions under which the judgments of a Chamber become final. If a request by a party for referral under Article 43 has been accepted, Article 44 can only be understood as meaning that the entire judgment of the Chamber will be set aside in order to be replaced by the new judgment of the Grand Chamber envisaged by Article 43(3). This being so, the 'case' referred to the Grand Chamber necessarily embraces all aspects of the application previously examined by the Chamber in its judgment, and not only the serious 'question' or 'issue' at the basis of the referral. In sum, there is no basis for a merely partial referral of the case to the Grand Chamber.

141. The Court would add, for the sake of clarification, that the 'case' referred to the Grand Chamber is the application in so far as it has been declared admissible (see, *mutatis mutandis*, the *Ireland v UK* judgment (1978) A.25 para 157). This does not mean, however, that the Grand Chamber may not also examine, where appropriate, issues relating to the admissibility of the application in the same manner as this is possible in normal Chambers proceedings, for example by virtue of Article 35(4) *in fine* of the Convention (which empowers the Court to 'reject any application which it considers inadmissible ... at any stage of the proceedings') or where such issues have been joined to the merits or where they are otherwise relevant at the merits stage.

This means that the Grand Chamber will examine all the applicant's admissible complaints *de novo*. The Grand Chamber will allow 'new materials' (i.e. information not presented to the national courts or the Chamber) to be introduced by the parties before the Grand Chamber. Citing judgments of the original Court, including, *Cruz Varas and Others v Sweden* (1991) A.201, the Grand Chamber held that; '146. .... the Court is not prevented from taking into account any additional information and fresh arguments in determining the merits of the applicants' complaints under the Convention if it considers them relevant.' The Grand Chamber will normally hold a public hearing during the examination of the merits of the case.

A rare example of the Grand Chamber determining that an Article 43 case should be declared inadmissible occurred in *Azinas v Cyprus*, judgment of 28 April 2004. A large majority of the Grand Chamber, twelve votes to five, accepted the Government's submission that the applicant had not exhausted domestic remedies (by failing to raise the issue of the right to property before the Cypriot courts).

The saga of *Hatton and Others v United Kingdom* (below, p 547) illustrates the ability of the Grand Chamber to overrule an earlier judgment of a Chamber. The successes of States in cases such as *Hatton* and *Azinas* reveals why they were so keen to establish the Article 43 referral procedure.

(VIII) EXECUTION OF JUDGMENTS

Where a Chamber judgment is not subject to referral to the Grand Chamber (or the screening panel refuses to accept the referral) or the Grand Chamber delivers a judgment then the judgment becomes final (under Article 44). The respondent State is bound to abide by that judgment (Article 46(1)). The Committee of Ministers is responsible, under Article 46(2), for supervising the execution of all judgments. Rules have been adopted by the Committee of Ministers (the latest version, which anticipates the coming into effect of Protocol 14, was agreed in May 2006) governing the application of Article 46(2). The rules provide that supervision of the execution of judgments will normally take place during special human rights meetings with a public agenda. If the Chair of the Committee is held by a representative of a State which is subject to a judgment being supervised, under Article 46(2), the Chair must relinquish that position whilst the case is being discussed. Once a judgment (where the Court has found a breach of the Convention/Protocols) has been transmitted to the Committee of Ministers, the latter invites the respondent State to inform it: (a) whether any just satisfaction has been paid, (b) whether any 'individual' measures (i.e. those concerning the applicant) have been taken and (c) whether any 'general' measures (i.e. those concerning a wider group of persons) have been adopted. Until the respondent State has confirmed that the just satisfaction award has been paid or individual measures have been taken the case is maintained on the agenda of each relevant meeting of the Committee of Ministers. Where a respondent State informs the Committee of Ministers that it has not yet been able to take necessary general measures then the Committee will normally examine the case every six months. Communications from the applicant, regarding the payment of just satisfaction or individual measures, will be brought to the attention of the Committee of Ministers via the secretariat.

During the course of its supervision of the execution of a case the Committee of Ministers may issue interim resolutions. These have the purposes of: (a) providing information regarding the progress in execution of the judgment, (b) to express concern or (c) make suggestions. A dramatic example of an interim resolution falling into category (b) was Interim Resolution ResDH (2001)80, adopted on 26 June 2001, concerning the judgment in *Loizidou v Turkey* (see below, p 922):

... Having regard to the judgment of the European Court of Human Rights ('the Court' below) of 28 July 1998 which ordered Turkey to pay to the applicant before 28 October 1998 specific sums for damages and for costs and expenses;

Recalling its Interim Resolution DH (2000) 105, in which it declared that the refusal of Turkey to execute the judgment of the Court demonstrated a manifest disregard for Turkey's international obligations, both as a High Contracting Party to the Convention and as a Member State of the Council of Europe, and strongly insisted that, in view of the gravity of the matter, Turkey comply fully and without any further delay with this judgment;

Very deeply deploring the fact that, to date, Turkey has still not complied with its obligations under this judgment;

Stressing that every Member State of the Council of Europe must accept the principles of the rule of law and of the enjoyment by all persons within its jurisdiction of human rights and fundamental freedoms;

Stressing that acceptance of the Convention, including the compulsory jurisdiction of the Court and the binding nature of its judgments, has become a requirement for Membership of the Organisation;

Stressing that the Convention is a system for the collective enforcement of the rights protected therein,

Declares the Committee's resolve to ensure, with all means available to the Organisation, Turkey's compliance with its obligations under this judgment,

Calls upon the authorities of the Member States to take such action as they deem appropriate to this end.

Eventually, on 2 December 2003, the Chair of the Committee of Ministers announced that Turkey had executed the judgment by paying Mrs Loizidou 450,000 Cypriot Pounds as just satisfaction (for damages and costs/expenses). The Chair observed that this conclusion was the result of efforts by all Member States.

The Directorate General of Human Rights (of the Council of Europe) assists the Committee of Minister in the execution of judgments. This can be by advice to the Committee and/or by consideration of possible solutions with a respondent State. According to the Committee of Ministers, '[i]n practice, the Committee of Ministers very seldom needs to exert political and diplomatic pressure but functions as a forum for constructive dialogue, thus helping States find satisfactory solutions enabling them to execute the Court's judgments.' Clearly, supervising the execution of *Loizidou* fell into the exceptional category. Ultimately, a recalcitrant respondent State could face suspension or expulsion from the Council of Europe if it did not comply with its obligations under Article 46.

An example of an individual measure, taken as part of the execution of a judgment, was the granting of indefinite leave to remain in the UK (where he would continue to receive medical treatment/palliative care) to D in *D v United Kingdom* (below, p 205): see Res DH (98)10, adopted on 18 February 1998 by the Committee of Ministers. An illustration of a general measure was the enactment of the Interception of Communications Act 1985 (creating a statutory framework for the interception of postal and telephonic communications) in response to *Malone v United Kingdom* (below, p 561): Res DH (86)1. Once the Committee of Ministers has been satisfied that the respondent State has taken all necessary measures then it adopts a resolution (such as those in the preceding examples) stating that its functions under Article 46(2) have been exercised.

Philip Leach, a commentator with considerable experience of litigating at Strasbourg, has supported calls for the Committee of Ministers to involve civic groups, such as interested non-governmental organisations, and the Parliamentary Assembly of the Council of Europe, in the implementation of judgments. 'The Effectiveness of the Committee of Ministers in supervising the enforcement of judgments of the European Court of Human Rights' [2006] *Public Law* 443.

The Protocol 14 system

Within a few months of the full-time Court beginning to operate under the Protocol 11 system President Wildhaber started publicly expressing concern about the rising caseload facing the Court. In June 1999 he issued a press release noting:

... The volume of work is already daunting but is set to become more challenging still, especially as applications come in from countries which ratified the ECHR in the late 1990s.

One year later he called upon Member States to appoint a 'committee of wise persons' to consider further major reform of the Convention's enforcement system. The Committee of Ministers responded by establishing an Evaluation Group [Chaired by Mr Justin Harman (Ambassador of Ireland to the Council of Europe), President Wildhaber and Mr Hans-Christian Kruger (Deputy Secretary General of the Council of Europe)], in February 2001 to:

(a) examine matters concerning the observed and expected growth in the number of applications to the European Court of Human Rights and the Court's capacity to deal with this growth; and

(b) consider all potential means of guaranteeing the continued effectiveness of the Court with a view, if appropriate, to making proposals concerning the need for reform and report thereon to the Committee of Ministers.

The Group submitted its *Report of the Evaluation Group to the Committee of Ministers on the European Court of Human Rights* (EGCourt(2001)1) in September 2001. The Court was found to be facing an ever increasing growth of individual applications (in 1988 there were 1,013 applications registered, in 1999 there were 10,486 and 7,909 in the first seven months of

2001). This produced an expanding backlog of registered applications (from 12,635 in 1999 to 18,292 in July 2001). The Group considered that one significant reason for the growth in applications was the 'snowball' effect of media coverage given to leading judgments by the Court.

3.9. It is abundantly clear from the foregoing that immediate and urgent action is indispensable if the Court is to remain effective. If no steps are taken, the situation will simply deteriorate, with the Court having no prospect of 'catching-up' with its ever-increasing arrears of work. It will no longer be able to determine all cases within a reasonable time, its public image will suffer and it will gradually lose credibility. Moreover, constant seeking for greater 'productivity' obviously entails the risk that applications will not receive sufficient, or sufficient collective, consideration, to the detriment of the quality of judgments; on this account as well, the credibility and authority of the Court would suffer. Finally, it should be reMembered that the problem cannot be seen solely in terms of statistics; the figures quoted say nothing as to the ratio of 'more difficult' to 'less difficult' cases, even though it may be that this will remain constant.

The Report adopted three premises in respect of possible solutions to the workload crisis. First, that there should be no reduction in the substantive rights guaranteed by the Convention and its Protocols. Secondly, the right of individual application must be preserved in its essence. Thirdly, the Court must be able to dispose of applications within a reasonable time and maintain the quality of its judgments. The Report then identified five avenues of potential reforms and improvements to the current enforcement system. The first type of measures were those to be taken at a national level, such as the provision of effective domestic remedies to prevent and redress breaches of the Convention. The Report emphasised the subsidiary role of the Court in protecting Convention rights and the primary responsibility of Member States' domestic authorities.

The second avenue of reform was concerned with the execution of judgments. The Group identified a 'serious defect' in the operation of the current system through the frequency with which the Court has had to deal with 'repetitive' applications, defined as those 'raising an issue identical or very similar to one already determined in a judgment finding a violation of the Convention'. The Group observed that if appropriate general measures had been taken by the various respondent States after the initial judgments then further applications would not have been necessary. The Report proposed the creation of a special procedure to deal with such cases. When the Court gave a judgment finding a violation in a particular case if the Registry was aware that there were a number of other applications raising a similar issue it would notify the Committee of Ministers. The later body would deal with the execution of the judgment in the lead case by an expedited process. In the meantime all the similar pending applications would be stayed by the Court for an (unspecified) period of time to allow the respondent State to take the necessary corrective measures. The Group believed that this new procedure would allow the Committee of Ministers 'to exert special pressure on the State concerned and could reduce the need for the Court to deliver a series of purely repetitive judgments on the merits'.

The third category of reforms were those which could be taken by the Court without the need for amendment of the Convention. The Report endorsed proposals emerging from the Court to provide variable levels of treatment for cases depending upon their nature and content; e.g. applications which were obviously far-fetched and those not satisfying the Rules of Court would no longer be registered. The Report also supported the idea that the Court should become more 'pro-active' in seeking to encourage the friendly settlement of cases; e.g. financial incentives for applicants to settle 'might be reinforced if there was a practice on the part of the Court of depriving them—in its awards of "just satisfaction"—of part of their costs in cases where they had declined a settlement offer deemed by the Court to be reasonable'.

The fourth avenue of reform was concerned with financial resources. The Report recommended a phased expansion of Registry personnel by approximately 50 per cent over the next four years. Under this proposal the Registry would contain 189 lawyers and ninety-five secretaries by 2005.

The final, and most dramatic, reforms proposed by the Report involved amendments to the Convention. These were necessary because even if the above procedural reforms and extra resources were implemented the Court would soon reach saturation point and the quality of its judgments could be in danger. The Court should be given the discretion to focus its detailed attention on those cases which merited such consideration. Therefore, the Report recommended that the Convention be amended to empower the Court 'to decline to examine in detail applications which raise no substantial issue under the Convention'. Also, the term of office of the judges should be extended to a single fixed term of not less than nine years. Thereby, strengthening the independence and continuity of the Court (see further: A. Mowbray, 'Proposals for Reform of the European Court of Human Rights' [2002] *Public Law* 252).

The Committee of Ministers issued a Declaration *On the protection of Human Rights in Europe Guaranteeing the long-term effectiveness of the European Court of Human Rights* (8 November 2001), 'warmly welcoming' the Report of the Evaluation Group. The Ministers' Deputies were instructed to 'pursue urgent consideration' of the recommendations in the Report. Subsequently, the Steering Committee of Human Rights (CDDH), a group of experts appointed by the Committee of Ministers, began considering detailed reforms. The CDDH submitted concrete proposals to the Committee of Ministers in April 2003. Their *Final Report Containing Proposals of the CDDH* (4 April 2003) identified two main areas of workload problems for the Court. Dealing with thousands of applications which are eventually determined without a judgment on their merits and adjudicating upon repetitive cases. The Report considered that in the light of these statistics a 'thorough re-assessment of the manner in which the Convention system works' was needed. The three judge Committees of the Court, which under Protocol 11 are empowered to unanimously declare an application inadmissible, should have their jurisdiction extended to allow them to (unanimously) rule on the merits of *manifestly well-founded* applications where the subject matter of the particular case is already governed by established jurisprudence of the Court. A study by the Registry of the Court calculated that the implementation of this proposal could apply to more than 50 per cent of cases dealt with by Chambers of the Court (consisting of seven judges). Hence there would be a considerable efficiency gain in judicial time. The Report accepted that this proposal would end the mandatory participation of the 'national' judge in all cases concerning his/her home State. However, the Report considered that such participation is 'often unnecessary' as these cases would be limited to those governed by established jurisprudence of the Court. Also, national judges could be invited to join a Committee in exceptional situations. The emerging practice of Chambers giving a joint decision on admissibility and merits should be codified in an amendment to Article 29 of the Convention. As fewer separate admissibility decisions would be taken in the future and it is the determining of the admissibility of an application that triggers the current power of the Court to seek to achieve a friendly settlement of the case, the Report endorsed a new Article on friendly settlements which would allow the Court to place itself at the disposal of the parties with a view to securing a friendly settlement at any stage of proceedings.

By far the most controversial recommendation in the Report concerning the processing of cases by the Court was directed at adding a further criterion of admissibility. The CDDH rejected the earlier Evaluation Group's suggestion that the Court be granted the power not to examine in detail applications raising no substantial issue under the Convention. In the opinion of the CDDH such a formulation would accord 'too wide a discretion to the Court enabling it to pick and choose the cases it would wish to deal with'. The CDDH proposed that the new discretion should be circumscribed by reference to objective factors. These would include both the general interest and circumstances of the applicant. A 'large majority' of the CDDH favoured the addition of the following criterion to Article 35 of the Convention:

3. The Court shall declare inadmissible any individual application . . .
b. if the applicant has not suffered a significant disadvantage and if the case raises neither a serious question affecting the interpretation or application of the Convention or the protocols thereto, nor a serious issue of general importance.

The thrust behind this proposal was to save the Court from having to determine 'minor' complaints, examples being length of civil proceedings cases involving less than 500 Euros or disputes between neighbours. A study by the Registry of the Court calculated that adopting a 'conservative' interpretation of this new criterion could result in a reduction of about 5 per cent in the current caseload of the Court with a further 'considerable' saving in the time of the Registry. 'Several' Members of the CDDH favoured a wider definition of the new criterion that would allow the Court to declare inadmissible applications 'if such a decision does not place the applicant at a significant disadvantage . . .'

The third category of proposed reforms were measures designed to improve and accelerate the execution of judgments. They included developing the procedures of the Committee of Ministers to prioritise the supervision of the execution of Court judgments disclosing systemic defects in Member States. Amending the Convention to enable the Committee of Ministers to supervise the execution of friendly settlement *decisions* reached by the Court. And, most importantly, giving the Committee of Ministers the power to institute infringement proceedings, before the Grand Chamber of the Court, against any State which persistently fails to comply with a judgment of the Court. The CDDH envisaged that such a procedure could lead to the Grand Chamber imposing financial penalties on a recalcitrant State. Whilst the CDDH acknowledged that the creation of this new mechanism needed further consideration it believed that such a procedure, and the threat of recourse to it, ought to be a 'significant and effective' incentive for compliance by the minority of States who do not currently do so.

The Committee of Ministers considered the CDDH Report at its May 2003 meeting and issued a Declaration 'welcoming' and 'endorsing' the Report (*Guaranteeing the long-term effectiveness of the European Court of Human Rights* CM (2003) 62). The Committee of Ministers expressed the wish to consider a draft amending Protocol to the Convention, based upon the CDDH recommendations, in one year's time. In the meantime the Minister's Deputies were instructed to work on the draft Protocol with further consideration being given to, *inter alia*, the Committee of Ministers being empowered to supervise the execution of friendly settlements and bring infringement proceedings against States which persistently refused to comply with Court judgments.

The CDDH presented the Committee of Ministers with its *Final Activity Report* in April 2004. The Report contained, *inter alia*, a draft Protocol 14 and an Explanatory Report concerning the draft Protocol. The latter Report explained that the draft Protocol did not make 'radical' changes to the existing Strasbourg enforcement system, but sought to improve the operation of that system so as to allow the Court to concentrate upon the most important cases. The Committee of Ministers invited the Parliamentary Assembly to give its opinion on the draft Protocol. The Assembly delivered its Opinion (No 251, on 28 April 2004), in which it, *inter alia*, criticized the proposed new admissibility criterion and complained that it had only been given two weeks notice of the draft Protocol. The Committee of Ministers agreed the final text of Protocol 14 at its meeting on 12 May 2004 and the Protocol was opened for signature the next day.

Three significant changes in the Court's handling of cases were introduced in Protocol 14. First, a new decision-making entity 'the single-judge formation' is created under revised Article 26 of the Convention. Such entities, under revised Article 27 of the Convention, will be empowered to declare inadmissible or strike out individual applications where such decisions 'can be taken without further examination'. The Explanatory Report notes that single-judge formations will only reach such decisions 'in clear-cut cases, where the inadmissibility of the application is manifest from the outset'. Under revised Article 26 of the Convention single-judge formations will not determine applications concerning the State in respect of which the judges have been elected. The single-judge formation will be assisted by 'rapporteurs' drawn from the Court's Registry. The single judge will have sole responsibility for making determinations but, according to the Explanatory Report:

58. ... it will be indispensable to create these rapporteur functions in order to achieve the significant potential increase in filtering capacity which the institution of single-judge formations aims at. The Members of the Registry exercising rapporteur functions will assist the new single-judge formations. In principle, the single judge should be assisted by a rapporteur with knowledge of the language and the legal system of the respondent Party. The function of rapporteur will never be carried out by a judge in this context.

The Court will be responsible for determining the number of rapporteurs to be appointed together with the manner and length of their appointments. It is envisaged that rapporteurs may be fixed-term appointments from lawyers having practical experience of Member States' legal systems. Of course, according to the Explanatory Report, '... it is understood that the new function of rapporteur should be conferred on persons with a solid legal experience, expertise in the Convention and its case-law and a very good knowledge of at least one of the two official languages of the Council of Europe and who, like the other staff of the Registry, meet the requirements of independence and impartiality'.

The single-judge formation is a novel method of increasing the efficiency of the Court in processing many of the vast majority of applications which are inadmissible. As we have examined above, under Protocol 11, this task has to be undertaken by a three-judge Committee. Hence re-allocating the function to a single-judge formation maximises the productivity of judges. Furthermore, they will be supported in the handling of these clearly inadmissible applications by the new rapporteurs. This group of Registry staff are the successors of the earlier idea of 'assessors' taking on a filtering role. Whereas, Protocol 14 has reserved formal decision-making on matters of admissibility for the judges of the Court, thereby avoiding the creation of a second category of judicial decision-makers within the Court.

The second major change introduced by the Protocol is the expansion of the powers of three-judge Committees. Under revised Article 28 of the Convention these Committees will be able to unanimously declare admissible and give a judgment on the merits, at the same time, in respect of cases where the complaint 'is already the subject of well-established case-law of the Court'. The Explanatory Report interprets the phrase as normally meaning: '... case-law which has been consistently applied by a Chamber. Exceptionally, however, it is conceivable that a single judgment on a question of principle may constitute "well-established case-law", particularly when the Grand Chamber has rendered it'. This new power of Committees is aimed at enabling the efficient judicial processing of the numerous admissible cases which raise structural problems in Member States that have been previously examined by the Court (e.g. the infamous delays in Italian criminal and civil proceedings breaching the reasonable time guarantee contained in Article 6(1) of the Convention). The national judge of the respondent State will not automatically be a Member of the Committee as his/her presence is not generally required due to lack of novelty in the substance of the application. However, Committees are given the power to invite the national judge to replace one of the existing Members of the Committee. An express factor in Committees' decisions to seek the participation of national judges is whether the respondent State has contested the use of the expedited decision-making process, for example on the ground that the application is materially distinguishable from previous cases. If a Committee is not of the unanimous view that the expedited process should be used then the application is sent to a Chamber, of seven judges, for determination.

The above expansion of the powers of Chambers is another strategy designed to increase the efficiency of the Court by enabling three-judge Committees to determine straightforward applications concerning previously examined structural problems in Member States. Applicants should benefit from obtaining swifter judgments on the merits of their complaints and States will also be alerted to the ongoing problems in their domestic systems.

The third major reform introduced by Protocol 14 is much more controversial as it involves the addition of a new admissibility criterion for individual applications. The new provision states:

The Court shall declare inadmissible any individual application submitted under Article 34 if it considers that: ... (b.) the applicant has not suffered a significant disadvantage, unless respect for human rights as defined in the Convention and the Protocols thereto requires an examination of the application on the merits and provided that no case may be rejected on this ground which has not been duly considered by a domestic tribunal.

It will be for the Grand Chamber and Chambers to elaborate the meaning of 'a significant disadvantage'. Indeed, under Article 20(2) of Protocol 14, for two years following the Protocol's entry into force single-judge formations and Committees will be prevented from utilising this new criterion. The final element of Article 35(3)(b) is a safeguard that provides, according to the Explanatory Report:

It will never be possible for the Court to reject an application on account of its trivial nature if the case has not been duly considered by a domestic tribunal. This clause, which reflects the principle of subsidiarity, ensures that, for the purposes of the application of the new admissibility criterion, every case will receive a judicial examination whether at the national level or at the European level.

The Committee on Legal Affairs and Human Rights of the Parliamentary Assembly proposed the addition of this safeguard after noting that many non-governmental organisations (including Amnesty International) were strongly opposed to the creation of a new admissibility criterion (*Report Draft Protocol 14*, Doc 10147, 23 April 2004). The Parliamentary Assembly formally objected to the addition of the new criterion because, '... it is vague, subjective and liable to do the applicant a serious injustice ... [i]n addition, it may have the unintended effect of discriminating against female applicants to the Court, by, for example, putting a premium on financial disadvantage suffered'. (Opinion No. 251, at para 11). However, the need to allow the Court greater latitude to focus its resources on the most significant complaints resulted in the Committee of Ministers approving the new criterion with the inclusion of the domestic consideration safeguard.

Protocol 14 also seeks to enhance the effectiveness of the supervision of the execution of the Court's judgments (finding States in breach of the Convention) by the Committee of

Ministers. Two new powers are created by the Protocol. First, the Committee of Ministers may, by a vote of two-thirds of representatives, seek a ruling from the Court on the interpretation of a judgment which is problematic (revised Article 46(3) of the Convention). This measure will be used when there is disagreement as to the meaning of the original judgment. Secondly, the ability to bring infringement proceedings against a recalcitrant State has been conferred upon the Committee of Ministers, by revised Article 46(4) of the Convention.

If the Committee of Ministers considers that a High Contracting Party refuses to abide by a final judgment in a case to which it is a party, it may, after serving formal notice on that Party and by a decision adopted by a majority vote of two-thirds of the representatives entitled to sit on the Committee, refer to the Court the question whether that Party has failed to fulfil its obligation under paragraph 1.

The Grand Chamber will then examine whether the respondent State has failed to abide by the original judgment of the Court and inform the Committee of Ministers if there has been a breach of Article 46(1) by the State. According to the Explanatory Report it is envisaged that infringement proceedings will only be necessary in 'exceptional circumstances' but 'the procedure's mere existence, and the threat of using it, should act as an effective new incentive to execute the Court's judgments'. It is noteworthy that the procedure created by Protocol 14 does not authorize the Court, or the Committee of Ministers, to impose any financial penalties if the former concludes that the respondent State has failed to abide by the original judgment. Political pressure on the State generated by the initiation of infringement proceedings and the Grand Chamber's judgment was seen as being sufficient.

Other institutional reforms include according the Council of Europe's Commissioner for Human Rights the right to participate, either via written comments or orally in hearings, in all cases being examined by Chambers or the Grand Chamber. Such interventions may help the Court to identify structural defects in respondent States (and other Member States). The Convention is also amended to allow the possible future accession of the European Union, though such a development will also require further modifications of the Convention. The term of office of Court judges is altered to a single period of nine years. This is a welcome reversion to the term of office held by judges in the original Court, with the adaptation that under Protocol 14 judges will not be eligible for re-election. Increasing the period of office and preventing re-election should help to enhance the perceived (and possibly the actual) independence of the judges from influence by States. The Parliamentary Assembly has campaigned for a long time for such a period of office [the above examination of the creation of Protocol 14 draws heavily upon my writings on the topic in the *Human Rights Law Review*].

Protocol 14 will come into force three months after all Member States have ratified it. The United Kingdom ratified it in January 2005. By the time of the 116th Session of the Committee of Ministers, in May 2006, all Member States had signed the Protocol and 40 States had ratified it.

Ominously, even before the Committee of Ministers had adopted the text of Protocol 14, President Wildhaber issued a press release (on 21 April 2004) warning that:

... the reform, even if it is a step in the right direction, is not going to solve all the Court's problems. Even with the new reform, the Court will continue to have an excessive workload. We shall continue to do everything we can to maintain the efficiency of our work.

Steven Greer, having interviewed some of the Court's judges and officials, concluded that:

Although it may not solve the current case overload crisis, Protocol 14 has, nevertheless, probably bought extra time for further reflection on the Court's future, 'Protocol 14 and the Future of the European Court of Human Rights' [2005] *Public Law* 83 at p. 104.

In his speech at the opening of the judicial year (on 21 January 2005) President Wildhaber observed:

Indeed the adoption of Protocol No 14 provides an appropriate opportunity for a brief stocktaking of what has been achieved by the new Court set up in November 1998 by Protocol No 11. This Protocol marked a huge leap forward in terms of principle, in fully judicialising the international control machinery: it merged the former Court and the Commission and made the new Court a permanent institution, it made the right of individual petition mandatory and abolished the adjudicative role of the Committee of Ministers, all elements which today are considered cornerstones of the Strasbourg system, taken for granted by everybody, but which came into being only six years ago.

But Protocol No 11 has also been a success in practice in that the single, permanent Court in Strasbourg has shown itself able to cope with a much heavier caseload than its two predecessors, while maintaining the authority and quality of the case-law in the substantial cases. I do not intend to bore you with a long list of statistics, so I will confine myself to giving you just three figures covering the last five years: in that period the number of applications lodged has increased by 99%—a frightening figure in itself—but the number of applications finally disposed of has risen by nearly five times that figure, that is by 470%, and this against the background of a growth in the budget of smaller proportions, amounting to 72%.

In 2004 the Court terminated 21,100 cases, by delivering 20,348 decisions and 739 judgments, an output which represents an increase of 18% on the 2003 output and was achieved under difficult circumstances, and with means which all in all appear quite modest when compared with those of other international courts. This output is the result of a collective and sustained effort by a highly dedicated Court assisted by an equally motivated and competent Registry, to which I would like to pay tribute here. Unfortunately, however, all productivity gains achieved over the years have been eaten up by the constant rise in the number of incoming cases. The desire of more and more European citizens to seek justice on an international level as regards their enjoyment of their basic human rights has outstripped the benefits of the structural innovations introduced by Protocol No 11.

...

The Court, for its part, will do its utmost to use to the full all the instruments contained in Protocol No 14, just as it did with Protocol No 11. In an effort to anticipate formal entry into force, the Court has even begun adapting some of its procedures to reflect the scheme foreseen in the Protocol. Preparations with a view to adjusting our structure and working methods in time for the entry into force of Protocol No 14 are under way.

Yet, as I have repeatedly said, Protocol No 14 is unlikely to be the end of the story, as it might well not be sufficient to get the caseload problem under control. For there is one thing which—despite all its potential and all our efforts—Protocol No. 14 will not do—and the Court has always been very clear about that: it will not itself reduce the volume of cases coming to Strasbourg; it will not turn off the tap; it will not even slow down the flow.

On the other hand, ceaselessly raising judicial productivity has its limits, if only physical limits; nor can it be a dictate which the Court should continue to yield to at all costs, as this would amount not only to an interference with the Court's independence in organising its judicial work, but would also be wrong in principle. Indeed the main aim of the Convention is not to have as many applications as possible declared inadmissible, but rather to secure effective protection of human rights in the Member States. Driving up the statistics of terminated cases every year can only be achieved by concentrating on the easier, more numerous inadmissible applications—which will inevitably be at the expense of the more complex, meritorious applications.

To keep the priorities right, the Court recently decided, in line with the objectives pursued by Protocol No 14, to devote more attention to adjudicating on the meritorious cases, the ones where the applicant will often have a serious claim of being the victim of a human rights violation. This may well result in the future in what could at first sight appear as a stagnating or even lower overall productivity. In reality, however, the figures, if compared category by category, should then indicate that the Court is progressively reverting to its core business, to the substantial cases, cases which actually contribute to enhancing the protection of human rights throughout the Council of Europe States and even beyond.

...

In April 2005 the Court submitted a *Memorandum* to the Third Summit of the Council of Europe, in which the Court warned that the increase in its caseload meant that now, 'the system's effectiveness is seriously jeopardised, despite the remarkable progress which the Court has achieved in its output'. In the view of the Court:

... further measures, going beyond a constant search for improvements in working methods and internal organisation, are likely to be necessary if the human rights protection system set up by the ECHR is to remain effective over the long term. In addition to a rapid ratification of Protocol No 14, **the Governments therefore need to start reflecting on the long-term options** available for further action capable of ensuring a stable, practicable system providing the highest possible effective protection, while preserving the basic philosophy underlying the ECHR. Fundamentally, the Governments are faced with a choice about the nature of the international protection machinery which must be provided to individuals in the Europe of the 21st century.

The Court proposed that 'an independent group of eminent and experienced national and international judges and other experts' be appointed to consider these issues and identify 'possible scenarios' (with their relative costs and benefits). Governments could then consider the group's findings.

The *Warsaw Declaration* (CM (2005) 79final), issued by the Heads of State and Government of the Council of Europe at the conclusion of the Third Summit restated 'the indispensable role of the ECHR and the Court in formulating, promoting and implementing human rights standards, it is essential to guarantee their effectiveness. Therefore, the Summit agreed to establish a 'group of wise persons to draw up a comprehensive strategy to secure the effectiveness of the system in the longer term'. In September 2005 the Committee of Ministers announced the names of the eleven wise persons and they included the former Lord Chief Justice (of England and Wales) Lord Woolf.

Separately from the establishment of the wise persons review of long-term reforms, the Secretary General of the Council of Europe and the President of the Court (in July 2005) invited Lord Woolf, assisted by a team of persons with expertise in the administration of courts, to conduct a review of the working methods of the Court. Lord Woolf published his seventy-six page *Review of the Working Methods of the European Court of Human Rights* during December 2005. The *Review* was designed to identify administrative steps that could be taken by the Court and its Registry to respond to the growing caseload prior to the implementation of Protocol 14 and future amendments of the Convention. Lord Woolf reported that there were 82,100 cases pending before the Court and this backlog was projected to increase to 250,000 by 2010. He recommended seven main changes to the working of the Court. (1) The Court should redefine what constitutes an application to encompass only those made by submission of a properly completed application form. (2) Satellite Offices of the Registry should be established in Warsaw and two or three other Member States from where there are significant numbers of applications (and those States have effective ombudsman to resolve human rights complaints). These offices would provide advice to persons on the admissibility criteria of the Court and the availability of national remedies. The Offices would also undertake the initial processing of applications made against the relevant State. (3) The Council of Europe and the Court should encourage greater use of national ombudsman and other methods of alternative dispute resolution to resolve human rights complaints. A 'Friendly Settlement Unit' should be established within the Registry to proactively identify a greater number of cases suitable for resolution by this means. (4) The Court's use of the pilot judgment procedure should be increased and an 'Article 41 Unit' should be created in the Registry that would produce guidelines (which could be published) on suitable amounts of compensation. A separate backlog secretariat should be established to tackle the reduction of pending cases. (5) A second Deputy Registrar (for Management) should be appointed to oversee the recruitment and training of Registry staff. (6) A central unit for the training of Registry lawyers should be introduced (7) A compulsory formal induction programme for judges on the Convention and working of the Court should be introduced, together with language training (in English and/or French) for those judges who need greater proficiency in both working languages of the Court. We can detect echoes in the Review from Lord Woolf's earlier major examination of English civil law proceedings, *Access to Justice: Final Report* (HMSO 1996), which led to significant changes in civil cases. For instance, Lord Woolf had advocated the use of alternative dispute resolution procedures, including ombudsmen, as a prelude to persons seeking judicial review of the lawfulness of the decisions of public authorities.

In May 2006 the group of wise persons submitted an interim report (Cm(2006)88) to the Committee of Ministers. The report explained the progress that the group had made and its provisional views. Whilst the group considered that the changes introduced by Protocol 14 will 'no doubt be extremely useful' it cautioned that they 'will not be sufficient for the Court to find any long lasting solution to its problem of congestion'. Estimates from the Court suggested that the Protocol 14 reforms may increase the productivity of the Court by between 20 and 25 per cent. Therefore, the group needed to make 'radical' recommendations to ensure the Court's effective long-term functioning. The group had decided not to pursue the idea of the creation of regional courts of first instance, due to the risk of the emergence of divergent case law and on grounds of cost. The Court also rejected the idea of giving the Court discretion to select cases for examination as it would be 'totally alien to the philosophy of the European human rights protection system' and 'would tend to politicise the system as the Court would have to select cases for examination'. Amongst the possible reforms being contemplated by the group was the creation of a 'Judicial Committee' attached to the Court that would deal with the large numbers of applications which are inadmissible on formal grounds (e.g. where domestic remedies have not been exhausted). The ability of the Court to give 'judgments of principle' which would be binding on all Member States and thereby enhance the 'constitutional' role of the Court whilst reducing the need for separate judgments in respect of individual States. Although the group believed that the EU preliminary ruling mechanism was not suitable for the ECHR system, the wise persons were examining whether national supreme courts should be allowed to seek consultative opinions on questions of Convention interpretation from the Court and whether the Court could be empowered to remit certain issues to national courts (e.g. how much compensation should be paid to a successful complainant). These deliberations build upon ideas (e.g. the creation of a new filtering body) that have been circulating in Strasbourg for some years. The Committee of Ministers requested the wise persons to produce a final report by the end of 2006.

3 ARTICLE 1 OBLIGATION TO RESPECT HUMAN RIGHTS

Assanidze v Georgia judgment of 8 April 2004
European Court of Human Rights

The applicant was a Georgian national, and former senior local politician, imprisoned in Batumi, the capital of the Ajarian Autonomous Republic in Georgia (an area historically ruled by the Ottoman and Russian Empires which during the period of the Union of Soviet Socialist Republics had been an autonomous part of Georgia, its precise status within independent Georgia had not been resolved at the time of the Court's judgment). He had been convicted of unlawful financial dealings in 1994 and sentenced to eight years' imprisonment. In 1999 he had been given a pardon suspending the remaining period of his imprisonment by the President of Georgia. The Ajarian authorities did not release him. New criminal charges were brought against him and in 2000 the Ajarian High Court sentenced him to twelve years' imprisonment (backdated to the time of his original arrest/detention in 1993). Assanidze appealed to the Georgian Supreme Court and in 2001 that Court quashed his convictions and ordered his immediate release. Despite numerous requests from the Georgian central government the Ajarian authorities refused to release Assanidze. He complained to the European Court of Human Rights alleging, *inter alia*, a violation of his right to liberty under Article 5.

A crucial aspect of the case concerned the responsibility of the Government of Georgia, under Article 1 of the Convention, for the applicant's continued detention by the Ajarian authorities. The Government accepted that the Ajarian Autonomous Republic was an integral part of Georgia, Ajaria did not have separatist ambitions and apart from the applicant's case (which had significant political elements) there were no problems of judicial co-operation between the central and Ajarian authorities.

The Grand Chamber held that:

137. Article 1 of the Convention requires the State Parties to 'secure to everyone within their jurisdiction the rights and freedoms defined in Section I of th[e] Convention'. It follows from this provision that the State Parties are answerable for any violation of the protected rights and freedoms of anyone within their 'jurisdiction'—or competence—at the time of the violation.

In certain exceptional cases, jurisdiction is assumed on the basis of non-territorial factors, such as: acts of public authority performed abroad by diplomatic and consular representatives of the State; the criminal activities of individuals overseas against the interests of the State or its nationals; acts performed on board vessels flying the State flag or on aircraft or spacecraft registered there; and particularly serious international crimes (universal jurisdiction).

However, as a general rule, the notion of 'jurisdiction' within the meaning of Article 1 of the Convention must be considered as reflecting the position under public international law (*Gentilhomme and Others v France*, Nos 48205/99, 48207/99 and 48209/99, § 20, 14 May 2002; *Bankovic and Others v Belgium and 16 Other Contracting States* (dec.) [GC], No 52207/99, §§ 59–61, ECHR 2001-XII). That notion is 'primarily' or 'essentially' territorial (see *Bankovic* cited above).

138. In addition to the State territory proper, territorial jurisdiction extends to any area which, at the time of the alleged violation, is under the 'overall control' of the State concerned (*Loizidou v Turkey* (preliminary objections) judgment of 23 March 1995, Series A No 310), notably occupied territories (*Cyprus v Turkey* [GC], No 25781/94, ECHR-2001-IV), to the exclusion of areas outside such control (see *Bankovic* cited above).

. . .

146. . . . the sole issue of relevance is the State's international responsibility, irrespective of the national authority to which the breach of the Convention in the domestic system is imputable (see, *mutatis mutandis*, *Foti and Others v Italy*, judgment of 10 December 1982, Series A No 56, p 21, § 63; *Zimmermann and Steiner v Switzerland*, judgment of 13 July 1983, Series A No 66, p 13, § 32; and *Lingens v Austria*, judgment of 8 July 1986, Series A No 103, p 28, § 46).

Even though it is not inconceivable that States will encounter difficulties in securing compliance with the rights guaranteed by the Convention in all parts of their territory, each State Party to the Convention nonetheless remains responsible for events occurring anywhere within its national territory.

Further, the Convention does not merely oblige the higher authorities of the Contracting States to respect for their own part the rights and freedoms it embodies; it also has the consequence that, in order to secure the enjoyment of those rights and freedoms, those authorities must prevent or remedy any breach at subordinate levels (*Ireland v the United Kingdom*, judgment of 18 January 1978, Series A No 25, pp 90–1, § 239). The higher authorities of the State are under a duty to require their subordinates to comply with the Convention and cannot shelter behind their inability to ensure that it is respected (ibid, p. 64, § 159).

147. Despite the malfunctioning of parts of the State machinery in Georgia and the existence of territories with special status, the Ajarian Autonomous Republic is in law subject to the control of the Georgian State. The relationship existing between the local Ajarian authorities and the central government is such that only a failing on the part of the latter could make the continued breach of the provisions of the Convention at the local level possible. The general duty imposed on the State by Article 1 of the Convention entails and requires the implementation of a national system capable of securing compliance with the Convention throughout the territory of the State for everyone. That is confirmed by the fact that, firstly, Article 1 does not exclude any part of the Member States' 'jurisdiction' from the scope of the Convention and, secondly, it is with respect to their 'jurisdiction' as a whole—which is often exercised in the first place through the Constitution—that Member States are called on to show compliance with the Convention (*United Communist Party of Turkey and Others v Turkey*, judgment of 30 January 1998, *Reports* 1998-I, pp 17–18, § 29).

. . .

149. The Court thus emphasises that the higher authorities of the Georgian State are strictly liable under the Convention for the conduct of their subordinates (*Ireland v the United Kingdom*, cited above, p 64, § 159). It is only the responsibility of the Georgian State itself—not that of a domestic authority or organ—that is in issue before the Court. It is not the Court's role to deal with a multiplicity of national authorities or courts or to examine disputes between institutions or over internal politics.

150. The Court therefore finds that the actual facts out of which the allegations of violations arose were within the 'jurisdiction' of Georgia within the meaning of Article 1 of the Convention and that, even though within the domestic system those matters are directly imputable to the local authorities of the

Ajarian Autonomous Republic, it is solely the responsibility of the Georgian State that is engaged under the Convention.

In respect of the applicant's continued imprisonment since the Georgian Supreme Court ordered his immediate release in 2001:

173. As to the conformity of the applicant's detention with the aim of Article 5 to protect against arbitrariness, the Court observes that it is inconceivable that in a State subject to the rule of law a person should continue to be deprived of his liberty despite the existence of a court order for his release.

174. As the documents in the case file show, the central State authorities themselves pointed out on a number of occasions that there was no basis for the applicant's detention. The central judicial and administrative authorities were forthright in telling the Ajarian authorities that the applicant's deprivation was arbitrary for the purposes of domestic law and Article 5 of the Convention. However, their numerous reminders and calls for the applicant's release went unanswered . . .

175. The Court considers that to detain a person for an indefinite and unforeseeable period, without such detention being based on a specific statutory provision or judicial decision, is incompatible with the principle of legal certainty (see, *mutatis mutandis, Jecius v Lithuania*, No 34578/97, § 62, ECHR 2000-IX) and arbitrary, and runs counter to the fundamental aspects of the rule of law.

. . .

FOR THESE REASONS, THE COURT

. . . .

2. *Holds* unanimously that the matters complained of are within the 'jurisdiction' of Georgia within the meaning of Article 1 of the Convention and that only the responsibility of the Georgian State is engaged under the Convention (see paragraph 150 above);

. . . .

5. *Holds* unanimously that since 29 January 2001 the applicant has been held arbitrarily in breach of the provisions of Article 5 (1) of the Convention . . .

NOTES

1   The Grand Chamber was composed of President Wildhaber and Judges: Rozakis, Costa, Ress, Bratza, Caflisch, Loucaides, Cabral Barreto, Straznicka, Jungwiert, Casadevall, Zupanic, Thomassen, Botoucharova, Ugrekhelidze, Zagrebelsky, and Mularoni.

2   The judgment in *Assanidze* demonstrated that the Court interprets the concept of jurisdiction under Article 1 in accordance with the principles of public international law to normally encompass the national territory of the respondent State. Furthermore, central governments are accountable, under the Convention, for securing respect for Convention rights and freedoms in all parts of their territories and by sub-national tiers of government. These are important rulings as they seek to ensure that persons will be guaranteed their Convention rights and freedoms throughout the territories of Member States. It is vital that the central governments of Member States ensure that their subordinate authorities fully respect the Convention and *de facto* zones of non-compliance do not emerge within national territories.

3   Another Grand Chamber emphasized the continuing responsibility of a Member State under the Convention even in respect of part of its territory which is under the *de facto* control of a separatist regime in *Ilascu and Others v Moldova and Russia*, judgment of 8 July 2004. The four applicants had been arrested, convicted and detained by the authorities of the 'Moldavian

Republic of Transdniestria' (MRT), a region in the east of Moldova which proclaimed its independence in 1991 but which is not recognized by the international community. The Grand Chamber held that:

333. The Court considers that where a Contracting State is prevented from exercising its authority over the whole of its territory by a constraining *de facto* situation, such as obtains when a separatist regime is set up, whether or not this is accompanied by military occupation by another State, it does not thereby cease to have jurisdiction within the meaning of Article 1 of the Convention over that part of its territory temporarily subject to a local authority sustained by rebel forces or by another State.

Nevertheless such a factual situation reduces the scope of that jurisdiction in that the undertaking given by the State under Article 1 must be considered by the Court only in the light of the Contracting State's positive obligations towards persons within its territory. The State in question must endeavour, with all the legal and diplomatic means available to it vis-à-vis foreign States and international organisations, to continue to guarantee the enjoyment of the rights and freedoms guaranteed by the Convention.

A large majority, eleven votes to six, consequently determined that the applicants fell within the jurisdiction of Moldova. The majority considered that Moldova had not taken 'effective measures' to bring to an end the continuing detention and mal-treatment of the three applicants who remained in the custody of the MRT after the release of Ilascu in 2001 (note, Judges Casadevall, Ress, Birsan, Tulkens, and Fura-Sandstrom believed that the Government of Moldova had adopted 'a rather acquiescent attitude' towards the plight of the applicants since 1992). Judge Bratza, joined by Judges Rozakis, Hedigan, Thomassen, and Pantiru, dissented regarding the jurisdictional responsibility of Moldova.

8. . . . I have difficulty in accepting the proposition that those within a part of the territory of a State over which, as a result of its unlawful occupation by a separatist administration, the State is prevented from exercising any authority or control may nevertheless be said to be within the 'jurisdiction' of that State according to the autonomous meaning of that term in Article 1 of the Convention, which term presupposes that the State has the power 'to secure to everyone . . . the rights and freedoms' defined therein. I find it equally difficult to accept the conclusion of the majority of the Court that in such a factual situation those within the territory remain 'within [the] jurisdiction' of the State but that the scope of that 'jurisdiction' is reduced, the State continuing to owe positive obligations with regard to the Convention rights of everyone in the territory. The very use of the term 'the positive obligations of the State' and the reliance placed in the judgment on the case-law of the Court under Article 1 concerning such obligations appears to me to be both misleading and unhelpful in the present context. That case-law—with its references to the fair balance to be struck between the general interest and the interests of the individual and the choices to be made in terms of priorities and resources—was developed in a factual context where the respondent State exercised full and effective control over all parts of its territory and where individuals within that territory were indisputably within the 'jurisdiction' of the State for Convention purposes. The Court's reasoning cannot in my view be readily adapted to the fundamentally different context in which a State is prevented by circumstances outside its control from exercising any authority within the territory and where the very issue is whether individuals within the territory are to be regarded as within the 'jurisdiction' of the State for Convention purposes.

I am unable to accept that in such a situation responsibility for a violation of the Convention rights of individuals within the territory may attach to the State merely because of a failure on its part to establish that it had made sufficient efforts on the legal or diplomatic plane to guarantee those rights. In the specific context of the present case, the responsibility of a State in respect of the wrongful detention of persons detained within territory outside its effective control cannot in my view depend on whether at any particular point of time the State is, in the estimation of the Court, making sufficiently concerted efforts to secure their release. Nor can I accept an interpretation of the Convention which would require the Court to make an assessment, in a complex and fluctuating international situation, as to whether particular legal or diplomatic measures would be effective to restore constitutional rule within the territory, whether such measures were in practice possible and whether they were adequately implemented by the State concerned.

9. I can agree that, where a State is prevented from exercising any authority or control over territory within its borders, the inaction of the State concerned may nevertheless be held to engage its responsibility under the Convention in respect of those within the territory. However, such responsibility could in my view only attach in exceptional circumstances where the evidence before the Court clearly demonstrates such a lack of commitment or effort on the part of the State concerned to reassert its authority or to reinstitute constitutional order within the territory as to amount to a tacit acquiescence in the continued exercise of authority or 'jurisdiction' within the territory by the unlawful administration.

The majority's innovative use of the concept of positive obligations (see further below note 12) had as its objective the desirable goal, examine above in the comments on *Assanidze*, of seeking to ensure that geographical areas of non-compliance/enforcement are not tolerated within the territories of Member States. Do you agree with Judge Bratza's view that the majority's approach requires the Court to become too involved in evaluating governments' diplomatic strategies? For an examination of the jurisdictional responsibility of Russia in respect of the applicants see below Note 7.

4   In exceptional situations, a wider notion of jurisdiction applies. For example, in *Loizidou v Turkey (Preliminary Objections)* A.310 (1995) a Grand Chamber held, by sixteen votes to two, that:

62. . . . Bearing in mind the object and purpose of the Convention, the responsibility of a Contracting Party may also arise when as a consequence of military action—whether lawful or unlawful—it exercises effective control of an area outside its national territory.

The obligation to secure, in such an area, the rights and freedoms set out in the Convention derives from the fact of such control whether it be exercised directly, through its armed forces, or through a subordinate local administration.

63. In this connection the respondent Government have acknowledged that the applicant's loss of control of her property stems from the occupation of the northern part of Cyprus by Turkish troops and the establishment there of the 'TRNC' [Turkish Republic of Northern Cyprus—an entity not recognized by the general international community]. Furthermore, it has not been disputed that the applicant was prevented by Turkish troops from gaining access to her property.

64. It follows that such acts are capable of falling within Turkish 'jurisdiction' within the meaning of Article 1 of the Convention. . . .

In the subsequent judgment on the merits of Mrs Loizidou's complants (see below pp 544 and 922, Article 8 and A1P1) the Grand Chamber held, by eleven votes to six, that:

56. It is not necessary to determine whether, as the applicant and the Government of Cyprus have suggested, Turkey actually exercises detailed control over the policies and actions of the authorities of the 'TRNC'. It is obvious from the large number of troops engaged in active duties in northern Cyprus . . . that her army exercises effective overall control over that part of the island. Such control, according to the relevant test and in the circumstances of the case, entails her responsibility for the policies and actions of the 'TRNC' . . . Those affected by such policies or actions therefore come within the 'jurisdiction' of Turkey for the purposes of Article 1 of the Convention. Her obligation to secure to the applicant the rights and freedoms set out in the Convention therefore extends to the northern part of Cyprus.

In view of this conclusion the Court need not pronounce itself on the arguments which have been adduced by those appearing before it concerning the alleged lawfulness or unlawfulness under international law of Turkey's military intervention in the island in 1974 since, as noted above, the establishment of State responsibility under the Convention does not require such an enquiry . . . It suffices to recall in this context its finding that the international community considers that the Republic of Cyprus is the sole legitimate Government of the island and has consistently refused to accept the legitimacy of the 'TRNC' as a State within the meaning of international law . . .

57. It follows from the above considerations that the continuous denial of the applicant's access to her property in northern Cyprus and the ensuing loss of all control over the property is a matter which falls within Turkey's 'jurisdiction' within the meaning of Article 1 and is thus imputable to Turkey.

5   In the later, rare, inter-State case of *Cyprus v Turkey* ECHR 2001-IV (see below p 119 [A 2]), another Grand Chamber, by sixteen votes to one, confirmed the *Loizidou* approach to jurisdiction in the context of the Turkish military occupation of northern Cyprus.

77. It is of course true that the Court in the *Loizidou* case was addressing an individual's complaint concerning the continuing refusal of the authorities to allow her access to her property. However, it is to be observed that the Court's reasoning is framed in terms of a broad statement of principle as regards Turkey's general responsibility under the Convention for the policies and actions of the 'TRNC' authorities. Having effective overall control over northern Cyprus, its responsibility cannot be confined to the acts of its own soldiers or officials in northern Cyprus but must also be engaged by virtue of the acts of the local administration which survives by virtue of Turkish military and other support. It follows that, in terms of Article 1 of the Convention, Turkey's 'jurisdiction' must be considered to extend to securing the entire range of substantive rights set out in the Convention and those additional Protocols which she has ratified, and that violations of those rights are imputable to Turkey.

The Grand Chamber, with the dissent of the Turkish ad-hoc judge, went on to find breaches of a number of Convention rights including failure to conduct effective investigations into disappeared persons (Articles 2 and 5), the subjection of civilians to trials before military courts in northern Cyprus (Article 6), the denial of access to displaced persons (Greek Cypriots) to their homes in northern Cyprus (Article 8 and Article 1 of Protocol No 1) and unjustifiable restrictions on the freedom to manifest their religion and freedom of expression of Greek Cypriots in northern Cyprus (Articles 9 and 10).

6   In *Bankovic and Others v Belgium and 16 Other Contracting States* ECHR 2001-XII, the six applicants were nationals of the Federal Republic of Yugoslavia (FYR) whose relatives were among the victims of the firing of a missile by a NATO aircraft at the Radio Television Serbia headquarters in Belgrade on 23 April 1999. The military action was part of a campaign of NATO air strikes on Serbia between March and June 1999 taken because the Government of Serbia refused to accept a political solution to the crisis in Kosovo between Serbian and Kosovar Albanian forces in 1998–9. The attack on the Radio Television Serbia building resulted in the deaths of sixteen persons and a similar number of seriously injured persons. The applicants brought a complaint before the Strasbourg Court alleging that the seventeen respondent States (who were members of NATO and parties to the Convention) had breached, *inter alia*, their relatives right to life (Article 2). The respondent States contended that applicants' complaints fell outside their jurisdiction under Article 1 and therefore were inadmissible. The Chamber determining the admissibility of the complaints relinquished the matter to the Grand Chamber. In its decision the latter noted the drafting history of Article 1.

19. The text prepared by the Committee of the Consultative Assembly of the Council of Europe on legal and administrative questions provided, in what became Article 1 of the Convention, that the

'Member States shall undertake to ensure to all persons residing within their territories the rights . . . '. The Expert Intergovernmental Committee, which considered the Consultative Assembly's draft, decided to replace the reference to 'all persons residing within their territories' with a reference to persons 'within their jurisdiction'. The reasons were noted in the following extract from the *Collected Edition of the* Travaux Préparatoires *of the European Convention on Human Rights* (vol III, p 260):

> 'The Assembly draft had extended the benefits of the Convention to "all persons residing within the territories of the signatory States". It seemed to the Committee that the term "residing" might be considered too restrictive. It was felt that there were good grounds for extending the benefits of the Convention to all persons in the territories of the signatory States, even those who could not be considered as residing there in the legal sense of the word. The Committee therefore replaced the term "residing" by the words "within their jurisdiction" which are also contained in Article 2 of the Draft Covenant of the United Nations Commission.'

20. The next relevant comment prior to the adoption of Article 1 of the Convention, made by the Belgian representative on 25 August 1950 during the plenary sitting of the Consultative Assembly, was to the effect that

> 'henceforth the right of protection by our States, by virtue of a formal clause of the Convention, may be exercised with full force, and without any differentiation or distinction, in favour of individuals of whatever nationality, who on the territory of any one of our States, may have had reason to complain that [their] rights have been violated'.

21. The *travaux préparatoires* go on to note that the wording of Article 1 including 'within their jurisdiction', did not give rise to any further discussion and the text as it was (and is now) was adopted by the Consultative Assembly on 25 August 1950 without further amendment (the *Collected Edition of the Travaux Préparatoire* s (vol VI, p 132)).

The Grand Chamber then held that:

67. In keeping with the essentially territorial notion of jurisdiction, the Court has accepted only in exceptional cases that acts of the Contracting States performed, or producing effects, outside their territories can constitute an exercise of jurisdiction by them within the meaning of Article 1 of the Convention.

. . .

71. In sum, the case-law of the Court demonstrates that its recognition of the exercise of extra-territorial jurisdiction by a Contracting State is exceptional: it has done so when the respondent State, through the effective control of the relevant territory and its inhabitants abroad as a consequence of military occupation or through the consent, invitation or acquiescence of the Government of that territory, exercises all or some of the public powers normally to be exercised by that Government.

. . .

75. . . . . the applicants suggest a specific application of the 'effective control' criteria developed in the northern Cyprus cases. They claim that the positive obligation under Article 1 extends to securing the Convention rights in a manner proportionate to the level of control exercised in any given extra-territorial situation. The Governments contend that this amounts to a 'cause-and-effect' notion of jurisdiction not contemplated by or appropriate to Article 1 of the Convention. The Court considers that the applicants' submission is tantamount to arguing that anyone adversely affected by an act imputable to a Contracting State, wherever in the world that act may have been committed or its consequences felt, is thereby brought within the jurisdiction of that State for the purpose of Article 1 of the Convention.

. . .

79. . . . the applicants maintain that any failure to accept that they fell within the jurisdiction of the respondent States would defeat the *ordre public* mission of the Convention and leave a regrettable vacuum in the Convention system of human rights' protection.

80. The Court's obligation, in this respect, is to have regard to the special character of the Convention as a constitutional instrument of *European* public order for the protection of individual human beings and its role, as set out in Article 19 of the Convention, is to ensure the observance of *the engagements undertaken* by the Contracting Parties (the above-cited Loizidou judgment (*preliminary objections*), at § 93). It is therefore difficult to contend that a failure to accept the extra-territorial jurisdiction of the respondent States would fall foul of the Convention's *ordre public* objective, which itself underlines the essentially regional vocation of the Convention system, or of Article 19 of the Convention which does not shed any particular light on the territorial ambit of that system.

It is true that, in its above-cited *Cyprus v Turkey* judgment (at § 78), the Court was conscious of the need to avoid 'a regrettable vacuum in the system of human-rights protection' in northern Cyprus. However, and as noted by the Governments, that comment related to an entirely different situation to the present: the inhabitants of northern Cyprus would have found themselves excluded from the benefits of the Convention safeguards and system which they had previously enjoyed, by Turkey's 'effective control' of the territory and by the accompanying inability of the Cypriot Government, as a Contracting State, to fulfil the obligations it had undertaken under the Convention.

In short, the Convention is a multi-lateral treaty operating, subject to Article 56 of the Convention, in an essentially regional context and notably in the legal space (*espace juridique*) of the Contracting States. The FRY clearly does not fall within this legal space. The Convention was not designed to be applied throughout the world, even in respect of the conduct of Contracting States. Accordingly, the desirability of avoiding a gap or vacuum in human rights' protection has so far been relied on by the Court in favour of establishing jurisdiction only when the territory in question was one that, but for the specific circumstances, would normally be covered by the Convention.

Consequently, the Grand Chamber was unanimous in determining that there was no jurisdictional link between the applicants' relatives and the respondent States and the application was declared inadmissible.

Happold has commented that:

Nor is this to say that *Bankovic et al* were legally unprotected. A body of law exists which regulates the conduct of hostilities in international armed conflicts: international humanitarian law. Indeed, there existed a court with jurisdiction over violations of that body of law in the former Yugoslavia at the time of the attack: the International Criminal Tribunal for the Former Yugoslavia. That the Prosecutor of the ICTY declined to bring proceedings with regard to the bombing of [Radio Television Serbia] is not something that can be laid at the door of the European Court of Human Rights, nor should the Court have stepped in to do the Tribunal's work. [M Happold, 'Bankovic v Belgium and the Territorial Scope of the ECHR' 3 (1) *Human Rights Law Review* 77 at p 90 (2003)].

7   The Grand Chamber, subject to the dissent of Judge Kovler—the Judge of Russian nationality, in *Ilascu and Others* (above Note 3) concluded that the applicants also came within the jurisdiction of Russia.

380. The Court observes that during the Moldovan conflict in 1991–92 forces of the former Fourteenth Army (which owed allegiance to the USSR, the CIS and the Russian Federation in turn) stationed in Transdniestria, an integral part of the territory of the Republic of Moldova, fought with and on behalf of the Transdniestrian separatist forces. Moreover, large quantities of weapons from the stores of the Fourteenth Army (which later became the ROG [Russian Operational Group]) were voluntarily transferred to the separatists, who were also able to seize possession of other weapons unopposed by Russian soldiers.

The Court notes that from December 1991 onwards the Moldovan authorities systematically complained, to international bodies among others, of what they called 'the acts of aggression' of the former Fourteenth Army against the Republic of Moldova and accused the Russian Federation of supporting the Transdniestrian separatists.

Regard being had to the principle of States' responsibility for abuses of authority, it is of no consequence that, as the Russian Government submitted, the former Fourteenth Army did not participate as such in the military operations between the Moldovan forces and the Transdniestrian insurgents.

381. Throughout the clashes between the Moldovan authorities and the Transdniestrian separatists the leaders of the Russian Federation supported the separatist authorities by their political declarations. The Russian Federation drafted the main lines of the ceasefire agreement of 21 July 1992, and moreover signed it as a party.

382. In the light of all these circumstances the Court considers that the Russian Federation's responsibility is engaged in respect of the unlawful acts committed by the Transdniestrian separatists, regard being had to the military and political support it gave them to help them set up the separatist regime and the participation of its military personnel in the fighting. In acting thus the authorities of the Russian Federation contributed both militarily and politically to the creation of a separatist regime in the region of Transdniestria, which is part of the territory of the Republic of Moldova.

The Court next notes that even after the ceasefire agreement of 21 July 1992 the Russian Federation continued to provide military, political and economic support to the separatist regime, thus enabling it to survive by strengthening itself and by acquiring a certain amount of autonomy vis-à-vis Moldova.

383. The Court further notes that in the context of the events mentioned above the applicants were arrested in June 1992 with the participation of soldiers of the Fourteenth Army (subsequently the ROG). The first three applicants were then detained on Fourteenth Army premises and guarded by Fourteenth Army troops. During their detention these three applicants were interrogated and subjected to treatment which could be considered contrary to Article 3 of the Convention. They were then handed over into the charge of the Transdniestrian police.

Similarly, after his arrest by soldiers of the Fourteenth Army, the fourth applicant was handed over to the Transdniestrian separatist police, then detained, interrogated and subjected on police premises to treatment which could be considered contrary to Article 3 of the Convention.

384. The Court considers that on account of the above events the applicants came within the jurisdiction of the Russian Federation within the meaning of Article 1 of the Convention, although at the time when they occurred the Convention was not in force with regard to the Russian Federation.

This is because the events which gave rise to the responsibility of the Russian Federation must be considered to include not only the acts in which the agents of that State participated, like the applicants' arrest and detention, but also their transfer into the hands of the Transdniestrian police and regime, and the subsequent ill-treatment inflicted on them by those police, since in acting in that way the agents of the Russian Federation were fully aware that they were handing them over to an illegal and unconstitutional regime.

In addition, regard being had to the acts the applicants were accused of, the agents of the Russian Government knew, or at least should have known, the fate which awaited them.

385. In the Court's opinion, all of the acts committed by Russian soldiers with regard to the applicants, including their transfer into the charge of the separatist regime, in the context of the Russian authorities' collaboration with that illegal regime, are capable of engaging responsibility for the acts of that regime.

It remains to be determined whether that responsibility remained engaged and whether it was still engaged at the time of the ratification of the Convention by the Russian Federation.

(B) AFTER RATIFICATION OF THE CONVENTION BY THE RUSSIAN FEDERATION

386. With regard to the period after ratification of the Convention, on 5 May 1998, the Court notes the following.

387. The Russian army is still stationed in Moldovan territory in breach of the undertakings to withdraw them completely given by the Russian Federation at the OSCE summits in Istanbul (1999) and Porto (2001). Although the number of Russian troops stationed in Transdniestria has in fact fallen significantly since 1992, the Court notes that the ROG's weapons stocks are still there.

Consequently, in view of the weight of this arsenal, the ROG's military importance in the region and its dissuasive influence persist.

388. The Court further observes that by virtue of the agreements between the Russian Federation, on the one hand, and the Moldovan and Transdniestrian authorities respectively, on the other the 'MRT' authorities were supposed to acquire the infrastructure and arsenal of the ROG at the time of its total withdrawal. It should be noted in that connection that the interpretation given by the Russian Government of the term 'local administrative authorities' of the region of Transdniestria, to be found, among other places, in the agreement of 21 October 1994 is different from that put forward by the Moldovan Government, a fact which enabled the 'MRT' regime to acquire that infrastructure.

389. As regards military relations, the Court notes that the Moldovan delegation to the Joint Control Commission constantly raised allegations of collusion between the ROG personnel and the Transdniestrian authorities regarding transfers of weapons to the latter. It notes that the ROG personnel denied those allegations in the presence of the delegates, declaring that some equipment could have found its way into the separatists' hands as a result of thefts.

Taking into account the accusations made against the ROG and the dangerous nature of its weapons stocks, the Court finds it hard to understand why the ROG troops do not have effective legal resources to prevent such transfers or thefts, as is apparent from their witness evidence to the delegates.

390. The Court attaches particular importance to the financial support enjoyed by the 'MRT' by virtue of the following agreements it has concluded with the Russian Federation:

— the agreement signed on 20 March 1998 between the Russian Federation and the representative of the 'MRT', which provided for the division between the 'MRT' and the Russian Federation of part of the income from the sale of the ROG's equipment;

— the agreement of 15 June 2001, which concerned joint work with a view to using armaments, military technology and ammunition;

— the Russian Federation's reduction by 100 million US dollars of the debt owed to it by the 'MRT'; and

— the supply of Russian gas to Transdniestria on more advantageous financial terms than those given to the rest of Moldova.

The Court further notes the information supplied by the applicants and not denied by the Russian Government to the effect that companies and institutions of the Russian Federation normally controlled by the State, or whose policy is subject to State authorisation, operating particularly in the military field, have been able to enter into commercial relations with similar firms in the 'MRT'.

391. The Court next notes that, both before and after 5 May 1998, in the security zone controlled by the Russian peacekeeping forces, the 'MRT' regime continued to deploy its troops illegally and to manufacture and sell weapons in breach of the agreement of 21 July 1992.

392. All of the above proves that the 'MRT', set up in 1991–1992 with the support of the Russian Federation, vested with organs of power and its own administration, remains under the effective authority, or at the very least under the decisive influence, of the Russian Federation, and in any event

that it survives by virtue of the military, economic, financial and political support given to it by the Russian Federation.

393. That being so, the Court considers that there is a continuous and uninterrupted link of responsibility on the part of the Russian Federation for the applicants' fate, as the Russian Federation's policy of support for the regime and collaboration with it continued beyond 5 May 1998, and after that date the Russian Federation made no attempt to put an end to the applicants' situation brought about by its agents, and did not act to prevent the violations allegedly committed after 5 May 1998.

Regard being had to the foregoing, it is of little consequence that since 5 May 1998 the agents of the Russian Federation have not participated directly in the events complained of in the present application.

394. In conclusion, the applicants therefore come within the 'jurisdiction' of the Russian Federation for the purposes of Article 1 of the Convention and its responsibility is engaged with regard to the acts complained of.

This analysis reveals how a Member State can be held responsible for actions occurring within the territory of another Member State where there has not been a military invasion/occupation.

In his dissenting opinion Judge Kovler stated:

In view of the particular nature of the case, in which the applicants' situation is indissociable from an extremely complex geopolitical context, the Court finds itself in new territory, given the lack of applicable case-law. The Court's judgment in this case could have set a precedent for similar situations in other zones of conflict within the Member States of the Council of Europe, including those which have joined recently. The historical roots of the conflict in which the countries of the region were involved and the 'fragmenting-empire' effect are features which bring to mind conflicts such as the not-so-very distant Balkans or Caucasus have seen.

However, the Court (wrongly in my opinion) preferred to see the situation in terms of a Cyprus-type conflict, following its corresponding case-law and falling into the trap that that case-law represented. To my mind that was a methodological error. The superficial similarities between the present case and the *Loizidou* case are deceptive. The only point in common (to which I will return) is the source of the conflict, namely the prospect for a sizeable community of being attached to another country from which it is radically differentiated by its historical, economic and cultural ties. Hence the reactions and counter-reactions of the participants in the conflict, which took violent forms and led to human tragedies.

He disagreed with the Court's explanation of the historical background to the emergence of the 'MRT' as he traced Russian/Slavic influence over the territory back to the early nineteenth century. Also he considered that Russia could not be held responsible for acts of the 'MRT' as the latter was proclaimed one year before the USSR broke up. Furthermore:

I have not found in the factual material concerning the military, political and economic aspects any valid evidence capable of establishing a limited or continuing intervention by Russia in favour of Transdniestria, or proof of the 'MRT's' military, political or economic dependence on Russia.

See below p 169 [Art 3] for further consideration of the case.

8   A unanimous Chamber found that a number of Iraqi shepherds shot and mutilated in northern Iraq at a time when there was a large-scale Turkish military operation, involving over 35,000 ground troops, into Iraq for six weeks in the spring of 1995 were not within the jurisdiction of Turkey in *Issa and Others v Turkey*, judgment of 16 November 2004. The six applicants, wives/mothers of the deceased, claimed that the latter had been killed by Turkish soldiers. The Turkish Government acknowledged that its forces had undertaken an anti-terrorist operation in northern Iraq, but denied that Turkish troops had been in the area where the shepherds had been killed. Applying *Bankovic and Loizidou* the Chamber held that:

74. The Court does not exclude the possibility that, as a consequence of this military action, the respondent State could be considered to have exercised, temporarily, effective overall control of a particular portion of the territory of northern Iraq. Accordingly, if there is a sufficient factual basis for holding that, at the relevant time, the victims were within that specific area, it would follow logically that they were within the jurisdiction of Turkey . . .

However, given, *inter alia*, the lack of independent eye-witnesses accounts of the presence of Turkish forces near the applicant's village the Chamber concluded that it was not satisfied 'beyond reasonable doubt' that the deceased were within the jurisdiction of Turkey at the time of their deaths. This judgment shows that the Court is very circumspect in holding member States liable for acts occurring outside their national territorial boundaries. The judgment in *Issa* also disclosed that at the time of the killings there was intense fighting between the PKK (Kurdistan Workers Party) and KDP (Kurdistan Democratic Party) in the area where the deceased were working.

9 The use of the term 'everyone' in Article 1 means that non-nationals within the jurisdiction of a Member state can claim the protection of the rights and guarantees elaborated in the Convention, see for example *Soering v United Kingdom* below p 192.

10 A Grand Chamber examined the overlapping responsibilities of a Member state under the Convention and to the European Union in *Bosphorus Hava Yollari Turizm ve Ticaret Anonim Sirketi v Ireland*, judgment of 30 June 2005. The applicant Turkish company had leased two aircraft from Yugoslav Airlines (the national airline of the former Yugoslavia) in 1992. In April 1993 the Security Council of the United Nations adopted a Resolution requiring all States to impound aircraft in their territories in which a controlling interest was held by a person/undertaking from Yugoslavia (this Resolution was part of an ongoing sanctions strategy aimed at the human rights violations taking place in Yugoslavia). The European Community implemented that Resolution by an EC Regulation later that month. In May 1993 the applicant arranged for one of the lease aircraft to be serviced by a company in Ireland. After the aircraft had been serviced (and payment made by the applicant) the Irish Department of Transport impounded the aircraft in accordance with the EC Regulation. The applicant challenged that decision before the Irish courts and the issue was referred to the European Court of Justice for a preliminary ruling as to whether the aircraft came within the Regulation and if so whether the impounding violate the applicant's fundamental rights. The ECJ ruled that the Regulation applied to the aircraft and that the impounding was in furtherance of important international goals and did not constitute a disproportionate measure. Subsequently, the Irish Supreme Court upheld the lawfulness of the impounding. Before the Grand Chamber the applicant company alleged that the actions of the Irish authorities constituted a violation of its rights under Article 1 of Protocol No 1. The Government submitted that its compliance with its international obligations in respect of the sanctions imposed upon Yugoslavia justified any interference with the applicant's property rights.

152. The Convention does not, on the one hand, prohibit Contracting Parties from transferring sovereign power to an international (including a supranational) organisation in order to pursue co-operation in certain fields of activity (the *M. & Co.* [v *Germany*, No 13258/87 64 DR 138] at p 144 and *Matthews* [v *UK* ECHR 1999-I] at § 32. Moreover, even as the holder of such transferred sovereign power, that organisation is not itself held responsible under the Convention for proceedings before, or decisions

of, its organs as long as it is not a Contracting Party (see *CFDT v European Communities*, No 8030/77, Commission decision of 10 July 1978, DR 13, p. 231; *Dufay v European Communities*, No 13539/88, Commission decision of 19 January 1989; the above-cited *M. & Co.* case, at p 144 and the above-cited *Matthews* judgment, at § 32).

153. On the other hand, it has also been accepted that a Contracting Party is responsible under Article 1 of the Convention for all acts and omissions of its organs regardless of whether the act or omission in question was a consequence of domestic law or of the necessity to comply with international legal obligations. Article 1 makes no distinction as to the type of rule or measure concerned and does not exclude any part of a Contracting Party's 'jurisdiction' from scrutiny under the Convention (*United Communist Party of Turkey and Others v Turkey* judgment of 30 January 1998, Reports, 1998-I, § 29).

154. In reconciling both these positions and thereby establishing the extent to which State action can be justified by its compliance with obligations flowing from its membership of an international organisation to which it has transferred part of its sovereignty, the Court has recognised that absolving Contracting States completely from their Convention responsibility in the areas covered by such a transfer would be incompatible with the purpose and object of the Convention: the guarantees of the Convention could be limited or excluded at will thereby depriving it of its peremptory character and undermining the practical and effective nature of its safeguards (*M. & Co* . at p 145 and *Waite and Kennedy* [*v Germany* ECHR 1999-I] at § 67). The State is considered to retain Convention liability in respect of treaty commitments subsequent to the entry into force of the Convention (*mutatis mutandis*, the above-cited *Matthews v the United Kingdom* judgment, at §§ 29 and 32–4, and *Prince Hans-Adam II of Liechtenstein v Germany* [GC], No 42527/98, § 47, ECHR 2001-VIII).

155. In the Court's view, State action taken in compliance with such legal obligations is justified as long as the relevant organisation is considered to protect fundamental rights, as regards both the substantive guarantees offered and the mechanisms controlling their observance, in a manner which can be considered at least equivalent to that for which the Convention provides (see the above-cited *M. & Co.* decision, at p 145, an approach with which the parties and the European Commission agreed). By 'equivalent' the Court means 'comparable': any requirement that the organisation's protection be 'identical' could run counter to the interest of international co-operation pursued (paragraph 150 above). However, any such finding of equivalence could not be final and would be susceptible to review in the light of any relevant change in fundamental rights' protection.

156. If such equivalent protection is considered to be provided by the organisation, the presumption will be that a State has not departed from the requirements of the Convention when it does no more than implement legal obligations flowing from its membership of the organisation.

However, any such presumption can be rebutted if, in the circumstances of a particular case, it is considered that the protection of Convention rights was manifestly deficient. In such cases, the interest of international co-operation would be outweighed by the Convention's role as a 'constitutional instrument of European public order' in the field of human rights (*Loizidou v Turkey (preliminary objections)*, judgment of 23 March 1995, Series A No 310, § 75).

157. It remains the case that a State would be fully responsible under the Convention for all acts falling outside its strict international legal obligations.

. . .

158. Since the impugned act constituted solely compliance by Ireland with its legal obligations flowing from membership of the EC, the Court will now examine whether a presumption arises that Ireland complied with its Convention requirements in fulfilling such obligations and whether any such presumption has been rebutted in the circumstances of the present case.

(B) WAS THERE A PRESUMPTION OF CONVENTION COMPLIANCE AT THE RELEVANT TIME?

159. The Court has described (at paragraphs 73–81 above) the fundamental rights guarantees of the EC which govern Member States, Community institutions together with natural and legal persons ('individuals').

While the constituent EC treaty did not initially contain express provisions for the protection of fundamental rights, the ECJ subsequently recognised that such rights were enshrined in the general principles of Community law protected by it and that the Convention had a 'special significance' as a source of such rights. Respect for fundamental rights has become 'a condition of the legality of Community acts' (paragraphs 73–5 above, together with the opinion of the AG in the present case at paragraphs 45–50 above) and in carrying out this assessment the ECJ refers extensively to Convention provisions and to this Court's jurisprudence. At the relevant time, these jurisprudential developments had been reflected in certain treaty amendments (notably those aspects of the Single European Act 1986 and of the TEU . . .).

This evolution has continued thereafter. The Treaty of Amsterdam 1997 is referred to at paragraph 79 above. Although not fully binding, the provisions of the Charter of Fundamental Rights of the European Union were substantially inspired by those of the Convention and the Charter recognises the Convention as establishing the minimum human rights standards. Article I-9 of the later Treaty establishing a Constitution for Europe (not in force) provides for the Charter to become primary law of the European Union and for the Union to accede to the Convention (see paragraphs 80–1 above).

160. However, the effectiveness of such substantive guarantees of fundamental rights depends on the mechanisms of control in place to ensure observance of such rights.

161. The Court has referred (at paragraphs 86–90 above) to the jurisdiction of the ECJ in, *inter alia*, annulment actions (Article 173, now Article 230), in actions against Community institutions for failure to perform Treaty obligations (Article 175, now Article 232), to hear related pleas of illegality under Article 184 (now Article 241) and in cases against Member States for failure to fulfil Treaty obligations (Articles 169, 170, and 171, now Articles 226, 227, and 228).

162. It is true that access of individuals to the ECJ under these provisions is limited: they have no *locus standi* under Articles 169 and 170; their right to initiate actions under Articles 173 and 175 is restricted as is, consequently, their right under Article 184; and they have no right to take an action against another individual.

163. It nevertheless remains the case that actions initiated before the ECJ by the Community institutions or a Member state constitute important control of compliance with Community norms to the indirect benefit of individuals. Individuals can also bring an action for damages before the ECJ in respect of the non-contractual liability of the institutions.

164. Moreover, it is essentially through the national courts that the Community system provides a remedy to individuals against a Member state or another individual for a breach of EC law. Certain EC Treaty provisions envisaged a complementary role for the national courts in the Community control mechanisms from the outset, notably Article 189 (the notion of direct applicability, now Article 249) and Article 177 (the preliminary reference procedure, now Article 234). It was the development by the ECJ of important notions such as the supremacy of EC law, direct effect, indirect effect and State liability which greatly enlarged the role of the domestic courts in the enforcement of Community law and its fundamental rights' guarantees.

The ECJ maintains its control on the application by national courts of EC law, including its fundamental rights guarantees, through the procedure for which Article 177 of the EC Treaty provides . . . While the ECJ's role is limited to responding to the interpretative or validity question referred by the domestic court, the response will often be determinative of the domestic proceedings (as, indeed, it was in the present case) and detailed guidelines on the timing and content of a preliminary reference have been laid down by the EC treaty provision and developed by the ECJ in its case-law. The parties to the domestic proceedings have the right to put their case to the ECJ during the Article 177 process. It is further recalled that national courts operate in legal systems into which the Convention has been incorporated, albeit to differing degrees.

165. In such circumstances, the Court finds that the protection of fundamental rights by EC law can be considered to be, and to have been at the relevant time, 'equivalent' (within the meaning of paragraph 155 above) to that of the Convention system. Consequently, the presumption arises that Ireland did not depart from the requirements of the Convention when it implemented legal obligations flowing from its membership of the EC (see paragraph 156).

(C) HAS THAT PRESUMPTION BEEN REBUTTED IN THE PRESENT CASE?

166. The Court has had regard to the nature of the interference, to the general interest pursued by the impoundment and by the sanctions regime and to the ruling of the ECJ (in the light of the opinion of the AG), a ruling with which the Supreme Court was obliged to and did comply. It considers it clear that there was no dysfunction of the mechanisms of control of the observance of Convention rights.

In the Court's view, therefore, it cannot be said that the protection of the applicant's Convention rights was manifestly deficient with the consequence that the relevant presumption of Convention compliance by the respondent State has not been rebutted.

4. Conclusion under Article 1 of Protocol No 1

167. It follows that the impoundment of the aircraft did not give rise to a violation of Article 1 of Protocol No. 1 to the Convention.

Judges Rozakis, Tulkens, Traja, Botoucharova, Zagrebelsky, and Garlicki issued a joint concurring opinion in which they expressed a more cautious attitude towards the protection of fundamental rights by the EU system.

On the other hand, as the judgment itself acknowledges, individuals' access to the Community court is 'limited' (see paragraph 162). Yet, as the Court reiterated in the *Mamatkulov and Askarov v Turkey* judgment ([GC], Nos 46827/99 and 46951/99, 4 February 2005), the right of individual application 'is one of the keystones in the machinery for the enforcement of the rights and freedoms set forth in the Convention' (see § 122 of that judgment). Admittedly, judicial protection under Community law is based on a plurality of appeals, among which the reference to the Court of Justice for a preliminary ruling has an important role. However, it remains that case that, despite its value, a reference for a preliminary ruling entails an internal, a priori review. It is not of the same nature and does not replace the external, a posteriori supervision of the European Court of Human Rights, carried out following an individual application.

The right of individual application is one of the basic obligations assumed by the States on ratifying the Convention. It is therefore difficult to accept that they should have been able to reduce the effectiveness of this right for persons within their jurisdiction on the ground that they have transferred certain powers to the European Communities. For the Court to leave to the EU's judicial system the task of ensuring 'equivalent protection', without retaining a means of verifying on a case-by-case basis that that protection is indeed 'equivalent', would be tantamount to consenting tacitly to substitution, in the field of Community law, of Convention standards by a Community standard which might be inspired by Convention standards but whose equivalence with the latter would no longer be subject to authorised scrutiny.

4. Admittedly, the judgment states that such *in concreto* review would remain possible, since the presumption could be rebutted if, in the circumstances of a particular case, the Court considered that 'the protection of Convention rights was manifestly deficient' (see paragraph 156).

In spite of its relatively undefined nature, the criterion 'manifestly deficient' appears to establish a relatively low threshold, which is in marked contrast to the supervision generally carried out under the European Convention on Human Rights. Since the Convention establishes a minimum level of protection (Article 53), any equivalence between it and the Community's protection can only ever be in terms of the means, not of the result. Moreover, it seems all the more difficult to accept that Community law could be authorised, in the name of 'equivalent protection', to apply standards that are less stringent than those of the European Convention on Human Rights when we consider that the latter were formally drawn on in the Charter of Fundamental Rights of the European Union, itself an integral part of the Union's Treaty establishing a Constitution for Europe. Although these texts have not (yet) entered into force, Article II-112(3) of the Treaty contains a rule whose moral weight would already appear to be binding on any future legislative or judicial developments in European Union law: 'Insofar as this Charter contains rights which correspond to rights guaranteed by the Convention for the Protection of Human Rights and Fundamental Freedoms, the meaning and scope of those rights shall be the same as those laid down by the said Convention.'

Thus, in order to avoid any danger of double standards, it is necessary to remain vigilant. If it were to materialise, such a danger would in turn create different obligations for the Contracting Parties to the European Convention on Human Rights, divided into those which had acceded to international conventions and those which had not. In another context, that of reservations, the Court has raised the possibility of inequality between Contracting States and reiterated that this would 'run counter to the aim, as expressed in the Preamble to the Convention, to achieve greater unity in the maintenance and further realisation of human rights' (*Loizidou v Turkey* (preliminary objections), judgment of 23 March 1995, Series A No 310, § 77).

In his concurring opinion Judge Ress expressed the belief that,

One would conclude that the protection of the Convention right would be manifestly deficient if, in deciding the key question in a case, the ECJ were to depart from the interpretation or the application of the Convention or the Protocols that had already been the subject of well-established ECHR case-law.

The judgment in *Bosphorus* was intended to maintain a harmonious relationship between the Strasbourg Court and the ECJ. President Wildhaber described it as a 'landmark judgment in the history of the relations between the two European Courts'. However, he noted that as applicants to the Strasbourg Court could seek to argue that in their particular cases they had not received 'equivalent' protection of Convention rights in domestic proceedings implementing EC law such applications were not in principle inadmissible *ratione materiae*. L Wildhaber, 'The Coordination of the Protection of Fundamental Rights in Europe', *Geneva*, 8 September 2005.

Cathryn Costello has observed:

To date, the comity between Strasbourg and Luxembourg has markedly increased the quality of Luxembourg's jurisprudence, in that the latter cites and examines Strasbourg case-law explicitly, rather than making elliptical assertions of fundamental rights compliance. Luxembourg has explicitly revised its stance on a number of fundamental rights rulings. It remains to be seen whether and to what extent Strasbourg will push Luxembourg further, by engaging in review of actual individual decisions. Its reluctance to do so in *Bosphorus* is explicable in light of the timing of the case and its inherently incrementalist approach to asserting control over the ECJ. 'The *Bosphorus* Ruling of the European Court of Human Rights: Fundamental Rights and Blurred Boundaries in Europe' (2006) 6(1) *Human Rights Law Review* 87 at p 129.

11   A unanimous Chamber determined that the arrest, detention and trial of the former President of Iraq did not occur within the jurisdiction of a Member state in *Saddam Hussein v Albania and 20 other States*, Decision of 14 March 2006. The applicant contended that the respondent Member States were partners with the United States in the coalition that invaded Iraq during 2003 and therefore accountable, under the Convention, for his capture and handing over to the Iraqi Government for trial. After observing that the coalition partners had military responsibility for different geographical zones of Iraq and that the applicant had been arrested and detained by United States' forces, the Chamber determine that:

In such circumstances, the Court considers that the applicant has not established that he fell within the jurisdiction of the respondent States on any of the bases alleged. The Court considers that he has not demonstrated that those States had jurisdiction on the basis of their control of the territory where the alleged violations took place (*Loizidou v Turkey*, judgment of 18 December 1996, *Reports of Decision and Judgments* 1996 VI and *Cyprus v Turkey* [GC], No 25781/94, ECHR 2001). Even if he could have fallen within a State's jurisdiction because of his detention by it, he has not shown that any one of the respondent States had any responsibility for, or any involvement or role in, his arrest and subsequent detention (*Issa and Others v Turkey*, No 31821/96, §§ 71–82, 16 November 2004 and *Öcalan v Turkey* [GC], No 46221/99, § 91, ECHR 2005 . . .). This failure to substantiate any such involvement also constitutes a response to his final submission to the effect that the respondent States were responsible for the acts of their military agents abroad. Finally, there is no basis in the Convention's jurisprudence and the applicant has not invoked any established principle of international law which would mean that he fell within the respondent States' jurisdiction on the sole basis that those States allegedly formed part (at varying unspecified levels) of a coalition with the US, when the impugned actions were carried out by the US, when security in the zone in which those actions took place was assigned to the US and when the overall command of the coalition was vested in the US.

Accordingly, the Court does not consider it to be established that there was or is any jurisdictional link between the applicant and the respondent States or therefore that the applicant was capable of falling within the jurisdiction of those States, within the meaning of Article 1 of the Convention.

Therefore, the application was declared inadmissible. The latter part of the decision indicates that participation in an overseas military campaign involving multi-national forces does not *per se* attract jurisdictional responsibility under the Convention for all the acts of the coalition.

12   The Court has utilized Article 1 combined with other Articles providing substantive rights as the jurisprudential basis for a number of implied positive obligations upon Member States. Examples include the duty to undertake effective investigations into killings first recognised in *McCann v United Kingdom* at paragraph 161 (see below p 77 and p 124 [section on investigation duty]), and the obligation to take measures to protect vulnerable persons from torture, inhuman or degrading treatment/punishment by other private persons: see *A v United Kingdom* at paragraph 22 (below p 158). For a detailed analysis of this topic see, A. Mowbray, *The Development of Positive Obligations under the European Convention on Human Rights by the European Court of Human Rights* (Hart Publishing, Oxford, 2004).

4 ARTICLE 2 RIGHT TO LIFE

The Court's general approach

....

McCann v UK A.324 (1995) 21 EHRR 97
European Court of Human Rights

In early 1988 the British, Spanish and Gibraltar authorities became aware that the Provisional Irish Republican Army (IRA) were planning a terrorist attack on Gibraltar. Intelligence suggested that it was to centre on the assembly area where the British army changed the guard every Tuesday morning. An advisory group, consisting of inter alios Special Air Service (SAS) personnel, British Security Service officers and a bomb-disposal officer, was sent to Gibraltar to assist the Gibraltar Commissioner of Police. Three suspected terrorists (members of an Active Service Unit) were sighted in Malaga (Spain) on 4 March. At midnight on 5 March the Commissioner of Police held a briefing during which representatives of the Security Services stated that in their opinion: the IRA intended to attack the changing of the guard ceremony on 8 March; the ASU comprised Daniel McCann (previously convicted of possessing explosives), Mairead Farrell (previously convicted of causing explosions) and Sean Savage (described as an expert bomb-maker); the attack would be by way of a car bomb; the use of a radio-operated remote-control device to detonate the bomb was thought likely; the placing of a 'blocking' car to reserve a parking space for the car containing the bomb was considered unlikely and the suspects were believed to be dangerous, almost certainly armed and likely to use their weapons if confronted by the security forces. A detective from Gibraltar went to the Spanish immigration post on the border with Gibraltar to keep a look-out for the suspects. Customs and police officers on duty at the Gibraltar border were not informed of the operation in order to reduce the number of persons with knowledge of the counter-terrorism plan (but an arrest team was located nearby). A person, thought to be Savage, was seen parking a white Renault car in the assembly area at about 12:30. At about 14:00 hours he was confirmed to be Savage. Thirty minutes later Farrell and McCann were identified crossing the border into Gibraltar on foot. At about 15:00 hours the three suspects were seen, by surveillance officers, together looking at the parked car in the assembly area. The police considered whether to arrest the suspects, but they started to move away from the car. The British bomb-disposal adviser spent two minutes looking at the exterior of the car and he noted that the car aerial was out of place (it was rusty while the car was not old). He reported to the Police Commissioner that it was 'a suspect car' (he meant that it was a car parked in suspicious circumstances where there was every reason to believe that it contained a bomb). The Commissioner decided that the suspects should be arrested on suspicion of conspiracy to murder and he signed an order requesting the military to intercept and apprehend the suspects. Two SAS soldiers, in plain clothes and each armed with a pistol, moved within 10 metres behind McCann and Farrell. The former turned round (he may have heard a police car siren in the distance) and Soldier A. considered that McCann made an aggressive movement (A. thought McCann was going to press a remote control device to detonate a bomb) so A. opened fire on McCann. Soldier A. also thought Farrell was reaching for a similar device in her handbag so he fired at her too. Soldier B. also shot at both suspects. The two soldiers fired a total of twelve shots. Two other SAS soldiers (also in plain clothes and armed) were following Savage a short distance away. When the shooting began Savage turned around, one of the soldiers shouted out 'Stop' and Savage moved his arm down to his hip. Soldier D. believed Savage was going for a radio detonator and so the former opened fire (from a distance of about two to three metres). Likewise soldier C. also fired at Savage. Fifteen bullets were fired into Savage. All three suspects were killed. No weapons or detonation devices were found on the suspects' bodies. Nor was a bomb found in the Renault car. However, keys found in Farrell's handbag led Spanish police to another car parked in Marbella which contained an explosive device (consisting of 64 kg of Semtex explosive surrounded by 200 rounds of ammunition—designed to explode as shrapnel—attached to two timers).

An inquest into the killings was held by the Gibraltar Coroner in September 1988. After nineteen days of hearings, during which seventy-nine witnesses were heard (including the soldiers, security and police officers involved in the operation), the jury (by nine to two) returned verdicts of lawful killing. The applicants, representatives of the estates of the deceased suspects, sought to bring civil actions against the Ministry of Defence in the Northern Ireland High Court; however their action was struck-out. The applicants then complained to the Commission alleging that the planning and execution of the above counter-terrorist operation was in breach of Article 2. By eleven votes six, the Commission found that there had been no breach.

A. INTERPRETATION OF ARTICLE 2 (ART 2)

1. GENERAL APPROACH

146. The Court's approach to the interpretation of Article 2 (art 2) must be guided by the fact that the object and purpose of the Convention as an instrument for the protection of individual human beings requires that its provisions be interpreted and applied so as to make its safeguards practical and effective (see, inter alia, the *Soering v UK* judgment of 7 July 1989, Series A No 161, p 34, para 87, and the *Loizidou v Turkey (Preliminary Objections)* judgment of 23 March 1995, Series A No 310, p 27, para 72).

147. It must also be borne in mind that, as a provision (art 2) which not only safeguards the right to life but sets out the circumstances when the deprivation of life may be justified, Article 2 (art 2) ranks as one of the most fundamental provisions in the Convention—indeed one which, in peacetime, admits of no derogation under Article 15 (art 15). Together with Article 3 (art 15+3) of the Convention, it also enshrines one of the basic values of the democratic societies making up the Council of Europe (see the above-mentioned *Soering* judgment, p 34, para 88). As such, its provisions must be strictly construed.

148. The Court considers that the exceptions delineated in paragraph 2 (art 2-2) indicate that this provision (art 2-2) extends to, but is not concerned exclusively with, intentional killing. As the Commission has pointed out, the text of Article 2 (art 2), read as a whole, demonstrates that paragraph 2 (art 2-2) does not primarily define instances where it is permitted intentionally to kill an individual, but describes the situations where it is permitted to 'use force' which may result, as an unintended outcome, in the deprivation of life. The use of force, however, must be no more than 'absolutely necessary' for the achievement of one of the purposes set out in sub-paragraphs (a), (b) or (c) (art 2-2-a, art 2-2-b, art 2-2-c) (see application No 10044/82, *Stewart v UK*, 10 July 1984, Decisions and Reports 39, pp 169–71).

149. In this respect the use of the term 'absolutely necessary' in Article 2 para 2 (art 2-2) indicates that a stricter and more compelling test of necessity must be employed from that normally applicable when

determining whether State action is 'necessary in a democratic society' under paragraph 2 of Articles 8 to 11 (art 8-2, art 9-2, art 10-2, art 11-2) of the Convention. In particular, the force used must be strictly proportionate to the achievement of the aims set out in sub-paragraphs 2 (a), (b) and (c) of Article 2 (art 2-2-a-b-c).

150. In keeping with the importance of this provision (art 2) in a democratic society, the Court must, in making its assessment, subject deprivations of life to the most careful scrutiny, particularly where deliberate lethal force is used, taking into consideration not only the actions of the agents of the State who actually administer the force but also all the surrounding circumstances including such matters as the planning and control of the actions under examination.

2. THE OBLIGATION TO PROTECT LIFE IN ARTICLE 2 PARA 1 (ART 2-1)

(a) Compatibility of national law and practice with Article 2 (art 2) standards

151. The applicants submitted under this head that Article 2 para 1 (art 2-1) of the Convention imposed a positive duty on States to 'protect' life. In particular, the national law must strictly control and limit the circumstances in which a person may be deprived of his life by agents of the State. The State must also give appropriate training, instructions and briefing to its soldiers and other agents who may use force and exercise strict control over any operations which may involve the use of lethal force.

In their view, the relevant domestic law was vague and general and did not encompass the Article 2 (art 2) standard of absolute necessity. This in itself constituted a violation of Article 2 para 1 (art 2-1). There was also a violation of this provision (art 2-1) in that the law did not require that the agents of the State be trained in accordance with the strict standards of Article 2 para 1 (art 2-1).

152. For the Commission, with whom the Government agreed, Article 2 (art 2) was not to be interpreted as requiring an identical formulation in domestic law. Its requirements were satisfied if the substance of the Convention right was protected by domestic law.

153. The Court recalls that the Convention does not oblige Contracting Parties to incorporate its provisions into national law (see, inter alia, the *James v UK* judgment of 21 February 1986, Series A No 98, p 47, para 84, and *The Holy Monasteries v Greece* judgment of 9 December 1994, Series A No 301-A, p 39, para 90). Furthermore, it is not the role of the Convention institutions to examine in *abstracto* the compatibility of national legislative or constitutional provisions with the requirements of the Convention (see, for example, the *Klass v Germany* judgment of 6 September 1978, Series A No 28, p 18, para 33).

154. Bearing the above in mind, it is noted that Article 2 of the Gibraltar Constitution ... is similar to Article 2 (art 2) of the Convention with the exception that the standard of justification for the use of force which results in the deprivation of life is that of 'reasonably justifiable' as opposed to 'absolutely necessary' in paragraph 2 of Article 2 (art 2-2). While the Convention standard appears on its face to be stricter than the relevant national standard, it has been submitted by the Government that, having regard to the manner in which the standard is interpreted and applied by the national courts ... there is no significant difference in substance between the two concepts.

155. In the Court's view, whatever the validity of this submission, the difference between the two standards is not sufficiently great that a violation of Article 2 para 1 (art 2-1) could be found on this ground alone.

156. As regards the applicants' arguments concerning the training and instruction of the agents of the State and the need for operational control, the Court considers that these are matters which, in the context of the present case, raise issues under Article 2 para 2 (art 2-2) concerning the proportionality of the State's response to the perceived threat of a terrorist attack. It suffices to note in this respect that the rules of engagement issued to the soldiers and the police in the present case provide a series of rules governing the use of force which carefully reflect the national standard as well as the substance of the Convention standard ...

(b) Adequacy of the inquest proceedings as an investigative mechanism

157. The applicants also submitted under this head ... that the State must provide an effective *ex post facto* procedure for establishing the facts surrounding a killing by agents of the State through an independent judicial process to which relatives must have full access.

Together with the *amici curiae*, Amnesty International and British-Irish Rights Watch and Others, they submitted that this procedural requirement had not been satisfied by the inquest procedure because of a combination of shortcomings. In particular, they complained that no independent police investigation took place of any aspect of the operation leading to the shootings; that normal scene-of-crime procedures were not followed; that not all eyewitnesses were traced or interviewed by the police; that the Coroner sat with a jury which was drawn from a 'garrison' town with close ties to the military; that the Coroner refused to allow the jury to be screened to exclude members who were Crown servants; that the public interest certificates issued by the relevant Government authorities effectively curtailed an examination of the overall operation.

They further contended that they did not enjoy equality of representation with the Crown in the course of the inquest proceedings and were thus severely handicapped in their efforts to find the truth since, inter alia, they had had no legal aid and were only represented by two lawyers; witness statements had been made available in advance to the Crown and to the lawyers representing the police and the soldiers but, with the exception of ballistic and pathology reports, not to their lawyers; they did not have the necessary resources to pay for copies of the daily transcript of the proceedings which amounted to £500–£700.

158. The Government submitted that the inquest was an effective, independent and public review mechanism which more than satisfied any procedural requirement which might be read into Article 2 para 1 (art 2-1) of the Convention. In particular, they maintained that it would not be appropriate for the Court to seek to identify a single set of standards by which all investigations into the circumstances of death should be assessed. Moreover, it was important to distinguish between such an investigation and civil proceedings brought to seek a remedy for an alleged violation of the right to life. Finally, they invited the Court to reject the contention by the intervenors British-Irish Rights Watch and Others that a violation of Article 2 para 1 (art 2-1) will have occurred whenever the Court finds serious differences between the UN Principles on Extra-Legal Executions and the investigation conducted into any particular death ...

159. For the Commission, the inquest subjected the actions of the State to extensive, independent and highly public scrutiny and thereby provided sufficient procedural safeguards for the purposes of Article 2 (art 2) of the Convention.

160. The Court considers that it is unnecessary to decide in the present case whether a right of access to court to bring civil proceedings in connection with deprivation of life can be inferred from Article 2 para 1 (art 2-1) since this is an issue which would be more appropriately considered under Articles 6 and 13 (art 6, art 13) of the Convention—provisions (art 6, art 13) that have not been invoked by the applicants.

161. The Court confines itself to noting, like the Commission, that a general legal prohibition of arbitrary killing by the agents of the State would be ineffective, in practice, if there existed no procedure for reviewing the lawfulness of the use of lethal force by State authorities. The obligation to protect the right to life under this provision (art 2), read in conjunction with the State's general duty under Article 1 (art 2+1) of the Convention to 'secure to everyone within their jurisdiction the rights and freedoms defined in [the] Convention', requires by implication that there should be some form of effective official investigation when individuals have been killed as a result of the use of force by, inter alios, agents of the State.

162. However, it is not necessary in the present case for the Court to decide what form such an investigation should take and under what conditions it should be conducted, since public inquest proceedings,

at which the applicants were legally represented and which involved the hearing of seventy-nine witnesses, did in fact take place. Moreover, the proceedings lasted nineteen days and, as is evident from the inquest's voluminous transcript, involved a detailed review of the events surrounding the killings. Furthermore, it appears from the transcript, including the Coroner's summing-up to the jury, that the lawyers acting on behalf of the applicants were able to examine and cross-examine key witnesses, including the military and police personnel involved in the planning and conduct of the anti-terrorist operation, and to make the submissions they wished to make in the course of the proceedings.

163. In light of the above, the Court does not consider that the alleged various shortcomings in the inquest proceedings, to which reference has been made by both the applicants and the intervenors, substantially hampered the carrying out of a thorough, impartial and careful examination of the circumstances surrounding the killings.

164. It follows that there has been no breach of Article 2 para 1 (art 2-1) of the Convention on this ground.

B. APPLICATION OF ARTICLE 2 (ART 2) TO THE FACTS OF THE CASE

1. GENERAL APPROACH TO THE EVALUATION OF THE EVIDENCE

165. While accepting that the Convention institutions are not in any formal sense bound by the decisions of the inquest jury, the Government submitted that the verdicts were of central importance to any subsequent examination of the deaths of the deceased. Accordingly, the Court should give substantial weight to the verdicts of the jury in the absence of any indication that those verdicts were perverse or ones which no reasonable tribunal of fact could have reached. In this connection, the jury was uniquely well placed to assess the circumstances surrounding the shootings. The members of the jury heard and saw each of the seventy-nine witnesses giving evidence, including extensive cross-examination. With that benefit they were able to assess the credibility and probative value of the witnesses' testimony. The Government pointed out that the jury also heard the submissions of the various parties, including those of the lawyers representing the deceased.

166. The applicants, on the other hand, maintained that inquests are by their very nature ill-equipped to be full and detailed inquiries into controversial killings such as in the present case. Moreover, the inquest did not examine the killings from the standpoint of concepts such as 'proportionality' or 'absolute necessity' but applied the lesser tests of 'reasonable force' or 'reasonable necessity'. Furthermore, the jury focused on the actions of the soldiers as they opened fire as if it were considering their criminal culpability and not on matters such as the allegedly negligent and reckless planning of the operation.

167. The Commission examined the case on the basis of the observations of the parties and the documents submitted by them, in particular the transcript of the inquest. It did not consider itself bound by the findings of the jury.

168. The Court recalls that under the scheme of the Convention the establishment and verification of the facts is primarily a matter for the Commission (Articles 28 para 1 and 31) (art 28-1, art 31). Accordingly, it is only in exceptional circumstances that the Court will use its powers in this area. The Court is not, however, bound by the Commission's findings of fact and remains free to make its own appreciation in the light of all the material before it (see, inter alia, the *Cruz Varas v Sweden* judgment of 20 March 1991, Series A No 201, p 29, para 74, and the *Klaas v Germany* judgment of 22 September 1993, Series A No 269, p 17, para 29).

169. In the present case neither the Government nor the applicants have, in the proceedings before the Court, sought to contest the facts as they have been found by the Commission although they differ fundamentally as to the conclusions to be drawn from them under Article 2 (art 2) of the Convention.

Having regard to the submissions of those appearing before the Court and to the inquest proceedings, the Court takes the Commission's establishment of the facts and findings ... to be an accurate and reliable account of the facts underlying the present case.

170. As regards the appreciation of these facts from the standpoint of Article 2 (art 2), the Court observes that the jury had the benefit of listening to the witnesses at first hand, observing their demeanour and assessing the probative value of their testimony.

Nevertheless, it must be borne in mind that the jury's finding was limited to a decision of lawful killing and, as is normally the case, did not provide reasons for the conclusion that it reached. In addition, the focus of concern of the inquest proceedings and the standard applied by the jury was whether the killings by the soldiers were reasonably justified in the circumstances as opposed to whether they were 'absolutely necessary' under Article 2 para 2 (art 2-2) in the sense developed above ...

171. Against this background, the Court must make its own assessment whether the facts as established by the Commission disclose a violation of Article 2 (art 2) of the Convention.

172. The applicants further submitted that in examining the actions of the State in a case in which the use of deliberate lethal force was expressly contemplated in writing, the Court should place on the Government the onus of proving, beyond reasonable doubt, that the planning and execution of the operation was in accordance with Article 2 (art 2) of the Convention. In addition, it should not grant the State authorities the benefit of the doubt as if its criminal liability were at stake.

173. The Court, in determining whether there has been a breach of Article 2 (art 2) in the present case, is not assessing the criminal responsibility of those directly or indirectly concerned. In accordance with its usual practice therefore it will assess the issues in the light of all the material placed before it by the applicants and by the Government or, if necessary, material obtained of its own motion (see the *Ireland v UK* judgment of 18 January 1978, Series A No 25, p 64, para 160, and the above-mentioned *Cruz Varas* judgment, p 29, para 75).

2. APPLICANTS' ALLEGATION THAT THE KILLINGS WERE PREMEDITATED

174. The applicants alleged that there had been a premeditated plan to kill the deceased. While conceding that there was no evidence of a direct order from the highest authorities in the Ministry of Defence, they claimed that there was strong circumstantial evidence in support of their allegation. They suggested that a plot to kill could be achieved by other means such as hints and innuendoes, coupled with the choice of a military unit like the SAS which, as indicated by the evidence given by their members at the inquest, was trained to neutralise a target by shooting to kill. Supplying false information of the sort that was actually given to the soldiers in this case would render a fatal shooting likely. The use of the SAS was, in itself, evidence that the killing was intended.

175. They further contended that the Gibraltar police would not have been aware of such an unlawful enterprise. They pointed out that the SAS officer E gave his men secret briefings to which the Gibraltar police were not privy. Moreover, when the soldiers attended the police station after the shootings, they were accompanied by an army lawyer who made it clear that the soldiers were there only for the purpose of handing in their weapons. In addition, the soldiers were immediately flown out of Gibraltar without ever having been interviewed by the police.

176. The applicants referred to the following factors, among others, in support of their contention:
— The best and safest method of preventing an explosion and capturing the suspects would have been to stop them and their bomb from entering Gibraltar. The authorities had their photographs and knew their names and aliases as well as the passports they were carrying;
— If the suspects had been under close observation by the Spanish authorities from Malaga to Gibraltar, as claimed by the journalist, Mr Debelius, the hiring of the white Renault car would have been seen and it would have been known that it did not contain a bomb ... ;

— The above claim is supported by the failure of the authorities to isolate the bomb and clear the area around it in order to protect the public. In Gibraltar there were a large number of soldiers present with experience in the speedy clearance of suspect bomb sites. The only explanation for this lapse in security procedures was that the security services knew that there was no bomb in the car;

— Soldier G, who was sent to inspect the car and who reported that there was a suspect car bomb, admitted during the inquest that he was not an expert in radio signal transmission . . . This was significant since the sole basis for his assessment was that the radio aerial looked older than the car. A real expert would have thought of removing the aerial to nullify the radio detonator, which could have been done without destabilising the explosive, as testified by Dr Scott. He would have also known that if the suspects had intended to explode a bomb by means of a radio signal they would not have used a rusty aerial—which would reduce the capacity to receive a clear signal—but a clean one. . . . It also emerged from his evidence that he was not an explosives expert either. There was thus the possibility that the true role of Soldier G was to report that he suspected a car bomb in order to induce the Gibraltar police to sign the document authorising the SAS to employ lethal force.

177. In the Government's submission it was implicit in the jury's verdicts of lawful killing that they found as facts that there was no plot to kill the three terrorists and that the operation in Gibraltar had not been conceived or mounted with this aim in view. The aim of the operation was to effect the lawful arrest of the three terrorists and it was for this purpose that the assistance of the military was sought and given. Furthermore, the jury must have also rejected the applicants' contention that Soldiers A, B, C and D had deliberately set out to kill the terrorists, whether acting on express orders or as a result of being given 'a nod and a wink'.

178. The Commission concluded that there was no evidence to support the applicants' claim of a premeditated plot to kill the suspects.

179. The Court observes that it would need to have convincing evidence before it could conclude that there was a premeditated plan, in the sense developed by the applicants.

180. In the light of its own examination of the material before it, the Court does not find it established that there was an execution plot at the highest level of command in the Ministry of Defence or in the Government, or that Soldiers A, B, C and D had been so encouraged or instructed by the superior officers who had briefed them prior to the operation, or indeed that they had decided on their own initiative to kill the suspects irrespective of the existence of any justification for the use of lethal force and in disobedience to the arrest instructions they had received. Nor is there evidence that there was an implicit encouragement by the authorities or hints and innuendoes to execute the three suspects.

181. The factors relied on by the applicants amount to a series of conjectures that the authorities must have known that there was no bomb in the car. However, having regard to the intelligence information that they had received, to the known profiles of the three terrorists, all of whom had a background in explosives, and the fact that Mr Savage was seen to 'fiddle' with something before leaving the car . . . the belief that the car contained a bomb cannot be described as either implausible or wholly lacking in foundation.

182. In particular, the decision to admit them to Gibraltar, however open to criticism given the risks that it entailed, was in accordance with the arrest policy formulated by the Advisory Group that no effort should be made to apprehend them until all three were present in Gibraltar and there was sufficient evidence of a bombing mission to secure their convictions . . .

183. Nor can the Court accept the applicants' contention that the use of the SAS, in itself, amounted to evidence that the killing of the suspects was intended. In this respect it notes that the SAS is a special unit which has received specialist training in combating terrorism. It was only natural, therefore, that in light of the advance warning that the authorities received of an impending terrorist attack they would

resort to the skill and experience of the SAS in order to deal with the threat in the safest and most informed manner possible.

184. The Court therefore rejects as unsubstantiated the applicants' allegations that the killing of the three suspects was premeditated or the product of a tacit agreement among those involved in the operation.

3. CONDUCT AND PLANNING OF THE OPERATION

(a) Arguments of those appearing before the Court

(1) The Applicants

185. The applicants submitted that it would be wrong for the Court, as the Commission had done, to limit its assessment to the question of the possible justification of the soldiers who actually killed the suspects. It must examine the liability of the Government for all aspects of the operation. Indeed, the soldiers may well have been acquitted at a criminal trial if they could have shown that they honestly believed the ungrounded and false information they were given.

186. The soldiers had been told by Officer E (the attack commander) that the three suspects had planted a car bomb in Gibraltar, whereas Soldier G—the bomb-disposal expert—had reported that it was merely a suspect bomb; that it was a remote-control bomb; that each of the suspects could detonate it from anywhere in Gibraltar by the mere flicking of a switch and that they would not hesitate to do so the moment they were challenged. In reality, these 'certainties' and 'facts' were no more than suspicions or at best dubious assessments. However, they were conveyed as facts to soldiers who not only had been trained to shoot at the merest hint of a threat but also, as emerged from the evidence given during the inquest, to continue to shoot until they had killed their target.

In sum, they submitted that the killings came about as a result of incompetence and negligence in the planning and conduct of the anti-terrorist operation to arrest the suspects as well as a failure to maintain a proper balance between the need to meet the threat posed and the right to life of the suspects.

(2) The Government

187. The Government submitted that the actions of the soldiers were absolutely necessary in defence of persons from unlawful violence within the meaning of Article 2 para 2 (a) (art 2-2-a) of the Convention. Each of them had to make a split-second decision which could have affected a large number of lives. They believed that the movements which they saw the suspects make at the moment they were intercepted gave the impression that the terrorists were about to detonate a bomb. This evidence was confirmed by other witnesses who saw the movements in question. If it is accepted that the soldiers honestly and reasonably believed that the terrorists upon whom they opened fire might have been about to detonate a bomb by pressing a button, then they had no alternative but to open fire.

188. They also pointed out that much of the information available to the authorities and many of the judgments made by them proved to be accurate. The three deceased were an IRA active service unit which was planning an operation in Gibraltar; they did have in their control a large quantity of explosives which were subsequently found in Spain; and the nature of the operation was a car bomb. The risk to the lives of those in Gibraltar was, therefore, both real and extremely serious.

189. The Government further submitted that in examining the planning of the anti-terrorist operation it should be borne in mind that intelligence assessments are necessarily based on incomplete information since only fragments of the true picture will be known. Moreover, experience showed that the IRA were exceptionally ruthless and skilled in counter-surveillance techniques and that they did their best to conceal their intentions from the authorities. In addition, experience in Northern Ireland showed

that the IRA is constantly and rapidly developing new technology. They thus had to take into account the possibility that the terrorists might be equipped with more sophisticated or more easily conceal-able radio-controlled devices than the IRA had previously been known to use. Finally, the conse-quences of underestimating the threat posed by the active service unit could have been catastrophic. If they had succeeded in detonating a bomb of the type and size found in Spain, everyone in the car-park would have been killed or badly maimed and grievous injuries would have been caused to those in adjacent buildings, which included a school and an old-people's home.

190. The intelligence assessments made in the course of the operation were reasonable ones to make in the light of the inevitably limited amount of information available to the authorities and the poten-tially devastating consequences of underestimating the terrorists' abilities and resources. In this regard the Government made the following observations:

— It was believed that a remote-controlled device would be used because it would give the terrorists a better chance of escape and would increase their ability to maximise the proportion of military rather than civilian casualties. Moreover, the IRA had used such a device in Brussels only six weeks before.

— It was assumed that any remote-control such as that produced to the Court would be small enough to be readily concealed about the person. The soldiers themselves successfully con-cealed radios of a similar size about their persons.

— As testified by Captain Edwards at the inquest, tests carried out demonstrated that a bomb in the car-park could have been detonated from the spot where the terrorists were shot ...

— Past experience strongly suggested that the terrorists' detonation device might have been operated by pressing a single button.

— As explained by Witness O at the inquest, the use of a blocking car would have been unnecessary because the terrorists would not be expected to have any difficulty in finding a free space on 8 March. It was also dangerous because it would have required two trips into Gibraltar, thereby sig-nificantly increasing the risk of detection ...

— There was no reason to doubt the *bona fides* of Soldier G's assessment that the car was a suspect car bomb. In the first place his evidence was that he was quite familiar with car bombs. Moreover, the car had been parked by a known bomb-maker who had been seen to 'fiddle' with something between the seats and the car aerial appeared to be out of place. IRA car bombs had been known from experience to have specially-fitted aerials and G could not say for certain from an external examination that the car did not contain a bomb ... Furthermore, all three suspects appeared to be leaving Gibraltar. Finally the operation of cordoning off the area around the car began only twenty minutes after the above assessment had been made because of the shortage of available manpower and the fact that the evacuation plans were not intended for implementation until 7 or 8 March.

— It would have been reckless for the authorities to assume that the terrorists might not have deto-nated their bomb if challenged. The IRA were deeply committed terrorists who were, in their view, at war with the United Kingdom and who had in the past shown a reckless disregard for their own safety. There was still a real risk that if they had been faced with a choice between an explosion causing civilian casualties and no explosion at all, the terrorists would have preferred the former.

(3) The Commission

191. The Commission considered that, given the soldiers' perception of the risk to the lives of the people of Gibraltar, the shooting of the three suspects could be regarded as absolutely necessary for the legitimate aim of the defence of others from unlawful violence. It also concluded that, having regard to the possibility that the suspects had brought in a car bomb which, if detonated, would have occasioned the loss of many lives and the possibility that the suspects could have been able to detonate it when

confronted by the soldiers, the planning and execution of the operation by the authorities did not disclose any deliberate design or lack of proper care which might have rendered the use of lethal force disproportionate to the aim of saving lives.

(b) The Court's assessment

(1) Preliminary considerations

192. In carrying out its examination under Article 2 (art 2) of the Convention, the Court must bear in mind that the information that the United Kingdom authorities received that there would be a terrorist attack in Gibraltar presented them with a fundamental dilemma. On the one hand, they were required to have regard to their duty to protect the lives of the people in Gibraltar including their own military personnel and, on the other, to have minimum resort to the use of lethal force against those suspected of posing this threat in the light of the obligations flowing from both domestic and international law.

193. Several other factors must also be taken into consideration.
In the first place, the authorities were confronted by an active service unit of the IRA composed of persons who had been convicted of bombing offences and a known explosives expert. The IRA, judged by its actions in the past, had demonstrated a disregard for human life, including that of its own members.

Secondly, the authorities had had prior warning of the impending terrorist action and thus had ample opportunity to plan their reaction and, in co-ordination with the local Gibraltar authorities, to take measures to foil the attack and arrest the suspects. Inevitably, however, the security authorities could not have been in possession of the full facts and were obliged to formulate their policies on the basis of incomplete hypotheses.

194. Against this background, in determining whether the force used was compatible with Article 2 (art 2), the Court must carefully scrutinise, as noted above, not only whether the force used by the soldiers was strictly proportionate to the aim of protecting persons against unlawful violence but also whether the anti-terrorist operation was planned and controlled by the authorities so as to minimise, to the greatest extent possible, recourse to lethal force. The Court will consider each of these points in turn.

(2) Actions of the soldiers

195. It is recalled that the soldiers who carried out the shooting (A, B, C and D) were informed by their superiors, in essence, that there was a car bomb in place which could be detonated by any of the three suspects by means of a radio-control device which might have been concealed on their persons; that the device could be activated by pressing a button; that they would be likely to detonate the bomb if challenged, thereby causing heavy loss of life and serious injuries, and were also likely to be armed and to resist arrest . . .

196. As regards the shooting of Mr McCann and Ms Farrell, the Court recalls the Commission's finding that they were shot at close range after making what appeared to Soldiers A and B to be threatening movements with their hands as if they were going to detonate the bomb . . . The evidence indicated that they were shot as they fell to the ground but not as they lay on the ground. Four witnesses recalled hearing a warning shout . . . Officer P corroborated the soldiers' evidence as to the hand movements . . . Officer Q and Police Constable Parody also confirmed that Ms Farrell had made a sudden, suspicious move towards her handbag . . .

197. As regards the shooting of Mr Savage, the evidence revealed that there was only a matter of seconds between the shooting at the Shell garage (McCann and Farrell) and the shooting at Landport tunnel (Savage). The Commission found that it was unlikely that Soldiers C and D witnessed the first shooting before pursuing Mr Savage who had turned around after being alerted by either the police siren or the shooting . . .

Soldier C opened fire because Mr Savage moved his right arm to the area of his jacket pocket, thereby giving rise to the fear that he was about to detonate the bomb. In addition, Soldier C had seen something bulky in his pocket which he believed to be a detonating transmitter. Soldier D also opened fire believing that the suspect was trying to detonate the supposed bomb. The soldiers' version of events was corroborated in some respects by Witnesses H and J, who saw Mr Savage spin round to face the soldiers in apparent response to the police siren or the first shooting ...

The Commission found that Mr Savage was shot at close range until he hit the ground and probably in the instant as or after he had hit the ground ... This conclusion was supported by the pathologists' evidence at the inquest ...

198. It was subsequently discovered that the suspects were unarmed, that they did not have a detonator device on their persons and that there was no bomb in the car ...

199. All four soldiers admitted that they shot to kill. They considered that it was necessary to continue to fire at the suspects until they were rendered physically incapable of detonating a device ...

200. The Court accepts that the soldiers honestly believed, in the light of the information that they had been given, as set out above, that it was necessary to shoot the suspects in order to prevent them from detonating a bomb and causing serious loss of life ... The actions which they took, in obedience to superior orders, were thus perceived by them as absolutely necessary in order to safeguard innocent lives.

It considers that the use of force by agents of the State in pursuit of one of the aims delineated in paragraph 2 of Article 2 (art 2-2) of the Convention may be justified under this provision (art 2-2) where it is based on an honest belief which is perceived, for good reasons, to be valid at the time but which subsequently turns out to be mistaken. To hold otherwise would be to impose an unrealistic burden on the State and its law-enforcement personnel in the execution of their duty, perhaps to the detriment of their lives and those of others.

It follows that, having regard to the dilemma confronting the authorities in the circumstances of the case, the actions of the soldiers do not, in themselves, give rise to a violation of this provision (art 2-2).

201. The question arises, however, whether the anti-terrorist operation as a whole was controlled and organised in a manner which respected the requirements of Article 2 (art 2) and whether the information and instructions given to the soldiers which, in effect, rendered inevitable the use of lethal force, took adequately into consideration the right to life of the three suspects.

(3) Control and organisation of the operation

202. The Court first observes that, as appears from the operational order of the Commissioner, it had been the intention of the authorities to arrest the suspects at an appropriate stage. Indeed, evidence was given at the inquest that arrest procedures had been practised by the soldiers before 6 March and that efforts had been made to find a suitable place in Gibraltar to detain the suspects after their arrest ...

203. It may be questioned why the three suspects were not arrested at the border immediately on their arrival in Gibraltar and why, as emerged from the evidence given by Inspector Ullger, the decision was taken not to prevent them from entering Gibraltar if they were believed to be on a bombing mission. Having had advance warning of the terrorists' intentions it would certainly have been possible for the authorities to have mounted an arrest operation. Although surprised at the early arrival of the three suspects, they had a surveillance team at the border and an arrest group nearby ... In addition, the Security Services and the Spanish authorities had photographs of the three suspects, knew their names as well as their aliases and would have known what passports to look for ...

204. On this issue, the Government submitted that at that moment there might not have been sufficient evidence to warrant the detention and trial of the suspects. Moreover, to release them, having alerted them to the authorities' state of awareness but leaving them or others free to try again, would obviously increase the risks. Nor could the authorities be sure that those three were the only terrorists they had to deal with or of the manner in which it was proposed to carry out the bombing.

205. The Court confines itself to observing in this respect that the danger to the population of Gibraltar—which is at the heart of the Government's submissions in this case—in not preventing their entry must be considered to outweigh the possible consequences of having insufficient evidence to warrant their detention and trial. In its view, either the authorities knew that there was no bomb in the car—which the Court has already discounted ... or there was a serious miscalculation by those responsible for controlling the operation. As a result, the scene was set in which the fatal shooting, given the intelligence assessments which had been made, was a foreseeable possibility if not a likelihood.

The decision not to stop the three terrorists from entering Gibraltar is thus a relevant factor to take into account under this head.

206. The Court notes that at the briefing on 5 March attended by Soldiers A, B, C, and D it was considered likely that the attack would be by way of a large car bomb. A number of key assessments were made. In particular, it was thought that the terrorists would not use a blocking car; that the bomb would be detonated by a radio-control device; that the detonation could be effected by the pressing of a button; that it was likely that the suspects would detonate the bomb if challenged; that they would be armed and would be likely to use their arms if confronted ...

207. In the event, all of these crucial assumptions, apart from the terrorists' intentions to carry out an attack, turned out to be erroneous. Nevertheless, as has been demonstrated by the Government, on the basis of their experience in dealing with the IRA, they were all possible hypotheses in a situation where the true facts were unknown and where the authorities operated on the basis of limited intelligence information.

208. In fact, insufficient allowances appear to have been made for other assumptions. For example, since the bombing was not expected until 8 March when the changing of the guard ceremony was to take place, there was equally the possibility that the three terrorists were on a reconnaissance mission. While this was a factor which was briefly considered, it does not appear to have been regarded as a serious possibility ...

In addition, at the briefings or after the suspects had been spotted, it might have been thought unlikely that they would have been prepared to explode the bomb, thereby killing many civilians, as Mr McCann and Ms Farrell strolled towards the border area since this would have increased the risk of detection and capture ... It might also have been thought improbable that at that point they would have set up the transmitter in anticipation to enable them to detonate the supposed bomb immediately if confronted ...

Moreover, even if allowances are made for the technological skills of the IRA, the description of the detonation device as a 'button job' without the qualifications subsequently described by the experts at the inquest ... of which the competent authorities must have been aware, over-simplifies the true nature of these devices.

209. It is further disquieting in this context that the assessment made by Soldier G, after a cursory external examination of the car, that there was a 'suspect car bomb' was conveyed to the soldiers, according to their own testimony, as a definite identification that there was such a bomb ... It is recalled that while Soldier G had experience in car bombs, it transpired that he was not an expert in radio communications or explosives; and that his assessment that there was a suspect car bomb, based on his observation that the car aerial was out of place, was more in the nature of a report that a bomb could not be ruled out ...

210. In the absence of sufficient allowances being made for alternative possibilities, and the definite reporting of the existence of a car bomb which, according to the assessments that had been made, could be detonated at the press of a button, a series of working hypotheses were conveyed to Soldiers A, B, C and D as certainties, thereby making the use of lethal force almost unavoidable.

211. However, the failure to make provision for a margin of error must also be considered in combination with the training of the soldiers to continue shooting once they opened fire until the suspect was

dead. As noted by the Coroner in his summing-up to the jury at the inquest, all four soldiers shot to kill the suspects ... Soldier E testified that it had been discussed with the soldiers that there was an increased chance that they would have to shoot to kill since there would be less time where there was a 'button' device . . Against this background, the authorities were bound by their obligation to respect the right to life of the suspects to exercise the greatest of care in evaluating the information at their disposal before transmitting it to soldiers whose use of firearms automatically involved shooting to kill.

212. Although detailed investigation at the inquest into the training received by the soldiers was prevented by the public interest certificates which had been issued ... it is not clear whether they had been trained or instructed to assess whether the use of firearms to wound their targets may have been warranted by the specific circumstances that confronted them at the moment of arrest.

Their reflex action in this vital respect lacks the degree of caution in the use of firearms to be expected from law enforcement personnel in a democratic society, even when dealing with dangerous terrorist suspects, and stands in marked contrast to the standard of care reflected in the instructions in the use of firearms by the police which had been drawn to their attention and which emphasised the legal responsibilities of the individual officer in the light of conditions prevailing at the moment of engagement ...

This failure by the authorities also suggests a lack of appropriate care in the control and organisation of the arrest operation.

213. In sum, having regard to the decision not to prevent the suspects from travelling into Gibraltar, to the failure of the authorities to make sufficient allowances for the possibility that their intelligence assessments might, in some respects at least, be erroneous and to the automatic recourse to lethal force when the soldiers opened fire, the Court is not persuaded that the killing of the three terrorists constituted the use of force which was no more than absolutely necessary in defence of persons from unlawful violence within the meaning of Article 2 para 2 (a) (art 2-2-a) of the Convention.

214. Accordingly, the Court finds that there has been a breach of Article 2 (art 2) of the Convention. . . .

FOR THESE REASONS, THE COURT

Holds by ten votes to nine that there has been a violation of Article 2 of the Convention;
. . .

NOTES

1   The Court was composed of Judges: Russo, Spielmann, Valticos, Morenilla, Lopes Rocha, Mifsud Bonnici, Makarczyk, Repik, Kuris, and Lohmus.

2   The nine dissenting judges (President Ryssdal and Judges: Bernhardt, Thor Vilhjalmsson, Gölcüklü, Palm, Pekkanen, Freeland, Baka, and Jambrek) issued a joint dissenting opinion. They disagreed with the majority's evaluation of the planning and control of the counter-terrorism operation in Gibraltar.

8. Before turning to the various aspects of the operation which are criticised in the judgment, we would underline three points of a general nature.

First, in undertaking any evaluation of the way in which the operation was organised and controlled, the Court should studiously resist the temptations offered by the benefit of hindsight. The authorities had at the time to plan and make decisions on the basis of incomplete information. Only the suspects knew at all precisely what they intended; and it was part of their purpose, as it had no doubt been part of their training, to ensure that as little as possible of their intentions was revealed. It would be wrong to conclude in retrospect that a particular course would, as things later transpired, have been better than one adopted at the time under the pressures of an ongoing anti-terrorist operation and that the latter course must therefore be regarded as culpably mistaken. It should not be so regarded unless it is established that in the circumstances as they were known at the time another course should have been preferred.

9. Secondly, the need for the authorities to act within the constraints of the law, while the suspects were operating in a state of mind in which members of the security forces were regarded as legitimate targets and incidental death or injury to civilians as of little consequence, would inevitably give the suspects a tactical advantage which should not be allowed to prevail. The consequences of the explosion of a large bomb in the centre of Gibraltar might well be so devastating that the authorities could not responsibly risk giving the suspects the opportunity to set in train the detonation of such a bomb. Of course the obligation of the United Kingdom under Article 2 para 1 (art 2-1) of the Convention extended to the lives of the suspects as well as to the lives of all the many others, civilian and military, who were present in Gibraltar at the time. But, quite unlike those others, the purpose of the presence of the suspects in Gibraltar was the furtherance of a criminal enterprise which could be expected to have resulted in the loss of many innocent lives if it had been successful. They had chosen to place themselves in a situation where there was a grave danger that an irreconcilable conflict between the two duties might arise.

10. Thirdly, the Court's evaluation of the conduct of the authorities should throughout take full account of (a) the information which had been received earlier about IRA intentions to mount a major terrorist attack in Gibraltar by an active service unit of three individuals; and (b) the discovery which (according to evidence given to the inquest by Witness O) had been made in Brussels on 21 January 1988 of a car containing a large amount of Semtex explosive and four detonators, with a radio-controlled system— equipment which, taken together, constituted a device familiar in Northern Ireland.

In the light of (a), the decision that members of the SAS should be sent to take part in the operation in response to the request of the Gibraltar Commissioner of Police for military assistance was wholly justifiable. Troops trained in a counter-terrorist role and to operate successfully in small groups would clearly be a suitable choice to meet the threat of an IRA active service unit at large in a densely populated area such as Gibraltar, where there would be an imperative need to limit as far as possible the risk of accidental harm to passers-by.

The detailed operational briefing on 5 March 1988 . . . shows the reasonableness, in the circumstances as known at the time, of the assessments then made. The operational order of the Gibraltar Commissioner of Police, which was drawn up on the same day, expressly proscribed the use of more force than necessary and required any recourse to firearms to be had with care for the safety of persons in the vicinity. It described the intention of the operation as being to protect life; to foil the attempt; to arrest the offenders; and the securing and safe custody of the prisoners . . .

All of this is indicative of appropriate care on the part of the authorities. So, too, is the cautious approach to the eventual passing of control to the military on 6 March 1988 . . .

11. As regards the particular criticisms of the conduct of the operation which are made in the judgment, foremost among them is the questioning (in paragraphs 203–05) of the decision not to prevent the three suspects from entering Gibraltar. It is pointed out in paragraph 203 that, with the advance information which the authorities possessed and with the resources of personnel at their disposal, it would have been possible for them 'to have mounted an arrest operation' at the border.

The judgment does not, however, go on to say that it would have been practicable for the authorities to have arrested and detained the suspects at that stage. Rightly so, in our view, because at that stage there might not be sufficient evidence to warrant their detention and trial. To release them, after having alerted them to the state of readiness of the authorities, would be to increase the risk that they or other IRA members could successfully mount a renewed terrorist attack on Gibraltar. In the circumstances as then known, it was accordingly not 'a serious miscalculation' for the authorities to defer the arrest rather than merely stop the suspects at the border and turn them back into Spain.

12. Paragraph 206 of the judgment then lists certain 'key assessments' made by the authorities which, in paragraph 207, are said to have turned out, in the event, to be erroneous, although they are accepted

as all being possible hypotheses in a situation where the true facts were unknown and where the authorities were operating on the basis of limited intelligence information. Paragraph 208 goes on to make the criticism that 'insufficient allowances appear to have been made for other assumptions'.

13. As a first example to substantiate this criticism, the paragraph then states that since the bombing was not expected until 8 March 'there was equally the possibility that the ... terrorists were on a reconnaissance mission'.

There was, however, nothing unreasonable in the assessment at the operational briefing on 5 March that the car which would be brought into Gibraltar was unlikely, on the grounds then stated, to be a 'blocking' car ... So, when the car had been parked in the assembly area by one of the suspects and all three had been found to be present in Gibraltar, the authorities could quite properly operate on the working assumption that it contained a bomb and that, as the suspects were unlikely to risk two visits, it was not 'equally' possible that they were on a reconnaissance mission.

In addition, Soldier F, the senior military adviser to the Gibraltar Commissioner of Police, gave evidence to the inquest that, according to intelligence information, reconnaissance missions had been undertaken many times before: reconnaissance was, he had been told, complete and the operation was ready to be run. In these circumstances, for the authorities to have proceeded otherwise than on the basis of a worst-case scenario that the car contained a bomb which was capable of being detonated by the suspects during their presence in the territory would have been to show a reckless failure of concern for public safety.

14. Secondly, it is suggested in the second sub-paragraph of paragraph 208 that, at the briefings or after the suspects had been spotted, 'it might have been thought unlikely that they would have been prepared to explode the bomb, thereby killing many civilians, as Mr McCann and Ms Farrell strolled towards the border area since this would have increased the risk of detection and capture'.

Surely, however, the question is rather whether the authorities could safely have operated on the assumption that the suspects would be unlikely to be prepared to explode the bomb when, even if for the time being moving in the direction of the border, they became aware that they had been detected and were faced with the prospect of arrest. In our view, the answer is clear: certainly, previous experience of IRA activities would have afforded no reliable basis for concluding that the killing of many civilians would itself be a sufficient deterrent or that the suspects, when confronted, would have preferred no explosion at all to an explosion causing civilian casualties. It is relevant that, according to Soldier F's evidence at the inquest, part of the intelligence background was that he had been told that the IRA were under pressure to produce a 'spectacular'. He also gave evidence of his belief that, when cornered, the suspects would have no qualms about pressing the button to achieve some degree of propaganda success: they would try to derive such a success out of having got a bomb into Gibraltar and that would outweigh in their minds the propaganda loss arising from civilian casualties.

15. The second sub-paragraph of paragraph 208 goes on to suggest that it 'might also have been thought improbable that at that point'—that is, apparently, as McCann and Farrell 'strolled towards the border'—'[the suspects] would have set up the transmitter in anticipation to enable them to detonate the supposed bomb immediately if confronted'.

Here, the question ought, we consider, to be whether the authorities could prudently have proceeded otherwise than on the footing that there was at the very least a possibility that, if not before the suspects became aware of detection then immediately afterwards, the transmitter would be in a state of readiness to detonate the bomb.

16. It is next suggested, in the third sub-paragraph of paragraph 208, that 'even if allowances are made for the technological skills of the IRA, the description of the detonation device as a 'button job' without the qualifications subsequently described by the experts at the inquest ... , of which the competent authorities must have been aware, over-simplifies the true nature of these devices'. The exact purport of this criticism is perhaps open to some doubt. What is fully clear, however, is that, as the applicants' own expert witness accepted at the inquest, a transmitter of the kind which was thought likely to be

used in the present case could be set up so as to enable detonation to be caused by pressing a single button; and in the light of past experience it would have been most unwise to discount the possibility of technological advance in this field by the IRA.

17. Paragraph 209 of the judgment expresses disquiet that the assessment made by Soldier G that there was a 'suspect car bomb' was conveyed to the soldiers on the ground in such a way as to give them the impression that the presence of a bomb had been definitely identified. But, given the assessments which had been made of the likelihood of a remote control being used, and given the various indicators that the car should indeed be suspected of containing a bomb, the actions which the soldiers must be expected to have taken would be the same whether their understanding of the message was as it apparently was or whether it was in the sense which Soldier G apparently intended. In either case, the existence of the risk to the people of Gibraltar would have been enough, given the nature of that risk, justifiably to prompt the response which followed.

18. Paragraph 209, in referring to the assessment made by Soldier G, also recalls that while he had experience with car bombs, he was not an expert in radio communications or explosives. In considering that assessment, it would, however, be fair to add that, although his inspection of the car was of brief duration, it was enough to enable him to conclude, particularly in view of the unusual appearance of its aerial in relation to the age of the car and the knowledge that the IRA had in the past used cars with aerials specially fitted, that it was to be regarded as a suspect car bomb.

The authorities were, in any event, not acting solely on the basis of Soldier G's assessment. There had also been the earlier assessment, to which we have referred in paragraph 13 above, that a 'blocking' car was unlikely to be used. In addition, the car had been seen to be parked by Savage, who was known to be an expert bomb-maker and who had taken some time (two to three minutes, according to one witness) to get out of the car, after fiddling with something between the seats.

19. Paragraph 210 of the judgment asserts, in effect, that the use of lethal force was made 'almost unavoidable' by the conveyance to Soldiers A, B, C and D of a series of working hypotheses which were vitiated by the absence of sufficient allowances for alternative possibilities and by 'the definite reporting ... of a car bomb which ... , could be detonated at the press of a button'.

We have dealt in paragraphs 13–16 with the points advanced in support of the conclusion that insufficient allowance was made for alternative possibilities; and in paragraphs 17 and 18 with the question of reporting as to the presence of a car bomb.

We further question the conclusion that the use of lethal force was made 'almost unavoidable' by failings of the authorities in these respects. Quite apart from any other consideration, this conclusion takes insufficient account of the part played by chance in the eventual outcome. Had it not been for the movements which were made by McCann and Farrell as Soldiers A and B closed on them and which may have been prompted by the completely coincidental sounding of a police car siren, there is every possibility that they would have been seized and arrested without a shot being fired; and had it not been for Savage's actions as Soldiers C and D closed on him, which may have been prompted by the sound of gunfire from the McCann and Farrell incident, there is every possibility that he, too, would have been seized and arrested without resort to shooting.

20. The implication at the end of paragraph 211 that the authorities did not exercise sufficient care in evaluating the information at their disposal before transmitting it to soldiers 'whose use of firearms automatically involved shooting to kill' appears to be based on no more than 'the failure to make provision for a margin of error' to which the beginning of the paragraph refers. We have dealt already with the 'insufficient allowances for alternative possibilities' point (see, again, paragraphs 13–16 above), which we take to be the same as the alleged failure to provide for a margin of error which is referred to here. Any assessment of the evaluation by the authorities of the information at their disposal should, in any event, take due account of their need to reckon throughout with the incompleteness of that information (see paragraph 8 above); and there are no cogent grounds for any suggestion that there was information which they ought reasonably to have known but did not.

21. Paragraph 212, after making a glancing reference to the restrictive effect of the public interest certificates and saying that it is not clear 'whether the use of firearms to wound their targets may have been warranted by the specific circumstances that confronted them at the moment of arrest', goes on to say that 'their reflex action in this vital respect lacks the degree of caution ... to be expected from law-enforcement personnel in a democratic society, even when dealing with dangerous terrorist suspects, and stands in marked contrast to the standard of care reflected in the instructions in the use of firearms by the police'. It concludes with the assertion that this 'failure by the authorities also suggests a lack of appropriate care in the control and organisation of the arrest operation'.

22. As regards any suggestion that, if an assessment on the issue had been required by their training or instruction to be carried out by the soldiers, shooting to wound might have been considered by them to have been warranted by the circumstances at the time, it must be recalled that those circumstances included a genuine belief on their part that the suspects might be about to detonate a bomb by pressing a button. In that situation, to shoot merely to wound would have been a highly dangerous course: wounding alone might well not have immobilised a suspect and might have left him or her capable of pressing a button if determined to do so.

23. More generally as regards the training given, there was in fact ample evidence at the inquest to the effect that soldiers (and not only these soldiers) would be trained to respond to a threat such as that which was thought to be posed by the suspects in this case—all of them dangerous terrorists who were believed to be putting many lives at immediate risk—by opening fire once it was clear that the suspect was not desisting; that the intent of the firing would be to immobilise; and that the way to achieve that was to shoot to kill. There was also evidence at the inquest that soldiers would not be accepted for the SAS unless they displayed discretion and thoughtfulness; that they would not go ahead and shoot without thought, nor did they; but they did have to react very fast. In addition, evidence was given that SAS members had in fact been successful in the past in arresting terrorists in the great majority of cases.

24. We are far from persuaded that the Court has any sufficient basis for concluding, in the face of the evidence at the inquest and the extent of experience in dealing with terrorist activities which the relevant training reflects, that some different and preferable form of training should have been given and that the action of the soldiers in this case 'lacks the degree of caution in the use of firearms to be expected of law-enforcement personnel in a democratic society'. (We also question, in the light of the evidence, the fairness of the reference to 'reflex action in this vital respect'—underlining supplied. To be trained to react rapidly and to do so, when the needs of the situation require, is not to take reflex action.)

Nor do we accept that the differences between the guide to police officers in the use of firearms ... and the 'Firearms—rules of engagement' annexed to the Commissioner's operational order ... when the latter are taken together (as they should be) with the Rules of Engagement issued to Soldier F by the Ministry of Defence ... can validly be invoked to support a contention that the standard of care enjoined upon the soldiers was inadequate. Those differences are no doubt attributable to the differences in backgrounds and requirements of the recipients to whom they were addressed, account being taken of relevant training previously given to each group (it is to be noted that, according to the evidence of Soldier F at the inquest, many lectures are given to SAS soldiers on the concepts of the rule of law and the use of minimum force). We fail to see how the instructions for the soldiers could themselves be read as showing a lack of proper caution in the use of firearms.

Accordingly, we consider the concluding stricture, that there was some failure by the authorities in this regard suggesting a lack of appropriate care in the control and organisation of the arrest operation, to be unjustified.

25. The accusation of a breach by a State of its obligation under Article 2 (art 2) of the Convention to protect the right to life is of the utmost seriousness. For the reasons given above, the evaluation in paragraphs 203 to 213 of the judgment seems to us to fall well short of substantiating the finding that

there has been a breach of the Article (art 2) in this case. We would ourselves follow the reasoning and conclusion of the Commission in its comprehensive, painstaking and notably realistic report. Like the Commission, we are satisfied that no failings have been shown in the organisation and control of the operation by the authorities which could justify a conclusion that force was used against the suspects disproportionately to the purpose of defending innocent persons from unlawful violence. We consider that the use of lethal force in this case, however regrettable the need to resort to such force may be, did not exceed what was, in the circumstances as known at the time, 'absolutely necessary' for that purpose and did not amount to a breach by the United Kingdom of its obligations under the Convention.

3 The British government, and significant sections of the British media, were highly critical of the majority's judgment. In response to a question about the case from the Shadow Attorney General (Mr John Morris), the Attorney General (Sir Nicholas Lyell) stated:

that judgment caused a great deal of proper public unease. I would have expected the right hon and learned Gentleman to have commended the views of the minority in the court. He will remember that the decision was made by only 10 to nine, and that the president of the court took a fundamentally different view from the majority and set it out in concise reasoning with which, in my opinion, every sensible person should agree. [H C Deb 265 (1994–5) col 14]

Do you think it was significant that the minority was composed of, inter alios, the four most senior members of the Court?

4 *McCann* was the first case in which the Court had to interpret and apply Article 2, therefore it is very important to appreciate that all the judges were in agreement about a number of fundamental aspects of the Article. For example, (a) that Article 2(2) applies to non-intentional killings (para 148), (b) the strict test of 'absolutely necessary' force in Article 2(2) (para 149), (c) the need for the Court to examine both the actions of State agents (such as police officers or soldiers) who are directly responsible for a death, and the planning and control of those operations when determining if a State is in breach of Article 2 (para 150), (d) that when evaluating the lawfulness of the State agents' actions the Court will have regard to the contemporary honest belief (perceived for good reasons) of those persons regarding the circumstances at the time of the killing (para 200), and (e) that Article 2(1) contains an implied obligation upon States to conduct effective official investigations into the killings of persons by State agents (para 161).

5 The divisions within the Court when applying the above principles to specific circumstances were further illustrated in the later case of *Andronicou and Constantinou v Cyprus* (1997) 25 EHRR 491, 1997-VI. Lefteris Andronicou and Elsie Constantinou announced their engagement on 22 December 1993. In the morning of 24 December 1993 neighbours heard a woman calling for help from inside Andronicou's flat. The police were called and Andronicou threatened to shoot the officer unless he left. During the afternoon the local police director called the chief of police about the hostage situation and the latter sent the platoon of Police Special Forces ('MMAD') to deal with the matter. The head of the MMAD platoon informed its members that Andronicou was armed with a double-barrelled hunting gun and that he might have other weapons. The MMAD officers were armed with pistols and machine guns (with torches attached). They were instructed to use proportionate force and fire only if Constantinou or their lives were in danger. Andronicou informed his doctor that he would release Constantinou at midnight and then commit suicide. At 23.00 hours food was delivered to the flat (the police had arranged for the food to be drugged with a sedative). However, Constantinou was still heard screaming that Andronicou was going to kill her. The senior police officers came to the view that Andronicou was planning to kill her and then himself. At 23.55 the MMAD officers forced their way into Andronicou's flat. The first officer to enter was shot, in the shoulder, by Andronicou who then shot Constantinou (in the hands and shoulder). Two other officers shot Andronicou dead (he was hit by at least twenty five bullets). Constantinou was hit by two bullets from the police machine guns. She was taken to hospital in a police car (no ambulance was present at the scene), but despite emergency surgery she died (from injuries caused by the police bullets) several hours later. Subsequently, the government appointed a Commission of Inquiry, chaired by the President of the Supreme Court, Mr Loizou (who also served as a judge at the European Court), to investigate the deaths of Andronicou and Constantinou. The Commission reported, in June 1994, that the MMAD officers had used no more force than was 'absolutely necessary' in order to try and rescue Constantinou and that no criticism could be made of the police operation. The applicants, relatives of the deceased, complained to the Commission alleging, *inter alia*, that the killings violated Andronicou and Constantinou's right to life guaranteed by Article 2. The Commission, by fifteen votes to three, found that the authorities' planning and control of the operation (especially deploying the MMAD unit to end a domestic dispute) violated that Article. A majority, of five judges, of the Chamber that heard the case held that:

182. In carrying out its assessment of the planning and control phase of the operation from the standpoint of Article 2 of the Convention, the Court must have particular regard to the context in which the incident occurred as well as to the way in which the situation developed over the course of the day.

183. As to the context, the authorities clearly understood that they were dealing with a young couple and not with hardened criminals or terrorists. The negotiations and the resolve to negotiate up until the last possible moment clearly indicate that the authorities never lost sight of the fact that the incident had its origins in a 'lovers' quarrel' and that this factor had to be taken into account if, in the final analysis, it transpired that force had to be used to free Elsie Constantinou. It was not unreasonable in view of the context for the authorities to enlist the help of the family and friends of Lefteris Andronicou in order to bring the situation to an end. It is also to be noted that the authorities tried to bring an end to the incident through persuasion and dialogue right up to the last possible moment. The police negotiator continued his attempts in the later phase of the incident to assure Lefteris Andronicou that no harm would come to him if he were to release the young woman. Instructions were in fact given at a meeting which ended at 11pm to delay the involvement of the *MMAD* officers as much as possible to enable negotiations to continue … This sustained effort by the authorities to resolve the situation through negotiations illustrates a deep concern on the part of the authorities to deploy the *MMAD* officers only as a last resort. While there may have been shortcomings as regards, for example, the lack of crowd control or the absence of a dedicated telephone line between the police negotiator and Lefteris Andronicou, the Court considers nevertheless that the negotiations were in general conducted in a manner which can be said to be reasonable in the circumstances.

184. Irrespective of the domestic nature of the incident, the situation progressively developed in the eyes of the authorities present into a situation fraught with danger and in which critical decisions had to be taken. Lefteris Andronicou's intransigence in the face of negotiations, his threatening tone as well as the young woman's shouts for help persuaded the authorities that he intended to kill her and commit suicide at midnight. Admittedly, Lefteris Andronicou never announced that he would kill Elsie Constantinou and he only threatened to shoot her if the police broke into his flat. Nevertheless, the authorities could not reasonably ignore her shouts that her life was in danger. It must be emphasised that one hour before midnight she was repeatedly heard screaming that Lefteris Andronicou was going to kill her … and that Lefteris Andronicou had already shown his capacity for violence by beating her …In these circumstances and in the knowledge that Lefteris Andronicou was armed, the authorities could reasonably consider that as midnight approached the negotiations had failed and that an attempt had to be made to get into the flat, disarm and arrest him and free Elsie Constantinou.

185. In the Court's view the authorities' decision to use the *MMAD* officers in the circumstances as they were known at the time was justified. Recourse to the skills of a highly professionally trained unit like the *MMAD* would appear to be quite natural given the nature of the operation which was contemplated.

The decision to use the *MMAD* officers was a considered one of last resort. It was discussed both at the highest possible level in the police chain of command and at ministerial level … and only implemented when the negotiations failed and, as noted above, in view of a reasonably held belief that the young woman's life was in imminent danger. While it is true that the officers deployed were trained to shoot to kill if fired at, it is to be noted that they were issued with clear instructions as to when to use their weapons. They were told to use only proportionate force and to fire only if Elsie Constantinou's life or their own lives were in danger … It is to be noted that no use of weapons was ever intended and in fact the authorities were deeply anxious to avoid any harm to the couple … However, it was not unreasonable to alert the officers to the dangers which awaited them and to direct them carefully on firearms use. Furthermore, it must be stressed that the officers were not in fact informed that Lefteris Andronicou was in possession of weapons in addition to the shotgun. They were told that this possibility could not be excluded … Seen in these terms the message could reasonably be considered to be a warning to the officers to use extreme caution when effecting the operation. As to the decision to arm the officers with machine guns, it must be emphasised once again that the use of any firearm was never intended in the execution of the plan. However, given that Lefteris Andronicou was armed with a double-barrelled shotgun and it was not to be excluded that he had other weapons, the authorities had to anticipate all possible eventualities. It might be added that the machine guns had the advantage that they were fitted with flashlights which would enable the officers to overcome any difficulties encountered in identifying the precise location of the young woman in a dark room filled with tear gas and at the same time leave their hands free to control their weapons in the event of coming under fire. Furthermore, the use by the officers of their machine guns was subject to the same clear instructions as applied to the use of their pistols …

186. Having regard to the above considerations the Court is of the view that it has not been shown that the rescue operation was not planned and organised in a way which minimised to the greatest extent possible any risk to the lives of the couple.

Consequently, the majority determined that there had been no breach of Article 2. The four dissentients considered that the planning and control of the operation did not satisfy the requirements of Article 2. They were particularly concerned about the deployment of the MMAD officers and their use of machine guns to end the hostage taking. 'The use of machine guns in the circumstances of the present case seems to me to be an excessive use of force. The use of that kind of fire power against a frightened young man cannot be considered to be absolutely necessary even if he had the possibility to fire two shots with his hunting gun', *per* Judge Pekkanen, Partly Dissenting Opinion, para 6. Is it possible to reconcile the Court's decisions in *McCann* and *Andronicou and Constantinou*? Is it significant that the MMAD officers only opened fire after they had been shot at by Andronicou? Why did the Cypriot police not remove the public from outside Andronicou's building or have medical facilities on standby at the scene in case persons were injured?

6 The Court was, however, united in finding a breach Article 2 in respect of the lack of sufficient care in the planning and control of a security forces operation against suspected armed PKK (Workers' Party of Kurdistan) members in *Ergi v Turkey, Reports* 1998-IV. The applicant alleged that his sister (Havva Ergi) had been killed by shots fired by Turkish security forces when they conducted an ambush of PKK members at the deceased's village. The Commission, unanimously, found a breach of Article 2 regarding, *inter alia*, the planning of the ambush. The Court held that:

79. … the responsibility of the State is not confined to circumstances where there is significant evidence that misdirected fire from agents of the State has killed a civilian. It may also be engaged where they fail to take all feasible precautions in the choice of means and methods of a security operation

mounted against an opposing group with a view to avoiding and, in any event, to minimising, incidental loss of civilian life. Thus, even though it has not been established beyond reasonable doubt that the bullet which killed Havva Ergi had been fired by the security forces, the Court must consider whether the security forces' operation had been planned and conducted in such a way as to avoid or minimise, to the greatest extent possible, any risk to the lives of the villagers, including from the fire-power of the PKK members caught in the ambush.

80. Turning to the particular circumstances of the case, the Court observes, on the one hand, that the Commission stated that its ability to make an assessment of how the operation had been planned and executed had been limited due to the lack of information provided by the Government. It had no information as to who took part in the operation, in what circumstances the security forces had opened fire and what steps had been taken by the security forces once the clash had developed … On the other hand, the gendarmerie officers' testimonies to the Commission had suggested that the ambush was organised in the north-west of the village without the distance between the village and the ambush being known. It was to be anticipated that PKK terrorists could have approached the village either following the path from the north or proceeding down the river bed to the north-east and in the latter event, they would have been able to penetrate to the edge of the village without being seen by the security forces to the north-west. The Commission found on the evidence that security forces had been present in the south … In these circumstances, the villagers had been placed at considerable risk of being caught in cross-fire between security forces and any PKK terrorists who had approached from the north or north-east. Even if it might be assumed that the security forces would have responded with due care for the civilian population in returning fire against terrorists caught in the approaches to the village, it could not be assumed that the terrorists would have responded with such restraint. There was no information to indicate that any steps or precautions had been taken to protect the villagers from being caught up in the conflict. Accordingly, in the absence of evidence from gendarmes involved in the planning and conduct of the operation, the Commission was not satisfied that the ambush operation carried out close to Kesentas village had been implemented with the requisite care for the lives of the civilian population.

81. The Court, having regard to the Commission's findings … and to its own assessment, considers that it was probable that the bullet which killed Havva Ergi had been fired from the south or south-east, that the security forces had been present in the south and that there had been a real risk to the lives of the civilian population through being exposed to cross-fire between the security forces and the PKK. In the light of the failure of the authorities of the respondent State to adduce direct evidence on the planning and conduct of the ambush operation, the Court, in agreement with the Commission, finds that it can reasonably be inferred that insufficient precautions had been taken to protect the lives of the civilian population.

The judgment is also important for requiring States to have regard to the dangers posed to innocent bystanders from both State personnel and non-State actors (eg terrorists or criminals) when planning security force operations. State authorities are under a stringent Convention duty to 'take all feasible precaution' to avoid or minimise 'incidental loss of civilian life' in the planning and implementation of such operations.

7   In two of the full-time Court's initial judgments concerning the actions of Federal military/security forces in Chechnya, a unanimous Chamber found breaches of Russia's obligation to protect the life of the applicants through a lack of the requisite care for civilian life in the planning and execution of military operations against insurgent fighters. In *Isayeva, Yusupova and Bazayeva v Russia*, judgment of 24 February 2005, the applicants were members of a large convoy of vehicles containing persons trying to flee the fighting between Federal forces and insurgents in Grozny during October 1999. The convoy was turned back at a military roadblock and during the return journey two military planes fired twelve air-to-ground

missiles at the convoy. The pilots claimed that they were responding to gunfire directed at them from insurgents in lorries. The missiles caused the deaths of sixteen civilians (including two children of the applicants). The Chamber stated that:

178. The Court accepts that the situation that existed in Chechnya at the relevant time called for exceptional measures on behalf of the State in order to regain control over the Republic and to suppress the illegal armed insurgency. These measures could presumably include employment of military aviation equipped with heavy combat weapons. The Court is also prepared to accept that if the planes were attacked by illegal armed groups, that could have justified use of lethal force, thus falling within paragraph 2 of Article 2.

179. However, in the present case, the Government failed to produce convincing evidence which would have supported such findings. The testimonies submitted by the two pilots and the air traffic controller are the only mention of such an attack. These testimonies were collected in October and December 2000, i.e. over a year after the attack. They are incomplete and refer to other statements made by these witnesses during the course of the investigation, which the Government failed to disclose. They are made in almost identical terms and contain a very brief and incomplete account of the events.

Taking account of the 'extremely powerful weapon' used by the military (i.e. missiles which had an impact radius of between 300 and 800 metres, within which thousands of pieces of shrapnel were created by the explosive force of the missiles) in the vicinity of a large convoy of civilian vehicles the Chamber concluded that the applicants had suffered a violation of Article 2. Similarly, in *Isayeva v Russia*, judgment of 24 February 2005, the applicant and her family were in a civilian vehicle trying to escape from fighting in their home town (where the Federal forces had trapped many armed insurgents). Military planes dropped high explosive bombs which caused the death of the applicant's son and three of her nieces. The Chamber found that:

190. Once the fighters' presence and significant number had become apparent to the authorities, the operation's commanders proceeded with the variant of the plan which involved a bomb and missile strike at Katyr-Yurt [the applicant's home town]. Between 8 and 9 a.m. on 4 February 2000 Major-General Nedobitko called in fighter jets, without specifying what load they should carry. The planes, apparently by default, carried heavy free-falling high-explosion aviation bombs FAB-250 and FAB-500 with a damage radius exceeding 1,000 metres. According to the servicemen's statements, bombs and other non-guided heavy combat weapons were used against targets both in the centre and on the edges of the village.

191. The Court considers that using this kind of weapon in a populated area, outside wartime and without prior evacuation of the civilians, is impossible to reconcile with the degree of caution expected from a law-enforcement body in a democratic society. No martial law and no state of emergency has been declared in Chechnya, and no derogation has been made under Article 15 of the Convention. The operation in question therefore has to be judged against a normal legal background. Even when faced with a situation where, as the Government submit, the population of the village had been held hostage by a large group of well-equipped and well-trained fighters, the primary aim of the operation should be to protect lives from unlawful violence. The massive use of indiscriminate weapons stands in flagrant contrast with this aim and cannot be considered compatible with the standard of care prerequisite to an operation of this kind involving the use of lethal force by State agents.

So, the death of the applicant's relatives amounted to a breach of Article 2. Both these cases reveal the Federal forces using combat weapons in areas with many civilians and with little regard for the protection of the life of ordinary persons, including children.

8 The Court has found a Member State liable for the actions of civilian volunteers acting in association with the professional security forces in *Avsar v Turkey*, judgment of 10 July 2001. The case primarily concerned the actions of village guards who are civilians appointed by the

Council of Elders in particular villages or civilians who volunteer themselves and are appointed by provincial governors. Village guards are armed and have the duties of protecting the life, honour and property of persons within the boundaries of their villages. They have also been used for a wider range of security activities, such as reporting on strangers visiting their villages and preventing attacks on the national infrastructure (roads, bridges and dams etc.). The district gendarme commander is responsible for the training and supervision of the village guards in his area. The Avsar family lived in south-east Turkey and they were regarded by the authorities as having a history of involvement with the PKK. In April 1994 Abdulkerim Avsar was in prison awaiting trial on charges of terrorism. On 22 April five village guards accompanied by a former PKK member (a 'confessor') and another unidentified man (who acted with authority as a member of the security forces) entered the Avsar family shop. They insisted that one of the Avsar brothers go with them to make a statement for Abdulkerim. After some resistance Mehmet Avsar agreed to accompany them. He was taken to a gendarmerie. Later he was removed by two of the village guards, the confessor, and the unidentified person. On the 7 May the body of Mehmet, (he had been shot) was found outside the city of Diyarbakir. Nearly six years later one of the village guards was convicted of murdering Mehmet whilst the other four guards and the confessor were convicted of abduction. The brother of Mehmet complained to Strasbourg alleging, *inter alia*, a breach of Article 2 as Mehmet was in the custody of security officials and killed in circumstances that fell outside Article 2(2). The Court, by six votes to one, upheld this claim.

412. The Court is satisfied that Mehmet Şerif Avşar may be regarded as having died after having been taken into custody by agents of the State. It does not accept the Government's submission that the crime was committed by persons acting in their private capacity without the knowledge of the authorities and thereby beyond the scope of the State's responsibility.

413. The village guards enjoyed an official position, with duties and responsibilities. They had been sent to Diyarbakır to participate in the apprehension of suspects and they held themselves out to the Avşar family as acting on authority. The seventh person, a security officer, also held himself out as acting officially. The participants were, and purported to act as, agents of the State, and made use of their position in forcing Mehmet Şerif Avşar to go with them. In these circumstances, the Government is answerable for their conduct.

414. In that context, the Court has already found that there was a lack of accountability as regarded the security forces in south-east Turkey in or about 1993.... This case additionally highlights the risks attaching to the use of civilian volunteers in a quasi-police function. Notwithstanding the official denials that guards were used outside their own villages, it has been established in this case that guards were used regularly on a variety of official operations, including the apprehension of suspects. According to the regulations provided by the Government, village guards were hierarchically subordinate to the district gendarme commander. However, it is not apparent what supervision was, or could be exerted over guards who were engaged in duties outside the jurisdiction of the district gendarme commander. Nor, as the village guards were outside the normal structure of discipline and training applicable to gendarmes and police officers, is it apparent what safeguards there were against wilful or unintentional abuses of position carried out by the village guards either on their own initiative or under the instructions of security officers who themselves were acting outside the law. ...

416. No justification for the killing of Mehmet Şerif Avşar being provided, the Court concludes that the Government are liable for his death.

There has accordingly been a breach of Article 2 in this respect.

This ruling is to be welcomed as it seeks to ensure that States are accountable for both the regular security forces and also civilian volunteers. Indeed, the judgment highlights the potential dangers to respect for human rights posed by the latter category of persons. This is increased where the civilian volunteers are armed, operate in areas where they have strong personal relationships with victims and suspects, and are subject to limited supervision. Clearly if States wish to use civilian volunteers they must provide them with rigorous training as to the proper use and limitations of their legal powers and subject them to effective supervision and discipline.

9   Where an applicant alleges that State agents have killed a person in violation of Article 2, the Court will have to be satisfied that there is sufficient evidence 'to enable it to conclude beyond all reasonable doubt' (para 97 of judgment in *Yasa*) that the State was responsible for the death before it can hold the State directly accountable under the Convention. In a number of Turkish cases the Court has been unable to determine who was directly responsible for the killing (eg as in *Ergi*, above) and/or that there was insufficient evidence to hold the State directly accountable for the death(s) (e.g. *Yasa*). The applicant (a newsagent) in *Yasa v Turkey* (1998) 28 EHRR 408, *Reports* 1998-VI, claimed that his uncle had been shot dead by members of the Turkish security forces because the applicant had been selling the pro-Kurdish newspaper *Ozgur Gundem* (see below p 627, for the paper's successful complaint under Article 10). The Commission was not able to establish beyond all reasonable doubt that security or police officers had been implicated in the shooting. Consequently, the Court found Turkey not to have violated Article 2 in regard to the actual shooting. Even though the Court has not always been able to determine who was actually responsible for a particular killing it may find a State liable for breaching other aspects of Article 2 (such as failing to take proper care in the planning of a security operation as in *Ergi* or failing to conduct an effective investigation into the death as in *Yasa*).

10   Where a person has been detained by State agents and subsequently disappears without ever being seen again and no body is found the Court may judge the existence of sufficient circumstantial evidence to determine the State liable under Article 2. For example in *Ipek v Turkey*, judgment of 17 February 2004, the applicant complained about the disappearance of his two sons. The Court found that they were amongst a group of six young men detained by soldiers during a military raid on their village in 1994. The six detainees were taken to a military establishment in a nearby town. On their arrival at the establishment the men were split into two groups of three. Members of one of these groups were released the next day. The other group (including the applicant's sons) were never seen again and their bodies were never found. Citing the earlier judgment of *Timurtas v Turkey*, ECHR 2000-VI, the Court held that:

166. ...'Whether the failure on the part of the authorities to provide a plausible explanation as to a detainee's fate, in the absence of a body, might also raise issues under Article 2 of the Convention will depend on all the circumstances of the case, and in particular on the existence of sufficient circumstantial evidence, based on concrete elements, from which it may be concluded to the requisite standard of proof that the detainee must be presumed to have died in custody.... In this respect the period of time which has elapsed since the person was placed in detention, although not decisive in itself, is a relevant factor to be taken into account. It must be accepted that the more time goes by without any news of the detained person, the greater the likelihood that he or she has died. The passage of time may therefore to some extent affect the weight to be attached to other elements of circumstantial evidence before it can be concluded that the person concerned is to be presumed dead....'

Applying this approach the judges went on to find that the applicant's sons were seen being taken away by soldiers, they were subsequently taken to a military establishment and no information regarding their whereabouts has subsequently come to light in over nine years. Therefore, the Court was united in concluding that:

168.... Servet and Ikram Ipek must be presumed dead following their unacknowledged detention by the security forces. Consequently, the responsibility of the respondent State for their death is engaged.

Noting that the authorities have not provided any explanation as to what occurred following the Ipek brothers' apprehension, and that they do not rely on any ground of justification in respect of any use of lethal force by their agents, it follows that liability for their death is attributed to the respondent Government. Accordingly, there has been a violation of Article 2 on that account.

Eyewitness testimony, especially from third-parties, supporting applicants' assertions that their relatives were last seen in the custody of State agents coupled with long periods of disappearance are crucial elements in allowing the Court to determine that States should be held liable under this Article in respect of disappeared persons.

11 The former Commission did not provide a definitive answer to the question whether foetuses/unborn children possess rights under Article 2. In *X v UK*, 19 DR 244 (1980), the applicant was a married man whose wife had undergone a lawful abortion in England. Previously, the applicant had sought an injunction from the High Court to prevent the abortion taking place, but that had been refused (the High Court held that under domestic law the foetus did not have legal rights until it was born and had a separate existence from its mother). He then alleged, *inter alia*, a breach of Article 2 as English law denied the foetus any rights. The Commission was of the view that, ' ... both the general usage of the term 'everyone' in the Convention and the context in which this term is employed in Article 2 tend to support the view that it does not include the unborn.' (para 9) Furthermore, the Commission rejected the contention that a foetus has an absolute right to life under Article 2.

20. The Commission finds that such an interpretation would be contrary to the object and purpose of the Convention. It notes that, already at the time of the signature of the Convention, all High Contracting Parties, with one possible exception, permitted abortion when necessary to save the life of the mother and that, in the meanwhile, the national law on termination of pregnancy has shown a tendency towards further liberalisation.

Also,

22. ... the Commission is in the present case not concerned with the broad question whether Article 2 recognises a 'right to life' of the foetus during the whole period of the pregnancy but only with the narrower issue whether such a right is to be assumed for the initial stage of the pregnancy. Moreover, as regards implied limitations of a 'right to life' of the foetus at the initial stage, only the limitation protecting the life and health of the pregnant woman, the so-called 'medical indication', is relevant for the determination of the present case and the question of other possible limitations (ethic indication, eugenic indication, social indication, time limitation) does not arise.

23. The Commission considers that it is not in these circumstances called upon to decide whether Article 2 does not cover the foetus at all or whether it recognises a 'right to life' of the foetus with implied limitations. It finds that the authorisation, by the United Kingdom authorities, of the abortion complained of is compatible with Article 2(1), first sentence because, if one assumes that this provision applies at the initial stage of the pregnancy, the abortion is covered by an implied limitation, protecting the life and health of the woman at that stage, of the 'right to life' of foetus.

24. The Commission concludes that the applicant's complaint under Article 2 is inadmissible as being manifestly ill-founded within the meaning of Article 27(2).

For other cases dealing with abortion see below, p 497 (A.8 *Bruggemann* and A.10 *Open Door*).

12 Similarly, a Grand Chamber declined to provide a definitive answer to the question whether an unborn child is a 'person' for the purposes of Article 2 in *Vo v France*, judgment of 8 July 2004. The applicant, Mrs Thi-Nho Vo, was a 24-year-old French national of Vietnamese origin. In 1991 she went to Lyons General Hospital for a scheduled medical examination as she was six months pregnant. On the same day a Mrs Thi Thanh Van Vo was due to have a coil removed at the hospital. The doctor responsible for the removal of the coil called out the name of 'Mrs Vo' in the waiting room. The applicant answered (the doctor noted that she had problems understanding French). He then consulted the notes for Mrs Van Vo and, without examining the applicant, sought to remove a coil. In undertaking this procedure the doctor pierced the applicant's amniotic sac and caused the loss of considerable fluid with the consequence that the applicant had to undergo an (unwanted) termination of her pregnancy several days later. The applicant, and her partner, made a criminal complaint against the doctor. He was charged with unintentional homicide (of the foetus) and unintentional injury of the applicant. The latter charge was later dropped in the light of a statutory amnesty. Eventually, the Court of Cassation ruled that the former offence had to be construed strictly and did not encompass the foetus. The applicant lodged a complaint at Strasbourg contending, *inter alia*, that the failure of French law to classify the taking of her unborn child's life as unintentional homicide amounted to a breach of Article 2. In her view a child that had not yet been born was a person. The Government responded that 'neither metaphysics nor medicine' had provided a definitive answer to when a foetus became a human being and Article 2 did not protect a foetus' right to life as a person. The Court held that:

75. Unlike Article 4 of the American Convention on Human Rights, which provides that the right to life must be protected 'in general, from the moment of conception', Article 2 of the Convention is silent as to the temporal limitations of the right to life and, in particular, does not define 'everyone' ('*toute personne*') whose 'life' is protected by the Convention. The Court has yet to determine the issue of the 'beginning' of 'everyone's right to life' within the meaning of this provision and whether the unborn child has such a right.

To date it has been raised solely in connection with laws on abortion. Abortion does not constitute one of the exceptions expressly listed in paragraph 2 of Article 2 but the Commission has expressed the opinion that it is compatible with the first sentence of Article 2 § 1 in the interests of protecting the mother's life and health because 'if one assumes that this provision applies at the initial stage of the pregnancy, the abortion is covered by an implied limitation, protecting the life and health of the woman at that stage, of the "right to life" of the foetus' (see *X v the United Kingdom*, Commission decision [(1980) 19 DR 244] at p 253).

76. Having initially refused to examine *in abstracto* the compatibility of abortion laws with Article 2 of the Convention (see *X v Norway*, No 867/60, Commission decision of 29 May 1961, Collection of Decisions 6, p. 34, and *X v Austria*, No 7045/75, Commission decision of 10 December 1976, DR 7, p 87), the Commission acknowledged in the case of *Brüggemann and Scheuten v the Federal Republic of Germany* [10 D&R 100 (1977)] that women complaining under Article 8 of the Convention about the Constitutional Court's decision restricting the availability of abortions had standing as victims. It stated on that occasion: 'pregnancy cannot be said to pertain uniquely to the sphere of private life. Whenever a woman is pregnant her private life becomes closely connected with the developing foetus' (ibid, at p 116, § 59). However, the Commission did not find it 'necessary to decide, in this context, whether the unborn child is to be considered as "life" in the sense of Article 2 of the Convention, or whether it could be regarded as an entity which under Article 8 § 2 could justify an interference "for the protection of others"' (ibid, at p 116, § 60). It expressed the opinion that there had been no violation of Article 8 of the Convention because 'not every regulation of the termination of unwanted pregnancies constitutes an interference with the right to respect for the private life of the mother' (ibid, at pp 116–17, § 61), while emphasising: 'There is no evidence that it was the intention of the Parties to the Convention to bind themselves in favour of any particular solution' (ibid, at pp 117–18, § 64).

. . .

78. In the case of *H. v Norway*, concerning an abortion carried out on non-medical grounds against the father's wishes, the Commission added that Article 2 required the State not only to refrain from taking

a person's life intentionally but also to take appropriate steps to safeguard life (see *H. v Norway* [73 D&R 155 (1992)] at p 167). It considered that it did not have to decide 'whether the foetus may enjoy a certain protection under Article 2, first sentence', but did not exclude the possibility that 'in certain circumstances this may be the case notwithstanding that there is in the Contracting States a considerable divergence of views on whether or to what extent Article 2 protects the unborn life' (ibid). It further noted that in such a delicate area the Contracting States had to have a certain discretion, and concluded that the mother's decision, taken in accordance with Norwegian legislation, had not exceeded that discretion (ibid, p. 168).

79. The Court has only rarely had occasion to consider the application of Article 2 to the foetus. In the case of *Open Door and Dublin Well Woman* [A.246-A (1992)] the Irish Government relied on the protection of the life of the unborn child to justify their legislation prohibiting the provision of information concerning abortion facilities abroad. The only issue that was resolved was whether the restrictions on the freedom to receive and impart the information in question had been necessary in a democratic society, within the meaning of paragraph 2 of Article 10 of the Convention, to pursue the 'legitimate aim of the protection of morals of which the protection in Ireland of the right to life of the unborn is one aspect' (see *Open Door and Dublin Well Woman*, cited above, pp 27–8, § 63), since the Court did not consider it relevant to determine 'whether a right to abortion is guaranteed under the Convention or whether the foetus is encompassed by the right to life as contained in Article 2' (ibid, p 28, § 66). Recently, in circumstances similar to those in the above-mentioned case of *H. v Norway*, where a woman had decided to terminate her pregnancy against the father's wishes, the Court held that it was not required to determine 'whether the foetus may qualify for protection under the first sentence of Article 2 as interpreted [in the case-law relating to the positive obligation to protect life]', and continued: 'Even supposing that, in certain circumstances, the foetus might be considered to have rights protected by Article 2 of the Convention, . . . in the instant case . . . [the] pregnancy was terminated in conformity with section 5 of Law No 194 of 1978'—a law which struck a fair balance between the woman's interests and the need to ensure protection of the foetus (see *Boso v Italy* (dec.), No 50490/99, ECHR 2002-VII).

80. It follows from this recapitulation of the case-law that in the circumstances examined to date by the Convention institutions—that is, in the various laws on abortion—the unborn child is not regarded as a 'person' directly protected by Article 2 of the Convention and that if the unborn do have a 'right' to 'life', it is implicitly limited by the mother's rights and interests. The Convention institutions have not, however, ruled out the possibility that in certain circumstances safeguards may be extended to the unborn child. That is what appears to have been contemplated by the Commission in considering that 'Article 8 §1 cannot be interpreted as meaning that pregnancy and its termination are, as a principle, solely a matter of the private life of the mother' (see *Brüggeman and Scheuten*, cited above, at pp 116–17, § 61) and by the Court in the above-mentioned *Boso* decision. It is also clear from an examination of these cases that the issue has always been determined by weighing up various, and sometimes conflicting, rights or freedoms claimed by a woman, a mother or a father in relation to one another or vis-à-vis an unborn child.

2. APPROACH IN THE INSTANT CASE

81. The special nature of the instant case raises a new issue. The Court is faced with a woman who intended to carry her pregnancy to term and whose unborn child was expected to be viable, at the very least in good health. Her pregnancy had to be terminated as a result of an error by a doctor and she therefore had to have a therapeutic abortion on account of negligence by a third party. The issue is consequently whether, apart from cases where the mother has requested an abortion, harming a foetus should be treated as a criminal offence in the light of Article 2 of the Convention, with a view to protecting the foetus under that Article. This requires a preliminary examination of whether it is advisable for the Court to intervene in the debate as to who is a person and when life begins, in so far as Article 2 provides that the law must protect 'everyone's right to life'.

82. As is apparent from the above recapitulation of the case-law, the interpretation of Article 2 in this connection has been informed by a clear desire to strike a balance, and the Convention institutions' position in relation to the legal, medical, philosophical, ethical or religious dimensions of defining the human being has taken into account the various approaches to the matter at national level. This has been reflected in the consideration given to the diversity of views on the point at which life begins, of legal cultures and of national standards of protection, and the State has been left with considerable discretion in the matter, as the opinion of the European Group on Ethics at Community level appositely puts it: 'the ... Community authorities have to address these ethical questions taking into account the moral and philosophical differences, reflected by the extreme diversity of legal rules applicable to human embryo research. ... It is not only legally difficult to seek harmonisation of national laws at Community level, but because of lack of consensus, it would be inappropriate to impose one exclusive moral code' [23 November 1998].

It follows that the issue of when the right to life begins comes within the margin of appreciation which the Court generally considers that States should enjoy in this sphere, notwithstanding an evolutive interpretation of the Convention, a 'living instrument which must be interpreted in the light of present-day conditions' (see *Tyrer v the United Kingdom*, judgment of 25 April 1978, Series A No 26, pp 15–16, §31, and subsequent case-law). The reasons for that conclusion are, firstly, that the issue of such protection has not been resolved within the majority of the Contracting States themselves, in France in particular, where it is the subject of debate ... and, secondly, that there is no European consensus on the scientific and legal definition of the beginning of life. ...

83. The Court observes that the French Court of Cassation, in three successive judgments delivered in 1999, 2001 and 2002, considered that the rule that offences and punishment must be defined by law, which required criminal statutes to be construed strictly, excluded acts causing a fatal injury to a foetus from the scope of Article 221-6 of the Criminal Code, under which unintentional homicide of 'another' is an offence. However, if, as a result of unintentional negligence, the mother gives birth to a live child who dies shortly after being born, the person responsible may be convicted of the unintentional homicide of the child. The first-mentioned approach, which conflicts with that of several courts of appeal, was interpreted as an invitation to the legislature to fill a legal vacuum. That was also the position of the Criminal Court in the instant case: 'The court ... cannot create law on an issue which [the legislature has] not yet succeeded in defining.' The French parliament attempted such a definition in proposing to create the offence of involuntary termination of pregnancy but the Bill containing that proposal was lost, on account of the fears and uncertainties that the creation of the offence might arouse as to the determination of when life began, and the disadvantages of the proposal, which were thought to outweigh its advantages. The Court further notes that alongside the Court of Cassation's repeated rulings that Article 221-6 of the Criminal Code does not apply to foetuses, the French parliament is currently revising the 1994 bioethics laws, which added provisions to the Criminal Code on the protection of the human embryo and required re-examination in the light of scientific and technological progress. It is clear from this overview that in France, the nature and legal status of the embryo and/or the foetus are currently not defined and that the manner in which it is to be protected will be determined by very varied forces within French society.

84. At European level, the Court observes that there is no consensus on the nature and status of the embryo and/or foetus although they are beginning to receive some protection in the light of scientific progress and the potential consequences of research into genetic engineering, medically assisted procreation or embryo experimentation. At best, it may be regarded as common ground between States that the embryo/foetus belongs to the human race. The potentiality of that being and its capacity to become a person—enjoying protection under the civil law, moreover, in many States, such as France, in the context of inheritance and gifts, and also in the United Kingdom—require protection in the name of human dignity, without making it a 'person' with the 'right to life' for the purposes of Article 2. The Oviedo Convention on Human Rights and Biomedicine, indeed, is careful not to give a definition of the

term 'everyone' and its explanatory report indicates that, in the absence of a unanimous agreement on the definition, the member States decided to allow domestic law to provide clarifications for the purposes of the application of that Convention. The same is true of the Additional Protocol on the Prohibition of Cloning Human Beings and the draft Additional Protocol on Biomedical Research, which do not define the concept of 'human being'. It is worth noting that the Court may be requested under Article 29 of the Oviedo Convention to give advisory opinions on the interpretation of that instrument.

85. Having regard to the foregoing, the Court is convinced that it is neither desirable, nor even possible as matters stand, to answer in the abstract the question whether the unborn child is a person for the purposes of Article 2 of the Convention ('*personne*' in the French text). As to the instant case, it considers it unnecessary to examine whether the abrupt end to the applicant's pregnancy falls within the scope of Article 2, seeing that, even assuming that that provision was applicable, there was no failure on the part of the respondent State to comply with the requirements relating to the preservation of life in the public-health sphere. With regard to that issue, the Court has considered whether the legal protection afforded the applicant by France in respect of the loss of the unborn child she was carrying satisfied the procedural requirements inherent in Article 2 of the Convention.

A large majority of the Grand Chamber, fourteen votes to three, went on to conclude (assuming Article 2 applied) that the option of bringing an action for damages against the doctor/hospital in the French administrative courts, which the applicant had not pursued, would have enabled her to obtain full redress for the damage caused by the doctor's negligence and therefore the procedural requirements were satisfied.

Judge Costa issued a separate opinion in which he expressed the view that:

17. In sum, I see no good legal reason or decisive policy consideration for not applying Article 2 in the present case. On a general level, I believe (in company with many senior judicial bodies in Europe) that there is life before birth, within the meaning of Article 2, that the law must therefore protect such life, and that if a national legislature considers that such protection cannot be absolute, then it should only derogate from it, particularly as regards the voluntary termination of pregnancy, within a regulated framework that limits the scope of the derogation. The actual circumstances of Mrs Vo's case made it all the more appropriate to find that Article 2 was applicable: she was six months pregnant (contrast this—purely for illustration purposes—with the German Federal Constitutional Court's view that life begins after fourteen days gestation), there was every prospect that the foetus would be born viable and, lastly, the pregnancy was clearly ended by an act of negligence, against the applicant's wishes.

18. I have nothing further to add, since, with minor differences, I agree with what the judgment has to say in finding that there has been no violation of Article 2.

Judge Rozakis, joined by Judges Caflisch, Fischbach, Lorenzen and Thomassen, produced a separate opinion in which he stated that:

It consequently transpires from the present stage of development of the law and morals in Europe that the life of the unborn child, although protected in some attributes, cannot be equated to post-natal life, and, therefore, does not enjoy a right in the sense of 'a right to life', as protected by Article 2 of the Convention.

Judge Ress dissented because:

4. ... Historically, lawyers have understood the notion of 'everyone' as including the human being before birth and, above all, the notion of 'life' as covering all human life commencing with conception, that is to say from the moment an *independent existence* develops until it ends with death, birth being but a stage in that development.

...

8. There can be no margin of appreciation on the issue of the applicability of Article 2. A margin of appreciation may, in my opinion, exist to determine the measures that should be taken to discharge the positive obligation that arises because Article 2 is applicable, but it is not possible to restrict the applicability of Article 2 by reference to a margin of appreciation. The question of the interpretation or applicability of Article 2 (an absolute right) cannot depend on a margin of appreciation. If Article 2 is applicable, any margin of appreciation will be confined to the effect thereof.

9. Since I consider that Article 2 applies to human beings even before they are born, an interpretation which seems to me to be consistent with the approach of the Charter of Fundamental Rights of the European Union, and since France does not afford sufficient protection to the foetus against the negligent acts of third parties, I find that there has been a violation of Article 2 of the Convention. As regards the specific measures necessary to discharge that positive obligation, that is a matter for the respondent State, which should either take strict disciplinary measures or afford the protection of the criminal law (against unintentional homicide).

Judge Mularoni, joined by Judge Straznicka, dissented as she considered that the remedy of an action before the French administrative courts did not provide an adequate level of protection for the loss of the applicant's 'child' and:

Although legal personality is only acquired at birth, this does not to my mind mean that there must be no recognition or protection of 'everyone's right to life' before birth. Indeed, this seems to me to be a principle that is shared by all the member States of the Council of Europe, as domestic legislation permitting the voluntary termination of pregnancy would not have been necessary if the foetus was not regarded as having a life that should be protected. Abortion therefore constitutes an exception to the rule that the right to life should be protected, even before birth.

Given the Grand Chamber's findings of the absence of a European consensus regarding the precise time at which the right to life begins or the legal status of embryos/foetuses we can understand why the Court has not felt able to give general rulings on the applicability of Article 2 to such entities. However, the judgment in *Vo* demonstrates that the Court is willing to examine complaints brought on behalf of the unborn. A. Plomer evaluates the judgment in a comparative context in 'A Foetal Right to Life? The Case of Vo France' (2005) 5(2) *Human Rights Law Review* 311.

13 A Grand Chamber examined the division between the ambit of Article 2 and Article 3 in the context of serious ill-treatment of persons by State agents in *Ilhan v Turkey*, judgment of 27 June 2000. The applicant's brother ran away when gendarmes came to his village in 1992. A group of gendarmes found him and subjected him to a severe beating, including hitting him with their rifles and kicking him. These injuries resulted in him suffering brain damage resulting in a loss of 60 per cent of the function of his left side. Despite the gravity of these injuries, described as life threatening by the doctors on his admission to hospital, the gendarmes did not take him to hospital until thirty-six hours after his arrest/assault. The applicant contended that the assault on his brother constituted a breach of Article 2 as that provision applied to the use of both lethal force and potentially lethal force (i.e. force that could foreseeably result in death). A large majority of the Grand Chamber (twelve votes to five) held that:

76. . . . it is only in exceptional circumstances that physical ill-treatment by State officials which does not result in death may disclose a breach of Article 2 of the Convention. . . . In almost all cases where a person is assaulted or maltreated by police or soldiers, their complaints will fall to be examined rather under Article 3 of the Convention.

Therefore, the majority did not consider that the force used by the gendarmes on the applicant's brother was of such a nature or degree to breach Article 2. The dissentients believed that as Article 2 protects the right to life and the injuries inflicted on the applicant's brother were life threatening that Article was applicable to his mal-treatment. Furthermore, given the gravity of the victim's injuries, the dissentients questioned what other 'exceptional circumstances' were required to be present for a serious mal-treatment case not resulting in death to be examined under Article 2? The Grand Chamber was, however, unanimous that the applicant's brother had suffered torture (in violation of Article 3) in respect of his severe ill-treatment by the gendarmes and their delay in ensuring that he received proper medical treatment. The majority's approach was to essentially confine Article 2 to cases where officials' mal-treatment of persons resulted in the death of the latter. This may be partially explained by the Court's contemporaneous widening of the scope of torture under Article 3 (see below p 166).

14   A later, rare, example of the Court finding the use of non-lethal force by State agents to have violated Article 2 occurred in *Makaratzis v Greece*, judgment of 20 December 2004. In September 1995 the applicant drove through red traffic lights, near the American embassy, in central Athens. He was chased by over thirty police officers, some of whom participated of their accord, in cars and on motorcycles. The applicant drove through five police roadblocks and collided with several non-police vehicles, injuring two civilians. The police thereupon opened fire on the applicant's car with handguns and submachine guns. He stopped his car at a petrol station and the police continued to fire at his car. The applicant would not leave his car, so the police forced their way into the car (one officer smashed the windscreen by throwing a plant pot at it). The applicant was then arrested. No weapon was found in his possession. He was taken to hospital and treated for gunshot wounds (he had been injured in the arm, foot, buttock, and chest). Subsequently, he was convicted of, *inter alia*, causing bodily injury to others by his negligence and sentenced to forty days' imprisonment. An administrative investigation was also carried out and it found sixteen bullet holes in the applicant's car. Twenty-nine police officers were identified as having taken part in the operation against the applicant but in addition an unknown number of other officers had participated of their own accord and they had left the scene without identifying themselves or handing in their weapons (to determine if they had been fired). The public prosecutor charged seven of the identified police officers with causing serious bodily harm and unauthorized use of weapons. However, they were later acquitted by the Athens First-Instance Criminal Court (because it had not been proven that the accused had injured the applicant and the court held that the police officers had only used their weapons to try and immobilize a car whose driver they believed to be a dangerous criminal). The applicant complained to the European Court alleging breaches of Article 2, because the police had used unnecessary and disproportionate force against him and there had not been an effective investigation into the actions of the police. The Grand Chamber held that:

51. On the other hand, the case-law establishes that it is only in exceptional circumstances that physical ill-treatment by State officials which does not result in death may disclose a violation of Article 2 of the Convention. It is correct that in the proceedings brought under the Convention the criminal responsibility of those concerned in the use of the impugned force is not in issue. Nonetheless, the degree and type of force used and the intention or aim behind the use of force may, among other factors, be relevant in assessing whether in a particular case the State agents' actions in inflicting injury short of death are such as to bring the facts within the scope of the safeguard afforded by Article 2 of the Convention, having regard to the object and purpose pursued by that Article. In almost all cases where a person is assaulted or ill-treated by the police or soldiers, their complaints will rather fall to be examined under Article 3 of the Convention (see *Ilhan v Turkey*, cited above, § 76).

52. What the Court must therefore determine in the present case, where State officials were implicated in the applicant's wounding, is whether the force used against the applicant was potentially lethal and

what kind of impact the conduct of the officials concerned had not only on his physical integrity but also on the interest which the right to life is intended to protect.

53. It is common ground that the applicant was chased by a large number of police officers who made repeated use of revolvers, pistols and submachine guns.

It is clear from the evidence adduced before the Court that the police used their weapons in order to immobilise the applicant's car and effect his arrest, this being one of the instances contemplated by the second paragraph of Article 2 when the resort to lethal, or potentially lethal, force may be legitimate. As far as the ill-treatment proscribed by Article 3 is concerned, at no time could there be inferred from the police officers' conduct an intention to inflict pain, suffering, humiliation or debasement on him (see, as a recent authority, *Ilascu and Others v Moldova and Russia* [GC], §§ 425–8, ECHR 2004-VII). In particular, on the material before it the Court cannot find that the applicant's allegation as to the shooting of his foot after his removal from his car has been substantiated.

54. The Court likewise accepts the Government's submission that the police did not intend to kill the applicant. It observes, however, that the fact that the latter was not killed was fortuitous. According to the findings of the ballistic report, there were sixteen holes in the car caused by bullets following a horizontal or an upward trajectory to the car driver's level. There were three holes and a mark on the car's front windscreen caused by bullets which came through the rear plate glass; the latter was broken and had fallen in. In the end, the applicant was injured in the right arm, the right foot, the left buttock and the right side of the chest and was hospitalised for nine days. The seriousness of his injuries is not in dispute between the parties.

55. In the light of the above circumstances, and in particular the degree and type of force used, the Court concludes that, irrespective of whether or not the police actually intended to kill him, the applicant was the victim of conduct which, by its very nature, put his life at risk, even though, in the event, he survived. Article 2 is thus applicable in the instant case. Furthermore, given the context in which his life was put at risk and the nature of the impugned conduct of the State officials concerned, the Court is satisfied that the facts call for examination under Article 2.

The Grand Chamber then examined the domestic law governing the use of weapons by police officers and the police operation to arrest the applicant.

62. At the time of the events in issue, however, the applicable legislation was Law No 29/1943, dating from the Second World War when Greece was occupied by the German armed forces. That statute listed a wide range of situations in which a police officer could use firearms without being liable for the consequences. In 1991, a presidential decree authorised the use of firearms in the circumstances set forth in the 1943 statute 'only when absolutely necessary and when all less extreme methods have been exhausted'. No other provisions regulating the use of weapons during police actions and laying down guidelines on planning and control of police operations were contained in Greek law. On its face, the above, somewhat slender, legal framework would not appear sufficient to provide the level of protection 'by law' of the right to life that is required in present-day democratic societies in Europe.

63. This conclusion as to the state of Greek law is confirmed by the evidence before the Court of the bearing which the legal and administrative framework at the material time had on the way in which the potentially lethal police operation culminating in the applicant's arrest was conducted.

64. Turning to the facts of the present case, and having regard to the findings of the domestic court, the Court accepts that the applicant was driving his motor car in the centre of Athens at excessive speed in an uncontrolled and dangerous manner, thereby putting the lives of bystanders and police officers at risk; the police were thus entitled to react on the basis that he was manoeuvring a life-endangering object in a public place. Alternative means to stop him were tried but failed; this was accompanied by an escalation of the havoc that the applicant was causing and by the lethal threat that he was posing by

his criminal conduct to innocent people. Further, the police officers pursuing the applicant had been informed by the control centre that he might well be armed and dangerous; they also believed that the movements which they saw the applicant make when he stopped his car were consistent with his being armed.

65. Another important factor must also be taken into consideration, namely the prevailing climate at that time in Greece, which was marked by terrorist activities against foreign interests. For example, a group called the 'Revolutionary Organisation 17 November', established in 1975, had committed, until it was dismantled in 2002, numerous crimes, including the assassination of US officials. This, coupled with the fact that the event took place at night, near the US Embassy, contributed to the applicant being perceived as a greater threat in the eyes of the police.

66. Consequently, like the national court, the Court finds in the circumstances that the police could reasonably have considered that there was a need to resort to the use of their weapons in order to immobilise the car and neutralise the threat posed by its driver, and not merely a need to arrest a motorist who had driven through a red traffic light. Therefore, even though it was subsequently discovered that the applicant was unarmed and that he was not a terrorist, the Court accepts that the use of force against him was based on an honest belief which was perceived, for good reasons, to be valid at the time. To hold otherwise would be to impose an unrealistic burden on the State and its law-enforcement personnel in the execution of their duty, perhaps to the detriment of their lives and those of others (see *McCann and Others v the United Kingdom*, cited above, pp 58–9, §200).

67. However, although the recourse as such to some potentially lethal force in the present case can be said to have been compatible with Article 2 of the Convention, the Court is struck by the chaotic way in which the firearms were actually used by the police in the circumstances. It may be recalled that an unspecified number of police officers fired volleys of shots at the applicant's car with revolvers, pistols and submachine guns. No less than sixteen gunshot impacts were counted on the car, some being horizontal or even upwards, and not downwards as one would expect if the tyres, and only the tyres, of the vehicle were being shot at by the pursuing police. Three holes and a mark had damaged the car's front windscreen and the rear plate glass was broken and had fallen in. In sum, it appears from the evidence produced before the Court that large numbers of police officers took part in a largely uncontrolled chase.

68. Serious questions therefore arise as to the conduct and the organisation of the operation. Admittedly some directions were given by the control centre to some police officers who had been expressly contacted, but some others ran of their own accord to their colleagues' assistance, without receiving any instructions. The absence of clear chains of command is a factor which by its very nature must have increased the risk of some police officers shooting erratically.

69. The Court evidently does not overlook the fact that the applicant was injured in the course of an unplanned operation which gave rise to developments to which the police was called upon to react without prior preparation (see, *a contrario, Rehbock v Slovenia*, No 29462/95, §§71–2, ECHR 2000-XII). Bearing in mind the difficulties in policing modern societies, the unpredictability of human conduct and the operational choices which must be made in terms of priorities and resources, the positive obligation must be interpreted in a way which does not impose an impossible burden on the authorities (see, *mutatis mutandis, Mahmut Kaya v Turkey*, No 22535/93, §86, ECHR 2000-III).

70. Nonetheless, while accepting that the police officers who were involved in the incident did not have sufficient time to evaluate all the parameters of the situation and carefully organise their operation, the Court considers that the degeneration of the situation, which some of the police witnesses themselves described as chaotic, was largely due to the fact that at that time neither the individual police officers nor the chase, seen as a collective police operation, had the benefit of the appropriate

structure which should have been provided by the domestic law and practice. In fact, the Court points out that in 1995, when the event took place, an admittedly obsolete and incomplete law for a modern democratic society was still regulating the use of weapons by State officials. The system in place did not afford to law-enforcement officials clear guidelines and criteria governing the use of force in peacetime. It was thus unavoidable that the police officers who chased and eventually arrested the applicant enjoyed a greater autonomy of action and were able to take unconsidered initiatives, which they would probably not have displayed had they had the benefit of proper training and instructions. The absence of clear guidelines could further explain why other police officers took part in the operation spontaneously without reporting to a central command.

71. In the light of the above, the Court considers that as far as their positive obligation under the first sentence of Article 2 § 1 to put in place an adequate legislative and administrative framework was concerned, the Greek authorities had not, at the relevant time, done all that could be reasonably expected of them to afford to citizens, and in particular to those, such as the applicant, against whom potentially lethal force was used, the level of safeguards required and to avoid real and immediate risk to life which they knew was liable to arise, albeit only exceptionally, in hot-pursuit police operations (see, *mutatis mutandis, Osman v United Kingdom*, cited above, p 3160, § 116 *in fine*).

72. Accordingly, the applicant has been the victim of a violation of Article 2 of the Convention on this ground. In view of this conclusion, it is not necessary to examine the life-threatening conduct of the police under the second paragraph of Article 2.

President Wildhaber, joined by Judges Kovler and Mularoni, dissented as they considered that the police had responded to 'the irresponsible and dangerous behaviour of the applicant' and, in their opinion, Greek law laid down 'in an absolutely clear fashion' the standard for the use of force by police officers. However, the Grand Chamber was unanimous in concluding that that there had been a procedural breach of Article 2 due to serious defects, including failing to identify all the police officers who participated in the operation against the applicant, in the administrative inquiry into the shooting of the applicant.

The willingness of the overwhelming majority in *Makaratzis* to find a breach of the substantive requirements of Article 2, although the applicant had not been killed, can be explained in terms of both the nature and scale of the police response to his illegal (and dangerous) behaviour (i.e. over thirty officers firing numerous shots at his car) and the existing vague legal restrictions governing the use of firearms by police officers. These features were sufficient for the Grand Chamber to apply the *Ilhan* test of 'exceptional circumstances' to justify the application of Article 2. For an examination of the application of Article 2(2) to the use of firearms resulting in the death of suspects see *Nachova and Others v Bulgaria*, below p 140.

15 The outer boundaries of the right to life were delimited in the tragic case of *Pretty v United Kingdom*, judgment of 29 April 2002. The applicant was a 43-year old woman suffering from advanced motor neurone disease (an incurable terminal illness resulting in the progressive weakening of muscles leading to respiratory failure). Mrs Pretty had been diagnosed with the disease in 1999 and it progressed rapidly so that by the time of the Court's judgment she was paralysed from the neck down but her intellect and ability to make decisions were not impaired. She was distressed at the suffering she would endure if the disease was allowed to progress to her death. Therefore, she wishes her husband to help her commit suicide at the time of her choosing (because of the effects of her disease she needed the physical help of another person to commit suicide). She requested the Director of Public Prosecutions to undertake that he would not prosecute her husband (under the Suicide Act 1961 it is an offence to assist another person to commit suicide) if he helped her. The DPP refused to give such an undertaking and the applicant's claim for judicial review of that decision was ultimately rejected by the House of Lords (*R (Pretty) v DPP* [2001] 3 WLR 1598). Before the Court her lawyers contended, *inter alia*, that Article 2 protected not only the right to life but also the right to choose whether to go on living. In a unanimous judgment the Court held that:

37. The Court's case-law accords pre-eminence to Article 2 as one of the most fundamental provisions of the Convention (see the *McCann and Others v the United Kingdom* judgment of 27 September 1995, Series A No 324, §§ 146–7). It safeguards the right to life, without which enjoyment of any of the other rights and freedoms in the Convention is rendered nugatory. It sets out the limited circumstances when deprivation of life may be justified and the Court has applied a strict scrutiny when those exceptions have been invoked by respondent Governments (*McCann and Others v the United Kingdom*, op cit., §§ 149–50).

. . .

39. The consistent emphasis in all the cases before the Court has been the obligation of the State to protect life. The Court is not persuaded that 'the right to life' guaranteed in Article 2 can be interpreted as involving a negative aspect. While, for example, in the context of Article 11 of the Convention, the freedom of association was found to involve not only a right to join an association but a corresponding right not to be forced to join an association, the Court observes that the notion of a freedom implies some measure of choice as to its exercise (see the *Young, James and Webster v the United Kingdom* judgment of 13 August 1981, Series A No 44, § 52, and *Sigurður A. Sigurjónsson v Iceland* judgment of 30 June 1993, Series A No 264, pp 15–16, § 35). Article 2 of the Convention is phrased in different terms. It is unconcerned with issues to do with the quality of living or what a person chooses to do with his or her life. To the extent that these aspects are recognised as so fundamental to the human condition that they require protection from State interference, they may be reflected in the rights guaranteed by other Articles of the Convention, or in other international human rights instruments. Article 2 cannot, without a distortion of language, be interpreted as conferring the diametrically opposite right, namely a right to die; nor can it create a right to self-determination in the sense of conferring on an individual the entitlement to choose death rather than life.

40. The Court accordingly finds that no right to die, whether at the hands of a third person or with the assistance of a public authority, can be derived from Article 2 of the Convention. It is confirmed in this view by the recent Recommendation 1418 (1999) of the Parliamentary Assembly of the Council of Europe.

Consequently, the Court found no breach of Article 2 (or any other right under the Convention). The applicant decided not to request a re-hearing before the Grand Chamber and she died in a hospice a few weeks after the delivery of the above judgment. Her lawyers' attempts to persuade the Court to recognize an implicit 'right to die' within Article 2 would have required the latter to legislate on a very sensitive topic in a manner contrary to the domestic and European consensus (reflected in Recommendation 1418 which sought to uphold 'the prohibition against intentionally taking the life of terminally ill or dying persons ... '). In May 2006 a majority of peers (148 to 100) voted to block the Assisted Dying for the Terminally Ill Bill (introduced by the independent Lord Joffe), that would have allowed competent terminally ill adults to end their lives with medication supplied by a doctor. A pressure group, Care not Killing, comprising churches and others campaigned against the Bill. *The Times* newspaper reported (13/5/2006) that the Roman Catholic Church had sent out 500,000 letters and DVDs to its members asking them to protest against the Bill. The Church of England peers also played a leading role in opposing the Bill.

Article 2(1)

States' positive obligations

1   The Court implied that Article 2(1) imposed positive obligations upon States to protect the lives of individuals within their jurisdictions in *LCB v UK* (1998) 27 EHRR 212, *Reports* 1998-III. The applicant's father, in his capacity as a catering assistant in the Royal Air Force, was present during four atmospheric nuclear bomb tests conducted at Christmas Island (located in the Pacific Ocean) during 1957–8. The applicant was born in 1966 and during 1970 she was diagnosed as having leukaemia. She received chemotherapy, which lasted until she was 10 years old. In 1992 she became aware of a report, produced by the British Nuclear Tests Veterans' Association, indicating a high incidence of cancers in children of Christmas Island veterans. Thereupon, she complained to the Commission alleging, inter alia, that the British government's failure to warn her parents of the possible risk to her health caused by her father's participation in the nuclear tests violated Article 2. The Commission was unanimous in finding no breach of that provision. The Court was also unanimous in determining that:

36. ... the first sentence of Article 2 § 1 enjoins the State not only to refrain from the intentional and unlawful taking of life, but also to take appropriate steps to safeguard the lives of those within its jurisdiction (cf the Court's reasoning in respect of Article 8 in the *Guerra v Italy* judgment of 19 February 1998, *Reports* 1998-I, p 227, § 58, and see also the decision of the Commission on the admissibility of application No 7154/75 of 12 July 1978, Decisions and Reports 14, p 31). It has not been suggested that the respondent State intentionally sought to deprive the applicant of her life. The Court's task is, therefore, to determine whether, given the circumstances of the case, the State did all that could have been required of it to prevent the applicant's life from being avoidably put at risk ...

39. Having examined the expert evidence submitted to it, the Court is not satisfied that it has been established that there is a causal link between the exposure of a father to radiation and leukaemia in a child subsequently conceived. As recently as 1993, the High Court judge sitting in the cases of *Reay* and *Hope v British Nuclear Fuels plc* ([1994] Medical Law Reports 1), having examined a considerable amount of expert evidence, found that 'the scales tilt[ed] decisively' in favour of a finding that there was no such causal link ... The Court could not reasonably hold, therefore, that, in the late 1960s, the United Kingdom authorities could or should, on the basis of this unsubstantiated link, have taken action in respect of the applicant.

40. Finally, in the light of the conflicting evidence of Dr Bross and Professor Eden ... and as the Commission also found ... it is clearly uncertain whether monitoring of the applicant's health *in utero* and from birth would have led to earlier diagnosis and medical intervention such as to diminish the severity of her disease. It is perhaps arguable that, had there been reason to believe that she was in danger of contracting a life-threatening disease owing to her father's presence on Christmas Island, the State authorities would have been under a duty to have made this known to her parents whether or not they considered that the information would assist the applicant. However, this is not a matter which the Court is required to decide in view of its above findings ...

41. In conclusion, the Court does not find it established that, given the information available to the State at the relevant time ... concerning the likelihood of the applicant's father having been exposed to dangerous levels of radiation and of this having created a risk to her health, it could have been expected to act of its own motion to notify her parents of these matters or to take any other special action in relation to her.

It follows that there has been no violation of Article 2.

2   The nature and extent of States' positive obligations arising from Article 2(1) were elaborated by the Court in *Osman v UK* (1998) 29 EHRR 245, *Reports* 1998-VIII. The applicants were Mrs Osman and her son, Ahmet. During 1986 the headmaster of the state school attended by Ahmet, who was then 14 years old, noted that one of the teachers (Paul Paget-Lewis) had formed an attachment to Ahmet. After some months the deputy headmaster (Mr Perkins) suggested that Paget-Lewis seek psychiatric help. The police were informed of Paget-Lewis's attachment, but concluded that the matter should be dealt with by the school as there was no sexual element to the attachment. In April 1987, Paget-Lewis changed his name, by deed poll, to Paul Ahmet Yildirim Osman. In May, the police held further discussions with the school during which it was noted that Paget-Lewis had previously adopted that name after a pupil he had taught at another school. Paget-Lewis was seen by an education authority psychiatrist who recommended that he remain teaching at the school, but that he should receive counselling/psychotherapy. The applicants' house and car were attacked. In June Paget-Lewis was designated unfit to work and took medical leave. Throughout the remainder of the year other criminal acts were committed against the applicants' property. In January 1988 Paget-Lewis stole a shotgun. On 7 March Paget-Lewis went to the Osman home and shot dead Mr Osman and seriously wounded Ahmet. He then drove to Mr Perkin's home where he wounded him and killed his son. Paget-Lewis was arrested the next day and subsequently convicted of two charges of manslaughter (he pleaded guilty on grounds of diminished responsibility and was sentenced to be detained, without limit of time, in a secure mental hospital). The applicants sought to sue the Metropolitan Police Commissioner for alleged negligence in failing to prevent Paget-Lewis committing his killings/assaults. The Court of Appeal held that public policy required the police to be immune from such actions (*Osman v Ferguson* [1993] 4 All ER 344). Later the applicants complained to the Commission alleging, *inter alia*, that the police had failed to protect the lives of Mr Osman and Ahmet as required by Article 2. By ten votes to seven the Commission found no breach of that Article. The Court noted:

115. ... that the first sentence of Article 2 § 1 enjoins the State not only to refrain from the intentional and unlawful taking of life, but also to take appropriate steps to safeguard the lives of those within its jurisdiction (see the *L C B v UK* judgment of 9 June 1998, *Reports of Judgments and Decisions* 1998-III, p 1403, § 36). It is common ground that the State's obligation in this respect extends beyond its primary duty to secure the right to life by putting in place effective criminal-law provisions to deter the commission of offences against the person backed up by law-enforcement machinery for the prevention, suppression and sanctioning of breaches of such provisions. It is thus accepted by those appearing before the Court that Article 2 of the Convention may also imply in certain well-defined circumstances a positive obligation on the authorities to take preventive operational measures to protect an individual whose life is at risk from the criminal acts of another individual. The scope of this obligation is a matter of dispute between the parties.

116. For the Court, and bearing in mind the difficulties involved in policing modern societies, the unpredictability of human conduct and the operational choices which must be made in terms of priorities and resources, such an obligation must be interpreted in a way which does not impose an impossible or disproportionate burden on the authorities. Accordingly, not every claimed risk to life can entail for the authorities a Convention requirement to take operational measures to prevent that risk from materialising. Another relevant consideration is the need to ensure that the police exercise their powers to control and prevent crime in a manner which fully respects the due process and other guarantees which legitimately place restraints on the scope of their action to investigate crime and bring offenders to justice, including the guarantees contained in Articles 5 and 8 of the Convention. In the opinion of the Court where there is an allegation that the authorities have violated their positive obligation to protect the right to life in the context of their above-mentioned duty to prevent and suppress offences against the person (see paragraph 115 above), it must be established to its satisfaction that

the authorities knew or ought to have known at the time of the existence of a real and immediate risk to the life of an identified individual or individuals from the criminal acts of a third party and that they failed to take measures within the scope of their powers which, judged reasonably, might have been expected to avoid that risk. The Court does not accept the Government's view that the failure to perceive the risk to life in the circumstances known at the time or to take preventive measures to avoid that risk must be tantamount to gross negligence or wilful disregard of the duty to protect life ... Such a rigid standard must be considered to be incompatible with the requirements of Article 1 of the Convention and the obligations of Contracting States under that Article to secure the practical and effective protection of the rights and freedoms laid down therein, including Article 2 (see, *mutatis mutandis*, the ... *McCann* judgment, p 45, § 146). For the Court, and having regard to the nature of the right protected by Article 2, a right fundamental in the scheme of the Convention, it is sufficient for an applicant to show that the authorities did not do all that could be reasonably expected of them to avoid a real and immediate risk to life of which they have or ought to have knowledge. This is a question which can only be answered in the light of all the circumstances of any particular case. On the above understanding the Court will examine the particular circumstances of this case. ...

121. In the view of the Court the applicants have failed to point to any decisive stage in the sequence of the events leading up to the tragic shooting when it could be said that the police knew or ought to have known that the lives of the Osman family were at real and immediate risk from Paget-Lewis. While the applicants have pointed to a series of missed opportunities which would have enabled the police to neutralise the threat posed by Paget-Lewis, for example by searching his home for evidence to link him with the graffiti incident or by having him detained under the Mental Health Act 1983 or by taking more active investigative steps following his disappearance, it cannot be said that these measures, judged reasonably, would in fact have produced that result or that a domestic court would have convicted him or ordered his detention in a psychiatric hospital on the basis of the evidence adduced before it. As noted earlier (see paragraph 116 above), the police must discharge their duties in a manner which is compatible with the rights and freedoms of individuals. In the circumstances of the present case, they cannot be criticised for attaching weight to the presumption of innocence or failing to use powers of arrest, search and seizure having regard to their reasonably held view that they lacked at relevant times the required standard of suspicion to use those powers or that any action taken would in fact have produced concrete results.

122. For the above reasons, the Court concludes that there has been no violation of Article 2 of the Convention in this case.

Seventeen judges agreed with the above conclusion, while three dissentients considered that the British authorities had not complied with their obligations under that Article.

The judgment clearly reveals that States are required by Article 2 to protect persons' right to life by: (a) creating effective criminal law measures, (b) providing policing and criminal justice systems to enforce those measures and (c) taking reasonable operational measures where there is a 'real and immediate' risk to the life of a particular individual from the criminal acts of another person. However, as the *Osman* case illustrates, the Court is very cautious about finding a breach of the latter requirement.

3 An example of the extreme circumstances required by the Court, before it is willing to find a State in breach of its positive obligations to protect the life of a particular individual, occurred in *Mahmut Kaya v Turkey* (28 March 2000). The applicant's brother (Hasan Kaya) was a medical doctor who practised in south-east Turkey. At Christmas 1992, Hasan told the applicant that he believed his life was in danger and the police were keeping him under surveillance. On 21 February 1993 Hasan, and another man, went to treat a wounded member of the PKK. Neither returned home. Six days later the bodies of Hasan and the other man were found under a bridge over 130 kilometres away. Both men had been shot in the head and had their hands tied. The applicant claimed that, *inter alia*, the Turkish authorities had failed to protect his brother's life in breach of Article 2. In support of his argument the applicant relied, in part, on the *Susurluk Report* (a 1998 report from the Vice-President of the Board of Inspectors within the Prime Minister's Office, which detailed unlawful dealings between political figures, government institutions and clandestine groups in south-east Turkey). The Court, by six votes to one, held that:

87. In the present case, the Court recalls that it has not been established beyond reasonable doubt that any State agent was involved in the killing of Hasan Kaya. There are however strong inferences that can be drawn on the facts of this case that the perpetrators of the murder were known to the authorities. The Court refers to the circumstance that Metin Can and Hasan Kaya were transported by their kidnappers ... over 130 kilometres through a series of official checkpoints. It notes also the evidence in the investigation file that a suspected terrorist who claimed involvement in the killing was seen by two witnesses to receive assistance from gendarmes in Pertek. ... Furthermore, the *Susurluk* report took the position that the murder of Metin Can, and therefore impliedly that of Hasan Kaya, was one of the extra-judicial executions carried out to the knowledge of the authorities. The question to be determined by the Court is whether in the circumstances the authorities failed in a positive obligation to protect Hasan Kaya from a risk to his life.

88. It notes that Hasan Kaya believed that his life was at risk and that he was under surveillance by the police. He was, according to Bira Zordag, under suspicion by the police of treating wounded members of the PKK. His friend Metin Can, a lawyer who had acted for PKK suspects and for prisoners detained in Tunceli prison, as well as being President of the [Human Rights Association] which was regarded as suspect by the authorities, had also received threats and feared that he was under surveillance.

89. The Government have claimed that Hasan Kaya was not at more risk than any other person, or doctor, in the south-east region. The Court notes the tragic number of victims to the conflict in that region. It recalls however that in 1993 there were rumours current alleging that contra-guerrilla elements were involved in targeting persons suspected of supporting the PKK. It is undisputed that there were a significant number of killings which became known as the 'unknown perpetrator killing' phenomenon and which included prominent Kurdish figures such as Mr Musa Anter as well as other journalists (see ... the *Yasa v Turkey* judgment ...). The Court is satisfied that Hasan Kaya as a doctor suspected of aiding and abetting the PKK was at this time at particular risk of falling victim to an unlawful attack. Moreover, this risk could in the circumstances be regarded as real and immediate.

90. The Court is equally satisfied that the authorities must be regarded as being aware of this risk. It has accepted the Commission's assessment of the evidence of Bira Zordag, who recounted that the police at Elazig questioned him about Hasan Kaya and Metin Can and made threats that they would be punished.

91. Furthermore, the authorities were aware, or ought to have been aware of the possibility that this risk derived from the activities of persons or groups acting with the knowledge or acquiescence of elements in the security forces. A 1993 report by a Parliamentary Investigation Commission ... stated that it had received information that a Hizbollah training camp was receiving aid and training from the security forces and concluded that some officials might be implicated in the 908 unsolved killings in the south-east region. The *Susurluk* report, published in January 1998, informed the Prime Minister's Office that the authorities were aware of killings being carried out to eliminate alleged supporters of the PKK, including the murders of Musa Anter and Metin Can. The Government insisted that this report did not have any judicial or evidential value. However, even the Government described the report as providing information on the basis of which the Prime Minister was to take further appropriate measures. It may therefore be regarded as a significant document. The Court does not rely on the report as establishing

that any State official was implicated in any particular killing. The report does however provide further strong substantiation for allegations, current at the time and since, that 'contra-guerrilla' groups involving confessors or terrorist groups were targeting individuals perceived to be acting against the State interests with the acquiescence, and possible assistance, of members of the security forces.

92. The Court has considered whether the authorities did all that could be reasonably expected of them to avoid the risk to Hasan Kaya.

93. It recalls that, as the Government submit, there were large numbers of security forces in the south-east region pursuing the aim of establishing public order. They faced the difficult task of countering the armed and violent attacks of the PKK and other groups. There was a framework of law in place with the aim of protecting life. The Turkish penal code prohibited murder and there were police and gendarmerie forces with the functions of preventing and investigating crime, under the supervision of the judicial branch of public prosecutors. There were also courts applying the provisions of the criminal law in trying, convicting and sentencing offenders.

94. The Court observes however that the implementation of the criminal law in respect of unlawful acts allegedly carried out with the involvement of the security forces discloses particular characteristics in the south-east region in this period.

95. Firstly, where offences were committed by State officials in certain circumstances, the public prosecutor's competence to investigate was removed to administrative councils which took the decision whether to prosecute ... These councils were made up of civil servants, under the orders of the Governor, who was himself responsible for the security forces whose conduct was in issue. The investigations which they instigated were often carried out by gendarmes linked hierarchically to the units concerned in the incident. The Court accordingly found in two cases that the administrative councils did not provide an independent or effective procedure for investigating deaths involving members of the security forces (*Güleç v Turkey* judgment of 27 July 1998, *Reports* 1998-IV, pp 1731–3, §§ 77–82 ...).

96. Secondly, the cases examined by the Convention organs concerning the region at this time have produced a series of findings of failures by the authorities to investigate allegations of wrongdoing by the security forces, both in the context of the procedural obligations under Article 2 of the Convention and the requirement of effective remedies imposed by Article 13 of the Convention (see concerning Article 2, *Kaya v Turkey* judgment of 19 February 1998, *Reports* 1998-I, §§ 86–92, *Ergi v Turkey* judgment of 28 July 1998, *Reports* 1998-IV, §§ 82–5, *Yasa v Turkey* judgment of 2 September 1998, *Reports* 1998-VI, §§ 98–108 ...). A common feature of these cases is a finding that the public prosecutor failed to pursue complaints by individuals claiming that the security forces were involved in an unlawful act, for example not interviewing or taking statements from implicated members of the security forces, accepting at face-value the reports of incidents submitted by members of the security forces and attributing incidents to the PKK on the basis of minimal or no evidence.

97. Thirdly, the attribution of responsibility for incidents to the PKK has particular significance as regards the investigation and judicial procedures which ensue since jurisdiction for terrorist crimes has been given to the State Security Courts ... In a series of cases, the Court has found that the State Security Courts do not fulfil the requirement of independence imposed by Article 6 of the Convention, due to the presence of a military judge whose participation gives rise to legitimate fears that the court may be unduly influenced by considerations which had nothing to do with the nature of the case (see *Incal v Turkey* judgment of 9 June 1998, *Reports* 1998-IV, pp 1571–3, §§ 65–73).

98. The Court finds that these defects undermined the effectiveness of criminal law protection in the south-east region during the period relevant to this case. It considers that this permitted or fostered a lack of accountability of members of the security forces for their actions which, as the Commission stated in its report, was not compatible with the rule of law in a democratic society respecting the fundamental rights and freedoms guaranteed under the Convention.

99. Consequently, these defects removed the protection which Hasan Kaya should have received by law.

100. The Government have disputed that they could in any event have effectively provided protection against attacks. The Court is not convinced by this argument. A wide range of preventive measures would have been available to the authorities regarding the activities of their own security forces and those groups allegedly acting under their auspices or with their knowledge. The Government have not provided any information concerning steps taken by them prior to the *Susurluk* report to investigate the existence of contra-guerrilla groups and the extent to which State officials were implicated in unlawful killings carried out during this period, with a view to instituting any appropriate measures of protection.

101. The Court concludes that in the circumstances of this case the authorities failed to take reasonable measures available to them to prevent a real and immediate risk to the life of Hasan Kaya. There has, accordingly, been a violation of Article 2 of the Convention.

Hence, the Court found that Turkey had failed to comply with its positive obligations to protect Hasan Kaya's right to life by not having an effective criminal law regime operating in south-east Turkey in 1993 and by not taking preventive measures to protect him from the real threats to his life (from the unlawful groups carrying out hundreds of killings in the region at that time). These were very serious breaches of Article 2 and reflect the virtual breakdown of the rule of law in that area.

Likewise, in *Gongadze v Ukraine*, judgment of 8 November 2005, the Chamber found that the killing of an investigative journalist (there was strong evidence of police officers involvement in the murder) had taken place at a time when other journalists had also been killed. Furthermore, the deceased had complained to the Prosecutor General about threats and surveillance from persons following him. But, the authorities provided him with no protection and he disappeared two months later. His decapitated body was found a few weeks later. The Chamber was unanimous in finding the respondent State had failed to protect the deceased's life. This case disclosed significant allegations of major criminal behaviour amongst a number of senior officials and politicians (including the former President of Ukraine) and an era of apparent violence towards critics of the regime.

4   The positive obligation of protection was applied to a prisoner by a unanimous Chamber in *Paul and Audrey Edwards v United Kingdom*, judgment of 14 March 2002. The applicants' 30-year-old son had been remanded in custody by magistrates for making inappropriate comments to women in the street (he had a history of mental illness). He was later transferred to Chelmsford Prison and placed in a cell. Another remand prisoner (Linford), who had previously been diagnosed as suffering from schizophrenia, was also placed in the same cell (because of a shortage of cells). A few hours later Linford killed the applicants' son in a violent attack. Subsequently, Linford was convicted of manslaughter by reason of diminished responsibility. The applicants' contended, *inter alia*, that the relevant authorities had failed to protect the life of their son in breach of their obligations under Article 2. After citing *Osman* the Court held that;

56. [i]n the context of prisoners, the Court has had previous occasion to emphasise that persons in custody are in a vulnerable position and that the authorities are under a duty to protect them.

The judges went on to find that many public agencies (including doctors, the police, the Crown Prosecution Service and the courts) had failed to pass on information about the health and background of Linford to the prison authorities and the latter had undertaken an inadequate screening of him when he arrived at Chelmsford Prison. Cumulatively, these failures amounted to a breach of the state's obligation to protect the life of the applicants' son under

Article 2. The tragic facts of *Edwards* demonstrate that it is not only the police who may be liable to provide protection to persons from the known (or constructively known) real threats posed by others. Where persons are imprisoned the public authorities (widely drawn in *Edwards*) having responsibility for the care of detainees are under a similar obligation. This is a highly desirable extension of *Osman* as prisoners obviously have limited abilities to protect themselves (e.g. they normally have no choice of whom they live with).

5 A failure by police officers to secure the provision of timely and adequate medical care to a seriously injured detainee, who subsequently died from his injuries, was found to constitute a breach of Article 2 by a unanimous Chamber in *Anguelova v Bulgaria*, judgment of 13 June 2002. The applicant's 17-year-old son had been arrested by the police on suspicion of theft. After a few hours in police detention it became apparent that his health had greatly deteriorated (he had injuries on his forehead and was breathing deeply). The officers at the police station did not call for an ambulance but recalled from patrol those officers who had arrested the detainee. Then the arresting officers went to the hospital and escorted an ambulance back to the police station to collect the detainee. The detainee was found to be dead by the time he arrived at the hospital. The Court found that the behaviour of the police officers and the absence of action taken against those officers by the authorities constituted a violation of '130. ... the State's obligation to protect the lives of persons in custody.' The behaviour of the police officers was both suspicious and obviously well below the standard of reasonable care for a seriously ill detainee.

6 A Grand Chamber developed the application of the obligation of protection in the context of a scheme for the early release of prisoners in *Mastromatteo v Italy*, judgment of 24 October 2002. The applicant's son had been shot dead by a bank robber, as the robber tried to escape from the crime scene. The robber and two of his accomplices were serving prison sentences, for violent crimes, at the time of the robbery. However, they had been granted either prison leave or discharge to a semi-custodial regime by the judiciary. The applicant contended that the State had failed to protect the life of his son in breach of its positive obligations under Article 2. After referring to *Osman* and *Edwards* the Court held that:

69. ... The instant case differs from those cases in that it is not a question here of determining whether the responsibility of the authorities is engaged for failing to provide personal protection to [the applicant's son]; what is at issue is the obligation to afford general protection to society against the potential acts of one or of several persons serving a prison sentence for a violent crime and the determination of the scope of that protection.

The judgment acknowledged that whilst one of the basic purposes of imprisonment was to protect society, '72. at the same time the Court recognises the legitimate aim of a policy of progressive social reintegration of persons sentenced to imprisonment.' Taking account of the key features of the Italian prisoner release scheme (including the need for eligible prisoners to have served a minimum period of imprisonment, to have a record of good behaviour whilst in prison and for a judge to assess the danger to society if a particular prisoner was to be released), together with statistical evidence on the criminal behaviour of prisoners given early release (showing, for example, that the percentage of prisoner on leave who absconded was about 1 per cent) the Court, unanimously, concluded that the Italian scheme was compatible with the State's obligations under Article 2. Also the individual judicial decisions to grant leave to the prisoners involved in the robbery and subsequent killing of the applicant's son were found to be in conformity with Article 2 because:

76. The Court considers that there was nothing in the material before the national authorities to alert them to the fact that the release of M.R. or G.M. would pose a real and immediate threat to life, still less that it would lead to the tragic death of A. Mastromatteo as a result of the chance sequence of events

which occurred in the present case. Nor was there anything to alert them to the need to take additional measures to ensure that, once released, the two did not represent a danger to society.

The judgment in *Mastromatteo* sought to achieve a delicate balance between the desirability of promoting social reintegration amongst prisoners and the need to protect the general public from the foreseeable risks of violent crimes being committed by prisoners given early release or home leave. The Court subjected the Italian scheme's criteria and operation to a thorough scrutiny for their conformity with the obligation upon States to protect life under Article 2. Statistically the scheme generated only a very small risk to the public. Furthermore, the Court was careful not to apply the benefit of hindsight when evaluating the release decisions taken by the Italian judiciary.

7   One, of the numerous (see also below p 125 [investigation duties]), complaints made by the applicant State in *Cyprus v Turkey*, ECHR 2001-IV, alleged that the authorities in northern Cyprus had failed to provide (or allowed the receipt of) adequate medical services to the several hundred Greek Cypriots and Maronites still living in the northern region thereby breaching Article 2. The Grand Chamber, by sixteen votes to one, held that:

219. The Court observes that an issue may arise under Article 2 of the Convention where it is shown that the authorities of a Contracting State put an individual's life at risk through the denial of health care which they have undertaken to make available to the population generally. It notes in this connection that Article 2 § 1 of the Convention enjoins the State not only to refrain from the intentional and unlawful taking of life, but also to take appropriate steps to safeguard the lives of those within its jurisdiction (see the *L.C.B. v the United Kingdom* judgment of 9 June 1998, *Reports* 1998-III, p 1403, § 36). It notes, however, that the Commission was unable to establish on the evidence that the 'TRNC' [Turkish Republic of Northern Cyprus] authorities deliberately withheld medical treatment from the population concerned or adopted a practice of delaying the processing of requests of patients to receive medical treatment in the south. It observes that during the period under consideration medical visits were indeed hampered on account of restrictions imposed by the 'TRNC' authorities on the movement of the populations concerned and that in certain cases delays did occur. However, it has not been established that the lives of any patients were put in danger on account of delay in individual cases. It is also to be observed that neither the Greek-Cypriot nor Maronite populations were prevented from availing themselves of medical services including hospitals in the north. The applicant Government are critical of the level of health care available in the north. However, the Court does not consider it necessary to examine in this case the extent to which Article 2 of the Convention may impose an obligation on a Contracting State to make available a certain standard of health care. . . .

221. The Court concludes that no violation of Article 2 of the Convention has been established by virtue of an alleged practice of denying access to medical services to Greek Cypriots and Maronites living in northern Cyprus.

Whilst the Court did not find a breach regarding the above health care complaints, the *Cyprus* judgment refined the earlier *L.C.B.* ruling to expressly provide that States may be liable under Article 2 for withholding from an individual life-saving medical care which they have promised to make generally available. The significance of this obligation is that it is left up to particular States to define their own level of health care provision. Only if a State fails to meet its own declared standard, in a life threatening case, could Article 2 be invoked. However, the Court went on tantalisingly to suggest that Article 2 may also require the provision of a minimum level of health care by Member States. Therefore, the positive obligation regarding the provision of medical care by States is at an early stage of development under Article 2.

8   The nature of States' obligations to regulate the provision of private medical services was considered by a Grand Chamber in *Calvelli and Ciglio v Italy*, judgment of 17 January 2002.

The applicants' baby had died two days after birth in a private clinic. Six years later the responsible doctor (and joint owner of the clinic) was found guilty of involuntary manslaughter. He successfully appealed against his conviction to the Court of Cassation and by the time his case was sent back for retrial it had become statute barred. The applicants, who had been civil parties to the criminal proceedings, settled their claims against the doctor/clinic when the latter's insurers agreed to pay them 95 million Lire compensation. The applicants claimed that, *inter alia*, the inability to prosecute the doctor, because of delays in the proceedings and the time-bar, constituted a violation of Article 2. After referring to *McCann* and *L.C.B.*, the Court stated that:

49. ... The aforementioned positive obligations therefore require States to make regulations compelling hospitals, whether public or private, to adopt appropriate measures for the protection of patients' lives. They also require an effective independent judicial system to be set up so that the cause of death of patients in the care of the medical profession, whether in the public or the private sector, can be determined and those responsible made accountable ...

The Court then examined the Italian judicial response to the death of the applicants' baby:

51. ... if the infringement of the right to life or to personal integrity is not caused intentionally, the positive obligation imposed by Article 2 to set up an effective judicial system does not necessarily require the provision of a criminal-law remedy in every case. In the specific sphere of medical negligence the obligation may for instance also be satisfied if the legal system affords victims a remedy in the civil courts, either alone or in conjunction with a remedy in the criminal courts, enabling any liability of the doctors concerned to be established and any appropriate civil redress, such as an order for damages and for the publication of the decision, to be obtained. Disciplinary measures may also be envisaged.

According to a large majority, fourteen votes to three, as the applicants had entered into a voluntary settlement of their civil proceedings against the doctor they had deprived themselves of the best means of a judicial determination of the doctor's responsibility and could no longer claim to be a 'victim' of a breach of the Convention. The determination in *Calvelli and Ciglio* was rather lenient to the State as the delayed and eventually time-barred prosecution of the doctor was not considered to amount to a breach of Article 2. In their joint dissenting opinion Judges Rozakis and Bonello expressed the belief that, '... considering civil proceedings as a satisfactory means of recourse satisfying the requirements of Article 2 amounts to a debasement of the protection of the right to life provided for by this Article; it amounts to a "privatisation" of the protection of the right to life.' However, at least the Grand Chamber held States are under a general obligation to regulate the provision of medical services.

9 A unanimous Grand Chamber found a breach of the positive obligation to protect life in the context of a failure by public authorities to safeguard persons from a lethal explosion at a hazardous waste site in *Oneryildiz v Turkey*, judgment of 30 November 2004. The applicant, his wife and ten children and his concubine(!) started living in a house, which had been constructed without official authorization on government-owned land, in 1988. The house was located in a 'slum quarter' of a district on Istanbul. Furthermore, the house was next to a municipal household-rubbish tip that had been in operation since the early 1970s. In 1991 the local District Council applied to the District Court for experts to be appointed to examine whether the rubbish tip complied with national environmental regulations. A committee of experts, including a professor of environmental engineering, were appointed. Their report, of May 1991, concluded that the rubbish tip did not comply with the relevant technical regulations and posed a major health risk (involving twenty contagious diseases) to local inhabitants. Also the site had no system for safely burning off the methane gas created by the decomposition of the rubbish and therefore created a serious risk of an explosion occurring. The report stated, 'May God preserve us, as the damage could be very substantial given the neighbouring dwellings ... ' The four local councils were informed of the report as was the governor and the central government. Two of the local councils applied to the court for the report to be set aside, as they claimed they had not been consulted about the establishment of the expert committee. The national Environment Office recommended, in June 1991, that Istanbul Governor and City Council and local councils take action to remedy the problems identified in the report. In August 1992 one of the local Mayors applied to the District Court for temporary orders to prevent other local authorities using the refuse tip. Istanbul Council opposed the request noting that a tender had been invited for redevelopment of the tip. On the morning of 28 April 1993 a methane explosion occurred at the tip causing the eruption of waste and a landslide which covered ten dwellings in the adjoining slum, including the applicant's house. Thirty-nine people died, including the applicant's wife, seven of their children and his concubine. The applicant complained, *inter alia*, that the authorities, in breach of Article 2, had tolerated the development of the slum dwellings next to the tip, had taken no action to counteract the known dangers posed by the tip and had not warned the slum residents of those dangers. The Grand Chamber held that:

89. The positive obligation to take all appropriate steps to safeguard life for the purposes of Article 2 entails above all a primary duty on the State to put in place a legislative and administrative framework designed to provide effective deterrence against threats to the right to life ...

90. This obligation indisputably applies in the particular context of dangerous activities, where, in addition, special emphasis must be placed on regulations geared to the special features of the activity in question, particularly with regard to the level of the potential risk to human lives. They must govern the licensing, setting up, operation, security and supervision of the activity and must make it compulsory for all those concerned to take practical measures to ensure the effective protection of citizens whose lives might be endangered by the inherent risks.

Among these preventive measures, particular emphasis should be placed on the public's right to information, as established in the case-law of the Convention institutions. The Grand Chamber agrees with the Chamber (see paragraph 84 of the Chamber judgment) that this right, which has already been recognised under Article 8 (see *Guerra and Others* [v Italy 1998-I] § 60), may also, in principle, be relied on for the protection of the right to life ...

...

100. The Court considers that neither the reality nor the immediacy of the danger in question is in dispute, seeing that the risk of an explosion had clearly come into being long before it was highlighted in the report of 7 May 1991 and that, as the site continued to operate in the same conditions, that risk could only have increased during the period until it materialised on 28 April 1993.

101. The Grand Chamber accordingly agrees with the Chamber (see paragraph 79 of the Chamber judgment) that it was impossible for the administrative and municipal departments responsible for supervising and managing the tip not to have known of the risks inherent in methanogenesis or of the necessary preventive measures, particularly as there were specific regulations on the matter. Furthermore, the Court likewise regards it as established that various authorities were also aware of those risks, at least by 27 May 1991, when they were notified of the report of 7 May 1991 ...

It follows that the Turkish authorities at several levels knew or ought to have known that there was a real and immediate risk to a number of persons living near the Ümraniye municipal rubbish tip. They consequently had a positive obligation under Article 2 of the Convention to take such preventive operational measures as were necessary and sufficient to protect those individuals, especially as they themselves had set up the site and authorised its operation, which gave rise to the risk in question.

102. However, it appears from the evidence before the Court that the city council in particular not only failed to take the necessary urgent measures, either before or after 14 March 1991, but also—as the Chamber observed—opposed the recommendation to that effect by the Prime Minister's Environment Office.

103. The city council also opposed the final attempt by the mayor of Ümraniye to apply to the courts, on 27 August 1992, for the temporary closure of the waste-collection site ...

Besides that ground, the Government also relied on the conclusions of the *Chapman v the United Kingdom* [2001-I] judgment and criticised the applicant for having knowingly chosen to break the law and live in the vicinity of the rubbish tip.

However, those arguments do not stand up to scrutiny for the following reasons.

104. In the instant case, the Court has examined the provisions of domestic law regarding the transfer to third parties of public property, whether inside or outside the 'slum rehabilitation and clearance zones' ...

The Court concludes from these legal considerations that in spite of the statutory prohibitions in the field of town planning, the State's consistent policy on slum areas encouraged the integration of such areas into the urban environment and hence acknowledged their existence and the way of life of the citizens who had gradually caused them to build up since 1960, whether of their own free will or simply as a result of that policy. Seeing that this policy effectively established an amnesty for breaches of town-planning regulations, including the unlawful occupation of public property, it must have created uncertainty as to the extent of the discretion enjoyed by the administrative authorities responsible for applying the measures prescribed by law, which could not therefore have been regarded as foreseeable by the public.

105. This interpretation is, moreover, borne out in the instant case by the administrative authorities' attitude towards the applicant.

The Court observes that between the unauthorised construction of the house in issue in 1988 and the accident of 28 April 1993, the applicant remained in possession of his dwelling, despite the fact that during that time his position remained subject to the rules laid down in Law no. 775, in particular section 18, by which the municipal authorities could have destroyed the dwelling at any time. Indeed, this was what the Government suggested, although they were unable to show that in the instant case the relevant authorities had even envisaged taking any such measure against the applicant.

The authorities let the applicant and his close relatives live entirely undisturbed in their house, in the social and family environment they had created. Furthermore, regard being had to the concrete evidence adduced before the Court and not rebutted by the Government, there is no cause to call into question the applicant's assertion that the authorities also levied council tax on him and on the other inhabitants of the Ümraniye slums and provided them with public services, for which they were charged.

106. In those circumstances, it would be hard for the Government to maintain legitimately that any negligence or lack of foresight should be attributed to the victims of the accident of 28 April 1993, or to rely on the Court's conclusions in the case of *Chapman v the United Kingdom*, in which the British authorities were not found to have remained passive in the face of Mrs Chapman's unlawful actions.

It remains for the Court to address the Government's other arguments relating, in general, to: the scale of the rehabilitation projects carried out by the city council at the time in order to alleviate the problems caused by the Ümraniye waste-collection site; the amount invested, which was said to have influenced the way in which the national authorities chose to deal with the situation at the site; and, lastly, the humanitarian considerations which at the time allegedly precluded any measure entailing the immediate and wholesale destruction of the slum areas.

107. The Court acknowledges that it is not its task to substitute for the views of the local authorities its own view of the best policy to adopt in dealing with the social, economic and urban problems in this part of Istanbul. It therefore accepts the Government's argument that in this respect, an impossible or

disproportionate burden must not be imposed on the authorities without consideration being given, in particular, to the operational choices which they must make in terms of priorities and resources (see *Osman* [v UK 1998-VIII] §116); this results from the wide margin of appreciation which States enjoy, as the Court has previously held, in difficult social and technical spheres such as the one in issue in the instant case (see *Hatton and Others v the United Kingdom* [GC], No 36022/97, §§100–1, ECHR 2003-VIII).

However, even when seen from this perspective, the Court does not find the Government's arguments convincing. The preventive measures required by the positive obligation in question fall precisely within the powers conferred on the authorities and may reasonably be regarded as a suitable means of averting the risk brought to their attention. The Court considers that the timely installation of a gas-extraction system at the Ümraniye tip before the situation became fatal could have been an effective measure without diverting the State's resources to an excessive degree in breach of Article 65 of the Turkish Constitution or giving rise to policy problems to the extent alleged by the Government. Such a measure would not only have complied with Turkish regulations and general practice in the area, but would also have been a much better reflection of the humanitarian considerations which the Government relied on before the Court.

108. The Court will next assess the weight to be attached to the issue of respect for the public's right to information (see paragraph 90 above). It observes in this connection that the Government were unable to show that any measures were taken in the instant case to provide the inhabitants of the Ümraniye slums with information enabling them to assess the risks they might run as a result of the choices they had made. In any event, the Court considers that in the absence of more practical measures to avoid the risks to the lives of the inhabitants of the Ümraniye slums, even the fact of having respected the right to information would not have been sufficient to absolve the State of its responsibilities.

109. In the light of the foregoing, the Court cannot see any reason to cast doubt on the domestic investigating authorities' findings of fact and considers that the circumstances examined above show that in the instant case the State's responsibility was engaged under Article 2 in several respects.

Firstly, the regulatory framework proved defective in that the Ümraniye municipal waste-collection site was opened and operated despite not conforming to the relevant technical standards and there was no coherent supervisory system to encourage those responsible to take steps to ensure adequate protection of the public and coordination and cooperation between the various administrative authorities so that the risks brought to their attention did not become so serious as to endanger human lives.

That situation, exacerbated by a general policy which proved powerless in dealing with general town-planning issues and created uncertainty as to the application of statutory measures, undoubtedly played a part in the sequence of events leading to the tragic accident of 28 April 1993, which ultimately claimed the lives of inhabitants of the Ümraniye slums, because the State officials and authorities did not do everything within their power to protect them from the immediate and known risks to which they were exposed.

110. Such circumstances give rise to a violation of Article 2 of the Convention in its substantive aspect ...

Hence Member States must ensure that they have appropriate domestic laws regulating the location, use and safety requirements of hazardous facilities/activities. The domestic authorities are also obliged to ensure these provisions are observed and enforced. Local residents must be provided with information about the risks presented by potentially hazardous facilities. Furthermore, States must take reasonable preventive measures (such as the installation of methane extraction equipment at waste tips) to protect the lives of persons known to be at risk from such facilities/activities. These legal and operational requirements vividly demonstrate the extensive substantive positive obligations upon States under Article 2.

For an examination of the Court's jurisprudence concerning States' responsibilities in the context of non-lethal environmental pollution see below p 546.

The duty on States to undertake effective investigations into killings

1   The types of investigations required by this implied duty, derived from the judgment in *McCann*, were elaborated by the Court in *Kaya v Turkey* (1998) 28 EHRR 1, *Reports* 1998-I. The applicant complained to the Commission that his brother (Abdulmenaf Kaya), a farmer, had been deliberately killed by Turkish security forces on 25 March 1993. The Government contended that the deceased was a terrorist who had been killed when he engaged the security forces. The Commission concluded that it was not proved beyond reasonable doubt that Abdulmenaf had been deliberately killed by soldiers in the circumstances alleged by the applicant. However, there had been a breach of Article 2 because of the inadequacy of the investigation conducted by the authorities into Abdulmenaf's death (twenty-seven votes to three). An overwhelming majority of the Court (eight votes to one) also found that there had been an ineffective investigation.

87. The Court observes that the procedural protection of the right to life inherent in Article 2 of the Convention secures the accountability of agents of the State for their use of lethal force by subjecting their actions to some form of independent and public scrutiny capable of leading to a determination of whether the force used was or was not justified in a particular set of circumstances. . . .

89. The Court is struck in particular by the fact that the public prosecutor would appear to have assumed without question that the deceased was a terrorist who had died in a clash with the security forces. No statements were taken from any of the soldiers at the scene and no attempt was made to confirm whether there were spent cartridges over the area consistent with an intense gun battle having been waged by both sides as alleged. As an independent investigating official he should have been alert to the need to collect evidence at the scene, to make his own independent reconstruction of the events and to satisfy himself that the deceased, despite being dressed as a typical farmer, was in fact a terrorist as alleged. There are no indications that he was prepared in any way to scrutinise the soldiers' account of the incident. His readiness to accept at face value the information given by the military may also explain why no tests were carried out on the deceased's hands or clothing for gunpowder traces or why the weapon was not dusted for fingerprints. In any event, these shortcomings must be considered particularly serious in view of the fact that the corpse was later handed over to villagers, thereby rendering it impossible to conduct any further analyses, including of the bullets lodged in the body. The only exhibits which were taken from the scene for further examination were the weapon and ammunition allegedly used by the deceased. However, whatever the merits of this initiative as an investigative measure at the time, it is to be noted that the public prosecutor issued his decision of non-jurisdiction without awaiting the findings of the ballistics experts ... The autopsy report provided the sole record of the nature, severity and location of the bullet wounds sustained by the deceased. The Court shares the concern of the Commission about the incompleteness of this report in certain crucial respects, in particular the absence of any observations on the actual number of bullets which struck the deceased and of any estimation of the distance from which the bullets were fired. It cannot be maintained that the perfunctory autopsy performed or the findings recorded in the report could lay the basis for any effective follow-up investigation or indeed satisfy even the minimum requirements of an investigation into a clear-cut case of lawful killing since they left too many critical questions unanswered. The Court acknowledges that the on-the-spot post-mortem and forensic examination were conducted in an area prone to terrorist violence, which may have made it extremely difficult to comply with standard practices. . . . It is therefore surprising that neither the doctor nor the public prosecutor requested that the body be flown to a safer location to allow more detailed analyses to be made of the body, the clothing and the bullet wounds.

90. No concrete measures were taken thereafter by the public prosecutor to investigate the death of the applicant's brother, for example by verifying whether the deceased was in fact an active member of

the PKK or by questioning villagers living in the vicinity of Dolunay to ascertain whether they heard the sound of a gun battle on the day in question or by summoning members of the security forces involved to his office to take statements. The public prosecutor's firm conviction that the deceased was a terrorist killed in an armed clash with the security forces was never in fact tested against any other evidence and the terms of his non-jurisdiction decision effectively excluded any possibility that the security forces might somehow have been culpable, including with respect to the proportionality of the force used in the circumstances of the alleged armed attack . . .

91. The Court notes that loss of life is a tragic and frequent occurrence in view of the security situation in south-east Turkey . . . However, neither the prevalence of violent armed clashes nor the high incidence of fatalities can displace the obligation under Article 2 to ensure that an effective, independent investigation is conducted into deaths arising out of clashes involving the security forces, more so in cases such as the present where the circumstances are in many respects unclear.

92. Having regard to the above considerations the Court, like the Commission, concludes that the authorities failed to carry out an effective investigation into the circumstances surrounding the death of the applicant's brother. There has accordingly been a violation of Article 2 of the Convention in that respect.

The Court requires the investigation to be conducted by an independent person exercising a critical assessment of all the relevant evidence (including that provided by State officials). Depending on the circumstances appropriate forensic tests (such as checks on clothing and bodies for traces of explosives or gunpowder) must also be undertaken. If investigations are to satisfy the requirements of Article 2 they must be genuinely rigorous and not merely ritualistic charades.

2   In *Yasa v Turkey* (above, p 100), the Court widened the circumstances where States are required to conduct investigations into deaths by holding that:

the obligation is not confined to cases where it has been established that the killing was caused by an agent of the State. Nor is the issue of whether members of the deceased's family or others have lodged a formal complaint about the killing with the competent investigatory authorities decisive. In the case under consideration, the mere fact that the authorities were informed of the murder of the applicant's uncle gave rise *ipso facto* to an obligation under Article 2 to carry out an effective investigation . . . (para 100)

As no 'concrete and credible progress' had been made in the investigation after five years, the Court (by eight votes to one) found a violation of Article 2. The above rulings are to be welcomed as they seek to ensure that States conduct effective investigations into killings irrespective of the background/position held by the perpetrator(s) and that duty applies once the State becomes aware of the killing.

3   A Grand Chamber of the full-time Court in *Cyprus v Turkey* (see above p 119 [A2 PO]), further extended the duty to undertake effective investigations to situations where it has not been conclusively established that a person has been killed. The applicant State contended, *inter alia*, that there had been no such investigations into the fate of about 1,500 persons alleged to have be killed or detained by Turkish military forces, or their supporters, during the military occupation of northern Cyprus in 1974. The Grand Chamber did not consider that the evidence before it justified a finding that those persons had been unlawfully killed. But the obligation to conduct an effective investigation, '132. . . . also arises upon proof of an arguable claim that an individual who was last seen in the custody of the state, subsequently disappeared in a context which may be considered life-threatening.' By an overwhelming majority of sixteen votes to one (the Turkish national judge being the dissentient) the Grand

Chamber found that the evidence demonstrated that many persons had been detained by Turkish/Turkish-Cypriot forces during military operations and the context of their detention could be classified as life-threatening. Consequently, the respondent State was under a duty to undertake effective investigations into the claims of the missing persons' relatives that the former had disappeared in life-threatening circumstances. No effective investigations had been held into the whereabouts and fate of the missing Greek-Cypriots, therefore the Grand Chamber found a breach of this duty under Article 2.

4 The Court requires that investigations into arguable claims of killings by State agents must satisfy four institutional and procedural requirements if they are to be classified as effective. These requirements were articulated in *Kelly and Others v United Kingdom*, judgment of 4 May 2001.

95. ... it may generally be regarded as necessary for the persons responsible for and carrying out the investigation to be independent from those implicated in the events ... This means not only a lack of hierarchical or institutional connection but also a practical independence (see, for example, the case of *Ergi* v *Turkey* judgment of 28 July 1998, *Reports* 1998-IV, §§ 83–4 where the public prosecutor investigating the death of a girl during an alleged clash showed a lack of independence through his heavy reliance on the information provided by the gendarmes implicated in the incident).

96. The investigation must also be effective in the sense that it is capable of leading to a determination of whether the force used in such cases was or was not justified in the circumstances ... and to the identification and punishment of those responsible. This is not an obligation of result, but of means. The authorities must have taken the reasonable steps available to them to secure the evidence concerning the incident, including inter alia eye witness testimony, forensic evidence and, where appropriate, an autopsy which provides a complete and accurate record of injury and an objective analysis of clinical findings, including the cause of death ... Any deficiency in the investigation which undermines its ability to establish the cause of death or the person responsible will risk falling foul of this standard.

97. A requirement of promptness and reasonable expedition is implicit in this context ... It must be accepted that there may be obstacles or difficulties which prevent progress in an investigation in a particular situation. However, a prompt response by the authorities in investigating a use of lethal force may generally be regarded as essential in maintaining public confidence in their adherence to the rule of law and in preventing any appearance of collusion in or tolerance of unlawful acts.

98. For the same reasons, there must be a sufficient element of public scrutiny of the investigation or its results to secure accountability in practice as well as in theory. The degree of public scrutiny required may well vary from case to case. In all cases, however, the next of kin of the victim must be involved in the procedure to the extent necessary to safeguard his or her legitimate interests ...

The Court was unanimous in finding a breach of the obligation to hold an effective investigation into the killings of the applicants' nine relatives who had been shot dead by SAS soldiers during an ambush of a terrorist attack on an RUC police station at Loughgall in Northern Ireland. The domestic investigation failed to satisfy the first requirement of independence as it had been undertaken by RUC officers and other members of that force had been involved in the ambush operation. The judgment of the Court indicates that it requires a clear institutional independence of investigators from those State agents implicated in the killing. Public acceptance of the legitimacy of investigations will be enhanced where the investigators are seen to have no connection with the subjects of the investigation.

5 Article 2 can require the effective prosecution of public officials whose gross negligence has contributed to the death of other persons. In *Oneryildiz v Turkey*, see above p 120, the applicant contended that there had been a breach of the procedural positive obligation upon

Turkey to take effective judicial proceedings against those officials who allowed the refuse tip to continue operating in a dangerous manner. He argue that the Istanbul Criminal Court's fining of two local mayors, the equivalent sum of 9.7 euros (these fines were suspended), for negligent omissions in the performance of their duties regarding the operation of the refuse tip did not satisfy the demands of Article 2. The Grand Chamber held that:

93. ... Where it is established that the negligence attributable to State officials or bodies on that account goes beyond an error of judgment or carelessness, in that the authorities in question, fully realising the likely consequences and disregarding the powers vested in them, failed to take measures that were necessary and sufficient to avert the risks inherent in a dangerous activity (see, *mutatis mutandis, Osman*, § 116), the fact that those responsible for endangering life have not been charged with a criminal offence or prosecuted may amount to a violation of Article 2, irrespective of any other types of remedy which individuals may exercise on their own initiative ...

94. To sum up, the judicial system required by Article 2 must make provision for an independent and impartial official investigation procedure that satisfies certain minimum standards as to effectiveness and is capable of ensuring that criminal penalties are applied where lives are lost as a result of a dangerous activity if and to the extent that this is justified by the findings of the investigation (see, *mutatis mutandis, Hugh Jordan v the United Kingdom*, No 24746/94, §§ 105–9, ECHR 2001-III, and *Paul and Audrey Edwards*, cited above, §§ 69–73). In such cases, the competent authorities must act with exemplary diligence and promptness and must of their own motion initiate investigations capable of, firstly, ascertaining the circumstances in which the incident took place and any shortcomings in the operation of the regulatory system and, secondly, identifying the State officials or authorities involved in whatever capacity in the chain of events in issue.

95. That said, the requirements of Article 2 go beyond the stage of the official investigation, where this has led to the institution of proceedings in the national courts; the proceedings as a whole, including the trial stage, must satisfy the requirements of the positive obligation to protect lives through the law.

96. It should in no way be inferred from the foregoing that Article 2 may entail the right for an applicant to have third parties prosecuted or sentenced for a criminal offence (see, *mutatis mutandis, Perez v France* [GC], No 47287/99, § 70, ECHR 2004-I) or an absolute obligation for all prosecutions to result in conviction, or indeed in a particular sentence (see, *mutatis mutandis, Tanlı v Turkey*, No 26129/95, § 111, ECHR 2001-III).

On the other hand, the national courts should not under any circumstances be prepared to allow life-endangering offences to go unpunished. This is essential for maintaining public confidence and ensuring adherence to the rule of law and for preventing any appearance of tolerance of or collusion in unlawful acts (see, *mutatis mutandis, Hugh Jordan*, cited above, §§ 108 and 136–40). The Court's task therefore consists in reviewing whether and to what extent the courts, in reaching their conclusion, may be deemed to have submitted the case to the careful scrutiny required by Article 2 of the Convention, so that the deterrent effect of the judicial system in place and the significance of the role it is required to play in preventing violations of the right to life are not undermined.

By an overwhelming majority, sixteen votes to one, the Grand Chamber concluded that:

117. Accordingly, it cannot be said that the manner in which the Turkish criminal-justice system operated in response to the tragedy secured the full accountability of State officials or authorities for their role in it and the effective implementation of provisions of domestic law guaranteeing respect for the right to life, in particular the deterrent function of the criminal law.

118. In short, it must be concluded in the instant case that there has been a violation of Article 2 of the Convention in its procedural aspect also, on account of the lack, in connection with a fatal accident provoked by the operation of a dangerous activity, of adequate protection 'by law' safeguarding the right to life and deterring similar life-endangering conduct in future.

Judge Turmen dissented because:

First of all, the majority are of the opinion that there has been a violation of the procedural aspect of Article 2, not because of the lack of an effective investigation, but because of the judicial proceedings or, more precisely, the application of domestic legislation. This is a wholly new approach which does not have any precedent in the Court's case-law.

The effect of the Grand Chamber's judgment is to extend the temporal scope of the implied procedural obligation to encompass the domestic judicial proceedings that should follow where an effective investigation has revealed evidence that State personnel and/or bodies may be guilty of gross negligence in the death(s) of persons. This is a logical development of the positive procedural obligation under Article 2 which has as one of its objectives the deterring of unlawful killings.

The death penalty

Because this judicial penalty was still used in Member States when the Convention was drafted (e.g. the death penalty imposed on Marshall Petain, the leader of the Vichy government in France that collaborated with the Nazis, after the liberation of France see *Lehideux and Isorni v France*, below p 651) the power of States to retain its use was enshrined in Article 2(1). Subsequently, as increasing numbers of European States abandoned the death penalty, the Council of Europe developed a policy opposing the death penalty. This development was reflected in Protocol No 6 that enables State parties to the ECHR to formally agree to abolish the use of the death penalty in peacetime. Protocol 6 came into effect in March 1985 (when five States had ratified it). The UK ratified it in May 1999. By July 2006, only Russia had not ratified it. Protocol No 13 strengthens the European prohibition on the death penalty by extending the abolition of the penalty to both times of war and peace. It came into force in July 2003 (when ten States had ratified the Protocol). The UK ratified Protocol No 13 in October 2003. Thirty-six States had ratified the Protocol by July 2006 (but neither Russia or Azerbaijan had signed it).

Applicants have asked the Court to interpret Article 2, and Article 3, to accord with the contemporary European disapproval of the death penalty. The original Court addressed this issue in *Soering v UK*, see below p 192. The full-time Court examined the matter in judgments by a Chamber (given on 12 March 2003) and then a Grand Chamber (under Article 43) in *Ocalan v Turkey*.

Ocalan v Turkey judgment of 12 May 2005
European Court of Human Rights

The applicant Abdullah Ocalan, before his arrest, was the leader of the PKK (Workers' Party of Kurdistan) terrorist/political organization. The contentious factual background involved the applicant being expelled from Syria, where he had been resident for several years, in early October 1998. He sought political asylum in Greece, this was refused, and Ocalan was flown to Russia in an aircraft chartered by the Greek secret services. The Russian Duma (Parliament) accepted Ocalan's request for political asylum, however the Prime Minister did not act on that decision. Two days later the applicant travelled to Rome where he, again, applied for political asylum. He was placed under house arrest, but the authorities declined to extradite him to Turkey. Ocalan's application for political asylum was rejected and he left Italy for a brief stay in Russia. He returned to Greece in early February 1999 and was almost immediately taken to Kenya. Officials from the Greek embassy met him at Nairobi airport and he was accommodated in the Greek Ambassador's residence (whilst there Ocalan made another application for political asylum in Greece, but he did not receive an answer).

The Kenyan Ministry of Foreign Affairs announced, on 15 February 1999, that Ocalan had entered Kenyan territory, on 2 February 1999, accompanied by Greek officials without declaring his identity or going through passport control. The Foreign Minister had summoned the Greek Ambassador to a meeting during which the latter, after initial denials, admitted that the relevant person was Ocalan. The Minister expressed the view that Ocalan's presence in Kenya constituted a major security risk. The Ambassador informed the Minister that authorities in Athens would arrange for Ocalan's departure from Kenya. The Kenyan Government expressed serious reservations about the credibility of the Ambassador and requested his immediate recall. The Minister stated that the Kenyan authorities played no part in the, subsequent, arrest of Ocalan and had no say in his destination.

After his meeting with the Minister, the Ambassador informed Ocalan that he was free to leave Kenya for the destination of his choice and the Netherlands was willing to accept him. Later that day, 15 February, Kenyan officials arrived at the Greek embassy to take Ocalan to the airport. The Ambassador sought to accompany Ocalan, but the latter went in a car driven by a Kenyan official. At Nairobi airport the car transporting Ocalan left the convoy and went through a route reserved for security personnel. He was driven to an aircraft, in which Turkish security personnel were waiting, they arrested him (Turkish courts had issued seven warrants for his arrest in respect of various alleged acts of terrorism) when he boarded the plane (at about 8 p.m.). During the flight to Turkey Ocalan was handcuffed and blindfolded (according to the Turkish Government the blindfold was removed when the aircraft reached Turkish airspace). A Turkish army doctor was present during the flight. Ocalan claimed that he had been given tranquillizers (probably at the Greek embassy!).

Ocalan was taken to Imrali prison, located on an island off the coast of Turkey, on 16 February. All the other inmates had just been moved to different prisons. The island was declared to be a prohibited military zone, as the Government considered that special measures were necessary to ensure the safety of Ocalan. Members of the security forces interrogated Ocalan at the prison. Four days later a judge determined, on the basis of the case file, that Ocalan should remain in custody as his interrogation had not been completed. Judges and prosecutors, from the Ankara State Security Court, arrived on the island on 21 February. Ocalan claimed that sixteen lawyers instructed by his family were denied access to him on the island on 22 and 23 February. On 22 February 1999 the Public Prosecutor at the Ankara State Security Court questioned the applicant and took a statement from him as an accused. The applicant told the prosecutor that he was the founder of the PKK and its current leader. Initially, his and the PKK's aim had been to found an independent Kurdish State, but with the passage of time they had changed their objective and sought to secure a share of power for the Kurds as a free people who had played an important role in the founding of the Republic. The applicant confessed that village guards were a prime target for the PKK. He also confirmed that the PKK used violent methods against the civil population, in particular from 1987 onwards; he was personally opposed to such methods and had tried in vain to prevent their being used. He told the prosecutor that the warlords who wanted to seize power within the PKK had exerted some of their pressure on the Kurdish population; some of them had been tried and found guilty by the PKK and had been executed with his personal approval. He acknowledged that the Turkish Government's estimate of the number of those killed [4,472 civilians, 3,874 soldiers, 247 policemen and 1,225 village guards from 1978 until the time of

Ocalan's arrest] or wounded as a result of the PKK's activities was fairly accurate; that the actual number might even be higher; and that he had ordered the attacks as part of the armed struggle being waged by the PKK. He added that he had decided in 1993 to declare a ceasefire, acting on a request by the Turkish President, Mr Özal.

On 23 February Ocalan was brought before a judge of the Ankara State Security Court. He repeated his statement given to the Prosecutor. The judge ordered that Ocalan should be detained pending trial. Ocalan was allowed to see two of his lawyers on 25 February. Ocalan's conversation with his lawyers took place in the presence of a judge and members of the security forces wearing masks. Ocalan claimed that subsequently he had only been allowed to meet with his lawyers twice a week for one hour at a time. He asserted that the discussions were monitored by officials behind glass panels and filmed on video. The Government retorted that no restrictions were placed on the number or length of Ocalan's discussions with his lawyers and that the interviews were held in accordance with the Code of Criminal Procedure.

Delegates of the European Committee for the Prevention of Torture and Inhuman or Degrading Treatment or Punishment (the CPT) visited Imrali prison in early March 1999. They informed the Turkish Government that they had found Ocalan to be in physically good health and that he had told them that he had not been ill-treated since his arrest. His cell was of a high standard. The delegates expressed the view that Ocalan's solitary confinement and limited access to open air could affect him psychologically. Imrali prison was again visited by delegates of the CPT in September 2001. They found Ocalan's cell to have washing and toilet facilities together with an air-conditioning system. He had access to books, newspapers, and a radio. Doctors gave him twice daily medical checks and he was visited by his lawyers once a week.

The Public Prosecutor at the Ankara State Security Court submitted an indictment, on 24 April 1999, accusing Ocalan of activities carried out for the purpose of bringing about the secession of part of Turkish national territory. The Prosecutor sought the death penalty. The case file concerning Ocalan combined seven sets of existing proceedings against him and amounted to 17,000 pages. Ocalan's lawyers were given access to the case file on 7 May, but the authorities did not supply them with a copy (Ocalan's lawyers had to use their own photocopier and it took them until 15 May to copy the case file).

The Ankara Sate Security Court held two hearings, in Ankara without the presence of Ocalan, at the end of March to determine procedural matters (including requests from third-parties to intervene in the proceedings against Ocalan). The Security Court, composed of two civilian and one military judge, held nine hearings, on the island of Imrali, between 31 May and 29 June 1999. Ocalan attended those hearings. He repeated his statement given to the Prosecutor. His lawyers contended that the Security Court was not an 'independent and impartial tribunal' as required by Article 6 of the Convention. Ocalan stated that he accepted the Security Court's jurisdiction. He promised to halt the PKK's armed struggle. Whilst accepting political responsibility for the PKK's general strategy he denied criminal responsibility for acts of violence which went beyond the organization's declared policy.

On 18 June 1999, the Turkish Parliament amended the constitution to exclude military personnel from being members of State Security Courts. The Security Court hearing the case against Ocalan sat without a military judge from 23 June 1999 (the new additional civilian judge had attended earlier proceedings). Ocalan's counsel unsuccessfully challenged this judge's appointment. The Security Court, on 29 June, found Ocalan guilty of carrying out acts designed to bring about the secession of part of Turkey's territory. It sentenced him to death and Ocalan appealed. In November 1999, the Court of Cassation affirmed the judgment. The European Court requested the Turkish Government to ensure that the death penalty was not implemented in order to enable the Court to examine Ocalan's complaints under the Convention. In January 2000, the Turkish Prime Minister stated that the applicant's file would be sent to the Turkish Parliament, which was empowered to approve/disapprove enforcement of the death penalty, when the Strasbourg proceedings were completed.

In October 2001 the Turkish Constitution was amended to abolish the death penalty except in times of war/imminent threat of war or for acts of terrorism. The Turkish Parliament legislated, in August 2002, to abolish the death penalty in peacetime. The Turkish Government informed the European Court, in September 2002, that Ocalan no longer faced the implementation of the death penalty imposed upon him by the domestic courts. During the following month the Ankara State Security Court commuted Ocalan's death sentence to life imprisonment. A Turkish political party's challenge to the legislation abolishing the death penalty in peacetime was rejected by the Turkish Constitutional Court in December 2002. In January 2003 Turkey signed Protocol 6 of the Convention and went on to ratify the Protocol in November 2003.

Before the Chamber of the European Court the applicant's lawyers sought to contend, *inter alia*, that Article 2 should be interpreted as no longer permitting capital punishment and that such punishment was inhuman and degrading in violation of Article 3. The Chamber, by six votes to one, found that the imposition of the death penalty on Ocalan, following an unfair trial that breached the requirements of Article 6, amounted to inhuman treatment. Subsequently, both the applicant and the Government requested that the case be referred to the Grand Chamber. These requests were accepted by a panel of the Grand Chamber.

A. IMPLEMENTATION OF THE DEATH PENALTY

151. In his initial application, the applicant complained that any recourse to the death penalty would violate both Articles 2 and 3 of the Convention.

152. In its judgment, the Chamber said that it considered that the threat of implementation of the death sentence had been effectively removed (see paragraphs 184–5 of the Chamber judgment).

153. The parties did not comment on this issue in the subsequent proceedings.

154. In that connection, the Court notes that the death penalty has been abolished in Turkey and the applicant's sentence has been commuted to one of life imprisonment. Furthermore, on 12 November 2003 Turkey ratified Protocol No 6 to the Convention for the Protection of Human Rights and Fundamental Freedoms concerning the abolition of the death penalty.

155. In these circumstances, the complaints which the applicant made in his initial application of violations of Articles 2, 3 and 14 on account of the implementation of the death penalty must be dismissed. Accordingly, there has been no violation of those provisions on that account.

B. IMPOSITION OF THE DEATH PENALTY

156. The Grand Chamber agrees with the Chamber that no separate issue arises under Article 2 with respect to the imposition of the death penalty. It will therefore examine this point under Article 3.

1. Submissions of the parties

(a) The applicant

157. The applicant asked the Grand Chamber to pursue the reasoning of the Chamber as regards the abolitionist trend established by the practice of the Contracting States and to take it a stage further by concluding that the States had, by their practice, abrogated the exception set out in the second sentence of Article 2 §1 of the Convention and that the death penalty constituted inhuman and degrading treatment within the meaning of Article 3. In that connection, he repeated the observations he had submitted to the Chamber (see paragraphs 175–9 of the judgment of 12 March 2003).

When the Convention was signed in 1950, the death penalty was not perceived as a degrading and inhuman penalty in Europe and was provided for in the legislation of a number of States. Since that time there had been *de facto* abolition throughout Europe. Such developments should be seen as an agreement by Contracting States to amend Article 2 § 1.

158. No construction of Article 2 should permit a State to inflict inhuman and degrading treatment since the death penalty *per se* constituted such treatment in breach of Article 3 of the Convention. In that latter respect the following submissions were made.

159. Developments in international and comparative law showed that the death penalty could also be seen to be contrary to international law. In that respect, reference was made, *inter alia*, to a judgment of the South African Constitutional Court in which it was held that the death penalty was contrary to the South African Constitution's prohibition of cruel, inhuman or degrading treatment (*S v Makwanyane* (1995) (6) Butterworths Constitutional Law Reports 665), and to the judgment of the Canadian Supreme Court in *US v Burns* (2001) SCC 7, where that Court, in a case concerning the extradition of a fugitive to the United States of America, considered capital punishment to amount to cruel and unusual punishment. The United Nations Human Rights Committee had also held that execution of a death sentence constituted cruel and inhuman treatment contrary to Article 6 of the International Covenant on Civil and Political Rights [*Reid v Jamaica* (No 250/1987)]. Reference was also made to similar statements by the Hungarian Constitutional Court and the Constitutional Courts of Ukraine, Albania, Lithuania and *Republika Srpska* (within Bosnia-Herzegovina).

160. Finally the applicant maintained that the imposition of the death penalty by a Court which failed to satisfy the requisite standards of the Convention and which permitted violations of the applicant's rights under Article 6 also violated Articles 2 and 3.

(b) The Government

161. The Government disagreed with the Chamber's finding that the imposition of the death penalty following an unfair trial constituted a violation of Article 3. They observed, firstly, that neither the applicant nor his lawyers had presented any argument on this point. Secondly, even assuming that the Court had decided of its own motion to examine the case under Article 3, it would be difficult if not impossible to do so in view of the nature of Article 3. Inhuman treatment within the meaning of Article 3 was based on a subjective concept, that is to say fear and anguish felt by the applicant that reached the level proscribed by Article 3. In the absence of such a complaint, it was not possible for the Court to stand in the applicant's shoes.

In the Government's submission, the conclusion reached by the Chamber was contrary to an earlier admissibility decision of the Commission in the case of *Çınar v Turkey* (No 17864/91, Commission decision of 5 September 1994, DR 79, p 5) and the *Abbas Sertkaya v Turkey* decision (No 77113/01, 11 December 2003, p 4). In those decisions, the Convention institutions found that the applicants had not felt fear or anguish as the moratorium on the implementation of the death penalty had eliminated any risk of their being executed.

The applicant's situation was identical to that of Mr Çınar and Mr Abbas Sertkaya, and the guarantees that the death penalty would not be carried out were, if anything, firmer in his case: as the applicant's case file had never been sent to the Parliament, the procedure allowing the death penalty to be implemented was never set in motion. In addition, the Turkish Government's moratorium on the implementation of the death penalty was unconditional and no offences or individuals were excluded from its scope. The Government had complied with the interim measure ordered by the Court under Rule 39 requiring them to stay the applicant's execution. There was a broad consensus in the Turkish Parliament that the applicant should not be executed, the composition of the Parliament at the material time being the same as when Parliament abolished the death penalty.

The Government submitted that there was no evidential basis for the Chamber's finding, nor could it be justified by the Court's request for a stay of execution of the death penalty.

Lastly, the Turkish Government's decision to comply with the European norms on capital punishment had eliminated all risk that the applicant would be executed.

2. The Court's assessment

(a) Legal significance of the practice of the Contracting States as regards the death penalty

162. The Court must first address the applicant's submission that the practice of the Contracting States in this area can be taken as establishing an agreement to abrogate the exception provided for in the second sentence of Article 2 §1, which explicitly permits capital punishment under certain conditions. In practice, if Article 2 is to be read as permitting capital punishment, notwithstanding the almost universal abolition of the death penalty in Europe, Article 3 cannot be interpreted as prohibiting the death penalty since that would nullify the clear wording of Article 2 § 1 (see *Soering v the United Kingdom*, judgment of 7 July 1989, Series A No 161, p 40, §103).

163. The Grand Chamber agrees with the following conclusions of the Chamber on this point (see paragraphs 189–196 of the Chamber judgment):

' ... the Court must first address the applicant's submission that the practice of the Contracting States in this area can be taken as establishing an agreement to abrogate the exception provided for in the second sentence of Article 2 § 1, which explicitly permits capital punishment under certain conditions.

' ... The Court reiterates that it must be mindful of the Convention's special character as a human-rights treaty and that the Convention cannot be interpreted in a vacuum. It should so far as possible be interpreted in harmony with other rules of public international law of which it forms part (see, *mutatis mutandis*, *Al-Adsani v the United Kingdom* [GC], No 35763/97, § 55, ECHR 2001-XI; and *Loizidou v Turkey*, judgment of 18 December 1996, Reports 1996-VI, p 2231, § 43). It must, however, confine its primary attention to the issues of interpretation and application of the provisions of the Convention which arise in the present case.

' ... It is recalled that the Court accepted in its *Soering v the United Kingdom* judgment that an established practice within the Member States could give rise to an amendment of the Convention. In that case the Court accepted that subsequent practice in national penal policy, in the form of a generalised abolition of capital punishment, could be taken as establishing the agreement of the Contracting States to abrogate the exception provided for under Article 2 § 1 and hence remove a textual limit on the scope for evolutive interpretation of Article 3 (see the above-cited judgment, § 103). It was found, however, that Protocol No 6 showed that the intention of the States was to adopt the normal method of amendment of the text in order to introduce a new obligation to abolish capital punishment in time of peace and to do so by an optional instrument allowing each State to choose the moment when to undertake such an engagement. The Court accordingly concluded that Article 3 could not be interpreted as generally prohibiting the death penalty (ibid §§ 103–4).

' ... The applicant takes issue with the Court's approach in the *Soering* judgment. His principal submission was that the reasoning is flawed since Protocol No. 6 represents merely one yardstick by which the practice of the States may be measured and that the evidence shows that all members of the Council of Europe have, either *de facto* or *de jure*, effected total abolition of the death penalty for all crimes and in all circumstances. He contended that as a matter of legal theory there was no reason why the States should not be capable of abolishing the death penalty both by abrogating the right to rely on the second sentence of Article 2 § 1 through their practice and by formal recognition of that process in the ratification of Protocol No 6.

' ... The Court reiterates that the Convention is a living instrument which must be interpreted in the light of present-day conditions and that the increasingly high standard being required in the area of the protection of human rights and fundamental liberties correspondingly and inevitably requires greater firmness in assessing breaches of the fundamental values of democratic societies (see *Selmouni v France*, judgment of 28 July 1999, *Reports* 1999-V, § 101).

' ... It reiterates that in assessing whether a given treatment or punishment is to be regarded as inhuman or degrading for the purposes of Article 3 it cannot but be influenced by the developments and commonly accepted standards in the penal policy of the member States of the Council of Europe in this field (see *Soering*, judgment cited above, p 40, § 102). Moreover, the concepts of inhuman and degrading treatment and punishment have evolved considerably since the Convention came into force in 1950 and indeed since the Court's *Soering v the United Kingdom* judgment in 1989.

' ... Equally the Court observes that the legal position as regards the death penalty has undergone a considerable evolution since the *Soering* case was decided. The *de facto* abolition noted in that case in respect of twenty-two Contracting States in 1989 has developed into a *de jure* abolition in forty-three of the forty-four Contracting States and a moratorium in the remaining State which has not yet abolished the penalty, namely Russia. This almost complete abandonment of the death penalty in times of peace in Europe is reflected in the fact that all the Contracting States have signed Protocol No 6 and forty-one States have ratified it, that is to say, all except Turkey, Armenia and Russia. It is further reflected in the policy of the Council of Europe which requires that new member States undertake to abolish capital punishment as a condition of their admission into the organisation. As a result of these developments the territories encompassed by the member States of the Council of Europe have become a zone free of capital punishment.

' ... Such a marked development could now be taken as signalling the agreement of the Contracting States to abrogate, or at the very least to modify, the second sentence of Article 2 § 1, particularly when regard is had to the fact that all Contracting States have now signed Protocol No 6 and that it has been ratified by forty-one States. It may be questioned whether it is necessary to await ratification of Protocol No 6 by the three remaining States before concluding that the death penalty exception in Article 2 has been significantly modified. Against such a consistent background, it can be said that capital punishment in peacetime has come to be regarded as an unacceptable ... form of punishment which is no longer permissible under Article 2.'

164. The Court notes that by opening for signature Protocol No. 13 concerning the abolition of the death penalty in all circumstances the Contracting States have chosen the traditional method of amendment of the text of the Convention in pursuit of their policy of abolition. At the date of this judgment, three member States have not signed this Protocol and sixteen have yet to ratify it. However, this final step toward complete abolition of the death penalty—that is to say both in times of peace and in times of war—can be seen as confirmation of the abolitionist trend in the practice of the Contracting States. It does not necessarily run counter to the view that Article 2 has been amended in so far as it permits the death penalty in times of peace.

165. For the time being, the fact that there are still a large number of States who have yet to sign or ratify Protocol No. 13 may prevent the Court from finding that it is the established practice of the Contracting States to regard the implementation of the death penalty as inhuman and degrading treatment contrary to Article 3 of the Convention, since no derogation may be made from that provision, even in times of war. However, the Grand Chamber agrees with the Chamber that it is not necessary for the Court to reach any firm conclusion on these points since, for the following reasons, it would be contrary to the Convention, even if Article 2 were to be construed as still permitting the death penalty, to implement a death sentence following an unfair trial.

(b) Unfair proceedings and the death penalty

(i) Under Article 2

166. As regards the reference in Article 2 of the Convention to "the execution of a sentence of a court", the Grand Chamber agrees with the Chamber's reasoning (see paragraphs 201–204 of the Chamber judgment):

' ... Since the right to life in Article 2 of the Convention ranks as one of the most fundamental provisions of the Convention—one from which there can be no derogation in peacetime under Article 15—and enshrines one of the basic values of the democratic societies making up the Council of

Europe, its provisions must be strictly construed (see, *mutatis mutandis, McCann v the United Kingdom*, judgment of 27 September 1995, Series A No 324, pp 45–46, § 147), *a fortiori* the second sentence of Article 2.

' ... Even if the death penalty were still permissible under Article 2, the Court considers that an arbitrary deprivation of life pursuant to capital punishment is prohibited. This flows from the requirement that "Everyone's right to life shall be protected by law". "An arbitrary act cannot be lawful under the Convention" (*Bozano v France*, judgment cited above, §§ 54 and 59).

' ... It also follows from the requirement in Article 2 § 1 that the deprivation of life be pursuant to the "execution of a sentence of a court", that the "court" which imposes the penalty be an independent and impartial tribunal within the meaning of the Court's case-law (*İncal v Turkey*, cited above; *Çıraklar v Turkey*, cited above; *Findlay v the United Kingdom*, 25 February 1997, *Reports* 1997-I; *Hauschildt v Denmark*, 24 May 1989, Series A No 154) and that the most rigorous standards of fairness are observed in the criminal proceedings both at first instance and on appeal. Since the execution of the death penalty is irreversible, it can only be through the application of such standards that an arbitrary and unlawful taking of life can be avoided (see, in this connection, Article 5 of ECOSOC Resolution 1984/50 and the decisions of the UN Human Rights Committee— ... ; also the Advisory Opinion OC-16/99 of 1 October 1999 of the Inter-American Court of Human Rights on 'The right to information on consular assistance in the framework of the guarantee of due process of law', §§ 135–6, and *Hilaire, Constantine and Benjamin et al v Trinidad and Tobago*, § 148– ...). Lastly, the requirement in Article 2 § 1 that the penalty be 'provided by law' means not only that there must exist a basis for the penalty in domestic law but that the requirement of the quality of the law be fully respected, namely that the legal basis be 'accessible' and 'foreseeable' as those terms are understood in the case-law of the Court (see *Amann v Switzerland* [GC], No 27798/95, § 56, ECHR 2000-II; *Rotaru v Romania* [GC], No 28341/95, § 52, ECHR 2000-V).

' ... It follows from the above construction of Article 2 that the implementation of the death penalty in respect of a person who has not had a fair trial would not be permissible.'

(ii) Under Article 3

167. The above conclusion concerning the interpretation of Article 2 where there has been an unfair trial must inform the opinion of the Court when it considers under Article 3 the question of the imposition of the death penalty in such circumstances.

168. As the Court has previously noted in connection with Article 3, the manner in which the death penalty is imposed or executed, the personal circumstances of the condemned person and a disproportionality to the gravity of the crime committed, as well as the conditions of detention awaiting execution, are examples of factors capable of bringing the treatment or punishment received by the condemned person within the proscription under Article 3 (see *Soering*, cited above, p 41, § 104).

169. In the Court's view, to impose a death sentence on a person after an unfair trial is to subject that person wrongfully to the fear that he will be executed. The fear and uncertainty as to the future generated by a sentence of death, in circumstances where there exists a real possibility that the sentence will be enforced, must give rise to a significant degree of human anguish. Such anguish cannot be dissociated from the unfairness of the proceedings underlying the sentence which, given that human life is at stake, becomes unlawful under the Convention.

(iii) Application of these principles to the present case

170. The Court notes that there has been a moratorium on the implementation of the death penalty in Turkey since 1984 and that in the present case the Turkish Government complied with the Court's interim measure pursuant to Rule 39 to stay the execution. It is further noted that the applicant's file was not sent to Parliament for approval of the death sentence as was then required by the Turkish Constitution.

171. The Court has also had regard, in this context, to the case of *Çınar* (cited above, p 5) in which the Commission rejected a claim that Article 3 had been violated in the case of an applicant who had been

sentenced to death in Turkey. In its reasoning, the Commission took into account the long-standing moratorium on the death penalty and concluded in the circumstances of that case that the risk of the penalty being implemented was illusory.

172. The Grand Chamber agrees with the Chamber that the special circumstances of the instant case prevent it from reaching the same conclusion as that reached in *Çınar*. The applicant's background as the leader and founder of the PKK, an organisation which had been engaged in a sustained campaign of violence causing many thousands of casualties, had made him Turkey's most wanted person. In view of the fact that the applicant has been convicted of the most serious crimes existing in the Turkish Criminal Code and of the general political controversy in Turkey—prior to the decision to abolish the death penalty—surrounding the question of whether he should be executed, it is not possible to rule out the possibility that the risk that the sentence would be implemented was a real one. In practical terms, the risk remained for more than three years of the applicant's detention in İmralı from the date of the Court of Cassation's judgment of 25 November 1999 affirming the applicant's conviction until the Ankara State Security Court's judgment of 3 October 2002 which commuted the death penalty to which the applicant had been sentenced to one of life imprisonment.

173. As to the nature of the applicant's trial, the Court refers to its conclusions on the applicant's complaints under Article 6 of the Convention. It has found that the applicant was not tried by an independent and impartial tribunal within the meaning of Article 6 § 1 and that there has been a breach of the rights of the defence under Article 6 § 1, taken together with Article 6 §§ 3 (b) and (c), as the applicant had no access to a lawyer while in police custody and was unable to communicate with his lawyers out of the hearing of officials, restrictions had been imposed on the number and length of his lawyers' visits to him, he was unable to consult the case-file until an advanced stage of the proceedings and his lawyers did not have sufficient time to consult the file properly.

174. The death penalty has thus been imposed on the applicant following an unfair procedure which cannot be considered to conform with the strict standards of fairness required in cases involving a capital sentence. Moreover, he had to suffer the consequences of the imposition of that sentence for nearly three years.

175. Consequently, the Court concludes that the imposition of the death sentence on the applicant following an unfair trial by a court whose independence and impartiality were open to doubt amounted to inhuman treatment in violation of Article 3.

....

FOR THESE REASONS, THE COURT

...

7. *Holds* unanimously that there has been no violation of Article 2 of the Convention;

8. *Holds* unanimously that there has been no violation of Article 14 of the Convention, taken together with Article 2, as regards the implementation of the death penalty;

9. *Holds* unanimously that there has been no violation of Article 3 of the Convention as regards the complaint concerning the implementation of the death penalty;

10. *Holds* by thirteen votes to four that there has been a violation of Article 3 as regards the imposition of the death penalty following an unfair trial;

....

NOTES

1   The Court was composed of President Wildhaber and Judges: Rozakis, Costa, Ress, Bratza, Palm, Caflisch, Loucaides, Turmen, Straznicka, Lorenzen, Butkevych, Hedigan, Ugrekehelidze, Garlicki, Borrego Borrego, and Gyulumyan.

2 Judges Costa, Caflisch, Turmen, and Borrego Borrego issued a joint partly dissenting opinion in which they noted:

The majority accepts that Article 3 cannot be interpreted as prohibiting the death penalty since that would nullify the clear wording of Article 2 (paragraph 162 of the judgment). In other words, according to the majority, while the death penalty itself does not constitute a violation of Article 3, a procedural defect in respect of impartiality and independence of the court which imposes the death penalty constitutes a violation of Article 3.

However, the dissentients considered that there was no evidence that Ocalan had suffered fear and anguish, due to the (disputed) lack of independence/impartiality of the State Security Court, and there was no 'real and immediate risk' that he would be executed as no person had been executed in Turkey since 1984. Indeed, the dissenters believed that Ocalan's political background made his execution less likely due to the political consequences his execution might have produced.

3 Judge Garlicki produced a partly concurring/dissenting opinion in which he expressed the view:

1. I am writing this separate opinion because I feel that, in this case, the Court should have decided, in the operative provisions of its judgment, that Article 3 had been violated because any imposition of the death penalty represents *per se* inhuman and degrading treatment prohibited by the Convention. Thus, while correct, the majority's conclusion that the imposition of the death penalty following an unfair trial represents a violation of Article 3 seems to me to stop short of addressing the real problem.

2. It is true that the majority's conclusion was sufficient to establish a violation in the instant case and that it was not absolutely necessary to produce any firm conclusion on the—more general—point whether the implementation of the death penalty should now be regarded as inhuman and degrading treatment contrary to Article 3 in all circumstances. I accept that there are many virtues in judicial self restraint, but am not persuaded that this was the best occasion to exercise it.

I am fully aware that the original text of the Convention allowed capital punishment provided the guarantees referred to in Article 2 § 1 were in place. I am also aware that in its 1989 *Soering* judgment this Court declined to hold that the new international context permitted it to conclude that the exception provided for in the second section of Article 2 § 1 had been abrogated. Today the Court, while agreeing that 'it can be said that capital punishment in peacetime has come to be regarded as an unacceptable ... form of punishment which is no longer permissible under Article 2' (see paragraph 163 of the judgment), seems to be convinced that there is no room for the death penalty even within the original text of the Convention. But, at the same time, it has chosen not to express that position in a universally binding manner. In my opinion, there are some arguments suggesting that the Court could and should have gone further in this case.

3. First of all, there seems to be no dispute over the substance of the problem. The Court was clearly right in observing that, over the past fifteen years, the territories encompassed by the member States of the Council of Europe have become a zone free of capital punishment and that such a development could now be taken as signalling the agreement of the Contracting States to abrogate, or at the very least to modify, the second sentence of Article 2 § 1. It is not necessary to recapitulate here all the relevant developments in Europe; it seems sufficient to quote the 2002 Opinion of the Parliamentary of the Council of Europe Assembly in which it recalled that in its most recent resolutions 'it reaffirmed its beliefs that the application of the death penalty constitutes inhuman and degrading punishment and a violation of the most fundamental right, right to life itself, and that capital punishment has no place in civilised, democratic societies governed by the rule of law'. Thus, today, in 2005, condemnation of the death penalty has become absolute and even fairness of the highest order at trial cannot legitimate the imposition of such a penalty. In other words, it is possible to conclude that the member States have

agreed through their practice to modify the second sentence of Article 2 § 1. The only problem is: who shall have the power to declare, in a binding manner, that such modification has taken place? So, this is a problem not of substance, but of jurisdiction (competence). In consequence, the only question which remains is whether the Court has the power to state the obvious truth, namely that capital punishment has now become an inhuman and degrading punishment *per se*.

4. In answering this question, it is necessary to bear in mind that the Convention, as an international treaty, should be applied and interpreted in accordance with general rules of international law, in particular Article 39 of the Vienna Convention. This suggests that the only way to modify the Convention is to follow the 'normal procedure of amendment' (see §§ 103–4 of the *Soering* judgment and §§ 164–5 of the present judgment).

But the Convention represents a very distinct form of international instrument and—in many respects—its substance and process of application are more akin to those of national constitutions than to those of 'typical' international treaties. The Court has always accepted that the Convention is a living instrument and must be interpreted in the light of present-day conditions. This may result (and, in fact, has on numerous occasions resulted) in judicial modifications of the original meaning of the Convention. From this perspective, the role of our Court is not very different from the role of national constitutional courts whose mandate is not only to defend constitutional provisions on human rights, but also to develop them. The Strasbourg Court has demonstrated such a creative approach to the text of the Convention many times, holding that the Convention rights and freedoms are applicable to situations which were not envisaged by the original drafters. Thus, it is legitimate to assume that, as long as the member States have not clearly rejected a particular judicial interpretation of the Convention (as occurred in relation to the expulsion of aliens, which became the subject of regulation by Protocols Nos 4 and 7), the Court has power to determine the actual meaning of words and phrases which were inserted into the text of the Convention more than fifty years ago. In any event, and this seems to be the situation with regard to the death penalty, the Court may so proceed when its interpretation remains in harmony with the values and standards that have been endorsed by the member States.

5. This Court has never denied that the 'living-instrument approach' may lead to a judicial imposition of new, higher standards of human-rights protection. However, with respect to capital punishment, it adopted—in the *Soering* judgment—'a doctrine of pre-emption'. As I have mentioned above, the Court found that since the member States had decided to address the problem of capital punishment by way of formal amendments to the Convention, this matter became the 'preserve' of the States and the Court was prevented from applying its living-instrument doctrine.

I am not sure whether such an interpretation was correct in *Soering* or applicable to the present *Öcalan* judgment.

The *Soering* judgment was based on the fact that, although Protocol No 6 had provided for the abolition of the death penalty, several member States had yet to ratify it in 1989. Thus, it would have been premature for the Court to take any general position as to the compatibility of capital punishment with the Convention. Now, the majority raises basically the same argument with respect to Protocol No 13 which, it is true, remains in the process of ratification.

But this may only demonstrate a hesitation on the part of certain member States over the best moment to irrevocably abolish the death penalty. At the same time, it can no longer be disputed that—on the European level—there is a consensus as to the inhuman nature of the death penalty. Therefore, the fact that governments and politicians are preparing a formal amendment to the Convention may be understood more as a signal that capital punishment should no longer exist than as a decision preempting the Court from acting on its own initiative.

That is why I am not convinced by the majority's replication of the *Soering* approach. I do not think that there are any legal obstacles to this Court's taking a decision with respect to the nature of capital punishment.

6. Such a decision would have universal applicability; in particular, it would prohibit any imposition of the death penalty, not only in times of peace but also in wartime or other warlike situations. But it should not stop the Court from taking this decision today. It may be true that the history of Europe demonstrates that there have been wars, like the Second World War, during which (or after which) there was justification for capital punishment. I do not think, however, that the present interpretation of the Convention should provide for such exceptions: it would be rather naïve to believe that, if a war of a similar magnitude was to break out again, the Convention as a whole would be able to survive, even if concessions were made with regard to the interpretation of capital punishment. On the other hand, if there is a war or armed conflict of a local dimension only—and this has been the experience of the last five decades in Europe—the international community could and should insist on respect for basic values of humanity, inter alia, on the prohibition of capital punishment. The same reasoning should apply to other 'wars', like—in particular—the 'war on terror', in which there is today no place for capital punishment (see Article X § 2 of the 2002 'Guidelines on Human Rights and the Fight Against Terrorism' issued by the Committee of Ministers of the Council of Europe).

Furthermore, it is notable that, as the Statute of the recently established International Criminal Court shows, the international community is of the opinion that even the most dreadful crimes can be dealt with without resorting to capital punishment.

7. Within the last fifteen years several constitutional courts in Europe have been invited to take a position on capital punishment. The courts of Hungary, Lithuania, Albania and Ukraine had no hesitation in decreeing that capital punishment was no longer permitted under the Constitutions of their respective countries, even if this was not clearly stated in the written text of those documents. The Constitutional Courts have, nevertheless, adopted the position that the inability of the political branches of government to take a clear decision on the matter should not impede the judicial branch from doing so. A similar approach was taken by the Constitutional Court of South Africa.

I am firmly convinced that the European Court of Human Rights should have followed the same path in the *Öcalan* judgment.

. . . .

4   The Grand Chamber judgment in *Ocalan* (at paragraph 164) indicated that whilst the Court was not unsympathetic to the view that State practice had amended Article 2 so as to abolish the death penalty, at least in peacetime, the Court would not make such a definitive ruling given Member States choice to abolish the use of the death penalty via Protocols 6 and 13. Nevertheless, the imposition or implementation of a particular death penalty might be contrary to Article 3.

5   In *Bader and Others v Sweden*, judgment of 8 November 2005, a unanimous Chamber extended the *Soering* approach to deportations under Article 3 (see below p 192) to Article 2. The applicants claimed that if they were deported back to Syria (their country of origin) the first applicant would face execution as he had been convicted and sentenced to death in respect of his (alleged) involvement in the killing of his brother-in-law. The Chamber held that:

42. . . . It follows that an issue may arise under Articles 2 and 3 of the Convention if a Contracting State deports an alien who has suffered or risks suffering a flagrant denial of a fair trial in the receiving State, the outcome of which was or is likely to be the death penalty.

Finding major defects in the Syrian trial of the first applicant, including the absence of him or his lawyer, and the failure of Sweden to secure guarantees that his case would be re-opened with the prosecutor not seeking the death penalty; the Chamber determined that the deportation of the applicants to Syria would breach Articles 2 and 3. Interestingly, Judge Cabral Barreto issued a Concurring Opinion in which he expressed the view that Sweden would breach Protocol 13 if it deported the applicants.

... The States which have already ratified Protocol No 13 wished to replace the obligation arising under Article 2 of the Convention by a stronger one, namely an obligation to abolish the death penalty in all circumstances.

The second sentence of Article 2 has, as it were, been abrogated, or at least rendered redundant, by the entry into force of Protocol No 13.

The States which have ratified Protocol No 13 have undertaken not only never to implement capital punishment but also not to put anyone at risk of incurring that penalty.

Consequently, there is no need to examine the trial or the situation of the person sentenced to death prior to the sentence being carried out because there will always be a violation of Article 1 of Protocol No 13.

Sweden has already ratified Protocol No 13.

I would therefore prefer to find that, in the instant case, the applicants' expulsion to Syria would entail a violation of Article 1 of Protocol No 13, in addition to a violation of Article 3.

Article 2(2)

Defence of persons from unlawful violence (Article 2(2)(a))

This exception was invoked in *McCann* (above).

To effect a lawful arrest or to prevent the escape of a person lawfully detained (Article 2(2)(b))

A unanimous Chamber elaborated important limitations upon the use of this exception in *Nachova and Others v Bulgaria*, judgment of 26 February 2004. The applicants complained to the Court about the shooting dead of two of their family members. The deceased were non-violent and unarmed fugitive conscripts, of Roma ethic origin, who had escaped from custody. Four military police officers, equipped with handguns and Kalashnikov automatic rifles, were sent to arrest the fugitives. Military police regulations authorized the use of firearms to apprehend a person serving in the army where, *inter alia*, that person had committed a publicly prosecutable offence, did not surrender, an oral warning had been given and a warning shot fired in the air. The deceased tried to run away from the house they had been hiding in when the military police arrived. The senior officer, a major, gave chase and after shouting at the fugitives to stop and firing a warning shot he opened fire with his Kalashnikov rifle killing both fugitives. A neighbour claimed that the major then pointed the weapon at him and said 'You damn Gypsies!'

103. The Court considers that, balanced against the imperative need to preserve life as a fundamental value, the legitimate aim of effecting a lawful arrest cannot justify putting human life at risk where the fugitive has committed a non-violent offence and does not pose a threat to anyone. Any other approach would be incompatible with the basic principles of democratic societies, as universally accepted today (see the relevant provisions of the United Nations Basic Principles on the Use of Force and Firearms by Law Enforcement Officials ... and, *mutatis mutandis*, the Court's reasoning in *Öcalan v Turkey*, No 46221/99, § 196, 12 March 2003).

104. It is only in subparagraphs (a) and (c) of Article 2 § 2 that violence (in the form of unlawful violence, a riot or an insurrection) is expressly made a condition that will justify the use of potentially lethal force.

However, the principle of strict proportionality as enshrined in Article 2 of the Convention cannot be read in dissociation from the purpose of that provision: the protection of the right to life. This implies that a similar condition applies to cases under subparagraph (b).

105. The use of potentially lethal firearms inevitably exposes human life to danger even when there are rules designed to minimise the risks. Accordingly, the Court considers that it can in no circumstances be 'absolutely necessary' within the meaning of Article 2 § 2 of the Convention to use such firearms to arrest a person suspected of a non-violent offence who is known not to pose a threat to life or limb, even where a failure to do so may result in the opportunity to arrest the fugitive being lost ...

Furthermore, the Chamber believed that excessive force had been used by the military police against the deceased, e.g. the major opening fire when other options were available (such as using the military police jeep to chase the fugitives) and the major choosing to fire his rifle in automatic mode when he had a handgun. Hence there had been a breach of Article 2. The Chamber's unequivocal ruling that the use of firearms to arrest non-violent suspects is not lawful under Article 2 should be commended. This provides clear guidance to Member states and they must ensure that all their law enforcement personnel are trained to observe this limitation. The right to life has to take precedence over the risk that non-violent offenders may (temporarily) escape arrest where resort to the use of firearms is prohibited under Article 2. Subsequently, a unanimous Grand Chamber confirmed this approach during a re-hearing of the case under Article 43 in *Nachova and Others v Bulgaria*, judgment of 6 July 2005.

95. Accordingly, and with reference to Article 2(2)(b) of the Convention, the legitimate aim of effecting a lawful arrest can only justify putting human life at risk in circumstances of absolute necessity. The Court considers that in principle there can be no such necessity where it is known that the person to be arrested poses no threat to life or limb and is not suspected of having committed a violent offence, even if a failure to use lethal force may result in the opportunity to arrest the fugitive being lost ...

In regard to the alleged racist overtones of the killings in *Nachova* see below p 823 [A14].

Action lawfully taken to quell a riot or insurrection (Article 2(2)(c))

1 The Court examined this exception in *Güleç v Turkey* (1998) 28 EHRR 121, *Reports* 1998-IV. The applicant claimed that his 15-year-old son (Ahmet) had been killed by the security forces who opened fire on about 3,000 demonstrators to make them disperse. According to the applicant, Ahmet was trying to return home from school. The Government asserted that Ahmet had been killed by a bullet fired by armed demonstrators shooting at the security forces. The Commission found that the security forces had opened fire, either in the air or at the ground, in order to disperse the demonstrators using a machine gun on an armoured vehicle and that Ahmet had been hit by a fragment of a bullet (that had ricocheted off the ground or a wall) from that weapon. The Commission did not believe the machine gun had been used to intentionally kill demonstrators. However, by thirty-one votes to one, the Commission concluded that there had been a breach of Article 2 as the use of a combat weapon to restore order during a demonstration could not be regarded as proportionate. The Court was unanimous in finding a violation of that Article.

70. The file on the present case has not revealed any reason to cast doubt on the establishment of the facts as set out in the Commission's report. As the Commission rightly pointed out, the demonstration was far from peaceful, as was evidenced by the damage to moveable and immoveable property in the town and the injuries sustained by some gendarmes. Confronted with acts of violence which were, admittedly, serious, the security forces, who were not present in sufficient strength, called for

reinforcements, and at least two armoured vehicles were deployed. Whereas the driver of the Condor, warrant-officer Nazim Ayhan, asserted that he had fired into the air, several witnesses, including some of the leading citizens of the town, said that shots had been fired at the crowd. Although this allegation was categorically denied by the Government, it is corroborated by the fact that nearly all the wounded demonstrators were hit in the legs; this would be perfectly consistent with ricochet wounds from bullets with a downward trajectory which could have been fired from the turret of an armoured vehicle.

71. The Court, like the Commission, accepts that the use of force may be justified in the present case under paragraph 2 (c) of Article 2, but it goes without saying that a balance must be struck between the aim pursued and the means employed to achieve it. The gendarmes used a very powerful weapon because they apparently did not have truncheons, riot shields, water cannon, rubber bullets or tear gas. The lack of such equipment is all the more incomprehensible and unacceptable because the province . . . , as the Government pointed out, is in a region in which a state of emergency has been declared, where at the material time disorder could have been expected.

72. As to the question whether there were armed terrorists among the demonstrators, the Court notes that the Government produced no evidence to support that assertion. In the first place, no gendarme sustained a bullet wound either in the place where the applicant's son died or in other places passed by the demonstration. Secondly, no weapons or spent cartridges supposed to have belonged to PKK members were found on the spot. Moreover, prosecutions brought in the Diyarbakir National Security Court against the owners of thirteen rifles confiscated after the incidents, from which spent cartridges had been collected by the security forces, ended in acquittals, because the defendants had not taken part in the events in issue . . .

73. In conclusion, the Court considers that in the circumstances of the case the force used to disperse the demonstrators, which caused the death of Ahmet Güleç, was not absolutely necessary within the meaning of Article 2.

Unfortunately, this case provides a dramatic example of excessive (disproportionate) use of force by State personnel.

2   The use of plastic baton rounds, commonly referred to as 'plastic bullets', by the security forces in Northern Ireland to deal with public disorder was considered by the Commission in *Stewart v UK*, 39 DR 162 (1984). The applicant's thirteen-year-old son (Brian) participated in a riot (with about 150 other persons) directed towards eight soldiers patrolling the Turf Lodge area of Belfast in October 1976. After stones and bottles were thrown by the rioters at the soldiers the Lieutenant, commanding the soldiers, ordered that one baton round be fired. However, this did not stop the rioters, therefore the officer ordered another baton round be fired at the leader of the rioters. The responsible soldier aimed at the leader's legs, but he was struck by two missiles (thrown by the rioters) as he fired. The assaults caused the soldier to jerk and his baton round hit Brian on the head. Brian died several days later as a result of his injuries. Brian's mother sued the Ministry of Defence, but the High Court found that the firing of the baton round was reasonable for the prevention of crime. She then complained to the Commission arguing that Article 2 had been violated by the security forces using such a deadly and dangerous weapon for crowd control and that the shooting of Brian was not absolutely necessary. Between 1970 and 1975 the security forces in Northern Ireland fired approximately 55,000 'rubber bullets'. Three persons were killed and numerous persons were seriously injured (blinded) by the use of rubber bullets. From 1973 the security forces began to use plastic baton rounds instead of rubber bullets (the former are fired from a more accurate gun). At the time of the Commission's ruling 11 persons (including Brian) had been killed by plastic baton

rounds. The Commission based its decision upon the facts found by the domestic courts, no new evidence had been presented to the Commission.

The Commission notes that the use of the plastic baton round in Northern Ireland has given rise to much controversy and that it is a dangerous weapon which can occasion serious injuries and death, particularly if it strikes the head. However, information provided by the parties concerning casualties, compared with the number of baton rounds discharged, shows that the weapon is less dangerous than alleged.

It recalls that the group of soldiers were confronted with a hostile and violent crowd of 150 persons who were attacking them with stones and other missiles, and, further, that the soldier's aim was disturbed at the moment of discharge when he was struck by several missiles.

The Commission is of the opinion, taking account of all the surrounding circumstances, referred to above, that the death of Brian Stewart resulted from the use of force which was no more than 'absolutely necessary' 'in action lawfully taken for the purpose of quelling a riot . . . (paras 28–30)

Therefore, the Commission declared the application inadmissible. This case is also an example of an unintentional killing being evaluated under Article 2 by the Commission.

5 | ARTICLE 3 PROHIBITION OF TORTURE

The Court's general approach

Ireland v UK A.25 (1978) 2 EHRR 25
European Court of Human Rights

Soon after the creation of the Irish Free State in 1921, six counties in the north opted to remain within the United Kingdom. These counties became Northern Ireland and until 1972 it had a separate Parliament (which was constitutionally subordinate to the Westminster Parliament) and Government. In the words of the Court:

Northern Ireland is not a homogeneous society. It consists of two communities divided by deep and long-standing antagonisms. One community is variously termed Protestant, Unionist or Loyalist, the other is generally labelled as Catholic, Republican or Nationalist. About two-thirds of the population of one and a half million belong to the Protestant community, the remaining third to the Catholic community. The majority group is descended from Protestant settlers who emigrated in large numbers from Britain to Northern Ireland during the seventeenth century. The now traditional antagonism between the two groups is based both on religion and on social, economic and political difference. In particular, the Protestant community has consistently opposed the idea of a united Ireland independent of the United Kingdom, whereas the Catholic community has traditionally supported it. (para 15)

From 1963 a campaign for 'civil rights' (demanding the ending of discrimination against Catholics in the allocation of public sector housing, local authority appointments, and the manipulation of electoral boundaries) began to gather momentum in Northern Ireland. Marches in support of the campaign started in 1968 and some ended in rioting. In November 1968 the Northern Ireland Government announced a reform programme to deal with the minority community's grievances. However, the protest marches continued with escalating public disorder in the province. In the spring of 1969 explosive devices were detonated (probably by Loyalist terrorists) at public utility facilities in Northern Ireland and British troops were sent to the province. At about the same time the IRA (the Irish Republican Army 'a clandestine organisation with quasi-military dispositions') secretly reactivated its members. During 1970 the IRA began a terrorist campaign of bombing buildings and attacking members of the security forces in Northern Ireland. Simultaneously Loyalist terrorists were killing Catholics and bombing their premises. The terrorist violence escalated in 1971 with the IRA being responsible for the majority of incidents. In August 1971 the Government of Northern Ireland, after discussions with the UK Government, brought into operation extra-judicial measures of detention and internment to try and reduce the level of terrorist violence. The authorities introduced these measures because they believed that; (1) the ordinary criminal justice system was unable to deal with IRA terrorism, (2) widespread intimidation of the population made it impossible to secure convictions against IRA terrorists and (3) the border with the Republic of Ireland made it easy for terrorists to escape from one jurisdiction to the other. In the weeks preceding the introduction of internment the security forces prepared lists of persons who were suspected of being involved with or having knowledge about IRA terrorism.

Starting at 4 am on Monday, 9 August 1971, the army, with police officers occasionally acting as guides, mounted an operation ('Demetrius') to arrest the 452 persons whose names appeared on the final list. In the event some 350 persons were arrested in accordance with the Special Powers Regulations. The arrested persons were taken to one of the three regional holding centres (Malligan Weekend Training Centre in County Londonderry, Ballykinder Weekend Training Centre in County Down and Girdwood Park territorial Army Centre in Belfast) that had been set up to receive the prisoners during 48 hours. All those arrested were subjected to interrogation by police officers of the Royal Ulster Constabulary (RUC). 104 persons were released within 48 hours. Those who were to be detained were sent on to the prison ship 'Maidstone' or to Crumlin Road prison, both in Belfast. Prior to being lodged in detention, 12 individuals were moved to one or more unidentified centres for 'interrogation in depth' extending over several days. (para 39)

Subsequently other persons held and interrogated under the extra-judicial measures were processed at Palace Barracks (Holywood, County Down), Gough (County Armagh), Girdwood Park and Ballykelly (County Londonderry). Internment resulted in serious rioting and increased terrorist activity. In March 1972, due to the deteriorating security situation, direct rule was established over Northern Ireland by the United Kingdom Government (the Northern Ireland Parliament was prorogued and the executive powers of the Northern Ireland Government transferred to the Secretary of State for Northern Ireland). One of the first actions taken under direct rule was to release over 250 detainees. Loyalist terrorism, however, began to increase, especially in the form of sectarian assassinations. In 1973 the first Loyalists were interned. Political reforms were unsuccessfully attempted in Northern Ireland and in 1975 the last extra-judicial detainees were released. By March 1975, according to the UK Government, 1,100 people had been killed, 11,500 injured and £140 million worth of property destroyed by terrorism and public disorder in Northern Ireland.

In December 1971 the Irish Government lodged a complaint with the Commission against the UK, alleging a number of breaches of the Convention in respect of, inter alia, the treatment of persons detained under the extra-judicial powers in Northern Ireland. The applicant Government submitted written evidence in respect of 228 cases concerning incidents between 1971 and 1974. The Commission examined in detail the evidence relating to sixteen 'illustrative' cases selected by the Irish Government. Also 41 further cases were considered by the Commission. The applicant Government was particularly concerned about the use of 'interrogation in depth' techniques, for several days, on fourteen persons in 1971 at unidentified interrogation centres. The 'five techniques' consisted of the following sensory deprivation methods which were used in combination:

(a) wall-standing: forcing the detainees to remain for periods of some hours in a 'stress position', described by those who underwent it as being 'spreadeagled against the wall, with their fingers put high above the head against the wall, the legs spread apart and the feet back, causing them to stand on their toes with the weight of the body mainly on the fingers';

(b) hooding: putting a black or navy coloured bag over the detainees' heads and, at least initially, keeping it there all the time except during interrogation;

(c) subjection to noise: pending their interrogations, holding the detainees in a room where there was a continuous loud and hissing noise;

(d) deprivation of sleep pending their interrogations, depriving the detainees of sleep;

(e) deprivation of food and drink: subjecting the detainees to a reduced diet during their stay at the centre and pending interrogations. (para 96)

The applicant Government also made a number of allegations of violent assaults by members of the security forces against detainees. In its report (February 1976) the Commission found, inter alia, that the combined use of the five techniques in the cases before it constituted a practice of inhuman treatment and of torture in breach of Article 3 (unanimously).

AS TO THE LAW

....

I. ON ARTICLE 3 (ART 3)

150. Article 3 (art 3) provides that 'no one shall be subjected to torture or to inhuman or degrading treatment or punishment'.

A. PRELIMINARY QUESTIONS

151. In their memorial of 26 October 1976 and at the hearings in February 1977, the United Kingdom Government raised two preliminary questions on the alleged violations of Article 3 (art 3). The first concerns the violations which they no longer contest, the second certain of the violations whose existence they dispute.

1. Preliminary question on the non-contested violations of Article 3 (art 3)

152. The United Kingdom Government contest neither the breaches of Article 3 (art 3) as found by the Commission . . . nor—a point moreover that is beyond doubt—the Court's jurisdiction to examine such breaches. However, relying *inter alia* on the case-law of the International Court of Justice (*Northern Cameroons* case, judgment of 2 December 1963, and *Nuclear Tests* cases, judgments of 20 December 1974), they argue that the European Court has power to decline to exercise its jurisdiction where the objective of an application has been accomplished or where adjudication on the merits would be devoid of purpose. Such, they claim, is the situation here. They maintain that the findings in question not only are not contested but also have been widely publicised and that they do not give rise to problems of interpretation or application of the Convention sufficiently important to require a decision by the Court. Furthermore, for them the subject-matter of those findings now belongs to past history in view of the abandonment of the five techniques (1972), the solemn and unqualified undertaking not to reintroduce these techniques (8 February 1977) and the other measures taken by the United Kingdom to remedy, impose punishment for, and prevent the recurrence of, the various violations found by the Commission.

This argument is disputed by the applicant Government. Neither is it accepted in a general way by the delegates of the Commission; they stated, however, that they would express no conclusion as to whether or not the above-mentioned undertaking had deprived the claim concerning the five techniques of its object.

153. The Court takes formal note of the undertaking given before it, at the hearing on 8 February 1977, by the United Kingdom Attorney-General on behalf of the respondent Government. The terms of this undertaking were as follows:

'The Government of the United Kingdom have considered the question of the use of the 'five techniques' with very great care and with particular regard to Article 3 (art 3) of the Convention. They now give this unqualified undertaking, that the 'five techniques' will not in any circumstances be reintroduced as an aid to interrogation.'

The Court also notes that the United Kingdom has taken various measures designed to prevent the recurrence of the events complained of and to afford reparation for their consequences. For example, it has issued to the police and the army instructions and directives on the arrest, interrogation and treatment of persons in custody, reinforced the procedures for investigating complaints, appointed commissions of enquiry and paid or offered compensation in many cases . . .

154. Nevertheless, the Court considers that the responsibilities assigned to it within the framework of the system under the Convention extend to pronouncing on the non-contested allegations of violation of Article 3 (art 3). The Court's judgments in fact serve not only to decide those cases brought before the Court but, more generally, to elucidate, safeguard and develop the rules instituted by the Convention, thereby contributing to the observance by the States of the engagements undertaken by them as Contracting Parties (Article 19) (art 19).

The conclusion thus arrived at by the Court is, moreover, confirmed by paragraph 3 of Rule 47 of the Rules of Court. If the Court may proceed with the consideration of a case and give a ruling thereon even in the event of a 'notice of discontinuance, friendly settlement, arrangement' or 'other fact of a kind to provide a solution of the matter', it is entitled *a fortiori* to adopt such a course of action when the conditions for the application of this Rule are not present.

155. Accordingly, that part of the present case which concerns the said allegations cannot be said to have become without object; the Court considers that it should rule thereon, notwithstanding the initiatives taken by the respondent State. . . .

B. QUESTIONS OF PROOF

160. In order to satisfy itself as to the existence or not in Northern Ireland of practices contrary to Article 3 (art 3), the Court will not rely on the concept that the burden of proof is borne by one or other of the two Governments concerned. In the cases referred to it, the Court examines all the material before it, whether originating from the Commission, the Parties or other sources, and, if necessary, obtains material *proprio motu*.

161. The Commission based its own conclusions mainly on the evidence of the one hundred witnesses heard in, and on the medical reports relating to, the sixteen 'illustrative' cases it had asked the applicant Government to select. The Commission also relied, but to a lesser extent, on the documents and written comments submitted in connection with the '41 cases' and it referred to the numerous 'remaining cases' (see paragraph 93 above). As in the '*Greek case*' (Yearbook of the Convention, 1969, *The Greek* case, p 196, para 30), the standard of proof the Commission adopted when evaluating the material it obtained was proof 'beyond reasonable doubt'.

The Irish Government see this as an excessively rigid standard for the purposes of the present proceedings. They maintain that the system of enforcement would prove ineffectual if, where there was a *prima facie* case of violation of Article 3 (art 3), the risk of a finding of such a violation was not borne by a State which fails in its obligation to assist the Commission in establishing the truth (Article 28, sub-paragraph (a) in fine, of the Convention) (art 28-a). In their submission, this is how the attitude taken by the United Kingdom should be described.

The respondent Government dispute this contention and ask the Court to follow the same course as the Commission. The Court agrees with the Commission's approach regarding the evidence on which to base the decision whether there has been violation of Article 3 (art 3). To assess this evidence, the Court adopts the standard of proof 'beyond reasonable doubt' but adds that such proof may follow from the coexistence of sufficiently strong, clear and concordant inferences or of similar unrebutted presumptions of fact. In this context, the conduct of the Parties when evidence is being obtained has to be taken into account.

C. QUESTIONS CONCERNING THE MERITS

162. As was emphasised by the Commission, ill-treatment must attain a minimum level of severity if it is to fall within the scope of Article 3 (art 3). The assessment of this minimum is, in the nature of things,

relative; it depends on all the circumstances of the case, such as the duration of the treatment, its physical or mental effects and, in some cases, the sex, age and state of health of the victim, etc.

163. The Convention prohibits in absolute terms torture and inhuman or degrading treatment or punishment, irrespective of the victim's conduct. Unlike most of the substantive clauses of the Convention and of Protocols Nos. 1 and 4 (P1, P4), Article 3 (art 3) makes no provision for exceptions and, under Article 15 para 2 (art 15–2), there can be no derogation therefrom even in the event of a public emergency threatening the life of the nation.

164. In the instant case, the only relevant concepts are 'torture' and 'inhuman or degrading treatment', to the exclusion of 'inhuman or degrading punishment'.

1. The unidentified interrogation centre or centres

(a) The 'five techniques'

165. . . . In the Commission's estimation, those facts constituted a practice not only of inhuman and degrading treatment but also of torture. The applicant Government ask for confirmation of this opinion which is not contested before the Court by the respondent Government.

166. The police used the five techniques on fourteen persons in 1971 . . . Although never authorised in writing in any official document, the five techniques were taught orally by the English Intelligence Centre to members of the RUC at a seminar held in April 1971. There was accordingly a practice.

167. The five techniques were applied in combination, with premeditation and for hours at a stretch; they caused, if not actual bodily injury, at least intense physical and mental suffering to the persons subjected thereto and also led to acute psychiatric disturbances during interrogation. They accordingly fell into the category of inhuman treatment within the meaning of Article 3 (art 3). The techniques were also degrading since they were such as to arouse in their victims feelings of fear, anguish and inferiority capable of humiliating and debasing them and possibly breaking their physical or moral resistance.

On these two points, the Court is of the same view as the Commission.

In order to determine whether the five techniques should also be qualified as torture, the Court must have regard to the distinction, embodied in Article 3 (art 3), between this notion and that of inhuman or degrading treatment.

In the Court's view, this distinction derives principally from a difference in the intensity of the suffering inflicted.

The Court considers in fact that, while there exists on the one hand violence which is to be condemned both on moral grounds and also in most cases under the domestic law of the Contracting States but which does not fall within Article 3 (art 3) of the Convention, it appears on the other hand that it was the intention that the Convention, with its distinction between 'torture' and 'inhuman or degrading treatment', should by the first of these terms attach a special stigma to deliberate inhuman treatment causing very serious and cruel suffering.

Moreover, this seems to be the thinking lying behind Article 1 in fine of Resolution 3452 (XXX) adopted by the General Assembly of the United Nations on 9 December 1975, which declares:

> 'Torture constitutes an aggravated and deliberate form of cruel, inhuman or degrading treatment or punishment'.

Although the five techniques, as applied in combination, undoubtedly amounted to inhuman and degrading treatment, although their object was the extraction of confessions, the naming of others and/or information and although they were used systematically, they did not occasion suffering of the particular intensity and cruelty implied by the word torture as so understood.

168. The Court concludes that recourse to the five techniques amounted to a practice of inhuman and degrading treatment, which practice was in breach of Article 3 (art 3).

(B) Ill-Treatment alleged to have accompanied the use of the five techniques

...

2. Palace Barracks

173. The Commission came to the view that inhuman treatment had occurred at Palace Barracks in September, October and November 1971 in seven of the nine 'illustrative' cases it examined . . . It considered that these cases, combined with other indications, showed that there had been in these Barracks, in the autumn of 1971, a practice in connection with the interrogation of prisoners by members of the RUC which was inhuman treatment.

The British Government do not contest these conclusions; the Irish Government ask the Court to confirm them but also to supplement them in various respects.

(A) Autumn 1971

174. Insofar as the Commission has found that a practice of inhuman treatment was followed in the autumn of 1971 . . . The evidence before the Court reveals that, at the time in question, quite a large number of those held in custody at Palace Barracks were subjected to violence by members of the RUC. This violence, which was repeated violence occurring in the same place and taking similar forms, did not amount merely to isolated incidents; it definitely constituted a practice. It also led to intense suffering and to physical injury which on occasion was substantial; it thus fell into the category of inhuman treatment.

According to the applicant Government, the violence in question should also be classified, in some cases, as torture.

On the basis of the data before it, the Court does not share this view. Admittedly, the acts complained of often occurred during interrogation and, to this extent, were aimed at extracting confessions, the naming of others and/or information, but the severity of the suffering that they were capable of causing did not attain the particular level inherent in the notion of torture as understood by the Court (see paragraph 167 above). . . .

3. Other Places

178. According to the applicant Government, a practice or practices in breach of Article 3 (art 3) existed in Northern Ireland from 1971 to 1974, for example at Girdwood Park and at Ballykinler; this allegation is denied by the respondent Government.

The Commission was of the opinion that T 16 and T 7 had been victims of treatment that was both inhuman and degrading and T 11 of treatment that was inhuman: T 16 on 13 August 1971 at Girdwood Park, T 7 on 28 October 1971 in a street in Belfast and T 11 on 20 December 1971 at Albert Street Barracks, also in Belfast. However, the Commission considered that no practice in breach of Article 3 (art 3) had been established in relation to these cases, including the general conditions at Girdwood Park . . . and, further, that the conditions of detention at Ballykinler did not disclose a violation of that Article (art 3) (ibid).

(A) Ballykinler

. . .

180. The RUC, with the assistance of the army, used Ballykinler as a holding and interrogation centre for a few days early in August 1971. Some dozens of people arrested in the course of Operation Demetrius were held there in extreme discomfort and were made to perform irksome and painful exercises . . .

There was thus a practice rather than isolated incidents. The Court found confirmation of this in the judgment of 18 February 1972 in the Moore case.

181. The Court has to determine whether this practice violated Article 3 (art 3). Clearly, it would not be possible to speak of torture or inhuman treatment, but the question does arise whether there was not

degrading treatment. The Armagh County Court granted Mr Moore £300 by way of damages, the maximum amount it had jurisdiction to award. This fact shows that the matters of which Mr Moore complained were, if nothing else, contrary to the domestic law then in force in the United Kingdom. Furthermore, the way in which prisoners at Ballykinler were treated was characterised in the judgment of 18 February 1972 as not only illegal but also harsh. However, the judgment does not describe the treatment in detail; it concentrates mainly on reciting the evidence tendered by the witnesses and indicates that the judge rejected that given on behalf of the defence. The Compton Committee for its part considered that, although the exercises which detainees had been made to do involved some degree of compulsion and must have caused hardship, they were the result of lack of judgment rather than an intention to hurt or degrade.

To sum up, the RUC and the army followed at Ballykinler a practice which was discreditable and reprehensible but the Court does not consider that they infringed Article 3 (art 3).

(B) Miscellaneous places

182. There remain the various other places referred to by the Irish Government . . . The information before the Court concerning these places—for example the large number of cases in which compensation was paid by the British authorities and the many criminal or disciplinary sanctions imposed on members of the security forces . . . suggests that there must have been individual violations of Article 3 (art 3) in Northern Ireland over and above the breaches already noted by the Court. However, the Commission did not regard this information . . . as being sufficient to disclose a practice or practices in breach of Article 3 (art 3).

The Court shares this view. Admittedly, the evidence before the Court bears out the Commission's opinion . . . However, these were incidents insufficiently numerous and inter-connected to amount to a practice . . . the preventive measures taken by the United Kingdom . . . at first sight render hardly plausible, especially as regards the period after the introduction of direct rule (30 March 1972), if not the suggestion of individual violations of Article 3 (art 3)—on which the Court does not have to give a specific ruling . . . at least the suggestion of the continuation or commencement of a practice or practices in breach of that Article (art 3). Furthermore, anyone claiming to be the victim of a breach of Article 3 (art 3) in Northern Ireland is entitled to exercise the domestic remedies open to him (Article 26 the Convention) (art 26) and subsequently, if need be, to apply to the Commission whose competence to receive 'individual' petitions has been recognised by the United Kingdom (Article 25) (art 25); this in fact often happened. Finally, the findings made in connection with the five techniques and Palace Barracks, henceforth embodied in a binding judgment of the Court, provide a far from negligible guarantee against a return to the serious errors of former times.

In these circumstances, the interests protected by the Convention do not compel the Court to undertake lengthy researches that would delay the Court's decision . . . .

185. In conclusion, the Court does not find, as regards the places concerned, any practice in breach of Article 3 (art 3).

4. The Irish request for a consequential order

186. In a letter dated 5 January 1977, the applicant Government requested the Court to order that the respondent Government

— refrain from reintroducing the five techniques, as a method of interrogation or otherwise;

— proceed as appropriate, under the criminal law of the United Kingdom and the relevant disciplinary code, against those members of the security forces who have committed acts in breach of Article 3 (art 3) referred to in the Commission's findings and conclusions, and against those who condoned or tolerated them.

At the hearings, the applicant Government withdrew the first request following the solemn undertaking given on behalf of the United Kingdom Government on 8 February 1977 . . . on the other hand, the second request was maintained.

187. The Court does not have to consider in these proceedings whether its functions extend, in certain circumstances, to addressing consequential orders to Contracting States. In the present case, the Court finds that the sanctions available to it do not include the power to direct one of those States to institute criminal or disciplinary proceedings in accordance with its domestic law. ...

V. ON ARTICLE 50 (ART 50)

245. The President, acting on behalf of the Court, instructed the Registrar to ask the Agent of the Irish Government to indicate 'as soon as possible whether it would be correct to assume, particularly in the light' of certain passages in the Commission's decision on the admissibility of the application and in the verbatim report of the public hearings held in February 1977, 'that [his] Government [were not inviting] the Court, should it find a violation of the Convention, to afford just satisfaction within the meaning of Article 50 (art 50)'. This the Registrar did by letter of 8 August 1977. On 14 October 1977, the Agent of the applicant Government replied as follows:

> '... the applicant Government, while not wishing to interfere with the de bene esse jurisdiction of the Court, have not as an object the obtaining of compensation for any individual person and do not invite the Court to afford just satisfaction under Article 50 (art 50), of the nature of monetary compensation, to any individual victim of a breach of the Convention ....'

246. The Court accordingly considers that it is not necessary to apply Article 50 (art 50) in the present case.

FOR THESE REASONS, THE COURT

I. ON ARTICLE 3 (art 3)

1. holds unanimously that, although certain violations of Article 3 (art 3) were not contested, a ruling should nevertheless be given thereon;

2. holds unanimously that it has jurisdiction to take cognisance of the cases of alleged violation of Article 3 (art 3) to the extent that the applicant Government put them forward as establishing the existence of a practice;

3. holds by sixteen votes to one that the use of the five techniques in August and October 1971 constituted a practice of inhuman and degrading treatment, which practice was in breach of Article 3 (art 3);

4. holds by thirteen votes to four that the said use of the five techniques did not constitute a practice of torture within the meaning of Article 3 (art 3);

5. holds by sixteen votes to one that no other practice of ill-treatment is established for the unidentified interrogation centres;

6. holds unanimously that there existed at Palace Barracks in the autumn of 1971 a practice of inhuman treatment, which practice was in breach of Article 3 (art 3);

7. holds by fourteen votes to three that the last-mentioned practice was not one of torture within the meaning of Article 3 (art 3);

8. holds unanimously that it is not established that the practice in question continued beyond the autumn of 1971;

9. holds by fifteen votes to two that no practice in breach of Article 3 (art 3) is established as regards other places;

10. holds unanimously that it cannot direct the respondent State to institute criminal or disciplinary proceedings against those members of the security forces who have committed the breaches of Article 3 (art 3) found by the Court and against those who condoned or tolerated such breaches; ...

IV. ON ARTICLE 50 (art 50)

18. holds unanimously that it is not necessary to apply Article 50 (art 50) in the present case.

....

NOTES

1 The plenary Court was composed of President Balladore Pallieri and Judges: Wiarda, Zekia, Cremona, O'Donoghue, Pedersen, Thor Vilhjalmsson, Ryssdal, Ganshof Van Der Meersch, Fitzmaurice, Bindschedler-Robert, Evrigenis, Teitgen, Lagergren, Liesch, Gölcüklü, and Matscher.

2 Judge Zekia issued a separate opinion in which he set out his conception of torture.

Admittedly the word 'torture' included in Article 3 of the Convention is not capable of an exact and comprehensive definition. It is undoubtedly an aggravated form of inhuman treatment causing intense physical and/or mental suffering. Although the degree of intensity and the length of such suffering constitute the basic elements of torture, a lot of other relevant factors had to be taken into account. Such as: the nature of ill-treatment inflicted, the means and methods employed, the repetition and duration of such treatment, the age, sex and health condition of the person exposed to it, the likelihood that such treatment might injure the physical, mental and psychological condition of the person exposed and whether the injuries inflicted caused serious consequences for short or long duration are all relevant matters to be considered together and arrive at a conclusion whether torture has been committed.

It seems to me permissible, in ascertaining whether torture or inhuman treatment has been committed or not, to apply not only the objective test but also the subjective test.

As an example I can refer to the case of an elderly sick man who is exposed to a harsh treatment—after being given several blows and beaten to the floor, he is dragged and kicked on the floor for several hours. I would say without hesitation that the poor man has been tortured. If such treatment is applied on a wrestler or even a young athlete, I would hesitate a lot to describe it as inhuman treatment and I might regard it as mere rough handling.

3 Judge O'Donoghue, the judge of Irish nationality, dissented on a number of grounds.

For my part I agree with the unanimous finding of the Commission that the use of the five techniques constituted 'torture' in breach of the Convention. . . . One is not bound to regard torture as only present in a mediaeval dungeon where the appliances of rack and thumbscrew or similar devices were employed. Indeed in the present-day world there can be little doubt that torture may be inflicted in the mental sphere.

4 Judge Sir Gerald Fitzmaurice, the judge of British nationality, was the dissenter who did not consider that the five techniques constituted a practice of inhuman and degrading treatment. Generally, he took a more restrictive view of the scope of Article 3 than the Court.

It would be reasonable to suppose that, at the date when the Convention was framed, during the aftermath of war and atrocity, it would have been the severer forms of ill-treatment that the Parties would have had in mind.

Subjection to the five techniques was certainly harsh treatment, ill-treatment, maltreatment, and other descriptions could be found; but the 'inhuman' involves a totally different order or category of concept to which, in my opinion, the five techniques, even used in combination, do not properly belong . . . if standing someone against a wall in a strained position over a considerable period, or keeping him with a hood over his head for a certain time, amounts to 'inhuman' treatment, what language should be used to describe kicking a man in the groin, or placing him in a blacked-out cell in the company of a bevy of starving rats? . . .

In the present context it can be assumed that [degrading treatment] is, or should be, intended to denote something seriously humiliating, lowering as to human dignity, or disparaging, like having one's head shaved, being tarred and feathered, smeared with filth, pelted with muck, paraded naked in front of strangers, forced to eat excreta, deface the portrait of one's sovereign or head of State, or dress up in a way calculated to provoke ridicule or contempt . . .

. . . not only must a certain intensity of suffering be caused before the process can be called torture, but also that torture involves a wholly different order of suffering from what falls short of it. It amounts not to a mere difference of degree but to a difference of kind. If the five techniques are to be regarded as involving torture, how does one characterize eg having one's finger-nails torn out, being slowly impaled on a stake through the rectum, or roasted over an electric grid? . . .

5 Judge Evrigenis took a diametrically opposite approach to Judge Fitzmaurice:

The Court's interpretation in this case seems also to be directed to a conception of torture based on methods of inflicting suffering which have already been overtaken by the ingenuity of modern techniques of oppression. Torture no longer presupposes violence, a notion to which the judgment refers expressly and generically. Torture can be practised—and indeed is practised—by using subtle techniques developed in multidisciplinary laboratories which claim to be scientific. By means of new forms of suffering that have little in common with the physical pain caused by conventional torture it aims to bring about, even if only temporarily, the disintegration of an individual's personality, the shattering of his mental and psychological equilibrium and the crushing of his will. I should very much regret it if the definition of torture which emerges from the judgment could not cover these various forms of technologically sophisticated torture. Such an interpretation would overlook the current situation and the historical prospects in which the European Convention on Human Rights should be implemented.

6 For Judge Matscher:

the distinguishing feature of the notion of torture is the systematic, calculated (hence deliberate) and prolonged application of treatment causing physical or psychological suffering of a certain intensity, the aim of which may be to extort confessions, to obtain information or simply to break a person's will in order to compel him to do something he would not otherwise do, or again, to make a person suffer for other reasons (sadism, aggravation of a punishment, etc.).

7 While the above judicial opinions indicate the difficulties inherent in determining if a particular form of maltreatment falls within any of the specific categories prescribed by Article 3 (for further guidance on how these categories have been applied by the Court see the cases extracted and discussed below), the Court's judgment in *Ireland* emphasises some of the basic certainties of the Article. Hence a victim's conduct does not permit a State to subject him or her to treatment prohibited by Article 3 (even if the victim is a terrorist or a major criminal). Furthermore, the Article is not subject to exceptions and cannot be derogated from under Article 15 (even where there is a public emergency threatening the life of the nation).

8 The Court's elaboration of the idea of 'a practice' which is incompatible with the Convention and its importance in the determination of the admissibility of a complaint has been examined above, p 26.

9 The Commission has expressed the view that legal persons cannot claim to be the victims of a violation of Article 3. In *Verein Kontakt-Information-Therapie and Hagen v Austria* 57 DR 81 (1988), the first applicant was a private association which ran rehabilitation centres for young drug abusers. The domestic courts ordered two therapists (including the second applicant), employed by the association, to give evidence in criminal proceedings for alleged drug abuse against a former patient. The therapists, with the support of the first applicant, refused to disclose confidential information about the former patient. The courts fined the therapists

5,000AS each and obliged the association to collect the fine by attachment of their earnings. The applicants complained, inter alia, of a breach of Article 3. The Commission declared the application inadmissible noting that the rights protected by Article 3 '... are by their very nature not susceptible of being exercised by a legal person such as a private association.' (p 162) Also the treatment of the second applicant involving 'the obligation to give the required evidence did not attain the level of severity which is required by this provision.' (p 163) Conceptually it is nonsensical to characterize the treatment of a legal entity as 'torture' or 'inhuman'.

10 The Court has interpreted Article 3 so as to impose a duty on Member states to undertake an effective official investigation where a person makes an arguable claim that he or she has been subject to serious maltreatment by public officials. This procedural obligation mirrors the similar duty created by Article 2, in cases where a person has been killed in circumstances governed by that provision, (see above, p 124). In *Assenov and others v Bulgaria* 1998-VIII, the first applicant was a Bulgarian of Roma origin. In 1992, when he was 14 years old, he was caught gambling in a market square by an off-duty police officer. The officer arrested the applicant and took him to a nearby bus station, where the officer called for additional police help. The applicant's parents were working at the bus station and they sought his release. To show that he would punish the applicant, his father hit the applicant with a strip of plywood. Subsequently, the applicant claimed that he was, inter alia, beaten with truncheons by three police officers. The Commission did not find a breach of Article 3 (sixteen votes to one) as it was not able to establish who had caused the bruises on the applicant. The Court, unanimously, held that:

102.....where an individual raises an arguable claim that he has been seriously ill-treated by the police or other such agents of the State unlawfully and in breach of Article 3, that provision, read in conjunction with the State's general duty under Article 1 of the Convention to 'secure to everyone within their jurisdiction the rights and freedoms defined in ... [the] Convention', requires by implication that there should be an effective official investigation. This investigation, as with that under Article 2, should be capable of leading to the identification and punishment of those responsible (see, in relation to Article 2 of the Convention, the *McCann and Others v the United Kingdom* judgment of 27 September 1995, Series A No 324, p 49 ...). If this were not the case, the general legal prohibition of torture and inhuman and degrading treatment and punishment, despite its fundamental importance ... would be ineffective in practice and it would be possible in some cases for agents of the State to abuse the rights of those within their control with virtual impunity.

103. The Court notes that following [the applicant's mother's] complaint, the State authorities did carry out some investigation into the applicant's allegations. It is not, however, persuaded that this investigation was sufficiently thorough and effective to meet the above requirements of Article 3. In this respect it finds it particularly unsatisfactory that the ... investigator was prepared to conclude that Mr Assenov's injuries had been caused by his father ... despite the lack of any evidence that the latter had beaten his son with the force which would have been required to cause the bruising described in the medical certificate. Although this incident had taken place in public view at the bus station, and although, according to the statements of the police officers concerned, it was seen by approximately fifteen to twenty Roma and twenty bus drivers, no attempt appears to have been made to ascertain the truth through contacting and questioning these witnesses in the immediate aftermath of the incident, when memories would have been fresh. Instead, at that time a statement was taken from only one independent witness, who was unable to recall the events in question ...

104. The initial investigation carried out by the regional military prosecution office (RMPO) and that of the general military prosecution office (GMPO) were even more cursory. The Court finds it particularly

striking that the GMPO could conclude, without any evidence that Mr Assenov had not been compliant, and without any explanation as to the nature of the alleged disobedience, that 'even if the blows were administered on the body of the juvenile, they occurred as a result of disobedience to police orders' . . . To make such an assumption runs contrary to the principle under Article 3 that, in respect of a person deprived of his liberty, recourse to physical force which has not been made strictly necessary by his own conduct is in principle an infringement of his rights . . .

106. Against this background, in view of the lack of a thorough and effective investigation into the applicant's arguable claim that he had been beaten by police officers, the Court finds that there has been a violation of Article 3 of the Convention.

The articulation of this implicit duty of investigation is valuable for two reasons. First, it seeks to ensure that victims of unlawful maltreatment by public officials will be able to demand an effective domestic inquiry, potentially leading to the punishment of the culpable officials. Secondly, the Convention duty to conduct such an inquiry may act as a deterrent, to prevent ill-treatment, as officials may fear discovery and punishment when an inquiry is held.

Subsequently, the application and development of this positive obligation by the full-time Court has demonstrated some uncertainty. For example, in *Ilhan v Turkey*, judgment of 27 June 2000 (and see above p 106 [A2]), a Grand Chamber sought to discourage the consideration of such investigation obligations under Article 3.

89. In the *Assenov* case . . . the Court made a finding of a procedural breach of Article 3 due to the inadequate investigation made by the authorities into the applicant's complaints that he had been severely ill-treated by the police. It had regard, in doing so, to the importance of ensuring that the fundamental prohibition against torture and inhuman and degrading treatment and punishment be effectively secured in the domestic system.

90. However, in that case, the Court had been unable to reach any conclusion as to whether the applicant's injuries had in fact been caused by the police as he alleged. The inability to make any conclusive findings of fact in that regard derived at least in part from the failure of the authorities to react effectively to those complaints at the relevant time . . .

91. Procedural obligations have been implied in varying contexts under the Convention, where this has been perceived as necessary to ensure that the rights guaranteed under the Convention are not theoretical or illusory but practical and effective. The obligation to provide an effective investigation into the death caused, *inter alios*, by the security forces of the State was for this reason implied under Article 2 which guarantees the right to life (see *McCann and Others v the United Kingdom* . . .). This provision does however include the requirement that the right to life be 'protected by law'. It also may concern situations where the initiative must rest on the State for the practical reason that the victim is deceased and the circumstances of the death may be largely confined within the knowledge of state officials.

92. Article 3 however is phrased in substantive terms. Furthermore, though the victim of an alleged breach of this provision may be in a vulnerable position, the practical exigencies of the situation will often differ from cases of the use of lethal force or suspicious deaths. The Court considers that the requirement under Article 13 of the Convention for a person with an arguable claim of a violation of Article 3 to be provided with an effective remedy will generally provide both redress to the applicant and the necessary procedural safeguards against abuses by state officers. The Court's case-law establishes that the notion of effective remedy in this context includes the duty to carry out a thorough and effective investigation capable of leading to the identification and punishment of those responsible for any ill-treatment and permitting effective access for the complainant to the investigatory procedure, (see *Aksoy v Turkey* . . .). Whether it is appropriate or necessary to find a procedural breach of Article 3 will therefore depend on the circumstances of the particular case.

93. In the present case, the Court has found that the applicant has suffered torture at the hands of the security forces. His complaints concerning the lack of any effective investigation by the authorities into the cause of his injuries fall to be dealt with in this case under Article 13 of the Convention.

This judgment indicated that the Court would only consider complaints, under Article 3, that there had not been effective investigations into arguable claims of serious mal-treatment by State agents in exceptional cases. The Grand Chamber's judgment linked the Court's inability to make a conclusive finding of a breach of the substantive provisions of Article 3 with a willingness to hold that there had been a violation of the effective investigation obligation. But in later cases (including *Satik and Others v Turkey*, judgment of 10 October 2000 and *Toteva v Bulgaria*, judgment of 19 May 2004) unanimous Chambers have reached judgments finding States liable for both substantive and procedural (effective investigation) breaches of Article 3. Indeed, in the latter case the Court clearly stated that:

62. Where an individual raises an arguable claim that she has been seriously ill-treated by the police in breach of Article 3, that provision, read in conjunction with the State's general duty under Article 1 of the Convention to 'secure to everyone within their jurisdiction the rights and freedoms defined in . . . [the] Convention', requires by implication that there should be an effective official investigation. This investigation should be capable of leading to the identification and punishment of those responsible.

A united Chamber also found a breach of this effective investigation obligation in conjunction with Article 14 where the authorities had failed to examine possible racist motivation behind acts of police brutality: *Bekos and Koutropoulos v Greece*, judgment of 13 December 2005 (below, p 826).

A broadening of the scope of the effective investigation obligation under this Article to encompass complaints about serious (criminal) ill-treatment by private persons has been endorsed by a unanimous Chamber in *MC v Bulgaria*, judgment of 4 December 2003. The applicant was born in 1980 and she alleged that on 31 July and 1 August 1995, when she was 14 years and 10 months old (the age of consent in Bulgaria is 14), she had been raped by two men. She had been waiting to enter a local disco bar on the evening of 31 July 1995 when three men (P. aged 21, A. aged 20, and V. A. of unknown age) arrived in a car. The applicant knew P. and A. They invited her to go to another disco bar in a town some distance away and she agreed. On the return journey they went to a reservoir as A. wished to swim (the applicant subsequently stated that she had objected to the detour). She remained in the car whilst the men went for a swim. P. returned to the car and started kissing her. She claimed that she had refused his advances and asked him to leave her alone. She contended that he then held her hands against her back. She did not have the strength to physically resist or scream. P. then had sexual intercourse with her. P. later claimed that the applicant had consented to sex. She alleged that afterwards she had been very disturbed and cried. In the early morning of 1 August the group went to a nearby town where relatives of V.A. had a house. The applicant went into the house with A. and V.A. She asserted that A. had pushed her down on a bed she was sitting on and forced her to have sexual intercourse with him (she claimed that she did not have the strength to resist). The applicant's mother found her in the house and took her directly to the local hospital. The medical examiner confirmed that the applicant had recently lost her virginity. One day later P. visited the applicant's home and (according to the applicant and her mother) had asked for forgiveness and promised that he would marry the applicant when she became of age. The applicant's mother considered this a suitable arrangement. Subsequently, the applicant went out with P. the following evening. On 10 August the applicant's father returned home. The family then decided to file a complaint with the authorities.

During 11 August 1995 the applicant made a written statement to the police. Later that day the police arrested P. and A. The men claimed that she had consented to sex and were subsequently released by the police. On 14 November 1995 the District Prosecutor opened criminal proceedings concerning the alleged rapes and referred the case to an investigator. No action was taken by the authorities for one year and then, in November 1996, the investigator questioned the parties and one month later produced a report recommending the termination of proceedings against P. and A. (as there was no evidence that they had used threats or violence towards the applicant). The District Prosecutor, in January 1997, ordered a further investigation (as the initial one had not been objective and thorough). The investigator sought the advice of a psychiatrist and a psychologist regarding the behaviour of the applicant at the time of the alleged rapes. They considered that she was psychologically sound but of a credulous nature. She did not appear to have been in a state of shock during the events as she had a clear recollection of them. Her subsequent socializing with P. could be explained by the family's wish to present a socially acceptable image of the events. In February 1997 the investigator produced a second report which again proposed terminating the proceedings (he considered that the experts' opinions did not undermine his earlier finding that there was no evidence of force or threats having been used against the applicant). The District Prosecutor terminated the proceedings in March 1997 as he concluded that the use of force or threats by P. and A. had not been established beyond reasonable doubt and no resistance by the applicant or attempts to seek help from others had been established. Appeals to the Regional and Chief Public Prosecutor, by the applicant, were rejected.

The applicant contended that, *inter alia*, the authorities had not effectively investigated the events of 31 July and 1 August 1995. The Court held that:

151. In a number of cases Article 3 of the Convention gives rise to a positive obligation to conduct an official investigation (see *Assenov v Bulgaria* . . .). Such positive obligations cannot be considered in principle to be limited solely to cases of ill-treatment by State agents . . .

The Court went on to find that the Bulgarian authorities had insufficiently investigated the surrounding circumstances of the applicant's allegations and placed undue emphasis on the absence of 'direct' proof of rape (i.e. the lack of evidence that the applicant had 'resisted' the men). Consequently, a violation of the respondent State's positive obligations under Article 3 (and Article 8) were found to have occurred. This extension of *Assenov* is a further enhancement of the procedural protection given to individuals under Article 3. The perpetrators of serious ill-treatment should be sought via effective investigations whether they be State agents or private individuals. More generally, it is to be hoped that the Court becomes as consistently vigorous in the application of this obligation as it has been in respect of the corresponding duty under Article 2.

11   Although the vast majority of cases relying upon Article 3 involve allegations against the actions of state officials, the Court has interpreted this provision to require States to take positive steps, such as the enactment of appropriate criminal offences, to protect persons from being subject to Article 3 maltreatment by other private persons. In *A v UK* (1998) 27 EHRR 611, 1998-VI, the applicant was a young person born in 1984. In 1993 the applicant's stepfather was charged with assault occasioning actual bodily harm in respect of his beating of the applicant. The stepfather admitted that on several occasions he had caned (ie hit on the bottom and back of the legs with a garden cane) the applicant, because the latter was a difficult boy who did not respond to parental or school discipline. To secure a conviction it was necessary for the prosecution to prove that the stepfather's punishment was not reasonable. The jury, by a majority verdict, found the stepfather not guilty. The applicant complained to the

Commission alleging, inter alia, that the Government had failed to protect him from ill-treatment by his stepfather in breach of Article 3. The Commission was unanimous in upholding that claim. The Court was also unanimous in its judgment that the beating of the applicant was sufficiently serious to fall within the scope of Article 3 (note, the Court did not specify what element of Article 3 had been infringed, e.g. whether it was degrading or inhuman treatment or punishment).

22. It remains to be determined whether the State should be held responsible, under Article 3, for the beating of the applicant by his stepfather. The Court considers that the obligation on the High Contracting Parties under Article 1 of the Convention to secure to everyone within their jurisdiction the rights and freedoms defined in the Convention, taken together with Article 3, requires States to take measures designed to ensure that individuals within their jurisdiction are not subjected to torture or inhuman or degrading treatment or punishment, including such ill-treatment administered by private individuals (see, *mutatis mutandis*, the *HLR v France* judgment of 29 April 1997, *Reports* 1997-III, p 758, § 40). Children and other vulnerable individuals, in particular, are entitled to State protection, in the form of effective deterrence, against such serious breaches of personal integrity (see, *mutatis mutandis*, the *X and Y v Netherlands* judgment of 26 March 1985, Series A No 91, pp 11–13, §§ 21–7; the *Stubbings v UK* judgment of 22 October 1996, *Reports* 1996-IV, p 1505, §§ 62–4; and also the United Nations Convention on the Rights of the Child, Articles 19 and 37).

23. The Court recalls that under English law it is a defence to a charge of assault on a child that the treatment in question amounted to 'reasonable chastisement' . . . The burden of proof is on the prosecution to establish beyond reasonable doubt that the assault went beyond the limits of lawful punishment. In the present case, despite the fact that the applicant had been subjected to treatment of sufficient severity to fall within the scope of Article 3, the jury acquitted his stepfather, who had administered the treatment.

24. In the Court's view, the law did not provide adequate protection to the applicant against treatment or punishment contrary to Article 3. Indeed, the Government have accepted that this law currently fails to provide adequate protection to children and should be amended. In the circumstances of the present case, the failure to provide adequate protection constitutes a violation of Article 3 of the Convention.

The Court went on to award the applicant £10,000 compensation for non-pecuniary damage. Would it be stretching the reasoning in the above judgment too far to require States to protect individuals from Article 3 maltreatment inflicted by legal persons, e.g. what of dangerous or humiliating working conditions (the Court used the phrase 'ill-treatment administered by private individuals')?

The Children Act 2004, section 58, removed the defence of reasonable punishment in respect of battery of a child amounting to the offences of wounding and causing grievous bodily harm, assault occasioning actual bodily harm and cruelty to a person under the age of 16. Also, battery causing actual bodily harm to a child cannot be justified in any civil proceedings as constituting reasonable punishment. These limitations, which apply to England and Wales, the Scottish Parliament having previously introduced similar legislation, came into effect in January 2005. They were designed to allow parents to administer mild physical punishment to their children provided that bruising and cuts were not inflicted. Leading child protection charities, including the NSPCC, criticized the amendments because, *inter alia*, they believed that it was as wrong to hit a child as to hit an adult. Proponents of physical chastisement criticized the legislation as being impossible to police.

12   A unanimous Grand Chamber applied the reasoning in *A v UK* to a local authority's failure to take prompt action to safeguard children from serious neglect by their parents in *Z and*

Others v United Kingdom, judgment of 10 May 2001. The four applicants were siblings, born between 1982 and 1988. From 1987 their local social services department were aware of concerns about the children's welfare (reports from their neighbours and teachers indicated that the children were not being properly fed and cared for by their parents). In 1989 a social work assistant was assigned to help the parents care for the applicants (social services had concluded that the parents should be aided to look after the applicants rather than the latter being taken away from them into public care). In 1992 the applicants were taken into public care when their mother informed the social services that she could not cope and would batter them. Subsequently, the applicants complained that the social services had failed to protect them from being subject to inhuman and degrading treatment by their parents. The Grand Chamber held that:

73. ... The obligation on High Contracting Parties under Article 1 of the Convention to secure to everyone within their jurisdiction the rights and freedoms defined in the Convention, taken together with Article 3, requires States to take measures designed to ensure that individuals within their jurisdiction are not subjected to torture or inhuman or degrading treatment, including such ill-treatment administered by private individuals (see *A v the United Kingdom* judgment of 23 September 1998, *Reports of Judgments and Decisions* 1998-VI, § 22). These measures should provide effective protection, in particular, of children and other vulnerable persons and include reasonable steps to prevent ill-treatment of which the authorities had or ought to have had knowledge (*mutatis mutandis*, the *Osman v the United Kingdom* judgment of 28 October 1998, *Reports* 1998-VIII, § 116).

74. There is no dispute in the present case that the neglect and abuse suffered by the four child applicants reached the threshold of inhuman and degrading treatment ... This treatment was brought to the local authority's attention, at the earliest in October 1987. It was under a statutory duty to protect the children and had a range of powers available to them, including removal from their home. The children were however only taken into emergency care, at the insistence of the mother, in 30 April 1992. Over the intervening period of four and a half years, they had been subject in their home to what the child consultant psychiatrist who examined them referred to as horrific experiences. ... The Criminal Injuries Compensation Board had also found that the children had been subject to appalling neglect over an extended period and suffered physical and psychological injury directly attributable to a crime of violence ... The Court acknowledges the difficult and sensitive decisions facing social services and the important countervailing principle of respecting and preserving family life. The present case however leaves no doubt as to the failure of the system to protect these child applicants from serious, long-term neglect and abuse.

75. Accordingly, there has been a violation of Article 3 of the Convention.

Each of the applicants was awarded £32,000 non-pecuniary damages in respect of pain and suffering experienced through the local authority's failure to protect them from abuse. In addition they were awarded individual sums, ranging from £4,000 to £100,00 pecuniary damages to compensate them for their loss of employment opportunities and future medical costs attributable to their suffering.

The above judgment expanded the protective measures obligation upon States to encompass the speedy physical intervention of State officials to protect children known to be at risk of serious risk of harm from their parents/carers.

13 The Court has refused to accept that States are under a positive obligation to permit/aid the assisted suicide of a competent adult in the final stages of a terminal illness. In *Pretty v United Kingdom*, judgment of 29 April 2002 (and see above p 110 for the Article 2 aspects of her case), the applicant submitted that the domestic authorities were under an Article 3 duty to so protect her from death caused by motor neurone disease.

55. The Court cannot but be sympathetic to the applicant's apprehension that without the possibility of ending her life she faces the prospect of a distressing death. It is true that she is unable to commit suicide herself due to physical incapacity and that the state of law is such that her husband faces the risk of prosecution if he renders her assistance. Nonetheless, the positive obligation on the part of the State which is invoked in the present case would not involve the removal or mitigation of harm by, for instance, preventing any ill-treatment by public bodies or private individuals or providing improved conditions or care. It would require that the State sanction actions intended to terminate life, an obligation that cannot be derived from Article 3 of the Convention.

56. The Court therefore concludes that no positive obligation arises under Article 3 of the Convention to require the respondent Government either to give an undertaking not to prosecute the applicant's husband if he assists her to commit suicide or to provide a lawful opportunity for any other form of assisted suicide. There has, accordingly, been no violation of this provision.

This interpretation of Article 3 was a logical consequence of the Court's earlier ruling that there was no right to die recognized under Article 2 of the Convention.

Torture

Aksoy v Turkey 1996-VI 2287, (1996) 23 EHRR 553
European Court of Human Rights

The applicant was a Turkish national who had been born in 1963 and lived in South East Turkey. In 1994 he was shot dead, but his father continued his application before the Strasbourg authorities. The applicant alleged that on the night of 24 November 1992 approximately 20 police officers came to his home, accompanied by a detainee who claimed that the applicant was a member of the PKK (Workers' Party of Kurdistan). The applicant was arrested and taken to Mardin Anti-terrorist Headquarters. He was interrogated about the man who identified him (the applicant claimed not to know the man) and threatened with torture. On the second day of his detention the applicant claimed that he was stripped naked, his hands were tied behind his back and he was strung up by his arms in the form of torture known as 'Palestinian hanging'. While he was hanging, the police connected electrodes to his genitals and threw water over him while they electrocuted him. He was blindfolded during this torture, which lasted for about half an hour. During the next two days he was regularly beaten by the police officers. The applicant claimed that the hanging resulted in him losing the movement of his arms and hands. He asked to see a doctor, but his request was denied. He was released from detention on 10 December 1992 and no charges were brought against him. On the 15 December 1992 he was admitted to the Dicle University Hospital where he was diagnosed as suffering from bilateral radial paralysis (paralysis of both arms caused by nerve damage in the upper arms). He discharged himself on the 31 December 1992, taking his medical file with him. The applicant complained to the Commission alleging, inter alia, that he had suffered maltreatment in breach of Article 3 during his detention. Delegates of the Commission held evidentiary hearings in Turkey. The Commission found, inter alia, that there was no evidence that the applicant was suffering from any disability prior to his arrest. The medical evidence showed that he was suffering from radial paralysis in both arms (an uncommon condition, but consistent with having been subject to 'Palestinian hanging') soon after his release. The Government had supplied no alternative explanation for the applicant's injuries. There was insufficient evidence for the Commission to reach any conclusions regarding the applicant's contentions that he had been electrocuted and beaten. By fifteen votes to one the Commission expressed the opinion that there had been a breach of Article 3.

... THE MERITS ...

60. The applicant complained of having been ill-treated in different ways. He claimed to have been kept blindfolded during interrogation, which caused disorientation; to have been suspended from his arms, which were tied together behind his back ('Palestinian hanging'); to have been given electric shocks, which were exacerbated by throwing water over him; and to have been subjected to beatings, slapping and verbal abuse. He referred to medical evidence from Dicle University Medical Faculty which showed that he was suffering from a bilateral brachial plexus injury at the time of his admission to hospital ... This injury was consistent with Palestinian hanging.

He submitted that the treatment complained of was sufficiently severe as to amount to torture; it was inflicted with the purpose of inducing him to admit that he knew the man who had identified him.

In addition, he contended that the conditions in which he was detained ... and the constant fear of torture which he suffered while in custody amounted to inhuman treatment.

61. The Court, having decided to accept the Commission's findings of fact ... considers that where an individual is taken into police custody in good health but is found to be injured at the time of release, it is incumbent on the State to provide a plausible explanation as to the causing of the injury, failing which a clear issue arises under Article 3 of the Convention (art 3) (see the *Tomasi v France* judgment of 27 August 1992, Series A No 241-A, pp 40–1, paras 108–11 and the *Ribitsch v Austria* judgment of 4 December 1995, Series A No 336, p 26, para 34).

62. Article 3 (art 3), as the Court has observed on many occasions, enshrines one of the fundamental values of democratic society. Even in the most difficult of circumstances, such as the fight against organised terrorism and crime, the Convention prohibits in absolute terms torture or inhuman or degrading treatment or punishment. Unlike most of the substantive clauses of the Convention and of Protocols Nos. 1 and 4 (P1, P4), Article 3 (art 3) makes no provision for exceptions and no derogation from it is permissible under Article 15 (art 15) even in the event of a public emergency threatening the life of the nation (see the *Ireland v the United Kingdom* judgment of 18 January 1978, Series A No 25, p 65, para 163, the *Soering v United Kingdom* judgment of 7 July 1989, Series A No 161, p 34, para 88, and the *Chahal v United Kingdom* judgment of 15 November 1996, Reports 1996-V, p 1855, para 79).

63. In order to determine whether any particular form of ill-treatment should be qualified as torture, the Court must have regard to the distinction drawn in Article 3 (art 3) between this notion and that of inhuman or degrading treatment. As it has remarked before, this distinction would appear to have been embodied in the Convention to allow the special stigma of 'torture' to attach only to deliberate inhuman treatment causing very serious and cruel suffering (see the *Ireland v United Kingdom* judgment previously cited, p 66, para 167).

64. The Court recalls that the Commission found, inter alia, that the applicant was subjected to 'Palestinian hanging', in other words, that he was stripped naked, with his arms tied together behind his back, and suspended by his arms ...

In the view of the Court this treatment could only have been deliberately inflicted; indeed, a certain amount of preparation and exertion would have been required to carry it out. It would appear to have been administered with the aim of obtaining admissions or information from the applicant. In addition to the severe pain which it must have caused at the time, the medical evidence shows that it led to a paralysis of both arms which lasted for some time ... The Court considers that this treatment was of such a serious and cruel nature that it can only be described as torture.

In view of the gravity of this conclusion, it is not necessary for the Court to examine the applicant's complaints of other forms of ill-treatment.

In conclusion, there has been a violation of Article 3 of the Convention (art 3).

...

IV. APPLICATION OF ARTICLE 50 OF THE CONVENTION (ART 50)

110. Under Article 50 of the Convention (art 50),

> 'If the Court finds that a decision or a measure taken by a legal authority or any other authority of a High Contracting Party is completely or partially in conflict with the obligations arising from the . . . Convention, and if the internal law of the said Party allows only partial reparation to be made for the consequences of this decision or measure, the decision of the Court shall, if necessary, afford just satisfaction to the injured party.'

111. In his memorial the applicant claimed compensation for pecuniary damage caused by his detention and torture, consisting of medical expenses of 16,635,000 Turkish liras and loss of earnings amounting to £40 (sterling).

In addition he sought non-pecuniary damages of £25,000 . . .

He also requested payment of his legal fees and expenses which totalled £20,710.

112. The Government offered no comment either in its memorial or during the hearing before the Court as regards these claims.

A. DAMAGE

113. In view of the extremely serious violations of the Convention suffered by Mr Zeki Aksoy and the anxiety and distress that these undoubtedly caused to his father, who has continued with the application after his son's death . . . the Court has decided to award the full amounts of compensation sought as regards pecuniary and non-pecuniary damage. In total this amounts to 4,283,450,000 (four thousand two hundred and eighty-three million, four hundred and fifty thousand) Turkish liras (based on the rate of exchange applicable on the date of adoption of the present judgment).

B. COSTS AND EXPENSES

114. The Court considers that the applicant's claim for costs and expenses is reasonable and awards it in full, less the amounts received by way of legal aid from the Council of Europe which have not already been taken into account in the claim.

C. DEFAULT INTEREST

115. With regard to the sum awarded in Turkish liras, default interest is to be payable at the rate of 30% per annum, which, according to the information available to the Court, is the statutory rate of interest applicable in Turkey at the date of adoption of the present judgment.

As the award in respect of costs and expenses is to be made in pounds sterling, the Court considers it appropriate that interest should be payable on this sum at the rate of 8% per annum, which, according to the information available to it, is the statutory rate applicable in England and Wales at the date of adoption of the present judgment.

FOR THESE REASONS, THE COURT

2. Holds by eight votes to one that there has been a violation of Article 3 of theConvention (art 3); . . .

NOTES

1   The Court was composed of President Ryssdal and Judges: Thor Vilhjalmsson, Gölcüklü, Pettiti, De Meyer, Morenilla, Baka, Makarczyk, and Lohmus.

Judge Gölcüklü, the Judge of Turkish nationality, dissented because he did not believe that the applicant had exhausted domestic remedies. Therefore he was dispensed from considering the merits of the case.

This was the first case where the Court found maltreatment by State officials amounted to torture. Even where the applicant suffered such horrendous treatment the level of compensation payable under Article 50 was not that large in absolute terms. However, the relative value of the just satisfaction award was greater when compared with the applicant's wage level (he claimed only £40 for several weeks loss of earnings). The effect upon the international reputation of a member-State found responsible for acts of torture by the Court is, of course, very significant.

2   The Commission had found a practice of torture inflicted on political detainees by the Athens Security Police in the earlier *Greek Case* 12 *Yearbook of the European Convention on Human Rights* (1969). From 1965 until 1967 there was political instability and some public disorder in Greece. During 1967 senior military officers staged a *coup d'etat* and subsequently a number of persons were detained. Widespread allegations of serious ill-treatment of detainees by security officials were made. Denmark, Norway and Sweden lodged an inter-State application against Greece in respect of the latter's treatment of political detainees. A few days later the Netherlands also made a similar application. The Commission joined the cases and a Sub-Commission went to Greece to conduct on-the-spot inquiries and hear witnesses. The Commission's report found that:

Falanga or bastinado has been a method of torture known for centuries. It is the beating of the feet with a wooden or metal stick or bar which, if skilfully done, breaks no bones, makes no skin lesions, and leaves no permanent and recognisable marks, but causes intense pain and swelling of the feet. The use of *falanga* has been described in a variety of situations: on a bench or chair or on a car-seat; with or without shoes on. Sometimes water has been thrown over the feet and sometimes the victim has been made to run around between beatings. Victims have also been gagged. . . .

While *falanga* and severe beatings of all parts of the body are the commonest forms of torture or ill-treatment that appear in the evidence before the Sub-Commission, other forms have been described: for example, the application of electric shock, squeezing of the head in a vice, pulling out of hair from the head or pubic region, or kicking of the male genital organs, dripping water on the head, and intense noises to prevent sleep. . . .

there has since April 1967 been a practice of torture and ill-treatment by the Athens Security Police, Bouboulinas Street, of persons arrested for political reasons, and that:

(a)   this torture and ill-treatment has most often consisted in the application of '*falanga*' or severe beatings of all parts of the body;

(b)   its purpose has been the extraction of information including confessions concerning the political activities and associations of the victims and other persons considered to be subversive . . . (pp 499, 500 and 504)

The Commission's report was transmitted to the Committee of Ministers on 18 November 1969. On 12 December 1969 the Government of Greece denounced the Convention (under former Article 65 the denunciation would take effect after six months: ie 13 June 1970) and refused to participate in further proceedings relating to the report. Therefore, the Committee issued Resolution DH70(1):

. . . Agreeing with the opinion of the Commission, Decides:

(a)   that the Government of Greece has violated Articles 3 . . .

19. Considering that these circumstances and communications clearly established that the Greek Government is not prepared to comply with its continuing obligations under the Convention and thus with the system of collective protection of human rights established thereby, and that accordingly the

Committee of Ministers is called upon to deal with the case in conditions which are not precisely those envisaged in the Convention;

20. Concludes that in the present case there is no basis for further action under paragraph 2 of Article 32 (art 32–2) of the Convention;

21. Concludes that it must take a decision, in accordance with paragraph 3 of Article 32 (arts 32–3) of the Convention, about the publication of the report of the Commission;

22. Decides to make public forthwith the report drawn up by the Commission on the above-mentioned Applications;

23. Urges the Government of Greece to restore, without delay, human rights and fundamental freedoms in Greece, in accordance with the Convention . . .

24. Also urges the Government of Greece, in particular, to abolish immediately torture and other ill-treatment of prisoners and to release immediately persons detained under administrative order;

25. And accordingly resolves to follow developments in Greece in this respect.

In 1974 constitutional government was restored in Greece and the Government sought readmission to the Council of Europe. The *Greek Case* reveals both the strengths and weaknesses of the Convention system for protecting human rights. The undemocratic military Government withdrew from the Council of Europe rather than face censure under the Convention for its practice of torturing political opponents. Yet diplomatic pressures encouraged the restoration of democracy in Greece and readmission to the Council of Europe (together with a renewed accession to the Convention) within a few years.

3 A Grand Chamber of the Court found an act of rape committed by a State official on a detainee to be torture in *Aydin v Turkey* (1997) 25 EHRR 251, 1997-VI 1889. The applicant, who was seventeen at the time of her detention, had never travelled outside her village before her arrest by the security forces. On the 29 June 1993 she alleged that village guards and a gendarme arrived at her village and arrested her, her father and her sister-in-law. They were questioned about visits to her family home by members of the PKK (as in *Aksoy* above). The three of them were then blindfolded and taken to the gendarmerie headquarters in Derik. The applicant was taken alone into a room, stripped, put in a car tyre and spun round, beaten, sprayed with cold water and raped by a man in military clothing. The applicant and her relatives were released from custody on 2 July 1993. She complained to the Commission alleging, inter alia, a breach of Article 3. Delegates of the Commission visited Turkey to hear witnesses and the Commission found the applicant's allegations to be established beyond reasonable doubt. By twenty-six votes to one the Commission expressed the opinion that there had been a violation of Article 3. A majority of the Court (fourteen votes to seven) determined that:

83. While being held in detention the applicant was raped by a person whose identity has still to be determined. Rape of a detainee by an official of the State must be considered to be an especially grave and abhorrent form of ill-treatment given the ease with which the offender can exploit the vulnerability and weakened resistance of his victim. Furthermore, rape leaves deep psychological scars on the victim which do not respond to the passage of time as quickly as other forms of physical and mental violence. The applicant also experienced the acute physical pain of forced penetration, which must have left her feeling debased and violated both physically and emotionally.

84. The applicant was also subjected to a series of particularly terrifying and humiliating experiences while in custody at the hands of the security forces at Derik gendarmerie headquarters having regard to her sex and youth and the circumstances under which she was held. She was detained over a period

of three days during which she must have been bewildered and disoriented by being kept blindfolded, and in a constant state of physical pain and mental anguish brought on by the beatings administered to her during questioning and by the apprehension of what would happen to her next. She was also paraded naked in humiliating circumstances thus adding to her overall sense of vulnerability and on one occasion she was pummelled with high-pressure water while being spun around in a tyre.

85. The applicant and her family must have been taken from their village and brought to Derik gendarmerie headquarters for a purpose, which can only be explained on account of the security situation in the region . . . and the need of the security forces to elicit information. The suffering inflicted on the applicant during the period of her detention must also be seen as calculated to serve the same or related purposes.

86. Against this background the Court is satisfied that the accumulation of acts of physical and mental violence inflicted on the applicant and the especially cruel act of rape to which she was subjected amounted to torture in breach of Article 3 of the Convention. Indeed the Court would have reached this conclusion on either of these grounds taken separately.

87. In conclusion, there has been a violation of Article 3 of the Convention. . . .

The Court went on to award the applicant £25,000 just satisfaction for non-pecuniary damage, 'having regard to the seriousness of the violation of the Convention suffered by the applicant while in custody and the enduring psychological harm which she may be considered to have suffered on account of being raped . . .'. (para 131) The dissenters did not consider that the applicant's allegations had been established with sufficient proof. As a matter of law the Court's decision clearly defines the rape of detainees as a particularly serious breach of Article 3.

4   A Grand Chamber of the full-time Court, unanimously, adopted a new approach to assessing whether particular maltreatment should be classified as torture in *Selmouni v France* (1999) 29 EHRR 403. The implication of the Court's statement that in the future 'greater firmness in assessing breaches' (para 101, below) is required, suggests that the Court will be more willing to categorize serious acts of maltreatment as torture. In that case the applicant was a Netherlands and Moroccan national (born in 1942) who had been arrested by the police in France, after he was implicated in drug-trafficking by a fellow suspect. The applicant was held in police custody from 8.30 pm on 25 November 1991 until 7 pm on 28 November 1991. During his detention he was questioned by a number of officers from the Seine-Saint-Denis Criminal Investigation Department. The applicant claimed that during his detention the investigating officers subjected him to a number of forms of serious maltreatment including: repeated assaults (with fists, kicks and a baseball bat), pulling of his hair, forcing the applicant to kneel down in front of a woman while being verbally abused by an officer, having an officer urinate over him, being threatened with a blowlamp and having a truncheon inserted into his anus. Later the applicant was convicted of drugs offences and sentenced to thirteen years' imprisonment and fined 24 million Francs. The applicant complained to the authorities about the abuse that he had suffered while being questioned and medical reports were obtained. These confirmed that he had many bruises and wounds over his body. However, by the time the applicant alleged that he had been sexually abused by the officers it was too late for medical investigations to establish the truth of his claim. Eventually several police officers were convicted of assaulting and wounding the applicant (the senior officer in charge was sentenced to eighteen months' imprisonment—of which fifteen months were suspended, another officer was given a fifteen months suspended sentence and another a twelve months' suspended sentence). The applicant complained to the Commission alleging, inter alia, a breach of Article 3. The Commission was unanimous in finding that the deliberate maltreatment of

the applicant was of such a serious and cruel nature as to be classified as torture. The Court held that:

96. In order to determine whether a particular form of ill-treatment should be qualified as torture, the Court must have regard to the distinction, embodied in Article 3, between this notion and that of inhuman or degrading treatment. As the European Court has previously found, it appears that it was the intention that the Convention should, by means of this distinction, attach a special stigma to deliberate inhuman treatment causing very serious and cruel suffering (see the *Ireland v United Kingdom* judgment . . .).

97. The United Nations Convention against Torture and Other Cruel, Inhuman or Degrading Treatment or Punishment, which came into force on 26 June 1987, also makes such a distinction, as can be seen from Articles 1 and 16:

Article 1:

'1. For the purposes of this Convention, the term "torture" means any act by which severe pain or suffering, whether physical or mental, is intentionally inflicted on a person for such purposes as obtaining from him or a third person information or a confession, punishing him for an act he or a third person has committed or is suspected of having committed, or intimidating or coercing him or a third person, or for any reason based on discrimination of any kind, when such pain or suffering is inflicted by or at the instigation of or with the consent or acquiescence of a public official or other person acting in an official capacity.

. . .

Article 16, paragraph 1:

'1. Each State Party shall undertake to prevent in any territory under its jurisdiction other acts of cruel, inhuman or degrading treatment or punishment which do not amount to torture as defined in Article 1, when such acts are committed by or at the instigation of or with the consent or acqui-escence of a public official or other person acting in an official capacity. In particular, the obligations contained in Articles 10, 11, 12 and 13 shall apply with the substitution for references to torture of references to other forms of cruel, inhuman or degrading treatment or punishment.'

98. The Court finds that all the injuries recorded in the various medical certificates . . . and the applicant's statements regarding the ill-treatment to which he had been subjected while in police custody . . . establish the existence of physical and—undoubtedly (notwithstanding the regrettable failure to order a psychological report on Mr Selmouni after the events complained of)—mental pain and suffering. The course of the events also shows that pain and suffering were inflicted on the applicant intentionally for the purpose of, inter alia, making him confess to the offence which he was suspected of having committed. Lastly, the medical certificates annexed to the case file show clearly that the numerous acts of violence were directly inflicted by police officers in the performance of their duties.

99. The acts complained of were such as to arouse in the applicant feelings of fear, anguish and inferiority capable of humiliating and debasing him and possibly breaking his physical and moral resistance. The Court therefore finds elements which are sufficiently serious to render such treatment inhuman and degrading (see the *Ireland v UK* judgment, p 66, § 167, and the *Tomasi v France* judgment p 42, § 115). In any event, the Court reiterates that, in respect of a person deprived of his liberty, recourse to physical force which has not been made strictly necessary by his own conduct diminishes human dignity and is in principle an infringement of the right set forth in Article 3 (see the *Ribitsch v Austria* judgment of 4 December 1995, Series A No 336, p 26, § 38) . . . .

100. In other words, it remains to establish in the instant case whether the 'pain or suffering' inflicted on Mr Selmouni can be defined as 'severe' within the meaning of Article 1 of the United Nations

Convention. The Court considers that this 'severity' is, like the 'minimum severity' required for the application of Article 3, in the nature of things, relative; it depends on all the circumstances of the case, such as the duration of the treatment, its physical or mental effects and, in some cases, the sex, age and state of health of the victim, etc.

101. The Court has previously examined cases in which it concluded that there had been treatment which could only be described as torture (see the *Aksoy v Turkey* judgment 2279, § 64, and the *Aydin v Turkey* judgment, pp 1892–3, §§ 83–4 and 86). However, having regard to the fact that the Convention is a 'living instrument which must be interpreted in the light of present-day conditions' (see, among other authorities, the following judgments: *Tyrer v UK*, 25 April 1978, Series A No 26, p 15, § 31; *Soering v UK*, p 40, § 102; and *Loizidou v Turkey*, 23 March 1995, Series A No 310, p 26, § 71), the Court considers that certain acts which were classified in the past as 'inhuman and degrading treatment' as opposed to 'torture' could be classified differently in future. It takes the view that the increasingly high standard being required in the area of the protection of human rights and fundamental liberties correspondingly and inevitably requires greater firmness in assessing breaches of the fundamental values of democratic societies.

102. The Court is satisfied that a large number of blows were inflicted on Mr Selmouni. Whatever a person's state of health, it can be presumed that such intensity of blows will cause substantial pain. Moreover, a blow does not automatically leave a visible mark on the body. However, it can be seen from Dr Garnier's medical report of 7 December 1991 . . . that the marks of the violence Mr Selmouni had endured covered almost all of his body.

103. The Court also notes that the applicant was dragged along by his hair; that he was made to run along a corridor with police officers positioned on either side to trip him up; that he was made to kneel down in front of a young woman to whom someone said 'Look, you're going to hear somebody sing'; that one police officer then showed him his penis, saying 'Look, suck this', before urinating over him; and that he was threatened with a blowlamp and then a syringe . . . Besides the violent nature of the above acts, the Court is bound to observe that they would be heinous and humiliating for anyone, irrespective of their condition.

104. The Court notes, lastly, that the above events were not confined to any one period of police custody during which—without this in any way justifying them—heightened tension and emotions might have led to such excesses. It has been clearly established that Mr Selmouni endured repeated and sustained assaults over a number of days of questioning . . .

105. Under these circumstances, the Court is satisfied that the physical and mental violence, considered as a whole, committed against the applicant's person caused 'severe' pain and suffering and was particularly serious and cruel. Such conduct must be regarded as acts of torture for the purposes of Article 3 of the Convention.

3. CONCLUSION

There has therefore been a violation of Article 3 . . .

Having regard to the 'extreme seriousness of the violations of the Convention of which Mr Selmouni was a victim' (para 123), the Court awarded him 500,000 Francs just satisfaction in respect of personal and non-pecuniary injury.

This was the first case in which the Court (both in its part-time and current form) found a European Union Member state to have committed acts of torture. The judgment indicates the evidential necessity for victims of maltreatment by officials to obtain expeditious and comprehensive medical reports of their physical and mental conditions. If such reports are not obtained the Court is constrained in its ability to determine the occurrence and effects of the maltreatment.

5 A Grand Chamber cited *Selmouni* when it unanimously found that the physical assaults on a young man by gendarmes, which resulted in him suffering considerable permanent brain damage, combined with a thirty-six hour delay in taking him to a hospital amounted to torture in *Ilhan v Turkey*, judgment of 27 June 2000 (see also above p 156 [A3]).

6 Another Grand Chamber, by sixteen votes to one, found Russia liable for, *inter alia*, the torture of the first applicant by the separatist regime of the 'Moldavian Republic of Transdniestria' (MRT) in *Ilascu and Others v Moldova and Russia* (above p 69 [Art. 1]).

434. The applicant was sentenced to death on 9 December 1993 and detained until his release on 5 May 2001.

The Court reiterates that the Convention is not binding on Contracting States save in respect of events that have occurred since its entry into force, the relevant dates being 12 September 1997 for Moldova and 5 May 1998 for the Russian Federation. However, in order to assess the effect on the applicant of his conditions of detention, which remained more or less identical throughout the time he spent in prison, the Court may also take into consideration the whole of the period in question, including that part of it which preceded the Convention's entry into force with regard to each of the respondent States.

435. During the very long period he spent on death row the applicant lived in the constant shadow of death, in fear of execution. Unable to exercise any remedy, he lived for many years, including the time after the Convention's entry into force, in conditions of detention apt to remind him of the prospect of his sentence being enforced.

In particular, the Court notes that after sending a letter to the Moldovan Parliament in March 1999 Mr Ilaşcu was savagely beaten by the warders at Tiraspol Prison, who threatened to kill him. After that incident he was denied food for two days and light for three.

As to the mock executions which took place before the Convention's entry into force, there is no doubt that the effect of such barbaric acts was to increase the anxiety felt by the applicant throughout his detention about the prospect of his execution.

436. The anguish and suffering he felt were aggravated by the fact that the sentence had no legal basis or legitimacy for Convention purposes. The 'Supreme Court of the MRT' which passed sentence on Mr Ilaşcu was set up by an entity which is illegal under international law and has not been recognised by the international community. That 'court' belongs to a system which can hardly be said to function on a constitutional and legal basis reflecting a judicial tradition compatible with the Convention. That is evidenced by the patently arbitrary nature of the circumstances in which the applicants were tried and convicted, as they described them in an account which has not been disputed by the other parties and as described and analysed by the institutions of the OSCE.

437. The judgment of the Supreme Court of Moldova setting aside the applicant's conviction confirmed the unlawful and arbitrary nature of the judgment of 9 December 1993.

438. As regards the applicant's conditions of detention while on death row, the Court notes that Mr Ilaşcu was detained for eight years, from 1993 until his release in May 2001, in very strict isolation: he had no contact with other prisoners, no news from the outside—since he was not permitted to send or receive mail—and no right to contact his lawyer or receive regular visits from his family. His cell was unheated, even in severe winter conditions, and had no natural light source or ventilation. The evidence shows that Mr Ilaşcu was also deprived of food as a punishment and that in any event, given the restrictions on receiving parcels, even the food he received from outside was often unfit for consumption. The applicant could take showers only very rarely, often having to wait several months between one and the next. On this subject the Court refers to the conclusions in the report produced by the CPT following its visit to Transdniestria in 2000, in which it described isolation for so many years as indefensible.

The applicant's conditions of detention had deleterious effects on his health, which deteriorated in the course of the many years he spent in prison. Thus, he did not receive proper care, having been deprived of regular medical examinations and treatment and dietetically appropriate meals. In addition, owing to the restrictions on receiving parcels, he could not be sent medicines and food to improve his health.

439. The Court notes with concern the existence of rules granting a discretionary power in relation to correspondence and prison visits, exercisable by both prison warders and other authorities, and emphasises that such rules are arbitrary and incompatible with the appropriate and effective safeguards against abuses which any prison system in a democratic society must put in place. Moreover, in the present case, such rules made the applicant's conditions of detention even harsher.

440. The Court concludes that the death sentence imposed on the applicant coupled with the conditions he was living in and the treatment he suffered during his detention after ratification, account being taken of the state he was in after spending several years in those conditions before ratification, were particularly serious and cruel and must accordingly be considered acts of torture within the meaning of Article 3 of the Convention.

There has therefore been a failure to observe the requirements of Article 3.

441. As Mr Ilaşcu was detained at the time when the Convention came into force with regard to the Russian Federation, on 5 May 1998, the latter is responsible, for the reasons set out above . . . on account of his conditions of detention, the treatment inflicted on him and the suffering caused to him in prison.

Mr Ilaşcu was released in May 2001 and it is only from that date on that Moldova's responsibility is engaged on account of the acts complained of for failure to discharge its positive obligations . . . Consequently, there has been no violation of Article 3 of the Convention by Moldova with regard to Mr Ilaşcu.

442. In conclusion, the violation of Article 3 of the Convention with regard to Mr Ilaşcu is imputable only to the Russian Federation.

The above findings are a truly appalling catalogue of abuse.

7 A unanimous Chamber found that the forced-feeding of a mentally competent remand prisoner, who was engaging in a hunger strike (to protest about the length and conditions of his detention), constituted torture in *Nevmerzhitsky v Ukraine*, judgment of 5 April 2005.

94. The Court reiterates that a measure which is of therapeutic necessity from the point of view of established principles of medicine cannot in principle be regarded as inhuman and degrading. The same can be said about force-feeding that is aimed at saving the life of a particular detainee who consciously refuses to take food. The Convention organs must nevertheless satisfy themselves that the medical necessity has been convincingly shown to exist (see *Herczegfalvy v Austria*, judgment of 24 September 1992, Series A No 244, p 26, § 83). Furthermore, the Court must ascertain that the procedural guarantees for the decision to force-feed are complied with. Moreover, the manner in which the applicant is subjected to force-feeding during the hunger strike shall not trespass the threshold of a minimum level of severity envisaged by the Court's case law under Article 3 of the Convention. The Court will examine these elements in turn.

95. At the outset, the Court notes that the applicant did not claim that he should have been left without any food or medicine regardless of the possible lethal consequences. However, he claimed that there had been no medical necessity to force-feed him, as there had been no medical examinations, relevant tests or other documents that sufficiently proved that necessity. He claimed that the decision to subject him to force-feeding had been based on the analysis of the acetone level in his urine. He further maintained that the force-feeding had been aimed at his humiliation and punishment, as its purpose

had been to make him stop the hunger strike and, in the event of his refusal, to subject him to severe physical suffering.

96. The Court observes the statement of the Government with regard to the satisfactory state of health of the applicant in detention ... In view of the failure of the Government to provide 'the written report of the medical commission establishing a life-threatening decrease in the state of health of the applicant' and 'the decision of the head of the [detention] institution' that were obligatory under the decree of 4 March 1992 ... the Court concludes that the Government have not demonstrated that there was a 'medical necessity' established by the domestic authorities to force-feed the applicant. It can only therefore be assumed that the force-feeding was arbitrary. Procedural safeguards were not respected in the face of the applicant's conscious refusal to take food, when dispensing forced treatment against his will. Accordingly, it cannot be said that the authorities acted in the applicant's best interests in subjecting him to force-feeding.

97. As to the manner in which the applicant was fed, the Court assumes, in view of the submissions of the parties, that the authorities complied with the manner of force-feeding prescribed by decree. However, in themselves the restraints applied—handcuffs, a mouth-widener, a special rubber tube inserted into the food channel—in the event of resistance, with the use of force, could amount to torture within the meaning of Article 3 of the Convention, if there is no medical necessity ...

98. In the instant case, the Court finds that the force-feeding of the applicant, without any medical justification having been shown by the Government, using the equipment foreseen in the decree, but resisted by the applicant, constituted treatment of such a severe character warranting the characterisation of torture.

99. In the light of the above, the Court considers that there has been a violation of Article 3 of the Convention.

Consequently, States must be able to demonstrate that there is a medical necessity to force-feed a detainee in order to preserve his/her life. The respondent State had not provided evidence of the existence of such dire circumstances at the time the decision was made to force-feed the applicant. Furthermore, the relevant domestic procedure, specified in a Decree of the Ministry of Internal Affairs, governing the resort to force-feeding of detainees had not been complied with. For an examination, by the original Court, of the lawfulness under the Convention of the forced-feeding of a mentally ill detainee see *Herczegfalvy v Austria*, A.244, below p 186.

8   The interrogation of a detainee, a young off-duty police officer, involving the use of a device that sent an electrical current to his ears which caused him such anguish that he attempted to commit suicide, by jumping out of a second floor window at the police station, was found to constitute torture by a unanimous Chamber in *Mikheyev v Russia*, judgment of 26 January 2006.

135. ... the Court is prepared to accept that while in custody the applicant was seriously ill-treated by agents of the State, with the aim of extracting a confession or information about the offences of which he was suspected. The ill-treatment inflicted on him caused such severe physical and mental suffering that the applicant attempted suicide, resulting in a general and permanent physical disability. In view of the Convention case-law in this respect and in particular the criteria of severity and the purpose of the ill-treatment (see, among other authorities, *Ilhan v Turkey* [GC], No 22277/93, § 85, ECHR 2000-VII), the Court concludes that the ill-treatment at issue amounted to torture within the meaning of Article 3 of the Convention.

Taking account of the fact that he had broken his spine and was subsequently confined to a wheel chair the Chamber awarded him 130,000 euros compensation for pecuniary damage (loss of earnings and medical care) and 120,000 euros non-pecuniary damage.

Inhuman treatment

Physical violence

As we have already seen in *Ireland v UK* (above, p 145), the subjection of detainees to physical violence by State officials can amount to inhuman treatment within Article 3. For example, the kicking and punching of detainees by members of the security forces at Palace Barracks was determined to be inhuman treatment by the Court, because the maltreatment led to intense suffering and physical injury (para 174).

Tomasi v France A.241-A (1992) 15 EHRR 1
European Court of Human Rights

In February 1982 the Corsican National Liberation Front (a movement seeking independence from France) claimed responsibility for an armed attack upon a Foreign Legion rest centre in which one soldier was killed and another seriously injured. The applicant, a shopkeeper resident in the same region of Corsica, was an active member of a Corsican political organization. The police suspected the applicant of having taken part in the attack on the rest centre and on 23 March 1983 they arrested him. He was taken to Bastia police station and held for questioning until 25 March. During this period of detention the applicant claimed that the police, inter alia, knocked his head against a wall, hit him in the stomach, slapped and kicked him, and left him naked in front of a window for several hours. Medical reports confirmed that he had bruises on different parts of his body. Subsequently he was remanded in custody, by an investigating judge, and in October 1988 he was acquitted of the charge of murder. The applicant complained to the Commission alleging, inter alia, that he had suffered inhuman and degrading treatment by the police. The Commission, by twelve votes to two, found a breach of Article 3.

B. MERITS OF THE COMPLAINT

107. In the circumstances of this case Mr Tomasi's complaint raises two issues, which are separate although closely linked: firstly that of the causal connection between the treatment which the applicant allegedly suffered during his police custody and the injuries noted subsequently by the investigating judge and the doctors; and, secondly and if necessary, the gravity of the treatment inflicted.

1. THE CAUSAL CONNECTION BETWEEN THE TREATMENT COMPLAINED OF AND THE INJURIES NOTED

108. According to the applicant, the observation made on 25 March 1983 by the Bastia investigating judge and the reports drawn up by various doctors at the end of his police custody . . . confirmed his statements, even though it was, he said, to be regretted that the prison authorities had failed to communicate the X-rays effected on 2 April 1983 at Bastia Hospital . . . His body had borne marks which had only one origin, the ill-treatment inflicted on him for a period of forty odd hours by some of the police-officers responsible for his interrogation: he had been slapped, kicked, punched and given forearm blows, made to stand for long periods and without support, hands handcuffed behind the back; he had been spat upon, made to stand naked in front of an open window, deprived of food, threatened with a firearm and so on.

109. The Government acknowledged that they could give no explanation as to the cause of the injuries, but they maintained that they had not resulted from the treatment complained of by Mr Tomasi. The medical certificates showed, in their opinion, that the slight bruises and abrasions noted were totally inconsistent with the acts of violence described by the applicant; the certificate of the Chief Medical Officer of Bastia Prison of 4 July 1989 had been drawn up a long time after the event and was in complete contradiction with the earlier certificates. The chronology of the interrogation sessions, which had not been contested by the applicant, in no way corresponded to the allegations. Finally, the five other persons in police custody at the time had neither noticed nor heard anything, and although one of them referred to Mr Tomasi's losing a tooth, this fact was not mentioned by a doctor until six years later. In short, a clear doubt subsisted, which excluded any presumption of the existence of a causal connection.

110. Like the Commission, the Court bases its view on several considerations.

In the first place, no one has claimed that the marks noted on the applicant's body could have dated from a period prior to his being taken into custody or could have originated in an act carried out by the applicant against himself or again as a result of an escape attempt.

In addition, at his first appearance before the investigating judge, he drew attention to the marks which he bore on his chest and his ear; the judge took note of this and immediately designated an expert...

Furthermore, four different doctors—one of whom was an official of the prison authorities—examined the accused in the days following the end of his police custody. Their certificates contain precise and concurring medical observations and indicate dates for the occurrence of the injuries which correspond to the period spent in custody on police premises...

111. This conclusion makes it unnecessary for the Court to inquire into the other acts which it is claimed the officials in question carried out.

2. THE GRAVITY OF THE TREATMENT COMPLAINED OF

112. Relying on the *Ireland v UK* judgment of 18 January 1978 (Series A No 25), the applicant maintained that the blows which he had received constituted inhuman and degrading treatment. They had not only caused him intense physical and mental suffering; they had also aroused in him feelings of fear, anguish and inferiority capable of humiliating him and breaking his physical or moral resistance...

113. The Commission stressed the vulnerability of a person held in police custody and expressed its surprise at the times chosen to interrogate the applicant. Although the injuries observed might appear to be relatively slight, they nevertheless constituted outward signs of the use of physical force on an individual deprived of his liberty and therefore in a state of inferiority. The treatment had therefore been both inhuman and degrading.

114. According to the Government, on the other hand, the 'minimum level of severity' required by the Court's case-law (see the *Ireland v the UK* judgment cited above and the *Tyrer v the UK* judgment of 25 April 1978, Series A No 26) had not been attained. It was necessary to take into account not only that the injuries were slight, but also the other facts of the case: Mr Tomasi's youth and good state of health, the moderate length of the interrogations (fourteen hours, three of which were during the night), 'particular circumstances' obtaining in Corsica at the time and the fact that he had been suspected of participating in a terrorist attack which had resulted in the death of one man and grave injuries to another. In the Government's view, the Commission's interpretation of Article 3 (art 3) in this case was based on a misunderstanding of the aim of that provision.

115. The Court cannot accept this argument... It finds it sufficient to observe that the medical certificates and reports, drawn up in total independence by medical practitioners, attest to the large number of blows inflicted on Mr Tomasi and their intensity; these are two elements which are sufficiently

serious to render such treatment inhuman and degrading. The requirements of the investigation and the undeniable difficulties inherent in the fight against crime, particularly with regard to terrorism, cannot result in limits being placed on the protection to be afforded in respect of the physical integrity of individuals.

3. CONCLUSION

116. There has accordingly been a violation of Article 3 (art 3)....

FOR THESE REASONS, THE COURT UNANIMOUSLY

Holds that there has been a violation of . . . Article 3 . . .

NOTES

1   The Court was composed of President Ryssdal and Judges: Bernhardt, Gölcüklü, Matscher, Pettiti, Russo, Spielmann, De Meyer and Morenilla.

The Court awarded the applicant 700,000 Francs just satisfaction in respect of pecuniary and non-pecuniary damage (he had already received 300,00 Francs compensation from the French authorities).

The judgment indicates that the infliction of significant physical violence on a detainee by State officials, even where no serious long-term injuries are caused, will be classified as inhuman treatment. Indeed, Judge De Meyer went further in his Concurring Opinion where he expressed the view that:

Any use of physical force in respect of a person deprived of his liberty which is not made strictly necessary as a result of his own conduct (for instance in the case of an escape attempt or an act carried out against himself..) violates human dignity and must therefore be regarded as a breach of the right guaranteed under Article 3 of the Convention.

2   In the later case of *Ribitsch v Austria* A.336 (1995) 21 EHRR 573, the Court stated that although: ' . . . in principle it is not its task to substitute its own assessment of the facts for that of the domestic courts . . . it is not bound by the domestic courts' findings any more than it is by those of the Commission. . . . Its vigilance must be heightened when dealing with rights such as those set forth in Article 3 of the Convention, which prohibits in absolute terms torture and inhuman or degrading treatment or punishment, irrespective of the victim's conduct.' (para 32) A majority of the Court, six votes to three, went on to uphold the applicant's claim of inhuman and degrading treatment even though the relevant police officers had been acquitted by the Austrian courts. The applicant had been arrested and his home searched, 0.5g. of hashish was found, by members of the Security Branch of the Vienna Federal Police Authority who suspected that he had supplied heroin to persons who had died of overdoses. Ribitsch was held in custody at the headquarters of the Security Branch from 12.30 pm on 31 May 1988 until 9.30 am on 2 June 1988. According to Ribitsch while he was being questioned by the police several officers assaulted him (by punching him in the head, kidneys and on the arm; kicking him; pulling his hair and banging his head on the floor). After his release from police custody the applicant sought medical treatment. A hospital report confirmed that he had several bruises on his right arm. The media gave coverage to Ribitsch's allegations of police maltreatment and in response the police began an inquiry into the officers' conduct. In 1989 the District Criminal Court found one officer guilty of assault occasioning bodily harm (he was given a suspended sentence of two months' imprisonment) and acquitted two other

officers. The convicted officer appealed claiming that Ribitsch had sustained his injuries by falling against a car door while being transported during his detention. The Regional Criminal Court allowed the appeal, noting that Ribitsch had been fined for drug offences and was unemployed. The Constitutional Court found that the arrest of Ribitsch, the search of his home and his detention had been unlawful. However, Ribitsch's allegations of maltreatment by the police had not been proved beyond doubt. The applicant complained to the Commission asserting that he had been subject to inhuman and degrading treatment by the police. By ten votes to six the Commission reported that there had been a breach of Article 3. The Court determined that:

34. It is not disputed that Mr Ribitsch's injuries were sustained during his detention in police custody, which was in any case unlawful, while he was entirely under the control of police officers. Police Officer Markl's acquittal in the criminal proceedings by a court bound by the principle of presumption of innocence does not absolve Austria from its responsibility under the Convention. The Government were accordingly under an obligation to provide a plausible explanation of how the applicant's injuries were caused. But the Government did no more than refer to the outcome of the domestic criminal proceedings, where the high standard of proof necessary to secure a criminal conviction was not found to have been satisfied. It is also clear that, in that context, significant weight was given to the explanation that the injuries were caused by a fall against a car door. Like the Commission, the Court finds this explanation unconvincing . . .

On the basis of all the material placed before it, the Court concludes that the Government have not satisfactorily established that the applicant's injuries were caused otherwise than—entirely, mainly or partly—by the treatment he underwent while in police custody.

35. . . . a number of witnesses had confirmed that the applicant had sustained physical injuries and was suffering from considerable psychological trauma . . .

38. The Court emphasises that, in respect of a person deprived of his liberty, any recourse to physical force which has not been made strictly necessary by his own conduct diminishes human dignity and is in principle an infringement of the right set forth in Article 3 of the Convention . . .

39. In the instant case the injuries suffered by Mr Ribitsch show that he underwent ill-treatment which amounted to both inhuman and degrading treatment.

Ribitsch was awarded 100,000 ATS just satisfaction in respect of non-pecuniary damage. Significantly, the judgment of the Court (of which Judge De Meyer was a member), at paragraph 38, incorporated Judge De Meyer's principle (enunciated in his Concurring Opinion in *Tomasi*, above Note 1) that the use of any physical force on a detainee, not strictly necessary to respond to actions of the detainee (such as attacking other detainees) is a breach of Article 3. This jurisprudential evolution of Article 3 is a very important Convention safeguard for detainees who are potentially in a highly vulnerable position vis à vis the public officials overseeing their detention and questioning.

3 The *Ribitsch* obligation upon States to provide a plausible explanation for injuries sustained by an individual during a period of detention was extended to injuries arising during a person's arrest in *Rehbock v Slovenia*, judgment of 28 November 2000. The applicant was a former German body-building champion whom the Slovenia authorities suspected of being a drugs dealer. Therefore, the authorities planned to arrest him in Slovenia during a drugs smuggling journey. Given the physical strength of the applicant thirteen police officers were deployed to arrest him. He was arrested by six officers, dressed in black and wearing masks, armed with a shotgun and pistols. After his arrest it was discovered that the applicant had suffered a double fracture to his jaw and facial cuts (subsequently he was sentenced to one year's imprisonment for unauthorized production and dealing in narcotics and of smuggling). A large majority, six votes to one, determined:

76. . . . that the Government have not furnished convincing or credible arguments which would provide a basis to explain or justify the degree of force used during the arrest operation. Accordingly, the force used was excessive and unjustified in the circumstances.

77. Such use of force had as a consequence injuries which undoubtedly caused serious suffering to the applicant of a nature amounting to inhuman treatment.

78. There has therefore been a violation of Article 3 of the Convention on account of the treatment to which the applicant was subjected during his arrest.

4 A majority (ten votes to seven) of the Grand Chamber in *Jalloh v Germany*, judgment of 11 July 2006, held that the forced administration of emetics to a suspected drugs dealer, in order to physically induce him to regurgitate a packet of cocaine that he had swallowed, amounted to inhuman and degrading treatment.

82. Having regard to all the circumstances of the case, the Court finds that the impugned measure attained the minimum level of severity required to bring it within the scope of Article 3. The authorities subjected the applicant to a grave interference with his physical and mental integrity against his will. They forced him to regurgitate, not for therapeutic reasons, but in order to retrieve evidence they could equally have obtained by less intrusive methods. The manner in which the impugned measure was carried out was liable to arouse in the applicant feelings of fear, anguish and inferiority that were capable of humiliating and debasing him. Furthermore, the procedure entailed risks to the applicant's health, not least because of the failure to obtain a proper anamnesis [assessment of his medical history] beforehand. Although this was not the intention, the measure was implemented in a way which caused the applicant both physical pain and mental suffering. He therefore has been subjected to inhuman and degrading treatment contrary to Article 3.

The policy of the public prosecutor in Wuppertal to order the use of emetics to secure evidence against suspected drugs offenders was not in accordance with the general practice in Member States (only Germany, Luxembourg, Norway, and Macedonia forcibly administered emetics against the wishes of a suspect).

Mental suffering

1 In the Court's judgment in *Ireland v UK* (above, p 145), the deliberate infliction of 'intense physical and mental suffering' leading to 'acute psychiatric disturbances during interrogation' of detainees, by the use of the five techniques, was characterised as inhuman treatment (para 167).

2 The 'severe mental distress and anguish' experienced, over a number of years, by a close relative of a 'disappeared' person was also classified as inhuman treatment by the Commission in *Kurt v Turkey* (1998) 27 EHRR 91, 1998-III 1187. The Commission found that in November 1993 gendarmes and village guards conducted an anti-terrorist operation against the PKK in the applicant's village. The last time the applicant, or any other member of her family or the village, saw the applicant's son (Uzeyir Kurt) was on the morning of 25 November 1993, when he was surrounded by members of the security forces. Despite the applicant's subsequent numerous inquiries of various officials, all of them denied any knowledge of the whereabouts or condition of Uzeyir. In May 1994 the applicant complained, on behalf of her son and herself, to the Commission alleging a number of breaches of the Convention. The latter body, by nineteen votes to five, expressed the opinion, inter alia, that the applicant had been subject to inhuman and degrading treatment through the 'uncertainty, doubt and apprehension' caused to her by the disappearance of her son for which the Turkish authorities were responsible. The Court, by six votes to three, agreed that there had been a breach of Article 3. But the Court did not specify which particular element of that Article had been infringed.

133. The Court notes that ill-treatment must attain a minimum level of severity if it is to fall within the scope of Article 3 . . . It recalls in this respect that the applicant approached the public prosecutor in the days following her son's disappearance in the definite belief that he had been taken into custody. She had witnessed his detention in the village with her own eyes and his non-appearance since that last sighting made her fear for his safety . . . However, the public prosecutor gave no serious consideration to her complaint . . . As a result, she has been left with the anguish of knowing that her son has been detained and that there is a complete absence of official information as to his subsequent fate. This anguish has endured over a prolonged period of time.

134. Having regard to the circumstances described above as well as to the fact that the complainant was the mother of the victim of a human rights violation and herself the victim of the authorities' complacency in the face of her anguish and distress, the Court finds that the respondent State is in breach of Article 3 in respect of the applicant.

Turkey was order to pay the applicant £10,000 compensation.

Regrettably, in the later case of *Cakici v Turkey* (8/7/1999), a large majority (fourteen votes to three) of a Grand Chamber took a restrictive view of the judgment in *Kurt* by emphasising that there must be 'special factors' present before a family member of a disappeared person can claim to be a victim of a breach of Article 3. The applicant, a resident of South East Turkey complained to the Commission (on behalf of his brother Ahmet and himself) regarding the disappearance of Ahmet. The Turkish security authorities suspected Ahmet of being involved in PKK terrorist activities and on 8 November 1993 gendarmes arrested him. Other detainees reported that they had seen Ahmet in a bad condition after he had been tortured. The authorities denied that they had detained Ahmet. Subsequently, the Government claimed that Ahmet had been killed during a clash between the security forces and the PKK in February 1995. The Commission expressed the opinion that, inter alia, there had been a breach of Article 2 in respect of Ahmet (unanimously) and a breach of Article 3 in respect of the applicant (twenty seven votes to three). The Court held that:

98. . . . in the *Kurt* case . . . which concerned the disappearance of the applicant's son during an unacknowledged detention, it found that the applicant had suffered a breach of Article 3 having regard to the particular circumstances of the case. It referred particularly to the fact that she was the mother of a victim of a serious human rights violation and herself the victim of the authorities' complacency in the face of her anguish and distress. The *Kurt* case does not however establish any general principle that a family member of a 'disappeared person' is thereby a victim of treatment contrary to Article 3. Whether a family member is such a victim will depend on the existence of special factors which gives the suffering of the applicant a dimension and character distinct from the emotional distress which may be regarded as inevitably caused to relatives of a victim of a serious human rights violation. Relevant elements will include the proximity of the family tie—in that context, a certain weight will attach to the parent-child bond—the particular circumstances of the relationship, the extent to which the family member witnessed the events in question, the involvement of the family member in the attempts to obtain information about the disappeared person and the way in which the authorities responded to those enquiries. The Court would further emphasise that the essence of such a violation does not so much lie in the fact of the 'disappearance' of the family member but rather concerns the authorities' reactions and attitudes to the situation when it is brought to their attention. It is especially in respect of the latter that a relative may claim directly to be a victim of the authorities' conduct.

99. In the present case, the applicant was the brother of the disappeared person. Unlike the applicant in the *Kurt* case, he was not present when the security forces took his brother, as he lived with his own family in another town. It appears also that, while the applicant was involved in making various petitions and enquiries to the authorities, he did not bear the brunt of this task, his father Tevfik Çakici taking the initiative in presenting the petition of 22 December 1993 to the Diyarbakir State Security Court. Nor have any aggravating features arising from the response of the authorities been brought to the attention of the Court in this case. Consequently, the Court perceives no special features existing in this case which would justify finding an additional violation of Article 3 of the Convention in relation to the applicant himself. Accordingly, there has been no breach of Article 3 as concerns the applicant in this case.

Judge Thomassen, joined by Judges Jungwiert and Fischbach, did not express an opinion on the merits of the majority's criterion of the existence of special factors. However, the dissenters considered that this criterion was satisfied in respect of the applicant because, 'a brother can also suffer deeply in face of the uncertainty of the fate of a sibling'. Furthermore:

. . . from the moment of the disappearance of his brother the applicant was actively involved in submitting various petitions and enquiries to the authorities and . . . he made the application to our Court. The Turkish Government have been found responsible for one of the gravest possible violations of human rights, a failure to respect the right to life. Moreover, they left the applicant in uncertainty, doubt and apprehension about his brother for more than five and a half years. In doing so, they demonstrated a cruel disregard for his feelings and his efforts to find out about his brother's fate. Apart from failing in their obligation to respect his brother's right to life, the Government must also be held responsible for the severe mental distress and anguish the applicant has suffered for a prolonged and continuing period of time as a consequence of their acts and negligence. I find that these are factors which do amount to a violation of Article 3 in relation to the applicant himself.

In *Cicek v Turkey*, judgment of 27 February 2001, a unanimous Chamber found a breach of Article 3 in regard to the authorities persistent refusals to explain to a mother the whereabouts/fate of her adult sons who had 'disappeared' after being taken into custody by gendarmes.

173. It recalls in this respect that the applicant and her daughter made several applications to the public prosecutor and the gendarme commander following her sons' disappearance in the definite belief that they had been kept in custody in the Lice Regional Boarding School [where the gendarmes were based]. However, the public prosecutor and the gendarmerie commander gave no serious consideration to her complaint. The Court observes that the applicant has had no news of her sons for almost six years. She has been living with the fear that her sons are dead and has made attempts before the public prosecutor and requested the authorities to be at least given their bodies. The uncertainty, doubt and apprehension suffered by the applicant over a prolonged and continuing period of time has undoubtedly caused her severe mental distress and anguish.

174. Having regard to the circumstances described above as well as to the fact that the complainant is the mother of victims of grave human rights violations and herself the victim of the authorities' complacency in the face of her anguish and distress, the Court finds that the respondent State is in breach of Article 3 in respect of the applicant.

A similar breach was found in the case of a father who had made many attempts to discover the whereabouts/fate of his 'disappeared' sons in *Ipek v Turkey*, judgment of 17 February 2004 (see also above p 100 for the Article 2 aspects of this case).

182. In the present case, the Court notes that the applicant is the father of the disappeared Ipek brothers. The applicant witnessed the impugned events and his sons being taken away by soldiers almost

nine years ago and he has never heard from them since. It further appears from the documents submitted by him that the applicant bore the weight of having to make numerous futile enquiries in order to find out what had happened to his two sons. Despite his tireless endeavours to discover the fate of his sons, the applicant has never received any plausible explanation or information from the authorities as to what became of his sons following their apprehension by the soldiers. Conversely, the authorities' reaction to the applicant's grave concerns was limited to denials that the İpek brothers had ever been detained by the security forces. It is to be noted that the applicant was not even informed of the outcome of the investigations pursued in respect of his complaints. Furthermore, the Court considers that the applicant's anguish about the fate of his sons must have been exacerbated by the destruction of his family home.

183. In view of the above, the Court finds that the applicant suffered, and continues to suffer, distress and anguish as a result of the disappearance of his two sons and of his inability to find out what had happened to them. The manner in which his complaints have been dealt with by the authorities must be considered to constitute inhuman treatment contrary to Article 3.

The Court concludes therefore that there has been a violation of Article 3 of the Convention in respect of the applicant.

Hence, the greater the length of time (normally amounting to many years) parents have persisted in their attempts to discover the whereabouts/fate of their 'disappeared' children, combined with lack of cooperation from the authorities, the greater the likelihood that the Court will conclude that the parents have suffered a violation of Article 3.

In *Tanis and Others v Turkey*, judgment of 2 August 2005, a unanimous Chamber found that the wives/partner of two politicians who 'disappeared' after being summoned to a gendarmerie station had suffered inhuman/degrading treatment due to the distress and anxiety caused to them by the authorities failure over four years to provide a plausible explanation for the fate of their relatives or undertake an effective investigation into the disappearances (the disappearances were found to involve breaches of both substantive and procedural aspects of Article 2).

3 In *V v UK* (1999) 30 EHRR 121, the applicant (born in 1982) had played truant from school with another 10-year-old boy (the applicant in the related case of *T v UK* (1999) 30 EHRR 121 one day during February 1993. While truanting T and V abducted a 2-year-old boy from a shopping centre, took him on a journey of a couple of miles, battered him to death and then left his body to be run over by a train. The applicants were arrested and charged with murder. Their trial took place in public before Preston Crown Court over three weeks in November 1993.

In the two months preceding the trial, each applicant was taken by social workers to visit the courtroom and was introduced to trial procedures and personnel by way of a 'child witness pack' containing books and games. The trial was preceded and accompanied by massive national and international publicity. Throughout the criminal proceedings, the arrival of the defendants was greeted by a hostile crowd. On occasion, attempts were made to attack the vehicles bringing them to court. In the courtroom, the press benches and public gallery were full. The trial was conducted with the formality of an adult criminal trial. The judge and counsel wore wigs and gowns. The procedure was, however, modified to a certain extent in view of the defendants' age. They were seated next to social workers in a specially raised dock. Their parents and lawyers were seated nearby. The hearing times were shortened to reflect the school day (10.30 am to 3.30 pm, with an hour's lunch break), and a ten-minute interval was taken every hour. During adjournments the defendants were allowed to spend time with their parents and social workers in a play area. The judge made it clear that he would adjourn whenever the social workers or defence lawyers told him that one of the defendants was showing signs of tiredness or stress. This occurred on one occasion.

At the opening of the trial on 1 November 1993 the judge made an order under section 39 of the Children and Young Persons Act 1933 . . . that there should be no publication of the names, addresses or other identifying details of the applicant or T. or publication of their photographs. On the same day, the applicant's counsel made an application for a stay of the proceedings, on the grounds that the trial would be unfair due to the nature and extent of the media coverage. After hearing argument, the judge found that it was not established that the defendants would suffer serious prejudice to the extent that no fair trial could be held. He referred to the warning that he had given to the jury to put out of their minds anything which they might have heard or seen about the case outside the courtroom.

The jury convicted the applicants of murder and the judge sentenced them, as required by law, to detention during Her Majesty's pleasure. Subsequently, the judge recommended that the applicants serve eight years detention in order to satisfy the requirements of retribution and deterrence (the 'tariff' period). The Lord Chief Justice recommended a tariff of ten years. The Home Secretary received considerable correspondence from members of the public, including a petition signed by nearly 300,000 people and 21,000 coupons from the *Sun* newspaper, calling for the applicants to be detained for the rest of their lives. The Home Secretary allowed the applicants' lawyers to make representations to him and then (July 1994) informed the applicant that his tariff period should be fifteen years. The applicant sought to challenge that decision in judicial review proceedings and the House of Lords (by a majority) ruled that the Home Secretary had acted unlawfully by giving weight to the public protests about the applicants' tariff. At the time of the Court's judgment the Home Secretary had not set a new tariff for the applicant (in part because he was still awaiting representations from T.). The applicant complained to the Commission alleging, inter alia, that his trial before an adult court in public and his sentence amounted to inhuman and degrading treatment in breach of Article 3. The Commission, by 17 votes to 2, found no breach of that provision. A majority of the Court (twelve votes to five and ten votes to seven) also found no violations of Article 3 in respect of the applicant's trial or sentence.

63. The applicant alleged that the cumulative effect of the age of criminal responsibility, the accusatorial nature of the trial, the adult proceedings in a public court, the length of the trial, the jury of twelve adult strangers, the physical lay-out of the courtroom, the overwhelming presence of the media and public, the attacks by the public on the prison van which brought him to court and the disclosure of his identity, together with a number of other factors linked to his sentence . . . gave rise to a breach of Article 3 . . . .

72. The Court has considered first whether the attribution to the applicant of criminal responsibility in respect of acts committed when he was ten years old could, in itself, give rise to a violation of Article 3. In doing so, it has regard to the principle, well established in its case-law that, since the Convention is a living instrument, it is legitimate when deciding whether a certain measure is acceptable under one of its provisions to take account of the standards prevailing among the member States of the Council of Europe (see the *Soering* judgment . . . p 40, § 102; and also the *Dudgeon v UK* judgment of 22 October 1981, Series A No 45, and the *X, Y and Z v UK* judgment of 22 April 1997, *Reports* 1997-II).

73. In this connection, the Court observes that, at the present time, there is not yet a commonly accepted minimum age for the imposition of criminal responsibility in Europe. While most of the Contracting States have adopted an age-limit which is higher than that in force in England and Wales, other States, such as Cyprus, Ireland, Liechtenstein and Switzerland, attribute criminal responsibility from a younger age. Moreover, no clear tendency can be ascertained from examination of the relevant international texts and instruments . . . . Rule 4 of the Beijing Rules which, although not legally

binding, might provide some indication of the existence of an international consensus, does not specify the age at which criminal responsibility should be fixed but merely invites States not to fix it too low, and Article 40(3)(a) of the UN Convention requires States Parties to establish a minimum age below which children shall be presumed not to have the capacity to infringe the criminal law, but contains no provision as to what that age should be.

74. The Court does not consider that there is at this stage any clear common standard among the member States of the Council of Europe as to the minimum age of criminal responsibility. Even if England and Wales is among the few European jurisdictions to retain a low age of criminal responsibility, the age of ten cannot be said to be so young as to differ disproportionately from the age-limit followed by other European States. The Court concludes that the attribution of criminal responsibility to the applicant does not in itself give rise to a breach of Article 3 of the Convention.

75. The second part of the applicant's complaint under Article 3 concerning the trial relates to the fact that the criminal proceedings took place over three weeks in public in an adult Crown Court with attendant formality, and that, after his conviction, his name was permitted to be published.

76. The Court notes in this connection that one of the minimum guarantees provided by Article 40(2)(b) of the UN Convention to children accused of crimes is that they should have their privacy fully respected at all stages of the proceedings. Similarly, Rule 8 of the Beijing Rules states that 'the juvenile's privacy shall be respected at all stages' and that 'in principle, no information that may lead to the identification of a juvenile offender shall be published'. Finally, the Committee of Ministers of the Council of Europe recommended in 1987 that member States should review their law and practice with a view to avoiding committing minors to adult courts where juvenile courts exist and to recognising the right of juveniles to respect for their private lives . . .

77. The Court considers that the foregoing demonstrates an international tendency in favour of the protection of the privacy of juvenile defendants, and it notes in particular that the UN Convention is binding in international law on the United Kingdom in common with all the other member States of the Council of Europe . . . Moreover, Article 6 § 1 of the Convention states that 'the press and public may be excluded from all or part of the trial . . . where the interests of juveniles . . . so require'. However, while the existence of such a trend is one factor to be taken into account when assessing whether the treatment of the applicant can be regarded as acceptable under the other Articles of the Convention, it cannot be determinative of the question whether the trial in public amounted to ill-treatment attaining the minimum level of severity necessary to bring it within the scope of Article 3 . . .

78. The Court recognises that the criminal proceedings against the applicant were not motivated by any intention on the part of the State authorities to humiliate him or cause him suffering. Indeed, special measures were taken to modify the Crown Court procedure in order to attenuate the rigours of an adult trial in view of the defendants' young age . . .

79. Even if there is evidence that proceedings such as those applied to the applicant could be expected to have a harmful effect on an eleven-year-old child . . . the Court considers that any proceedings or inquiry to determine the circumstances of the acts committed by T. and the applicant, whether such inquiry had been carried out in public or in private, attended by the formality of the Crown Court or informally in the Youth Court, would have provoked in the applicant feelings of guilt, distress, anguish and fear. The psychiatric evidence shows that before the trial commenced he was suffering from the post-traumatic effects of the offence; that he cried inconsolably and found it difficult and distressing when asked to talk about what he and T. had done to the two-year-old, and that he suffered fears of punishment and terrible retribution . . . While the public nature of the proceedings may have exacerbated to a certain extent these feelings in the applicant, the Court is not convinced that the particular features of the trial process as applied to him caused, to a significant degree, suffering going beyond that which would inevitably have been engendered by any attempt by the authorities to deal with the applicant following the commission by him of the offence in question . . .

80. In conclusion, therefore, the Court does not consider that the applicant's trial gave rise to a violation of Article 3 of the Convention. ...

93. The applicant argued that, in view of his age at the time of the offence, the sentence of detention during Her Majesty's pleasure was severely disproportionate and in breach of Article 3 of the Convention ...

98. The Court recalls that States have a duty under the Convention to take measures for the protection of the public from violent crime (see, for example, the *A v UK* judgment of 23 September 1998, *Reports* 1998-VI, p 2699, § 22, and the *Osman v UK* judgment of 28 October 1998, *Reports* 1998-VIII, p 3159, § 115). It does not consider that the punitive element inherent in the tariff approach itself gives rise to a breach of Article 3, or that the Convention prohibits States from subjecting a child or young person convicted of a serious crime to an indeterminate sentence allowing for the offender's continued detention or recall to detention following release where necessary for the protection of the public (see the *Hussain* judgment ... p 269, § 53).

99. The applicant has not yet reached the stage in his sentence where he is able to have the continued lawfulness of his detention reviewed with regard to the question of dangerousness, and although he has not yet been notified of any new tariff, it can be assumed that he is currently detained for the purposes of retribution and deterrence. Until a new tariff has been set, it is not possible to draw any conclusions regarding the length of punitive detention to be served by the applicant. At the time of adoption of the present judgment he has been detained for six years since his conviction in November 1993. The Court does not consider that, in all the circumstances of the case including the applicant's age and his conditions of detention, a period of punitive detention of this length can be said to amount to inhuman or degrading treatment.

100. Finally, the Court observes that it cannot be excluded, particularly in relation to a child as young as the applicant at the time of his conviction, that an unjustifiable and persistent failure to fix a tariff, leaving the detainee in uncertainty over many years as to his future, might also give rise to an issue under Article 3. In the present case, however, in view of the relatively short period of time during which no tariff has been in force and the need to seek the views, inter alia, of both the applicant and T. ... no such issue arises.

101. It follows that there has been no violation of Article 3 in respect of the applicant's sentence.

The above judgment indicates that the effects of a trial and a subsequent sentence of imprisonment on a person's mental well-being will have to be devastating before the Court is likely to find suffering of an intensity that violates Article 3 (note, the Court found the applicant's trial and the setting of his tariff to be in breach of Articles 6 and 5). An expert child law practitioner made the following comments on the previous judgment:

There should be no delay in establishing a therapeutic environment from the moment a child is identified as an offender, a child centred trial system and a proper programme of care for a detained young person who passes into adulthood. None of these were in place in 1993 and we have made remarkably little progress since. It is as if we have reluctantly awaited an adverse decision. The key and difficult question whether such trials should be in public or private has been little debated. If there had been progress on these issues, the present decision might have looked less out of place. [R White (2000) *New Law Journal* 19.]

In February 2000 a new Practice Note (Crown Court: trial of children and young persons) was issued [2000] 2 All ER 284. The Direction emphasised that all possible steps should be taken to assist the young defendant to understand and participate in his/her trial. The proceedings should not expose the defendant to avoidable intimidation, humiliation or distress. Special arrangements should be made for the trials of juveniles in the Crown Court including: cousel not wearing robes and wigs, police presence in the courtroom should not normally be recognizable and restricting the numbers of reporters present in the courtroom (if appropriate the proceedings could be relayed to another room to which the media would have access). In March 2000 the Home Secretary (Mr Jack Straw) referred the cases of Robert Thompson and Jon Venables to the Lord Chief Justice for the latter to determine the tariff to be served before their cases would be considered by the Parole Board.

In October 2000 Lord Woolf ruled that the parole process could begin for both Thompson and Venables. During June 2001 the Parole Board authorised their release on life licences as they were no longer deemed to pose a danger to society. However, because of their notoriety and threats made against them they were given new secret identities on their release.

Destruction of homes

The Court, by eight votes to one, has held that the burning of people's homes, by members of the security forces of a member State, can be so serious in its effects as to amount to inhuman treatment. In *Selcuk and Asker v Turkey* (1998) 26 EHRR 477, 1998-II, the Court determined that:

77. . . . Mrs Selçuk and Mr Asker were aged respectively 54 and 60 at the time and had lived in the village . . . all their lives . . . . Their homes and most of their property were destroyed by the security forces, depriving the applicants of their livelihoods and forcing them to leave their village. It would appear that the exercise was premeditated and carried out contemptuously and without respect for the feelings of the applicants. They were taken unprepared; they had to stand by and watch the burning of their homes; inadequate precautions were taken to secure the safety of Mr and Mrs Asker; Mrs Selçuk's protests were ignored, and no assistance was provided to them afterwards.

78. Bearing in mind in particular the manner in which the applicants' homes were destroyed . . . and their personal circumstances, it is clear that they must have been caused suffering of sufficient severity for the acts of the security forces to be categorised as inhuman treatment within the meaning of Article 3.

79. The Court recalls that the Commission made no finding as regards the underlying motive for the destruction of the applicants' property. However, even if it were the case that the acts in question were carried out without any intention of punishing the applicants, but instead to prevent their homes being used by terrorists or as a discouragement to others, this would not provide a justification for the ill-treatment.

80. In conclusion, the Court finds that the particular circumstances of this case disclose a violation of Article 3.

In the light of the applicants' property losses the Court awarded Mrs Selcuk £17,760 and Mr Asker £22,408 compensation for pecuniary damage. In addition Turkey was ordered to pay each applicant £10,000 in respect of non-pecuniary damage to compensate for their suffering. Where the circumstances and effects of the deliberate destruction of homes is not quite so traumatic the Court will find such conduct to be a breach of Article 8 (right to respect for a person's home), see below p 553.

Conditions of detention

1   The Commission articulated its understanding of the requirements of Article 3 in the context of extreme prison conditions in the case of *Krocher and Moller v Switzerland* 34 DR 24

(1982). The applicants were suspected political terrorists, from Germany, who were believed to have committed violent crimes. They were arrested in the border area of Switzerland after they had fired shots at customs officers. During their remand in custody (from 21 December 1977 to 30 June 1978) awaiting trial the Swiss authorities placed the applicants under severe conditions of security. The applicants were placed in separate non-adjacent cells with no other prisoners on the same floor. The cells above and below their cells were empty. The applicants were kept under constant surveillance by closed circuit television. The windows of their cells were blocked and a light was kept on at all times. They were not allowed newspapers, books, television or radio. They were not allowed contact with each other, other prisoners or visitors. Over several months the conditions of detention were relaxed to allow, inter alia, two one-hour visits weekly by their lawyers, the switching off of their cell lights at night (from 17 February 1978, but an infra-red surveillance system was installed which allowed constant monitoring of the applicants) and permission to listen to supplied radios and newspapers (from 7 June 1978). On 30 June 1978 the applicants were convicted of attempting to murder the Swiss customs officers and sentenced to eleven and fifteen years' imprisonment. In August 1978 they were allowed to receive visits from close relatives and correspond with other persons (subject to strict supervision). The applicants complained to the Commission alleging that the conditions of their detention were inhuman or degrading. The Commission noted that:

... [it] has already had occasion to recall that the segregation of a prisoner from the prison community does not in itself constitute a form of inhuman treatment. In many States Parties to the Convention, more stringent security measures exist for dangerous prisoners. . . . It has on other occasions stated that complete sensory isolation coupled with total social isolation, can destroy the personality and constitutes a form of treatment which cannot be justified by the requirements of security or any other reason. It has moreover drawn a distinction between this and removal from association with other prisoners for security, disciplinary or protective reasons, and has not considered that this form of segregation from the prison community amounts to inhuman or degrading treatment or punishment . . . In making an assessment in a given case, regard must be had to the surrounding circumstances including the particular conditions, the stringency of the measure, its duration, the objective pursued and its effects on the person concerned. (p 53)

The Commission took account of the 'climate of terrorism' at that time (including the kidnapping and murder of a prominent German businessman, the hijacking of an aircraft and the deaths in prison of founder members of a German terrorist group). In the opinion of the Commission (by eight votes to five):

Having regard to all the circumstances of the case and in particular to the fact that the Swiss authorities saw fit gradually to relax the arrangements for the applicants' detention, and to the behaviour of the latter in refusing certain opportunities for contact, the Commission is unable to affirm that the applicants were subject to a form of physical or moral suffering designed to punish them, destroy their personality or break their resistance . . . The Commission therefore considers that the special conditions imposed on the applicants could not be construed as inhuman or degrading treatment within the meaning of Article 3 of the Convention. (p 57)

While the above opinion (which was approved by the Committee of Ministers: Resolution DH(83)15) showed that States could subject detainees to stringent security measures where there was a grave danger of detainees escaping or injuring themselves, the Commission would not accept prison conditions which destroyed the personality of detainees as being compatible with Article 3.

2   A unanimous Chamber found the severe regime of imprisonment in which a convicted multiple child murderer had been held for over three years amounted to inhuman and degrading treatment in *Iorgov v Bulgaria*, Judgment of 11 March 2004. The applicant who had been sentenced to death, but after the introduction of a *de facto* moratorium on executions, was imprisoned alone in a cell for twenty-three hours per day. Food was served in his cell and he was not allowed to eat with other prisoners. Apart from two visits per month his only contacts with other persons were with prison staff and conversations with other prisoners during a daily one-hour walk.

84. The Court notes that although the damaging effects of the impoverished regime to which the applicant was subject were known, that regime was maintained for many years .... Furthermore, it is significant that the Government have not invoked any particular security reasons requiring the applicant's isolation and have not mentioned why it was not possible to revise the regime of prisoners in the applicant's situation so as to provide them with adequate possibilities for human contact and sensible occupation ....

86. In sum, the Court considers that the stringent custodial regime to which the applicant was subjected after 1995 and the material conditions in which he was detained must have caused him suffering exceeding the unavoidable level inherent in detention. The Court thus concludes that the minimum threshold of severity under Article 3 of the Convention has been reached and that the applicant has been subjected to inhuman and degrading treatment.

This case is distinguishable from *Krocher and Moller* due to the absence of any security threats posed by the prisoner and the much longer time period that he was subjected to the severe regime.

3   A Chamber was very divided on the issue whether the detention of the notorious terrorist Ilich Ramirez, popularly known as 'Carlos the Jackal', in solitary confinement for over eight years amounted to inhuman treatment. In *Ramirez Sanchez v France*, judgment of 27 January 2005, the applicant complained about his detention in a 7 sq. m. cell; he was allowed two hours of walking in a prison exercise yard per day and access to newspapers and television. He was not allowed to associate with other prisoners but was visited by a doctor twice a week, a cleric once a month, and his lawyer (who had become his partner) visited him 640 times during five years. The applicant was in good physical and mental health. The authorities sought to justify the stringent conditions of detention because of the exceptional level of danger he posed (he was deemed to be the most dangerous terrorist in the world at the time of his capture in the mid-1990s; in 1997 he had been sentenced to life imprisonment for the murder of three French police officers in 1975—part of his terrorists group's campaign of violence which included the seizure of OPEC ministers and the hi-jacking of an Air France aeroplane). The Chamber, by four votes to three, found that given his personality and the extreme level of danger he posed the conditions of his detention did not amount to inhuman treatment. On a referral under Article 43 the Grand Chamber (judgment of 4 July 2006) by a large majority (twelve votes to five) found that, having regard to the applicant's character and the danger he posed, his solitary confinement did not amount to a breach of Article 3. However, the Grand Chamber emphasized that solitary confinement should not be imposed on a prisoner indefinitely. Since the beginning of 2006 he had been detained under normal prison conditions and the Grand Chamber expressed the view that should continue.

4   The routine subjection of a prisoner to strip-searches, combined with a very strict security regime (e.g. limited physical contact allowed with visiting close family members), was found to constitute inhuman or degrading treatment by a united Chamber in *Van Der Ven v Netherlands*,

judgment of 4 February 2003. The applicant was detained on remand, in an ordinary prison, during September 1995 accused of having committed murder, rape, and narcotics offences. The next month he was transferred to an 'Extra-Security Institution' ('EBI') after the authorities concluded that he was planning to escape from custody. The 'EBI' was part of a large prison complex. As the applicant had threatened to commit suicide if transferred to the 'EBI' he was placed under a high security regime in the institution. His cell was searched at least on a weekly basis and each time that occurred he was subject to a strip-search (involving an external inspection of his body orifices—including an anal inspection—by an officer of the same gender in a closed room). The applicant was subject to this regime for over three and a half years. The European Committee for the Prevention of Torture had reported that in its view the systematic strip-searching of detainees in the 'EBI' did not appear to be justified in accordance with legitimate security requirements.

61. In the present case, the Court is struck by the fact that the applicant was submitted to the weekly strip-search in addition to all the other strict security measures within the EBI. In view of the fact that the domestic authorities, through the reports drawn up by the Psychological Department of their Penitentiary Selection Centre, were well aware that the applicant was experiencing serious difficulties coping with the regime, and bearing in mind that at no time during the applicant's stay in the EBI did it appear that anything untoward was found in the course of a strip-search, the Court is of the view that the systematic strip-searching of the applicant required more justification than has been put forward by the Government in the present case.

62. The Court considers that in the situation where the applicant was already subjected to a great number of control measures, and in the absence of convincing security needs, the practice of weekly strip-searches that was applied to the applicant for a period of approximately three and a half years diminished his human dignity and must have given rise to feelings of anguish and inferiority capable of humiliating and debasing him. The applicant himself confirmed that this was indeed the case in a meeting with a psychiatrist, during which he also stated that he would forsake, for instance, going to the hairdresser's so as not to have to undergo a strip-search . . .

63. Accordingly, the Court concludes that the combination of routine strip-searching with the other stringent security measures in the EBI amounted to inhuman or degrading treatment in violation of Article 3 of the Convention. There has thus been a breach of this provision.

The above judgment does not prevent States from subjecting detainees to strip-searches but recourse to them must be justifiable on legitimate security grounds in the case of each person undergoing such a search (see also *Iwanczuk v Poland*, below p 212). [degrading treatment]. More generally, once again, in *Van Der Ven* it was the prison regime, rather than the physical conditions of incarceration, that led the Court to find a breach of Article 3.

5   The forced-feeding, physical restraint and forced administration of sedatives to a mentally ill person who was compulsorily detained in a psychiatric hospital and a special prison were found not to have breached Article 3 in *Herczegfalvy v Austria* A.242-B (1992) 15 EHRR 437. The applicant had been proven to have assaulted fellow prisoners and prison wardens together with threatening judges, but the court found that he was 'dangerous and not criminally responsible for his acts' due to a mental illness (paranoia querulans). Therefore, he was detained in a special prison and later a psychiatric hospital.

After several weeks of the applicant being on a hunger strike the director of the hospital ordered that he be force fed. The applicant was also given sedatives, against his will, on a number of occasions. For two days he was also attached to a security bed by means of straps and a net. The applicant claimed that this treatment was inhuman. The Commission, unanimously, agreed that it was in breach of Article 3. However, the Court, also unanimously, took a different view.

79. Mr Herczegfalvy also complained of his medical treatment. In that he had been forcibly administered food and neuroleptics [tranquillizers], isolated and attached with handcuffs to a security bed . . . he had been subjected to brutal treatment incompatible with Article 3 . . .

80. The Commission considered that the manner in which the treatment was administered had not complied with the requirements of Article 3 (art 3): the various measures complained of had been violent and excessively prolonged, and taken together had amounted to inhuman and degrading treatment, and even contributed to the worsening of the patient's condition.

81. In the Government's opinion, on the other hand, the measures were essentially the consequence of the applicant's behaviour, as he had refused medical treatment which was urgent in view of the deterioration in his physical and mental health.

Thus when Mr Herczegfalvy returned to the hospital on 10 September 1979 it proved to be necessary to feed him artificially, in view of his extremely weak state caused by his refusal to take any food . . . Later on, it was partly at his own request that he was fed through a tube, while continuing—at least ostensibly—with his hunger strike.

Similarly, it was only his resistance to all treatment, his extreme aggressiveness and the threats and acts of violence on his part against the hospital staff which explained why the staff had used coercive measures including the intramuscular injection of sedatives and the use of handcuffs and the security bed. These measures had been agreed to by Mr Herczegfalvy's curator, their sole aim had always been therapeutic, and they had been terminated as soon as the state of the patient permitted this.

Finally, the Government claimed that the isolation complained of had in fact consisted of being placed in an individual cell, in accordance with Mr Herczegfalvy's wishes. He had had contact with doctors and nurses, and had been able to receive visits and even walk in the garden.

82. The Court considers that the position of inferiority and powerlessness which is typical of patients confined in psychiatric hospitals calls for increased vigilance in reviewing whether the Convention has been complied with. While it is for the medical authorities to decide, on the basis of the recognised rules of medical science, on the therapeutic methods to be used, if necessary by force, to preserve the physical and mental health of patients who are entirely incapable of deciding for themselves and for whom they are therefore responsible, such patients nevertheless remain under the protection of Article 3 (art 3), whose requirements permit of no derogation.

The established principles of medicine are admittedly in principle decisive in such cases; as a general rule, a measure which is a therapeutic necessity cannot be regarded as inhuman or degrading. The Court must nevertheless satisfy itself that the medical necessity has been convincingly shown to exist.

83. In this case it is above all the length of time during which the handcuffs and security bed were used . . . which appears worrying. However, the evidence before the Court is not sufficient to disprove the Government's argument that, according to the psychiatric principles generally accepted at the time, medical necessity justified the treatment in issue. Moreover, certain of the applicant's allegations are not supported by the evidence. This is the case in particular with those relating to . . . the extent of the isolation.

84. No violation of Article 3 (art 3) has thus been shown.

Hence the Court will permit the compulsory medical treatment of mentally ill patients who cannot make rational decisions about their own treatment. But, States will have to be able to show that any particular course of treatment was medically necessary. The Court's 'vigilance' in ensuring that the Convention rights of these patients have been respected is a vital

European safeguard to prevent States abusing their extensive domestic powers over a potentially vulnerable group.

6   The failure of the authorities to provide a detained person, who had been injured during his arrest, with prompt medical treatment was considered to be inhuman treatment by the Commission, unanimously, in *Hurtado v Switzerland* A.280A (1994). The applicant, a suspected member of a drugs smuggling gang, had been arrested by a police special task force who used a stun grenade in order to overpower him. Two days after his arrest and detention the applicant asked to see a doctor. However, he was not examined by a doctor for another six days at which time X-rays revealed that the applicant had a fracture of the ninth left rib.

The Commission considers that in a situation of such gravity, resulting from the use of force by the police, Article 3 of the Convention requires the State authorities to adopt measures to safeguard the physical well-being of a person placed in the charge of the police, judicial or prison authorities. Under Article 3 of the Convention the State has a specific positive obligation to protect the physical well-being of persons deprived of their liberty. The lack of adequate medical treatment in such a situation must be classified as inhuman treatment. (para 79)

Later the applicant and the respondent State agreed a friendly settlement in which the latter paid the former an *ex gratia* sum of 14,000 SF (while not admitting that there had been a breach of the Convention).

7   The Court applied *Hurtado* when determining that the lack of appropriate specialist medical care, together with the imposition of a disciplinary period of solitary confinement, for a prisoner with a long history of serous mental illness who committed suicide amounted to inhuman and degrading treatment in *Keenan v United Kingdom*, judgment of 3 April 2001. The applicant's son, Mark, had a history of mental illness, including symptoms of paranoia, violence, and deliberate self-harm. In April 1993 he was convicted of assaulting his former girlfriend and sentenced to four months' imprisonment. He was admitted to Exeter Prison and sent to the prison health centre. The prison's senior doctor consulted the psychiatrist who had been treating Mark. Several attempts were made to transfer Mark to the ordinary cells but he resisted (by barricading himself in the ward on one occasion). At the end of April the prison's visiting psychiatrist recommended a change in Mark's medication. The next day Mark's condition deteriorated and a prison doctor, with no psychiatric training, ordered a return to his original medication. Later that day Mark assaulted two prison hospital officers (one was seriously injured). The next day another prison doctor, who had six months psychiatric training, certified Mark as being fit for disciplinary proceedings in respect of the assaults and for placement in the segregation unit within the prison's punishment block. A deputy governor ordered Mark's placement in the segregation unit, where he was locked up for twenty-three hours each day. He was visited each day by a doctor, the prison chaplain and the prison governor. Mark asked to see a prisoner trained by the Samaritans (to counsel inmates who may be suicidal) and threatened to harm himself. He was put on a fifteen-minute watch by prison staff. Prison doctors recorded that he was a hazard to staff. No further entries were made in Mark's medical record from 3 May 1993. However, the segregation unit's occurrence book had several entries regarding his behaviour, stating that he was being aggressive to staff and acting strangely. On 14 May he was subject to a disciplinary adjudication, after being certified as medically fit for the hearing by one of the prison doctors, and found guilty of assaulting the officers. The deputy governor sentenced him to twenty-eight additional days in prison and seven days in the segregation unit. During the next day Mark was visited by a friend and he appeared to be in good spirits. However, that evening Mark was found hanged in his cell

(the relevant prison officer had been absent in the toilet for a few minutes prior to the discovery of Mark's suicide). The applicant contended that, *inter alia*, there had been wholly insufficient psychiatric care given to her son whilst in prison and that violated his rights under Article 3. The Court, by five votes to two, held that:

110. It is relevant in the context of the present application to recall also that the authorities are under an obligation to protect the health of persons deprived of liberty (*Hurtado v Switzerland*, Comm. Report 8 July 1993, Series A No 280, p 16, § 79). The lack of appropriate medical treatment may amount to treatment contrary to Article 3 (see *Ilhan v Turkey* [GC] No 22277/93, ECHR 2000-VII, § 87). In particular, the assessment of whether the treatment or punishment concerned is incompatible with the standards of Article 3 has, in the case of mentally ill persons, to take into consideration their vulnerability and their inability, in some cases, to complain coherently or at all about how they are being affected by any particular treatment (see e.g. the *Herczegfalvy v Austria* judgment of 24 September 1992, Series A no. 244, § 82; the *Aerts v Belgium* judgment of 30 July 1998, *Reports* 1998-V, p 1966, § 66).

113. In this case, the Court is struck by the lack of medical notes concerning Mark Keenan, who was an identifiable suicide risk and undergoing the additional stresses that could be foreseen from segregation and, later, disciplinary punishment. From 5 May to 15 May 1993, when he died, there were no entries in his medical notes. Given that there were a number of prison doctors who were involved in caring for Mark Keenan, this shows an inadequate concern to maintain full and detailed records of his mental state and undermines the effectiveness of any monitoring or supervision process. The Court does not find the explanation of Dr Keith—that an absence of notes indicates that there was nothing to record—a satisfactory answer in the light of the occurrence book entries for the same period.

114. Further, while the prison senior medical officer consulted Mark Keenan's doctor on admission and the visiting psychiatrist, who also knew Mark Keenan, had been called to see Mark Keenan on 29 April 1993, the Court notes that there was no subsequent reference to a psychiatrist. Even though Dr Rowe had warned on 29 April 1993 that Mark Keenan should be kept from association until his paranoid feelings had died down, the question of returning to normal location was raised with him the next day. When his condition proceeded to deteriorate, a prison doctor, unqualified in psychiatry, reverted to Mark Keenan's previous medication without reference to the psychiatrist who had originally recommended a change. The assault on the two prison officers followed. Though Mark Keenan asked the prison doctor to point out to the governor at the adjudication that the assault occurred after a change in medication, there was no reference to a psychiatrist for advice either as to his future treatment or his fitness for adjudication and punishment.

115. The lack of effective monitoring of Mark Keenan's condition and the lack of informed psychiatric input into his assessment and treatment disclose significant defects in the medical care provided to a mentally ill person known to be a suicide risk. The belated imposition on him in those circumstances of a serious disciplinary punishment—seven days' segregation in the punishment block and an additional twenty-eight days to his sentence imposed two weeks after the event and only nine days before his expected date of release—which may well have threatened his physical and moral resistance, is not compatible with the standard of treatment required in respect of a mentally ill person. It must be regarded as constituting inhuman and degrading treatment and punishment within the meaning of Article 3 of the Convention.

Accordingly, the Court finds a violation of this provision.

This judgment is important for indicating the Court's increasing concern that States must provide adequate medical care for mentally ill prisoners, especially those who may commit suicide.

8 The failure to accurately monitor and adequately treat a new inmate experiencing serious withdrawal symptoms from heroin addiction were found to constitute inhuman and degrading treatment in *McGlinchey and Others v UK*, judgment of 29 April 2003. The applicants were the mother and children of Judith McGlinchey, born in 1968, who had a long history of drug addiction. On 7 December 1998 she was sentenced to four months' imprisonment for theft. On her arrival, at New Hall Prison Wakefield, she weighed 50 kg and complained of withdrawal symptoms (she was vomiting frequently). The next day the prison doctor examined her and prescribed medication to reduce the symptoms of withdrawal. On the 9th her weight was recorded as 43 kg and she was given an anti-nausea drug. The following day she telephoned her mother to complain about the lack of treatment she was receiving. On the 11th she was found to be 'opiate positive'. For the next two days her pulse and blood pressure readings were within normal limits. However, on the 14th she collapsed and was taken to hospital. Subsequently she suffered a cardiac arrest and died on 3 January 1999. The autopsy found brain damage and multiple organ failure and recorded her weight as being 41 kg. An inquest jury was unanimous in reaching an open verdict in respect of her death. The applicants complained that the authorities subjected-Judith-to inhuman and degrading treatment by, *inter alia*, permitting her to de-hydrate and leaving he to clean up her vomit. The Chamber, by six votes to one, concluded that:

57. The evidence indicates to the Court that by the morning of 14 December 1998 Judith McGlinchey, a heroin addict whose nutritional state and general health were not good on admission to prison, had suffered serious weight loss and was dehydrated. This was the result of a week of largely uncontrolled vomiting symptoms and an inability to eat or hold down fluids. This situation, in addition to causing Judith McGlinchey distress and suffering, posed very serious risks to her health, as shown by her subsequent collapse. Having regard to the responsibility owed by prison authorities to provide the requisite medical care for detained persons, the Court finds that in the present case there was a failure to meet the standards imposed by Article 3 of the Convention. It notes in this context the failure of the prison authorities to provide accurate means of establishing Judith McGlinchey's weight loss, which was a factor that should have alerted the prison to the seriousness of her condition, but was largely discounted due to the discrepancy of the scales. There was a gap in the monitoring of her condition by a doctor over the weekend when there was a further significant drop in weight and a failure of the prison to take more effective steps to treat Judith McGlinchey's condition, such as her admission to hospital to ensure the intake of medication and fluids intravenously, or to obtain more expert assistance in controlling the vomiting.

58. The Court concludes that the prison authorities' treatment of Judith McGlinchey contravened the prohibition against inhuman or degrading treatment contained in Article 3 of the Convention.

In this case, as in *Keenan*, the victim sadly died.

9   The full-time Court found no breach of Article 3 in respect of the forced medical treatment of a convicted murder being held on 'death row' (his sentence was commuted to life imprisonment four years later) in *Naumenko v Ukraine*, judgment of 10 February 2004. During his detention on 'death row' he was diagnosed as being psychopathic, he attempted to commit suicide several times and was aggressive. A psychiatrist prescribed neuroleptic and psychoactive drugs. The applicant complained, *inter alia*, that he was being subject to radiation from a 'psychoactive drugs generator'. A delegation from the Court took evidence from the applicant and witnesses at the prison he was being held in. In its judgment the Court repeated that domestic authorities were under a duty to protect the health of prisoners and therapeutic treatment, no matter how disagreeable, could not be regarded as breaching Article 3 if it was shown to be necessary on medical grounds. Although the Court was critical of the lack of detail in the medical records kept on the applicant by the prison authorities, the judges were unanimous in finding no credible evidence that the authorities had acted wrongly in making the applicant take the above medication. Also, there was no evidence that he had been subject to treatment from a 'psychoactive drugs generator'. This judgment adopted a similar approach to the compulsory treatment of a mentally ill detainee as that applied by the original Court in *Herczegfalvy* (above Note 5).

10 In *Iorgov v Bulgaria* (above Note 2) the applicant also alleged that surgery on a swollen gland had been unduly delayed because of hostility to him by the prison medical staff and administration. The Court stated that:

85. As regards the quality of the health care provided to the applicant, the Court notes that his health was regularly monitored and in most cases the necessary treatment was provided. However, the evidence about the treatment of the applicant's swollen salivary gland, although not conclusive, suggests that there had been an unwarranted delay in providing adequate medical assistance. It must be stressed in this respect that the applicant's alleged rude behaviour towards medical staff and, indeed, any violation of prison rules and discipline by a detainee, can in no circumstances warrant a refusal to provide medical assistance.

Cleary, denial or delay in the provision of necessary medical care must not be used as a form of (official or unofficial) punishment of detainees.

11 A united Grand Chamber determined that the high security conditions in which the former leader of a terrorist/political organization (described as a 'warlord' by President Wildhaber in his joint partly dissenting opinion) was serving his life sentence did not constitute inhuman or degrading treatment in *Ocalan v Turkey*, see above p 128.

192. In the present case, it is true that the applicant's detention posed exceptional difficulties for the Turkish authorities. The applicant, as the leader of a large, armed separatist movement, is considered in Turkey to be the most dangerous terrorist in the country. Reactions to his arrest and differences of opinion that have come to light within his own movement show that his life is genuinely at risk. It is also a reasonable presumption that his supporters will seek to help him escape from prison. In those circumstances, it is understandable that the Turkish authorities should have found it necessary to take extraordinary security measures to detain the applicant.

193. The applicant's prison cell is indisputably furnished to a standard that is beyond reproach. From the photographs in its possession and the findings of the delegates of the CPT [European Committee for the Prevention of Torture], who inspected the applicant's prison during their visit to Turkey from 2 to 14 September 2001, the Court notes that the cell which the applicant occupies alone is large enough to accommodate a prisoner and furnished with a bed, table, armchair and bookshelves. It is also air-conditioned, has washing and toilet facilities and a window overlooking an inner courtyard. The applicant appears to be under medical supervision that is both strict and regular. The Court considers that these conditions do not give rise to any issue under Article 3 of the Convention.

194. Further, the Court considers that the applicant cannot be regarded as being kept in sensory isolation or cellular confinement. It is true that, as the sole inmate, his only contact is with prison staff. He has books, newspapers and a radio at his disposal. He does not have access to television programmes or a telephone. He does, however, communicate with the outside world by letter. He sees a doctor every day and his lawyers and members of his family once a week (his lawyers were allowed to see him twice a week during the trial). The difficulties in gaining access to İmralı Prison in adverse weather conditions appear to have been resolved, as the prison authorities were provided with a suitable craft at the end of 2004.

195. The Court notes the CPT's recommendations that the applicant's relative social isolation should not be allowed to continue for too long and that its effects should be attenuated by giving him access to a television and to telephone communications with his lawyers and close relatives. However, like the Chamber, the Grand Chamber is also mindful of the Government's concerns that the applicant may

seek to take advantage of communications with the outside world to renew contact with members of the armed separatist movement of which he was the leader. These concerns cannot be said to be unfounded. An added consideration is the Government's fear that it would be difficult to protect the applicant's life in an ordinary prison.

196. While concurring with the CPT's recommendations that the long-term effects of the applicant's relative social isolation should be attenuated by giving him access to the same facilities as other high security prisoners in Turkey, such as television and telephone contact with his family, the Grand Chamber agrees with the Chamber that the general conditions in which he is being detained at İmralı Prison have not thus far reached the minimum level of severity required to constitute inhuman or degrading treatment within the meaning of Article 3 of the Convention. Consequently, there has been no violation of that provision on that account.

12　The chaining of the legs of unconscious prisoners (undertaking a hunger strike) to their beds in a hospital was held to constitute inhuman treatment by a unanimous Chamber in *Avci and Others v Turkey*, judgment of 27 June 2006. The Court found that given their weak medical condition the risk of the prisoners absconding was non-existent (they were also guarded by gendarmes) and therefore the restraint was disproportionate.

Extradition or deportation

Soering v United Kingdom　A.161 (1989) 11 EHRR 439
European Court of Human Rights

The applicant, Jens Soering, is a German national born in 1966. In March 1985 the parents of his girlfriend were brutally killed in their home in Virginia (USA). The applicant and his girlfriend disappeared together from Virginia in October 1985 and were subsequently arrested in England, during April 1986, in connection with cheque fraud. The applicant was interviewed, in England, by a Virginia police officer and admitted that he had killed his girlfriend's parents because they were opposed to his relationship with her. In June 1986 a Virginia grand jury indicted Soering on capital murder charges in respect of the killings. Two months later the Government of the United States of America requested the applicant's extradition (and that of the girlfriend) under the terms of the 1972 Extradition Treaty between the USA and the UK. The UK Government began extradition proceedings against the applicant in September 1986 and shortly afterwards the British Embassy in Washington made the following request of the US authorities:

Because the death penalty has been abolished in Great Britain, the Embassy has been instructed to seek an assurance, in accordance with the terms of ... the Extradition Treaty, that, in the event of Mr Soering being surrendered and being convicted of the crimes for which he has been indicted ..., the death penalty, if imposed, will not be carried out. Should it not be possible on constitutional grounds for the United States Government to give such an assurance, the United Kingdom authorities ask that the United States Government undertake to recommend to the appropriate authorities that the death penalty should not be imposed or, if imposed, should not be executed.

In December 1986 a German prosecutor interviewed the applicant and in February 1987 a court in Bonn issued a warrant for Soering's arrest in respect of the alleged murders. This was followed by the German Government requesting his extradition to Germany under the terms of the 1872 Extradition Treaty between Germany and the UK. The UK Government replied that as the US authorities had already submitted a request for Soering's extradition those proceedings should be allowed to continue. The prosecuting attorney in Virginia swore an affidavit that:

I hereby certify that should Jens Soering be convicted of the offence of capital murder as charged in Bedford County, Virginia . . . a representation will be made in the name of the United Kingdom to the judge at the time of sentencing that it is the wish of the United Kingdom that the death penalty should not be imposed or carried out.

However, he intended to seek the death penalty. After a hearing the Chief Magistrate at Bow Street Magistrates' Court committed the applicant to await the Home Secretary's order for his return to the US. Soering was unsuccessful in challenging that decision in judicial review proceedings. While awaiting extradition, in July 1987, Soering applied to the Commission alleging that if he was to be extradited to the US there was a serious likelihood that he would be sentenced to death and that consequently he would be subject to inhuman and degrading treatment and punishment contrary to Article 3 (particularly through exposure to the 'death row phenomenon'). The Commission requested the UK not to extradite Soering until the application had been determined. Subsequently, the Commission (by six votes to five) expressed the opinion that there had been no breach of Article 3. The Commission, UK and German Governments referred the case to the Court.

A. APPLICABILITY OF ARTICLE 3 (ART 3) IN CASES OF EXTRADITION

81. The alleged breach derives from the applicant's exposure to the so-called 'death row phenomenon'. This phenomenon may be described as consisting in a combination of circumstances to which the applicant would be exposed if, after having been extradited to Virginia to face a capital murder charge, he were sentenced to death.

82. In its report (at paragraph 94) the Commission reaffirmed 'its case-law that a person's deportation or extradition may give rise to an issue under Article 3 (art 3) of the Convention where there are serious reasons to believe that the individual will be subjected, in the receiving State, to treatment contrary to that Article (art 3)'.

The Government of the Federal Republic of Germany supported the approach of the Commission, pointing to a similar approach in the case-law of the German courts.

The applicant likewise submitted that Article 3 (art 3) not only prohibits the Contracting States from causing inhuman or degrading treatment or punishment to occur within their jurisdiction but also embodies an associated obligation not to put a person in a position where he will or may suffer such treatment or punishment at the hands of other States. For the applicant, at least as far as Article 3 (art 3) is concerned, an individual may not be surrendered out of the protective zone of the Convention without the certainty that the safeguards which he would enjoy are as effective as the Convention standard.

83. The United Kingdom Government, on the other hand, contended that Article 3 (art 3) should not be interpreted so as to impose responsibility on a Contracting State for acts which occur outside its jurisdiction. In particular, in their submission, extradition does not involve the responsibility of the extraditing State for inhuman or degrading treatment or punishment which the extradited person may suffer outside the State's jurisdiction. To begin with, they maintained, it would be straining the language of Article 3 (art 3) intolerably to hold that by surrendering a fugitive criminal the extraditing State has 'subjected' him to any treatment or punishment that he will receive following conviction and sentence in the receiving State. Further arguments advanced against the approach of the Commission were that it interferes with international treaty rights; it leads to a conflict with the norms of international judicial process, in that it in effect involves adjudication on the internal affairs of foreign States not Parties to the Convention or to the proceedings before the Convention institutions; it entails grave difficulties of

evaluation and proof in requiring the examination of alien systems of law and of conditions in foreign States; the practice of national courts and the international community cannot reasonably be invoked to support it; it causes a serious risk of harm in the Contracting State which is obliged to harbour the protected person, and leaves criminals untried, at large and unpunished.

In the alternative, the United Kingdom Government submitted that the application of Article 3 (art 3) in extradition cases should be limited to those occasions in which the treatment or punishment abroad is certain, imminent and serious. In their view, the fact that by definition the matters complained of are only anticipated, together with the common and legitimate interest of all States in bringing fugitive criminals to justice, requires a very high degree of risk, proved beyond reasonable doubt, that ill-treatment will actually occur.

84. The Court will approach the matter on the basis of the following considerations.

85. As results from Article 5 § 1 (f) (art 5–1-f), which permits 'the lawful . . . detention of a person against whom action is being taken with a view to . . . extradition', no right not to be extradited is as such protected by the Convention. Nevertheless, in so far as a measure of extradition has consequences adversely affecting the enjoyment of a Convention right, it may, assuming that the consequences are not too remote, attract the obligations of a Contracting State under the relevant Convention guarantee (see, *mutatis mutandis*, the *Abdulaziz, Cabales and Balkandali* judgment of 25 May 1985, Series A No 94, pp 31–2, §§ 59–60—in relation to rights in the field of immigration). What is at issue in the present case is whether Article 3 (art 3) can be applicable when the adverse consequences of extradition are, or may be, suffered outside the jurisdiction of the extraditing State as a result of treatment or punishment administered in the receiving State.

86. Article 1 (art 1) of the Convention, which provides that 'the High Contracting Parties shall secure to everyone within their jurisdiction the rights and freedoms defined in Section I', sets a limit, notably territorial, on the reach of the Convention. In particular, the engagement undertaken by a Contracting State is confined to 'securing' ('*reconnaître*' in the French text) the listed rights and freedoms to persons within its own 'jurisdiction'. Further, the Convention does not govern the actions of States not Parties to it, nor does it purport to be a means of requiring the Contracting States to impose Convention standards on other States. Article 1 (art 1) cannot be read as justifying a general principle to the effect that, notwithstanding its extradition obligations, a Contracting State may not surrender an individual unless satisfied that the conditions awaiting him in the country of destination are in full accord with each of the safeguards of the Convention. Indeed, as the United Kingdom Government stressed, the beneficial purpose of extradition in preventing fugitive offenders from evading justice cannot be ignored in determining the scope of application of the Convention and of Article 3 (art 3) in particular.

In the instant case it is common ground that the United Kingdom has no power over the practices and arrangements of the Virginia authorities which are the subject of the applicant's complaints. It is also true that in other international instruments cited by the United Kingdom Government—for example the 1951 United Nations Convention relating to the Status of Refugees (Article 33), the 1957 European Convention on Extradition (Article 11) and the 1984 United Nations Convention against Torture and Other Cruel, Inhuman and Degrading Treatment or Punishment (Article 3)—the problems of removing a person to another jurisdiction where unwanted consequences may follow are addressed expressly and specifically.

These considerations cannot, however, absolve the Contracting Parties from responsibility under Article 3 (art 3) for all and any foreseeable consequences of extradition suffered outside their jurisdiction.

87. In interpreting the Convention regard must be had to its special character as a treaty for the collective enforcement of human rights and fundamental freedoms (see the *Ireland v UK* judgment of 18 January 1978, Series A No 25, p 90, § 239). Thus, the object and purpose of the Convention as an instrument for the protection of individual human beings require that its provisions be interpreted and applied so as to make its safeguards practical and effective (see, inter alia, *the Artico* judgment of

13 May 1980, Series A No 37, p 16, § 33). In addition, any interpretation of the rights and freedoms guaranteed has to be consistent with 'the general spirit of the Convention, an instrument designed to maintain and promote the ideals and values of a democratic society' (see *the Kjeldsen, Busk Madsen and Pedersen* judgment of 7 December 1976, Series A No 23, p 27, § 53).

88. Article 3 (art 3) makes no provision for exceptions and no derogation from it is permissible under Article 15 (art 15) in time of war or other national emergency. This absolute prohibition of torture and of inhuman or degrading treatment or punishment under the terms of the Convention shows that Article 3 (art 3) enshrines one of the fundamental values of the democratic societies making up the Council of Europe. It is also to be found in similar terms in other international instruments such as the 1966 International Covenant on Civil and Political Rights and the 1969 American Convention on Human Rights and is generally recognised as an internationally accepted standard.

The question remains whether the extradition of a fugitive to another State where he would be subjected or be likely to be subjected to torture or to inhuman or degrading treatment or punishment would itself engage the responsibility of a Contracting State under Article 3 (art 3). That the abhorrence of torture has such implications is recognised in Article 3 of the United Nations Convention Against Torture and Other Cruel, Inhuman or Degrading Treatment or Punishment, which provides that 'no State Party shall ... extradite a person where there are substantial grounds for believing that he would be in danger of being subjected to torture'. The fact that a specialised treaty should spell out in detail a specific obligation attaching to the prohibition of torture does not mean that an essentially similar obligation is not already inherent in the general terms of Article 3 (art 3) of the European Convention. It would hardly be compatible with the underlying values of the Convention, that 'common heritage of political traditions, ideals, freedom and the rule of law' to which the Preamble refers, were a Contracting State knowingly to surrender a fugitive to another State where there were substantial grounds for believing that he would be in danger of being subjected to torture, however heinous the crime allegedly committed. Extradition in such circumstances, while not explicitly referred to in the brief and general wording of Article 3 (art 3), would plainly be contrary to the spirit and intendment of the Article, and in the Court's view this inherent obligation not to extradite also extends to cases in which the fugitive would be faced in the receiving State by a real risk of exposure to inhuman or degrading treatment or punishment proscribed by that Article (art 3).

89. What amounts to 'inhuman or degrading treatment or punishment' depends on all the circumstances of the case (see paragraph 100 below). Furthermore, inherent in the whole of the Convention is a search for a fair balance between the demands of the general interest of the community and the requirements of the protection of the individual's fundamental rights. As movement about the world becomes easier and crime takes on a larger international dimension, it is increasingly in the interest of all nations that suspected offenders who flee abroad should be brought to justice. Conversely, the establishment of safe havens for fugitives would not only result in danger for the State obliged to harbour the protected person but also tend to undermine the foundations of extradition. These considerations must also be included among the factors to be taken into account in the interpretation and application of the notions of inhuman and degrading treatment or punishment in extradition cases.

90. It is not normally for the Convention institutions to pronounce on the existence or otherwise of potential violations of the Convention. However, where an applicant claims that a decision to extradite him would, if implemented, be contrary to Article 3 (art 3) by reason of its foreseeable consequences in the requesting country, a departure from this principle is necessary, in view of the serious and irreparable nature of the alleged suffering risked, in order to ensure the effectiveness of the safeguard provided by that Article (art 3) (see paragraph 87 above).

91. In sum, the decision by a Contracting State to extradite a fugitive may give rise to an issue under Article 3 (art 3), and hence engage the responsibility of that State under the Convention, where substantial grounds have been shown for believing that the person concerned, if extradited, faces a real

risk of being subjected to torture or to inhuman or degrading treatment or punishment in the request-ing country. The establishment of such responsibility inevitably involves an assessment of conditions in the requesting country against the standards of Article 3 (art 3) of the Convention. Nonetheless, there is no question of adjudicating on or establishing the responsibility of the receiving country, whether under general international law, under the Convention or otherwise. In so far as any liability under the Convention is or may be incurred, it is liability incurred by the extraditing Contracting State by reason of its having taken action which has as a direct consequence the exposure of an individual to proscribed ill-treatment.

B. APPLICATION OF ARTICLE 3 (ART 3) IN THE PARTICULAR CIRCUMSTANCES OF THE PRESENT CASE

92. The extradition procedure against the applicant in the United Kingdom has been completed, the Secretary of State having signed a warrant ordering his surrender to the United States authorities . . . this decision, albeit as yet not implemented, directly affects him. It therefore has to be determined on the above principles whether the foreseeable consequences of Mr Soering's return to the United States are such as to attract the application of Article 3 (art 3). This inquiry must concentrate firstly on whether Mr Soering runs a real risk of being sentenced to death in Virginia, since the source of the alleged inhuman and degrading treatment or punishment, namely the 'death row phenomenon', lies in the imposition of the death penalty. Only in the event of an affirmative answer to this question need the Court examine whether exposure to the 'death row phenomenon' in the circumstances of the appli-cant's case would involve treatment or punishment incompatible with Article 3 (art 3).

1. WHETHER THE APPLICANT RUNS A REAL RISK OF A DEATH SENTENCE AND HENCE OF EXPOSURE TO THE 'DEATH ROW PHENOMENON'

93. The United Kingdom Government, contrary to the Government of the Federal Republic of Germany, the Commission and the applicant, did not accept that the risk of a death sentence attains a sufficient level of likelihood to bring Article 3 (art 3) into play. Their reasons were fourfold.

Firstly, as illustrated by his interview with the German prosecutor where he appeared to deny any intention to kill . . . the applicant has not acknowledged his guilt of capital murder as such.

Secondly, only a *prima facie* case has so far been made out against him. In particular, in the United Kingdom Government's view the psychiatric evidence . . . is equivocal as to whether Mr Soering was suffering from a disease of the mind sufficient to amount to a defence of insanity under Virginia law . . .

Thirdly, even if Mr Soering is convicted of capital murder, it cannot be assumed that in the general exercise of their discretion the jury will recommend, the judge will confirm and the Supreme Court of Virginia will uphold the imposition of the death penalty . . . The United Kingdom Government referred to the presence of important mitigating factors, such as the applicant's age and mental condition at the time of commission of the offence and his lack of previous criminal activity, which would have to be taken into account by the jury and then by the judge in the separate sentencing proceedings.

Fourthly, the assurance received from the United States must at the very least significantly reduce the risk of a capital sentence either being imposed or carried out . . .

At the public hearing the Attorney General nevertheless made clear his Government's understand-ing that if Mr Soering were extradited to the United States there was 'some risk', which was 'more than merely negligible', that the death penalty would be imposed.

94. As the applicant himself pointed out, he has made to American and British police officers and to two psychiatrists admissions of his participation in the killings of the Haysom parents, although he appeared to retract those admissions somewhat when questioned by the German prosecutor . . . It is not for the European Court to usurp the function of the Virginia courts by ruling that a defence of insan-ity would or would not be available on the psychiatric evidence as it stands. The United Kingdom Government are justified in their assertion that no assumption can be made that Mr Soering would cer-tainly or even probably be convicted of capital murder as charged . . . Nevertheless, as the Attorney

General conceded on their behalf at the public hearing, there is 'a significant risk' that the applicant would be so convicted.

95. Under Virginia law, before a death sentence can be returned the prosecution must prove beyond reasonable doubt the existence of at least one of the two statutory aggravating circumstances, namely future dangerousness or vileness (see paragraph 43 above). In this connection, the horrible and brutal circumstances of the killings . . . would presumably tell against the applicant, regard being had to the case-law on the grounds for establishing the 'vileness' of the crime . . .

Admittedly, taken on their own the mitigating factors do reduce the likelihood of the death sentence being imposed. No less than four of the five facts in mitigation expressly mentioned in the Code of Virginia could arguably apply to Mr Soering's case. These are a defendant's lack of any previous criminal history, the fact that the offence was committed while a defendant was under extreme mental or emotional disturbance, the fact that at the time of commission of the offence the capacity of a defendant to appreciate the criminality of his conduct or to conform his conduct to the requirements of the law was significantly diminished, and a defendant's age . . .

96. These various elements arguing for or against the imposition of a death sentence have to be viewed in the light of the attitude of the prosecuting authorities.

97. The Commonwealth's Attorney for Bedford County, Mr Updike, who is responsible for conducting the prosecution against the applicant, has certified that 'should Jens Soering be convicted of the offence of capital murder as charged . . . a representation will be made in the name of the United Kingdom to the judge at the time of sentencing that it is the wish of the United Kingdom that the death penalty should not be imposed or carried out' . . . The Court notes, like Lord Justice Lloyd in the Divisional Court . . . that this undertaking is far from reflecting the wording of Article IV of the 1972 Extradition Treaty between the United Kingdom and the United States, which speaks of 'assurances satisfactory to the requested Party that the death penalty will not be carried out' . . . However, the offence charged, being a State and not a Federal offence, comes within the jurisdiction of the Commonwealth of Virginia; it appears as a consequence that no direction could or can be given to the Commonwealth's Attorney by any State or Federal authority to promise more; the Virginia courts as judicial bodies cannot bind themselves in advance as to what decisions they may arrive at on the evidence; and the Governor of Virginia does not, as a matter of policy, promise that he will later exercise his executive power to commute a death penalty . . . This being so, Mr Updike's undertaking may well have been the best 'assurance' that the United Kingdom could have obtained from the United States Federal Government in the particular circumstances. According to the statement made to Parliament in 1987 by a Home Office Minister, acceptance of undertakings in such terms 'means that the United Kingdom authorities render up a fugitive or are prepared to send a citizen to face an American court on the clear understanding that the death penalty will not be carried out . . . It would be a fundamental blow to the extradition arrangements between our two countries if the death penalty were carried out on an individual who had been returned under those circumstances' . . . Nonetheless, the effectiveness of such an undertaking has not yet been put to the test.

98. The applicant contended that representations concerning the wishes of a foreign government would not be admissible as a matter of law under the Virginia Code or, if admissible, of any influence on the sentencing judge.

Whatever the position under Virginia law and practice . . . and not withstanding the diplomatic context of the extradition between the United Kingdom and the United States, objectively it cannot be said that the undertaking to inform the judge at the sentencing stage of the wishes of the United Kingdom eliminates the risk of the death penalty being imposed. In the independent exercise of his discretion the Commonwealth's Attorney has himself decided to seek and to persist in seeking the death penalty because the evidence, in his determination, supports such action . . . If the national authority with responsibility for prosecuting the offence takes such a firm stance, it is hardly open to the Court to hold that there are no substantial grounds for believing that the applicant faces a real risk of being sentenced to death and hence experiencing the 'death row phenomenon'.

99. The Court's conclusion is therefore that the likelihood of the feared exposure of the applicant to the 'death row phenomenon' has been shown to be such as to bring Article 3 (art 3) into play.

2. WHETHER IN THE CIRCUMSTANCES THE RISK OF EXPOSURE TO THE 'DEATH ROW PHENOMENON' WOULD MAKE EXTRADITION A BREACH OF ARTICLE 3 (ART 3)

(a) General considerations

100. As is established in the Court's case-law, ill-treatment, including punishment, must attain a minimum level of severity if it is to fall within the scope of Article 3 (art 3). The assessment of this minimum is, in the nature of things, relative; it depends on all the circumstances of the case, such as the nature and context of the treatment or punishment, the manner and method of its execution, its duration, its physical or mental effects and, in some instances, the sex, age and state of health of the victim (see the . . . *Ireland v UK* judgment, Series A No 25, p 65, § 162; and the *Tyrer* judgment of 25 April 1978, Series A No 26, pp 14–15, §§ 29 and 30).

Treatment has been held by the Court to be both 'inhuman' because it was premeditated, was applied for hours at a stretch and 'caused, if not actual bodily injury, at least intense physical and mental suffering', and also 'degrading' because it was 'such as to arouse in [its] victims feelings of fear, anguish and inferiority capable of humiliating and debasing them and possibly breaking their physical or moral resistance' (see the above-mentioned *Ireland v UK* judgment, p 66, § 167). In order for a punishment or treatment associated with it to be 'inhuman' or 'degrading', the suffering or humiliation involved must in any event go beyond that inevitable element of suffering or humiliation connected with a given form of legitimate punishment (see the *Tyrer* judgment, loc. cit.). In this connection, account is to be taken not only of the physical pain experienced but also, where there is a considerable delay before execution of the punishment, of the sentenced person's mental anguish of anticipating the violence he is to have inflicted on him.

101. Capital punishment is permitted under certain conditions by Article 2 § 1 (art 2–1) of the Convention, which reads:

'Everyone's right to life shall be protected by law. No one shall be deprived of his life intentionally save in the execution of a sentence of a court following his conviction of a crime for which this penalty is provided by law.'

In view of this wording, the applicant did not suggest that the death penalty *per se* violated Article 3 (art 3). He, like the two Government Parties, agreed with the Commission that the extradition of a person to a country where he risks the death penalty does not in itself raise an issue under either Article 2 (art 2) or Article 3 (art 3). On the other hand, Amnesty International in their written comments . . . argued that the evolving standards in Western Europe regarding the existence and use of the death penalty required that the death penalty should now be considered as an inhuman and degrading punishment within the meaning of Article 3 (art 3).

102. Certainly, 'the Convention is a living instrument which . . . must be interpreted in the light of present-day conditions'; and, in assessing whether a given treatment or punishment is to be regarded as inhuman or degrading for the purposes of Article 3 (art 3), 'the Court cannot but be influenced by the developments and commonly accepted standards in the penal policy of the member States of the Council of Europe in this field' (see the above-mentioned *Tyrer* judgment, Series A No 26, pp 15–16, § 31). *De facto* the death penalty no longer exists in time of peace in the Contracting States to the Convention. In the few Contracting States which retain the death penalty in law for some peacetime offences, death sentences, if ever imposed, are nowadays not carried out. This 'virtual consensus in Western European legal systems that the death penalty is, under current circumstances, no longer

consistent with regional standards of justice', to use the words of Amnesty International, is reflected in Protocol No 6 (P6) to the Convention, which provides for the abolition of the death penalty in time of peace. Protocol No 6 (P6) was opened for signature in April 1983, which in the practice of the Council of Europe indicates the absence of objection on the part of any of the Member States of the Organisation; it came into force in March 1985 and to date has been ratified by thirteen Contracting States to the Convention, not however including the United Kingdom.

Whether these marked changes have the effect of bringing the death penalty *per se* within the prohibition of ill-treatment under Article 3 (art 3) must be determined on the principles governing the interpretation of the Convention.

103. The Convention is to be read as a whole and Article 3 (art 3) should therefore be construed in harmony with the provisions of Article 2 (art 2) (see, *mutatis mutandis*, the *Klass* judgment of 6 September 1978, Series A No 28, p 31, § 68). On this basis Article 3 (art 3) evidently cannot have been intended by the drafters of the Convention to include a general prohibition of the death penalty since that would nullify the clear wording of Article 2 § 1 (art 2-1).

Subsequent practice in national penal policy, in the form of a generalised abolition of capital punishment, could be taken as establishing the agreement of the Contracting States to abrogate the exception provided for under Article 2 § 1 (art 2-1) and hence to remove a textual limit on the scope for evolutive interpretation of Article 3 (art 3). However, Protocol No 6 (P6), as a subsequent written agreement, shows that the intention of the Contracting Parties as recently as 1983 was to adopt the normal method of amendment of the text in order to introduce a new obligation to abolish capital punishment in time of peace and, what is more, to do so by an optional instrument allowing each State to choose the moment when to undertake such an engagement. In these conditions, notwithstanding the special character of the Convention (see paragraph 87 above), Article 3 (art 3) cannot be interpreted as generally prohibiting the death penalty.

104. That does not mean however that circumstances relating to a death sentence can never give rise to an issue under Article 3 (art 3). The manner in which it is imposed or executed, the personal circumstances of the condemned person and a disproportionality to the gravity of the crime committed, as well as the conditions of detention awaiting execution, are examples of factors capable of bringing the treatment or punishment received by the condemned person within the proscription under Article 3 (art 3). Present-day attitudes in the Contracting States to capital punishment are relevant for the assessment whether the acceptable threshold of suffering or degradation has been exceeded.

(b) The particular circumstances

105. The applicant submitted that the circumstances to which he would be exposed as a consequence of the implementation of the Secretary of State's decision to return him to the United States, namely the 'death row phenomenon', cumulatively constituted such serious treatment that his extradition would be contrary to Article 3 (art 3). He cited in particular the delays in the appeal and review procedures following a death sentence, during which time he would be subject to increasing tension and psychological trauma; the fact, so he said, that the judge or jury in determining sentence is not obliged to take into account the defendant's age and mental state at the time of the offence; the extreme conditions of his future detention on 'death row' in Mecklenburg Correctional Center, where he expects to be the victim of violence and sexual abuse because of his age, colour and nationality; and the constant spectre of the execution itself including the ritual of execution. He also relied on the possibility of extradition or deportation, which he would not oppose, to the Federal Republic of Germany as accentuating the disproportionality of the Secretary of State's decision.

The Government of the Federal Republic of Germany took the view that, taking all the circumstances together, the treatment awaiting the applicant in Virginia would go so far beyond treatment inevitably connected with the imposition and execution of a death penalty as to be 'inhuman' within the meaning of Article 3 (art 3).

On the other hand, the conclusion expressed by the Commission was that the degree of severity contemplated by Article 3 (art 3) would not be attained.

The United Kingdom Government shared this opinion. In particular, they disputed many of the applicant's factual allegations as to the conditions on death row in Mecklenburg and his expected fate there.

I. Length of detention prior to execution

106. The period that a condemned prisoner can expect to spend on death row in Virginia before being executed is on average six to eight years.... This length of time awaiting death is, as the Commission and the United Kingdom Government noted, in a sense largely of the prisoner's own making in that he takes advantage of all avenues of appeal which are offered to him by Virginia law. The automatic appeal to the Supreme Court of Virginia normally takes no more than six months... The remaining time is accounted for by collateral attacks mounted by the prisoner himself in *habeas corpus* proceedings before both the State and Federal courts and in applications to the Supreme Court of the United States for *certiorari* review, the prisoner at each stage being able to seek a stay of execution... The remedies available under Virginia law serve the purpose of ensuring that the ultimate sanction of death is not unlawfully or arbitrarily imposed.

Nevertheless, just as some lapse of time between sentence and execution is inevitable if appeal safeguards are to be provided to the condemned person, so it is equally part of human nature that the person will cling to life by exploiting those safeguards to the full. However well-intentioned and even potentially beneficial is the provision of the complex of post-sentence procedures in Virginia, the consequence is that the condemned prisoner has to endure for many years the conditions on death row and the anguish and mounting tension of living in the ever-present shadow of death.

II. Conditions on death row

107. As to conditions in Mecklenburg Correctional Center, where the applicant could expect to be held if sentenced to death, the Court bases itself on the facts which were uncontested by the United Kingdom Government, without finding it necessary to determine the reliability of the additional evidence adduced by the applicant, notably as to the risk of homosexual abuse and physical attack undergone by prisoners on death row...

... In this connection, the United Kingdom Government drew attention to the necessary requirement of extra security for the safe custody of prisoners condemned to death for murder. While it might thus well be justifiable in principle, the severity of a special regime such as that operated on death row in Mecklenburg is compounded by the fact of inmates being subject to it for a protracted period lasting on average six to eight years.

III. The applicant's age and mental state

108. At the time of the killings, the applicant was only 18 years old and there is some psychiatric evidence, which was not contested as such, that he 'was suffering from [such] an abnormality of mind ... as substantially impaired his mental responsibility for his acts'...

Unlike Article 2 (art 2) of the Convention, Article 6 of the 1966 International Covenant on Civil and Political Rights and Article 4 of the 1969 American Convention on Human Rights expressly prohibit the death penalty from being imposed on persons aged less than 18 at the time of commission of the offence. Whether or not such a prohibition be inherent in the brief and general language of Article 2 (art 2) of the European Convention, its explicit enunciation in other, later international instruments, the former of which has been ratified by a large number of States Parties to the European Convention, at the very least indicates that as a general principle the youth of the person concerned is a circumstance which is liable, with others, to put in question the compatibility with Article 3 (art 3) of measures connected with a death sentence.

It is in line with the Court's case-law (as summarised above at paragraph 100) to treat disturbed mental health as having the same effect for the application of Article 3 (art 3).

109. Virginia law, as the United Kingdom Government and the Commission emphasised, certainly does not ignore these two factors. Under the Virginia Code account has to be taken of mental disturbance in

a defendant, either as an absolute bar to conviction if it is judged to be sufficient to amount to insanity or, like age, as a fact in mitigation at the sentencing stage ... Additionally, indigent capital murder defendants are entitled to the appointment of a qualified mental health expert to assist in the preparation of their submissions at the separate sentencing proceedings ... These provisions in the Virginia Code undoubtedly serve, as the American courts have stated, to prevent the arbitrary or capricious imposition of the death penalty and narrowly to channel the sentencer's discretion. ... They do not however remove the relevance of age and mental condition in relation to the acceptability, under Article 3 (art 3), of the 'death row phenomenon' for a given individual once condemned to death.

Although it is not for this Court to prejudge issues of criminal responsibility and appropriate sentence, the applicant's youth at the time of the offence and his then mental state, on the psychiatric evidence as it stands, are therefore to be taken into consideration as contributory factors tending, in his case, to bring the treatment on death row within the terms of Article 3 (art 3).

IV. Possibility of extradition to the Federal Republic of Germany

110. For the United Kingdom Government and the majority of the Commission, the possibility of extraditing or deporting the applicant to face trial in the Federal Republic of Germany ... where the death penalty has been abolished under the Constitution ... is not material for the present purposes. Any other approach, the United Kingdom Government submitted, would lead to a 'dual standard' affording the protection of the Convention to extraditable persons fortunate enough to have such an alternative destination available but refusing it to others not so fortunate.

This argument is not without weight. Furthermore, the Court cannot overlook either the horrible nature of the murders with which Mr Soering is charged or the legitimate and beneficial role of extradition arrangements in combating crime. The purpose for which his removal to the United States was sought, in accordance with the Extradition Treaty between the United Kingdom and the United States, is undoubtedly a legitimate one. However, sending Mr Soering to be tried in his own country would remove the danger of a fugitive criminal going unpunished as well as the risk of intense and protracted suffering on death row. It is therefore a circumstance of relevance for the overall assessment under Article 3 (art 3) in that it goes to the search for the requisite fair balance of interests and to the proportionality of the contested extradition decision in the particular case (see paragraphs 89 and 104 above).

(c) Conclusion

111. For any prisoner condemned to death, some element of delay between imposition and execution of the sentence and the experience of severe stress in conditions necessary for strict incarceration are inevitable. The democratic character of the Virginia legal system in general and the positive features of Virginia trial, sentencing and appeal procedures in particular are beyond doubt. The Court agrees with the Commission that the machinery of justice to which the applicant would be subject in the United States is in itself neither arbitrary nor unreasonable, but, rather, respects the rule of law and affords not inconsiderable procedural safeguards to the defendant in a capital trial. Facilities are available on death row for the assistance of inmates, notably through provision of psychological and psychiatric services ... However, in the Court's view, having regard to the very long period of time spent on death row in such extreme conditions, with the ever present and mounting anguish of awaiting execution of the death penalty, and to the personal circumstances of the applicant, especially his age and mental state at the time of the offence, the applicant's extradition to the United States would expose him to a real risk of treatment going beyond the threshold set by Article 3 (art 3). A further consideration of relevance is that in the particular instance the legitimate purpose of extradition could be achieved by another means which would not involve suffering of such exceptional intensity or duration.

Accordingly, the Secretary of State's decision to extradite the applicant to the United States would, if implemented, give rise to a breach of Article 3 (art 3).

This finding in no way puts in question the good faith of the United Kingdom Government, who have from the outset of the present proceedings demonstrated their desire to abide by their Convention obligations, firstly by staying the applicant's surrender to the United States authorities in accord with the interim measures indicated by the Convention institutions and secondly by themselves referring the case to the Court for a judicial ruling . . .

FOR THESE REASONS, THE COURT UNANIMOUSLY

I. Holds that, in the event of the Secretary of State's decision to extradite the applicant to the United States of America being implemented, there would be a violation of Article 3; . . .

NOTES

1 The plenary Court was composed of President Ryssdal and Judges: Cremona, Thor Vilhjalmsson, Gölcüklü, Matscher, Pettiti, Walsh, Evans, Macdonald, Russo, Bernhardt, Spielmann, De Meyer, Carrillo Salcedo, Valticos, Martens, Palm, and Foighel.

Soering was eventually extradited to the United States after the UK received an assurance that he would not be prosecuted on capital charges.

The British Parliament abolished the death penalty for the remaining civilian offences of treason and piracy (Crime and Disorder Act 1998) and for military offences, in times of peace and war (Human Rights Act 1998) during 1998. Subsequently, the United Kingdom ratified Protocol 6 (abolition of the death penalty in peacetime) on 20 May 1999 and Protocol 13 (abolition of the death penalty in all circumstances) on 10 October 2003.

2 The *Soering* principle has been extended by the Court to cover Member States' decisions to deport or expel aliens in *Cruz Varas v Sweden* A.201 (1991) 14 EHRR 1. The applicants were a husband, wife and their son all of whom held Chilean citizenship. The husband arrived in Sweden in January 1987 and applied for political asylum. At first he claimed that he had been a member of various left-wing political groups in Chile in the 1960s and 1970s, but that he left Chile for financial reasons. The Swedish National Immigration Board and the Government rejected his request for asylum. Some months later he informed the Swedish authorities that he had been tortured by members of the Chilean security forces in 1986. The Swedish Government decided to continue with his expulsion and he was expelled from Sweden (to Chile) in October 1989. He complained to the Commission alleging, inter alia, a breach of Article 3. A majority of that body, eight votes to five, found no breach of Article 3. The Court held:

69. In its *Soering* judgment of 7 July 1989 the Court held that the decision by a Contracting State to extradite a fugitive may give rise to an issue under Article 3 (art 3), and hence engage the responsibility of that State under the Convention, where substantial grounds have been shown for believing that the person concerned, if extradited, faces a real risk of being subjected to torture or to inhuman or degrading treatment or punishment in the requesting country (Series A No 161, p 35, § 91).

Although the establishment of such responsibility involves an assessment of conditions in the requesting country against the standards of Article 3 (art 3), there is no question of adjudicating on or establishing the responsibility of the receiving country, whether under general international law, under the Convention or otherwise. In so far as any liability under the Convention is or may be incurred, it is liability incurred by the extraditing Contracting State by reason of its having taken action which has as a direct consequence the exposure of an individual to proscribed ill-treatment (ibid, p 36, § 91).

70. Although the present case concerns expulsion as opposed to a decision to extradite, the Court considers that the above principle also applies to expulsion decisions and *a fortiori* to cases of actual expulsion.

75. In determining whether substantial grounds have been shown for believing in the existence of a real risk of treatment contrary to Article 3 (art 3) the Court will assess the issue in the light of all the material placed before it or, if necessary, material obtained *proprio motu* (see the *Ireland v UK* judgment of 18 January 1978, Series A No 25, p 64, § 160).

76. Since the nature of the Contracting States' responsibility under Article 3 (art 3) in cases of this kind lies in the act of exposing an individual to the risk of ill-treatment, the existence of the risk must be assessed primarily with reference to those facts which were known or ought to have been known to the Contracting State at the time of the expulsion; the Court is not precluded, however, from having regard to information which comes to light subsequent to the expulsion. This may be of value in confirming or refuting the appreciation that has been made by the Contracting Party or the well-foundedness or otherwise of an applicant's fears.

A majority of the Court, eighteen votes to one, went on to find that the principle's requirements had not been satisfied in this case because, inter alia, of doubts regarding the credibility of the applicant's claims regarding his alleged maltreatment in Chile, the re-emergence of democracy in Chile and the thorough examination of the applicant's case by the Swedish immigration authorities. Therefore, no breach of Article 3 had occurred.

3 The Court has held that mere membership of a minority group, which is caught up in a foreign civil conflict, is not of itself enough to satisfy the *Soering* principle. The evidence must show that there were substantial grounds for believing that the particular applicant was at real risk of being subject to prohibited treatment if he/she was to be deported back to the State where the conflict was occurring. In *Vilvarajah v UK*, A.215 (1991) 14 EHRR 248, the applicants were Sri Lankan citizens of Tamil ethnic origin. Tamils make up about 20 per cent of the population of Sri Lanka and there has been ethnic conflict between the majority Sinhalese and the minority Tamils for several decades. The applicants were refused political asylum in the UK and returned to Sri Lanka where several of them claimed to have been seriously mistreated by security officials (one applicant alleged that he was beaten with belts and kicked for about half an hour by police officers). Subsequently, the British authorities allowed them to return to stay in the UK. The Commission, on the casting vote of the President, expressed the opinion that there had been no breach of Article 3 in respect of the UK's original decisions to deport the applicants. A majority of the Court, eight votes to one, upheld that finding.

111. The evidence before the Court concerning the background of the applicants, as well as the general situation, does not establish that their personal position was any worse than the generality of other members of the Tamil community or other young male Tamils who were returning to their country. Since the situation was still unsettled there existed the possibility that they might be detained and ill-treated as appears to have occurred previously in the cases of some of the applicants . . . A mere possibility of ill-treatment, however, in such circumstances, is not in itself sufficient to give rise to a breach of Article 3.

4 The Court ruled in *Chahal v UK* (1996) 23 EHRR 413, 1996-V, that the conduct of the individual was not a relevant factor in the application of the *Soering* principle. Mr Chahal is an Indian citizen who illegally entered the UK in 1971. Three years later he was given indefinite leave to remain under the terms of an amnesty for illegal entrants. Subsequently he married another Indian citizen and she came to live with him in the UK. They had two children born in the UK (who have British citizenship). In the early 1980s Mr Chahal visited the Punjab province and was baptised into Sikhism. At this time there was considerable violence taking place between Sikh separatists, who wanted an independent State, and Indian security forces; since 1984 over 20,000 people have been killed in this conflict. When he returned to the UK Mr Chahal became a leading figure in the Sikh community and he organised protests against the Indian government. He was arrested several times, on suspicion of conspiring to kill the Indian Prime Minister and moderate Sikhs in the UK, but he was released without charge. In 1990 the Home Secretary decided that Mr Chahal ought to be deported as his presence in the UK was contrary to the public good for reasons of national security and the international fight against terrorism. The Secretary ordered the detention of Chahal who sought, unsuccessfully, to challenge that decision before an advisory panel and in judicial review proceedings. Chahal complained to the Commission and it requested the UK to stay the deportation of the applicant. Later the Commission expressed the unanimous opinion that, inter alia, there would be a breach of Article 3 if the applicant were to be deported to India because of the applicant's notoriety and the level of violence against Sikh separatists and their supporters in that country. Before the Court, the British Government argued that the guarantees under Article 3 were not absolute where the applicant posed a threat to the national security of the member State. However, this limitation was not accepted by the Court:

79. Article 3 (art 3) enshrines one of the most fundamental values of democratic society (see ... *Soering* judgment, p 34, para 88). The Court is well aware of the immense difficulties faced by States in modern times in protecting their communities from terrorist violence. However, even in these circumstances, the Convention prohibits in absolute terms torture or inhuman or degrading treatment or punishment, irrespective of the victim's conduct. Unlike most of the substantive clauses of the Convention and of Protocols Nos. 1 and 4 (P1, P4), Article 3 (art 3) makes no provision for exceptions and no derogation from it is permissible under Article 15 (art 15) even in the event of a public emergency threatening the life of the nation (see the *Ireland v UK* judgment of 18 January 1978, Series A No 25, p 65, para 163, and also the *Tomasi v France* judgment of 27 August 1992, Series A No 241-A, p 42, para 115).

80. The prohibition provided by Article 3 (art 3) against ill-treatment is equally absolute in expulsion cases. Thus, whenever substantial grounds have been shown for believing that an individual would face a real risk of being subjected to treatment contrary to Article 3 (art 3) if removed to another State, the responsibility of the Contracting State to safeguard him or her against such treatment is engaged in the event of expulsion (see the ... *Vilvarajah* judgment, p 34, para 103). In these circumstances, the activities of the individual in question, however undesirable or dangerous, cannot be a material consideration ...

81. Paragraph 88 of the Court's above-mentioned *Soering* judgment, which concerned extradition to the United States, clearly and forcefully expresses the above view. It should not be inferred from the Court's remarks concerning the risk of undermining the foundations of extradition, as set out in paragraph 89 of the same judgment, that there is any room for balancing the risk of ill-treatment against the reasons for expulsion in determining whether a State's responsibility under Article 3 (art 3) is engaged.

82. It follows from the above that it is not necessary for the Court to enter into a consideration of the Government's untested, but no doubt *bona fide*, allegations about the first applicant's terrorist activities and the threat posed by him to national security.

C. APPLICATION OF ARTICLE 3 (ART 3) IN THE CIRCUMSTANCES OF THE CASE

1. THE POINT OF TIME FOR THE ASSESSMENT OF THE RISK

83. Although there were differing views on the situation in India and in Punjab ... it was agreed that the violence and instability in that region reached a peak in 1992 and had been abating ever since. For this reason, the date taken by the Court for its assessment of the risk to Mr Chahal if expelled to India is of importance.

84. The applicant argued that the Court should consider the position in June 1992, at the time when the decision to deport him was made final ... The purpose of the stay on removal requested by the Commission ... was to prevent irremediable damage and not to afford the High Contracting Party with an opportunity to improve its case. Moreover, it was not appropriate that the Strasbourg organs should be involved in a continual fact-finding operation.

85. The Government, with whom the Commission agreed, submitted that because the responsibility of the State under Article 3 of the Convention (art 3) in expulsion cases lies in the act of exposing an individual to a real risk of ill-treatment, the material date for the assessment of risk was the time of the proposed deportation. Since Mr Chahal had not yet been expelled, the relevant time was that of the proceedings before the Court.

86. ... as far as the applicant's complaint under Article 3 (art 3) is concerned, the crucial question is whether it has been substantiated that there is a real risk that Mr Chahal, if expelled, would be subjected to treatment prohibited by that Article (art 3). Since he has not yet been deported, the material point in time must be that of the Court's consideration of the case. It follows that, although the historical position is of interest in so far as it may shed light on the current situation and its likely evolution, it is the present conditions which are decisive ....

A majority of the Court, 12 votes to 7, went on to determine that the evidence showed that the contemporary involvement of the Indian security forces in killings and serious human rights violations associated with the problems in the Punjab meant that there was a real risk of Mr Chahal being subject to treatment contrary to Article 3 if he were to be deported to India. Therefore, the UK would violate Article 3 if it were to implement the Home Secretary's deportation order.

In addition to reinforcing the absolute nature of the guarantees contained in Article 3, the above judgment also provides valuable guidance regarding the time at which the risk to the applicant should be assessed. Where the applicant has been extradited/deported the date of that action will be appropriate, but where the applicant has not yet been expelled the Court will consider the risk at the time of the determination of the case at Strasbourg.

5   The nature and sources of the prohibited forms of treatment which fall within the *Soering* principle were defined very broadly by the unanimous Court in *D v UK* (1997) 24 EHRR 423, 1997-III. The applicant was a citizen of St Kitts who was in the terminal stages of AIDS (Acquired Immunodeficiency Syndrome). He had sought to enter the UK in 1993, but was found to be in possession of a large quantity of cocaine. He was formally refused entry to the UK and arrested. Subsequently, he pleaded guilty to being knowingly involved in the fraudulent evasion of the prohibition on the importation of controlled drugs into the UK. He was sentenced to six years' imprisonment. While in prison it was discovered that the applicant was HIV (Human Immunodeficiency Virus) positive, the infection appeared to have occurred at some time prior to his arrival in the UK. He was given medical treatment and allowed a period of compassionate leave in 1995. Prior to his release from prison in January 1996 (on licence because of his good behaviour) the immigration authorities gave directions for his deportation to St Kitts. The applicant's lawyers sought leave for him to remain in the UK on compassionate grounds as they argued that he would not be able to receive the same specialist medical care in St Kitts that he was currently receiving in the UK, thereby shortening his life expectancy. The Chief Immigration Officer refused the request and judicial review proceedings were also unsuccessful. The applicant complained to the Commission and it requested the UK not to deport him while his case was being examined. The Commission, by eleven votes to seven, expressed the opinion that there would be a breach of Article 3 if the applicant were to be deported. Before the Court, the applicant's lawyers argued that his removal to St Kitts would condemn him to an even earlier death in conditions of squalor and destitution (as he had no close relatives or friends to care for him and expensive drug therapies were not available to patients with HIV/AIDS in St Kitts).

B. THE COURT'S ASSESSMENT

46. The Court recalls at the outset that Contracting States have the right, as a matter of well-established international law and subject to their treaty obligations including the Convention, to control the entry, residence and expulsion of aliens. It also notes the gravity of the offence which was committed by the applicant and is acutely aware of the problems confronting Contracting States in their efforts to combat the harm caused to their societies through the supply of drugs from abroad. The administration of severe sanctions to persons involved in drug trafficking, including expulsion of alien drug couriers like the applicant, is a justified response to this scourge.

47. However, in exercising their right to expel such aliens Contracting States must have regard to Article 3 of the Convention (art 3), which enshrines one of the fundamental values of democratic societies. It is precisely for this reason that the Court has repeatedly stressed in its line of authorities involving extradition, expulsion or deportation of individuals to third countries that Article 3 (art 3) prohibits in absolute terms torture or inhuman or degrading treatment or punishment and that its guarantees apply irrespective of the reprehensible nature of the conduct of the person in question . . .

48. The Court observes that the above principle is applicable to the applicant's removal under the Immigration Act 1971. Regardless of whether or not he ever entered the United Kingdom in the technical sense . . . is to be noted that he has been physically present there and thus within the jurisdiction of the respondent State within the meaning of Article 1 of the Convention (art 1) since 21 January 1993. It is for the respondent State therefore to secure to the applicant the rights guaranteed under Article 3 (art 3) irrespective of the gravity of the offence which he committed.

49. It is true that this principle has so far been applied by the Court in contexts in which the risk to the individual of being subjected to any of the proscribed forms of treatment emanates from intentionally inflicted acts of the public authorities in the receiving country or from those of non-State bodies in that country when the authorities there are unable to afford him appropriate protection . . . Aside from these situations and given the fundamental importance of Article 3 (art 3) in the Convention system, the Court must reserve to itself sufficient flexibility to address the application of that Article (art 3) in other contexts which might arise. It is not therefore prevented from scrutinising an applicant's claim under Article 3 (art 3) where the source of the risk of proscribed treatment in the receiving country stems from factors which cannot engage either directly or indirectly the responsibility of the public authorities of that country, or which, taken alone, do not in themselves infringe the standards of that Article (art 3). To limit the application of Article 3 (art 3) in this manner would be to undermine the absolute character of its protection. In any such contexts, however, the Court must subject all the circumstances surrounding the case to a rigorous scrutiny, especially the applicant's personal situation in the expelling State.

50. Against this background the Court will determine whether there is a real risk that the applicant's removal would be contrary to the standards of Article 3 (art 3) in view of his present medical condition. In so doing the Court will assess the risk in the light of the material before it at the time of its consideration of the case, including the most recent information on his state of health . . .

51. The Court notes that the applicant is in the advanced stages of a terminal and incurable illness. At the date of the hearing, it was observed that there had been a marked decline in his condition and he had to be transferred to a hospital. His condition was giving rise to concern . . . . The limited quality of life he now enjoys results from the availability of sophisticated treatment and medication in the United Kingdom and the care and kindness administered by a charitable organisation. He has been counselled on how to approach death and has formed bonds with his carers.

52. The abrupt withdrawal of these facilities will entail the most dramatic consequences for him. It is not disputed that his removal will hasten his death. There is a serious danger that the conditions of adversity which await him in St Kitts will further reduce his already limited life expectancy and subject him to

acute mental and physical suffering. Any medical treatment which he might hope to receive there could not contend with the infections which he may possibly contract on account of his lack of shelter and of a proper diet as well as exposure to the health and sanitation problems which beset the population of St Kitts . . . While he may have a cousin in St Kitts . . . no evidence has been adduced to show whether this person would be willing or in a position to attend to the needs of a terminally ill man. There is no evidence of any other form of moral or social support. Nor has it been shown whether the applicant would be guaranteed a bed in either of the hospitals on the island which, according to the Government, care for AIDS patients . . .

53. In view of these exceptional circumstances and bearing in mind the critical stage now reached in the applicant's fatal illness, the implementation of the decision to remove him to St Kitts would amount to inhuman treatment by the respondent State in violation of Article 3 (art 3).

The Court also notes in this respect that the respondent State has assumed responsibility for treating the applicant's condition since August 1994. He has become reliant on the medical and palliative care which he is at present receiving and is no doubt psychologically prepared for death in an environment which is both familiar and compassionate. Although it cannot be said that the conditions which would confront him in the receiving country are themselves a breach of the standards of Article 3 (art 3), his removal would expose him to a real risk of dying under most distressing circumstances and would thus amount to inhuman treatment . . . .

54. Against this background the Court emphasises that aliens who have served their prison sentences and are subject to expulsion cannot in principle claim any entitlement to remain in the territory of a Contracting State in order to continue to benefit from medical, social or other forms of assistance provided by the expelling State during their stay in prison.

However, in the very exceptional circumstances of this case and given the compelling humanitarian considerations at stake, it must be concluded that the implementation of the decision to remove the applicant would be a violation of Article 3 (art 3) . . . .

Clearly the Court was motivated by the extreme plight of the applicant's situation in concluding that deportation to his country of birth would amount to inhuman treatment. Given the increase in HIV/AIDS in many countries it is, sadly, not surprising that other non-nationals infected with HIV have contended that their deportation from Member States to their home States would violate Article 3. The Court has responded by emphasizing the 'very exceptional circumstances' in *D*. For example, in *Amegnigan v Netherlands*, decision of 25 November 2004, a unanimous Chamber determined the applicant's claim to be inadmissible. Amegnigan was a 24-year-old Togolese national who had been refused asylum on three occasions by the Dutch authorities. Whilst those applications were being determined the applicant was found to be infected with HIV and he was placed on antiretroviral medication. His condition stabilized but his doctor noted that if the medication were stopped the applicant would regress to the advanced stage of the disease. The applicant complained that if he were returned to Togo, given the difficulty of obtaining suitable medication there, his life expectancy would be considerable reduced and therefore deportation would amount to a breach of Article 3. The Chamber concluded that:

The Court has found no indication in the applicant's submissions that he has reached the stage of full-blown AIDS or that he is suffering from any HIV-related illness. Whilst acknowledging the assessment of the applicant's treating specialist doctor that the applicant's health condition would relapse if treatment would be discontinued, the Court notes that adequate treatment is in principle available in Togo, albeit at a possibly considerable cost.

In these circumstances the Court considers that, unlike the situation in the above-cited case of *D. v the United Kingdom* or in the case of *B.B. v France* (No 39030/96, Commission's report of 9 March 1998, subsequently struck out by the Court by judgment of 7 September 1998, *Reports* 1998-VI, p 2595), it does not appear that the applicant's illness has attained an advanced or terminal stage, or that he has no prospect of medical care or family support in Togo where his mother and a younger brother are residing. The fact that the applicant's circumstances in Togo would be less favourable than those he enjoys in the Netherlands cannot be regarded as decisive from the point of view of Article 3 of the Convention.

Accordingly, although the Court accepts the seriousness of the applicant's medical condition, it does not find that the circumstances of his situation are of such an exceptional nature that his expulsion would amount to treatment proscribed by Article 3 of the Convention.

It follows that the application is manifestly ill-founded within the meaning of Article 35 § 3 of the Convention and must be rejected pursuant to Article 35 § 4 of the Convention.

6   One day after giving judgment in the case of *D v UK*, the Court further broadened the scope of the *Soering* principle by stating that the source of the risk of an applicant being subject to treatment contrary to Article 3 could arise from the actions of private persons, such as organised criminals. In *HLR v France, Reports of Judgments and Decisions* 1997–111 758, the applicant was a Colombian national who was arrested at a French airport in possession of 580 grammes of cocaine. While being questioned by the police the applicant provided officers with information on other persons involved in the smuggling of drugs. This information facilitated the conviction of another person for drugs smuggling in Germany. The applicant was convicted of drugs offences and sentenced to five years' imprisonment and permanent exclusion from French territory. After the applicant had served his sentence the French authorities began the process of deporting him. He complained to the Commission alleging that if he were to be returned to Colombia he would face a real risk of serious injury or death at the hands of the drug traffickers whom he had informed on. The Commission, by nineteen votes to ten, expressed the opinion that if France were to deport the applicant in these circumstances it would amount to a breach of Article 3. The Court held that:

40. Owing to the absolute character of the right guaranteed, the Court does not rule out the possibility that Article 3 of the Convention (art 3) may also apply where the danger emanates from persons or groups of persons who are not public officials. However, it must be shown that the risk is real and that the authorities of the receiving State are not able to obviate the risk by providing appropriate protection.

41. Like the Commission, the Court can but note the general situation of violence existing in the country of destination. It considers, however, that this circumstance would not in itself entail, in the event of deportation, a violation of Article 3 (art 3).

42. The documents from various sources produced in support of the applicant's memorial provide insight into the tense atmosphere in Colombia, but do not contain any indication of the existence of a situation comparable to his own. Although drug traffickers sometimes take revenge on informers, there is no relevant evidence to show in H.L.R.'s case that the alleged risk is real. His aunt's letters cannot by themselves suffice to show that the threat is real. Moreover, there are no documents to support the claim that the applicant's personal situation would be worse than that of other Colombians, were he to be deported.

Amnesty International's reports for 1995 and 1996 do not provide any information on the type of situation in which the applicant finds himself. They describe acts of the security forces and guerrilla movements. Only in the 1995 report is there any reference, in a context which is not relevant to the present case, to criminal acts attributable to drug trafficking organisations.

43. The Court is aware, too, of the difficulties the Colombian authorities face in containing the violence. The applicant has not shown that they are incapable of affording him appropriate protection.

44. In the light of these considerations, the Court finds that no substantial grounds have been established for believing that the applicant, if deported, would be exposed to a real risk of being subjected to inhuman or degrading treatment within the meaning of Article 3 (art 3). It follows that there would be no violation of Article 3 (art 3) if the order for the applicant's deportation were to be executed.

Six judges dissented as they believed that the risk to the applicant was sufficient to satisfy the *Soering* test.

The deportation of aliens may also raise Convention issues under Article 8 (right to respect for family life), see below p 526.

7   A unanimous Chamber distinguished *D v UK* in *Bensaid v United Kingdom*, judgment of 6 February 2001. The applicant was an Algerian national whom the authorities decided to deport in 1997 after enquiries indicated that he had obtained leave to remain in the UK by deception (through a marriage of convenience). Since 1994 he had developed schizophrenia and had been prescribed anti-psychotic medication by the national health service. Bensaid contended that if he were removed to Algeira he would not receive the same level of medical care that he was receiving in the UK and consequently he would suffer a real risk of a relapse of his illness. The British Government submitted evidence that the drugs the applicant was currently receiving were available (freely under the Algerian national social insurance fund) at a hospital 75 km from his home village.

38. The Court observes, however, that the applicant faces the risk of relapse even if he stays in the United Kingdom as his illness is long term and requires constant management. Removal will arguably increase the risk, as will the differences in available personal support and accessibility of treatment. The applicant has argued, in particular, that other drugs are less likely to be of benefit to his condition, and also that the option of becoming an inpatient should be a last resort. Nonetheless, medical treatment is available to the applicant in Algeria. The fact that the applicant's circumstances in Algeria would be less favourable than those enjoyed by him in the United Kingdom is not decisive from the point of view of Article 3 of the Convention.

39. The Court finds that the risk that the applicant would suffer a deterioration in his condition if he were returned to Algeria and that, if he did, he would not receive adequate support or care is to a large extent speculative. The arguments concerning the attitude of his family as devout Muslims, the difficulty of travelling to Blida [where the nearest hospital was located] and the effects on his health of these factors are also speculative. The information provided by the parties does not indicate that travel to the hospital is effectively prevented by the situation in the region. The applicant is not himself a likely target of terrorist activity. Even if his family does not have a car, this does not exclude the possibility of other arrangements being made.

40. The Court accepts the seriousness of the applicant's medical condition. Having regard, however, to the high threshold set by Article 3, particularly where the case does not concern the direct responsibility of the Contracting State for the infliction of harm, the Court does not find that there is a sufficiently real risk that the applicant's removal in these circumstances would be contrary to the standards of Article 3. The case does not disclose the exceptional circumstances of *D. v the United Kingdom* (cited above), where the applicant was in the final stages of a terminal illness, Aids, and had no prospect of medical care or family support on expulsion to St Kitts.

41. The Court finds, therefore, that the implementation of the decision to remove the applicant to Algeria would not violate Article 3 of the Convention.

The decisive factors in *Bensaid* were that his illness, although serious, was not terminal and he would be able to receive appropriate medical treatment together with family support in his home State.

8   In *D. and Others v Turkey*, judgment of 22 June 2006, a unanimous Chamber held that the deportation of a married woman (together with her husband and child) to her home State of Iran where she had been sentenced to 100 lashes for fornication (she had married her husband in a Sunni ceremony without the consent of her father, a Shia) would constitute inhuman treatment. The Chamber expressed the view that where a legal system permitted such physical violence, even if it was imposed by a symbolic punishment using a special lash with 100 tails, the sentence was 'inhuman'.

For earlier case law involving corporal punishment see the section below on Degrading punishment.

Degrading treatment

Yankov v Bulgaria judgment of 11 December 2003
European Court of Human Rights

The applicant, a Bulgarian national born in 1943, had a doctorate in economics and was the executive director of an agricultural investment fund and a financial company. In March 1996 he had been arrested and detained in respect of alleged criminal dereliction of his professional duties. He was subsequently held in custody pending his trial. Whilst in prison, on 10 March 1998, prior to a meeting with his lawyers the applicant was searched. The officers found and confiscated a manuscript from the applicant. The manuscript was read and it contained an account of the applicant's prosecution and imprisonment by the authorities. Parts of the manuscript were highly critical of officials: e.g. 'The search [in the apartment] was conducted by police officer [B.]. His inexperience was betrayed by his behaviour, he was a provincial parvenu ... The [prison] wardens, most of whom are simple villagers and are better paid than teachers, doctors and engineers, 'work' 24 hours and then have a 72-hour rest ... ' On the same day the prison governor ordered that the applicant be placed in an isolation cell for seven days as punishment for having made offensive remarks about public officials. The applicant contended that the manuscript was the draft of a book he had been writing and he had merely intended to read parts of the manuscript to his lawyers, while the prison officer who seized the manuscript claimed that the applicant had planned to transmit it to his lawyer. Prior to being placed in the isolation cell the applicant's head was shaved (no other prisoners had witnessed the shaving). Two days after being released from the isolation cell the applicant was brought before a public hearing of the District Court and the fact that his head had been shaved was noticeable. Subsequently the applicant lodged a complaint with the Strasbourg authorities alleging, *inter alia*, that the shaving of his head amounted to a breach of Article 3.

105. In considering whether treatment is 'degrading' within the meaning of Article 3, the Court will have regard to whether its object is to humiliate and debase the person concerned and whether, as far as the consequences are concerned, it adversely affected his or her personality in a manner incompatible with Article 3. Even the absence of such a purpose cannot conclusively rule out a finding of a violation of Article 3 (see, for example, *Peers v Greece*, No 28524/95, § 74, ECHR 2001-III; and *Kalashnikov v Russia*, No 47095/99, § 101, ECHR 2002-VI).

106. Ill-treatment must attain a minimum level of severity if it is to fall within the scope of Article 3 of the Convention. The assessment of this minimum level of severity is relative; it depends on all the circumstances of the case, such as the duration of the treatment, its physical and mental effects and, in some

cases, the sex, age and state of health of the victim (see *Ireland v the United Kingdom*, judgment of 18 January 1978, Series A No 25, p. 65, § 162).

107. The Court has consistently stressed that the suffering and humiliation involved must go beyond that inevitable element of suffering or humiliation connected with a given form of legitimate treatment or punishment. Measures depriving a person of his liberty may often involve such an element. The State must ensure that a person is detained in conditions which are compatible with respect for his human dignity, that the manner and method of the execution of the measure do not subject him to distress or hardship of an intensity exceeding the unavoidable level of suffering inherent in detention and that, given the practical demands of imprisonment, his health and well-being are adequately secured (*Kudla v Poland* [GC], No 30210/96, §§ 93–4, ECHR 2000-XI).

2. Application of those principles in the present case

108. The Court notes that the applicant's hair was shaved off before his placement in an isolation cell.

109. The Court has not had occasion to rule on whether or not the forced shaving off of a prisoner's hair may constitute degrading treatment contrary to Article 3 of the Convention.

112. A particular characteristic of the treatment complained of, the forced shaving off of a prisoner's hair, is that it consists in a forced change of the person's appearance by the removal of his hair. The person undergoing that treatment is very likely to experience a feeling of inferiority as his physical appearance is changed against his will.

113. Furthermore, for at least a certain period of time a prisoner whose hair has been shaved off carries a mark of the treatment he has undergone. The mark is immediately visible to others, including prison staff, co-detainees and visitors or the public, if the prisoner is released or brought into a public place soon thereafter. The person concerned is very likely to feel hurt in his dignity by the fact that he carries a visible physical mark.

114. The Court thus considers that the forced shaving off of detainees' hair is in principle an act which may have the effect of diminishing their human dignity or may arouse in them feelings of inferiority capable of humiliating and debasing them. Whether or not the minimum threshold of severity is reached and, consequently, whether or not the treatment complained of constitutes degrading treatment contrary to Article 3 of the Convention will depend on the particular facts of the case, including the victim's personal circumstances, the context in which the impugned act was carried out and its aim.

115. The Court rejects as being unsubstantiated the Government's allegation that the applicant's hair was shaved off as a hygienic measure. It has not been alleged that a problem of infestation existed in the particular detention facility. It is also unclear why the hygienic requirements for entry into the isolation cell would differ from those concerning other cells in the same detention facility.

116. The Government have not offered any other explanation. Therefore, even assuming that there was a practice of shaving off of the hair of prisoners punished by confinement in an isolation cell . . . the act complained of had no legal basis and valid justification.

117. The Court thus considers that even if it was not intended to humiliate, the removal of the applicant's hair without specific justification contained in itself an arbitrary punitive element and was therefore likely to appear in his eyes to be aimed at debasing and/or subduing him.

118. Furthermore, in the particular case the applicant must have had reasons to believe that the aim had been to humiliate him, given the fact that his hair was shaved off by the prison administration in the context of a punishment imposed on him for writing critical and offensive remarks about prison warders, among others.

119. Additional factors to be taken into consideration in the present case are the applicant's age—55 at the relevant time—and the fact that he appeared at a public hearing nine days after his hair had been shaved off.

120. Having regard to the foregoing, the Court considers that in the particular circumstances of the present case the shaving off of the applicant's hair in the context of his punishment by confinement in an isolation cell for writing critical and offensive remarks about prison warders and State organs constituted an unjustified treatment of sufficient severity to be characterised as degrading within the meaning of Article 3 of the Convention.

121. It follows that there has been a violation of Article 3 of the Convention on account of the forced removal of the applicant's hair.

FOR THESE REASONS, THE COURT UNANIMOUSLY

1. *Holds* that there has been a violation of Article 3 of the Convention;

NOTES

1 The Court was composed of President Rozakis and Judges: Tulkens, Vajic, Levits, Botoucharova, Kovler, and Zagrebelsky.

2 *Yankov* reveals that degrading treatment can occur via intentionally humiliating acts or by subjecting a person to degrading conditions. For a consideration of the Article 10 aspects of the judgment see below p 648.

3 An example of State officials intentionally subjecting a person to degrading treatment occurred in *Iwanczuk v Poland*, judgment of 15 November 2001. The applicant was a remand prisoner awaiting trial on charges of misappropriation. At 9.30 pm on 19 September 1993 he asked the Wroclaw prison authorities to allow him to visit the voting facilities in the prison, so that he might cast his vote in the parliamentary elections. A prison officer took him to the guards' room and four guards told him that he would have to undress and undergo a body search in order to be allowed to vote. The applicant removed all his clothes, except his underwear, and the guards verbally abused him (in part by making humiliating comments about his body). The guards ordered that he strip naked. The applicant refused. He also refused to undergo a body search. Consequently the guards denied him the opportunity to vote and took him back to his cell. Iwanczuk subsequently lodged a complaint with the Strasbourg authorities alleging, *inter alia*, that the guards' behaviour constituted degrading treatment in breach of Article 3. The Court determined that the guards' order that the applicant undergo a body search as a precondition to being allowed to enter the voting area in the prison was not necessary. Relevant factors included his peaceful behaviour during his entire period of detention, the nature of the charges against him (not involving allegations of violence) and the absence of previous convictions against the applicant. The Court held that:

59. . . . whilst strip searches may be necessary on occasions to ensure prison security or prevent disorder in prisons, they must be conducted in an appropriate manner. In the present case, the prison's guards verbally abused and derided the applicant. Their behaviour was intended to cause in the applicant feelings of humiliation and inferiority. This, in the Court's view, showed a lack of respect for the applicant's human dignity.

Therefore, by six votes to one, the Court determined that the applicant had been subjected to degrading treatment. Here the guards' behaviour was unjustified/unprofessional and suggests that they were seeking to humiliate him as a response to his request to vote during the late evening. For the Court's consideration of a high security regime involving regular strip-searches see *Van Der Ven v Netherlands* (above p 185).

4   In recent years the Court has found that poor physical conditions of detention in a number of States constituted degrading treatment even though there was no intention to humiliate detainees. Examples include: *Dougoz v Greece*, judgment of 6 March 2001, where a convicted foreign drugs offender was held for ten months in Drapetsona detention centre and for eight months in Alexandras Avenue police headquarters (both locations were severely overcrowded and there were no beds, mattresses or blankets). The Court, unanimously, determined that:

46. . . . conditions of detention may sometimes amount to inhuman or degrading treatment. In the *Greek case* (Yearbook of the European Convention on Human Rights No 12, 1969), the Commission reached this conclusion regarding overcrowding and inadequate facilities for heating, sanitation, sleeping arrangements, food, recreation and contacts with the outside world. When assessing conditions of detention, account has to be taken of the cumulative effects of these conditions, as well as of specific allegations made by the applicant. In the present case, although the Court has not conducted an on-site visit, it notes that the applicant's allegations are corroborated by the conclusions of the CPT [the European Committee for the Prevention of Torture and Inhuman or Degrading Treatment or Punishment] report of 29 November 1994 regarding the Police Headquarters in Alexandras Avenue. In its report the CPT stressed that the cellular accommodation and detention regime in that place were quite unsuitable for a period in excess of a few days, the occupancy levels being grossly excessive and the sanitary facilities appalling. Although the CPT had not visited the Drapetsona detention centre at that time, the Court notes that the Government had described the conditions in Alexandras as being the same as in Drapetsona, and the applicant himself conceded that the former were slightly better with natural light, air in the cells and adequate hot water.

47. Furthermore, the Court does not lose sight of the fact that in 1997 the CPT visited both the Alexandras Police Headquarters and the Drapetsona detention centre and felt it necessary to renew its visit to both places in 1999. The applicant was detained in the interim from July 1997 to December 1998.

48. In the light of the above, the Court considers that the conditions of detention of the applicant in the Alexandras Police Headquarters and the Drapetsona detention centre, in particular the serious overcrowding and absence of sleeping facilities, combined with the inordinate length of the period during which he was detained in such conditions, amounted to degrading treatment contrary to Article 3.

Shortly afterwards the segregation unit of Koridallos prison was found to breach this element of Article 3 in *Peers v Greece*, judgment of 19 April 2001. The applicant was a British drug addict who had been convicted of drugs offences. He was detained in the segregation unit for two months while he underwent drugs withdrawal. During that time he had to share a single person cell with another prisoner and they had to use an open toilet (with no screen from the sleeping area) in their cell. A united Court concluded that:

74. . . . in the present case there is no evidence that there was a positive intention of humiliating or debasing the applicant. However, the Court notes that, although the question whether the purpose of the treatment was to humiliate or debase the victim is a factor to be taken into account, the absence of any such purpose cannot conclusively rule out a finding of violation of Article 3 (*V. v the United Kingdom* [GC], No 24888/94, § 71, ECHR-IX).

75. Indeed, in the present case, the fact remains that the competent authorities have taken no steps to improve the objectively unacceptable conditions of the applicant's detention. In the Court's view, this

omission denotes lack of respect for the applicant. The Court takes particularly into account that, for at least two months, the applicant had to spend a considerable part of each 24-hour period practically confined to his bed in a cell with no ventilation and no window which would at times become unbearably hot. He also had to use the toilet in the presence of another inmate and be present while the toilet was being used by his cellmate. The Court is not convinced by the Government's allegation that these conditions have not affected the applicant in a manner incompatible with Article 3. On the contrary, the Court is of the opinion that the prison conditions complained of diminished the applicant's human dignity and arose in him feelings of anguish and inferiority capable of humiliating and debasing him and possibly breaking his physical or moral resistance. In sum, the Court considers that the conditions of the applicant's detention in the segregation unit of the Delta wing of the Koridallos prison amounted to degrading treatment within the meaning of Article 3 of the Convention.

A few days detention of a severely disabled person was found to breach this provision in *Price v United Kingdom*, judgment of 10 July 2001. The applicant was a four-limb deficient victim of Thalidomide. In 1995 she refused to answer questions regarding her financial position during civil proceedings. The judge found her in contempt of court and ordered that she be committed to prison for seven days. She was held in the cells of Lincoln police station that night, as it was too late to send her to a prison. Price had to sleep in her wheelchair (she claimed that she could not sleep on the wooden bed as it would have been too painful for her hips) and was cold (extra blankets were provided and a doctor attended her). The next day she was moved to the health centre of New Hall Women's Prison, in Wakefield. Her cell had a wider wheelchair door access, hand pulls on the toilet, and a hydraulic hospital bed. Constant nursing care was provided. Male officers were required to help the nurse lift Price on and off the toilet. She was released after four days (due to the rules on remission of sentences). Price alleged that her treatment during detention breached Article 3. The Court, unanimously, found that:

30. There is no evidence in this case of any positive intention to humiliate or debase the applicant. However, the Court considers that to detain a severely disabled person in conditions where she is dangerously cold, risks developing sores because her bed is too hard or unreachable, and is unable to go to the toilet or keep clean without the greatest of difficulty, constitutes degrading treatment contrary to Article 3.

The judgment in *Price* indicates that States must ensure that the conditions of detention are appropriate for disabled detainees (the Court was critical of the domestic judge for not checking to confirm that there would be suitable facilities for the care of Price before he ordered her incarceration).

The dire conditions of detention in Russia were first examined by the Court in *Kalashnikov v Russia*, judgment of 15 July 2002. The applicant, a businessman charged with fraud, had been held on remand in a detention centre in Magadan for over four years. His cell was so overcrowded that the inmates had to share each bed amongst three detainees (on an eight-hour shift system), the light was constantly on in the cell and between eleven and twenty-four inmates had to share the toilet in the corner of the cell. Furthermore, the cell was infested with pests and some of the inmates had serious contagious diseases (e.g. tuberculosis). Consequently, the Court, unanimously, ruled that:

102. . . . the applicant's conditions of detention, in particular the severely overcrowded and insanitary environment and its detrimental effect on the applicant's health and well-being, combined with the length of the period during which the applicant was detained in such conditions, amounted to degrading treatment.

Very significantly during the Strasbourg proceedings the respondent Government had acknowledged that the conditions of the applicant's detention were no worse than those of most detainees in Russia and that, because of economic difficulties, such conditions were below those acceptable to the Council of Europe.

In the subsequent case of *Poltoratskiy v Ukraine*, judgment of 29 April 2003, the Court held that a State's economic problems cannot be used to justify bad conditions of detention which infringe Article 3. The applicant was convicted, in December 1995, of the murder of four persons. He was sentenced to death. In February 1996 he was moved to one of the cells in Ivano-Frankivsk prison where convicted prisoners awaiting execution were detained. A moratorium on executions was announced by the President of Ukraine in March 1997 and in December 1999 the Constitutional Court of Ukraine ruled that the death penalty was contrary to the Constitution. In June 2000 the applicant's sentence was commuted to life imprisonment. He alleged a number of breaches of his Convention rights before the Strasbourg authorities.

145. The Court views with particular concern the fact that, until at earliest May 1998, the applicant, in common with other prisoners detained in the prison under a death sentence, was locked up for 24 hours a day in cells which offered only a very restricted living space, that the windows of the cells were covered with the consequence that there was no access to natural light, that there was no provision for any outdoor exercise and that there was little or no opportunity for activities to occupy himself or for human contact. In common with the observations of the CPT concerning the subjection of death row prisoners in Ukraine to similar conditions, the Court considers that the detention of the applicant in unacceptable conditions of this kind amounted to degrading treatment in breach of Article 3 of the Convention. In the case of the present applicant, the situation was aggravated by the fact that in the period between 24 February and 24 March 1998, he was detained in a cell where there was no water tap or washbasin but only a small pipe on the wall near the toilet, and where the water supply could only be turned on from the corridor, where the walls were covered with faeces and where the bucket for flushing the toilet had been taken away. The applicant' situation was further aggravated by the fact that he was throughout the period in question subject to a death sentence, although . . . a moratorium had been in effect since 11 March 1997.

146. The Court considers that in the present case there is no evidence that there was a positive intention of humiliating or debasing the applicant. However, although the question whether the purpose of the treatment was to humiliate or debase the victim is a factor to be taken into account, the absence of any such purpose cannot conclusively rule out a finding of a violation of Article 3 of the Convention (see *V. v the United Kingdom* [GC], No 24888/94, § 71, ECHR 1999-IX; and *Kalashnikov*, cited above, § 101). It considers that the conditions of detention, which the applicant had to endure in particular until May 1998, must have caused him considerable mental suffering, diminishing his human dignity.

147. The Court acknowledges that following May 1998 substantial and progressive improvements had taken place, both in the general conditions of the applicant's detention and in the regime applied within the prison. In particular, the coverings over the windows of the cells were removed, daily outdoor walks were introduced and the rights of prisoners to receive visits and to correspond were enhanced. Nevertheless, the Court observes that, by the date of introduction of these improvements, the applicant had already been detained in these deleterious conditions for a period of nearly 30 months, including a period of 8 months after the Convention had come into force in respect of Ukraine.

148. The Court has also borne in mind, when considering the material conditions in which the applicant was detained and the activities offered to him, that Ukraine encountered serious socio-economic problems in the course of its systemic transition and that prior to the summer of 1998 the prison authorities were both struggling under difficult economic conditions and occupied with the implementation of new national legislation and related regulations. However, the Court observes that lack of resources cannot in principle justify prison conditions which are so poor as to reach the threshold of treatment contrary to Article 3 of the Convention. Moreover, the economic problems faced by Ukraine cannot in

any event explain or excuse the particular conditions of detention which it has found in paragraph 145 to be unacceptable in the present case.

149. There has, accordingly, been a violation of Article 3 of the Convention in this respect.

If the Court had allowed a plea of State economic hardship to justify very poor prison conditions it would have undermined the potential protection of Article 3 for many detainees across Europe and reduced the external incentive upon States to improve their conditions of detention.

We can note that in many of the above prison condition cases the judgments have reflected a symbiotic relationship between the Court's role in applying and interpreting the Convention rights of detainees and the work of it sister organisation the European Committee for the Prevention of Torture and Inhuman or Degrading Treatment or Punishment (the 'CPT'). Published reports by the latter on its inspections of particular places of detention are of great help to the Court in reaching findings of fact in respect of applicants who allege breaches of their Convention rights concerning their treatment in those institutions. Also adverse comments by the CPT regarding conditions in an institution may encourage the Court to find a breach of Article 3 where an inmate, who has suffered from those conditions, lodges a complaint under the Convention.

5   The conditions in which a prisoner was repeatedly transported from a remand facility to the courthouse were held to violate Article 3 by a unanimous Chamber in *Khudoyorov v Russia*, judgment of 8 November 2005. On 205 occasions the applicant was transported to and from the Regional Court, a journey that took an hour, in a prison van where he occupied a compartment of about one square metre. The applicant had to share that compartment with another prisoner, there was only one seat and the occupants had to take turns sitting on the other's lap. During the days that he was taken to the Regional Court the applicant was given no food or outdoor exercise. The Chamber had regard to the CPT's published views that transportation compartments for individual prisoners up to 0.8 square metres were unsuitable (irrespective of the duration of the journey). Therefore, given the size of the compartment used to transport the applicant and another prisoner, the lack of adequate seating and the absence of food and exercise the Chamber concluded that Article 3 had been breached. The Court did not specify which element of the Article had been violated. Again, we see the significance of the CPT's expertise being used by the Court in the application of Article 3.

6   The delayed release of a very ill elderly prisoner was found to constitute degrading treatment by a Chamber (six votes to one) in *Farbtuhs v Latvia*, judgment of 2 December 2004. The applicant had been sentenced to five years' imprisonment in 2000, when he was aged 84, in respect of acts of genocide and crimes against humanity he committed when an official of the Soviet Union after the latter's annexation of Latvia in 1940. Prior to beginning his imprisonment he was examined by medical experts who reported that he was paraplegic and suffered from a number of other serious ailments. Because of his ill-health he was detained in the prison infirmary. In February 2001 the medical experts recommended that, given his ill-health and age, he should be released on licence. Three days later the prison governor applied for the applicant's release to the District Court. His request was refused. In March 2002 the Regional Court authorized the applicant's release in the light of evidence that he had developed two further illnesses, including diabetes, whilst in prison. The applicant was then released. The Chamber expressed grave concern that the applicant's release from prison had been delayed for over one year despite expert medical advice that his declining health merited immediate release. Furthermore, the Chamber was critical of the limited professional medical

care given to Farbtuhs whilst he was being detained. Outside working hours he had to rely on fellow prisoners, sometimes acting on a voluntary basis, to care for him. This judgment indicates that States ought not to continue the detention of persons where independent medical opinion clearly supports their immediate release on health grounds.

7   Latvia's failure to provide adequate food to a remand prisoner on the days when he was taken to court for hearings constituted degrading treatment according to the unanimous Chamber in *Moisejevs v Latvia*, judgment of 15 June 2006. The applicant was taken to court for hearings on seventy-two days and on those occasions he was not given a normal lunch, but only a slice of bread, an onion, and a piece of fish or a meatball. The Chamber considered that this was insufficient nutrition to meet his needs (especially having regard to the stresses he faced during trial hearings). Furthermore, on the hearing days when he was returned to prison in the evening he frequently was not given a meal, but just a bread roll.

8   In *Hurtado v Switzerland*, A.280A (1994), above p 188, the effects of the stun grenade and the police officers' use of physical force to arrest the applicant were to cause him to defecate in his trousers. He was not allowed to change into clean clothing for over twenty-four hours, during which time he was questioned by the police and brought before an investigating judge. The Commission, by fifteen votes to one, found this treatment to be degrading contrary to Article 3.

67. The Commission reiterates that treatment is considered 'degrading' when it is such as to arouse in its victims feelings of fear, anguish and inferiority capable of humiliating and debasing them and possibly breaking their physical or moral resistance (Court's judgments in *Ireland v UK* p 66 para 167 and *Soering v UK* p 39 para 100).

68. The Commission considers that the conduct of the authorities, who neglected to take the most elementary hygiene measures by failing to make available to the applicant clean clothes to replace those soiled as a result of their action, was humiliating and debasing for the applicant and therefore degrading within the meaning of Article 3 of the Convention.

9   The Commission found racial discrimination in British immigration restrictions amounted to degrading treatment in *East African Asians v UK* (1973) 3 EHRR 76. By the 1960s there were several hundred thousand citizens of the United Kingdom and colonies, many of whom were of Asian ethnic origin, resident in East Africa. As British colonies in that region gained their independence their new national governments began various 'Africanisation' policies; the effects of these programmes were to deprive many of the Asians of their livelihoods (eg by withdrawing their trading licences) and render them destitute. Consequently, significant numbers of the Asians sought to enter and settle in the UK. In 1968 Parliament enacted the Commonwealth Immigrants Act 1968 which had the effect of prohibiting the East African Asians from entering or settling in the UK. Twenty-five such persons, who had been refused entry into the UK, complained to the Commission alleging, inter alia, a breach of Article 3. In its report the Commission concluded that:

207.... the legislation applied in the present case discriminated against the applicants on the grounds of their colour or race. It has also confirmed the view, which it expressed at the admissibility stage, that discrimination based on race could, in certain circumstances, of itself amount to degrading treatment within the meaning of Article 3 of the Convention. The Commission recalls in this connection that, as generally recognised, a special importance should be attached to discrimination based on race; that publicity [sic.] to single out a group of persons for differential treatment on the basis of race might, in certain circumstances, constitute a special form of affront to human dignity; and that differential treatment of a group of persons on the basis of race might therefore be capable of constituting degrading treatment when differential treatment on some other ground would raise no such question.

208. The Commission considers that the racial discrimination, to which the applicants have been publicly subjected by the application of the above immigration legislation, constitutes an interference with their human dignity which, in the special circumstances described above, amounted to 'degrading treatment' in the sense of Article 3 of the Convention.

209. It therefore *concludes*, by six votes against three votes [in addition two other members of the Commission, who were not present when the vote was taken, expressed their agreement with the majority], that Article 3 has been violated in the present case.

The special circumstances identified by the Commission included the fact that the applicants were not aliens in British law, yet the 1968 Act denied them entry to the UK, and the difficult situation the applicants faced in East Africa because of the local 'Africanisation' programmes. Subsequently the British Government allowed the applicants to enter the UK and introduced a special voucher scheme that allowed entry for other persons in the same predicament. In 1977 the Committee of Ministers was unable to reach a two-thirds majority decision on the application and, therefore, resolved that no further action was called for (Resolution DH(77)2). In 1994, at the request of the British Government, the Committee of Ministers finally resolved to formally publish the above report of the Commission (Resolution DH(94)30). The failure of the Committee of Ministers to reach a conclusive determination of the case illustrates the problematic role played by that institution under the former Strasbourg supervisory system.

10 The Court did not find racial or sexual discrimination which breached Article 3 in *Abdulaziz, Cabales and Balkandali v UK* A.94 (1985) 7 EHRR 471, and see below p 525. The applicants, who were aliens, were lawfully resident in the UK and under existing immigration rules they were unable to gain entry to the UK for their foreign husbands. The Court, unanimously, held that: '... the difference of treatment complained of did not denote any contempt or lack of respect for the personality of the applicants and that it was not designed to, and did not, humiliate or debase...' (para 91) Hence, the Court will examine the justifications and effects of any alleged discriminatory action when assessing if it is serious enough to constitute degrading treatment.

11 A unanimous Chamber of the full-time Court determined that racially discriminatory comments by domestic courts and public officials against members of the minority Roma community contributed towards the latter suffering degrading treatment in *Moldovan and Others v Romania (No 2)*, judgment of 12 July 2005. The seven Roma applicants had their homes and personal property destroyed by a mob, including police officers, who also murdered three Roma involved in a fight with non-Roma villagers which had led to the death of a villager. For many years after the destruction of their homes the applicants were forced to live in hen-houses, pigsties, and cellars. During the criminal proceedings against the villagers the court stated that, *inter alia*, the Roma living in the village '...rejected the moral values accepted by the rest of the population.... Most of the Roma have no occupation and earn their living by doing odd jobs, stealing and engaging in all kinds of illicit activity.' The applicants complained to Strasbourg. The Chamber held that:

111. In addition, the remarks concerning the applicants' honesty and way of life made by some authorities dealing with the applicants' grievances ... appear to be, in the absence of any substantiation on behalf of those authorities, purely discriminatory. In this connection the Court reiterates that discrimination based on race can of itself amount to degrading treatment within the meaning of Article 3 of the Convention (see *East African Asians v the United Kingdom*, Commission Report, 14 December 1973, DR 78, p 5, at p 62).

Such remarks should therefore be taken into account as an aggravating factor in the examination of the applicants' complaint under Article 3 of the Convention.

113. In the light of the above, the Court finds that the applicants' living conditions and the racial discrimination to which they have been publicly subjected by the way in which their grievances were dealt with by the various authorities, constitute an interference with their human dignity which, in the special circumstances of this case, amounted to 'degrading treatment' within the meaning of Article 3 of the Convention.

114. Accordingly, there has also been a violation of Article 3 of the Convention.

12 The types of discrimination which can potentially violate Article 3 were extended to encompass sexual orientation in *Smith and Grady v UK* (1999) 29 EHRR 493, extracted and discussed below p 489. The Court, unanimously, held that:

121. . . . Moreover, the Court would not exclude that treatment which is grounded upon a predisposed bias on the part of a heterosexual majority against a homosexual minority of the nature described above could, in principle, fall within the scope of Article 3 (see *mutatis mutandis*, the *Addulaziz, Cabales and Balkandali v UK* A.94 p 42, paras 90–1).

122. However, while accepting that the policy, together with the investigation and discharge which ensued, were undoubtedly distressing and humiliating for each of the applicants, the Court does not consider, having regard to all the circumstances of the case, that the treatment reached the minimum level of severity which would bring it within the scope of Article 3 of the Convention.

Degrading punishment

....

Tyrer v UK A.26 (1978) 2 EHRR 1
European Court of Human Rights

The applicant was born on the Isle of Man (a dependency of the British Crown with its own government, legislature and courts) in 1956. In early March 1972 he pleaded guilty to a charge of unlawful assault occasioning actual bodily harm to a fellow pupil at school (who had earlier reported the applicant for bringing beer into the school). The juvenile court sentenced him to three strokes of the birch (local regulations specified that the birch rod should have a maximum length of 40 inches with a spray circumference not exceeding 6 inches). The applicant appealed against the sentence to the High Court of Justice of the Isle of Man. On the morning of 28 April 1972 the court ordered Tyrer to be examined by a doctor to determine if he was fit to receive the punishment. The doctor reported that he was fit. In the afternoon the court dismissed Tyrer's appeal. After waiting in a police station for some time for a doctor to arrive, Tyrer was birched later that day. The doctor and Tyrer's father were present. Tyrer was made to take down his trousers and underpants and bend over a table; he was held by two policemen while a third officer administered the birching. After the first stroke pieces of the birch rod were broken by the force of the impact on Tyrer. The applicant's father thereupon 'went for' one of the policemen and had to be restrained. The birching did not cut the applicant's skin, but he was sore for about one and a half weeks after the punishment. Judicial corporal punishment of adults and juveniles was abolished in England, Wales and Scotland in 1948 and in

Northern Ireland in 1968. The applicant complained to the Commission in 1972 arguing, inter alia, that his punishment violated Article 3. In January 1976 the applicant sought to withdraw his application. However, the Commission refused his request because, 'the case raised questions of a general character affecting the observance of the Convention which necessitated a further examination of the issues involved'. Thereafter the applicant took no further part in the proceedings. In its December 1976 report the Commission, by fourteen votes to one, found the punishment to be degrading and in breach of Article 3.

II. ON ARTICLE 3 (ART 3)

29. The Court shares the Commission's view that Mr Tyrer's punishment did not amount to 'torture' within the meaning of Article 3 (art 3). The Court does not consider that the facts of this particular case reveal that the applicant underwent suffering of the level inherent in this notion as it was interpreted and applied by the Court in its judgment of 18 January 1978 (*Ireland v UK*, Series A No 25, pp 66–67 and 68, paras 167 and 174).

That judgment also contains various indications concerning the notions of 'inhuman treatment' and 'degrading treatment' but it deliberately left aside the notions of 'inhuman punishment' and 'degrading punishment' which alone are relevant in the present case (ibid, p 65, para 164). Those indications accordingly cannot, as such, serve here. Nevertheless, it remains true that the suffering occasioned must attain a particular level before a punishment can be classified as 'inhuman' within the meaning of Article 3 (art 3). Here again, the Court does not consider on the facts of the case that that level was attained and it therefore concurs with the Commission that the penalty imposed on Mr Tyrer was not 'inhuman punishment' within the meaning of Article 3 (art 3). Accordingly, the only question for decision is whether he was subjected to a 'degrading punishment' contrary to that Article (art 3).

30. The Court notes first of all that a person may be humiliated by the mere fact of being criminally convicted. However, what is relevant for the purposes of Article 3 (art 3) is that he should be humiliated not simply by his conviction but by the execution of the punishment which is imposed on him. In fact, in most if not all cases this may be one of the effects of judicial punishment, involving as it does unwilling subjection to the demands of the penal system.

However, as the Court pointed out in its judgment of 18 January 1978 in the case of *Ireland v UK* (Series A No 25, p 65, para 163), the prohibition contained in Article 3 (art 3) of the Convention is absolute: no provision is made for exceptions and, under Article 15 (2) (art 15-2) there can be no derogation from Article 3 (art 3). It would be absurd to hold that judicial punishment generally, by reason of its usual and perhaps almost inevitable element of humiliation, is 'degrading' within the meaning of Article 3 (art 3). Some further criterion must be read into the text. Indeed, Article 3 (art 3), by expressly prohibiting 'inhuman' and 'degrading' punishment, implies that there is a distinction between such punishment and punishment in general.

In the Court's view, in order for a punishment to be 'degrading' and in breach of Article 3 (art 3), the humiliation or debasement involved must attain a particular level and must in any event be other than that usual element of humiliation referred to in the preceding subparagraph. The assessment is, in the nature of things, relative: it depends on all the circumstances of the case and, in particular, on the nature and context of the punishment itself and the manner and method of its execution.

31. The Attorney-General for the Isle of Man argued that the judicial corporal punishment at issue in this case was not in breach of the Convention since it did not outrage public opinion in the Island. However, even assuming that local public opinion can have an incidence on the interpretation of the concept of 'degrading punishment' appearing in Article 3 (art 3), the Court does not regard it as established that judicial corporal punishment is not considered degrading by those members of the Manx population who favour its retention: it might well be that one of the reasons why they view the penalty as an effective deterrent is precisely the element of degradation which it involves. As regards their belief that judicial corporal punishment deters criminals, it must be pointed out that a punishment does not lose its

degrading character just because it is believed to be, or actually is, an effective deterrent or aid to crime control. Above all, as the Court must emphasise, it is never permissible to have recourse to punishments which are contrary to Article 3 (art 3), whatever their deterrent effect may be.

The Court must also recall that the Convention is a living instrument which, as the Commission rightly stressed, must be interpreted in the light of present-day conditions. In the case now before it the Court cannot but be influenced by the developments and commonly accepted standards in the penal policy of the member States of the Council of Europe in this field. Indeed, the Attorney-General for the Isle of Man mentioned that, for many years, the provisions of Manx legislation concerning judicial corporal punishment had been under review.

32. As regards the manner and method of execution of the birching inflicted on Mr Tyrer, the Attorney-General for the Isle of Man drew particular attention to the fact that the punishment was carried out in private and without publication of the name of the offender.

Publicity may be a relevant factor in assessing whether a punishment is 'degrading' within the meaning of Article 3 (art 3), but the Court does not consider that absence of publicity will necessarily prevent a given punishment from falling into that category: it may well suffice that the victim is humiliated in his own eyes, even if not in the eyes of others.

The Court notes that the relevant Isle of Man legislation, as well as giving the offender a right of appeal against sentence, provides for certain safeguards. Thus, there is a prior medical examination; the number of strokes and dimensions of the birch are regulated in detail; a doctor is present and may order the punishment to be stopped; in the case of a child or young person, the parent may attend if he so desires; the birching is carried out by a police constable in the presence of a more senior colleague.

33. Nevertheless, the Court must consider whether the other circumstances of the applicant's punishment were such as to make it 'degrading' within the meaning of Article 3 (art 3).

The very nature of judicial corporal punishment is that it involves one human being inflicting physical violence on another human being. Furthermore, it is institutionalised violence, that is in the present case violence permitted by the law, ordered by the judicial authorities of the State and carried out by the police authorities of the State . . . . Thus, although the applicant did not suffer any severe or long-lasting physical effects, his punishment—whereby he was treated as an object in the power of the authorities—constituted an assault on precisely that which it is one of the main purposes of Article 3 (art 3) to protect, namely a person's dignity and physical integrity. Neither can it be excluded that the punishment may have had adverse psychological effects.

The institutionalised character of this violence is further compounded by the whole aura of official procedure attending the punishment and by the fact that those inflicting it were total strangers to the offender.

Admittedly, the relevant legislation provides that in any event birching shall not take place later than six months after the passing of sentence. However, this does not alter the fact that there had been an interval of several weeks since the applicant's conviction by the juvenile court and a considerable delay in the police station where the punishment was carried out. Accordingly, in addition to the physical pain he experienced, Mr Tyrer was subjected to the mental anguish of anticipating the violence he was to have inflicted on him.

34. In the present case, the Court does not consider it relevant that the sentence of judicial corporal punishment was imposed on the applicant for an offence of violence. Neither does it consider it relevant that, for Mr Tyrer, birching was an alternative to a period of detention: the fact that one penalty may be preferable to, or have less adverse effects or be less serious than, another penalty does not of itself mean that the first penalty is not 'degrading' within the meaning of Article 3 (art 3).

35. Accordingly, viewing these circumstances as a whole, the Court finds that the applicant was subjected to a punishment in which the element of humiliation attained the level inherent in the notion of 'degrading punishment' as explained at paragraph 30 above. The indignity of having the punishment

administered over the bare posterior aggravated to some extent the degrading character of the applicant's punishment but it was not the only or determining factor.

The Court therefore concludes that the judicial corporal punishment inflicted on the applicant amounted to degrading punishment within the meaning of Article 3 (art 3) of the Convention.

FOR THESE REASONS, THE COURT

...

2. holds by six votes to one that the judicial corporal punishment inflicted on Mr Tyrer amounted to degrading punishment within the meaning of Article 3; ...

NOTES

1   The Court was composed of President Balladore Pallieri and Judges: Cremona, Pedersen, Vilhjalmsson, Teitgen, and Matscher.

Judge Fitzmaurice dissented as he did not consider that judicial corporal punishment was degrading when applied to juveniles. Furthermore:

9. The 'other' circumstances (Judgment, paragraph 33 et seq.)—I have noted the following:

(i) In paragraph 33, much stress is placed on the fact that the 'violence' was 'institutionalised', ie 'permitted by law' and 'carried out by the police authorities'. For my part, I cannot see the relevance of this criterion, ie that the punishment was degrading because 'institutionalised', or more degrading on that account that if it had not been.

To be 'institutionalised' is, in an ordered society, inseparable from any punishment for crime, since non-institutionalised punishment, except such as the law tolerates, must be illegal. Therefore I do not follow (and it is not explained) why institutionalised violence must necessarily be degrading, if non-institutionalised is not, or be more degrading than the latter. Indeed, it is not at all clear what form of non-institutionalised violence the Court had in mind which, by comparison, would not be regarded as degrading to the recipient. Possibly it was desired to imply (though this is not stated) that, for instance, a beating administered by a parent to a child would not degrade the latter,—whereas a 'judicial' one would. I do not believe in these subtleties. In my view neither punishment (so long as administered in private) can be considered as inherently degrading where a juvenile is concerned, unless other factors over and above the beating as such are involved. The State is, in a certain sense, in loco parentis in such a situation.

(ii) Next (third section of paragraph 33), the alleged effect of the institutionalisation is said to be 'compounded' by 'the whole aura of official procedure attending the punishment'—(but how could the procedure not be official if there was institutionalisation?—the one is, or entails, the other)—and also compounded 'by the fact that those inflicting [the punishment] were total strangers to the offender'. As to this last objection, leaving aside the question whether, in the restricted community of Castletown, Isle of Man, the police officers concerned were 'total strangers' to the boy, I for my part fail to see how it can be any more degrading to be beaten by strangers than non-strangers. Many would, I believe, think it less so.

...

11. ... Modern opinion has come to regard corporal punishment as an undesirable form of punishment; and this, whatever the age of the offender. But the fact that a certain form of punishment is an undesirable form of punishment does not automatically turn it into a degrading one. A punishment may well have an undesirable character without being in the least degrading—or at any rate not more so than punishment in general is. And hitherto, whatever may have been felt about corporal punishment from such standpoints as whether it really deters, whether it may not have a brutalising effect, whether it harms the psyche of those who carry it out, etc., it has not been generally regarded as

degrading when applied to juveniles and young offenders, in the same way as it is considered so to be in the case of adults. In that respect, the two things have never been regarded as being quite of the same order or as being on the same plane. This last is the real point—for to put it in terms of the criterion adopted by the Court, and assuming that corporal punishment does involve some degree of degradation, it has never been seen as doing so for a juvenile to anything approaching the same manner or extent as for an adult. Put in terms of the Convention and of the Court's criterion, therefore, such punishment does not, in the case of a juvenile, attain the level of degradation needed to constitute it a breach of Article 3 (art 3), unless of course seriously aggravating circumstances are present over and above the simple fact of the corporal character of the punishment. This is why I could have understood it if the Court had regarded the infliction of the blows on the bare posterior as bringing matters up to the required level of degradation. I would not necessarily have agreed with that view, but it would have been tenable. However, the Court held that this was not a determining element: the punishment was in any event degrading. This means, in effect, that any judicial corporal punishment meted out to a juvenile is degrading and a breach of Article 3 (art 3). It is this view (in my opinion far too dogmatic and sweeping) that I cannot agree with. That such punishments may be undesirable and ought perhaps to be abolished is, as I have said, quite another matter: they are not ipso facto degrading on that account in the case of juvenile offenders.

12. I have to admit that my own view may be coloured by the fact that I was brought up and educated under a system according to which the corporal punishment of schoolboys (sometimes at the hands of the senior ones—prefects or monitors—sometimes by masters) was regarded as the normal sanction for serious misbehaviour, and even sometimes for what was much less serious. Generally speaking, and subject to circumstances, it was often considered by the boy himself as preferable to probable alternative punishments such as being kept in on a fine summer's evening to copy out 500 lines or learn several pages of Shakespeare or Virgil by heart, or be denied leave of absence on a holiday occasion. Moreover, these beatings were carried out without any of the safeguards attendant on Mr Tyrer's: no parents, nurses or doctors were ever present. They also not infrequently took place under conditions of far greater intrinsic humiliation than in his case. Yet I cannot remember that any boy felt degraded or debased. Such an idea would have been thought rather ridiculous. The system was the same for all until they attained a certain seniority. If a boy minded, and resolved not to repeat the offence that had resulted in a beating, this was simply because it had hurt, not because he felt degraded by it or was so regarded by his fellows: indeed, such is the natural perversity of the young of the human species that these occasions were often seen as matters of pride and congratulation,—not unlike the way in which members of the student corps in the old German universities regarded their duelling scars as honourable—(though of course that was, in other respects, quite a different case).

13. In conclusion, I must insist that I am not seeking to maintain that the state of affairs I have just described was necessarily a good one, though it had, and has, many supporters. I am not advocating corporal punishment. I am simply saying that it is not degrading for juvenile offenders—or (to such extent as it is), does not, in their case, involve the level of degradation required to constitute it a breach of Article 3 (art 3) of the European Human Rights Convention, when inflicted under proper restrictions and safeguards in consequence of a regularly pronounced judicial sentence, traditionally sanctioned for certain offences by the law of the community to which the offender belongs, and by its public opinion. No juvenile is or need feel 'degraded' under those conditions ....

The dissent is notable for the candour with which Sir Gerald Fitzmaurice acknowledged the effects of his public school upbringing upon his personal conception of degrading punishment. For a contrasting (and more contemporary) account of the consequences of corporal punishment in a British non-state school see *Costello-Roberts*, below Note 3.

In 1993 the Parliament of the Isle of Man (Tynwald) enacted legislation abolishing judicial corporal punishment.

The judgment of the Court in *Tyrer* also has an enduring importance, extending beyond the definition of Article 3, through the judiciary's articulation of the 'living instrument' doctrine regarding the interpretation and application of the rights guaranteed by the Convention. This evolutionary approach enables the Court to take account of changes in social and economic relationships, cultural values and governmental structures since the time of the Convention's drafting in the immediate post-Second World War era.

In an analysis of the doctrine I have observed that it has been used by the Court to:

... creatively update the interpretation of a number of Convention Articles in varied situations. These judgment have, *inter alia*, prohibited judicial corporal punishment (*Tyrer v UK*), limited the role of a government minister in determining the release of a prisoner (*Stafford v UK*), contributed to reducing the 'democratic deficit' in the European Union (*Matthews v UK*), recognised a right not to be compelled to belong to a trade union/employers' association (*Sigurjonsson v Iceland*) and required the legal recognition of the new identity of post-operative transsexuals (*Christine Goodwin v UK*). In utilising this doctrine the Court has had regard to a wide range of factors when determining what contemporary conditions necessitate. The common approach of member States has been relied upon (e.g. in *Tyrer* and *Pretty v UK*), whilst similar developments in a number of non-member States were noted in *Christine Goodwin*. The rulings of other international bodies were cited in support of the Court's interpretation of Article 11 in *Sigurjonsson*. 'The Creativity of the European Court of Human Rights' (2005) 5:1 *Human Rights Law Review* 57 at p 69.

2   Corporal punishment in state funded schools was challenged by two Scottish mothers in *Campbell and Cosans v UK*, A.48 (1982) 4 EHRR 293. Mrs Campbell's son, who was aged six at the time of the application to the Commission, attended a Roman Catholic primary school in the Strathclyde Region Education Authority area. The school used corporal punishment, in the form of the striking of the palm of the pupil's hand with a leather strap called a tawse, for disciplinary purposes. Mrs Campbell's son never received such punishment while he attended that school, but the Authority refused her request that it guarantee that he would not be so punished. Mrs Cosans' son, Jeffrey who was born in 1961, attended a High School in the Fife Region Education Authority area. In September 1976 Jeffrey was ordered to report to the Assistant Headmaster to receive corporal punishment (the tawse) for having tried to take a prohibited route, through a cemetery, on his way home from school. On his father's advice, Jeffrey reported to the Assistant Headmaster, but refused to accept the punishment. Jeffrey was immediately suspended from the school and he never returned as his parents continued to object to him receiving corporal punishment (in May 1977 he ceased to be of compulsory school age). Both mothers complained to the Commission that the use of corporal punishment in the schools attended by their sons violated, inter alia, Article 3. By thirteen votes to one, the Commission found no breach of that Article. The Court was unanimous in also finding no violation of that provision on the facts of the applicants' cases.

25. Neither Gordon Campbell nor Jeffrey Cosans was, in fact, strapped with the tawse. Accordingly, the Court does not in the present case have to consider under Article 3 (art 3) an actual application of corporal punishment.

26. However, the Court is of the opinion that, provided it is sufficiently real and immediate, a mere threat of conduct prohibited by Article 3 (art 3) may itself be in conflict with that provision. Thus, to threaten an individual with torture might in some circumstances constitute at least 'inhuman treatment'.

27. Although the system of corporal punishment can cause a certain degree of apprehension in those who may be subject to it, the Court nevertheless shares the Commission's view that the situation in which the applicants' sons found themselves did not amount to 'torture' or 'inhuman treatment',

within the meaning of Article 3 (art 3): there is no evidence that they underwent suffering of the level inherent in these notions as they were interpreted and applied in the Court's *Ireland v UK* judgment of 18 January 1978 (Series A No 25, pp 66–7 and 68, paras 167 and 174).

28. The Court's judgment of 25 April 1978 in the *Tyrer* case does indicate certain criteria concerning the notion of 'degrading punishment' (Series A No 26, p 15, par 30). In the present case, no 'punishment' has actually been inflicted. Nevertheless, it follows from that judgment that 'treatment' itself will not be 'degrading' unless the person concerned has undergone—either in the eyes of others or in his own eyes (ibid, p 16, para 32)—humiliation or debasement attaining a minimum level of severity. That level has to be assessed with regard to the circumstances of the case (see the above-mentioned *Ireland v UK* judgment, p 65, para 162, p 66, para 167, and pp 69–70, paras 179–181).

29. Corporal chastisement is traditional in Scottish schools and, indeed, appears to be favoured by a large majority of parents . . . Of itself, this is not conclusive of the issue before the Court for the threat of a particular measure is not excluded from the category of 'degrading', within the meaning of Article 3 (art 3), simply because the measure has been in use for a long time or even meets with general approval (see, *mutatis mutandis*, the above-mentioned *Tyrer* judgment, p 15, para 31).

However, particularly in view of the above-mentioned circumstances obtaining in Scotland, it is not established that pupils at a school where such punishment is used are, solely by reason of the risk of being subjected thereto, humiliated or debased in the eyes of others to the requisite degree or at all.

30. As to whether the applicants' sons were humiliated or debased in their own eyes, the Court observes first that a threat directed to an exceptionally insensitive person may have no significant effect on him but nevertheless be incontrovertibly degrading; and conversely, an exceptionally sensitive person might be deeply affected by a threat that could be described as degrading only by a distortion of the ordinary and usual meaning of the word. In any event, in the case of these two children, the Court, like the Commission, notes that is has not been shown by means of medical certificates or otherwise that they suffered any adverse psychological or other effects . . .

Jeffrey Cosans may well have experienced feelings of apprehension or disquiet when he came close to an infliction of the tawse . . . but such feelings are not sufficient to amount to degrading treatment, within the meaning of Article 3 (art 3).

The same applies, *a fortiori*, to Gordon Campbell since he was never directly threatened with corporal punishment . . . It is true that counsel for his mother alleged at the hearings that group tension and a sense of alienation in the pupil are induced by the very existence of this practice but, even if this be so, these effects fall into a different category from humiliation or debasement.

31. To sum up, no violation of Article 3 (art 3) is established . . . .

Hence the fact that neither of the applicants' sons had actually received corporal punishment was the decisive element in the Court's determination that the minimum threshold of Article 3 had not been infringed in these circumstances (for discussion of the applicants' successful invocation of Article 2 of Protocol No 1 see below p 963).

Subsequently, a number of other complaints were made to the Commission by parents, and their children, concerning the existence and use of corporal punishment in state funded schools. These cases, where admissible, were subject to friendly settlements. A major component in the friendly settlements was the enactment of the Education (No 2) Act 1986, which ended corporal punishment in state funded schools (by abolishing teachers' reasonable punishment defence to criminal charges or civil actions brought in respect of corporal punishment in such schools). See for example, *Durairaj, Townend and Brant v UK* (1987), European Commission of Human Rights, *Stock-taking on the ECHR: Supplement 1987*, p 26.

3 Corporal punishment in non-state funded schools, where the parents paid for the educa-tion of their children, was considered by the Court in *Costello-Roberts v UK*, A.247-C (1993) 19 EHRR 112. In September 1985 Mrs Costello-Roberts sent her son, Jeremy, aged seven to an independent boarding preparatory school (the school received no financial support from the Government). The school's prospectus stated that a high standard of discipline was main-tained, but it did not mention the use of corporal punishment. In fact the school operated a demerit marks system whereby pupils were given demerit marks each time they broke a school rule. When five demerit marks had been accumulated the pupil was subject to corporal pun-ishment. By early October 1985 Jeremy had acquired five demerit marks, for talking in the cor-ridor and being late for bed. The headmaster discussed the matter with colleagues and decided to punish Jeremy. Three days later the headmaster 'whacked' Jeremy three times on the bottom through his shorts with a rubber-soled gym shoe. No other person was present when the pun-ishment was administered. Afterwards, Jeremy wrote to his mother several time complaining about the 'slippering'. In early November Mrs Costello-Roberts wrote to the school's Governors expressing her 'grave concern' about the use of such a 'barbaric practice'. She also informed the headmaster that she did not want her son to be subject to any further corporal punishment. He replied that as she wished Jeremy to be exempt from the 'framework of discipline and pun-ishment that is acceptable to all other parents at the school' it would be best if Jeremy were to be removed from the school at the end of term. Mrs Costello-Roberts also complained to the police regarding Jeremy's punishment, but they said that action could not be taken as there was no evidence of bruising on his buttocks. Jeremy was removed from the school in November 1985 by his mother. Mrs Costello-Roberts and Jeremy complained to the Commission alleg-ing, inter alia, that the headmaster's punishment violated Article 3. The Commission declared Mrs Costello-Roberts' application inadmissible and that Jeremy had not suffered a breach of Article 3 (by nine votes to four). The Court held that the Government was responsible under the Convention for the actions of the school because, inter alia, States are obliged (by Article 2 of Protocol 1) to secure to children their right to education and they cannot absolve them-selves from responsibility by devolving authority to private persons/bodies. However, a major-ity, of five judges, determined that there had been no breach of Article 3.

31. The circumstances of the applicant's punishment may be distinguished from those of Mr Tyrer's which was found to be degrading within the meaning of Article 3 (art 3). Mr Costello-Roberts was a young boy punished in accordance with the disciplinary rules in force within the school in which he was a boarder. This amounted to being slippered three times on his buttocks through his shorts with a rub-ber-soled gym shoe by the headmaster in private . . . Mr Tyrer, on the other hand, was a young man sen-tenced in the local juvenile court to three strokes of the birch on the bare posterior. His punishment was administered some three weeks later in a police station where he was held by two policemen while a third administered the punishment, pieces of the birch breaking at the first stroke.

32. Beyond the consequences to be expected from measures taken on a purely disciplinary plane, the applicant has adduced no evidence of any severe or long-lasting effects as a result of the treatment complained of. A punishment which does not occasion such effects may fall within the ambit of Article 3 (art 3) (see the *Tyrer* judgment, Series A No 26, pp 16–17, para 33), provided that in the particular cir-cumstances of the case it may be said to have reached the minimum threshold of severity required. While the Court has certain misgivings about the automatic nature of the punishment and the three-day wait before its imposition, it considers that minimum level of severity not to have been attained in this case.

Accordingly, no violation of Article 3 (art 3) has been established.

Is the Court's distinction between the context and nature of the punishments in the above case and *Tyrer* convincing? Four judges dissented.

However, in the present case, the ritualised character of the corporal punishment is striking. After a three-day gap, the headmaster of the school 'whacked' a lonely and insecure 7-year-old boy. A spanking on the spur of the moment might have been permissible, but in our view, the official and formalised nature of the punishment meted out, without adequate consent of the mother, was degrading to the applicant and violated Article 3 (art 3).

The School Standards and Framework Act 1998 abolished corporal punishment in all schools.

4 Yutaka Arai-Takahashi has commented that:

Degrading treatment or punishment, set as the 'lowest' form of an absolute right on the graded scale of ill-treatment under Article 3 of the ECHR, offers a string of practical advantages to the decision-making policy of the Strasbourg organs. First, in view of its low intensity requirement, degrading treatment or punishment allows the Court to address multiple issues in diverse fields, some of which may never be condemned as worthy of a stigma associated with the inkling of torture. Second, since the ascertainment of a minimum threshold of severity is a malleable process susceptible to evolving perceptions of common European human rights standards, the benchmark of degrading treatment can be adapted to capture a greater number of claims, including even those that were previously declared inadmissible *ratione materiae* in the initial screening phase.... Third, an extensive coverage of issues under the rubric of degrading treatment can be undertaken without compromising the non-derogable nature of Article 3. 'Grading Scale of Degradation: Identifying the Threshold of Degrading Treatment or Punishment Under Article 3 ECHR', (2003) 21 (3) *Netherlands Quarterly of Human Rights* 385 at pp 420–1.

<table>
<tr><td>6</td><td>

ARTICLE 4
PROHIBITION OF
SLAVERY AND
FORCED LABOUR

</td></tr>
</table>

Van der Mussele v Belgium A.70 (1983) 6 EHRR 163
European Court of Human Rights

The profession of avocat in Belgium is regulated by the Ordre des avocats, a public law body that is independent of the executive. The Ordre determines who is qualified to be entered on the register of avocats. Avocats, including pupil avocats, enjoy an exclusive right of audience before the courts. At the time of this case the Belgian Judicial Code subjected the Ordre to a duty to make provision for the assistance of persons of insufficient means by establishing a 'Legal Advice and Defence Office'. In criminal cases the Office had to make an officially appointed ('pro Deo') avocat available to any indigent accused who so requested at least three days before his/her hearing. The Office generally appointed pupil avocats and they would normally spend about one quarter of their working time dealing with such cases during their three years of training. Appointed avocats were not entitled to remuneration or reimbursement of their expenses incurred in defending the poor. If a pupil avocat had not acted as an officially appointed avocat for a sufficient number of defendants the Ordre would not register that person as a qualified avocat.

The applicant was enrolled as a pupil avocat in September 1976. During July 1979, the Legal Advice and Defence Office of the Antwerp Bar appointed him to defend a Gambian national (Ebrima) arrested on suspicion of theft. The applicant represented Ebrima throughout his trial and appeal. After the latter was released from prison in December 1979, following representations from the applicant, the Office discharged the applicant from the case. Although the applicant had spent about eighteen hours working for Ebrima he was allocated no fees or expenses (the applicant calculated these involving: 250BF for preparation of the case file, 1,800BF for correspondence, 1,300BF for travel to and from the prison and courts, and 50BF in respect of court costs) by the Office due to Ebrima's impecuniosity. The applicant was registered as a qualified avocat by the Ordre in October 1979. During his three years of pupillage he handled about 250 cases of which approximately fifty were in the capacity as an officially appointed avocat.

In 1980 an Act was passed that provided for governmental funding to pay pupil avocats for their defence work undertaken at the direction of the Legal Advice and Defence Office. However, because of budgetary reasons, the Act had not been implemented at the time of the Court's judgment.

The applicant complained to the Commission that his appointment by the Office to represent Ebrima, without remuneration and with sanctions in respect of his career if he refused, amounted to forced or compulsory labour contrary to Article 4. By ten votes to four, the Commission found no breach of that Article.

II. RESPONSIBILITY OF THE BELGIAN STATE

28. Before the Commission and in their memorial to the Court, the Government submitted that there was no primary or subordinate legislation that obliged avocats to accept work entrusted to them by a Legal Advice and Defence Office: their duty to act for indigent persons was said to derive solely from professional rules freely adopted by the Ordres des avocats themselves. According to the Government, the Belgian State did not prescribe either how appointments were to be made or their effects; it was therefore not answerable for any infringements of the Convention's guarantees that might be occasioned by implementation of the professional rules.

29. This argument, to which counsel for the Government did not revert at the hearings before the Court, was not accepted by the applicant or the Commission. Neither does it convince the Court.

Under the Convention, the obligation to grant free legal assistance arises, in criminal matters, from Article 6 § 3 (c) (art 6-3-c); in civil matters, it sometimes constitutes one of the means of ensuring a fair trial as required by Article 6 § 1 (art 6-1) (see the Airey judgment of 9 October 1979, Series A No 32, pp 14–16, § 26). This obligation is incumbent on each of the Contracting Parties. The Belgian State— and this was not contested by the Government—lays the obligation by law on the Ordres des avocats, thereby perpetuating a state of affairs of long standing; under Article 455, first paragraph, of the Judicial Code, the Councils of the Ordres are to make provision for the assistance of indigent persons by setting up Legal Advice and Defence Offices ... As was pointed out by the applicant, the Councils have 'no discretion as regards the principle itself': legislation 'compels them to compel' members of the Bar to 'defend indigent persons'. Such a solution cannot relieve the Belgian State of the responsibilities it would have incurred under the Convention had it chosen to operate the system itself.

Moreover, the Government recognised at the hearings that 'the obligation', for pupil avocats, 'to act as defence counsel in cases assigned by the Legal Advice and Defence Office' arose from Article 455 of the Judicial Code; in paragraph 21 of their memorial, they had already conceded that Belgian law, by not making any provision for indemnifying pupil avocats, acknowledged at least implicitly that the latter have to bear the expenses incurred in dealing with the cases in question.

In addition, the Belgian Bars, bodies that are associated with the exercise of judicial power, are, without prejudice to the basic principle of independence necessary for the accomplishment of their important function in the community, subject to the requirements of the law. The relevant legislation states their objects and establishes their institutional organs; it endows with legal personality in public law each of the Councils of the twenty-seven local Ordres and the General Council of the National Ordre ...

30. The responsibility of the Belgian State being thus engaged in the present case, it has to be ascertained whether that State complied with the provisions of the Convention and of Protocol No 1 art 4, art 14, P1-1) relied on by Mr Van der Mussele.

III. ALLEGED VIOLATION OF ARTICLE 4 OF THE CONVENTION, TAKEN ALONE (ART 4)

31. The applicant maintained that he had had to perform forced or compulsory labour incompatible with Article 4 (art 4) of the Convention. Under that Article (art 4) ...

Four members of the Commission considered that this had been the case, but a majority of ten of their colleagues arrived at the opposite conclusion. The Government contended, as their principal submission, that the labour in question was not 'forced or compulsory' or, in the alternative, that it formed part of the applicant's 'normal civic obligations'.

32. Article 4 (art 4) does not define what is meant by 'forced or compulsory labour' and no guidance on this point is to be found in the various Council of Europe documents relating to the preparatory work of the European Convention.

As the Commission and the Government pointed out, it is evident that the authors of the European Convention—following the example of the authors of Article 8 of the draft International Covenant on

Civil and Political Rights—based themselves, to a large extent, on an earlier treaty of the International Labour Organisation, namely Convention No 29 concerning Forced or Compulsory Labour.

Under the latter Convention (which was adopted on 28 June 1930, entered into force on 1 May 1932 and was modified—as regards the final clauses—in 1946), States undertook 'to suppress the use of forced or compulsory labour in all its forms within the shortest possible period' (Article 1 § 1); with a view to 'complete suppression' of such labour, States were permitted to have recourse thereto during a 'transitional period', but 'for public purposes only and as an exceptional measure, subject to the conditions and guarantees' laid down in Articles 4 et seq. (Article 1 § 2). The main aim of the Convention was originally to prevent the exploitation of labour in colonies, which were still numerous at that time. Convention No 105 of 25 June 1957, which entered into force on 17 January 1959, complemented Convention No 29, by prescribing 'the immediate and complete abolition of forced or compulsory labour' in certain specified cases.

Subject to Article 4 § 3 (art 4-3), the European Convention, for its part, lays down a general and absolute prohibition of forced or compulsory labour.

The Court will nevertheless take into account the above-mentioned ILO Conventions—which are binding on nearly all the member States of the Council of Europe, including Belgium—and especially Convention No 29. There is in fact a striking similarity, which is not accidental, between paragraph 3 of Article 4 (art 4-3) of the European Convention and paragraph 2 of Article 2 of Convention No 29. Paragraph 1 of the last-mentioned Article provides that 'for the purposes' of the latter Convention, the term 'forced or compulsory labour' shall mean 'all work or service which is exacted from any person under the menace of any penalty and for which the said person has not offered himself voluntarily'. This definition can provide a starting-point for interpretation of Article 4 (art 4) of the European Convention. However, sight should not be lost of that Convention's special features or of the fact that it is a living instrument to be read 'in the light of the notions currently prevailing in democratic States' (see, inter alia, the *Guzzardi* judgment of 6 November 1980, Series A No 39, p 34, § 95).

33. It was common ground between those appearing before the Court that the services rendered by Mr Van der Mussele to Mr Ebrima amounted to 'labour' for the purposes of Article 4 § 2 (art 4-2). It is true that the English word 'labour' is often used in the narrow sense of manual work, but it also bears the broad meaning of the French word 'travail' and it is the latter that should be adopted in the present context. The Court finds corroboration of this in the definition included in Article 2 § 1 of Convention No 29 ('all work or service', 'tout travail ou service'), in Article 4 § 3 (d) (art 4-3-d) of the European Convention ('any work or service', 'tout travail ou service') and in the very name of the International Labour Organisation (Organisation internationale du Travail), whose activities are in no way limited to the sphere of manual labour.

34. It remains to be ascertained whether there was 'forced or compulsory' labour. The first of these adjectives brings to mind the idea of physical or mental constraint, a factor that was certainly absent in the present case. As regards the second adjective, it cannot refer just to any form of legal compulsion or obligation. For example, work to be carried out in pursuance of a freely negotiated contract cannot be regarded as falling within the scope of Article 4 (art 4) on the sole ground that one of the parties has undertaken with the other to do that work and will be subject to sanctions if he does not honour his promise. On this point, the minority of the Commission agreed with the majority. What there has to be is work 'exacted . . . under the menace of any penalty' and also performed against the will of the person concerned, that is work for which he 'has not offered himself voluntarily'.

35. The definition given in Article 2 § 1 of ILO Convention No 29 leads the Court to inquire firstly whether there existed in the circumstances of the present case 'the menace of any penalty'.

Had Mr Van der Mussele refused without good reason to defend Mr Ebrima, his refusal would not have been punishable with any sanction of a criminal character. On the other hand, he would have run the risk of having the Council of the Ordre strike his name off the roll of pupils or reject his application for entry on the register of avocats . . . these prospects are sufficiently daunting to be capable of constituting 'the menace of [a] penalty', having regard both to the use of the adjective 'any' in the definition and to the standards adopted by the ILO on this point ('Abolition of Forced Labour': General Survey by the Committee of Experts on Application of Conventions and Recommendations, 1979, paragraph 21).

36. It must next be determined whether the applicant 'offered himself voluntarily' for the work in question.

According to the majority of the Commission, the applicant had consented in advance to the situation he complained of, so that it ill became him to object to it subsequently. Their argument ran as follows. On the eve of embarking on his career, the future avocat will make 'a kind of prospective assessment': he will weigh up the pros and cons, setting the 'advantages' of the profession against the 'drawbacks' it entails. And here the drawbacks were 'perfectly foreseeable' by the future avocat since he was not unaware either of the existence or of the scope of the obligations he would have to bear as regards defending clients free of charge, obligations that were 'limited' both in quantity (about fourteen cases each year) and in time (the period of pupillage). He also had knowledge of the corresponding advantages: the freedom he would enjoy in carrying out his duties and the opportunity he would have of familiarising himself with life in the courts and of 'establishing for himself a paying clientele'. One of the distinctive features of compulsory labour was therefore lacking and this was sufficient to establish that there had not been a violation of Article 4 § 2 (art 4-2).

This argument, which was supported by the Government, correctly reflects one aspect of the situation; nevertheless, the Court cannot attach decisive weight thereto. Mr Van der Mussele undoubtedly chose to enter the profession of avocat, which is a liberal profession in Belgium, appreciating that under its rules he would, in accordance with a long-standing tradition, be bound on occasions to render his services free of charge and without reimbursement of his expenses. However, he had to accept this requirement, whether he wanted to or not, in order to become an avocat and his consent was determined by the normal conditions of exercise of the profession at the relevant time. Nor should it be overlooked that what he gave was an acceptance of a legal régime of a general character.

The applicant's prior consent, without more, does not therefore warrant the conclusion that the obligations incumbent on him in regard to legal aid did not constitute compulsory labour for the purposes of Article 4 § 2 (art 4-2) of the Convention. Account must necessarily also be taken of other factors.

37. On the basis of jurisprudence of its own which dates back to 1963 (admissibility decision on application No 1468/62, *Iversen v Norway*, Yearbook of the Convention, vol. 6, pp 327–9) and which it has subsequently re-affirmed, the Commission expressed the opinion that for there to be forced or compulsory labour, for the purposes of Article 4 § 2 (art 4–2) of the European Convention, two cumulative conditions have to be satisfied: not only must the labour be performed by the person against his or her will, but either the obligation to carry it out must be 'unjust' or 'oppressive' or its performance must constitute 'an avoidable hardship', in other words be 'needlessly distressing' or 'somewhat harassing'. After examining the issue 'as a supplementary consideration', the Commission concluded by a majority that the second condition was no more satisfied than the first condition.

The Court would observe that the second criterion thus applied is not stated in Article 2 § 1 of ILO Convention No 29. Rather it is a criterion that derives from Article 4 and the following Articles of that Convention, which are not concerned with the notion of forced or compulsory labour but lay down the requirements to be met for the exaction of forced or compulsory labour during the transitional period provided for under Article 1 § 2 (see 'ILO-internal minute—January 1966', paragraph 2).

Be that as it may, the Court prefers to adopt a different approach. Having held that there existed a risk comparable to 'the menace of [a] penalty' (see paragraph 35 above) and then that relative weight is to be attached to the argument regarding the applicant's 'prior consent' (see paragraph 36 above), the Court will have regard to all the circumstances of the case in the light of the underlying objectives of Article 4 (art 4) of the European Convention in order to determine whether the service required of

Mr Van der Mussele falls within the prohibition of compulsory labour. This could be so in the case of a service required in order to gain access to a given profession, if the service imposed a burden which was so excessive or disproportionate to the advantages attached to the future exercise of that profession, that the service could not be treated as having been voluntarily accepted beforehand; this could apply, for example, in the case of a service unconnected with the profession in question.

38. The structure of Article 4 (art 4) is informative on this point. Paragraph 3 (art 4-3) is not intended to 'limit' the exercise of the right guaranteed by paragraph 2 (art 4-2), but to 'delimit' the very content of this right, for it forms a whole with paragraph 2 (art 4-2) and indicates what 'the term 'forced or compulsory labour' shall not include' (ce qui 'n'est pas considéré comme 'travail forcé ou obligatoire'). This being so, paragraph 3 (art 4-3) serves as an aid to the interpretation of paragraph 2 (art 4-2).

The four sub-paragraphs of paragraph 3 (art 4-3-a, art 4-3-b, art 4-3-c, art 4-3-d), notwithstanding their diversity, are grounded on the governing ideas of the general interest, social solidarity and what is in the normal or ordinary course of affairs. The final sub-paragraph, namely sub-paragraph (d) (art 4-3-d) which excludes 'any work or service which forms part of normal civil obligations' from the scope of forced or compulsory labour, is of especial significance in the context of the present case.

39. When viewed in the light of the foregoing considerations, the circumstances complained of can be seen to be characterised by several features, each of which provides a standard of evaluation.

The services to be rendered did not fall outside the ambit of the normal activities of an avocat; they differed from the usual work of members of the Bar neither by their nature nor by any restriction of freedom in the conduct of the case.

Secondly, a compensatory factor was to be found in the advantages attaching to the profession, including the exclusive right of audience and of representation enjoyed by avocats in Belgium as in several other countries ...

In addition, the services in question contributed to the applicant's professional training in the same manner as did the cases in which he had to act on the instructions of paying clients of his own or of his pupil-master. They gave him the opportunity to enlarge his experience and to increase his reputation. In this respect, a certain degree of personal benefit went hand in hand with the general interest which was foremost.

Moreover, the obligation to which Mr Van der Mussele objected constituted a means of securing for Mr Ebrima the benefit of Article 6 § 3 (c) (art 6-3-c) of the Convention. To this extent, it was founded on a conception of social solidarity and cannot be regarded as unreasonable. By the same token, it was an obligation of a similar order to the 'normal civic obligations' referred to in Article 4 § 3 (d) (art 4-3-d). ©The Court is not required on the present occasion to rule on the correctness of the argument of the minority of the Commission to the effect that the almost routine allocation of pro-Deo cases to pupil avocats might not be fully consonant with the need to provide effective legal aid to impecunious litigants (see the *Artico* judgment of 13 May 1980, Series A No 37, pp 15–16, § 33).

Finally, the burden imposed on the applicant was not disproportionate. According to his own evidence, acting for Mr Ebrima accounted for only seventeen or eighteen hours of his working time ... Even if one adds to this the other cases in which he was appointed to act during his pupillage— about fifty in three years, representing, so he said, a total of some seven hundred and fifty hours ...— it can be seen that there remained sufficient time for performance of his paid work (approximately two hundred cases).

40. In point of fact, the applicant did not challenge the principle, as such, of the obligation in question; his complaint was limited to two aspects of the manner in which the obligation was implemented, namely the absence of fees and more especially the non-reimbursement of incurred expenditure ... He felt it unjust—and on this the minority of the Commission concurred with him—to entrust the free representation of the most needy citizens to pupil avocats who themselves were in receipt of insufficient

resources and to make them bear the cost of a public service instituted by law. He drew attention to the fact that for many years the successive chairmen of the Ordre des avocats in Belgium have regarded such a state of affairs as intolerable.

For their part, the Government acknowledged that the practice complained of was inspired by a 'paternalism' that was now 'outmoded'. They asserted that the traditional stance of a profession jealous of its independence accounted for the fact that Belgium had delayed in 'endeavouring', by means of the Act of 9 April 1980 . . . 'to bring its standards' in this sphere to 'the level of other States, notably European': until recent times, so the Government stated, the Bar had viewed with 'distrust' State-payment of pupil avocats, the idea of an official scale of fees inspiring deep-rooted hostility among its members.

The Commission also described as unfortunate a legal situation which in its opinion, while being compatible with Article 4 (art 4), no longer meets 'the requirements of modern life'. Pointing out that if pupil avocats were remunerated their professional training would not suffer thereby, the Commission expressed the wish for a prompt and effective implementation of the Act of 9 April 1980.

The Court has not overlooked this aspect of the problem. While remunerated work may also qualify as forced or compulsory labour, the lack of remuneration and of reimbursement of expenses constitutes a relevant factor when considering what is proportionate or in the normal course of affairs. In this connection, it is noteworthy that the respective laws of numerous Contracting States have evolved or are evolving, albeit in varying degrees, towards the assumption by the public purse of the cost of paying lawyers or trainee lawyers appointed to act for indigent litigants. The Belgian Act of 9 April 1980 is an example of this development; that Act, once it has been implemented, should bring about a significant improvement, without thereby threatening the independence of the Bar.

At the relevant time, the state of affairs complained of undoubtedly caused Mr Van der Mussele some prejudice by reason of the lack of remuneration and of reimbursement of expenses, but that prejudice went hand in hand with advantages (see paragraph 39 above) and has not been shown to be excessive. The applicant did not have a disproportionate burden of work imposed on him (ibid) and the amount of expenses directly occasioned by the cases in question was relatively small . . .

The Court would recall that Mr Van der Mussele had voluntarily entered the profession of avocat with knowledge of the practice complained of. This being so, a considerable and unreasonable imbalance between the aim pursued—to qualify as an avocat—and the obligations undertaken in order to achieve that aim would alone be capable of warranting the conclusion that the services exacted of Mr Van der Mussele in relation to legal aid were compulsory despite his consent. No such imbalance is disclosed by the evidence before the Court, notwithstanding the lack of remuneration and of reimbursement of expenses—which in itself is far from satisfactory.

Having regard, furthermore, to the standards still generally obtaining in Belgium and in other democratic societies, there was thus no compulsory labour for the purposes of Article 4 § 2 (art 4–2) of the Convention.

41. In view of this conclusion, the Court need not determine whether the work in question was in any event justified under Article 4 § 3 (d) (art 4–3-d) as such and, in particular, whether the notion of 'normal civic obligations' extends to obligations incumbent on a specific category of citizens by reason of the position they occupy, or the functions they are called upon to perform, in the community.

IV. ALLEGED VIOLATION OF ARTICLE 14 OF THE CONVENTION, TAKEN TOGETHER WITH ARTICLE 4 (ART 14+4)

42. The applicant also invoked Article 14 read in conjunction with Article 4 (art 14+4)

. . .

43. Article 14 (art 14) complements the other substantive provisions of the Convention and the Protocols. It may be applied in an autonomous manner as breach of Article 14 (art 14) does not

presuppose breach of those other provisions. On the other hand, it has no independent existence since it has effect solely in relation to 'the enjoyment of the rights and freedoms' safeguarded by the other substantive provisions (see, inter alia, the *Marckx* judgment of 13 June 1979, Series A No 31, pp 15–16, § 32). As the Court has found that there was no forced or compulsory labour for the purposes of Article 4 (art 4), the question arises whether the facts in issue fall completely outside the ambit of that Article (art 4) and, hence, of Article 14 (art 14). However, such reasoning would be met by one major objection. The criteria which serve to delimit the concept of compulsory labour include the notion of what is in the normal course of affairs (see paragraph 38 above). Work or labour that is in itself normal may in fact be rendered abnormal if the choice of the groups or individuals bound to perform it is governed by discriminatory factors, which was precisely what the applicant contended had occurred in the present circumstances.

Consequently, this is not a case where Article 14 (art 14) should be held inapplicable; the Government, moreover, did not contest the point.

44. In a memorial of 27 October 1980 filed before the Commission, Mr Van der Mussele stated that he was not complaining of any discrimination between pupil avocats and avocats entered on the register. He did not alter his attitude before the Court, and the Court sees no reason for examining the issue of its own motion.

45. On the other hand, in the applicant's submission, Belgian avocats are subject, in respect of the matters under consideration, to less favourable treatment than that of members of a whole series of other professions. In legal aid cases, the State accords remuneration to judges and registrars, pays the emoluments of interpreters (Article 184 bis of the Code of Criminal Procedure and Article 691 of the Judicial Code) and, 'in lieu of the legally aided person', advances 'the travel and subsistence expenses of judicial, public or publicly appointed officers, the costs and fees of experts, the allowances of witnesses . . . , the disbursements and one quarter of the salaries of bailiffs as well as the disbursements of other public or publicly appointed officers' (Article 692 of the Judicial Code) . . . Medical practitioners, veterinary surgeons, pharmacists and dentists, for their part, are not required to provide their services free of charge to indigent persons. According to the applicant, these all represented instances of arbitrary inequality, being devoid of any 'objective and reasonable justification' (see the judgment of 23 July 1968 in the '*Belgian Linguistic*' case, Series A No 6, p 34, § 10); they thereby contravened Articles 14 and 4 (art 14+4) taken together. The minority of the Commission shared this view, at least to a large extent.

46. Article 14 (art 14) safeguards individuals, placed in analogous situations, from discrimination (see the above-mentioned *Marckx* judgment, Series A No 31, p 15, § 32). Yet between the Bar and the various professions cited by the applicant, including even the judicial and parajudicial professions, there exist fundamental differences to which the Government and the majority of the Commission rightly drew attention, namely differences as to legal status, conditions for entry to the profession, the nature of the functions involved, the manner of exercise of those functions, etc. The evidence before the Court does not disclose any similarity between the disparate situations in question: each one is characterised by a corpus of rights and obligations of which it would be artificial to isolate one specific aspect.

On the basis of the applicant's grievances, the Court accordingly does not find any breach of Articles 14 and 4 taken together (art 14+4).

. . .

FOR THESE REASONS, THE COURT UNANIMOUSLY
Holds that there has been no breach of Article 4 of the Convention, taken on its own or in conjunction with Article 14 . . .

NOTES

1   The Court was composed of President Wiarda and Judges: Ryssdal, Thor Vilhjalmsson, Ganshof van der Meersch, Bindschedler-Robert, Evrigenis, Lagergren, Liesch, Gölcüklü, Matscher, Garcia de Enterria, Pettiti, Walsh, Evans, Russo, and Gersing.

The judgment is very important for explaining the origins of the terms used in Article 4 and the way in which they should be interpreted. The Court also set out the relationship between the constituent paragraphs of the Article. The judges were not willing to follow the Commission's established approach to Article 4(2) and introduced a proportionality test as an element in assessing the extent and lawfulness of the burdens placed upon individuals required to undertake work by States.

2   The notion of 'servitude' in Article 4(1) was considered in the case of *Van Droogenbroeck v Belgium*, A.44 (1982) 4 EHRR 443. The applicant was a recidivist who had been convicted of a number of thefts. In 1970 he was sentenced to two years' imprisonment for theft and also 'placed at the Government's disposal' for ten years pursuant to the Social Protection Act 1964. The latter order was classified as a penalty, but had the objective of trying to rehabilitate frequent offenders. After the applicant completed his prison sentence the authorities attempted to secure training and employment for the applicant on a number of occasions, however he continued to engage in criminal activity and was recalled to prison a number of times during the period of his placement. The applicant complained to the Commission alleging, inter alia, that he had been held in servitude and forced to work contrary to paragraphs (1) and (2) of Article 4. The Commission was unanimous in finding no breach of Article 4. Likewise the Court was united in rejecting the applicant's complaints under this Article:

58. The applicant's first allegation was that by being placed at the Government's disposal he was held in 'servitude', contrary to paragraph 1, in that he was subjected 'to the whims of the administration'.

The situation complained of did not violate Article 5 par. 1 [as it was justified under Article 5(1)(a), being a lawful detention after conviction by a competent court]. Accordingly, it could have been regarded as servitude only if it involved a 'particularly serious' form of 'denial of freedom' (see paragraphs 79–80 of the Commission's report), which was not so in the present case.

59. Mr Van Droogenbroeck further complained that, contrary to paragraph 2 of Article 4 (art 4–2), he was 'forced' to work in order to save 12,000 BF. According to the Government, he was simply 'invited' to work.

The Court considers that it may leave this question of fact open. In practice, once release is conditional on the possession of savings from pay for work done in prison . . . one is not far away from an obligation in the strict sense of the term.

However, it does not follow that the complaint is well-founded . . . the latter Article authorises, in paragraph 3 (a) (art 4-3-a), work required to be done in the ordinary course of detention which has been imposed, as was here the case, in a manner that does not infringe paragraph 1 of Article 5 (art 5-1). Moreover, the work which Mr Van Droogenbroeck was asked to do did not go beyond what is 'ordinary' in this context since it was calculated to assist him in reintegrating himself into society and had as its legal basis provisions which find an equivalent in certain other member States of the Council of Europe . . .

60. Accordingly, the Belgian authorities did not fail to observe the requirements of Article 4 (art 4).

Hence, forms of punishment and prison work which are within the bounds of contemporary European practices will not generally violate Article 4.

3   A unanimous Chamber of the full-time Court held that States are under positive obligations to adopt and effectively implement criminal law provisions prohibiting the practices proscribed by Article 4 in *Siliadin v France*, judgment of 26 July 2005. In 1994, when she was 15 years old, the applicant, a Togolese national, was brought to France by a relative of her father. The relative, who had acquired French nationality, had undertaken to regularize the applicant's immigration status in France and arrange for her education. In return the applicant was to undertake housework for the relative until she had earned enough to pay back the cost of her airfare to France. The relative confiscated the applicant's passport. Ten months after the applicant arrived in France the relative 'lent' the applicant to a couple of friends in order that she could help them with household tasks. The applicant was retained by the couple as a 'maid of all work' for nearly four years. During that time she worked from 7.30 am to 10.30 pm, with no days off (she was given permission to attend church on certain Sundays) for no pay. She slept on a mattress on the floor and wore old clothes. Eventually, the applicant informed a neighbour of her situation and the matter was referred to the public prosecutor. The couple were charged and convicted of, *inter alia*, wrongfully obtaining unpaid services from a vulnerable person. The couple successfully appealed against their conviction. However, they were ordered to pay the applicant 15,000 euros in damages and an employment tribunal later awarded her 31,000 euros in salary arrears against them. The Chamber characterized the treatment of the applicant as amounting to forced labour in that she was required to work for years, against her will, on behalf of the couple without being paid. Furthermore, given the applicant's status as a minor and the coercion exercised over her by the couple (her passport had been confiscated, her immigration status had never been regularized and she was afraid of being arrested by the police) the Chamber found that she had also been held in servitude. Given the couple's acquittal and subsequent criticism of the relevant criminal law provisions by the National Assembly, the Chamber concluded that there had been a breach of Article 4 by the respondent State as its law had not provided the applicant with adequate protection. The horrifying facts of this case amply illustrate why States must take appropriate measures to ensure that vulnerable persons within their jurisdiction are not abused by other exploitative persons.

4   The authority of States to require persons to undertake compulsory military or civilian service, recognized by Article 4(3)(b), was considered by the Commission in *Johansen v Norway*, 44 DR 155 (1985). The Norwegian Constitution imposed a general duty on male citizens to perform military service. However, since 1922 conscientious objection to military service has been recognized. When a person objects to military service on grounds of conscience then he will be required to undertake civilian service (normally involving work in the health or social services). If a person refuses to perform his civilian service then his case will be referred to the courts and if he is found to be in breach of his legal duties then he may be ordered to work at a special camp (doing administrative or agricultural work) for the duration of his civilian service. If such a person does not attend the camp or refuses to perform the work assigned to him then he will be held in prison for the remainder of his period of civilian service. The applicant, a pacifist, was opposed to both military service and civilian service (which he considered to have the purpose of upholding respect for military service). The authorities recognised him as a conscientious objector and required him to perform civilian service. The applicant refused to carry out any form of civilian service. His case was referred to the District Court which found him in breach of his legal duties. The applicant then complained to the Commission alleging a breach of a number of Convention rights. The Commission declared his application inadmissible because the duty to perform civilian service:

... is an obligation fully compatible with the Convention. The Convention does not oblige the Contracting States to make available for conscientious objectors to military service any substitute civilian service.

In States which recognise conscientious objectors and provide for alternative service it is fully compatible with the Convention to require the objectors to perform alternative service. This is clear from the text of Article 4(3)(b) of the Convention which specifically sets out that service extracted from conscientious objectors instead of compulsory military service is not to be regarded as 'forced or compulsory labour'. (p 162)

As regards the applicant's argument that compulsory civilian service violated his freedom of conscience under Article 9, the Commission stated that:

When interpreting this provision, the Commission has taken into consideration Article 4(3)(b) of the Convention ... Since the Convention thus expressly recognises that conscientious objectors may be required to perform civilian service it is clear that the Convention does not guarantee a right to be exempted from civilian service ... The Convention does not prevent a state from taking measures to enforce performance of civilian service, or from imposing sanctions on those who refuse such service. (p 165)

For another example of the failure of an application by a conscientious objector to a different form of civilian obligation see *Fadini v Switzerland*, below p 605.

5 The Court interpreted Article 4(3)(d) as encompassing the duty on men to serve in the local fire brigade, or pay a financial contribution instead of actual service, in Baden-Wurttemberg: *Schmidt v Germany*, A.291-B (1994) 18 EHRR 513.

23. Like the participants in the proceedings, the Court considers that compulsory fire service such as exists in Baden-Württemberg is one of the 'normal civic obligations' envisaged in Article 4 para 3 (d) (art 4–3-d). It observes further that the financial contribution which is payable—in lieu of service—is, according to the Federal Constitutional Court ... a 'compensatory charge'. The Court therefore concludes that, on account of its close links with the obligation to serve, the obligation to pay also falls within the scope of Article 4 para 3 (d) (art 4-3-d).

By holding that the liability for the financial payment was also covered by Article 4 the Court was able to go on and find unlawful sex discrimination in breach of Article 14, because only men were liable (see below, p 814).

6 The approach of the original Court to the interpretation of paragraph 3 of Article 4 in *Schmidt* was followed by the Chamber in *Zarb Adami v Malta*, judgment of 20 June 2006. In the latter case the applicant complained that men were much more likely to be called for jury service then women (in 1996: 147 women were placed on the lists of jurors whilst 4,298 men were placed on the lists). The Chamber (six votes to one) held that:

46 .... Therefore, the fact that a situation corresponds to the notion of a normal civic obligation within the meaning of paragraph 3 is not an obstacle to the applicability of Article 4 of the Convention, read in conjunction with Article 14.

47. Like the participants in the proceedings, the Court considers that compulsory jury service such as exists in Malta is one of the 'normal civic obligations' envisaged in Article 4 § 3(d). It observes further that the applicant did not offer himself voluntarily for jury service and that his failure to appear led to the imposition of a fine, which could be converted into a term of imprisonment. On account of its close links with the obligation to serve, the obligation to pay the fine also falls within the scope of Article 4 § 3(d) (see, *mutatis mutandis*, *Karlheinz Schmidt*, judgment cited above, p 32, § 23).

...

49. It follows that the facts in issue fall within the ambit of Article 4. Article 14 of the Convention is accordingly applicable.

The Chamber then found that the Government had not been able to provide any proper justification for the low number of women registered on the lists of jurors and consequently there had been a breach of Article 14 read in conjunction with Article 4(3)(d). However, several judges expressed varying degrees of disquiet about the established interpretation of the ambit of Article 4. Judge Bratza in his concurring opinion stated that he did not find the reasoning in *Schmidt* 'to be entirely convincing or satisfactory'. Whilst Judge Garlicki in his concurring opinion was not convinced by the earlier reasoning. He believed that:

...it is possible to read Article 4, taken as a whole, in a broader way, not only as prohibiting any forms of forced or compulsory labour but also as regulating State prerogatives in establishing different forms of compulsory works and services. In other words, Article 4 may also be read as setting a general framework of duties which may be imposed on an individual. Article 4 empowers the State to establish such duties and services, but—by the very fact of their enumeration—Article 4 also absorbs (includes) them into the realm of the Convention. One of the consequences of such inclusion is that those duties and services must be formulated in a manner compatible with the Convention, its Article 14 included. It should not be forgotten that Article 4 is drafted in a particular manner: no other substantive provision of the Convention contains enumerations of such kind. This may suggest that the drafters of the Convention envisaged that Article 4 might be interpreted in a particular way.

Several arguments may warrant this broad reading of Article 4. First of all, it would reflect the particular rank of Article 4 as 'one of the fundamental values of democratic societies'. Secondly, it would correspond better to the concept of positive duties of the State: the State is not only prohibited from introducing any form of forced or compulsory labour, but is also required to regulate the scope and manner of what remains imposable on individual citizens. Finally, it would respond to the developing trends of modern societies: whilst it is now very difficult to find situations of 'classic' forced labour or servitude (the 2005 *Siliadin v France* case being the only recent example), there may be more controversies surrounding obligations enumerated in paragraph 3 of Article 4.

Judge Casadevall dissented:

2. Like the dissenting judges in the case of *Karlheinz Schmidt* (a judgment that is now twelve years old), I fail to see how Article 14, which is dependent for its existence on a recognised right (see paragraph 42 of the judgment), can be linked to subparagraph (d) of Article 4 § 3 for the following reasons:

(a)   subparagraph (d) actually constitutes an exception to the general rule prohibiting forced or compulsory labour;

(b)   the expression 'forced or compulsory labour' in Article 4 does not include 'any work or service which forms part of normal civic obligations' (see paragraph 43 of the judgment); and

(c)   it is accepted that the obligation to serve as a juror in Malta forms part of the 'normal civic obligations' (see paßragraph 47 of the judgment).

3. It is quite clear that Mr Zarb Adami has not been required to perform forced or compulsory labour within the meaning of Article 4 § 2 and that the service he was asked to perform constituted a civic obligation, such as serving the administration of criminal justice. Since the applicant is unable to assert a substantive right protected by the Convention (Article 4 does not prohibit civic obligations of this type) Article 14 cannot come into play.

Furthermore, he considered the applicant's complaint to be 'frivolous'. Given these diverging views in the Chamber, the Grand Chamber may reconsider the interpretation of Article 4(2) and (3) in the future.

7 ARTICLE 5 RIGHT TO LIBERTY AND SECURITY

Introduction

The concept of liberty

Guzzardi v Italy A.39 (1980) 3 EHRR 333
European Court of Human Rights

The applicant was suspected by the police of engaging in very serious illegal activities and belonging to a band of Mafia. Under legislation making provision for various preventive measures which could be taken against 'persons presenting a danger for security and public morality', the Milan Regional Court directed that the applicant be placed under special supervision and combined this with an obligation of confinement to a part of an island (Asinara) allocated for compulsory residents. Accordingly, for sixteen months the applicant was confined to a special area of approximately 2.5 sq km, viz a hamlet (Cala Reale) on the island consisting of a former medical establishment and certain other buildings, including a police station where he had to report twice daily. He was subject to a curfew between 10 pm and 7 am but otherwise there were significant elements of the confinement which distinguished it from normal prison detention.

The applicant alleged breaches of Articles 3, 8, 9, and Article 2 of Protocol 1. The Commission of its own initiative examined the case from the perspective of Article 5. It was unanimously of the opinion that there had been a breach of Article 5(1), but not of any other Articles.

JUDGMENT OF THE COURT

92. The Court recalls that in proclaiming the 'right to liberty', paragraph 1 of Article 5 is contemplating the physical liberty of the person; its aim is to ensure that no one should be dispossessed of this liberty in an arbitrary fashion. As was pointed out by those appearing before the Court, the paragraph is not concerned with mere restrictions on liberty of movement; such restrictions are governed by Article 2 of Protocol No 4 which has not been ratified by Italy. In order to determine whether someone has been 'deprived of his liberty' within the meaning of Article 5, the starting point must be his concrete situation and account must be taken of a whole range of criteria such as the type, duration, effects and manner of implementation of the measure in question (see the *Engel* judgment of 8 June 1976, Series A No 22, p 24, §§ 58–9).

93. The difference between deprivation of and restriction upon liberty is nonetheless merely one of degree or intensity, and not one of nature or substance. Although the process of classification into one or other of these categories sometimes proves to be no easy task in that some borderline cases are a matter of pure opinion, the Court cannot avoid making the selection upon which the applicability or inapplicability of Article 5 depends.

94. As provided for under the 1956 Act . . . , special supervision accompanied by an order for compulsory residence in a specified district does not of itself come within the scope of Article 5. The Commission acknowledged this: it focused its attention on Mr Guzzardi's 'actual position' at Cala Reale . . . and pointed out that on 5 October 1977 it had declared inadmissible application no 7960/77 lodged by the same individual with regard to his living conditions at Force . . . .

[However it] does not follow that 'deprivation of liberty' may never result from the manner of implementation of such a measure, and in the present case the manner of implementation is the sole issue that falls to be considered . . . .

95. The Government's reasoning is not without weight. It demonstrates very clearly the extent of the difference between the applicant's treatment on Asinara and classic detention in prison or strict arrest imposed on a serviceman (see the above-mentioned *Engel* judgment, p 26, § 63). Deprivation of liberty may, however, take numerous other forms. Their variety is being increased by developments in legal standards and in attitudes; and the Convention is to be interpreted in the light of the notions currently prevailing in democratic States (see notably the *Tyrer* judgment of 25 April 1978, Series A No 26, pp 15–16, § 31).

Whilst the area around which the applicant could move far exceeded the dimensions of a cell and was not bounded by any physical barrier, it covered no more than a tiny fraction of an island to which access was difficult and about nine-tenths of which was occupied by a prison. Mr Guzzardi was housed in part of the hamlet of Cala Reale which consisted mainly of the buildings of a former medical establishment which were in a state of disrepair or even dilapidation, a *carabinieri* station, a school and a chapel. He lived their principally in the company of other persons subjected to the same measure and of policemen. The permanent population of Asinara resided almost entirely at Cala d'Oliva, which Mr Guzzardi could not visit, and would appear to have made hardly any use of its right to go to Cala Reale. Consequently, there were few opportunities for social contacts available to the applicant other than with his near family, his fellow 'residents' and the supervisory staff. Supervision was carried out strictly and on an almost constant basis. Thus, Mr Guzzardi was not able to leave his dwelling between 10 pm and 7 am without giving prior notification to the authorities in due time. He had to report to the authorities twice a day and inform them of the name and number of his correspondent whenever he wished to use the telephone. He needed the consent of the authorities for each of his trips to Sardinia or the mainland, trips which were rare and, understandably, made under the strict supervision of the *carabinieri*. He was liable to punishment by 'arrest' if he failed to comply with any of his obligations. Finally, more than sixteen months elapsed between his arrival at Cala Reale and his departure for Force . . . .

It is admittedly not possible to speak of 'deprivation of liberty' on the strength of any one of these factors taken individually, but cumulatively and in combination they certainly raise an issue of categorisation from the viewpoint of Article 5. In certain respects the treatment complained of resembles detention in an 'open prison' or committal to a disciplinary unit (see the above-mentioned *Engel* judgment, p 26, § 64) . . . .

The Court considers on balance that the present case is to be regarded as one involving deprivation of liberty . . . .

96. It remains to be determined whether the situation was one of those, exhaustively listed in Article 5 § 1 of the Convention (see the *Winterwerp* judgment of 24 October 1979, Series A No 33, p 16, § 37), in which the Contracting States reserve the right to arrest or detain individuals . . . .

[*The Court rejected a government argument that the applicant was a vagrant within Article 5(1)(e).*]

100. On a true analysis, the order for Mr Guzzardi's compulsory residence was not a punishment for a specific offence but a preventive measure taken on the strength of indications of a propensity to crime . . . .

In the Court's opinion, comparison of Article 5 § 1(a) with Articles 6 § 2 and 7 § 1 shows that for Convention purposes there cannot be a '*condamnation*' (in the English text: 'conviction') unless it has been established in accordance with the law that there has been an offence—either criminal or, if appropriate, disciplinary (see the above-mentioned *Engel* judgment, p 27, § 68). Moreover, to use 'conviction' for a preventive or security measure would be consonant neither with the principle of narrow interpretation to be observed in this area (see paragraph 98 above) nor with the fact that that word implies a finding of guilt. . . .

101. The deprivation of liberty complained of was not covered by *sub-paragraph (b)* either.

Admittedly, under the procedure laid down by the 1956 Act judicial decisions are a kind of sanction for failure to heed a prior warning (*deffida*), but the warning is not indispensable if, as in the present case, recourse is had to the 1965 Act; moreover, the warning is issued by the Chief of Police and so does not constitute an 'order of a court'. . . .

As regards the words 'to secure the fulfilment of any obligation prescribed by law', they concern only those cases where the law permits the detention of a person to compel him to fulfil a 'specific and concrete' obligation which he has failed to satisfy (see the above-mentioned *Engel* judgment, p 28, § 69). However, as the Commission rightly emphasised, the 1956 and 1965 Acts impose general obligations . . . .

102. Neither was the applicant in one of the situations dealt with by *sub-paragraph (c)*.

It is true that there was 'reasonable suspicion of [his] having committed an offence' and that he remained subject to charges throughout the time he spent on Asinara, but the decisions of the Regional Court (30 January 1975), the Court of Appeal (12 March 1975) and the Court of Cassation (6 October 1975) [authorising his detention as Asinara] had no connection in law with the investigation being pursued in his respect: they were based on the 1956 and 1965 Acts which are applicable irrespective of whether or not there has been a charge and do not prescribe any subsequent appearance 'before the competent legal authority' . . . .

At first sight, a more likely hypothesis is that the measure complained of was taken because it was 'reasonably considered necessary to prevent [Mr Guzzardi's] committing an offence' or, at the outside, 'fleeing after having done so'. However, in that case as well a question would arise as to the measure's 'lawfulness' since, solely on the basis of the 1956 and 1965 Acts, an order for compulsory residence as such, leaving aside the manner of its implementation, does not constitute deprivation of liberty (see paragraph 94 above). It would also be necessary to consider whether the requirements of paragraph 3 of Article 5 had been observed (see the *Lawless* judgment of 1 July 1961, Series A No 3, pp 51–3, §§ 13–14). In any event, the phrase under examination is not adapted to a policy of general prevention directed against an individual or a category of individuals who, like *mafiosi*, present a danger on account of their continuing propensity to crime; it does no more than afford the Contracting States a means of preventing a concrete and specific offence. This can be seen both from the use of the singular ('an offence', '*celle-ci*' in the French text; see the *Matznetter* judgment of 10 November 1969, Series A No 10, pp 40 and 43, separate opinions of Mr Balladore Palliere and Mr Zekia) and from the object of Article 5, namely to ensure that no one should be dispossessed of his liberty in an arbitrary fashion (see the above-mentioned *Winterwerp* judgment, p 16, § 37). . . .

FOR THESE REASONS, THE COURT . . .

4. Holds by eleven votes to seven that there was in the instant case deprivation of liberty within the meaning of Article 5 of the Convention;

5. Holds unanimously that the said deprivation of liberty was not justified under sub-paragraph (e) of Article 5 § 1 or under sub-paragraph (b);

6. Holds by sixteen votes to two that the said deprivation of liberty was also not justified under sub-paragraph (a);

7. Holds by twelve votes to six that the said deprivation of liberty was not justified under sub-paragraph (c) either;

8. Holds, to sum up, by ten votes to eight, that from 8 February 1975 to 22 July 1976 the applicant was the victim of a breach of Article 5 § 1; ...

Dissenting Opinion of Judge Sir Gerald Fitzmaurice:

8. Basically what happened to the applicant was not that he was imprisoned or confined, but that he was banished to an island on which he was assigned a place of residence (an ordinary house) and restricted to an area sufficiently big for him to be able to live a normal life except that he could not leave it without permission, and was (and for that purpose had to be) under surveillance. To me all this has very much more the flavour of Article 2 of the [Fourth] Protocol than of Article 5 of the Convention, even if a residue of doubt may remain—but in that event, is it right to condemn a Government for breach of the Convention in the presence of a very reasonable doubt as to whether any has occurred? ...

11. In this connexion, and in general, I consider that the Court failed to give any adequate weight—if weight at all—to the fact that the applicant was a terrorist and *mafioso*. Naturally these factors would not justify treating him in a manner clearly, or at any rate substantially, contrary to the Convention. But where there are grounds for genuine doubt whether any contravention has in fact occurred, such factors, though in no way conclusive *per se*, may legitimately be taken into account (I do not put it any higher than that) in deciding how to set about resolving the doubt—again I put it no higher. In the present case, however, the Court completely ignored the plea of the Italian Government to the effect that public order in Italy at this time was seriously menaced by threats coming essentially from political terrorism and the mafia, and that the authorities were under strong pressure to combat these evils by draconian measures—pressure which they had so far resisted, as was exemplified in the case of Guzzardi by the relative leniency of his original treatment as described in paragraph 8 above. ...

12. The process of simply ignoring the whole context in which a case occurs is bound to lead to injustices and absurdities ... The present case in fact bristles with absurdities. Another instance of this is that, as pointed out by the Italian Government, whereas by reason of sub-paragraph (e) of Article 5 § 1 of the Convention, a vagrant can, merely by reason of his being such, be placed under detention without any contravention of the Convention, a known terrorist cannot even have his movements restricted under the conditions applied to Guzzardi without such a breach resulting—if the judgment of the Court is correct. To be sure, modern terrorism was an evil not specifically present to the minds of those who drafted the Convention, or they would doubtless have provided for it. Again, it is admittedly for governments and none other to remedy this defect: the Court cannot do so by deeming a terrorist to be a vagrant even though he is in fact much worse than a vagrant (who may well be a harmless individual, which a terrorist never is). But this does not alter the fact that, according to the order of things resulting from the Court's judgment, a terrorist may be much better off than a vagrant. (He may even be paid a million lire!). All these absurdities could have been avoided by an attitude of greater realism against the background of the case, leading to the conclusion—for which there was ample warrant on the facts—that the case was basically one of restriction on movement and place of residence and not one of deprivation of liberty under Article 5 of the Convention, interpreted, as it has to be, in the light of the existence of Article 2 of Protocol No 4.

NOTES

1 The Court was composed of President Wiarda and Judges Balladore Pallieri, Zekia, Cremona, Vilhjálmsson, Ryssdal, Van der Meersch, Sir Gerald Fitzmaurice, Bindschedler-Robert, Evrigenis, Teitgen, Lagergren, Liesch, Gölcüklü, Matscher, Pinheiro Farinha, García de Enterría, and Walsh.

In addition to Judge Fitzmaurice dissenting opinions were given by Judges: Balladore Pallieri, Zekia, Cremona, Bindschedler-Robert, Teitgen and García de Enterría, and Pinheiro Farinha. Judge Matscher issued a partly dissenting opinion.

2 As the *Guzzardi* case indicates, the distinction between the deprivation of liberty in the sense of Article 5, ECHR and a limitation upon freedom of movement, which is subject only to Article 2, 4th Protocol to the ECHR, is a matter of the 'degree and intensity' of the confinement. In Application 7960/77, to which the Court refers, the same applicant had been restricted to a village on the mainland where his living conditions were those of other inhabitants. The Commission considered that this case did not involve sufficiently close detention for Article 5 to apply.

3 There are other cases in which the closeness of confinement has been an issue. In *Engel v Netherlands*, A 22 (1976) 1 EHRR 647, in the context of disciplinary offences, the detention of a soldier in a locked cell ('strict arrest') fell within Article 5, but confinement during off duty hours to an unlocked building in the barracks ('aggravated arrest') did not.

4 In *Amuur v France* (1996) 22 EHRR 533, 1996-III 826, the applicant Somali nationals arrived at Orly airport in Paris, having fled from Somalia (via Syria) in fear of their lives after a revolution. They were refused entry into France because their passports were false. While their applications for asylum were being considered, they were kept in the international transit area at the airport. After 20 days, their applications were refused and they were put on a flight back to Syria. During the whole of this time, they were free to leave the airport on a flight of their choice for another state that would receive them. The European Court held unanimously that the applicants were being detained in the sense of Article 5 during the 20-day period. It stated:

43. Holding aliens in the international zone does indeed involve a restriction upon liberty, but one which is not in every respect comparable to that which obtains in centres for the detention of aliens pending deportation. Such confinement, accompanied by suitable safeguards for the persons concerned, is acceptable only in order to enable States to prevent unlawful immigration while complying with their international obligations, particularly under the 1951 Geneva Convention Relating to the Status of Refugees and the European Convention on Human Rights. States' legitimate concern to foil the increasingly frequent attempts to circumvent immigration restrictions must not deprive asylumseekers of the protection afforded by these conventions.

Such holding should not be prolonged excessively, otherwise there would be a risk of it turning mere restriction on liberty—inevitable with a view to organising the practical details of the alien's repatriation or, where he has requested asylum, while his application for leave to enter the territory for that purpose is considered—into a deprivation of liberty. In that connection account should be taken of the fact that the measure is applicable not to those who have committed criminal offences but to aliens who, often fearing for their lives, have fled from their own country.

Although by the force of circumstances the decision to order holding must necessarily be taken by the administrative or police authorities, its prolongation requires speedy review by the courts, the traditional guardians of personal liberties. Above all, such confinement must not deprive the asylum-seeker of the right to gain effective access to the procedure for determining refugee status. . . .

45. The Court notes that for the greater part of the above period [20 days] the applicants, who claimed to be refugees, were left to their own devices. They were placed under strict and constant police surveillance and had no legal and social assistance—particularly with a view to completing the formalities relating to an application for political refugee status—until 24 March, when a humanitarian association, which had in the meantime been informed of their presence in the international zone, put them in contact with a lawyer. Moreover, until 26 March neither the length nor the necessity of their confinement were reviewed by a court. . . .

48. The mere fact that it is possible for asylum-seekers to leave voluntarily the country where they wish to take refuge cannot exclude a restriction on liberty, the right to leave any country, including one's own, being guaranteed, moreover, by Protocol No 4 to the Convention. Furthermore, this possibility becomes theoretical if no other country offering protection comparable to the protection they expect to find in the country where they are seeking asylum is inclined or prepared to take them in.

Sending the applicants back to Syria only became possible, apart from the practical problems of the journey, following negotiations between the French and Syrian authorities. The assurances of the latter were dependent on the vagaries of diplomatic relations, in view of the fact that Syria was not bound by the Geneva Convention relating to the Status of Refugees.

49. The Court concludes that holding the applicants in the transit zone of Paris-Orly Airport was equivalent in practice, in view of the restrictions suffered, to a deprivation of liberty. Article 5 § 1 is therefore applicable to the case. . . .

The Court then held unanimously that Article 5(1) had been infringed. It stated:

50. . . . In laying down that any deprivation of liberty must be effected 'in accordance with a procedure prescribed by law', Article 5 § 1 primarily requires any arrest or detention to have a legal basis in domestic law. However, these words do not merely refer back to domestic law; like the expressions 'in accordance with the law' and 'prescribed by law' in the second paragraphs of Articles 8 to 11, they also relate to the quality of the law, requiring it to be compatible with the rule of law, a concept inherent in all the Articles of the Convention.

In order to ascertain whether a deprivation of liberty has complied with the principle of compatibility with domestic law, it therefore falls to the Court to assess not only the legislation in force in the field under consideration, but also the quality of the other legal rules applicable to the persons concerned. Quality in this sense implies that where a national law authorises deprivation of liberty—especially in respect of a foreign asylum-seeker—it must be sufficiently accessible and precise, in order to avoid all risk of arbitrariness. These characteristics are of fundamental importance with regard to asylum-seekers at airports, particularly in view of the need to reconcile the protection of fundamental rights with the requirements of States' immigration policies. . . .

52. The Court notes that even though the applicants were not in France within the meaning of the Ordinance of 2 November 1945, holding them in the international zone of Paris-Orly Airport made them subject to French law.

Despite its name, the international zone does not have extraterritorial status. In its decision of 25 February 1992 the Constitutional Council did not challenge the legislature's right to lay down rules governing the holding of aliens in that zone. For example, the Law of 6 July 1992 . . . provides, *inter alia*, for the intervention of the ordinary courts to authorise holding for more than four days, the assistance of an interpreter and a doctor and the possibility of communicating with a lawyer. The Decree of 15 December 1992 . . . lays down the procedural rules applicable to proceedings brought in accordance with that Law. The Decree of 2 May 1995 . . . gives the delegate of the United Nations High Commissioner for Refugees or his representatives and humanitarian associations permanent access to the zone.

However, these rules—which postdate the facts of the case—were not applicable at the time to the applicants.

53. The Court emphasises that from 9 to 29 March 1992 the applicants were in the situation of asylum-seekers whose application had not yet been considered. In that connection, neither the Decree of 27 May 1982 nor the—unpublished—circular of 26 June 1990 (the only text at the material time which specifically dealt with the practice of holding aliens in the transit zone) constituted a 'law' of sufficient 'quality' within the meaning of the Court's case-law; there must be adequate legal protection in domestic law against arbitrary interferences by public authorities with the rights safeguarded by the Convention (see the *Malone v UK* judgment of 2 August 1984, Series A No 82, p 32, § 67). In any event,

the Decree of 27 May 1982 did not concern holding aliens in the international zone. The above-mentioned circular consisted, by its very nature, of instructions given by the Minister of the Interior to Prefects and Chief Constables concerning aliens refused leave to enter at the frontiers. It was intended to provide guidelines for immigration control at ports and airports. Moreover, the brief section it devoted to holding in the international zone and aliens' rights contains no guarantees comparable to those introduced by the Law of 6 July 1992. At the material time none of these texts allowed the ordinary courts to review the conditions under which aliens were held or, if necessary, to impose a limit on the administrative authorities as regards the length of time for which they were held or, if necessary, to impose a limit on the administrative authorities as regards the length of time for which they were held. They did not provide for legal, humanitarian and social assistance, nor did they lay down procedures and time-limits for access to such assistance so that asylum seekers like the applicants could take the necessary steps.

54. The French legal rules in force at the time, as applied in the present case, did not sufficiently guarantee the applicants' right to liberty.

There has accordingly been a breach of Article 5(1).

5 In *Nielsen v Denmark*, A.144 (1988) 11 EHRR 175 a 12-year-old boy was confined to a child psychiatric ward for five months at the request of his mother, who held sole parental rights, following medical advice that the child was developing 'nervously'. The parents were separated and the child had indicated that he wanted to live with his father. The European Court held, by nine votes to five, that Article 5 did not apply. It stated:

72. The Court accepts, with the Government, that the rights of the holder of parental authority cannot be unlimited and that it is incumbent on the State to provide safeguards against abuse. However, it does not follow that the present case falls within the ambit of Article 5.

The restrictions imposed on the applicant were not of a nature or degree similar to the cases of deprivation of liberty specified in paragraph 1 of Article 5. In particular, he was not detained as a person of unsound mind so as to bring the case within paragraph 1(e). Not only was the child not mentally ill within the meaning of the 1938 Act, but the Psychiatric Ward at the Hospital was in fact not used for the treatment of patients under the 1938 Act or of patients otherwise suffering from mental illnesses of a psychotic nature. Indeed, the restrictions to which the applicant was subject were no more than the normal requirements for the care of a child of 12 years of age receiving treatment in hospital. The conditions in which the applicant stayed thus did not, in principle, differ from those obtaining in many hospital wards where children with physical disorders are treated.

Regarding the weight which should be given to the applicant's views as to his hospitalisation, the Court considers that he was still of an age at which it would be normal for a decision to be made by the parent even against the wishes of the child. There is no evidence of bad faith on the part of the mother. Hospitalisation was decided upon by her in accordance with expert medical advice. It must be possible for a child like the applicant to be admitted to hospital at the request of the holder of parental rights, a case which clearly is not covered by paragraph 1 of Article 5.

Nor did the intervention of the police, which would have been appropriate for the return of any runaway child of that age even to parental custody, throw a different light on the situation.

73. The Court concludes that the hospitalisation of the applicant did not amount to a deprivation of liberty within the meaning of Article 5, but was a responsible exercise by his mother of her custodial rights in the interest of the child. Accordingly, Article 5 is not applicable in the case.

The crucial factors for the Court were the nature of the restrictions placed upon the child, his age, and the medical view of his health.

6 A unanimous Chamber of the full-time Court held that the deprivation of liberty under Article 5 involved both objective and subjective elements in *Storck v Germany*, judgment of

16 June 2005. When the applicant was 18 years old, in 1977, she was placed in a private psychiatric clinic (located in Bremen) at the demand of her father. She was forced to remain in the clinic and receive medication for nearly two years. During that period she was brought back to the clinic by the police after she escaped. She contended that during her time in the clinic she was given psychotropic drugs and had been physically attached to beds, chairs and radiators. Subsequently, she received extensive medical treatment at a number of hospitals and at the Bremen clinic. From 1980 until 1991 she lost the ability to speak. In the 1990s she obtained two reports from expert psychiatrists that she had never suffered from schizophrenia and that in the 1970s she had had experienced an 'identity crisis'. At the time of the proceedings before the Court she was classified as 100 per cent handicapped and received an invalidity pension. After a number of actions in the lower courts the German Constitutional Court determined that she had not demonstrated a violation of her constitutional rights in respect of her treatment in the private clinic. The Chamber ruled that:

74. However, the notion of deprivation of liberty within the meaning of Article 5 § 1 does not only comprise the objective element of a person's confinement to a certain limited place for a not negligible length of time. A person can only be considered as being deprived of his or her liberty if, as an additional subjective element, he has not validly consented to the confinement in question (see, *mutatis mutandis*, *H.M. v Switzerland* [ECHR 2002-II] § 46). The Court notes that in the present case, it is disputed between the parties whether the applicant had consented to her stay in the clinic.

75. Having regard to the national courts' related findings of fact and to the factors which are undisputed between the parties, the Court observes that the applicant had attained majority at the time of her admission to the clinic and had not been placed under guardianship. Therefore, she had been considered to have the capacity to consent or object to her admission and treatment in hospital. It is undisputed that she had not signed the clinic's admission form prepared on the day of her arrival. It is true that she had presented herself to the clinic, accompanied by her father. However, the right to liberty is too important in a democratic society for a person to lose the benefit of the Convention protection for the single reason that he may have given himself up to be taken into detention (see *De Wilde, Ooms and Versyp v Belgium*, judgment of 18 June 1971, Series A No 12, p. 36, § 65; *H.L. v the United Kingdom* [ECHR 2004-IX] § 90).

76. Having regard to the continuation of the applicant's stay in the clinic, the Court considers the key factor in the present case to be that—which is uncontested—the applicant, on several occasions, had tried to flee from the clinic. She had to be fettered in order to prevent her from absconding and had to be brought back to the clinic by the police when she had managed to escape on one occasion. Under these circumstances, the Court is unable to discern any factual basis for the assumption that the applicant—presuming her capacity to consent—had agreed to her continued stay in the clinic. In the alternative, assuming that the applicant had no longer been capable of consenting following her treatment with strong medicaments, she could, in any event, not be considered as having validly agreed to her stay in the clinic.

77. Indeed, a comparison of the facts of this case with those in *H.L. v the United Kingdom* (cited above) cannot but confirm this finding. That case concerned the confinement of an individual who was of age but lacked the capacity to consent in a psychiatric institution which he had never attempted to leave, and in which the Court had found that there had been a deprivation of liberty. In the present case, *a fortiori*, a deprivation of liberty must be found. The applicant's lack of consent must also be regarded as the decisive feature distinguishing the present case from the case of *H.M. v Switzerland* (cited above, § 46). In that case, it was held that the placing of an elderly person in a foster home, to ensure necessary medical care, had not amounted to a deprivation of liberty. However, that applicant, who had been legally capable of expressing a view, had been undecided as to whether or not she wanted to stay in the nursing home. The clinic could then draw the conclusion that she did not object.

78. The Court therefore concludes that the applicant had been deprived of her liberty within the meaning of Article 5 § 1 of the Convention.

The Chamber then found that the State was responsible, under Article 5, for the applicant's deprivation of liberty in the private clinic on several grounds. First, through the involvement of public authorities, as the police had returned her to the clinic after she had escaped. Secondly, the German courts had failed to interpret the civil law in accordance with the 'spirit' of Article 5 in the actions brought by the applicant. Thirdly, through the State's failure to comply with its positive obligation to protect the applicant's liberty from being interfered with by private persons.

101. The Court has consistently held that the responsibility of a State is engaged if a violation of one of the rights and freedoms defined in the Convention is the result of non-observance by that State of its obligation under Article 1 to secure those rights and freedoms in its domestic law to everyone within its jurisdiction (see, *inter alia*, *Costello-Roberts v. the United Kingdom*, judgment of 25 March 1993, Series A No 247-C, p 57, § 26; *Woś v Poland* (dec.), No 22860/02, § 60, 1 March 2005). Consequently, the Court has expressly found that Article 2 (see, amongst others, *L.C.B. v the United Kingdom*, judgment of 9 June 1998, *Reports of Judgments and Decisions* 1998-III, p 1403, § 36), Article 3 (see, *inter alia*, *Costello-Roberts*, cited above, pp 57–8, §§ 26 and 28) and Article 8 of the Convention (see, *inter alia*, *X and Y v The Netherlands*, judgment of 26 March 1985, Series A No 91, p 11, § 23; *Costello-Roberts*, ibid) enjoin the State not only to refrain from an active infringement by its representatives of the rights in question, but also to take appropriate steps to provide protection against an interference with those rights either by State agents or private parties.

102. Having regard to this, the Court considers that Article 5 § 1, first sentence, of the Convention must equally be considered as laying down a positive obligation on the State to protect the liberty of its citizens. Any conclusion to the effect that this was not the case would not only be inconsistent with the Court's case-law, notably under Articles 2, 3 and 8 of the Convention. It would, moreover, leave a sizeable gap in the protection from arbitrary detention, which would be inconsistent with the importance of personal liberty in a democratic society. The State is, therefore, obliged to take measures providing effective protection of vulnerable persons, including reasonable steps to prevent a deprivation of liberty of which the authorities have or ought to have knowledge (see, *mutatis mutandis, Z and Others v the United Kingdom* [GC], No 29392/95, § 73, ECHR 2001-V; *Ilaşcu and Others v Moldova and Russia* [GC], No 48787/99, §§ 332–52, 464, ECHR 2004-VII).

103. With respect to persons in need of psychiatric treatment in particular, the Court observes that the State is under an obligation to secure to its citizens their right to physical integrity under Article 8 of the Convention. For this purpose there are hospitals run by the State which coexist with private hospitals. The State cannot completely absolve itself from its responsibility by delegating its obligations in this sphere to private bodies or individuals (see, *mutatis mutandis, Van der Mussele v Belgium*, judgment of 23 November 1983, Series A No 70, pp 14–15, §§ 28–30; *Woś*, cited above, § 60). The Court recalls that in the case of *Costello-Roberts* (cited above, p 58, §§ 27–8) the State was held responsible for the act of a headmaster of an independent school due to its obligation to secure to pupils their rights guaranteed by Articles 3 and 8 of the Convention. The Court finds that, similarly, in the present case the State remained under a duty to exercise supervision and control over private psychiatric institutions. These institutions, in particular those where persons are held without a court order, need not only a licence, but a competent supervision on a regular basis of the justification of the confinement and medical treatment.

105. Turning to the present case, the Court notes that, under German law, the confinement of a person to a psychiatric hospital had to be ordered by a judge if the person concerned either did not or was unable to consent. In this case, the competent health authority also had supervisory powers to control the execution of these court orders. However, in the applicant's case, the clinic, despite the lack of the

applicant's consent, had not obtained the necessary court order. Therefore, no public health officer had ever assessed whether the applicant—what was more than doubtful—posed a serious threat to public safety or order within the meaning of Article 2 of the Act of the *Land* Bremen on the detention of mentally insane persons, mentally deficient persons and drug addicts. Consequently, the State also did not exercise any supervisory control over the lawfulness of the applicant's detention in the clinic for some 20 months.

106. It is true, though, that, with deprivation of liberty being a crime punishable with up to ten years' imprisonment, German law retrospectively provided sanctions with a deterring effect. Moreover, a victim could, under German civil law, claim compensation in tort for damage caused by an unlawful detention. However, the Court, having regard to the importance of the right to liberty, does not consider such retrospective measures alone as providing effective protection for individuals in such a vulnerable position as the applicant. It notes that particularly in the Act of the *Land* Bremen on the detention of mentally insane persons, mentally deficient persons and drug addicts, there were numerous— necessary—safeguards for persons detained in a mental institution following a court order. However, these safeguards did not apply in the more critical cases of persons confined to a psychiatric institution without such an order. It must be borne in mind that the applicant, once detained and treated with strong antipsychotic medicaments, had no longer been in a position to secure independent outside help.

106. The lack of any effective State control is most strikingly shown by the fact that on 4 March 1979 the police, by the use of force, had brought back the applicant to her place of detention from which she had escaped. Thereby, public authorities, as already shown above, had been involved in the applicant's detention in the clinic, without her flight and obvious unwillingness to return having entailed any control of the lawfulness of her forced stay in the clinic. This discloses the great danger of abuse in this field, notably in cases like that of the applicant, in which family conflicts and an identity crisis had been at the root of her troubles and long detention in a psychiatric hospital. The Court is therefore not convinced that the control exercised by State authorities merely in connection with the issuing of a licence for the conduct of a private clinic pursuant to Section 30 of the Act regulating the Conduct of Trade sufficed to ensure a competent and regular supervisory control against a deprivation of liberty in such a clinic. Moreover, Section 30 of the Act regulating the Conduct of Trade as such had not been in force at the beginning of the applicant's detention in the clinic.

107. The Court observes that shortly after the end of the applicant's detention in the private clinic, further safeguards have been introduced by Section 34 of the Act on Measures of Aid and Protection with respect to Mental Disorders for individuals detained in psychiatric institutions, responding to the lack of sufficient protection in this field. In particular, visiting commissions were created to inspect psychiatric institutions, to control whether the rights of patients were respected and to give patients the opportunity to raise complaints. However, these mechanisms came too late for the applicant.

108. Therefore, the Court concludes that the respondent State has violated its existing positive obligation to protect the applicant against interferences with her liberty carried out by private persons from July 1977 to April 1979. Consequently, there has been a violation of Article 5 § 1, first sentence, of the Convention.

The Chamber went on to conclude that the applicant's detention in the private clinic could not be justified under Article 5(1)(e) as it had not been 'lawful' due to the fact that she had not consented and no court order had been obtained (as was required by Lander law).

The judgment in *Storck* should be welcomed for the robust protection of the right to liberty taken by the Chamber. It is particularly noteworthy that the Chamber decisively rejected the Government's assertion that it was 'questionable' whether States were under a positive obligation to protect persons from being deprived of their liberty by other private persons. Paragraph 102 of the judgment elaborates the scope of this positive obligation in terms similar to those of analogous obligations under other Articles, therefore it should not be unduly burdensome for States.

The obligation to account for a person in custody

Kurt v Turkey 1998-III 1187, (1998) 27 EHRR 91
European Court of Human Rights

The facts of this case are set out above, p 176.

JUDGMENT OF THE COURT

122. The Court notes at the outset the fundamental importance of the guarantees contained in Article 5 for securing the right of individuals in a democracy to be free from arbitrary detention at the hands of the authorities. It is precisely for that reason that the Court has repeatedly stressed in its case-law that any deprivation of liberty must not only have been effected in conformity with the substantive and procedural rules of national law but must equally be in keeping with the very purpose of Article 5, namely to protect the individual from arbitrariness (see, among many other authorities, the *Chahal v UK* judgment of 15 November 1996, Reports 1996-IV, p 1864, § 118). This insistence on the protection of the individual against any abuse of power is illustrated by the fact that Article 5 § 1 circumscribes the circumstances in which individuals may be lawfully deprived of their liberty, it being stressed that these circumstances must be given a narrow interpretation having regard to the fact that they constitute exceptions to the most basic guarantee of individual freedom (see, *mutatis mutandis*, the *Quinn v France* judgment of 22 March 1995, Series A No 311, p 17, § 42).

123. It must also be stressed that the authors of the Convention reinforced the individual's protection against arbitrary deprivation of his or her liberty by guaranteeing a corpus of substantive rights which are intended to minimise the risks of arbitrariness by allowing the act of deprivation of liberty to be amenable to independent judicial scrutiny and by securing the accountability of the authorities for that act. The requirements of Article 5 §§ 3 and 4 with their emphasis on promptitude and judicial control assume particular importance in this context. Prompt judicial intervention may lead to the detection and prevention of life-threatening measures or serious ill-treatment which violate the fundamental guarantees contained in Articles 2 and 3 of the Convention (see, *mutatis mutandis*, the above-mentioned *Aksoy* judgment, p 2282, § 76). What is at stake is both the protection of the physical liberty of individuals as well as their personal security in a context which, in the absence of safeguards, could result in a subversion of the rule of law and place detainees beyond the reach of the most rudimentary forms of legal protection.

124. The Court emphasises in this respect that the unacknowledged detention of an individual is a complete negation of these guarantees and a most grave violation of Article 5. Having assumed control over that individual it is incumbent on the authorities to account for his or her whereabouts. For this reason, Article 5 must be seen as requiring the authorities to take effective measures to safeguard against the risk of disappearance and to conduct a prompt effective investigation into an arguable claim that a person has been taken into custody and has not been seen since.

125. Against that background, the Court recalls that it has accepted the Commission's finding that Üzeyir Kurt was held by soldiers and village guards on the morning of 25 November 1993. His detention at that time was not logged and there exists no official trace of his subsequent whereabouts or fate. That fact in itself must be considered a most serious failing since it enables those responsible for the act

of deprivation of liberty to conceal their involvement in a crime, to cover their tracks and to escape accountability for the fate of the detainee. In the view of the Court, the absence of holding data recording such matters as the date, time and location of detention, the name of the detainee as well as the reasons for the detention and the name of the person effecting it must be seen as incompatible with the very purpose of Article 5 of the Convention.

126. Furthermore, the Court considers that having regard to the applicant's insistence that her son was detained in the village the public prosecutor should have been alert to the need to investigate more thoroughly her claim. He had the powers under the Code of Criminal Procedure to do so. . . . However, he did not request her to explain why she was so adamant in her belief that he was in detention. She was neither asked to provide a written statement nor interviewed orally. Had he done so he may have been able to confront the military personnel involved in the operation in the village with her eye-witness account. However, that line of enquiry was never opened and no statements were taken from any of the soldiers or village guards present in the village at the time. The public prosecutor was unwilling to go beyond the gendarmerie's assertion that the custody records showed that Üzeyir Kurt had neither been held in the village nor was in detention. He accepted without question the explanation that Üzeyir Kurt had probably been kidnapped by the PKK during the military operation and this explanation shaped his future attitude to his enquiries and laid the basis of his subsequent non-jurisdiction decision.

127. The Court, like the Commission, also considers that the alleged PKK involvement in the disappearance of the applicant's son lacked any firm and plausible evidentiary basis. As an explanation it was advanced too hastily by the gendarmerie in the absence of any corroborating evidence; nor can it be maintained that the statements given by the three villagers to the gendarme officers on 28 February 1994 lent credence to what was in effect mere supposition as to the fate of Üzeyir Kurt. The questions put to the villagers can only be described as formulated in a way designed to elicit responses which could enhance the credibility of the PKK kidnapping theory . . . . Furthermore, and as noted earlier . . . , the Government's other contention that the applicant's son had left the village to join the PKK also lacks any firm evidentiary basis.

128. Having regard to these considerations, the Court concludes that the authorities have failed to offer any credible and substantiated explanation for the whereabouts and fate of the applicant's son after he was detained in the village and that no meaningful investigation was conducted into the applicant's insistence that he was in custody and that she was concerned for his life. They have failed to discharge their responsibility to account for him and it must be accepted that he has been held in unacknowledged detention in the complete absence of the safeguards contained in Article 5.

129. The Court, accordingly, like the Commission, finds that there has been a particularly grave violation of the right to liberty and security of person guaranteed under Article 5 raising serious concerns about the welfare of Üzeyir Kurt. . . .

FOR THESE REASONS, THE COURT . . .

5. Holds by six votes to three that there has been a violation of Article 5 of the Convention; . . .

NOTES

1   The Court was composed of President Bernhardt and Judges: Foighel, Morenilla, Bonnici, Jungwiert, and Lohmus. Judges Matscher, Golcuklu, and Pettiti issued dissenting opinions in which they expressed the view that the applicant had not established the truth of her allegations beyond all reasonable doubt.

2   In most cases under Article 5, the State acknowledges that the person concerned is in its custody. In the *Kurt* case, the Court accepted the Commission's finding of fact the son had

been detained by state agents, despite the state's denial. In this situation, the question is not one of testing compliance with the particular guarantees listed in Article 5, but of a State obligation to account for a person in its detention that is implicit in Article 5. Following from this general obligation, are particular implied obligations to keep records of persons detained and to investigate allegations of detention.

3   A unanimous Chamber found a breach of the *Kurt* record-keeping obligation in *Anguelova v Bulgaria*, judgment of 13 June 2002 (see above p 118 for the Article 2 aspect of this case). The police station's register did not contain an original record of the detention of the applicant's son and a forged entry was later added to the register. Accordingly, the Chamber found a violation of the '157. . . . requirements implicit in Article 5 of the Convention for the proper recording of deprivations of liberty.'

4   Grave systematic failings were found in the custody records of Turkish gendarme stations in *Orhan v Turkey*, judgment of 18 June 2002. The applicant contended that three of his close relatives had been taken away by gendarmes in 1994 and those persons had never been seen again. The Chamber was united in concluding that serious deficiencies were present in the practice of recording custody in gendarme stations.

372. . . . The first established deficiency is not allowed by domestic law namely, the gendarme practice of detaining persons for various reasons in their stations without being entered in the custody records. The second and third failing further underline the unreliability of custody records as those records will not show whether one is apprehended by military forces and may not show the date of release from the gendarme station. These three deficiencies attest to the absence of effective measures to safeguard against the risk of disappearances of individuals in detention.

Consequently, the Court concluded that the applicant's two brothers and son had been held in unacknowledged detention in violation of Article 5. The above findings indicated both weaknesses in the scope of domestic custody records and a flouting of existing requirements by military personnel.

5   A Grand Chamber held that the implied obligation upon States to undertake effective investigations into the whereabouts and fate of persons whom, it is arguably claimed, have disappeared after being detained by State agents is a continuing duty in *Cyprus v Turkey*, judgment of 10 May 2001 (and see above p 125 for the Article 2 aspects of the case). The applicant government asserted that the Turkish authorities had failed to effectively investigate (in both occupied northern Cyprus and in Turkey) the detention and subsequent disappearance of many hundreds of Greek-Cypriots who had disappeared during the military invasion of 1974. The Grand Chamber, subject to the dissent of the Turkish *ad-hoc* judge, determine that, '150. . . . there has been a continuing violation of Article 5 of the Convention by virtue of the failure of the authorities of the respondent State to conduct an effective investigation in to the whereabouts and fate of the missing Greek-Cypriot persons in respect of whom there is an arguable claim that they were in custody at the time they disappeared.' This was an important clarification of the extent of the effective investigation duty and ought to provide some satisfaction to the relatives of 'disappeared' persons whose legitimate wish to discover the fate of their family members is an enduring goal.

6   In the autumn of 2005 reports began to appear in the American media (led by the *Washington Post*) of secret Central Intelligence Agency (CIA) detention centres in European States (Romania and Poland were named) where suspects in the United States' 'War on Terror' were being held and interrogated. The Legal Affairs Committee of the Parliamentary Assembly

(Council of Europe) appointed Senator Dick Marty, a former prosecutor, to undertake an inquiry into alleged secret detentions in Member States. Allegations also emerged of clandestine CIA aircraft flights using European airports and airspace for the transportation of detainees as part of the American global programme of 'extraordinary rendition', involving terrorist suspects being secretly sent for interrogation by officials in other States where they have no rights under American law. In November 2005 the Council of Europe's Secretary General, Terry Davis, invoked his (rarely used) power under Article 52 of the ECHR to request all Member states to inform him how their domestic laws prevented the unacknowledged deprivation of liberty and the giving of aid to foreign agents to undertake such acts. Article 52 provides that: 'On receipt of a request from the Secretary General of the Council of Europe any High Contracting Party shall furnish an explanation of the manner in which its internal law ensures the effective implementation of any of the provisions of the Convention.' The Secretary General published his report (1 March 2006) on the replies received. He stated:

... I strongly support cooperation between Europe and the United States of America on all issues and especially the fight against terrorism but I also insist that European governments should have sufficient confidence to participate in such cooperation as equal partners and not play the role of the proverbial three brass monkeys [who could not hear, see or speak].

... For the time being, the analysis of the replies received already indicates that there are several areas of general concern. Firstly, it would appear that most of Europe is a happy hunting ground for foreign security services. Whilst most of our member States have mechanisms to supervise the activities of their domestic intelligence agencies as well as the presence of foreign police officers on their territory, hardly any country, with the exception of Hungary, has any legal provisions to ensure an effective oversight over the activities of foreign security services on their territory. ...

The second concern is that Europe's skies appear to be excessively open. Very few countries seem to have adopted an adequate and effective way to monitor who and what is transiting through their airports and airspace. Indeed, no member State appears to have established any kind of procedure in order to assess whether civil aircraft are used for purposes which would be incompatible with internationally recognised human rights standards. This is alarming because the explanations provided on the specific point of controls over aircraft allegedly used for rendition show that existing procedures do not provide adequate safeguards against abuse.

The third general concern arising from the analysis of the replies is related to the existing rules on jurisdiction and state immunity, which create considerable obstacles for effective law enforcement in relation to the activities of foreign agents, especially when they are accredited as diplomatic or consular agents. ...

The Secretary General considered that the replies by Bosnia and Herzegovina, Italy, the former Yugoslav republic of Macedonia and Poland were not adequate. He intended to continue his inquiries in respect of those States and more generally to consider what action the Council of Europe should take to deal with the problems identified in his report.

At a meeting of the Legal Affairs Committee, on 7 June 2006, Mr Marty reported that his investigations had found 'converging elements' indicating that 'landing points in Romania and Poland were detainee drop-off points near to secret detention centres'. In his opinion '... the authorities in several European countries actively participated with the CIA in these unlawful activities. Other countries ignored them knowingly, or did not want to know.' Spain, Turkey, Germany, and Cyprus provided 'staging posts' for rendition operations and the UK, Portugal, Ireland, and Greece were 'stopping-off points' during the transportation of detainees. Italy, Sweden, Macedonia, and Bosnia-Herzegovina allowed the Americans to abduct persons from their territories. On the same day, BBC news reported that it was unlikely that any secret American detention centres were still operating in Europe and they had probably been relocated to northern Africa.

So far it has been the parliamentary and administrative institutions of the Council of Europe that have played the leading roles in the investigations into these serious allegations. Presumably, the nature of the Americans' detention and treatment of any individual detainees has created practical obstacles preventing them from invoking the judicial remedies under the ECHR.

In accordance with a procedure prescribed by law

Article 5 requires that all deprivations of liberty must satisfy this condition. A unanimous Grand Chamber of the full-time Court explained the meaning of this requirement in *Ocalan v Turkey*, see above p 128. The following extracts deal with the applicant's complaint that his detention in Kenya amounted to abduction by Turkish officials in breach of international law.

83. . . . On the question whether detention is 'lawful', including whether it complies with 'a procedure prescribed by law', the Convention refers back essentially to national law and lays down the obligation to conform to the substantive and procedural rules thereof. However, it requires in addition that any deprivation of liberty should be consistent with the purpose of Article 5, namely to protect individuals from arbitrariness. What is at stake here is not only the 'right to liberty' but also the 'right to security of person' (see, among other authorities, *Bozano* [*v France*, A.111 (1986)], p 23, § 54; and *Wassink v The Netherlands*, judgment of 27 September 1990, Series A No 185-A, p 11, § 24).

84. It is in the first place for the national authorities, notably the courts, to interpret and apply domestic law. However, since under Article 5 § 1 failure to comply with domestic law entails a breach of the Convention, it follows that the Court can and should exercise a certain power to review whether this law has been complied with (see *Benham v the United Kingdom*, judgment of 10 June 1996, *Reports of Judgments and Decisions* 1996-III, p 753, § 41; and *Bouamar v Belgium*, judgment of 29 February 1988, Series A No 129, p 21, § 49).

85. An arrest made by the authorities of one State on the territory of another State, without the consent of the latter, affects the person concerned's individual rights to security under Article 5 § 1 (see, to the same effect, *Stocké v Germany*, 12 October 1989, Series A No 199, opinion of the Commission, p 24, § 167).

86. The Convention does not prevent cooperation between States, within the framework of extradition treaties or in matters of deportation, for the purpose of bringing fugitive offenders to justice, provided that it does not interfere with any specific rights recognised in the Convention (see *Stocké*, opinion of the Commission cited above, pp 24–5, § 169).

87. As regards extradition arrangements between States when one is a party to the Convention and the other not, the rules established by an extradition treaty or, in the absence of any such treaty, the cooperation between the States concerned are also relevant factors to be taken into account for determining whether the arrest that has led to the subsequent complaint to the Court was lawful. The fact that a fugitive has been handed over as a result of cooperation between States does not in itself make the arrest unlawful or, therefore, give rise to any problem under Article 5 (see *Freda v Italy*, No 8916/80, Commission decision of 7 October 1980, DR 21, p 250; *Klaus Altmann (Barbie) v France*, No 10689/83, Commission decision of 4 July 1984, DR 37, p 225; *Luc Reinette v France*, No 14009/88, Commission decision of 2 October 1989, DR 63, p 189).

88. Inherent in the whole of the Convention is a search for a fair balance between the demands of the general interest of the community and the requirements of the protection of the individual's fundamental rights. As movement about the world becomes easier and crime takes on a larger international dimension, it is increasingly in the interest of all nations that suspected offenders who flee abroad

should be brought to justice. Conversely, the establishment of safe havens for fugitives would not only result in danger for the State obliged to harbour the protected person but also tend to undermine the foundations of extradition (see *Soering v the United Kingdom*, judgment of 7 July 1989, Series A No 161, p. 35, § 89).

89. The Convention contains no provisions concerning the circumstances in which extradition may be granted, or the procedure to be followed before extradition may be granted. Subject to its being the result of cooperation between the States concerned and provided that the legal basis for the order for the fugitive's arrest is an arrest warrant issued by the authorities of the fugitive's State of origin, even an atypical extradition cannot as such be regarded as being contrary to the Convention (see *Illich Ramirez Sánchez* [v *France*, Commission Decision of 24 June 1996, DR 86], p. 155).

90. Irrespective of whether the arrest amounts to a violation of the law of the State in which the fugitive has taken refuge—a question which only falls to be examined by the Court if the host State is a party to the Convention—the Court requires proof in the form of concordant inferences that the authorities of the State to which the applicant has been transferred have acted extra-territorially in a manner that is inconsistent with the sovereignty of the host State and therefore contrary to international law (see, *mutatis mutandis*, *Stocké v Germany*, judgment of 19 March 1991, Series A No 199, p 19, § 54). Only then will the burden of proving that the sovereignty of the host State and international law have been complied with shift to the respondent Government. However, the applicant is not required to adduce proof 'beyond all reasonable doubt' on this point, as was suggested by the Chamber (judgment of 12 March 2003, § 92).

(B) APPLICATION OF THE PRINCIPLES TO THE PRESENT CASE

(i) Whether the arrest complied with Turkish law

91. The Court notes that the applicant was arrested by members of the Turkish security forces inside an aircraft registered in Turkey in the international zone of Nairobi Airport.

It is common ground that, directly after being handed over to the Turkish officials by the Kenyan officials, the applicant was under effective Turkish authority and therefore within the 'jurisdiction' of that State for the purposes of Article 1 of the Convention, even though in this instance Turkey exercised its authority outside its territory. It is true that the applicant was physically forced to return to Turkey by Turkish officials and was under their authority and control following his arrest and return to Turkey (see, in this respect, the aforementioned decisions in the cases of *Illich Ramirez Sánchez v France* and *Freda v Italy*; and, by converse implication, the *Banković and Others v Belgium and 16 Other Contracting States* decision ((dec.) [GC], No 52207/99, ECHR 2001-XII)).

92. As to whether the arrest complied with Turkish domestic law, the Court notes that the Turkish criminal courts had issued seven warrants for the applicant's arrest while Interpol had circulated a wanted notice ('red notice'). In each of these documents, the applicant was accused of criminal offences under the Turkish Criminal Code, namely founding an armed gang with a view to undermining the territorial integrity of the State and instigating a series of terrorist acts that had resulted in the loss of life. Following his arrest and on the expiry of the statutory period for which he could be held in police custody the applicant was brought before a court. Subsequently, he was charged, tried and convicted of offences under Article 125 of the Criminal Code. It follows that his arrest and detention complied with orders that had been issued by the Turkish courts 'for the purpose of bringing him before the competent legal authority on reasonable suspicion of having committed an offence'.

(ii) Interception by Kenyan agents

93. The Court must decide in the light of the parties' arguments whether the applicant's interception in Kenya immediately before he was handed over to Turkish officials on board the aircraft at Nairobi

Airport was the result of acts by Turkish officials that violated Kenyan sovereignty and international law (as the applicant submitted) or of cooperation between the Turkish and Kenyan authorities in the absence of any extradition treaty between Turkey and Kenya laying down a formal procedure (as the Government submitted).

94. The Court will begin by examining the evidence on the role in fact played by the Kenyan authorities in the present case. The applicant entered Kenya without declaring his identity to the immigration officers. However, once they had been informed of the applicant's presence at the Greek Embassy in Nairobi, the Kenyan authorities invited the Greek Ambassador, with whom the applicant was staying in Nairobi, to arrange for the applicant to leave Kenyan territory. Shortly before the applicant was due to leave Kenya, more precisely as he was being transferred from the Greek Embassy to the airport, Kenyan officials intervened and separated the applicant from the Greek Ambassador. The car in which the applicant was travelling was driven by a Kenyan official, who took him to the aircraft in which Turkish officials were waiting to arrest him.

95. The Kenyan authorities did not perceive the applicant's arrest by the Turkish officials on board an aircraft at Nairobi Airport as being in any way a violation of Kenyan sovereignty. In sum, neither aspect of the applicant's detention—whether his interception by the Kenyan authorities before his transfer to the airport, or his arrest by the Turkish officials in the aircraft—led to an international dispute between Kenya and Turkey or to any deterioration in their diplomatic relations. The Kenyan authorities did not lodge any protest with the Turkish Government on these points or claim any redress from Turkey, such as the applicant's return or compensation.

96. The Kenyan authorities did, however, issue a formal protest to the Greek Government, accompanied by a demand for the Greek Ambassador's immediate recall, on the grounds that the applicant had entered Kenya illegally with the help of Greek officials and was unlawfully staying there. The applicant was not welcome in Kenya and the Kenyan authorities were anxious for him to leave.

97. These aspects of the case lead the Court to accept the Government's version of events: it considers that at the material time the Kenyan authorities had decided either to hand the applicant over to the Turkish authorities or to facilitate such a handover.

98. The applicant has not adduced evidence enabling concordant inferences (see paragraph 90 above) to be drawn that Turkey failed to respect Kenyan sovereignty or to comply with international law in the present case. The Grand Chamber agrees with the Chamber's finding that:

'. . . The Court is not persuaded by the statement by the Kenyan Minister of Foreign Affairs on 16 February 1999 that, contrary to what the applicant maintained, the Kenyan authorities had had no involvement in the applicant's arrest or transfer . . . While it is true that the applicant was not arrested by the Kenyan authorities, the evidence before the Court indicates that Kenyan officials had played a role in separating the applicant from the Greek Ambassador and in transporting him to the airport immediately preceding his arrest on board the aircraft.' (see paragraph 100 of the Chamber judgment)

99. Consequently, the applicant's arrest on 15 February 1999 and his detention were in accordance with 'a procedure prescribed by law' for the purposes of Article 5 § 1 of the Convention. There has, therefore, been no violation of that provision.

Hence, this phrase demands that States comply with national law and international law, where appropriate (e.g. when extraditing individuals), regarding the detention of persons. Also, States must not act in an 'arbitrary' manner, that is contrary to the ethos of the right to liberty guaranteed by Article 5 (see *Bozano* below p 290). Do you agree with the Grand Chamber that the Turkish authorities did not violate these standards in *Ocalan*?

Article 5(1): Permissible grounds for arrest and detention

Article 5(1)(a): Conviction by a competent court

Van Droogenbroeck v Belgium A.50 (1982) 4 EHRR 443
European Court of Human Rights

The applicant was convicted of theft by the Bruges criminal court and sentenced to two years' imprisonment. In the light of prior convictions, he was also ordered by the court to be 'placed at the Government's disposal' for a further 10 years as a recidivist, pursuant to the 1964 Social Protection Act. The first instance decision was confirmed by the Ghent Court of Appeal. On completion of his two-year sentence, the applicant was released. Thereafter, within the pre-scribed ten-year period, he was detained and released several times by the Minister of Justice under the court order because of later offences of theft and his failure to respond to rehabilitation measures.

The applicant alleged breaches, *inter alia*, of Articles 5(1) and 5(4) resulting respectively from the periods of detention ordered by the Minister of Justice and the absence of satisfactory remedies to challenge their legality. The Commission expressed the opinion unanimously that there had been a violation of Article 5(4), but, by ten votes to two, that the detention could be justified under Article 5(1)(a).

JUDGMENT OF THE COURT

35. The Court has to determine whether those periods of detention occurred 'after conviction' by the Ghent Court of Appeal.

Having regard to the French text, the word 'conviction', for the purposes of Article 5 § 1(a), has to be understood as signifying both a 'finding of guilt', after 'it has been established in accordance with the law that there has been an offence' (see the *Guzzardi* judgment of 6 November 1980, Series A No 39, p 37, § 100), and the imposition of a penalty or other measure involving deprivation of liberty. These conditions are satisfied in the instant case.

The word 'after' does not simply mean that the 'detention' must follow the 'conviction' in point of time: in addition, the 'detention' must result from, 'follow and depend upon' or occur 'by virtue of' the 'conviction' (see the *X v UK* judgment of 5 November 1981, Series A No 46, p 17, § 39; the *Engel* judgment of 8 June 1976, Series A, No 22, p 27, § 68) . . .

37. The Ministerial decisions . . . revoking the conditional release granted to Mr Van Droogenbroeck did order that he be 'detained' . . .

38. Be that as it may, one must look beyond the appearances and the language used and concentrate on the realities of the situation (see notably, *mutatis mutandis*, the *Deweer* judgment of 27 February 1980, Series A No 35, p 23, § 44).

This is a matter in which the Government enjoy a wide measure of discretion. Case-law and practice certainly confirm the meaning suggested by the text of section 25 of the 1964 Act ('if necessary') and the actual phrase 'placing at disposal'. In a judgment of 4 April 1978, the Belgian Court of Cassation observed that 'execution of the penalty' in question 'is to a large extent a matter for the discretion' of the Minister of Justice (*Pasicrisie* 1978, I, p 861). One finds that far less fetters are imposed on Ministerial decisions by a court's decision to apply the Social Protection Act than in the analogous area of the system of placing vagrants 'at the Government's disposal' (Act of 27 November 1891; see the *De Wilde, Ooms and Versyp* judgment of 18 June 1971, Series A No 12, pp 24–25, § 37, and pp 33–34, § 61). In short, to adopt the language used by the Commission's Delegate, 'the court decision does not order the detention' of recidivists and habitual offenders: it 'authorises' it.

39. In these circumstances, the Court has to consider whether there was a sufficient connection, for the purposes of Article 5, between the last-mentioned decision and the deprivation of liberty at issue.

This question must receive an affirmative reply since the Minister's discretion is exercised within a framework set both by the Act and by the sentence pronounced by the 'competent court'. In this respect, the Court notes that, according to Belgian case-law, a judgment which sentences the person concerned to imprisonment and, by way of a supplementary or accessory penalty, places him at the Government's disposal pursuant to section 22 or section 23 of the 1964 Act constitutes 'an inseparable whole' (Court of Cassation, 17 June 1975, *Pasicrisie* 1975, I, p 999). There are two components to the judgment: the first is a penalty involving deprivation of liberty which the offender must undergo for a period specified in the court decision, and the second is the placing of the offender at the Government's disposal, the execution of which may take different forms ranging from remaining at liberty under supervision to detention.

The choice between these forms of execution is a matter for the discretion of the Minister of Justice. Nevertheless he does not enjoy an unlimited power in making his decision: within the bounds laid down by the Act, he must assess the degree of danger presented by the individual concerned and the short- to medium-term prospects of reintegrating him into society.

40. In fact, sight must not be lost of what the title and general structure of the 1964 Act, the drafting history and Belgian case-law show to be the objectives of this statute, that is to say not only 'to protect society against the danger presented by recidivists and habitual offenders' but also 'to provide [the Government] with the possibility of endeavouring to reform [them]' (Court of Cassation, 11 December 1933, *Pasicrisie* 1934, I, p 99). Attempting to achieve these objectives requires that account be taken of circumstances that, by their nature, differ from case to case and are susceptible of modification. At the time of its decision, the court can, in the nature of things, do no more than estimate how the individual will develop in the future. The Minister of Justice, for his part, is able, through and with the assistance of his officials, to monitor that development more closely and at frequent intervals but this very fact means that with the passage of time the link between his decisions not to release or to re-detain and the initial judgment gradually becomes less strong. The link might eventually be broken if a position were reached in which those decisions were based on grounds that had no connection with the objectives of the legislature and the court or on an assessment that was unreasonable in terms of those objectives. In those circumstances, a detention that was lawful at the outset would be transformed into a deprivation of liberty that was arbitrary and, hence, incompatible with Article 5 (see, notably, the above-mentioned *X v UK* judgment, Series A No 46, p 19, § 43).

Such a situation did not obtain in the present case. The Belgian authorities showed patience and trust towards Mr Van Droogenbroeck: notwithstanding his conduct, they gave him several opportunities to mend his ways. . . . The manner in which they exercised their discretion respected the requirements of the Convention, which allows a measure of indeterminacy in sentencing and does not oblige the Contracting States to entrust to the courts the general supervision of the execution of sentences. . . .

42. There has accordingly been no violation of Article 5 § 1. . . .

[*The Court then considered the claim under Article 5(4), as to which see below, p 227.*]

FOR THESE REASONS, THE COURT UNANIMOUSLY

1. Holds that there has not been a violation of Article 5(1) of the Convention;

2. Holds that there has been a violation of Article 5(4); ...

NOTES

1 The Court was composed of President Wiarda and Judges: Zekia, Cremona, Van der Meersch, Bindschedler-Robert, Evrigenis, Lagergren, Liesch, Gölcüklü, Matscher, Pinheiro Farinha, García de Enterría, Pettiti, Walsh, Sir Vincent Evans, Russo, Bernhardt, and Gersing.

2 The 'sufficient connection' test that was adopted by the Court in the *Van Droogenbroeck* case was followed in *Weeks v UK*, the facts of which are summarised below, p 327, where the case is considered under Article 5(4). The *Weeks* case concerned the recall by the Home Secretary of a convicted person who had been given a discretionary life sentence. Holding that Article 5(1) had not been infringed, the Court stated:

46. ... The intention [in giving him a discretionary life sentence] was to make the applicant, who was qualified both by the trial judge and by the Court of Appeal as a 'dangerous young man', subject to a continuing security measure in the interests of public safety'.

... In substance, Mr Weeks was being put at the disposal of the State because he needed continued supervision in custody for an unforeseeable length of time and, as a corollary, periodic reassessment in order to ascertain the most appropriate manner of dealing with him.

The grounds expressly relied on by the sentencing courts for ordering this form of deprivation of liberty against Mr Weeks are by their very nature susceptible of change with the passage of time, whereas the measure will remain in force for the whole of his life. In this, his sentence differs from a life sentence imposed on a person because of the gravity of the offence.

47. In this sense, the measure ordered against Mr Weeks is thus comparable to the Belgian measure at issue in the *Van Droogenbroeck* case, that is the placing of a recidivist or habitual offender at the disposal of the Government—although in the present case the placement was for a whole lifetime and not for a limited period (Series A No 50, especially at pp 21–2, § 40). The legitimate aim (of social protection and the rehabilitation of offenders) pursued by the measure and its effect on the convicted person are substantially the same in both cases. ...

49. Applying the principles stated in the *Van Droogenbroeck* judgment, the formal legal connection between Mr Weeks' conviction in 1966 and his recall to prison some ten years later is not on its own sufficient to justify the contested detention under Article 5 § 1(a). The causal link required by sub-paragraph (a) ... might eventually be broken if a position were reached in which a decision not to release or to re-detain was based on grounds that were inconsistent with the objectives of the sentencing court. 'In those circumstances, a detention that was lawful at the outset would be transformed into a deprivation of liberty that was arbitrary and, hence, incompatible with Article 5' (Series A No 50, pp 21–2, § 40). ...

It remains to examine the sufficiency of the grounds on which his re-detention in June 1977 and thereafter was based. In this area, as in many others, the national authorities are to be recognised as having a certain discretion since they are better placed than the international judge to evaluate the evidence in a particular case (see, *inter alia*, the *X v UK* judgment of 5 November 1981, Series A No 46, p 20, § 43, and the *Luberti* judgment of 23 February 1984, Series A No 75, p 12, § 27). ...

51. ... In view of [his] unstable, disturbed and aggressive behaviour, there were grounds for the Home Secretary to have considered that the applicant's continued liberty would constitute a danger to the public and to himself. The Minister's decision to re-detain remained.

In the Court's view, therefore, a sufficient connection, for the purposes of sub-paragraph (a) of Article 5 § 1, existed between his conviction in 1966 and his recall to prison in 1977.

3 In *Monnell and Morris v UK*, A.115 (1987) 10 EHRR 205, the Court of Appeal directed that the time between a conviction and the rejection of a frivolous appeal should not count towards the sentence. The European Court held that detention during the period of the appeal was justified under Article 5(1)(a) since it followed from the conviction.

4 In *Tsirlis and Kouloumpas v Greece*, 1997-III 909, (1997) 25 EHRR 198, the applicants were ministers of the Jehovah's Witnesses who were convicted for insubordination by a military tribunal and sentenced to four years' imprisonment for refusing to perform military service, the tribunal considering that Jehovah's Witnesses were not a 'known religion'. In convicting the applicants, the tribunal ignored Greek judicial decisions establishing that Jehovah's Witnesses were a 'known religion', so that their ministers were exempt from military service. Eventually, the applicants' convictions were quashed by the Supreme Administrative Court and the applicants were released after detention for thirteen and twelve months respectively. Holding that the applicants' detention was not 'lawful' under Article 5(1)(a), the European Court stated:

56. It must therefore be established whether Mr Tsirlis's detention between 30 April 1990 and 30 May 1991 as well as Mr Kouloumpas's detention between 30 May 1990 and 29 May 1991 were 'in accordance with a procedure prescribed by law' and 'lawful' within the meaning of Article 5 § 1 of the Convention. The Court reiterates that the Convention here essentially refers back to domestic law and states the obligation to conform to the substantive and procedural rules thereof; but it requires in addition that any deprivation of liberty should be consistent with the purpose of Article 5, namely to protect individuals from arbitrariness (see, among many other authorities, the *Bozano v France* judgment of 18 December 1986, Series A No 111, p 23, § 54, and the *Lukanov v Bulgaria* judgment of 20 March 1997, *Reports of Judgments and Decisions* 1997-II, pp 543–4, § 41).

57. It is in the first place for the national authorities, notably the courts, to interpret and apply domestic law. However, since under Article 5 § 1 failure to comply with domestic law entails a breach of the Convention, it follows that the Court can and should exercise a certain power to review whether this law has been complied with (see the *Bouamar v Belgium* judgment of 29 February 1988, Series A No 129, p 21, § 49).

58. Detention will in principle be lawful if it is carried out pursuant to a court order. A subsequent finding that the court erred under domestic law in making the order will not necessarily retrospectively affect the validity of the intervening period of detention. For this reason, the Strasbourg organs have consistently refused to uphold applications from persons convicted of criminal offences who complain that their convictions or sentences were found by the appellate courts to have been based on errors of fact or law (see the *Benham v UK* judgment of 10 June 1996, Reports 1996-III, p 753, § 42).

59. The Court notes that section 6 of the 1988 Law refers to ministers of all 'known religions'. As early as 1975, the Supreme Administrative Court acknowledged that the Jehovah's Witnesses were to be considered as such, and this case-law could unquestionably be regarded as established by 1990. . . . It was not disputed throughout the domestic proceedings that the applicants were ministers of that religion. However, in deciding on the issue of the applicants' criminal liability, and thus on the lawfulness of their detention, the military authorities blatantly ignored this case-law. As a result, Mr Tsirlis and Mr Kouloumpas spent thirteen and twelve months in detention respectively.

60. Furthermore, the relevant authorities' persistence not to recognise Jehovah's Witnesses as a 'known religion' and the disregard of the applicants' right to liberty that followed, were of a discriminatory nature when contrasted with the way in which ministers of the Greek Orthodox Church obtain exemption . . . .

61. It is no answer to these failings that, as the Government have submitted, the question of the applicants' position as ministers of religion lay outside the scope of the case before the military courts, whose jurisdiction only extended itself to the alleged offence of insubordination. . . . In the first place, it is clear from the repeated adjournments of the applicants' cases by the Military Appeal Court in order to clarify whether Jehovah's Witnesses ministers were under an obligation to perform military service . . . that this latter issue was of central importance to the appeals. In the second place, the appellate courts acquitted the applicants immediately after the Supreme Administrative Court had quashed the Director for Recruitment's decision not to grant exemption from military duties on the grounds that the applicants were ministers of a 'known religion'.

62. Against this background, the Court finds that the applicants' detention following their conviction on charges of insubordination had no basis under domestic law and was arbitrary. It cannot accordingly be considered to have been 'lawful' for the purposes of Article 5 § 1.

5 A Grand Chamber found that the detention of the applicants after their 'conviction', following an arbitrary trial, by a 'court' established by a separatist regime not recognized by the international community violated Article 5(1)(a) in *Ilascu and Others v Moldova and Russia*, judgment of 8 July 2004 (and see above p 169 in respect of Article 3 aspects of the case).

461. The requirement of lawfulness laid down by Article 5 § 1 (a) ('lawful detention' ordered 'in accordance with a procedure prescribed by law') is not satisfied merely by compliance with the relevant domestic law; domestic law must itself be in conformity with the Convention, including the general principles expressed or implied in it, particularly the principle of the rule of law, which is expressly mentioned in the Preamble to the Convention. The notion underlying the expression 'in accordance with a procedure prescribed by law' is one of fair and proper procedure, namely that any measure depriving a person of his liberty should issue from and be executed by an appropriate authority and should not be arbitrary (see, among other authorities, *Winterwerp v The Netherlands*, judgment of 24 October 1979, Series A No 33, § 45).

In addition, as the purpose of Article 5 is to protect the individual from arbitrariness (see, among other authorities, *Stafford v the United Kingdom* [GC], No 46295/99, § 63, ECHR 2002-IV), a 'conviction' cannot be the result of a flagrant denial of justice (see, *mutatis mutandis*, *Drozd and Janousek v France and Spain*, judgment of 26 June 1992, Series A No 240, § 110).

The Court also refers to its conclusions under Article 3 of the Convention regarding the nature of the proceedings in the 'Supreme Court of the MRT'.

462. The Court accordingly finds that none of the applicants was convicted by a 'court', and that a sentence of imprisonment passed by a judicial body such as the 'Supreme Court of the MRT' at the close of proceedings like those conducted in the present case cannot be regarded as 'lawful detention' ordered 'in accordance with a procedure prescribed by law'.

463. That being so, the deprivation of liberty suffered by the applicants during the period covered by the Court's jurisdiction *ratione temporis* in respect of the respondent States (namely, as regards Mr Ilaşcu, from 12 September 1997 to 5 May 2001 for Moldova, and from 5 May 1998 to 5 May 2001 for Russia and, as regards the other applicants, from the date of ratification by each of the respondent States to the present date) cannot satisfy the conditions laid down in paragraph 1 (a) of Article 5 of the Convention.

It follows that there was a violation of Article 5 § 1 of the Convention until May 2001 as regards Mr Ilaşcu [when he was released], and that there has been and continues to be a violation of that provision as regards the three applicants still detained.

464. Having regard to the fact that the applicants were detained at the time of the Convention's entry into force with regard to the Russian Federation, and taking into account its findings above . . . the Court concludes that the conduct constituting a violation of Article 5 is imputable to the Russian Federation as regards all the applicants.

Taking into account its conclusion above . . . that the responsibility of the Republic of Moldova by virtue of its positive obligations is engaged from May 2001, the Court concludes that there has been no violation of Article 5 by Moldova as regards Mr Ilaşcu. On the other hand, there has been a violation of that provision by Moldova as regards the other three applicants.

Hence trials and 'convictions' by bodies that fail to comply with the constitutional and procedural norms of the Convention will not be recognized by the Court as justifying the detention of persons under Article 5.

Article 5(1)(b): Non-compliance with a court order or failure to fulfil an obligation prescribed by law

....

McVeigh, O'Neill and Evans v UK Article 31 Report. 25 DR 15 (1981)
European Commission of Human Rights

The applicants were arrested when they arrived at Liverpool on a boat from Ireland as it was apparently suspected that they were involved in terrorist activities. They were held for some 45 hours, after which they were released and allowed freely to enter Great Britain. They were arrested under powers conferred by the Prevention of Terrorism (Temporary Provisions) Act 1976 and the Prevention of Terrorism (Supplemental Temporary Provisions) Order 1976. Article 10(1) of the Order permitted detention of a person 'under the authority of an examining officer pending his examination'. This was the reason given to the applicants for their detention, the formal notification for which stated that they would be detained 'pending further examination'. Article 5(1) of the Order permitted detention in order to determine (a) whether the person examined appeared to be concerned in terrorism, (b) whether he was subject to an exclusion order, or (c) whether there were grounds for suspecting that he had committed an offence relating to non-compliance with exclusion orders and failure to disclose information concerning terrorism. Domestic law required no suspicion of any of the above; the purpose of the detention was to allow an 'examination' in order to ascertain whether grounds for suspicion existed sufficient to justify a criminal charge or an exclusion order.

During their detention the applicants were searched, questioned, photographed and fingerprinted. No evidence was adduced before the Commission, nor was it there alleged by the respondent government, that the applicants had in fact actually been involved in terrorist activities.

The applicants alleged a breach, *inter alia*, of Article 5(1). In the following extract from its Article 31 Report on the merits of the case, the Commission considered whether the detention was justified under Article 5(1)(b) as being 'in order to secure the fulfilment of an obligation prescribed by law'.

REPORT OF THE COMMISSION

170. . . . The only question is whether there was 'lawful arrest or detention . . . in order to secure the fulfilment of any obligation prescribed by law'. . . .

171. As both parties have pointed out, the Court held in the *Engel* case that these words 'concern only cases where the law permits the detention of a person to compel him to fulfil a specific and concrete obligation which he has until then failed to satisfy' (Judgment, para 69). Both the Commission and the Court have consistently rejected a wide interpretation of the phrase such as would, for instance, authorise administrative internment for the purpose of compelling a citizen to comply with general

obligations arising from criminal law (see eg *Lawless* Case, Report of Commission, Series B, p 64; *Engel* case, Judgment of Court, sup cit; *Guzzardi* case, Report of Commission, para 103, Judgment of Court, para 101).

172. Although the 'obligation' must thus be 'specific and concrete', Article 5(1)(b) does not require that it should arise from a court order. ...

173. The applicants submit . . . that the obligation in question must be an antecedent one and some voluntary failure to comply with it must already have taken place before detention to secure its fulfilment is justified. The Commission considers that there is much force in the argument, which is supported by the above-quoted *dicta* of the Court in the *Engel* Case, and particularly the Court's use of the words 'négligé . . . de remplir' and 'failed to satisfy' in the passages referred to. This branch of Article 5(1)(b) is primarily intended, in the Commission's opinion, to cover the case where the law permits detention as a coercive measure to induce a person to perform a specific obligation which he has wilfully or negligently failed to perform hitherto.

174. Nonetheless, the wording of Article 5(1)(b) does not expressly require that there should have been such deliberate or negligent failure on the part of the detainee. It requires only that the purpose of the detention should be to secure the fulfilment of the obligation. This does not expressly exclude the possibility of detention in the absence of a prior breach of legal duty. However in the Commission's opinion the mere combination of an unfulfilled obligation (even if 'specific and concrete'), coupled with the relevant purpose, is not enough for the purposes of Article 5(1)(b). To hold that it was would open up a clear possibility of arbitrary detention, thus ignoring the object and purpose of Article 5(1) and the importance of the right to liberty in a democratic society (cf *Winterwerp* Case, Series A, Vol 33, p 16, para 37).

175. In the Commission's opinion there must accordingly be specific circumstances such as to warrant the use of detention as a means of securing the fulfilment of an obligation before detention on this ground can be justified under Article 5(1)(b). In this respect the Commission follows the Court's approach in the *Winterwerp* Case where it held that the nature and degree of a mental disorder must be such as to warrant detention before a person could be detained as being of 'unsound mind' under Article 5(1)(f) (sup cit, p 18, para 39). The mere existence of a mental disorder was not itself enough. Similarly the mere fact that an unfulfilled obligation is incumbent on a person is not enough to justify detention in order to secure its fulfilment. In the Commission's opinion the person concerned must normally have had a prior opportunity to fulfil the 'specific and concrete' obligation incumbent on him and have failed, without proper excuse, to do so before it can be said in good faith that his detention is 'in order to secure the fulfilment' of the obligation. However, there may, in the Commission's opinion, be other limited circumstances of a pressing nature which could warrant detention in order to secure fulfilment of an obligation.

176. Finally, on the general question of interpretation, the Commission notes that the nature of the obligation whose fulfilment is sought must itself be compatible with the Convention. The obligation in question cannot, in particular, consist in substance merely of an obligation to submit to detention.

177. As to the present case, the Commission has first examined the 'obligations' arising from the relevant legislation. ...

178. In the Commission's view these provisions create an overall obligation arising in specified circumstances, to submit to 'examination'. Where a person is examined he is subject to subsidiary obligations to provide information, to submit to being searched etc.

179. The concept of 'examination' is not expressly defined in the legislation. However, it clearly includes questioning and searching of the examinee for the purpose of determining the matters set out in sub-paras (a)–(c) of Article 5(1) of the Order. If the person examined is detained it may also include

measures such as fingerprinting and photography. In practice it also includes checking of police records and other external investigations. In essence it is thus a process of investigation or a form of security check limited in scope *inter alia* by the purposes set out in Article 5(1) of the Order. ...

...

181. The Commission finds that the purpose of the detention 'pending ... examination' of the present applicants was essentially to secure their compliance with the overall obligation to submit to examination. It was not based on any specific failure on their part to fulfil the legal obligations incumbent on them in connection with their initial examination. The basis of the arrest was not, for instance, any refusal or failure to answer questions or produce evidence of their identity. The examining officer may have suspected that they had not answered his initial questions correctly, but he was not in a position to say with any certainty that this was the case. The purpose of their arrest was not therefore to compel them to rectify any specific prior breach of legal duty. It was to compel them to submit to the further examination which the examining officer considered necessary.

182. In these circumstances the Commission must first consider whether the obligation was sufficiently 'concrete and specific' to be capable in principle of falling within the scope of Article 5(1)(b), and if so whether there were circumstances sufficient to warrant the applicants' detention in order to secure its fulfilment. ...

184. In the Commission's opinion the obligation to submit to examination is, as a matter of both form and substance, distinct from the obligation to submit to detention. As it has already noted, detention is not an inherent feature of examination (para 176 above).

185. The obligation to submit to examination incumbent on the applicants was not a general obligation arising under criminal or disciplinary law comparable to those considered by the Commission and Court in other cases (see eg para 103 of the Commission's Report in the *Guzzardi* Case and other cases referred to in para 171 above). It arose only in circumstances specified by law, in this case on the applicants' entry into Great Britain, and on the requirement of an examining officer. It can to some extent be seen as comparable in character to other obligations to produce evidence of identity, to make customs declarations or tax returns, or the obligation to furnish an affidavit referred to by the Government. On the other hand in the present case the information to be furnished is not precisely specified in a comparable manner to the above cases. Furthermore the Commission has already noted that 'examination' involves a process of investigation going beyond questioning and eliciting information from the person examined (para 179 above). It is clear that an important part of the process consists in the checking of records and the verification of information given by the person examined. There is therefore also a certain analogy between the detention power at issue in the present case and the powers of initial arrest and detention for interrogation and investigation purposes which were at issue in the case of *Ireland v UK* (see Report of the Commission, p 88) and to which the applicants have referred. However, the powers at issue in the present case are more closely circumscribed, *inter alia* as to their purpose, and neither analogy is thus precise.

186. The obligation to submit to examination does not amount to a general obligation to submit to questioning or interrogation on any occasion, or for any purpose. ... It is in essence an obligation to submit to a security check (if so required) on entering or leaving Great Britain. The purpose of the check is limited to determining the matters set out in Article 5 of the 1976 Order. The scope of the obligation is furthermore effectively limited by the limitation set on the duration of detention permitted under Article 10 of the 1976 Order. At the relevant time the maximum period permitted on the authority of an examining officer was seven days. Whilst this could be extended by the Secretary of State, his power to do so was not exercised in the present case, which in any event concerns a period of some 45 hours only. The Commission is only called upon to express an opinion in relation to the actual period at issue here. ...

188. In all the circumstances, the Commission considers that the obligation imposed on the present applicants to submit to examination was a specific and concrete obligation and that the UK authorities were therefore **in principle** entitled under Article 5(1)(b) to resort to detention to secure its fulfilment. In reaching this conclusion the Commission has particularly taken into account the fact that the obligation in question arises only in limited circumstances, namely in the context of passage over a clear geographical or political boundary. Furthermore the purpose of the examination is limited and directed towards an end of evident public importance in the context of a serious and continuing threat from organised terrorism.

189. However, as the Commission has already observed, the mere existence of an unfulfilled obligation (albeit 'specific and concrete') is not of itself enough to justify arrest or detention under Article 5(1)(b). There must be specific circumstances which warrant the use of detention as a means of securing the fulfilment of the obligation. …

190. The Commission has already observed that the applicants' detention was not based on any prior voluntary failure to fulfil obligations incumbent on them such as a refusal to co-operate in the initial examination. It reiterates that in the absence of such circumstances detention cannot normally be justified under Article 5(1)(b). In general only a person's refusal or neglect to comply with an obligation can justify his detention in order to secure its fulfilment. However as the Commission has indicated above, the possibility that there may be other circumstances justifying detention under this provision is not excluded by the wording of Article 5(1)(b) and in its view there may be other limited circumstances of a pressing nature which could justify such detention.

191. In considering whether such circumstances exist, account must be taken, in the Commission's opinion, of the nature of the obligation. It is necessary to consider whether its fulfilment is a matter of immediate necessity and whether the circumstances are such that no other means of securing fulfilment is reasonably practicable. A balance must be drawn between the importance in a democratic society of securing the immediate fulfilment of the obligation in question, and the importance of the right to liberty. The duration of the period of detention is also a relevant factor in drawing such a balance.

192. The Commission has already noted that the obligation imposed on the applicants in the present case was, in essence, an obligation to submit to a security check on entering Great Britain, the scope of the check being limited (broadly speaking) to the prevention of terrorism. The importance in present day conditions of controlling the international movement of terrorists has been widely recognised in Western Europe, in particular by the Parliamentary Assembly of the Council of Europe. (See Report of Political Affairs Committee of 5 December 978, Doc 4258, para 17; Recommendation 852 (1979), para 15 (ix).) In the particular context of the UK there is also evident importance in controlling and detecting the movement of terrorists not only between the UK and the Republic of Ireland but also between Great Britain and Ireland as a whole, including Northern Ireland. The necessary checks must obviously be carried out as the person concerned enters or leaves the territory in question and there is a legitimate need to obtain immediate fulfilment of the obligation to submit to such checks.

193. The Commission further notes that, from the information before it, it appears that the powers of examination are, so far as reasonably practicable, exercised without resort to detention, the majority of persons examined being subjected only to a relatively short examination at the port of entry or departure. It is true that where the authorities consider a prolonged examination to be necessary, detention is apparently used invariably. There is no provision for release on bail pending examination, in contrast to the position under the normal immigration legislation in the UK. (Immigration Act 1971, Schedule 2, Article 22(1)). However, release on bail scarcely seems compatible with the effective operation of the limited security check at issue in the present case.

194. It takes into account furthermore the practice whereby an examining officer does not exercise the powers of arrest and detention unless he is left in some suspicion as to the matters specified in Articles 5(1)(a)–(c) of the Order. In the context of such a security check it is obvious that a person

engaged in terrorist activity is unlikely openly to refuse to reply to questions or otherwise fail to comply with the obligations incumbent on him. However he may well give false or incomplete information. Accordingly in order effectively to secure the fulfilment of the obligation in question it may therefore be necessary to resort to detention even where it cannot be said with certainty that there has already been any culpable failure on the part of the detainee to fulfil the obligations incumbent on him.

195. The Commission finds no indication that the detention of the present applicants was arbitrary or effected for any improper purpose. It accepts that it was based on the examining officer's appreciation on the basis of the information available to him, that there was a necessity to examine them in greater depth than was practicable at the port. In the exceptional context of the case it concludes that there were thus sufficient circumstances to warrant their arrest and detention for some 45 hours for the purpose of securing fulfilment of the obligation incumbent on them to submit to examination.

196. It is not in dispute that the arrest and detention were in accordance with domestic law and the Commission finds nothing to suggest that it was not both 'in accordance with a procedure prescribed by law' and 'lawful' as these concepts in Article 5(1) have been interpreted by the Court (see eg *Winterwerp* Case, sup cit, paras 39 and 45). It concludes that their arrest and detention were justified under Article 5(1)(b) in order to secure the fulfilment of an obligation prescribed by law.

NOTES

1 In *Benham v UK* (1996) 22 EHRR 293, 1996 III 738, a magistrates' court ordered the applicant to be imprisoned for one month because his failure to pay his community charge had been due to his culpable neglect. On appeal, the Divisional Court held that the magistrates' court had been mistaken: there was no evidence on the basis of which they could properly have found culpable neglect. The European Court held that the applicant's detention on the basis of the court order was justified by Article 5(1)(b), and that this was so even though the order had been set aside on appeal. It stated:

42. A period of detention will in principle be lawful if it is carried out pursuant to a court order. A subsequent finding that the court erred under domestic law in making the order will not necessarily retrospectively affect the validity of the intervening period of detention. For this reason, the Strasbourg organs have consistently refused to uphold applications from persons convicted of criminal offences who complain that their convictions or sentences were found by the appellate courts to have been based on errors of fact or law (see the *Bozano v France* judgment of 18 December 1986, Series A No 111, p 23, § 55, and the report of the Commission of 9 March 1978 on application no 7629/76, *Krzycki v Germany*, Decisions and Reports 13, pp 60–1).

43. It was agreed by those appearing before the Court that the principles of English law which should be taken into account in this case distinguished between acts of a magistrates' court which were within its jurisdiction and those which were in excess of jurisdiction. The former were valid and effective unless or until they were overturned by a superior court, whereas the latter were null and void from the outset....

46. It cannot be said with any degree of certainty that . . . the magistrates acted in excess of jurisdiction within the meaning of English law. It follows that the Court does not find it established that the order for detention was invalid, and thus that the detention which resulted from it was unlawful under national law (see the above-mentioned *Bouamar* judgment p 21, § 49). The mere fact that the order was set aside on appeal did not in itself affect the lawfulness of the detention (see paragraph 42 above).

47. Nor does the Court find that the detention was arbitrary. It has not been suggested that the magistrates who ordered Mr Benham's detention acted in bad faith, nor that they neglected to attempt to apply the relevant legislation correctly (see the above-mentioned *Bozano* judgment, pp 25–6, § 59)....

Accordingly, the Court finds no violation of Article 5 § 1 of the Convention.

In the later case of *Beet and Others v UK*, judgment of 1 March 2005, a unanimous Chamber applied *Benham* to determine that as the magistrates had failed to undertake a proper inquiry into the applicant's means, before imprisoning her due to her arrears in the payment of the community charge, this omission resulted in the magistrates' order being made in excess of jurisdiction. Consequently, it was unlawful and therefore the applicant had been detained in breach of Article 5(1).

2 A unanimous Chamber of the full-time Court found a violation of this provision in *Vasileva v Denmark*, judgment of 25 September 2003. The applicant was a 67-year-old Bulgarian citizen. On 11 August 1995 she had a dispute with a ticket inspector on a bus in Arhus. The inspector accused her of travelling without a valid ticket and sought to issue her with a penalty fare. However, she refused to disclose her identity. The police were called and they requested that she disclose her identity, under section 750 of the Administration of Justice Act everyone is under a duty to disclose his/her name, address and date of birth to the police upon request (failure to do so is punishable with a fine). She refused to provide the police with this information and so they arrested her, under the same Act, at 9.30 pm. She was taken to the police station and placed in a waiting room. Vasileva continued to refuse to identify herself (and she had no documents in her possession which contained such information). At 11 pm she was placed in a cell. From 6.30 am the next day the police sought to persuade the applicant to disclose her identity. She eventually did so at 10.45 am and she was then released at 11 am. Immediately after her release she collapsed and was hospitalized for three days diagnosed with high blood pressure. She was not charged with the offence of refusing to provide details of her identity to the police. After failing to secure compensation from the police in the domestic courts she complained to Strasbourg alleging a breach of Article 5. The Government sought to justify her detention under Article 5(1)(b) in order to secure the fulfilment of her specific legal obligation under Danish law to identify herself to the police when so requested. The Court held that:

36. ... detention is authorised under sub-paragraph (b) of Article 5 § 1 only to 'secure the fulfilment' of the obligation prescribed by law. It follows that, at the very least, there must be an unfulfilled obligation incumbent on the person concerned and the arrest and detention must be for the purpose of securing its fulfilment and not punitive in character. As soon as the relevant obligation has been fulfilled, the basis for detention under Article 5 § 1 (b) ceases to exist.

37. Finally, a balance must be drawn between the importance in a democratic society of securing the immediate fulfilment of the obligation in question, and the importance of the right to liberty . . . The duration of detention is also a relevant factor in drawing such a balance (see *McVeigh and Others v the United Kingdom*, Applications Nos 8022/77, 8025/77, 8027/77, Commission decision of 18 March 1981, DR 25, pp 37–8 and 42; *Johansen v Norway*, Application No 10600/83, Commission decision of 14 October 1985, DR 44, p 162).

41. ... In the present case the applicant was deprived of her liberty for thirteen and a half hours. The Court notes that the police several times in vain requested that she reveal her identity in the period from 9.30 until 11.00 p.m. on 11 August 1995, and from 6.30 until 10.45 a.m. on 12 August 1995, and relying on the findings of the domestic courts, the Court is satisfied that the applicant was not in possession of any documentation, which could have revealed her identity. Also, it notes that it appears to be common ground that no efforts were made to identify her in the period between 11.00 p.m. and 6.30 a.m. The Government allege that the reason therefore can be attributed to considerations as to the applicant's need for sleep. While accepting that such considerations may be relevant in certain circumstances, it is in the Court's opinion not established that this was so in the present case. Furthermore, the Court would be reluctant to accept that such considerations could generally be given

priority over the obligation to secure that the detention did not exceed a period proportionate to the cause of the detention. The Court notes in addition, having regard to the fact that the Chief Constable of Århus on 18 July 1996 found reason to regret that the applicant during her detention had not been attended to by a doctor as promised, that the involvement of such a third person might have broken the impasse, which the communication between the police and the applicant obviously had reached. Moreover, having regard to its finding above as to the applicant and the circumstances leading to her detention, and to the fact that the applicant's failure to comply with the obligation prescribed in section 750 of the Administration of Justice Act was a minor offence, which could carry only a fine, the Court considers that her detention in any event should not have been maintained for a longer period of time. It finds that the deprivation of the applicant's liberty for thirteen and a half hours exceeded a period proportionate to the cause of her detention.

42. In the light of the above elements, the Court considers that the authorities by extending the applicant's detention to thirteen and a half-hour failed to strike a fair balance between the need to ensure the fulfilment of the obligation and the right to liberty.

43. There has, accordingly, been a violation of Article 5 § 1 of the Convention.

The obligation upon the applicant to identify herself to the police was a clear example of the type of specific duty falling within Article 5(1)(b). However, in assessing the proportionality of a period of detention utilized to secure the fulfilment of such a duty the Court examined, *inter alia*, the nature/purpose of the obligation, the action/inaction of the police to secure the fulfilment of that obligation during the period of detention and the duration of the period of detention. Here the combination of the minor nature of the applicant's suspected criminal conduct, the overnight hiatus in the attempts by the police to discover the applicant's identity and the length of her detention resulted in the Court's finding a breach of Article 5. Do you agree with the Court's assessment that the police were at fault for allowing the applicant to sleep during the night and not continuing to try and discover her identity?

Article 5(1)(c): Reasonable suspicion of a criminal offence, etc

....

K-F v Germany 1997-VII 2657, (1997) 26 EHRR 390
European Court of Human Rights

In the light of allegations that he was attempting to leave a holiday home without paying bills and initial inquiries casting doubts over his home address and revealing prior investigations for fraud, the applicant was arrested at 9.45 pm on 4 July 1991 by the police. He was taken to the local police station for questioning and to verify his identity. The police report drawn up that night expressed the view that there was a strong suspicion of rent fraud and a fear that he would abscond. After the applicant had spent the night at the police station, at 9.25 am on 5 July 1991 the Public Prosecutor informed the police that he did not intend to issue a warrant for the applicant's arrest. He was released at 10.30 am.

The applicant alleged, *inter alia*, that his detention had been 'unlawful' as it had exceeded the twelve-hour limit in German law, so that it was not justified by Article 5(1)(c). The Commission expressed the opinion, by seven votes to six, that there had been no violation of Article 5(1) on the basis that practical reasons may excuse the delay in releasing an individual beyond the legal time limit.

JUDGMENT OF THE COURT

63. Lastly, the Court must determine whether the applicant's arrest and detention were 'lawful', including whether they were effected 'in accordance with a procedure prescribed by law'. It reiterates that the Convention here refers essentially to national law and lays down an obligation to comply with its substantive and procedural provisions, but also requires that any measure depriving the individual of his liberty must be compatible with the purchase of Article 5, namely to protect the individual from arbitrariness (see, for example, the *Lukanov v Bulgaria* judgment of 20 March 1997, Reports 1997-II, pp 543–4, § 41; and the *Giulia Manzoni v Italy* judgment of 1 July 1997, Reports 1997-IV, p 1190, §21). In order to resolve that issue, the Court will consider in turn the various grounds for arrest and detention put forward by the Government. . . .

67. The Court observes, firstly, that the Court of Appeal, a national court which is in a better position than the Convention institutions to verify compliance with domestic law, found that the applicant's arrest and detention were lawful. . . . The Court sees no reason to come to a different conclusion.

68. The Court of Appeal left open the question whether it was necessary to hold the applicant until the following morning 'as, on grounds of intent at least, the potential defendants' conviction on a charge of false imprisonment [was] unlikely'. It has been established, however, that the police continued to make inquiries throughout the night and up until the applicant's release, partly in order to check whether an arrest warrant had been issued against him. . . . Having regard to those circumstances, the Court concludes that the applicant's detention from 9.45 pm on 4 July to 9.45 am the following day was justifiable.

69. On the other hand, it notes that the length of time the applicant spent in detention exceeded the legal maximum laid down by article 163 c § 3 of the Code of Criminal Procedure. . . . The Koblenz Court of Appeal came to the same conclusion in its judgment of 30 November 1993. . . : 'A person affected by a measure taken under Article 163 for the purposes of checking his identity cannot be deprived of his liberty for more than twelve hours in all. The applicant was detained at 9.45 pm on 4 July 1991 (. . .) and released at 10.30 am on 5 July 1991 (. . .). For this detention, which lasted for more than twelve hours, Superintendent Blang was responsible.'

70. The Court reiterates in this connection that the list of exceptions to the right to liberty secured in Article 5 § 1 is an exhaustive one and only a narrow interpretation of those exceptions is consistent wit the aim of that provision, namely to ensure that no one is arbitrarily deprived of his or her liberty (see, as the most recent authority, the *Giulia Manzoni* judgment cited above, p 1191, § 25).

71. It is true that the Court has accepted that, in certain circumstances, there may be some limited delay before a detained person is released. However, this has been in cases where the period of detention was not laid down in advance by statute and ended as a result of a court order. Practical considerations relating to the running of the courts and the completion of special formalities mean that the execution of such a court order may take time (see the *Quinn v France* judgment of 22 March 1995, Series A No 311, p 17, § 42, and the *Giulia Manzoni* judgment cited above, p 1191, § 25).

72. However, in the instant case, the maximum period of twelve hours' detention for the purposes of checking identity was laid down by law and was absolute. Since the maximum period of detention was known in advance, the authorities responsible for the detention were under a duty to take all necessary precautions to ensure that the permitted duration was not exceeded. That applies also to the recording of Mr K-F's personal details, which—being included among the measures for checking identity—should have been carried out during the period of detention allotted for that purpose.

73. Having regard to those factors, the Court holds that, because the maximum period laid down by law for detaining the applicant was exceeded, there has been a breach of Article 5 § 1 (c).

FOR THESE REASONS, THE COURT

...

2. Holds unanimously that there has been a violation of Article 5 § 1(c) of the Convention.

NOTES

1 The Court was composed of President Ryssdal and Judges Bernhardt, Russo, Valticos, Palm, Bonnici, Repik, Jungweirt and Lohmus.

2 This extract from the *K-F* case concerns the requirement in Article 5(1)(c) that an arrest or detention must be 'lawful'. The same requirement was in issue in *Loukanov v Bulgaria* (1997) 24 EHRR 121, 1997-II 529. There the Prosecutor-General had instituted criminal proceedings against the applicant for misappropriating public funds while holding high government office in the 1980s. The Court held unanimously that the applicant's detention could not be justified under Article 5(1)(c) because it was not 'lawful' under Bulgarian law. The Court stated:

42. Turning to the particular circumstances of the case, the Court observes that it is undisputed that the applicant had, as a member of the Bulgarian Government, taken part in the decisions—granting funds in assistance and loans to certain developing countries—which had given rise to the charges against him.

43. However, none of the provisions of the Criminal Code relied on to justify the detention—Articles 201 to 203, 219 and 282—specified or even implied that anyone could incur criminal liability by taking part in collective decisions of this nature. Moreover, no evidence has been adduced to show that such decisions were unlawful, that is to say contrary to Bulgaria's Constitution or legislation, or more specifically that the decisions were taken in excess of powers or were contrary to the law on the national budget.

In the light of the above, the Court is not persuaded that the conduct for which the applicant was prosecuted constituted a criminal offence under Bulgarian law at the relevant time.

....

Fox, Campbell and Hartley v UK A.182 (1990) 13 EHRR 157
European Court of Human Rights

The applicants were arrested in Northern Ireland by a police constable exercising his statutory power under s 11, Northern Ireland (Emergency Provisions) Act 1978 'to arrest without warrant any person whom he suspects of being a terrorist'. This power had been interpreted in *McKee v Chief Constable for Northern Ireland* [1984] 1 WLR 1358, HL, as incorporating a subjective test, so that an arrest was permissible if the policeman had an 'honestly held suspicion'. On their arrest, the applicants were told only that they were being arrested under s 11 on suspicion of being terrorists; they were given no facts in support of the suspicion. The applicants claimed, *inter alia*, that Articles 5(1)(c) and 5(2) had been infringed. In its report, the Commission expressed the opinion, by seven votes to five, that both provisions had been infringed in respect of all three applicants.

JUDGMENT OF THE COURT

32. The 'reasonableness' of the suspicion on which an arrest must be based forms an essential part of the safeguard against arbitrary arrest and detention which is laid down in Article 5 § 1(c). The Court agrees with the Commission and the Government that having a 'reasonable suspicion' presupposes

the existence of facts or information which would satisfy an objective observer that the person concerned may have committed the offence. What may be regarded as 'reasonable' will however depend upon all the circumstances.

In this respect, terrorist crime falls into a special category. Because of the attendant risk of loss of life and human suffering, the police are obliged to act with utmost urgency in following up all information, including information from secret sources. Further, the police may frequently have to arrest a suspected terrorist on the basis of information which is reliable but which cannot, without putting in jeopardy the source of the information, be revealed to the suspect or produced in court to support a charge.

As the Government pointed out, in view of the difficulties inherent in the investigation and prosecution of terrorist-type offences in Northern Ireland, the 'reasonableness of the suspicion justifying such arrests cannot always be judged according to the same standards as are applied in dealing with conventional crime'. Nevertheless, the exigencies of dealing with terrorist crime cannot justify stretching the notion of 'reasonableness' to the point where the essence of the safeguard secured by article 5 § 1(c) is impaired.

...

34. Certainly Article 5 § 1(c) of the Convention should not be applied in such a manner as to put disproportionate difficulties in the way of the police authorities of the Contracting States in taking effective measures to counter organised terrorism (see, *mutatis mutandis*, the *Klaas* judgment of 6 September 1978, Series A No 28, pp 27 and 30–1, §§ 58 and 68). It follows that the Contracting States cannot be asked to establish the reasonableness of the suspicion grounding the arrest of a suspected terrorist by disclosing the confidential sources of supporting information or even facts which would be susceptible to indicating such sources or their identity.

Nevertheless the Court must be enabled to ascertain whether the essence of the safeguard afforded by Article 5 § 1(c) has been secured. Consequently the respondent Government have to furnish at least some facts or information capable of satisfying the Court that the arrested person was reasonably suspected of having committed the alleged offence. This is all the more necessary where, as in the present case, the domestic law does not require reasonable suspicion, but sets a lower threshold by merely requiring honest suspicion.

35. The Court accepts that the arrest and detention of each of the present applicants was based on a *bona fide* suspicion that he or she was a terrorist, and that each of them, including Mr Hartley, was questioned during his or her detention about specific terrorist acts of which he or she was suspected.

The fact that Mr Fox and Ms Campbell both have previous convictions for acts of terrorism connected with the IRA . . . , although it could reinforce a suspicion linking them to the commission of terrorist-type offences, cannot form the sole basis of a suspicion justifying their arrest in 1986, some seven years later.

The fact that all the applicants, during their detention, were questioned about specific terrorist acts, does no more than confirm that the arresting officers had a genuine suspicion that they had been involved in those acts, but it cannot satisfy an objective observer that the applicants may have committed these acts.

The aforementioned elements on their own are insufficient to support the conclusion that there was 'reasonable suspicion'. The Government have not provided any further material on which the suspicion against the applicants was based. Their explanations therefore do not meet the minimum standard set by Article 5(1)(c) for judging the reasonableness of a suspicion for the arrest of an individual. . . .

FOR THESE REASONS, THE COURT

1. Holds by four votes to three that there has been a breach of Article 5 § 1; . . .

JOINT DISSENTING OPINION OF JUDGES SIR VINCENT EVANS, BERNHARDT AND PALM

We are unable to agree with the finding of the majority of the Court that there has been a violation of Article 5 § 1(c) in this case . . .

The majority accept—and on this we agree—that the arrest and detention of each of the applicants was based on a *bona fide* suspicion that he or she was a terrorist and that each of them was questioned during his or her detention about specific terrorist acts of which he or she was suspected. But, in the opinion of the majority, the latter fact does no more than confirm that the arresting officers had a genuine suspicion and a genuine suspicion was not the equivalent of a reasonable suspicion.

In our view the 'genuine suspicion' on the part of the arresting officers that the applicants were involved in the specific terrorist acts about which they were questioned must have had some basis in information received by them, albeit from sources which the Government maintain that they are unable to disclose for security reasons. In the situation in Northern Ireland the police must have a responsibility to follow up such information of involvement in terrorist activities and, if circumstances so warrant, to arrest and detain the suspect for further investigation.

In cases such as these it is not possible to draw a sharp distinction between genuine suspicion and reasonable suspicion. Having regard to all the circumstances and to the facts and information between the Court, including in the case of Mr Fox and Ms Campbell the fact that they had previously been involved in and convicted of terrorist activities, we are satisfied that there were reasonable grounds for suspicion justifying the arrest and detention of the applicants in accordance with Article 5 § 1(c). . . .

NOTES

1   The Court was composed of President Ryssdal and Judges Cremona, Pinheiro Farinha, Sir Vincent Evans, Bernhardt, Martens and Palm.

2   The *Fox, Campbell and Hartley* cases spell out the meaning of 'reasonable suspicion' in Article 5(1)(c). The objective test that it states was not complied with on the facts, even with the special allowance that the Court was prepared to make in the special context of terrorist offences. The test was complied with in the later terrorist case of *Murray (Margaret) v UK* A.300 (1994) 19 EHRR 193. In that case, the first applicant was arrested by a member of the armed forces under s 14, Northern Ireland (Emergency Provisions) Act 1978 on suspicion of having committed an offence involving the collection of funds for the Provisional IRA. Confirming the approach it had taken in the *Fox, Campbell and Hartley* case, and adding that the length of time for which the person might be detained (four hour maximum under s 14) was relevant to the level of suspicion required, the Court stated:

61. It cannot be excluded that all or some of the evidence adduced before the national courts in relation to the genuineness of the suspicion on the basis of which Mrs Murray was arrested may also be material to the issue whether the suspicion was 'reasonable' for the purposes of Article 5 § 1(c) of the Convention. At the very least the honesty and *bona fides* of a suspicion constitute one indispensable element of its reasonableness.

In the action brought by Mrs Murray against the Ministry of Defence for false imprisonment and other torts, the High Court judge, after having heard the witnesses and assessed their credibility, found that she had genuinely been suspected of having been involved in the collection of funds for the purchase of arms in the USA for the Provisional IRA. . . . The judge believed the evidence of the arresting officer, Corporal D, who was described as a 'transparently honest witness', as to what she had been told at her briefing before the arrest. . . . Likewise as found by the judge, although the interview at the Army centre was later in time than the arrest, the line of questioning pursued by the interviewer also tends to support the conclusion that Mrs Murray herself was suspected of the commission of a special criminal offence. . . .

62. Some weeks before her arrest two of Mrs Murray's brothers had been convicted in the USA of offences connected with purchase of arms for the Provisional IRA. . . . As she disclosed in her evidence to the High Court, she had visited the USA and had contacts with her brothers there. . . . The offences of which her brothers were convicted were ones that implied collaboration with 'trustworthy' persons residing in Northern Ireland.

63. Having regard to the level of factual justification required at the stage of suspicion and to the special exigencies of investigating terrorist crime, the Court finds, in the light of all the above considerations, that there did exist sufficient facts or information which would provide a plausible and objective basis for a suspicion that Mrs Murray may have committed the offence of involvement in the collection of funds for the Provisional IRA. On the particular facts of the present case, therefore, the Court is satisfied that, notwithstanding the lower standard of suspicion under domestic law, Mrs Murray can be said to have been arrested and detained on 'reasonable suspicion' of the commission of a criminal offence, within the meaning of sub-paragraph (c) of Article 5 § 1.

3 'Reasonable suspicion' was also in issue in *Loukanov v Bulgaria*, above, p 271. There the Court said:

44. . . . the public prosecutor's order of detention of 9 July 1992 and the Supreme Court's decision of 13 July upholding the order referred to Articles 201 to 203 of the Criminal Code. . . . As appears from the case-law supplied to the Court, a constituent element of the offence of misappropriation under Articles 201 to 203 of the Criminal Code was that the offender had sought to obtain for himself or herself or for a third party an advantage. . . . The order of 9 July in addition referred to Article 282 which specifically makes it an offence for a public servant to abuse his or her power in order to obtain such advantage . . . .

However, the Court has not been provided with any fact or information capable of showing that the applicant was at the time reasonably suspected of having sought to obtain for himself or a third party an advantage from his participation in the allocation of funds in question (see, for instance, the *Murray v UK* judgment of 28 October 1994, Series A No 300-A, p 25, § 51). In this connection it is to be noted that the Government's submission that there had been certain 'deals' was found by the Commission to be unsubstantiated and was not reiterated before the Court. Indeed, it was not contended before the Convention institutions that the funds had not been received by the States concerned.

45. In these circumstances, the Court does not find that the deprivation of the applicant's liberty during the period under consideration was 'lawful detention' effected 'on reasonable suspicion of [his] having committed an offence'.

4 In *Brogan v UK* below, p 300, it was held that Article 5(1)(c) may justify an arrest or detention even though no criminal proceedings are eventually brought, provided that there is 'reasonable suspicion' that an offence has been committed when the arrest is made.

5 The 'prevention of an offence' ground for arrest or detention in Article 5(1)(c) does not authorize preventive detention: see the *Guzzardi* case, above, p 241, and *Lawless v Ireland*, A 1 (1961).

6 A 'breach of the peace' is an 'offence' for the purposes of Article 5(1)(c) even though it is not a criminal offence in English law: *Steel v UK* (1998) 28 EHRR 603, 1998 VII 2719.

7 The full-time Court examined another Northern Irish suspected terrorist arrest in *O'Hara v United Kingdom*, judgment of 16 October 2001. The applicant was a well-known member of 'Sinn Fein'. In November 1985 a German national, Kurt Konig, who worked for the caterers supplying food to police stations in Londonderry was murdered (the Provisional IRA claimed responsibility for his killing). The Northern Irish Special Branch received intelligence from four informants (none of whom had criminal records and whose previous information had proved reliable) stating that the applicant and three other persons were responsible for the murder of Konig. The Special branch briefed Detective Superintendent R. of the Royal Ulster Constabulary that the applicant was a member of the Provisional IRA and had been implicated in the murder. Superintendent R. subsequently briefed Inspector B. who then briefed Detective Constable S. On 28 December 1985 the latter went to the applicant's home and arrested him. The applicant was informed by S. that he was being arrested under section 12(1)(b) of the

Prevention of Terrorism (Temporary Provisions) Act 1984 (which authorized a police officer to arrest a person whom he had reasonable grounds for suspecting of being concerned in the commission, preparation, or instigation of acts of terrorism). The applicant was taken to Castlereagh Detention Centre and held for six days and thirteen hours during which he interviewed thirty-four times (he did not answer any questions). He was released without charge. The applicant sued the Chief Constable for, *inter alia*, seizure of documents and unlawful arrest. The High Court in Northern Ireland heard evidence from Detective Constable S. that Inspector B. had, prior to the arrest of the applicant, briefed him that there were reasonable grounds for suspecting the applicant to be involved in the murder of Konig. The trial judge considered that he only had 'scanty' evidence of the matters disclosed to Detective Constable S. but that he was 'just satisfied' of the legality of the arrest. On appeal both the Court of Appeal and the House of Lords upheld the lawfulness of the arrest. Before the Court the applicant contended that he had never been a member of the IRA or been involved in the murder of Konig and therefore the police could not have received reliable information to that effect.

34. The Court emphasises that the 'reasonableness' of the suspicion on which an arrest must be based forms an essential part of the safeguard against arbitrary arrest and detention laid down in Article 5 § 1 (c) of the Convention. This requires the existence of some facts or information which would satisfy an objective observer that the person concerned may have committed the offence, though what may be regarded as reasonable will depend on all the circumstances of the case (see *Fox, Campbell and Hartley v the United Kingdom*, judgment of 30 August 1990, Series A No 182, p 16, § 32).

35. In that context, terrorist crime poses particular problems, as the police may be called upon, in the interests of public safety, to arrest a suspected terrorist on the basis of information which is reliable but which cannot be disclosed to the suspect or produced in court without jeopardising the informant. However, though Contracting States cannot be required to establish the reasonableness of the suspicion grounding the arrest of a suspected terrorist by disclosing confidential sources of information, the Court has held that the exigencies of dealing with terrorist crime cannot justify stretching the notion of 'reasonableness' to the point where the safeguard secured by Article 5 § 1 (c) is impaired. Even in those circumstances, the respondent Government have to furnish at least some facts or information capable of satisfying the Court that the arrested person was reasonably suspected of having committed the alleged offence (see *Fox, Campbell and Hartley*, cited above, pp 16–18, §§ 32–4).

36. It may also be observed that the standard imposed by Article 5 § 1 (c) does not presuppose that the police have sufficient evidence to bring charges at the time of arrest. The object of questioning during detention under sub-paragraph (c) of Article 5 § 1 is to further the criminal investigation by way of confirming or dispelling the concrete suspicion grounding the arrest. Thus facts which raise a suspicion need not be of the same level as those necessary to justify a conviction, or even the bringing of a charge which comes at the next stage of the process of criminal investigation (see *Brogan and Others v the United Kingdom*, judgment of 29 November 1988, Series A No 145-B, p 29, § 53, and *Murray v the United Kingdom*, judgment of 28 October 1994, Series A No 300-A, p 27, § 55).

...

42. The suspicion in the present case was based on information passed on at a police briefing by informers who identified the applicant as one of a number of persons suspected of involvement in a specific terrorist event, the murder of Mr Konig. There is no basis in the material provided for the Court to reject the Government's submissions on this point. The arrest was therefore a pre-planned operation, more akin to the arrest in *Murray*, and was based on slightly more specific detail than in *Fox, Campbell and Hartley*. In these circumstances...the Court considers that the domestic courts' approach—that the judge was entitled on the sparse materials before him to infer the existence of reasonable grounds of suspicion—was not incompatible with the standard imposed by Article 5 § 1 (c) of the Convention.

43. The applicant argued, with some force, that police officers should not be able to hide behind references to anonymous informants by way of justifying abuse of their power of arrest. The Court reiterates, however, that in the domestic proceedings the applicant did not attempt to raise any complaints concerning bad faith or oppression. His claim was based on the narrow legal argument concerning the state of mind of the arresting officer relevant under section 12(1)(b) of the 1984 Act. Nor is the Court persuaded that there was any immunity conferred on other police officers, as a result of the finding by the domestic courts, that the arresting officer had the required suspicion. If the briefing officer or any other superior officer had deliberately passed on misleading or inaccurate information to the arresting officer, the police authorities would have been liable for wrongful arrest or false imprisonment in respect of that misconduct.

44. The Court does not find, therefore, that the approach of the domestic courts to the standard of suspicion in this case removed the accountability of the police for arbitrary arrest, or conferred on the police any impunity with regard to arrests conducted on the basis of confidential information. In the circumstances, the suspicion against the applicant reached the required level as it was based on specific information that he was involved in the murder of Kurt Konig and the purpose of the deprivation of liberty was to confirm or dispel that suspicion. The applicant can accordingly be said to have been arrested and detained on 'reasonable suspicion' of a criminal offence, within the meaning of subparagraph (c) of Article 5 § 1.

Accordingly, there has been no violation of that provision.

Judge Loucaides dissented as he considered that:

. . . this case is nearer to *Fox, Campbell and Hartley* than to *Murray*, the reason being that both in this case and in the first-mentioned case no grounds at all in support of the reasonableness of the suspicion were submitted to the domestic courts, while in *Murray* certain facts in support of the suspicion were in fact adduced in the competent national courts.

The judgment in *O'Hara* reveals the Court treading a fine line between requiring the production of information justifying the reasonableness of an arrest of a suspected terrorist by States and recognition of the security implications of such disclosures in the increasingly important battle against all forms of terrorism. Do you agree with the Court's assessment of the sufficiency of the information against O'Hara?

8   The Court considered Article 5(1)(c) and Article 18 in the politically and economically high profile case of *Gusinskiy v Russia*, judgment of 19 May 2004, see below p 863.

Article 5(1)(d): Educational supervision, etc, of minors

Bouamar v Belgium A.129 (1988) 11 EHRR 1
European Court of Human Rights

The applicant was a seriously disturbed, delinquent 16-year-old who was detained by court order in a remand prison that provided no educational facilities for periods amounting to 119 days during most of one year. The orders were made under a 1965 Act, the purpose of which was to cause juveniles who committed criminal offences to be placed in juvenile reformatories with educational facilities instead of being tried and convicted by a criminal court. The Act allowed a juvenile to be placed in a remand prison for up to 15 days when it was 'materially impossible' to find him a place in a reformatory immediately. In the applicant's case, no open reformatory with the necessary educational facilities was willing to take him because of his behavioural problems and there was no suitable closed reformatory in the French-speaking region. In these circumstances, orders for his detention in a remand prison for 15-day periods were regularly renewed.

The applicant alleged that his detention was in breach of Article 5(1), not being justifiable under Article 5(1)(d). Having found that the detention was not in breach of Belgian law (since 'material impossibility' had been interpreted as extending to the juvenile's behavioural problems) and hence was not unlawful contrary to Article 5(1) on this basis, the Court continued as follows.

JUDGMENT OF THE COURT

50. 'Lawfulness', however, also implies that the deprivation of liberty is in keeping with the purpose of the restrictions permissible under Article 5 § 1 of the Convention. . . .

The Court notes that the confinement of a juvenile in a remand prison does not necessarily contravene sub-paragraph (d), even if it is not in itself such as to provide for the person's 'educational supervision'. As is apparent from the words 'for the purpose of' ('pour'), the 'detention' referred to in the text is a means of ensuring that the person concerned is placed under 'educational supervision', but the placement does not necessarily have to be an immediate one. Just as Article 5 § 1 recognises—in sub-paragraphs (c) and (a)—the distinction between pre-trial detention and detention after conviction, so sub-paragraph (d) does not preclude an interim custody measure being used as a preliminary to a regime of supervised education, without itself involving any supervised education. In such circumstances, however, the imprisonment must be speedily followed by actual application of such a regime in a setting (open or closed) designed and with sufficient resources for the purpose.

51. In the instant case the applicant was, as it were, shuttled to and fro between the remand prison at Lantin and his family. In 1980 alone, the juvenile courts ordered his detention nine times and then released him on or before the expiry of the statutory limit of fifteen days; in all, he was thus deprived of his liberty for 119 days during the period of 291 days from 18 January to 4 November 1980. . . .

52. In the Government's submission, the placements complained of were part of an educative programme initiated by the courts, and Mr Bouamar's behaviour during the relevant time enabled them to gain a clearer picture of his personality.

The Court does not share this view. The Belgian State chose the system of educational supervision with a view to carrying out its policy on juvenile delinquency. Consequently it was under an obligation to put in place appropriate institutional facilities which met the demands of security and the educational objectives of the 1965 Act, in order to be able to satisfy the requirements of Article 5 § 1(d) of the Convention (see, among other authorities and mutatis mutandis, the Guincho judgment of 10 July 1984, Series A No 81, p 16, § 38, and the De Cubber judgment of 26 October 1984, Series A No 86, p 20, § 35).

Nothing in the evidence, however, shows that this was the case. At the time of the events in issue, Belgium did not have—at least in the French-speaking region in which the applicant lived—any closed institution able to accommodate highly disturbed juveniles (see paragraph 28 above). The detention of a young man in a remand prison in conditions of virtual isolation and without the assistance of staff with educational training cannot be regarded as furthering any educational aim. . . .

53. The Court accordingly concludes that the nine placement orders, taken together, were not compatible with sub-paragraph (d). Their fruitless repetition had the effect of making them less and less 'lawful' under sub-paragraph (d), especially as Crown Counsel never instituted criminal proceedings against the applicant in respect of the offences alleged against him.

There was therefore a breach of Article 5 § 1 of the Convention. . . .

FOR THESE REASONS, THE COURT

1. Holds unanimously that there was a breach of paragraph 1 of Article 5; . . .

NOTES

1 The Court was composed of President Ryssdal and Judges Vilhjálmsson, Walsh, Sir Vincent Evans, Macdonald, Russo, and De Meyer.

2 The full-time Court followed the approach of *Bouamar* in the case of *D.G. v Ireland*, judgment of 16 May 2002. The applicant had been in the care of public authorities since he was two years old due to his father's imprisonment for life and his mother's inability to care for him or his siblings. The applicant committed a number of crimes and after serving several periods of detention he was released in March 1997 when he was 16 years old. A case conference determined that he needed to live in a high support therapeutic unit for 16–18 year olds but that no such facility existed in Ireland. In the following month his guardian *ad litem* brought judicial review proceedings against the authorities claiming that in failing to provide him with suitable care and accommodation they were violating his constitutional rights. The High Court initially ordered that the applicant be accommodated in a hostel but that option became impossible when the applicant made threats of violence. Thereupon the High Court concluded that as the applicant had a serious personality order, which meant that he was a danger to himself and others, and as no secure therapeutic unit existed in Ireland he should be detained in St Patrick's Institution (an institution for the detention of males between 16 and 21 years of age being held on remand or after sentencing). The applicant was detained in St Patrick's from 27 June to 28 July 1997 when he was placed in special accommodation under twenty-four hour supervision. The applicant complained to Strasbourg that his detention in St Patrick's violated Article 5(1)(d). The Government responded that his detention there had been for the lawful purpose of 'educational supervision'. The Court was unanimous in holding that:

80. It is also accepted that, in the context of the detention of minors, the words 'educational supervision' must not be equated rigidly with notions of classroom teaching: in the context of a young person in local authority care, educational supervision must embrace many aspects of the exercise, by the local authority, of parental rights for the benefit and protection of the person concerned . . .

81. However, the Court does not consider, and indeed, it does not appear to be argued by the Government, that St Patrick's itself constituted 'educational supervision'. As noted above, it was a penal institution and the applicant was subjected to its disciplinary regime. The educational and other recreation services were entirely voluntary and the applicant's history was demonstrative of an unwillingness to cooperate with the authorities: indeed the Government accept that he did not avail himself of the educational facilities. There is no entry in the applicant's 'prison' file, in the medical or psychiatric reports submitted or any specific submission by the Government detailing any instruction received by the applicant during his detention in St Patrick's. The only indication of his participation in recreational activities is a brief reference to his playing football in a medical report. Most importantly, the High Court itself was convinced that St Patrick's could not guarantee his constitutional educational right or provide the special care he required: even with the special conditions the High Court attached to his detention, the High Court considered St Patrick's to be the best of four inappropriate options and that, accordingly, his detention there should be temporary.

Consequently, the applicant's detention was not compatible with Article 5(1)(d).

This judgment, again, demonstrates the need for States to establish specialist facilities for the care and education of severely disturbed young persons.

Article 5(1)(e): infectious diseases, mentally disordered, alcoholics, vagrants etc.

Enhorn v Sweden 25 January 2005
European Court of Human Rights

The applicant, born in 1947, was a homosexual. In 1994 he was diagnosed as being infected with the HIV virus. It was also discovered that he had infected a 19-year-old, with whom he had first had sex in 1990. In September 1994 the relevant county medical officer issued a number of instructions to the applicant, under the Infectious Diseases Act 1988, designed to minimize the risks of the applicant transmitting the virus to other persons (they included: not to have sexual intercourse without first telling his partner about his HIV infection, using a condom, abstaining from consuming alcohol in amounts that would impair his judgment, informing medical staff about his condition if he had to have an operation etc., and to attend medical appointments scheduled by the county medical officer). At first the applicant attended his scheduled medical appointments, but he then failed to attend five appointments in October and November 1994. In February 1995 the county medical officer applied to the County Administrative Court, under the 1988 Act, for an order that the applicant be compulsorily isolated in a hospital for three months (on the grounds that he was not complying with the practical instructions issued to him to prevent the spreading of a 'disease dangerous to society' and there was a 'manifest risk of the infection being spread'). The Administrative Court granted the order. The applicant failed to go to the hospital and some weeks later he was arrested by the police and taken there. The domestic courts regularly renewed the compulsory isolation orders until December 2001. However, during those years the applicant absconded from the hospital on a number of occasion and he actually spent a total of one and a half years in compulsory isolation. During the remainder of the time, when he was absent without permission from the hospital, he claimed that he had not had any sexual relationships and there was no evidence that he had infected any other persons. In his complaint to the European Court the applicant contended that the issuing of the compulsory isolation orders against him had not been a proportionate response to his situation. The Government replied that the orders had been made with the aim of supporting a person having a dangerous infection to change their lifestyle and that no coercive medical treatment had been given to the applicant whilst he was isolated in the hospital.

43. Moreover, Article 5 § 1 (e) of the Convention refers to several categories of individuals, namely persons spreading infectious diseases, persons of unsound mind, alcoholics, drug addicts and vagrants. There is a link between all those persons in that they may be deprived of their liberty either in order to be given medical treatment or because of considerations dictated by social policy, or on both medical and social grounds. It is therefore legitimate to conclude from this context that a predominant reason why the Convention allows the persons mentioned in paragraph 1 (e) of Article 5 to be deprived of their liberty is not only that they are dangerous for public safety but also that their own interests may necessitate their detention (see *Guzzardi v Italy*, judgment of 6 November 1980, Series A No 39, pp. 36–7, § 98 *in fine*, and *Witold Litwa* [*v Poland* ECHR 2000-III] § 60).

44. Taking the above principles into account, the Court finds that the essential criteria when assessing the 'lawfulness' of the detention of a person 'for the prevention of the spreading of infectious diseases'

are whether the spreading of the infectious disease is dangerous for public health or safety, and whether detention of the person infected is the last resort in order to prevent the spreading of the disease, because less severe measures have been considered and found to be insufficient to safeguard the public interest. When these criteria are no longer fulfilled, the basis for the deprivation of liberty ceases to exist.

45. Turning to the instant case, it is undisputed that the first criterion was fulfilled, in that the HIV virus was and is dangerous for public health and safety.

46. It thus remains to be examined whether the applicant's detention could be said to be the last resort in order to prevent the spreading of the virus, because less severe measures had been considered and found to be insufficient to safeguard the public interest.

47. In a judgment of 16 February 1995, the County Administrative Court ordered that the applicant should be kept in compulsory isolation for up to three months under section 38 of the 1988 Act. Thereafter, orders to prolong his deprivation of liberty were continuously issued every six months until 12 December 2001, when the County Administrative Court turned down the county medical officer's application for an extension of the detention order. Accordingly, the order to deprive the applicant of his liberty was in force for almost seven years.

Admittedly, since the applicant absconded several times, his actual deprivation of liberty lasted from 16 March 1995 until 25 April 1995, 11 June 1995 until 27 September 1995, 28 May 1996 until 6 November 1996, 16 November 1996 until 26 February 1997, and 26 February 1999 until 12 June 1999—almost one and a half years altogether.

48. The Government submitted that a number of voluntary measures had been attempted in vain during the period between September 1994 and February 1995 to ensure that the applicant's behaviour would not contribute to the spread of the HIV infection. Also, they noted the particular circumstances of the case, notably as to the applicant's personality and behaviour, as described by various physicians and psychiatrists; his preference for teenage boys; the fact that he had transmitted the HIV virus to a young man; and the fact that he had absconded several times and refused to cooperate with the staff at the hospital. Thus, the Government found that the involuntary placement of the applicant in hospital had been proportionate to the purpose of the measure, namely to prevent him from spreading the infectious disease.

49. The Court notes that the Government have not provided any examples of less severe measures which might have been considered for the applicant in the period from 16 February 1995 until 12 December 2001, but were apparently found to be insufficient to safeguard the public interest.

50. It is undisputed that the applicant failed to comply with the instruction issued by the county medical officer on 1 September 1994, which stated that he should visit his consulting physician again and keep to appointments set up by the county medical officer. Although he kept to three appointments with the county medical officer in September 1994 and one in November 1994, and received two home visits by the latter, on five occasions during October and November 1994 the applicant failed to appear as summoned.

51. Another of the practical instructions issued by the council medical officer on 1 September 1994 was that, if the applicant was to have a physical examination, an operation, a vaccination or a blood test or was bleeding for any reason, he was obliged to tell the relevant medical staff about his infection. Also, he was to inform his dentist about his HIV infection. In April 1999, before the County Administrative Court, the county medical officer stated that during the last two years, while on the run, the applicant had sought medical treatment twice and that it had been established that both times he had said that he had the HIV virus, as opposed to the period when he had absconded between September 1995 and May 1996, during which the applicant had failed on three occasions to inform medical staff about his virus.

52. Yet another of the practical instructions issued by the county medical officer on 1 September 1994 required the applicant to abstain from consuming such an amount of alcohol that his judgment would thereby be impaired and others put at risk of being infected with HIV. However, there were no instructions to abstain from alcohol altogether or to undergo treatment against alcoholism. Nor did the domestic courts justify the deprivation of the applicant's liberty with reference to his being an 'alcoholic' within the meaning of Article 5 § 1(e) and the requirements deriving from that provision.

53. Moreover, although the county medical officer stated before the County Administrative Court in February 1995 that, in his opinion, it was necessary for the applicant to consult a psychiatrist in order to alter his behaviour, undergoing psychiatric treatment was not among the practical instructions issued by the county medical officer on 1 September 1994. Nor did the domestic courts during the proceedings justify the deprivation of the applicant's liberty with reference to his being of 'unsound mind' within the meaning of Article 5 § 1(e) and the requirements deriving from that provision.

54. The instructions issued on 1 September 1994 prohibited the applicant from having sexual intercourse without first having informed his partner about his HIV infection. Also, he was to use a condom. The Court notes in this connection that, despite his being at large for most of the period from 16 February 1995 until 12 December 2001, there is no evidence or indication that during that period the applicant transmitted the HIV virus to anybody, or that he had sexual intercourse without first informing his partner about his HIV infection, or that he did not use a condom, or that he had any sexual relationship at all for that matter. It is true that the applicant infected the 19-year-old man with whom he had first had sexual contact in 1990. This was discovered in 1994, when the applicant himself became aware of his infection. However, there is no indication that the applicant transmitted the HIV virus to the young man as a result of intent or gross neglect, which in many of the Contracting States, including Sweden, would have been considered a criminal offence under the Criminal Code.

55. In these circumstances, the Court finds that the compulsory isolation of the applicant was not a last resort in order to prevent him from spreading the HIV virus because less severe measures had been considered and found to be insufficient to safeguard the public interest. Moreover, the Court considers that by extending over a period of almost seven years the order for the applicant's compulsory isolation, with the result that he was placed involuntarily in a hospital for almost one and a half years in total, the authorities failed to strike a fair balance between the need to ensure that the HIV virus did not spread and the applicant's right to liberty.

56. There has accordingly been a violation of Article 5 § 1 of the Convention.

...

FOR THESE REASONS, THE COURT UNANIMOUSLY

1. *Holds* that there has been a violation of Article 5(1) of the Convention;

NOTES

1 The Court was composed of President Costa and Judges: Baka, Cabral Barreto, Turmen, Ugrekhelidze, Fura-Sandstrom, and Jociene.

2 This was the first case where the Court examined, in detail, the infectious diseases ground of detention. The judgment clearly demonstrates that even in respect of a serious infection, such as HIV, compulsory hospitalisation is a measure of last resort. Such an approach is in conformity with the United Nations' *International Guidelines on HIV/Aids and Human Rights* (1998) which state that: '112. In exceptional cases involving objective judgments concerning deliberate and dangerous behaviour, restrictions on liberty may be imposed. Such exceptional

cases should be handled under ordinary provisions of public health, or criminal laws, with appropriate due process protection.'

Johnson v UK 1997-VII 2391, (1997) 27 EHRR 296
European Court of Human Rights

After being diagnosed as suffering from 'mental illness' and in accordance with the appropriate procedures under the Mental Health Act 1983, the applicant was transferred from Leicester Prison to Rampton Hospital, a maximum security psychiatric institution.

The applicant's detention was reviewed regularly by a Mental Health Review Tribunal. On the basis of psychiatric reports, in 1989 the Tribunal ruled that, although no longer suffering from mental illness, the applicant, having been a resident at Rampton for five years, had an unrealistic opinion of his ability to live on his own and that he required rehabilitation under medical supervision in a hostel environment. In the interests of the applicant himself and of the public, a conditional discharge was ordered, one condition of which was residence in an approved hostel under psychiatric supervision.

Discharge from Rampton proved impossible, however, because, despite considerable efforts, a suitable hostel that was willing to take the applicant could not be found. A trial period in a less secure hospital began in September 1990 but the applicant was returned to Rampton six weeks later after a drinking bout which lead to the assault of one patient and the terrorising of nursing staff. Thereafter, in the continued absence of a suitable hostel, the applicant remained in detention in Rampton until the Tribunal ordered his absolute discharge into the community in 1993.

JUDGMENT OF THE COURT

50. The applicant complained that his detention between 15 June 1989, the date when the Tribunal first found him to be no longer suffering from mental illness, and 12 January 1993, the date when his absolute discharge was ordered, was in violation of Article 5 § 1 of the Convention. . . .

58. The Court considers at the outset that it is appropriate to examine the lawfulness of the applicant's continued detention after 15 June 1989 under Article 5 § 1(e) alone of the Convention, even if the lawfulness of his detention, at least up until that date, could also possibly be grounded on Article 5 § 1(a) since it resulted from a 'conviction' by a 'competent court' within the meaning of that sub-paragraph. While the applicability of one ground listed in Article 5 § 1 does not necessarily preclude the applicability of another and a detention may be justified under more than one sub-paragraph of that provision (see the *Eriksen v Norway* judgment of 27 May 1997, *Reports of Judgments and Decisions* 1997-III, pp 861–2, § 76), it is to be noted that the applicant was detained at Rampton Hospital on the basis of a hospital and a restriction order without limit in time made under the Mental Health Act 1983 in order to undergo psychiatric treatment . . .

59. The Court also notes that those appearing before it have not contested that the applicant's continued detention was lawful under domestic law, having regard to the Tribunal's powers under section 73(2) and (7) of the 1983 Act to impose conditions on the discharge of patients who are no longer mentally ill within the meaning of section 1(2) of that Act and to defer a discharge until those conditions have been fulfilled. . . .

60. The Court stresses, however, that the lawfulness of the applicant's continued detention under domestic law is not in itself decisive. It must also be established that his detention after 15 June 1989 was in conformity with the purpose of Article 5 § 1 of the Convention, which is to prevent persons from

being deprived of their liberty in an arbitrary fashion (see, among many authorities, the *Wassink v Netherlands* judgment of 27 September 1990, Series A No 185-A, p 11, § 24) and with the aim of the restriction contained in sub-paragraph (e) (see the above-mentioned *Winterwerp* judgment, p 17, § 39). In this latter respect the Court recalls that, according to its established case-law, an individual cannot be considered to be of 'unsound mind' and deprived of his liberty unless the following three minimum conditions are satisfied: firstly, he must reliably be shown to be of unsound mind; secondly, the mental disorder must be of a kind or degree warranting compulsory confinement; thirdly, and of sole rele-vance to the case at issue, the validity of continued confinement depends upon the persistence of such a disorder (see the *Winterwerp* judgment cited above, pp 21–2, § 40; and the *Luberti v Italy* judgment of 23 February 1984, Series A No 75, pp 12–13, § 27).

61. By maintaining that the 1989 Tribunal was satisfied that he was no longer suffering from the mental illness which led to his committal to Rampton Hospital, Mr Johnson is arguing that the above-mentioned third condition as to the persistence of mental disorder was not fulfilled and he should as a consequence have been immediately and unconditionally released from detention.

The Court cannot accept that submission. In its view it does not automatically follow from a find-ing by an expert authority that the mental disorder which justified a patient's compulsory confine-ment no longer persists, that the latter must be immediately and unconditionally released into the community . . . .

62. It is to be recalled in this respect that the Court in its *Luberti* judgment (cited above, pp 13–15, § 29) accepted that the termination of the confinement of an individual who has previously been found by a court to be of unsound mind and to present a danger to society is a matter that concerns, as well as that individual, the community in which he will live if released. Having regard to the pressing nature of the interests at stake, and in particular the very serious nature of the offence committed by Mr Luberti when mentally ill, it was accepted in that case that the responsible authority was entitled to proceed with caution and needed some time to consider whether to terminate his confinement, even if the medical evidence pointed to his recovery.

63. In the view of the Court it must also be acknowledged that a responsible authority is entitled to exercise a similar measure of discretion in deciding whether in the light of all the relevant circum-stances and the interests at stake it would in fact be appropriate to order the immediate and absolute discharge of a person who is no longer suffering from the mental disorder which led to his confine-ment. That authority should be able to retain some measure of supervision over the progress of the person once he is released into the community and to that end make his discharge subject to condi-tions. It cannot be excluded either that the imposition of a particular condition may in certain circum-stances justify a deferral of discharge from detention, having regard to the nature of the condition and to the reasons for imposing it. It is, however, of paramount importance that appropriate safeguards are in place so as to ensure that any deferral of discharge is consonant with the purpose of Article 5 § 1 and with the aim of the restriction in sub-paragraph (e) (see paragraph 60 above) and, in particular, that discharge is not unreasonably delayed.

64. Having regard to the above considerations, the Court is of the opinion that the 1989 Tribunal could in the exercise of its judgment properly conclude that it was premature to order Mr Johnson's absolute and immediate discharge from Rampton Hospital. . . .

It was not . . . unreasonable for the Tribunal to consider, having regard to the views of Dr Wilson and Dr Cameron, that the applicant should be placed under psychiatric and social-worker supervision and required to undergo a period of rehabilitation in a hostel on account of the fact that 'the recurrence of mental illness requiring recall to hospital cannot be excluded' . . . . The Tribunal was also in principle justified in deferring the applicant's release in order to enable the authorities to locate a hostel which best suited his needs and provided him with the most appropriate conditions for his successful rehabilitation. . . .

66. However, while imposing the hostel residence requirement on the applicant and deferring his release until the arrangements had been made to its satisfaction, the Tribunal lacked the power to guarantee that the applicant would be relocated to a suitable post-discharge hostel within a reasonable period of time. The onus was on the authorities to secure a hostel willing to admit the applicant. It is to be observed that they were expected to proceed with all reasonable expedition in finalising the arrangements for a placement. . . . While the authorities made considerable efforts to this end, these efforts were frustrated by the reluctance of certain hostels to accept the applicant as well as by the latter's negative with respect to the options available. . . . They were also constrained by the limited number of available placements. Admittedly, a suitable hostel may have been located within a reasonable period of time had the applicant adopted a more positive approach to his rehabilitation. However, this cannot refute the conclusion that neither the Tribunal nor the authorities possessed the necessary powers to ensure that the condition could be implemented within a reasonable time. . . .

67. In these circumstances, it must be concluded that the imposition of the hostel residence condition by the June 1989 Tribunal led to the indefinite deferral of the applicant's release from Rampton Hospital, especially since the applicant was unwilling after October 1990 to co-operate further with the authorities in their efforts to secure a hostel, thereby excluding any possibility that the condition could be satisfied. While the 1990 and 1991 Tribunals considered the applicant's case afresh, they were obliged to order his continued detention since he had not yet fulfilled the terms of the conditional discharge imposed by the June 1989 Tribunal.

Having regard to the situation which resulted from the decision taken by the latter Tribunal and to the lack of adequate safeguards, including provision for judicial review to ensure that the applicant's release from detention would not be unreasonably delayed, it must be considered that his continued confinement after 15 June 1989 cannot be justified on the basis of Article 5 § 1(e) of the Convention (see paragraph 63 above).

For these reasons, the Court concludes that the applicant's continued detention after 15 June 1989 constituted a violation of Article 5 § 1 of the Convention . . . .

FOR THESE REASONS, THE COURT UNANIMOUSLY

1. Holds that there has been a breach of Article 5 § 1 of the Convention. . . .

NOTES

1 The Court was composed of President Ryssdal and Judges Gölcüklü, Spielmann, Valticos, Sir John Freeland, Baka, Kuris, Levits, and Van Dijk.

2 The three requirements justifying the detention of persons of 'unsound mind' (see para 60, judgment) were first set out by the Court in the *Winterwerp* case, below, p 319.

3 Although Article 5(1) does not guarantee a right to treatment (see the *Winterwerp* case, below, p 319), a person of 'unsound mind' must be detained in an appropriate institution. In *Aerts v Belgium* (1998) 29 EHRR 50, 1998 V 1939, there was a breach of Article 5(1) when there was some delay in finding the applicant an appropriate hospital. The Court stated:

46. . . . there must be some relationship between the ground of permitted deprivation of liberty relied on and the place and conditions of detention. In principle, the 'detention' of a person as a mental health patient will only be 'lawful' for the purposes of subparagraph (e) of paragraph 1 if effected in a hospital, clinic or other appropriate institution (see the *Ashingdane v UK* judgment of 28 May 1985, Series A No 93, p 21, § 44).

47. In the present case, on 15 January 1993, the Committals Chamber decided to order Mr Aerts's detention and stated that, pending a decision by the Mental Health Board designating the institution in which he was to be detained, he would be detained provisionally in the psychiatric wing of Lantin

Prison. On 22 March 1993 the Mental Health Board designed the Paifve Social Protection Centre as the place of detention. As there were no spare places at Paifve, the applicant continued to be detained at Lantin for seven months, his transfer not being effected until 27 October 1993. . . .

48. The Court notes that the length of provisional detention pending transfer is not specified by any statutory or other provision. Nevertheless, it must determine whether, in view of the purpose of the detention order, the continuation of provisional detention for such a lengthy period can be regarded as lawful.

49. The reports of 10 and 15 January 1990, which reflect the situation obtaining in 1990 . . . , the CPT's [the European Committee for the Prevention of Torture's] report . . . and the observations on that report made by the Belgian Government . . . show sufficiently clearly that the Lantin psychiatric wing could not be regarded as an institution appropriate for the detention of persons of unsound mind, the latter not receiving either regular medical attention or a therapeutic environment. On 2 August 1993, in response to an application for leave lodged by Mr Aerts, the Mental Health Board expressed the view that the situation was harmful to the applicant, who was not receiving the treatment required by the condition that had given rise to his detention. Moreover, the Government did not deny that the applicant's treatment in Lantin had been unsatisfactory from a therapeutic point of view. The proper relationship between the aim of the detention and the conditions in which it took place was therefore deficient.

See also on the detention of persons of 'unsound mind' *Ashingdane v UK*, A.93 (1985) 7 EHRR 528.

4 A unanimous Chamber found the English practice of detaining mentally incapacitated persons as 'informal' patients under common law failed to satisfy the procedural safeguards inherent within Article 5(1) in *H.L. v UK*, judgment of 5 October 2004. The applicant had suffered from autism since his birth in 1949. He cannot speak and has limited understanding. Therefore, he is unable to consent/object to medical treatment. He is often agitated and prone to self-harm. For over thirty years he was cared for in a national health service hospital (Bournewood). Since 1977 his responsible medical officer has been Dr M (a Consultant Psychiatrist). In 1994 he was discharged to reside with paid carers, though the hospital remained responsible for his care and treatment. H.L. attended a weekly day-care centre run by his local authority. On 22 July 1997, whilst at the day-care centre, he became very agitated (hitting his head against the wall and with his fists). His carers could not be contacted so the centre called a local doctor who administered a sedative to H.L. He was then taken to the accident and emergency unit of the hospital where an Acting Consultant Psychiatrist assessed H.L. as requiring in-patient treatment. H.L. was moved, with the physical support of two members of staff, to the hospital's intensive behavioural unit. H.L. made no attempt to leave the unit. Dr M decided not to order the compulsory detention of H.L. under the Mental Health Act 1983 as he had not resisted his admission to the hospital. He was therefore, admitted as an 'informal' patient. Dr M decided to discourage H.L.'s carers from visiting him to prevent him, and them, becoming distressed. In August 1997 Dr M reported to the local health authority that the hospital was coming to the view that H.L. suffered from a mood disorder as well as autism and that his immediate discharge would be against medical opinion. Another Consultant Psychiatrist, who examined H.L. on behalf of his carers, reached similar conclusions but recommended closer cooperation between H.L.'s doctors and his carers. In September 1997 the applicant, via his cousin, applied for judicial review of the hospital's decision to admit him in July. The High Court rejected the application finding that H.L. had been informally admitted to the hospital and the common law principle of necessity had been satisfied. On appeal the Court of Appeal found that as the applicant did not have the capacity to consent to his admission he had been detained unlawfully. On the same day a doctor ordered H.L.'s compulsory detention under the Mental Health Act 1983. That decision was confirmed by two other doctors in accordance with the statutory procedure two days later. At the beginning of November 1997 H.L.'s carers were allowed to visit him for the first time since his hospitalization. In December 1997 the hospital formally discharged H.L. to his carers. Subsequently, the House of Lords allowed an appeal by the health authority against the judgment of the Court of Appeal.

Before the Court the applicant contended that his detention in the hospital between July and October 1997 as an 'informal' patient violated Article 5(1) as he was not of unsound mind, the common law principle of necessity lacked precision and there had been inadequate safeguards against arbitrary detention. The Government responded that the admission of informal patients (who were incapacitated) respected their dignity and the authorities wished to avoid having to utilize formal statutory procedures of compulsory committal wherever possible. The Court considered that H.L. had been deprived of his liberty, for the purposes of Article 5(1) because:

91. ...the health care professionals treating and managing the applicant exercised complete and effective control over his care and movements from the moment he presented acute behavioural problems on 22 July 1997 to the date he was compulsorily detained on 29 October 1997.

Applying the well-established test, derived from *Winterwerp v Netherlands*, the Court found that he was of unsound mind as the evidence established H.L.:

101. ... to have been suffering from a mental disorder of a kind or degree warranting compulsory confinement which persisted during his detention between 22 July and 5 December 1997.

The Court did not reach a conclusion in regard to the applicant's argument that the common law doctrine of necessity was too vague to satisfy the requirement of reasonable foreseeability under Article 5(1). This was because the judges found the common law provided insufficient safeguards against the arbitrary detention of informal patients.

120. In this latter respect, the Court finds striking the lack of any fixed procedural rules by which the admission and detention of compliant incapacitated persons is conducted. The contrast between this dearth of regulation and the extensive network of safeguards applicable to psychiatric committals covered by the 1983 [Mental Health] Act is, in the Court's view, significant.

In particular and most obviously, the Court notes the lack of any formalised admission procedures which indicate who can propose admission, for what reasons and on the basis of what kind of medical and other assessments and conclusions. There is no requirement to fix the exact purpose of admission (for example, for assessment or for treatment) and, consistently, no limits in terms of time, treatment or care attach to that admission. Nor is there any specific provision requiring a continuing clinical assessment of the persistence of a disorder warranting detention. The nomination of a representative of a patient who could make certain objections and applications on his or her behalf is a procedural protection accorded to those committed involuntarily under the 1983 Act and which would be of equal importance for patients who are legally incapacitated and have, as in the present case, extremely limited communication abilities.

121. As a result of the lack of procedural regulation and limits, the Court observes that the hospital's health care professionals assumed full control of the liberty and treatment of a vulnerable incapacitated individual solely on the basis of their own clinical assessments completed as and when they considered fit ... While the Court does not question the good faith of those professionals or that they acted in what they considered to be the applicant's best interests, the very purpose of procedural safeguards

is to protect individuals against any 'misjudgements and professional lapses' (Lord Steyn [in the House of Lords judgment]).

. . .

123. The Government's submission that detention could not be arbitrary within the meaning of Article 5 § 1 because of the possibility of a later review of its lawfulness disregards the distinctive and cumulative protections offered by paragraphs 1 and 4 of Article 5 of the Convention: the former strictly regulates the circumstances in which one's liberty can be taken away whereas the latter requires a review of its legality thereafter.

124. The Court therefore finds that this absence of procedural safeguards fails to protect against arbitrary deprivations of liberty on grounds of necessity and, consequently, to comply with the essential purpose of Article 5 § 1 of the Convention. On this basis, the Court finds that there has been a violation of Article 5 § 1 of the Convention.

The domestic rights of vulnerable persons were enhanced by the Mental Capacity Act 2005. Furthermore, in June 2006, the Department of Health published proposals to add further statutory measures of protection for persons in circumstances similar to those of H.L. (*Bournewood Briefing Sheet*).

....

Witold Litwa v Poland judgment of 4 April 2000
European Court of Human Rights

Accompanied by a friend, the applicant, whose sight was severely impaired, went with his guide dog to the Post Office to check his post box. Finding that it was open and empty, he complained to the Post Office clerks, who then called the police alleging that the applicant was drunk and had behaved offensively. Since the applicant smelt of alcohol, the police took him to the Krakow Sobering-up Centre. After being medically examined by a doctor and assessed to be 'moderately intoxicated', he was detained at the Centre for six and a half hours. The Commission was of the opinion, by 21 votes to 5, that the detention was justified under Article 5(1)(e) on the basis that the applicant was lawfully detained as an alcoholic.

JUDGMENT OF THE COURT

57. The Court affirms that, in ascertaining the Convention meaning of the term 'alcoholics', it will be guided by Articles 31 to 33 of the Vienna Convention of 23 May 1969 on the Law of Treaties, as it has repeatedly been in other cases where an interpretation of the Convention was required (see, for instance, the *Johnston v Ireland* judgment of 18 December 1986, Series A No 112, p 24, § 51 et seq and the *Lithgow v UK* judgment of 8 July 1986, Series A No 102, p 48 § 114 *in fine* and p 49 § 117).

58. In that respect, the Court reiterates that, in the way it is presented in the general rule of interpretation laid down in Article 31 of the Vienna Convention, the process of discovering and ascertaining the true meaning of the terms of the treaty is a unity, a single combined operation. This general rule, closely integrated, places on the same footing the various elements enumerated in the four paragraphs of that Article (see the *Golder v UK* judgment of 21 February 1975, Series A No 18, p 14, §§ 29–30).

59. The sequence in which those elements are listed in Article 31 of the Vienna Convention stipulates, however, the order which the process of interpretation of the treaty should follow. That process must start from ascertaining the ordinary meaning of the terms of a treaty—in their context and in the light of its object and purpose, as laid down in paragraph 1 of Article 31. This is particularly so in relation to the provisions which, like Article 5 § 1 of the Convention, refer to exceptions to a general rule and

which, for this very reason, cannot be given an extensive interpretation (see the *De Wilde, Ooms and Versyp v Belgium* judgment of 18 June 1971, Series A No 12, p 37, § 68 and the *Winterwerp v Netherlands* judgment of 24 October 1979, Series A No 33, p 16, § 37).

60. The Court observes that the word 'alcoholics', in its common usage, denotes persons who are addicted to alcohol. On the other hand, in Article 5 § 1 of the Convention this term is found in a context that includes a reference to several other categories of individuals, that is, persons spreading infectious diseases, persons of unsound mind, drug addicts and vagrants. There is a link between all those persons in that they may be deprived of their liberty either in order to be given medical treatment or because of considerations dictated by social policy, or on both medical and social grounds. It is therefore legitimate to conclude from this context that a predominant reason why the Convention allows the persons mentioned in paragraph 1(e) of Article 5 to be deprived of their liberty is not only that they are dangerous for public safety but also that their own interests may necessitate their detention (see the *Guzzardi v Italy* judgment of 6 November 1980, Series A No 39, p 37, § 98 *in fine*).

61. This *ratio legis* indicates how the expression 'alcoholics' should be understood in the light of the object and purpose of Article 5 § 1(e) of the Convention. It indicates that the object and purpose of this provision cannot be interpreted as only allowing the detention of 'alcoholics' in the limited sense of persons in a clinical state of 'alcoholism'. The Court considers that, under Article 5 § 1(e) of the Convention, persons who are not medically diagnosed as 'alcoholics', but whose conduct and behaviour under the influence of alcohol pose a threat to public order or themselves, can be taken into custody for the protection of the public or their own interests, such as their health or personal safety.

62. That does not mean that Article 5 § 1(e) of the Convention can be interpreted as permitting the detention of an individual merely because of his alcohol intake. However, the Court considers that in the text of Article 5 there is nothing to suggest that this provision prevents that measure from being applied by the State to an individual abusing alcohol, in order to limit the harm caused by alcohol to himself and the public, or to prevent dangerous behaviour after drinking. On this point, the Court observes that there can be no doubt that the harmful use of alcohol poses a danger to society and that a person who is in a state of intoxication may pose a danger to himself and others, regardless of whether or not he is addicted to alcohol.

63. The Court further finds that this meaning of the term 'alcoholics' is confirmed by the preparatory work of the Convention. . . . In that regard, the Court observes that in the commentary on the preliminary draft Convention it is recorded that the text of the relevant Article covered the right of the signatory States to take measures to combat vagrancy and 'drunkenness' ('*l'alcoolisme*' in French). It is further recorded that the Committee of Experts had no doubt that this could be agreed 'since such restrictions were justified by the requirements of public morality and order'.

64. On this basis, the Court concludes that the applicant's detention fell within the ambit of Article 5 § 1(e) of the Convention. . . .

72. The Court reiterates that under Article 5 of the Convention any deprivation of liberty must be 'lawful', which includes a requirement that it must be effected 'in accordance with a procedure prescribed by law'. On this point, the Convention essentially refers to national law and lays down an obligation to comply with its substantive and procedural provisions.

73. It also requires that any measure depriving the individual of his liberty must be compatible with the purpose of Article 5, namely to protect the individual from arbitrariness (see the *K-F v Germany* judgment of 27 November 1997, *Reports* 1997-VII, p 2674, § 63).

74. In the present case, the Court notes that there is no dispute as to the fact that the police, when arresting the applicant and taking him to the sobering-up centre, followed the procedure provided for by Section 40 of the Law of 26 October 1982. The Court considers therefore that the applicant's detention had a legal basis in Polish law.

75. The Court further notes that the essential statutory conditions for the application of the measures laid down in Section 40 of the Law of 26 October 1982 are, first, that the person concerned is intoxicated and, second, that either his behaviour is offensive or his condition is such as to endanger his own or other persons' life or health. . . .

76. It is not for the Court to review whether the domestic authorities have taken correct decisions under Polish law. Its task is to establish whether the applicant's detention was 'the lawful detention' of an 'alcoholic', within the autonomous meaning of the Convention as the Court has explained it above in paragraphs 57 to 63.

77. In this respect, the Court entertains serious doubts as to whether it can be said that the applicant behaved in such a way, influenced by alcohol, that he posed a threat to the public or himself, or that his own health, well-being or personal safety were endangered. The Court's doubts are reinforced by the rather trivial factual basis for the detention and the fact that the applicant is almost blind.

78. The Court reiterates that a necessary element of the 'lawfulness' of the detention within the meaning of Article 5 § 1(e) is the absence of arbitrariness. The detention of an individual is such a serious measure that it is only justified where other, less severe measures have been considered and found to be insufficient to safeguard the individual or public interest which might require that the person concerned be detained. That means that it does not suffice that the deprivation of liberty is executed in conformity with national law but it must also be necessary in the circumstances.

79. However, in the applicant's case no consideration appears to have been given to the fact that Section 40 of the Law of 26 October 1982 provides for several different measures which may be applied to an intoxicated person, among which detention in a sobering-up centre is the most extreme one. Indeed, under that section, an intoxicated person does not necessarily have to be deprived of his liberty since he may well be taken by the police to a public-care establishment or to his place of residence. . . .

80. The absence of any such considerations in the present case, although expressly foreseen by the domestic law, has finally persuaded the Court that the applicant's detention cannot be considered 'lawful' under Article 5 § 1(e). There has therefore been a breach of that provision. . . .

FOR THESE REASONS THE COURT

Holds by six votes to one that there has been a violation of Article 5 § 1 of the Convention.
. . . .

NOTES

1   The Court was composed of President of the Chamber Fischbach and Judges Conforti, Bonello, Stráznická, Tsatsa-Nivolovska, Baka, and Levits. Judge Baka issued a dissenting opinion in which he agreed with the Court's interpretation of the term 'alcoholics' but he considered that there had been an adequate basis for the detention of the applicant (he had been causing a public nuisance and a doctor diagnosed him as being moderately intoxicated).

2   The *Litwa* concept of 'alcoholics' was subsequently applied in *Hilda Hafsteinsdottir v Iceland*, judgment of 8 June 2004. The applicant was a woman in her forties who developed a habit of going, when intoxicated, to her local police station and verbally/physically abusing the police officers! On each occasion she was arrested, detained overnight and then released without charge. She contended that she had suffered violations of Article 5(1) as the deprivation of her liberty had not been authorised under any statutory provisions. The Court found:

42. . . . it established that the applicant's conduct and behaviour were under the strong influence of alcohol and could reasonably be considered to entail a threat to public order. It is further satisfied that

the purpose of the measures was to avert that kind of threat. In other words, the matter was covered by the notion of 'alcoholic' in sub-paragraph (e), which is therefore applicable.

As to whether her detention was 'lawful' the Court stated that:

51. . . . where deprivation of liberty is concerned it is particularly important that the general principle of legal certainty be satisfied. It is therefore essential that the conditions for deprivation of liberty under domestic law be clearly defined and that the law itself be foreseeable in its application, so that it meets the standard of 'lawfulness' set by the Convention, a standard which requires that all law be sufficiently accessible and precise to allow the person—if necessary with appropriate advice—to foresee, to a degree that is reasonable in the circumstances the consequences which a given action may entail . . .

A large majority of the Court, five votes to two, concluded that:

56. . . . at the time of the six disputed events, in one essential respect, namely the duration of the relevant type of detention, the scope and the manner of exercise of the police's discretion were governed by administrative practice alone and, in the absence of precise statutory provisions or case-law, lacked the necessary regulatory framework (see the *Kruslin v France* and *Huvig v France* judgments of 24 April 1990, Series A No 176-A and –B, respectively §§ 35 and 34). Moreover, it appears that, at the time of the first event in January 1988, before the entry into force on 1 July 1988 of the 1988 Rules, not only the duration of the detention but also the decision to detain suffered from that defect.

Moreover the Court is not convinced that the more detailed provisions contained in the above-mentioned instructions had been made accessible to the public.

For these reasons, the Court is not satisfied that the law, as applicable at the material time, was sufficiently precise and accessible to avoid all risk of arbitrariness. Accordingly, it finds that the applicant's deprivation of liberty was not 'lawful' within the autonomous meaning of Article 5 § 1 of the Convention, which has therefore been violated.

The judgments in *Litwa* and *Hafsteinsdottir* demonstrate the Court adopting a broad and purposive interpretation of the term 'alcoholics', but this is counterbalanced by the strict examination of the question whether the detention of such persons was 'lawful', i.e. was it a proportional response to the danger those persons posed to others or themselves and was the domestic law sufficiently clear/accessible. This is a well-balanced analytical framework that seeks to protect the interests of both society and intoxicated persons.

3   On the detention of vagrants consistently with Article 5(1)(e), see the *Vagrancy* cases, below p 312.

Article 5(1)(f): Deportation or extradition

Bozano v France A.111 (1986) 9 EHRR 297
European Court of Human Rights

The applicant, an Italian national, was tried in absentia by an Italian court for abduction and murder and sentenced to life imprisonment. Three years later, he was arrested in France by the police, but a formal request for extradition was refused by the Limoges Court of Appeal as the conviction in absentia was incompatible with French public policy. The applicant remained in residence in the Limoges area awaiting trial by the French courts for other offences. On the day that an order was made committing him for trial, the applicant was abducted by French policemen, served with a deportation order (which was over one month old) and forcibly taken to the Swiss border where he was handed over to the Swiss authorities. Following proceedings in Switzerland, he was extradited to Italy, under a standing agreement between the two countries, where he was imprisoned for the conviction by the Italian courts.

After his abduction, the applicant's lawyers pursued various remedies in the French courts, including the summoning of the Minister of the Interior before the Paris *tribunal de grande instance* where they sought an injunction requiring him to apply for the applicant's return. Although the tribunal held that it had no competence to meet the request, it noted the 'manifest and very serious irregularities' behind what appeared 'not a straightforward expulsion on the basis of the deportation order, but ... a prearranged handing over to the Swiss police ...'. The Limoges Administrative Court subsequently quashed the deportation order on the basis that the Minister of the Interior had committed 'a manifest error of judgment' and the administrative authorities an 'abuse of powers'.

The Commission concluded, by eleven votes to two, that there had been a violation of Article 5(1).

JUDGMENT OF THE COURT

58. Where the Convention refers directly back to domestic law, as in Article 5, compliance with such law is an integral part of Contracting States' 'engagements' and the Court is accordingly competent to satisfy itself of such compliance where relevant (Article 19); the scope of its task in this connection, however, is subject to limits inherent in the logic of the European system of protection, since it is in the first place for the national authorities, notably the courts, to interpret and apply domestic law (see, *inter alia* and *mutatis mutandis*, the *Winterwerp* judgment of 24 October 1976 Series A No 33, p 20, § 46).

Several points of French law have been disputed in the instant case. Even if the arguments of those appearing before the Court and the other information in the file are not absolutely conclusive in the Court's view, they provide sufficient material for the Court to have the gravest doubts whether the contested deprivation of liberty satisfied the legal requirements in the respondent State.

59. 'Lawfulness', in any event, also implies absence of any arbitrariness. ... In this respect, the Court attaches great weight to the circumstances in which the applicant was forcibly conveyed to the Swiss border.

Firstly, the relevant authorities waited for more than a month before serving the deportation order of 17 September 1979 on Mr Bozano, although there was no difficulty about finding him in Limoges, where he was in pre-trial detention until 19 September and subsequently under judicial supervision. ... The authorities thus prevented him from making any effective use of the remedies theoretically available to him.

What is more serious is that the authorities gave every appearance of having wanted to ensure that Mr Bozano did not find out about the action they were preparing to take against him, so that they could the more effectively face him with a *fait accompli* thereafter. ...

To this must be added the suddenness with which the applicant was apprehended by the police on the evening of 26 October and, more striking still, the way in which the Minister of the Interior's decision was carried out. From what their own Agent himself indicated, the Government had contacted only Switzerland, a State which had an extradition treaty with Italy and where since April 1976 there had been a warrant out for the applicant's arrest with a view to extradition, as was recorded in the Swiss Police Gazette (*Moniteur suisse de police*). ... Mr Bozano was not even able to speak to his wife or his lawyer and at no time was any offer made to him that he should be expelled—if necessary under supervision—across the frontier of his choice or even across the nearest frontier, the Spanish border. On the contrary, he was forced to travel from Limoges to the customs post at Moillesulaz—some twelve hours and several hundred kilometres away—, handcuffed and flanked by policemen who in due course handed him over to Swiss colleagues. ... Mr Bozano's precise, detailed description of the events strongly suggests that this is what happened. His account seems plausible in the absence of any evidence or explanation to the contrary. . . .

60. Viewing the circumstances of the case as a whole and having regard to the volume of material pointing in the same direction, the Court consequently concludes that the applicant's deprivation of liberty in the night of 26 to 27 October 1975 was neither 'lawful', within the meaning of Article 5 § 1(f), nor compatible with the 'right to security of person'. Depriving Mr Bozano of his liberty in this way amounted in fact to a disguised form of extradition designed to circumvent the negative ruling of 15 May 1979 by the Indictment Division of the Limoges Court of Appeal, and not to 'detention' necessary in the ordinary course of 'action . . . taken with a view to deportation'. The findings of the presiding judge of the Paris *tribunal de grande instance*—even if *obiter*—and of the Limoges Administrative Court, even if that court had only to determine the lawfulness of the order of 17 September 1979, are of the utmost importance in the Court's view; they illustrate the vigilance displayed by the French courts. . . .

FOR THESE REASONS, THE COURT UNANIMOUSLY

. . .

Holds that there has been a breach of Article 5(1) of the Convention.

. . .

NOTES

1   The Court was composed of President Ryssdal and Judges Cremona, Pinheiro Farinha, Pettiti, Sir Vincent Evans, Russo, and Gersing.

2   The *Bozano* case concerned the 'lawfulness' of the detention pending deportation. Although the grounds for deporting or extraditing a person who is detained pending his removal may not be challenged under Article 5, the unreasonable length of time taken to complete deportation or extradition proceedings may mean that the detention is not justified by Article 5(1)(f). In *Quinn v France*, A.311 (1995) 21 EHRR 529, the applicant was detained for almost two years while extradition proceedings were pending. The applicant alleged that the reason for this was to keep him in detention after a French court had ordered his release on bail in connection with criminal proceedings against him which later led to his conviction and a sentence of imprisonment, which he completed before he was extradited. The Court found a breach of Article 5(1). Holding that the detention was not justified by Article 5(1)(f), it stated:

47. . . . Unlike the Commission, the Court does not discern in the present case any evidence to suggest that the detention pending extradition pursued an aim other than that for which it was ordered and that it was pre-trial detention in disguise. In particular the circumstances of Mr Quinn's arrest and the fact that proceedings were conducted concurrently cannot in themselves warrant the conclusion that there was abuse, for purposes relating to national law, of the extradition procedure and accordingly that the detention ordered in response to the request of the Geneva investigating judge was unlawful.

48. The Court notes nevertheless that the applicant's detention with a view to extradition was unusually long. He was detained in connection with the extradition proceedings from 4 August 1989 to 10 July 1991, almost two years. . . . Thereafter he served the sentence imposed by the Paris Court of Appeal until 24 September 1992, on which date he was surrendered to the Swiss authorities pursuant to the order of 24 January 1991.

It is clear from the wording of both the French and the English versions of Article 5 § 1(f) that deprivation of liberty under this sub-paragraph will be justified only for as long as extradition proceedings are being conducted. It follows that if such proceedings are not being prosecuted with due diligence, the detention will cease to be justified under Article 5 § 1(f). The Court notes that, at the different stages of the extradition proceedings, there were delays of sufficient length to render the total duration of those proceedings excessive: the first decision on the merits, a preliminary decision, was given on 2 November 1989, three months after the applicant had been placed in detention pending extradition, and the extradition order was not made until 24 January 1991, ten months after the Indictment Division's favourable opinion. . . . The remedies of which Mr Quinn availed himself over this period (three appeals on points of law against the decisions dismissing applications for release and one appeal on points of law against the Indictment Division's opinion) . . . did not significantly delay the proceedings.

The detention with a view to extradition continued until 10 July 1991, well after the adoption of the extradition order, as the applicant's surrender to the Swiss authorities was postponed, in accordance with Article 19 § 1 of the European Convention on Extradition, on account of the criminal proceedings conducted in France at the same time. It is not the Court's role to determine what measures the national authorities should have taken in these circumstances to ensure that the detention pending extradition, which had already exceeded a reasonable time by 24 January 1991, did not last even hours after the Indictment Division's decision directing that he be released 'forthwith', without that decision being notified to him or any move being made to commence its execution.

Mr Quinn's continued detention on 4 August 1989 was clearly not covered by subparagraph (c) of paragraph 1 of Article 5 and did not fall within the scope of any other of the sub-paragraphs of that provision.

3   In contrast, the detention of the applicant for three and a half years pending deportation in *Chahal v UK* (1996) 23 EHRR 413, 1996-IV 1864, did not prevent the detention being justifiable under Article 5(1)(f). There was, however, a breach of Article 5(4): see below, p 316. For the facts of the case, see above, p 203. On compliance with Article 5(1)(f), the Court stated:

115. . . . As regards the decisions taken by the Secretary of State to refuse asylum, it does not consider that the periods (that is, 16 August 1990–27 March 1991 and 2 December 1991–1 June 1992) were excessive, bearing in mind the detailed and careful consideration required for the applicant's request for political asylum and the opportunities afforded to the latter to make representations and submit information. . . .

116. In connection with the judicial review proceedings before the national courts, it is noted that Mr Chahal's first application was made on 9 August 1991 and that a decision was reached on it by Mr Justice Popplewell on 2 December 1991. He made a second application on 16 July 1992, which was heard between 18 and 21 December 1992, judgment being given on 12 February 1993. The Court of Appeal dismissed the appeal against this decision on 22 October 1993 and refused him leave to appeal to the House of Lords. The House of Lords similarly refused leave to appeal on 3 March 1994. . . .

117. As the Court has observed in the context of Article 3, Mr Chahal's case involves considerations of an extremely serious and weighty nature. It is neither in the interests of the individual applicant nor in the general public interest in the administration of justice that such decisions be taken hastily, without due regard to all the relevant issues and evidence.

Against this background, and bearing in mind what was at stake for the applicant and the interest that he had in his claims being thoroughly examined by the courts, none of the periods complained of can be regarded as excessive, taken either individually or in combination. Accordingly, there has been no violation of Article 5 § 1 (f) of the Convention on account of the diligence, or lack of it, with which the domestic procedures were conducted.

118. It also falls to the Court to examine whether Mr Chahal's detention was 'lawful' for the purposes of Article 5 § 1(f), with particular reference to the safeguards provided by the national system. . . .

119. There is no doubt that Mr Chahal's detention was lawful under national law and was effected 'in accordance with a procedure prescribed by law'. . . . However, in view of the extremely long period during which Mr Chahal has been detained, it is also necessary to consider whether there existed sufficient guarantees against arbitrariness.

120. In this context, the Court observes that the applicant has been detained since 16 August 1990 on the ground, essentially, that successive Secretaries of State have maintained that, in view of the threat to national security represented by him, he could not safely be released. … The applicant has, however, consistently denied that he posed any threat whatsoever to national security, and has given reasons in support of this denial. …

121. The Court further notes that, since the Secretaries of State asserted that national security was involved, the domestic courts were not in a position effectively to control whether the decisions to keep Mr Chahal in detention were justified, because the full material on which these decisions were based was not made available to them. …

122. However, in the context of Article 5 § 1 of the Convention, the advisory panel procedure … provided an important safeguard against arbitrariness. This panel, which included experienced judicial figures … was able fully to review the evidence relating to the national security threat represented by the applicant. Although its report has never been disclosed, at the hearing before the Court the Government indicated that the panel had agreed with the Home Secretary that Mr Chahal ought to be deported on national security grounds. The Court considers that this procedure provided an adequate guarantee that there were at least prima facie grounds for believing that, if Mr Chahal were at liberty, national security would be put at risk and thus that the executive had not acted arbitrarily when it ordered him to be kept in detention.

123. In conclusion, the Court recalls that Mr Chahal has undoubtedly been detained for a length of time which is bound to give rise to serious concern. However, in view of the exceptional circumstances of the case and the facts that the national authorities have acted with due diligence throughout the deportation proceedings against him and that there were sufficient guarantees against the arbitrary deprivations of his liberty, this detention complied with the requirements of Article 5 § 1(f).

4   A unanimous chamber of the full-time Court found that the use of deception by public authorities to secure the attendance at a police station of illegal immigrants, so that the latter could be arrested and detained pending deportation was a breach of Article 5(1) in *Conka v Belgium*, judgment of 5 February 2002. The applicants were a family of Slovakian nationals of Roma ethnicity. Their claims for political asylum in Belgium had been rejected but the applicants did not leave that country. Therefore, the authorities planned a large-scale operation to deport many Slovakian Roma living illegally in Ghent back to Slovakia. The Roma were each sent a letter inviting them to attend Ghent police station to enable their files to be completed. At the station the Roma were arrested and, whilst some were released, seventy, including the applicants, were detained and then deported a few days later.

38. The Court notes that it is common ground that the applicants were arrested so that they could be deported from Belgium. Article 5 § 1(f) of the Convention is thus applicable in the instant case. Admittedly, the applicants contest the necessity of their arrest for that purpose; however, Article 5 § 1(f) does not require that the detention of a person against whom action is being taken with a view to deportation be reasonably considered necessary, for example to prevent his committing an offence or fleeing. In this respect, Article 5 § 1(f) provides a different level of protection from Article 5 § 1(c): all that is required under sub-paragraph (f) is that 'action is being taken with a view to deportation' (see *Chahal v the United Kingdom*, judgment of 15 November 1996, *Reports of Judgments and Decisions* 1996-V, p 1862, § 112).

39. Where the 'lawfulness' of detention is in issue, including the question whether 'a procedure prescribed by law' has been followed, the Convention refers essentially to the obligation to conform to the substantive and procedural rules of national law, but it requires in addition that any deprivation of liberty should be in keeping with the purpose of Article 5, namely to protect the individual from arbitrariness (see, among other authorities, *Bozano v France*, judgment of 18 December 1986, Series A No 111, p 23, § 54, and *Chahal*, cited above, p 1864, § 118).

40. In the present case, the applicants received a written notice at the end of September 1999 inviting them to attend Ghent police station on 1 October to 'enable the file concerning their application for asylum to be completed'. On their arrival at the police station they were served with an order to leave the territory dated 29 September 1999 and a decision for their removal to Slovakia and for their arrest for that purpose. A few hours later they were taken to a closed transit centre at Steenokkerzeel.

41. The Court notes that, according to the Government, while the wording of the notice was admittedly unfortunate, as had indeed been publicly recognised by the Minister of the Interior . . . that did not suffice to vitiate the entire arrest procedure, or to warrant its being qualified as an abuse of power.

While the Court has reservations about the compatibility of such practices with Belgian law, particularly as the practice in the instant case was not reviewed by a competent national court, the Convention requires that any measure depriving an individual of his liberty must be compatible with the purpose of Article 5, namely to protect the individual from arbitrariness (see paragraph 39 above). Although the Court by no means excludes its being legitimate for the police to use stratagems in order, for instance, to counter criminal activities more effectively, acts whereby the authorities seek to gain the trust of asylum-seekers with a view to arresting and subsequently deporting them may be found to contravene the general principles stated or implicit in the Convention.

In that regard, there is every reason to consider that while the wording of the notice was 'unfortunate', it was not the result of inadvertence; on the contrary, it was chosen deliberately in order to secure the compliance of the largest possible number of recipients. At the hearing, counsel for the Government referred in that connection to a 'little ruse', which the authorities had knowingly used to ensure that the 'collective repatriation' they had decided to arrange was successful.

42. The Court reiterates that the list of exceptions to the right to liberty secured in Article 5 § 1 is an exhaustive one and only a narrow interpretation of those exceptions is consistent with the aim of that provision (see, *mutatis mutandis*, *K.-F. v Germany*, judgment of 27 November 1997, *Reports* 1997-VII, p. 2975, § 70). In the Court's view, that requirement must also be reflected in the reliability of communications such as those sent to the applicants, irrespective of whether the recipients are lawfully present in the country or not. It follows that, even as regards overstayers, a conscious decision by the authorities to facilitate or improve the effectiveness of a planned operation for the expulsion of aliens by misleading them about the purpose of a notice so as to make it easier to deprive them of their liberty is not compatible with Article 5.

. . .

Consequently, there has been a violation of Article 5 § 1 of the Convention.

The above judgment also discloses that States have wider powers of arrest/detention in respect of persons arrested/detained under Article 5(1)(f) than with regard to suspected criminals arrested/detained under Article 5(1)(c).

5   A Chamber held that States are not required to justify the necessity of detaining a person claiming asylum whilst their claim was being processed through an expedited process in *Saadi v United Kingdom*, judgment of 11 July 2006. The applicant was detained in Oakington Reception Centre for seven days whilst his claim was considered via a fast-track procedure.

44. . . . Accordingly, and this finding does no more than apply to the first limb of Article 5 § 1(f) the ruling the Court has already made as regards the second limb of the provision, there is no requirement in Article 5 § 1(f) that the detention of a person to prevent his effecting an unauthorised entry into the country be reasonably considered necessary, for example to prevent his committing an offence or fleeing. All that is required is that the detention should be a genuine part of the process to determine whether the individual should be granted immigration clearance and/or asylum, and that it should not otherwise be arbitrary, for example on account of its length.

The majority (of four) determined that the applicant's detention had not been excessive and therefore no breach of Article 5(1)(f) had occurred. Whereas, the three dissentients believed that as the applicant had been granted temporary admission to the UK for a few days prior to his detention at Oakington, he was no longer liable to be detained under Article 5(1)(f) as a person effecting an 'unauthorized entry' to the country.

Article 5(2): Reasons for detention

Fox, Campbell and Hartley v UK A.182 (1990) 13 EHRR 157
European Court of Human Rights

For the facts of this case, see above, p 271 under Article 5(1)(c).

JUDGMENT OF THE COURT

40. Paragraph 2 of Article 5 contains the elementary safeguard that any person arrested should know why he is being deprived of his liberty. This provision is an integral part of the scheme of protection afforded by Article 5: by virtue of paragraph 2 any person arrested must be told, in simple, non-technical language that he can understand, the essential legal and factual grounds for his arrest, so as to be able, if he sees fit, to apply to a court to challenge its lawfulness in accordance with paragraph 4. . . . Whilst this information must be conveyed 'promptly' (in French: 'dans le plus court delai'), it need not be related in its entirety by the arresting officer at the very moment of the arrest. Whether the content and promptness of the information conveyed were sufficient is to be assessed in each case according to its special features. . . .

41. On being taken into custody, Mr Fox, Ms Campbell and Mr Hartley were simply told by the arresting officer that they were being arrested under section 11(1) of the 1978 Act on suspicion of being terrorists. . . . This bare indication of the legal basis for the arrest, taken on its own, is insufficient for the purposes of Article 5 § 2, as the Government conceded.

However, following their arrest all of the applicants were interrogated by the police about their suspected involvement in specific criminal acts and their suspected membership of proscribed organisations. . . . There is no ground to suppose that these interrogations were not such as to enable the applicants to understand why they had been arrested. The reasons why they were suspected of being terrorists were thereby brought to their attention during their interrogation.

42. Mr Fox and Ms Campbell were arrested at 3.40 pm on 5 February 1986 at Woodbourne RUC station and then separately questioned the same day between 8.15 pm and 10.00 pm at Castlereagh Police Office. . . . Mr Hartley, for his part, was arrested at his home at 7.55 am on 18 August 1986 and taken to Antrim Police Station where he was questioned between 11.05 am and 12.15 pm. . . . In the context of the present case these intervals of a few hours cannot be regarded as falling outside the constraints of time imposed by the notion of promptness in Article 5 § 2. . . .

FOR THESE REASONS, THE COURT . . .

Holds unanimously that there has been no breach of Article 5 § 2; . . .

NOTES

1   For the composition of the Court, see above, p 273.

2   The *Fox, Campbell and Hartley* case was followed on the matter of the information to be given to the arrested person in the *Murray (Margaret)* case, above, p 273, another Northern

Ireland terrorist case. There the arrested person was only told at the time of arrest of the section of the 1978 Act under which she was arrested, but the questions put to her during interrogation some two hours later meant that overall Article 5(2) was complied with. The Court stated:

In the Court's view, it must have been apparent to Mrs Murray that she was being questioned about her possible involvement in the collection of funds for the purchase of arms for the Provisional IRA by her brothers in the United States. Admittedly, 'there was never any probing examination of her collecting money'—to use the words of the trial judge—but, as the national courts noted, this was because of Mrs Murray's declining to answer any questions at all beyond giving her name. The Court therefore finds that the reasons for her arrest were sufficiently brought to her attention during her interview.

3   Should it be sufficient, as the Court allows in the *Fox, Campbell and Hartley* case, that a person may infer the information required by Article 5(2) from what might be said during questioning? Might the Court have been unduly influenced by the terrorist context of the case when stating what appears to intend as an interpretation of Article 5(2) of general application?

4   The original Court greatly widened the scope of this obligation to encompass persons detained under civil law powers in *Van der Leer v Netherlands*, A.170 (1990). The applicant was detained in a psychiatric hospital on the orders of the local Burgomaster. A few days later the District Court refused to confirm his order. However, the applicant remained in the hospital as a voluntary patient. Two months later another court, at the request of the applicant's husband, ordered her compulsory confinement in the hospital for six months. The applicant was not told of the order and only learnt of it ten days later when she was placed in isolation within the hospital. She immediately contacted her lawyer and after various court proceedings the order was revoked some months later. Before the Court, the Government submitted that Article 5(2) only applied to detentions under criminal law. The unanimous Court held that:

27. The Court is not unmindful of the criminal-law connotation of the words used in Article 5(2). However, it agrees with the Commission that they should be interpreted 'autonomously', in particular in accordance with the aim and purpose of Article 5, which are to protect everyone from arbitrary deprivations of liberty. Thus the 'arrest' referred to in paragraph 2 of Article 5 extends beyond the realm of criminal-law measures. Similarly, in using the words 'any charge' ('tout accusation') in this provision, the intention of the drafters was not to lay down a condition for its applicability, but to indicate an eventuality of which it takes account.

28. The close links between paragraphs 2 and 4 of Article 5 supports this interpretation. Any person who is entitled to take proceedings to have the lawfulness of his detention decided speedily cannot make effective use of that right unless he is promptly and adequately informed of the reasons why he has been deprived of his liberty . . .

Paragraph 4 does not make any distinction as between persons deprived of their liberty on the basis of whether they have been arrested or detained. There are therefore no grounds for excluding the latter from the scope of paragraph 2.

The Court concluded that neither the manner nor timing of the applicant becoming aware of the order satisfied the requirements of Article 5(2). This judgment represented a valuable expansion of the ambit of this provision to potentially vulnerable persons being detained under civil law powers.

5   A unanimous Chamber of the full-time Court found a breach of this obligation when the immigration authorities took seventy-six hours to inform an asylum seeker of the reasons why he was being detained in a special immigration centre for the fast processing of his claim: *Saadi v United Kingdom* (see above p 295)

Article 5(3): Pre-trial detention and trial within a reasonable time

Assenov and others v Bulgaria 1998-VIII 3264
European Court of Human Rights

The applicant alleged, *inter alia*, that he had not been brought promptly before 'a judge or other officer authorised to exercise judicial power', as required by Article 5(3). The facts of the case, so far as relevant to this allegation, are set out in the following extract.

JUDGMENT OF THE COURT

32. In January 1995, Mr Assenov was questioned by the Shoumen prosecuting authorities in connection with an investigation into a series of thefts and robberies.

33. He was arrested on 27 July 1995 and the following day, in the presence of his lawyer and a prosecutor ('K'), he was questioned by an investigator and formally charged with ten or more burglaries, allegedly committed between 9 January and 2 May 1995, and six robberies committed between 10 September 1994 and 24 July 1995, all involving attacks on passers-by on the street. Mr Assenov admitted most of the burglaries but denied having committed the robberies.

The decision was taken to detain him on remand. This decision was approved the same day by another prosecutor, 'A.' . . .

144. The Government submitted that the various prosecutors who considered Mr Assenov's applications for release were 'officer[s] authorised by law to exercise judicial power' within the meaning of Article 5 § 3, since under Bulgarian law a prosecutor was fully independent, under a duty to protect the public interest and authorised to decide on a number of questions arising in criminal proceedings, including whether or not to detain an accused on remand.

145. The Commission, with whom the applicant agreed, noted that although under Bulgarian law investigators were institutionally independent, in practice they were subject to the control of prosecutors with regard to every question concerning the conduct of an investigation, including whether or not to detain a suspect on remand. There was, therefore, a strong objective appearance that the investigator who dealt with Mr Assenov lacked independence from the prosecuting authorities, which were subsequently to act as the opposing party in criminal proceedings.

146. The Court reiterates that judicial control of interferences by the executive with the individual's right to liberty is an essential feature of the guarantee embodied in Article 5 § 3 (see the above-mentioned *Aksoy* judgment, p 2282, § 76). Before an 'officer' can be said to exercise 'judicial power' within the meaning of this provision, he or she must satisfy certain conditions providing a guarantee to the person detained against any arbitrary or unjustified deprivation of liberty (see the *Schiesser v Switzerland* judgment of 4 December 1979, Series A No 34, p 13, § 31).

Thus, the 'officer' must be independent of the executive and the parties (ibid). In this respect, objective appearances at the time of the decision on detention are material: if it appears at that time that the 'officer' may later intervene in subsequent criminal proceedings on behalf of the prosecuting authority, his independence and impartiality may be open to doubt (see the *Huber v Switzerland* judgment of 23 October 1990, Series A No 188, p 18, § 43 and the *Brincat v Italy* judgment of 26 November 1992, Series A No 249-A, p 12, § 21). The 'officer' must hear the individual brought before him in person and review, by reference to legal criteria, whether or not the detention is justified. If it is not so justified, the 'officer' must have the power to make a binding order for the detainee's release (see the above-mentioned *Schiesser* judgment, pp 13–14, § 31, and the *Ireland v UK* judgment of 18 January 1978, Series A No 25, p 76, § 199).

147. The Court notes at the outset that Mr Assenov's application for release was not considered by a judge until 19 September 1995 . . . three months into his detention. This was clearly insufficiently 'prompt' for the purposes of Article 5 § 3 (see, for example, the *Brogan v UK* judgment of 29 November 1988, Series A No 145, p 33, § 62), and indeed it has not been argued that this procedure was adequate to satisfy the requirements of this provision.

148. The Court recalls that on 28 July 1995 Mr Assenov was brought before an investigator who questioned him, formally charged him, and took the decision to detain him on remand. . . . It notes that, under Bulgarian law, investigators do not have the power to make legally binding decisions as to the detention or release of a suspect. Instead, any decision made by an investigator is capable of being overturned by the prosecutor, who may also withdraw a case from an investigator if dissatisfied with the latter's approach. . . . It follows that the investigator was not sufficiently independent properly to be described as an 'officer authorised by law to exercise judicial power' within the meaning of Article 5 § 3.

149. Mr Assenov was not heard in person by prosecutor A, who approved the investigator's decision . . . or by any of the other prosecutors who later decided that he should continue to be detained. In any case, since any one of these prosecutors could subsequently have acted against the applicant in criminal proceedings . . . they were not sufficiently independent or impartial for the purposes of Article 5 § 3.

150. The Court considers, therefore, that there has been a violation of Article 5 § 3 on the grounds that the applicant was not brought before an 'officer authorised by law to exercise judicial power'. . . .

FOR THESE REASONS THE COURT . . .

Holds unanimously that there has been a violation of Article 5(3) of the Convention in that Mr Assenov was not brought promptly before a judge or other officer authorised by law to exercise judicial power. . . .

NOTES

1 The Court was composed of President Bernhardt and Judges Petitti, Palm, Baka, Bonnici, Makarczyk, Gotchev, Van Dijk, and Toumanov.

2 In the Bulgarian system of criminal investigation under examination in the *Assenov* case, the investigation into offences was the responsibility of investigators from the state funded central investigation service or the competent regional investigation department, which were institutionally separate from the police and the prosecutor's department. However, as the European Court judgment notes, the investigators were subject to the control of the prosecutor's department in the conduct of the investigation and the taking of remand decisions. Bulgarian law has been reformed so that remand decisions are now taken by a judge.

3 In *Hood v UK* (1999) The Times, 11 March, the Court held that a decision by his commanding officer ordering the detention of a soldier pending trial was in breach of Article 5(3). The Court stated:

57. As to the applicant's substantive complaint about the commanding officer's impartiality in the context of the Rule 4 hearing, according to the case-law of the Convention bodies, if it appears at the time

the decision on pre-trial detention is taken that the 'officer authorised by law to exercise judicial power' is liable to intervene in the subsequent proceedings as a representative of the prosecuting authority, then he could not be regarded as independent of the parties at that preliminary stage as it is possible for him to become one of the parties at a later stage (see the *Huber v Switzerland* judgment of 23 October 1990, Series A No 188, p 18, §§ 42–3 and the *Brincat v Italy* judgment of 26 November 1992, Series A No 249-A, pp 11–12, §§ 20–1).

The Court has noted the powers and duties of the commanding officer outlined, in particular, at paragraphs 23, 27, 28, 32 and 34 above, which would arise subsequent to that officer's conduct of the hearing pursuant to Rule 4 of the 1972 Rules. This being so, the commanding officer was liable to play a central role in the subsequent prosecution of the case against the applicant. Although the unit adjutant often carries out certain of these functions of the commanding officer (and, indeed, did so in the present case), it is clear that the adjutant does so on behalf of the commanding officer to whom he is directly subordinate in rank. Moreover, the judge advocate confirmed during the applicant's court martial that the unit adjutant is generally nominated prosecuting or assistant prosecuting officer and, in the present case, he carried out the latter function.

In such circumstances, the Court concludes that the applicant's misgivings about his commanding officer's impartiality must be taken to be objectively justified.

58. The Court also considers, as did the Commission, that the commanding officer's concurrent responsibility for discipline and order in his command would provide an additional reason for an accused reasonably to doubt that officer's impartiality when deciding on the necessity of the pre-trial detention of an accused in his command. This view is reinforced by paragraph 6.005 of the Queen's Regulations (see paragraph 36 above), which allows for the commanding officer to refuse the pre-trial release of an accused if he is of the view that it is undesirable 'in the interests of discipline' that the accused be at large or be allowed to consort with his comrades.

Brogan v UK A.145 (1988) 11 EHRR 117
European Court of Human Rights

The four applicants were arrested by the police in Northern Ireland under section 12, Prevention of Terrorism (Temporary Provisions) Act 1984 as persons suspected on reasonable grounds of being 'concerned in the commission, preparation or instigation of acts of terrorism' connected with the affairs of Northern Ireland. They were then questioned in respect of specific criminal offences resulting from terrorist activities and of membership of proscribed organisations. All four applicants were later released without being charged with any offence, having been detained for periods ranging from four days and six hours to six days and sixteen and a half hours. Under the 1984 Act, it was lawful to detain a person for an initial period of 48 hours and, on the authorisation of the Secretary of State for Northern Ireland, for up to five more days, making a total of seven days' detention, without bringing him before a magistrate. In this case, the applicants alleged, *inter alia*, breaches of Article 5(1)(c), 5(3), 5(4), and 5(5), ECHR. As to Article 5(4), the Court held, unanimously, that habeas corpus provided the remedy required by Article 5(4). The following extract from the Court's judgment concerns Article 5(3), (5). The Commission had expressed the opinion in its report that Article 5(3) had been infringed in respect of the two applicants who had been detained for over five days because they had not been brought 'promptly before a judge', but not in respect of the two who had been detained for four to five days. The Commission had also expressed the opinion that Article 5(5) had been infringed in respect of the first two applicants.

JUDGMENT OF THE COURT

57. The Commission, in its report, cited its established case-law to the effect that a period of four days in cases concerning ordinary criminal offences and of five days in exceptional cases could be considered compatible with the requirement of promptness in Article 5 § 3 (see respectively the admissibility decisions in *application no 2864/66, X v Netherlands*, Yearbook of the Convention, Vol 9, p 568 [1966], and in *application No 4960/71, X v Belgium*, Collection of Decisions, Vol 42, pp 54–5 [1973]). In the Commission's opinion, given the context in which the applicants were arrested and the special problems associated with the investigation of terrorist offences, a somewhat longer period of detention than in normal cases was justified. The Commission concluded that the periods of four days and six hours (Mr McFadden) and four days and eleven hours (Mr Tracey) did satisfy the requirement of promptness, whereas the periods of five days and eleven hours (Mr Brogan) and six days and sixteen and a half hours (Mr Coyle) did not.

58. The fact that a detained person is not charged or brought before a court does not in itself amount to a violation of the first part of Article 5 § 3. No violation of Article 5 § 3 can arise if the arrested person is released 'promptly' before any judicial control of his detention would have been feasible (see the *de Jong, Baljet and van den Brink* judgment of 22 May 1984, Series A No 77, p 25, § 52). If the arrested person is not released promptly, he is entitled to a prompt appearance before a judge or judicial officer.

The assessment of 'promptness' has to be made in the light of the object and purpose of Article 5. ... The Court has regard to the importance of this Article in the Convention system: it enshrines a fundamental human right, namely the protection of the individual against arbitrary interferences by the State with his right to liberty (see the *Bozano* judgment of 18 December 1986, Series A No 111, p 23, § 54). Judicial control of interferences by the executive with the individual's right to liberty is an essential feature of the guarantee embodied in Article 5 § 3, which is intended to minimise the risk of arbitrariness. ...

59. The obligation expressed in English by the word 'promptly' and in French by the word '*aussitôt*' is clearly distinguishable from the less strict requirement in the second part of paragraph 3 ('reasonable time' / '*délai raisonnable*') and even from that in paragraph 4 of Article 5 ('speedily'/'*à bref délai*'). The term 'promptly' also occurs in the English text of paragraph 2, where the French text uses the words '*dans le plus court délai*'. As indicated in the *Ireland v UK* judgment (18 January 1978, Series A No 25, p 76, § 199), 'promptly' in paragraph 3 may be understood as having a broader significance than '*aussitôt*', which literally means immediately. Thus confronted with versions of a law-making treaty which are equally authentic but not exactly the same, the Court must interpret them in a way that reconciles them as far as possible and is most appropriate in order to realise the aim and achieve the object of the treaty (see, *inter alia*, the *Sunday Times* judgment of 26 April 1979, Series A No 30, p 30, § 48, and Article 33 § 4 of the Vienna Convention of 23 May 1969 on the Law of Treaties).

The use in the French text of the word '*aussitôt*', with its constraining connotation of immediacy, confirms that the degree of flexibility attaching to the notion of 'promptness' is limited, even if the attendant circumstances can never be ignored for the purposes of the assessment under paragraph 3. Whereas promptness is to be assessed in each case according to its special features (see the above-mentioned *de Jong, Baljet and van den Brink* judgment, Series A No 77, p 25, § 52), the significance to be attached to those features can never be taken to the point of impairing the very essence of the right guaranteed by Article 5 § 3, that is to the point of effectively negativing the State's obligation to ensure a prompt release or a prompt appearance before a judicial authority.

60. The instant case is exclusively concerned with the arrest and detention, by virtue of powers granted under special legislation, of persons suspected of involvement in terrorism in Northern Ireland. ... There is no call to determine in the present judgment whether in an ordinary criminal case any given period, such as four days, in police or administrative custody would as a general rule be capable of being compatible with the first part of Article 5 § 3.

None of the applicants was in fact brought before a judge or judicial officer during his time in custody. The issue to be decided is therefore whether, having regard to the special features relied on by the Government, each applicant's release can be considered as 'prompt' for the purposes of Article 5 § 3.

61. The investigation of terrorist offences undoubtedly presents the authorities with special problems. . . . The Court takes full judicial notice of the factors adverted to by the Government in this connection. It is also true that in Northern Ireland the referral of police requests for extended detention to the Secretary of State and the individual scrutiny of each police request by a Minister do provide a form of executive control. . . . In addition, the need for the continuation of the special powers has been constantly monitored by Parliament and their operation regularly reviewed by independent personalities. . . . The Court accepts that, subject to the existence of adequate safeguards, the context of terrorism in Northern Ireland has the effect of prolonging the period during which the authorities may, without violating Article 5 § 3, keep a person suspected of serious terrorist offences in custody before bringing him before a judge or other judicial officer.

The difficulties, alluded to by the Government, of judicial control over decisions to arrest and detain suspected terrorists may affect the manner of implementation of Article 5 § 3, for example in calling for appropriate procedural precautions in view of the nature of the suspected offences. However, they cannot justify, under Article 5 § 3, dispensing altogether with 'prompt' judicial control.

62. As indicated above (paragraph 59), the scope for flexibility in interpreting and applying the notion of 'promptness' is very limited. In the Court's view, even the shortest of the four periods of detention, namely the four days and six hours spent in police custody by Mr McFadden . . . , falls outside the strict constraints as to time permitted by the first part of Article 5 § 3. To attach such importance to the special features of this case as to justify so lengthy a period of detention without appearance before a judge or other judicial officer would be an unacceptably wide interpretation of the plain meaning of the word 'promptly'. An interpretation to this effect would import into Article 5 § 3 a serious weakening of a procedural guarantee to the detriment of the individual and would entail consequences impairing the very essence of the right protected by this provision. The Court thus has to conclude that none of the applicants was either brought 'promptly' before a judicial authority or released 'promptly' following his arrest. The undoubted fact that the arrest and detention of the applicants were inspired by the legitimate aim of protecting the community as a whole from terrorism is not on its own sufficient to ensure compliance with the specific requirements of Article 5 § 3.

There has thus been a breach of Article 5 § 3 in respect of all four applicants. . . .

FOR THESE REASONS, THE COURT . . .

Holds by twelve votes to seven that there has been a violation of Article 5 § 3 in respect of all four applicants; . . .

NOTES

1　The Court was composed of President Ryssdal and Judges Cremona, Vilhjálmsson, Bindschleder-Robert, Gölcüklü, Matscher, Pinheiro Farinha, Pettiti, Walsh, Evans, Macdonald, Russo, Bernhardt, Spielmann, Meyer, Carrilo Salcedo, Valticos, Martens, and Palm. A joint dissenting opinion was issued by Judges: Vilhjálmsson, Bindschleder-Robert, Gölcüklü, Matscher, and Valticos in which they expressed the view that taking account of the exceptional situation in Northern Ireland assessed against the established case law of the Commission they considered the applicants' periods of detention were justifiable.

2　The UK's response to the decision in the *Brogan* case was to derogate under Article 15 from its obligations under, *inter alia*, Article 5(3) in respect of the public emergency which it judged to exist in Northern Ireland. The UK had on several occasions previously derogated under Article 15 in respect of Northern Ireland. No such derogation was in operation at the time of the *Brogan* case. The UK decided upon this response to the *Brogan* case after failing to find a way of bringing its law into line with the judgment that was consistent with its traditions and that also allowed it to counteract sufficiently the threat posed by terrorism in Northern Ireland. In *Brannigan and McBride v UK* A.258-B (1993) (see below p 845 for the Article 15 aspects of this judgment), the Court held that the UK derogation notice was valid, so that the applicants could not complain that the detention of terrorist suspects under the same power as in the *Brogan* case and for similar periods was in breach of Article 5(3).

In February 2001 the Permanent Representative of the UK at the Council of Europe issued a Note Verbale to the Secretary General withdrawing the above derogation. This withdrawal was based upon the enactment of the Terrorism Act 2000 which provided, *inter alia*, that police officers could arrest and detain for up to forty-eight hours any person reasonably suspected of being concerned in the commission, preparation, or instigation of acts of terrorism. Thereafter, a judicial authority could extend the period of detention for up to a further five days (by section 306 of the Criminal Justice Act 2003 this period was increased to a maximum of fourteen days and after intense controversy this period was further extended to twenty-eight days by section 23 of the Terrorism Act 2006).

3 In *Aksoy v Turkey* (1996) 23 EHRR 553, 1996 VI 2260, the Court held that an Article 15 notice of derogation could not justify the applicant's detention for fourteen days without being brought before a judicial officer: it was not required by 'the exigencies of the situation' (Article 15(1)). The Court stated:

78. Although the Court is of the view—which it has expressed on several occasions in the past (see, for example, the above-mentioned *Brogan and Others* judgment)—that the investigation of terrorist offences undoubtedly presents the authorities with special problems, it cannot accept that it is necessary to hold a suspect for fourteen days without judicial intervention. This period is exceptionally long, and left the applicant vulnerable not only to arbitrary interference with his right to liberty but also to torture (see paragraph 64 above). Moreover, the Government have not adduced any detailed reasons before the Court as to why the fight against terrorism in South-East Turkey rendered judicial intervention impracticable. . . .

82. In its above-mentioned *Brannigan and McBride* judgment . . . , the Court was satisfied that there were effective safeguards in operation in Northern Ireland which provided an important measure of protection against arbitrary behaviour and incommunicado detention. For example, the remedy of habeas corpus was available to test the lawfulness of the original arrest and detention, there was an absolute and legally enforceable right to consult a solicitor forty-eight hours after the time of arrest and detainees were entitled to inform a relative or friend about their detention and to have access to a doctor (op cit pp 55–6, §§ 62–3).

83. In contrast, however, the Court considers that in this case insufficient safeguards were available to the applicant, who was detained over a long period of time. In particular, the denial of access to a lawyer, doctor, relative or friend and the absence of any realistic possibility of being brought before a court to test the legality of the detention meant that he was left completely at the mercy of those holding him.

4 The full-time Court applied its predecessor's approach to assessing the promptness of the release of a suspected terrorist in *O'Hara v United Kingdom* (see above p 274).

46. The Court notes that the Government have not disputed that the applicant was held for six days and thirteen hours before his eventual release and that this was not in compliance with the requirement to bring an arrested person promptly before an appropriate judicial officer. Having regard to its case-law (in particular *Brogan and Others* . . . where detention periods exceeding four days for terrorists

suspects were found not to be compatible with the requirement of prompt judicial control), the Court finds that there has in this respect been a violation of Article 5(3) of the Convention.

5 A Grand Chamber explained the purpose and requirements of the domestic judicial scrutiny mandated by Article 5(3) in respect of arrested criminal suspects in *T.W. v Malta*, judgment of 29 April 1999. One day after the applicant had been arrested he was brought before a magistrate. He pleaded not guilty to charges of physically and sexually abusing his daughter. The magistrate had no powers to order his release. He was eventually granted bail eighteen days later by another magistrate. The applicant contended that the inability of the first magistrate to review the merits of his continued detention and order his release on bail, if deemed appropriate, violated Article 5(3). The Grand Chamber was unanimous in holding that:

41. As the Court has pointed out on many occasions, Article 5 § 3 of the Convention provides persons arrested or detained on suspicion of having committed a criminal offence with a guarantee against any arbitrary or unjustified deprivation of liberty (see, *inter alia*, the *Assenov and Others v Bulgaria* judgment of 28 October 1998, *Reports of Judgments and Decisions* 1998-VIII, p 3187, § 146). It is essentially the object of Article 5 § 3, which forms a whole with paragraph 1 (c), to require provisional release once detention ceases to be reasonable. The fact that an arrested person had access to a judicial authority is not sufficient to constitute compliance with the opening part of Article 5 § 3. This provision enjoins the judicial officer before whom the arrested person appears to review the circumstances militating for or against detention, to decide by reference to legal criteria whether there are reasons to justify detention, and to order release if there are no such reasons . . . In other words, Article 5 § 3 requires the judicial officer to consider the merits of the detention.

42. To be in accordance with Article 5 § 3, judicial control must be prompt. Promptness has to be assessed in each case according to its special features . . . However, the scope of flexibility in interpreting and applying the notion of promptness is very limited (see the *Brogan and Others v the United Kingdom* judgment of 29 November 1988, Series A No 145-B, pp 33–4, § 62).

43. In addition to being prompt, the judicial control of the detention must be automatic . . . It cannot be made to depend on a previous application by the detained person. Such a requirement would not only change the nature of the safeguard provided for under Article 5 § 3, a safeguard distinct from that in Article 5 § 4, which guarantees the right to institute proceedings to have the lawfulness of detention reviewed by a court . . . It might even defeat the purpose of the safeguard under Article 5 § 3 which is to protect the individual from arbitrary detention by ensuring that the act of deprivation of liberty is subject to independent judicial scrutiny (see, *mutatis mutandis*, the *Kurt v Turkey* judgment of 25 May 1998, *Reports* 1998-III, p 1185, § 123). Prompt judicial review of detention is also an important safeguard against ill-treatment of the individual taken into custody (see the *Aksoy v Turkey* judgment of 18 December 1996, *Reports* 1996-VI, p 2282, § 76). Furthermore, arrested persons who have been subjected to such treatment might be incapable of lodging an application asking the judge to review their detention. The same could hold true for other vulnerable categories of arrested persons, such as the mentally weak or those who do not speak the language of the judicial officer.

44. Finally, by virtue of Article 5 § 3 the judicial officer must himself or herself hear the detained person before taking the appropriate decision . . .

Consequently, as the first magistrate had no power to undertake such a review there had been a breach of Article 5(3). This judgment clearly reveals the extent of the obligations upon domestic authorities—these include automatically and promptly bringing an arrested person before a judicial authority that has the power to review the merits of the continued detention of the suspect and ordering his/her release if detention is no longer reasonable. Hence this process must provide effective safeguards for arrested persons against the unnecessary prolongation of their detention.

Wemhoff v Federal Republic of Gemany A.7 (1968) 1 EHRR 55
European Court of Human Rights

The applicant, a West German national, was arrested on 9 November 1961, on suspicion of complicity in offences of breach of trust. The investigation of the case by the West Berlin Prosecutor's Office was completed on 24 February 1964. An indictment was filed on 23 April 1964, and on 17 July 1964 the applicant was committed for trial. The trial began in the Regional Court of Berlin on 9 November 1964, and the applicant was convicted on 7 April 1965 of a 'particularly serious case of prolonged abetment to breach of trust' for which he was sentenced to six-and-a-half-years' penal servitude. The period of time spent in detention pending trial was counted as a part of this sentence. The applicant's appeal against conviction was rejected on 17 December 1965. The applicant had remained in detention since he was first arrested. The case was very complicated. It involved 12 other accused and required the examination of a mass of bank accounts and transactions. The Commission admitted the application for consideration on its merits in respect of alleged violations by West Germany of Articles 5(3) and 6(1). In its report, the Commission expressed the opinion, by seven votes to three, that Article 5(3) had been violated because the applicant had not been brought to trial 'within a reasonable time' and, unanimously, that there had been no violation of the 'reasonable time' guarantee in Article 6(1). The Commission referred the case to the Court. The following extracts concern Article 5(3). The Court held unanimously that Article 6 had not been infringed.

JUDGMENT OF THE COURT

4. ... As the word 'reasonable' applies to the time within which a person is entitled to trial, a purely grammatical interpretation would leave the judicial authorities with a choice between two obligations, that of conducting the proceedings until judgment within a reasonable time or that of releasing the accused pending trial, if necessary against certain guarantees.

5. The Court is quite certain that such an interpretation would not conform to the intention of the High Contracting Parties. It is inconceivable that they should have intended to permit their judicial authorities, at the price of release of the accused, to protract proceedings beyond a reasonable time. This would, moreover, be flatly contrary to the provision in Article 6(1) cited above. ...

Article 5, which begins with an affirmation of the right of everyone to liberty and security of person, goes on to specify the situations and conditions in which derogations from this principle may be made. ... It is thus mainly in the light of the fact of the detention of the person being prosecuted that national courts, possibly followed by the European Court, must determine whether the time that has elapsed, for whatever reason, before judgment is passed on the accused has at some stage exceeded a reasonable limit, that is to say imposed a greater sacrifice than could, in the circumstances of the case, reasonably be expected of a person presumed to be innocent.

In other words it is the provisional detention of accused persons which must not, according to Article 5(3), be prolonged beyond a reasonable time. ...

6. Another question relating to the interpretation of Article 5(3) ... is that of the period of detention covered by the requirement of a 'reasonable time. ...'

The representative of the German Government expounded the reasons which led him to maintain the interpretation, accepted in the Commission's Report, that it is the time of appearance before the trial court that marks the end of the period with which Article 5(3) is concerned.

7. The Court cannot accept this restrictive interpretation. It is true that the English text of the Convention allows such an interpretation. ...

But while the English text permits two interpretations the French version, which is of equal authority, allows only one. According to it the obligation to release an accused person within a reasonable time continues until that person has been '*jugée*,' that is until the day of the judgment that terminates the trial. Moreover, he must be released '*pendant la procédure*,' a very broad expression which indubitably covers both the trial and the investigation.

8. Thus confronted with two versions of a treaty which are equally authentic but not exactly the same the Court must, following established international law precedents, interpret them in a way that will reconcile them as far as possible. Given that it is a law-making treaty, it is also necessary to seek the interpretation that is most appropriate in order to realise the aim and achieve the object of the treaty, not that which would restrict to the greatest possible degree the obligations undertaken by the Parties. It is impossible to see why the protection against unduly long detention on remand which Article 5 seeks to ensure for persons suspected of offences should not continue up to delivery of judgment rather than cease at the moment the trial opens.

9. It remains to ascertain whether the end of the period of detention with which Article 5(3) is concerned is the day on which a conviction becomes final or simply that on which the charge is determined, even if only by a court of first instance.

The Court finds for the latter interpretation.

One consideration has appeared to it as decisive, namely that a person convicted at first instance, whether or not he has been detained up to this moment, is in the position provided for by Article 5(1)(2)(a) which authorises deprivation of liberty '*after conviction*.' This last phrase cannot be interpreted as being restricted to the case of a final conviction, for this would exclude the arrest at the hearing of convicted persons who appeared for trial while still at liberty, whatever remedies are still open to them. Now, such a practice is frequently followed in many Contracting States and it cannot be believed that they intended to renounce it. It cannot be overlooked moreover that the guilt of a person who is detained during the appeal or review proceedings, has been established in the course of a trial conducted in accordance with requirements of Article 6. . . . A person who has cause to complain of the continuation of his detention after conviction because of delay in determining his appeal, cannot avail himself of Article 5(3) but could possibly allege a disregard of the 'reasonable time' provided for by Article 6(1). . . .

10. The reasonableness of an accused person's continued detention must be assessed in each case according to its special features. The factors which may be taken into consideration are extremely diverse. Hence the possibility of wide differences in opinion in the assessment of the reasonableness of a given detention. . . .

13. The arrest warrant taken out in Wemhoff's name on 9 November 1961 was based on the fear that if he were left at liberty, he would abscond and destroy the evidence against him, in particular by communicating with persons who might be involved. . . . Both of these reasons continued to be invoked until 5 August 1963 in the decisions of the courts rejecting Wemhoff's many applications for release pending trial.

On that date, however, although the investigation had yet to be concluded, the Court of Appeal accepted that there was some doubt as to whether any danger of suppression of evidence still existed, but it considered that the other reason was still operative . . . , and the same reasoning was repeated in later decisions dismissing the Applicant's appeals.

14. With regard to the existence of a danger of suppression of evidence, the Court regards this anxiety of the German courts to be justified in view of the character of the offences of which Wemhoff was suspected and the extreme complexity of the case.

As to the danger of flight, the Court is of opinion that, while the severity of the sentence which the accused may expect in the event of conviction may legitimately be regarded as a factor encouraging him to abscond—though the effect of such fear diminishes as detention continues and, consequently, the balance of the sentence which the accused may expect to have to serve is reduced, nevertheless the possibility of a severe sentence is not sufficient in this respect. The German courts have moreover been careful to support their affirmations that a danger of flight existed by referring at an early stage in the proceedings to certain circumstances relating to the material position and the conduct of the accused. . . .

15. The Court wishes, however, to emphasise that the concluding words of Article 5(3) of the Convention show that, when the only remaining reason for continued detention is the fear that the accused will abscond and thereby subsequently avoid appearing for trial, his release pending trial must be ordered if it is possible to obtain from him guarantees that will ensure such appearance.

It is beyond doubt that, in a financial case such as that in which Wemhoff was involved, an essential factor in such guarantees should have been the deposit by him of bail or the provision of security for a large amount. The positions successfully taken up by him on this matter (statement of the facts, paras 5 and 14) [in August 1962, the applicant offered to deposit 200,000 DM but withdrew the offer two days later, apparently before the court had considered it. After his conviction, an offer of 100,000 DM was accepted by the court, but then replaced by a much lower one which the court could not accept] are not such as to suggest that he would have been prepared to furnish such guarantees.

16. In these circumstances the Court could not conclude that there had been any breach of the obligations imposed by Article 5(3) unless the length of Wemhoff's provisional detention between 9 November 1961 and 7 April 1965 had been due either (a) to the slowness of the investigation, which was only completed at the end of February 1964, or (b) to the lapse of time which occurred either between the closing of the investigation and the preferment of the indictment (April 1964) or between then and the opening of the trial (9 November 1964) or finally (c) to the length of the trial (which lasted until 7 April 1965). It cannot be doubted that, even when an accused person is reasonably detained during these periods for reasons of the public interest, there may be a violation of Article 5(3) if, for whatever cause, the proceedings continue for a considerable length of time.

17. On this point the Court shares the opinion of the Commission that no criticism can be made of the conduct of the case by the judicial authorities. The exceptional length of the investigation and of the trial are justified by the exceptional complexity of the case and by further unavoidable reasons for delay. . . .

FOR THESE REASONS, THE COURT

Holds, by six votes to one, that there has been no breach of Article 5(3) of the Convention; . . .

INDIVIDUAL DISSENTING OPINION OF JUDGE ZEKIA

The legal system of a country, governing the provisions of the criminal law and procedure relating to pre-trial proceedings—such as preliminary enquiries, investigation and arraignment—as well as the presentation of a case to the court and the power of the court itself in reopening investigations, has a lot to do with the time taken in the conclusion of a trial. . . .

In [a common law system] . . . it is the police and the prosecution who conduct the enquiries and collect the evidence. They present the case to a court either for trial or—in indictable offences—for preliminary enquiries for the purpose of committal before the Assizes. Under [a civil law] . . . system the investigation is carried out by a judge and the trial of the accused is started after judicial investigations are closed and after the decision is taken for remitting the case before trial. . . .

While in the former system sufficient evidence to build up a prima facie case against the suspected person is normally expected to be available before he is charged and is taken into custody, in the latter case, ie continental system, it appears that the availability of such evidence at an early stage is not essential. Information to the satisfaction of the judicial officials seems to be sufficient for the arrest and detention of a suspect.

As a consequence of these basic divergences inherent in the two systems, suspected persons are, as a rule, kept in detention considerably longer on the continent than in the case of those in England or other countries where the system of common law prevails.

... My intention is neither to touch on the merits or demerits of either system. My digression from the track is to emphasise the fact that—if in England, a Member of the Council of Europe—the concept of 'reasonable time' regarding the period of detention of an unconvicted person awaiting his trial does not allow us to stretch the time beyond six months even in an exceptionally difficult and complicated case, could we say that, in the continent in a similar case, the period of detention might be six times longer and yet it could be considered as reasonable and therefore compatible with the Convention?

... it may fairly be inferred that the Governments' signatories of the Convention, intended amongst other things, to set a common standard of right to liberty, the scope of which could not differ so vastly from one country to another. ...

If a man, presumably innocent, is kept in custody for years, this is bound to ruin him. It is true in the case of Wemhoff that the trial ended with a conviction, but it might have ended with an acquittal as well...

I believe that in all systems of law there exist always ways and means of avoiding unreasonably long delayed trials. ...

NOTES

1   The Court was composed of President Rolin and Judges Rodenberg, Wold, Mosler, Zekia, Favre, and Bilge.

2   In deciding that the 'reasonable time' guarantee in Article 5(3) provided a basis for reviewing the *grounds* upon which a person detained pending trial under Article 5(1)(c) continues to be detained after his initial arrest as well as providing a means of control over the *length* of the procedure against a person detained pending trial, the Court clearly filled what would otherwise have been a significant gap in the Convention and made sense of an obscure text.

3   In *Stögmüller v Austria* A.9 (1969), the Court expressed the general test that should be applied in deciding whether the danger of the accused disappearing is too great to permit his release as follows:

There must be a whole set of circumstances... which give reason to suppose that the consequences and hazards of flight will seem to him [the accused] to be a lesser evil than continued imprisonment.

Apart from the dangers of flight and of the suppression of evidence, the Court also, in *Matznetter v Austria* A.10 (1969) by four votes to three, accepted prevention of crime as a permissible ground for detention 'in the special circumstances of the case'. These would seem to have been that there was good reason to believe that the accused, if released, would have committed an offence or offences of the same and serious kind as those with which he was already charged, although there was no particular offence which could be identified at the time that the question of release arose as one which it was reasonably believed he would commit.

4   A threat to public order may also justify the refusal of bail. In *Letellier v France*, A.207 (1991) 14 EHRR 83, the applicant ran a bar-restaurant at La Varenne Saint-Hilaire on the outskirts of Paris. She was accused of being an accessory to the murder of her second husband. The murderer and his accomplice claimed that the applicant had instructed and paid for the murder. Although she had at one stage been released on bail for one month, the applicant was detained again by court order on the ground that her detention was 'necessary to preserve public order from the disturbance caused by the offence' (Art 144, Code of Criminal Procedure).

The Court held that the detention was in breach of Article 5(3) because there was no evidence that the applicant's release would in fact have presented a public order problem. The Court stated:

51. The Court accepts that, by reason of their particular gravity and public reaction to them, certain offences may give rise to a social disturbance capable of justifying pre-trial detention, at least for a time. In exceptional circumstances this factor may therefore be taken into account for the purposes of the Convention, in any event in so far as domestic law recognises—as in Article 144 of the Code of Criminal Procedure—the notion of disturbance to public order caused by an offence.

However, this ground can be regarded as relevant and sufficient only provided that it is based on facts capable of showing that the accused's release would actually disturb public order. In addition detention will continue to be legitimate only if public order remains actually threatened; its continuation cannot be used to anticipate a custodial sentence.

In this case, these conditions were not satisfied. The indictments divisions assessed the need to continue the deprivation of liberty from a purely abstract point of view, taking into consideration only the gravity of the offence. This was despite the fact that the applicant had stressed in her memorials of 16 January 1986 and of 3 March and 10 April 1987 that the mother and sister of the victim had not submitted any observations when she filed her applications for release. . . .

5   In *Cabellero v UK* [2000] Crim LR 587, the European Court accepted a UK Government concession that the automatic refusal of bail to the applicant, who was charged with attempted rape, under s 25, Criminal Justice and Public Order Act 1994 was a breach of Article 5(3). Under s 25, an accused charged with murder, manslaughter, or rape, or attempted murder or rape, 'shall not be granted bail . . . only if he has been previously convicted . . . of any such offence or of culpable homicide and, in the case of a previous conviction of manslaughter or culpable homicide, if he was then sentenced to imprisonment or, if he was then a child or young person, to long term detention.'

Subsequently, in *S.C.B. v United Kingdom*, judgment of 19 June 2001, the Court examined the compatibility of section 25 with the requirements of Article 5(3) in the context of a person refused bail for six months who was subsequently acquitted of all the charges against him. Despite the Government, again, conceding a breach of Article 5(3) the Court determined that it should consider the applicant's complaints.

21. As to the merits of those complaints, the Court recalls that the Government's concession in the Caballero case was made following the adoption of the Commission's report in that case which concluded that the application of section 25 of the 1994 Act constituted a violation of Article 5 §§ 3 and 5 of the Convention.

22. The reasoning of the Commission in its report can be summarised as follows. It noted that judicial control of interference by the executive with an individual's right to liberty was an essential feature of the guarantees embodied in Article 5 § 3, the purpose being to minimise the risk of arbitrariness in the pre-trial detention of accused persons. Certain procedural and substantive guarantees ensure that judicial control: the judge (or other officer) before whom the accused is 'brought promptly' must be seen to be independent of the executive and of the parties to the proceedings; that judge, having heard the accused himself, must examine all the facts arguing for and against the existence of a genuine requirement of public interest justifying, with due regard to the presumption of innocence, a departure from the rule of respect for the accused's liberty, and that judge must have the power to order an accused's release. It not being disputed that Mr Caballero fell within the scope of section 25 of the 1994 Act, the Commission found that the possibility of any consideration by a Magistrate of his pre-trial release on bail had been excluded in advance by the legislature by section 25 of the 1994 Act. This removal of the judicial control of pre-trial detention required by Article 5 § 3 of the Convention was found by the Commission to amount to a violation of that Article. . . .

23. The Court sees no reason to disagree with the conclusions reached by the Commission in relation to Articles 5 and 13 in its report in the Cabellero case and, in this context, it finds no material difference between the relevant facts of the cases of Mr Caballero and the present applicant. It considers that section 25 of the 1994 Act applied in the applicant's case and that, by its terms, it removed the judicial control of his pre-trial detention which is required by Article 5 § 3 of the Convention.

24. Accordingly, the Court concludes that there has been a violation of Article 5 §§ 3 and 5 of the Convention.

Parliament had amended section 25 in 1998 (by the Crime and Disorder Act 1998, s. 56) so that, in respect of the listed charges, 'bail shall be granted . . . only if the court, or as the case may be, the constable, considering the grant of bail is satisfied that there are exceptional circumstances which justify it'.

Kalashnikov v Russia judgment of 15 July 2002
European Court of Human Rights

The applicant was the president of a bank in 1995. In February of that year criminal proceedings were begun against him in respect of embezzlement of bank funds and misappropriation of shares. In June 1995 he was arrested and held in detention on remand by order of the prosecutor, as it was alleged that Kalashnikov had obstructed the criminal investigation. Subsequently, the applicant's lawyer made numerous unsuccessful applications to the courts for Kalashnikov to be released on bail. In August 1999 he was convicted, by the Magadan City Court, of one count and acquitted on two others. The court sentenced him to five and a half years' imprisonment (starting from the time of his detention in 1995). He was released from prison, under an amnesty, in May 2000.

The applicant complained to the Court that, *inter alia*, his lengthy pre-trial detention violated Article 5(3).

114. The Court recalls that the question of whether or not a period of detention is reasonable cannot be assessed in the abstract. Whether it is reasonable for an accused to remain in detention must be examined in each case according to its special features. Continued detention can be justified in a given case only if there are specific indications of a genuine requirement of public interest which, notwithstanding the presumption of innocence, outweighs the rule of respect for individual liberty laid down in Article 5 of the Convention. . .

It falls in the first place to the national judicial authorities to ensure that, in a given case, the pre-trial detention of an accused person does not exceed a reasonable time. To this end they must, paying due regard to the principle of the presumption of innocence, examine all the facts arguing for or against the existence of the above-mentioned requirement of public interest justifying a departure from the rule in Article 5, and must set them out in their decisions on the applications for release. It is essentially on the basis of the reasons given in these decisions, and any well-documented facts stated by the applicant in his appeals, that the Court is called upon to decide whether or not there has been a violation of Article 5 § 3 . . .

The persistence of a reasonable suspicion that the person arrested has committed an offence is a condition *sine qua non* for the lawfulness of the continued detention, but after a certain lapse of time it no longer suffices. The Court must then establish whether the other grounds given by the judicial authorities continued to justify the deprivation of liberty. Where such grounds were 'relevant' and 'sufficient', the Court must also be satisfied that the national authorities displayed 'special diligence' in the conduct of the proceedings. The complexity and special characteristics of the investigation are factors to be considered in this respect . . .

(ii) Application of the above principles to the present case

(α) Grounds for detention

115. During the period covered by the Court's jurisdiction *ratione temporis* the Magadan City Court, in refusing to release the applicant, relied on the gravity of the charges against him and the danger of his obstructing the establishment of the truth while at liberty. The Court observes that similar grounds had been cited by the City Court earlier—on 27 December 1996 and 8 August 1997—to justify the applicant's continued detention.

It further notes that the principal reason for the decision to place the applicant in detention on remand on 29 June 1995 was that he had obstructed the investigation of the case by refusing to turn over certain bank documents necessary for the investigation, he had brought pressure to bear on witnesses and had allegedly tampered with the evidence. The decision also had regard to the gravity of the charges.

116. The Court recalls that the existence of a strong suspicion of the involvement of a person in serious offences, while constituting a relevant factor, cannot alone justify a long period of pre-trial detention ... As regards the other ground relied on by the Magadan City Court in prolonging the applicant's detention, namely the danger of obstructing the examination of the case, the Court notes that, unlike the order of the investigator of 29 June 1995, the City Court did not mention any factual circumstances underpinning its conclusions, which were identical both in 1996, 1997 and 1999. There is no reference in its rulings to any factor capable of showing that the risk relied on actually persisted during the relevant period.

117. The Court accepts that the interference with the investigation, along with the suspicion that the applicant had committed the offences with which he was charged, could initially suffice to warrant the applicant's detention. However, as the proceedings progressed and the collection of the evidence became complete that ground inevitably became less relevant.

118. In sum, the Court finds that the reasons relied on by the authorities to justify the applicant's detention, although relevant and sufficient initially, lost this character as time passed.

(β) Conduct of the proceedings

119. As regards the duration of the criminal investigation, the Court notes the findings of the domestic courts that the case was not particularly complex and that the investigation of the case had been of poor quality contributing to a delay in the proceedings. The Court finds no reason to come to a different conclusion. It also observes that, according to the domestic courts, the investigators had unjustifiably attempted to increase the number of counts in the indictment—a reproach which is borne out by the fact that only one of the nine charges against the applicant was found to be substantiated in the judgment of the Magadan City Court on 3 August 1999.

120. As regards the subsequent judicial proceedings, the Court observes that there were significant delays in the proceedings before the Magadan City Court. The trial, which had began on 11 November 1996, was adjourned on 7 May 1997 due to the removal from office of the presiding judge. It did not resume until 15 April 1999, although certain procedural steps were taken in July–August 1997 (the appointment of a new judge and scheduling of a hearing), May and July 1998 (the transfer of the case to another court), November 1998 (the scheduling of a hearing), January and March 1998 (decisions on the need for further investigation).

While it is true that the hearing scheduled for 8 August 1997 had to be postponed on account of the absence of the applicant's lawyer and the applicant objected to the transfer of his case to another court—a move destined to expedite the proceedings—the Court finds that the applicant did not substantially contribute to the length of the proceedings between the two trial periods, where there was no progress in the case.

It is thus apparent that the protracted proceedings are attributable neither to the complexity of the case nor the conduct of the applicant. Having regard to the characteristics of the investigation and the substantial delays in the court proceedings, the Court considers that the authorities did not act with all due expedition.

(γ) Conclusion

121. Against the above background, the Court finds that the period spent by the applicant in detention pending trial exceeded a 'reasonable time'. There has thus been a violation of Article 5 § 3 of the Convention.

...

FOR THESE REASONS, THE COURT UNANIMOUSLY

...

2. *Holds* that there has been a violation of Article 5(3) of the Convention;

NOTES

1 The Court was composed of President Costa and Judges: Fuhrmann, Loucaides, Bratza, Greve, Traja and Kovler.

2 The judgment demonstrates the contemporary approach of the full-time Court to assessing whether a (lengthy) period of pre-trial detention on remand is reasonable under Article 5(3). The Court will subject the reasons for the detention given by the domestic judiciary to a close and strict evaluation. National authorities must grant detainees bail unless there are convincing public interest grounds justifying pre-trial detention. Where such grounds exist the domestic courts must monitor the continuance of those grounds and order the detainees release as soon as they end. Furthermore, the prosecution and judicial authorities must process cases with reasonable expedition.

3 For the Article 3 aspects of *Kalashnikov* see above p 214.

Article 5(4): Remedy to challenge the legality of detention

....

De Wilde, Ooms and Versyp v Belgium (the 'Vagrancy' cases)
A.12 (1971) 1 EHRR 373
European Court of Human Rights

....

The applicants reported voluntarily to the police declaring that they had no home and were destitute. They were brought before a police court composed of a single magistrate who verified the 'identity, age, physical and mental state and manner of life' of the individuals and, after giving them an opportunity to reply, decided they were 'vagrants' as defined by Belgian law. Under an 1891 Act 'for the suppression of vagrancy and begging' the magistrate was therefore obliged to place the applicants 'at the disposal of the Government'. De Wilde and Versyp were ordered by the magistrate 'to be detained in a vagrancy centre for two years' (the minimum requirement) and Ooms was ordered 'to be detained in an assistance home' (under special provisions in the Act for alcoholism or begging). Although an appropriate note was put on their criminal records, domestic law did not treat the court's decision as a criminal conviction.

For this reason, no challenge or appeal was possible as legally the magistrates decision was viewed an administrative act, not a judgment.

Soon after their respective detention orders were issued, the applicants made a series of unsuccessful representations to the Minister of Justice complaining, *inter alia*, of the regime and conditions of work to which they were subject and requesting their release, *inter alia*, because of their changed circumstances, including the prospect of work in the community and the money that they had earned for their work in detention. The 1891 Act required release on the expiry of the term given by the court or at the discretion of the Minister of Justice, or additionally, for those detained in assistance homes only (ie Ooms), when an amount stated in advance by the Minister of Justice had been saved.

The applicants alleged, *inter alia*, breaches of Articles 5(1) and (4). The Commission expressed the opinion, *inter alia*, that there had been a violation of Article 5(4) (nine votes to two), but not of Article 5(1) (ten votes to one).

In the following extract, the Court first considered whether the detention of the applicants could be justified under Article 5(1)(e) on the basis that they were 'vagrants'. It then examined how Article 5(4) should be applied in a case where the detention is ordered not by a policeman or an administrator, but by a body that qualifies as a court in the sense of Article 5(4).

JUDGMENT OF THE COURT

64. The government stressed that the applicants had reported voluntarily to the police and that their admission to Wortel and Merksplas had been the result 'of an express or implicit request' on their part, express for Versyp and Ooms, implicit for De Wilde. According to the Government, such a 'voluntary reporting' can scarcely amount to being 'deprived of liberty' within the meaning of Article 5. From this it concluded that the Court ought to rule out forthwith any idea of a failure to comply with the requirements of the Convention, as regards both 'the detention itself' and 'the conditions of detention'.

65. The Court is not persuaded by this line of argument.

Temporary distress or misery may drive a person to give himself up to the police to be detained. This does not necessarily mean that the person so asking is in a state of vagrancy and even less that he is a professional beggar or that his state of vagrancy results from one of the circumstances—idleness, drunkenness or immorality—which, under Section 13 of the Belgian Act of 1891, may entail a more severe measure of detention.

Insofar as the wishes of the applicants were taken into account, they cannot in any event remove or disguise the mandatory, as opposed to contractual, character of the decisions complained of; this mandatory character comes out unambiguously in the legal texts (Sections 8, 13, 15, 16 and 18 of the 1891 Act) and in the documents before the Court.

Finally and above all, the right to liberty is too important in a 'democratic society' within the meaning of the Convention for a person to lose the benefit of the protection of the Convention for the single reason that he gives himself up to be taken into detention. Detention might violate Article 5 even although the person concerned might have agreed to it. When the matter is one which concerns *ordre public* within the Council of Europe, a scrupulous supervision by the organs of the Convention of all measures capable of violating the rights and freedoms which it guarantees is necessary in every case. Furthermore, Section 12 of the 1891 Act acknowledges the need for such supervision at national level: it obliges the magistrates to 'ascertain the identity, age, physical and mental state and manner of life of persons brought before the police court for vagrancy'. Nor does the fact that the applicants 'reported voluntarily' in any way relieve the Court of its duty to see whether there has been a violation of the Convention. . . .

67. The applicants were provisionally deprived of their freedom by the police superintendent to whom they presented themselves and they were brought by him within 24 hours, as provided by section 3 of the Act of 1 May 1849, before the magistrate, who placed them at the disposal of the Government. . . .

The lawfulness of the action of the police superintendents has not been challenged; as the persons concerned reported voluntarily and indicated that they were in a state of vagrancy, it was only normal that they should be brought before the magistrate for a decision. This action, moreover, was of a purely preliminary nature.

It was by virtue of the magistrates' orders that the detention took place. It is therefore by reference to these orders that the lawfulness of the detention of the three applicants must be assessed.

68. The Convention does not contain a definition of the term 'vagrant'. The definition in article 347 of the Belgian Criminal Code reads: 'vagrants are persons who have no fixed abode, no means of subsistence and no regular trade or profession'. Where these three conditions are fulfilled, they may lead the competent authorities to order that the persons concerned be placed at the disposal of the Government as vagrants. The definition quoted does not appear to be in any way irreconcilable with the usual means of the term 'vagrant', and the Court considers that a person who is a vagrant under the terms of Article 347 in principle falls within the exception provided for in article 5(1)(e) of the Convention.

In the present cases, the want of a fixed abode and of means of subsistence resulted not merely from the action of the persons concerned in reporting voluntarily to the police but from their own declarations made at the time: all three stated that they were without any employment. . . . As to the habitual character of this lack of employment, the magistrates at Charleroi, Namur and Brussels were in a position to deduce this from the information available to them concerning the respective applicants. . . .

69. Having thus the character of a 'vagrant', the applicants could, under Article 5(1)(e) of the Convention, be made the subject of a detention provided that it was ordered by the competent authorities and in accordance with the procedure prescribed by Belgian law.

[The Court then examined the procedures that had been followed and concluded that Belgian law had been complied with.]

70. The Court has, therefore, not found either irregularity or arbitrariness in the placing of the three applicants at the disposal of the Government and it has no reason to find the resulting detention incompatible with Article 5(1)(e) of the Convention. . . .

73. Although the Court has not found in the present cases any incompatibility with paragraph (1) of Article 5 . . . this finding does not dispense it from now proceeding to examine whether there has been any violation of paragraph (4). The latter is, in effect, a separate provision, and its observance does not result *eo ipso* from the observance of the former: 'everyone who is deprived of his liberty', lawfully or not, is entitled to a supervision of lawfulness by a court; a violation can therefore result either from a detention incompatible with paragraph (1) or from the absence of any proceedings satisfying paragraph (4), or even from both at the same time. . . .

75. The applicants were detained in execution of the magistrates' orders: their arrest by the police was merely a provisional act and no other authority intervened in the three cases. . . . A first question consequently arises. Does Article 5(4) require that two authorities should deal with the cases falling under it, that is, one which orders the detention and a second, having the attributes of a court, which examines the lawfulness of this measure on the application of the person concerned? Or, as against this, is it sufficient that the detention should be ordered by an authority which had the elements inherent in the concept of a 'court' within the meaning of Article 5(4)?

76. At first sight, the wording of Article 5(4) might make one think that it guarantees the right of the detainee always to have supervised by a court the lawfulness of a previous decision which has deprived him of his liberty. The two official tests do not however use the same terms, since the English text speaks of 'proceedings' and not of 'appeal', 'recourse' or 'remedy' (compare Articles 13 and 26). Besides, it is clear that the purpose of Article 5(4) is to assure to persons who are arrested and detained the right to a judicial supervision of the lawfulness of the measure to which they are thereby subjected; the word 'court' ('tribunal') is there found in the singular and not in the plural. Where the decision

depriving a person of his liberty is one taken by an administrative body, there is no doubt that Article 5(4) obliges the Contracting States to make available to the person detained a right of recourse to a court; but there is nothing to indicate that the same applies when the decision is made by a court at the close of judicial proceedings. In the latter case the supervision required by Article 5(4) is incorporated in the decision; this is so, for example, where a sentence of imprisonment is pronounced after 'conviction by a competent court' (Article 5(1)(a) of the Convention). It may therefore be concluded that Article 5(4) is observed if the arrest or detention of a vagrant, provided for in paragraph (1)(e), is ordered by a 'court' within the meaning of paragraph (4).

It results, however, from the purpose and object of Article 5, as well as from the very terms of paragraph (4) ('proceedings'/'*recours*'), that in order to constitute such a 'court' an authority must provide the fundamental guarantee of procedure applied in matters of deprivation of liberty. . . .

77. The Court has therefore enquired whether in the present case the magistrate possessed the character of a 'court' within the meaning of Article 5(4), and especially whether the applicants enjoyed, when appearing before him, the guarantees mentioned above. There is no doubt that, from an organisational point of view, the magistrate is a 'court. . . . The magistrate is independent both of the executive and of the parties to the case . . .

78. . . . The forms of the procedure required by the Convention need not, however, necessarily be identical in each of the cases where the intervention of a court is required. In order to determine whether a proceeding provides adequate guarantees, regard must be had to the particular nature of the circumstances in which such proceeding takes place. Thus, in the *Neumeister* case, the Court considered that the competent courts remained 'courts' in spite of the lack of 'equality of arms' between the prosecution and an individual who requested provisional release (*ibidem*); nevertheless, the same might not be true in a different context and, for example, in another situation which is also governed by Article 5(4).

79. . . . The deprivation of liberty complained of by De Wilde, Ooms and Versyp resembles that imposed by a criminal court. Therefore, the procedure applicable should not have provided guarantees markedly inferior to those existing in criminal matters in the member States of the Council of Europe.

According to Belgian law, every individual found in a state of vagrancy is arrested and then brought—within twenty-four hours as a rule—before the police court (Section 8 of the 1891 Act and Section 3 of the Act of 1st May 1849). Regarding the interrogation of this individual, the 1891 Act limits itself to specifying in Section 12 that the magistrate ascertains the identity, age, physical and mental state and manner of life of the person brought before him. Regarding the right of defence, the only relevant provision is found in Section 3 of the Act of 1st May 1849, which provides that the person concerned is granted a three-day adjournment if he so requests. According to information provided by the Government, the Code of Criminal Procedure does not apply to the detention of vagrants.

The procedure in question is affected by the administrative nature of the decision to be given. It does not ensure guarantees comparable to those which exist as regards detention in criminal cases, notwithstanding the fact that the detention of vagrants is very similar in many respects. It is hard to understand why persons arrested for simple vagrancy have to be content with such a summary procedure. . . . This procedure undoubtedly presents certain judicial features, such as the hearing taking place and the decision being given in public, but they are not sufficient to give the magistrate the character of a 'court' within the meaning of Article 5(4) when due account is taken of the seriousness of what is at stake, namely a long deprivation of liberty attended by various shameful consequences. Therefore it does not by itself satisfy the requirements of Article 5(4) and the Commission was quite correct in considering that a remedy should have been open to the applicants. The Court, however, has already held that De Wilde, Ooms and Versyp had no access either to a superior court or, at least in practice, to the Conseil d'Etat. . . .

80. The Court therefore reaches the conclusion that on the point now under consideration there has been a violation of Article 5(4) in that the three applicants did not enjoy the guarantees contained in that paragraph. . . .

FOR THESE REASONS, THE COURT,

Holds unanimously that the 'voluntary reporting' by the applicants does not suffice to establish the absence of any violation of the Convention;

Holds unanimously that there has been no breach of Article 5(1);

Holds by nine votes to seven that there has been a breach of Article 5(4) in that the applicants had no remedy open to them before a court against the decision ordering their detention; . . .

NOTES

1   The Court was composed of President Sir Humphrey Waldock and Judges Rolin, Cassin, Holmback, Verdross, Rodenbourg, Ross, Wold, Balladore Pallieri, Mosler, Zekia, Favre, Cremona, Bilge, Wiarda, and Sigurjónsson. Judges Balladore Pallieri and Verdross issued a joint separate opinion in which they considered that the possibility of the applicants' appealing to the Conseil d'Etat against the decisions of the magistrates satisfied the requirements of Article 5(4). A similar conclusion was reached in the collective separate opinion of Judges: Holmback, Rodenbourg, Ross, Favre, and Bilge.

2   The *Vagrancy* cases establish that where the decision to detain an individual is taken by a court—not by a police officer or an administrator—the judicial decision on the legality of the detention required by Article 5(4) is incorporated in the initial decision to detain. For the purpose of this 'incorporation' rule, and generally under Article 5(4), a 'court' is a body that is 'independent both of the executive and of the parties to the case': *Neumeister v Austria*, A.8 (1968) 1 EHRR 91. It must also be able to take a binding decision. This last requirement and the need for the remedy to be able to cover all aspects of the justification for detention led to the finding of a breach of Article 5(4) in *Chahal v UK* (1996) 23 EHRR 413, 1996-IV 1864. The Court stated:

129. The notion of 'lawfulness' in Article 5 § 1 (f) does not refer solely to the obligation to conform to the substantive and procedural rules of national law; it requires in addition that any deprivation of liberty should be in keeping with the purpose of Article 5. . . . The question therefore arises whether the available proceedings to challenge the lawfulness of Mr Chahal's detention and to seek bail provided an adequate control by the domestic courts.

130. The Court recollects that, because national security was involved, the domestic courts were not in a position to review whether the decisions to detain Mr Chahal and to keep him in detention were justified on national security grounds. . . . Furthermore, although the procedure before the advisory panel undoubtedly provided some degree of control, bearing in mind that Mr Chahal was not entitled to legal representation before the panel, that he was only given an outline of the grounds for the notice of intention to deport, that the panel had no power of decision and that its advice to the Home Secretary was not binding and was not disclosed . . . , the panel could not be considered as a 'court' within the meaning of Article 5 § 4 (see, *mutatis mutandis*, the *X v UK* judgment of 5 November 1981, Series A No 46, p 26, § 61).

131. The Court recognises that the use of confidential material may be unavoidable where national security is at stake. This does not mean, however, that the national authorities can be free from effective control by the domestic courts whenever they choose to assert that national security and terrorism are involved (see, *mutatis mutandis*, the *Fox, Campbell and Hartley v UK* judgment of 30 August 1990, Series A No 182, p 17, § 34, and the *Murray v UK* judgment of 28 October 1994, Series A No 300-A, p 27, § 58). The Court attaches significance to the fact that, as the intervenors pointed out in connection with Article 13 . . . , in Canada a more effective form of judicial control has been developed in cases of this type. This example illustrates that there are techniques which can be employed which both

accommodate legitimate security concerns about the nature and sources of intelligence information and yet accord the individual a substantial measure of procedural justice.

132. It follows that the Court considers that neither the proceedings for habeas corpus and for judicial review of the decision to detain Mr Chahal before the domestic courts, nor the advisory panel procedure, satisfied the requirements of Article 5 § 4. This shortcoming is all the more significant given that Mr Chahal has undoubtedly been deprived of his liberty for a length of time which is bound to give rise to serious concern. . . .

3   As established in the *Vagrancy* cases, and confirmed, *inter alia*, in the *Chahal* case, the 'court' before which a detained person must have a remedy must provide appropriate procedural guarantees, which may vary according to the kind of detention (of an accused, a person of 'unsound mind', a person being deported, etc). In *Sanchez-Reisse v Switzerland*, A 107 (1986) 9 EHRR 71, in a case concerning detention pending extradition, the applicant argued that he should have been given an opportunity to reply to the Federal Police Office's opinion on his release and of appearing in person. Holding that there had been a breach of Article 5(4), the Court stated:

51. In the Court's opinion, Article 5 § 4 required in the present case that Mr Sanchez-Reisse be provided, in some way or another, with the benefit of an adversarial procedure.

Giving him the possibility of submitting written comments on the Office's opinion would have constituted an appropriate means, but there is nothing to show that he was offered such a possibility. Admittedly, he had already indicated in his request the circumstances which, in his view, justified his release, but this of itself did not provide the 'equality of arms' that is indispensable: the opinion could subsequently have referred to new points of fact or of law giving rise, on the detainee's part, to reactions or criticisms or even to questions of which the Federal Court should have been able to take notice before rendering its decision.

The applicant's reply did not, however, necessarily have to be in writing: the result required by Article 5 § 4 could also have been attained if he had appeared in person before the Federal Court.

The possibility for a detainee 'to be heard either in person or, where necessary, through some form of representation' (see the above-mentioned *Winterwerp* judgment, Series A No 33, p 24, § 60) features in certain instances among the 'fundamental guarantees of procedure applied in matters of deprivation of liberty' (see the *De Wilde, Ooms and Versyp* judgment of 18 June 1971, Series A No 12, p 41, § 76). Despite the difference in wording between paragraph 3 (right to be brought before a judge or other officer) and paragraph 4 (right to take proceedings) of Article 5, the Court's previous decisions relating to these two paragraphs have hitherto tended to acknowledge the need for a hearing before the judicial authority (see, *inter alia*, in addition to the above-mentioned *Winterwerp* judgment, the *Schiesser* judgment of 4 December 1979, Series A No 34, p 13, §§ 30–1). These decisions concerned, however, only matters falling within the ambit of sub-paragraphs (c) and (e) *in fine* of paragraph 1. And, in fact, 'the forms of the procedure required by the Convention need not . . . necessarily be identical in each of the cases where the intervention of a court is required' (see the above-mentioned *De Wilde, Ooms and Versyp* judgment, Series A No 12, pp 41–2, § 78).

In the present case, the Federal Court was led to take into consideration the applicant's worsening state of health, a factor which might have militated in favour of his appearing in person, but it had at its disposal the medical certificates appended to the third request for provisional release from custody (see paragraph 28 above). There is no reason to believe that the applicant's presence could have convinced the Federal Court that he had to be released.

Nevertheless, it remains the case that Mr Sanchez-Reisse did not receive the benefit of a procedure that was really adversarial.

The full-time Court held that an oral hearing was required when the Parole Board considered the personality of a recalled life prisoner in order to determine his dangerousness. In

Waite v UK, judgment of 10 December 2002, the applicant had been convicted of murdering his grandmother when aged 16 in 1981. He was released on life licence in 1994 but recalled in July 1997, after he had been arrested on suspicion of possessing controlled drugs and had attempted to commit suicide. The Parole Board considered his recall in September 1997 by means of written representations from the applicant (though under administrative arrangements he should have been given an oral hearing). The Board determined that he was a danger to himself and the community and confirmed his recall. In October 1998 the Parole Board re-examined his case via an oral hearing, at which the applicant was represented and present. The Board concluded that he should be released on licence and that took place in November 1998. The applicant asserted, *inter alia*, a breach of Article 5(4) through the failure to provide him with an oral hearing before the Parole Board in September 1997. The Court, unanimously, held that:

59. . . . In matters of such crucial importance as the deprivation of liberty and where questions arise involving, for example, an assessment of the applicant's character or mental state, the Court's case-law indicates that it may be essential to the fairness of the proceedings that the applicant be present at an oral hearing. In such a case as the present, where characteristics pertaining to the applicant's personality and level of maturity and reliability are of importance in deciding on his dangerousness, Article 5 § 4 requires an oral hearing in the context of an adversarial procedure involving legal representation and the possibility of calling and questioning witnesses.

As such a procedure had not been followed there had been a breach of Article 5(4).

4 In *Kampanis v Greece*, A.325 (1995) 21 EHRR 43, the prosecutor was allowed to appear before the court deciding on the renewal of detention on remand when the accused was not. The European Court held that this lack of 'equality of arms' infringed Article 5(4). It stated:

56. The Court must bear in mind that the prosecutor essentially represents the interests of society in criminal proceedings. In connection with the application in issue, his task was to suggest to the Indictment Division either that the accused's detention be prolonged or that he be released. In the instant case he always submitted that detention should be prolonged.

57. Secondly, the Court acknowledges that the applicant filed a number of applications for release and a number of pleadings in support of them, both during the investigation and even after it had been closed. His arguments, which mostly concerned the legal classification of the offences he was accused of and the reasons given for his detention, were undoubtedly known to the prosecutor and the Indictment Division.

However, when he lodged the application in question, Mr Kampanis had been in prison for 25 months and 10 days pursuant to three successive orders, each of which fixed a different starting point for the calculation of his detention on remand; in two of these cases detention had been prolonged up to the maximum permitted under the Constitution. Moreover, in this particular application he criticised, *inter alia*, the incompatibility of the length of his detention with the Constitution and the Convention.

58. In the light of these considerations, the Court is of the view that to ensure equality of arms it was necessary to give the applicant the opportunity to appear at the same time as the prosecutor so that he could reply to his arguments.

5 In *Reinprecht v Austria*, judgment of 15 November 2005, a unanimous Chamber held that Article 5(4) does not impose a general requirement for the hearing of reviews of the lawfulness of pre-trial detention to be held in public. The applicant brought several challenges to his pre-trial detention before the Regional Court. The latter held hearings, at which the applicant and his lawyer were present, after which the Regional Court ordered the applicant's continued detention. He complained to Strasbourg arguing that Article 5(4) required the hearings to be held in public. The Helsinki Foundation for Human Rights, as a third party, supported his claim as they believed that public scrutiny of such hearings would help verify the independence of the court and ensure the absence of arbitrariness. The Government contended that requiring these hearings to be held in public could well cause delays (the hearings were often held in remand prisons and if the prisoner had to be taken to a court building for a public hearing that might result in delays). The Chamber concluded that the Court's existing case law did not oblige these hearings to be held in public and there was 'some force' in the Government's argument that requiring public hearings could have a negative impact on the speediness of reviews. Therefore, no breach of Article 5(4) had occurred.

6 The speediness of the judicial determination of a detainee's challenge to the lawfulness of his detention was examined by the full-time Court in *Rehbock v Slovenia*, judgment of 28 November 2000 (and see above p 175 for the Article 3 aspects of the case). The applicant was arrested by Slovenian police on 8 September 1995 for suspected drugs smuggling. On 10 September an investigating judge of the Slovenj Gradec Regional Court remanded him in custody. On 3 October the applicant, via his lawyer, lodged a request for his release on bail (he offered a security of 50,000 DEM). The Slovenj Gradec Regional Court dismissed his request on 26 October (the Court did not consider the applicant's offer of security as a sufficient guarantee that he would attend his trial). The Strasbourg Court was unanimous in concluding that the twenty-three days taken by the Regional Court to determine the applicant's request for release did not satisfy the requirement of speediness contained in Article 5(4).

Winterwerp v Netherlands A.33 (1979) 2 EHRR 387
European Court of Human Rights

In 1968, after events in which it was apparent that he was in some distress, the applicant was committed for a short term period to a psychiatric hospital by the direction of the local burgomaster in accordance with an emergency procedure provided for in Dutch law. Six weeks later, on his wife's application and following a medical report, the applicant was confined on a longer term basis following non-emergency procedures to the same hospital under an order made by the District Court. Thereafter the applicant regularly requested that he be discharged. His requests were passed by the hospital authorities to the public prosecutor. In 1969, in the exercise of his discretion, the public prosecutor referred the applicant's first request to the Regional Court where it was dismissed. As the law allowed, the prosecutor declined to refer the requests to the Regional Court in 1971, 1972 and again in 1973 on the basis that upon the evidence it appeared manifestly impossible that the Regional Court would grant the request.

The Commission expressed the unanimous opinion that there had been no breach of Article 5(1) but that there had been for Article 5(4). In the following extract, the Court considered whether the applicant's detention could be justified under Article 5(1)(e) on the basis that he was 'of unsound mind' and whether the failure to refer the applicant's requests for release to a court after 1969 amounted to a breach of Article 5(4) in a case where the facts justifying for the detention may change.

JUDGMENT OF THE COURT

37. The Convention does not state what is to be understood by the words 'persons of unsound mind'. This term is not one that can be given a definitive interpretation: as was pointed out by the Commission, the Government and the applicant, it is a term whose meaning is continually evolving

as research in psychiatry progresses, an increasing flexibility in treatment is developing and society's attitude to mental illness changes, in particular so that a greater understanding of the problems of mental patients is becoming more wide-spread.

In any event, sub-paragraph (e) of Article 5 § 1 obviously cannot be taken as permitting the detention of a person simply because his views or behaviour deviate from the norms prevailing in a particular society. To hold otherwise would not be reconcilable with the text of Article 5 § 1 which sets out an exhaustive list (see the *Engel* judgment of 8 June 1976, Series A No 22, p 24, § 57, and the *Ireland v UK* judgment of 18 January 1978, Series A No 25, p 74, § 194) of exceptions calling for a narrow interpretation (see, *mutatis mutandis*, the *Klass* judgment of 6 September 1978, Series A No 28, p 21, § 42, and the *Sunday Times* judgment of 26 April 1979, Series A No 30, p 41, § 65). Neither would it be in conformity with the object and purpose of Article 5 § 1, namely to ensure that no one should be dispossessed of his liberty in an arbitrary fashion (see the *Lawless* judgment of 1 July 1961, Series A No 3, p 52, and the above-mentioned *Engel* judgment, p 25, § 58). Moreover, it would disregard the importance of the right to liberty in a democratic society (see the *De Wilde, Ooms and Versyp* judgment of 18 June 1971, Series A No 12, p 36, § 65, and the above-mentioned *Engel* judgment, p 35, § 82 *in fine*).

38. Just as the Convention does not give any definition of 'persons of unsound mind', so the Netherlands legislation does not define 'mentally ill persons' (*krankzinnige*); what the legislation does is to lay down the grounds for committing such persons to a psychiatric hospital. . . .

[The Court examined the relevant Dutch law and practice.]

Having regard to the above-mentioned practice, the law in force does not appear to be in any way incompatible with the meaning that the expression 'persons of unsound mind' is to be given in the context of the Convention. The Court therefore considers that an individual who is detained under the Netherlands Mentally Ill Persons Act in principle falls within the ambit of Article 5 § 1(e).

39. The next issue to be examined is the 'lawfulness' of the detention for the purposes of Article 5 § 1(e). Such 'lawfulness' presupposes conformity with the domestic law in the first place and also, as confirmed by Article 18, conformity with the purpose of the restrictions permitted by Article 5 § 1(e); it is required in respect of both the ordering and the execution of the measures involving deprivation of liberty (see the above-mentioned *Engel and others* judgment, p 28, § 68, *in fine*).

As regards the conformity with the domestic law, the Court points out that the term 'lawful' covers procedural as well as substantive rules. There thus exists a certain overlapping between this term and the general requirement stated at the beginning of Article 5 § 1, namely observance of 'a procedure prescribed by law'. . . .

Indeed, these two expressions reflect the importance of the aim underlying Article 5 § 1 (see paragraph 37 above): in a democratic society subscribing to the rule of law (see the *Golder* judgment of 21 February 1975, Series A No 18, pp 16–17, § 34, and the above-mentioned *Klass* judgment, p 25, § 55), no detention that is arbitrary can ever be regarded as 'lawful'.

The Commission likewise stresses that there must be no element of arbitrariness; the conclusion it draws is that no one may be confined as 'a person of unsound mind' in the absence of medical evidence establishing that his mental state is such as to justify his compulsory hospitalisation. . . . The applicant and the Government both express similar opinions.

The Court fully agrees with this line of reasoning. In the Court's opinion, except in emergency cases, the individual concerned should not be deprived of his liberty unless he has been reliably shown to be of 'unsound mind'. The very nature of what has to be established before the competent authority— that is, a true mental disorder—calls for objective medical expertise. Further, the mental disorder must be of a kind or degree warranting compulsory confinement. What is more, the validity of continued confinement depends upon the persistence of such a disorder (see, *mutatis mutandis*, the *Stögmüller* judgment of 10 November 1969, Series A No 9, pp 39–40, § 4, and the above-mentioned *De Wilde, Ooms and Versyp* judgment, p 43, § 82).

40. The Court undoubtedly has the jurisdiction to verify the 'lawfulness' of the detention (see the above-mentioned *Engel* judgment, p 29, § 69). Mr Winterwerp in fact alleges unlawfulness by reason of procedural defects in the making of three of the detention orders under consideration. Those allegations are dealt with below in connection with the closely linked issue of compliance with 'a procedure prescribed by law'.... In the present context it suffices to add the following: in deciding whether an individual should be detained as a 'person of unsound mind', the national authorities are to be recognised as having a certain discretion since it is in the first place for the national authorities to evaluate the evidence adduced before them in a particular case; the Court's task is to review under the Convention the decisions of those authorities (see notably, *mutatis mutandis*, the *Handyside* judgment of 7 December 1976, Series A No 24, pp 22 and 23, §§ 48 and 50, the above-mentioned *Klass* judgment, p 23, § 49, and the above-mentioned *Sunday Times* judgment, p 36, § 59).

41. As to the facts of the instant case, the medical evidence submitted to the courts indicated in substance that the applicant showed schizophrenic and paranoiac reactions, that he was unaware of his pathological condition and that, on several occasions, he had committed some fairly serious acts without appreciating their consequences. In addition, various attempts at his gradual rehabilitation into society have failed....

42. Mr Winterwerp criticises the medical reports as unsatisfactory for the purposes of Article 5 § 1(e). In addition, he queries whether the burgomaster's initial direction to detain was founded on psychiatric evidence.

In the Court's view, the events that prompted the burgomaster's direction in May 1968 ... are of a nature to justify an 'emergency' confinement of the kind provided for at that time under section 14 of the Netherlands Act. While some hesitation may be felt as to the need for such confinement to continue for as long as six weeks, the period is not so excessive as to render the detention 'unlawful'. Despite the applicant's criticisms, the Court has no reason whatsoever to doubt the objectivity and reliability of the medical evidence on the basis of which the Netherlands courts, from June 1968 onwards, have authorised his detention as a person of unsound mind. Neither is there any indication that the contested deprivation of liberty was effected for a wrongful purpose.

43. The Court accordingly concludes that Mr Winterwerp's confinement, during all the various phases under consideration, constituted 'the lawful detention' of [a person] of unsound mind', within the meaning of sub-paragraph (e) of Article 5 § 1....

51. Mr Winterwerp argues that Article 5 § 1(e) entails, for any individual confined as a 'person of unsound mind', the right to appropriate treatment in order to ensure that he is not detained longer than absolutely necessary. As to his own situation, he complains that the meetings with his psychiatrist were too short and infrequent and that the medication administered to him was unduly made up of tranquillisers.

The Government categorically deny these allegations.

The Court considers, as does the Commission, that a mental patient's right to treatment appropriate to his condition cannot as such be derived from Article 5 § 1(e). Furthermore, the evidence contains no suggestion, as regards treatment, of a breach of any other provision in the Convention....

53. The applicant also relies on paragraph 4 of Article 5....

55. In the above-mentioned *De Wilde, Ooms and Versyp* judgment of 18 June 1971 (p 40, § 76), the Court stated:

'Where the decision depriving a person of his liberty is one taken by an administrative body, ... Article 5 § 4 obliges the Contracting States to make available to the person detained a right of recourse to a court; but there is nothing to indicate that the same applies when the decision is made by a court at the close of judicial proceedings. In the latter case the supervision required by Article 5 § 4 is incorporated in the decision; ...'

Citing its own case-law, the Commission puts forward the view that, as it stands, this conclusion by the Court cannot be sustained in the case of confinement of persons on the ground of 'unsound mind', at any rate when the confinement is for an indefinite period (see paragraph 95 of the report).

As is indicated earlier in the present judgment, . . . the reasons initially warranting confinement of this kind may cease to exist. . . . Consequently, it would be contrary to the object and purpose of Article 5 . . . to interpret paragraph 4 thereof, read in its context, as making this category of confinement immune from subsequent review of lawfulness merely provided that the initial decision issued from a court. The very nature of the deprivation of liberty under consideration would appear to require a review of lawfulness to be available at reasonable intervals. However, as the Commission states in paragraph 95 of its report, further examination of this question is superfluous without first establishing whether the relevant decisions affecting Mr Winterwerp were in fact take after 'proceedings [before] a court' ('*recours devant un tribunal*') within the meaning of Article 5 § 4.

56. Neither the burgomaster, who made the initial direction to detain, nor the public prosecutor, who prolonged its validity, can be regarded as possessing the characteristics of a 'court'. In contrast, there is no doubt that the District Court and the Regional Courts, which issued the various detention orders, are 'courts' from an organisational point of view: they are 'independent both of the executive and of the parties to the case' (see the above-mentioned *De Wilde, Ooms and Versyp* judgment, p 41, § 77).

57. Nevertheless, the intervention of such a body will satisfy Article 5 § 4 only on condition that 'the procedure followed has a judicial character and gives to the individual concerned guarantees appropriate to the kind of deprivation of liberty in question'; 'in order to determine whether a proceeding provides adequate guarantees, regard must be had to the particular nature of the circumstances in which such proceeding takes place' (see the last-mentioned judgment, pp 41 and 42, §§ 76 *in fine* and 78).

As the Government rightly stress, the 'detention of persons of unsound mind' (Article 5 § 1 (e) constitutes a special category. . . .'

60. The judicial proceedings referred to in Article 5 § 4 need not, it is true, always be attended by the same guarantees as those required under Article 6 § 1 for civil or criminal litigation (see the above-mentioned *De Wilde, Ooms and Versyp* judgment, p 42, § 78 *in fine*). Nonetheless, it is essential that the person concerned should have access to a court and the opportunity to be heard either in person or, where necessary, through some form of representation, failing which he will not have been afforded 'the fundamental guarantees of procedure applied in matters of deprivation of liberty' (see the last-mentioned judgment, p 41, § 76). Mental illness may entail restricting or modifying the manner of exercise of such a right (see, as regards Article 6 § 1, the above-mentioned *Golder* judgment, p 19, § 39), but it cannot justify impairing the very essence of the right. Indeed, special procedural safeguards may prove called for in order to protect the interests of persons who, on account of their mental disabilities, are not fully capable of acting for themselves.

61. Under sections 17, 23 and 24 of the Mentally Ill Persons Act as in force at the relevant times, neither the District Court nor the Regional Court was obliged to hear the individual whose detention was being sought. . . .

As to the particular facts, the applicant was never associated either personally or through a representative, in the proceedings leading to the various detention orders made against him: he was never notified of the proceedings or of their outcome; neither was he heard by the courts or given the opportunity to argue his case.

In this fundamental respect, the guarantees demanded by Article 5 § 4 of the Convention were lacking both in law and in practice. In spite of presenting some judicial features, the procedure followed by the District Court and the Regional Court for deciding the applications for his detention did not entitle Mr Winterwerp 'to take proceedings . . . [before] a court', within the meaning of Article 5 § 4 (see paragraph 57 above). Without in any way underestimating the value of the many guarantees provided under the Mentally Ill Persons Act, the Court finds that the said procedure did not meet the requirements of Article 5 § 4.

62. As concerns the applicant's requests for discharge [the] Government rightly insist on the need to take a comprehensive view of the whole system established under the Mentally Ill Persons Act. It therefore remains to determine whether the foregoing lacunae found by the Court are remedied in the procedure governing requests for discharge. . . .

63. While section 29 of the Act allows the person concerned to seek a review of his detention, his request for discharge is not necessarily decided on by a court. The request has to be addressed to the hospital authorities who transmit it, if they have received an unfavourable medical opinion, to the public prosecutor. The public prosecutor will in principle then refer the request to the Regional Court, but in certain cases he is not obliged to do so, in particular where it appears manifestly impossible to grant the request. The public prosecutor's decision can in no way be regarded as issuing from a court for the purposes of Article 5 § 4 of the Convention. Admittedly, limitations as to the intervals between applications for release may, according to the circumstances, constitute legitimate restrictions on access to the courts by persons of unsound mind (see paragraph 60 above). However, each time the public prosecutor declines to communicate a request to the Regional Court on the ground that it appears evidently ill-founded he is not merely restricting but effectively denying the right to court proceedings as embodied in Article 5 § 4.

The Regional Court, in those instances where the request has come before it for decision, is completely free in judging the desirability of hearing the detained person. A power of this kind does not assure the fundamental guarantees of procedure to be applied in matters of deprivation of liberty (see paragraphs 60 and 61 above).

64. Mr Winterwerp was in fact heard by the Regional Court in February 1969 when it examined his first request for release. . . . To this extent, he had been able to take proceedings before a court in order to test the lawfulness of his confinement.

In contrast, his subsequent requests in April 1971, July 1972 and February 1973 were not forwarded to the Regional Court since the public prosecutor rejected them as being devoid of any prospects of success. . . . The public prosecutor heard Mr Winterwerp each time and his decisions may well have been justified on the basis of the information at his disposal, but they cannot be qualified as decisions taken by a 'court' within the meaning of Article 5 § 4.

67. To sum up, the various decisions ordering or authorising Mr Winterwerp's detention issued from bodies which either did not possess the characteristics of a 'court' or, alternatively, failed to furnish the guarantees of judicial procedure required by Article 5 § 4; neither did the applicant have access to a 'court' or the benefit of such guarantees when his request which was rejected by the Regional Court in February 1969. Mr Winterwerp was accordingly the victim of a breach of Article 5 § 4.

FOR THESE REASONS, THE COURT UNANIMOUSLY

Holds that there has been no breach of Article 5(1);

Holds that there has been a breach of Article 5(4); . . .

NOTES

1 The Court was composed of President Pedersen and Judges Wiarda, Evrigenis, Teitgen, Lagergren, Liesch and Gölcüklü.

2 In the *Winterwerp* case the Court recognized that in some cases Article 5(4) requires a continuing remedy at reasonable intervals to check that the reasons justifying a person's detention continue to apply. The cases that follow in the remainder of this section are all concerned with this continuing remedy requirement.

X v UK A.46 (1981) 4 EHRR 188
European Court of Human Rights

Following his conviction by Sheffield Assizes in 1968 of wounding with intent to cause grievous bodily harm, X was ordered by the court to be detained in Broadmoor Hospital as a restricted offender patient under section 85, Mental Health Act 1959. In 1971, the Home Secretary, acting under section 66, 1959 Act, ordered X's conditional discharge on the ground that X's condition had improved. After some three years of normal life, X was recalled to Broadmoor by the Home Secretary, acting under section 66, 1959 Act, in the light of evidence that his condition had deteriorated. X at once applied to the High Court for habeas corpus, but his application was unsuccessful. After six months detention following his recall, X was entitled by section 66, 1959 Act to apply to the Mental Health Tribunal for a recommendation that he be released, which he did without success. Had the Tribunal recommended in his favour, the Home Secretary would have retained a discretion whether or not to accept the recommendation.

The applicant alleged breaches, *inter alia*, of Article 5(1) and (4). The Commission expressed the opinion, by 14 votes to two, that X's recall had not violated Article 5(1). It was of the unanimous opinion that Article 5(4) had been violated, since X had not been entitled to take proceedings by which the lawfulness of his detention consequent on his recall to hospital could be decided speedily by a court. In particular, an appeal to the Mental Health Review Tribunal to challenge the recall was only possible six months after it had occurred.

The Court held unanimously that Article 5(1) was not infringed. In the following passage from its judgment, the Court considered whether there was a breach of Article 5(4).

JUDGMENT OF THE COURT

50. As their main submission, the Government contended that the requirements of Article 5 § 4 were met by the proceedings before the Sheffield Assizes in 1968. In this connection, they relied on a passage from the *De Wilde, Ooms and Versyp* judgment of 18 June 1971 (Series A No 12, p 40, § 76):

> 'At first sight, the wording of Article 5 § 4 might make one think that it guarantees the right of the detainee always to have supervised by a court the lawfulness of a previous decision which has deprived him of his liberty. ... Where [this] decision ... is one taken by an administrative body, there is no doubt that Article 5 § 4 obliges the Contracting States to make available to the person detained a right of recourse to a court; but there is nothing to indicate that the same applies when the decision is made by a court at the close of judicial proceedings. In the latter case the supervision required by Article 5 § 4 is incorporated in the decision; this is so, for example, where a sentence of imprisonment is pronounced after 'conviction by a competent court' (Article 5 § 1(a) of the Convention).'

51. In point of fact, this passage speaks only of 'the decision depriving a person of his liberty'; it does not purport to deal with an ensuing period of detention in which new issues affecting the lawfulness of the detention might subsequently arise. The judgment of 18 June 1971 considered, for the purposes of Article 5 § 4, not only the initial decisions ordering detention for vagrancy taken in respect of three applicants (ibid, pp 40, 43, §§ 74–80), but also the procedure governing the examination of the applicants' requests for release (ibid, pp 43–4, §§ 81–4).

52. Furthermore, as the Government themselves pointed out the content of the obligation imposed on the Contracting States by Article 5 § 4 will not necessarily be the same in all circumstances and as regards every category of deprivation of liberty (see, *mutatis mutandis*, the above-mentioned *De Wilde, Ooms and Versyp* judgment, pp 41–2, § 78).

X's detention fell within the ambit of sub-paragraph (e) of Article 5 § 1 at least as much as within that of sub-paragraph (a). . . . The 'detention of persons of unsound mind' constitutes a special category with its own specific problems (see *Winterwerp* judgment, pp 23–24, §§ 57 and 60). In particular, 'the reasons initially warranting confinement of this kind may cease to exist'. This leads, so the *Winterwerp* judgment noted, to a consequence of some importance (p 23, § 55):

'. . . it would be contrary to the object and purpose of Article 5 . . . to interpret paragraph 4 . . . as making this category of confinement immune from subsequent review of lawfulness merely provided that the initial decision issued from a court. The very nature of the deprivation of liberty under consideration would appear to require a review of lawfulness to be available at reasonable intervals'.

By virtue of Article 5 § 4, a person of unsound mind compulsorily confined in a psychiatric institution for an indefinite or lengthy period is thus in principle entitled, at any rate where there is no automatic periodic review of a judicial character, to take proceedings at reasonable intervals before a court to put in issue the 'lawfulness'—within the meaning of the Convention (see paragraph 57 below)—of his detention, whether that detention was ordered by a civil or criminal court or by some other authority.

53. It is not within the province of the Court to inquire into what would be the best or most appropriate system of judicial review in this sphere, for the Contracting States are free to choose different methods of performing their obligations. Thus, in Article 5 § 4 the word 'court' is not necessarily to be understood as signifying a court of law of the classic kind, integrated within the standard judicial machinery of the country. This term, as employed in several Articles of the Convention including Article 5 § 4, serves to denote 'bodies which exhibit not only common fundamental features, of which the most important is independence of the executive and of the parties to the case . . . , but also the guarantees'—'appropriate to the kind of deprivation of liberty in question'—'of [a] judicial procedure', the forms of which may vary from one domain to another (see the above-mentioned *De Wilde, Ooms and Versyp* judgment, pp 41–2, §§ 76 and 78).

54. To sum up, during the period of his detention subsequent to his readmission to Broadmoor Hospital in April 1974 X should have been enabled to take proceedings attended by such 'guarantees'. At that stage, the proceedings that had been held in 1968 before the Sheffield Assizes were no longer sufficient to satisfy the requirements of Article 5 § 4. . . .

55. The Government maintained, in the alternative, that the 'lawfulness' of the said detention had in fact been 'decided speedily by a court', namely by the Divisional Court of the Queen's Bench Division when hearing X's application for a writ of habeas corpus. . . .

56. The habeas corpus proceedings brought by X are described above. . . . The case was considered by the Divisional Court on the basis of affidavits, including one by the applicant. Such medical evidence as there was before the Divisional Court . . . was obtained by X's solicitors. The Home Secretary was himself under no obligation to produce material justification for X's detention.

All this, however, followed from the nature of the remedy provided. In habeas corpus proceedings, in examining an administrative decision to detain, the court's task is to inquire whether the detention is in compliance with the requirements stated in the relevant legislation and with the applicable principles of the common law. According to these principles, such a decision—even though technically legal on its face—may be upset, *inter alia*, if the detaining authority misused its powers by acting in bad faith or capriciously or for a wrongful purpose, or if the decision is supported by no sufficient evidence or is one which no reasonable person could have reached in the circumstances. Subject to the foregoing, the court will not be able to review the grounds or merits of a decision taken by an administrative authority to the extent that under the legislation in question these are exclusively a matter for determination by that authority. As X's case well exemplifies, when the terms of a statute afford the executive a discretion, whether wide or narrow, the review exercisable by the courts in habeas corpus proceedings will bear solely upon the conformity of the exercise of that discretion with the empowering statute.

In the present case, once it was established that X was a patient who had been conditionally discharged whilst still subject to a restriction order, the statutory requirements for recall by warrant under section 66 § 3 of the 1959 Act were satisfied. This being so, it was then effectively up to X to show, within the limits permitted by English law, some reason why the apparently legal detention was unlawful. The evidence adduced by X did not disclose any such reason and the Divisional Court had no option but to dismiss the application.

57. Although X had access to a court which ruled that his detention was 'lawful' in terms of English law, this cannot of itself be decisive as to whether there was a sufficient review of 'lawfulness' for the purposes of Article 5 § 4. In paragraph 1(e) of Article 5 as interpreted by the Court (see the above-mentioned *Winterwerp* judgment, pp 17–18, § 39), . . . the Convention itself makes the 'lawfulness' of the kind of deprivation of liberty undergone by X subject to certain requirements over and above conformity with domestic law. Article 5 must be read as a whole and there is no reason to suppose that in relation to one and the same deprivation of liberty the significance of 'lawfulness' differs from paragraph 1(e) to paragraph 4.

58. Notwithstanding the limited nature of the review possible in relation to decisions taken under section 66 § 3 of the 1959 Act, the remedy of habeas corpus can on occasions constitute an effective check against arbitrariness in this sphere. It may be regarded as adequate, for the purposes of Article 5 § 4, for emergency measures for the detention of persons on the ground of unsoundness of mind. Such measures, provided they are of short duration (see the above-mentioned *Winterwerp* judgment, p 19, § 42), are capable of being 'lawful' under Article 5 § 1(e) even though not attended by the usual guarantees such as thorough medical examination (see paragraph 41 above). The authority empowered to order emergency detention of this kind must, in the nature of things, enjoy a wide discretion, and this inevitably means that the role of the courts will be reduced.

On the other hand, in the Court's opinion, a judicial review as limited as that available in the habeas corpus procedure in the present case is not sufficient for a continuing confinement such as the one undergone by X. Article 5 § 4, the Government are quite correct to affirm, does not embody a right to judicial control of such scope as to empower the court, on all aspects of the case, to substitute its own discretion for that of the decision-making authority. The review should, however, be wide enough to bear on those conditions which, according to the Convention, are essential for the 'lawful' detention of a person on the ground of unsoundness of mind, especially as the reasons capable of initially justifying such a detention may cease to exist . . . . This means that in the instant case, Article 5 § 4 required an appropriate procedure allowing a court to examine whether the patient's disorder still persisted and whether the Home Secretary was entitled to think that a continuation of the compulsory confinement was necessary in the interests of public safety (see, *mutatis mutandis*, the above-mentioned *De Wilde, Ooms and Versyp* judgment, pp 43–4, §§ 82–3).

59. The habeas corpus proceedings brought by X in 1974 did not therefore secure him the enjoyment of the right guaranteed by Article 5 § 4; this would also have been the case had he made any fresh application at a later date. . . .

61. The Government drew the Court's attention to four ways by which the continued need for detention may come to be reviewed by the Home Office, namely a recommendation from the responsible medical officer that the patient be discharged, the intervention of a Member of Parliament with the Home Secretary, a direct request by the patient to the Home Secretary asking for release or for his case to be referred to a Mental Health Review Tribunal. . . .

The first three do not, however, bring into play any independent review procedure, whether judicial or administrative.

The fourth calls for closer examination since, in relation to the confinement of restricted patients, the 1959 Act provides the opportunity for a periodic review on a comprehensive factual basis by Mental

Health Review Tribunals. There is nothing to preclude a specialised body of this kind being considered as a 'court' within the meaning of Article 5 § 4 provided it enjoys the necessary independence and offers sufficient procedural safeguards appropriate to the category of deprivation of liberty being dealt with (see paragraph 59 above and the above-mentioned *Winterwerp* judgment, p 24, § 20). Nonetheless, even supposing Mental Health Review Tribunals fulfilled these conditions, they lack the competence to decide 'the lawfulness of [the] detention' and to order release if the detention is unlawful, as they have advisory functions only. . . .

Therefore, without underestimating the undoubted value of the safeguards thereby provided, the Court does not find that the other machinery adverted to by the Government serves to remedy the inadequacy, for the purposes of Article 5 § 4, of the habeas corpus proceedings.

62. In conclusion, there has been a breach of Article 5 § 4. . . .

FOR THESE REASONS, THE COURT UNANIMOUSLY . . .

Holds that there has been a breach of Article 5(4); . . .

NOTES

1 The Court was composed of President Wiarda and Judges Zekia, Evrigenis, Matscher, Pinheiro Farinha, Walsh and Jennings (*ad hoc judge*).

2 To comply with Article 5(4), a remedy must allow a person to challenge the grounds for his detention as well as the legality of the procedures followed. Thus, in *X v UK*, habeas corpus was not a sufficient remedy. Nor was the possibility of recourse to a Mental Health Review Tribunal because, as the Court indicated, the Tribunal could only make a recommendation to the Home Secretary who took the final decision. In its report in the case, the Commission had expressed the opinion that the Tribunal remedy was insufficient also because it was only available after six months' detention, so that the question of release was not decided 'speedily'. The Mental Health (Amendment) Act 1982 brought English law into line with *X v UK*.

3 As *X v UK*, following the *Winterwerp* case, also indicates, Article 5(4) requires that in cases in which a detained person's condition or circumstances may change so that the justification for his detention may cease to exist, he must be provided with a remedy meeting the requirements of Article 5(4) on a continuing basis at reasonable intervals. This is the case where, as in *X v UK* and the *Winterwerp* case, the ground for detention is mental disorder.

....

Weeks v UK A.114 (1987) 10 EHRR 293
European Court of Human Rights

In 1966, when aged 17, the applicant had been given a discretionary life sentence for armed robbery after having stolen 35 pence from a shop with a starting pistol. The sentence had been imposed because the alternative was a definite term of imprisonment for a number of years and the judge had considered that the more merciful approach was to impose a life sentence so that the emotionally immature applicant could be released on licence when it was considered appropriate (i.e. when he was sufficiently responsible) and this might be earlier than in the case of a determinate sentence. In fact, the applicant was released by the Home Secretary, following a Parole Board recommendation, only in 1976 after a ten-year spell in detention. In 1977, following incidents involving minor offences, the Parole Board confirmed an order by the Home Secretary for the applicant's recall. Thereafter the applicant was twice released and recalled, following the same procedures and as a result of minor offences. The Court held that the recalls could be justified under Article 5(1)(a): see above, p 260. In this extract the Court considered whether the remedies available to challenge the legality of the recall satisfied Article 5(4).

JUDGMENT OF THE COURT

58. The Court has already held in the context of paragraph 1(a) of Article 5 [see above, p 163] that the stated purpose of social protection and rehabilitation for which the 'indeterminate' sentence was passed on Mr Weeks, taken together with the particular circumstances of the offence for which he was convicted, places the sentence in a special category . . . : unlike the case of a person sentenced to life imprisonment because of the gravity of the offence committed, the grounds relied on by the sentencing judges for deciding that the length of the deprivation of Mr Weeks' liberty should be subject to the discretion of the executive for the rest of his life are by their nature susceptible of change with the passage of time. The Court inferred from this that if the decisions not to release or to re-detain were based on grounds inconsistent with the objectives of the sentencing court, Mr Weeks' detention would no longer be 'lawful' for the purposes of sub-paragraph (a) of paragraph 1 of Article 5.

It follows that, by virtue of paragraph 4 of Article 5, Mr Weeks was entitled to apply to a 'court' having jurisdiction to decide 'speedily' whether or not his deprivation of liberty had become 'unlawful' in this sense; this entitlement should have been exercisable by him at the moment of any return to custody after being at liberty and also at reasonable intervals during the course of his imprisonment (see, *mutatis mutandis*, the above-mentioned *Van Droogenbroeck* judgment, Series A No 50, p 26, § 48 *in fine*).

59. Article 5 § 4 does not guarantee a right to judicial control of such scope as to empower the 'court', on all aspects of the case, including questions of expediency, to substitute its own discretion for that of the decision-making authority. The review should, however, be wide enough to bear on those conditions which, according to the Convention, are essential for the lawful detention of a person subject to the special kind of deprivation of liberty ordered against Mr Weeks (ibid, p 26, § 49). . . .

60. The Government submitted in the alternative that the requirements of Article 5 § 4 were sufficiently met by the Parole Board's jurisdiction, supplemented as it was by the availability of judicial review before the High Court. Both the applicant and the Commission disagreed with this analysis. . . .

61. The 'court' referred to in Article 5 § 4 does not necessarily have to be a court of law of the classic kind integrated within the standard judicial machinery of the country (see the above-mentioned *X v UK* judgment, Series A No 46, p 23, § 53). The term 'court' serves to denote 'bodies which exhibit not only common fundamental features, of which the most important is independence of the executive and of the parties to the case . . . , but also the guarantees'—'appropriate to the kind of deprivation of liberty in question'—'of [a] judicial procedure', the forms of which may vary from one domain to another (see the above-mentioned *De Wilde, Ooms and Versyp* judgment, Series A No 12, pp 41–2, §§ 76 and 78). In addition, as the text of Article 5 § 4 makes clear, the body in question must not have merely advisory functions but must have the competence to 'decide' the 'lawfulness' of the detention and to order release if the detention is unlawful.

There is thus nothing to preclude a specialised body such as the Parole Board being considered as a 'court' within the meaning of Article 5 § 4, provided it fulfils the foregoing conditions (see the above-mentioned *X v UK* judgment, Series A No 46, p 26, § 61). . . .

62. The applicant maintained that the Parole Board is not independent of the Home Secretary, primarily because he appoints the members of the Board, provides its staff and makes the rules under which it conducts its procedures.

The Parole Board sits in small panels, each of which in the case of life prisoners includes a High Court judge and a psychiatrist. . . . The manner of appointment of the Board's members does not, in the Court's opinion, establish a lack of independence on the part of the members (see, *mutatis mutandis*, the *Campbell and Fell* judgment of 28 June 1984, Series A No 80, p 40, § 79). Furthermore, the Court is satisfied that the judge member and the other members of the Board remain wholly independent of the executive and impartial in the performance of their duties.

There remains the question whether the Board presents an appearance of independence, notably to persons whose liberty it considers (ibid, pp 39–41, §§ 78 and 81). On this point, as the Government stated, the functions of the Board do not bring it into contact with officials of the prisons or of the Home Secretary in such a way as to identify it with the administration of the prison or of the Home Office.

The Court therefore sees no reason to conclude that the Parole Board and its members are not independent and impartial.

63. The Commission, together with the applicant, took the view that the Board lacked the necessary powers and procedural guarantees for the purposes of Article 5 § 4. The applicant further contended that the Board's proceedings were not 'speedy'. He pointed out that, whereas his licence was revoked in June 1977, the Board did not give its decision until December 1977. ...

64. According to the wording of the 1967 Act, the duty of the Parole Board is to 'advise' the Home Secretary on the exercise of his powers to release prisoners on licence and to revoke such licences, and its decisions take the form of 'recommendations' to the Home Secretary (sections 59(3), 61(1) and 62(1) and (5). ...

The Board's functions are without doubt purely advisory, both in law and in substance, as regards the periodic review that it carries out in relation to the question of the possible release on licence of a detained person serving a sentence of life imprisonment (section 61(1) of the 1967 Act). The Home Secretary may not, it is true, release on licence a life prisoner unless recommended to do so by the Parole Board (ibid). However, where the Board does recommend release of such prisoners, the Home Secretary must also consult the Lord Chief Justice, together with the trial judge if available (ibid); and, as demonstrated by the facts of Mr Weeks' own case . . . , the Home Secretary is free, in the light of all the material before him, not to accept the Board's recommendation. Quite apart from any consideration of procedural guarantees, the Board therefore lacks the power of decision required by Article 5 § 4 when dealing with this category of case.

On the other hand, the Board's recommendation to release is binding on the Home Secretary when the Board has to consider, as it did in December 1977 in relation to Mr Weeks, recall to prison after release on licence (section 62(5) of the 1967 Act). . . . The procedure applicable in the event of recall must therefore be examined. ...

65. The language of Article 5 § 4 speaks of the detained individual being entitled to initiate proceedings. Under the British system of parole of life prisoners, although only the Home Secretary may refer a case to the Board, referral is obligatory in recall cases except where a person recalled after a recommendation to that effect by the Board has chosen not to make written representations (section 62(4) of the 1967 Act). . . . In these circumstances, the recalled person can be considered as having sufficient access to the Parole Board for the purposes of Article 5 § 4 (see the above-mentioned *X v UK* judgment, Series A No 46, p 23, § 52).

66. The Board deals with individual cases on consideration of the documents supplied to it by the Home Secretary and of any reports, information or interviews with the individual concerned it has itself called for (section 59(4) and (5) of the 1967 Act). . . . The prisoner is entitled to make representations with respect to his recall, not only in writing to the Board but also orally to a member of the Local Review Committee (sections 59(5)–(6) and 62(3) of the 1967 Act). . . . The individual is free to take legal advice in preparing such representations. Furthermore, he must be sufficiently informed of the reasons for his recall in order to enable him to make sensible representations (section 62(3) of the 1967 Act and the judgments in the *Gunnell* and *Wilson* cases—ibid).

Whilst these safeguards are not negligible, there remains a certain procedural weakness in the case of a recalled prisoner. Thus, the Court of Appeal established in the *Gunnell* case that the duty on the

Board to act fairly, as required under English law by the principles of natural justice, does not entail an entitlement to full disclosure of the adverse material which the Board has in its possession . . . . The procedure followed does not therefore allow proper participation of the individual adversely affected by the contested decision, this being one of the principal guarantees of a judicial procedure for the purposes of the Convention, and cannot therefore be regarded as judicial in character (see, *mutatis mutandis*, the *Sanchez-Reisse* judgment of 21 October 1986, Series A No 107, p 19, § 51).

67. In view of this finding, the Court does not consider it necessary to rule on the remaining points raised by the applicant and the Commission, that is: firstly, whether, in relation to the special category of deprivation of liberty ordered against Mr Weeks, this requirement of a proper procedure calls for the holding of an oral hearing in addition to the existing possibility of making written submissions (see, *mutatis mutandis*, the above-mentioned *Sanchez-Reisse* judgment, Series A No 107, p 19, § 51); and, secondly, whether the proceedings before the Board were 'speedy'. . . .

68. Consequently, neither in relation to consideration of Mr Weeks' recall to prison in 1977 nor in relation to periodic examination of his detention with a view to release on licence can the Parole Board be regarded as satisfying the requirements of Article 5 § 4. . . .

69. The Court has in previous cases recognised the need to take a comprehensive view of the system in issue before it, as apparent short-comings in one procedure may be remedied by safeguards available in other procedures (see, for example, the above-mentioned *X v UK* judgment, Series A No 46, p 26, § 60). In this connection, an application for judicial review undoubtedly represents a useful supplement to the procedure before the Parole Board: it enables the individual concerned to obtain a control by the ordinary courts of both the Parole Board's decisions (see, for example, the judgment of the Queen's Bench Division in the *Wilson* case . . .) and the Home Secretary's decisions.

The applicant, adopting conclusions reached by the Commission in its report, argued that the remedy of judicial review did not meet the requirements of accessibility and effectiveness under Article 5 § 4 (see the above-mentioned *Van Droogenbroeck* judgment, Series A No 50, p 30, § 54).

The grounds on which judicial review lies, as summarised by Lord Diplock in his speech in the *Council of Civil Service Unions* case, are 'illegality', 'irrationality' and 'procedural impropriety'. By 'illegality' is meant incorrect application of the law governing the decision-making power and, in particular, breach of the relevant statutory requirements; 'irrationality' covers a decision that is so outrageous in its defiance of logic or of accepted moral standards that no sensible person who had applied his mind to the question to be decided could have arrived at it; and 'procedural impropriety' is a failure to observe expressly laid down procedural rules, a denial of natural justice or a lack of procedural fairness . . . .

As the Commission pointed out, the scope of the control afforded is thus not wide enough to bear on the conditions essential for the 'lawfulness', in the sense of Article 5 § 4 of the Convention, of Mr Weeks' detention, that is to say, whether it was consistent with and therefore justified by the objectives of the indeterminate sentence imposed on him (see paragraphs 58 and 59 above). In the Court's view, having regard to the nature of the control it allows, the remedy of judicial review can neither itself provide the proceedings required by Article 5 § 4 nor serve to remedy the inadequacy, for the purposes of that provision, of the procedure before the Parole Board. . . .

FOR THESE REASONS, THE COURT . . . .

Holds, by thirteen votes to four, that there has been a breach of Article 5 § 4;

NOTES

1 The Court was composed of President Ryssdal and Judges Cremona, Thor Vilhjálmsson, Bindschedler-Robert, Lagergren, Gölcüklü, Matscher, Pinheiro Farinha, Pettiti, Walsh, Sir Vincent Evans, Macdonald, Russo, Bernhardt, Gersing, Spielman, and De Mayer. Judges Vilhjalmsson, Lagergren, Evans, and Gersing issued a joint partly concurring/dissenting opinion in which they expressed the view that Weeks's original trial combined with the possibility of him challenging his recall via an action for judicial review satisfied the demands of Article 5(4).

2   The *Weeks* case was the first in a series of cases in which the European Court applied the continuing remedy requirement in Article 5(4) to the arrangements in English discretionary or indeterminate life sentences, mandatory life sentences and to the detention of juveniles during Her Majesty's Pleasure. As will be seen the involvement of the Home Secretary, who clearly is not a 'court', has become increasingly problematic and untenable in the judgments of the court.

Thynne, Wilson and Gunnell v UK A.190 (1990) 13 EHRR 666
European Court of Human Rights

The applicants had been convicted of very grave sex offences for which they would have been sentenced to long terms of imprisonment had definite terms been imposed. Instead, since the applicants were regarded as unstable and likely to commit other offences if released, they were, in accordance with established sentencing policy, given discretionary life sentences, which contained a number of years (the tariff period) calculated as punishment for the offence committed and thereafter were justified in terms of the public interest in keeping dangerous criminals secure. In all three cases, the applicants had moved from the punishment to the security phase of their life sentences and could be released on licence by the Home Secretary on the recommendation of the Parole Board if they were no longer thought a danger to society. The Commission expressed the opinion, by ten votes to two, that the remedies available to the applicant to challenge their continued detention after the end of the tariff period did not satisfy Article 5(4).

JUDGMENT OF THE COURT

68. It was held in the *De Wilde, Ooms and Versyp* judgment of 18 June 1971 that where a sentence of imprisonment is imposed after 'conviction by a competent court', the supervision required by Article 5 § 4 is incorporated in the decision of the court (Series A No 12, p 40, § 76). In subsequent cases the Court made it clear that this finding related only to 'the initial decision depriving a person of his liberty' and did not purport 'to deal with an ensuing period of detention in which new issues affecting the lawfulness of the detention might arise' (see, *inter alia*, the above-mentioned *Weeks* judgment, Series A No 114, p 28, § 56). In this connection the concept of lawfulness under Article 5 § 4 requires that the detention be in conformity not only with domestic law but also with the text of the Convention, the general principles embodied therein and the aim of the restrictions permitted by Article 5 § 1 (ibid, p 23, § 42, and p 28, § 57).

69. In cases concerning detention of persons of unsound mind under Article 5 § 1 (e) where the reasons initially warranting detention may cease to exist the Court has held that 'it would be contrary to the object and purpose of Article 5 . . . to interpret paragraph 4 . . . as making this category of confinement immune from subsequent review of lawfulness merely provided that the initial decision issued from a court . . .' (see the *X v UK* judgment of 5 November 1981, Series A No 46, pp 22–3, § 52). This interpretation of Article 5 § 4 has also, in certain circumstances, been applied to detention 'after conviction by a competent court' under Article 5 § 1 (a) (see, *inter alia*, the *Van Droogenbroeck* judgment of 24 June 1982, Series A No 50, pp 23–7, §§ 44–9, the above-mentioned *Weeks* judgment, Series A No 114, pp 28–9, §§ 55–9, and the *E v Norway* judgment of 29 August 1990, Series A No 181-A, pp 21–2, § 50). What is of importance in this context is the nature and purpose of the detention in question, viewed in

the light of the objectives of the sentencing court, and not the category to which it belongs under Article 5 § 1 (see the above-mentioned *Van Droogenbroeck* judgment, p 24, § 47).

70. Mr Weeks received a discretionary life sentence not because of the gravity of his offence but because of his dangerous and unstable personality and to enable the Home Secretary to monitor his progress and release him when he was no longer judged to represent a danger to the community (see Series A No 114, especially at pp 10–11, §§ 14–15).

The Court considered that the measure ordered against him was comparable to the measure of placement at the Government's disposal at issue in the *Van Droogenbroeck* case and, further, that the protective purpose underlying the life sentence, taken together with the particular circumstances of the offence for which he was convicted, placed the sentence in a special category to which Article 5 § 4 was applicable (ibid, pp 24–5, §§ 46–7, and pp 28–9, § 58). It was an important feature of this category that the grounds relied on by the sentencing judges as the reason for imposing a life sentence on Mr Weeks, namely his mental instability and dangerousness, were, by their nature, susceptible of change with the passage of time. The Court inferred from this that, if the decisions not to release or to re-detain were based on grounds inconsistent with the objectives of the sentencing court, his detention would no longer be 'lawful' for the purposes of Article 5 § 1(a) and the Court concluded that Mr Weeks was entitled, by virtue of Article 5 § 4, to have recourse to a court to decide on the lawfulness of his deprivation of liberty at the moment of any return to custody after being at liberty as well as at reasonable intervals during the course of his imprisonment (ibid, p 29, § 58).

71. The Court has had regard to the reasons given by the courts for the sentences imposed on each of the applicants in the present case and the nature and purpose of the discretionary life sentence under English law.

72. Mr Thynne was found to have a personality disorder which required observation and possibly operative treatment. The sentencing judge indicated that but for the psychiatric reports he would have imposed a very long prison sentence. . . . However, the Court of Appeal said that it did not 'see the life sentence in this case as necessarily involving detention in custodial conditions for a very long period of time'; it added that this was a case in which the offences were very grave indeed and society needed to be protected against 'outbursts of this nature which would very seriously affect other persons'. . . .

[The Court made similar analyses of the other two applicants' cases.]

Each of the applicants was thus sentenced to life imprisonment because, in addition to the need for punishment, he was considered by the courts to be suffering from a mental or personality disorder and to be dangerous and in need of treatment. Life imprisonment was judged to be the most appropriate sentence in the circumstances since it enabled the Secretary of State to assess their progress and to act accordingly. Thus the courts' sentencing objectives were in that respect similar to those in Weeks, but also took into account the much greater gravity of the offences committed.

73. As regards the nature and purpose of the discretionary life sentence under English law, the Government's main submission was that it is impossible to disentangle the punitive and security components of such sentences. The Court is not persuaded by this argument: the discretionary life sentence has clearly developed in English law as a measure to deal with mentally unstable and dangerous offenders; numerous judicial statements have recognised the protective purpose of this form of life sentence (see, in particular, the remarks by Lord Chief Justice Lane and Lord Justice Stuart-Smith in *R v Wilkinson* and *R v Secretary of State, ex p Bradley,* . . .). Although the dividing line may be difficult to draw in particular cases, it seems clear that the principles underlying such sentences, unlike mandatory life sentences, have developed in the sense that they are composed of a punitive element and subsequently of a security element designed to confer on the Secretary of State the responsibility for determining when the public interest permits the prisoner's release. This view is confirmed by the judicial description of the 'tariff' as denoting the period of detention considered necessary to meet the requirements of retribution and deterrence. . . .

75. It is clear from the judgments of the sentencing courts that in their view the three applicants, unlike Mr Weeks, had committed offences of the utmost gravity meriting lengthy terms of imprisonment. Nevertheless, the Court is satisfied that in each case the punitive period of the discretionary life sentence has expired. ....

76. Having regard to the foregoing, the Court finds that the detention of the applicants after the expiry of the punitive periods of their life sentences is comparable to that at issue in the *Van Droogenbroeck* and *Weeks* cases: the factors of mental instability and dangerousness are susceptible to change over the passage of time and new issues of lawfulness may thus arise in the course of detention. It follows that at that phase in the execution of their sentences, the applicants were entitled under Article 5 § 4 to take proceedings to have the lawfulness of their continued detention decided by a court at reasonable intervals and to have the lawfulness of any re-detention determined by a court.

77. The applicants and the Commission submitted that Article 5 § 4 should be considered to apply throughout the whole of the applicants' imprisonment because of the uncertainty of the 'tariff' period, which was not communicated directly to the applicants. Furthermore the applicants attached weight to the fact that the 'tariff' or punitive period was not stated in open court and subject to the normal process of appeal.

The Government argued that a life prisoner should not be placed in a better position than a prisoner who received a fixed-term sentence. The length of the 'tariff' can be deduced from the date when the first review is set. Article 5 § 4 should only apply, if at all, following the expiry of the 'tariff' period.

78. The Court does not consider that it is necessary to decide this question in the present case since it is clear that the punitive period of the three applicants' life sentences has expired (see paragraph 75 above). Accordingly the applicants were entitled to subsequent judicial control as guaranteed by Article 5 § 4. ....

79. Article 5 § 4 does not guarantee a right to judicial control of such scope as to empower the 'court' on all aspects of the case, including questions of expediency, to substitute its own discretion for that of the decision-making authority; the review should, nevertheless, be wide enough to bear on those conditions which, according to the Convention, are essential for the lawful detention of a person subject to the special type of deprivation of liberty ordered against these three applicants (see, *inter alia*, the above-mentioned *Weeks* judgment, Series A No 114, p 29, § 59, and the above-mentioned *E v Norway* judgment, Series A No 181-A, pp 21–2, § 50).

80. The Court sees no reason to depart from its finding in the *Weeks* judgment (pp 29–33, §§ 60–9) that neither the Parole Board nor judicial review proceedings—no other remedy of a judicial character being available to the three applicants—satisfy the requirements of Article 5 § 4. Indeed, this was not disputed by the Government. ....

FOR THESE REASONS, THE COURT

Holds by eighteen votes to one that there has been a violation of Article 5(4) in the case of all three applicants;

NOTES

1   The Court was composed of President Ryssdal and Judges Cremona, Vilhjálmsson, Gölcüklü, Matchser, Pinheiro Farinha, Pettiti, Walsh, Sir Vincent Evans, MacDonald, Russo, Bernhardt, Spielmann, De Meyer, Valticos, Martens, Pekkanen, Loizou, Morenilla Rodriguez. Judge Vilhjálmsson issued a dissenting opinion in which he stated that he considered the applicants' original trials provided the judicial review required by Article 5(4).

2   In *Oldham v UK*, judgment of 26 September 2000, the applicant, a post-tariff discretionary life prisoner, claimed the two-year period between reviews of his continuing detention did not

satisfy the requirements of Article 5(4). Oldham had been convicted of manslaughter, whilst suffering from a mental abnormality induced by alcohol, in 1970. He was released and recalled to prison several times from the late 1980s. In July 1996 he was recalled by the Home Secretary on the ground that he had injured his partner after a drinking binge. The Parole Board Discretionary Lifer Panel that examined his recall expressed the view that he should remain in custody, as he posed a risk to the public and that he should undertake work in respect of alcohol abuse and the management of anger. The Home Secretary informed Oldham that the Parole Board would review his detention in two years' time. Within eight months of his recall Oldham completed courses on the specified topics. In 1998 the applicant had another hearing before the Discretionary Lifer Panel and it recommended his release (the Homes Secretary duly released him on licence). Oldham contended that the delay in reviewing his detention was unreasonable and thereby violated Article 5(4). The Court stated that:

31. It is true that the question of whether periods comply with the requirement must—as with the reasonable time stipulation in Article 5 § 3 and Article 6 § 1—be determined in the light of the circumstances of each case (see the *Sanchez-Reisse* v *Switzerland* judgment of 21 October 1986, Series A No 107, p 55, § 55). It is therefore not for this Court to attempt to rule as to the maximum period of time between reviews which should automatically apply to this category of life prisoner as a whole. It notes that the system as applied in this case has a flexibility which must reflect the realities of the situation, namely, that there are significant differences in the personal circumstances of the prisoners under review.

After observing that Oldham had completed his courses within eight months of the previous review the Court concluded that his having to wait a further sixteen months before having his case reconsidered by the Discretionary Lifer Panel was not reasonable, hence the lawfulness of his continuing detention had not been decided 'speedily' as mandated by Article 5(4). This judgment indicates that national review procedures should not be primarily governed by automatic timetables but by the personal conditions of individual prisoners.

3   In the *Thynne, Wilson* and *Gunnell* cases, para 73, the European Court drew a distinction between discretionary and mandatory life sentences in the English system, with the result that a continuing remedy was not required under Article 5(4) in the case of the latter. The original Court confirmed this view in its ruling, by eighteen votes to one, in *Wynne v UK*, A.294 (1994) 19 EHRR 333, which concerned a mandatory life sentence on its facts. The Court stated:

35. . . . . However, the fact remains that the mandatory sentence belongs to a different category from the discretionary sentence in the sense that it is imposed automatically as the punishment for the offence of murder irrespective of considerations pertaining to the dangerousness of the offender. . . . That mandatory life prisoners do not actually spend the rest of their lives in prison and that a notional tariff period is also established in such cases—facts of which the Court was fully aware in *Thynne, Wilson* and *Gunnell* (loc cit, p 29, § 74)—does not alter this essential distinction between the two types of life sentence.

As observed by the House of Lords in *R v Secretary of State, ex p Doody*, while the two types of life sentence may now be converging there remains nonetheless, on the statutory framework, the underlying theory and the current practice, a substantial gap between them. . . . This is borne out by the very facts *inter alia* relied on by the applicant to support his case, namely that in mandatory life sentences the release of the prisoner is entirely a matter within the discretion of the Secretary of State who is not bound by the judicial recommendation as to the length of the tariff period and who is free under English law to have regard to other criteria than dangerousness, following the expiry of the 'tariff' period, in deciding whether the prisoner should be released. . . . It is further reflected in the decision of Parliament to limit the application of the new procedures in the 1991 Act to discretionary life sentences only, even in cases like the present where the prisoner is serving both a mandatory and a discretionary life sentence. . . .

36. Against the above background, the Court sees no cogent reasons to depart from the finding in the *Thynne, Wilson* and *Gunnell* case that, as regards mandatory life sentences, the guarantee of Article 5 § 4 was satisfied by the original trial and appeal proceedings and confers no additional right to challenge the lawfulness of continuing detention or re-detention following revocation of the life licence (see, *mutatis mutandis*, the *Cossey v UK* judgment of 27 September 1990, Series A No 184, p 14, § 35). Accordingly, in the circumstances of the present case, there are no new issues of lawfulness which entitle the applicant to a review of his continued detention under the original mandatory life sentence. . . .

However, in 2002 a Grand Chamber of the full-time Court declined to follow the approach in *Wynne. Stafford* v *UK*, judgment of 28 May 2002 concerned a person convicted of murder in 1967. He was released on licence in 1979 but broke his parole conditions by leaving the country. During 1989 he returned to the UK and was arrested in possession of a false passport. He was fined and remained in custody because his licence had been revoked. After eighteen months imprisonment the Parole Board recommended his release on licence. The Home Secretary authorized Stafford's release. In 1994 he was convicted of conspiracy to forge travellers' cheques and passports and sentence to six years' imprisonment. His licence was again revoked. In 1996 the Parole Board recommended his release on licence as it considered the risk of him re-offending was low. Nevertheless, the Home Secretary refused to release him. In July 1997 the applicant would have been released from prison in respect of his fraud sentence but he remained in custody due to the revocation of his life sentence licence. The Home Secretary approved his release on licence in December 1998. Stafford contended that the Court should reconsider the judgment in *Wynne* and hold that Article 5(4) required a judicial body to determine the continuing need for a mandatory lifer to be held in custody. The Court observed that:

78. . . . The abolition of the death penalty in 1965 and the conferring on the Secretary of State of the power to release convicted murderers represented, at that time, a major and progressive reform. However, with the wider recognition of the need to develop and apply, in relation to mandatory life prisoners, judicial procedures reflecting standards of independence, fairness and openness, the continuing role of the Secretary of State in fixing the tariff and in deciding on a prisoner's release following its expiry, has become increasingly difficult to reconcile with the notion of separation of powers between the executive and the judiciary, a notion which has assumed growing importance in the case-law of the Court (*mutatis mutandis*, the *Incal v Turkey* judgment of 9 June 1998, *Reports* 1998–IV).

79. The Court considers that it may now be regarded as established in domestic law that there is no distinction between mandatory life prisoners, discretionary life prisoners and juvenile murderers as regards the nature of tariff-fixing. It is a sentencing exercise. The mandatory life sentence does not impose imprisonment for life as a punishment. The tariff, which reflects the individual circumstances of the offence and the offender, represents the element of punishment. The Court concludes that the finding in *Wynne* that the mandatory life sentence constituted punishment for life can no longer be regarded as reflecting the real position in the domestic criminal justice system of the mandatory life prisoner.

Furthermore, the Grand Chamber determined that after the expiry of the tariff the continued detention of mandatory lifers depended upon:

87. . . . elements of dangerousness and risk associated with the objectives of the original sentence of murder. These elements may change with the course of time, and thus new issues of lawfulness arise requiring determination by a body satisfying the requirements of Article 5 § 4. It can no longer be maintained that the original trial and appeal proceedings satisfied, once and for all, issues of compatibility

of subsequent detention of mandatory life prisoners with the provisions of Article 5 § 1 of the Convention.

Consequently the Grand Chamber unanimously found a breach of Article 5(4) as Stafford had not had access to such a judicial body.

President Wildhaber speaking extra-judicially observed that in *Stafford*:

The Court took judicial notice of the evolving position of the British courts as to the nature of life sentences in an interesting example of a two-way process whereby developments in the domestic legal system influence Strasbourg to change its case-law, which in turn results in the consolidation of the evolution at national level, what one might call jurisprudential osmosis. (Speech by President Luzius Wildhaber to mark the opening of the judicial year: Strasbourg, 23 January 2003)

The Court's decision in *Stafford* can be welcomed on both constitutional and public policy grounds as individual sentencing decisions should be left to the independent judiciary and not rest with a minister subject to political pressures.

The Criminal Justice Act 2003 created a new system of sentencing adults subject to mandatory life sentences with the trial court determining the minimum term of imprisonment, having regard to the severity of the crime(s) assessed in the light of statutory criteria (Chapter 7 and Schedule 21 of the Act).

··

Hussain v UK 1996-I 252, (1996) 22 EHRR 1
European Court of Human Rights

At the age of 16, the applicant was convicted of murdering his 2-year-old brother. As he was a juvenile, he automatically received a mandatory sentence of detention 'during Her Majesty's Pleasure' pursuant to section 53(1) of the Children and Young Persons Act 1933. The effect was that he was 'liable to be detained in such a place and under such conditions as the [Home Secretary] may direct'. The release procedure for this type of detention was the same as for adults who had received mandatory life sentences, i.e. only after the expiry of the tariff (here fifteen years, as determined by the Home Secretary) and on the decision of the Home Secretary. The Parole Board undertook periodical reviews of the applicant's position with a view to his release on licence, but could only make recommendations to the Home Secretary. Following an English court decision in another case, the applicant was allowed to see the reports on him that had been placed before the Parole Board, but he was still not given the opportunity to appear in person before it. By the time the case reached the European Court the applicant had been detained for seventeen years.

JUDGMENT OF THE COURT

50. The Court notes at the outset that, as has been commonly accepted, the central issue in the present case is whether detention during Her Majesty's pleasure, given its nature and purpose, should be assimilated, under the case-law on the Convention, to a mandatory sentence of life imprisonment or rather to a discretionary sentence of life imprisonment. In dealing with this issue the Court must therefore decide whether the substance of a sentence of detention under section 53 is more closely related to that at the heart of the cases of *Weeks v UK* (judgment of 2 March 1987, Series A No 114) and *Thynne, Wilson* and *Gunnell* or to that in the more recent *Wynne* case. . . .

51. It is true, as submitted by the Government, that a sentence of detention during Her Majesty's pleasure is mandatory: it is fixed by law and is imposed automatically in all cases where persons under the age of 18 are convicted of murder, the trial judge having no discretion. It is also the case that the 1991

Act as well as recent policy statements treat the sentence at issue in the present case in an identical manner to mandatory life sentences as regards proceedings for release on licence and recall. . . .

On the other hand, it is undisputed that, in its statutory origins, the expression 'during Her Majesty's pleasure' had a clearly preventive purpose and that—unlike sentences of life custody or life imprisonment—the word 'life' is not mentioned in the description of the sentence.

52. Nevertheless, important as these arguments may be for the understanding of the sentence of detention under section 53 in English law, the decisive issue in the present context is whether the nature and, above all, the purpose of that sentence are such as to require the lawfulness of the continued detention to be examined by a court satisfying the requirements of Article 5 § 4.

53. It is recalled that the applicant was sentenced to be detained during Her Majesty's pleasure because of his young age at the time of the commission of the offence. In the case of young persons convicted of serious crimes, the corresponding sentence undoubtedly contains a punitive element and accordingly a tariff is set to reflect the requirements of retribution and deterrence. However an indeterminate term of detention for a convicted young person, which may be as long as that person's life, can only be justified by considerations based on the need to protect the public.

These considerations, centred on an assessment of the young offender's character and mental state and of his or her resulting dangerousness to society, must of necessity take into account any developments in the young offender's personality and attitude as he or she grows older. A failure to have regard to the changes that inevitably occur with maturation would mean that young persons detained under section 53 would be treated as having forfeited their liberty for the rest of their lives, a situation which, as the applicant and the Delegate of the Commission pointed out, might give rise to questions under Article 3 of the Convention.

54. Against this background the Court concludes that the applicant's sentence, after the expiration of his tariff, is more comparable to a discretionary life sentence. This was, albeit in a different context, the view expressed by the Divisional Court in its judgment of 20 April 1993 (R v Secretary of State for the Home Department, ex p Prem Singh). . . .

The decisive ground for the applicant's continued detention was and continues to be his dangerousness to society, a characteristic susceptible to change with the passage of time. Accordingly, new issues of lawfulness may arise in the course of detention and the applicant is entitled under Article 5 § 4 to take proceedings to have these issues decided by a court at reasonable intervals (see, mutatis mutandis, the above-mentioned Thynne, Wilson and Gunnell judgment, p 30, § 76). . . .

58. As in Thynne, Wilson and Gunnell (p 30, § 80) and despite the new policy allowing persons detained under section 53 of the 1933 Act the opportunity to see the material before the Parole Board . . . , the Court sees no reason to depart from its findings in the case of Weeks (cited above, pp 29–33, §§ 60–69) that the Parole Board does not satisfy the requirements of Article 5 § 4. Indeed, to the extent to which the Parole Board cannot order the release of a prisoner this is not contested by the Government. However, the lack of adversarial proceedings before the Parole Board also prevents it from being regarded as a court or court-like body for the purposes of Article 5 § 4.

59. The Court recalls in this context that, in matters of such crucial importance as the deprivation of liberty and where questions arise which involve, for example, an assessment of the applicant's character or mental state, it has held that it may be essential to the fairness of the proceedings that the applicant be present at an oral hearing (see, mutatis mutandis, the Kremzow v Austria judgment of 21 September 1993, Series A No 268-B, p 45, § 67).

60. The Court is of the view that, in a situation such as that of the applicant, where a substantial term of imprisonment may be at stake and where characteristics pertaining to his personality and level of maturity are of importance in deciding on his dangerousness, Article 5 § 4 requires an oral hearing in the context of an adversarial procedure involving legal representation and the possibility of calling and questioning witnesses.

61. It is not an answer to this requirement that the applicant might have been able to obtain an oral hearing by instituting proceedings for judicial review. In the first place, Article 5 § 4 presupposes the existence of a procedure in conformity with its requirements without the necessity of instituting separate legal proceedings in order to bring it about. In the second place, like the Delegate of the Commission, the Court is not convinced that the applicant's possibility of obtaining an oral hearing by way of proceedings for judicial review is sufficiently certain to be regarded as satisfying the requirements of Article 5 § 4 of the Convention. . . .

FOR THESE REASONS, THE COURT UNANIMOUSLY

Holds that there has been a violation of Article 5 § 4 of the Convention in that the applicant, after the expiry of his punitive period, was unable to bring the case of his continued detention before a court; . . .

NOTES

1 The Court was composed of President Ryssdal and Judges Golcuklu, MacDonald, Spielmann, Valticos, Palm, Bigi, Sir John Freeland, and Jambrek.

2 The *Hussain* case concerned remedies under Article 5(4) after the end of the tariff period. See also the similar case of *Singh v UK* (1996) The Times, 26 February, 1996-I 280. In *T v UK*, judgment of 16 December 1999, the Court held that Article 5(4) also required a continuing remedy to challenge the detention of a juvenile during Her Majesty's pleasure before the tariff period expired because the tariff had been set not by a court but by the Home Secretary. The Court stated:

118. The Court recalls that where a national court, after convicting a person of a criminal offence, imposes a fixed sentence of imprisonment for the purposes of punishment, the supervision required by Article 5 § 4 is incorporated in that court decision (see the *De Wilde, Ooms and Versyp v Belgium* judgment of 18 June 1971, Series A No 12, pp 40–1, § 76, and the *Wynne* judgment cited above, p 15, § 36). This is not the case, however, in respect of any ensuing period of detention in which new issues affecting the lawfulness of the detention may arise (see the *Weeks* judgment cited above, p 28, § 56, and the *Thynne, Wilson* and *Gunnell v UK* judgment of 25 October 1990, Series A No 190-A, pp 26–7, § 68). Thus, in the *Hussain* judgment (op cit, pp 269–70, § 54), the Court decided in respect of a young offender detained during Her Majesty's pleasure that, after the expiry of the tariff period, Article 5 § 4 required that he should be able periodically to challenge the continuing legality of his detention since its only justification could be dangerousness, a characteristic subject to change. In the *Hussain* case the Court was not called upon to consider the position under Article 5 § 4 prior to the expiry of the tariff (op cit, p 266, § 44).

119. The Court has already determined that the failure to have the applicant's tariff set by an independent tribunal within the meaning of Article 6 § 1 gives rise to a violation of that provision (see paragraph 113 above). Accordingly, given that the sentence of detention during Her Majesty's pleasure is indeterminate and that the tariff was initially set by the Home Secretary rather than the sentencing judge, it cannot be said that the supervision required by Article 5 § 4 was incorporated in the trial court's sentence (cf the *De Wilde, Ooms and Versyp* judgment and the *Wynne* judgment cited in paragraph 118 above).

120. Moreover, the Home Secretary's decision setting the tariff was quashed by the House of Lords on 12 June 1997 and no new tariff has since been substituted. This failure to set a new tariff means that the applicant's entitlement to access to a tribunal for periodic review of the continuing lawfulness of his detention remains inchoate.

121. It follows that the applicant has been deprived, since his conviction in November 1993, of the opportunity to have the lawfulness of his detention reviewed by a judicial body in accordance with Article 5 § 4. Against this background, the Court finds a violation of that Article.

See also the companion case of *V v UK* (1999) 30 EHRR 121.

Article 5(5) Right to compensation

Brogan v UK A.145 (1988)
European Court of Human Rights

As we have examined above (p 300) the plenary Court found a violation of Article 5(3), the applicants further contended that as they could not claim compensation under domestic law in respect of this violation there had also been a breach of Article 5(5).

VI. ALLEGED BREACH OF ARTICLE 5 PARA. 5

66. The applicants further alleged breach of Article 5 para. 5 which reads:

'Everyone who has been the victim of arrest or detention in contravention of the provisions of this Article shall have an enforceable right to compensation.'

A claim for compensation for unlawful deprivation of liberty may be made in the United Kingdom in respect of a breach of domestic law. As Article 5 is not considered part of the domestic law of the United Kingdom, no claim for compensation lies for a breach of any provision of Article 5 which does not at the same time constitute a breach of United Kingdom law.

The Government argued, inter alia, that the aim of paragraph 5 is to ensure that the victim of an 'unlawful' arrest or detention should have an enforceable right to compensation. In this regard, they have also contended that 'lawful' for the purposes of the various paragraphs of Article 5 is to be construed as essentially referring back to domestic law and in addition as excluding any element of arbitrariness. They concluded that even in the event of a violation being found of any of the first four paragraphs, there has been no violation of paragraph 5 because the applicants' deprivation of liberty was lawful under Northern Ireland law and was not arbitrary.

67. The Court, like the Commission, considers that such a restrictive interpretation is incompatible with the terms of paragraph 5 which refers to arrest or detention 'in contravention of the provisions of this Article'.

In the instant case, the applicants were arrested and detained lawfully under domestic law but in breach of paragraph 3 of Article 5. This violation could not give rise, either before or after the findings made by the European Court in the present judgment, to an enforceable claim for compensation by the victims before the domestic courts; this was not disputed by the Government.

Accordingly, there has also been a breach of paragraph 5 in this case in respect of all four applicants.

. . .

FOR THESE REASONS, THE COURT

. . .

4. Holds by thirteen votes to six that there has been a violation of Article 5 para. 5 in respect of all four applicants;

. . .

NOTES

1 The Court's rejection of the Government's narrow interpretation of Article 5(5) favours victims of breaches of earlier parts of this Article and is in accordance with the language of paragraph 5.

2   The Dutch Government was, however, successful in arguing that applicants must be able to show that they have suffered damage as a consequence of breaches of Article 5 rights if they are to be entitled to compensation under paragraph 5 in *Wassink v Netherlands*, A.185-A (1990). The applicant had been subject to confinement in a psychiatric hospital by his local burgo-master under emergency powers (he had attacked members of his family and a neighbour). A few days later the President of the District Court authorized the applicant's continued confine-ment in the hospital after a hearing, which the applicant and his representative had attended. Subsequently, the applicant challenged the lawfulness of the District Court's decision, before the Strasbourg authorities, arguing that it violated Article 5(1) as a registrar had not been pre-sent to record the proceedings in accordance with Dutch law. The Strasbourg Court found a breach of Article 5(1) by a large majority (six votes to one).

36. The applicant alleged a violation of Article 5 § 5, according to which:

> 'Everyone who has been the victim of arrest or detention in contravention of the provisions of this Article shall have an enforceable right to compensation.'

In his opinion, the sole provision of Netherlands law which he could have relied on in order to obtain compensation, Article 1401 of the Civil Code, only applied where damage could be shown. In this case, the existence of damage would have been almost impossible to prove because it could not be affirmed with absolute certainty that proceedings conducted in conformity with Article 5 of the Convention would have led to the desired result.

37. Unlike the Commission, the Government did not subscribe to this view. They considered that the right to compensation guaranteed in paragraph 5 of Article 5 was restricted to persons who had sus-tained damage, whether pecuniary or non-pecuniary, on account of the violation of another of the paragraphs of the Article; this was clear, in particular, from the use of the word 'victim'. Article 1401 of the Civil Code was therefore fully consistent with the Convention.

38. In the Court's view, paragraph 5 of Article 5 is complied with where it is possible to apply for com-pensation in respect of a deprivation of liberty effected in conditions contrary to paragraphs 1, 2, 3 or 4 (art. 5-1, art. 5-2, art. 5-3, art. 5-4). It does not prohibit the Contracting States from making the award of compensation dependent upon the ability of the person concerned to show damage resulting from the breach. In the context of Article 5 § 5, as for that of Article 25 (see, *inter alia*, the *Huvig* [v France] judgment of 24 April 1990, Series A No 176-B, pp 56–7, § 35), the status of 'victim' may exist even where there is no damage, but there can be no question of 'compensation' where there is no pecuniary or non-pecuniary damage to compensate.

More generally, the evidence provided to the Court does not lead to the conclusion that an action based on Article 1401 of the Netherlands Civil Code would have failed to satisfy the requirements of Article 5 § 5 of the Convention.

Therefore, the Court was unanimous in finding no breach of Article 5(5).

3   The full-time Court found a breach of Article 5(5) in *Beet and Others v UK*, above p 268. The Government submitted that from 2 October 2000, the date when the Human Rights Act 1998 came into force, anyone imprisoned in violation of Article 5(1) had a domestic right to claim compensation from the Crown.

ARTICLE 6 RIGHT TO A FAIR TRIAL

Article 6(1)

Civil rights and obligations

Ringeisen v Austria A.13 (1971) 1 EHRR 455
European Court of Human Rights

The applicant was an insurance agent and also dealt in real estate between 1958 and 1963. In 1961 he obtained general powers of attorney from Mr and Mrs Roth, who owned agricultural land in Upper Austria, and later that year he acquired an option to purchase their land. During February 1962 he made a contract with the Roths to purchase the land. From early 1962 Ringeisen had begun to sell part of the relevant land to various purchasers for building plots. In March 1962 Ringeisen submitted the Roths' contract for sale to the District Commission for its approval, this public authority had to be satisfied that the sale of agricultural land was in the public interest according to The Upper Austria Real Property Transactions Act. The District Commission refused to grant permission in September 1962 (it concluded the sale was for speculative building). Ringeisen then appealed to the Regional Real Property Trans-actions Commission, headed by a judge and seven other appointed persons. In May 1963 the Regional Commission dismissed his appeal. Ringeisen then successfully challenged the Regional Commission's conduct (some of the members had not fully participated in all the Commission's meetings) before the Constitutional Court. Ringeisen's appeal was remitted to the Regional Commission. He sought to challenge the composition of the Commission on the ground of bias, e.g. claiming that certain of the members had participated in the previous appeal. Ringeisen's challenges were dismissed and in February 1965 the Regional Commission rejected his appeal.

By early 1963 several persons, including the Roths, had laid criminal charges against Ringeisen in respect of his property dealings. The investigating judge first interviewed Ringeisen in February of that year. The indictment, containing charges of aggravated fraud and fraudulent conversion, was laid against him in April 1965. The trial began in December 1965 and was concluded in January 1966. Ringeisen was convicted of seventy-eight counts of fraud and sentenced to three years' severe imprisonment. After several appeals, the Supreme Court upheld his convictions in February 1968.

Ringeisen complained to the Commission alleging, *inter alia*, breaches of Article 6 in respect of both the civil proceedings he had brought to challenge the authorities' refusal to approve his contract with the Roths and the criminal proceedings brought against him. By seven votes to five, the Commission expressed the opinion that Article 6(1) did not apply to the contract approval proceedings as they were not concerned with 'civil rights and obliga-tions'. The Commission was also unanimous in concluding that the criminal proceedings against Ringeisen had been concluded within a reasonable time.

(C) AS TO THE QUESTION WHETHER THE PRESENT COMPLAINT INVOLVES THE DETERMINATION OF CIVIL RIGHTS AND OBLIGATIONS

94. For Article 6, paragraph (1) (art 6-1), to be applicable to a case ('contestation') it is not necessary that both parties to the proceedings should be private persons, which is the view of the majority of the Commission and of the Government. The wording of Article 6, paragraph (1) (art 6-1), is far wider; the French expression 'contestations sur (des) droits et obligations de caractère civil' covers all proceed-ings the result of which is decisive for private rights and obligations. The English text 'determination of . . . civil rights and obligations', confirms this interpretation.

The character of the legislation which governs how the matter is to be determined (civil, commercial, administrative law, etc.) and that of the authority which is invested with jurisdiction in the matter (ordin-ary court, administrative body, etc.) are therefore of little consequence.

In the present case, when Ringeisen purchased property from the Roth couple, he had a right to have the contract for sale which they had made with him approved if he fulfilled, as he claimed to do, the conditions laid down in the Act. Although it was applying rules of administrative law, the Regional Commission's decision was to be decisive for the relations in civil law ('de caractère civil') between Ringeisen and the Roth couple. This is enough to make it necessary for the Court to decide whether or not the proceedings in this case complied with the requirements of Article 6, paragraph (1) (art 6-1), of the Convention.

(D) AS TO WHETHER THE COMPLAINT THAT ARTICLE 6, PARAGRAPH (1) (ART 6-1), WAS NOT OBSERVED IS WELL-FOUNDED

95. The Court has not found any facts to prove that Ringeisen was not given a 'fair hearing' of his case. Besides, the Court observes that the Regional Commission is a 'tribunal' within the meaning of Article 6, paragraph (1) (art 6-1), of the Convention as it is independent of the executive and also of the parties, its members are appointed for a term of five years and the proceedings before it afford the necessary guarantees (see, *mutatis mutandis*, the *Neumeister* judgment of 27th June 1968, Series A, p 44, paragraph 24, and the *De Wilde, Ooms and Versyp* judgment of 18th June 1971, paragraph 78).

96. The applicant, however, accused six members of the Regional Commission of bias; when these complaints were brought before it, the Constitutional Court did not find it necessary to examine their substance for the reason that, as stated in its judgment of 27th September 1965, the question of bias had no bearing on the competence of the Regional Commission which was the only question submit-ted to its supervision . . .

97. It is not the function of the European Court to pronounce itself on the interpretation of Austrian law on which the said judgment is based or to express an opinion on the manner in which it was substanti-ated; on the other hand, it is the Court's duty to examine the grounds relied upon by Ringeisen and to determine whether or not the Regional Commission respected the rule of impartiality laid down in Article 6, paragraph (1) (art 6-1).

The Court finds that even if Ringeisen's assertions were in fact true they would not support the con-clusion that there was bias on the part of the Regional Commission. In the case of such a board with mixed membership comprising, under the presidency of a judge, civil servants and representatives of interested bodies, the complaint made against one member for the single reason that he sat as nom-inee of the Upper Austrian Chamber of Agriculture cannot be said to bear out a charge of bias. The same holds true for the complaint made against a member who was alleged by Ringeisen to have made certain statements the precise tenor of which the Regional Commission was, moreover, at pains to restore . . . As to the twofold fact that the president had represented the Regional Commission before the Constitutional Court in 1964 and that another member had been heard as a witness, this is obviously immaterial. Nor, finally, can any grounds of legitimate suspicion be found in the fact that two other members had participated in the first decision of the Regional Commission, for it cannot be stated as a general rule resulting from the obligation to be impartial that a superior court which sets aside an administrative or judicial decision is bound to send the case back to a different jurisdictional authority or to a differently composed branch of that authority.

98. Article 6, paragraph (1) (art 6-1), is not limited, however, to ensuring that in every determination of civil rights and obligations there must be a fair hearing within a reasonable time; it also requires, at least as a general rule, that the case be heard and the judgment pronounced in public.

The Court could have verified, even *proprio motu*—and subject to the reopening of the hearings on this point—whether the District and Regional Commissions had complied with this rule or whether they were entitled to depart from it.

The Court has not undertaken this examination because Austria's ratification of the Convention was made subject to the following reservation:

'... The provisions of Article 6 (art 6) of the Convention shall be so applied that there shall be no prejudice to the principles governing public court hearings (*im gerichtlichen Verfahren*) laid down in Article 90 of the 1929 version of the Federal Constitution Law. ...'

The said Article 90 is worded as follows:

'Hearings in civil and criminal cases (*in Zivil- und Strafrechtssachen*) by the trial court shall be oral and public. Exceptions may be prescribed by law. ...'

This reservation does not refer expressly to administrative proceedings but only to civil and criminal cases, that is, no doubt, the cases dealt with by the civil or criminal courts. Yet it must be accepted that the reservation covers *a fortiori* proceedings before administrative authorities where their subject matter is the determination of civil rights and where, therefore, the said authorities are considered to be tribunals within the meaning of Article 6, paragraph (1) (art 6-1). This is the case of the proceedings commenced by Ringeisen's request for approval on 30th March 1962.

99. For these reasons, the Court reaches the conclusion that there was no violation of Article 6, paragraph (1) (art 6-1), in the proceedings relating to that request.

III. AS TO THE QUESTION WHETHER THE DURATION OF THE CRIMINAL PROCEEDINGS AGAINST RINGEISEN EXCEEDED THE LIMITS OF A REASONABLE TIME AS LAID DOWN IN ARTICLE 6, PARAGRAPH (1) (ART 6-1)

110. The Court shares the Commission's opinion that the length of the fraud proceedings—preliminary investigations were opened on 21st February 1963 and the final decision was taken on 24th April 1968—resulted from both the complexity of the case and the innumerable requests and appeals made by Ringeisen not merely for his release, but also challenging most of the competent judges and for the transfer of the proceedings to different court areas. ... The Court therefore reaches the conclusion that there was no violation of Article 6, paragraph (1) (art 6-1).

FOR THESE REASONS, THE COURT,

I. As to the question whether Ringeisen was the victim of a violation of Article 6, paragraph (1) (art 6-1), in the proceedings he introduced to obtain approval of a transfer of real property consisting of farmland ...

3. Holds unanimously that Article 6, paragraph (1) (art 6-1), was applicable to the proceedings in question;

4. Holds unanimously that in the proceedings in question there has been no violation of Article 6, paragraph (1) (art 6-1); . . .

III. As to the question whether the duration of the criminal proceedings against Ringeisen exceeded the limits of a reasonable time as laid down in Article 6, paragraph (1) (art 6-1)

8. Holds unanimously that in the proceedings in question there has been no violation of Article 6, paragraph (1) (art 6-1).

NOTES

1 The Court was composed of President Rolin and Judges: Holmback, Verdross, Wold, Zekia, Favre, and Sigurjonsson.

2 The above judgment is crucial for articulating the essence of the Court's conception of what types of rights and duties fall within the Convention notion of 'civil rights and obligations'. The Court focuses upon the substance of the rights/duties at issue to determine if they are 'private rights and obligations', such as the contractual and property rights being asserted by Ringeisen. Furthermore, the Court held that all forms of legal proceedings, including those before administrative authorities and courts exercising public law jurisdictions, could fall within the ambit of Article 6(1) where their determinations were decisive for this class of rights and obligations (see further below, note 9).

3 The Court elaborated upon its conception of 'civil rights and obligations' in the subsequent case of *König v Germany*, A.27 (1978) 2 EHRR 170. The applicant opened a clinic, where he performed plastic surgery, at Bad Homburg in 1960. In 1962 the Regional Medical Society began proceedings against Dr Konig for unprofessional conduct and in 1964 he was declared unfit to practise. In April 1967 the Regierungsprasident in Wiesbaden (the senior officer of the provincial government), at the request of the Regional Medical Society, withdrew the applicant's authorization to run his clinic (an inspection had revealed numerous irregularities, including poor medical record keeping and an unclean operating theatre). The applicant filed an objection, which was rejected, and then he appealed (in November 1967) to the Frankfurt Administrative Court against the Regierungsprasident's decision. The appeal was dismissed in June 1977. Konig's appeal to the Hessen Administrative Court of Appeal was still pending when the European Court gave its judgment. In May 1971 the Regierungsprasident in Darmstadt withdrew Konig's authorization to practise medicine. Konig's objection to that decision was dismissed in September 1971, and he then appealed to the Administrative court (it was referred to another division of the Frankfurt Administrative Court). His appeal was dismissed in June 1976 (a further appeal by Konig to the Hessen Administrative Court of Appeal had not been finalized by the time of the European Court's decision). Konig complained to the Commission alleging that the dilatory nature of the Frankfurt Administrative Court's proceedings violated his right to the determination of his civil rights and obligations within a reasonable time as guaranteed by Article 6(1). The Commission, by nine votes to six—with one abstention, found a breach of that provision.

(A) ON THE APPLICABILITY OF ARTICLE 6 PARA 1 (ART 6-1) OF THE CONVENTION

86. The majority of the Commission is of the opinion that Article 6 para 1 (art 6-1) is applicable to the rights claimed by the applicant before the Frankfurt Administrative Court, namely the right to run his clinic and the right to exercise his profession of medical practitioner; it considers these rights to be 'civil' . . .

The correctness of this opinion is disputed by the Government.

87. The Court notes at the outset that, as is not contested, under the legislation of the State concerned the actions brought by the applicant before the German courts concern 'rights'. The difference of view between Commission and Government relates only to the question whether the present case involves disputes ('contestations') over civil rights within the meaning of Article 6 para 1 (art 6-1) of the Convention.

88. Both the Commission and the Government agree that the concept of 'civil rights and obligations' cannot be interpreted solely by reference to the domestic law of the respondent State.

The problem of the 'autonomy' of the meaning of the expressions used in the Convention, compared with their meaning in domestic law, has already been raised before the Court on several occasions. Thus, it has decided that the word 'charge' appearing in Article 6 para 1 (art 6-1) has to be understood 'within the meaning of the Convention' (*Neumeister* judgment of 27 June 1968, Series A No 8, p 41, para 18, as compared with the second sub-paragraph on p 28 and the first sub-paragraph on p 35; see also *Wemhoff* judgment of 27 June 1968, Series A No 7, pp 26–7, para 19; *Ringeisen* judgment of 16 July 1971, Series A No 13, p 45 para 110; *Engel* judgment of 8 June 1976, Series A No 22, p 34 para 81). The Court has also recognised, in the context of the case of *Engel*, the 'autonomy' of the concept of 'criminal' within the meaning of Article 6 para 1 (art 6–1) (above-mentioned *Engel* judgment, p 34, para 81). Again, the Court has already acknowledged, implicitly, that the concept of 'civil rights and obligations' is autonomous (above-mentioned *Ringeisen* judgment, p 39, para 94).

The Court confirms this case-law on the present occasion. Hence, it considers that the same principle of autonomy applies to the concept in question; any other solution might lead to results incompatible with the object and purpose of the Convention (see, *mutatis mutandis*, the above-mentioned *Engel* and others judgment, p 34, para 81).

89. While the Court thus concludes that the concept of 'civil rights and obligations' is autonomous, it nevertheless does not consider that, in this context, the legislation of the State concerned is without importance. Whether or not a right is to be regarded as civil within the meaning of this expression in the Convention must be determined by reference to the substantive content and effects of the right—and not its legal classification—under the domestic law of the State concerned. In the exercise of its supervisory functions, the Court must also take account of the object and purpose of the Convention and of the national legal systems of the other Contracting States (see, *mutatis mutandis*, the above-mentioned *Engel* and others judgment, p 35, para 82).

90. The Government submit that Article 6 para 1 (art 6-1) covers private-law disputes in the traditional sense, that is disputes between individuals or between an individual and the State to the extent that the latter had been acting as a private person, subject to private law; among other things, disputes between an individual and the State acting in its sovereign capacity would be excluded from the ambit of that Article (art 6-1).

As regards the field of application of Article 6 para 1 (art 6-1), the Court held in its *Ringeisen* judgment of 16 July 1971 that 'for Article 6 para 1 (art 6-1) to be applicable to a case ('contestation') it is not necessary that both parties to the proceedings should be private persons . . . The wording of Article 6 para 1 (art 6-1) is far wider; the French expression 'contestations sur (des) droits et obligations de caractère civil' covers all proceedings the result of which is decisive for private rights and obligations. The English text, 'determination of . . . civil rights and obligations', confirms this interpretation. The character of the legislation which governs how the matter is to be determined . . . and that of the authority which is invested with jurisdiction in the matter . . . are therefore of little consequence' (Series A No 13, p 39, para 94).

If the case concerns a dispute between an individual and a public authority, whether the latter had acted as a private person or in its sovereign capacity is therefore not conclusive.

Accordingly, in ascertaining whether a case ('contestation') concerns the determination of a civil right, only the character of the right at issue is relevant.

91. The Court recalls firstly that the applicant's appeals before the German administrative courts do not concern the right to be authorised to run a clinic and to be authorised to exercise the medical profession ... in challenging the withdrawal of his authorisations ordered by the competent authorities, Dr König is claiming the right to continue his professional activities for which he had obtained the necessary authorisations. If the proceedings before the administrative courts were successful, the applicant would not be granted new authorisations: the Court would simply annul the withdrawal decisions taken by the Regierungspräsidenten in Wiesbaden and Darmstadt ...

Therefore, it remains to be ascertained whether Dr König's right to continue to run a private clinic and his right to continue to exercise the medical profession are civil rights within the meaning of Article 6 para 1 (art 6-1).

92. The Court notes that, in the Federal Republic of Germany, the running of a private clinic is in certain respects a commercial activity carried on with a view to profit, classified by German law as a 'Gewerbe'. This activity is carried on in the private sector through the conclusion of contracts between the clinic and its patients and resembles the exercise of a private right in some ways akin to the right of property. Private clinics are certainly subject to supervision effected by the authorities in the public interest in order, inter alia, to protect health; supervision in the public interest, which moreover exists as a general rule for all private professional activities in the member States of the Council of Europe, cannot of itself lead to the conclusion that the running of a private clinic is a public-law activity. An activity presenting, under the law of the State concerned, the character of a private activity cannot automatically be converted into a public-law activity by reason of the fact that it is subject to administrative authorisations and supervision, including if appropriate the withdrawal of authorisations, provided for by law in the interests of public order and public health. The Court recalls in this context the *Ringeisen* case in which supervision by the public authorities concerned a contract for sale between private individuals: the Court nonetheless concluded that the right at issue had a civil character (above-mentioned judgment, p 39, para 94).

93. The medical profession counts, in the Federal Republic of Germany, among the traditional liberal professions ... Even under the national health scheme, the medical profession is not a public service: once authorised, the doctor is free to practise or not, and he provides treatment for his patients on the basis of a contract made with them. Of course, besides treating his patients, the medical practitioner, in the words of the above-mentioned Act, 'has the care of the health of the community as a whole'. This responsibility, which the medical profession bears towards society at large, does not, however, alter the private character of the medical practitioner's activity: while of great importance from the social point of view, that responsibility is accessory to his activity and its equivalent is to be found in other professions whose nature is undeniably private.

94. In these conditions, it is of little consequence that here the cases concern administrative measures taken by the competent bodies in the exercise of public authority. Neither does it appear pertinent that, under the law of the State concerned, it is for administrative courts to give the decision on these cases and to do so in proceedings which leave to the court the responsibility for the investigation and for the conduct of the trial. All that is relevant under Article 6 para 1 (art 6-1) of the Convention is the fact that the object of the cases in question is the determination of rights of a private nature.

95. Since it thus considers the rights affected by the withdrawal decisions and forming the object of the cases before the administrative courts to be private rights, the Court concludes that Article 6 para 1 (art 6-1) is applicable, without it being necessary in the present case to decide whether the concept of 'civil rights and obligations' within the meaning of that provision extends beyond those rights which have a private nature.

96. Before the Commission, the applicant claimed, in the alternative, that, in view of the nature of the complaints which led to the decisions he contests, he is in reality faced with a 'criminal charge' within the meaning of Article 6 para 1 (art 6-1) of the Convention. ... However, the Court does not consider that it has to examine whether in this case paragraph 1 of Article 6 (art 6-1) is also relevant under the

'criminal charge' head. For, although the requirements of Article 6 (art 6) as regards cases ('contest-ations') concerning civil rights are less onerous than they are for criminal charges, this difference is of no consequence here: all proceedings covered by Article 6 (art 6) are subject to the requirement of a 'reasonable time', whose observance by the German courts remains to be examined.

(B) ON THE OBSERVANCE OF ARTICLE 6 PARA 1 (ART 6-1) OF THE CONVENTION

97. According to the Commission, the duration of the proceedings instituted by the applicant before the administrative courts exceeded the 'reasonable time' stipulated by Article 6 para 1 (art 6-1) of the Convention. Before the Court, the Agent of the Government conceded that the length of those pro-ceedings was a serious matter. She referred, moreover, to certain proposals under discussion in the Federal Republic of Germany designed to accelerate the procedure before the administrative courts. Although she questions whether, in the circumstances of the case, it is possible to speak of a violation of the Convention, she leaves it to the Court to assess whether the duration of the proceedings was reasonable.

98. In order to be able to arrive at a decision, the Court must first specify the period to be taken into account in the application of Article 6 para 1 (art 6-1).

According to the Government and the Commission, time starts to run from the date of the filing of the appeals with the Administrative Court of first instance. The Court does not share this view. As the Court stated in its *Golder* judgment of 21 February 1975, 'it is conceivable . . . that in civil matters the reasonable time may begin to run, in certain circumstances, even before the issue of the writ com-mencing proceedings before the court to which the plaintiff submits the dispute' (Series A No 18, p 15, para 32). This is the situation in the applicant's case, since he could not seise the competent court before having the lawfulness and the expediency of the impugned administrative acts examined in pre-liminary proceedings (Vorverfahren) before the administrative authority . . . Consequently, in the pre-sent case, the reasonable time stipulated by Article 6 para 1 (art 6-1) starts to run on the day on which Dr König lodged an objection against the withdrawals of his authorisations.

As regards the period to which Article 6 (art 6) is applicable, the Court has held that in criminal matters this period covers the whole of the proceedings in question, including appeal proceedings (above-mentioned *Wemhoff* judgment, pp 26 and 27, paras 18 and 20; above-mentioned *Neumeister* judgment, p 41, para 19; *Delcourt* judgment of 17 January 1970, Series A No 11, pp 13–15, paras 25 and 26). The position—as, moreover, the Government concede—is no different in the case of disputes ('contestations') over civil rights and obligations for which Article 6 para 1 (art 6-1) likewise requires that there be—at first instance, on appeal or in cassation—a determination.

99. The reasonableness of the duration of proceedings covered by Article 6 para 1 (art 6-1) of the Convention must be assessed in each case according to its circumstances. When enquiring into the reasonableness of the duration of criminal proceedings, the Court has had regard, inter alia, to the complexity of the case, to the applicant's conduct and to the manner in which the matter was dealt with by the administrative and judicial authorities (above-mentioned *Neumeister* judgment, pp 42–3, paras 20–1; above-mentioned *Ringeisen* judgment, p 45, para 110). The Court, like those appearing before it, considers that the same criteria must serve in the present case as the basis for its examin-ation of the question whether the duration of the proceedings before the administrative courts exceeded the reasonable time stipulated by Article 6 para 1 (art 6-1).

100. Before embarking upon this examination, the Court wishes to emphasise that it is not its function to express an opinion on the German system of procedure before administrative courts which, as the Agent of the Government stated, enjoys a long tradition. Admittedly, the present system may appear complex on account of the number of courts and remedies but the Court is not unaware that the explanation for this situation is to be found in the eminently praiseworthy concern to reinforce the guarantees of individual rights. Should these efforts result in a procedural maze, it is for the State alone to draw the conclusions and, if need be, to simplify the system with a view to complying with Article 6 para 1 (art 6-1) of the Convention.

(i) The proceedings relative to the withdrawal of the authorisation to run the clinic

101. These proceedings, which began on 13 July 1967 when the applicant filed an objection against the withdrawal of the authorisation . . . have still not been concluded: the Hessen Administrative Court of Appeal has not yet ruled on Dr König's appeal against the judgment of 22 June 1977 of the 4th Chamber of the Frankfurt Administrative Court.

102. It is clearly a matter for serious concern—as the Government moreover admit—that more than ten years and ten months have elapsed without a decision on the merits of the case and that it was necessary to wait for almost ten years for the judgment at first instance.

It is true—and on this point the Court shares the Government's opinion—that the 4th Chamber of the Administrative Court encountered great difficulties in tracing witnesses several of whom had in the meantime changed name or address . . .

105. In an overall assessment of the various factors, the Court concludes that the delays occasioned by the difficulties in the investigation and by the applicant's behaviour do not of themselves justify the length of the proceedings. Without attaching decisive importance to any one step taken by the 4th Chamber rather than to another, the Court is in fact of the opinion that the principal reason for the length of the proceedings is to be found in the conduct of the case. The Court finds that it would have been possible for the 4th Chamber to bring the proceedings to an end at an earlier date. Taking into account the fact that the proceedings began on 13 July 1967 and ended on 22 June 1977, the Court concludes that the 'reasonable time' stipulated by Article 6 para 1 (art 6-1) was exceeded.

The Government stressed that Dr König's appeal had the effect of suspending enforcement of the withdrawal of the authorisation to run his clinic . . . and that this feature of the proceedings might have been to his advantage. The Court recognises that this suspensive effect may have a bearing on the interpretation of the concept of 'reasonable time'. However, in view of the total duration of the proceedings and the prolonged uncertainty in which the applicant found himself, the Court cannot depart, on the ground of the appeal's suspensive effect, from the assessment at which it has arrived above.

(ii) The proceedings relative to the withdrawal of the authorisation to practise

106. These proceedings began on 18 May 1971 when the applicant lodged his objection against the withdrawal of the authorisation to practise. The 2nd Chamber of the Frankfurt Administrative Court gave judgment on 9 June 1976, that is after more than five years of proceedings, and the Hessen Administrative Court of Appeal on 2 May 1978.

107. Although the length of these particular proceedings is not as great as that of the action relative to the withdrawal of the authorisation to run the clinic, it does not appear to the Court to be less serious.

This action seems less complex than the action before the 4th Chamber of the Administrative Court: not only did the 2nd Chamber encounter fewer difficulties as regards the hearing of the witnesses summoned, but also the enquiry was facilitated by the fact that, as early as 14 October 1970, the Regional Tribunal for the Medical Profession had declared Dr König unfit to practise . . .

111. In an overall assessment of the various factors and taking into account what was at stake in the proceedings, namely, Dr König's whole professional livelihood, the Court considers that, notwithstanding the delays attributable to the applicant's behaviour, the investigation of the case was not conducted with the necessary expedition. . . .

Accordingly, the Court considers that in this case the 'reasonable time' stipulated by Article 6 para 1 (art 6-1) of the Convention was exceeded.

. . .

FOR THESE REASONS, THE COURT

1. holds by fifteen votes to one that Article 6 para 1 (art 6-1) is applicable to the proceedings relative to the withdrawal of the applicant's authorisation to run his clinic;

2. holds by fourteen votes to two that Article 6 para 1 (art 6-1) is applicable to the proceedings relative to the withdrawal of the applicant's authorisation to practise;

3. holds by fifteen votes to one that there has been a violation of Article 6 para 1 (art 6-1) as regards the duration of the proceedings relative to the withdrawal of the authorisation to run the clinic;

4. holds by fifteen votes to one that there has been a violation of Article 6 para 1 (art 6-1) as regards the duration of the proceedings relative to the withdrawal of the authorisation to practise; . . .

By the time of this judgment the Court was willing to openly express the ruling that the concept of 'civil rights and obligations' was an autonomous one (for the identical approach to the notion of 'criminal charge' see the extracts in the following section of this chapter).

4 Domestic proceedings determining the existence of a right to a licence can also come within this limb of Article 6(1) according to the Court. In *Benthem v Netherlands*, A.97 (1985) 8 EHRR 1, the applicant had owned a garage, and during 1976 he applied to the municipal authority for a licence to build and operate a liquid petroleum gas installation at his garage. The municipal authority granted him the licence, however the Regional Health Inspector lodged an appeal with the Crown (i.e. central government) against the grant of the licence. The appeal was considered by the Administrative Litigation Division of the Council of State, which sought information from the Minister of Public Health and held a hearing (at which the applicant was heard). In June 1979 the Administrative Litigation Division sent an opinion to the Minister of Health recommending that the licence should be refused. A few weeks later the Crown issued a Decree quashing the municipal authority's decision to grant the licence to Benthem. The applicant complained to the Commision alleging that the dispute over his civil rights and obligations had not been heard by an independent and impartial tribunal in breach of Article 6(1). By nine votes to eight, the Commission considered that provision was not applicable to Benthem's case. After citing its understanding of 'civil rights and obligations' expressed in *Ringeisen* and *Konig*, the Court applied those principles to the facts of these proceedings.

36. The grant of the licence to which the applicant claimed to be entitled was one of the conditions for the exercise of part of his activities as a businessman. It was closely associated with the right to use one's possessions in conformity with the law's requirements. In addition, a licence of this kind has a proprietary character, as is shown, inter alia, by the fact that it can be assigned to third parties.

According to the Government, Mr Benthem was prevented only from exploiting an LPG installation on a site of his own choosing, and could have obtained a licence for another locality. The Court is not persuaded by this argument: a change of this kind—which anyway would have involved an element of chance since it would have required a fresh application whose success was in no way guaranteed in advance—might have had adverse effects on the value of the business and of the goodwill and also on Mr Benthem's contractual relations with his customers and his suppliers. This confirms the existence of direct links between the grant of the licence and the entirety of the applicant's commercial activities.

In consequence, what was at stake was a 'civil' right, within the meaning of Article 6 para 1 (art 6-1). That provision was therefore applicable to the proceedings in the appeal to the Crown.

II. COMPLIANCE WITH ARTICLE 6 PARA 1 (ART 6-1)

37. In order to determine whether the proceedings complained of were in conformity with Article 6 para 1 (art 6-1), two institutions fall to be considered, namely the Administrative Litigation Division of the Council of State and the Crown.

A. THE ADMINISTRATIVE LITIGATION DIVISION OF THE COUNCIL OF STATE

38. The applicant relied on the fact that the Division merely tendered an advice, which had no binding force; in addition, it did not, in his submission, constitute an independent and impartial tribunal. On technical matters, it consulted the department of the competent Minister; the latter could request

the Division to reconsider its draft Decree and was entitled, as a last resort, not to approve it. Moreover, the Division was not obliged to give its views within a specified time-limit and the text of its advice remained secret, being communicated neither to the appellant nor to the licence-holder nor to the issuing authority.

39. According to the Government, one had to look beyond the appearances in order to determine whether the proceedings in appeals to the Crown satisfied the requirements of Article 6 para 1 (art 6-1). Although the Division was not empowered to determine the dispute, it took cognisance of all the aspects of the case and not only of questions of law; in fact, it acted like a court, and only very rarely did the competent Minister not follow the Division's proposals to the letter.

40. The Court does not agree with this argument. It is true that, in order to decide whether the Convention rights have been infringed, one must frequently look beyond the appearances and the language used and concentrate on the realities of the situation (see, inter alia, as regards Article 5 para 1 (art 5-1), the *Van Droogenbroeck* judgment of 24 June 1982, Series A No 50, p 20, para 38). However, a power of decision is inherent in the very notion of 'tribunal' within the meaning of the Convention (see the *Sramek* judgment of 22 October 1984, Series A No 84, p 17, para 36). Yet the Division tenders only an advice. Admittedly, that advice is—as happened on the present occasion—followed in the great majority of cases, but this is only a practice of no binding force, from which the Crown can depart at any moment... The proceedings before the Administrative Litigation Division of the Council of State thus do not provide the 'determination by a tribunal of the matters in dispute' which is required by Article 6 para 1 (art 6-1) (see notably the ... *Albert and Le Compte* judgment, Series A No 58, p 16, para 29 in fine).

B. THE CROWN

41. According to the applicant, the proceedings in appeals to the Crown were of an administrative and not of a judicial nature, since there was a review not only of the lawfulness but also of the expediency of the decisions challenged.

In the present case, the appellant was the Regional Health Inspector; his superior was the Director General for Environmental Protection, and that official was also responsible for the department dealing with appeals to the Crown. Again, the technical opinion on which the Royal Decree was based reflected the provisional view of the Ministry and not of independent and impartial experts.

42. For the Government, on the other hand, the Crown was here exercising a function of an essentially judicial nature. Save very exceptionally, it followed the advice tendered by the Administrative Litigation Division of the Council of State and, indeed, had done so on this occasion. As for the Regional Inspector, he acted independently of the Minister where the entering of appeals was concerned.

43. It is true that the Crown, unlike the Administrative Litigation Division, is empowered to determine the dispute, but the Convention requires more than this: by the word 'tribunal', it denotes 'bodies which exhibit ... common fundamental features', of which the most important are independence and impartiality, and 'the guarantees of judicial procedure'. The Court refers on this point to its established case-law, and notably to its *De Wilde, Ooms and Versyp* judgment of 18 June 1971 (Series A No 12, p 41, para 78).

However, the Royal Decree by which the Crown, as head of the executive, rendered its decision constituted, from the formal point of view, an administrative act and it emanated from a Minister who was responsible to Parliament therefor. Moreover, the Minister was the hierarchical superior of the Regional Health Inspector, who had lodged the appeal, and of the Ministry's Director General, who had submitted the technical report to the Division.

Finally, the Royal Decree was not susceptible to review by a judicial body as required by Article 6 para 1 (art 6-1).

C. CONCLUSION

44. There was accordingly a violation of Article 6 para 1 (art 6-1)....

5   The ownership of real property, which was also an element in *Benthem*, has been held to be a 'civil right' in *Zander v Sweden*, A.279-B (1993) 18 EHRR 175. The applicants owned a piece of land which contained a well from which they drew their drinking water. In 1986 the National Licensing Board for Protection of the Environment granted a company permission to expand its household/industrial waste dump on land adjacent to the applicants' property. Under Swedish law there was no opportunity for the applicants to challenge that decision before the domestic courts. Therefore, the applicants complained to Strasbourg alleging a breach of Article 6(1). Both the Commission and the Court were unanimous in finding a breach of that provision. The Court held that, 'the right of property is clearly a 'civil right' within the meaning of Article 6(1)...' (para 27).

6   The Court has held that an increasing range of social insurance and welfare assistance entitlements can be classified as 'civil rights' for the purposes of Article 6. This trend began with *Feldbrugge v Netherlands*, A.99 (1986) 8 EHRR 425. During March 1978 the applicant's occupational insurance association determined that she was fit to resume work and therefore stopped paying her a sickness allowance. The applicant appealed, but the President of the Appeals Board, after considering medical reports, rejected her appeal. Mrs Feldbrugge also lost a further domestic appeal. She complained to the Commission alleging a breach of Article 6(1) in that she had not had a fair hearing of her appeals. The Commission, by eight votes to six, considered that her case did not fall within this Article. After citing its previous judgments in *Ringeisen* and *Konig*, the Court stated that:

27. As in previous cases, the Court does not consider that it has to give on this occasion an abstract definition of the concept of 'civil rights and obligations.'
   This being the first time that the Court has had to deal with the field of social security, and more particularly the sickness insurance scheme in the Netherlands, the Court must identify such relevant factors as are capable of clarifying or amplifying the principles stated above.

(B) SUPPLEMENTARY FACTORS DISCLOSED BY THE SUBJECT MATTER OF THE LITIGATION

28. Under Netherlands legislation, the right in issue is treated as a public-law right... This classification, however, provides only a starting point (see notably, *mutatis mutandis, the Engel* judgment of 8 June 1976, Series A No 22, p 35, para 82); it cannot be conclusive of the matter unless corroborated by other factors. In its *König* judgment of 28 June 1978, the Court stated in particular:

   'Whether or not a right is to be regarded as civil... must be determined by reference to the substantive content and effects of the right—and not its legal classification—under the domestic law of the State concerned. In the exercise of its supervisory functions, the Court must also take account of the object and purpose of the Convention and of the national legal systems of the other Contracting States....' (Series A No 27, p 30, para 89)

29. There exists great diversity in the legislation and case-law of the member States of the Council of Europe as regards the juridical nature of the entitlement to health insurance benefits under social security schemes, that is to say as regards the category of law to which such entitlement belongs. Some States—including the Netherlands—treat it as a public-law right, whereas others, on the contrary, treat it as a private-law right; others still would appear to operate a mixed system. What is more, even within the same legal order differences of approach can be found in the case-law. Thus, in some States where the public-law aspect is predominant, some court decisions have nonetheless held Article 6 para 1 (art 6-1) to be applicable to claims similar to the one in issue in the present case (for example, the

judgment of 11 May 1984 by the Brussels Labour Court, Journal des Tribunaux 1985, pp 168–169).
Accordingly, there exists no common standard pointing to a uniform European notion in this regard.

30. An analysis of the characteristics of the Netherlands system of social health insurance discloses
that the claimed entitlement comprises features of both public law and private law.

(i) Features of public law

31. A number of factors might tend to suggest that the dispute in question should be considered as one
falling within the sphere of public law.

(1) Character of the legislation

32. The first such factor is the character of the legislation. The legal rules governing social security benefits in the context of health insurance differ in many respects from the rules which apply to insurance in
general and which are part of civil law. The Netherlands State has assumed the responsibility of regulating the framework of the health insurance scheme and of overseeing the operation of that scheme.
To this end, it specifies the categories of beneficiaries, defines the limits of the protection afforded, lays
down the rates of the contributions and the allowances, etc.

    In several cases (see notably *König; Le Compte, Van Leuven and De Meyere; Benthem*), State inter-
vention by means of a statute or delegated legislation has nonetheless not prevented the Court from
finding the right in issue to have a private, and hence civil, character. In the present case likewise, such
intervention cannot suffice to bring within the sphere of public law the right asserted by the applicant.

(2) Compulsory nature of the insurance

33. A second factor of relevance is the obligation to be insured against illness or, more precisely, the
fact of being covered by insurance in the event of fulfilling the conditions laid down by the legislation
(see paragraph 38 below). In other words, those concerned can neither opt out of the benefits nor
avoid having to pay the relevant contributions.

    Comparable obligations can be found in other fields. Examples are provided by the rules making insur-
ance cover compulsory for the performance of certain activities—such as driving a motor vehicle—or
for householders. Yet the entitlement to benefits to which this kind of insurance contract gives rise cannot be qualified as a public-law right. The Court does not therefore discern why the obligation to belong
to a health insurance scheme should change the nature of the corresponding right.

(3) Assumption by the State of responsibility for social protection

34. One final aspect to be considered is the assumption, by the State or by public or semi-public institutions, of full or partial responsibility for ensuring social protection. This was what happened in the
present case by virtue of the health insurance scheme operated by the Occupational Association of the
Banking and Insurance, Wholesale Trade and Self-Employment Sector in Amsterdam. Whether viewed
as the culmination of or a stage in the development of the role of the State, such a factor implies, *prima
facie*, an extension of the public-law domain.

    On the other hand—and the Court will revert to the point later (see paragraph 39 below)—the pre-
sent case concerns a matter having affinities with insurance under the ordinary law, which insurance
is traditionally governed by private law. It thus seems difficult to draw from the consequences of the
extent of State intervention any firm conclusion as to the nature of the right in issue.

35. In sum, even taken together the three foregoing factors, on analysis, do not suffice to establish that
Article 6 (art 6) is inapplicable.

(ii) Features of private law

36. In contrast, various considerations argue in favour of the opposite conclusion.

(1) Personal and economic nature of the asserted right

37. To begin with, Mrs Feldbrugge was not affected in her relations with the public authorities as
such, acting in the exercise of discretionary powers, but in her personal capacity as a private individual.

She suffered an interference with her means of subsistence and was claiming a right flowing from specific rules laid down by the legislation in force.

For the individual asserting it, such a right is often of crucial importance; this is especially so in the case of health insurance benefits when the employee who is unable to work by reason of illness enjoys no other source of income. In short, the right in question was a personal, economic and individual right, a factor that brought it close to the civil sphere.

(2) Connection with the contract of employment

38. Secondly, the position of Mrs Feldbrugge was closely linked with the fact of her being a member of the working population, having been a salaried employee. The applicant was admittedly unemployed at the relevant time, but the availability of the health benefits was determined by reference to the terms of her former contract of employment and the legislation applicable to that contract.

The legal basis of the work that she had performed was a contract of employment governed by private law. While it is true that the insurance provisions derived directly from statute and not from an express clause in the contract, these provisions were in a way grafted onto the contract. They thus formed one of the constituents of the relationship between employer and employee.

In addition, the sickness allowance claimed by Mrs Feldbrugge was a substitute for the salary payable under the contract, the civil character of this salary being beyond doubt. This allowance shared the same nature as the contract and hence was also invested with a civil character for the purposes of the Convention.

(3) Affinities with insurance under the ordinary law

39. Finally, the Netherlands health insurance is similar in several respects to insurance under the ordinary law. Thus, under the Netherlands health insurance scheme recourse is had to techniques of risk covering and to management methods which are inspired by those current in the private insurance sphere. In the Netherlands, the occupational associations conduct their dealings, notably with those insured, in the same way as a company providing insurance under the ordinary law, for example as regards collection of contributions, calculation of risks, verification of fulfilment of the conditions for receipt of benefits, and payment of allowances.

There exists a further feature of relevance. Complementary insurance policies, taken out with friendly societies or private insurance companies, allow employees to improve their social protection at the price of an increased or fresh financial outlay; such policies constitute in sum an optional extension of compulsory insurance cover. Proceedings instituted in their connection are incontestably civil proceedings. Yet in both cases the risk insured against (for example, ill-health) is the same and, while the extent of the cover increases, the nature of the cover does not change.

Such differences as may exist between private sector insurance and social security insurance do not affect the essential character of the link between the insured and the insurer. Finally, the Court would draw attention to the fact that in the Netherlands, as in some other countries, the insured themselves participate in the financing of all or some of the social security schemes. Deductions at source are made from their salaries, which deductions establish a close connection between the contributions called for and the allowances granted. Thus, when Mrs Feldbrugge was working, her employer withheld from her pay a sum paid over to the Occupational Association ... In addition, her employer also bore a portion of the insurance contributions, which were included in the firm's accounts under the head of social insurance expenses. The Netherlands State, for its part, was not involved in the financing of the scheme.

(C) CONCLUSION

40. Having evaluated the relative cogency of the features of public law and private law present in the instant case, the Court finds the latter to be predominant. None of these various features of private law is decisive on its own, but taken together and cumulatively they confer on the asserted entitlement the character of a civil right within the meaning of Article 6 para 1 (art 6-1) of the Convention, which was thus applicable. ...

This view was supported by ten judges, while seven dissented arguing that the applicant's entitle-ment was not a 'civil right'. The majority went on to find a breach of Article 6(1) as the presi-dent of the Appeals Board had not allowed Mrs Feldbrugge to participate in the proceedings (by either oral or written pleadings). In the later case of *Salesi v Italy*, A.257-E (1990), a unani-mous Court applied the majority's analytical framework developed in *Feldbrugge* to a non-contributory welfare assistance entitlement. Mrs Salesi was refused a monthly disability allowance by the government. During February 1986 she began legal proceedings, in the Rome magistrate's court, to challenge that decision. The Court of Cassation finally determined the case in March 1992. She complained to the Commission claiming that the domestic courts had not determined her 'civil rights' within a reasonable time as required by Article 6(1). By thirteen votes to eight the Commission upheld her complaint.

19. The Court is here once again confronted with the issue of the applicability of Article 6 para 1 (art 6-1) to social security disputes. The question arose earlier in the cases of *Feldbrugge v the Netherlands* and *Deumeland v Germany*, in which it gave judgment on 29 May 1986 (Series A nos 99 and 100). At that time the Court noted that there was great diversity in the legislation and practice of the member States of the Council of Europe as regards the nature of the entitlement to insurance benefits under social security schemes. Nevertheless, the development in the law that was initiated by those judg-ments and the principle of equality of treatment warrant taking the view that today the general rule is that Article 6 para 1 (art 6-1) does apply in the field of social insurance.

  In the present case, however, the question arises in connection with welfare assistance and not, as in the cases previously cited, social insurance. Certainly there are differences between the two, but they cannot be regarded as fundamental at the present stage of development of social security law. This justifies following, in relation to the entitlement to welfare allowances, the opinion which emerges from the aforementioned judgments as regards the classification of the right to social insur-ance benefits, namely that State intervention is not sufficient to establish that Article 6 para 1 (art 6-1) is inapplicable.

  As in the two cases previously referred to, other considerations argue in favour of the applicability of Article 6 para 1 (art 6-1) in the instant case. The most important of these lies in the fact that despite the public law features pointed out by the Government, Mrs Salesi was not affected in her relations with the administrative authorities as such, acting in the exercise of discretionary powers; she suffered an inter-ference with her means of subsistence and was claiming an individual, economic right flowing from specific rules laid down in a statute giving effect to the Constitution ...

  The protection of this basic right is, moreover, organised in such a way that at the judicial stage dis-putes over it come within the jurisdiction of the ordinary court, the labour magistrate's court (*pretore del lavoro*).

  In sum, the Court sees no convincing reason to distinguish between Mrs Salesi's right to welfare benefits and the rights to social insurance benefits asserted by Mrs Feldbrugge and Mr Deumeland.

  Article 6 para 1 (art 6-1) therefore applies in the instant case. ...

As the domestic proceedings were not complex and the applicant had not contributed to the delay, the Court found that they had not been completed within a 'reasonable' time. In terms of the Court's application of the concept of 'civil rights' in the above cases the decisive con-sideration was that private law factors outweighed those of public law. How significant do you think it was that both Mrs Feldbrugge and Mrs Salesi had rights under domestic law to the social insurance and welfare assistance benefits they were claiming? The Court has also utilised the *Feldbrugge* method of analysis to determine that compulsory contributions to a social insurance scheme could be classified as 'civil rights and obligations' in *Schouten and Meldrum v Netherlands*, A.304 (1994) 19 EHRR 432. The applicants were physiotherapists and their occupational insurance association demanded that they pay health and disability insurance contributions in respect of other physiotherapists who used their premises. According to the applicants the time taken by the domestic tribunals to determine their appeals breached Article 6(1). The Court unanimously found that the duration of the proceedings (four years, three months and three years, three months) exceeded the 'reasonable time' requirement laid down in that provision.

The full-time Court has adopted an expansive approach to the classification of welfare benefits as 'possessions' falling within Article 1 of Protocol No 1, see *Stec and Others v United Kingdom*, below p 916.

7   Disputes between some public servants and governmental authorities are excluded from the category of 'civil rights and obligations'. The Court's contemporary approach to this issue was explained in *Pellegrin v France*, (8/12/1999). The applicant had been employed in the private sector, as a management/accountancy consultant, until 1989. Then in March 1989 the French Ministry of Cooperation and Development contracted him to work as an economic advisor to the government of Equatorial Guinea (he was to be responsible for drawing up the budget for state investment). After disagreements with the Guinean authorities the applicant returned to France in early 1990. In March of that year the Ministry informed the applicant that he was to be removed from its list of staff as medical reports had revealed that he was permanently unfit to serve overseas. The applicant sought to challenge that decision before the French courts, but in 1999 his action was still pending before the Paris Administrative Court of Appeal. He, therefore, complained to the Commission alleging that his case had not been determined within a reasonable time. By eighteen votes to fourteen, the Commission upheld his complaint.

58. The facts of the present case raise the problem of the applicability of Article 6 § 1 to disputes raised by servants of the State over their conditions of service.

1. EXISTING CASE LAW

59. As the Court has noted in previous cases, in the law of many member States of the Council of Europe there is a basic distinction between civil servants and employees governed by private law. This has led the Court to hold that 'disputes relating to the recruitment, careers and termination of service of civil servants are as a general rule outside the scope of Article 6 § 1' (see, for example, the *Massa v Italy* judgment of 24 August 1993, Series A No 265-B, p 20, § 26).

This general principle of exclusion has however been limited and clarified in a number of judgments. Thus, in the *Massa* case (*ibid*) the applicant applied for a reversionary pension following the death of his wife, who had been a headmistress. In the Francesco Lombardo case [*Lombardo v Italy*, A.249-B (1992)] a *carabiniere* who had been invalided out of the service because of disability and who maintained that the disability was 'due to his service' applied for an 'enhanced ordinary pension'. The Court considered that the applicants' complaints related neither to the 'recruitment' nor to the 'careers' of civil servants and only indirectly to 'termination of service' as they consisted in claims for purely pecuniary rights arising in law after termination of service. In those circumstances and in view of the fact that the Italian State was not using 'discretionary powers' in performing its obligation to pay the pensions in issue and could be compared to an employer who was a party to a contract of employment governed by private law, the Court held that the applicants' claims were civil ones within the meaning of Article 6 § 1.

In the *Neigel* case [*Neigel v France* 1997-II 411] on the other hand, the decision contested by the applicant, namely the refusal to reinstate her to a permanent post in the civil service, was held by the Court to concern 'her 'recruitment', her 'career' and the 'termination of [her] service'. The Court went on to say that the applicant's claim for payment of the salary she would have received if she had been reinstated did not make Article 6 § 1 applicable because an award of such compensation by the administrative court was 'directly dependent on a prior finding that the refusal to reinstate [had been] unlawful' (previously cited *Neigel* judgment, p 411, § 44). The Court accordingly decided that the dispute did not concern a 'civil' right within the meaning of Article 6 § 1. It should be noted that the administrative authorities' refusal to reinstate did not constitute exercise of any discretionary power on their part since, according to the applicable domestic law, either the post was vacant, in which case the applicant would have been entitled to reinstatement, or there was no vacancy and the authorities could not reinstate her.

According to other judgments, Article 6 § 1 applies where the claim in issue relates to a 'purely economic' right—such as payment of salary (see the *De Santa v Italy, Lapalorcia v Italy* and *Abenavoli v Italy* judgments of 2 September 1997, *Reports* 1997-V, at p 1663, § 18, p 1677, § 21, and p 1690, § 16, respectively)—or an 'essentially economic' one (see the *Nicodemo v Italy* judgment of 2 September 1997, *Reports* 1997-V, p 1703, § 18) and does not mainly call in question 'the authorities' discretionary powers' (see the following judgments: *Benkessiouer v France*, 24 August 1998, *Reports* 1998-V, p 2287, §§ 29–30; *Couez v France*, 24 August 1998, *Reports* 1998-V, p 2265, § 25 . . .

2. THE LIMITS OF THE PRESENT CASE-LAW AND ITS CONSEQUENCES

60. The Court considers that, as it stands, the above case-law contains a margin of uncertainty for Contracting States as to the scope of their obligations under Article 6 § 1 in disputes raised by employees in the public sector over their conditions of service.

In the *Neigel* case, for example, the criterion of the absence of discretionary power was not taken to be decisive for the applicability of Article 6 § 1 (see paragraph 59 above).

The criterion relating to the economic nature of a dispute, for its part, leaves scope for a degree of arbitrariness, since a decision concerning the 'recruitment', 'career' or 'termination of service' of a civil servant nearly always has pecuniary consequences. This being so, it is difficult to draw a distinction between proceedings of 'purely' or 'essentially' economic interest and other kinds of proceedings . . .

61. The Court therefore wishes to put an end to the uncertainty which surrounds application of the guarantees of Article 6 § 1 to disputes between States and their servants.

62. The parties in the present case derived argument from the distinction which exists in France, as in some other Contracting States, between two categories of staff at the service of the State, namely officials under contract and established civil servants . . . It is true that in some States officials under contract are governed by private law, unlike established civil servants, who are governed by public law. The Court notes, however, that in the current practice of the Contracting States established civil servants and officials under contract frequently perform equivalent or similar duties. Whether the applicable legal provisions form part of domestic public or private law cannot, according to the Court's established case-law, be decisive in itself, and it would in any event lead to inequality of treatment from one State to another and between persons in State service performing equivalent duties.

63. The Court accordingly considers that it is important, with a view to applying Article 6 § 1, to establish an autonomous interpretation of the term 'civil service' which would make it possible to afford equal treatment to public servants performing equivalent or similar duties in the States party to the Convention, irrespective of the domestic system of employment and, in particular, whatever the nature of the legal relation between the official and the administrative authority (whether stipulated in a contract or governed by statutory and regulatory conditions of service). In addition, this interpretation must take into account the disadvantages engendered by the Court's existing case-law (see paragraph 60 above).

3. NEW CRITERION TO BE APPLIED

64. To that end, in order to determine the applicability of Article 6 § 1 to public servants, whether established or employed under contract, the Court considers that it should adopt a functional criterion based on the nature of the employee's duties and responsibilities. In so doing, it must adopt a restrictive interpretation, in accordance with the object and purpose of the Convention, of the exceptions to the safeguards afforded by Article 6 § 1.

65. The Court notes that in each country's public-service sector certain posts involve responsibilities in the general interest or participation in the exercise of powers conferred by public law. The holders of such posts thus wield a portion of the State's sovereign power. The State therefore has a legitimate interest in requiring of these servants a special bond of trust and loyalty. On the other hand, in respect of other posts which do not have this 'public administration' aspect, there is no such interest.

66. The Court therefore rules that the only disputes excluded from the scope of Article 6 § 1 of the Convention are those which are raised by public servants whose duties typify the specific activities of the public service in so far as the latter is acting as the depositary of public authority responsible for protecting the general interests of the State or other public authorities. A manifest example of such activities is provided by the armed forces and the police. In practice, the Court will ascertain, in each case, whether the applicant's post entails—in the light of the nature of the duties and responsibilities appertaining to it—direct or indirect participation in the exercise of powers conferred by public law and duties designed to safeguard the general interests of the State or of other public authorities. In so doing, the Court will have regard, for guidance, to the categories of activities and posts listed by the European Commission in its communication of 18 March 1988 and by the Court of Justice of the European Communities . . .

67. Accordingly, no disputes between administrative authorities and employees who occupy posts involving participation in the exercise of powers conferred by public law attract the application of Article 6 § 1 since the Court intends to establish a functional criterion (see paragraph 64 above). Disputes concerning pensions all come within the ambit of Article 6 § 1 because on retirement employees break the special bond between themselves and the authorities; they, and *a fortiori* those entitled through them, then find themselves in a situation exactly comparable to that of employees under private law in that the special relationship of trust and loyalty binding them to the State has ceased to exist and the employee can no longer wield a portion of the State's sovereign power (see paragraph 65 above).

4. APPLICATION OF THE ABOVE CRITERION IN THE INSTANT CASE

68. The Court notes that at the material time the applicant was employed by the Ministry of Co-operation and Development. As one of the civilian co-operation staff in post in foreign States he was under specific obligations 'inherent in the public-service nature' of his duties, as defined in particular in section 3 of the Law of 13 July 1972 on the position of civilian cultural, scientific and technical co-operation staff in post in foreign States . . . As evidenced by those obligations, such an activity, which comes under the aegis of a government Ministry and partakes of the conduct of foreign relations, typifies the specific activities of the public service as defined above (see paragraph 66 above).

69. It remains for the Court to examine the particular nature of the applicant's duties and responsibilities in the course of his employment. In that connection, the Court is not persuaded by the applicant's submission . . . which was limited to the assertion that, since it had proved possible to entrust his duties to a private consultant, they did not involve powers conferred under public law. It accepts the Government's argument in so far as it is based on the nature of the work performed by the applicant in the States concerned . . .

70. The facts of the case show that the tasks assigned to the applicant . . . gave him considerable responsibilities in the field of the State's public finances, which is, *par excellence*, a sphere in which States exercise sovereign power. This entailed participating directly in the exercise of powers conferred by public law and the performance of duties designed to safeguard the general interests of the State.

71. Accordingly, Article 6 § 1 is not applicable in the present case . . .

The above judgment was endorsed by thirteen judges, while four dissented. It is now clear that the decisive criterion in determining if specific public servants' disputes fall within Article 6(1) is the type of duties they perform. Where such a person is exercising aspects of government's 'sovereign power' his/her disputes with the State over employment matters will not be subject to the requirements of Article 6(1). The judgment is interesting for linking the Court's classification of public servants in respect of Article 6(1) with the European Union's treatment of public sector workers for the purposes of freedom of movement (see paragraph 66 of the above judgment). The European Commission, in its March 1988 communication, stated that a number of groups of public servants came within Article 48(4) of the Treaty of Rome (derogation from the principle of freedom of movement of workers), because of their 'participation in the exercise of powers conferred by public law and duties designed to safeguard the general interests of the State'. Identified classes included: members of the diplomatic corps, tax authorities and local government officials involved in preparing legal acts and supervising subordinate bodies. The European Court of Justice has held that teachers and many positions in the public utilities (water supply etc) are not within the derogation classes: *EC Commission v Luxembourg*, (C-473/93) [1997] ECR I-3207. The decision in *Pellegrin* is also significant as it vividly demonstrates that the full-time Court is willing to depart from its predecessor's interpretations where the new body considers that the existing jurisprudence is defective. In subsequent cases the Court has held that senior officials within the Spanish Ministry of Foreign Affairs were exercising important public law powers and could not therefore bring their claims in respect of overseas allowances within Article 6 (*Martinez-Caro De La Concha Castaneda v Spain*, Decision of 7/3/2000); whereas a school caretaker was not exercising such powers and could invoke Article 6 in respect of her employment dispute (*Procaccini v Italy*, Decision of 30/3/2000), as could an applicant for a post of administrative assistant (the lowest grade) in the civil service (*Devlin v UK*, judgment of 30 October 2001).

8   A Grand Chamber, by eleven votes to six, confirmed the established approach of the Strasbourg institutions that tax proceedings do not fall within the scope of 'civil rights and obligations' in *Ferrazzini v Italy*, judgment of 12 July 2001. The applicant claimed that, *inter alia*, his capital-gains tax liabilities had not been determined by the domestic authorities in a reasonable time as required by Article 6(1).

21. The Government argued that Article 6 was inapplicable to the proceedings in question, considering that they did not concern a 'civil right'. The existence of an individual's tax obligation *vis-à-vis* the State belonged, in their submission, exclusively to the realm of public law. That obligation was part of the civic duties imposed in a democratic society and the purpose of the specific provisions of public law was to support national economic policy.

22. The applicant, for his part, stressed the pecuniary aspect of his claims and contended that the proceedings accordingly concerned 'civil rights and obligations'.

23. As it is common ground that there was a 'dispute' (*contestation*), the Court's task is confined to determining whether it was over 'civil rights and obligations'.

24. According to the Court's case-law, the concept of 'civil rights and obligations' cannot be interpreted solely by reference to the domestic law of the respondent State. The Court has on several occasions affirmed the principle that this concept is 'autonomous', within the meaning of Article 6 § 1 of the Convention (see, among other authorities, *König v Germany*, judgment of 28 June 1978, Series A No 27, pp 29–30, §§ 88–9, and *Baraona v Portugal*, judgment of 8 July 1987, Series A No 122, pp 17–18, § 42). The Court confirms this case-law in the instant case. It considers that any other solution is liable to lead to results that are incompatible with the object and purpose of the Convention (see, *mutatis mutandis*, *König*, cited above, pp 29–30, § 88, and *Maaouia v France* [GC], No 39652/98, § 34, ECHR 2000-X).

25. Pecuniary interests are clearly at stake in tax proceedings, but merely showing that a dispute is 'pecuniary' in nature is not in itself sufficient to attract the applicability of Article 6 § 1 under its 'civil' head (see *Pierre-Bloch v France*, judgment of 21 October 1997, *Reports of Judgments and Decisions* 1997-VI, p 2223, § 51, and *Pellegrin v France* [GC], No 28541/95, § 60, ECHR 1999-VIII; cf. *Editions Périscope v France*, judgment of 26 March 1992, Series A No 234-B, p 66, § 40). In particular, according to the traditional case-law of the Convention institutions:

'There may exist "pecuniary" obligations *vis-à-vis* the State or its subordinate authorities which, for the purpose of Article 6 § 1, are to be considered as belonging exclusively to the realm of public law and are accordingly not covered by the notion of "civil rights and obligations". Apart from fines imposed by way of "criminal sanction", this will be the case, in particular, where an obligation which is pecuniary in nature derives from tax legislation or is otherwise part of normal civic duties in a democratic society'. (See, among other authorities, *Schouten and Meldrum v The Netherlands*, judgment of 9 December 1994, Series A No 304, p 21, § 50; *Company S. and T. v Sweden*, No 11189/84, Commission decision of 11 December 1986, *Decisions and Reports* (DR) 50, p 121, at p 140; and *Kustannus oy Vapaa Ajattelija AB, Vapaa-Ajattelijain Liitto—Fritänkarnas Förbund r.y. and Kimmo Sundström v Finland*, No 20471/92, Commission decision of 15 April 1996, DR 85-A, p 29, at p 46).

26. The Convention is, however, a living instrument to be interpreted in the light of present-day conditions (see, among other authorities, *Johnston and Others v Ireland*, judgment of 18 December 1986, Series A No 112, pp 24–5, § 53), and it is incumbent on the Court to review whether, in the light of changed attitudes in society as to the legal protection that falls to be accorded to individuals in their relations with the State, the scope of Article 6 § 1 should not be extended to cover disputes between citizens and public authorities as to the lawfulness under domestic law of the tax authorities' decisions.

27. Relations between the individual and the State have clearly evolved in many spheres during the fifty years which have elapsed since the Convention was adopted, with State regulation increasingly intervening in private-law relations. This has led the Court to find that procedures classified under national law as being part of 'public law' could come within the purview of Article 6 under its 'civil' head if the outcome was decisive for private rights and obligations, in regard to such matters as, to give some examples, the sale of land, the running of a private clinic, property interests, the granting of administrative authorisations relating to the conditions of professional practice or of a licence to serve alcoholic beverages (see, among other authorities, *Ringeisen v Austria*, judgment of 16 July 1971, Series A No 13, p 39, § 94; *König*, cited above, p 32, §§ 94–5; *Sporrong and Lönnroth v Sweden*, judgment of 23 September 1982, Series A No 52, p 29, § 79; *Allan Jacobsson v Sweden (no. 1)*, judgment of 25 October 1989, Series A No 163, pp 20–1, § 73; *Benthem v The Netherlands*, judgment of 23 October 1985, Series A No 97, p 16, § 36; and *Tre Traktörer AB v Sweden*, judgment of 7 July 1989, Series A No 159, p 19, § 43). Moreover, the State's increasing intervention in the individual's day-to-day life, in terms of welfare protection for example, has required the Court to evaluate features of public law and private law before concluding that the asserted right could be classified as 'civil' (see, among other authorities, *Feldbrugge v The Netherlands*, judgment of 29 May 1986, Series A No 99, p 16, § 40; *Deumeland v Germany*, judgment of 29 May 1986, Series A No 100, p 25, § 74; *Salesi v Italy*, judgment of 26 February 1993, Series A No 257-E, pp 59–60, § 19; and *Schouten and Meldrum*, cited above, p 24, § 60).

28. However, rights and obligations existing for an individual are not necessarily civil in nature. Thus, political rights and obligations, such as the right to stand for election to the National Assembly (see *Pierre-Bloch*, cited above, p 2223, § 50), even though in those proceedings the applicant's pecuniary interests were at stake (ibid, § 51), are not civil in nature, with the consequence that Article 6 § 1 does not apply. Neither does that provision apply to disputes between administrative authorities and those of their employees who occupy posts involving participation in the exercise of powers conferred by public law (see *Pellegrin*, cited above, §§ 66–7). Similarly, the expulsion of aliens does not give rise to

disputes (*contestations*) over civil rights for the purposes of Article 6 § 1 of the Convention, which accordingly does not apply (see *Maaouia*, cited above, §§ 37–8).

29. In the tax field, developments which might have occurred in democratic societies do not, however, affect the fundamental nature of the obligation on individuals or companies to pay tax. In comparison with the position when the Convention was adopted, those developments have not entailed a further intervention by the State into the 'civil' sphere of the individual's life. The Court considers that tax matters still form part of the hard core of public-authority prerogatives, with the public nature of the relationship between the taxpayer and the community remaining predominant. Bearing in mind that the Convention and its Protocols must be interpreted as a whole, the Court also observes that Article 1 of Protocol No 1, which concerns the protection of property, reserves the right of States to enact such laws as they deem necessary for the purpose of securing the payment of taxes (see, *mutatis mutandis*, *Gasus Dosier und Fördertechnik GmbH v The Netherlands*, judgment of 23 February 1995, Series A No 306-B, pp. 48–9, § 60). Although the Court does not attach decisive importance to that factor, it does take it into account. It considers that tax disputes fall outside the scope of civil rights and obligations, despite the pecuniary effects which they necessarily produce for the taxpayer.

30. The principle according to which the autonomous concepts contained in the Convention must be interpreted in the light of present-day conditions in democratic societies does not give the Court power to interpret Article 6 § 1 as though the adjective 'civil' (with the restriction that that adjective necessarily places on the category of 'rights and obligations' to which that Article applies) were not present in the text.

31. Accordingly, Article 6 § 1 of the Convention does not apply in the instant case.

Of course, if penal tax proceedings satisfy the *Engel* criteria (see below p 365) they can be classified as involving a 'criminal charge' and fall under that limb of Article 6: see, for example, *Bendenoun v France*, judgment of 24 February 1994, where the Court found proceedings involving the imposition of substantial tax surcharges (totalling nearly £100,000) should be so categorized.

9 In order to be able to invoke this limb of Article 6(1) applicants must be able to satisfy the Court that there is (or had been) a 'contestation' (dispute) regarding their 'civil rights and obligations' at the domestic level. The Court elaborated its understanding of this requirement in *Le Compte, Van Leuven and De Meyere v Belgium*, A.43 (1981) 4 EHRR 1. The applicants were medical doctors who had been found to have breached professional rules, governing contempt for the *Ordre* and fellow doctors, by the Provincial Council and Appeals Council of the *Ordre des medecins* (Belgian Medical Association). The applicants' appeals to the courts against those findings and the related suspensions of their rights to practise (three months for Dr Le Compte and fifteen days for the other applicants) were unsuccessful. They complained to the Commission alleging, *inter alia*, breaches of their right to a fair hearing under Article 6(1) in respect of the domestic proceedings. The Commission, by eight votes to three, found a violation of the right to a public hearing contained in that provision.

1. THE EXISTENCE OF 'CONTESTATIONS' (DISPUTES) OVER 'CIVIL RIGHTS AND OBLIGATIONS'

44. In certain respects, the meaning of the words 'contestations' (disputes) over 'civil rights and obligations' has been clarified in the *Ringeisen* judgment of 16 July 1971 and the *König* judgment of 28 June 1978.

According to the first of these judgments, the phrase in question covers 'all proceedings the result of which is decisive for private rights and obligations', even if the proceedings concern a dispute between an individual and a public authority acting in its sovereign capacity; the character 'of the legislation which governs how the matter is to be determined' and of the 'authority' which is invested with jurisdiction in the matter are of little consequence (Series A No 13, p 39, par 94).

The very notion of 'civil rights and obligations' lay at the heart of the *König* case. The rights at issue included the right 'to continue his professional activities' as a medical practitioner 'for which he had obtained the necessary authorisations'. In the light of the circumstances of that case, the Court classified this right as private, and hence as civil for the purposes of Article 6 par 1 (art 6-1) (*loc. cit.*, pp 29–32, par 88–91 and 93–5).

The ramifications of this line of authority are again considerably extended as a result of the Golder judgment of 21 February 1975. The Court concluded that 'Article 6 par 1 (art 6-1) secures to everyone the right to have any claim relating to his civil rights and obligations brought before a court or tribunal' (Series A No 18, p 18, par 36). One consequence of this is that Article 6 par 1 (art 6-1) is not applicable solely to proceedings which are already in progress: it may also be relied on by anyone who considers that an interference with the exercise of one of his (civil) rights is unlawful and complains that he has not had the possibility of submitting that claim to a tribunal meeting the requirements of Article 6 par 1 (art 6-1).

45. In the present case, a preliminary point needs to be resolved: can it be said that there was a veritable 'contestation' (dispute), in the sense of 'two conflicting claims or applications' (oral submissions of counsel for the Government)?

Conformity with the spirit of the Convention requires that this word should not be construed too technically and that it should be given a substantive rather than a formal meaning; besides, it has no counterpart in the English text of Article 6 par 1 (art 6-1) ('In the determination of his civil rights and obligations'; cf Article 49 (art 49): 'dispute').

Even if the use of the French word 'contestation' implies the existence of a disagreement, the evidence clearly shows that there was one in this case. The Ordre des médecins alleged that the applicants had committed professional misconduct rendering them liable to sanctions and they denied those allegations. After the competent Provincial Council had found them guilty of that misconduct and ordered their suspension from practice—decisions that were taken in absentia in the case of Dr Le Compte (West Flanders) and after hearing submissions on issues of fact and of law from Dr Van Leuven and Dr De Meyere in their cases (East Flanders)—the applicants appealed to the Appeals Council. They all appeared before that Council where, with the assistance of lawyers, they pleaded among other things Articles 6 par 1 and 11 (art 6-1, art 11). In most respects their appeals proved unsuccessful, whereupon they turned to the Court of Cassation relying once more, *inter alia*, on the Convention . . .

46. In addition, it must be shown that the 'contestation' (dispute) related to 'civil rights and obligations', in other words that the 'result of the proceedings' was 'decisive' for such a right (see the above-mentioned *Ringeisen* judgment).

According to the applicants, what was at issue was their right to continue to exercise their profession; they maintained that this had been recognised to be a 'civil' right in the *König* judgment of 28 June 1978 (loc. cit., pp 31–2, paragraphs 91 and 93).

According to the Government, the decisions of the Provincial and Appeals Councils had but an 'indirect effect' in the matter. It was argued that these organs, unlike the German administrative courts in the *König* case, did not review the lawfulness of an earlier measure withdrawing the right to practise but had instead to satisfy themselves that breaches of the rules of professional conduct, of a kind justifying disciplinary sanctions, had actually occurred. A 'contestation' (dispute) over the right to continue to exercise the medical profession was said to have arisen, if at all, 'at a later stage', that is when Dr Le Compte, Dr Van Leuven and Dr De Meyere contested before the Court of Cassation the lawfulness of the measures imposed on them. The Government further submitted that this right was not 'civil' and invited the Court not to follow the decision which it took in this respect in the König judgment.

47. As regards the question whether the dispute related to the above-mentioned right, the Court considers that a tenuous connection or remote consequences do not suffice for Article 6 par 1 (art 6-1), in either of its official versions ('contestation sur', 'determination of'): civil rights and obligations must be the object—or one of the objects—of the 'contestation' (dispute); the result of the proceedings must be directly decisive for such a right.

While the Court agrees with the Government on this point, it does not agree that in the present case there was not this kind of direct relationship between the proceedings in question and the right to continue to exercise the medical profession. The suspensions ordered by the Provincial Council on 30 June 1971 (Dr Le Compte) and on 24 October 1973 (Dr Van Leuven and Dr De Meyere) were to deprive them temporarily of their rights to practise. That right was directly in issue before the Appeals Council and the Court of Cassation, which bodies had to examine the applicants' complaints against the decisions affecting them.

48. Furthermore, it is by means of private relationships with their clients or patients that medical practitioners in private practice, such as the applicants, avail themselves of the right to continue to practise; in Belgian law, these relationships are usually contractual or quasi-contractual and, in any event, are directly established between individuals on a personal basis and without any intervention of an essential or determining nature by a public authority. Accordingly, it is a private right that is at issue, notwithstanding the specific character of the medical profession—a profession which is exercised in the general interest—and the special duties incumbent on its members.

The Court thus concludes that Article 6 par 1 (art 6-1) is applicable; as in the *König* case (see the above-mentioned judgment, p 32, par 95), it does not have to determine whether the concept of 'civil rights' extends beyond those rights which have a private nature.

49. Two members of the Commission, Mr Frowein and Mr Polak, emphasised in their dissenting opinion that the present proceedings did not concern a withdrawal of the authorisation to practise, as did the König case, but a suspension for a relatively short period—three months for Dr Le Compte and fifteen days for Dr Van Leuven and Dr de Meyere. These members maintained that a suspension of this kind did not impair a civil right but was to be regarded as no more than a limitation inherent therein.

The Court is not convinced by this argument, which the Government adopted as a further alternative plea in paragraph 19 of their memorial. Unlike certain other disciplinary sanctions that might have been imposed on the applicants (warning, censure and reprimand . . .), the suspension of which they complained undoubtedly constituted a direct and material interference with the right to continue to exercise the medical profession. The fact that the suspension was temporary did not prevent its impairing that right (see, *mutatis mutandis*, the above-mentioned *Golder* judgment, p 13, par 26); in the 'contestations' (disputes) contemplated by Article 6 par 1 (art 6-1) the actual existence of a 'civil' right may, of course, be at stake but so may the scope of such a right or the manner in which the beneficiary may avail himself thereof.

50. Since the dispute over the decisions taken against the applicants has to be regarded as a dispute relating to 'civil rights and obligations', it follows that they were entitled to have their case (in French: 'cause') heard by 'a tribunal' satisfying the conditions laid down in Article 6 par 1 (art 6-1) (see the above-mentioned *Golder* judgment, p 18, par 36).

51. In fact, their case was dealt with by three bodies—the Provincial Council, the Appeals Council and the Court of Cassation. The question therefore arises whether those bodies met the requirements of Article 6 par 1 (art 6-1).

(a) The Court does not consider it indispensable to pursue this point as regards the Provincial Council. While Article 6 par 1 (art 6-1) embodies the 'right to a court' (see paragraph 44 above), it nevertheless does not oblige the Contracting States to submit 'contestations' (disputes) over 'civil rights and obligations' to a procedure conducted at each of its stages before 'tribunals' meeting the Article's various requirements. Demands of flexibility and efficiency, which are fully compatible with the protection of human rights, may justify the prior intervention of administrative or professional bodies and, *a fortiori*, of judicial bodies which do not satisfy the said requirements in every respect; the legal tradition of many Member states of the Council of Europe may be invoked in support of such a system...

(b) Once the Provincial Council had imposed on Dr Le Compte, Dr Van Leuven and Dr De Meyere a temporary ban on the exercise of their profession, they appealed to the Appeals Council which thus had to determine the dispute over the right in question.

According to the Government, the Appeals Council nevertheless did not have to meet the conditions contained in Article 6 par 1 (art 6-1) since an appeal on a point of law against its decision lay to the Court of Cassation and that Court's procedure certainly did satisfy those conditions.

The Court does not agree. For civil cases, just as for criminal charges (see the *Deweer* judgment of 27 February 1980, Series A No 35, pp 24–5, par 48), Article 6 par 1 (art 61) draws no distiction between questions of fact and questions of law. Both categories of question are equally crucial for the outcome of proceedings relating to 'civil rights and obligations'. Hence, the 'right to a court' (see the above-mentioned *Golder* judgment, p 18, par 36) and the right to a judicial determination of the dispute (see the above-mentioned *König* judgment, p 34, par 98 in fine) cover questions of fact just as much as questions of law. Yet the Court of Cassation does not have jurisdiction to rectify factual errors or to examine whether the sanction is proportionate to the fault... It follows that Article 6 par 1 (art 6-1) was not satisfied unless its requirements were met by the Appeals Council itself....

B. COMPLIANCE WITH ARTICLE 6 PAR 1 (ART 6-1)

54. Having regard to the conclusion at paragraph 51 above, it has to be established whether in the exercise of their jurisdiction both the Appeals Council and the Court of Cassation met the conditions laid down by Article 6 par 1 (art 6-1), the former because it alone fully examined measures affecting a civil right and the latter because it conducted a final review of the lawfulness of those measures...

59. Under the Royal Decree of 6 February 1970, all publicity before the Appeals Council is excluded in a general and absolute manner, both for the hearings and for the pronouncement of the decision...

Article 6 par 1 (art 6-1) of the Convention does admittedly provide for exceptions to the rule requiring publicity—at least in respect of the trial of the action—, but it makes them subject to certain conditions. However, there is no evidence to suggest that any of these conditions was satisfied in the present case. The very nature both of the misconduct alleged against the applicants and of their own complaints against the Ordre was not concerned with the medical treatment of their patients. Consequently, neither matters of professional secrecy nor protection of the private life of these doctors themselves or of patients were involved; the Court does not concur with the Government's argument to the contrary. Furthermore, there is nothing to indicate that other grounds, among those listed in the second sentence of Article 6 par 1 (art 61), could have justified sitting in camera; the Government, moreover, did not rely on any such ground.

Dr Le Compte, Dr Van Leuven and Dr de Meyere were thus entitled to have the proceedings conducted in public. Admittedly, neither the letter nor the spirit of Article 6 par 1 (art 6-1) would have prevented them from waiving this right of their own free will, whether expressly or tacitly (cf the above-mentioned *Deweer* judgment, p 26, par 49); conducting disciplinary proceedings of this kind in private does not contravene the Convention, provided that the person concerned consents. In the present case, however, the applicants clearly wanted and claimed a public hearing. To refuse them such a hearing was not permissible under Article 6 par 1 (art 6-1), since none of the circumstances set out in its second sentence existed.

60. The public character of the proceedings before the Belgian Court of Cassation cannot suffice to remedy this defect. In fact, the Court of Cassation 'shall not take cognisance of the merits of cases' (Article 95 of the Constitution and Article 23 of Royal Decree No 79); this means that numerous issues arising in 'contestations' (disputes) concerning 'civil rights and obligations' fall outside its jurisdiction... On the issues of this nature arising in the present case, there was neither a public hearing nor a decision pronounced publicly as required by Article 6 par 1 (art 6-1).

61. To sum up, the applicants' case (in French: 'cause') was not heard publicly by a tribunal competent to determine all the aspects of the matter. In this respect, there was, in the particular circumstances, a breach of Article 6 par 1 (art 6-1). . . .

Sixteen judges agreed with the above conclusion and four dissented. The Court was willing to find the existence of a 'contestation' regarding 'civil rights and obligations' where domestic proceedings were decisive for a range of issues associated with such entitlements and duties (including the scope and availability of these provisions). The Article 11 aspects of this case are also examined below, at p 744.

10 The full-time Court, unanimously, found disciplinary proceedings taken against the applicant (a former accountant) by the Chamber of Accountants fell within the civil limb of Article 6(1) and breached the reasonable time guarantee as they took nearly eleven years to be concluded in *Luksch v Austria*, judgment of 13 December 2001.

11 A unanimous Grand Chamber announced a new approach to the analysis under Article 6(1) of civil party proceedings, claims for compensation by the victims lodged during criminal cases, available in several continental jurisdiction in *Perez v France*, judgment of 12 February 2004. The applicant filed a criminal complaint with her local gendarmerie that her son and daughter had injected her with a sedative drug (Valium). During the subsequent judicial investigation she applied to join the proceedings as a civil party. The investigating judge determined that there was no case to answer, as there was insufficient evidence of a crime having been committed. The applicant unsuccessfully challenged the judge's ruling before the Court of Cassation. She then complained to Strasbourg that the procedure and judgment of the Court of Cassation had violated Article 6(1). The Grand Chamber held that:

56. The Court thus wishes to end the uncertainty surrounding the applicability of Article 6 § 1 to civil-party proceedings, particularly since a number of other High Contracting Parties to the Convention have similar systems.

iii. A new approach

57. The Court notes that although it has found the concept of 'civil rights and obligations' to be autonomous, it has also held that, in this context, the legislation of the State concerned is not without importance. (see *König v Germany*, judgment of 28 June 1987, Series A No 27, p 30, § 89). Whether or not a right is to be regarded as civil within the meaning of that term in the Convention must be determined by reference not only to its legal classification but also to its substantive content and effects under the domestic law of the State concerned. Moreover the Court, in the exercise of its supervisory function, must also take account of the object and purpose of the Convention.

58. The Court considers it necessary to examine the domestic legislation on civil-party applications in the French criminal courts.

59. In French law victims of an offence may, under Article 4 § 1 of the Code of Criminal Procedure, pursue a civil action separately from the prosecution, in the civil courts. They may also pursue it in the criminal courts simultaneously with the prosecution, under Article 3 § 1 of that Code. Article 3 § 2 specifies that a civil claim is admissible in respect of all the damage caused by the offence being prosecuted.

60. French law thus gives the victim of an offence the option of choosing between civil and criminal proceedings. Under the civil option, the fact that the damage is caused by a criminal offence means that civil procedure is only applied subject to certain rules: irrevocability of the choice (Article 5 of the Code of Criminal Procedure), the principle whereby 'civil proceedings must await the outcome of criminal proceedings' and 'a final criminal judgment prevails over a civil claim'.

61. The criminal option, with which the Court is concerned here, is exercised by way of a civil-party complaint, which is subject to certain conditions and produces certain consequences. Civil-party proceedings are brought either 'by intervention', after the prosecution has already started, by means of an application to the investigating judge or the trial court for leave to join the proceedings, or 'by instigation', or in other words by means of a civil-party complaint or a direct summons before the trial court. Although a civil-party victim faces certain constraints in as much as he can no longer testify and is exposed to sanctions for failure or abuse, he enjoys the benefit of being a party to the criminal trial, is kept informed of the steps in the proceedings, may file requests for documents and lodge appeals and, above all, may obtain compensation from the criminal courts for the damage he has suffered.

62. In view of the foregoing, there can be no doubt that civil-party proceedings constitute, in French law, a civil action for reparation of damage caused by an offence. In these circumstances the Court therefore sees no reason, a priori, to consider it otherwise for the purposes of applying Article 6 § 1 of the Convention.

The Grand Chamber went on to rule that in general, except where the applicant was seeking to bring the proceedings for the purposes of 'private revenge' or as an *action popularis*, civil party proceedings should be classified as within the 'civil rights and obligations' limb of Article 6(1). However, in the applicant's case there had been no breach of the requirements of Article 6(1) by the Court of Cassation. This judgment demonstrates the complex intertwining that may exist between civil rights and criminal proceedings in Member States.

12   A unanimous Chamber held that the claims of Polish victims of forced labour under Nazi Germany seeking compensation from the Polish–German Reconciliation Foundation (established under a 1991 agreement between the Federal Republic of Germany and Poland) were asserting a civil right in *Wos v Poland*, judgment of 8 June 2006. As the Polish courts had declined to review the determinations of the Foundation (whose adjudicative bodies did not meet the requirements of Article 6(1)) the Chamber held that the applicant had been denied the right of access to a court in breach of Article 6(1).

Criminal charge

....

Engel v The Netherlands A.22 (1976) 1 EHRR 647
European Court of Human Rights

The five applicants were conscript soldiers serving in the Netherlands' armed forces. Under the Military Discipline Act 1903 they were subject to disciplinary law, which was a separate body of law from that of military criminal law. Each of the applicants was found to be in breach of disciplinary law and punished by the relevant military authorities. Mr Engel was sentenced, by the Supreme Military Court, to two days' 'strict arrest' (ie locked in a cell) for disregarding previous lesser punishments (imposed for having been absent without authorisation). Mr van der Wiel was sentenced, by the Supreme Military Court, to four days' 'light arrest' (ie confined to barracks, during off-duty hours he could freely move around the barracks and use the facilities: such as the camp cinema) for being four hours late for duty. The same Court sentenced Mr de Wit to twelve days' 'aggravated arrest' (ie confined to a specially designated, but unlocked, place in the barracks during off-duty hours) for failures to observe discipline, including driving a military jeep in an irresponsible manner. Messrs. Dona and Schul were committed to a disciplinary unit (a separate military establishment where soldiers were subject to a stricter disciplinary regime and locked in cells during the night) for three months, by the Supreme Military Court, for editing a journal (published by the Conscript Servicemen's Association) considered to undermine military discipline. The applicants complained to the Commission alleging breaches of a number of Convention provisions, including Article 6 in respect of the proceedings before the Supreme Military Court in each of their cases. By ten votes to one, the Commission concluded that Article 6 was not applicable to any of the disciplinary proceedings against the applicants.

79. ... the Court will first investigate whether the said proceedings concerned 'any criminal charge' within the meaning of this text; for, although disciplinary according to Netherlands law, they had the aim of repressing through penalties offences alleged against the applicants, an objective analogous to the general goal of the criminal law.

1. ON THE APPLICABILITY OF ARTICLE 6 (ART 6)

(A) ON THE EXISTENCE OF 'ANY CRIMINAL CHARGE'

80. All the Contracting States make a distinction of long standing, albeit in different forms and degrees, between disciplinary proceedings and criminal proceedings. For the individuals affected, the former usually offer substantial advantages in comparison with the latter, for example as concerns the sentences passed. Disciplinary sentences, in general less severe, do not appear in the person's criminal record and entail more limited consequences. It may nevertheless be otherwise; moreover, criminal proceedings are ordinarily accompanied by fuller guarantees.

It must thus be asked whether or not the solution adopted in this connection at the national level is decisive from the standpoint of the Convention. Does Article 6 (art 6) cease to be applicable just because the competent organs of a Contracting State classify as disciplinary an act or omission and the proceedings it takes against the author, or does it, on the contrary, apply in certain cases notwithstanding this classification? This problem, the importance of which the Government acknowledge, was rightly raised by the Commission; it particularly occurs when an act or omission is treated by the domestic law of the respondent State as a mixed offence, that is both criminal and disciplinary, and where there thus exists a possibility of opting between, or even cumulating, criminal proceedings and disciplinary proceedings.

81. The Court has devoted attention to the respective submissions of the applicants, the Government and the Commission concerning what they termed the 'autonomy' of the concept of a 'criminal charge' ...

In the Neumeister judgment of 27 June 1968, the Court has already held that the word 'charge' must be understood 'within the meaning of the Convention' (Series A No 8, p 41, para 18 . . .) . . .

The question of the 'autonomy' of the concept of 'criminal' does not call for exactly the same reply.

The Convention without any doubt allows the States, in the performance of their function as guardians of the public interest, to maintain or establish a distinction between criminal law and disciplinary law, and to draw the dividing line, but only subject to certain conditions. The Convention leaves the States free to designate as a criminal offence an act or omission not constituting the normal exercise of one of the rights that it protects. This is made especially clear by Article 7 (art 7). Such a choice, which has the effect of rendering applicable Articles 6 and 7 (art 6, art 7), in principle escapes supervision by the Court.

The converse choice, for its part, is subject to stricter rules. If the Contracting States were able at their discretion to classify an offence as disciplinary instead of criminal, or to prosecute the author of a 'mixed' offence on the disciplinary rather than on the criminal plane, the operation of the fundamental clauses of Articles 6 and 7 (art 6, art 7) would be subordinated to their sovereign will. A latitude extending thus far might lead to results incompatible with the purpose and object of the Convention. The

Court therefore has jurisdiction, under Article 6 (art 6) and even without reference to Articles 17 and 18 (art 17, art 18), to satisfy itself that the disciplinary does not improperly encroach upon the criminal.

In short, the 'autonomy' of the concept of 'criminal' operates, as it were, one way only.

82. Hence, the Court must specify, limiting itself to the sphere of military service, how it will determine whether a given 'charge' vested by the State in question—as in the present case—with a disciplinary character nonetheless counts as 'criminal' within the meaning of Article 6 (art 6).

In this connection, it is first necessary to know whether the provision(s) defining the offence charged belong, according to the legal system of the respondent State, to criminal law, disciplinary law or both concurrently. This however provides no more than a starting point. The indications so afforded have only a formal and relative value and must be examined in the light of the common denominator of the respective legislation of the various Contracting States.

The very nature of the offence is a factor of greater import. When a serviceman finds himself accused of an act or omission allegedly contravening a legal rule governing the operation of the armed forces, the State may in principle employ against him disciplinary law rather than criminal law. In this respect, the Court expresses its agreement with the Government.

However, supervision by the Court does not stop there. Such supervision would generally prove to be illusory if it did not also take into consideration the degree of severity of the penalty that the person concerned risks incurring. In a society subscribing to the rule of law, there belong to the 'criminal' sphere deprivations of liberty liable to be imposed as a punishment, except those which by their nature, duration or manner of execution cannot be appreciably detrimental. The seriousness of what is at stake, the traditions of the Contracting States and the importance attached by the Convention to respect for the physical liberty of the person all require that this should be so (see, *mutatis mutandis, the De Wilde, Ooms and Versyp* judgment of 18 June 1971, Series A No 12, p 36, last sub-paragraph, and p 42 in fine).

83. It is on the basis of these criteria that the Court will ascertain whether some or all of the applicants were the subject of a 'criminal charge' within the meaning of Article 6 para 1 (art 6-1).

In the circumstances, the charge capable of being relevant lay in the decision of the commanding officer as confirmed or reduced by the complaints officer. It was undoubtedly this decision that settled once and for all what was at stake, since the tribunal called upon to give a ruling, that is the Supreme Military Court, had no jurisdiction to pronounce a harsher penalty . . .

84. The offences alleged against Mr Engel, Mr van der Wiel, Mr de Wit, Mr Dona and Mr Schul came within provisions belonging to disciplinary law under Netherlands legislation (the 1903 Act and Regulations on Military Discipline), although those to be answered for by Mr Dona and Mr Schul (Article 147 of the Military Penal Code), and perhaps even by Mr Engel and Mr de Wit (Articles 96 and 114 of the said Code according to Mr van der Schans, hearing on 28 October 1975), also lent themselves to criminal proceedings. Furthermore, all the offences had amounted, in the view of the military authorities, to contraventions of legal rules governing the operation of the Netherlands armed forces. From this aspect, the choice of disciplinary action was justified.

85. The maximum penalty that the Supreme Military Court could pronounce consisted in four days' light arrest for Mr van der Wiel, two days' strict arrest for Mr Engel (third punishment) and three or four months' committal to a disciplinary unit for Mr de Wit, Mr Dona and Mr Schul.

Mr van der Wiel was therefore liable only to a light punishment not occasioning deprivation of liberty . . .

For its part, the penalty involving deprivation of liberty that in theory threatened Mr Engel was of too short a duration to belong to the 'criminal' law. He ran no risk, moreover, of having to undergo this penalty at the close of the proceedings instituted by him before the Supreme Military Court on 7 April 1971, since he had already served it from 20 to 22 March . . .

On the other hand, the 'charges' against Mr de Wit, Mr Dona and Mr Schul did indeed come within the 'criminal' sphere since their aim was the imposition of serious punishments involving deprivation of liberty . . . The Supreme Military Court no doubt sentenced Mr de Wit to twelve days' aggravated arrest only, that is to say, to a penalty not occasioning deprivation of liberty . . . but the final outcome of the appeal cannot diminish the importance of what was initially at stake.

The Convention certainly did not compel the competent authorities to prosecute Mr de Wit, Mr Dona and Mr Schul under the Military Penal Code before a court martial . . . a solution which could have proved less advantageous for the applicants. The Convention did however oblige the authorities to afford them the guarantees of Article 6 (art 6).

. . .

88. In short, it is the duty of the Court to examine under Article 6 (art 6) the treatment meted out to Mr de Wit, Mr Dona and Mr Schul, but not that complained of by Mr Engel and Mr van der Wiel.

2. ON COMPLIANCE WITH ARTICLE 6 (ART 6)

89. The Supreme Military Court, before which appeared Mr de Wit, Mr Dona and Mr Schul, constitutes an 'independent and impartial tribunal established by law' . . . and there is nothing to indicate that it failed to give them a 'fair hearing'. For its part, the 'time' that elapsed between the 'charge' and the final decision appears 'reasonable'. It did not amount to six weeks for Mr Dona and Mr Schul (8 October–17 November 1971) and hardly exceeded two months for Mr de Wit (22 February–28 April 1971). Furthermore, the sentence was 'pronounced publicly'.

In contrast, the hearings in the presence of the parties had taken place in camera in accordance with the established practice of the Supreme Military Court in disciplinary proceedings . . . In point of fact, the applicants do not seem to have suffered on that account; indeed the said Court improved the lot of two of their number, namely Mr Schul and, to an even greater extent, Mr de Wit. Nevertheless, in the field it governs, Article 6 para 1 (art 6-1) requires in a very general fashion that judicial proceedings be conducted in public. Article 6 (art 6) of course makes provision for exceptions which it lists, but the Government did not plead, and it does not emerge from the file, that the circumstances of the case amounted to one of the occasions when the Article allows 'the press and the public (to be) excluded'. Hence, on this particular point, there has been violation of paragraph 1 of Article 6 (art 6-1).

. . .

FOR THESE REASONS, THE COURT,

. . . Holds, by eleven votes to two, that Article 6 was not applicable to Mr Engel on the ground of the words 'criminal charge';

Holds, unanimously, that neither was it applicable to Mr van der Wiel;

Holds, by eleven votes to two, that there was a breach of Article 6 para 1 in the case of Mr de Wit, Mr Dona and Mr Schul insofar as hearings before the Supreme Military Court took place in camera; . . .

NOTES

1 The Court was composed of President Mosler and Judges: Verdross, Wiarda, Vilhjalmsson, Petren, Bozer, Ganshof Van Der Meersch, Bindschedler-Robert, and Evrigenis. Judges O'Donoghue and Pedersen issued a separate opinion in which they expressed the view that the proceedings against all the applicants were 'predominantly' disciplinary offences and therefore fell outside the ambit of criminal charges under Article 6. Judges Zekia and Cremona also produced separate opinions in which they argued that where soldiers were charged with an offence punishable with loss of liberty (even of short duration) Article 6(1) was applicable to those proceedings.

2 The Court's judgment in *Engel* is very important because it establishes the autonomous nature of the Convention term 'criminal'. As the Court explained, in paragraph 81, where

domestic law does not characterise a charge as being criminal that of itself is not decisive for the application of Article 6 by the Strasbourg control system. In such circumstances the Court will make its own assessment as to whether the national proceedings should be classified as criminal. In reaching such a determination the Court has regard to the three criteria identified in paragraph 82, of the above judgment. First, the type of national law embodying the relevant offence (and how other Member States' legal systems characterise similar offences). Secondly, the nature of the conduct prohibited by the offence. Finally, the severity of the punishment attached to the offence (more than minimal loss of liberty is likely to result in the Court ruling that the offence is criminal). Having regard to these criteria, especially the last one, do you agree with the majority's determination that the proceedings against Engel did not involve a criminal charge? The Article 10 aspects of *Engel* are examined below (at p 703).

3   In subsequent cases the Court has applied the three criteria established in *Engel* to decide if particular domestic proceedings fall within Article 6's 'criminal' category. The second criterion was accorded greater significance, than the first, when the Court evaluated the German programme of decriminalisation of minor road traffic offences in *Öztürk v Germany*, A.73 (1984) 6 EHRR 409. The applicant, a Turkish citizen living and working in Germany, drove his car into another car and caused DM 5,000 worth of damage. The owner of the other car called the police and they sent a report on the incident to the local administrative authority (Heilbronn). Two months later, in April 1978, the administrative authorities imposed a fine (of DM 60) on the applicant for careless driving under the authority of the Regulatory Offences Act 1968/1975. The Act removed petty offences from the sphere of the criminal law and substituted 'regulatory offences', which were punishable by the imposition of fines. The applicant, through his lawyer, lodged an objection against the administrative authority's decision in his case. In August 1978, the Heilbronn District Court heard the applicant, who was assisted by an interpreter, and three witnesses. Thereupon the applicant withdrew his objection. The District Court ordered that the applicant should bear the court costs (DM 185, of which DM 64 related to the interpreter's fees) and his own expenses. The applicant appealed against his liability to pay the interpreter's fees based upon Article 6(3)(e) of the Convention. However, his appeal was dismissed. The court costs, including the interpreter's fees, were paid by the applicant's insurance company. The applicant complained to the Commission alleging that the order to pay the interpreter's fees violated his right to free interpretation in criminal proceedings guaranteed by Article 6. A majority of the Commission, eight votes to five, found a violation of subparagraph (3)(e). Before the Court, the Government contended that Article 6 was not applicable to Mr Ozturk as he had not been charged with a criminal offence. The decriminalisation of minor road traffic offences meant that he had been found liable for a 'regulatory offence', which was subject to a different procedure and consequences, than an ordinary criminal offence.

48. The Court was confronted with a similar issue in the case of *Engel* and others, which was cited in argument by the representatives. The facts of that case admittedly concerned penalties imposed on conscript servicemen and treated as disciplinary according to Netherlands law. In its judgment delivered on 8 June 1976 in that case, the Court was careful to state that it was confining its attention to the sphere of military service (Series A No 22, p 34, § 82). The Court nevertheless considers that the principles set forth in that judgment (ibid, §§ 80–2) are also relevant, *mutatis mutandis*, in the instant case.

49. The Convention is not opposed to States, in the performance of their task as guardians of the public interest, both creating or maintaining a distinction between different categories of offences for the purposes of their domestic law and drawing the dividing line, but it does not follow that the classification thus made by the States is decisive for the purposes of the Convention.

By removing certain forms of conduct from the category of criminal offences under domestic law, the law-maker may be able to serve the interests of the individual (see, *mutatis mutandis*, the above-mentioned *Engel* and others judgment, ibid, p 33, § 80) as well as the needs of the proper administration of justice, in particular in so far as the judicial authorities are thereby relieved of the task of prosecuting and punishing contraventions—which are numerous but of minor importance—of road traffic rules. The Convention is not opposed to the moves towards 'decriminalisation' which are taking place—in extremely varied forms—in the member States of the Council of Europe. The Government quite rightly insisted on this point. Nevertheless, if the Contracting States were able at their discretion, by classifying an offence as 'regulatory' instead of criminal, to exclude the operation of the fundamental clauses of Articles 6 and 7 (art 6, art 7), the application of these provisions would be subordinated to their sovereign will. A latitude extending thus far might lead to results incompatible with the object and purpose of the Convention.

50. Having thus reaffirmed the 'autonomy' of the notion of 'criminal' as conceived of under Article 6 (art 6), what the Court must determine is whether or not the 'regulatory offence' committed by the applicant was a 'criminal' one within the meaning of that Article (art 6). For this purpose, the Court will rely on the criteria adopted in the above-mentioned *Engel* and others judgment (ibid, pp 34–5, § 82). The first matter to be ascertained is whether or not the text defining the offence in issue belongs, according to the legal system of the respondent State, to criminal law; next, the nature of the offence and, finally, the nature and degree of severity of the penalty that the person concerned risked incurring must be examined, having regard to the object and purpose of Article 6 (art 6), to the ordinary meaning of the terms of that Article (art 6) and to the laws of the Contracting States.

51. Under German law, the facts alleged against Mr Öztürk—non-observance of Regulation 1 § 2 of the Road Traffic Regulations—amounted to a 'regulatory offence' (Regulation 49 § 1, No 1, of the same Regulations). They did not fall within the ambit of the criminal law, but of section 17 of the Ordnungswidrigkeitengesetz and of section 24 sub-section 2 of the Road Traffic Act . . . The 1968/1975 legislation marks an important step in the process of 'decriminalisation' of petty offences in the Federal Republic of Germany. Although legal commentators in Germany do not seem unanimous in considering that the law on 'regulatory offences' no longer belongs in reality to criminal law, the drafting history of the 1968/1975 Act nonetheless makes it clear that the offences in question have been removed from the criminal law sphere by that Act (see Deutscher Bundestag, Drucksache V/1269 and, inter alia, the judgment of 16 July 1969 by the Constitutional Court, Entscheidungen des Bundesverfassungsgerichts, vol 27, pp 18–36).

While the Court thus accepts the Government's arguments on this point, it has nonetheless not lost sight of the fact that no absolute partition separates German criminal law from the law on 'regulatory offences', in particular where there exists a close connection between a criminal offence and a 'regulatory offence' . . . Nor has the Court overlooked that the provisions of the ordinary law governing criminal procedure apply by analogy to 'regulatory' proceedings . . . notably in relation to the judicial stage, if any, of such proceedings.

52. In any event, the indications furnished by the domestic law of the respondent State have only a relative value. The second criterion stated above—the very nature of the offence, considered also in relation to the nature of the corresponding penalty—represents a factor of appreciation of greater weight.

In the opinion of the Commission—with the exception of five of its members—and of Mr Öztürk, the offence committed by the latter was criminal in character.

For the Government in contrast, the offence in question was beyond doubt one of those contraventions of minor importance—numbering approximately five million each year in the Federal Republic of Germany—which came within a category of quite a different order from that of criminal offences. The Government's submissions can be summarised as follows. By means of criminal law, society endeavoured to safeguard its very foundations as well as the rights and interests essential for the life of the community. The law on Ordnungswidrigkeiten, on the other hand, sought above all to maintain public order. As a general rule and in any event in the instant case, commission of a 'regulatory offence' did not involve a degree of ethical unworthiness such as to merit for its perpetrator the moral value-judgment of reproach (*Unwerturteil*) that characterised penal punishment (*Strafe*). The difference between 'regulatory offences' and criminal offences found expression both in procedural terms and in relation to the attendant penalties and other legal consequences.

In the first place, so the Government's argument continued, in removing 'regulatory offences' from the criminal law the German legislature had introduced a simplified procedure of prosecution and punishment conducted before administrative authorities save in the event of subsequent appeal to a court. Although general laws on criminal procedure were in principle applicable by analogy, the procedure laid down under the 1968/1975 Act was distinguishable in many respects from criminal procedure. For example, prosecution of Ordnungswidrigkeiten fell within the discretionary power of the competent authorities and the 1968/1975 Act greatly limited the possibilities of restricting the personal liberty of the individual at the stage of the preliminary investigations . . .

In the second place, instead of a penal fine (*Geldstrafe*) and imprisonment the legislature had substituted a mere 'regulatory' fine (*Geldbusse* . . .). Imprisonment was not an alternative (*Ersatzfreiheitsstrafe*) to the latter type of fine as it was to the former and no coercive imprisonment (*Erzwingungshaft*) could be ordered unless the person concerned had failed to pay the sum due without having established his inability to pay . . . Furthermore, a 'regulatory offence' was not entered in the judicial criminal records but solely, in certain circumstances, on the central traffic register . . .

The reforms accomplished in 1968/1975 thus, so the Government concluded, reflected a concern to 'decriminalise' minor offences to the benefit not only of the individual, who would no longer be answerable in criminal terms for his act and who could even avoid all court proceedings, but also of the effective functioning of the courts, henceforth relieved in principle of the task of dealing with the great majority of such offences.

53. The Court does not underestimate the cogency of this argument. The Court recognises that the legislation in question marks an important stage in the history of the reform of German criminal law and that the innovations introduced in 1968/1975 represent more than a simple change of terminology.

Nonetheless, the Court would firstly note that, according to the ordinary meaning of the terms, there generally come within the ambit of the criminal law offences that make their perpetrator liable to penalties intended, inter alia, to be deterrent and usually consisting of fines and of measures depriving the person of his liberty.

In addition, misconduct of the kind committed by Mr Öztürk continues to be classified as part of the criminal law in the vast majority of the Contracting States, as it was in the Federal Republic of Germany until the entry into force of the 1968/1975 legislation; in those other States, such misconduct, being regarded as illegal and reprehensible, is punishable by criminal penalties.

Moreover, the changes resulting from the 1968/1975 legislation relate essentially to procedural matters and to the range of sanctions, henceforth limited to Geldbussen. While the latter penalty appears less burdensome in some respects than Geldstrafen, it has nonetheless retained a punitive character, which is the customary distinguishing feature of criminal penalties. The rule of law infringed by the applicant has, for its part, undergone no change of content. It is a rule that is directed, not towards a given group possessing a special status—in the manner, for example, of disciplinary law—but towards all citizens in their capacity as road-users; it prescribes conduct of a certain kind and makes the resultant requirement subject to a sanction that is punitive. Indeed, the sanction—and this the Government did not contest—seeks to punish as well as to deter. It matters little whether the legal provision contravened by Mr Öztürk is aimed at protecting the rights and interests of others or solely at meeting the demands of road traffic. These two ends are not mutually exclusive. Above all, the general character of the rule and the purpose of the penalty, being both deterrent and punitive, suffice to show that the offence in question was, in terms of Article 6 (art 6) of the Convention, criminal in nature.

The fact that it was admittedly a minor offence hardly likely to harm the reputation of the offender does not take it outside the ambit of Article 6 (art 6). There is in fact nothing to suggest that the criminal offence referred to in the Convention necessarily implies a certain degree of seriousness. In this connection, a number of Contracting States still draw a distinction, as did the Federal Republic at the time when the Convention was opened for the signature of the Governments, between the most serious offences (crimes), lesser offences (*délits*) and petty offences (contraventions), while qualifying them all as criminal offences. Furthermore, it would be contrary to the object and purpose of Article 6 (art 6), which guarantees to 'everyone charged with a criminal offence' the right to a court and to a fair trial, if the State were allowed to remove from the scope of this Article (art 6) a whole category of offences merely on the ground of regarding them as petty. Nor does the Federal Republic deprive the presumed perpetrators of Ordnungswidrigkeiten of this right since it grants them the faculty—of which the applicant availed himself—of appealing to a court against the administrative decision.

54. As the contravention committed by Mr Öztürk was criminal for the purposes of Article 6 (art 6) of the Convention, there is no need to examine it also in the light of the final criterion stated above (at paragraph 50). The relative lack of seriousness of the penalty at stake . . . cannot divest an offence of its inherently criminal character.

55. The Government further appeared to consider that the applicant did not have the status of a person 'charged with a criminal offence' because the 1968/1975 Act does not provide for any 'Beschuldigung' ('charge') and does not employ the terms 'Angeschuldigter' ('person charged') or 'Angeklagter' ('the accused'). On this point, the Court would simply refer back to its well-established case-law holding that 'charge', for the purposes of Article 6 (art 6), may in general be defined as 'the official notification given to an individual by the competent authority of an allegation that he has committed a criminal offence', although 'it may in some instances take the form of other measures which carry the implication of such an allegation and which likewise substantially affect the situation of the suspect' (see, as the most recent authorities, the *Foti* judgment of 10 December 1982, Series A No 56, p 18, § 52, and the *Corigliano* judgment of the same date, Series A No 57, p 13, § 34). In the present case, the applicant was 'charged' at the latest as from the beginning of April 1978 when the decision of the Heilbronn administrative authorities was communicated to him . . .

56. Article 6 § 3 (e) (art 6-3-e) was thus applicable in the instant case. It in no wise follows from this, the Court would want to make clear, that the very principle of the system adopted in the matter by the German legislature is being put in question. Having regard to the large number of minor offences, notably in the sphere of road traffic, a Contracting State may have good cause for relieving its courts of the task of their prosecution and punishment. Conferring the prosecution and punishment of minor offences on administrative authorities is not inconsistent with the Convention provided that the person concerned is enabled to take any decision thus made against him before a tribunal that does offer the guarantees of Article 6 . . .

II. COMPLIANCE WITH ARTICLE 6 § 3 (E) (ART 6-3-E)

57. Invoking the above-cited *Luedicke, Belkacem and Koç* judgment of 28 November 1978 [(A.29)], the applicant submitted that the decision whereby the Heilbronn District Court had made him bear the costs incurred in having recourse to the services of an interpreter at the hearing on 3 August 1978 was in breach of Article 6 § 3 (e) (art 6-3-e).

The Commission's opinion was to the same effect. The Government, for their part, maintained that there had been no violation, but concentrated their arguments on the issue of the applicability of Article 6 § 3 (e) (art 6-3-e), without discussing the manner in which the Court had construed this text in 1978.

58. On the basis of the above-cited judgment, the Court finds that the impugned decision of the Heilbronn District Court violated the Convention: 'the right protected by Article 6 § 3 (e) (art 6-3-e) entails, for anyone who cannot speak or understand the language used in court, the right to receive the free assistance of an interpreter, without subsequently having claimed back from him the payment of the costs thereby incurred' (Series A No 29, p 19, § 46).

. . .

FOR THESE REASONS, THE COURT

...

Holds, by twelve votes to six, that there has been a breach of the said Article (6(3)(e)); ...

The judgment reveals that when applying the second *Engel* criterion, the nature of the offence at issue, the Court is likely to conclude that the proceedings are 'criminal' where the provision applies to a large section of the public and the relevant sanction has a punitive aim. From a wider policy perspective the Court, in paragraph 56, upheld the ability of States to engage in decriminalisation programmes regarding the determination and punishment of less serious offences, provided that affected individuals have an ultimate right of recourse to a body complying with the institutional and procedural safeguards laid down by Article 6. This is a fair balance between the efficiency goals of governments and the due process rights of individuals.

4   The Court was, however, united in determining that breach of privilege proceedings brought by a national parliament against a satirical journalist were 'criminal' in *Demicoli v Malta*, A.210 (1991) 14 EHRR 47. The applicant edited a political periodical in which he published a satirical review of a parliamentary debate. The article, headed 'The Parliamentary Clown', ridiculed the speeches of two members of the Maltese House of Representatives (Mr Debono Grech and Mr Bartolo). The two members brought the article to the attention of the House and the Speaker found it to be a *prima facie* case of breach of privilege. The same day the House, on a proposal from Mr Debono Grech, passed a resolution holding the article to be in breach of parliamentary privilege. Several weeks later the House passed a motion, seconded by Mr Debono Grech, summoning the applicant to appear before the House '... to state why he should not be found guilty of breach of privilege ...'. Together with his lawyer, the applicant appeared before the House; however he refused to answer whether he was guilty or not. The House found him guilty. After the Constitutional Court upheld the legality of the House's proceedings, the latter body fined Demicoli 250 Maltese liri and ordered him to publish details of the House's findings in his periodical. The two criticized members participated in the House proceedings against Demicoli. The Commission expressed the unanimous view that Maltese proceedings violated the applicant's right to a fair trial under Article 6(1). The Court began by applying the *Engel* criteria.

32. It must first be ascertained whether the provisions defining the offence in issue belong, according to the legal system of the respondent State, to criminal law, disciplinary law or both concurrently.

The legal basis of the proceedings taken against Mr Demicoli was provided by section 11 of the Ordinance ... The applicant argued that the origin of the Maltese law of Parliamentary privilege is to be found in United Kingdom law and that breaches of privilege are referred to as crimes in certain textbooks on English law. As noted by the Commission and the Government, breach of Parliamentary privilege is not formally classified as a crime in Maltese law ... The Constitutional Court, in its judgment of 13 October 1986, did not find it necessary to decide whether 'the act constituting the contempt or breach of privilege amounts to a criminal act or not.'

33. However ... the indication afforded by national law is not decisive for the purpose of Article 6 (art 6). A factor of greater importance is 'the very nature of the offence' in question (see, inter alia, the ... *Campbell and Fell* judgment, Series A No 80, p 36, para 71 ...

In this context the applicant quoted from the records of the Parliamentary sittings of 4, 17, 18 and 19 March 1986 to highlight the fact that certain Members of the House equated the proceedings taken against him with criminal proceedings ...

The Government, on the other hand, submitted that, although some breaches of privilege may also constitute criminal offences, Parliamentary privilege, being concerned with respect for the dignity of the House, pursued a different aim from that of the criminal law. ...

Mr Demicoli was not a Member of the House. In the Court's view, the proceedings taken against him in the present case for an act of this sort done outside the House are to be distinguished from other types of breach of privilege proceedings which may be said to be disciplinary in nature in that they relate to the internal regulation and orderly functioning of the House. Section 11(1)(k) potentially affects the whole population since it applies whether the alleged offender is a Member of the House or not and irrespective of where in Malta the publication of the defamatory libel takes place. For the offence thereby defined the Ordinance provides for the imposition of a penal sanction and not a civil claim for damages. From this point of view, therefore, the particular breach of privilege in question is akin to a criminal offence . . .

34. The third criterion is the degree of severity of the penalty that the person concerned risks incurring. The Court notes that in the present case, while the House imposed a fine of 250 Maltese liri on the applicant which has not yet been paid or enforced, the maximum penalty he risked was imprisonment for a period not exceeding sixty days or a fine not exceeding 500 Maltese liri or both. What was at stake was thus sufficiently important to warrant classifying the offence with which the applicant was charged as a criminal one under the Convention . . .

35. In conclusion, Article 6 applied in the present case.

B. COMPLIANCE WITH ARTICLE 6 PARA 1 (ART 6-1)

36. The applicant submitted that in the proceedings before the House of Representative she did not receive a fair hearing by an independent and impartial tribunal. The political context in which the proceedings against him were conducted 'made a mockery of the whole concept of the independence and the impartiality of the judiciary'. This, he claimed, was evident from statements made by Members of the House in relation to his case in the official record of the Parliamentary sittings . . . He maintained that in breach of privilege proceedings Members of Parliament sit as victims, accusers, witnesses and judges. In his case it was the privilege of the individual Members concerned that was in issue and not, as the Government suggested, that of the whole House. Even if the Government's view on this point were accepted, that would mean, in his view, that 'each and every Member of the House of Representatives is a *judex in causa sua*'.

37. The Government argued that the House of Representatives was 'an independent and impartial tribunal established by law' for the purpose of hearing the disciplinary charge against Mr Demicoli. The Maltese House of Representatives was an independent authority 'par excellence'. The House was independent of the executive and of the parties, its Members were elected for a term of five years and its proceedings afforded the necessary guarantees. Accordingly it fulfilled all the requirements of a tribunal set out in the *Ringeisen* judgment of 16 July 1971 (Series A No 13, p 39, para 95). The independence of the House was sufficient to exclude any legitimate doubt as to its impartiality. Moreover, the Members directly satirised by the article intervened to defend the dignity of the House and not just their own reputations.

38. The Commission took the view that the House of Representatives could not be considered to be a court and did not fulfil the requirements of the Convention as to independence or impartiality.

39. The Court, like the Commission, notes that the power of the Maltese Parliament to impose disciplinary measures and to govern its own internal affairs is not in issue. Moreover, the Court's task is not to review the relevant law and practice in *abstracto*, but to determine whether the manner in which the proceedings against Mr Demicoli were conducted gave rise to a violation of Article 6 para 1 (art 6-1).

According to its case-law, 'a 'tribunal' is characterised in the substantive sense of the term by its judicial function, that is to say determining matters within its competence on the basis of rules of law and after proceedings conducted in a prescribed manner . . . It must also satisfy a series of further requirements—independence, in particular of the executive; impartiality; duration of its members' terms of office; guarantees afforded by its procedure—several of which appear in the text of Article 6 para 1 (art 6-1) itself' (see the *Belilos* judgment of 29 April 1988, Series A No 132, p 29, para 64).

40. In the circumstances of the present case the House of Representatives undoubtedly exercised a judicial function in determining the applicant's guilt. The central issue raised in this case is whether the requirement of impartiality was duly respected. For the purposes of Article 6 para 1 (art 6-1) this must be determined according to a subjective test, that is on the basis of the personal conviction or interest of a particular judge in a given case, and according to an objective test, namely ascertaining whether the judge offered guarantees sufficient to exclude any legitimate doubt in this respect. In this context even appearances may be of a certain importance, particularly as far as criminal proceedings are concerned (see, among other authorities, the *Hauschildt* judgment of 24 May 1989, Series A No 154, p 21, paras 46–8).

41. The two Members of the House whose behaviour in Parliament was criticised in the impugned article and who raised the breach of privilege in the House . . . participated throughout in the proceedings against the accused, including the finding of guilt and (except for one of them who had meanwhile died) the sentencing.

Already for this reason, the impartiality of the adjudicating body in these proceedings would appear to be open to doubt and the applicant's fears in this connection were justified . . .

42. Accordingly, there has been a breach of Article 6 para 1 (art 6-1) of the Convention on the point considered. It is therefore not necessary to go into other aspects of this provision. . . .

The decisive factors in the Court classifying these proceedings as 'criminal' were the general applicability of the privilege norms (i.e. they encompassed the public outside the House, rather than being internal principles governing members' behaviour) and the potential severity of the punishments available (including imprisonment for up to almost two months).

5   The Court has also decided that the term 'charge' has an autonomous meaning (i.e. the Court is not bound to accept national interpretations of the concept). The authoritative definition of this term was given in *Deweer v Belgium*, A.35 (1980) 2 EHRR 439. The applicant had owned a butcher's shop in Louvain since 1935. On 18 September 1974 an official from the Economic Inspectorate General visited the shop. The inspector concluded that the applicant had not reduced the price of his pigmeat by 6.5 per cent as required by a Ministerial Decree issued a few weeks earlier. The applicant claimed that he had made a mistake in good faith and immediately reduced the price. The inspector later produced a formal report (called a *pro-justitia*) of his visit and sent it to the procureur du Roi attached to the Louvain Court of First Instance. On 30 September the procureur ordered the provisional closure of the applicant's shop within forty-eight hours of the notification of his decision, under powers granted by the Economic Regulation and Prices Act 1945. The same day the procureur wrote a letter to the applicant informing him of the closure order and stating that if he paid 10,000F, as a friendly settlement, the closure order would be terminated. The police delivered the letter to the applicant on the 1 October and he replied on 3 October. The applicant wrote that he was paying the sum to avoid the costs of closure of his business pending a subsequent criminal trial. The applicant complained to the Commission alleging that the procureur's making of the provisional closure order combined with the offer of a financial settlement violated his right to a fair hearing in the determination of any criminal charge against him guaranteed by Article 6(1). The Commission unanimously found a breach of that right. The Court held that:

46. . . . The 'charge' could, for the purposes of Article 6 par 1 (art 6-1), be defined as the official notification given to an individual by the competent authority of an allegation that he has committed a criminal offence. In several decisions and opinions the Commission has adopted a test that appears to be

fairly closely related, namely whether 'the situation of the [suspect] has been substantially affected' (*Neumeister* case, Series B No 6, p 81; case *of Huber v Austria*, Yearbook of the Convention, vol 18, p 356, 67; case of *Hätti v Federal Republic of Germany*, ibid, vol 19, p 1064, 50, etc). Under these circumstances, the Court considers that as from 30 September 1974 the applicant was under a 'criminal charge'.

Furthermore, the Court was unanimous that the procureur's actions had deprived the applicant of his right to a fair trial and thereby breached Article 6(1). We have already seen the Court's utilization of this definition of a criminal 'charge' in the context of German road traffic proceedings: *Ozturk* para 55 (above).

6 In *V v UK*, (see above, p 179) the Court held that in criminal cases Article 6(1) covers the whole of the proceedings, including the determination of sentence. The Court, therefore, concluded that the Home Secretary's role in determining the tariff period (ie the minimum term of imprisonment necessary to satisfy the requirements of retribution and deterrence) of juvenile murderers, sentenced to detention during Her Majesty's pleasure, violated the 'independent tribunal' element of Article 6(1). As the Court noted, the Home Secretary 'was clearly not independent of the executive'. (para 114)

7 Two convicted prisoners successfully contended that the power of English prison governors to determine 'disciplinary' offences and award extra days custody (i.e. to delay their final release date) of prisoners found guilty, amounted to the determination of 'criminal charges' within the meaning of Article 6(1) in *Ezeh and Connors v United Kingdom*, Chamber judgment of 15 July 2002 and Grand Chamber Judgment of 9 October 2003. The first applicant was alleged to have threatened to kill his probation officer during a meeting with her in prison. His case was heard by a prison governor who refused the applicant's request to have legal representation. The governor found him guilty of using threatening words (this was his seventh offence of threatening to kill or injure a member of staff) and sentenced him to, *inter alia*, forty days' additional custody. The second applicant was charged with assaulting a prison officer, by deliberately running into him in the exercise yard of the prison. The prison governor also refused his request for legal representation. The governor found him guilty (it was Connors's thirty-seventh offence against discipline) and awarded him seven days' additional custody. Both applicants complained to Strasbourg alleging a breach of the right to legal representation in respect of persons charged with a criminal offence under Article 6(3)(c). The Chamber, unanimously, applied the *Engel* criteria to classify the proceedings before the governors as involving 'criminal charges' and concluded that Article 6(3)(c) had been violated. The Government petitioned the Grand Chamber to re-hear the case under Article 43 on the ground that the Article 6 did not apply to these proceedings. Before the Grand Chamber, the Government argued that the Chamber, when applying the *Engel* criteria, had not accorded sufficient weight to the needs of maintaining effective discipline within prisons. The Court, by eleven votes to six, held that:

85. . . . as in the *Campbell and Fell* [v U.K. A.80 (1984).] judgment, the Grand Chamber agrees with the Chamber that it is correct to apply the '*Engel* criteria' to the facts of the present cases in determining where to place the dividing line between the 'criminal' and the 'disciplinary'. The Court will do so in a manner consistent with the object and purpose of Article 6 of the Convention, while making 'due allowance' for the prison context and for the 'practical reasons and reasons of policy' in favour of establishing a special prison disciplinary regime.

86. In addition, it is the Court's established jurisprudence that the second and third criteria laid down in the *Engel* judgment are alternative and not necessarily cumulative: for Article 6 to be held applicable, it suffices that the offence in question is by its nature to be regarded as 'criminal' from the point of view

of the Convention, or that the offence made the person liable to a sanction which, by its nature and degree of severity, belongs in general to the 'criminal' sphere (*Öztürk v Germany*, judgment of 21 February 1984, Series A No 73, § 54, and *Lutz v Germany*, judgment of 25 August 1987, Series A No 123, § 55). This does not exclude that a cumulative approach may be adopted where separate analysis of each criterion does not make it possible to reach a clear conclusion as to the existence of a criminal charge (*Bendenoun v France*, judgment of 24 February 1994, Series A No 284, § 47; *Benham v the United Kingdom*, judgment of 10 June 1996, *Reports of Judgments and Decisions* 1996-III, § 56; *Garyfallou AEBE v Greece*, judgment of 24 September 1997, *Reports* 1997-V, § 33; *Lauko v Slovakia*, judgment of 2 September 1998, *Reports* 1998-VI, § 57).

87. The Court would also make certain observations on the more general submissions of the parties concerning the application of the *Engel* criteria to a prison environment.

88. In the first place, the Court notes that the Government's central submission was that the necessity of maintaining an effective prison disciplinary regime had to weigh heavily in determining where the dividing line between the criminal and disciplinary lay. As in its *Campbell and Fell* judgment, the Court would not question the importance of preserving an effective system of order and control in prison. However, it does not find compelling the Government's argument that the loss by the governor of the power to award 'additional days' would undermine the prison disciplinary regime in England and Wales.

In this regard, the Court notes that other sanctions were available to the governor at the relevant times (including forfeiture of privileges, exclusion from associated work and cellular confinement) and that the range and severity of sanctions other than additional days has been extended and increased since the applicants' adjudication proceedings, most recently in August 2002. The Court considers that it has not been convincingly explained why these other sanctions would not have an impact comparable to awards of additional days in maintaining the effectiveness of the prison disciplinary system, including the authority of the prison management. In this regard, the Government did not address how a sanction with immediate application would be less effective than an award of additional days which is not served until a prisoner's early release date (set pursuant to section 33 of the [Criminal Justice] 1991 Act) and which in many cases will be therefore served some time, even years, after the adjudication hearing. Further, the Court does not consider that the Government have convincingly demonstrated significant material differences between the disciplinary needs in Scottish prisons, where use of additional days was suspended almost two years ago, and those needs in prisons in England and Wales.

...

The first of the Engel criteria—the domestic classification of the offences

90. The offences with which the applicants were charged were classified by domestic law as disciplinary: paragraphs 1 and 17 of Rule 47 state that the relevant conduct on the part of a prisoner shall be 'an offence against discipline' and the Prison Rules go on to provide how such offences shall be dealt with under the prison disciplinary regime by adjudication before the governor.

Thus, as the Chamber noted, according to national law the adjudication of such offences was treated as a disciplinary matter and was designed to maintain order within the confines of the prison. The fact, as pointed out by the Government, that a governor's findings would not form part of the applicants' criminal records is simply a natural consequence of the disciplinary classification of the offence.

91. However, the indications so afforded by the national law have only a formal and relative value; the 'very nature of the offence is a factor of greater import' (the above-cited *Engel and Others* judgment, at § 82).

The second of the Engel criteria—the nature of the charge

...

103. In the present cases, the Court notes, in the first place, that the offences in question were directed towards a group possessing a special status, namely prisoners, as opposed to all citizens. However, the Court does not accept the Government's submission that this fact renders the nature of the offences

prima facie disciplinary. It is but one of the 'relevant indicators' in assessing the nature of the offence (the *Campbell and Fell* judgment, cited above, at § 71).

104. Secondly, it was not disputed before the Grand Chamber that the charge against the first applicant corresponded to an offence in the ordinary criminal law (sections 4 and 5 of the [Public Order]1986 Act). It is also clear that the charge of assault against the second applicant is an offence under the criminal law as well as under the Prison Rules. It is true that the latter charge involved a relatively minor incident of deliberately colliding with a prison officer which may not necessarily have led to prosecution outside the prison context. It is also true that the extreme gravity of the offence may be indicative of its criminal nature, as indicated in the *Campbell and Fell* judgment. However, that does not conversely mean that the minor nature of an offence can, of itself, take it outside of the ambit of Article 6 as there is nothing in the Convention to suggest that the criminal nature of an offence, within the meaning of the second of the *Engel* criteria, necessarily requires a certain degree of seriousness (the above-cited *Öztürk* judgment, § 53). The reliance on the severity of the penalty in the *Campbell and Fell* judgment (at § 72) was a matter relevant to the third of the *Engel* criteria as opposed to a factor defining the nature of the offence.

Relying on Convention case-law, the Government contested the weight to be attached to this concurrent criminal and disciplinary liability. However, in the case most directly in point, the *Campbell and Fell* judgment (at § 71), the Court referred to even a 'theoretical' possibility of the impugned acts being the subject of concurrent criminal and disciplinary pursuit as a relevant factor in the assessment of the nature of the offence and it did so independently of the gravity of the offences in question. Accordingly, and even noting the prison context of the charges, the theoretical possibility of concurrent criminal and disciplinary liability is, at the very least, a relevant point which tends to the classification of the nature of both offences as 'mixed' offences.

105. Thirdly, the Government submit that disciplinary rules and sanctions in prison are designed primarily to ensure the successful operation of a system of early release so that the 'punitive' element of the offence is secondary to the primary purpose of 'prevention' of disorder. The Court considers that awards of additional days were, on any view, imposed after a finding of culpability (*Benham v the United Kingdom*, cited above, at § 56) to punish the applicants for the offences they had committed and to prevent further offending by them and other prisoners. It does not find persuasive the Government's argument distinguishing between the punishment and deterrent aims of the offences in question, these objectives not being mutually exclusive (the above-cited *Öztürk* judgment, at § 53) and being recognised as characteristic features of criminal penalties).

106. Accordingly, the Court considers that these factors, even if they were not of themselves sufficient to lead to the conclusion that the offences with which the applicants were charged are to be regarded as 'criminal' for Convention purposes, clearly gives them a certain colouring which does not entirely coincide with that of a purely disciplinary matter.

107. The Court finds, as did the Chamber, that it is therefore necessary to turn to the third criterion: the nature and degree of severity of the penalty that the applicants risked incurring (the *Engel and Others* judgment, § 82, and the *Campbell and Fell* judgment, § 72, both cited above).

The third of the Engel criteria—the nature and severity of the penalty

...

123. ... The reality of awards of additional days was that prisoners were detained in prison beyond the date on which they would otherwise have been released, as a consequence of separate disciplinary proceedings which were legally unconnected to the original conviction and sentence.

124. Accordingly, the Court finds that awards of additional days by the governor constitute fresh deprivations of liberty imposed for punitive reasons after a finding of culpability (see paragraph 105 above). The Court finds further support for this view in the provisions of Rule 54(1) of the Prison Rules which allow for the imposition of additional days during a prisoner's detention on remand and, therefore, prior to any conviction, although such days would not be served in the event of acquittal.

125. This being so, the mere fact, emphasised by the Government, that at the time of the governor's decision the applicants were prisoners serving a lawfully imposed prison sentence does not, in the view of the Court, serve to distinguish their case from that of civilians or military personnel at liberty. It is, moreover, for this reason that the question of the procedural protections to be accorded to prison adjudication proceedings is one properly considered under Article 6 and not, as the Government suggest, under the provisions of Article 5 of the Convention.

It is true that in its *Campbell and Fell* judgment the Court concluded that the penalty imposed 'came close to, even if it did not technically constitute' a deprivation of liberty. However, the Court was constrained to so frame its finding since it was examining a 'loss of remission' as opposed to an 'award of additional days' for which the later 1991 Act provided.

126. It is recalled that, in its *Engel and Others* judgment, the Court found (at § 82) as follows:

'In a society subscribing to the rule of law, there belong to the "criminal" sphere deprivations of liberty liable to be imposed as a punishment, except those which by their nature, duration or manner of execution cannot be appreciably detrimental. The seriousness of what is at stake, the traditions of the Contracting States and the importance attached by the Convention to respect for the physical liberty of the person all require that this should be so.'

Accordingly, given the deprivations of liberty, liable to be and actually imposed on the present applicants, there is a presumption that the charges against them were criminal within the meaning of Article 6, a presumption which could be rebutted entirely exceptionally, and only if those deprivations of liberty could not be considered 'appreciably detrimental' given their nature, duration or manner of execution.

127. As to whether the presumption can be rebutted in the present cases, the Chamber could not find much guidance from the Court's *Campbell and Fell* judgment and the Grand Chamber agrees. In that judgment the Court concluded that the level of 'remission lost' by Mr Campbell (570 days) involved 'such serious consequences as regards the length of his detention' that that penalty had to be regarded as 'criminal' for the purposes of Article 6 of the Convention. It was not therefore relevant, in the *Campbell and Fell* case, to apply the 'appreciably detrimental' test.

128. In the present cases, it is observed that the maximum number of additional days which could be awarded to each applicant by the governor was 42 for each offence (Rule 50 of the Prison Rules). The first applicant was awarded 40 additional days and this was to be his twenty-second offence against discipline and his seventh offence involving violent threats. The second applicant was awarded 7 additional days' detention and this was to be his thirty-seventh offence against discipline. The awards of 40 and 7 additional days constituted the equivalent, in duration, of sentences handed down by a domestic court of approximately 11 and 2 weeks' imprisonment, respectively, given the provisions of section 33 (1) of the 1991 Act.

The Court also observes that there was nothing before the Chamber, and nothing was submitted to the Grand Chamber, to suggest that awards of additional days would be served other than in prison and under the same prison regime as would apply until the normal release date set by section 33 of the 1991 Act.

129. In these circumstances, the Court finds that the deprivations of liberty which were liable to be, and which were actually, imposed on the applicants cannot be regarded as sufficiently unimportant or inconsequential as to displace the presumed criminal nature of the charges against them.

The Court notes that the maximum penalty that could have been awarded against *Mr Engel* and the actual penalty imposed on him—2 days' strict arrest in both respects—was found to be of too short a duration to belong to the criminal sphere. However, it observes that, in any event even the lowest penalty imposed in the present cases was substantially greater than that in Mr *Engel*'s case.

The Court's conclusion

130. In such circumstances, the Court concludes as did the Chamber that the nature of the charges together with the nature and severity of the penalties, were such that the charges against the applicants

constituted criminal charges within the meaning of Article 6 of the Convention, which Article applied to their adjudication hearings.

The Court went on to conclude that Article 6(3)(c) had been breached in the governors' proceedings against both applicants.

In his dissenting opinion Judge Pellonpaa (joined by President Wildhaber and Judges Palm and Caflisch) stated:

... I also disagree with the view of the majority that 'the mere fact' that 'the applicants were prisoners serving a lawfully imposed sentence does not ... serve to distinguish their case from that of civilians or military personnel at liberty' (paragraph 125). To me, the difference is fundamental. This also leads me to conclude that the additional days awarded cannot be regarded as 'appreciably detrimental' within the meaning of paragraph 82 of the *Engel* judgment. I note that even the imposition of the maximum penalty of 42 days would not as such have prevented the applicants' release long—indeed, several years—before the expiry of their respective sentences.

The British Government is to be credited for swiftly responding to the Chamber's judgment in *Ezeh and Connors* by introducing a new system of prison discipline in August 2002. If the governor considers that a charge against a prisoner is serious enough to warrant the imposition of additional days punishment if proven the governor must refer the case to an independent adjudicator (a District Judge) appointed by the Home Secretary. Prisoners are given the opportunity to be legally represented before adjudicators. Adjudicators can impose an award of up to 42 additional days' in prison (together with any other punishment available to governors *e.g.* loss of privileges) where they find a prisoner guilty. Charges not meriting the award of additional days continue to be determined by governors.

8 Lustration proceedings to determine if a person had collaborated with the security services of a State during the era of communist totalitarianism were held to fall within the criminal limb of Article 6 by a unanimous Chamber in *Matyjek v Poland*, decision of 29 June 2006. The applicant, a former member of the Polish Parliament, submitted a lustration declaration, as required by legislation passed in 1997, stating that he had not collaborated with the communist security services. Later, the Warsaw Court of Appeal ruled that he had lied in his lustration declaration and, in accordance with the 1997 legislation, he was prohibited from holding a number of specified public positions for ten years. The Chamber considered that having regard to the nature and severity of the penalty imposed on the applicant the lustration proceedings should be classified as criminal under Article 6 and his complaints about the fairness of the domestic hearings would be declared admissible. The application of Article 8 to lustration proceedings conducted by another former communist State are considered below in *Turek v Slovakia* (see p 503).

Fair hearing

RIGHT TO A COURT

Golder v UK A.18 (1975) 1 EHRR 524
European Court of Human Rights

In 1965 the applicant had been sentenced to 15 years' imprisonment for robbery. During October 1969 a serious disturbance took place in Parkhurst prison where Golder was serving his sentence. After the authorities had restored order in the prison one officer (Laird) made a statement identifying Golder as a participant in the violence. A few days later that officer qualified his accusation against Golder and another officer reported that Golder had not participated in the prisoners' violence. The authorities did not bring any disciplinary charges against Golder. Subsequently he applied to the Home Secretary for permission to consult a solicitor with a view to suing Laird for libel in respect of the latter's accusations against him. The Home Secretary refused Golder's request. The applicant then complained to the Commission alleging, *inter alia*, that the Home Secretary's refusal violated his right of access to a court guaranteed by Article 6(1). The Commission, unanimously, upheld his complaint.

27. One point has not been put in issue and the Court takes it for granted: the 'right' which Golder wished, rightly or wrongly, to invoke against Laird before an English court was a 'civil right' within the meaning of Article 6 para 1 (art 6-1).

28. Again, Article 6 para 1 (art 6-1) does not state a right of access to the courts or tribunals in express terms. It enunciates rights which are distinct but stem from the same basic idea and which, taken together, make up a single right not specifically defined in the narrower sense of the term. It is the duty of the Court to ascertain, by means of interpretation, whether access to the courts constitutes one factor or aspect of this right.

29. The submissions made to the Court were in the first place directed to the manner in which the Convention, and particularly Article 6 para 1 (art 6-1), should be interpreted. The Court is prepared to consider, as do the Government and the Commission, that it should be guided by Articles 31 to 33 of the Vienna Convention of 23 May 1969 on the Law of Treaties. That Convention has not yet entered into force and it specifies, at Article 4, that it will not be retroactive, but its Articles 31 to 33 enunciate in essence generally accepted principles of international law to which the Court has already referred on occasion....

30. In the way in which it is presented in the 'general rule' in Article 3l of the Vienna Convention, the process of interpretation of a treaty is a unity, a single combined operation...

31. The terms of Article 6 para 1 (art 6-1) of the European Convention, taken in their context, provide reason to think that this right is included among the guarantees set forth.

32. The clearest indications are to be found in the French text, first sentence. In the field of 'contestations civiles' (civil claims) everyone has a right to proceedings instituted by or against him being conducted in a certain way—'équitablement' (fairly), 'publiquement' (publicly), 'dans un délai raisonnable' (within a reasonable time), etc—but also and primarily 'à ce que sa cause soit entendue' (that his case be heard) not by any authority whatever but 'par un tribunal' (by a court or tribunal) within the meaning of Article 6 para 1 (art 6-1) (*Ringeisen* judgment of 16 July 1971, Series A No 13, p 39, para 95). The Government have emphasised rightly that in French 'cause' may mean 'procès qui se plaide' (Littré, Dictionnaire de la langue française, tome I, p 509, 5'). This, however, is not the sole ordinary sense of this noun; it serves also to indicate by extension 'l'ensemble des intérêts à soutenir, à faire prévaloir' (Paul Robert, Dictionnaire alphabétique et analogique de la langue française, tome I, p 666, II–2'). Similarly, the 'contestation' (claim) generally exists prior to the legal proceedings and is a concept independent of them. As regards the phrase 'tribunal indépendant et impartial établi par la loi' (independent and impartial tribunal established by law), it conjures up the idea of organisation rather than that of functioning, of institutions rather than of procedure.

The English text, for its part, speaks of an 'independent and impartial tribunal established by law'. Moreover, the phrase 'in the determination of his civil rights and obligations', on which the Government have relied in support of their contention, does not necessarily refer only to judicial proceedings already pending; as the Commission have observed, it may be taken as synonymous with 'wherever his civil rights and obligations are being determined' (paragraph 52 of the report). It too would then imply the right to have the determination of disputes relating to civil rights and obligations made by a court or 'tribunal'.

The Government have submitted that the expressions 'fair and public hearing' and 'within a reasonable time', the second sentence in paragraph 1 ('judgment', 'trial'), and paragraph 3 of Article 6 (art 6-1, art 6-3) clearly presuppose proceedings pending before a court.

While the right to a fair, public and expeditious judicial procedure can assuredly apply only to proceedings in being, it does not, however, necessarily follow that a right to the very institution of such proceedings is thereby excluded . . . Besides, in criminal matters, the 'reasonable time' may start to run from a date prior to the seisin of the trial court, of the 'tribunal' competent for the 'determination . . . of (the) criminal charge' (*Wemhoff* judgment of 27 June 1968, Series A No 7, pp 26–7, para 19; *Neumeister* judgment of 27 June l968, Series A No 8, p 41, para 18; *Ringeisen* judgment of 16 July 1971, Series A No 13, p 45, para 110). It is conceivable also that in civil matters the reasonable time may begin to run, in certain circumstances, even before the issue of the writ commencing proceedings before the court to which the plaintiff submits the dispute. . . .

34. As stated in Article 31 para 2 of the Vienna Convention, the preamble to a treaty forms an integral part of the context. Furthermore, the preamble is generally very useful for the determination of the 'object' and 'purpose' of the instrument to be construed.

In the present case, the most significant passage in the Preamble to the European Convention is the signatory Governments declaring that they are 'resolved, as the Governments of European countries which are like-minded and have a common heritage of political traditions, ideals, freedom and the rule of law, to take the first steps for the collective enforcement of certain of the Rights stated in the Universal Declaration' of 10 December 1948. . . . And in civil matters one can scarcely conceive of the rule of law without there being a possibility of having access to the courts.

35. . . . The principle whereby a civil claim must be capable of being submitted to a judge ranks as one of the universally 'recognised' fundamental principles of law; the same is true of the principle of international law which forbids the denial of justice. Article 6 para 1 (art 6-1) must be read in the light of these principles.

Were Article 6 para 1 (art 6-1) to be understood as concerning exclusively the conduct of an action which had already been initiated before a court, a Contracting State could, without acting in breach of that text, do away with its courts, or take away their jurisdiction to determine certain classes of civil actions and entrust it to organs dependent on the Government. Such assumptions, indissociable from a danger of arbitrary power, would have serious consequences which are repugnant to the aforementioned principles and which the Court cannot overlook (*Lawless* judgment of 1 July 1961, Series A No 3, p 52, and *Delcourt* judgment of 17 January 1970, Series A No 11, pp 14–15).

It would be inconceivable, in the opinion of the Court, that Article 6 para 1 (art 6-1) should describe in detail the procedural guarantees afforded to parties in a pending lawsuit and should not first protect that which alone makes it in fact possible to benefit from such guarantees, that is, access to a court. The fair, public and expeditious characteristics of judicial proceedings are of no value at all if there are no judicial proceedings.

36. Taking all the preceding considerations together, it follows that the right of access constitutes an element which is inherent in the right stated by Article 6 para 1 (art 6-1). This is not an extensive interpretation forcing new obligations on the Contracting States: it is based on the very terms of the first sentence of Article 6 para 1 (art 6-1) read in its context and having regard to the object and purpose of the Convention, a lawmaking treaty (see the *Wemhoff* judgment of 27 June 1968, Series A No 7, p 23, para 8), and to general principles of law.

The Court thus reaches the conclusion, without needing to resort to 'supplementary means of interpretation' as envisaged at Article 32 of the Vienna Convention, that Article 6 para 1 (art 6-1) secures to everyone the right to have any claim relating to his civil rights and obligations brought before a court or tribunal. In this way the Article embodies the 'right to a court', of which the right of access, that is the right to institute proceedings before courts in civil matters, constitutes one aspect only. To this are added the guarantees laid down by Article 6 para 1 (art 6–1) as regards both the organisation and composition of the court, and the conduct of the proceedings. In sum, the whole makes up the right to a fair hearing. The Court has no need to ascertain in the present case whether and to what extent Article 6 para 1 (art 6-1) further requires a decision on the very substance of the dispute (English 'determination', French 'décidera').

B. ON THE 'IMPLIED LIMITATIONS'

37. Since the impediment to access to the courts . . . affected a right guaranteed by Article 6 para 1 (art 6-1), it remains to determine whether it was nonetheless justifiable by virtue of some legitimate limitation on the enjoyment or exercise of that right.

38. The Court considers, accepting the views of the Commission and the alternative submission of the Government, that the right of access to the courts is not absolute. As this is a right which the Convention sets forth (see Articles 13, 14, 17 and 25) (art 13, art 14, art 17, art 25) without, in the narrower sense of the term, defining, there is room, apart from the bounds delimiting the very content of any right, for limitations permitted by implication. . . .

39. The Government and the Commission have cited examples of regulations, and especially of limitations, which are to be found in the national law of states in matters of access to the courts, for instance regulations relating to minors and persons of unsound mind. Although it is of less frequent occurrence and of a very different kind, the restriction complained of by Golder constitutes a further example of such a limitation.

It is not the function of the Court to elaborate a general theory of the limitations admissible in the case of convicted prisoners, nor even to rule in abstracto on the compatibility of . . . the Prison Rules 1964 with the Convention. Seised of a case which has its origin in a petition presented by an individual, the Court is called upon to pronounce itself only on the point whether or not the application of those Rules in the present case violated the Convention to the prejudice of Golder (*De Becker* judgment of 27 March 1962, Series A No 4, p 26).

40. In this connection, the Court confines itself to noting what follows.

In petitioning the Home Secretary for leave to consult a solicitor with a view to suing Laird for libel, Golder was seeking to exculpate himself of the charge made against him by that prison officer on 25 October 1969 and which had entailed for him unpleasant consequences . . . Furthermore, the contemplated legal proceedings would have concerned an incident which was connected with prison life and had occurred while the applicant was imprisoned. Finally, those proceedings would have been directed against a member of the prison staff who had made the charge in the course of his duties and who was subject to the Home Secretary's authority.

In these circumstances, Golder could justifiably wish to consult a solicitor with a view to instituting legal proceedings. It was not for the Home Secretary himself to appraise the prospects of the action contemplated; it was for an independent and impartial court to rule on any claim that might be brought. In declining to accord the leave which had been requested, the Home Secretary failed to respect, in the person of Golder, the right to go before a court as guaranteed by Article 6 para 1 (art 6-1). . . .

FOR THESE REASONS, THE COURT,

Holds by nine votes to three that there has been a breach of Article 6(1); . . .

NOTES

1   The Court was composed of President Balladore Pallieri and Judges: Mosler, Rodenbourg, Cremona, Pedersen, Vilhjalmsson, Ryssdal, Bozer and Ganshof van der Meersch. Judges Verdross,

Zekia, and Fitzmaurice issued dissenting opinions in which they concluded that if the contracting States had intended to include a right of access to the civil courts in the Convention, they would have expressly embodied such a provision in the text of the Convention.

2   The above judgment is very significant for a number of reasons. First, it revealed the general principles and methodology the Court will utilise to interpret the rights contained within the Convention (particularly relying upon the guidelines elaborated by the Vienna Convention on the Law of Treaties). Secondly, the Court's interpretation of Article 6(1) demonstrated a generous approach that facilitated the protection of implicit, as well as express, rights concerned with a fair hearing/trial. Thirdly, the decision reflected a concern to protect the rights of prisoners, a group of persons who have historically not possessed many domestic legal rights in States such as the United Kingdom (for further cases involving prisoners see below, p 565, Ch 10).

3   The Court refined the right of access to a domestic court in its subsequent jurisprudence and ruled that Article 6(1) guaranteed effective access. This elaboration of the right could necessitate positive action by States, to facilitate individuals' access to their courts. In *Airey v Ireland*, A.32 (1979) 2 EHRR 305, the applicant was a married woman, of humble background and modest means (her net weekly wage was £40), who had been trying for a number of years to obtain a decree of judicial separation from her husband (who had been convicted of assaulting her). Under Irish law such an order could only be obtained from the High Court and the legal costs involved varied between £500–1,200. As there was no civil legal aid in Ireland the applicant had not been able to find a lawyer willing to act for her. She, therefore, complained to the Commission alleging, *inter alia*, that her right of access to a court was effectively denied to her by the Irish legal system. The Commission was unanimous in finding a breach of Article 6(1). By five votes to two, the Court also upheld her claim.

24. The Government contend that the applicant does enjoy access to the High Court since she is free to go before that court without the assistance of a lawyer.

The Court does not regard this possibility, of itself, as conclusive of the matter. The Convention is intended to guarantee not rights that are theoretical or illusory but rights that are practical and effective (see, *mutatis mutandis*, the judgment of 23 July 1968 in the *'Belgian Linguistic'* case, Series A No 6, p 31, paras 3 in fine and 4; the above-mentioned *Golder* judgment, p 18, para 35) . . . This is particularly so of the right of access to the courts in view of the prominent place held in a democratic society by the right to a fair trial . . . It must therefore be ascertained whether Mrs Airey's appearance before the High Court without the assistance of a lawyer would be effective, in the sense of whether she would be able to present her case properly and satisfactorily.

Contradictory views on this question were expressed by the Government and the Commission during the oral hearings. It seems certain to the Court that the applicant would be at a disadvantage if her husband were represented by a lawyer and she were not. Quite apart from this eventuality, it is not realistic, in the Court's opinion, to suppose that, in litigation of this nature, the applicant could effectively conduct her own case, despite the assistance which, as was stressed by the Government, the judge affords to parties acting in person.

In Ireland, a decree of judicial separation is not obtainable in a District Court, where the procedure is relatively simple, but only in the High Court. A specialist in Irish family law, Mr Alan J Shatter, regards the High Court as the least accessible court not only because 'fees payable for representation before it are very high' but also by reason of the fact that 'the procedure for instituting proceedings . . . is complex particularly in the case of those proceedings which must be commenced by a petition', such as those for separation (Family Law in the Republic of Ireland, Dublin 1977, p 21).

Furthermore, litigation of this kind, in addition to involving complicated points of law, necessitates proof of adultery, unnatural practices or, as in the present case, cruelty; to establish the facts, expert evidence may have to be tendered and witnesses may have to be found, called and examined. What is more, marital disputes often entail an emotional involvement that is scarcely compatible with the degree of objectivity required by advocacy in court.

For these reasons, the Court considers it most improbable that a person in Mrs Airey's position ... can effectively present his or her own case. This view is corroborated by the Government's replies to the questions put by the Court, replies which reveal that in each of the 255 judicial separation proceedings initiated in Ireland in the period from January 1972 to December 1978, without exception, the petitioner was represented by a lawyer ...

The Court concludes from the foregoing that the possibility to appear in person before the High Court does not provide the applicant with an effective right of access ...

25. The Government seek to distinguish the *Golder* case on the ground that, there, the applicant had been prevented from having access to court by reason of the positive obstacle placed in his way by the State in the shape of the Home Secretary's prohibition on his consulting a solicitor. The Government maintain that, in contrast, in the present case there is no positive obstacle emanating from the State and no deliberate attempt by the State to impede access; the alleged lack of access to court stems not from any act on the part of the authorities but solely from Mrs Airey's personal circumstances, a matter for which Ireland cannot be held responsible under the Convention.

Although this difference between the facts of the two cases is certainly correct, the Court does not agree with the conclusion which the Government draw therefrom. In the first place, hindrance in fact can contravene the Convention just like a legal impediment (above-mentioned *Golder* judgment, p 13, para 26). Furthermore, fulfilment of a duty under the Convention on occasion necessitates some positive action on the part of the State; in such circumstances, the State cannot simply remain passive and 'there is ... no room to distinguish between acts and omissions' (see, *mutatis mutandis*, the above-mentioned *Marckx* judgment, p 15, para 31) ... The obligation to secure an effective right of access to the courts falls into this category of duty.

26. The Government's principal argument rests on what they see as the consequence of the Commission's opinion, namely that, in all cases concerning the determination of a 'civil right', the State would have to provide free legal aid. In fact, the Convention's only express provision on free legal aid is Article 6 para 3 (c) (art 6-3-c) which relates to criminal proceedings and is itself subject to limitations; what is more, according to the Commission's established case law, Article 6 para 1 (art 6-1) does not guarantee any right to free legal aid as such. The Government add that since Ireland, when ratifying the Convention, made a reservation to Article 6 para 3 (c) (art 6-3-c) with the intention of limiting its obligations in the realm of criminal legal aid, *a fortiori* it cannot be said to have implicitly agreed to provide unlimited civil legal aid. Finally, in their submission, the Convention should not be interpreted so as to achieve social and economic developments in a Contracting State; such developments can only be progressive.

The Court is aware that the further realisation of social and economic rights is largely dependent on the situation—notably financial—reigning in the State in question. On the other hand, the Convention must be interpreted in the light of present-day conditions (above-mentioned *Marckx* judgment, p 19, para 41) and it is designed to safeguard the individual in a real and practical way as regards those areas with which it deals (see paragraph 24 above). While the Convention sets forth what are essentially civil and political rights, many of them have implications of a social or economic nature. The Court therefore considers, like the Commission, that the mere fact that an interpretation of the Convention may extend into the sphere of social and economic rights should not be a decisive factor against such an interpretation; there is no watertight division separating that sphere from the field covered by the Convention.

The Court does not, moreover, share the Government's view as to the consequence of the Commission's opinion.

It would be erroneous to generalise the conclusion that the possibility to appear in person before the High Court does not provide Mrs Airey with an effective right of access; that conclusion does not hold good for all cases concerning 'civil rights and obligations' or for everyone involved therein. In certain eventualities, the possibility of appearing before a court in person, even without a lawyer's assistance, will meet the requirements of Article 6 para 1 (art 6-1); there may be occasions when such a possibility secures adequate access even to the High Court. Indeed, much must depend on the particular circumstances.

In addition, while Article 6 para 1 (art 6-1) guarantees to litigants an effective right of access to the courts for the determination of their 'civil rights and obligations', it leaves to the State a free choice of the means to be used towards this end. The institution of a legal aid scheme—which Ireland now envisages in family law matters . . . constitutes one of those means but there are others such as, for example, a simplification of procedure. In any event, it is not the Court's function to indicate, let alone dictate, which measures should be taken; all that the Convention requires is that an individual should enjoy his effective right of access to the courts in conditions not at variance with Article 6 para 1 (art 6-1) . . .

The conclusion appearing at the end of paragraph 24 above does not therefore imply that the State must provide free legal aid for every dispute relating to a 'civil right'.

To hold that so far-reaching an obligation exists would, the Court agrees, sit ill with the fact that the Convention contains no provision on legal aid for those disputes, Article 6 para 3 (c) (art 6-3-c) dealing only with criminal proceedings. However, despite the absence of a similar clause for civil litigation, Article 6 para 1 (art 6-1) may sometimes compel the State to provide for the assistance of a lawyer when such assistance proves indispensable for an effective access to court either because legal representation is rendered compulsory, as is done by the domestic law of certain Contracting States for various types of litigation, or by reason of the complexity of the procedure or of the case.

As regards the Irish reservation to Article 6 para 3 (c) (art 6-3-c), it cannot be interpreted as affecting the obligations under Article 6 para 1 (art 6-1); accordingly, it is not relevant in the present context.

27. The applicant was unable to find a solicitor willing to act on her behalf in judicial separation proceedings. The Commission inferred that the reason why the solicitors she consulted were not prepared to act was that she would have been unable to meet the costs involved. The Government question this opinion but the Court finds it plausible and has been presented with no evidence which could invalidate it.

28. Having regard to all the circumstances of the case, the Court finds that Mrs Airey did not enjoy an effective right of access to the High Court for the purpose of petitioning for a decree of judicial separation. There has accordingly been a breach of Article 6 para 1 . . .

The Court's focus upon the practicality of a specific person's right of access to a court was a very welcome development. The full-time Court's analysis of the circumstances where States are obliged to provide legal assistance for impecunious civil defendants can be seen in *Steel and Morris v UK* below p 407.

4   The Court's approach to restrictions on persons' right of access to a court was explained in *Stubbings v UK* (1996) 23 EHRR 213, 1996-IV. Ms Stubbings was born in 1957 and adopted when she was 3 years old. From 1976 she experienced serious psychological problems and in 1984, following treatment by a family psychiatrist, she allegedly realised that there might be a connection between her mental health problems and childhood sexual abuse that she claimed to have suffered from members of her adoptive family. In 1987 she commenced civil proceedings against her adoptive father and brother seeking damages for the alleged assaults. The defendants sought to have her claim dismissed as time-barred under the Limitation Act 1980. Eventually, the House of Lords determined that her claim was subject to a six-year limitation period that began on her eighteenth birthday. As she had only begun her action in 1987, her claim was dismissed as being out of time (*Stubbings v Webb* [1993] 1 All ER 322). She, and three other women whose alleged sexual abuse claims were also dismissed as time-barred, complained to the Commission alleging breaches of their right of access to a court. The Commission, unanimously, found a breach of Article 14 in combination with Article 6(1). The Court, by seven votes to two, stated that:

47. The applicants submitted that the very essence of their right of access to court had been impaired by the limitation period of six years from the age of majority applied in their cases. One of the effects of

the sexual abuse each applicant suffered was to prevent her from appreciating that it was the cause of her psychological problems until after the expiry of the limitation period ... Expert evidence showed that the victims of child sexual abuse might commonly be unable to perceive the causal connection between the abuse and their psychological problems without medical assistance. Thus, each applicant's claim for damages for the injuries caused by the abuse became time-barred before she had even realised she had a cause of action. ...

50. The Court recalls that Article 6 para 1 (art 6-1) embodies the 'right to a court', of which the right of access, that is, the right to institute proceedings before a court in civil matters, constitutes one aspect.

However, this right is not absolute, but may be subject to limitations; these are permitted by implication since the right of access by its very nature calls for regulation by the State. In this respect, the Contracting States enjoy a certain margin of appreciation, although the final decision as to the observance of the Convention's requirements rests with the Court. It must be satisfied that the limitations applied do not restrict or reduce the access left to the individual in such a way or to such an extent that the very essence of the right is impaired. Furthermore, a limitation will not be compatible with Article 6 para 1 (art 6-1) if it does not pursue a legitimate aim and if there is not a reasonable relationship of proportionality between the means employed and the aim sought to be achieved ...

51. It is noteworthy that limitation periods in personal injury cases are a common feature of the domestic legal systems of the Contracting States. They serve several important purposes, namely to ensure legal certainty and finality, protect potential defendants from stale claims which might be difficult to counter and prevent the injustice which might arise if courts were required to decide upon events which took place in the distant past on the basis of evidence which might have become unreliable and incomplete because of the passage of time.

52. In the instant case, the English law of limitation allowed the applicants six years from their eighteenth birthdays in which to initiate civil proceedings. In addition, subject to the need for sufficient evidence, a criminal prosecution could be brought at any time and, if successful, a compensation order could be made ... Thus, the very essence of the applicants' right of access to a court was not impaired.

53. The time-limit in question was not unduly short; indeed it was longer than the extinction periods for personal injury claims set by some international treaties ... Moreover, it becomes clear that the rules applied were proportionate to the aims sought to be achieved (see paragraph 50 above) when it is considered that if the applicants had commenced actions shortly before the expiry of the period, the courts would have been required to adjudicate on events which had taken place approximately twenty years earlier.

54. The time bar in the applicants' cases commenced from the age of majority and could not be waived or extended ... It appears from the material available to the Court that there is no uniformity among the member States of the Council of Europe with regard either to the length of civil limitation periods or the date from which such periods are reckoned. In many States, the period is calculated from the date of the accrual of the cause of action, while in other jurisdictions time only starts to run from the date when the material facts in the case were known, or ought to have been known, to the plaintiff. This second principle applies in England and Wales to civil claims based on negligence (sections 11 (4) (b) and 14 of the 1980 Act ...). However, it cannot be said at the present time that this principle is commonly accepted in European States in cases such as that in issue.

55. The Contracting States properly enjoy a margin of appreciation in deciding how the right of access to court should be circumscribed. It is clear that the United Kingdom legislature has devoted a substantial amount of time and study to the consideration of these questions. Since 1936, there have been four statutes to amend and reform the law of limitation and six official bodies have reviewed aspects of it ... The decision of the House of Lords, of which the applicants complain ... that a fixed six-year period should apply in cases of intentionally caused personal injury, was not taken arbitrarily,

but rather followed from the interpretation of the Limitation Act 1980 in the light of the report of the Tucker Committee upon which the Act had been based ...

56. There has been a developing awareness in recent years of the range of problems caused by child abuse and its psychological effects on victims, and it is possible that the rules on limitation of actions applying in member States of the Council of Europe may have to be amended to make special provision for this group of claimants in the near future.

   However, since the very essence of the applicants' right of access was not impaired and the restrictions in question pursued a legitimate aim and were proportionate, it is not for the Court to substitute its own view for that of the State authorities as to what would be the most appropriate policy in this regard.

57. Accordingly, taking into account in particular the legitimate aims served by the rules of limitation in question and the margin of appreciation afforded to States in regulating the right of access to a court (see paragraphs 50–1 above), the Court finds that there has been no violation of Article 6 para 1 of the Convention taken alone (art 6-1) ...

The Court, by eight votes to one, also found no breach of Article 14 taken in conjunction with Article 6(1). To what extent do you think the above judgment was influenced by the lack of consensus among Member States regarding the starting time and duration of limitation periods for civil actions? A unanimous Court applied the criteria outlined in paragraph 50 of the *Stubbings* judgment when evaluating ministerial certificates preventing the continuation of alleged religious/political discrimination proceedings in Northern Ireland. The applicants in *Tinnelly & Sons Ltd and McElduff v UK* (1998) 27 EHRR 249, 1998-IV, complained to the Fair Employment Commission/Fair Employment Tribunal that they had been refused contracts or security clearance with public bodies because of religious/political discrimination contrary to the Fair Employment (Northern Ireland) Act 1976. The Secretary of State issued certificates under section 42 of the Act stating that action taken in respect of the applicants had been done 'for the purposes of safeguarding national security'. The certificates had the effect of terminating the applicants' complaints before domestic tribunals/courts. The Commission, unanimously, found a violation of Article 6(1). The Court held that:

61. ... the 1976 Act guaranteed persons a right not to be discriminated against on grounds of religious belief or political opinion in the job market including, and of relevance to the instant case, when bidding for a public works contract or subcontract. In the opinion of the Court that clearly defined statutory right, having regard to the context in which it applied and to its pecuniary nature, can be classified as a 'civil right' within the meaning of Article 6(1) of the Convention. ...

77. ... the conclusive nature of the section 42 certificates had the effect of preventing a judicial determination of the merits of the applicants' complaints that they were victims of unlawful discrimination. The Court would observe that such a complaint can properly be submitted for an independent judicial determination even if national security considerations are present and constitute a highly material aspect of the case. The right guaranteed to an applicant under Article 6 § 1 of the Convention to submit a dispute to a court or tribunal in order to have a determination of questions of both fact and law cannot be displaced by the *ipse dixit* of the executive ...

Therefore, the issuing of the certificates constituted a disproportionate restriction on the applicants' right of access to a court. Clearly, the absolute effect of the certificates on the applicants' domestic proceedings was a dominant factor in the Court's determination. A similar conclusion was reached by the Court in respect of the public policy immunity of the English police from negligence actions concerning the investigation and suppression of crime. In *Osman v UK* (see above, p 60), the Court was united in finding a breach of Article 6(1):

150. Although the aim of such a rule may be accepted as legitimate in terms of the Convention, as being directed to the maintenance of the effectiveness of the police service and hence to the prevention of

disorder or crime, the Court must nevertheless, in turning to the issue of proportionality, have particular regard to its scope and especially its application in the case at issue. While the Government have contended that the exclusionary rule of liability is not of an absolute nature ... and that its application may yield to other public-policy considerations, it would appear to the Court that in the instant case the Court of Appeal proceeded on the basis that the rule provided a watertight defence to the police and that it was impossible to prise open an immunity which the police enjoy from civil suit in respect of their acts and omissions in the investigation and suppression of crime.

151. The Court would observe that the application of the rule in this manner without further enquiry into the existence of competing public-interest considerations only serves to confer a blanket immunity on the police for their acts and omissions during the investigation and suppression of crime and amounts to an unjustifiable restriction on an applicant's right to have a determination on the merits of his or her claim against the police in deserving cases. ...

Once again, it was the comprehensive nature of the immunity which led the Court to determine that the there had been a disproportionate limitation on the applicants' right of access to a court.

5   Three important judgments on the relationship between the international law rules on State (sovereign) immunity and the implied right of access to court were given by Grand Chambers on the same day in November 2001. In *Al-Adsani v United Kingdom,* judgment of 21 November 2001, the applicant was a dual British/Kuwaiti national. He claimed that during 1991 he went to Kuwait to assist in its defence against invasion by Iraq. After the latter's invasion he remained in Kuwait as a member of the resistance movement. He came into possession of sexual video tapes involving Sheikh Jaber Al-Sabah (a relative of the Emir of Kuwait). Somehow those tapes were circulated and the Sheikh held the applicant responsible for their distribution. In May 1991, after the Iraqui's had been expelled from Kuwait, the Sheikh together with two other persons entered the applicant's house, beat him and forced him to accompany them in a government vehicle. He was taken to the Kuwait State Security Prison and repeatedly beaten by guards over several days. Soon after his release the applicant was again forced to accompany the Sheikh in a government car to the palace of the Emir's brother. The applicant's head was held under the water of a swimming pool containing corpses and he was then taken to a room where the Sheikh set fire to the furniture causing Al-Adsani to receive burns on a quarter of his body's surface. Later that month the applicant returned to the UK for medical treatment. In August 1992 the applicant began civil proceedings against the Sheikh and the Government of Kuwait in respect of the injuries allegedly inflicted upon him in Kuwait. In December of that year Al-Adsani obtained a default judgment against the Sheikh. In 1993 the proceedings were re-issued to include two named individuals as defendants. In August the High Court granted the applicant leave to serve the proceedings upon the named individual defendants, but not on the Government of Kuwait. Subsequently the Court of Appeal granted the applicant leave to serve the writ on the Kuwait Government. However, the latter applied for an order striking the proceedings out on the grounds of State immunity. The UK has ratified, with seven other States, the Council of Europe's 1972 European Convention on State Immunity (Basle Convention) which provides that contracting States are entitled to immunity unless the proceedings relate to stated exceptions. Domestic law was brought into conformity with the Basle Convention by the State Immunity Act 1978. During 1996 the Court of Appeal held that the Government of Kuwait were entitled to assert State immunity under the 1978 Act.

The applicant later lodged a complaint at Strasbourg asserting that the striking out of his claim against the Government of Kuwait violated his right of access to a court for the determination of his civil rights guaranteed by Article 6(1) of the Convention. The Court held that his claim was for damages in respect of personal injuries a well established cause of action in England. Consequently, there existed a genuine dispute over 'civil rights' within the meaning of Article 6(1). The British Government argued that the restriction on the applicant's right of access was for the legitimate aim of complying with the universally applicable principles of public international law on State immunity as embodied in the Basle Convention. The Court acknowledged that:

53. The right of access to court is not, however, absolute, but may be subject to limitations; these are permitted by implication since the right of access by its very nature calls for regulation by the State. In this respect, the Contracting States enjoy a certain margin of appreciation, although the final decision as to the observance of the Convention's requirements rests with the Court. It must be satisfied that the limitations applied do not restrict or reduce the access left to the individual in such a way or to such an extent that the very essence of the right is impaired. Furthermore, a limitation will not be compatible with Article 6 § 1 if it does not pursue a legitimate aim and if there is no reasonable relationship of proportionality between the means employed and the aim sought to be achieved. . . .

A bare majority (nine votes to eight) determined that the striking out of the applicant's claim by the English courts was for a legitimate aim and proportionate to that objective. The former criterion was satisfied because, '54. . . . the grant of sovereign immunity to a State in civil proceedings pursues the legitimate aim of complying with international law to promote comity and good relations between States through the respect of another State's sovereignty.' As to the latter, the Court considered that:

55. . . . The Convention should so far as possible be interpreted in harmony with other rules of international law of which it forms part, including those relating to the grant of State immunity.

56. It follows that measures taken by a High Contracting Party which reflect generally recognised rules of public international law on State immunity cannot in principle be regarded as imposing a disproportionate restriction on the right of access to court as embodied in Article 6 § 1. Just as the right of access to court is an inherent part of the fair trial guarantee in that Article, so some restrictions on access must likewise be regarded as inherent, an example being those limitations generally accepted by the community of nations as part of the doctrine of State immunity.

The majority, however, rejected the applicant's contention that public international law now recognized a peremptory norm (*jus cogens*) that prevented States from claiming State immunity from civil proceedings in another State regarding acts of torture committed in the territory of the former.

61. While the Court accepts, on the basis of these authorities, that the prohibition of torture has achieved the status of a peremptory norm in international law, it observes that the present case concerns not, as in the [*Prosecutor v] Furundzija* [ICTY: (1999) 38 ILM 317] and *Pinochet* [*R. v Bow Street Metropolitan Stipendiary Magistrate and Others, ex parte Pinochet Ugarte (No 3)* [2000] AC 147] decisions, the criminal liability of an individual for alleged acts of torture, but the immunity of a State in a civil suit for damages in respect of acts of torture within the territory of that State. Notwithstanding the special character of the prohibition of torture in international law, the Court is unable to discern in the international instruments, judicial authorities or other materials before it any firm basis for concluding that, as a matter of international law, a State no longer enjoys immunity from civil suit in the courts of another State where acts of torture are alleged. In particular, the Court observes that none of the primary international instruments referred to (Article 5 of the Universal Declaration of Human Rights, Article 7 of the International Covenant on Civil and Political Rights and Articles 2 and 4 of the United Nations Convention against Torture) relates to civil proceedings or to State immunity.

62. It is true that in its Report on Jurisdictional Immunities of States and their Property the Working Group of the International Law Commission noted, as a recent development in State practice and legislation on the subject of immunities of States, the argument increasingly put forward that immunity should be denied in the case of death or personal injury resulting from acts of a State in violation of human rights norms having the character of *jus cogens*, particularly the prohibition on torture. However, as the Working Group itself acknowledged, while national courts had in some cases shown some sympathy for the argument that States were not entitled to plead immunity where there had been a violation of human rights norms with the character of *jus cogens*, in most cases (including those cited by the applicant in the domestic proceedings and before the Court) the plea of sovereign immunity had succeeded.

66. The Court, while noting the growing recognition of the overriding importance of the prohibition of torture, does not accordingly find it established that there is yet acceptance in international law of the proposition that States are not entitled to immunity in respect of civil claims for damages for alleged torture committed outside the forum State. The 1978 Act, which grants immunity to States in respect of personal injury claims unless the damage was caused within the United Kingdom, is not inconsistent with those limitations generally accepted by the community of nations as part of the doctrine of State immunity.

67. In these circumstances, the application by the English courts of the provisions of the 1978 Act to uphold Kuwait's claim to immunity cannot be said to have amounted to an unjustified restriction on the applicant's access to court.

It follows that there has been no violation of Article 6 § 1 in this case.

A dissenting opinion was given by Judges Rozarkis and Caflisch, joined by Judges Wildhaber, Costa, Cabral Barreto, and Vajic. They disagreed with the majority's distinction between criminal and civil proceedings involving allegations of State torture. In the dissentients' view it was significant that the British courts had not relied upon that distinction. Furthermore:

... the distinction made by the majority between civil and criminal proceedings, concerning the effect of the rule of the prohibition of torture, is not consonant with the very essence of the operation of the *jus cogens* rules. It is not the nature of the proceedings which determines the effects that a *jus cogens* rule has upon another rule of international law, but the character of the rule as a peremptory norm and its interaction with a hierarchically lower rule. The prohibition of torture, being a rule of *jus cogens*, acts in the international sphere and deprives the rule of sovereign immunity of all its legal effects in that sphere. The criminal or civil nature of the domestic proceedings is immaterial. The jurisdictional bar is lifted by the very interaction of the international rules involved, and the national judge cannot admit a plea of immunity raised by the defendant State as an element preventing him from entering into the merits of the case and from dealing with the claim of the applicant for the alleged damages inflicted upon him.

Under these circumstances we believe that the United Kingdom courts have erred in considering that they had no jurisdiction to entertain the applicant's claim because of the procedural bar of State immunity and the consequent application of the 1978 Act. Accordingly, the applicant was deprived of his right to have access to the British court to entertain his claim of damages for the alleged torture suffered by him in Kuwait, and Article 6 § 1, has, in our view, been violated.

Judge Pellonpaa, joined by Judge Bratza, issued a concurring opinion in which he elaborated the practical difficulties that would arise for member States if they were obliged to deny claims of State immunity in civil proceedings concerning extra-territorial allegations of torture.

The somewhat paradoxical result, had the minority's view prevailed, could have been that precisely those States which so far have been most liberal in accepting refugees and asylum seekers, would have had imposed upon them the additional burden of guaranteeing access to court for the determination of perhaps hundreds of refugees' civil claims for compensation for alleged torture. Even if the finding of a violation of Article 6 in this case had not had a 'chilling effect' on the readiness of the Contracting States to accept refugees—a consequence which I would not totally exclude—the question of the effectiveness of the access in the circumstances . . . would inevitably have arisen.

He noted that the Court's established jurisprudence concerning Article 6(1) required not merely access to a court but also execution of judgments involving the determination of 'civil rights'. Therefore, the dissentients' application of the *jus cogens* prohibition of torture to Article 6(1) would ultimately have required Member States to seek to enforce civil judgments against foreign States' property in the former's jurisdiction (possibly including embassies) with very serious consequences for diplomatic relations.

Although giving absolute priority to the prohibition of torture may at first sight seem very 'progressive', a more careful consideration tends to confirm that such a step would also run the risk of proving a sort of 'Pyrrhic victory'. International co-operation, including co-operation with a view to eradicating the vice of torture, presupposes the continuing existence of certain elements of a basic framework for the conduct of international relations. Principles concerning State immunity belong to that regulatory framework, and I believe it is more conducive to orderly international co-operation to leave this framework intact than to follow another course.

In my view this case leaves us with at least two important lessons. First, although consequences should not alone determine the interpretation of a given rule, one should never totally lose sight of the consequences of a particular interpretation one is about to adopt. Secondly, when having to touch upon central questions of general international law, this Court should be very cautious before taking upon itself the role of a forerunner.

The above case reveals the Court to be very divided in its assessments of the current requirements of public international law regarding claims of State immunity in the context of allegations of State torture. As Judge Pellonpaa warned the potential burdens placed on Member States by the dissentients' broad application of the *jus cogens* prohibition of torture could have been extensive and onerous. Apart from practical considerations another justification for the majority's cautious application of the right of access to a court is that it is an implied right and therefore as a judicial creation it needs to be applied with particular sensitivity to the legitimate needs of Member States.

The same Grand Chamber was, however, much more united in its assessment of the rules of State immunity regarding civil claims involving the employment of persons by foreign embassies. In *Fogarty v United Kingdom*, judgment of 21 November 2001, the applicant was an Irish national. Between November 1993 and February 1995 she had been employed as an administrative assistant in the Foreign Broadcasting Information Service (a subsidiary organisation of the Central Intelligence Agency) at the United States' embassy in London. Following her dismissal she brought proceedings against the United States Government before an Industrial Tribunal alleging that her dismissal had been the result of sex discrimination (contrary to the Sex Discrimination Act 1975). She claimed that she had been the victim of persistent sexual harassment by her supervisor. In June 1995 she obtained a twelve month contract as an administrative assistant with the Foreign Building Operations section of the United States' embassy. The Government of the United States did not claim State immunity before the Industrial Tribunal and in May 1996 the Tribunal upheld the applicant's claim. Compensation of £12,000 was agreed between the parties. In June and August 1996 the applicant unsuccessfully applied for secretarial posts within the United States' embassy. During September 1996 the applicant made a further application to the Industrial Tribunal asserting that the embassy's refusals to re-employ her were a consequence of her successful earlier sex discrimination claim and therefore constituted further acts of discrimination and victimisation contrary to the 1975 Act. Lawyers acting for the United States Government informed the Tribunal that the Government intended to claim immunity from these subsequent proceedings under the State Immunity Act 1978. The latter provides for the immunity of States in respect of the employment of members of foreign missions and consular facilities. Likewise the Basle Convention expressly preserves the privileges and immunities of diplomatic missions. Consequently, counsel advised the applicant that the United States Government was entitled to assert immunity and that she had no remedy in domestic law.

Before the Court the applicant complained that the doctrine of State immunity recognised by English law denied her access to a court in breach of Article 6(1). Following the method of analysis used in *Al-Adsani*, the Court first examined whether the applicant had been seeking to assert a 'civil right' in the proceedings before the Industrial Tribunal.

26. Section 6 of the Sex Discrimination Act 1975 creates a statutory right which arises, *inter alia*, when an employer refuses to employ a woman on grounds of sex discrimination or by reason of the fact that she has already taken proceedings under the 1975 Act. Thus, the proceedings which the applicant intended to pursue were for damages for a cause of action well known to English law. The Court does not accept the Government's plea that because of the operation of State immunity she did not have a substantive right under domestic law. . . .

Secondly, did the restriction on the applicant's right to bring those proceedings against the United States Government pursue a legitimate aim? The Court held that it did because:

34. . . . sovereign immunity is a concept of international law, developed out of the principle *par in parem non habet imperium*, by virtue of which one State shall not be subject to the jurisdiction of another State. The Court considers that the grant of sovereign immunity to a State in civil proceedings pursues the legitimate aim of complying with international law to promote comity and good relations between States through the respect of another State's sovereignty.

Thirdly, it was necessary to determine if the restriction was a proportionate measure. An overwhelming majority (sixteen votes to one) considered that it was.

38. . . . Questions relating to the recruitment of staff to missions and embassies may by their very nature involve sensitive and confidential issues, related, *inter alia*, to the diplomatic and organisational policy of a foreign State. The Court is not aware of any trend in international law towards a relaxation of the rule of State immunity as regards issues of recruitment to foreign missions. . . .

39. In these circumstances, the Court considers that, in conferring immunity on the United States in the present case by virtue of the provisions of the 1978 Act, the United Kingdom cannot be said to have exceeded the margin of appreciation allowed to States in limiting an individual's access to court.

It follows that there has been no violation of Article 6 § 1 in this case.

Judge Loucaides dissented on the ground that the application of the doctrine of State immunity to the applicant's sex discrimination claim resulted in an absolute blocking of her proceedings without any consideration of the substance of her claim or the balancing of competing interests. He considered that such an absolute bar to proceedings was not a proportionate limitation of the right of access to a court.

The distinction between *Fogarty* and *Al-Adsani* was that in the former case the relevant rules of international law on State immunity, in respect of employment of embassy staff, were much more certain. Therefore, the Court was almost unanimous in holding that they were a legitimate and proportionate restriction on the Convention right of access to a court.

In *McElhinney v Ireland*, judgment of 21 November 2001, the Court was faced with a respondent State that was not a party to the Basle Convention. The applicant was a police officer in Ireland. Late one evening in March 1991, whilst off-duty, the applicant drove a vehicle pulling a trailer into the barrier of a United Kingdom vehicle checkpoint in County Derry (Northern Ireland). The checkpoint was staffed by armed British soldiers. A corporal in the military police approached the applicant's vehicle and was hit by the trailer. The applicant drove off into Ireland and the soldier climbed onto the tow-bar of the applicant's vehicle. The soldier fired six shots, hitting the exhaust pipe and rear window of the applicant's vehicle. The applicant claimed that he heard the shots and believed that he was under attack from a terrorist. Therefore, he drove for about two miles until he reached an Irish police station. When he stopped the soldier ordered him, and his passengers, to stand against a wall with their hands in the air. According to the applicant the soldier tried to shoot him, but his gun jammed. The applicant was arrested by Irish police officers on suspicion of driving having consumed excess alcohol. He refused to provide either blood or urine samples and was later convicted for failing to do so. The applicant alleged that he suffered severe post-traumatic shock as a result of the soldier's actions. In 1993 he began an action in the Irish High Court against the soldier and the (British) Secretary of State for Northern Ireland claiming damages for assault. In 1994 the Secretary of State applied for the summons to be set aside on the ground of sovereign immunity. The High Court granted the Secretary's request. On appeal the Supreme Court upheld the lower court's ruling, as the soldier was carrying out governmental/sovereign activities at the checkpoint his actions had to be regarded as *de jure imperii*. Furthermore, it had not been established that the principles of sovereign immunity in public international no longer applied to the tortious acts of a foreign State's agent within the sphere of *de jure imperii*. The applicant did not pursue his action against the corporal nor did he initiate civil proceedings in the courts of Northern Ireland.

At Strasbourg the Court held that the applicant had been seeking to assert 'civil rights' in his action against the British Government, because his claims of assault, trespass to the person, negligence and breach of duty were well known causes of action in Ireland. However, the setting aside of his proceedings had been for the legitimate aim of complying with international law. A large majority of the Court (twelve votes to five) also concluded that the Irish courts' termination of the proceedings, in deference to the doctrine of sovereign immunity, was a proportionate measure.

38. The Court observes that, on the material before it ... there appears to be a trend in international and comparative law towards limiting State immunity in respect of personal injury caused by an act or omission within the forum State, but that this practice is by no means universal. Further, it appears ... that the trend may primarily refer to 'insurable' personal injury, that is incidents arising out of ordinary road traffic accidents, rather than matters relating to the core area of State sovereignty such as the acts of a soldier on foreign territory which, of their very nature, may involve sensitive issues affecting diplomatic relations between States and national security. Certainly, it cannot be said that Ireland is alone in holding that immunity attaches to suits in respect of such torts committed by *acta jure imperii* or that, in affording this immunity, Ireland falls outside any currently accepted international standards. The Court agrees with the Supreme Court in the present case ... that it is not possible, given the present state of the development of international law, to conclude that Irish law conflicts with its general principles.

40. In these circumstances, the decisions of the Irish courts upholding the United Kingdom's claim to immunity cannot be said to have exceeded the margin of appreciation allowed to States in limiting an individual's right to access to court.

It follows that there has been no violation of Article 6 § 1 in this case.

Judges Caflisch, Cabral Barreto and Vajic issued a dissenting opinion in which they expressed the belief that international law had evolved further in the limitation of claims of sovereign immunity than the position recognised by the majority.

... This convergence is sufficiently powerful to suggest, at any rate, that at present there is no international *duty*, on the part of States, to grant immunity to other States in matters of torts caused by the latter's agents.

There was, consequently, no conflict between the international law on sovereign immunity and the right of access to domestic courts guaranteed by Article 6 § 1 of the Convention. It follows that the Court, in our view, should have held Article 6 § 1 to apply to the present case. It could then have found that the Republic of Ireland should have allowed the applicant to have access to its courts. By not doing so, it disproportionately restricted the applicant's rights under the Convention.

In his dissent Judge Loucaides emphasised the distinct nature of the Convention's legal regime and sought to distance it from the universal principles of international law.

In a case like the one before the Court, the *lex specialis* is the European Convention of Human Rights. General principles of international law are not embodied in the Convention except insofar as reference is expressly made to them by the Convention (see, for example, Articles 15, 35 § 1 and 53 of the Convention and Article 1 of Protocol No 1). Therefore, one should be reluctant to accept restrictions on Convention rights derived from principles of international law such as those establishing immunities which are not even part of the *jus cogens* norms.

In the above three cases the variable sizes of the majorities and minorities in the Court reflected the different contexts in which claims for State/sovereign immunity were being claimed and the judges disagreements over the requirements of contemporary international law. The fact that the latter body of law is evolving in its treatment of State/sovereign immunity claims added to the complexity of the task facing the Court. Nevertheless, it is a tribute to the creativity of the Court, since the landmark judgment of the original Court in *Golder* articulated the implied right of access to a court under Article 6(1), that the above three applicants were able to challenge the invocation of State/sovereign immunity in domestic proceedings before a supra-national court. Although the Court did not uphold the applicants' complaints, the existence of support for their contentions amongst a number of judges (especially the substantial group of dissentients in *Al-Adsani*) suggests that not all claims of State/sovereign immunity may be held to be compatible with Article 6(1) in the future. See also, E. Bates, 'The Al-Adsani Case, State Immunity and the International Legal Prohibition on Torture', 3(1) *Human Rights Law Review* 193 (2003).

6   The absolute privilege given to debates in the House of Commons, by Article 9 of the Bill of Rights 1689, was challenged in *A. v UK*, judgment of 17 December 2002. The applicant's Member of Parliament (MP) initiated a debate on public sector housing in which he described the applicant and her family as neighbours from hell giving detailed allegations of anti-social behaviour caused by her family. The MP identified the applicant and gave her address in his speech. The speech was given wide publicity in the local press and subsequently the applicant received hate mail and was harassed to the extent that she was re-housed. She contended that her inability to bring civil proceedings against the MP violated her right of access to court. The Chamber, by six votes to one, held that:

77. The Court concludes that the parliamentary immunity enjoyed by the MP in the present case pursued the legitimate aims of protecting free speech in Parliament and maintaining the separation of powers between the legislature and the judiciary.

78. The Court must next assess the proportionality of the immunity enjoyed by the MP. In this regard, the Court notes that the immunity concerned was absolute in nature and applied to both criminal and

civil proceedings. The Court agrees with the applicant's submission that the broader an immunity, the more compelling must be its justification in order that it can be said to be compatible with the Convention. However, . . . its absolute nature cannot be decisive. Thus, for example, in the above-mentioned *Al-Adsani* case, the Court stated that measures taken by signatory States which reflected generally recognised rules of public international law on State immunity could not in principle be regarded as imposing a disproportionate restriction on the right of access to court as embodied in Article 6 § 1 (see also *Fogarty v the United Kingdom* [GC], No 37112/97, § 36, ECHR 2001-XI; *McElhinney v Ireland* [GC], No 31253/96, § 37, ECHR 2001-XI).

79. It is also recalled that, in the recent case of *Jerusalem v Austria* (No 26958/95, §§ 36 and 40, ECHR 2001-II), the Court stated that, while freedom of expression is important for everybody, it is especially so for an elected representative of the people. He or she represents the electorate, draws attention to their preoccupations and defends their interests. In a democracy, Parliament or such comparable bodies are the essential *fora* for political debate. Very weighty reasons must be advanced to justify interfering with the freedom of expression exercised therein.

80. The Court notes that most, if not all, signatory States to the Convention have in place some form of immunity for members of their national legislatures. In particular, the domestic law of each of the eight States to have made a third-party intervention in the present case makes provision for such an immunity . . . although the precise detail of the immunities concerned varies.

81. Measures are also in place granting privileges and immunities to, *inter alios*, Representatives to the Consultative Assembly of the Council of Europe and Members of the European Parliament.

. . .

83. In light of the above, the Court believes that a rule of parliamentary immunity, which is consistent with and reflects generally recognised rules within signatory States, the Council of Europe and the European Union, cannot in principle be regarded as imposing a disproportionate restriction on the right of access to court as embodied in Article 6 § 1 (see, *mutatis mutandis*, the above-mentioned *Al-Adsani* judgment, § 56). Just as the right of access to court is an inherent part of the fair trial guarantee in that Article, so some restrictions on access must likewise be regarded as inherent, an example being those limitations generally accepted by signatory States as part of the doctrine of parliamentary immunity (ibid).

84. Furthermore, the immunity afforded to MPs in the United Kingdom appears to the Court to be in several respects narrower than that afforded to members of national legislatures in certain other signatory States and those afforded to Representatives to the Consultative Assembly of the Council of Europe and Members of the European Parliament. In particular, the immunity attaches only to statements made in the course of parliamentary debates on the floor of the House of Commons or House of Lords. No immunity attaches to statements made outside Parliament, even if they amount to a repetition of statements made during the course of Parliamentary debates on matters of public interest. Nor does any immunity attach to an MP's press statements published prior to parliamentary debates, even if their contents are repeated subsequently in the debate itself.

85. The absolute immunity enjoyed by MPs is moreover designed to protect the interests of Parliament as a whole as opposed to those of individual MPs. This is illustrated by the fact that the immunity does not apply outside Parliament. In contrast, the immunity which protects those engaged in the reporting of parliamentary proceedings, and that enjoyed by elected representatives in local government, are each qualified in nature.

86. The Court observes that victims of defamatory misstatement in Parliament are not entirely without means of redress. In particular, such persons can, where it is their own MP who has made the offending remarks, petition the House through any other MP with a view to securing a retraction. In extreme cases, deliberately misleading statements may be punishable by Parliament as a contempt. General control is

exercised over debates by the Speaker of each House. The Court considers that all of these factors are of relevance to the question of proportionality of the immunity enjoyed by the MP in the present case.

87. It follows that, in all the circumstances of this case, the application of a rule of absolute Parliamentary immunity cannot be said to exceed the margin of appreciation allowed to States in limiting an individual's right of access to court.

88. The Court agrees with the applicant's submissions to the effect that the allegations made about her in the MP's speech were extremely serious and clearly unnecessary in the context of a debate about municipal housing policy. The MP's repeated reference to the applicant's name and address was particularly regrettable. The Court considers that the unfortunate consequences of the MP's comments for the lives of the applicant and her children were entirely foreseeable. However, these factors cannot alter the Court's conclusion as to the proportionality of the parliamentary immunity at issue, since the creation of exceptions to that immunity, the application of which depended upon the individual facts of any particular case, would seriously undermine the legitimate aims pursued.

89. There has, accordingly, been no violation of Article 6 § 1 of the Convention as regards the parliamentary immunity enjoyed by the MP.

The concluding comments of the Court indicate that it did not approve of the way in which the MP (Michael Stern) had used his freedom of speech in Parliament.

The Court has not always upheld claims of parliamentary immunity. For example, in the subsequent case of *Cordova (No 1) v Italy*, judgment of 30 January 2003, the applicant was a prosecutor who had been investigating a person associated with Francesco Cossiga (a former President of Italy and a 'senator for life'). Cosigga sent the applicant several sarcastic letters and toys. The applicant lodged criminal and civil complaints against Cossgia for allegedly insulting a public official. However, the Senate considered that Cossiga's acts were covered by a constitutional immunity as his opinions had been expressed in the performance of his parliamentary duties. Therefore, the court held that Cossiga had no case to answer. The Strasbourg Court was unanimous in concluding that the absence of an obvious link between Cossiga's acts and any kind of parliamentary activity meant that the resolution of the Senate and ruling of the court that he had no case to answer upset the fair balance between the interests of the community and the rights of the applicant and consequently a breach of Article 6(1) had occurred. Hence, only comments/actions directly connected with parliamentary affairs are likely to be recognised as deserving absolute immunity by the Court.

7   In *Roche v United Kingdom*, judgment of 19 October 2005, the Grand Chamber confirmed the distinction, under Article 6(1), between 'substantive' and 'procedural' limitations on the right of access to a civil court. The former concern the existence and scope of 'civil rights' within national law, whilst the latter govern the ability of litigants to bring proceedings in domestic courts to enforce 'civil rights'. The Grand Chamber repeated that Article 6(1) does not guarantee any particular content of 'civil rights', that is a matter for national law. Hence, national law delimiting the scope of a particular 'civil right' will not constitute a breach of the right of access to a court. Whereas, procedural limitations on the enforcement of a recognized 'civil right' may breach Article 6(1); as in *Tinnelly*, above Note 4. Roche complained that section 10 of the Crown Proceedings Act 1947, which prevented military personnel from generally suing the Crown in respect of alleged torts, violated his right of access to a court. The Grand Chamber was deeply divided on whether section 10 should be classified as a substantive or procedural limitation. The majority, of nine judges, accorded significant weight to the unanimous decision of the House of Lords in *Matthews v Ministry of Defence* [2003] UKHL 4, that section 10 was a substantive limitation that did not infringe Article 6(1).

120. In assessing therefore whether there is a civil 'right' and in determining the substantive or procedural characterisations to be given to the impugned restriction, the starting point must be the provisions of the relevant domestic law and their interpretation by the domestic courts ...

Consequently, the majority found no breach of Article 6(1). Whereas, the eight dissentients believed that section 10 should be classified as a procedural limitation that violated Article 6(1) by denying Roche access to the courts to challenge the lawfulness of the poison gas tests he had been subject to whilst serving in the British army during the 1960s.

Providing for a condition such as certification by the Secretary of State, rather than defining a series of exceptions and leaving the question of their existence in any particular case to be decided by the courts, lends support to the view that the relevant restriction on the right of access to the court is procedural in nature.

Roche vividly disclosed how difficult it can be in practice to distinguish between substantive and procedural limitations. Indeed, Judge Zupancic, one of the dissenters, described it as being an 'artificial separation'.

8   Excessive court fees have been found to violate the right of access to a court. For example, in *Kreuz v Poland*, judgment of 19 June 2001, the applicant was a businessman who sued his local council regarding their refusal to confirm his planning permission to construct a carwash. The domestic court ordered that he pay 100 million PLZ (roughly the average annual salary in Poland at that time) as a fee for lodging his claim. Despite his contention that he could not afford that sum, the court ruled that as a businessman he should have ensured that he had adequate funds available to conduct litigation concerning his venture. He did not pay the fee and his proceedings were terminated. In response to his claim of a breach of Article 6(1) the Court, unanimously, held that:

60. .... the requirement to pay fees to civil courts in connection with claims they are asked to determine cannot be regarded as a restriction on the right of access to a court that is incompatible *per se* with Article 6(1) of the Convention. It reiterates, however, that the amount of the fees assessed in the light of the particular circumstances of a given case, including the applicant's ability to pay them, and the phase of the proceedings at which that restriction has been imposed are factors which are material in determining whether or not a person enjoyed his right of access ...

66. Assessing the facts of the case as a whole and having regard to the prominent place held by the right to a court in a democratic society, the Court considers that the judicial authorities have failed to secure a proper balance between, on the one hand, the interest of the State in collecting court fees for dealing with claims and, on the other hand, the interest of the applicant in vindicating his claim through the courts.

   The fee required from the applicant for proceeding with his action was excessive. It resulted in his desisting from his claim and in his case never being heard by a court. That, in the Court's opinion, impaired the very essence of his right of access.

67. For the above reasons, the Court concludes that the imposition of the court fees on the applicant constituted a disproportionate restriction on his right of access to a court. It accordingly finds that there has been a breach of Article 6(1) of the Convention.

The Polish courts had clearly failed to give sufficient weight to the actual financial resources available to Kreuz when determining the amount of fees he should be required to pay to bring his action.

9   The failure of State authorities to take adequate steps to enforce court judgments is another type of breach. For example, in *Sirbu and Others v Moldova*, judgment of 15 June 2004, the six applicants were civil servants who had obtained final court judgments against the Ministry of Internal Affairs requiring the payment to them of allowances. Despite the issuing of enforcement warrants the Ministry refused to pay the sums due because of alleged lack of funds. After the applicants lodged their complaints at Strasbourg the Ministry executed the judgments (over five years after the domestic judgments against the Ministry). The Court, unanimously, ruled that:

23. . . . Article 6 § 1 secures to everyone the right to have any claim relating to his civil rights and obligations brought before a court or tribunal; in this way it embodies the 'right to a court', of which the right of access, that is the right to institute proceedings before courts in civil matters, constitutes one aspect. However, that right would be illusory if a Contracting State's domestic legal system allowed a final, binding judicial decision to remain inoperative to the detriment of one party. It would be inconceivable that Article 6 § 1 should describe in detail procedural guarantees afforded to litigants—proceedings that are fair, public and expeditious—without protecting the implementation of judicial decisions; to construe Article 6 as being concerned exclusively with access to a court and the conduct of proceedings would be likely to lead to situations incompatible with the principle of the rule of law which the Contracting States undertook to respect when they ratified the Convention. Execution of a judgment given by any court must therefore be regarded as an integral part of the 'trial' for the purposes of Article 6 (see the *Hornsby v Greece* judgment of 19 March 1997, *Reports* 1997-II, p 510, § 40).

24. It is not open to a State authority to cite lack of funds as an excuse for not honouring a judgment. Admittedly, a delay in the execution of a judgment may be justified in particular circumstances. But the delay may not be such as to impair the essence of the right protected under Article 6 § 1 of the Convention (see *Immobiliare Saffi v Italy* [GC], No 22774/93, § 74, ECHR 1999-V). In the instant case, the applicants should not have been prevented from benefiting from the success of the litigation, which concerned the payment of compensation.

25. The Court notes that the Centru District Court's judgments of 1 and 18 August 1997 remained unenforced for more than five years and a half (until after the cases had been communicated to the Government by the Court, on 15 May 2003).

26. By failing for years to take the necessary measures to comply with the final judgments in the instant case, the Moldovan authorities deprived the provisions of Article 6 § 1 of the Convention of all useful effect.

27. There has accordingly been a violation of Article 6 § 1 of the Convention. It is noteworthy that the Court expressly rejected the suggestion that lack of public funds is an excuse for domestic authorities not complying with a financial judgment against them.

EQUALITY OF ARMS

....

Rowe and Davis v UK [2000] Crim LR 584
European Court of Human Rights

During the night of 15–16 December 1988 a series of serious offences occurred in Surrey. Around 1.30 am two men were attacked in a field near Fickleshall, one of the men (Hurburgh) was killed. The victim's car was also stolen. Two hours later three masked men armed with a knife and a gun entered a house in Oxted, robbed the occupants of jewellery, stabbed one occupant (Timothy Napier) and stole the latter's car. Hurburgh's car was abandoned near the Napier home. A few hours afterwards three masked men broke into a house in Fetcham, bound the occupants, stole jewellery and a car. Timothy's car was left nearby. There was great media coverage of these crimes and a large reward (£25,000) offered for information leading to the conviction of the offenders. On 18 December information was given to the police that the offenders were living in a specific house in south London. The police obtained search warrants and carried out a search of the premises (flats) on 19 December. The premises were occupied by Rowe and Davis (who were black) and the 'Jobbins group' (Jobbins, Duncan and Griffin; all of whom had criminal records and were white). A brooch from the Fetcham robbery was found in Rowe's wastepaper basket together with a blood stained jacket. Rowe, Davis, Jobbins and Griffin were arrested on suspicion of aggravated burglary. Rowe's 16-year-old girlfriend gave the police other items of jewellery stolen from the Fetcham robbery which she claimed Rowe had given her. Johnson was arrested, carrying a gun, a couple of weeks later and he admitted that he had been at the south London house on the night of the offences, but he denied any involvement in the crimes. Rowe, Davis and Johnson were tried at the Old Bailey in February 1990. The prosecution relied heavily on the evidence of the Jobbins group having helped the defendants commit the crimes on the night in question. The defendants denied involvement in the offences. The jury, unanimously, found the defendants guilty of murder, grievous bodily harm and robbery. They were given life sentences. On appeal the prosecution gave the court a document which the defendants/appellants were not allowed to see. The Court of Appeal refused to order disclosure of the document and dismissed the appeal. In 1997 the new Criminal Cases Commission ordered an investigation into the case and it was revealed that one member of the Jobbins group (Duncan) was a long-standing police informant who had provided the police with the information about the applicants. Duncan received £10,000 reward and immunity from prosecution in respect of his involvement in the crimes. These facts had not been disclosed to the defence on grounds of public interest immunity. The Criminal Cases Commission referred the applicants' convictions back to the Court of Appeal. The applicants complained to the European Commission alleging that the prosecution's failure to disclose the information about Duncan undermined their right to a fair trial. The Commission was unanimous in finding a breach of Article 6(1) in conjunction with Article 6(3)(b) and(d).

59. The Court recalls that the guarantees in paragraph 3 of Article 6 are specific aspects of the right to a fair trial set out in paragraph 1 . . . In the circumstances of the case it finds it unnecessary to examine the applicants' allegations separately from the standpoint of paragraph 3(b) and (d), since they amount to a complaint that the applicants did not receive a fair trial. It will therefore confine its examination to the question whether the proceedings in their entirety were fair . . .

60. It is a fundamental aspect of the right to a fair trial that criminal proceedings, including the elements of such proceedings which relate to procedure, should be adversarial and that there should be equality of arms between the prosecution and defence. The right to an adversarial trial means, in a criminal case, that both prosecution and defence must be given the opportunity to have knowledge of and comment on the observations filed and the evidence adduced by the other party (see the *Brandstetter v Austria* judgment of 28 August 1991, Series A No 211, §§ 66, 67). In addition Article 6 § 1 requires, as indeed does English law . . . that the prosecution authorities should disclose to the defence all material evidence in their possession for or against the accused . . .

61. However, as the applicants recognised . . . the entitlement to disclosure of relevant evidence is not an absolute right. In any criminal proceedings there may be competing interests, such as national security or the need to protect witnesses at risk of reprisals or keep secret police methods of investigation of crime, which must be weighed against the rights of the accused (see, for example, the *Doorson v Netherlands* judgment of 26 March 1996, *Reports of Judgments and Decisions* 1996-II, § 70). In some cases it may be necessary to withhold certain evidence from the defence so as to preserve the fundamental rights of another individual or to safeguard an important public interest.

However, only such measures restricting the rights of the defence which are strictly necessary are permissible under Article 6 § 1 (see the *Van Mechelen v Netherlands* judgment of 23 April 1997, *Reports* 1997-III, § 58). Moreover, in order to ensure that the accused receives a fair trial, any difficulties caused to the defence by a limitation on its rights must be sufficiently counterbalanced by the procedures followed by the judicial authorities (see the above-mentioned *Doorson* judgment, § 72 and the above-mentioned *Van Mechelen* judgment, § 54).

62. In cases where evidence has been withheld from the defence on public interest grounds, it is not the role of this Court to decide whether or not such non-disclosure was strictly necessary since, as a general rule, it is for the national courts to assess the evidence before them ... Instead, the European Court's task is to ascertain whether the decision-making procedure applied in each case complied, as far as possible, with the requirements of adversarial proceedings and equality of arms and incorporated adequate safeguards to protect the interests of the accused.

63. During the applicants' trial at first instance the prosecution decided, without notifying the judge, to withhold certain relevant evidence on grounds of public interest. Such a procedure, whereby the prosecution itself attempts to assess the importance of concealed information to the defence and weigh this against the public interest in keeping the information secret, cannot comply with the above-mentioned requirements of Article 6 § 1. Indeed this principle is recognised by the English case-law from the Court of Appeal's judgment in *Ward* (*R v Ward* [1993] 2 All ER 577) onwards ...

64. It is true that at the commencement of the applicants' appeal prosecution counsel notified the defence that certain information had been withheld, without however revealing the nature of this material, and that on two separate occasions the Court of Appeal reviewed the undisclosed evidence and, in *ex parte* hearings with the benefit of submissions from the Crown but in the absence of the defence, decided in favour of non-disclosure.

65. However, the Court does not consider that this procedure before the appeal court was sufficient to remedy the unfairness caused at the trial by the absence of any scrutiny of the withheld information by the trial judge. Unlike the latter, who saw the witnesses give their testimony and was fully versed in all the evidence and issues in the case, the judges in the Court of Appeal were dependent for their understanding of the possible relevance of the undisclosed material on transcripts of the Crown Court hearings and on the account of the issues given to them by prosecuting counsel. In addition, the first instance judge would have been in a position to monitor the need for disclosure throughout the trial, assessing the importance of the undisclosed evidence at a stage when new issues were emerging, when it might have been possible through cross-examination seriously to undermine the credibility of key witnesses and when the defence case was still open to take a number of different directions or emphases. In contrast, the Court of Appeal was obliged to carry out its appraisal *ex post facto* and may even, to a certain extent, have unconsciously been influenced by the jury's verdict of guilty into underestimating the significance of the undisclosed evidence.

66. In conclusion, therefore, the prosecution's failure to lay the evidence in question before the trial judge and to permit him to rule on the question of disclosure deprived the applicants of a fair trial ... It follows that there has been a violation of Article 6 § 1 of the Convention.

...

FOR THESE REASONS THE COURT UNANIMOUSLY

Holds that there has been a violation of Article 6(1) of the Convention ...

NOTES

1   The Court was composed of President Wildhaber and Judges: Palm, Ferrari Bravo, Caflisch, Costa, Fuhrmann, Jungwiert, Fischbach, Zupanoio, Vajio, Hedigan, Thomassen, Tsatsa-Nikolovska, Pantiru, Levits, Traja, and Laws.

2 The Criminal Procedure and Investigations Act 1996 introduced a new system of prosecution disclosures and defence statements for trials in England and Wales. Under the statutory scheme prosecution disclosure decisions may be challenged by the defence and reviewed by the trial judge.

3 In July 2000, the Court of Appeal quashed the convictions of Rowe, Davis and Johnson. The court ruled that the collusion between the police and Duncan was one of three 'material irregularities' that made the jury's verdicts unsafe. However, the court stated that the case against all three was 'formidable' and in respect of the charge of robbery against Rowe the evidence was 'overwhelming'. The Lord Justices expressed the view that the Court's judgment 'is not a finding of innocence, far from it.' The court also considered the relationship between the European Court of Human Rights' finding of a breach of Article 6(1) in an English criminal case and the Court of Appeal's duty to determine the 'safety' of that conviction. Mantell LJ ruled that: '...a finding of a breach of Article 6(1) would not lead inexorably to the quashing of the conviction. The effect of any unfairness upon the safety of a conviction would vary according to its nature and degree.' *R v Davis, R v Rowe and R v Johnson* (2000) The Times, 25 July.

4 Two persons who had been convicted, after their trial judges allowed *ex parte* applications by the prosecution to withhold evidence from the defence on public interest grounds, successfully invoked Article 6(1) to challenge their inability during their trials to establish whether the involvement of *agents provocateurs* in the alleged offences made the proceedings against them unfair in *Edwards and Lewis v UK*, judgment of 22 July 2003. The first applicant had been arrested, following a police undercover operation, in a van with nearly 5 kg of heroin accompanied by 'Graham' (an undercover policed officer). Edwards subsequently came to suspect that a number of the other participants in the drugs transaction were either undercover police officers or police informers. He was sentenced to nine years' imprisonment for possessing a Class A drug with intent to supply. The second applicant was arrested when he showed two undercover police officers counterfeit notes that he was willing to supply. Lewis was sentenced to four and a half years' imprisonment. Before the Chamber the applicants contended that their trials had been unfair as their trial judges, who had to determine if the applicants had been entrapped, had heard prosecution requests for the withholding of evidence without any adversarial processes.

49. The applicants claim to have been victims of entrapment. The Court recalls that, although the admissibility of evidence is primarily a matter for regulation by national law, the requirements of a fair criminal trial under Article 6 entail that the public interest in the fight against crime cannot justify the use of evidence obtained as a result of police incitement... In *Teixeira de Castro* [v *Portugal*, Reports 1998-IV] the Court found that the activities of the two police officers had gone beyond that of undercover agents, in that they had not 'confined themselves to investigating the applicant's criminal activity in an essentially passive manner', but had 'exercised an influence such as to incite the commission of the offence'. Their actions had 'gone beyond those of undercover agents because they instigated the offence and there is nothing to suggest that without their intervention it would have been committed' (ibid, § 39).

In arriving at this conclusion the Court laid stress on a number of features of the case before it, particularly the facts that the intervention of the two officers had not been part of a judicially supervised operation and that the national authorities had had no good reason to suspect the applicant of prior involvement in drug trafficking: he had no criminal record and there was nothing to suggest that he had a predisposition to become involved in drug dealing until he was approached by the police (ibid, §§ 37–8).

50. Under English law, although entrapment does not constitute a substantive defence to a criminal charge, it does place the judge under a duty either to stay the proceedings as an abuse of process or

to exclude any evidence obtained by entrapment on the grounds that its admission would have such an adverse effect on the fairness of the proceedings that the court could not admit it (see *R. v Looseley* [[2001] UKHL 53], and the earlier case-law referred to therein).

51. As the applicants point out, it is impossible for this Court to determine whether or not either applicant was the victim of entrapment, contrary to Article 6, because the relevant information has not been disclosed by the prosecuting authorities. It is, therefore, essential that the Court examine the procedure whereby the plea of entrapment was determined in each case, to ensure that the rights of the defence were adequately protected ...

52. It is in any event a fundamental aspect of the right to a fair trial that criminal proceedings, including the elements of such proceedings which relate to procedure, should be adversarial and that there should be equality of arms between the prosecution and defence. The right to an adversarial trial means, in a criminal case, that both prosecution and defence must be given the opportunity to have knowledge of and comment on the observations filed and the evidence adduced by the other party ... In addition Article 6 § 1 requires that the prosecution authorities should disclose to the defence all material evidence in their possession for or against the accused ...

53. The entitlement to disclosure of relevant evidence is not, however, an absolute right. In any criminal proceedings there may be competing interests, such as national security or the need to protect witnesses at risk of reprisals or keep secret police methods of investigation of crime, which must be weighed against the rights of the accused. In some cases it may be necessary to withhold certain evidence from the defence so as to preserve the fundamental rights of another individual or to safeguard an important public interest. Nonetheless, only such measures restricting the rights of the defence which are strictly necessary are permissible under Article 6 § 1. Furthermore, in order to ensure that the accused receives a fair trial, any difficulties caused to the defence by a limitation on its rights must be sufficiently counterbalanced by the procedures followed by the judicial authorities ...

54. In cases where evidence has been withheld from the defence on public interest grounds, it is not the role of this Court to decide whether or not such non-disclosure was strictly necessary since, as a general rule, it is for the national courts to assess the evidence before them. In any event, in many cases, including the present, where the evidence in question has never been revealed, it would not be possible for the Court to attempt to weigh the public interest in non-disclosure against that of the accused in having sight of the material. It must therefore scrutinise the decision-making procedure to ensure that, as far as possible, the procedure complied with the requirements to provide adversarial proceedings and equality of arms and incorporated adequate safeguards to protect the interests of the accused ...

57. In the present case, however, it appears that the undisclosed evidence related, or may have related, to an issue of fact decided by the trial judge. Each applicant complained that he had been entrapped into committing the offence by one or more undercover police officers or informers, and asked the trial judge to consider whether prosecution evidence should be excluded for that reason. In order to conclude whether or not the accused had indeed been the victim of improper incitement by the police, it was necessary for the trial judge to examine a number of factors, including the reason for the police operation, the nature and extent of police participation in the crime and the nature of any inducement or pressure applied by the police ... Had the defence been able to persuade the judge that the police had acted improperly, the prosecution would, in effect, have had to be discontinued. The applications in question were, therefore, of determinative importance to the applicants' trials, and the public interest immunity evidence may have related to facts connected with those applications.

58. Despite this, the applicants were denied access to the evidence. It was not, therefore, possible for the defence representatives to argue the case on entrapment in full before the judge. Moreover, in each case the judge, who subsequently rejected the defence submissions on entrapment, had already seen prosecution evidence which may have been relevant to the issue. ...

59. In these circumstances, the Court does not consider that the procedure employed to determine the issues of disclosure of evidence and entrapment complied with the requirements to provide adversarial proceedings and equality of arms and incorporated adequate safeguards to protect the interests of the accused. It follows that there has been a violation of Article 6 § 1 in this case.

The unanimous judgment was another condemnation by the Court of the common law procedure governing disclosure of evidence. The Government sought a referral of the Chamber's judgment in *Edwards and Lewis* for a re-hearing by a Grand Chamber under Article 43. The latter granted permission in December 2003. However, in April 2004 the Government wrote to the Grand Chamber that:

Having now had the opportunity to give even fuller consideration to the judgment of the Chamber of the Court of 22 July 2003 and its implications, the Government have decided that they no longer wish to pursue the referral of this application to the Grand Chamber which was accepted on 3 December 2002 at the request of the Government.

In the circumstances the Government accept that it is open to the Grand Chamber to endorse the judgment of the Chamber of 22 July 2003, and confirm that they are content that the Grand Chamber should now do so.

Subsequently, the Grand Chamber, unanimously ruled that:

48. Having examined the issues raised by the case in the light of the Chamber's judgment, the Grand Chamber sees no reason to depart from the Chamber's findings. It therefore concludes that there has been a violation of Article 6 § 1, for the reasons elaborated by the Chamber.

We may speculate that the Government decided not to pursue the re-hearing because of the House of Lords's judgment, pronounced on 5 February 2004, in *R. v H. and R. v C.* [2004] UKHL 3. The House, unanimously, endorsed the appointment of special counsel to represent the interests of defendants in criminal trials where the prosecution sought non-disclosure of sensitive information to the defendants or their ordinary lawyers. But, according to their Lordships:

22. ... Such an appointment will always be exceptional, never automatic; a course of last and never first resort. It should not be ordered unless and until the trial judge is satisfied that no other course will adequately meet the overriding requirement of fairness to the defendant. ...'

Two criminal evidence scholars have observed that:

An accused who is denied access to crucial information cannot have a fair trial, either under common law or under Article 6 of the ECHR. In cases where the extreme sensitivity of the information in question is regarded as an absolutely insurmountable obstacle to its public disclosure, the prosecution's ultimate fallback option is to abandon criminal proceedings entirely. This is a distasteful outcome if it means that victims of crime are left without redress and an offender goes unpunished. But it may be the lesser of all evils, where the irresistible force of the accused's right to a fair trial meets the immovable object of public interest immunity. P. Roberts and A. Zuckerman, *Criminal Evidence* (2004) at p 241.

5   The principle of equality of arms is not only concerned with matters of court procedure but also institutional arrangements. For example, in *Borgers v Belgium*, A.214-A (1991) 15 EHRR 92, the applicant complained about the role of the avocat general in the determination of cases by the Belgian Court of Cassation. The avocat general provided advice to the court on whether a particular appeal should be allowed or dismissed and participated in the court's deliberations. The applicant's appeal against his forgery conviction was opposed by the avocat general and dismissed by the Court of Cassation. He then alleged that the functions of the avocat general violated the equality of arms principle (the Commission found a breach of

Article 6(1) by fourteen votes to one). A large majority of the Court, eighteen votes to four, also found a violation.

26. No one questions the objectivity with which the procureur général's department at the Court of Cassation discharges its functions. This is shown by the consensus which has existed in Belgium in relation to it since its inception and by its approval by Parliament on various occasions.

Nevertheless the opinion of the procureur général's department cannot be regarded as neutral from the point of view of the parties to the cassation proceedings. By recommending that an accused's appeal be allowed or dismissed, the official of the procureur général's department becomes objectively speaking his ally or his opponent. In the latter event, Article 6 para 1 (art 6-1) requires that the rights of the defence and the principle of equality of arms be respected.

27. In the present case the hearing on 18 June 1985 before the Court of Cassation concluded with the avocat général's submissions to the effect that Mr Borger's appeal should not be allowed . . . At no time could the latter reply to those submissions: before hearing them, he was unaware of their contents because they had not been communicated to him in advance; thereafter he was prevented from doing so by statute. Article 1107 of the Judicial Code prohibits even the lodging of written notes following the intervention of the member of the procureur général's department . . .

The Court cannot see the justification for such restrictions on the rights of the defence. Once the avocat général had made submissions unfavourable to the applicant, the latter had a clear interest in being able to submit his observations on them before argument was closed. The fact that the Court of Cassation's jurisdiction is confined to questions of law makes no difference in this respect.

28. Further and above all, the inequality was increased even more by the avocat général's participation, in an advisory capacity, in the Court's deliberations. Assistance of this nature, given with total objectivity, may be of some use in drafting judgments, although this task falls in the first place to the Court of Cassation itself. It is however hard to see how such assistance can remain limited to stylistic considerations, which are in any case often indissociable from substantive matters, if it is in addition intended, as the Government also affirmed, to contribute towards maintaining the consistency of the case-law. Even if such assistance was so limited in the present case, it could reasonably be thought that the deliberations afforded the avocat général an additional opportunity to promote, without fear of contradiction by the applicant, his submissions to the effect that the appeal should be dismissed.

29. In conclusion, having regard to the requirements of the rights of the defence and of the principle of the equality of arms and to the role of appearances in determining whether they have been complied with, the Court finds a violation of Article 6 para 1 (art 6-1). . . .

In the very early case of *Delcourt v Belgium*, A.11 (1970) 1 EHRR 355, the Court had upheld the independence and impartiality of the Court of Cassation and its procureur general's department. However, the Court adopted a more rigorous stance in *Borgers*, because the concept of a fair trial, ' . . . has undergone a considerable evolution in the Court's case-law, notably in respect of the importance attached to appearances and to the increased sensitivity of the public to the fair administration of justice . . .' (para 24).

6 The Court has held that the principle of equality of arms extends to civil proceedings. In *Dombo Beheer BV v Netherlands*, A.274 (1993) 18 EHRR 213, the applicant company had sued its bank after the latter had allegedly frozen Dombo's accounts. The bank disputed the company's allegations. Before the domestic courts Dombo sought to call it former managing director as a witness (he had been directly involved in the company's dealing with the bank). The bank objected to the admissibility of his evidence (under the Civil Code a person who was substantively a party to litigation could not be heard as a witness in his/her own case). The court agreed with the bank and refused to allow the former managing director to testify.

However, the bank was able to call its local bank manager to give evidence on its behalf. The Dutch courts decided in favour of the bank. Dombo then complained to the Commission alleging a breach of the equality of arms principle. By fourteen votes to five, the Commission upheld the complaint. The Court determined that:

32. The requirements inherent in the concept of 'fair hearing' are not necessarily the same in cases concerning the determination of civil rights and obligations as they are in cases concerning the determination of a criminal charge. This is borne out by the absence of detailed provisions such as paragraphs 2 and 3 of Article 6 (art 6-2, art 6-3) applying to cases of the former category. Thus, although these provisions have a certain relevance outside the strict confines of criminal law (see, *mutatis mutandis, the Albert and Le Compte v Belgium* judgment of 10 February 1983, Series A No 58, p 20, para 39), the Contracting States have greater latitude when dealing with civil cases concerning civil rights and obligations than they have when dealing with criminal cases.

33. Nevertheless, certain principles concerning the notion of a 'fair hearing' in cases concerning civil rights and obligations emerge from the Court's case-law. Most significantly for the present case, it is clear that the requirement of 'equality of arms', in the sense of a 'fair balance' between the parties, applies in principle to such cases as well as to criminal cases . . .

The Court agrees with the Commission that as regards litigation involving opposing private interests, 'equality of arms' implies that each party must be afforded a reasonable opportunity to present his case—including his evidence—under conditions that do not place him at a substantial disadvantage vis-à-vis his opponent.

It is left to the national authorities to ensure in each individual case that the requirements of a 'fair hearing' are met.

34. In the instant case, it was incumbent upon the applicant company to prove that there was an oral agreement between it and the Bank to extend certain credit facilities. Only two persons had been present at the meeting at which this agreement had allegedly been reached, namely Mr van Reijendam (the former managing director) representing the applicant company and Mr van W. representing the Bank. Yet only one of these two key persons was permitted to be heard, namely the person who had represented the Bank. The applicant company was denied the possibility of calling the person who had represented it, because the Court of Appeal identified him with the applicant company itself.

35. During the relevant negotiations Mr van Reijendam and Mr van W. acted on an equal footing, both being empowered to negotiate on behalf of their respective parties. It is therefore difficult to see why they should not both have been allowed to give evidence.

The applicant company was thus placed at a substantial disadvantage vis-à-vis the Bank and there has accordingly been a violation of Article 6 para 1 (art 6-1). . . .

Four judges dissented as they considered that the applicant company had an equal opportunity to submit its evidence (both written and oral) during the domestic proceedings. Two months after Dombo lost its final appeal before the Supreme Court, the Dutch Civil Code was amended to allow parties to give evidence as witnesses in their own cases.

7   The full-time Court has followed *Dombo Beheer*, for example in *Komanicky v Slovakia*, judgment of 4 June 2002. The applicant was involved in protracted litigation concerning his former employment. The domestic courts held several hearings at which the applicant was not present (even when he had given prior notice of his inability to attend due to ill-health). A unanimous Chamber held that:

45. The Court recalls that the principle of equality of arms—one of the elements of the broader concept of fair trial—requires that each party should be afforded a reasonable opportunity to present his or her case under conditions that do not place him or her at a substantial disadvantage *vis-à-vis* his or

her opponent (see the *Dombo Beheer B.V. v The Netherlands* judgment of 27 October 1993, Series A No 274, p. 19, § 33; *Ankerl v Switzerland* judgment of 23 October 1996, *Reports of Judgments and Decisions* 1996-V, pp 1567–8, § 38).

46. The concept of a fair hearing also implies the right to adversarial proceedings, according to which the parties must have the opportunity not only to make known any evidence needed for their claims to succeed, but also to have knowledge of, and comment on, all evidence adduced or observations filed, with a view to influencing the court's decision (see the *Nideröst-Huber v Switzerland* judgment of 18 February 1997, *Reports* 1997-I, p 108, § 24, and the *Mantovanelli v France* judgment of 18 March 1997, *Reports* 1997-II, p 436, § 33).

47. The Court's role is to ascertain whether the proceedings considered as a whole were fair as required by Article 6 § 1. In this context, importance is to be attached to the appearance of the fair administration of justice. However, it is not the Court's function to deal with errors of fact or law allegedly committed by a national court unless and in so far as they may have infringed rights and freedoms protected by the Convention. Moreover, while Article 6 of the Convention guarantees the right to a fair hearing, it does not lay down any rules on the admissibility of evidence or the way it should be assessed, which are therefore primarily matters for regulation by national law and the national courts (see, *mutatis mutandis*, the *Schenk v Switzerland* judgment of 12 July 1988, Series A No 140, p 29, § 46; the *Borgers v Belgium* judgment of 30 October 1991, Series A No 214-B, p 31, § 24 and the *Garcia Ruiz v Spain* judgment of 21 January 1999, *Reports* 1999-I, pp 98–9, § 28).

. . .

55. In these circumstances, and having regard to the requirements of the principle of the equality of arms and to the role of appearances in determining whether they have been complied with, the Court finds that the procedure followed did not enable the applicant to participate properly in the proceedings and thus deprived him of a fair hearing within the meaning of Article 6 § 1 of the Convention. In conclusion, there has been a violation of this provision.

8   A unanimous Chamber found a breach of the equality of arms principle in the well publicised case of *Steel and Morris v UK*, judgment of 15 February 2005 (often referred to as the 'McLibel' case in the British media). The applicants were two campaigners (on low income/ state benefits) who, according to the High Court, were responsible for the publication of several thousand copies of a leaflet, distributed in the UK, which made serious allegations about, *inter alia*, the health and environmental implications of eating McDonald's food and the working practices within the company. In 1990 the American and UK divisions of McDonald's brought libel proceedings against the applicants claiming £100,000 damages for the alleged defamation caused by the production and distribution of the leaflets. Civil legal aid was not available for defamation proceedings in England and the applicants had to defend themselves, with some *pro bono* assistance from various lawyers, in what became the longest trial (civil or criminal) in English legal history. The High Court proceedings involved 313 court days (with 40,000 pages of documentary evidence, 130 witnesses gave oral evidence and it was estimated that McDonald's spent over £10 million on their legal expenses/representation for the action). In June 1997, after six month's deliberation, the judge delivered his 762-page judgment finding that a number of the allegations in the leaflets were untrue and he awarded McDonald's damages of £60,000 against the applicants (McDonald's did not seek to require the applicants to pay their legal costs as they could have). The applicants appealed to the Court of Appeal and after a hearing of twenty-three days the Court of Appeal delivered its 301-page judgment in March 1999. The Court of Appeal allowed some of the applicants grounds of appeal. Before the European Court the applicants contended, *inter alia*, that the denial of legal aid to help them defend themselves from McDonald's resulted in them facing an unfair trial. The Court held that:

61. The question whether the provision of legal aid is necessary for a fair hearing must be determined on the basis of the particular facts and circumstances of each case and will depend *inter alia* upon the importance of what is at stake for the applicant in the proceedings, the complexity of the relevant law and procedure and the applicant's capacity to represent him or herself effectively ...

McDonald's were seeking substantial damages against the applicants, the case involved complex factual and legal issues and whilst the applicants were articulate and resourceful:

69. ... the disparity between the respective levels of legal assistance enjoyed by the applicants and McDonald's was of such a degree that it could not have failed, in this exceptionally demanding case, to have given rise to unfairness, despite the best efforts of the judges at first instance and on appeal.

....

72. In conclusion, therefore, the Court finds that the denial of legal aid to the applicants deprived them of the opportunity to present their case effectively before the court and contributed to an unacceptable inequality of arms with McDonald's. There has, therefore, been a violation of Article 6(1).

Whilst the above judgment maintains the approach of the original Court, that States are not obliged to establish general civil legal aid schemes under Article 6, it demonstrates that gross inequalities in the resources of parties can require the authorities to provide legal assistance for impecunious defendants in specific cases.

THE RIGHT TO SILENCE/PRIVILEGE AGAINST SELF-INCRIMINATION

John Murray v UK (1996) 22 EHRR 29
European Court of Human Rights

The applicant was arrested in a house by Northern Irish police officers at 5.40pm on 7 January 1990. He was cautioned that he did not have to say anything, but that adverse inferences might be drawn at his trial if he failed to mention any facts he later relied on as part of his defence. Almost as soon as he arrived at the police station he stated that he wished to consult a solicitor. Half an hour later, a detective superintendent authorized the delaying of the applicant's access to a solicitor for forty-eight hours under powers granted by emergency legislation. Murray was subsequently interviewed by the police on ten occasions. He did not answer any of the questions put to him. After forty-eight hours he was allowed to consult a solicitor. Afterwards he continued to refuse to reply to police questions. In May 1991, Murray was tried (before the Lord Chief Justice of Northern Ireland) on charges of, *inter alia*, conspiracy to murder and unlawful imprisonment. Murray did not give any evidence and no witnesses were called on his behalf. The prosecution alleged that Murray was one of a group of persons who had imprisoned a suspected IRA informer, they were interrogating him and planned to have him killed. Murray had been arrested in the house where the police also found the victim. The Lord Chief Justice found Murray guilty of unlawful imprisonment and in doing so drew 'very strong inferences against' his failure to explain to the police his presence in the house and give evidence in his own defence. Under the Criminal Evidence (Northern Ireland) Order 1988, a defendant could not be convicted solely on the basis of adverse inferences from silence, but trial courts could take account of such inferences in specified circumstances (e.g. where a defendant failed to explain his/her presence at a particular place). Murray was sentenced to eight years' imprisonment. He later complained to the Commission alleging that he was deprived of the right to silence in breach of Article 6(1) and that delaying his access to a solicitor violated Article 6(3). The Commission rejected the first complaint (by fifteen votes to two) and upheld the latter (by thirteen votes to four).

45. Although not specifically mentioned in Article 6 (art 6) of the Convention, there can be no doubt that the right to remain silent under police questioning and the privilege against self-incrimination are generally recognised international standards which lie at the heart of the notion of a fair procedure under Article 6 (art 6) (see the *Funke v France* judgment [A.256-A (1993)]). By providing the accused with protection against improper compulsion by the authorities these immunities contribute to avoiding miscarriages of justice and to securing the aims of Article 6 (art 6).

46. The Court does not consider that it is called upon to give an abstract analysis of the scope of these immunities and, in particular, of what constitutes in this context 'improper compulsion'. What is at stake in the present case is whether these immunities are absolute in the sense that the exercise by an accused of the right to silence cannot under any circumstances be used against him at trial or, alternatively, whether informing him in advance that, under certain conditions, his silence may be so used, is always to be regarded as 'improper compulsion'.

47. On the one hand, it is self-evident that it is incompatible with the immunities under consideration to base a conviction solely or mainly on the accused's silence or on a refusal to answer questions or to give evidence himself. On the other hand, the Court deems it equally obvious that these immunities cannot and should not prevent that the accused's silence, in situations which clearly call for an explanation from him, be taken into account in assessing the persuasiveness of the evidence adduced by the prosecution.

Wherever the line between these two extremes is to be drawn, it follows from this understanding of 'the right to silence' that the question whether the right is absolute must be answered in the negative.

It cannot be said therefore that an accused's decision to remain silent throughout criminal proceedings should necessarily have no implications when the trial court seeks to evaluate the evidence against him. In particular, as the Government have pointed out, established international standards in this area, while providing for the right to silence and the privilege against self-incrimination, are silent on this point.

Whether the drawing of adverse inferences from an accused's silence infringes Article 6 (art 6) is a matter to be determined in the light of all the circumstances of the case, having particular regard to the situations where inferences may be drawn, the weight attached to them by the national courts in their assessment of the evidence and the degree of compulsion inherent in the situation.

48. As regards the degree of compulsion involved in the present case, it is recalled that the applicant was in fact able to remain silent. Notwithstanding the repeated warnings as to the possibility that inferences might be drawn from his silence, he did not make any statements to the police and did not give evidence during his trial. Moreover under Article 4 (5) of the Order he remained a non-compellable witness . . . Thus his insistence in maintaining silence throughout the proceedings did not amount to a criminal offence or contempt of court. Furthermore, as has been stressed in national court decisions, silence, in itself, cannot be regarded as an indication of guilt . . .

49. The facts of the present case accordingly fall to be distinguished from those in *Funke* . . . where criminal proceedings were brought against the applicant by the customs authorities in an attempt to compel him to provide evidence of offences he had allegedly committed. Such a degree of compulsion in that case was found by the Court to be incompatible with Article 6 (art 6) since, in effect, it destroyed the very essence of the privilege against self-incrimination.

50. Admittedly a system which warns the accused—who is possibly without legal assistance (as in the applicant's case)—that adverse inferences may be drawn from a refusal to provide an explanation to

the police for his presence at the scene of a crime or to testify during his trial, when taken in conjunction with the weight of the case against him, involves a certain level of indirect compulsion. However, since the applicant could not be compelled to speak or to testify, as indicated above, this factor on its own cannot be decisive. The Court must rather concentrate its attention on the role played by the inferences in the proceedings against the applicant and especially in his conviction.

51. In this context, it is recalled that these were proceedings without a jury, the trier of fact being an experienced judge. Furthermore, the drawing of inferences under the Order is subject to an important series of safeguards designed to respect the rights of the defence and to limit the extent to which reliance can be placed on inferences.

In the first place, before inferences can be drawn under Article 4 and 6 of the Order appropriate warnings must have been given to the accused as to the legal effects of maintaining silence. . . . The question in each particular case is whether the evidence adduced by the prosecution is sufficiently strong to require an answer. The national court cannot conclude that the accused is guilty merely because he chooses to remain silent. It is only if the evidence against the accused 'calls' for an explanation which the accused ought to be in a position to give that a failure to give any explanation 'may as a matter of common sense allow the drawing of an inference that there is no explanation and that the accused is guilty'. Conversely if the case presented by the prosecution had so little evidential value that it called for no answer, a failure to provide one could not justify an inference of guilt . . . In sum, it is only common-sense inferences which the judge considers proper, in the light of the evidence against the accused, that can be drawn under the Order.

In addition, the trial judge has a discretion whether, on the facts of the particular case, an inference should be drawn. As indicated by the Court of Appeal in the present case, if a judge accepted that an accused did not understand the warning given or if he had doubts about it, 'we are confident that he would not activate Article 6 against him' . . . Furthermore in Northern Ireland, where trial judges sit without a jury, the judge must explain the reasons for the decision to draw inferences and the weight attached to them. The exercise of discretion in this regard is subject to review by the appellate courts.

52. In the present case, the evidence presented against the applicant by the prosecution was considered by the Court of Appeal to constitute a 'formidable' case against him . . . It is recalled that when the police entered the house some appreciable time after they knocked on the door, they found the applicant coming down the flight of stairs in the house where Mr L had been held captive by the IRA. Evidence had been given by Mr L—evidence which in the opinion of the trial judge had been corroborated—that he had been forced to make a taped confession and that after the arrival of the police at the house and the removal of his blindfold he saw the applicant at the top of the stairs. He had been told by him to go downstairs and watch television. The applicant was pulling a tape out of a cassette. The tangled tape and cassette recorder were later found on the premises. Evidence by the applicant's co-accused that he had recently arrived at the house was discounted as not being credible . . .

53. The trial judge drew strong inferences against the applicant under Article 6 of the Order by reason of his failure to give an account of his presence in the house when arrested and interrogated by the police. He also drew strong inferences under Article 4 of the Order by reason of the applicant's refusal to give evidence in his own defence when asked by the court to do so . . .

54. In the Court's view, having regard to the weight of the evidence against the applicant, as outlined above, the drawing of inferences from his refusal, at arrest, during police questioning and at trial, to provide an explanation for his presence in the house was a matter of common sense and cannot be regarded as unfair or unreasonable in the circumstances

57. Against the above background, and taking into account the role played by inferences under the Order during the trial and their impact on the rights of the defence, the Court does not consider that the criminal proceedings were unfair or that there had been an infringement of the presumption of innocence . . .

58. Accordingly, there has been no violation of Article 6 paras 1 and 2 (art 6-1, art 6-2) of the Convention.

B. ACCESS TO LAWYER

59. The applicant submitted that he was denied access to a lawyer at a critical stage of the criminal proceedings against him. He pointed out that in Northern Ireland the initial phase of detention is of crucial importance in the context of the criminal proceedings as a whole because of the possibility of inferences being drawn under Articles 3, 4 and 6 of the Order. . . .

62. The Court observes that it has not been disputed by the Government that Article 6 (art 6) applies even at the stage of the preliminary investigation into an offence by the police. In this respect it recalls its finding in the *Imbrioscia v Switzerland* judgment of 24 November 1993 that Article 6 (art 6)—especially paragraph 3 (art 6-3)—may be relevant before a case is sent for trial if and so far as the fairness of the trial is likely to be seriously prejudiced by an initial failure to comply with its provisions (art 6-3) (Series A No 275, p 13, para 36). As it pointed out in that judgment, the manner in which Article 6 para 3 (c) (art 6-3-c) is to be applied during the preliminary investigation depends on the special features of the proceedings involved and on the circumstances of the case (loc cit, p 14, para 38).

63. National laws may attach consequences to the attitude of an accused at the initial stages of police interrogation which are decisive for the prospects of the defence in any subsequent criminal proceedings. In such circumstances Article 6 (art 6) will normally require that the accused be allowed to benefit from the assistance of a lawyer already at the initial stages of police interrogation. However, this right, which is not explicitly set out in the Convention, may be subject to restrictions for good cause. The question, in each case, is whether the restriction, in the light of the entirety of the proceedings, has deprived the accused of a fair hearing.

64. In the present case, the applicant's right of access to a lawyer during the first 48 hours of police detention was restricted under section 15 of the Northern Ireland (Emergency Provisions) Act 1987 on the basis that the police had reasonable grounds to believe that the exercise of the right of access would, inter alia, interfere with the gathering of information about the commission of acts of terrorism or make it more difficult to prevent such an act. . . .

66. The Court is of the opinion that the scheme contained in the Order is such that it is of paramount importance for the rights of the defence that an accused has access to a lawyer at the initial stages of police interrogation. It observes in this context that, under the Order, at the beginning of police interrogation, an accused is confronted with a fundamental dilemma relating to his defence. If he chooses to remain silent, adverse inferences may be drawn against him in accordance with the provisions of the Order. On the other hand, if the accused opts to break his silence during the course of interrogation, he runs the risk of prejudicing his defence without necessarily removing the possibility of inferences being drawn against him.

Under such conditions the concept of fairness enshrined in Article 6 (art 6) requires that the accused has the benefit of the assistance of a lawyer already at the initial stages of police interrogation. To deny access to a lawyer for the first 48 hours of police questioning, in a situation where the rights of the defence may well be irretrievably prejudiced, is—whatever the justification for such denial—incompatible with the rights of the accused under Article 6 (art 6) . . . .

70. There has therefore been a breach of Article 6 para 1 in conjunction with paragraph 3 (c) (art 6-1 art 6-3-c) of the Convention as regards the applicant's denial of access to a lawyer during the first 48 hours of his police detention.

FOR THESE REASONS, THE COURT

Holds by fourteen votes to five that there has been no violation of Article 6(1) and (2) of the Convention arising out of the drawing of adverse inferences on account of the applicant's silence;

Holds by twelve votes to seven that there has been a violation of Article 6(1) in conjunction with 6(3)(c) as regards the applicant's lack of access to a lawyer during the first 48 hours of his police detention; . . .

NOTES

1 The Court was composed of Judges: Bernhardt, Pettiti, Walsh, Valticos, Martens, Pekkanen, Loizou, Bigi, Lopes Rocha, Makarczyk, Gotchev, and Lohmus. President Ryssdal and Judges: Matscher, Palm, Foighel, Freeland, Wildhaber, and Jungwiert issued a Joint Partly Dissenting Opinion in which they expressed the view that in the context of the terrorist situation prevailing in Northern Ireland during the 1990s it was not unreasonable for senior police officers to possess a statutory power to delay arrested terrorist suspects access to a lawyer for not more than forty-eight hours.

2 The Court's judgment in *Murray* reflects a deft balancing exercise. Adverse inferences can in certain circumstances (relevant factors are elaborated in paragraph 47) be drawn in respect of a suspect/defendant's silence. However, where national law allows such inferences to be drawn in regard to a suspect's refusal to answer police questions then there is a corresponding implied right for suspects to have access to a lawyer (paragraph 63).

3 The Court first recognised the implied right to silence/privilege against self-incrimination in *Funke v France*, A.256-A (1993) 16 EHRR 297. French courts had ordered Mr Funke to produce foreign bank account details to the customs authorities (they suspected him of unlawful foreign financial dealings) and imposed a daily fine of 50 Francs payable by him until he delivered the documents to the authorities. By eight votes to one, the Court found a breach of Article 6(1).

44. The Court notes that the customs secured Mr Funke's conviction in order to obtain certain documents which they believed must exist, although they were not certain of the fact. Being unable or unwilling to procure them by some other means, they attempted to compel the applicant himself to provide the evidence of offences he had allegedly committed. The special features of customs law . . . cannot justify such an infringement of the right of anyone 'charged with a criminal offence', within the autonomous meaning of this expression in Article 6, to remain silent and not to contribute to incriminating himself.

It is interesting to observe that the Court in *Funke* provided no clear justification for recognizing these implicit rights/privileges. But in *Murray* the Court was more forthcoming (see paragraph 45) about the origins and objectives of these implied safeguards.

4 In the later case of *Saunders v UK* (1996) 23 EHRR 313, 1996-VI, the Court referred to the 'right' not to incriminate oneself and elaborated the purposes served by this provision. The applicant had been the chief executive of Guinness plc during its contentious take-over of another drinks company (Distillers Company plc). Rumours of misconduct during the take-over led the Secretary of State for Trade and Industry to appoint inspectors to investigate the affair. The inspectors had statutory powers to require witnesses to answer their questions. The applicant, accompanied by his lawyers, was interviewed by the inspectors on nine occasions. Subsequently he was charged with a number of financial crimes. During his trial the prosecution read out extracts of the applicant's answers to the inspectors' questions. The jury convicted him of twelve counts of conspiracy, false accounting and theft. He was sentenced to five years' imprisonment. The Commission upheld his complaint under Article 6(1), by fourteen votes to one. Likewise the Court, by sixteen votes to four, determined that there was a violation of that provision.

68. The Court recalls that, although not specifically mentioned in Article 6 of the Convention (art 6), the right to silence and the right not to incriminate oneself are generally recognised international standards which lie at the heart of the notion of a fair procedure under Article 6 (art 6). Their rationale lies, inter alia, in the protection of the accused against improper compulsion by the authorities thereby contributing to the avoidance of miscarriages of justice and to the fulfilment of the aims of Article 6 (art 6) (see the . . . *John Murray* judgment, p 49, para 45, and the . . . *Funke* judgment, p 22, para 44). The right not to incriminate oneself, in particular, presupposes that the prosecution in a criminal case seek to prove their case against the accused without resort to evidence obtained through methods of coercion or oppression in defiance of the will of the accused. In this sense the right is closely linked to the presumption of innocence contained in Article 6 para 2 of the Convention (art 6-2).

69. The right not to incriminate oneself is primarily concerned, however, with respecting the will of an accused person to remain silent. As commonly understood in the legal systems of the Contracting Parties to the Convention and elsewhere, it does not extend to the use in criminal proceedings of material which may be obtained from the accused through the use of compulsory powers but which has an existence independent of the will of the suspect such as, inter alia, documents acquired pursuant to a warrant, breath, blood and urine samples and bodily tissue for the purpose of DNA testing.

In the present case the Court is only called upon to decide whether the use made by the prosecution of the statements obtained from the applicant by the inspectors amounted to an unjustifiable infringement of the right. This question must be examined by the Court in the light of all the circumstances of the case. In particular, it must be determined whether the applicant has been subject to compulsion to give evidence and whether the use made of the resulting testimony at his trial offended the basic principles of a fair procedure inherent in Article 6 para 1 (art 6-1) of which the right not to incriminate oneself is a constituent element.

70. It has not been disputed by the Government that the applicant was subject to legal compulsion to give evidence to the inspectors. He was obliged under sections 434 and 436 of the Companies Act 1985 . . . to answer the questions put to him by the inspectors in the course of nine lengthy interviews of which seven were admissible as evidence at his trial. A refusal by the applicant to answer the questions put to him could have led to a finding of contempt of court and the imposition of a fine or committal to prison for up to two years . . . and it was no defence to such refusal that the questions were of an incriminating nature . . .

However, the Government have emphasised, before the Court, that nothing said by the applicant in the course of the interviews was self-incriminating and that he had merely given exculpatory answers or answers which, if true, would serve to confirm his defence. In their submission only statements which are self-incriminating could fall within the privilege against self-incrimination.

71. The Court does not accept the Government's premise on this point since some of the applicant's answers were in fact of an incriminating nature in the sense that they contained admissions to knowledge of information which tended to incriminate him . . . In any event, bearing in mind the concept of fairness in Article 6 (art 6), the right not to incriminate oneself cannot reasonably be confined to statements of admission of wrongdoing or to remarks which are directly incriminating. Testimony obtained under compulsion which appears on its face to be of a non-incriminating nature—such as exculpatory remarks or mere information on questions of fact—may later be deployed in criminal proceedings in support of the prosecution case, for example to contradict or cast doubt upon other statements of the accused or evidence given by him during the trial or to otherwise undermine his credibility. Where the credibility of an accused must be assessed by a jury the use of such testimony may be especially harmful. It follows that what is of the essence in this context is the use to which evidence obtained under compulsion is put in the course of the criminal trial.

72. In this regard, the Court observes that part of the transcript of answers given by the applicant was read to the jury by counsel for the prosecution over a three-day period despite objections by the applicant. The fact that such extensive use was made of the interviews strongly suggests that the

prosecution must have believed that the reading of the transcripts assisted their case in establishing the applicant's dishonesty. This interpretation of the intended impact of the material is supported by the remarks made by the trial judge in the course of the voir dire concerning the eighth and ninth interviews to the effect that each of the applicant's statements was capable of being a 'confession' for the purposes of section 82(1) of the Police and Criminal Evidence Act 1984 . . . Similarly, the Court of Appeal considered that the interviews formed 'a significant part' of the prosecution's case against the applicant . . . Moreover, there were clearly instances where the statements were used by the prosecution to incriminating effect in order to establish the applicant's knowledge of payments to persons involved in the share-support operation and to call into question his honesty . . . They were also used by counsel for the applicant's co-accused to cast doubt on the applicant's version of events . . .

In sum, the evidence available to the Court supports the claim that the transcripts of the applicant's answers, whether directly self-incriminating or not, were used in the course of the proceedings in a manner which sought to incriminate the applicant. . . .

74. Nor does the Court find it necessary, having regard to the above assessment as to the use of the interviews during the trial, to decide whether the right not to incriminate oneself is absolute or whether infringements of it may be justified in particular circumstances.

It does not accept the Government's argument that the complexity of corporate fraud and the vital public interest in the investigation of such fraud and the punishment of those responsible could justify such a marked departure as that which occurred in the present case from one of the basic principles of a fair procedure. Like the Commission, it considers that the general requirements of fairness contained in Article 6 (art 6), including the right not to incriminate oneself, apply to criminal proceedings in respect of all types of criminal offences without distinction from the most simple to the most complex. The public interest cannot be invoked to justify the use of answers compulsorily obtained in a non-judicial investigation to incriminate the accused during the trial proceedings. It is noteworthy in this respect that under the relevant legislation statements obtained under compulsory powers by the Serious Fraud Office cannot, as a general rule, be adduced in evidence at the subsequent trial of the person concerned. Moreover the fact that statements were made by the applicant prior to his being charged does not prevent their later use in criminal proceedings from constituting an infringement of the right.

75. It follows from the above analysis and from the fact that section 434(5) of the Companies Act 1985 authorises, as noted by both the trial judge and the Court of Appeal, the subsequent use in criminal proceedings of statements obtained by the inspectors that the various procedural safeguards to which reference has been made by the respondent Government . . . cannot provide a defence in the present case since they did not operate to prevent the use of the statements in the subsequent criminal proceedings.

76. Accordingly, there has been an infringement in the present case of the right not to incriminate oneself.

Mr Saunders was controversially given early release from prison, on the grounds of ill-health, and subsequently resumed working in the world of business. In September 2000 three of Saunders' co-defendants successfully argued that the prosecution's use of statements, which they had been compelled to give to the DTI inspectors, violated their right to a fair trial: *IJL, GMR and AKP v UK*, (19/9/2000). The applicants were identified by *The Times* (20 September 2000) as Jack Lyons, Gerald Ronson, and Anthony Parnes. The applicants were businessmen whom the prosecution alleged had engaged in an illegal share support operation designed to help Guinness acquire Distillers. In the light of the Court's earlier ruling in *Saunders*, the British Government conceded that the prosecution's use of the statements violated Article 6(1). The Court rejected the applicants' other complaints. Significantly, the Court did not award the applicants any compensation for pecuniary or non-pecuniary damage. Under Schedule 3 of the Youth Justice and Criminal Evidence Act 1999, which came into effect during April 2000, the prosecution are generally prohibited from using statements obtained from defendants under compulsory powers in the field of company and business inquiries.

5 A unanimous Court found a breach of the right to silence where an English judge failed to direct a jury to exercise sufficient caution when drawing adverse inferences from the silence of two suspects, who were undergoing heroin withdrawal symptoms, while being questioned by the police. The husband and wife applicants in *Condron v UK* (2 May 2000), were suspected of aiding a neighbour in the supply of unlawful drugs (police videos showed them passing suspicious items between their adjoining flats). The applicants were arrested and sixteen 'wraps' (individual sachets) of heroin were found in their flat. Several hours later when the police proposed to interview the applicants, at the police station, their solicitor formed the view that because the applicants were undergoing the effects of drug withdrawal (they were both heroin addicts) they were unfit to be questioned. However, the force's doctor examined the applicants and determined that they were fit to be questioned. Each of the applicants was cautioned by the police that 'you do not have to say anything but it may harm your defence if you do not mention when questioned something which you later rely on in court. ...' The police also advised them that if they felt unwell during the interviews they could ask for them to be stopped. Their solicitor was present throughout the separate interviews of each applicant. Both applicants replied 'no comment' when asked about their activities with their neighbour. They were tried on charges of possession and supply of heroin. The applicants gave evidence at their trial that the heroin in the flat was for their own consumption and they had not helped their neighbour supply drugs. They stated that they had not answered the police questions because their solicitor had advised them that they were not fit to do so. The judge directed the jury that under the Criminal Justice and Public Order Act 1994: 'The law is ... that you may draw such inferences as appear proper from a defendant's failure to mention the points ... referred to in their respective interviews. ... You do not have to hold it against him or her. It is for you to decide whether it is proper to do so. Failure to mention the points in interview cannot on its own prove guilt but depending on the circumstances you may hold it against him or her when deciding whether he or she is guilty. ...' Both applicants were convicted by majority (nine to one) verdicts and sentenced to four and three years' imprisonment. Although the Court of Appeal expressed some criticism of the judge's direction it upheld the applicants' convictions. The European Court reiterated its approach to the right to silence articulated in *Murray*.

57. The Court observes that there are features of the applicants' case which distinguish it from that of the applicant John Murray. In particular, unlike John Murray, the applicants gave evidence at their trial and their case was conducted before a jury which required direction by the trial judge on how to approach the issue of their silence during police interview. Moreover, the applicants, contrary to the stance adopted by John Murray at his trial, offered an explanation at their trial for their silence at the police station. For the Court, these and other distinguishing features fall to be considered from the standpoint of 'all the circumstances of the case' ... Accordingly, the fact that the applicants' exercised their right to silence at the police station is relevant to the determination of the fairness issue. However, that fact does not of itself preclude the drawing of an adverse inference, it being observed that the principles laid down in the John Murray judgment addressed the drawing of inferences under both Articles 4 and 6 of the Criminal Evidence (Northern Ireland) Order 1988. Similarly, the fact that the issue of the applicants' silence was left to a jury cannot of itself be considered incompatible with the requirements of a fair trial. It is, rather, another relevant consideration to be weighed in the balance when assessing whether or not it was fair to do so in the circumstances. ...

60. It must also be observed that the applicants' solicitor was present throughout the whole of their interviews and was able to advise them not to volunteer any answers to the questions put to them. The

fact that an accused person who is questioned under caution is assured access to legal advice, and in the applicants' case the physical presence of a solicitor during police interview, must be considered a particularly important safeguard for dispelling any compulsion to speak which may be inherent in the terms of the caution. . . .

61. It is to be noted that the trial judge directed the jury on the issue of the applicants' silence in accordance with the terms of the relevant specimen direction at the time . . . The Court notes, however, that the formula employed by the trial judge cannot be said to reflect the balance which the Court in its John Murray judgment sought to strike between the right to silence and the circumstances in which an adverse inference may be drawn from silence, including by a jury. It reiterates that the Court stressed in that judgment that, provided appropriate safeguards were in place, an accused's silence, in situations which clearly call for an explanation, could be taken into account in assessing the persuasiveness of the evidence adduced by the prosecution against him . . . The Court further noted, with reference to Articles 4 and 6 of the Criminal Evidence (Northern Ireland) Order 1988, that those provisions only permitted a judge to draw common-sense inferences which he considered proper in the light of the evidence against the accused . . . However, in the instant case the applicants put forward an explanation for their failure to mention during the police interview why certain items were exchanged between them and their co-accused, Mr Curtis . . . They testified that they acted on the strength of the advice of their solicitor who had grave doubts about their fitness to cope with police questioning . . . Their solicitor confirmed this in his testimony in the *voir dire* proceedings . . . Admittedly the trial judge drew the jury's attention to this explanation. However he did so in terms which left the jury at liberty to draw an adverse inference notwithstanding that it may have been satisfied as to the plausibility of the explanation. It is to be observed that the Court of Appeal found the terms of the trial judge's direction deficient in this respect . . . In the Court's opinion, as a matter of fairness, the jury should have been directed that if it was satisfied that the applicants' silence at the police interview could not sensibly be attributed to their having no answer or none that would stand up to cross-examination it should not draw an adverse inference. . . .

The judgment reveals that the Court demands clear guidance be given by trial judges on the limited circumstances where it is permissible for juries to draw adverse inferences from defendants' silences. In England, the Judicial Studies Board provides guideline directions, taking account of the Court of Appeal's evolving case law on the 1994 Act, for judges to use when juries may have to consider a particular defendant's silence.

6   The full-time Court, unanimously, rejected the Government's defence that the fight against Irish terrorism justified compelling arrested persons to explain their conduct during a specified period of time in *Heaney and McGuinness v Ireland*, judgment of 21 December 2000. The applicants had been arrested in connection with a nearby bombing of a checkpoint on the border with Northern Ireland at which a number of persons had been killed. The applicants refused to answer police questions whereupon the latter invoked section 52 of the Offences Against the State Act 1939 (which provided that if detainees held under the Act refused to account for their movements and actions during a specified timeframe they were guilty of an offence punishable with up to six months' imprisonment). The applicants failed to provide the required information and were subsequently convicted and sentenced to the maximum term of imprisonment. In response to the applicants' contention that they had suffered an infringement of their right to silence under Article 6(1) the Government submitted that section 52 was a proportionate response to the continuing threat from terrorism. However, the Court held that:

55. . . . the 'degree of compulsion', imposed on the applicants by s.52 of the 1939 Act with a view to compelling them under that Act, in effect, destroyed the very essence of their privilege against self-incrimination and their right to remain silent.

. . .

58. The Court, accordingly, finds that the security and public order concerns of the Government cannot justify a provision which extinguishes the very essence of the applicants' right to silence and against self-incrimination guaranteed by Article 6(1) of the Convention.

59. It concludes therefore that there has been a violation of the applicants' right to silence and their right not to incriminate themselves guaranteed by Article 6(1) of the Convention.

The above case can be distinguished from *John Murray* because in the former the applicants had been convicted and punished for remaining silent as opposed to having adverse inferences drawn from their silence in respect of a specific substantive crime.

7   A Chamber was closely divided in respect of the conviction of the registered owner of a car for failing to provide accurate information concerning the driver of the car at a specified time/place in *Weh v Austria*, judgment of 8 April 2004. The Bregenz District Authority began criminal proceedings against unknown offenders in regard to the driver of a car, registered in the applicant's name, which allegedly exceeded the city speed limit. The Authority issued a statutory order against the applicant, as the registered owner, to disclose who had been driving the car. He replied giving a person's name and address as being 'USA/University of Texas'. The Authority then served a penal order on the applicant sentencing him to a fine of 900 ATS (with 24 hours' imprisonment in default) for supplying inaccurate information. The applicant, a lawyer, appealed to the Voralberg Independent Administrative Panel which, after a hearing, dismissed his appeal noting that the applicant's reply had been inaccurate as the University of Texas has fourteen locations in Texas. The applicant was not prosecuted for speeding. The applicant complained to the Court contending that the statutory obligation upon him to disclose the identity of the driver violated his right to remain silent/privilege against self-incrimination. A bare majority (four votes to three) of the Chamber considered that:

41. A perusal of the Court's case-law shows that there are two types of cases in which it found violations of the right to silence and the privilege against self-incrimination.

42. First, there are cases relating to the use of compulsion for the purpose of obtaining information which might incriminate the person concerned in pending or anticipated criminal proceedings against him, or -in other words- in respect of an offence with which that person has been "charged" within the autonomous meaning of Article 6 § 1 (see *Funke*, p 22, § 44; *Heaney and McGuinness*, §§ 55–9; *J.B.*, §§ 66–71).

43. Second, there are cases concerning the use of incriminating information compulsorily obtained outside the context of criminal proceedings in a subsequent criminal prosecution (*Saunders*, cited above, p 2064, § 67, *I.J.L. and Others v the United Kingdom*, No 29522/95, § 82–3, 2000-IX).

44. However, it also follows from the Court's case-law that the privilege against self-incrimination does not per se prohibit the use of compulsory powers to obtain information outside the context of criminal proceedings against the person concerned.

50. The heart of the applicant's complaint is that he was punished for failure to give information which may have incriminated him in the context of criminal proceedings for speeding. However, neither at the time when the applicant was requested to disclose the driver of his car nor thereafter were these proceedings conducted against him.

51. Thus, the present case is not one concerned with the use of compulsorily obtained information in subsequent criminal proceedings (see the cases referred to above, paragraph 43).

52. Moreover, the present case differs from the group of cases in which persons, against whom criminal proceedings were pending or were at least anticipated, were compelled on pain of a penalty to give

potentially incriminating information. . . . In *Funke* and in *Heaney and McGuinnes* (both cited above) criminal proceedings were anticipated, though they had not been formally opened, at the time the respective applicants were required to give potentially incriminating information. In *Funke* the customs authorities had a specific suspicion against the applicant, in *Heaney and McGuinness* the applicants had been arrested on suspicion of terrorist offences.

53. In the present case the proceedings for speeding were conducted against unknown offenders, when the authorities requested the applicant under section 103 § 2 of the Motor Vehicles Act to disclose who had been driving his car on 5 March 1995. There were clearly no proceedings for speeding pending against the applicant and it cannot even be said that they were anticipated as the authorities did not have any element of suspicion against him.

54. There is nothing to show that the applicant was 'substantially affected' so as to consider him being 'charged' with the offence of speeding within the autonomous meaning of Article 6 § 1 (see *Heaney and McGuinness*, cited above, § 41 . . . It was merely in his capacity as the registered car owner that he was required to give information. Moreover, he was only required to state a simple fact—namely who had been the driver of his car—which is not in itself incriminating.

. . .

56. The Court reiterates that it is not called upon to pronounce on the existence or otherwise of potential violations of the Convention (see *mutatis mutandis, Soering v the United Kingdom*, judgment of 7 July 1989, Series A No 161, p 35, § 90). It considers that, in the present case, the link between the applicant's obligation under section 130 § 2 of the Motor Vehicles Act to disclose the driver of his car and possible criminal proceedings for speeding against him remains remote and hypothetical. However, without a sufficiently concrete link with these criminal proceedings the use of compulsory powers (i.e. the imposition of a fine) to obtain information does not raise an issue with regard to the applicant's right to remain silent and the privilege against self-incrimination.

57. Accordingly, there has been no violation of Article 6 § 1 of the Convention.

However, the three dissentients took a diametrically opposite view of the applicants position *vis-à-vis* the domestic authorities:

1. . . . Looking behind the appearances at the reality of the situation, criminal proceedings for speeding were with some probability contemplated against the applicant.

. . .

4. Finally, we are not convinced by the Government's argument that the registered car owner's obligation to divulge the driver was a proportionate response to the public interest in the prosecution of speeding which outweighs a car owner's interest in not being compelled to incriminate himself of having committed such an offence. The general requirements of fairness contained in Article 6 including the right not to incriminate oneself, apply to criminal proceedings in respect of all types of criminal offences without distinction from the most simple to the most complex (see *Saunders*, cited above, p 2066, § 74). It certainly should not be overlooked that the prosecution of traffic offences like speeding, though they are in themselves often of a minor nature, serves to prevent traffic accidents and thus to prevent injury and loss of life. Nevertheless, a provision like section 103 § 2 of the Motor Vehicles Act possibly obliges the registered car owner, on pain of a fine, to admit to having driven the car at the time a specific offence was committed. He will thus have to provide the prosecution with a major element of evidence, being left with limited possibilities of defence in the subsequent criminal proceedings. Seen in this light the infringement of the right to remain silent does not appear proportionate. Consequently, the vital public interest in the prosecution of traffic offences cannot in our opinion justify the departure from one of the basic principles of a fair procedure (see, *mutatis mutandis, Saunders*, cited above, § 74. relating to corporate fraud and *Heaney and McGuinness*, cited above, § 58, relating to terrorist offences).

75. In conclusion, we find that there has been a violation of the applicant's right to remain silent and his right not to incriminate himself guaranteed by Article 6 § 1 of the Convention.

The above judgments disclose profound disagreement within the Court as to the acceptability under Article 6(1) of potentially incriminating disclosure obligations upon registered car owners.

8 A large majority (11 votes to 6) of the Grand Chamber in *Jalloh v Germany* (see above p 176) considered that allowing the use at the applicant's trial of evidence (a packet of cocaine he had swallowed) obtained by the forced application of emetics to him was both an infringement of his right to a fair trial and his right not to incriminate himself.

105. As noted above, the use of evidence obtained in violation of Article 3 in criminal proceedings raises serious issues as to the fairness of such proceedings. The Court has not found in the instant case that the applicant was subjected to torture. In its view, incriminating evidence—whether in the form of a confession or real evidence—obtained as a result of acts of violence or brutality or other forms of treatment which can be characterised as torture—should never be relied on as proof of the victim's guilt, irrespective of its probative value. Any other conclusion would only serve to legitimate indirectly the sort of morally reprehensible conduct which the authors of Article 3 of the Convention sought to proscribe or, as it was so well put in the US Supreme Court's judgment in the *Rochin* [v California (342 U.S. 165 (1952)] case, to 'afford brutality the cloak of law'. It notes in this connection that Article 15 of the UN Convention against Torture and Other Cruel, Inhuman or Degrading Treatment or Punishment provides that statements which are established to have been made as a result of torture shall not be used in evidence in proceedings against the victim of torture.

106. Although the treatment to which the applicant was subjected did not attract the special stigma reserved to acts of torture, it did attain in the circumstances the minimum level of severity covered by the ambit of the Article 3 prohibition. It cannot be excluded that on the facts of a particular case the use of evidence obtained by intentional acts of ill-treatment not amounting to torture will render the trial against the victim unfair irrespective of the seriousness of the offence allegedly committed, the weight attached to the evidence and the opportunities which the victim had to challenge its admission and use at his trial.

107. In the present case, the general question whether the use of evidence obtained by an act qualified as inhuman and degrading treatment automatically renders a trial unfair can be left open. The Court notes that, even if it was not the intention of the authorities to inflict pain and suffering on the applicant, the evidence was obtained by a measure which breached one of the core rights guaranteed by the Convention. Furthermore, it was common ground between the parties that the drugs obtained by the impugned measure were the decisive element in securing the applicant's conviction. It is true that, as was equally uncontested, the applicant was given the opportunity, which he took, of challenging the use of the drugs obtained by the impugned measure. However, any discretion on the part of the national courts to exclude that evidence could not come into play as they considered the administration of emetics to be authorised by the domestic law. Moreover, the public interest in securing the applicant's conviction cannot be considered to have been of such weight as to warrant allowing that evidence to be used at the trial. As noted above, the measure targeted a street dealer selling drugs on a relatively small scale who was finally given a six months' suspended prison sentence and probation.

108. In these circumstances, the Court finds that the use in evidence of the drugs obtained by the forcible administration of emetics to the applicant rendered his trial as a whole unfair.

Regarding the principle against self-incrimination the majority considered that the extent of force used on the applicant '118 .... significantly interfered with his physical and mental integrity.' He was only suspected of small scale drugs dealing and the evidence obtained by the use of emetics was decisive in securing his conviction. Therefore, the obtaining of this evidence could be distinguished from the permissible compulsory acquisition of blood *etc* samples mentioned in para 69 of *Saunders* (above). As we have discovered in respect of the Article 3 aspect of *Jalloh*, the forcible use of emetics to obtain physical evidence from inside the bodies of suspects in some regions of Germany was contrary to the practice of the overwhelming majority of Member States.

THE RIGHT OF DEFENDANTS TO PARTICIPATE EFFECTIVELY IN THEIR CRIMINAL TRIALS

V v UK (1999) 30 EHRR 121
European Court of Human Rights

The background to this case has already been explained (above, at p 179). One of the applicant's complaints was that he had not received a fair trial. The Commission, by fifteen votes to four, agreed that there had been a breach of Article 6(1).

85. The Court notes that Article 6, read as a whole, guarantees the right of an accused to participate effectively in his criminal trial (see the *Stanford judgment* [*Stanford v UK*, A.282-A (1994)]). It has not until the present time been called upon to consider how this Article 6 § 1 guarantee applies to criminal proceedings against children, and in particular whether procedures which are generally considered to safeguard the rights of adults on trial, such as publicity, should be abrogated in respect of children in order to promote their understanding and participation . . .

86. The Court recalls its above findings that there is not at this stage any clear common standard among the member States of the Council of Europe as to the minimum age of criminal responsibility and that the attribution of criminal responsibility to the applicant does not in itself give rise to a breach of Article 3 of the Convention . . . Likewise, it cannot be said that the trial on criminal charges of a child, even one as young as eleven, as such violates the fair trial guarantee under Article 6 § 1. The Court does, however, agree with the Commission that it is essential that a child charged with an offence is dealt with in a manner which takes full account of his age, level of maturity and intellectual and emotional capacities, and that steps are taken to promote his ability to understand and participate in the proceedings.

87. It follows that, in respect of a young child charged with a grave offence attracting high levels of media and public interest, it would be necessary to conduct the hearing in such a way as to reduce as far as possible his or her feelings of intimidation and inhibition. In this connection it is noteworthy that in England and Wales children charged with less serious crimes are dealt with in special Youth Courts, from which the general public is excluded and in relation to which there are imposed automatic reporting restrictions on the media . . . Moreover, the Court has already referred to the international tendency towards the protection of the privacy of child defendants . . . It has considered carefully the Government's argument that public trials serve the general interest in the open administration of justice . . . and observes that, where appropriate in view of the age and other characteristics of the child and the circumstances surrounding the criminal proceedings, this general interest could be satisfied by a modified procedure providing for selected attendance rights and judicious reporting.

88. The Court notes that the applicant's trial took place over three weeks in public in the Crown Court. Special measures were taken in view of the applicant's young age and to promote his understanding of the proceedings: for example, he had the trial procedure explained to him and was taken to see the courtroom in advance, and the hearing times were shortened so as not to tire the defendants excessively. Nonetheless, the formality and ritual of the Crown Court must at times have seemed incomprehensible and intimidating for a child of eleven, and there is evidence that certain of the modifications to the courtroom, in particular the raised dock which was designed to enable the defendants to see what

was going on, had the effect of increasing the applicant's sense of discomfort during the trial, since he felt exposed to the scrutiny of the press and public. The trial generated extremely high levels of press and public interest, both inside and outside the courtroom, to the extent that the judge in his summing-up referred to the problems caused to witnesses by the blaze of publicity and asked the jury to take this into account when assessing their evidence.

89. There is considerable psychiatric evidence relating to the applicant's ability to participate in the proceedings. Thus, Dr Susan Bailey (a consultant psychiatrist from the Adolescent Forensic Service of the Home Office) gave evidence during the trial in November 1993 that on each occasion when she had seen the applicant prior to the trial he had cried inconsolably and had not been able to talk about the circumstances of the offence in any useful way... Dr Bentovim (a defence expert from the Great Ormond Street Hospital for Children) similarly found in his report of September 1993 that the applicant was suffering from post-traumatic effects and found it very difficult and distressing to think or talk about the events in question, making it impossible to ascertain many aspects... Subsequent to the trial, in January 1995, the applicant told Dr Bentovim that he had been terrified of being looked at in court and had frequently found himself worrying what people were thinking about him. He had not been able to pay attention to the proceedings and had spent time counting in his head or making shapes with his shoes. Dr Bentovim considered that, in view of V.'s immaturity, it was 'very doubtful' that he understood the situation and was able to give informed instruction to his lawyers... The report of Dr Bailey dated November 1997 also described the applicant's attempts to distract himself during the trial, his inability to listen to what was said and the distress caused to him by the public nature of the proceedings...

90. In such circumstances the Court does not consider that it was sufficient for the purposes of Article 6 § 1 that the applicant was represented by skilled and experienced lawyers. This case is different from that of *Stanford*... where the Court found no violation arising from the fact that the accused could not hear some of the evidence given at trial, in view of the fact that his counsel, who could hear all that was said and was able to take his client's instructions at all times, chose for tactical reasons not to request that the accused be seated closer to the witnesses. Here, although the applicant's legal representatives were seated, as the Government put it, 'within whispering distance', it is highly unlikely that the applicant would have felt sufficiently uninhibited, in the tense courtroom and under public scrutiny, to have consulted with them during the trial or, indeed, that, given his immaturity and his disturbed emotional state, he would have been capable outside the courtroom of cooperating with his lawyers and giving them information for the purposes of his defence.

91. In conclusion, the Court considers that the applicant was unable to participate effectively in the criminal proceedings against him and was, in consequence, denied a fair hearing in breach of Article 6 § 1.

NOTES

1   The Court was composed of President Wildhaber and Judges: Palm, Rozakis, Pastor Ridruejo, Ress, Makarczyk, Kuris, Turmen, Costa, Tulkens, Birsan, Lorenzen, Fischbach, Butkevych, Casadevall and Reed. Judge Baka dissented because in his opinion the authorities had sufficiently adapted the ordinary court proceedings to take account of the applicant's young age.

2   The changes in the institutional arrangements and procedures for dealing with subsequent trials of juvenile defendants facing serious criminal charges have been outlined during our previous examination of the Article 3 aspects of this case. The modified process was found by a Chamber, five votes to two, not to satisfy the right to participate effectively of an 11-year-old with a limited intellectual capacity in *S.C. v UK*, judgment of 15 June 2004. The applicant, with a 14-year-old accomplice, attempted to snatch the bag of an elderly woman causing her

to fracture her arm. He was charged with attempted robbery. Having regard to his previous criminal history (including robbery, burglary, and arson) the Youth Court committed him for trial at the Crown Court. Two expert reports were commissioned and one found that he was capable of entering a pleas whilst another determined that he had a significant degree of learning difficulty (with cognitive abilities of a 6- to 8-year-old). The judge ruled that he should stand trial in the Crown Court adopting an informal procedure (S.C. did not sit in the dock and was accompanied by his social worker, wigs and gowns were dispensed with and frequent breaks were taken by the court). The trial lasted one day and the applicant gave evidence (he was legally represented). He was convicted and sentenced to two and a half year's detention. The Chamber held that:

29. The Court accepts the Government's argument that Article 6 § 1 does not require that a child on trial for a criminal offence should understand or be capable of understanding every point of law or evidential detail. Given the sophistication of modern legal systems, many adults of normal intelligence are unable fully to comprehend all the intricacies and exchanges which take place in the courtroom: this is why the Convention, in Article 6 § 3(c), emphasises the importance of the right to legal representation. However, 'effective participation' in this context presupposes that the accused has a broad understanding of the nature of the trial process and of what is at stake for him or her, including the significance of any penalty which may be imposed. It means that he or she, if necessary with the assistance of, for example, an interpreter, lawyer, social worker or friend, should be able to understand the general thrust of what is said in court. The defendant should be able to follow what is said by the prosecution witnesses and, if represented, to explain to his own lawyers his version of events, point out any statements with which he disagrees and make them aware of any facts which should be put forward in his defence . . .

35. The Court considers that, when the decision is taken to deal with a child, such as the applicant, who risks not being able to participate effectively because of his young age and limited intellectual capacity, by way of criminal proceedings rather than some other form of disposal directed primarily at determining the child's best interests and those of the community, it is essential that he be tried in a specialist tribunal which is able to give full consideration to and make proper allowance for the handicaps under which he labours, and adapt its procedure accordingly.

36. . . . Dr Brennan found that, 'on balance', the applicant probably did have sufficient intelligence to understand that what he had done was wrong, and that he was therefore fit to plead. The Court is not, however, convinced, in the circumstances of the present case, that it follows that the applicant was capable of participating effectively in his trial to the extent required by Article 6(1).

37. There has therefore been a violation of that provision.

Judges Pellonpaa and Bratza dissented as they believed that sufficient precautions had been taken to accommodate the applicant's youth and mental development. Whilst S.C.'s trial had not been accompanied by any of the media interest or public outrage present in V.'s, the very low intellectual development of the former was the decisive factor for the majority in concluding that S.C. had not been accorded a trial process in which he was able to participate effectively. Is it realistic to expect that young children/juveniles can participate effectively as defendants in trials held by the ordinary criminal courts?

3 In the earlier case of *Stanford v UK*, A.282-A (1994), the Court articulated its understanding of the basis and scope of this implied right in the following terms:

Nor is it in dispute that Article 6, read as whole, guarantees the right of an accused to participate effectively in a criminal trial. In general this includes, inter alia, not only his right to be present but also, to hear and follow the proceedings. Such rights are implicit in the very notion of an adversarial procedure and can also be derived from the guarantees contained in sub-paragraphs (c), (d) and (e) of paragraph 3 of Article 6 . . . (para 26)

Stanford had been tried at Norwich Crown Court in respect of a number of serious sexual and violent crimes. During his trial he sat in a glass-fronted dock and he was unable to hear all the witnesses' testimony. He complained about the poor acoustics to his solicitor and counsel but, for tactical reasons, they did not pass his concern on to the trial judge. Stanford was convicted of rape, kidnapping and making threats to kill for which he was sentenced to a total of ten years' imprisonment. The Court was unanimous in finding no breach of Article 6 because, *inter alia*, he was represented by experienced counsel who heard all the testimony and was able to discuss it with him and expert reports indicated that the glass screen only caused a minimal loss of sound in the courtroom. The practical significance of the judgment was that the increasing need for more elaborate security features in domestic criminal courtrooms would not be allowed by the Court to undermine defendants' basic right of participation either personally or via their lawyers.

Overall assessment

When determining if there has been a breach of the right to a fair hearing the Court makes an evaluation of the fairness of the entire domestic proceedings. For example, in *Barberà, Messegué and Jabardo v Spain*, A.146 (1988) 11 EHRR 360, the applicants made a number of complaints about the trial that led to their conviction and imprisonment for involvement in a terrorist murder. The Court determined that:

89. Having regard to the belated transfer of the applicants from Barcelona to Madrid, the unexpected change in the court's membership immediately before the hearing opened, the brevity of the trial and, above all, the fact that very important pieces of evidence were not adequately adduced and discussed at the trial in the applicants' presence and under the watchful eye of the public, the Court concludes that proceedings in question, taken as a whole, did not satisfy the requirements of a fair and public hearing. Consequently, there was a violation of Article 6(1).

This approach also enables the Court to consider whether defects in first instance proceedings have been rectified by subsequent appellate hearings. In *Edwards v UK*, A.247-B (1992) 15 EHRR 417, the applicant had been convicted at Sheffield Crown Court of robbery and burglary. Subsequently, Edwards complained to the Home Secretary about the conduct of the police investigation into those crimes. The Home Secretary referred Edwards' case back to the Court of Appeal. The latter found that police officers testifying at Edward's trial had not stated that another person's (the neighbour's) fingerprints had been found at the crime scene, however the applicant's conviction was not 'unsafe or unsatisfactory'. Edwards then alleged a breach of Article 6 before the Strasbourg authorities. The Court found no violation because, '. . . the defects of the original trial were remedied by the subsequent procedure before the Court of Appeal . . .' (para 39).

4 A unanimous Chamber found a breach of this requirement in *Ziliberberg v Moldova*, judgment of 1 February 2005. The applicant, a student, had been fined by the Centru District Court for participating in an unauthorized demonstration. He appealed against that decision. However, he did not receive notification of the date/time of his appeal hearing until after it had taken place. Consequently, he was unable to attend the hearing. The appeal court considered his appeal, in his absence, and dismissed it. The Chamber found that the applicant had thereby been denied the opportunity to participate in his appeal and that constituted a breach of Article 6(1).

Public hearing

We have already examined several cases which involved this right. The Court found a breach of this provision in *Le Compte, Van Leuven and De Meyere v Belgium* (above, p 360), because the disciplinary hearings before the Provincial Council and the Appeals Council of the Belgian Medical Association were held in private. The Court noted that if the disciplinary charges had involved allegations of malpractice involving patients (rather than accusations of contempt of the Association) then it would have been appropriate to invoke the Article 6(1) exception to a public hearing for the 'protection of the private life' of the patients. Conversely, in *Campbell and Fell v UK* A.80 (1984), the Court held that the prison authorities were justified, on the grounds of 'public order and security', in excluding the press and public from the disciplinary hearings involving prisoners conducted inside prisons. We should also note that the wide access of the public and press to the trial of the juvenile defendant in *V v UK* (above, p 420), was one of the factors which led the Court to conclude that he had been unable to participate effectively in his trial.

The full-time Court revealed a far more protective attitude, than its predecessor, towards the right to public hearings of prisoners facing criminal charges in *Riepan v Austria*, judgment of 14 February 2001. The applicant had been convicted of murder and during his subsequent imprisonment he was alleged to have made a number of threats against prison officers. The authorities responded by charging him with the crime of dangerous menace. The local Regional Court decided to hold the applicant's trial in the closed area of the prison where he was serving his existing sentence. As usual, in the week before the trial, the Public Prosecutor's Office at the Regional Court distributed a list of forthcoming cases (and their locations) including the applicant's to the media and made the list available to the public. The hearing took place in a small room within the prison. The applicant, represented by counsel, pleaded not guilty. After hearing from the relevant prison officers the judge found the applicant guilty and sentenced him to ten months' imprisonment. The trial lasted about half an hour and no members of the media/public were present. Before the Court the applicant complained that his trial breached the public hearing obligation under Article 6(1). A united Court held that:

27. . . . The public character of the proceedings assumes particular importance in a case such as the present where the defendant in the criminal proceedings is a prisoner, where the charges relate to the making of threats against prison officers and where the witnesses are officers of the prison in which the defendant is detained.

28. It was undisputed in the present case, that the publicity of the hearing was not formally excluded. However, hindrance in fact can contravene the Convention just like a legal impediment (see the *Airey v Ireland* judgment of 9 October 1979, Series A No 32, p. 14, § 25). The Court considers that the mere fact that the trial took place in the precincts of Garsten Prison does not lead necessarily to the conclusion that it lacked publicity. Nor did the fact that any potential spectators would have had to undergo certain identity and possibly security checks in itself deprive the hearing of its public nature . . .

29. Nevertheless, it must be borne in mind that the Convention is intended to guarantee not rights that are theoretical or illusory but rights that are practical and effective (see the *Artico v Italy* judgment of 13 May 1980, Series A No 37, p 16, § 33). The Court considers a trial will only comply with the requirement of publicity if the public is able to obtain information about its date and place and if this place is easily accessible to the public. In many cases these conditions will be fulfilled by the simple fact that a hearing is held in a regular court room large enough to accommodate spectators. However, the Court observes that the holding of a trial outside a regular court room, in particular in a place like a prison to

which the general public on principle has no access, presents a serious obstacle to its public character. In such a case, the State is under an obligation to take compensatory measures in order to ensure that the public and the media are duly informed about the place of the hearing and are granted effective access.

The Court did not find that such measures, for example directions in a special public/media notice issued by the Public Prosecutor as to how the media/public could reach the prison and what access conditions would apply, had been taken. Consequently, the Court determined that there had been a violation of the public hearing requirement of Article 6(1). Although *Riepan* concerned a criminal trial being held in a prison and *Campbell and Fell* dealt with 'criminal' disciplinary charges the full-time Court was, rightfully, concerned to ensure that adequate publicity and accessibility applied to proceedings involving a serious charge of misbehaviour against a prisoner.

An examination, by the full-time Court, of the obligation to hold public hearings for civil proceedings occurred in *B. and P. v United Kingdom*, judgment of 24 July 2001. The applicants were fathers whose children resided with their mothers. Both applicants applied to the courts for residency orders in respect of their sons. The applicants requested that the proceedings be conducted in open court, however their requests were rejected by the judges as the Children Act 1989 established a presumption that such proceedings should be conducted in private. The applicants complained that the presumption violated the right to a public hearing in Article 6(1). The Court explained the justification for the public hearing obligation as being:

36. . . . The public character of proceedings protects litigants against the administration of justice in secret with no public scrutiny; it is also one of the means whereby confidence in the courts can be maintained. By rendering the administration of justice visible, publicity contributes to the achievement of the aim of Article 6 § 1, a fair hearing, the guarantee of which is one of the foundations of a democratic society . . .

As to whether States could establish predetermined exceptions to the public hearing obligation the Court was divided. A majority, five votes to two, held that:

39. . . . while the Court agrees that Article 6 § 1 states a general rule that civil proceedings, *inter alia*, should take place in public, it does not find it inconsistent with this provision for a State to designate an entire class of case as an exception to the general rule where considered necessary in the interests of morals, public order or national security or where required by the interests of juveniles or the protection of the private life of the parties . . . although the need for such a measure must always be subject to the Court's control . . . The English procedural law can therefore be seen as a specific reflection of the general exceptions provided for by Article 6 § 1.

From this perspective there had been no violation of the applicants' right to a public hearing. However, the dissentients, Judges Loucaides and Tulkens, believed that; '. . . the general legal rule against public hearings applied in these cases is incompatible not only with the wording but also with the basic objective and philosophy of the requirement for public hearings under Article 6 . . .' The approach of the majority allows States considerable freedom to establish broad class exemptions from the obligation to hold public hearings, but individuals should be able to apply to the national courts for their particular cases to be heard in public (as the applicants were able to do in this case). If the individuals consider that the domestic procedural rulings are not compatible with Article 6(1), e.g. their cases do not fall within the exceptions specified in the Article, then they have the possibility of making a complaint to Strasbourg.

Within a reasonable time

1   The criteria that the Court applies when evaluating whether a civil or criminal court has determined proceedings (falling within Article 6(1)) within a reasonable time were articulated in paragraph 99 of the *Konig* judgment (above, p 344). That case also established that where national legal systems provide appellate courts which are competent to determine 'civil rights and obligations' or 'criminal charges' their proceedings come within this Convention right.

2   In *Robins v UK* (1997) 26 EHRR 527, 1997-V, the Court ruled that judicial decisions regarding legal costs, made after the substantive dispute had been decided, could be subject to this right. During May 1991 Exeter County Court gave judgment against the applicants in a civil action they had brought against their neighbours over alleged sewage pollution. Subsequent hearings were held into the applicants' liability to pay the defendants' legal costs. In November 1992 the County Court ordered that the applicants should pay approximately £10,000 to the defendants. The applicants appealed to the Court of Appeal which confirmed the costs award in June 1995. The applicants complained that their liability to pay costs had not been determined within a reasonable time. In a unanimous judgment:

28. The Court recalls that Article 6(1) requires that all stages of legal proceedings for the 'determination of . . . civil rights and obligations', not excluding stages subsequent to judgment on the merits, be resolved within a reasonable time . . .

29. The Court observes that the legal costs which formed the subject matter of the proceedings in question were incurred during the resolution of a dispute between neighbours which undoubtedly involved 'the determination of . . . civil rights and obligations' . . . the Court considers that the costs proceedings, even though separately decided, must be seen as a continuation of the substantive litigation and accordingly as part of a 'determination of . . . civil rights and obligations' . . .

The Court went on to find a violation of this right due to two periods (lasting ten months and 16 months) of inactivity by the State authorities preceding the Court of Appeal's resolution of the appeal.

3   The attitude of the Court towards States' obligation to operate effective domestic judicial systems was expressed in the following terms:

51. . . . The Court points out that the Convention places a duty on the contracting States to organise their legal systems so as to allow the courts to comply with the requirements of Article 6(1), including that of trial within a 'reasonable time'. Nonetheless, a temporary backlog of business does not involve liability on the part of the Contracting States provided they have taken reasonably prompt remedial action to deal with an exceptional situation of this kind. (*Buchholz v Germany*, A.42 (1981))

In that case the Court was unanimous in finding no breach of this right, despite the fact that it took nearly five years for the German Labour courts to determine the applicant's claim of unjust dismissal. The Court took account of the sudden economic recession that occurred during the mid-1970s, when the applicant brought his claim, which resulted in a 60 per cent increase in cases before the Labour courts. Furthermore, the Government had appointed 30 per cent more judges during this period to deal with the backlog of cases. Although other States have sought to argue that delays in their judicial systems were also temporary backlogs, the Court has been strict in assessing whether they have taken adequate remedial action to deal with the problem. For example, in *Zimmermann and Steiner v Switzerland*, A.66 (1983) 6 EHRR 17, the Federal Court took almost three and a half years to determine the applicants' claims for compensation in respect of noise pollution from a public airport. The Government submitted evidence that public law appeals had risen by 86 per cent during the 1970s. Some extra judges had been appointed to the relevant Swiss courts, but the Court (unanimously) concluded that:

31. ... although the steps taken during the period ending on [the date of the final determination of the applicants' cases] reflected a genuine willingness to tackle the problem, they did not give sufficient weight to the structural aspect and therefore only produced results that were not very satisfactory.

Therefore, the Court found a breach of the reasonable time guarantee. Similarly in *Guincho v Portugal*, A.81 (1984) 7 EHRR 223, the Government sought to contend that exceptional circumstances (including the restoration of democracy in 1974 and the repatriation of many former colonists) excused the four-year time period taken to determine the applicant's civil action (in respect of injuries suffered in a road accident). In a unanimous judgment it was stated that, 'the Court would once more draw attention to the extreme importance of this requirement for the proper administration of justice' (para 38). Furthermore, the Court concluded that the Government's response (appointing a few extra judges) was 'insufficient and belated'. Therefore, the applicant's complaint of a violation of Article 6(1) was upheld.

4 The State that has been found to be in breach of the reasonable time guarantee most frequently is Italy. In *Bottazzi v Italy*, ECHR 1999-V, a Grand Chamber found the continuing failure of Italian courts to determine cases within a reasonable time amounted to a 'practice' in breach of the Convention. The applicant complained that it had taken the Court of Audit nearly seven years to determine his claim for a pension.

22. The Court notes at the outset that Article 6 § 1 of the Convention imposes on the Contracting States the duty to organise their judicial systems in such a way that their courts can meet the requirements of this provision (see the *Salesi v Italy* judgment of 26 February 1993, Series A No 257-E, p 60, § 24). It wishes to reaffirm the importance of administering justice without delays which might jeopardise its effectiveness and credibility (see the *Katte Klitsche de la Grange v Italy* judgment of 27 October 1994, Series A No 293-B, p 39, § 61). It points out, moreover, that the Committee of Ministers of the Council of Europe, in its Resolution DH (97) 336 of 11 July 1997 (Length of civil proceedings in Italy: supplementary measures of a general character), considered that 'excessive delays in the administration of justice constitute an important danger, in particular for the respect of the rule of law'.

The Court next draws attention to the fact that since 25 June 1987, the date of the *Capuano v Italy* judgment (Series A No 119), it has already delivered 65 judgments in which it has found violations of Article 6 § 1 in proceedings exceeding a 'reasonable time' in the civil courts of the various regions of Italy. Similarly, under former Articles 31 and 32 of the Convention, more than 1,400 reports of the Commission resulted in resolutions by the Committee of Ministers finding Italy in breach of Article 6 for the same reason.

The frequency with which violations are found shows that there is an accumulation of identical breaches which are sufficiently numerous to amount not merely to isolated incidents. Such breaches reflect a continuing situation that has not yet been remedied and in respect of which litigants have no domestic remedy.

This accumulation of breaches accordingly constitutes a practice that is incompatible with the Convention.

Therefore, the judges were united in concluding that the applicant had suffered a breach of Article 6(1). Unfortunately, the number of complaints against Italy alleging breaches of this guarantee (in respect of both civil and criminal proceedings) continued to grow. According to the Evaluation Group, set up to examine the workload crisis facing the Court, by July 2001 there were 10,000 provisional applications pending against Italy alleging violations of this right (*Report of the Evaluation Group to the Committee of Ministers on the ECtHR*, September

2001, para 22). The Committee of Ministers responded to this systemic problem of the Italian judicial system by initiating, from 2002, an annual examination of the general measures taken by Italy to deal with the problem of delays in its courts. The 'Pinto Act' was enacted by Italy in 2001 to enable persons subject to excessive delays in domestic courts to seek compensation. However, the Committee of Ministers, in Interim Resolution ResDH (2005) 114 concerning the judgments of the European Court of Human Rights and decisions by the Committee of Ministers in 2,183 cases against Italy relating to the excessive length of judicial proceedings, noted that:

... despite the efforts undertaken, numerous elements still indicate that the solution to the problem will not be found in the near future (as evidenced in particular by the statistical data, the new cases before both domestic courts and the European Court, the information contained in the annual reports submitted by the government to the Committee and in the reports of the Prosecutor General at the Court of Cassation) ...

Stressing the importance the Convention attaches to the right to fair administration of justice in a democratic society and recalling that the problem of the excessive length of judicial proceedings, by reason of its persistence and extent, constitutes a real danger for the respect of the rule of law in Italy ... URGES the Italian authorities to enhance their political commitment and make it their effective priority to meet Italy's obligation under the Convention and the Court's judgments, to secure the right to a fair trial within a reasonable time to all persons under Italy's jurisdiction ...

The continuing problems of Italian judicial delays were highlighted in the Grand Chamber case of *Riccardi Pizzati v Italy*, judgment of 29 March 2006 (one of nine joined Grand Chamber judgments involving the Pinto Act). The Court was confronted with an elderly applicant (aged 82) who had waited twenty-six years for a first-instance court to determine her civil claim against a neighbour in respect of sewage pollution. She had applied, in October 2001, under the Pinto Act for compensation of 103,000 euros (in respect of non-pecuniary damage). In January 2002 the Court of Appeal found that the first-instance proceedings had been excessively long and awarded her 5,000 euros compensation. She appealed the level of damages to the Court of Cassation which dismissed her appeal, for being out of time, in November 2002. The authorities did not pay her compensation until December 2003. Before the Grand Chamber, the Government disputed the existence of a 'practice' of unreasonable delays in Italian trials given the enactment of the Pinto Act. The Grand Chamber was unanimous in finding that:

115. ... Like the applicant, the Court does not see how the introduction of the Pinto remedy at domestic level has solved the problem of excessively lengthy proceedings. It has admittedly saved the Court the trouble of finding these violations, but the task has simply been transferred to the courts of appeal, which were already overburdened. ...

116. The Court emphasises once again that Article 6(1) of the Convention obliges the Contracting States to organise their legal systems so as to enable the courts to comply with its various requirements. It wishes to reaffirm the importance of administering justice without delays which might jeopardise its effectiveness and credibility (see *Bottazzi*, para 22). Italy's position in this regard has not changed sufficiently to call into question the conclusion that this accumulation of breaches constitutes a practice that is incompatible with the Convention.

Regarding the payment of compensation in respect of lengthy proceedings the Grand Chamber held that:

88. ... The Court can accept that the authorities need time in which to make payment. However, in respect of a compensatory remedy designed to redress the consequences of excessively lengthy

proceedings that period should not generally exceed six months from the date on which the decision awarding compensation becomes final.

Overall, the Grand Chamber concluded that the complainant's first-instance proceedings had not been determined in a reasonable time and that breach of Article 6(1) had been aggravated by the delay in the payment of (inadequate) compensation under the Pinto Act. As there were 'hundreds' of cases pending before the Court in respect of awards made under the Pinto Act the Grand Chamber invited Italy; '127 . . . . to take all measures necessary to ensure that the domestic decisions are not only in conformity with the case-law of this Court but also executed within six months of being deposited with the registry.'

So, the Grand Chamber has found serious defects in the Italian remedial measure designed to compensate victims of lengthy proceedings. For an examination of how the Court calculates the amount of non-pecuniary damage suffered by such an applicant see below p 880.

An independent and impartial tribunal

McGonnell v UK (2000) The Times, 22 February
European Court of Human Rights

In 1982 the applicant bought the Calais Vinery on Guernsey. A few years later he started to live in a converted packing shed on that land. During 1988, through an advocate, he made representations to a planning inquiry that was considering the draft Detailed Development Plan No 6 (DDP6). The inspector rejected the applicant's arguments that his land should be subject to development. In 1990 the States of Deliberation (the Parliament of Guernsey) presided over by the Deputy Bailiff (the Bailiff is President of the States of Deliberation, President of the island's Royal Court and a senior figure in the government of Guernsey), Mr Graham Dorey, adopted DDP6 and continued to zone the applicant's land as agricultural. In 1995 the applicant brought legal proceedings to challenge the authorities' refusal to allow him to build on his land. His appeal was heard by the Royal Court, composed of its President (the new Bailiff, Sir Graham Dorey) and seven Jurats (lay persons). The appeal was dismissed unanimously. The applicant complained to the Commission alleging that his appeal had not been heard by an independent and impartial tribunal because of the participation of the Bailiff. By 25 votes to five the Commission considered that there had been a breach of Article 6(1).

46. The applicant pointed to the non-judicial functions of the Bailiff, contending that they gave rise to such close connections between the Bailiff as a judicial officer and the legislative and executive functions of government that the Bailiff no longer had the independence and impartiality required by Article 6. . . .

48. The Court recalls that it found in its *Findlay v UK* judgment (judgment of 25 February 1997, *Reports* 1997-I, p 198, § 73) that:

> in order to establish whether a tribunal can be considered as 'independent', regard must be had, inter alia, to the manner of appointment of its members and their term of office, the existence of guarantees against outside pressures and the question whether the body presents an appearance of independence . . .
>
> As to the question of 'impartiality', there are two aspects to this requirement. First, the tribunal must be subjectively free of personal prejudice or bias. Secondly, it must also be impartial from an

objective viewpoint, that is, it must offer sufficient guarantees to exclude any legitimate doubt in this respect . . . The concepts of independence and objective impartiality are closely linked . . .

49. In the present case, too, the concepts of independence and objective impartiality are closely linked, and the Court will consider them together.

50. The Court first observes that there is no suggestion in the present case that the Bailiff was subjectively prejudiced or biased when he heard the applicant's planning appeal in June 1995. It has not been alleged that the Bailiff's participation as Deputy Bailiff in the adoption of DDP6 in 1990 gives rise to actual bias on his part: the applicant states that it is not possible to ascertain whether there was actual bias because of the Bailiff's various functions, but he does not contend that the Bailiff was subjectively biased or prejudiced.

51. The Court can agree with the Government that neither Article 6 nor any other provision of the Convention requires States to comply with any theoretical constitutional concepts as such. The question is always whether, in a given case, the requirements of the Convention are met. The present case does not, therefore, require the application of any particular doctrine of constitutional law to the position in Guernsey: the Court is faced solely with questions of whether the Bailiff had the required 'appearance' of independence, or the required 'objective' impartiality.

52. In this connection, the Court notes that the Bailiff's functions are not limited to judicial matters, but that he is also actively involved in non-judicial functions on the island. The Court does not accept the Government's analysis that when the Bailiff acts in a non-judicial capacity he merely occupies positions rather than exercising functions: even a purely ceremonial constitutional role must be classified as a 'function'. The Court must determine whether the Bailiff's functions in his non-judicial capacity were, or were not, compatible with the requirements of Article 6 as to independence and impartiality.

53. The Court observes that the Bailiff in the present case had personal involvement with the planning matters at the heart of the applicant's case on two occasions. The first occasion was in 1990, when, as Deputy Bailiff, he presided over the States of Deliberation at the adoption of DDP6. The second occasion was on 6 June 1995, when he presided over the Royal Court in the determination of the applicant's planning appeal.

55. . . . As the Court has noted above, the Bailiff's non-judicial constitutional functions cannot be accepted as being merely ceremonial. With particular respect to his presiding, as Deputy Bailiff, over the States of Deliberation in 1990, the Court considers that any direct involvement in the passage of legislation, or of executive rules, is likely to be sufficient to cast doubt on the judicial impartiality of a person subsequently called on to determine a dispute over whether reasons exist to permit a variation from the wording of the legislation or rules at issue. . . .

57. The Court thus considers that the mere fact that the Deputy Bailiff presided over the States of Deliberation when DDP6 was adopted in 1990 is capable of casting doubt on his impartiality when he subsequently determined, as the sole judge of the law in the case, the applicant's planning appeal. The applicant therefore had legitimate grounds for fearing that the Bailiff may have been influenced by his prior participation in the adoption of DDP6. That doubt in itself, however slight its justification, is sufficient to vitiate the impartiality of the Royal Court, and it is therefore unnecessary for the Court to look into the other aspects of the complaint. It follows that there has been a breach of Article 6 § 1. . . .

NOTES

1 The unanimous Court was composed of President Costa and Judges: Kuris, Tulkens, Fuhrmann, Jungwiert, Greve and Laws.

2 In advance of the full implementation of the Human Rights Act 1998, the Lord Chancellor, Lord Irvine of Lairg, announced that he would not sit in the Judicial Committee of the House

of Lords when it heard cases involving legislation which he had been directly concerned with or cases directly involving the Government (HL Deb, Vol 610, col WA33: 23 February 2000). The Constitutional Reform Act 2005 provides, *inter alia*, for the creation of a Supreme Court of the United Kingdom to replace the Judicial Committee of the House of Lords. The Lord Chancellor, who need no longer be a qualified lawyer, will not be a member of the new Supreme Court. Furthermore, The Lord Chancellor (Transfer of Functions and Supplementary Provisions) (No 2) Order 2006 SI 1016/2006 abolished the Lord Chancellor's position as a Lord of Appeal.

3   *McGonnell* was distinguished in the subsequent case of *Pabla Ky v Finland*, judgment of 22 June 2004. The applicant company had unsuccessfully sued its landlord in the specialist Housing Court Division of the Court of Appeal (composed of two experts and three professional judges). The applicant company subsequently challenged the objective impartiality of one of the expert members (M.P.) of the Court of Appeal on the basis that he was a member of the Finnish Parliament at the time of the judgment. The Strasbourg Court, by six votes to one, held that:

29. This case also raises issues concerning the role of a member of the legislature in a judicial context. Although the notion of the separation of powers between the political organs of government and the judiciary has assumed growing importance in the Court's case-law (see *Stafford v the United Kingdom* [GC], No 46295/99, § 78, ECHR 2002-IV), neither Article 6 nor any other provision of the Convention requires States to comply with any theoretical constitutional concepts regarding the permissible limits of the powers' interaction. The question is always whether, in a given case, the requirements of the Convention are met. As in the other cases examined by the Court, the present case does not, therefore, require the application of any particular doctrine of constitutional law. The Court is faced solely with the question whether, in the circumstances of the case, the Court of Appeal had the requisite 'appearance' of independence, or the requisite 'objective' impartiality (see *McGonnell v the United Kingdom*, No 28488/95, ECHR 2000-II, § 51 . . .

31. The Court notes, first of all, that there is no indication that M.P. was actually, or subjectively, biased against the applicant when sitting in the Court of Appeal in his case. The only issue is whether due to his position as a member of the legislature his participation cast legitimate doubt on the objective impartiality or structural impartiality of the court which decided the applicant's appeal.

32. There is no objection *per se* to expert lay members participating in the decision-making in a court. The domestic legislation of the Council of Europe's member States affords many examples of tribunals in which professional judges sit alongside specialists in a particular sphere whose knowledge is desirable and even essential in settling the disputes (see, e.g., *Ettl v Austria*, judgment of 23 April 1994, Series A No 117, §§ 38–40 *Debled v Belgium*, judgment of 22 September 1994, Series A No 292-B, §36). The Court recalls that M.P. had sat on the Court of Appeal as an expert in rental matters since 1974 and had, in the Government's view, accrued considerable experience valuable in contributing to adjudicating in these types of cases. The Court notes in that regard that two expert members sat alongside a majority of three judges in the composition of the Court of Appeal in such cases.

33. While the applicant points to M.P.'s political affiliation, the Court does not find that there is any indication in the present case that M.P.'s membership of a particular political party had any connection or link with any of the parties in the proceedings or the substance of the case before the Court of Appeal (*mutatis mutandis*, *Holm v Sweden*, judgment of 25 November 1995, Series A No 279-A, §§ 32–3). Nor is there any indication that M.P. played any role in respect of the legislation which was in issue in the case. The Act on Commercial Leases had been submitted by the Government for adoption by Parliament on 21 November 1994 and it had been adopted on 17 February 1995 before M.P. had been elected for his second term of office on 19 March 1995. Even assuming therefore that participation by

a Member of Parliament in, for example, the adoption of a general legislative measure could cast doubts on later judicial functions, it cannot be asserted in this case that M.P. was involved in any other capacity with the subject-matter of the applicant's case through his position as Member of Parliament.

34. Accordingly, the Court concludes that, unlike the situation examined by it in the cases of *Procola v Luxembourg* 28 September 1985, Series A No 326, and *McGonnell v the United Kingdom*, cited above, M.P. had not exercised any prior legislative, executive or advisory function in respect of the subject-matter or legal issues before the Court of Appeal for decision in the applicant's appeal. The judicial proceedings therefore cannot be regarded as involving 'the same case' or 'the same decision' in the sense which was found to infringe Article 6 § 1 in the two judgments cited above. The Court is not persuaded that the mere fact that M.P. was a member of the legislature at the time when he sat on the applicant's appeal is sufficient to raise doubts as to the independence and impartiality of the Court of Appeal. While the applicant relies on the theory of separation of powers, this principle is not decisive in the abstract.

35. In these circumstances, the Court is of the opinion that the applicant's fear as to a lack of independence and impartiality of the Court of Appeal, due to the participation of an expert member who was also a Member of Parliament, cannot be regarded as being objectively justified. Consequently, there has been no violation of Article 6 § 1 of the Convention.

The dissentient, Judge Borrego Borrego, stated:

I would refer here to Montesquieu, father of the theory of separation of powers:

> 'Nor is there liberty if the power of judging is not separate from legislative power and from executive power. If it were joined to legislative power, the power over the life and liberty of the citizens would be arbitrary, for the judge would be the legislator. If it were joined to executive power, the judge could have the force of an oppressor'.

I believe that this is the first time the Court has examined a complaint concerning the simultaneous exercise of legislative and judicial functions by the same person. I consider—humbly, as befits a minority voice, yet with strong conviction—that in the present case the requirement of independence of the courts from the legislature, as set forth in our case-law, was not observed.

Do you agree with the pragmatic approach of the majority?

4 The conflicting functions of court martial 'convening officers' were at the heart of the *Findlay v UK* (1997) 24 EHRR 221, 1997-I, case. The applicant was a former lance-sergeant who in 1990, after a heavy drinking session, held members of his unit at gunpoint and threatened to kill some of them and himself. Subsequent, psychiatric evidence disclosed that he was suffering from post-traumatic stress disorder caused by his experiences in the Falklands war. The General Officer Commanding London District, a Major-General, assumed the duties of convening officer (including remanding the applicant for trial on eight charges, appointing the members of the court martial, appointing the prosecuting and defending officers) and later confirming the sentence. The applicant pleaded guilty to seven charges (including threatening to kill) and was sentenced by the court martial to, *inter alia*, two years' imprisonment. The Major General confirmed this sentence. The applicant complained that because of the influence of the convening officer over the court martial process he had not received a fair hearing by an independent and impartial tribunal. The Commission, unanimously, found a breach of Article 6(1). Likewise the Court upheld his complaint because:

76. In order to maintain confidence in the independence and impartiality of the court, appearances may be of importance. Since all the members of the court martial which decided Mr Findlay's case were subordinate in rank to the convening officer and fell within his chain of command, Mr Findlay's doubts about the tribunal's independence and impartiality could be objectively justified . . .

77. In addition, the Court finds it significant that the convening officer also acted as 'confirming officer'. Thus, the decision of the court martial was not effective until ratified by him, and he had the power to vary the sentence imposed as he saw fit ... This is contrary to the well-established principle that the power to give a binding decision which may not be altered by a non-judicial authority is inherent in the very notion of 'tribunal' and can also be seen as a component of the 'independence' required by Article 6 para 1. ...

80. For all these reasons, and in particular the central role played by the convening officer in the organisation of the court martial, the Court considers that Mr Findlay's misgivings about the independence and impartiality of the tribunal which dealt with his case were objectively justified. ...

The Armed Forces Act 1996 abolished the role of convening officer and allocated the functions to separate bodies within the military (a 'higher authority' decides whether a case should be referred to a prosecuting authority within the Services' legal branches and court administration officers (independent of the higher and prosecuting authorities) are responsible for organizing individual court martial hearings).

4   The revised courts martial systems, as used by the different armed services, have received mixed responses in subsequent cases at Strasbourg. In *Morris v UK*, judgment of 26 February 2002, a Chamber was unanimous in finding structural violations of Article 6(1) in the army system. These included the absence of sufficient safeguards to guarantee the independence of the two junior officers who sat *ad hoc* on the applicant's court martial. '72. In particular, it notes that those officers had no legal training, that they remained subject to arm discipline and reports, and that there was no statutory or other bar to their being made subject to external army influence when sitting on the case.' However, the next year in *Cooper v UK*, judgment of 16 December 2003, a Grand Chamber, unanimously, found no breach of Article 6(1) in respect of a Royal Air Force court martial. The Grand Chamber took account of new submissions by the Government and concluded that it should depart from the conclusions in *Morris*. Regarding the independence of the *ad hoc* officers the Grand Chamber found that they were provided with detailed written guidance on their roles prior to the trial and that they could not be subject to disciplinary reporting on their judicial performance. '126. For these reasons, the Court finds that there were sufficient safeguards of the independence of the ordinary members of the applicant's court martial.' But, the same Grand Chamber was united in finding a breach of Article 6(1) by a Royal Navy court martial in *Grieves v UK*, judgment of 16 December 2003. The applicant, a former member of the Royal Navy, had been convicted of malicious wounding by a court-martial and sentenced to three year's imprisonment and dismissal from the service.

74. The present applicant raised the same complaint as in the *Cooper* case but in relation to a naval court-martial. Naval courts-martial differ in certain important respects from the air-force system examined in the *Cooper* case and the Court has considered whether those distinctions are such as to lead to a conclusion in the present case different from that in the *Cooper* judgment.

...

80. Fourthly, the post of PPCM [Permanent President of Court-Martial] does not exist in the naval system, the President of a naval court-martial being appointed for each court-martial as it is convened. The applicant pointed out that, as a result, the entire court-martial was convened on an *ad hoc* basis. The Government explained that, since there were less naval courts-martial, there was no need for a group of officers with the sole task of acting as PPCMs and considered that the naval court-martial complied with Article 6 § 1 even without PPCMs.

81. The Court considers that the absence of a full-time PPCM, with no hope of promotion and no effective fear of removal and who was not subject to report on his judicial decision-making (the *Cooper* judgment, § 118) deprives naval courts-martial of what was considered, in the air-force context, to be an important contribution to the independence of an otherwise *ad hoc* tribunal.

82. Fifthly, and most importantly, the Judge Advocate [the legal expert to the court-martial] in a naval court-martial is a serving naval officer who, when not sitting in a court-martial, carries out regular naval duties. In contrast, the Judge Advocate in the air-force is a civilian working full-time on the staff of the Judge Advocate General, himself a civilian.

83. The applicant considered this distinction sufficient of itself to conclude as to the lack of independence of naval courts-martial. He maintained that it was inevitable that the JAF's [Judge Advocate of the Fleet] comments on the Judge Advocate's conduct of the court-martial would be taken into account in the wider service evaluation of that officer for promotion. Whether or not there was at the time a regulation excluding reporting in the service on a Judge Advocate's judicial decision-making, he submitted that it was unreal to consider that the service would genuinely separate his judicial and other service functions. . . .

84. The Government maintained that a service Judge Advocate is no less a safeguard than the civilian one sitting in air-force courts-martial because, *inter alia*, of the following matters: the Judge Advocate is ticketed [appointed] only with the consent of the JAF (a civilian judge), he can only be removed by the JAF and on the same grounds as those for a civilian judge; he is responsible solely to the JAF in the performance of his duties as Judge Advocate; he receives no extra pay for acting as Judge Advocate and neither his pay nor promotion are affected by his performance as Judge Advocate; the Judge Advocate in the applicant's court-martial was not reported on as regards his performance as Judge Advocate (a practice now enshrined in Queen's Regulation 3630) . . . there is *de facto* security of tenure since a ticketed Judge Advocate remains as such indefinitely; a Judge Advocate takes a particular form of oath; he sits apart from court-martial members and his only contact with them (apart from deliberations on sentence) is in open court . . .

85. The Court notes that, as in the air-force, the naval Judge Advocate fulfils a pivotal role in the court-martial but that, unlike his air-force equivalent, he is a serving naval officer in a post which may or may not be a legal one and who, although 'ticketed' indefinitely, sits in courts-martial only from time to time. As to the Government's reliance on the involvement of a civilian JAF, the Court observes that the JAF has no input into naval court-martial proceedings, his principal role being to report to the Reviewing Authority on those proceedings. Further, it is not the JAF but the CNJA [Chief Naval Judge Advocate] (a naval officer) who is responsible for the initial 'ticketing' of a Judge Advocate (albeit with the agreement of the JAF).

86. Moreover, the Court notes with some concern certain reporting practices as regards Judge Advocates which applied at the relevant time. The JAF could pass comments about a Judge Advocate's court-martial performance to the CNJA. It may be that the CNJA had no control over promotions but the CNJA remained a senior service officer whose main functions included the appointment of legally trained service officers to legal posts in the service and who was answerable as regards those duties to the senior Admiral responsible for personnel policy. In addition, at the relevant time the JAF's report on a Judge Advocate's judicial performance could be forwarded to the Judge Advocate's service reporting officer. While this may not actually have happened in the present case, the Judge Advocate took up his duties in the applicant's court-martial at a time when his performance in those proceedings could, in principle, have been the subject of a report to his evaluating service officer. . . .

87. For these reasons, the Court considers that, even if the naval Judge Advocate appointed to the applicant's court-martial could be considered to have been independent despite the reporting matters highlighted in the preceding paragraph, the position of naval Judge Advocates cannot be considered to constitute a strong guarantee of the independence of a naval court-martial.

88. Moreover, the Court finds unconvincing the Government's explanations as to why a serving officer was to be preferred as Judge Advocate in naval courts-martial whereas the JAG and the Judge Advocates involved air-force courts-martial were civilians.

The Government referred, in the first place, to the relatively small number of naval courts-martial. However, the Court considers that this only means that fewer naval Judge Advocates would be required. They also relied upon the knowledge a naval officer would have of the unique language, customs and environment of the Royal Navy. However, since the essential function of the Judge Advocate is to ensure the lawfulness and fairness of the court-martial and to direct the court on points of law, it is difficult to understand why a detailed knowledge of the way of life and language of the navy should be called for, particularly where, as in the present case, the offence with which the applicant was charged was the ordinary criminal offence of malicious wounding. In any event, the Court is not persuaded that a civilian Judge Advocate would have more difficulty in following naval language or customs than a trial judge would have with complex expert evidence in a civilian case.

The Government further relied on the need for the naval court-martial system to be 'flexible' and 'portable' because of the particularly mobile nature of the navy. Naval Judge Advocates were therefore preferable as, *inter alia*, they would have 'ready access' to the area in question and would be better prepared for the difficulties and dangers of working at sea. However, the Court does not find this relevant given the Government's clarification (in response to questions at the oral hearing) that naval courts-martial have in fact been held on land since 1986 in two trial centres (Portsmouth and Plymouth) regardless of the part of the world in which the offence was alleged to have been committed.

89. Accordingly, the lack of a civilian in the pivotal role of Judge Advocate deprives a naval court-martial of one of the most significant guarantees of independence enjoyed by other services' courts-martial (army and air-force court-martial systems being the same for all relevant purposes—the *Cooper* judgment, § 107), for the absence of which the Government have offered no convincing explanation.

90. Sixthly and finally, the Court considers the Briefing Notes sent to members of naval courts-martial to be substantially less detailed and significantly less clear than the CMAU (RAF) Briefing Notes examined in detail in the above-cited *Cooper* case (see paragraphs 45–62 of that judgment). The Court considers that they are consequently less effective in safeguarding the independence of the ordinary members of courts-martial from inappropriate outside influence.

91. The Court accordingly finds that the distinctions between the air-force court-martial system assessed in the above-cited *Cooper* case and naval court-martial system at issue in the present case are such that the present applicant's misgivings about the independence and impartiality of his naval court-martial, convened under the 1996 Act, can be considered to be objectively justified. His court-martial proceedings were consequently unfair (see, for example, *Smith and Ford v the United Kingdom*, Nos 37475/97 and 39036/97, § 25, 29 September 1999 and *Moore and Gordon v the United Kingdom*, Nos 36529/97 and 37393/97, § 24, 29 September 1999).

There has therefore been a violation of Article 6 § 1 of the Convention.

5   The subjective and objective approaches to evaluating whether a particular judge/tribunal is impartial were explained, in the context of a continental criminal trial, in *Piersack v Belgium*, A.53 (1982) 5 EHRR 169. The applicant had been arrested on suspicion of murder. His prosecution was handled by a section of the office of the Brussels public prosecutor. Mr Van de Walle was the head of that section. Subsequently, Mr Van de Walle was appointed to the Brussels Court of Appeal and presided over the applicant's trial (the jury found him guilty by a majority of seven votes to five). Judge Van de Walle sentenced the applicant to eighteen years' hard labour. The Commission was unanimous in finding a breach of the independent and impartial tribunal guarantee. A united Court held that:

30. While impartiality normally denotes absence of prejudice or bias, its existence or otherwise can, notably under Article 6 § 1 (art 6-1) of the Convention, be tested in various ways. A distinction can be

drawn in this context between a subjective approach, that is endeavouring to ascertain the personal conviction of a given judge in a given case, and an objective approach, that is determining whether he offered guarantees sufficient to exclude any legitimate doubt in this respect.

(a) As regards the first approach, the Court notes that the applicant is pleased to pay tribute to Mr Van de Walle's personal impartiality; it does not itself have any cause for doubt on this score and indeed personal impartiality is to be presumed until there is proof to the contrary (see the *Le Compte, Van Leuven and De Meyere* judgment of 23 June 1981, Series A No 43, p 25, § 58).

However, it is not possible to confine oneself to a purely subjective test. In this area, even appearances may be of a certain importance (see the *Delcourt* judgment of 17 January 1970, Series A No 11, p 17, § 31). As the Belgian Court of Cassation observed in its judgment of 21 February 1979 ... any judge in respect of whom there is a legitimate reason to fear a lack of impartiality must withdraw. What is at stake is the confidence which the courts must inspire in the public in a democratic society.

(b) It would be going too far to the opposite extreme to maintain that former judicial officers in the public prosecutor's department were unable to sit on the bench in every case that had been examined initially by that department, even though they had never had to deal with the case themselves. So radical a solution, based on an inflexible and formalistic conception of the unity and indivisibility of the public prosecutor's department, would erect a virtually impenetrable barrier between that department and the bench. It would lead to an upheaval in the judicial system of several Contracting States where transfers from one of those offices to the other are a frequent occurrence. Above all, the mere fact that a judge was once a member of the public prosecutor's department is not a reason for fearing that he lacks impartiality; the Court concurs with the Government on this point. ...

31. ... Yet previously and until November 1977, Mr Van de Walle had been the head of section B of the Brussels public prosecutor's department, which was responsible for the prosecution instituted against Mr Piersack. As the hierarchical superior of the deputies in charge of the file, Mrs del Carril and then Mr De Nauw, he had been entitled to revise any written submissions by them to the courts, to discuss with them the approach to be adopted in the case and to give them advice on points of law ... Besides, the information obtained by the Commission and the Court ... tends to confirm that Mr Van de Walle did in fact play a certain part in the proceedings. ... It is sufficient to find that the impartiality of the 'tribunal' which had to determine the merits (in the French text: 'bien-fondé') of the charge was capable of appearing open to doubt.

32. In this respect, the Court therefore concludes that there was a violation of Article 6 § 1 (art 6-1)...

The acceptability under the Convention of transfers between domestic prosecution services and the judiciary, provided that judges do not hear cases in which they had a prior involvement as a prosecutor, is very important for those Member States that have a career judicial system in which transfers between these organisations is a common occurrence.

6   The difficulty of establishing subjective bias was illustrated by the case of *Sander v UK* (2000) The Times, 12 May. The applicant was an Asian who was tried for conspiracy to defraud before a judge and jury at Birmingham Crown Court. During the judge's summing up a juror sent the judge a note in which he/she alerted the judge that two other jurors had allegedly made racist jokes. The writer of the note was separated from the rest of the jury. The judge then adjourned proceedings and asked the jurors to let him know if they could not try the case fairly. The next day all the jurors wrote a collective note in which they assured the court that they would try the case without racial bias. One juror sent another note to the judge in which he/she apologised for having given any offence and claimed that he/she was not racially biased. The judge concluded that in the light of the above events, '... it is quite clear to me that each and every one of you are conscious of the oath or affirmation that you have taken and are dutifully

prepared to abide by it.' The jury convicted the applicant, but acquitted a fellow defendant who was also Asian. The applicant complained that he was not tried by an impartial tribunal. A majority of the Court (four) concluded that:

22. The Court recalls that it is of fundamental importance in a democratic society that the courts inspire confidence in the public and above all, as far as criminal proceedings are concerned, in the accused. To that end it has constantly stressed that a tribunal, including a jury, must be impartial from a subjective as well as an objective point of view . . .

23. The Court also recalls that the present case concerns clear and precise allegations that racist comments had been made by jurors called upon to try an Asian accused. The Court considers this to be a very serious matter given that, in today's multicultural European societies, the eradication of racism has become a common priority goal for all Contracting States (see, inter alia, Declarations of the Vienna and Strasbourg Summits of the Council of Europe).

24. The Court notes that the allegations in question led the applicant to the conclusion that he was tried by a racially prejudiced jury. The applicant's complaint is, therefore, that there was subjective bias on the part of some jurors.

25. The Court recalls that the personal impartiality of a judge must be presumed until there is proof to the contrary (see the Piersack v Belgium judgment of 1 October 1982, Series A No 53, pp 14–15, § 30). The same holds true in respect of jurors.

26. In the circumstances of the applicant's case, a member of the jury submitted a note alleging that two fellow jurors '[had] been making openly racist remarks and jokes' and stating that he feared that 'they [were] going to convict the defendants not on the evidence but because they were Asian'. Another juror, being confronted with these allegations, accepted that 'he might have done so' and stated that 'he was sorry if he had given any offence'. The Court, therefore, considers that it was established that at least one juror had made comments that could be understood as jokes about Asians. In the Court's view, this does not on its own amount to evidence that the juror in question was actually biased against the applicant. Moreover, the Court notes that it was not possible for the trial judge to question the jurors about the true nature of these comments and the exact context in which they had been made. It follows that it has not been established that the court that tried the applicant was lacking in impartiality from a subjective point of view.

27. This is not, however, the end of the Court's examination of the applicant's complaint. The Court must also examine whether the court was impartial from an objective point of view, ie whether in the circumstances there were sufficient guarantees to exclude any objectively justified or legitimate doubts as to the impartiality of the court. Although the standpoint of the accused is important in this connection, it cannot be decisive . . .

34. The Court has accepted that, although discharging the jury may not always be the only means to achieve a fair trial, there are certain circumstances where this is required by Article 6 § 1 of the Convention . . . In the present case the judge was faced with a serious allegation that the applicant risked being condemned because of his ethnic origin. Moreover, one of the jurors indirectly admitted to making racist comments. Given the importance attached by all Contracting States to the need to combat racism . . . the Court considers that the judge should have reacted in a more robust manner than merely seeking vague assurances that the jurors could set aside their prejudices and try the case solely on the evidence. By failing to do so, the judge did not provide sufficient guarantees to exclude any objectively justified or legitimate doubts as to the impartiality of the court. It follows that the court that condemned the applicant was not impartial from an objective point of view.

35. There was, therefore, a violation of Article 6 § 1 of the Convention.

Three judges dissented as they considered that the judge's actions had been sufficient to satisfy the objective requirements of Article 6(1). Apart from demonstrating the Court's caution in finding sufficient evidence of subjective bias, the judgment more positively confirms that jurors fall within the scope of this part of Article 6. Professor Zander has, however, been very critical of the majority's decision:

The decision in *Sander* is disturbing since it suggests that the Strasbourg court does not sufficiently understand or value the jury system. The great strength of the system is that generally the verdict of twelve ordinary citizens is felt to be understandable in terms of either of the evidence or of the jury's sense of equity. This is despite the fact that most jurors probably have prejudices, which will often include racial prejudice. To pretend otherwise is naïve. But the process of deliberation in the jury room tends to neutralise individual prejudices. The possibility of a majority verdict provides an additional safeguard against the effect of prejudice but in fact in the great majority of cases the verdict is unanimous. . . . The Court's decision in *Sander* seems to owe more to political correctness than to serious assessment of either the actual risk or the appearance of bias. [M Zander, 'The Complaining Juror' (2000) New Law Journal 723.]

7 A unanimous Chamber found the substantial financial dealings between a bank and the husband of a judge, at a time when the judge was hearing a case against the bank, amounted to a breach of the objective test in *Sigurdsson v Iceland*, judgment of 10 April 2003. The applicant, a lawyer, sued the National Bank of Iceland. Whilst Sigurdsson's case was before the Supreme Court the bank reached an agreement with the husband of Mrs Justice Erlendsdottir which, *inter alia*, involved the bank waiving 75 per cent of the debt (totalling 190,000 euros) he owed them and mortgages being granted on two properties owned by her. Mrs Justice Erlensdsdottir voted with the majority of the Supreme Court (three to two) to dismiss the applicant's claim against the bank. Sigurdsson contended before the Court that the massive relinquishment of debt by the bank meant that the judge and her husband were under a lifelong obligation of gratitude to the bank with the consequence that his case had not been determined by an independent and impartial tribunal.

37. The Court considers that it is essentially the requirement of 'impartiality' that is in issue in the present case . . . The existence of impartiality for the purposes of Article 6 § 1 of the Convention must be determined according to a subjective test, that is on the basis of the personal conviction of a particular judge in a given case, and also according to an objective test, that is, by ascertaining whether the judge offered guarantees sufficient to exclude any legitimate doubt in this respect . . .

As to the subjective test, the personal impartiality of a judge must be presumed until there is proof to the contrary; the applicant has adduced no evidence to suggest that Mrs Justice Guðrún Erlendsdóttir was personally biased . . .

Under the objective test, it must be determined whether, quite apart from the judge's personal conduct, there are ascertainable facts which may raise doubts as to his impartiality. In this respect even appearances may be of a certain importance. What is at stake is the confidence which the courts in a democratic society must inspire in the public. Accordingly, any judge in respect of whom there is a legitimate reason to fear a lack of impartiality must withdraw. This implies that in deciding whether in a given case there is a legitimate reason to fear that a particular judge lacks impartiality, the standpoint of the party concerned is important but not decisive. What is decisive is whether this fear can be held to be objectively justified . . .

43. The Court appreciates that Mr Örn Clausen's [the judge's husband] difficulties in May 1996 did not stem directly from his own personal financial situation but from that of an insolvent third party, Mr Edvard Lövdal, for whom he was a guarantor, as well as from the inability of other guarantors to honour their guarantees.

It remains, however, that Mr Örn Clausen had a legal obligation to cover claims from the twenty-one creditors totalling approximately ISK 50,000,000, including ISK 16,000,000 (approximately EUR 190,000) to the National Bank ... Yet a further consequence was the fact that Mr Örn Clausen's debts to the National Bank had decreased to an ordinary level by April 1997, which state of affairs could not have been unrelated to the settlement with the National Bank in June 1996.

In view of the above, the Court is not persuaded by the Government's argument that the debt settlement agreement between Mr Örn Clausen and the National Bank as well as other creditors, securing the latter recovery of 25% of the debts, was for them an attractive alternative to declaring him bankrupt and one that could not be viewed as a favour towards him personally. On the contrary, even assuming that the solution reached suited creditors, it finds that the cancellation of 75% of such large debts must be considered a favourable treatment of Mr Örn Clausen.

44. It should also be noted that when the four mortgage certificates were brokered by Landsbréf and the debt settlement agreement was concluded with the National Bank, the applicant's case, in which the National Bank was an opposing party, was already pending before the Supreme Court.

45. Against this background, there was at least the appearance of a link between the steps taken by Mrs Justice Guðrún Erlendsdóttir in favour of her husband and the advantages he obtained from the National Bank. The Court will not speculate as to whether she derived any personal benefit from the operation and finds no reason to believe that either she or her husband had any direct interest in the outcome in the case between the applicant and the National Bank. However, the judge's involvement in the debt settlement, the favours received by her husband and his links to the National Bank were of such a nature and amplitude and were so close in time to the Supreme Court's examination of the case that the applicant could entertain reasonable fears that it lacked the requisite impartiality (see, *mutatis mutandis*, *Holm v Sweden*, judgment of 25 November 1993, Series A No 279-A, pp 15–16, §§ 32–3).

46. Accordingly, the Court finds that there has been a violation of Article 6 § 1 of the Convention in the present case.

8 Assize Court judges were found not to have been subjectively impartial when convicting a defence lawyer for contempt in the face of the court in *Kyprianou v Cyprus*, judgment of 15 December 2005. The Assize Court had questioned the way the applicant was cross examining a prosecution witness and he had retorted that the judges had been passing 'ravasakia' (translated as love letters/notes) amongst themselves. After a short adjournment the judges found the applicant (who had been practising law for forty years with an unblemished professional reputation) guilty of contempt and sentenced him to five days' imprisonment (to begin immediately). This was the first time that a lawyer had been imprisoned for contempt of court in Cyprus. Subsequently, before the Grand Chamber, the applicant contended that the Assize judges had acted with personal bias when convicting him.

130. This limb of the applicant's complaint was therefore directed at the judges' personal conduct. The Court will accordingly examine a number of aspects of the judges' conduct which are capable of raising an issue under the subjective test.

Firstly, the judges in their decision sentencing the applicant acknowledged that they had been 'deeply insulted' 'as persons' by the applicant. Even though the judges proceeded to say that this had been the least of their concerns, in the Court's view this statement in itself shows that the judges had been personally offended by the applicant's words and conduct and indicates personal embroilment on the part of the judges.

Secondly, the emphatic language used by the judges throughout their decision conveyed a sense of indignation and shock, which runs counter to the detached approach expected of judicial pronouncements. In particular, the judges stated that they could not 'conceive of another occasion of such a manifest and unacceptable contempt of court by any person, let alone an advocate' and that 'if the court's reaction is not immediate and drastic, we feel that justice will have suffered a disastrous blow'.

Thirdly, they then proceeded to impose a sentence of five days' imprisonment, enforced immediately, which they deemed to be the 'only adequate response'. In the judges' opinion, 'an inadequate reaction on the part of the lawful and civilised order, as expressed by the courts would mean accepting that the authority of the courts be demeaned'.

Fourthly, the judges expressed the opinion early on in their discussion with the applicant that they considered him guilty of the criminal offence of contempt of court. After deciding that the applicant had committed the above offence they gave the applicant the choice, either to maintain what he had said and to give reasons why a sentence should not be imposed on him or to retract. He was, therefore, in fact asked to mitigate 'the damage he had caused by his behaviour' rather than defend himself.

131. Although the Court does not doubt that the judges were concerned with the protection of the administration of justice and the integrity of the judiciary and that for this purpose they felt it appropriate to initiate the *instanter* summary procedure, it finds, in view of the above considerations, that they did not succeed in detaching themselves sufficiently from the situation.

132. This conclusion is reinforced by the speed with which the proceedings were carried out and the brevity of the exchanges between the judges and Mr Kyprianou.

132. Against this background and having regard in particular to the different elements of the judges' personal conduct taken together, the Court finds that the misgivings of Mr Kyprianou about the impartiality of the Limassol Assize Court were also justified under the subjective test.

This was a rare example of an allegation of subjective bias being upheld by the European Court. Indeed, the Grand Chamber observed that, '119. . . . the Court has recognised the difficulty of establishing a breach of Article 6 on account of subjective partiality and for this reason has in the vast majority of cases raising impartiality issues focused on the objective test.' In *Kyprianou* the Grand Chamber also found that the Assize judges had violated the objective standard of impartiality. However, the Grand Chamber emphasised that it was only ruling on the facts of this case and '125. . . . the Court does not regard it as necessary or desirable to review generally the law on contempt and the practice of summary proceedings in Cyprus and other common law systems'. Thereby leaving open the potential lawfulness under Article 6 of trial court judges dealing summarily with certain types of contempt in the face of the court (e.g. the refusal of a witness to give evidence).

9　All the judges were united in finding that the Home Secretary's determination of the tariff (period of imprisonment for the purposes of retribution and deterrence) for juvenile murderers violated the 'independent' tribunal requirement in *V v UK* (above, p 420).

114. The Court notes that Article 6(1) guarantees, inter alia, 'a fair . . . hearing . . . by an independent and impartial tribunal . . .'. 'Independent' in this context means independent of the parties to the case and also of the executive . . . The Home Secretary, who set the applicant's tariff, was clearly not independent of the executive, and it follows that there has been a violation of Article 6(1).

10　A majority of the Court, twelve votes to eight, found a violation of the right to an independent and impartial tribunal when an opposition politician was tried before a special court (composed of two civilian judges and a military judge) for distributing a leaflet critical of the authorities' treatment of Kurds: *Incal v Turkey* (see below, p 644).

67. The Court notes that the status of military judges sitting as members of National Security Courts provides certain guarantees of independence and impartiality. For example, military judges follow the same professional training as their civilian counterparts, which gives them the status of regular members of the Military Legal Service. When sitting as members of National Security Courts, military judges enjoy

constitutional safeguards identical to those of civilian judges . . . as full members of a National Security Court they sit as individuals, according to the Constitution, they must be independent and no public authority may give them instructions concerning their judicial activities or influence them in the performance of their duties.

68. On the other hand, other aspects of these judges' status make it questionable. Firstly, they are servicemen who still belong to the army, which in turn takes its orders from the executive. Secondly, they remain subject to military discipline and assessment reports are compiled on them by the army for that purpose . . . Decisions pertaining to their appointment are to a great extent taken by the army's administrative authorities . . . Lastly, their term of office as National Security Court judges is only four years and can be renewed.

72. . . . the Court attaches great importance to the fact that a civilian had to appear before a court composed, even if only in part, of members of the armed forces. It follows that the applicant could legitimately fear that because one of the judges of the Izmir National Security Court was a military judge it might allow itself to be unduly influenced by considerations which had nothing to do with the nature of the case. . . .

73. In conclusion, the applicant had legitimate cause to doubt the independence and impartiality of the Izmir national Security Court. . . .

Do you think the nature of the accusations against the applicant exacerbated the dangers of the military judge undermining the independence and impartiality of the National Security Court?

Subsequently, a number of other persons convicted by the Turkish Security Courts successfully invoked this aspect of Article 6 before the European Court. In *Ocalan v Turkey*, see above p 128, the applicant complained that a judge holding the military rank of a colonel sat as one of the members of the State Security Court that tried and convicted him. The Government responded that the military judge was replaced by a civilian judge during the course of the trial. The Grand Chamber, eleven votes to six, found that the applicant had not been tried by an independent and impartial tribunal.

112. The Court has consistently held that certain aspects of the status of military judges sitting as members of the State Security Courts made their independence from the executive questionable (see *Incal v Turkey*, judgment of 9 June 1998, *Reports* 1998-IV, § 68; and *Çiraklar v Turkey*, judgment of 28 October 1998, *Reports of Judgments and Decisions* 1998-VII, § 39).

113. It is understandable that the applicant—prosecuted in a State Security Court for serious offences relating to national security—should have been apprehensive about being tried by a bench which included a regular army officer belonging to the military legal service. On that account he could legitimately fear that the State Security Court might allow itself to be unduly influenced by considerations which had nothing to do with the nature of the case (see, among other authorities, *Iprahim Ülger v Turkey*, No 57250/00, 29 July 2004).

114. As to whether the military judge's replacement by a civilian judge in the course of the proceedings before the verdict was delivered remedied the situation, the Court considers, firstly, that the question whether a court is seen to be independent does not depend solely on its composition when it delivers its verdict. In order to comply with the requirements of Article 6 regarding independence, the court concerned must be seen to be independent of the executive and the legislature at each of the three stages of the proceedings, namely the investigation, the trial and the verdict (those being the three stages in Turkish criminal proceedings according to the Government).

115. Secondly, when a military judge has participated in one or more interlocutory decisions that continue to remain in effect in the criminal proceedings concerned, the accused has reasonable cause for

concern about the validity of the entire proceedings, unless it is established that the procedure subsequently followed in the state security court sufficiently disposed of that concern. More specifically, where a military judge has participated in an interlocutory decision that forms an integral part of proceedings against a civilian the whole proceedings are deprived of the appearance of having been conducted by an independent and impartial court.

116. In its previous judgments, the Court attached importance to the fact that a civilian had to appear before a court composed, even if only in part, of members of the armed forces (see, among other authorities, *Incal*, cited above, § 72). Such a situation seriously affects the confidence which the courts must inspire in a democratic society (see, *mutatis mutandis*, *Piersack v Belgium*, judgment of 1 October 1982, Series A No 53, pp 14–15, § 30).

117. In the instant case, the Court notes that before his replacement on 23 June 1999 the military judge was present at two preliminary hearings and six hearings on the merits when interlocutory decisions were taken. It further notes that none of the decisions were renewed after the replacement of the military judge and that all were validated by the replacement judge.

118. In these circumstances, the Court cannot accept that the replacement of the military judge before the end of the proceedings disposed of the applicant's reasonably held concern about the trial court's independence and impartiality. Insofar as the decision or reasoning in the case of *Imrek v Turkey* [(dec.) No 57175/00, 28 January 2003] may be regarded as inconsistent with this conclusion, the Grand Chamber would not follow the decision and the reasoning in that case.

Consequently, there has been a violation of Article 6 § 1 on this point.

President Wildhaber, joined by Judges: Costa, Caflisch, Turmen, Garlicki, and Borrego Borrego, issued a joint partly dissenting opinion in which they expressed the view that:

1. The majority of the Court found that in the present case the Ankara State Security Court was not an independent and impartial court, owing to the presence of a military judge on the bench. We disagree with that conclusion for the following reasons.

2. It is true that since *Incal* (judgment of 9 June 1998, *Reports* 1998-IV, p 1548) the principle followed by the Court in this type of case is that an applicant has legitimate cause to doubt the independence and impartiality of a state security court when a military judge sits alongside two civilian judges. The Court was divided in *Incal* and decided the point by a majority of twelve to eight (see for the opposite view the opinion of the judges in the minority, *Reports* 1998-IV, pp 1578 and 1579).

3. It is equally true that the *Incal* precedent has since been followed in a number of judgments (including *Sürek v Turkey (No 1)* [GC], No 26682/95, ECHR 1999-IV—see Mr Wildhaber's declaration and the dissenting opinion of Mr Gölçüklü).

4. However, things have changed. Within a very short space of time, Turkey took remedial action following the *Incal* judgment and did not hesitate to amend its Constitution (and subsequently its legislation) so that now only civilian judges sit in the state security courts (which have since been abolished). By 18 June 1999 the Constitution had already been amended and the legislative amendments followed just four days later, with immediate effect (see paragraphs 53 and 54 of the judgment in the present case). It would be desirable for all States Parties to the Convention to comply with the Court's judgments within such a reasonable period.

5. The amended legislation was immediately applied to the applicant's trial, with the third civilian judge replacing the military judge the day after it entered into force. It should be noted that the replacement judge had been present throughout the proceedings and had attended all the hearings of the State Security Court from the start of the trial, that the State Security Court noted that he had read the file and the transcripts (see paragraph 44 of the judgment) and, lastly, that he was at liberty to request additional evidence or investigations.

6. Thus the State Security Court's verdict and sentence were handed down by a court composed entirely of civilian judges, all three of whom had taken part in the entire trial. To say that the presence of a military judge, who was replaced under new rules (that were introduced to comply with the case-law of the European Court of Human Rights) made the State Security Court appear not to be independent and impartial is to take the 'theory' of appearances very far. That, in our opinion at least, is neither realistic, nor even fair.

7. For this reason we consider that the Court's approach in the *Imrek* case was wiser. In that case, against the same background and in view of the Turkish authorities' positive response to the *Incal* line of authority, it held that the complaint was manifestly ill-founded, as the problem had been solved by the military judge's replacement by a civilian judge during the course of the trial (see the inadmissibility decision of 28 January 2003, application No 57175/00).

8. In addition, in Mr Öçalan's case, and without departing from the principles established in the *Incal* judgment itself, it is hard to agree with what is said in paragraph 116 of the judgment. The applicant is there described as a civilian (or equated to a civilian). However, he was accused of instigating serious terrorist crimes leading to thousands of deaths, charges which he admitted at least in part. He could equally well be described as a warlord, which goes a long way to putting into perspective the fact that at the start of his trial one of the three members of the court before which he appeared was himself from the military.

9. Inherent in a system based on the principle of subsidiarity is loyal cooperation between a supranational judicial body such as this Court and the States which have adhered to the system. Imposing standards that are too high does not appear to us to be the best way of encouraging such cooperation or of expressing satisfaction to the States which provide it.

Do you agree with the dissentients that the majority were being too stringent in their application of the requirements of independence/impartiality to the domestic court?

11 The range of bodies classified as 'tribunals' for the purposes of this provision has been drawn widely by the Court. For example, we have already seen that the Court found a lack of impartiality on the part of the Maltese House of Representatives in seeking to punish a journalist in *Demicoli v Malta* (above, p 373). The Court's conception of a 'tribunal' was explained in paragraph 39 of that judgment.

Public pronouncement of judgment

1 The Court was unanimous in finding no breach of this requirement in respect of the Italian Court of Cassation's procedure of depositing its judgments in the court registry (members of the public could consult/obtain copies of judgments from the registry): *Pretto v Italy*, A.71 (1983) 6 EHRR 182. The first applicant, a tenant farmer, had brought proceedings in the Vicenza Regional Court and the Venice Court of Appeal to acquire the land he farmed. The latter court decided in favour of the landlord and Mr Pretto appealed on points of law to the Court of Cassation. His appeal was dismissed and the Court of Cassation deposited its full judgment in the court registry. The applicant complained to the Commission alleging, *inter alia*, a breach of this right. By twelve votes to three the Commission found no violation of this provision. The Court held that:

21. The public character of proceedings before the judicial bodies referred to in Article 6 § 1 (art 6-1) protects litigants against the administration of justice in secret with no public scrutiny; it is also one of the means whereby confidence in the courts, superior and inferior, can be maintained. By rendering the administration of justice visible, publicity contributes to the achievement of the aim of Article 6 § 1

(art 6-1), namely a fair trial, the guarantee of which is one of the fundamental principles of any democratic society, within the meaning of the Convention (see the *Golder* judgment of 21 February 1975, Series A No 18, p 18, § 36, and also the *Lawless* judgment of 14 November 1960, Series A No 1, p 13).

22. While the member States of the Council of Europe all subscribe to this principle of publicity, their legislative systems and judicial practice reveal some diversity as to its scope and manner of implementation, as regards both the holding of hearings and the 'pronouncement' of judgments. The formal aspect of the matter is, however, of secondary importance as compared with the purpose underlying the publicity required by Article 6 § 1 (art 6-1). The prominent place held in a democratic society by the right to a fair trial impels the Court, for the purposes of the review which it has to undertake in this area, to examine the realities of the procedure in question . . .

24. In accordance with Article 133 of the Code of Civil Procedure, the judgment adopted on 19 October 1976 by the Court of Cassation was simply deposited in the court registry, with written notification of the operative provisions being given to the parties, but not pronounced in open court . . . It therefore has to be determined whether, as the applicants and a minority of the Commission contended, this state of affairs violated the Convention.

25. The terms used in the second sentence of Article 6 § 1 (art 6-1)—'judgment shall be pronounced publicly', 'le jugement sera rendu publiquement'—might suggest that a reading out aloud of the judgment is required. Admittedly the French text employs the participle 'rendu' (given), whereas the corresponding word in the English version is 'pronounced' (prononcé), but this slight difference is not sufficient to dispel the impression left by the language of the provision in question: in French, 'rendu publiquement'—as opposed to 'rendu public' (made public)—can very well be regarded as the equivalent of 'prononcé publiquement'.

At first sight, Article 6 § 1 (art 6-1) of the European Convention would thus appear to be stricter in this respect than Article 14 § 1 of the 1966 International Covenant on Civil and Political Rights, which provides that the judgment 'shall be made public', 'sera public'.

26. However, many member States of the Council of Europe have a long-standing tradition of recourse to other means, besides reading out aloud, for making public the decisions of all or some of their courts, and especially of their courts of cassation, for example deposit in a registry accessible to the public. The authors of the Convention cannot have overlooked that fact, even if concern to take it into account is not so easily identifiable in their working documents as in the travaux préparatoires of the 1966 Covenant (see, for instance, document A/4299 of 3 December 1959, pp 12, 15 and 19, §§ 38 (b), 53 and 63 (c) in fine).

The Court therefore does not feel bound to adopt a literal interpretation. It considers that in each case the form of publicity to be given to the 'judgment' under the domestic law of the respondent State must be assessed in the light of the special features of the proceedings in question and by reference to the object and purpose of Article 6 § 1 (art 6-1).

27. . . . the Court of Cassation took its decision after holding public hearings and, although the judgment dismissing the appeal on points of law was not delivered in open court, anyone may consult or obtain a copy of it on application to the court registry . . .

In the opinion of the Court, the object pursued by Article 6 § 1 (art 6-1) in this context—namely, to ensure scrutiny of the judiciary by the public with a view to safeguarding the right to a fair trial—is, at any rate as regards cassation proceedings, no less achieved by a deposit in the court registry, making the full text of the judgment available to everyone, than by a reading in open court of a decision dismissing an appeal or quashing a previous judgment, such reading sometimes being limited to the operative provisions.

28. The absence of public pronouncement of the Court of Cassation's judgment therefore did not contravene the Convention in the present case. . . .

Hence the Court, sensibly, focused upon the substantive goal of ensuring that the domestic court's reasoning and decision was subject to public scrutiny.

2   A majority of the full-time Court, five votes to two, found the English system of restricted access to civil judgments concerning children to be compatible with the public judgments obligation in *B. and P. v United Kingdom*, judgment of 24 July 2001 (and see above p 425 in respect of the public hearing aspect of the case). Generally court orders and judgments concerning children are not made public, but any person with a legitimate interest can apply to the relevant court for permission to see and copy the text of orders and judgments. Also judgments of legal importance are published, in an anonymous form, in the law reports. In the light of these practices the Court held that:

48. . . . a literal interpretation of the terms of Article 6 § 1 concerning the pronouncement of judgments would not only be unnecessary for the purposes of public scrutiny but might even frustrate the primary aim of Article 6 § 1, which is to secure a fair hearing . . .

49. The Court thus concludes that the Convention did not require making available to the general public the residence judgments in the present cases, and that there has been no violation of Article 6 § 1 in this respect.

Judges Loucaides and Tulkens dissented as they considered that the obligation to pronounce judgments was expressed in unqualified terms by Article 6(1).

In an ideal world all judgments should be made generally available to the public (technically more feasible in the modern digital era) with appropriate deletions of sensitive information (e.g. the identities of persons in family disputes).

Article 6(2)

....

Minelli v Switzerland A.62 (1983) 5 EHRR 554
European Court of Human Rights

The applicant was a journalist who published an article in a Swiss newspaper in January 1972 accusing a company, Tele-Repertoire SA, and its director, Mr Vass, of fraud. The accusation involved the same allegations as another journalist, Mr Furst, had published a few days earlier in a different newspaper. The company and Mr Vass brought a criminal complaint of defamation against both journalists. Proceedings against the applicant were suspended in July 1974, at the request of Mr Vass, until the complaint against Mr Furst had been completed. In September 1975 Mr Furst was convicted, fined and ordered to pay costs. In May 1976 the Zurich Assize Court held that it could not hear the complaint against the applicant because the absolute limitation period of four years had expired. However, the court ordered that he should pay two-thirds of the court's costs and 1,200 SF towards the costs incurred by the complainants, because if it had not been for the expiry of the limitation period the complaint would 'very probably have led to the conviction of the accused . . .'. The applicant complained to the Commission that the court's order to pay costs amounted to a violation of the presumption of innocence contained in Article 6(2). The Commission was unanimous in finding a violation of that right.

30. In the Court's opinion, Article 6 § 2 (art 6-2) governs criminal proceedings in their entirety, irrespective of the outcome of the prosecution, and not solely the examination of the merits of the charge...

In the Canton of Zürich, a decision on the apportionment of costs is a normal part of criminal proceedings for defamation and is designed to settle certain consequences thereof. In this connection, it is of little moment that the decision was adopted after the ruling on the merits or that its text appears in a separate document.

II. COMPLIANCE WITH ARTICLE 6 § 2 (ART 6-2)

A. LIMITS OF THE COURT'S TASK

34. The applicant and the Government agreed that the case raised a question of principle: is it consonant with the presumption of innocence to direct that a person shall pay court costs and compensation in respect of expenses where he has been acquitted or where the case has been discontinued, discharged or, as here, terminated on account of limitation?

As the Government emphasised by way of alternative plea, the system which permits the adoption of such a solution in certain cases is deeply rooted in Swiss legal tradition: it is enshrined in Federal legislation and in that of most Cantons, including the Canton of Zürich, and has been developed by case-law and practice. According to Mr Minelli, on the other hand, it is the State which should bear all the risks of criminal proceedings, not only as regards evidence but also as regards costs.

In the Commission's view, the system in question could not of itself run counter to Article 6 § 2 (art 6-2) of the Convention; however, a problem arose if the reasons for the court's decision or some other precise and conclusive evidence showed that the apportionment of costs resulted from an appraisal of the guilt of the accused.

35. The Court in principle concurs with the Commission. However, it would point out, in conformity with its established jurisprudence, that in proceedings originating in an individual application, it has to confine itself, as far as possible, to an examination of the concrete case before it... Accordingly, it has to give a ruling not on the Zürich legislation and practice in abstracto but solely on the manner in which they were applied to the applicant.

...

37. In the Court's judgment, the presumption of innocence will be violated if, without the accused's having previously been proved guilty according to law and, notably, without his having had the opportunity of exercising his rights of defence, a judicial decision concerning him reflects an opinion that he is guilty. This may be so even in the absence of any formal finding; it suffices that there is some reasoning suggesting that the court regards the accused as guilty. The Court has to ascertain whether this was the case on 12 May 1976.

38. The Chamber of the Assize Court based its decision on Article 293 of the Zürich Code of Criminal Procedure, which, in the case of a private prosecution for defamation, permits a departure, in special circumstances, from the rule that the losing party is to bear the court costs and pay compensation to the other party in respect of his expenses... In the light of Zürich case-law, it found that in the present case 'the incidence of the costs and expenses should depend on the judgment that would have been delivered' had the statutory period of limitation not expired. To decide this point, it had regard to four matters... the fact that the case was virtually identical to that of the journalist Fust, which had resulted on 2 September 1975 in a conviction... the seriousness of the applicant's accusations against Mr Vass; the applicant's failure to verify his allegations; and the negative outcome of the 1972 prosecution of Mr Vass...

For these reasons, which were set out at length and cannot be dissociated from the operative provisions... the Chamber of the Assize Court concluded that, in the absence of limitation, the 'National Zeitung' article complained of would 'very probably have led to the conviction' of the applicant. In setting out those reasons, the Chamber treated the conduct denounced by the private prosecutors as having been proved; furthermore, the reasons were based on decisions taken in two other cases to which, although they concerned the same facts, Mr Minelli had not been a party and which, in law, were distinct from his case.

In this way the Chamber of the Assize Court showed that it was satisfied of the guilt of Mr Minelli, an accused who, as the Government acknowledged, had not had the benefit of the guarantees contained in paragraphs 1 and 3 of Article 6 (art 6-1, art 6-3). Notwithstanding the absence of a formal finding and despite the use of certain cautious phraseology ('in all probability', 'very probably'), the Chamber proceeded to make appraisals that were incompatible with respect for the presumption of innocence.

...

41. Accordingly, there has been a violation of Article 6(2). . . .

NOTES

1   The Court was composed of President Wiarda, and Judges: Bindschedler-Robert, Lagergren, Gölcüklü, Matscher, Macdonald, and Russo.

2   Subsequently, the Court has held that statements by public officials, as well as judicial determinations, can violate this right. In *Allenet de Ribemont v France*, A.308 (1995), on 24 December 1976 a member of the French Parliament was murdered outside the applicant's home. The applicant had financial dealings with the victim. On 29 December the Paris police arrested the applicant in connection with the murder. During that day the Minister of the Interior held a press conference regarding the police budget. He was accompanied by senior police officers involved in the murder investigation. During the conference a journalist asked who was the key figure in the case and Mr Ducret, Director of the Paris Criminal Investigation Department, replied 'The instigator, Mr De Varga, and his acolyte, Mr de Ribemont, were the instigators of the murder.' On 14 January 1977 the applicant was charged with aiding and abetting intentional homicide. Three years later a discharge order was issued against him. The applicant complained that the comments made at the press conference infringed Article 6(2). The Commission unanimously upheld his complaint.

32. The Government contested, in substance, the applicability of Article 6 para 2 (art 6-2), relying on the *Minelli v Switzerland* judgment of 25 March 1983 (Series A No 62). They maintained that the presumption of innocence could be infringed only by a judicial authority, and could be shown to have been infringed only where, at the conclusion of proceedings ending in a conviction, the court's reasoning suggested that it regarded the defendant as guilty in advance.

33. The Commission acknowledged that the principle of presumption of innocence was above all a procedural safeguard in criminal proceedings, but took the view that its scope was more extensive, in that it imposed obligations not only on criminal courts determining criminal charges but also on other authorities.

34. The Court's task is to determine whether the situation found in this case affected the applicant's right under Article 6 para 2 . . .

35. The presumption of innocence enshrined in paragraph 2 of Article 6 (art 6-2) is one of the elements of the fair criminal trial that is required by paragraph 1 (art 6-1) (see, among other authorities, the . . . *Minelli* judgment previously cited, p 15, para 27). It will be violated if a judicial decision concerning a person charged with a criminal offence reflects an opinion that he is guilty before he has been proved guilty according to law. It suffices, even in the absence of any formal finding, that there is some reasoning suggesting that the court regards the accused as guilty (see the *Minelli* judgment previously cited, p 18, para 37).

However, the scope of Article 6 para 2 (art 6-2) is not limited to the eventuality mentioned by the Government . . . Moreover, the Court reiterates that the Convention must be interpreted in such a way as to guarantee rights which are practical and effective as opposed to theoretical and illusory . . .

36. The Court considers that the presumption of innocence may be infringed not only by a judge or court but also by other public authorities.

37. At the time of the press conference of 29 December 1976 Mr Allenet de Ribemont had just been arrested by the police . . . Although he had not yet been charged with aiding and abetting intentional homicide . . . his arrest and detention in police custody formed part of the judicial investigation begun a few days earlier by a Paris investigating judge and made him a person 'charged with a criminal offence' within the meaning of Article 6 para 2 (art 6-2). The two senior police officers present were conducting the inquiries in the case. Their remarks, made in parallel with the judicial investigation and supported by the Minister of the Interior, were explained by the existence of that investigation and had a direct link with it. Article 6 para 2 (art 6-2) therefore applies in this case.

B. COMPLIANCE WITH ARTICLE 6 PARA 2 (ART 6-2)

1. Reference to the case at the press conference

38. Freedom of expression, guaranteed by Article 10 (art 10) of the Convention, includes the freedom to receive and impart information. Article 6 para 2 (art 6-2) cannot therefore prevent the authorities from informing the public about criminal investigations in progress, but it requires that they do so with all the discretion and circumspection necessary if the presumption of innocence is to be respected.

2. Content of the statements complained of

39. Like the applicant, the Commission considered that the remarks made by the Minister of the Interior and, in his presence and under his authority, by the police superintendent in charge of the inquiry and the Director of the Criminal Investigation Department, were incompatible with the presumption of innocence. It noted that in them Mr Allenet de Ribemont was held up as one of the instigators of Mr de Broglie's murder.

40. The Government maintained that such remarks came under the head of information about criminal proceedings in progress and were not such as to infringe the presumption of innocence, since they did not bind the courts and could be proved false by subsequent investigations. The facts of the case bore this out, as the applicant had not been formally charged until two weeks after the press conference and the investigating judge had eventually decided that there was no case to answer.

41. The Court notes that in the instant case some of the highest-ranking officers in the French police referred to Mr Allenet de Ribemont, without any qualification or reservation, as one of the instigators of a murder and thus an accomplice in that murder . . . This was clearly a declaration of the applicant's guilt which, firstly, encouraged the public to believe him guilty and, secondly, prejudged the assessment of the facts by the competent judicial authority. There has therefore been a breach of Article 6 para 2 (art 6-2). . . .

Do you think the Court would have found a breach if the statements had been made by a junior police officer?

3 Comments made by the Chairman of the Lithuanian Seimas (Parliament) were found to violate this provision in *Butkevicius v Lithuania*, judgment of 26 March 2002. The applicant was the Minister of Defence and a Member of the Seimas from 1996 to 2000. In 1997 he was arrested by intelligence officers while accepting $15,000 from a businessman. After criminal

proceedings were initiated against Butkevicius the Chairman made several comments to the press about him including calling him a 'bribe-taker'. The applicant was later convicted and sentenced to five years' imprisonment for attempting to obtain property by deception. The Court, unanimously, accepted that:

50. … the fact that the applicant was an important political figure at the time of the alleged offence required the highest State officials, including the Prosecutor General and the Chairman of the Seimas, to keep the public informed of the alleged offence and the ensuing criminal proceedings. However, it cannot agree with the Government's argument that this circumstance could justify any use of words chosen by the officials in their interviews with the press.

53. … While the impugned remarks of the Chairman of the Seimas were in each case brief and made on separate occasions, in the Court's opinion they amounted to declarations by a public official of the applicant's guilt, which served to encourage the public to believe him guilty and prejudged the assessment of the facts by the competent judicial authority.

54. There has therefore been a breach of Article 6(2) of the Convention.

Clearly, the Chairman's position as a State office holder brought him within the ambit of Article 6(2). Similar comments by a political opponent of the applicant would not have infringed this provision.

4   The Court has also ruled that presumptions of law or fact imposed on persons in defined circumstances by domestic criminal law provisions may be compatible with Article 6(2). For example, in *Salabiaku v France*, A.141-A (1988) 13 EHRR 379, the applicant had gone to collect a parcel at Roissy airport. He was unable to find the parcel but directed to a trunk (which had not been collected and had no name on it). An airline official advised him to leave the trunk where it was. However, the applicant removed the trunk and took it through the 'green' (nothing to declare) customs exit. He was detained by customs officials outside the airport building who opened the trunk and found a false bottom with 10 kg cannabis hidden inside. The applicant was eventually convicted of the customs offence of smuggling prohibited goods because: '… any person in possession of goods which he or she has brought into France without declaring them to customs is presumed to be legally liable unless he or she can prove specific event of *force majeure* exculpating him; such *force majeure* may arise only as a result of an event beyond human control which could be neither foreseen nor averted …' The applicant complained that his conviction under the Customs Code violated Article 6(2). The Commission, by nine votes to four, found no breach of this right. A united Court rejected the applicant's complaint.

27. As the Government and the Commission have pointed out, in principle the Contracting States remain free to apply the criminal law to an act where it is not carried out in the normal exercise of one of the rights protected under the Convention (*Engel* judgment of 8 June 1976, Series A No 22, p 34, para 81) and, accordingly, to define the constituent elements of the resulting offence. In particular, and again in principle, the Contracting States may, under certain conditions, penalise a simple or objective fact as such, irrespective of whether it results from criminal intent or from negligence. Examples of such offences may be found in the laws of the Contracting States.

28. … Presumptions of fact or of law operate in every legal system. Clearly, the Convention does not prohibit such presumptions in principle. It does, however, require the Contracting States to remain within certain limits in this respect as regards criminal law. If, as the Commission would appear to

consider (paragraph 64 of the report), paragraph 2 of Article 6 (art 6-2) merely laid down a guarantee to be respected by the courts in the conduct of legal proceedings, its requirements would in practice overlap with the duty of impartiality imposed in paragraph 1 (art 6-1). Above all, the national legislature would be free to strip the trial court of any genuine power of assessment and deprive the presumption of innocence of its substance, if the words 'according to law' were construed exclusively with reference to domestic law. Such a situation could not be reconciled with the object and purpose of Article 6 (art 6), which, by protecting the right to a fair trial and in particular the right to be presumed innocent, is intended to enshrine the fundamental principle of the rule of law (see, inter alia, the *Sunday Times* judgment of 26 April 1979, Series A No 30, p 34, para 55).

Article 6 para 2 (art 6-2) does not therefore regard presumptions of fact or of law provided for in the criminal law with indifference. It requires States to confine them within reasonable limits which take into account the importance of what is at stake and maintain the rights of the defence. The Court proposes to consider whether such limits were exceeded to the detriment of Mr Salabiaku.

. . . .

30. . . . It is clear from the judgment of 27 March 1981 and that of 9 February 1982, that the courts in question were careful to avoid resorting automatically to the presumption laid down in Article 392 para 1 of the Customs Code. As the Court of Cassation observed in its judgment of 21 February 1983, they exercised their power of assessment 'on the basis of the evidence adduced by the parties before [them]'. They inferred from the 'fact of possession a presumption which was not subsequently rebutted by any evidence of an event responsibility for which could not be attributed to the perpetrator of the offence or which he would have been unable to avoid' . . . Moreover, as the Government said, the national courts identified in the circumstances of the case a certain 'element of intent', even though legally they were under no obligation to do so in order to convict the applicant.

It follows that in this instance the French courts did not apply Article 392 para 1 of the Customs Code in a way which conflicted with the presumption of innocence. . . .

Hence, offences of strict liability will not necessarily be incompatible with the Convention.

5 An example of the Court finding an unacceptable re-allocation of the burden of proof onto the defence occurred in *Telfner v Austria*, judgment of 20 March 2001. A person had been slightly injured one night by being hit by a car. The victim had noted the registration number of the car, but he had not been able to identify the driver. The next morning the police found the car, registered to the applicant's mother, outside the family home. The mother informed the police that she had not been driving the car and the applicant was not yet home. She said that the car was frequently used by different members of her family. Subsequently the applicant was charged with causing injury by negligence. He pleaded not guilty and stated that he had not been driving the car at the time of the accident. His mother and sister exercised their right not to testify. The District Court found the applicant guilty on the basis that, according to the local police, '. . . it was common knowledge that the vehicle in question was mainly driven by the accused'. Therefore, the District Court concluded that the applicant was the driver who caused the accident/injury. He was sentenced to a fine of 24,000 Austrian schillings. His appeal was dismissed by the Regional Court. The European Court, unanimously, determined that:

18. In the present case, both the District Court and the Regional Court relied in essence on a report of the local police station that the applicant was the main user of the car and had not been home on the night of the accident. However, the Court cannot find that these elements of evidence, which were moreover not corroborated by evidence taken at the trial in an adversarial manner, constituted a case against the applicant which would have called for an explanation from his part. In this context, the Court notes, in particular, that the victim of the accident had not been able to identify the driver, nor

even to say whether the driver had been male or female, and that the Regional Court, after supplementing the proceedings, found that the car in question was also used by the applicant's sister. In requiring the applicant to provide an explanation although they had not been able to establish a convincing prima facie case against him, the courts shifted the burden of proof from the prosecution to the defence.

. . .

20. In conclusion, the Court finds that there has been a violation of Article 6(2) of the Convention.

6 The Court, by a large majority of five to two, concluded that Article 6(2) did not apply to financial confiscation proceedings brought against a convicted drugs smuggler in *Phillips v UK*, judgment of 5 July 2001. The applicant had been found guilty of importing a large amount of cannabis resin into the UK and sentenced to nine years' imprisonment. Soon after his conviction, in June 1996, the Customs and Excise began confiscation proceedings, under the Drug Trafficking Act 1994, against the applicant. Under that Act all property held or expenditure by a convicted drugs trafficker up to six years prior to the start of the criminal proceedings was assumed to have been obtained from the proceeds of drugs trafficking. The value of that property/expenditure was liable to be confiscated by the court that tried the offender unless the latter was able to establish, on the balance of probabilities that the property/expenditure was not so obtained. In December 1996 the trial court ordered that the applicant should pay £91,400 compensation in respect of property acquired as a result of drugs trafficking (or serve a further two years' imprisonment in default of payment). The applicant contended before the European Court that the statutory assumption utilised by the trial court violated his right to the presumption of innocence. The Court held that:

34. . . . the purpose of the procedure under the 1994 Act was to enable the national court to assess the amount at which the confiscation order should properly be fixed. The Court considers that this procedure was analogous to the determination by a court of the amount of a fine or the length of a period of imprisonment to impose upon a properly convicted offender. . . .

35. . . . Once an accused has properly been proved guilty of that offence, Article 6(2) can have no application in relation to allegations made about the accused's character and conduct as part of the sentencing process, unless such accusations are of such a nature and degree as to amount to the bringing of a new "charge" within the autonomous Convention meaning . . .

36. In conclusion, therefore, the Court holds that Article 6(2) was not applicable to the confiscation proceedings brought against the applicant.

For an examination of the Court's consideration of earlier financial confiscation powers applicable to drugs offenders under Article 7 see below p 481.

7 The relationship between criminal and compensation proceedings relating to the same event was examined in *Y. v Norway*, judgment of 11 February 2003. The applicant, when aged 18, was alleged to have committed a violent sexual assault on his 17-year-old cousin which resulted in her death. He was convicted of her homicide by the District Court and sentenced to fourteen years' imprisonment. The District Court ordered him to pay the victim's parents 100,000 NOK compensation under the Damage Compensation Act 1969. The Act provided that, *inter alios*, the parents of a deceased person could claim compensation, for pecuniary/non-pecuniary damage, from the alleged perpetrator who had caused the death intentionally or by gross negligence. Regardless of the outcome of criminal proceedings against the alleged perpetrator, in the compensation proceedings the claimants bore the burden of proof, on the balance of probabilities. The applicant appealed to the High Court where the jury found him not guilty. However, after submissions by counsel for the victim's parents and the applicant the High Court ordered that the District Court's compensation award should be upheld. The applicant's appeal to the Supreme Court was rejected. He then lodged a complaint at Strasbourg contending that the upholding of the compensation award against him violated his presumption of innocence under Article 6(2). A united Chamber held that:

39. The Court reiterates that the concept of a 'criminal charge' in Article 6 is an autonomous one. According to its established case-law there are three criteria to be taken into account when deciding whether a person was 'charged with a criminal offence' for the purposes of Article 6, namely the classification of the proceedings under national law, their essential nature and the type and severity of the penalty that the applicant risked incurring (see *Phillips v the United Kingdom* . . .). Moreover, the scope of Article 6 § 2 is not limited to criminal proceedings that are pending (see *Allenet de Ribemont v France*, judgment of 10 February 1995, Series A No 308, p 16, § 35). In certain instances, the Court has also found the provision applicable to judicial decisions taken after the discontinuation of such proceedings (see in particular the following judgments: *Minelli v Switzerland*, 25 March 1983, Series A No 62, and *Lutz, Englert and Nölkenbockhoff v Germany*, 25 August 1987, Series A No 123), or following an acquittal . . . Those judgments concerned proceedings related to such matters as an accused's obligation to bear court costs and prosecution expenses, a claim for reimbursement of his (or his heirs') necessary costs, or compensation for detention on remand, and which were found to constitute a –consequence and the concomitant of the criminal proceedings.

Accordingly, the Court will examine whether the compensation proceedings in the present case gave rise to a 'criminal charge' against the applicant and, in the event that this was not the case, whether the compensation case nevertheless was linked to the criminal trial in such a way as to fall within the scope of Article 6 § 2.

40. Turning to the first of the above-mentioned criteria, the classification of the proceedings under national law, the Court notes the applicant's argument that, formally speaking, he remained 'charged' until the acquittal gained legal force. However, this concerned only the initial criminal charges of which he was acquitted; it was of no relevance to the compensation claim. The Court notes that the latter had its legal basis in Chapter 3 of the Damage Compensation Act 1969, which sets out the general principles of the national law on torts applicable to personal injuries. It is clear from both the wording of Article 3-5 and Norwegian case-law that criminal liability is not a prerequisite for liability to pay compensation. Even where, as here, the victim had opted for joining the compensation claim to the criminal trial, pursuant to Article 3 of the Code of Criminal Procedure, the claim would still be considered a 'civil' one. This also transpires from the Supreme Court's judgment in the applicant's case, which described the claim as 'civil'. Thus, the Court finds that the compensation claim in issue was not viewed as a 'criminal charge' under the relevant national law.

41. As regard the second and third criteria, the nature of the proceedings and the type and severity of the 'penalty' (i.e. in the instant case the allegedly punitive award of compensation), the Court observes that, while the conditions for civil liability could in certain respects overlap, depending on the circumstances, with those for criminal liability, the civil claim was nevertheless to be determined on the basis of the principles that were proper to the civil law of tort. The outcome of the criminal proceedings was not decisive for the compensation case. The victim had a right to claim compensation regardless of whether the defendant was convicted or, as here, acquitted, and the compensation issue was to be the subject of a separate legal assessment based on criteria and evidentiary standards which in several important respects differed from those applicable to criminal liability.

In the view of the Court, the fact that an act which may give rise to a civil compensation claim under the law of tort is also covered by the objective constitutive elements of a criminal offence could not, notwithstanding its gravity, provide a sufficient ground for regarding the person allegedly responsible for the act in the context of a tort case as being 'charged with a criminal offence'. Nor could the fact that evidence from the criminal trial is used to determine civil law consequences of the act warrant such characterisation. Otherwise, as rightly pointed out by the Government, Article 6 § 2 would give a criminal acquittal the undesirable effect of pre-empting the victim's possibilities of claiming compensation under the civil law of tort, entailing an arbitrary and disproportionate limitation on his or her right of access to court under Article 6 § 1 of the Convention. This again could give an acquitted perpetrator, who would be deemed responsible according the civil burden of proof, the undue advantage of avoiding any responsibility for his or her actions. Such an extensive interpretation would not be supported either by the wording of Article 6 § 2 or any common ground in the national legal systems within the Convention community. On the contrary, in a significant number of Contracting States, an acquittal does not preclude establishing civil liability in relation to the same facts.

Thus, the Court considers that, while the acquittal from criminal liability ought to be maintained in the compensation proceedings, it should not preclude the establishment of civil liability to pay compensation arising out of the same facts on the basis of a less strict burden of proof (see, *mutatis mutandis*, *X v Austria*, No 9295/81, Commission decision of 6 October 1992, *Decisions and Reports* (D.R.) 30, p 227; *M.C. v the United Kingdom*, No 11882/85, decision of 7 October 1987, D.R. 54, p 162).

42. However, if the national decision on compensation contains a statement imputing the criminal liability of the respondent party, this could raise an issue falling within the ambit of Article 6 § 2 of the Convention.

43. The Court will therefore examine the question whether the domestic courts acted in such a way or used such language in their reasoning as to create a clear link between the criminal case and the ensuing compensation proceedings as to justify extending the scope of the application of Article 6 § 2 to the latter.

44. The Court notes that the High Court opened its judgment with the following finding:

> 'Considering the evidence adduced in the case as a whole, the High Court **finds it clearly probable that [the applicant] has committed the offences against Ms T.** with which he was charged and that an award of compensation to her parents should be made under Article 3-5 (2) of the Damage Compensation Act. . . .' (emphasis added)

45. This judgment was upheld by the majority of the Supreme Court, albeit using more careful language. However, that judgment, by not quashing the former, did not rectify the issue, which in the Court's opinion, thereby arises.

46. The Court is mindful of the fact that the domestic courts took note that the applicant had been acquitted of the criminal charges. However, in seeking to protect the legitimate interests of the purported victim, the Court considers that the language employed by the High Court, upheld by the Supreme Court, overstepped the bounds of the civil forum, thereby casting doubt on the correctness of that acquittal. Accordingly, there was a sufficient link to the earlier criminal proceedings which was incompatible with the presumption of innocence.

47. In the light of these considerations, the Court concludes that Article 6 § 2 was applicable to the proceedings relating to the compensation claim against the present applicant and that this provision was violated in the instant case.

So, civil actions based on events which have been the subject of criminal proceedings will not infringe Article 6(2) provided the courts determining the civil claims do not attribute criminal liability to parties, who have not been convicted by the criminal courts. The Court delivered similar judgments in the parallel cases of *O. v Norway* and *Hammern v Norway*, judgments of 11 February 2003.

Article 6(3)

Article 6(3)(a)

Brozicek v Italy A.167 (1989) 12 EHRR 371
European Court of Human Rights

The applicant had been born in the former Czechoslovakia and was now a German national living in the latter country. In August 1975 he was arrested by the Italian police in Savona for allegedly tearing down flags erected by a political party. One of the police officers who detained him was allegedly injured by the applicant. In February 1976 the Savona Public Prosecutor's Office sent a registered letter, written in Italian, to the applicant's home in Germany informing him that criminal proceedings had been initiated against him for, *inter alia*, resisting the police and wounding. The applicant returned the letter to the prosecutor with a letter, written in German, requesting that the Italian authorities write to him in his mother-tongue or one of the official languages of the United Nations. The prosecutor did not reply and continued to send correspondence to the applicant written in Italian. In July 1981 the applicant was convicted, *in absentia*, by the Savona Regional Court. A majority of the Commission upheld the applicant's claim of a breach of Article 6(3)(a).

41. In the Court's opinion, it is necessary to proceed on the basis of the following facts. The applicant was not of Italian origin and did not reside in Italy. He informed the relevant Italian judicial authorities in an unequivocal manner that because of his lack of knowledge of Italian he had difficulty in understanding the contents of their communication. He asked them to send it to him either in his mother tongue or in one of the official languages of the United Nations.

On receipt of this request, the Italian judicial authorities should have taken steps to comply with it so as to ensure observance of the requirements of Article 6 § 3 (a) (art 6-3-a), unless they were in a position to establish that the applicant in fact had sufficient knowledge of Italian to understand from the notification the purport of the letter notifying him of the charges brought against him.

No such evidence appears from the documents in the file or the statements of the witnesses heard on 23 April 1989 . . . On this point there has therefore been a violation of Article 6 § 3 (a) (art 6-3-a).

42. On the other hand, the Court considers the allegation that the judicial notification of 23 February 1976 did not identify 'in detail . . . the nature and cause of the accusation' to be unfounded. This communication was intended to inform Mr Brozicek of the institution of proceedings against him; it sufficiently listed the offences of which he was accused, stated the place and the date thereof, referred to the relevant Articles of the Criminal Code and mentioned the name of the victim. . . .

NOTES

1 The Court was composed of President Ryssdal and Judges Cremona, Bindschedler-Robert, Gölcüklü, Matscher, Pinheiro-Farinha, Walsh, Evans, Macdonald, Bernhardt, Spielmann, Carrillo Salcedo, Martens, Palm, and Foighel.

2 Judges Thor Vilhjalmsson, Pettiti, Russo, De Meyer and Valticos issued a joint dissenting opinion in which they expressed the view that the applicant had not exhausted domestic remedies in Italy.

Article 6(3)(b)

A dramatic example of a breach of this provision was found by a unanimous Grand Chamber in *Ocalan v Turkey*, see above p 128. The Grand Chamber determined, *inter alia*, that the applicant/defendant was only given access to the case file against him (which comprised 17,000 pages) on 4 June 1999 and his trial was concluded on 29 June 1999. Furthermore, Ocalan's lawyers were only given access to the case file on the 7 May 1999 (they were not given a copy and it took them until 15 May 1999 to photocopy the contents of the case file).

Article 6(3)(c)

Artico v Italy A.37 (1980) 3 EHRR 1
European Court of Human Rights

The applicant was an accountant who had been convicted and imprisoned for various dishonesty offences. He appealed against his convictions and requested the Court of Cassation to provide him with free legal aid. In August 1972 the President of the Second Criminal Section of the court accepted the request and appointed a lawyer (Mr Della Rocca) as the applicant's legal aid lawyer. During the next month Mr Della Rocca informed the applicant that he could not accept the appointment due to other commitments. Subsequently, Mr Della Rocca stated that health reasons prevented him from taking on the onerous task of representing the applicant. Despite the applicant's numerous requests to the Court of Cassation for the appointment of another legal aid lawyer none was appointed. The Commission was unanimous in upholding the applicant's complaint under Article 6(3)(c).

32. Paragraph 3 of Article 6 (art 6-3) contains an enumeration of specific applications of the general principle stated in paragraph 1 of the Article (art 6-1). The various rights of which a non-exhaustive list appears in paragraph 3 reflect certain of the aspects of the notion of a fair trial in criminal proceedings ... When compliance with paragraph 3 is being reviewed, its basic purpose must not be forgotten nor must it be severed from its roots.

33. ... Mr Artico claimed to be the victim of a breach of this obligation. The Government, on the other hand, regarded the obligation as satisfied by the nomination of a lawyer for legal aid purposes, contending that what occurred thereafter was in no way the concern of the Italian Republic. According to them, although Mr Della Rocca declined to undertake the task entrusted to him on 8 August 1972 by the President of the Second Criminal Section of the Court of Cassation, he continued to the very end and 'for all purposes' to be the applicant's lawyer. In the Government's view, Mr Artico was, in short, complaining of the failure to appoint a substitute but this amounted to claiming a right which was not guaranteed.

   The Court recalls that the Convention is intended to guarantee not rights that are theoretical or illusory but rights that are practical and effective; this is particularly so of the rights of the defence in view of the prominent place held in a democratic society by the right to a fair trial, from which they derive (see the *Airey* judgment of 9 October 1979, Series A No 32, pp 12–13, par 24, and paragraph 32 above). As the Commission's Delegates correctly emphasised, Article 6 par 3 (c) (art 6-3-c) speaks of 'assistance' and not of 'nomination'. Again, mere nomination does not ensure effective assistance since the lawyer appointed for legal aid purposes may die, fall seriously ill, be prevented for a protracted period from acting or shirk his duties. If they are notified of the situation, the authorities must either replace him or cause him to fulfil his obligations. Adoption of the Government's restrictive interpretation would lead to results that are unreasonable and incompatible with both the wording of sub-paragraph (c) (art 6-3-c) and the structure of Article 6 (art 6) taken as a whole; in many instances free legal assistance might prove to be worthless.

In the present case, Mr Artico did not have the benefit of Mr Della Rocca's services at any point of time. From the very outset, the lawyer stated that he was unable to act. He invoked firstly the existence of other commitments and subsequently his state of health ... The Court is not called upon to enquire into the relevance of these explanations. It finds, as did the Commission ... that the applicant did not receive effective assistance before the Court of Cassation; as far as he was concerned, the above-mentioned decision of 8 August 1972 remained a dead letter.

34. Sub-paragraph (c) of Article 6 par 3 (art 6-3-c) does, nevertheless, make entitlement to the right it sets forth dependent on two conditions. While here there was no argument over the first condition—that the person charged with a criminal offence does not have sufficient means—, the Government denied that the second condition was satisfied: on their view, the 'interests of justice' did not require that Mr Artico be provided with free legal aid. The subject-matter of the Court of Cassation proceedings was, so the Government claimed, crystallized by the grounds adduced in support of the applications to quash, grounds that were filed by the applicant in December 1971 with the assistance of a lawyer of his own choice, Mr Ferri. However, the Government continued, the grounds related to an issue—the regularity of the summons to appear in court—that was of the utmost simplicity, so much so that the public pros-ecutor pleaded in July 1973 that the applications were manifestly ill-founded ... hence, a lawyer would have played but a 'modest' rôle, limited to receiving notification to the effect that the Court of Cassation would take its decision in chambers ...

In any event, here the interests of justice did require the provision of effective assistance. This would, according to Mr Della Rocca, have been a very demanding and onerous task ... At any rate, the written procedure, which is of prime importance before the Italian Court of Cassation, had not been concluded by 8 August 1972. A qualified lawyer would have been able to clarify the grounds adduced by Mr Artico and, in particular, to give the requisite emphasis to the crucial issue of statutory limitation which had hardly been touched on in the 'voluminous and verbose' declarations of 14/15 March 1972 ... In addi-tion, only a lawyer could have countered the pleadings of the public prosecutor's department by caus-ing the Court of Cassation to hold a public hearing devoted, among other things, to a thorough discussion of this issue ...

36. ... In reality, Mr Artico doggedly attempted to rectify the position: he multiplied his complaints and representations both to his official lawyer—to the extent of importuning and even finally exasperating him—and to the Court of Cassation ... Admittedly, a State cannot be held responsible for every short-coming on the part of a lawyer appointed for legal aid purposes but, in the particular circumstances, it was for the competent Italian authorities to take steps to ensure that the applicant enjoyed effectively the right to which they had recognised he was entitled. Two courses were open to the authorities: either to replace Mr Della Rocca or, if appropriate, to cause him to fulfil his obligations ... They chose a third course—remaining passive -, whereas compliance with the Convention called for positive action on their part (see the above-mentioned Airey judgment, p 14, par 25 in fine).

37. The Court thus concludes that there has been a breach of the requirements of Article 6 par 3 (c) (art 6-3-c) ....

NOTES

1   The Court was composed of President Wiarda and Judges: Balladore Pallieri, Zekia, Bindschedler-Robert, Liesch, Gölcüklü and Pinheiro-Farinha. The Court's focus upon the reality of whether the applicant had been provided with effective legal assistance was to be commended. If States could satisfy the requirements of this provision merely by designating a

legal aid lawyer the guarantee could become worthless in practice; as happened in the applicant's case.

2 In *Benham v UK*, 1996 III 738 (see above p 267), the Grand Chamber was unanimous in holding that, '61. . . . where deprivation of liberty is at stake, the interests of justice in principle call for legal representation'. As Benham was liable to be imprisoned for failing to pay his community charge ('poll tax') the Grand Chamber concluded that he should have received free legal representation and consequently the absence of such representation for him before the magistrates resulted in a breach of Article 6(3)(c). A unanimous Chamber of the full-time Court reached a similar conclusion in *Beet and Others v UK*, judgment of 1 March 2005. Legal aid was made available for such proceedings from 1 June 1997.

3 As we have already seen in *John Murray v UK*, (above, p 408), the denial of access to a lawyer for the first 48 hours of questioning (and detention) of a terrorist suspect was held to amount to a violation of this provision (at least where adverse inferences could be drawn from the detainee's silence).

4 In the later case of *Averill v UK*, (6 June 2000), the Court applied its reasoning in *John Murray* to hold that denying a detained terrorist suspect access to a lawyer for 24 hours was also a breach of this right.

5 The applicability of Article 6(3)(c) to significant pre-trial events was further confirmed in *Berlinski v Poland*, judgment of 20 June 2002. The two applicant body-builders refused to leave an athletics club with the consequence that the police were called. A violent struggle ensued with the applicants sustaining various injuries during their arrest by the police. Two days later the applicants requested that the prosecuting authorities appoint a free defence lawyer to help them. The prosecution did not respond. Some months later the applicants were charged with assaulting police officers. One year after the applicants had requested legal aid a court appointed a free lawyer to represent them. Two years later they were convicted and given suspended prison sentences. The applicants claimed, *inter alia*, to have suffered from a breach of Article 6(3)(c). A united Chamber held that:

> 75. The Court recalls that, even if the primary purpose of Article 6, as far as criminal matters are concerned, is to ensure a fair trial by a 'tribunal' competent to determine 'any criminal charge', it does not follow that this provision of the Convention has no application to pre-trial proceedings. Thus, Article 6—especially paragraph 3—may be relevant before a case is sent for trial if and so far as the fairness of the trial is likely to be seriously prejudiced by an initial failure to comply with its provisions. The manner in which Article 6 §§ 1 and 3 (c) is to be applied during the preliminary investigation depends on the special features of the proceedings involved and on the circumstances of the case . . .

> 77. The Court observes that it is undisputed that the applicants lacked means to employ a private representative in the context of criminal proceedings against them. It is also uncontested that the applicants' request for an official lawyer to be appointed was ignored by the authorities, with the result that they had no defence counsel for more than a year. Given that a number of procedural acts, including questioning of the applicants and their medical examinations, were carried out during that period . . . the Court finds no justification for this restriction which deprived the applicants of the right to adequately defend themselves during the investigation and trial.

Therefore a breach of Article 6(3)(c) had occurred. The greater the potential detriment to the defence of an impecunious suspect a pre-trial event poses the stronger such a person's claim to free legal assistance under this provision.

6 In *Krombach v France*, judgment of 13 February 2001 (see below p 1000), the respondent Government submitted that the term 'assistance' should be given a strict interpretation and distinguished from 'representation'; with the consequence that the applicant did not have a right to have his lawyer represent him at his trial when he was absent. A unanimous Chamber rejected this narrow interpretation:

89. . . . Although not absolute, the right of everyone charged with a criminal offence to be effectively defended by a lawyer, assigned officially if need be, is one of the fundamental features of a fair trial. A person charged with a criminal offence does not loose the benefit of this right merely on account of not being present at the trial. Even if the legislature must be able to discourage unjustified absences, it cannot penalise them by creating exceptions to the right to legal assistance.

The Court concluded that the penalisation of the applicant for his non-attendance at his trial by barring his lawyer from making any submissions on behalf of the applicant was 'manifestly disproportionate' and amounted to a breach of Article 6(1) in conjunction with Article 6(3)(c).

7 In *Ezeh and Connors v UK*, judgment of 9 October 2003 (see above p 376), the Grand Chamber concluded, by eleven votes to six, that there had been a breach of Article 6(3)(c) because of the governors' refusals to allow the applicant prisoners to have legal representation during the disciplinary hearings. However, the Grand Chamber declined to consider the applicants' contention that the interests of justice required that they should have been given free legal assistance under this provision.

8 In *Ocalan v Turkey*, see above p 128 the Grand Chamber emphasised the need for privileged communications between a defendant and his/her lawyers.

132. . . . the Grand Chamber endorses the Chamber's findings:

'. . . the applicant's first visit from his lawyers took place under the supervision and within sight and hearing of members of the security forces and a judge, all of whom were present in the same room as the applicant and his lawyers. The security forces restricted the visit to twenty minutes. The record of the visit was sent to the State Security Court.

'. . . As regards subsequent visits, . . . the Court accepts that meetings between the applicant and his lawyers after the initial visit took place within hearing of members of the security forces, even though the security officers concerned were not in the room where the meetings took place.'

133. The Grand Chamber agrees with the Chamber's assessment of the effects of the applicant's inability to consult his lawyers out of the hearing of third parties:

'. . . an accused's right to communicate with his legal representative out of hearing of a third person is part of the basic requirements of a fair trial in a democratic society and follows from Article 6 § 3 (c) of the Convention. If a lawyer were unable to confer with his client and receive confidential instructions from him without such surveillance, his assistance would lose much of its usefulness, whereas the Convention is intended to guarantee rights that are practical and effective (*S. v Switzerland*, judgment of 28 November 1991, Series A No 220, p. 16 § 48). The importance to the rights of the defence of ensuring confidentiality in meetings between the accused and his lawyers has been affirmed in various international instruments, including European instruments (see *Brennan v the United Kingdom*, No 39846/98, §§ 38–40, ECHR 2001-X). However, as stated above . . . restrictions may be imposed on an accused's access to his lawyer if good cause exists. The relevant issue is whether, in the light of the proceedings taken as a whole, the restriction has deprived the accused of a fair hearing.

'. . . In the present case, the Court accepts . . . that the applicant and his lawyers were unable to consult out of hearing of the authorities at any stage. It considers that the inevitable consequence of that restriction, which was imposed during both the preliminary investigation and the trial, was to prevent the applicant from conversing openly with his lawyers and asking them questions that [might prove] important to the preparation of his defence. The rights of the defence were thus significantly affected.

'... The Court observes in that connection that the applicant had already made statements by the time he conferred with his lawyers and made further statements at hearings before the State Security Court after consulting them. If his defence to the serious charges he was required to answer was to be effective, it was essential that those statements be consistent. Accordingly, the Court considers that it was necessary for the applicant to be able to speak with his lawyers out of hearing of third parties.

'... As to the Government's contention that the supervision of the meetings between the applicant and his lawyers was necessary to ensure the applicant's security, the Court observes that the lawyers had been retained by the applicant himself and that there was no reason to suspect that they had threatened their client's life. They were not permitted to see the applicant until they had undergone a series of searches. Mere visual surveillance by the prison officials, accompanied by other measures, would have sufficed to ensure the applicant's security.'

Consequently, the Court held that the fact that it was impossible for the applicant to confer with his lawyers out of the hearing of members of the security forces infringed the rights of the defence. The Grand Chamber, unanimously, went on to find a violation of Article 6(3)(c).

Article 6(3)(d)

Van Mechelen v The Netherlands 1997-III, (1997) 25 EHRR 647
European Court of Human Rights

The police received information that the four applicants were involved in a series of armed robberies. Teams of officers were deployed to keep the suspects under observation. The officers saw the applicants go, in three cars, to a post office where a robbery took place and the police gave chase. The robbers opened fire, with a sub-machine gun, on the police and some officers were wounded. Subsequently, the applicants were arrested and charged with attempted murder/manslaughter and robbery. The prosecution relied on written statements of anonymous police officers identifying the applicants as the persons involved in the robbery and shootings. The Regional Court convicted the applicants of attempted manslaughter and robbery. Each applicant was sentenced to 10 years' imprisonment. The applicants appealed to the Hertogenbosch Court of Appeal. The court ordered that the anonymous police officers should be questioned by the defence and prosecution through a sound link (the police witness was in one room with an investigating judge and registrar while the defendants, their lawyers and prosecution were in another room). Each anonymous police witnesses stated that he wished to remain anonymous to protect himself/his family. The officers repeated their evidence that the applicants had been participants in the robbery and shootings. The investigating judge reported that the officers appeared to be truthful. The Court of Appeal convicted the applicants of attempted murder and robbery and sentenced each of them to fourteen years' imprisonment. The applicants complained that their convictions, based to a decisive extent on the evidence of the anonymous police officers, violated Article 6(1) and 6(3)(d). By twenty votes to eight, the Commission found no breach of the Convention.

49. As the requirements of Article 6 para 3 (art 6-3) are to be seen as particular aspects of the right to a fair trial guaranteed by Article 6 para 1 (art 6-1), the Court will examine the complaints under Article 6 paras 1 and 3 (d) taken together (art 6-1+6-3-d) (see, among many other authorities, the above-mentioned Doorson judgment, pp 469–70, para 66).

50. The Court reiterates that the admissibility of evidence is primarily a matter for regulation by national law and as a general rule it is for the national courts to assess the evidence before them. The Court's task under the Convention is not to give a ruling as to whether statements of witnesses were properly admitted as evidence, but rather to ascertain whether the proceedings as a whole, including the way in which evidence was taken, were fair (see, among other authorities, the . . . Doorson judgment [Doorson v The Netherlands, 1996-II], p 470, para 67).

51. In addition, all the evidence must normally be produced at a public hearing, in the presence of the accused, with a view to adversarial argument. There are exceptions to this principle, but they must not infringe the rights of the defence; as a general rule, paragraphs 1 and 3 (d) of Article 6 (art 6-1, art 6-3-d) require that the defendant be given an adequate and proper opportunity to challenge and question a witness against him, either when he makes his statements or at a later stage . . .

52. As the Court had occasion to state in its Doorson judgment (ibid, p 470, para 69), the use of statements made by anonymous witnesses to found a conviction is not under all circumstances incompatible with the Convention.

53. In that same judgment the Court noted the following:

> It is true that Article 6 (art 6) does not explicitly require the interests of witnesses in general, and those of victims called upon to testify in particular, to be taken into consideration. However, their life, liberty or security of person may be at stake, as may interests coming generally within the ambit of Article 8 of the Convention (art 8). Such interests of witnesses and victims are in principle protected by other, substantive provisions of the Convention, which imply that Contracting States should organise their criminal proceedings in such a way that those interests are not unjustifiably imperilled. Against this background, principles of fair trial also require that in appropriate cases the interests of the defence are balanced against those of witnesses or victims called upon to testify. (See the above-mentioned Doorson judgment, p 470, para 70.)

54. However, if the anonymity of prosecution witnesses is maintained, the defence will be faced with difficulties which criminal proceedings should not normally involve. Accordingly, the Court has recognised that in such cases Article 6 para 1 taken together with Article 6 para 3 (d) of the Convention (art 6-1+6-3-d) requires that the handicaps under which the defence labours be sufficiently counterbalanced by the procedures followed by the judicial authorities (ibid, p 471, para 72).

55. Finally, it should be recalled that a conviction should not be based either solely or to a decisive extent on anonymous statements (ibid, p 472, para 76).

2. APPLICATION OF THE ABOVE PRINCIPLES

56. In the Court's opinion, the balancing of the interests of the defence against arguments in favour of maintaining the anonymity of witnesses raises special problems if the witnesses in question are members of the police force of the State. Although their interests—and indeed those of their families—also deserve protection under the Convention, it must be recognised that their position is to some extent different from that of a disinterested witness or a victim. They owe a general duty of obedience to the State's executive authorities and usually have links with the prosecution; for these reasons alone their use as anonymous witnesses should be resorted to only in exceptional circumstances. In addition, it is in the nature of things that their duties, particularly in the case of arresting officers, may involve giving evidence in open court.

57. On the other hand, the Court has recognised in principle that, provided that the rights of the defence are respected, it may be legitimate for the police authorities to wish to preserve the anonymity of an agent deployed in undercover activities, for his own or his family's protection and so as not to impair his usefulness for future operations . . .

58. Having regard to the place that the right to a fair administration of justice holds in a democratic society, any measures restricting the rights of the defence should be strictly necessary. If a less restrictive measure can suffice then that measure should be applied.

59. In the present case, the police officers in question were in a separate room with the investigating judge, from which the accused and even their counsel were excluded. All communication was via a sound link. The defence was thus not only unaware of the identity of the police witnesses but were also prevented from observing their demeanour under direct questioning, and thus from testing their reliability . . .

60. It has not been explained to the Court's satisfaction why it was necessary to resort to such extreme limitations on the right of the accused to have the evidence against them given in their presence, or why less far-reaching measures were not considered.

   In the absence of any further information, the Court cannot find that the operational needs of the police provide sufficient justification . . .

61. Nor is the Court persuaded that the Court of Appeal made sufficient effort to assess the threat of reprisals against the police officers or their families. It does not appear from that court's judgment that it sought to address the question whether the applicants would have been in a position to carry out any such threats or to incite others to do so on their behalf. Its decision was based exclusively on the seriousness of the crimes committed . . . In this connection, it is to be noted that Mr Engelen, a civilian witness who in the early stages of the proceedings had made statements identifying one of the applicants as one of the perpetrators, did not enjoy the protection of anonymity and it has not been claimed that he was at any time threatened.

62. It is true—as noted by the Government and the Commission . . .—that the anonymous police officers were interrogated before an investigating judge, who had himself ascertained their identity and had, in a very detailed official report of his findings, stated his opinion on their reliability and credibility as well as their reasons for remaining anonymous.

   However these measures cannot be considered a proper substitute for the possibility of the defence to question the witnesses in their presence and make their own judgment as to their demeanour and reliability. It thus cannot be said that the handicaps under which the defence laboured were counterbalanced by the above procedures.

63. Moreover, the only evidence relied on by the Court of Appeal which provided positive identification of the applicants as the perpetrators of the crimes were the statements of the anonymous police officers. That being so the conviction of the applicants was based 'to a decisive extent' on these anonymous statements.

64. In the Court's view, the present case falls to be distinguished from that of Doorson: in the latter case it was decided on the basis of information contained in the case file itself that the witnesses Y.15 and Y.16—who were both civilians, and who knew the accused personally—had sufficient reason to believe that he might resort to violence, and they were heard in the presence of counsel (see the above-mentioned Doorson judgment, pp 454–5, para 25, pp 455–6, para 28, and pp 470–1, paras 71 and 73).

   In addition, in the latter case other evidence providing positive identification of the accused as the perpetrator of the crimes charged was available from sources unrelated to the anonymous witnesses (ibid, pp 458–9, para 34, and p 472, para 76).

65. Against this background the Court cannot find that the proceedings taken as a whole were fair.

C. CONCLUSION

66. There has been a violation of Article 6 para 1 taken together with Article 6 para 3 (d) (art 6-1+6-3-d) ....

NOTES

1 The Court was composed of President Bernhardt and Judges: Russo, Foighel, Repik, Jungwiert and Levits. Judges Matscher, and Valticos issued a joint dissenting opinion in which they expressed the view that the case was a 'borderline' one. However, they found no violation of Article 6 because, '... this was a case of armed robbery and it is understandable that the witnesses—even though they were police officers—should be in fear of reprisals from trigger-happy criminals.' In his dissenting opinion Judge Van Dijk concluded that the applicants had received a fair trial as, *inter alia*, the police officers had been interrogated by the investigating judge and the Court of Appeal had assessed the threat of reprisals against the officers.

2 Should police officers generally be expected to identify themselves and give evidence in open court?

3 The fundamental criterion applied by the Court in the above judgment was that articulated in paragraph 55.

4 In the earlier case of *Doorson v Netherlands*, 1996-II, the police had launched an investigation into drug trafficking in Amsterdam. Drug users would only give the police information on their suppliers if the informants remained anonymous (in the light of past experience they feared violence from the suppliers). Information was given to the police regarding the applicant and he was arrested. He was eventually convicted, by the Amsterdam Regional Court, of drug trafficking on the basis of an identified witness who appeared in court and was subject to defence and prosecution questioning (his evidence was very equivocal) and two anonymous witnesses (Y.15 and Y.16) who had been heard by the investigating judge (the applicant's lawyer had left the hearing before they arrived, late, to give their evidence). The applicant appealed to the Amsterdam Court of Appeal and his lawyer was able to question Y.15 and Y.16 in the presence of the investigating judge (however their identities were not disclosed). Both these witnesses stated that the applicant had sold them illegal drugs. The Court of Appeal found the applicant guilty of selling heroin and cocaine on the basis of, *inter alia*, the evidence of Y.15 and Y.16, police information regarding his illegal activities, and the evidence of the identified witness before the Regional Court. The applicants complaint of a breach of Articles 6(1) and 6(3)(d) was rejected by the Commission (by fifteen votes to twelve). A large majority of the Court (seven votes to two) also found no breach of these provisions.

73. In the instant case the anonymous witnesses were questioned at the appeals stage in the presence of counsel by an investigating judge who was aware of their identity ... even if the defence was not. She noted, in the official record of her findings dated 19 November 1990, circumstances on the basis of which the Court of Appeal was able to draw conclusions as to the reliability of their evidence ... Counsel was not only present, but he was put in a position to ask the witnesses whatever questions he considered to be in the interests of the defence except in so far as they might lead to the disclosure of their identity, and these questions were all answered ...

74. While it would clearly have been preferable for the applicant to have attended the questioning of the witnesses, the Court considers, on balance, that the Amsterdam Court of Appeal was entitled to consider that the interests of the applicant were in this respect outweighed by the need to ensure the safety of the witnesses. More generally, the Convention does not preclude identification—for the purposes of Article 6 para 3 (d) (art 6-3-d)—of an accused with his counsel ...

75. In addition, although it is normally desirable that witnesses should identify a person suspected of serious crimes in person if there is any doubt about his identity, it should be noted in the present case that Y.15 and Y.16 identified the applicant from a photograph which he himself had acknowledged to be of himself... moreover, both gave descriptions of his appearance and dress...

It follows from the above considerations that in the circumstances the 'counterbalancing' procedure followed by the judicial authorities in obtaining the evidence of witnesses Y.15 and Y.16 must be considered sufficient to have enabled the defence to challenge the evidence of the anonymous witnesses and attempt to cast doubt on the reliability of their statements, which it did in open court by, among other things, drawing attention to the fact that both were drug addicts...

76. Finally, it should be recalled that even when 'counterbalancing' procedures are found to compensate sufficiently the handicaps under which the defence labours, a conviction should not be based either solely or to a decisive extent on anonymous statements. That, however, is not the case here: it is sufficiently clear that the national court did not base its finding of guilt solely or to a decisive extent on the evidence of Y.15 and Y.16...

Furthermore, evidence obtained from witnesses under conditions in which the rights of the defence cannot be secured to the extent normally required by the Convention should be treated with extreme care. The Court is satisfied that this was done in the criminal proceedings leading to the applicant's conviction, as is reflected in the express declaration by the Court of Appeal that it had treated the statements of Y.15 and Y.16 'with the necessary caution and circumspection'...

The applicant, through his lawyer, clearly had a greater opportunity to challenge the testimony and credibility of the anonymous witnesses (Y.15 and Y.16) in this case than the applicants did in *Van Mechelen* regarding the anonymous police officers.

5   The Committee of Ministers promulgated a Recommendation to member States ('Concerning Intimidation of Witnesses and the Rights of the Defence' R (97) 13) in 1997 to guide the latters' formulation of domestic criminal policy and legislation. The Recommendation stated that:

... 10. Where available and in accordance with domestic law, anonymity of persons who might give evidence should be an exceptional measure. Where the guarantee of anonymity has been requested by such persons and/or temporarily granted by the competent authorities, criminal procedural law should provide for a verification procedure to maintain a fair balance between the needs of criminal proceedings and the rights of the defence. The defence should, through this procedure, have the opportunity to challenge the alleged need for anonymity of the witness, his credibility and the origin of his knowledge.

11. Anonymity should only be granted when the competent judicial authority, after hearing the parties, finds that: i. the life or freedom of the person involved is seriously threatened or, in the case of an undercover agent, his potential to work in the future is seriously threatened; and ii. the evidence is likely to be significant and the person appears to be credible.

12. Where appropriate, further measures should be available to protect witnesses giving evidence, including preventing identification of the witness by the defence eg by using screens, disguising his face or distorting his voice.

13. When anonymity has been granted, the conviction shall not be based solely or to a decisive extent on the evidence of such persons.

14. Where appropriate, special programmes, such as witness protection programmes, should be set up and made available to witnesses who need protection. The main objective of these programmes should be to safeguard the life and personal security of witnesses, their relatives and other persons close to them.

15. Witness protection programmes should offer various methods of protection; this may include giving witnesses and their relatives and other persons close to them an identity change, relocation, assistance in obtaining new jobs, providing them with bodyguards and other physical protection. ...

464 • ARTICLE 6(3)

6 The full-time Court has followed the approach of its predecessor to Article 6(3)(d), for example in *Birutis and Others v Lithuania*, judgment of 28 June 2002. The three applicants/ prisoners were charged with organizing and participating in a prison riot. The evidence against the first applicant consisted of written statements obtained by the investigating authorities from seventeen anonymous witnesses, mostly other prisoners, statements made by three co-accused and evidence given at his trial by five members of the prison staff. The evidence against the second applicant was broadly the same, however the only evidence against the third applicant comprised of written statements by six anonymous witnesses. The trial court convicted all the applicants and imposed long prison sentences on them. The European Court held that:

28. ...as a general rule, paragraphs 1 and 3(d) of Article 6 require that the defendant be given an adequate and proper opportunity to challenge and question a witness against him, either when he makes his statements or at a later stage...

The judges were united in concluding that the conviction of the third applicant solely on the basis of anonymous evidence violated the *Doorson* principle. Furthermore, the trial court had failed to implement counterbalancing procedures, such as questioning the anonymous witnesses or scrutinizing how their evidence had been obtained, to safeguard the defence rights of the first and second applicants. Therefore, the Court found a breach of Article 6(3)(d) had occurred in respect of each applicant.

Article 6(3)(e)

Luedicke, Belkacem and Koc v Germany A.29 (1978) 2 EHRR 149
European Court of Human Rights

The three applicants were non-German nationals (respectively a British citizen, an Algerian citizen and a Turkish citizen) who had been convicted of various offences (a road traffic offence, assault and grievous bodily harm) by German courts. They were not fluent in German therefore interpreters had been provided for their trials. After conviction the courts ordered the applicants to pay the costs of interpretation. The applicants complained to the Commission which was unanimous in finding a violation of Article 6(3)(e).

38. ....In its report, the Commission expressed the unanimous opinion that the decisions challenged by the applicants were in breach of Article 6 para 3(e) (art 6-3-e). The Commission takes this provision to mean that every accused person who 'cannot understand or speak the language used in court' must be granted the free assistance of an interpreter and may not have payment of the resulting costs subsequently claimed back from him.

The Government contest the correctness of this opinion. They submit that while Article 6 para 3(e) (art 6-3-e) exempts the accused from paying in advance for the expenses incurred by using an interpreter, it does not prevent him from being made to bear such expenses once he has been convicted.

39. For the purposes of interpreting Article 6 para 3(e) (art 6-3-e), the Court will be guided, as also were the Government and the Commission, by Articles 31 to 33 of the Vienna Convention of 23 May 1969 on the Law of Treaties (see the *Golder* judgment of 21 February 1975, Series A No 18, p 14, para 29). In order to decide the issue arising in the present proceedings, the Court will therefore seek to ascertain 'the ordinary meaning to be given to the terms' of Article 6 para 3(e) (art 6-3-e) 'in their context and in the light of its object and purpose' (Article 31 para 1 of the Vienna Convention).

40. The Court finds, as did the Commission, that the terms 'gratuitement'/'free' in Article 6 para 3(e) (art 6-3-e) have in themselves a clear and determinate meaning. In French, 'gratuitement' signifies 'd'une manière gratuite, qu'on donne pour rien, sans rétribution' (*Littré, Dictionnaire de la langue française*), 'dont on jouit sans payer' (*Hatzfeld* et Darmesteter, *Dictionnaire général de la langue française*), 'à titre gratuit, sans avoir rien à payer', the opposite of 'à titre onéreux' (Larousse, *Dictionnaire de la langue française*), 'd'une manière gratuite; sans rétribution, sans contrepartie' (Robert, *Dictionnaire alphabétique et analogique de la langue française*). Similarly, in English, 'free' means 'without payment, gratuitous' (*Shorter Oxford Dictionary*), 'not costing or charging anything, given or furnished without cost or payment' (*Webster's Third New International Dictionary*).

Consequently, the Court cannot but attribute to the terms 'gratuitement' and 'free' the unqualified meaning they ordinarily have in both of the Court's official languages: these terms denote neither a conditional remission, nor a temporary exemption, nor a suspension, but a once and for all exemption or exoneration. It nevertheless remains to be determined whether, as the Government contend, the context as well as the object and purpose of the provision in issue negative the literal interpretation.

41. According to the Government, all the rights enumerated in Article 6 para 3 (art 6-3) are concerned with criminal proceedings and become devoid of substance once those proceedings, the fair conduct of which they are to guarantee, have been terminated by a final and binding judgment. The Government submitted that what are involved are certain minimum rights which—in specifying the content of the right to a fair trial as enshrined in Article 6 para 1 (art 6-1)—are granted only to an accused ('everyone charged with a criminal offence', 'tout accusé'). The Government likewise place reliance on the presumption of innocence, which is enunciated in Article 6 para 2 (art 6-2) and which is rebutted on the final and binding conviction of the accused. Their reasoning is that the various guarantees of a fair trial, because they are intended to enable the accused to preserve the presumption of innocence, lapse at the same time as that presumption. In the Government's submission, the costs of the proceedings constitute a consequence of the conviction and accordingly fall entirely outside the ambit of Article 6 (art 6).

42. The Court notes that, for the purpose of ensuring a fair trial, paragraph 3 of Article 6 (art 6-3) enumerates certain rights ('minimum rights'/'notamment') accorded to the accused (a person 'charged with a criminal offence'). Nonetheless, it does not thereby follow, as far as sub-paragraph (e) is concerned, that the accused person may be required to pay the interpretation costs once he has been convicted. To read Article 6 para 3(e) (art 6-3-e) as allowing the domestic courts to make a convicted person bear these costs would amount to limiting in time the benefit of the Article and in practice, as was rightly emphasised by the Delegates of the Commission, to denying that benefit to any accused person who is eventually convicted. Such an interpretation would deprive Article 6 para 3(e) (art 6-3-e) of much of its effect, for it would leave in existence the disadvantages that an accused who does not understand or speak the language used in court suffers as compared with an accused who is familiar with that language—these being the disadvantages that Article 6 para 3(e) (art 6-3-e) is specifically designed to attenuate.

Furthermore, it cannot be excluded that the obligation for a convicted person to pay interpretation costs may have repercussions on the exercise of his right to a fair trial as safeguarded by Article 6 (art 6) (see the *Golder* judgment of 21 February 1975, Series A No 18, p 18, para 36), even if, as in the Federal Republic of Germany, an interpreter is appointed as a matter of course to assist every accused person who is not conversant with the language of the court. Making such an appointment admittedly eliminates in principle the serious drawbacks that would arise were an accused to defend himself in person in a language he did not master or fully master rather than incurring additional costs. Nevertheless, as was pointed out by the Delegates of the Commission, the risk remains that in some borderline cases the appointment or not of an interpreter might depend on the attitude taken by the accused, which might in turn be influenced by the fear of financial consequences.

Hence, it would run counter not only to the ordinary meaning of the terms 'free'/'gratuitement' but also to the object and purpose of Article 6 (art 6), and in particular of paragraph 3(e) (art 6-3-e) thereof, if this latter paragraph were to be reduced to the guarantee of a right to provisional exemption from payment—not preventing the domestic courts from making a convicted person bear the interpretation costs—, since the right to a fair trial which Article 6 (art 6) seeks to safeguard would itself be adversely affected. . . .

48. Before the Court a difference of opinion emerged between the Government and the Commission as to which costs come within the scope of Article 6 para 3(e) (art 6-3-e). In the Government's submission, Article 6 para 3(e) (art 6-3-e) 'unambiguously and expressly settles the assistance of an interpreter at the oral hearing (audience)' but does not apply to other interpretation costs.

The Government's contention, the correctness of which is contested by the Delegates, cannot be accepted by the Court. Article 6 para 3(e) (art 6-3-e) does not state that every accused person has the right to receive the free assistance of an interpreter at the oral hearing (à l'audience); it states that this right is accorded to him 'if he cannot understand or speak the language used in court' ('s'il ne comprend pas ou ne parle pas la langue employée à l'audience'). As was pointed out by the Delegates, the latter words do no more than indicate the conditions for the granting of the free assistance of an interpreter. Furthermore, the English text 'used in court', being wider than the French expression 'employée à l'audience' (literally translated as 'used at the hearing'), furnishes an additional argument in this respect.

Construed in the context of the right to a fair trial guaranteed by Article 6, paragraph 3(e) (art 6-3-e) signifies that an accused who cannot understand or speak the language used in court has the right to the free assistance of an interpreter for the translation or interpretation of all those documents or statements in the proceedings instituted against him which it is necessary for him to understand in order to have the benefit of a fair trial.

49. In this connection, certain differences exist between the three cases.

Mr Luedicke had to pay DM 225.40 by way of interpretation costs, including DM 154.60 in respect of the oral hearing . . . The representatives appearing before the Court did not provide any details as to the nature of the remaining balance; accordingly, the Court cannot conclude that this balance falls outside the scope of the guarantee in Article 6 para 3(e) (art 6-3-e).

As regards Mr Koç, the interpretation costs are exclusively attributed to three hearings before the Assize Court attached to the Aachen Regional Court and amount respectively to DM 311.50 and DM 510.50 and DM 112.50 . . . Therefore, these costs indisputably come within the ambit of Article 6 para 3(e) (art 6-3-e).

The interpretation costs awarded against Mr Belkacem result from four distinct procedural steps, namely, the accused's appearance before the judge (DM 33.25), the review of his detention on remand (DM 67.60), the translation of the indictment (DM 90.20) and the trial hearing (DM 130.90) (see paragraph 22 above). In the Court's opinion, Article 6 para 3(e) (art 6-3-e) covers all these costs.

50. Accordingly, the Court concludes that the contested decisions of the German courts were in breach of Article 6 para 3(e) (art 6-3-e) of the Convention. . . .'

NOTES

1 The Court was composed of President Wiarda and Judges: Mosler, Pedersen, Bindschedler-Robert, Evrigenis, Teitgen, and Lagergren.

2 The Court's unwillingness to accept the Government's narrow conception of the scope of this right should be commended. In the Court's judgment the right encompasses the provision of translation/interpretation facilities covering more than just the oral aspects of a criminal trial (paragraph 48) and it is not conditional on the defendant being acquitted (paragraph 42). Once again, the Court's ruling sought to make Convention rights effective in practice.

3 The Court also found Germany to be in breach of this right in *Öztürk* (above, p 369).

4   The full-time Court has emphasized the fundamental role of trial judges in ensuring that defendants who do not understand the language of the court are provided with effective interpretation assistance. In *Cuscani v United Kingdom*, judgment of 24 September 2002, the applicant was an Italian national with a very limited command of English. He had been the manager of a restaurant in Newcastle-upon-Tyne. The authorities charged him with various offences involving the alleged evasion of hundreds of thousands of pounds of taxes. He was granted legal aid and represented by a Queen's Counsel, junior counsel and solicitors. At his trial Cuscani pleaded guilty, on the advice of his counsel. During that hearing his counsel informed the judge of Cuscani's poor English and asked the court to direct that an interpreter be present at subsequent hearings. The court so ordered. However, when the trial resumed a few weeks later for sentencing no interpreter was present. Cuscasni's counsel accepted that the hearing should proceed without an interpreter. The judge asked if there was anyone in court who knew the defendant and was fluent in Italian and English. Cuscani's counsel, without consulting him, replied that Cuscani's brother (who was present) could provide translation if required. In fact the brother was never asked to provide any interpretation during the subsequent hearing at which Cuscani was sentenced to four years' imprisonment. The European Court was unanimous in finding that those proceedings violated Article 6(3)(e).

38. ... in the Court's opinion the verification of the applicant's need for interpretation facilities was a matter for the judge to determine in consultation with the applicant, especially since he had been alerted to counsel's own difficulties in communicating with the applicant.

9 ARTICLE 7 NO PUNISHMENT WITHOUT LAW

Article 7(1)

....

CR v UK A.335-C (1995) 21 EHRR 363
European Court of Human Rights

The applicant married his wife in 1984. They separated for a short time in 1987, but were reconciled. On 21 October 1989 the applicant's wife left their home, with their son, and went to live with her parents. She left a note for the applicant informing him that she intended to seek a divorce. On 12 November 1989 the applicant forced his way into the parent's house and attempted to have sexual intercourse with the wife against her will. In the course of the attempt he assaulted her, by squeezing her neck with his hands. The applicant was charged with attempted rape (under section 1(1) of the Sexual Offences (Amendment) Act 1976 rape was defined as occurring when a man 'has unlawful sexual intercourse with a woman who at the time of the intercourse does not consent to it . . .') and assault occasioning actual bodily harm. At his trial, in the summer of 1990, the applicant submitted that the charge of rape was not one which was known to the law because the victim was his wife. He relied upon a statement by Sir Matthew Hale CJ in his 'History of the Pleas of the Crown' (published in 1736): 'But the husband cannot be guilty of rape committed by himself upon his lawful wife, for by their matrimonial consent and contract the wife hath given up herself in this kind unto her husband, which she cannot retract.' However, the trial judge, Owen J, cited more recent cases to support the view that in certain circumstances wives could revoke their consent to sexual intercourse with their husbands. He identified three such situations: (a) by a court order, (b) by agreement between the parties and (c) a withdrawal of either party from cohabitation accompanied by a clear indication that consent to sexual intercourse had been terminated. The judge considered that both (b) and (c) applied to the wife of the applicant. In the light of this ruling the applicant pleaded guilty and was sentenced to three years' imprisonment. His appeal was dismissed by a unanimous Court of Appeal. The House of Lords was also united in rejecting his final appeal (*R v R* [1991] 4 All ER 481). On behalf of the House Lord Keith of Kinkel stated that:

For over 150 years after the publication of Hale's work there appeared to have been no reported case in which judicial consideration was given to his proposition. The first such case was *R v Clarence* [1888] 22 Queen's Bench Division 23, [1886–90] All England Law Reports 133 . . . It may be taken that the proposition was generally regarded as an accurate statement of the common law of England. The common law is, however, capable of evolving in the light of changing social, economic and cultural developments. Hale's proposition reflected the state of affairs in these respects at the time it was enunciated. Since then the status of women, and particularly of married women, has changed out of all recognition in various ways which are very familiar and upon which it is unnecessary to go into detail. Apart from property matters and the availability of matrimonial remedies, one of the most important changes is that marriage is in modern times regarded as a partnership of equals, and no longer one in which the wife was the subservient chattel of the husband. Hale's proposition involves that by marriage a wife gives her irrevocable consent to sexual intercourse with her husband under all circumstances and irrespective of the state of her health or how she happens to be feeling at the time. In modern times any reasonable person must regard that conception as quite unacceptable....

The position then is that that part of Hale's proposition which asserts that a wife cannot retract the consent to sexual intercourse which she gives on marriage has been departed from in a series of decided cases. On grounds of principle there is no good reason why the whole proposition should not be held inapplicable in modern times. The only question is whether section 1(1) of the 1976 Act presents an insuperable obstacle to that sensible course. The argument is that 'unlawful' in that subsection means outside the bond of marriage.

... The fact is that it is clearly unlawful to have sexual intercourse with any woman without her consent, and that the use of the word in the subsection adds nothing. In my opinion there are no rational grounds for putting the suggested gloss on the word, and it should be treated as being mere surplusage in this enactment ...

I am therefore of the opinion that section 1 (1) of the 1976 Act presents no obstacle to this House declaring that in modern times the supposed marital exception in rape forms no part of the law of England. The Court of Appeal, Criminal Division, took a similar view [in the present case]. Towards the end of the judgment of that court Lord Lane CJ said ...:

> The remaining and no less difficult question is whether, despite that view, this is an area where the court should step aside to leave the matter to the parliamentary process. This is not the creation of a new offence, it is the removal of a common law fiction which has become anachronistic and offensive and we consider that it is our duty having reached that conclusion to act upon it.

I respectfully agree. (pp 483–490)

The applicant complained to the Commission alleging a breach of Article 7 in that he had been convicted of conduct, attempted rape of his wife, which he argued did not constitute a criminal offence at that time. By fourteen votes to three, the Commission considered that there had been no breach of Article 7. The Court held that:

A. GENERAL PRINCIPLES

32. The guarantee enshrined in Article 7 (art 7), which is an essential element of the rule of law, occupies a prominent place in the Convention system of protection, as is underlined by the fact that no derogation from it is permissible under Article 15 (art 15) in time of war or other public emergency. It should be construed and applied, as follows from its object and purpose, in such a way as to provide effective safeguards against arbitrary prosecution, conviction and punishment.

33. Accordingly, as the Court held in its *Kokkinakis v Greece* judgment of 25 May 1993 (Series A No 260-A, p 22, para 52), Article 7 (art 7) is not confined to prohibiting the retrospective application of the criminal law to an accused's disadvantage: it also embodies, more generally, the principle that only the law can define a crime and prescribe a penalty (nullum crimen, nulla poena sine lege) and the principle that the criminal law must not be extensively construed to an accused's detriment, for instance by analogy. From these principles it follows that an offence must be clearly defined in the law. In its aforementioned judgment the Court added that this requirement is satisfied where the individual can know from the wording of the relevant provision and, if need be, with the assistance of the courts' interpretation of it, what acts and omissions will make him criminally liable. The Court thus indicated that when speaking

of 'law' Article 7 (art 7) alludes to the very same concept as that to which the Convention refers elsewhere when using that term, a concept which comprises written as well as unwritten law and implies qualitative requirements, notably those of accessibility and foreseeability (see, as a recent authority, the *Tolstoy Miloslavsky v UK* judgment of 13 July 1995, Series A No 316-B, pp 71–2, para 37).

34. However clearly drafted a legal provision may be, in any system of law, including criminal law, there is an inevitable element of judicial interpretation. There will always be a need for elucidation of doubtful points and for adaptation to changing circumstances. Indeed, in the United Kingdom, as in the other Convention States, the progressive development of the criminal law through judicial law-making is a well entrenched and necessary part of legal tradition. Article 7 (art 7) of the Convention cannot be read as outlawing the gradual clarification of the rules of criminal liability through judicial interpretation from case to case, provided that the resultant development is consistent with the essence of the offence and could reasonably be foreseen.

B. APPLICATION OF THE FOREGOING PRINCIPLES

35. The applicant maintained that the general common law principle that a husband could not be found guilty of rape upon his wife, albeit subject to certain limitations, was still effective on 12 November 1989, when he committed the acts which gave rise to the charge of attempted rape . . . A succession of court decisions before and also after that date . . . had affirmed the general principle of immunity. It was clearly beyond doubt that as at 12 November 1989 no change in the law had been effected, although one was being mooted. The removal of the immunity by the Court of Appeal on 14 March 1991 and the House of Lords on 23 October 1991 occurred by way of direct reversal, not clarification, of the law.

When the House of Commons debated the Bill for the Sexual Offences (Amendment) Act 1976 . . . different views on the marital immunity were expressed. On the advice of the Minister of State to await a report of the Criminal Law Revision Committee, an amendment that would have abolished the immunity was withdrawn and never voted upon. In its report, which was not presented until 1984, the Criminal Law Revision Committee recommended that the immunity should be maintained and that a new exception should be created.

In 1988, when considering certain amendments to the 1976 Act, Parliament had the opportunity to take out the word 'unlawful' in section 1(1)(a) . . . or to introduce a new provision on marital intercourse, but took no action in this respect.

On 17 September 1990 the Law Commission provisionally recommended that the immunity rule be abolished . . . However, the debate was pre-empted by the Court of Appeal's and the House of Lords' rulings in the applicant's case . . . In the applicant's submission, these rulings altered the law retrospectively, which would not have been the case had the Law Commission's proposal been implemented by Parliament. Consequently, he concluded, when Parliament in 1994 removed the word 'unlawful' from section 1 of the 1976 Act . . . it did not merely restate the law as it had been in 1976.

36. The applicant further argued that in examining his complaint under Article 7 para 1 (art 7-1) of the Convention, the Court should not consider his conduct in relation to any of the exceptions to the immunity rule. The issue was never resolved by the national courts, as the sole ground on which the applicant's conviction rested was in fact the removal of the common law fiction by the Court of Appeal and the House of Lords.

37. Should a foreseeability test akin to that under Article 10 para 2 (art 10-2) apply in the instant case, the applicant was of the opinion that it had not been satisfied. Although the Court of Appeal and the House of Lords did not create a new offence or change the basic ingredients of the offence of rape, they were extending an existing offence to include conduct which until then was excluded by the common law. They could not be said to have adapted the law to a new kind of conduct but rather to a change of social attitudes. To extend the criminal law, solely on such a basis, to conduct which was previously lawful was precisely what Article 7 (art 7) of the Convention was designed to prevent. Moreover, the applicant stressed, it was impossible to specify with precision when the change in question had

occurred. In November 1989, change by judicial interpretation was not foreseen by the Law Commission, which considered that a parliamentary enactment would be necessary.

38. The Government and the Commission were of the view that by November 1989 there was significant doubt as to the validity of the alleged marital immunity for rape. This was an area where the law had been subject to progressive development and there were strong indications that still wider interpretation by the courts of the inroads on the immunity was probable. In particular, given the recognition of women's equality of status with men in marriage and outside it and of their autonomy over their own bodies, the adaptation of the ingredients of the offence of rape was reasonably foreseeable, with appropriate legal advice, to the applicant. He was not convicted of conduct which did not constitute a criminal offence at the time when it was committed.

In addition, the Government pointed out, on the basis of agreed facts Mr Justice Owen had found that there was an implied agreement between the applicant and his wife to separation and to withdrawal of the consent to intercourse. The circumstances in his case were thus covered by the exceptions to the immunity rule already stated by the English courts.

39. The Court notes that the applicant's conviction for attempted rape was based on the statutory offence of rape in section 1 of the 1956 Act, as further defined in section 1(1) of the 1976 Act . . . The applicant does not dispute that the conduct for which he was convicted would have constituted attempted rape within the meaning of the statutory definition of rape as applicable at the time, had the victim not been his wife. His complaint under Article 7 (art 7) of the Convention relates solely to the fact that he could not avail himself of the marital immunity under common law because, so he submitted, it had been retrospectively abolished.

40. It is to be observed that a crucial issue in the judgment of the Court of Appeal . . . related to the definition of rape in section 1(1)(a) of the 1976 Act: 'unlawful sexual intercourse with a woman who at the time of the intercourse does not consent to it'. The question was whether 'removal' of the marital immunity would conflict with the statutory definition of rape, in particular whether it would be prevented by the word 'unlawful'. The Court of Appeal carefully examined various strands of interpretation of the provision in the case-law, including the argument that the term 'unlawful' excluded intercourse within marriage from the definition of rape. In this connection, the Court recalls that it is in the first place for the national authorities, notably the courts, to interpret and apply national law (see, for instance, the *Kemmache v France (No 3)* judgment of 24 November 1994, Series A No 296-C, pp 86–7, para 37). It sees no reason to disagree with the Court of Appeal's conclusion, which was subsequently upheld by the House of Lords . . . that the word 'unlawful' in the definition of rape was merely surplusage and did not inhibit them from 'removing a common law fiction which had become anachronistic and offensive' and from declaring that 'a rapist remains a rapist subject to the criminal law, irrespective of his relationship with his victim' . . .

41. The decisions of the Court of Appeal and then the House of Lords did no more than continue a perceptible line of case-law development dismantling the immunity of a husband from prosecution for rape upon his wife . . . There was no doubt under the law as it stood on 12 November 1989 that a husband who forcibly had sexual intercourse with his wife could, in various circumstances, be found guilty of rape. Moreover, there was an evident evolution, which was consistent with the very essence of the offence, of the criminal law through judicial interpretation towards treating such conduct generally as within the scope of the offence of rape. This evolution had reached a stage where judicial recognition of the absence of immunity had become a reasonably foreseeable development of the law . . .

42. The essentially debasing character of rape is so manifest that the result of the decisions of the Court of Appeal and the House of Lords—that the applicant could be convicted of attempted rape, irrespective of his relationship with the victim—cannot be said to be at variance with the object and purpose of Article 7 (art 7) of the Convention, namely to ensure that no one should be subjected to arbitrary prosecution, conviction or punishment (see paragraph 32 above). What is more, the abandonment of the unacceptable idea of a husband being immune against prosecution for rape of his wife

was in conformity not only with a civilised concept of marriage but also, and above all, with the fundamental objectives of the Convention, the very essence of which is respect for human dignity and human freedom.

43. Having reached this conclusion, the Court does not find it necessary to enquire into whether the facts in the applicant's case were covered by the exceptions to the immunity rule already made by the English courts before 12 November 1989.

44. In short, the Court, like the Government and the Commission, finds that the national courts' decisions that the applicant could not invoke immunity to escape conviction and sentence for attempted rape upon his wife did not give rise to a violation of his rights under Article 7 para 1 (art 7-1) of the Convention.

FOR THESE REASONS, THE COURT UNANIMOUSLY

Holds that there has been no violation of Article 7 para 1 (art 7-1) of the Convention.

NOTES

1   The Court was composed of President Ryssdal and Judges: Gölcüklü, Russo, De Meyer, Martens, Bigi, Freeland, Jambrek, and Lohmus.

2   On the same day as the above judgement was delivered the Court issued an identical decision in the case of *S W v UK*, A.335-C (1995) 21 EHRR 363. The applicant raped his wife, after she told him that she was leaving him, in September 1990. At his trial, in April 1991, the jury found the applicant guilty of, *inter alia*, rape and he was sentenced to five years' imprisonment.

3   Parliament adopted a new, and wider, statutory definition of rape in the Criminal Justice and Public Order Act 1994: '1(1) It is an offence for a man to rape a woman or another man. (2) A man commits rape if—(a) he has sexual intercourse with a person ... who at the time of the intercourse does not consent to it ....'

4   The Court's judgments in *CR* and *SW* uphold the 'gradual clarification' of rules of criminal liability, provided the evolution is 'consistent with the essence of the offence and could reasonably be foreseen', as being compatible with the requirements of Article 7(1). However, determining whether a particular evolution is within these broad parameters is not an easy task. To what extent do you think the Court's conclusions in the above cases were influenced by its abhorrence of the act of rape?

5   The case of *Kokkinakis v Greece* is examined below (at p 595). The Court, by eight votes to one, found that the Greek offence of proselytism defined by Law No 1363/1938 did not breach the certainty requirements of Article 7(1).

....

Streletz, Kessler and Krenz v Germany judgment of 22 March 2001
European Court of Human Rights

The applicants were the former Deputy Defence Minister (from 1979 to 1989), the Minister of Defence (from 1985 to 1989) and President of the Council of State and the National Defence Council (October–December 1989) of the former German Democratic Republic (GDR). Between 1949 and the construction of the Berlin Wall in 1961 approximately two and a half million persons fled from East Germany to the Federal Republic of Germany (FRG). Thereafter, the GDR authorities maintained a highly sophisticated security system along the border with West Germany including anti-personnel minefields and automatic-fire installations. East German border guards through their training and political instruction were under orders 'not to permit border crossings, to arrest border violators or to annihilate them and to protect the State borders at all costs . . .' (para. 19 of the judgment). Western estimates of the numbers of persons killed whilst trying to cross the border varied between 264 and 938 due to the secrecy surrounding these events by the GDR authorities. Following the collapse of the GDR, in the autumn of 1989, a newly elected parliament requested the FRG to ensure that criminal prosecutions would be initiated against persons who had committed injustices under the rule of the East German Communist Party. In October 1990 Germany was reunited (under the FRG). Subsequently, during 1993, the Berlin Regional Court sentenced the first and second applicants to periods of imprisonment (five years and seven years) for incitement to commit intentional homicide on the grounds of shared responsibility for the deaths of a number of young persons killed (by anti-personnel mines or shot by border guards) between 1971 and 1989. The Regional Court initially applied the Criminal Code of the former GDR to determine the applicants' guilt and then substituted the FRG's Criminal Code as it was more lenient. The convictions were upheld by the Federal Court of Justice and the Federal Constitutional Court. The third applicant was sentenced to six years' imprisonment for intentional homicide as an indirect principal, on the basis of his participation in decisions of the Political Bureau and the National Defence Council (between 1984 and 1986) on the GDR's border-policing regime and the consequent deadly shooting of four young persons trying to cross to the West between 1984 and 1989). The Berlin Regional Court's decision was also upheld on appeal.

The applicants petitioned the former Commission alleging that their actions did not constitute offences, at the times when they were committed, under either national (i.e. GDR) or international law; and their convictions by FRG courts breached, *inter alia*, Article 7 (no punishment without law). The applications were transferred to the new Court where a Chamber, none of the parties objecting, relinquished them to the Grand Chamber. Before the Court the applicants argued that Article 7 had been violated because, *inter alia*, (1) their convictions after reunification were not foreseeable, (2) their actions did not constitute offences under GDR criminal law and (3) neither did their actions amount to offences under international law (in the majority of States access to borders was forbidden/strictly regulated and the use of firearms by border guards authorized)

51. . . . it notes that one special feature of the present case is that its background is the transition between two States governed by two different legal systems, and that after reunification the German courts convicted the applicants for crimes they had committed in their capacity as leaders of the GDR.

(A) NATIONAL LAW

73. The Court considers that recourse to anti-personnel mines and automatic-fire systems, in view of their automatic and indiscriminate effect, and the categorical nature of the border guards' orders to 'annihilate border violators (*Grenzverletzer*) and protect the border at all costs', flagrantly infringed the fundamental rights enshrined in Articles 19 and 30 of the GDR's Constitution, which were essentially confirmed by the GDR's Criminal Code (Article 213) and successive statutes on the GDR's borders (section 17(2) of the People's Police Act 1968 and section 27(2) of the State Borders Act 1982). This State practice was also in breach of the obligation to respect human rights and the other international obligations of the GDR, which, on 8 November 1974, had ratified the International Covenant on Civil and Political Rights, expressly recognising the right to life and to the freedom of movement . . . regard being had to the fact that it was almost impossible for ordinary citizens to leave the GDR legally. Even though

the use of anti-personnel mines and automatic-fire systems had ceased in about 1984, the border guards' orders remained unchanged until the fall of the Berlin Wall in November 1989.

74. The Court further notes that, in justification, the applicants relied on the order to fire which they themselves had issued to the border guards and on the ensuing practice, on account of which they had been convicted. However, according to the general principles of law, defendants are not entitled to justify the conduct which has given rise to their conviction simply by showing that such conduct did in fact take place and therefore formed a practice.

75. Moreover, irrespective of the GDR's responsibility as a State, the applicants' acts as individuals were defined as criminal by Article 95 of the GDR's Criminal Code, which already provided in its 1968 version, in terms repeated in 1977: 'Any person whose conduct violates human or fundamental rights . . . may not plead statute law, an order or written instructions in justification; he shall be held criminally responsible.'

76. There is accordingly no doubt that the applicants bore individual responsibility for the acts in question.

77. However, the applicants argued that in view of the reality of the situation in the GDR their conviction by the German courts had not been foreseeable and that it had been absolutely impossible for them to foresee that they would one day be called to account in a criminal court because of a change of circumstances.

78. The Court is not convinced by that argument. The broad divide between the GDR's legislation and its practice was to a great extent the work of the applicants themselves. Because of the very senior positions they occupied in the State apparatus, they evidently could not have been ignorant of the GDR's Constitution and legislation, or of its international obligations and the criticisms of its border-policing regime that had been made internationally . . . Moreover, they themselves had implemented or maintained that regime, by superimposing on the statutory provisions, published in the GDR's Official Gazette, secret orders and service instructions on the consolidation and improvement of the border-protection installations and the use of firearms. In the order to fire given to border guards they had insisted on the need to protect the GDR's borders 'at all costs' and to arrest 'border violators' or 'annihilate' them . . . The applicants were therefore directly responsible for the situation which obtained at the border between the two German States from the beginning of the 1960s until the fall of the Berlin Wall in 1989.

79. Moreover, the fact that the applicants had not been prosecuted in the GDR, and were not prosecuted and convicted by the German courts until after the reunification, on the basis of the legal provisions applicable in the GDR at the material time, does not in any way mean that their acts were not offences according to the law of the GDR.

80. In that connection, the Court notes that the problem Germany had to deal with after reunification as regards the attitude to adopt vis-à-vis persons who had committed crimes under a former regime has also arisen for a number of other States which have gone through a transition to a democratic regime.

80. The Court considers that it is legitimate for a State governed by the rule of law to bring criminal proceedings against persons who have committed crimes under a former regime; similarly, the courts of such a State, having taken the place of those which existed previously, cannot be criticised for applying and interpreting the legal provisions in force at the material time in the light of the principles governing a State subject to the rule of law. . . .

84. It should also be pointed out that the parliament of the GDR democratically elected in 1990 had expressly requested the German legislature to ensure that criminal prosecutions would be brought in respect of the injustices committed by the SED [East German Communist Party]. That makes it reasonable to suppose that, even if the reunification of Germany had not taken place, a democratic regime

taking over from the SED regime in the GDR would have applied the GDR's legislation and prosecuted the applicants, as the German courts did after reunification.

85. Moreover, regard being had to the pre-eminence of the right to life in all international instruments on the protection of human rights . . . including the Convention itself, in which the right to life is guaranteed by Article 2, the Court considers that the German courts' strict interpretation of the GDR's legislation in the present case was compatible with Article 7 § 1 of the Convention. . . .

87. The Court considers that a State practice such as the GDR's border-policing policy, which flagrantly infringes human rights and above all the right to life, the supreme value in the international hierarchy of human rights, cannot be covered by the protection of Article 7 § 1 of the Convention. That practice, which emptied of its substance the legislation on which it was supposed to be based, and which was imposed on all organs of the GDR, including its judicial bodies, cannot be described as "law" within the meaning of Article 7 of the Convention.

88. The Court accordingly takes the view that the applicants, who, as leaders of the GDR, had created the appearance of legality emanating from the GDR's legal system but then implemented or continued a practice which flagrantly disregarded the very principles of that system, cannot invoke the protection of Article 7 § 1 of the Convention. To reason otherwise would run counter to the object and purpose of that provision, which is to ensure that no one is subjected to arbitrary prosecution, conviction or punishment.

89. Having regard to all of the above considerations, the Court holds that at the time when they were committed the applicants' acts constituted offences defined with sufficient accessibility and foreseeability in GDR law.

(B) INTERNATIONAL LAW

i. Applicable rules

90. The Court considers that it is its duty to examine the present case from the standpoint of the principles of international law also, particularly those relating to the international protection of human rights, especially because the German courts used arguments grounded on those principles . . .

91. It is therefore necessary to consider whether, at the time when they were committed, the applicants' acts constituted offences defined with sufficient accessibility and foreseeability under international law, particularly the rules of international law on the protection of human rights.

ii. International protection of the right to life

92. The Court notes in the first place that in the course of the development of that protection the relevant conventions and other instruments have constantly affirmed the pre-eminence of the right to life.

93. Article 3 of the Universal Declaration on Human Rights of 10 December 1948, for example, provides: 'Everyone has the right to life.' That right was confirmed by the International Covenant on Civil and Political Rights of 16 December 1966, ratified by the GDR on 8 November 1974, Article 6 of which provides: 'Every human being has the inherent right to life' and 'No one shall be arbitrarily deprived of his life'. It is also included in the Convention, Article 2 § 1 of which provides:

> 'Everyone's right to life shall be protected by law. No one shall be deprived of his life intentionally save in the execution of a sentence of a court following his conviction of a crime for which this penalty is provided by law.'

94. The convergence of the above-mentioned instruments is significant: it indicates that the right to life is an inalienable attribute of human beings and forms the supreme value in the hierarchy of human rights.

95. However, the applicants alleged that their actions had been justified by the exceptions in Article 2 § 2 of the Convention, which provides:

'Deprivation of life shall not be regarded as inflicted in contravention of this article when it results from the use of force which is no more than absolutely necessary:

'(a) in defence of any person from unlawful violence;

'(b) in order to effect a lawful arrest or to prevent the escape of a person lawfully detained;

'(c) in action lawfully taken for the purpose of quelling a riot or insurrection.'

96. The Court considers that, regard being had to the arguments set out above, the deaths of the fugitives were in no sense the result of a use of force which was 'absolutely necessary'; the State practice implemented in the GDR by the applicants did not protect anyone against unlawful violence, was not pursued in order to make any arrest that could be described as 'lawful' according to the law of the GDR and had nothing to do with the quelling of a riot or insurrection, as the fugitives' only aim was to leave the country.

97. It follows that the applicants' acts were not justified in any way under Article 2 § 2 of the Convention.

iii. International protection of the freedom of movement

98. Like Article 2 § 2 of Protocol No. 4 to the Convention, Article 12 § 2 of the International Covenant on Civil and Political Rights provides: 'Everyone shall be free to leave any country, including his own.' Restrictions on that right are authorised only where they are provided by law, are necessary to protect national security, public order, public health or morals or the rights and freedoms of others, and are consistent with the other rights recognised in the Covenant.

99. The applicants relied on those restrictions to justify the introduction and continued operation the GDR's border-policing regime.

100. However, the Court considers that in the present case none of the above exceptions applied. Firstly, the acts in issue were orders, given and executed, which were not compatible with either the Constitution or statute law. Secondly, it cannot be contended that a general measure preventing almost the entire population of a State from leaving was necessary to protect its security, or for that matter the other interests mentioned. Lastly, the way in which the GDR put into practice the prohibition barring its nationals from leaving the country and punished contravention of that policy was contrary to another right secured under the Covenant, namely the right to life guaranteed by Article 6, for those who were its victims.

101. Still in connection with the right to freedom of movement, the Court points out that when Hungary opened its border with Austria on 11 September 1989 it denounced a bilateral agreement between itself and the GDR, referring expressly to Articles 6 and 12 of the International Covenant and to Article 62 (fundamental change of circumstances) of the Vienna Convention on the Law of Treaties.

iv. The GDR's State responsibility and the applicants' individual responsibility

102. Thus, by installing anti-personnel mines and automatic-fire systems along the border, and by ordering border guards to 'annihilate border violators and protect the border at all costs', the GDR had set up a border-policing regime that clearly disregarded the need to preserve human life, which was enshrined in the GDR's Constitution and legislation, and the right to life protected by the above-mentioned international instruments; that regime likewise infringed the right to the freedom of movement mentioned in Article 12 of the International Covenant on Civil and Political Rights.

103. The State practice in issue was to a great extent the work of the applicants themselves, who, as political leaders, knew—or should have known—that it infringed both fundamental rights and human rights, since they could not have been ignorant of the legislation of their own country. Articles 8 and 19

§ 2 of the 1968 Constitution already provided, respectively: 'The generally recognised rules of international law intended to promote peace and peaceful cooperation between peoples are binding on the State and every citizen' and 'Respect for and protection of the dignity and liberty of the person are required of all State bodies, all forces in society and every citizen'. Furthermore, as early as 1968 the first chapter of the Special Part of the Criminal Code included an introduction that provided: 'The merciless punishment of crimes against . . . humanity and human rights . . . is an indispensable prerequisite for stable peace in the world, for the restoration of faith in fundamental human rights and the dignity and worth of human beings, and for the preservation of the rights of all.'

Similarly, as noted above (paragraph 78), the applicants could not have been ignorant of the international obligations entered into by the GDR or of the repeated international criticism of its border-policing regime.

104. If the GDR still existed, it would be responsible from the viewpoint of international law for the acts concerned. It remains to be established that alongside that State responsibility the applicants individually bore criminal responsibility at the material time. Even supposing that such responsibility cannot be inferred from the above-mentioned international instruments on the protection of human rights, it may be deduced from those instruments when they are read together with Article 95 of the GDR's Criminal Code, which explicitly provided, and from as long ago as 1968 moreover, that individual criminal responsibility was to be borne by those who violated the GDR's international obligations or human rights and fundamental freedoms.

105. In the light of all of the above considerations, the Court considers that at the time when they were committed the applicants' acts also constituted offences defined with sufficient accessibility and foreseeability by the rules of international law on the protection of human rights.

106. In addition, the applicants' conduct could be considered, likewise under Article 7 § 1 of the Convention, from the standpoint of other rules of international law, notably those concerning crimes against humanity. However, the conclusion reached by the Court (see paragraph 105 above) makes consideration of that point unnecessary.

(C) CONCLUSION

107. Accordingly, the applicants' conviction by the German courts after the reunification was not in breach of Article 7 § 1.

108. In the light of that finding, the Court is not required to consider whether their convictions were justified under Article 7 § 2 of the Convention.

. . .

FOR THESE REASONS, THE COURT UNANIMOUSLY

1. *Holds* that there has been no violation of Article 7(1) of the Convention.

NOTES

1 The Grand Chamber was composed of President Wildhaber and Judges: Palm, Rozakis, Ress, Costa, Ferrari Bravo, Caflisch, Loucaides, Cabral Barreto, Jungwiert, Bratza, Zupancic, Vaji, Pellonpaa, Tsatsa-Nikolovska, Levits, and Kovler.

2 Judge Loucaides issued a concurring opinion in which he expressed the belief that the applicants' actions were also in breach of international criminal law. 'More specifically, I think that the conduct for which the applicants were convicted (as set out in the judgment), amounted to the international law crime known as a "crime against humanity", which at the time of such conduct, had already been established as part of the general principles of customary international law.' He referred to the Charter of the International (Nuremberg) Military Tribunal For the Prosecution of the Major War Criminals of the European Axis and Resolution 3074 of the UN General Assembly of 3 December 1973 (which proclaimed the need for international cooperation in the punishment of persons guilty of war crimes and crimes against humanity).

3   Two judges, with personal experiences of living under communist totalitarian governments, expressed their criticisms of the theories and practices of the 'legal systems' operating under those regimes in separate concurring opinions. Judge Zupancic, from Slovenia, observed:

'In terms of their own criminal law, the applicants were the co-conspirators in a large and consistent conspiracy to disregard the objective meaning of the law on the statute book, i.e. they co-conspired to create and maintain a two-faced situation in which the so-called "State practice" of impunity and even of rewarding the criminal behaviour of other co-conspirators was in unqualified contradiction with the formal language of the relevant criminal statutes. The distinctive characteristic of this case is that it was the applicants themselves who were 'the public officer[s] or [members of the] body charged by law with responsibility for the interpretation, administration or enforcement of the law defining the offence.'

Here there was a self-referential situation in which the very same people who were charged with responsibility for the interpretation, administration or enforcement of the law defining the offence propagated the 'State practice' which they now claim to have been the source of their own understanding of the law and thus of their excuse under the law? What is more, the applicants maintain that the GDR's State practice was part and parcel of contemporaneous objective impunity and that it is therefore unacceptable *ex post* to activate criminal liability for their acts.

Clearly, this raises the issue of the rule of law and more specifically the issue of the rule of substantive criminal law. For the European Court of Human Rights to accept this 'State practice' as an integral part of the 'law defining the offence' for the purposes of Article 7 § 1, or to accept the defence of mistake of law would seal this circuitous self-justification in contradiction to the rule of law.'

Judge Levits, from Latvia, was also concerned to emphasize that newly democratic States should not be constrained by their predecessor's legal structures when dealing with alleged breaches of human rights by former officials.

10. Consequently, interpretation and application of national or international legal norms according to socialist or other non-democratic methodology (with results intolerable for a democratic system) should from the standpoint of a democratic system be regarded as wrong. That applies both to *ex post facto* assessment of the legal practice of previous non-democratic regimes (as in the instant case, although the same situation may obviously arise in other new democracies) and to assessment of the actual legal practice (e.g. regarding the Covenant) of today's non-democratic regimes. That practice should be regarded as a misuse of law. After the change to a democratic political order the persons responsible cannot rely for justification of their conduct on the 'specific' way in which law is interpreted by non-democratic regimes.

11. In my view, that is a compelling conclusion, which derives from the inherent universality of human rights and democratic values, by which all democratic institutions are bound. At least since the time of the Nuremberg Tribunal that conception of the democratic order has been well understood in the world and it is therefore foreseeable for everybody. . . .

13. Paragraph 107 of the judgment confirms that the applicants' conduct could also be considered under Article 7 § 1 of the Convention from the standpoint of other rules of international law, notably

those concerning crimes against humanity, but that in view of the Court's findings after applying international human rights norms in conjunction with the norms of the former GDR's national law it is not necessary to examine this question.

14. In principle, I agree with that approach. However, the conclusions of the present judgment were reached mainly because the Constitution and other laws of the GDR were well-formulated in a language which was similar to the language of the constitutional and other legal provisions of democratic States governed by the rule of law (e.g. constitutional provisions on human rights). That was not the real intention of the non-democratic regime of the GDR. The human rights provisions in the constitutions of the former socialist states were rather of a propagandistic character. Nevertheless, the German domestic courts and this Court, for what in my view are compelling reasons, as explained above, have 'taken these rights seriously' (Ronald Dworkin) by giving them the meaning derived from the wording of the various legal norms as construed according to the methodology of application of the law inherent in the democratic system.

15. I think that the ability of courts in the newly established democracies to deal with the 'legacy' of former non-democratic regimes should not depend solely on the wording of the legal norms of the non-democratic regimes, formulated in the first place not for legal but rather for propagandistic purposes.

16. The judgment left the door open also for the examination of such conduct as the applicants' under the heading of a criminal offence under international law (paragraph 107).

17. In that connection, I would like to stress recent developments in international law in respect of the strengthening of the protection of human rights, including norms on crimes against humanity. Despite the fact that many legal problems in this field are not yet entirely resolved, the direction of these developments is obvious.

18. I therefore endorse the convincing analysis of Judge Loucaides in his separate opinion, that at the material time the applicants' conduct was not only a criminal offence under domestic law but could also be considered an offence under international law.

4   The judgment of the Grand Chamber, in the year of the fortieth anniversary of the construction of the Berlin wall, revealed a clear condemnation of the practical failure of the former GDR regime to respect the basic human rights (enshrined in international, regional and domestic legal rules) of its citizens. The irony of the applicants' complaints was that they were in essence challenging the application of their own regime's formal laws to (retrospectively) determine their criminal culpability. Of course, as the judgment vividly demonstrates, one of the great lies of the former communist regimes of eastern Europe was the fundamental difference between the formal legal provisions in those States and the norms actually applied. In contrast the value of the Strasbourg system is that it seeks to ensure that Member States give practical effect to those Convention rights that they have guaranteed to observe in their treatment of all persons within their jurisdictions. Consequently, the Court is a vital mechanism in ensuring that member governments do not develop a corrosive bifurcation between the public espousal of human rights and the neglect, or deliberate undermining, of those norms in official practices.

5   The same Grand Chamber delivered a similar judgment in the parallel case of *K-H.W. v Germany*, judgment of 22 March 2001. In this case the applicant was a former GDR border guard who, when aged 20, in 1972 had shot dead a person trying to swim across the border from East Berlin. The applicant was awarded an Order of Merit and given a bonus of 150 marks by the GDR authorities for his actions. After the re-unification of Germany, he was convicted in 1993 of intentional homicide by the Berlin Regional Court and sentenced to one year and ten months' juvenile detention suspended on probation. The Grand Chamber, by

fourteen votes to three, rejected the applicant's claim that his conviction violated Article 7. The dissentients, Judges Cabral Barreto, Pellonpaa, and Zupancic considered the applicant to be a low-level official who was a victim of the oppressive communist regime. In the words of Judge Cabral Barreto in his partly dissenting opinion:

6. In conclusion, I consider that in the present case there has been a violation of Article 7 of the Convention on account of the applicant's conviction for his actions in February 1972.

Lastly, I remain convinced that the applicant, who was then a young man without maturity or independence, and who had been indoctrinated in accordance with the dominant ideology, was rather the victim of a regime and a system which the Court, with my full support, has just censured today in the *Streletz, Kessler and Krenz* judgment.

....

Welch v UK A.307-A (1995) 20 EHRR 247
European Court of Human Rights

The applicant was arrested for suspected drugs offences in November 1986. On the day following his arrest he was charged with offences involving the importation of large amounts of cannabis. In February 1987 he was further charged with the offence of possession with intent to supply cocaine (alleged to have taken place on 3 November 1986) and in May 1987 he was also charged with conspiracy to obtain cocaine with intent to supply (between January and November 1986). In August 1987 he was found guilty on five counts and sentenced to twenty-two years' imprisonment. The judge also imposed a confiscation order, under the Drug Trafficking Offences Act 1986, on the applicant in the sum of £66,914 (in default of payment the applicant would be liable to serve a further period of two years' imprisonment). The Act came into force on 12 January 1987 and enabled the Crown Court to make confiscation orders in respect of 'any payment or other reward in connection with drug trafficking' received (whether before or after the commencement of the Act) by a person convicted of a drugs trafficking offence after 12 January 1987. Subsequently, the Court of Appeal slightly reduced his sentence and the amount of the confiscation order. The applicant complained to the Commission alleging that the imposition of the confiscation order on him amounted to a retrospective criminal penalty in breach of Article 7(1). By seven votes to seven with the casting vote of the Acting President, the Commission found no violation of that Article. The Court determined that:

26. The Court first observes that the retrospective imposition of the confiscation order is not in dispute in the present case. The order was made following a conviction in respect of drugs offences which had been committed before the 1986 Act came into force ... The only question to be determined therefore is whether the order constitutes a penalty within the meaning of Article 7 para 1 (art 7-1), second sentence.

27. The concept of a 'penalty' in this provision is, like the notions of 'civil rights and obligations' and 'criminal charge' in Article 6 para 1 (art 6-1), an autonomous Convention concept ... To render the protection offered by Article 7 (art 7) effective, the Court must remain free to go behind appearances and assess for itself whether a particular measure amounts in substance to a 'penalty' within the meaning of this provision ...

28. The wording of Article 7 para 1 (art 7-1), second sentence, indicates that the starting-point in any assessment of the existence of a penalty is whether the measure in question is imposed following conviction for a 'criminal offence'. Other factors that may be taken into account as relevant in this connection are the nature and purpose of the measure in question; its characterisation under national law; the procedures involved in the making and implementation of the measure; and its severity.

29. As regards the connection with a criminal offence, it is to be observed that before an order can be made under the 1986 Act the accused must have been convicted of one or more drug-trafficking offences (see section 1(1) of the 1986 Act) . . . This link is in no way diminished by the fact that, due to the operation of the statutory presumptions concerning the extent to which the applicant has bene-fited from trafficking, the court order may affect proceeds or property which are not directly related to the facts underlying the criminal conviction. While the reach of the measure may be necessary to the attainment of the aims of the 1986 Act, this does not alter the fact that its imposition is dependent on there having been a criminal conviction.

30. In assessing the nature and purpose of the measure, the Court has had regard to the background of the 1986 Act, which was introduced to overcome the inadequacy of the existing powers of forfeiture and to confer on the courts the power to confiscate proceeds after they had been converted into other forms of assets . . . The preventive purpose of confiscating property that might be available for use in future drug-trafficking operations as well as the purpose of ensuring that crime does not pay are evident from the ministerial statements that were made to Parliament at the time of the introduction of the legislation . . . However it cannot be excluded that legislation which confers such broad powers of confiscation on the courts also pursues the aim of punishing the offender. Indeed the aims of preven-tion and reparation are consistent with a punitive purpose and may be seen as constituent elements of the very notion of punishment.

31. In this connection, confiscation orders have been characterised in some United Kingdom court decisions as constituting 'penalties' and, in others, as pursuing the aim of reparation as opposed to punishment . . . Although on balance these statements point more in the direction of a confiscation order being a punitive measure, the Court does not consider them to be of much assistance since they were not directed at the point at issue under Article 7 (art 7) but rather made in the course of examin-ation of associated questions of domestic law and procedure.

32. The Court agrees with the Government and the Commission that the severity of the order is not in itself decisive, since many non-penal measures of a preventive nature may have a substantial impact on the person concerned.

33. However, there are several aspects of the making of an order under the 1986 Act which are in keep-ing with the idea of a penalty as it is commonly understood even though they may also be considered as essential to the preventive scheme inherent in the 1986 Act. The sweeping statutory assumptions in section 2 (3) of the 1986 Act that all property passing through the offender's hands over a six-year period is the fruit of drug trafficking unless he can prove otherwise . . . the fact that the confiscation order is directed to the proceeds involved in drug dealing and is not limited to actual enrichment or profit (see sections 1 and 2 of the 1986 Act . . .); the discretion of the trial judge, in fixing the amount of the order, to take into consideration the degree of culpability of the accused . . . and the possibility of imprisonment in default of payment by the offender . . . are all elements which, when considered together, provide a strong indication of, inter alia, a regime of punishment.

34. Finally, looking behind appearances at the realities of the situation, whatever the characterisation of the measure of confiscation, the fact remains that the applicant faced more far-reaching detriment as a result of the order than that to which he was exposed at the time of the commission of the offences for which he was convicted (see, *mutatis mutandis*, the *Campbell and Fell v UK* judgment of 28 June 1984, Series A No 80, p 38, para 72).

35. Taking into consideration the combination of punitive elements outlined above, the confiscation order amounted, in the circumstances of the present case, to a penalty. Accordingly, there has been a breach of Article 7 para 1 (art 7-1).

36. The Court would stress, however, that this conclusion concerns only the retrospective application of the relevant legislation and does not call into question in any respect the powers of confiscation conferred on the courts as a weapon in the fight against the scourge of drug trafficking.

. . .

FOR THESE REASONS, THE COURT UNANIMOUSLY

1. Holds that there has been a violation of Article 7 para 1 (art 7-1) of the Convention

...

NOTES

1   The Court was composed of President Ryssdal and Judges: Matscher, Macdonald, De Meyer, Foighel, Pekkanen, Freeland, Wildhaber, and Jungwiert.

2   In a separate judgment (*Welch v UK*, 1996-II) dealing with the applicant's claims for just satisfaction, the Court noted that the British authorities had not, and were not going to, enforce the compensation order against Welch. The Court dismissed the applicant's request for pecuniary and non-pecuniary damages.

3   In *Achour v France*, judgment of 29 March 2006, the applicant complained that the application of new legislative rules concerning recidivism to him violated Article 7. In 1984 he had been sentenced to three years' imprisonment for drug trafficking. In 1994 the Criminal Code was amended to provide that where a person had been convicted of a serious offence if they were subsequently convicted of a similar offence within ten years (of the expiry of the original sentence) the maximum sentence for the repeat offence should be doubled. In 1997 the applicant was convicted of further drug offences and sentenced to twelve years' under the amended Criminal Code. The Grand Chamber, by sixteen votes to one, found no breach of Article 7 as the French Court of Cassation had for over 100 years adopted the consistent view that new legislative rules on recidivism applied immediately and defendants could properly be sentenced, under the new rules, in respect of second offences committed after the date of entry into force of the new rules. Furthermore, there had been no retrospective application of the law in the applicant's case as he had simply been punished under a successive law.

Article 7(2)

The framers of the Convention included this provision to protect national laws enacted in the immediate aftermath of the Second World War to punish war crimes and other serious offences committed during that war.

10 ARTICLE 8 RIGHT TO RESPECT FOR PRIVATE AND FAMILY LIFE

Article 8(1)

Private life

Niemietz v Germany A.251B (1992) 16 EHRR 97
European Court of Human Rights

A fax was sent from the Freiburg post office to a District Court judge, who was hearing a criminal case involving the alleged non-payment of church tax. The fax accused the judge of abusing his office, by his conduct in the tax case, and was sent by 'Klaus Wegner' of the 'Freiburg Bunte Liste' (a local political party). The Munich public prosecutor's office began criminal proceedings against Wegner for insulting behaviour, but they were unable to serve a summons on him as his whereabouts was unknown and his identity may also have been false. Consequently, the prosecutor obtained a judicial warrant to search the law office of Mr Niemietz, a local lawyer and chairman of the Bunte Liste, because mail for the party was sent to his office and it was believed that Niemietz might have documents revealing the identity of Wegner. Police officers and officials from the public prosecutor's office carried out the search, which lasted for just over one hour. During the search a number of filing cabinets, containing details of clients' legal affairs, and the client index were examined. No documents disclosing any details of Wegner were found and nothing was seized by the authorities. Later, criminal proceedings were discontinued against Wegner for lack of evidence. Niemietz complained to the Commission that he had suffered a violation of his rights under Articles 8, 13 and Article 1, First Protocol. He also acknowledged that he had hidden and then destroyed documents identifying Wegner. The Commission expressed the unanimous opinion that Niemietz's rights to respect for his private life and home in Article 8 had been infringed. The Commission did not consider it necessary to examine the other complaints.

A. WAS THERE AN 'INTERFERENCE'?

29. The Court does not consider it possible or necessary to attempt an exhaustive definition of the notion of 'private life'. However, it would be too restrictive to limit the notion to an 'inner circle' in which the individual may live his own personal life as he chooses and to exclude therefrom entirely the outside world not encompassed within that circle. Respect for private life must also comprise to a certain degree the right to establish and develop relationships with other human beings.

There appears, furthermore, to be no reason of principle why this understanding of the notion of 'private life' should be taken to exclude activities of a professional or business nature since it is, after all, in the course of their working lives that the majority of people have a significant, if not the greatest, opportunity of developing relationships with the outside world. This view is supported by the fact that, as was rightly pointed out by the Commission, it is not always possible to distinguish clearly which of an individual's activities form part of his professional or business life and which do not. Thus, especially in the case of a person exercising a liberal profession, his work in that context may form part and parcel of his life to such a degree that it becomes impossible to know in what capacity he is acting at a given moment of time.

To deny the protection of Article 8 on the ground that the measure complained of related only to professional activities—as the Government suggested should be done in the present case—could moreover lead to an inequality of treatment, in that such protection would remain available to a person whose professional and non-professional activities were so intermingled that there was no means of distinguishing between them. In fact, the Court has not heretofore drawn such distinctions: it concluded that there had been an inference with private life even where telephone tapping covered both business and private calls (see the *Huvig v France* judgment of 24 April 1990, Series A No 176-B, p 41, § 8, and p 52, § 25); and where a search was directed solely against business activities, it did not rely on that fact as a ground for excluding the applicability of Article 8 under the head of 'private life' (see the *Chappell v UK* judgment of 30 March 1989, Series A No 152-A, pp 12–13, § 26, and pp 21–2, § 51.)

30. As regards the word 'home', appearing in the English text of Article 8, the Court observes that in certain Contracting States, notably Germany ..., it has been accepted as extending to business premises. Such an interpretation is, moreover, fully consonant with the French text, since the word '*domicile*' has a broader connotation than the word 'home' and may extend, for example, to a professional person's office.

In this context also, it may not always be possible to draw precise distinctions, since activities which are related to a profession or business may well be conducted from a person's private residence and activities which are not so related may well be carried on in an office or commercial premises. A narrow interpretation of the words 'home' and '*domicile*' could therefore give rise to the same risk of inequality of treatment as a narrow interpretation of the notion of 'private life' (see paragraph 29 above).

31. More generally, to interpret the words 'private life' and 'home' as including certain professional or business activities or premises would be consonant with the essential object and purpose of Article 8, namely to protect the individual against arbitrary interference by the public authorities (see, for example, the *Marckx v Belgium* judgment of 13 June 1979, Series A No 31, p 15, § 31). Such an interpretation would not unduly hamper the Contracting States, for they would retain their entitlement to 'interfere' to the extent permitted by paragraph 2 of Article 8; that entitlement might well be more far-reaching where professional or business activities or premises were involved than would otherwise be the case.
...

33. Taken together, the foregoing reasons lead the Court to find that the search of the applicant's office constituted an interference with his rights under Article 8.

...

D. WAS THE INTERFERENCE 'NECESSARY IN A DEMOCRATIC SOCIETY'?

37. [the Court] has formed the opinion that, as was contended by the applicant and as was found by the Commission, the measure complained of was not proportionate to those aims.

It is true that the offence in connection with which the search was effected, involving as it did not only an insult to but also an attempt to bring pressure on a judge, cannot be classified as no more than minor. On the other hand, the warrant was drawn in broad terms, in that it ordered a search for and seizure of 'documents', without any limitation, revealing the identity of the author of the offensive letter; this point is of special significance where, as in Germany, the search of a lawyer's office is not accompanied by any special procedural safeguards, such as the presence of an independent observer. More importantly, having regard to the materials that were in fact inspected, the search impinged on professional secrecy to an extent that appears disproportionate in the circumstances; it has, in this connection, to be recalled that, where a lawyer is involved, an encroachment on professional secrecy may have repercussions on the proper administration of justice and hence on the rights guaranteed by Article 6 of the Convention. In addition, the attendant publicity must have been capable of affecting adversely the applicant's professional reputation, in the eyes both of his existing clients and of the public at large.

FOR THESE REASONS, THE COURT UNANIMOUSLY [9-0]

1. *Holds* that there has been a violation of Article 8 of the Convention; . . .

NOTES

1 The Chamber was composed of President Ryssdal and Judges: Bernhart, Pettiti, Walsh, Russo, Spielmann, Valticos, Loizou, and Freeland.

2 Although the Court made clear in *Niemietz* that it was not going to provide a comprehensive definition of the concept of 'private life', other cases help to delimit the wide boundaries of this flexible notion.

3 In *X and Y v Netherlands*, A.191 (1985) 8 EHRR 235, the Court unanimously held that; '... private life', [is] a concept which covers the physical and moral integrity of the person, including his or her sexual life.' (para 22) In that case Article 8 was found to have been violated by the failure of Dutch criminal law to provide effective protection for a mentally handicapped 16-year-old who had been subjected to a serious sexual assault. For further details of this case see below p 568.

4 Similarly, in *Dudgeon v UK*, A.45 (1981) 4 EHRR 149, the Court treated a person's sexual life as an essential aspect of his/her private life. A majority (15 to 4) ruled that the criminal prohibition on homosexual conduct between consenting adults in private existing in Northern Ireland; '... constitutes a continuing interference with the applicant's right to respect for his private life (which includes his sexual life) within the meaning of Article 8(1).' (para 41) Furthermore, the majority did not consider that the interference could be justified under Article 8(2). Subsequently, analogous criminal laws were found by the Court to breach homosexuals' right to respect for their private lives in *Norris v Ireland* A.142 (1988) 13 EHRR 186 and *Modinos v Cyprus*, A.259 (1993) 16 EHRR 485.

Furthermore, in *Sutherland v UK* (1997) 24 EHRR CD22, the applicant successfully challenged the age of consent for male homosexuals in England before the Commission. Sutherland, who was born in 1977, became aware of attraction to other boys at about the age of 12 and had his first homosexual sexual relations (with another person of his own age) when he was 16. Under the Sexual Offences Act 1967, male homosexual acts were decriminalized where the parties were aged 21 or over and the conduct took place in private. By virtue of the earlier Sexual Offences Act 1956, the heterosexual age of consent is 16 and this also applies to sexual relations between lesbians. In 1981 the Policy Advisory Committee on Sexual Offences recommended to the Home Secretary that, in accordance with medical advice on the sexual maturity of males, the age of consent for male homosexuals should be reduced to 18. The Government did not act on this suggestion. However, in 1994 the British Medical Association, responding to new research that showed that sexual orientation is usually established before the age of puberty and growing concern that young male homosexuals were especially at risk from sexually transmitted infections (including HIV), recommended that the age of consent for male homosexuals should be reduced to 16. That year the House of Commons, on a free vote, passed an amendment to reduce the homosexual age of consent to 18 (by 427 votes to 162) and that was implemented by the Criminal Justice and Public Order Act 1994. The applicant complained to the Commission that the 1994 Act's homosexual age of consent was discriminatory when compare with the heterosexual (and lesbian) minimum age of 16 and therefore breached his rights under Articles 8 and 14. Even though Sutherland had not been threatened with prosecution, applying the Court's reasoning in *Dudgeon*, the Commission concluded that the applicant had been directly affected by the age of consent legislation and it constituted an interference with his right to respect for his private life. Consequently, it was necessary to examine whether the legislation was compatible with Articles 8(2) and 14. The Commission believed that the different ages of consent for heterosexual and homosexual sexual relations were a difference that fell within Article 14 as being based on 'sex' or 'other status' and that as this different treatment '... impinges on a most intimate aspect of affected individuals' private lives, the margin of appreciation must be relatively narrow.' (para 57) While the Commission acknowledged that it had upheld the 21-year-old age of homosexual consent in *X v UK* 19 DR 66 (1975), it considered that it was now time to reconsider its earlier case law in the light of modern circumstances. A majority of the Commission (fourteen votes to four) then found that (having regard to *inter alia* the view of the BMA and the fact that '... equality of treatment in respect of the age of consent is now recognised by the great majority of Member states of the Council of Europe.' (para 59)) there had been a violation of Article 8 taken in conjunction with Article 14. In the majority's opinion, '... no objective and reasonable justification exists for the maintenance of a higher minimum age of consent to male homosexual, than to heterosexual, acts and that the application discloses discriminatory treatment in the exercise of the applicant's right to respect for private life under Article 8 of the Convention.' (para 66) The dissenters felt that the homosexual age of consent established by Parliament in 1994 was within the domestic margin of appreciation and they also did not consider that there was a common European standard regarding the age of consent. In June 1998 the British Government reached an agreement with Sutherland and the House of Commons was given an opportunity to hold a free vote (on an amendment to the Crime and Disorder Bill) to reduce the homosexual age of consent to 16. The amendment was passed by the Commons but rejected by the House of Lords. Consequently, during December 1998, the Government introduced the Sexual Offences (Amendment) Bill which sought, *inter alia*, to harmonise the age of consent for homosexual and heterosexual relations at 16 for England, Wales and Scotland (it provided that in Northern Ireland the homosexual age of consent should be 17 as that is the existing heterosexual age of consent in the Province). However, the House of Lords, again, refuse to pass the Bill.

The Government responded by invoking the, rarely used, Parliament Acts 1911 and 1949 procedure (whereby approval by the House of Lords can be dispensed with). The House of Commons enacted (with Royal Assent) the Sexual Offences (Amendment) Act 2000 which implemented the above changes to the homosexual age of consent. In January 2001, after the Act was brought into effect, Sutherland applied to the Court for his case to be struck out. A unanimous Grand Chamber did so in *Sutherland v UK*, judgment of 27 March 2001, after noting the legislative changes and that the applicant's legal costs had been paid by the Government, the Court was satisfied that the complaint had been resolved.

The full-time Court, unanimously, found a breach of Article 14 in combination with Article 8 when a 41-year-old man had been prosecuted in 1998 (after the Commission gave its Opinion in *Sutherland*) for alleged buggery with a 16-year-old male. In *B.B. v UK*, judgment of 10 February 2004, the applicant had complained to the police, in January 1998, that he had been attacked by the 16-year-old male. However, it was B.B. who was prosecuted (he was formally acquitted in 1999 when the young person refused to testify). The Court found that that, '25. ... the existence of, and the applicant's prosecution under, the legislation applicable at the relevant time constituted a violation of Article 14 taken in conjunction with Article 8 of the Convention.'

5   The Court has unanimously found a breach of Article 8 in respect of the investigations into the sexual orientation and the subsequent discharge from the British armed forces of a number of homosexual (gay and lesbian) personnel: *Smith and Grady v UK* (1999) 29 EHRR 493 and in the simultaneous case *Lustig-Prean and Beckett v UK* (1999) 29 EHRR 548. Jeanette Smith joined the Royal Air Force, for a nine-year engagement, in 1989 as a nurse and she obtained the rank of senior aircraft woman. In June 1994 a woman telephoned the air force Provost and Security Service (the service police) alleging that Ms Smith was homosexual and was sexually harassing the caller. Subsequently, Smith was interviewed by the service police. Smith admitted that she was homosexual (she had her initial lesbian relationship during her first year in the air force) and that she had a current homosexual relationship (which had begun eighteen months previously) with a civilian. The service police then sought to question Smith about the intimate aspects of her homosexual relationships (the police stated that they had to verify Smith's statement about her sexual orientation in order to ensure that she was not seeking to obtain an early discharge from the service). She was asked, *inter alia*, the names of her previous partners, the extent of her relationship with her current partner, whether she and her current partner had a sexual relationship with their foster daughter, whether she had thought about HIV and whether she liked 'girlie games' such as hockey. Her partner was, voluntarily, also interviewed and she confirmed that they were involved in a full sexual relationship. A few months later Smith was given an administrative discharge from the air force in accordance with the armed forces' policy that homosexuality (male or female) is incompatible with service in those force. The Air Force had assessed Smith's trade proficiency and personal qualities as very good and her conduct as exemplary. Graeme Grady joined the RAF in 1980 and by 1993 he was a sergeant working as chief clerk to the British Defence Intelligence Liaison Service in Washington DC. In June 1994 the nanny to the wife of the head of the Liaison Service made disclosures which resulted in Sergeant Grady being sent back to a British air base and his questioning by the service police. At his first interview Grady denied he was homosexual. The next day, after seeking legal advice and ascertaining his financial position if he was to be given an administrative discharge, he admitted his homosexuality (he confirmed that he began homosexual relationships in the previous year). The police asked him a number of intimate questions including whether his wife knew he was homosexual, the names of his sexual partners and the nature of his relationships with them. In December 1994 Mr Grady was given an administrative discharge, his service record noted that he had displayed sound personal qualities and integrity throughout his service. The applicants sought to challenge their discharges through judicial review proceedings but the High Court and the Court of Appeal found that the authorities' actions did not violate the principles of legality including *Wednesbury* unreasonableness/irrationality (*R v Ministry of Defence, ex p Smith* [1996] 1 All ER 257). The applicants then complained to the Strasbourg institutions alleging a breach of their Convention rights including their right to respect for their private lives under Article 8. The Government accepted that there had been such interferences.

... In these circumstances, the Court is of the view that the investigations by the military police into the applicants' homosexuality, which included detailed interviews with each of them and with third parties on matters relating to their sexual orientation and practices, together with the preparation of a final report for the armed forces' authorities on the investigations, constituted a direct interference with the applicants' right to respect for their private lives. Their consequent administrative discharge on the sole ground of their sexual orientation also constituted an interference with that right (see the *Dudgeon v UK* judgment of 22 October 1981, Series A No 45, pp 18–19, § 41, and, *mutatis mutandis*, the *Vogt v Germany* judgment of 26 September 1995, Series A No 323, p 23, § 44). (para 71)

As the armed forces' policy of discharging homosexuals was endorsed by s 146 of the Criminal Justice and Public Order Act 1994, the Court found that the interferences were 'in accordance with the law'. Furthermore the authorities' actions pursued the legitimate aims of 'the interests of national security' and 'the prevention of disorder' under Article 8(2) as the Government contended that its policy towards homosexuality in the armed forces maintained the morale of service personnel and consequently the fighting power of the armed forces. The contentious issue was whether the interferences were 'necessary in a democratic society'. The Government, relying particularly on a 1996 internal review of the policy conducted by the 'Homosexuality Policy Assessment Team' (HPAT), argued that, *inter alia*, admitting homosexuals to the armed forces at the present time would have a significant and negative effect on the morale of those forces and that it was within the State's margin of appreciation to impose such limitations on the private lives of service personnel. The applicants contended, *inter alia*, that the Government had not produced any objective evidence to support its assertion that service morale would be damaged by altering the policy towards homosexuals.

(C) THE COURT'S ASSESSMENT

(I) APPLICABLE GENERAL PRINCIPLES

87. An interference will be considered 'necessary in a democratic society' for a legitimate aim if it answers a pressing social need and, in particular, is proportionate to the legitimate aim pursued (see the *Norris* judgment . . . , p 18, § 41). Given the matters at issue in the present case, the Court would underline the link between the notion of 'necessity' and that of a 'democratic society', the hallmarks of the latter including pluralism, tolerance and broadmindedness (see the *Vereinigung Demokratischer Soldaten Österreichs and Gubi* judgment . . . above, p 17, § 36, and the *Dudgeon* judgment . . . p 21, § 53).

88. The Court recognises that it is for the national authorities to make the initial assessment of necessity, though the final evaluation as to whether the reasons cited for the interference are relevant and sufficient is one for this Court. A margin of appreciation is left open to Contracting States in the context of this assessment, which varies according to the nature of the activities restricted and of the aims pursued by the restrictions (see the *Dudgeon* judgment . . . pp 21 and 23, §§ 52 and 59).

89. Accordingly, when the relevant restrictions concern 'a most intimate part of an individual's private life', there must exist 'particularly serious reasons' before such interferences can satisfy the requirements of Article 8 § 2 of the Convention (see the *Dudgeon* judgment . . . p 21, § 52). When the core of the national security aim pursued is the operational effectiveness of the armed forces, it is accepted that each State is competent to organise its own system of military discipline and enjoys a certain margin of appreciation in this respect (see the *Engel* judgment p 25, § 59). The Court also considers that it is open to the State to impose restrictions on an individual's right to respect for his private life where there is a real threat to the armed forces' operational effectiveness, as the proper functioning of an army is hardly imaginable without legal rules designed to prevent service personnel from undermining it. However, the national authorities cannot rely on such rules to frustrate the exercise by individual members of the armed forces of their right to respect for their private lives, which right applies to service personnel as it does to others within the jurisdiction of the State. Moreover, assertions as to a risk to operational effectiveness must be 'substantiated by specific examples' (see, *mutatis mutandis*, the

Vereinigung Demokratischer Soldaten Österreichs and Gubi judgment . . . , p 17, §§ 36 and 38, and the *Grigoriades* judgment . . . pp 2589–90, § 45).

(II) APPLICATION TO THE FACTS OF THE CASE

90. It is common ground that the sole reason for the investigations conducted and for the applicants' discharge was their sexual orientation. Concerning as it did a most intimate aspect of an individual's private life, particularly serious reasons by way of justification were required (see paragraph 89 above). In the case of the present applicants, the Court finds the interferences to have been especially grave for the following reasons.

91. In the first place, the investigation process . . . was of an exceptionally intrusive character. Anonymous telephone calls to Ms Smith and to the service police, and information supplied by the nanny of Mr Grady's commander, prompted the investigations into their sexual orientation, a matter which, until then, each applicant had kept private. The investigations were conducted by the service police, whose investigation methods were, according to the HPAT, based on criminal procedures and whose presence the HPAT described as widely publicised and strongly resented among the forces . . . Once the matter was brought to the attention of the service authorities, Mr Grady was required to return immediately (without his wife or children) to the United Kingdom. While he was in the United Kingdom, detailed investigations into his homosexuality began in the United States and included detailed and intrusive interviews about his private life with his wife, a colleague, the latter's husband and the nanny who worked with his commander's family. Both applicants were interviewed and asked detailed questions of an intimate nature about their particular sexual practices and preferences. Certain lines of questioning of both applicants were, in the Court's view, particularly intrusive and offensive and, indeed, the Government conceded that they could not defend the question put to Ms Smith about whether she had had a sexual relationship with her foster daughter. Ms Smith's partner was also interviewed. Mr Grady's accommodation was searched, many personal items (including a letter to his homosexual partner) were seized and he was later questioned in detail on the content of these items. After the interviews, a service police report was prepared for the air force authorities on each applicant's homosexuality and related matters.

92. Secondly, the administrative discharge of the applicants had, as Sir Thomas Bingham MR described, a profound effect on their careers and prospects. Prior to the events in question, both applicants enjoyed relatively successful service careers in their particular field. Ms Smith had over five years' service in the air force; she had been recommended for promotion, had been accepted for a training course which would facilitate this promotion and was about to complete the course final examinations. Her evaluations prior to and after her discharge were very positive. Mr Grady had served in the air force for fourteen years, being promoted to sergeant and posted to a high-security position in Washington in 1991. His evaluations prior to and after his discharge were also very positive with recommendations for further promotion. The Government accepted in their observations that neither the service records nor the conduct of the applicants gave any grounds for complaint and the High Court described their service records as 'exemplary'. The Court notes, in this respect, the unique nature of the armed forces (underlined by the Government in their pleadings before the Court) and, consequently, the difficulty in directly transferring essentially military qualifications and experience to civilian life. The Court recalls, in this respect that one of the several reasons why the Court considered Mrs Vogt's dismissal from her post as a school teacher to be a 'very severe measure', was its finding that school teachers in her situation would 'almost certainly be deprived of the opportunity to exercise the sole profession for which they have a calling, for which they have been trained and in which they have acquired skills and experience' (*Vogt* judgment . . . p 29, § 60). In this regard, the Court accepts that the applicants' training and experience would be of use in civilian life. However, it is clear that the applicants would encounter difficulty in obtaining civilian posts in their areas of specialisation which would reflect the seniority and status which they had achieved in the air force.

93. Thirdly, the absolute and general character of the policy which led to the interferences in question is striking (see the *Dudgeon* judgment ... p 24, § 61, and the *Vogt* judgment ... p 28, § 59). The policy results in an immediate discharge from the armed forces once an individual's homosexuality is established and irrespective of the individual's conduct or service record. With regard to the Government's reference to the *Kalaç* judgment, the Court considers that the compulsory retirement of Mr Kalaç is to be distinguished from the discharge of the present applicants, the former being dismissed on grounds of his conduct while the applicants were discharged on grounds of their innate personal characteristics.

94. Accordingly, the Court must consider whether, taking account of the margin of appreciation open to the State in matters of national security, particularly convincing and weighty reasons exist by way of justification for the interferences with the applicants' right to respect for their private lives.

95. The core argument of the Government in support of the policy is that the presence of open or suspected homosexuals in the armed forces would have a substantial and negative effect on morale and, consequently, on the fighting power and operational effectiveness of the armed forces. The Government rely in this respect on the report of the HPAT and, in particular, on Section F of the report. Although the Court acknowledges the complexity of the study undertaken by the HPAT, it entertains certain doubts as to the value of the HPAT report for present purposes. The independence of the assessment contained in the report is open to question given that it was completed by Ministry of Defence civil servants and service personnel ... In addition, on any reading of the report and the methods used ... only a very small proportion of the armed forces' personnel participated in the assessment. Moreover, many of the methods of assessment (including the consultation with policy-makers in the Ministry of Defence, one-to-one interviews and the focus group discussions) were not anonymous. It also appears that many of the questions in the attitude survey suggested answers in support of the policy.

96. Even accepting that the views on the matter which were expressed to the HPAT may be considered representative, the Court finds that the perceived problems which were identified in the HPAT report as a threat to the fighting power and operational effectiveness of the armed forces were founded solely upon the negative attitudes of heterosexual personnel towards those of homosexual orientation. The Court observes, in this respect, that no moral judgment is made on homosexuality by the policy, as was confirmed in the affidavit of the Vice Chief of the Defence Staff ... It is also accepted by the Government that neither the records nor conduct of the applicants nor the physical capability, courage, dependability and skills of homosexuals in general are in any way called into question by the policy.

97. The question for the Court is whether the above-noted negative attitudes constitute sufficient justification for the interferences at issue. The Court observes from the HPAT report that these attitudes, even if sincerely felt by those who expressed them, ranged from stereotypical expressions of hostility to those of homosexual orientation, to vague expressions of unease about the presence of homosexual colleagues. To the extent that they represent a predisposed bias on the part of a heterosexual majority against a homosexual minority, these negative attitudes cannot, of themselves, be considered by the Court to amount to sufficient justification for the interferences with the applicants' rights outlined above any more than similar negative attitudes towards those of a different race, origin or colour.

98. The Government emphasised that the views expressed in the HPAT report served to show that any change in the policy would entail substantial damage to morale and operational effectiveness. The applicants considered these submissions to be unsubstantiated.

99. The Court notes the lack of concrete evidence to substantiate the alleged damage to morale and fighting power that any change in the policy would entail. Thorpe LJ in the Court of Appeal found that

there was no actual or significant evidence of such damage as a result of the presence of homosexuals in the armed forces ... and the Court further considers that the subsequent HPAT assessment did not, whatever its value, provide evidence of such damage in the event of the policy changing. Given the number of homosexuals dismissed between 1991 and 1996 [30 officers and 331 persons of other rank] the number of homosexuals who were in the armed forces at the relevant time cannot be said to be insignificant. Even if the absence of such evidence can be explained by the consistent application of the policy, as submitted by the Government, this is insufficient to demonstrate to the Court's satisfaction that operational effectiveness problems of the nature and level alleged can be anticipated in the absence of the policy (see the *Vereinigung Demokratischer Soldaten Österreichs and Gubi* judgment ... p 17, § 38).

100. However, in the light of the strength of feeling expressed in certain submissions to the HPAT and the special, interdependent and closely knit nature of the armed forces' environment, the Court considers it reasonable to assume that some difficulties could be anticipated as a result of any change in what is now a long-standing policy. Indeed, it would appear that the presence of women and racial minorities in the armed forces led to relational difficulties of the kind which the Government suggest admission of homosexuals would entail ...

101. The applicants submitted that a strict code of conduct applicable to all personnel would address any potential difficulties caused by negative attitudes of heterosexuals. The Government, while not rejecting the possibility out of hand, emphasised the need for caution given the subject matter and the armed forces context of the policy and pointed out that this was one of the options to be considered by the next Parliamentary Select Committee in 2001.

102. The Court considers it important to note, in the first place, the approach already adopted by the armed forces to deal with racial discrimination and with racial and sexual harassment and bullying ... The January 1996 Directive, for example, imposed both a strict code of conduct on every soldier together with disciplinary rules to deal with any inappropriate behaviour and conduct. This dual approach was supplemented with information leaflets and training programmes, the army emphasising the need for high standards of personal conduct and for respect for others. The Government, nevertheless, underlined that it is 'the knowledge or suspicion of homosexuality' which would cause the morale problems and not conduct, so that a conduct code would not solve the anticipated difficulties. However, in so far as negative attitudes to homosexuality are insufficient, of themselves, to justify the policy (see paragraph 97 above), they are equally insufficient to justify the rejection of a proposed alternative. In any event, the Government themselves recognised during the hearing that the choice between a conduct code and the maintenance of the policy lay at the heart of the judgment to be made in this case. This is also consistent with the Government's direct reliance on Section F of the HPAT's report where the anticipated problems identified as posing a risk to morale were almost exclusively problems related to behaviour and conduct ... The Government maintained that homosexuality raised problems of a type and intensity that race and gender did not. However, even if it can be assumed that the integration of homosexuals would give rise to problems not encountered with the integration of women or racial minorities, the Court is not satisfied that the codes and rules which have been found to be effective in the latter case would not equally prove effective in the former. The 'robust indifference' reported by the HPAT of the large number of British armed forces' personnel serving abroad with allied forces to homosexuals serving in those foreign forces, serves to confirm that the perceived problems of integration are not insuperable ...

103. The Government highlighted particular problems which might be posed by the communal accommodation arrangements in the armed forces. Detailed submissions were made during the hearing, the parties disagreeing as to the potential consequences of shared single-sex accommodation and associated facilities. The Court notes that the HPAT itself concluded that separate accommodation for homosexuals would not be warranted or wise and that substantial expenditure would not, therefore,

have to be incurred in this respect. Nevertheless, the Court remains of the view that it has not been shown that the conduct codes and disciplinary rules referred to above could not adequately deal with any behavioural issues arising on the part either of homosexuals or of heterosexuals.

104. The Government, referring to the relevant analysis in the HPAT report, further argued that no worthwhile lessons could be gleaned from the relatively recent legal changes in those foreign armed forces which now admitted homosexuals. The Court disagrees. It notes the evidence before the domestic courts to the effect that the European countries operating a blanket legal ban on homosexuals in their armed forces are now in a small minority. It considers that, even if relatively recent, the Court cannot overlook the widespread and consistently developing views and associated legal changes to the domestic laws of Contracting States on this issue (see the *Dudgeon* judgment ... , pp 23–4, § 60).

105. Accordingly, the Court concludes that convincing and weighty reasons have not been offered by the Government to justify the policy against homosexuals in the armed forces or, therefore, the consequent discharge of the applicants from those forces.

106. While the applicants' administrative discharges were a direct consequence of their homosexuality, the Court considers that the justification for the investigations into the applicants' homosexuality requires separate consideration in so far as those investigations continued after the applicants' admissions of homosexuality. In Ms Smith's case her admission was immediate and Mr Grady admitted his homosexuality when his interview of 26 May 1994 commenced.

107. The Government maintained that investigations, including the interviews and searches, were necessary in order to detect false claims of homosexuality by those seeking administrative discharges from the armed forces. The Government cited five examples of individuals in the armed forces who had relatively recently made such false claims in order to obtain discharge. However, and despite the fact that Mr Grady's family life could have led to some doubts about the genuineness of the information received as to his homosexuality, it was and is clear, in the Court's opinion, that at the relevant time both Ms Smith and Mr Grady wished to remain in the air force. Accordingly, the Court does not find that the risk of false claims of homosexuality could, in the case of the present applicants, provide any justification for their continued questioning.

108. The Government further submitted that the medical, security and disciplinary concerns outlined by the HPAT justified certain lines of questioning of the applicants. However, the Court observes that, in the HPAT report, security issues relating to those suspected of being homosexual were found not to stand up to close examination as a ground for maintaining the policy. The Court is, for this reason, not persuaded that the risk of blackmail, being the main security ground canvassed by the Government, justified the continuation of the questioning of either of the present applicants. Similarly, the Court does not find that the clinical risks (which were, in any event, substantially discounted by the HPAT as a ground for maintaining the policy) justified the extent of the applicants' questioning. Moreover, no disciplinary issue existed in the case of either applicant.

109. The Government, referring to the cautions given to the applicants at the beginning of their interviews, further argued that the applicants were not obliged to participate in the interview process. Moreover, Ms Smith was asked to consent to her partner being interviewed and Mr Grady agreed to the search of his accommodation and to hand over his electronic diary. The Court considers, however, that the applicants did not have any real choice but to cooperate in this process. It is clear that the interviews formed a standard and important part of the investigation process which was designed to verify to 'a high standard of proof' the sexual orientation of the applicants ... Had the applicants not cooperated with the interview process, including with the additional elements of this process outlined above, the Court is satisfied that the authorities would have proceeded to verify the suspected homosexuality of the applicants by other means which were likely to be less discreet. That this was

the alternative open to the applicants in the event of their failing to cooperate was made clear to both applicants, and in particularly forthright terms to Mr Grady.

110. In such circumstances, the Court considers that the Government have not offered convincing and weighty reasons justifying the continued investigation of the applicants' sexual orientation once they had confirmed their homosexuality to the air force authorities.

111. In sum, the Court finds that neither the investigations conducted into the applicants' sexual orientation, nor their discharge on the grounds of their homosexuality in pursuance of the Ministry of Defence policy, were justified under Article 8 § 2 of the Convention.

112. Accordingly, there has been a violation of Article 8 of the Convention.

Clearly, the Court was not satisfied that the Government had provided credible justification for the armed forces' treatment of homosexual personnel. In reaching that conclusion the Court may have been influenced by a number of *dicta* in the domestic proceedings where several of the judges (including Simon Brown LJ and Thorpe LJ) expressed doubts about the durability of the armed forces' policy towards homosexuals. Within hours of the Court's judgment the Defence Secretary, Lord Robertson, announced that the armed forces would suspend current actions against homosexual personnel. After consulting the chiefs of the armed forces, ministers would make recommendations to Parliament regarding the policy to be adopted towards homosexuals in the forces. In January 2000, the new Defence Secretary (Geoffrey Hoon) announced to Parliament that the ban on homosexuals serving in the British armed forces had been ended. All service personnel would now be subject to a code of social conduct which prohibits 'social misconduct'. Commanding officers will be obliged to investigate the personal lives of their subordinates where the latter's actions or behaviour 'adversely impacted ... on the efficiency or operational effectiveness of the Service.' The code covers all forms of sexual activity and expressly prohibits, *inter alia*, 'displays of affection which might cause offence to others' or 'taking sexual advantage of subordinates'. On the same day as the Defence Secretary made the above announcement the Chief of the Defence Staff (General Sir Charles Guthrie) gave an interview (to *The Times* newspaper) in which he expressed his full support for the new policy. He described the code of conduct as 'sensible and pragmatic', and acknowledged that some of the earlier military police investigations into the sexual practices of service personnel 'went too far'. In July 2000, the Court awarded Ms Smith and Mr Grady £19,000 each in non-pecuniary damages to compensate them for 'the profoundly destabilising events' experienced during their investigations and discharges from the military. Smith was also awarded £59,000 pecuniary damages (in respect of past and future loss of earnings, loss of service pension benefits and interest), while Grady was allocated £40,000 in pecuniary damages (under the same heads). For other cases applying the Convention to military personnel see below p 703.

6 However, the Court has indicated in *obiter dicta* that there are limits as to the types of sexual conduct that fall within the protected concept of 'private life'. *Laskey, Jaggard and Brown v UK* (1997) 24 EHRR 39, 1997-I 120, concerned the conviction of a number of homosexual men for assaults occasioning actual bodily as a result of organised 'consensual' sado-masochistic encounters involving over 40 men during a 10-year period.

The Court observes that not every sexual activity carried out behind closed doors necessarily falls within the scope of Article 8. In the present case, the applicants were involved in consensual sado-masochistic activities for purposes of sexual gratification. There can be no doubt that sexual orientation and activity concern an intimate aspect of private life (see, *Dudgeon v UK*, A45 (1981)). However, a considerable number of people were involved in the activities in question which included, inter alia, the recruitment of new 'members', the provision of several specially-equipped 'chambers', and the shooting of many video-tapes which were distributed among the 'members'. It may thus be open to question whether the sexual activities of the applicants fell entirely within the notion of 'private life' in the particular circumstances of the case. (para 36)

But, as neither the British Government nor the Commission had raised this point, the Court was not willing to examine it of its own motion. Instead, the unanimous Court decided that the interferences with the applicants' private lives, brought about by the convictions, could be justified under Article 8(2) as being necessary in a democratic society for the protection of health (the applicants' conduct resulted in the flow of blood and left scarring). Moran has criticized the Court's judgment: 'In the final instance the decision appears to suggest that in matters of particular complexity specifically when concerned with morality or presented in terms of the protection of the vulnerable, the Strasbourg Court will be reluctant to intervene, thereby giving a State's paternalistic policy, decisions considerable latitude and the gloss of legitimacy associated with human rights.' (1998) 61 MLR 82.

In the later case of *ADT v UK* [2000] 2 FLR 697, a Chamber of the Court determined that consensual homosexual activity between five adult men in the applicant's home was a matter of private sexual behaviour protected by Article 8. During a lawful search of the applicant's home the police discovered video tapes which showed the applicant and up to four other men engaged in acts of oral sex and mutual masturbation (no physical harm was involved in the conduct). The applicant was subsequently convicted of gross indecency (prohibited by section 13 of the Sexual Offences Act 1956) and conditionally discharged for two years plus the seized materials were ordered to be destroyed. Under section 1 of the Sexual Offences Act 1967, if more than two persons take part or are present when consensual male homosexual acts occur those acts are deemed not to have taken place in private and are criminal. English law does not criminalise private homosexual acts between consenting adult women nor heterosexual acts between consenting adults. In response to the applicant's complaints that section 13 of the 1956 Act when combined with section 1 of the 1967 Act and his conviction violated his right to respect for his private life under Article 8, the Government sought to argue that following *Laskey* the applicant's sexual activity fell outside the scope of 'private life'. The Court was unanimous in rejecting the Government's contention:

25. As to the Government's comments in connection with the scope of 'private life' within the meaning of Article 8 of the Convention, the Court recalls that there was no dispute between the parties in the case of *Laskey, Jaggard and Brown* as to the existence of an interference ... In that case, the Court's comments did not go beyond raising a question 'whether the sexual activities of the applicants fell entirely within the notion of 'private life''. The sole element in the present case which could give rise to any doubt about whether the applicants' private lives were involved is the video recording of the activities. No evidence has been put before the Court to indicate that there was any actual likelihood of the contents of the tapes being rendered public, deliberately or inadvertently. In particular, the applicant's conviction related not to any offence involving the making or distribution of the tapes, but solely to the acts themselves. The Court finds it most unlikely that the applicant, who had gone to some lengths not to reveal his sexual orientation, and who has repeated his desire for anonymity before the Court, would knowingly be involved in any such publication.

26. The Court thus considers that the applicant has been the victim of an interference with his right to respect for his private life both as regards the existence of legislation prohibiting consensual sexual acts between more than two men in private, and as regards the conviction for gross indecency.

The Court went on to conclude that neither the legislation nor the applicant's conviction were 'necessary in a democratic society'.

37. The Court can agree with the Government that, at some point, sexual activities can be carried out in such a manner that State interference may be justified, either as not amounting to an interference with the right to respect for private life, or as being justified for the protection, for example, of health or morals. The facts of the present case, however, do not indicate any such circumstances. The applicant was involved in sexual activities with a restricted number of friends in circumstances in which it was most unlikely that others would become aware of what was going on. It is true that the activities were recorded on video tape, but the Court notes that the applicant was prosecuted for the activities themselves, and not for the recording, or for any risk of it entering the public domain. The activities were therefore genuinely 'private', and the approach of the Court must be to adopt the same narrow margin of appreciation as it found applicable in other cases involving intimate aspects of private life (as, for example, in the *Dudgeon* judgment, p 21, § 52).

38. Given the narrow margin of appreciation afforded to the national authorities in the case, the absence of any public health considerations and the purely private nature of the behaviour in the present case, the Court finds that the reasons submitted for the maintenance in force of legislation criminalising homosexual acts between men in private, and *a fortiori* the prosecution and conviction in the present case, are not sufficient to justify the legislation and the prosecution.

39. There has therefore been a violation of Article 8 of the Convention.

Significantly, the Government did not contest the applicant's claim for over £20,000 in just satisfaction, including £10,000 in respect of non-pecuniary loss. The Court considered his claim to be reasonable and awarded the full amount sought. This case can be distinguished from *Laskey* on a number of grounds, such as the nature of the sexual activities and numbers of persons involved. A few days before the Court issued its judgment in ADT, the Government published a report (*Setting the Boundaries*) from a group of experts it had appointed to review the law on sexual offences. The report made sixty-two recommendations for reform, including abolishing the offence of gross indecency. Most of these recommendations, including the abolition of the offence of gross indecency, were implemented by the Sexual Offences Act 2003.

In *K.A. and A.D. v Belgium*, judgment of 17 February 2005, a unanimous Chamber ruled that there had to be 'particularly serious reasons' to justify a State interfering with matters of sexuality. The first applicant, a judge, had been convicted of assault occasioning actual bodily harm and incitement to prostitution/immorality by facilitating his wife being used as a 'slave' for violent and extremely cruel sadomasochistic practices at a sadomasochism club. The second applicant, a doctor, had been convicted of assault occasioning actual bodily harm in respect of the sadomasochistic acts in which he engaged with the first applicant's wife at the club. The domestic court found that videotape evidence disclosed that the applicants had ignored the wife's pleas for the violent conduct to stop. The Chamber held that the applicants' freedom to engage in sexual behaviour had to respect the wishes of the 'victims' of such activities and that this had not occurred in the violent treatment of the first applicant's wife. Therefore, the applicants' convictions did not amount to a disproportionate interference with their right to respect for their private lives.

7   The Commission refrained from providing unequivocal guidance on the extent to which women can claim the right/freedom to abortions falls within their Convention right to respect for their 'private life'. In *Bruggemann and Scheuten v Germany* (1977) 10 DR 100, two women claimed that the German law regulating abortions violated their rights under Article 8. An Act

of 1974 allowed terminations within the first twelve weeks of pregnancy without requiring any particular reason of necessity. But, in 1975 the Federal Constitutional Court held that this part of the Act was void as it did not comply with the constitutional obligation to protect the unborn child. Thereupon, a new Act was passed in 1976 which, *inter alia*, permitted women to have abortions where: '... the termination of the pregnancy is advisable according to medical knowledge in order to avert a danger to her life or the danger of a serious prejudice to her physical or mental health, provided that the danger cannot be averted in any other way she can reasonably be expected to bear.' The applicants argued that the judgment of the Constitutional Court and the 1976 Act deprived them of their freedom of self-determination, as secured by the 1974 Act, and thereby interfered with their right under Article 8(1). The Commission expressed the opinion that:

... pregnancy cannot be said to pertain uniquely to the sphere of private life. Whenever a woman is pregnant her private life becomes closely connected with the developing foetus.

The Commission does not find it necessary to decide, in this context, whether the unborn child is to be considered as 'life' in the sense of Art 2 of the Convention, or whether it could be regarded as an entity which under Art 8(2) could justify an interference 'for the protection of others'. There can be no doubt that certain interests relating to pregnancy are legally protected, eg as shown by a survey of the legal order in 13 High Contracting Parties. This survey reveals that, without exception, certain rights are attributed to the conceived but unborn child, in particular the right to inherit. The Commission also notes that Art 6(5) of the United Nations Covenant on Civil and Political Rights prohibits the execution of death sentences on pregnant women.

The Commission therefore finds that not every regulation of the termination of unwanted pregnancies constitutes an interference with the right to respect for the private life of the mother. Art 8(1) cannot be interpreted as meaning that pregnancy and its termination are, as a principle, solely a matter of the private life of the mother. In this respect the Commission notes that there is not one Member State of the Convention which does not, in one way or another, set up legal rules in this matter. (paras 59–61)

Having regard to the circumstances where abortions were permitted under the 1976 Act, the Commission concluded that there was no breach of Article 8. Mr JES Fawcett issued a dissenting opinion in which he expressed the view that:

'Private life' in Art 8(1) must in my view cover pregnancy, its commencement and termination: indeed, it would be hard to envisage more essentially private elements in life. But pregnancy has also responsibilities for the mother towards the unborn child, at least when it is capable of independent life, and towards the father of the child, and for the father too towards both. But pregnancy, its commencement and its termination, as so viewed is still part of private and family life, calling for respect under Art 8(1). I am not then able to follow the Commission in holding, if I understand its reasoning correctly, that there are certain inherent limits to treating pregnancy and its termination as part of private life. Such limits, beyond those mentioned, at least in the form of intervention by legislation, must be found and justified in Art 8(2): in the absence of such limits, the decision to terminate a pregnancy remains a free part of private life. (para 1)

The case was not referred to the Court and the Committee of Ministers agreed with the Commission's opinion that there had been no violation of the Convention (Resolution DH (78)1). We should also note that the Court did not express a view on this question in *Open Door and Dublin Well Woman v Ireland* (1992) A.246 (below, p 707). The full-time Court applied *Bruggemann and Scheuten* when declaring inadmissible a husband's complaint that under Italian law he was unable to challenge his wife's decision to have an abortion. In *Boso v Italy*, Decision of 5 September 2002, the Court ruled:

... that any interpretation of a potential father's rights under Article 8 of the Convention when the mother intends to have an abortion should above all take into account her rights, as she is the person primarily concerned by the pregnancy and its continuation or termination.

As the Court noted above, the abortion in the instant case was carried out in accordance with Italian legislation and thus pursued the aim of protecting the mother's health.

Accordingly, any interference with the right protected under Article 8 which might be assumed in the circumstances of the case was justified as being necessary for the protection of the rights of another person ...

For an examination of the full-time Court's cautious stance on the status of foetuses/unborn children under Article 2 see *Vo v France*, above p 101.

8 The Court has expanded the 'physical and moral integrity' perspective on the meaning of private life to encompass the loss of liberty. In *Raninen v Finland* (1997) 26 EHRR 563, 1997-VIII 2804, it was stated that:

The Court further recognises that these aspects of the concept extends to situations of deprivation of liberty. Moreover, it does not exclude the possibility that there might be circumstances in which Article 8 could be regarded as affording a protection in relation to conditions during detention which do not attain the level of severity required by Article 3. (para 63)

The applicant was a young person who objected to military or civilian service and had, consequently, been convicted and imprisoned several times for failing to perform military service. On one occasion after a court hearing he was transported back to the prison to be released. At the prison a squad of military police were waiting for him and they handcuffed him in the prison courtyard (in full view of a group of the applicant's supporters). The applicant was then taken to a military hospital and released from the handcuffs. He was not medically examined. The next morning he was questioned by military personnel. The applicant, again, refused to perform his military service and he was then arrested. The Court (unanimously) found the transportation of the applicant, from the prison to the military hospital, to be in breach of Article 5(1); because his arrest and detention during this time was contrary to national law and therefore not 'lawful' under the Article. A majority of the Court (7 votes to 2) considered that the handcuffing of the applicant did not violate his right to respect for his private life under Article 8(1) as it had not been shown that this action had physically or mentally affected him. Therefore, applicants must show that they have suffered appreciable physical or psychological harm from the conditions of their detention if they are to satisfy the Court that a breach of Article 8 has occurred.

9 Another facet of private life is a person's name. In *Burghartz v Switzerland*, A.280B (1994) 18 EHRR 101, the applicant complained that his rights under Article 8 and Article 14 had been violated by the Swiss authorities' refusal to register his surname as Schnyder Burghartz after his family surname had been recorded as Burghartz (his wife's surname). A majority (6–3) of the Court held that:

Unlike some other international instruments, such as the International Covenant on Civil and Political Rights (Article 24(2)), the Convention on the Rights of the Child of 20 November 1989 (Articles 7 and 8) or the American Convention on Human Rights (Article 18), Article 8 of the Convention does not contain any explicit provisions on names. As a means of personal identification and of linking to a family, a person's name none the less concerns his or her private and family life. The fact that society and the State have an interest in regulating the use of names does not exclude this, since these public-law aspects are compatible with private life conceived of as including, to a certain degree, the right to establish and develop relationships with other human beings, in professional or business contexts as in others (see, *Niemietz v Germany* A.251B (1992)). In the instant case, the applicant's retention of the surname by which, according to him, he has become known in academic circles may significantly affect his career. Article 8 therefore applies. (para 24)

By a bare majority of one (five to four) the Court went on to decide that Switzerland had violated the applicant's rights under Article 14 taken together with Article 8, as there was no objective and reasonable justification why men could not combine their surnames with their wives' surnames when Swiss law allowed married women to combine their surnames with their husbands' surnames. In a later case the Court did not find a violation of Article 8 when a man was refused permission to change his surname, despite the fact that he claimed other people often misspelt his name. The unanimous view of the Court was that states had a wide margin of appreciation in regulating the changing of names, because there was little common ground in the domestic practices of Member states: see, *Stjerna v Finland*, A.299B (1994) 24 EHRR 195. In *Guillot v France*, 1996-V 1593, the Court held that forenames fall within the ambit of 'private life'. However, by a majority (7 to 2) the Court found that France had not violated the parents' rights, under Article 8, by refusing to register their daughter as 'Fleur de Marie' (a forename which was not listed in any calendar of saints' days). Instead, the authorities had registered the child's name as 'Fleur-Marie' and the majority considered that this did not cause the applicants sufficient inconvenience as to amount to a breach of their Convention rights. A unanimous Chamber of the full-time Court ruled that the tradition of demonstrating family unity by married women being obliged to adopt the surname of their husbands was no longer compatible with the Convention in *Unal Tekeli v Turkey*, judgment of 16 November 2004. The applicant married in 1990 and took her husband's surname in accordance with Turkish law. In 1995 she applied to the domestic courts for permission to use her maiden name (Unal). Her application was dismissed. In 1997 the Turkish Civil Code was amended to enable married women to put their maiden name before their husband's surname if they so wished (this provision was re-enacted in 2001). This reform did not satisfy the applicant's wish to only use her maiden name. She complained to the Court alleging a breach of Article 8 and Article 14. The Chamber held that:

61. Moreover, the Court notes the emergence of a consensus among the Contracting States of the Council of Europe in favour of choosing the spouses' family name on an equal footing.

Of the member states of the Council of Europe Turkey is the only country which legally imposes—even where the couple prefers an alternative arrangement—the husband's name as the couple's surname and thus the automatic loss of the woman's own surname on her marriage. Married women in Turkey cannot use their maiden name alone even if both spouses agree to such an arrangement. The possibility made available by the Turkish legislature on 22 November 2001 of putting the maiden name in front of the husband's surname does not alter that position. The interests of married women who do not want their marriage to affect their name have not been taken into consideration.

62. The Court observes, moreover, that Turkey does not position itself outside the general trend towards placing men and women on an equal footing in the family. Prior to the relevant legislative amendments, particularly those of 22 November 2001, the man's position in the family was the dominant one. The reflection of family unity through the husband's surname corresponded to the traditional conception of the family maintained by the Turkish legislature until then. The aim of the reforms of November 2001 was to place married women on an equal footing with their husband in representing the couple, in economic activities and in the decisions to be taken affecting the family and children. Among other things the husband's role as head of the family has been abolished. Both married partners have acquired the power to represent the family. Despite the enactment of the Civil Code in 2001, however, the provisions concerning the family name after marriage, including those obliging married women to take their husband's name, have remained unchanged.

63. The first question for the Court is whether the tradition of reflecting family unity through the husband's name can be regarded as a decisive factor in the present case. Admittedly, that tradition derives

from the man's primordial role and the woman's secondary role in the family. Nowadays the advancement of the equality of the sexes in the member states of the Council of Europe, including Turkey, and in particular the importance attached to the principle of non-discrimination, prevent States from imposing that tradition on married women.

64. In this context it should be recalled that while family unity can be reflected by choosing the husband's surname as the family name, it can be reflected just as well by choosing the wife's surname or a joint name chosen by the couple (see *Burghartz*, cited above, § 28).

65. The second question that the Court is asked to address is whether family unity has to be reflected by a joint family name and whether, in the event of disagreement between the married partners, one partner's surname can be imposed on the other.

66. The Court observes in this regard that, according to the practice of the Contracting States, it is perfectly conceivable that family unity will be preserved and consolidated where a married couple chooses not to bear a joint family name. Observation of the systems applicable in Europe supports this finding. The Government have not shown in the present case that concrete or substantial hardship for married partners and/or third parties or detriment to the public interest would be likely to flow from the lack of reflection of family unity through a joint family name. In these circumstances the Court considers that the obligation on married women, in the name of family unity, to bear their husband's surname—even if they can put their maiden name in front of it—has no objective and reasonable justification.

67. The Court does not underestimate the important repercussions which a change in the system, involving a transition from the traditional system of family name based on the husband's surname to other systems allowing the married partners either to keep their own surname or freely choose a joint family name, will inevitably have for keeping registers of births, marriages and deaths. However, it considers that society may reasonably be expected to tolerate a certain inconvenience to enable individuals to live in dignity and worth in accordance with the name they have chosen (see, *mutatis mutandis*, *Christine Goodwin v the United Kingdom* [GC], No 28957/95, § 91, ECHR 2002-VI).

68. Consequently, the objective of reflecting family unity through a joint family name cannot provide a justification for the gender-based difference in treatment complained of in the instant case.

Accordingly, the difference in treatment in question contravenes Article 14 taken in conjunction with Article 8.

69. Having regard to that conclusion, the Court does not consider it necessary to determine whether there has also been a breach of Article 8 taken alone.

This judgment discloses that the margin of appreciation for Member States to regulate the choice of family names has now been eliminated where national regulations are based upon gender discrimination.

10 The keeping and use of secret files on individuals by governmental bodies amounts to an interference with such persons' private lives. In *Leander v Sweden*, A.116 (1987) 9 EHRR 433, the applicant had been prevented from continuing to work at a naval museum, this job involved access to a neighbouring naval base, when the military authorities refused him a personnel control after seeing the contents of a secret file on him maintained by the National Police Board. Despite Leander's complaints to the authorities they would not allow him to see or comment upon the file concerning him. During proceedings before the Commission Leander explained that some years earlier he had been a member of the Swedish Communist Party, he had also been active in the soldiers' union and more recently in the Swedish Building

Workers' Association. His only criminal conviction was for being late for a military parade. The Court held that:

It is uncontested that the secret police-register contained information relating to Mr Leander's private life. Both the storing and the release of such information, which were coupled with a refusal to allow Mr Leander an opportunity to refute it, amounted to an interference with his right to respect for private life as guaranteed by Article 8(1). (para 48)

However, the Court, unanimously, went on to find that the Swedish secret police-register was necessary for the protection of national security and had sufficient procedural safeguards (including the involvement of parliamentarians) to satisfy the requirements of Article 8(2).

The Commission has expressed the opinion that:

... secret surveillance activities for the purpose of gathering and storing on file information concerning a person's private life also constitutes an interference with this right.' (*Hewitt and Harman v UK* 14 EHRR 657 at p. 663)

The applicants, former senior officers working for the National Council for Civil Liberties (now known as 'Liberty'), complained that the British Security Service had subjected them to secret surveillance and had kept files on them as 'communist sympathisers' and 'subversives'. A majority of the Commission (13 to 2) concluded that the likely actions of the Security Service violated the applicants' rights under Article 8(1) and could not be brought within the exceptions in Article 8(2), because the Security Service did not operate within a legal framework that was 'in accordance with the law'. The Committee of Ministers agreed with the Commission's opinion. However, it noted that the British Parliament had subsequently enacted the Security Service Act 1989, which placed the Service on a statutory basis and established an independent Commissioner and Tribunal to determine complaints against the Service; therefore, no further action was required by the Committee. In *Christie v UK* 78A DR E Com HR 119 (1994), the Commission declared inadmissible a complaint by a trade unionist, who had links with the former communist authorities of Eastern Europe, regarding alleged surveillance of him by the British Security Service. The Commission considered that in his case the provisions of the 1989 Act satisfied the requirements of Article 8(2). In July 1998 the British Government disclosed, for the first time, the numbers of files held by the British Security Service. The Home Secretary stated that the Service held a total of 440,000 files. 290,000 files related to persons who had at some time been the subject of inquiry or investigation by the Service. 75,000 concerned people or groups who had not been investigated by the Service, but had some connection with its work (e.g. they had been given security advice by the Service). 40,000 involved organisations and subjects studied by the Service. About 20,000 files were active dossiers of which one-third related to foreign nationals (e.g. members of foreign intelligence services) and the rest to British nationals (of whom over half were suspected terrorists): (1998) *Times*, 30 July.

The practice of the Swiss Federal Government compiling a card index of persons who had, *inter alia*, been in contact with staff at the former Soviet embassy was found to be in breach of Article 8 in the case of *Amann v Switzerland*, (16/2/2000). The applicant was a businessman who sold depilatory appliances. During 1981 a woman telephoned him from the former Soviet embassy in Berne to order one of his appliances. The telephone call was secretly intercepted by the Federal Public Prosecutor's Office, which then instigated an investigation into the applicant and his business. As a result of the investigation a card on the applicant was placed in the national security card index. The card stated 'from the Zurich Intelligence Service: A. identified as a contact with the Russian embassy according to ...'. In 1990 the applicant became aware of the index and sought a copy of his card. Subsequently, he brought legal proceedings against the Government for compiling and retaining the card, but the Federal Court dismissed his claims. He then complained to the Commission which, by nine votes to eight, concluded there had been a breach of the applicant's rights under Article 8. The Court was unanimous in concluding that:

... both the creation of the impugned card by the Public Prosecutor's Office and the storing of it in the Confederation's card index amounted to interference with the applicant's private life which cannot be considered to be 'in accordance with the law' since Swiss law does not indicate with sufficient clarity the scope and conditions of exercise of the authorities' discretionary power in the area under consideration. It follows that there has been a violation of Article 8 of the Convention. (para 80)

Hence, the storing of information regarding persons, and their businesses, by public authorities amounts to an 'interference' with their right to respect for their private lives, which States must justify under the conditions laid down in Article 8(2).

A Chamber has held that where Member states have introduced schemes to determine if persons have collaborated with former totalitarian regimes ('lustration measures') then affected persons should generally have access to the secret files upon which such decisions have been made. In *Turek v Slovakia*, judgment of 14 February 2006, the applicant had been issued with a certificate stating that he had collaborated with the former State Security Agency (StB) of Czechoslovakia. He challenged the certificate before the Slovak courts but they ruled that he had not proved that he not collaborated with the StB. The Chamber held that:

115. The Court recognises that, particularly in proceedings related to the operations of state security agencies, there may be legitimate grounds to limit access to certain documents and other materials. However, in respect of lustration proceedings, this consideration loses much of its validity. In the first place, lustration proceedings are, by their very nature, oriented towards the establishment of facts dating back to the communist era and are not directly linked to the current functions and operations of the security services. Thus, unless the contrary is shown on the facts of a specific case, it cannot be assumed that there remains a continuing and actual public interest in imposing limitations on access to materials classified as confidential under former regimes. Secondly, lustration proceedings inevitably depend on the examination of documents relating to the operations of the former communist security agencies. If the party to whom the classified materials relate is denied access to all or most of the materials in question, his or her possibilities to contradict the security agency's version of the facts would be severely curtailed. Finally, under the relevant laws, it is typically the security agency itself that has the power to decide what materials should remain classified and for how long. Since, it is the legality of the agency's actions which is in question in lustration proceedings, the existence of this power is not consistent with the fairness of the proceedings, including the principle of equality of arms. Thus, if a State is to adopt lustration measures, it must ensure that the persons affected thereby enjoy all procedural guarantees under the Convention in respect of any proceedings relating to the application of such measures.

By a large majority, six votes to one, the Chamber concluded that an unrealistic burden had been placed on the applicant to disprove his alleged collaboration with the StB and consequently he had not had access to a procedure which effectively protected his right to respect for his private life. This judgment is potentially very significant for ensuring that those States with lustration schemes provide adequate procedural safeguards for affected persons.

When States maintain secret security files on individuals the Court has held that the storage of such information must be supported by relevant and sufficient reasons. In a contemporary case involving the Swedish system a unanimous Chamber found that, *inter alia*, the retention of a record that a person participated in a political meeting in Poland during 1967 was no longer justified as regards the protection of national security and constituted a breach of Article 8: *Segerstedt-Wiberg and Others v Sweden*, judgment of 6 June 2006.

11 The disclosure of medical records and information concerning patients by State authorities will in principle amount to a breach of the right to respect for a person's 'private life' and can only be justified if the conditions of Article 8(2) are satisfied. In *Z v Finland* (1997) 25 EHRR 371, 1997-I 323, the applicant had been married to a man (X) who was originally charged with a series of serious sexual offences, later the prosecutors also charged him with several counts of attempted manslaughter on the basis that he knew/ought to have known that he was HIV positive at the time of the sexual crimes. A central element of the trial concerned the issue of when X became aware that he was HIV positive. The applicant exercised her right under Finnish law not to give evidence in a case concerning a spouse. Thereupon, the court ordered Z's doctor to provide evidence about her health and he disclosed that she too was HIV positive (all the proceedings were conducted *in camera*). Later the prosecution ordered the seizing and copying of the applicant's medical records. The court convicted X of three counts of attempted manslaughter and one count of rape, and sentenced him to seven years' imprisonment. Records of the proceedings were ordered by the court to be kept confidential for ten years. On appeal the Helsinki Court of Appeal gave a judgment, a copy of which was provided to the press, which found X guilty of five counts of attempted manslaughter and increased his sentence to eleven and a half years' imprisonment. The judgment identified the applicant by name and disclosed her HIV status. This information was published by several newspapers. She complained to the Commission which, unanimously, found a breach of Article 8. The Court also found breaches of that Article. The judgment focused on whether the Finnish authorities could justify their interferences with the applicant's right to respect for her privacy under Article 8(2).

In this connection, the Court will take into account that the protection of personal data, not least medical data, is of fundamental importance to a person's enjoyment of his or her right to respect for private and family life as guaranteed by Article 8 of the Convention. Respecting the confidentiality of health data is a vital principle in the legal systems of all the Contracting Parties to the Convention. It is crucial not only to respect the sense of privacy of a patient but also to preserve his or her confidence in the medical profession and in the health services in general.

Without such protection, those in need of medical assistance may be deterred from revealing such information of a personal and intimate nature as may be necessary in order to receive appropriate treatment and even, from seeking such assistance, thereby endangering their own health and, in the case of transmissible diseases, that of the community.

The domestic law must therefore afford appropriate safeguards to prevent any such communication or disclosure of personal health data as may be inconsistent with the guarantees in Article 8 of the Convention. The above considerations are especially valid as regards protection of the confidentiality of information about a person's HIV infection. The disclosure of such data may dramatically affect his or her private and family life, as well as social and employment situation, by exposing him or her to opprobrium and the risk of ostracism ...

In view of the highly intimate and sensitive nature of information concerning a person's HIV status, any state measures compelling communication or disclosure of such information without the consent of the patient call for the most careful scrutiny on the part of the Court, as do the safeguards designed to secure an effective protection.

At the same time, the Court accepts that the interests of a patient and the community as a whole in protecting the confidentiality of medical data may be outweighed by the interest in investigation and prosecution of crime and in the publicity of court proceedings.' (paras 95–7)

A majority of the Court (8 votes to 1) held that (a) the Finnish court's requirement for Z's doctors to give evidence regarding her medical condition and (b) the prosecution's seizure/copying of Z's medical records, were proportionate actions under Article 8(2) directed at the 'prevention of crime' and 'the protection of the rights and freedoms of others'. However, the Court, unanimously, found that (c) the limited (10 year) time limit on the confidentiality of the trial court's records and (d) the Court of Appeal's public judgment, could not be justified under Article 8(2). The exceptional circumstances of X's criminal behaviour and the trial court's confidential hearings undoubtedly constituted significant factors in the Court's application of Article 8 in this case. Indeed, the Court noted that the Committee of Ministers of the Council of Europe had issued guidance to Member states on the importance of confidentiality of medical data regarding HIV infections (Recommendation No R(89)14: 'The ethical issues of HIV infection in the health care and social settings'). States will also have to justify, under Article 8(2), any disclosure of medical records from public health bodies to other agencies of the state. In *MS v Sweden* (1997) 28 EHRR 313, 1997-IV 1437, the applicant allegedly injured herself at work and sought treatment at her regional hospital. She was unable to return to work because of serious back pain and later she received a disability pension. In 1991 she applied to the state Social Insurance Office for compensation regarding her alleged injury under the terms of the Industrial Injury Insurance Act. The Office obtained her medical records from the hospital, these included details of her subsequent treatments including an abortion. In the light of these medical details the Office rejected her claim on the basis that her ill health had not been caused by an industrial injury. The applicant complained to the Commission that the disclosure of her medical details to the Social Insurance Office by the hospital without her express consent amounted to a violation of her right to respect for her private life. The Commission (by twenty-two votes to five) found no violation. The Court (unanimously) also rejected her claim. However, the Court held that the disclosure of her medical records to a wider circle of public servants (albeit subject to similar duties of confidence regarding the contents of the records) combined with the different use of the data by the Social Insurance Office, amounted to a interference with the applicant's right to privacy under Article 8(1). But the Swedish authorities were able to justify the interference as being necessary for 'the protection of the economic well-being of the country' under Article 8(2), because they were seeking to ensure that public funds were only allocated to deserving claimants. The Court considered that all the medical records disclosed to the Office were relevant to determining the applicant's claim. Presumably, therefore, if State authorities disclose irrelevant confidential medical information to other public agencies, the individual concerned might be able to claim that the disclosure was not a proportionate interference and fell outside Article 8(2). For an individual's right of access to his/her own social or medical files see, *Gaskin* and *McGinley and Egan* (below, pp 574–5).

12 The covert recording of the voices of two suspects whilst at a police station, for the purposes of voice analysis to determine if they were involved in a planned robbery, was held to fall within the scope of private life in *P.G. and J.H. v UK*, judgment of 25 September 2001. Whilst the applicants were responding to formal charges and were talking in their cells their voices were secretly recorded. They subsequently convicted of conspiracy to commit armed robbery and sentenced to fifteen years' imprisonment. The Chamber, unanimously, ruled that:

59. The Court's case-law has, on numerous occasions, found that the covert taping of telephone conversations falls within the scope of Article 8 in both aspects of the right guaranteed, namely, respect for private life and correspondence. While it is generally the case that the recordings were made for the

purpose of using the content of the conversations in some way, the Court is not persuaded that recordings taken for use as voice samples can be regarded as falling outside the scope of the protection afforded by Article 8. A permanent record has nonetheless been made of the person's voice and it is subject to a process of analysis directly relevant to identifying that person in the context of other personal data. Though it is true that when being charged the applicants answered formal questions in a place where police officers were listening to them, the recording and analysis of their voices on this occasion must still be regarded as concerning the processing of personal data about the applicants.

60. The Court concludes therefore that the recording of the applicants' voices when being charged and when in their police cell discloses an interference with their right to respect for private life within the meaning of Article 8 § 1 of the Convention.

No precise domestic law authorized the police to make the recordings and therefore the Chamber found that the interference with the applicants' private lives had not been in accordance with the law as required by Article 8(2). Part II of the Regulation of Investigatory Powers Act 2000 sought to fill this lacunae by establishing a statutory scheme of authorisations for such forms of directed surveillance by senior police officers and independent Surveillance Commissioners (persons who hold or have held high judicial office). For an examination of the case law on the interception of telephone calls see below p 556.

13 A unanimous Chamber found that the disclosure to the media of pictures, derived from a closed circuit television system (CCTV) covering a town centre, by the local authority operating the system breached the right to respect for his private life of a person shown attempting to commit suicide in *Peck v UK*, judgment of 28 January 2003. The Council's CCTV operator saw a man walking down the High Street carrying a knife. The police were alerted and officers took the knife from the man (the applicant), gave him medical help and took him to the police station where he was detained under the Mental Health Act 1983. After being treated by a doctor he was released without charge. Subsequently, as part of the Council's policy to publicise the effectiveness of the CCTV system, the local authority authorised the release of photos taken by the CCTV cameras showing the applicant (but not him cutting his wrists) and the police response. These pictures were published in two local papers and on regional and national television programmes. The applicant's face was not masked in all these publications/broadcasts and people who knew him were able to identify the applicant from the pictures. The High Court found that the Council had acted lawfully, under the Criminal Justice Act 1994 and the Local Government Act 1972. The Chamber considered that:

59. The monitoring of the actions of an individual in a public place by the use of photographic equipment which does not record the visual data does not, as such, give rise to an interference with the individual's private life (see, for example, *Herbecq and the association 'Ligue des droits de l'homme' v Belgium*, applications Nos 32200/96 and 32201/96, Commission decision of 14 January 1998, DR 92-B, p 92). On the other hand, the recording of the data and the systematic or permanent nature of the record may give rise to such considerations. Accordingly, in both *Rotaru* and *Amann* (to which *P.G. and J.H.* [v UK ECHR 2001-IX] referred) the compilation of data by security services on particular individuals, even without the use of covert surveillance methods, constituted an interference with the applicants' private lives (*Rotaru v Romania* [GC], No 28341/95, §§ 43-4, ECHR 2000-V, and *Amann v Switzerland* [GC], No 27798/95, §§ 65-7, ECHR 2000-II). While the permanent recording of the voices of P.G. and J.H. was made while they answered questions in a police cell as police officers listened to them, the recording of their voices for further analysis was regarded as the processing of personal data about them amounting to an interference with their right to respect for their private lives (see *P.G. and J.H.*, cited above, §§ 59-60).

60. However, the Court notes that the present applicant did not complain that the collection of data through the CCTV-camera monitoring of his movements and the creation of a permanent record of itself amounted to an interference with his private life. Indeed, he admitted that that function of the CCTV system, together with the consequent involvement of the police, may have saved his life. Rather, he argued that it was the disclosure of that record of his movements to the public in a manner in which he could never have foreseen which gave rise to such an interference.

61. In this connection, the Court recalls both *Lupker* and *Friedl* decided by the Commission, which concerned the unforeseen use by the authorities of photographs which had been previously voluntarily submitted to them (*Lupker and Others v The Netherlands*, No 18395/91, Commission decision of 7 December 1992, unreported) and the use of photographs taken by the authorities during a public demonstration (*Friedl v Austria*, judgment of 31 January 1995, Series A No 305-B, opinion of the Commission, p 21, §§ 49–52). In those cases, the Commission attached importance to whether the photographs amounted to an intrusion into the applicant's privacy (as, for instance, by entering and taking photographs in a person's home), whether the photograph related to private or public matters and whether the material thus obtained was envisaged for a limited use or was likely to be made available to the general public. In *Friedl* the Commission noted that there was no such intrusion into the 'inner circle' of the applicant's private life, that the photographs taken of a public demonstration related to a public event and that they had been used solely as an aid to policing the demonstration on the relevant day. In this context, the Commission attached weight to the fact that the photographs taken remained anonymous in that no names were noted down, the personal data recorded and photographs taken were not entered into a data-processing system and no action had been taken to identify the persons photographed on that occasion by means of data processing (ibid). Similarly, in *Lupker*, the Commission specifically noted that the police used the photographs to identify offenders in criminal proceedings only and that there was no suggestion that the photographs had been made available to the general public or would be used for any other purpose.

62. The present applicant was in a public street but he was not there for the purposes of participating in any public event and he was not a public figure. It was late at night, he was deeply perturbed and in a state of distress. While he was walking in public wielding a knife, he was not later charged with any offence. The actual suicide attempt was neither recorded nor therefore disclosed. However, footage of the immediate aftermath was recorded and disclosed by the Council directly to the public in its *CCTV News* publication. In addition, the footage was disclosed to the media for further broadcasting and publication purposes. Those media included the audiovisual media: Anglia Television broadcast locally to approximately 350,000 people and the BBC broadcast nationally, and it is 'commonly acknowledged that the audiovisual media have often a much more immediate and powerful effect than the print media' (*Jersild v Denmark*, judgment of 23 September 1994, Series A No 298, pp 23–4, § 31). The *Yellow Advertiser* was distributed in the applicant's locality to approximately 24,000 readers. The applicant's identity was not adequately, or in some cases not at all, masked in the photographs and footage so published and broadcast. He was recognised by certain members of his family and by his friends, neighbours and colleagues.

As a result, the relevant moment was viewed to an extent which far exceeded any exposure to a passer-by or to security observation (as in *Herbecq and the association 'Ligue des droits de l'homme'*, cited above) and to a degree surpassing that which the applicant could possibly have foreseen when he walked in Brentwood on 20 August 1995.

63. Accordingly, the Court considers that the disclosure by the Council of the relevant footage constituted a serious interference with the applicant's right to respect for his private life.

The Chamber found that the Council's disclosure was in accordance with the law, as it had a statutory basis and was foreseeable. Also it had a legitimate aim, under Article 8(2) of promoting public safety, the prevention of disorder and crime and the protection of the rights of others. However the Chamber did not consider that the disclosure was necessary in a democratic society.

85. In sum, the Court does not find that, in the circumstances of this case, there were relevant or sufficient reasons which would justify the direct disclosure by the Council to the public of stills from the footage in its own *CCTV News* article without the Council obtaining the applicant's consent or masking his identity, or which would justify its disclosures to the media without the Council taking steps to ensure so far as possible that such masking would be effected by the media. The crime-prevention objective and context of the disclosures demanded particular scrutiny and care in these respects in the present case.

...

87. Accordingly, the Court considers that the disclosures by the Council of the CCTV material in the *CCTV News* and to the *Yellow Advertiser*, Anglia Television and the BBC were not accompanied by sufficient safeguards to prevent disclosure inconsistent with the guarantees of respect for the applicant' private life contained in Article 8. As such, the disclosure constituted a disproportionate and therefore unjustified interference with his private life and a violation of Article 8 of the Convention.

The Chamber awarded the applicant €11,800 compensation in respect of non-pecuniary damage.

Given the rapid expansion of public CCTV systems (and those of private sector bodies) over recent years the judgment in *Peck* is very important for articulating the Court's approach to the installation and use of such technology. Clearly the recording of images from such systems and their retention or distribution potentially fall within the ambit of relevant persons' private lives. In such circumstances the judgment requires that, *inter alia*, adequate procedural steps are taken to protect the identity of such persons from improper public disclosure.

Subsequently, another Chamber examined the modification and use of images obtained from a CCTV system located inside a police station in *Perry UK*, judgment of 17 July 2003. The applicant had been arrested on suspicion of committing a number of armed robberies. Later he failed to attend several identification parades. So the police arranged to have the surveillance camera at one of their custody suites adjusted to record detailed pictures. The applicant was then brought to the custody area and his picture was recorded by the camera. The recording was used by the police to compile a video identification and that evidence was used in his trial. He was convicted of three counts of robbery and sentenced to five years' imprisonment. Before the Court he argued that the filming of him in the above circumstances violated his right to respect for his private life. The Chamber, unanimously, held that:

40. As stated above, the normal use of security cameras *per se* whether in the public street or on premises, such as shopping centres or police stations where they serve a legitimate and foreseeable purpose, do not raise issues under Article 8 § 1 of the Convention. Here, however, the police regulated the security camera so that it could take clear footage of the applicant in the custody suite and inserted it in a montage of film of other persons to show to witnesses for the purposes of seeing whether they identified the applicant as the perpetrator of the robberies under investigation. The video was also shown during the applicant's trial in a public court room. The question is whether this use of the camera and footage constituted a processing or use of personal data of a nature to constitute an interference with respect for private life.

41. The Court recalls that the applicant had been brought to the police station to attend an identity parade and that he had refused to participate. Whether or not he was aware of the security cameras running in the custody suite, there is no indication that the applicant had any expectation that footage was being taken of him within the police station for use in a video identification procedure and, potentially, as evidence prejudicial to his defence at trial. This ploy adopted by the police went

beyond the normal or expected use of this type of camera, as indeed is demonstrated by the fact that the police were required to obtain permission and an engineer had to adjust the camera. The permanent recording of the footage and its inclusion in a montage for further use may therefore be regarded as the processing or collecting of personal data about the applicant.

42. The Government argued that the use of the footage was analogous to the use of photos in identification albums, in which circumstance the Commission had stated that no issue arose where they were used solely for the purpose of identifying offenders in criminal proceedings (*Lupker v The Netherlands*, No 18395/91, Commission decision of 7 December 1992, unreported). However, the Commission emphasised in that case that the photographs had not come into the possession of the police through any invasion of privacy, the photographs having been submitted voluntarily to the authorities in passport applications or having been taken by the police on the occasion of a previous arrest. The footage in question in the present case had not been obtained voluntarily or in circumstances where it could be reasonably anticipated that it would be recorded and used for identification purposes.

43. The Court considers therefore that the recording and use of the video footage of the applicant in this case discloses an interference with his right to respect for private life.

As the actions of the police were in breach of the requirements of the Code of Practice, issued under the Police and Criminal Evidence Act 1984, governing identification videos, the Chamber concluded that the measures taken against the applicant were not in accordance with the law and therefore violated Article 8. Perry was awarded €1,500 compensation in respect of non-pecuniary damage.

So, whilst the normal use of surveillance cameras within police stations (which may help to ensure the proper treatment of detainees as officers know their actions are being recorded and conversely help to protect officers from false accusations by detainees) will not fall within the scope of Article 8(1) their covert use, as in *Perry*, may do so.

14   The full-time Court has held that resolving questions of disputed paternity falls within the scope of the child's private life in *Mikulic v Croatia*, judgment of 7 February 2002. The applicant was born out of an extra-marital relationship in November 1996. Two months later she and her mother filed a paternity suit against a named man alleged to be her father. On six occasions the Zagreb Municipal Court scheduled appointments for that man to undergo DNA tests, to determine if he was the applicant's father. The man did not attend any of the appointments to provide a specimen of his DNA for analysis. In November 2001, the Municipal Court gave judgment finding that the man was the applicant's father, based upon his repeated avoidance of the DNA tests and the testimony of the applicant's mother. The man then appealed against the judgment. The applicant complained to the Strasbourg Court alleging, *inter alia*, that the Croatian judicial system had been inefficient in determining her paternity claim and thereby left her uncertain as to her personal identity in breach of her right to respect for her private life under Article 8. The Court accepted that her claim fell within the ambit of that right.

53. . . . . There appears, furthermore, to be no reason of principle why the notion of "private life" should be taken. to exclude the determination of the legal relationship between a child born out of wedlock and her natural father.

The Court then examined whether Croatia had complied with its positive obligations under Article 8. Having regard to the diversity of paternity procedures and evidential rules in Member states the Court concluded that Article 8 did not require states to compel alleged fathers to undergo DNA testing. However, if such testing was not compulsory in a particular State the legal system must provide '64. . . . alternative means enabling an independent authority to determine the paternity claim speedily.' That had not happened in the applicant's case therefore Article 8 had been violated.

In *Shofman v Russia*, judgment of 24 November 2005, a unanimous Chamber extended the ruling in *Mikulic* to encompass the 'private life' of a man who disputed his parentage of the child of his former wife. Under the law of the former Russian Soviet Federalist Socialist Republic, subsequently amended, actions contesting paternity were subject to a time limit of one year from the date the man was informed that he had been registered as the father. The applicant received no indications that his wife's child was not his until two years after he had been registered as the father. He then disputed paternity in the courts. Despite DNA evidence that the applicant was not the father the courts applied the time limit to reject the applicant's claim. The Chamber concluded that there had been a breach of the applicant's right to respect for his private life as the Russian Soviet law had not struck a fair balance between his interest and that of the general interest regarding legal certainty of family relationships.

For cases where persons seek information about their natural parents which is in the possession of public authorities see below p 574.

15   In *Pretty v UK*, judgment of 29 April 2002 (and see above p 110) the Chamber stated:

61. As the Court has had previous occasion to remark, the concept of 'private life' is a broad term not susceptible to exhaustive definition. . . . Though no previous case has established as such any right to self-determination as being contained in Article 8 of the Convention, the Court considers that the notion of personal autonomy is an important principle underlying the interpretation of its guarantees.

Therefore, the judges were not willing to exclude that the English law restrictions on the applicant's husband helping her to commit suicide interfered with Mrs Pretty's right to respect for her private life. However, those restrictions were in accordance with the law and had the legitimate aim of protecting the rights of others (vulnerable persons). Furthermore:

76. The Court does not consider therefore that the blanket nature of the ban on assisted suicide is disproportionate. The Government have stated that flexibility is provided for in individual cases by the fact that consent is needed from the DPP [Director of Public Prosecutions] to bring a prosecution and by the fact that a maximum sentence is provided, allowing lesser penalties to be imposed as appropriate. The Select Committee report indicated that between 1981 and 1992 in 22 cases in which 'mercy killing' was an issue, there was only one conviction for murder, with a sentence for life imprisonment, while lesser offences were substituted in the others and most resulted in probation or suspended sentences . . . It does not appear to be arbitrary to the Court for the law to reflect the importance of the right to life, by prohibiting assisted suicide while providing for a system of enforcement and adjudication which allows due regard to be given in each particular case to the public interest in bringing a prosecution, as well as to the fair and proper requirements of retribution and deterrence.

77. Nor in the circumstances is there anything disproportionate in the refusal of the DPP to give an advance undertaking that no prosecution would be brought against the applicant's husband. Strong arguments based on the rule of law could be raised against any claim by the executive to exempt individuals or classes of individuals from the operation of the law. In any event, the seriousness of the act for which immunity was claimed was such that the decision by the DPP to refuse the undertaking sought in the present case cannot be said to be arbitrary or unreasonable.

78. The Court concludes that the interference in this case may be justified as "necessary in a democratic society" for the protection of the rights of others and, accordingly, that there has been no violation of Article 8 of the Convention.

16   A unanimous Chamber determined that a gynaecological examination of a detainee, undertaken against her wishes, constituted an unlawful interference with her private life in

Y.F. v Turkey, judgment of 22 July 2003. The applicant and his wife were arrested by the police on suspicion of aiding the PKK. After four days detention the police took the applicant's wife to a gynaecologist and requested an examination to determine if she had been subject to sexual intercourse during her time in custody. The wife refused to consent to the examination, but the police officers insisted that it be undertaken and remained on the premises whilst the examination took place (the wife was examined in private). The doctor reported that there was no evidence of sexual intercourse having taken place during the period of detention. The applicant complained to the Court, on behalf of his wife. The Court held:

33. ... It reiterates in this connection that a person's body concerns the most intimate aspect of one's private life. Thus, a compulsory medical intervention, even if it is of minor importance, constitutes an interference with this right ...

43. ... Finally, while the Court accepts the Government's submission that the medical examination of detainees by a forensic medical doctor can prove to be a significant safeguard against sexual harassment or ill-treatment, it considers that any interference with the physical integrity of a person must be prescribed by law and requires the consent of that person. Otherwise, a person in a vulnerable situation, such as a detainee, would be deprived of legal guarantees against arbitrary acts. In the light of the foregoing, the Court finds that the interference at issue was not 'in accordance with the law'.

44. That finding suffices for the Court to hold that there has been a violation of Article 8.

This is obviously an important ruling that is designed to protect the dignity of detainees. In the later case of *Storck v Germany*, see above p 247 for the factual background and Article 5 aspects of the case, the Chamber found that the medical treatment of the applicant against her will in a private clinic also constituted a violation of her right to respect for her private life.

17 A Grand Chamber applied Article 8 in the politically highly sensitive context of the withdrawal of former Soviet Union military forces from the territory of an independent State that had previously been part of the Union of Soviet Socialist Republics (USSR) in *Slivenko v Latvia*, judgment of 9 October 2003. The first applicant, Tatjana Slivenko, had been born during 1959 in Estonia to the wife of a military officer serving in the forces of the USSR. One month after her birth the family moved to Latvia where her father was posted. Tatjana met her future husband in Latvia during the late 1970s and they married there in 1980. He was stationed in Latvia as an officer of the USSR military. Their daughter, Karina (the second applicant), was born in Latvia during 1981. Tatjana's father retired from military service in 1986 and remained living in Latvia. During 1991 Latvia regained its independence from the USSR and on 28 January 1992 the Russian Federation took control of the military forces of the former USSR. The applicants and Tatjana's parents were recorded as 'ex-USSR citizens' in the register of Latvian residents in March 1993. Tatjana's husband became a Russian citizen on an unspecified date in the early 1990s and continued to serve in the Russian army, based in Latvia, until his discharge in 1994. A treaty was signed between Latvia and Russia on 30 April 1994 providing for the complete withdrawal of Russian military troops (and members of their families) by 31 August 1994. Under the treaty the discharge of military personnel after 28 January 1992 (the date Russia assumed control over former USSR forces) was not to be regarded as constituting their withdrawal from Latvia.

In October 1994 Tatjana's husband applied to the Latvian Citizenship and Migration Authority (CMA) for a temporary residence permit in Latvia based on his marriage to a permanent resident of Latvia. The CMA refused his application as the Authority considered that he was a Russian military officer who was obliged to leave Latvia under the terms of the above treaty. Soon afterwards the CMA cancelled the applicants' entry in the register of Latvian residents on the basis of Tatjana's husband's status. He challenged the CMA's decision to refuse him a temporary residence permit in the Latvian courts. Eventually, in 1996, the Riga Regional Court upheld the lawfulness of the CMA's decision on the ground that he had been a Russian officer until June 1994 and therefore he was obliged to leave Latvia under the treaty. In August 1996 the Latvian immigration authorities issued a deportation order against the applicants and two days later the local authority issued an eviction order against them in respect of the flat that they rented (this order was never enforced). Tatjana's husband moved to Russia on an unspecified date in 1996.

The applicants brought legal proceedings in the Latvian courts arguing that they were permanent residents and could not be removed. Their claims were upheld by Riga District and Regional Courts but rejected by the Supreme Court (on the basis that the applicants had been provided with a flat in Russia and that they were subject to the 1994 treaty). In early October 1998 Tatjana submitted an appeal to the immigration authorities in respect of the deportation order against her and Karina. However, late on the evening of 28 October the police arrested the applicants at their flat on the basis that they had no valid documents justifying their presence in Latvia. They were released the next day following the intervention of the Director of the CMA. The latter wrote to the applicants in early February 1999 informing them that they were required to leave Latvia immediately. On 16 March 1999 the police arrested Karina, at her grandparents' home, and she was detained in a centre for illegal immigrants for thirty hours. The applicants moved to Russia, to join Tatjana's husband/Karina's father, on 11 July 1999. They adopted Russian citizenship in 2001. Tatjana's parents continued to live, lawfully, in Latvia. The Latvian authorities issued the applicants with visas allowing them to visit their parents/grandparents in late 2001.

The applicants complained to the Court that, *inter alia*, their removal from Latvia violated their right to respect for their private/family life and their home guaranteed by Article 8. In their contention they had been completely integrated into Latvian society (Tatjana had lived there since she was one month old, she had been educated in Latvia and had worked there since she was 17; Katrina had been born and educated in Latvia). The Government of Russia joined the proceedings as a third-party intervener under Article 36 of the Convention. The Chamber decided to relinquish jurisdiction over the complaint to the Grand Chamber in accordance with Article 30.

The Latvian Government submitted that the applicants' removal should be considered in the context of '76. .... the eradication of the consequences of the illegal occupation of Latvia by the Soviet Union, which had been completed by the withdrawal of Russian troops from the territory of Latvia'. Furthermore, their removal had been in accordance with the Latvian-Russian treaty of 1994 governing the withdrawal of the latter's troops and any interference with the applicants' rights had the legitimate aims, under Article 8(2) of the Convention, of protecting Latvian national security and preventing crime or disorder. The Government asserted that the applicants had never been integrated into Latvian society because: they had not chosen to live in Latvia but had been there in connection with the military service of members of their family, in their everyday life they had not had to deal with local inhabitants/authorities as their basic services (such as medical care) had been provided by the USSR military authorities and the applicants were not proficient in the Latvian language. The Russian Government claimed that the applicants had been completely integrated in to Latvian society as they had been nationals of the Latvian Soviet Socialist Republic and had lived almost all their lives in the country.

The Grand Chamber began its judgment by considering whether the applicants could claim that they had a 'private life', 'family life', or 'home' in Latvia.

96. … It is undisputed that the applicants left Latvia against their own will, as a result of the unsuccessful outcome of the legal proceedings concerning the legality of their stay in Latvia. They were thus removed from the country where they had developed, uninterruptedly since birth, the network of personal, social and economic relations that make up the private life of every human being. Furthermore, as a result of the removal the applicants lost the flat in which they had lived in Riga. In these circumstances, the Court cannot but find that the applicants' removal from Latvia constituted an interference with their 'private life' and their 'home' within the meaning of Article 8 paragraph 1 of the Convention.

However, the Grand Chamber did not consider that the removal of the applicants from Latvia was directed at breaking–up their 'family life'. This was because the whole family (husband, wife and daughter) were deported in consequence of the Latvian–Russian treaty.

97. … Furthermore, the existence of 'family life' could not be relied on by the applicants in relation to the first applicant's elderly parents, adults who did not belong to the core family and who have not been shown to have been dependent members of the applicants' family, the applicants' arguments in this respect not having been sufficiently substantiated. Nonetheless, the impact of the impugned measures on the applicants' family life—notably their ultimate enforced migration as a family unit to the Russian Federation—is a relevant factor for the Court's assessment of the case under Article 8 of the Convention. The Court will also take into account the applicants' link with the first applicant's parents (the second applicant's grandparents) under the head of the applicants' 'private' life within the meaning of Article 8 paragraph 1 of the Convention.

The Grand Chamber went on to find that the applicants' removal was 'in accordance with the law' under Article 8(2) on the basis that the Latvian court decisions concerning them were applying the Latvian–Russian treaty. As to whether the removal was for the legitimate aim, under Article 8(2), of safeguarding Latvia's national security:

111. The Court considers that the aim of the particular measures taken in respect of the applicants cannot be dissociated from the wider context of the constitutional and international law arrangements made after Latvia regained its independence in 1991. In this context it is not necessary to deal with the previous situation of Latvia under international law. It is sufficient to note that after the dissolution of the USSR former Soviet military troops remained in Latvia under Russian jurisdiction, at the time when both Latvia and Russia were independent States. The Court therefore accepts that by the Latvian-Russian treaty on the withdrawal of Russian troops and the measures for the implementation of this treaty, the Latvian authorities sought to protect the interest of the country's national security.

Therefore, the key issue for the Court was whether the applicants' removal was 'necessary in a democratic society'.

116. In the Court's view, the withdrawal of the armed forces of one independent State from the territory of another, following the dissolution of the State to which they both formerly belonged, constitutes, from the point of view of the Convention, a legitimate means of dealing with the various political, social and economic problems arising from that dissolution. The fact that in the present case the Latvian-Russian treaty provided for the withdrawal of all military officers who after 28 January 1992 had been placed under Russian jurisdiction, including those who had been discharged from the armed forces prior to the entry into force of the treaty (which in this respect therefore had retroactive effect), and that it also obliged their families to leave the country, is not in itself objectionable from the point of view of the Convention and in particular Article 8. Indeed, it can be said that this arrangement respected the family life of the persons concerned in that it did not interfere with the family unit and obliged Russia to

accept the whole family within its territory, irrespective of the origin or nationality of the individual family members.

117. In so far as the withdrawal of the Russian troops interfered with the private life and home of the persons concerned, this interference would normally not appear disproportionate, having regard to the conditions of service of military officers. This is true in particular in the case of active servicemen and their families. Their withdrawal can be treated as akin to a transfer to another place of service, which might have been ordered on other occasions in the course of their normal service. Moreover, it is evident that the continued presence of active servicemen of a foreign army, with their families, may be seen as being incompatible with the sovereignty of an independent State and as a threat to national security. The public interest in the removal of active servicemen and their families from the territory will therefore normally outweigh the individual's interest in staying. However, even in respect of such persons it is not to be excluded that the specific circumstances of their case might render the removal measures unjustified from the point of view of the Convention.

118. The justification of removal measures does not apply to the same extent to retired military officers and their families. After their discharge from the armed forces a requirement to move for reasons of service will normally no longer apply to them. While their inclusion in the treaty does not as such appear objectionable (see paragraph 116 above), the interests of national security will in the Court's view carry less weight in respect of this category of persons, while more importance must be attached to their legitimate private interests.

The Grand Chamber noted that the applicants' husband/father had retired from the Russian military by mid 1994. Also the Latvian authorities had permitted about 900 Latvian citizens/ close relatives of Latvian citizens to remain in Latvia despite the fact that they were family members of Russian military personnel obliged to leave under the terms of the Latvian–Russian treaty.

122. The Court considers that schemes such as the present one for the withdrawal of foreign troops and their families, based on a general finding that their removal is necessary for national security, cannot as such be deemed to be contrary to Article 8 of the Convention. However, application of such a scheme without any possibility of taking into account the individual circumstances of persons not exempted by the domestic law from removal is in the Court's view not compatible with the requirements of that Article. In order to strike a fair balance between the competing interests of the individual and the community the removal of a person should not be enforced where such measure is disproportionate to the legitimate aim pursued. In the present case the question is whether the applicants' specific situation was such as to outweigh any danger to national security based on their family ties with former foreign military officers.

A large majority of the Grand Chamber, eleven votes to six, concluded that the Latvian authorities had not achieved such a balance in forcing the applicants to leave Latvia. The majority found that the applicants had been integrated into Latvian society (they did not live in army barracks, nor did they work or study in a military institution and their language skills in Latvian were sufficient to allow them to participate in everyday life). The Latvian Government's refusal to make an exception in respect of the applicants' removal was because they were the daughter/granddaughter of a former USSR officer. However, the majority was unable to accept that this fact created a danger to the national security of Latvia (the applicants' father/grandfather was allowed to remain in Latvia). Consequently, the majority found a breach of Article 8, respect for private life/home, as the applicants' removal was not 'necessary in a democratic society'.

The applicants claimed 400,000 euros in respect of non-pecuniary damage caused by their enforced removal from their motherland. The Russian Government supported this claim, whilst the Latvian Government submitted that it was exorbitant. The Court, by eleven votes to six, awarded each applicant the much smaller sum of 10,000 euros compensation.

The six dissentients (President Wildhaber and Judges: Ress, Bratza, Cabral Barreto, Greve, and Maruste) issued a joint dissenting opinion in which they emphasised the significance of the origins and terms of the Latvian–Russian treaty as the decisive factors in assessing the proportionality, under Article 8 of the Convention, of the removal measures taken against the applicants.

4. We note at the outset the specific historical context and purpose for which the treaty was signed, namely the elimination of the consequences of the Soviet rule of Latvia. In the preamble of the treaty both parties to the agreement—Latvia and Russia—accepted that the withdrawal of the Russian troops was intended "to eradicate the negative consequences of their common history. The legitimacy of this purpose of the treaty is, in our view, of foremost importance in assessing the justification for an interference with the rights of individual members of the forces and of their families, who were subject to removal from the country under the treaty.

It is also significant to note that the treaty itself did not impose on the Latvian authorities an obligation to justify each measure taken by reference to the actual danger posed to national security by the specific individual concerned, particularly in relation to non-military family members. General schemes such as the present one for the withdrawal of foreign troops and their families do not easily accommodate procedures of individual, particularised justification on the merits of each and every case (see, *mutatis mutandis, James and Others v the United Kingdom*, judgment of 21 February 1986, Series A No 98, pp 41–2, § 68). In our view the approach of defining in the governing instrument the broad categories of troops, and the accompanying members of their family, to be withdrawn without reference to their personal history strikes the requisite fair balance between the competing interests of the individual and the community.

The dissenters also stressed the applicants' ties with Russia including the facts that: they were of Russian national origin, Russian speaking, had attended Russian-speaking educational institutions and eventually became Russian citizens.

11. In these circumstances, we are unable to conclude that the Latvian authorities overstepped the margin of appreciation afforded to them under Article 8 of the Convention in the particular context of the withdrawal of the Russian armed forces from the territory of Latvia after almost 50 years of Soviet presence there. The Latvian authorities were in our view entitled to consider that the impugned interference with the applicants' right to respect for their private life and their home was 'necessary in a democratic society'.

The dissenters placed the agreed removal of Russian forces (and their family members) from Latvia above the interests of the applicants being able to remain in Latvia. Given the seniority of many of the dissenters in the hierarchy of the Court (including the President of the Court and two Section Presidents) their views merit our respect, but the dissenting opinion may be unduly dismissive of the applicants' links with Latvia (the first applicant had spent all her life, bar one month, living in Latvia and the second applicant had been born there and lived all her life in that country). Prior to their removal, which they vigorously contested in the Latvian courts over several years, the applicants had not demonstrated any desire to re-locate to Russia. If their ties with Russia were as great as the dissenters contended then surely the applicants would have been keener to move to their true motherland?

18   A unanimous Chamber determined that the administration of diamorphine to a chronically ill 12-year-old (who was severely mentally and physically disabled) by doctors, against the wishes of the child's mother, amounted to an interference with the former's '70. . . . right to respect for his private life, and in particular his right to physical integrity': in *Glass v UK*,

judgment of 9 March 2004. The child had been admitted to hospital following respiratory failure and the doctors considered that he was dying from lung disease. To relieve his distress the doctors ordered that he be given diamorphine. The next day the child's condition had deteriorated significantly and his mother resuscitated him, whilst other family members assaulted the doctors. The child's condition subsequently improved and he was discharged from hospital later that day. The Chamber found a breach of Article 8 because the hospital authorities had not sought a ruling from the domestic court's regarding the appropriateness of treating the child with diamorphine against the wishes of his mother.

83. The Court considers that, having regard to the circumstances of the case, the decision of the authorities to override the [mother's] objection to the proposed treatment in the absence of authorisation by a court resulted in a breach of Article 8 of the Convention.

There have been several well-publicized domestic cases involving disputes between parents and doctors after *Glass*, including the treatment of Charlotte Wyatt by the same National Health Service Trust (Portsmouth Hospitals) that was involved in *Glass*.

19   The interpretation of 'private life' to encompass professional/business activities given in *Niemietz* was developed and applied by a Chamber of the full-time Court in *Sidabras and Dziautas v Lithuania*, judgment of 27 July 2004. The applicants had been employees of the Lithuanian branch of the KGB (Soviet Security Service) during the 1980s at a time when Lithuania had been a member of the USSR. Following the independence of Lithuania the applicants became a tax inspector and a public prosecutor. In 1998 the Lithuanian Parliament enacted a law which prohibited former members of the KGB from working as public officials and for banks, credit institutions, security companies and a number of other private sector businesses for ten years beginning in 1998. The applicants were dismissed from their public employment under the terms of the legislation. They then complained to the Court that the statutory ban on them working in the designated private sector businesses and occupations violated their rights under Article 8 in combination with Article 14. The Court held that:

47. Nevertheless, having regard in particular to the notions currently prevailing in democratic states, the Court considers that a far-reaching ban on taking up private-sector employment does affect 'private life'. It attaches particular weight in this respect to the text of Article 1 § 2 of the European Social Charter and the interpretation given by the European Committee of Social Rights as well as to the texts adopted by the ILO [International Labour Organization]. It further recalls that there is no watertight division separating the sphere of social and economic rights from the field covered by the Convention (see, *Airey v Ireland*, judgment of 9 October 1979, Series A No 32, § 26).

A majority of the Court, five votes to two, went on to find a breach of Article 14 in conjunction with Article 8 as the restrictions upon the applicants' employment were not proportionate to the legitimate aims of protecting national security and the economic well-being of Lithuania.

57. Even assuming that their lack of loyalty had been undisputed, it must be noted that the applicants' employment prospects were restricted not only in the State service but also in various spheres of the private sector. The Court reiterates that the requirement of an employee's loyalty to the State is an inherent condition of employment with State authorities responsible for protecting and securing the general interest. However, such a requirement is not inevitably the case for employment with private companies. Although the economic activities of private-sector actors undoubtedly affect and contribute to the functioning of the State, they are not depositaries of the sovereign power vested in the State. Moreover, private companies may legitimately engage in activities, notably financial and economic, which compete with the goals fixed for public authorities or State-run companies.

58. For the Court, State-imposed restrictions on the possibility for a person to find employment with a private company for reasons of lack of loyalty to the State cannot be justified from the Convention point of view in the same manner as restrictions governing access to their employment in the public service, regardless of the private company's importance to the State's economic, political or security interests.

The majority were also concerned that the legislation had not been enacted until eight years after Lithuania had regained its independence. The Court awarded each applicant 7,000 euros compensation for pecuniary and non-pecuniary damage. The two dissentients, Judges Loucaides and Thomassen believed that Article 8 alone had been violated.

A number of Member States that had formerly been members of the USSR have enacted laws seeking to curtail the employment prospects of former officials of the previous regimes (including Bulgaria, Czech Republic, and Latvia). Following *Sidabras and Dziautas* they will need to examine the scope of the prohibitions on private sector employment to ensure that they are sufficiently precise and limited to comply with the Convention requirement of proportionality.

Article 1(2) of the European Social Charter, referred to in the above judgment, provides that: 'With a view to ensuring the effective exercise of the right to work, the Parties undertake ... to protect effectively the right of the worker to earn his living in an occupation freely entered upon.'

20 A Chamber considered that the relationship between a mother and her stillborn child fell within the scope of the mother's 'private life' in *Znamenskaya v Russia*, judgment of 2 June 2005. However the Chamber was deeply divided on the extent of the State's obligations to respect the mother's private life. The applicant gave birth to a stillborn baby boy in August 1997 (in the thirty-fifth week of pregnancy). Since 1994 she had been living with a man (G) who she claimed was the father. In March 1997 she and her former husband had been divorced. The Civil Acts Registration Authority registered the stillbirth and entered the applicant's former husband as the father in the birth certificate and birth register during August 1997. G died in custody in October 1997. The applicant applied to the District Court, in 2000, for the recognition of G as the father of the stillborn child and for the latter to have G's surname and patronymic name. The District Court ordered the discontinuation of the proceedings as the claim was 'not fit for examination'. The applicant complained to the European Court alleging that the domestic authorities had failed in their positive obligation to respect her private and family life. The Court held that:

27. ... Bearing in mind that the applicant must have developed a strong bond with the embryo whom she had almost brought to full term and that she expressed the desire to give him a name and bury him, the establishment of his descent undoubtedly affected her 'private life', the respect for which is also guaranteed by Article 8. That provision is therefore applicable in the present case.

...

31. According to the Court's case-law, the situation where a legal presumption is allowed to prevail over biological and social reality, without regard to both established facts and the wishes of those concerned and without actually benefiting anyone, is not compatible, even having regard to the margin of appreciation left to the State, with the obligation to secure effective 'respect' for private and family life (*Kroon* [v The Netherlands A.297-C (1994)], para 40).

32. There has been therefore a violation of Article 8 of the Convention.

However, three judges dissented:

We are ready to accept the argument that the strong emotional bond of a mother with her stillborn child may be regarded as part of the mother's private life. However, we have difficulty in accepting that her private life encompasses a right to ask for recognition of the paternity of the stillborn child, as part of the State's positive obligations in guaranteeing the protection of private life offered by Article 8. Here, we are concerned with the private life of the mother, not that of the child—who could have had, if born alive, a legitimate expectation of being recognised by his biological father as part of his family and private life- and we are dealing not simply with a request to change the name of another person, but with the latter's recognition by a third person.

Whilst the death of G added to the complexity of the situation, presumably it would have been possible via DNA testing to ascertain the paternity of the applicant's stillborn child if any member of either G's or her former husband's (he had died in 2000) families had disputed the applicant's assertion of paternity? *Kroon* is examined below at p 523.

21 The seizure and retention of a national's passport for several years whilst criminal proceedings were pending against him was found to violate Article 8 in *Iletmis v Turkey*, judgment of 6 December 2005. The applicant had registered as a student at a German university in 1975. He married, a Turkish national, in 1979 and they had two children who lived with them in Germany. In 1984 a judicial investigation was opened by the Turkish authorities into the applicant's political activities. Whilst visiting his family in Turkey, during 1992, the applicant was arrested and his passport seized. He was charged, with separatist activities, and released on bail a few weeks later. However, the authorities would not return his passport. In 1999 he was acquitted and supplied with a passport. The Chamber, unanimously determined that the confiscation of the applicant's passport amounted to an interference with the applicant's right to respect for his private life and that it was a disproportionate act (given that he had no criminal record, there was never any evidence that he was a danger to national security and his family lived in Germany).

22 A Chamber held that the right to respect for a person's private life 'incorporates the right to respect for both the decisions to become and not to become a parent' in *Evans v United Kingdom*, judgment of 7 March 2006. The majority, five judges to two, went on to conclude that, given the lack of an international consensus regarding the regulation of *in vitro* fertilization treatment, the legislature's enactment of a clear rule that both the male and female partners could withdraw their consent to the implantation of an embryo at any time prior to implantation did not breach Article 8 regarding a woman whose former partner withdrew his consent with the consequence that she would not be able to have a child to whom she was biologically related. (Note, in July 2006 the Grand Chamber accepted the applicant's request for the case to be re-heard under Article 43.) A few weeks later another Chamber was very divided on the issue of the denial of permission for a prisoner to artificially inseminate his wife in *Dickson v United Kingdom*, judgment of 18 April 2006. The majority (of four) considered that this too was a topic on which there was no European consensus and therefore States should be accorded a wide margin of appreciation. Furthermore, the majority concluded that the authorities' decision in this case was not arbitrary or unreasonable. The three dissentients considered that the domestic policy of only granting prisoners permission for artificial insemination in exceptional cases was not compatible with the applicants' rights under Article 8 and 'paternalistic'.

23 Professor Feldman has cautioned against an excessive widening of the notion of private life.

... the idea of private life must not stretch to the point at which it subsumes other autonomy-related rights and loses its rationale. ... The differences between the interests protected by different Articles, and the varying levels of protection accorded to each under the Convention, must be respected, as in relation to the overlap between Articles 3 and 8. (D Feldman, 'The Developing Scope of Article 8 of the European Convention on Human Rights' [1997] European Human Rights Law Review 265 at p 273).

Family life

....

X, Y and Z v UK 1997-II 619 (1997) 24 EHRR 143
European Court of Human Rights

X was born in 1955 and is a female to male transsexual. In 1975, he (the male pronoun is used in accordance with the Court's judgment) began hormone treatment and started to live as a man. During 1979 he began to co-habit with Y, a 20-year-old woman, and a few months later he underwent gender reassignment surgery. Since that time X and Y have lived in a permanent and stable union. In 1990, X and Y applied for permission, from a hospital ethics committee, for Y to undergo Artificial Insemination by Donor (AID). After an appeal the committee granted permission and asked that X acknowledge himself to be the father of the child under section 28 of the Human Fertility and Embryology Act 1990 (which provides that where an unmarried woman gives birth as a result of AID with the involvement of her male partner, the latter, rather than the donor of the sperm, shall be treated for legal purposes as the father of the child). In 1992 Y gave birth to a girl (applicant Z). X sought to be registered as Z's father on her birth certificate. However, the Registrar General refused as he considered that only a biological man could be regarded as a father for the purpose of registration. In the register Z was given X's surname, while the identity of her father was left blank. The applicants petitioned the European Commission alleging that the refusal to register X as the father of Z amounted to a violation of Article 8 and unlawful discrimination (Articles 14 and 8). The Commission found a breach of Article 8 (13 votes to 5) and that it was not necessary to examine Article 14.

...

A. THE EXISTENCE OF 'FAMILY LIFE'

33. The applicants submitted that they had shared a 'family life' within the meaning of Article 8 since Z's birth. They emphasised that, according to the jurisprudence of the Commission and the Court, social reality, rather than formal legal status, was decisive. Thus, it was important to note that X had irrevocably changed many of his physical characteristics and provided financial and emotional support to Y and Z. To all appearances, the applicants lived as a traditional family.

34. The Government did not accept that the concept of 'family life' applied to the relationships between X and Y or X and Z. They reasoned that X and Y had to be treated as two women living together, because X was still regarded as female under domestic law and a complete change of sex was not medically possible. Case-law of the Commission indicated that a 'family' could not be based on two unrelated persons of the same sex, including a lesbian couple (see the Commission's decisions on admissibility in *X and Y v UK* application No 9369/81, Decisions and Reports 32, p 220, and *Kerkhoven v Netherlands*, application No 15666/89). Nor could X be said to enjoy 'family life' with Z since he was not related to the child by blood, marriage or adoption.

At the hearing before the Court, counsel for the Government accepted that if X and Y applied for and were granted a joint residence order in respect of Z ... , it would be difficult to maintain that there was no 'family life' for the purposes of Article 8.

35. The Commission considered that the relationship between X and Y could not be equated with that of a lesbian couple, since X was living in society as a man, having undergone gender reassignment

surgery. Aside from the fact that X was registered at birth as a woman and was therefore under a legal incapacity to marry Y or be registered as Z's father, the applicants' situation was indistinguishable from the traditional notion of 'family life'.

36. The Court recalls that the notion of 'family life' in Article 8 is not confined solely to families based on marriage and may encompass other de facto relationships (see the *Marckx v Belgium* judgment of 13 June 1979, Series A No 31, p 14, § 31; the *Keegan v Ireland* judgment of 26 May 1994, Series A No 290, p 17, § 44; and the *Kroon v Netherlands* judgment of 27 October 1994, Series A No 297-C, pp 55–6, § 30). When deciding whether a relationship can be said to amount to 'family life', a number of factors may be relevant, including whether the couple live together, the length of their relationship and whether they have demonstrated their commitment to each other by having children together or by any other means (see, for example, the above-mentioned *Kroon* judgment, loc cit).

37. In the present case, the Court notes that X is a transsexual who has undergone gender reassignment surgery. He has lived with Y, to all appearances as her male partner, since 1979. The couple applied jointly for, and were granted, treatment by AID to allow Y to have a child. X was involved throughout that process and has acted as Z's 'father' in every respect since the birth. ... In these circumstances, the Court considers the de facto family ties link the three applicants.

It follows that Article 8 is applicable.

B. COMPLIANCE WITH ARTICLE 8

...

2. THE COURT'S GENERAL APPROACH

44. The Court observes that there is no common European standard with regard to the granting of parental rights to transsexuals. In addition, it has not been established before the Court that there exists any generally shared approach amongst the High Contracting Parties with regard to the manner in which the social relationship between a child conceived by AID and the person who performs the role of father should be reflected in law. Indeed, according to the information available to the Court, although the technology of medically assisted procreation has been available in Europe for several decades, many of the issues to which it gives rise, particularly with regard to the question of filiation, remain the subject of debate. For example, there is no consensus amongst the Member states of the Council of Europe on the question whether the interests of a child conceived in such a way are best served by preserving the anonymity of the donor of the sperm or whether the child should have the right to know the donor's identity.

Since the issues in the case, therefore, touch on areas where there is little common ground amongst the Member states of the Council of Europe and, generally speaking, the law appears to be in a transitional stage, the respondent State must be afforded a wide margin of appreciation. ...

3. WHETHER A FAIR BALANCE WAS STRUCK IN THE INSTANT CASE

45. The applicants, with whom the Commission agreed, argued that a number of consequences flowed from the lack of legal recognition of X's role as father. Perhaps most importantly, the child's sense of security within the family might be undermined. Furthermore, the absence of X's name on her birth certificate might cause distress on those occasions when a full-length certificate had to be produced, for example on registration with a doctor or school, if an insurance policy was taken out on her life or when she applied for a passport. Although Z was a British citizen by birth and could trace connection through her mother in immigration and nationality matters, problems could still arise if X sought to work abroad. For example, he had already had to turn down an offer of employment in Botswana

because he had been informed that Y and Z would not have been recognised as his 'dependants' and would not, therefore, have been entitled to receive certain benefits (see paragraph 19 above). Moreover, in contrast to the position where a parent–child relationship was recognised by law, Z could not inherit from Y on intestacy or succeed to certain tenancies on X's death. The possibility of X obtaining a residence order in respect of Z ... did not satisfy the requirement of respect, since this would entail the incurring of legal expense and an investigation by a court welfare officer which might distress the child.

In their submission, it was apparent that the legal recognition sought would not interfere with the rights of others or require any fundamental reorganisation of the United Kingdom system of registration of births, since the Human Fertility and Embryology Act 1990 allowed a man who was not a transsexual to be registered as the father of a child born to his female partner by AID ...

46. The Government pointed out that the applicants were not restrained in any way from living together as a 'family' and they asserted that the concerns expressed by them were highly theoretical. Furthermore, X and Y could jointly apply for a residence order, conferring on them parental rights and duties in relation to Z ...

47. First, the Court observes that the community as a whole has an interest in maintaining a coherent system of family law which places the best interests of the child at the forefront. In this respect, the Court notes that, whilst it has not been suggested that the amendment to the law sought by the applicants would be harmful to the interests of Z or of children conceived by AID in general, it is not clear that it would necessarily be to the advantage of such children.

In these circumstances, the Court considers that the State may justifiably be cautious in changing the law, since it is possible that the amendment sought might have undesirable or unforeseen ramifications for children in Z's position. Furthermore, such an amendment might have implications in other areas of family law. For example, the law might be open to criticism on the ground of inconsistency if a female-to-male transsexual were granted the possibility of becoming a 'father' in law while still being treated for other legal purposes as female and capable of contracting marriage to a man.

48. Against these general interests, the Court must weigh the disadvantages suffered by the applicants as a result of the refusal to recognise X in law as Z's 'father'.

The applicants identify a number of legal consequences flowing from this lack of recognition (see paragraph 45 above). For example, they point to the fact that if X were to die intestate, Z would have no automatic right of inheritance. The Court notes, however, that the problem could be solved in practice if X were to make a will. No evidence has been adduced to show that X is the beneficiary of any transmissible tenancies of the type referred to; similarly, since Z is a British citizen by birth and can trace connection through her mother in immigration and nationality matters, she will not be disadvantaged in this respect by the lack of a legal relationship with X.

The Court considers, therefore, that these legal consequences would be unlikely to cause undue hardship given the facts of the present case.

49. In addition, the applicants claimed that Z might suffer various social or developmental difficulties. Thus, it was argued that she would be caused distress on those occasions when it was necessary to produce her birth certificate.

In relation to the absence of X's name on the birth certificate, the Court notes, first, that unless X and Y choose to make such information public, neither the child nor any third party will know that this absence is a consequence of the fact that X was born female. It follows that the applicants are in a similar position to any other family where, for whatever reason, the person who performs the role of the child's 'father' is not registered as such. The Court does not find it established that any particular stigma still attaches to children or families in such circumstances.

Secondly, the Court recalls that in the United Kingdom a birth certificate is not in common use for administrative or identification purposes and that there are few occasions when it is necessary to produce a full length certificate ...

50. The applicants were also concerned, more generally, that Z's sense of personal identity and security within her family would be affected by the lack of legal recognition of X as father.

   In this respect, the Court notes that X is not prevented in any way from acting as Z's father in the social sense. Thus, for example, he lives with her, providing emotional and financial support to her and Y, and he is free to describe himself to her and others as her 'father' and to give her his surname. . . . Furthermore, together with Y, he could apply for a joint residence order in respect of Z, which would automatically confer on them full parental responsibility for her in English law . . .

51. It is impossible to predict the extent to which the absence of a legal connection between X and Z will affect the latter's development. As previously mentioned, at the present time there is uncertainty with regard to how the interests of children in Z's position can best be protected (see paragraph 44 above) and the Court should not adopt or impose any single viewpoint.

52. In conclusion, given that transsexuality raises complex scientific, legal, moral and social issues, in respect of which there is no generally shared approach among the Contracting States, the Court is of the opinion that Article 8 cannot, in this context, be taken to imply an obligation for the respondent State formally to recognise as the father of a child a person who is not the biological father. That being so, the fact that the law of the United Kingdom does not allow special legal recognition of the relationship between X and Z does not amount to a failure to respect family life within the meaning of that provision.

It follows that there has been no violation of Article 8 of the Convention.

. . .

FOR THESE REASONS, THE COURT

1. Holds unanimously that Article 8 of the Convention is applicable in the present case;
2. Holds by fourteen votes to six that there has been no violation of Article 8; . . .

NOTES

1 The majority of the Grand Chamber on the Article 8 aspect of the case was comprised of President Ryssdal and Judges: Bernhart, Matscher, Pettiti, Spielmann, De Meyer, Valticos, Freeland, Baka, Lopes Rocha, Jungwiert, Kuris, Lohmus, and Levits. Six judges dissented for various reasons. Casadevall J. (joined by Russo and Makarczyk JJ.) considered that the UK was in breach of Article 8 because it had authorized, and financed, X's gender reassignment together with Y's AID, and 'it must accept the consequences and take all the measures needed to enable the applicants to live normal lives, without discrimination, under their new identity and with respect for their right to private and family life.' Thor Vilhjalmsson J. based his dissent on the consideration that the register of births may now lawfully contain statements that are not in conformity with biological facts (i.e. the identity of the 'father' of a child created via AID). Therefore, he felt that to refuse to register X as Z's 'father' amounted to a lack of respect for the applicants' family life. Foighel J. believed that the Government had not been able to justify its refusal to register X, an act which would have benefited him and harmed no other person. Gotchev J. held that as *de facto* family ties existed between the applicants, the Government was under a duty to facilitate Z's integration into the family unit, which entailed X being able to be recognised in law as her father.

2 The Court's willingness to recognise a broad spectrum of *de facto* relationships as capable of falling within the protected category of 'family life' under Article 8, demonstrates that the judges are interpreting this concept in accordance with evolving patterns of social behaviour. A dynamic interpretation helps to ensure that the rights guaranteed do not become redundant through social change. However, this evolutionary approach is counterbalance by the judiciary's granting of a wide margin of appreciation (note, this judicial creation is discussed below at p 629) to States in cases concerning social mores where there is no European consensus in the legal and administrative regulation of such relationships. In this case, the margin of appreciation was particularly extensive as the subject matter involved both transsexualism and the rapidly developing medical technology of AID. On the Court's jurisprudence regarding transsexuals see further below p 571.

3 Writing in her private capacity a member of the Commission commented that:

The X, Y and Z case clearly raised numerous moral and ethical problems, as was acknowledged by several of the dissenting judges. The end result is that although the meaning of 'family life' between parent-figure and child has been extended beyond relationships of blood, marriage or adoption into de facto relationships of a certain duration and commitment, the concept of what measures are called for to respect such family life may, apparently differ between the biological and the non-biological parent-figure in the areas of, for example, inheritance and the automatic effect or otherwise of legal measures to accord a degree of legal security to the father-figure in custodial matters. [Jane Liddy, 'The Concept of Family Life under the ECHR' [1998] EHRLR 15 at pp 23-4.]

4 In *Kroon v Netherlands*, A.297-C (1994) 19 EHRR 263, the applicants challenged the Dutch birth registration system. The first applicant (Mrs Kroon) had married a Moroccan national (Mr Omar M'Hallem-Driss) in 1979. By the end of 1980 the marriage had broken down and Mrs Kroon lived apart from her husband (official records showed that he left Amsterdam in 1986 and his whereabouts have remained unknown since that time). The second applicant (Mr Ali Zerrouk, also a Moroccan national) developed a stable relationship with the first applicant, although they did not live together, and in 1987 the third applicant (Samir M'Hallem-Driss) was born of the relationship. He was entered in the register of births as the son of Mrs Kroon and Mr M'Hallem-Driss. Mrs Kroon and Mr Zerrouk applied to the registrar for Samir to be registered as the son of Mr Zerrouk (his biological father), however their application was refused because under Dutch law only the married husband (Mr M'Hallem-Driss) could bring proceedings to deny the paternity of a child born to his wife. The applicants alleged that this ruling failed to respect their right to family life under Article 8. The Commission, by twelve votes to six, found a breach. The Court rejected the Government's argument that the applicants' relationship did not amount to 'family life' under Article 8(1).

Although, as a rule, living together may be a requirement for such a relationship, exceptionally other factors may also serve to demonstrate that a relationship has sufficient constancy to create de facto 'family ties'; such is the case here, as since 1987 four children have been born to Mrs Kroon and Mr Zerrouk. (para 30)

A majority, seven votes to two, went on to find in favour of the applicants because:

In the Court's opinion, 'respect' for 'family life' requires that biological and social reality prevail over a legal presumption which, as in the present case, flies in the face of both established fact and the wishes of those concerned without actually benefiting anyone. Accordingly, the Court concludes that, even having regard to the margin of appreciation left to the State, the Netherlands has failed to secure to the applicants the 'respect' for their family life to which they are entitled under the Convention. (para 40)

5 In *Marckx v Belgium*, A31 (1979) 2 EHRR 330, an unmarried mother and her infant daughter complained, *inter alia*, about the status of illegitimate children in Belgian law. Illegitimate children were only recognised as the children of their mothers if the latter formally recognized

their maternity and, in law, such children remained strangers to their parents' families. The Court held that:

By guaranteeing the right to respect for family life, Article 8 presupposes the existence of a family. The Court concurs entirely with the Commission's established case-law on a crucial point, namely that Article 8 makes no distinction between the 'legitimate' and the 'illegitimate' family. Such a distinction would not be consonant with the word 'everyone', and this is confirmed by Article 14 with its prohibition, in the enjoyment of the rights and freedoms enshrined in the Convention, of discrimination grounded on 'birth'. In addition, the Court notes that the Committee of Ministers of the Council of Europe regards the single woman and her child as one form of family no less than others (Resolution (70) 15 of 15 May 1970). . . . In the Court's opinion, 'family life' within the meaning of Article 8, includes at least the ties between near relatives, for instance those between grandparents and grandchildren, since such relatives may play a considerable part in family life. (paras 31 and 45)

By varying majorities the Court then held that Belgian law, regarding affiliation rules and family relationships, violated the applicants' rights under Article 8. A similar approach was followed in *Johnston v Ireland* A.112 (1986) 9 EHRR 203. The first applicant separated from his wife, they were unable to obtain a divorce as that was prohibited by the Irish Constitution, and since 1971 he had been living with the second applicant. The third applicant was their daughter who had been born in 1978. The applicants complained, *inter alia*, of a violation of Article 8 due to the lack of respect for their family life on account of the third applicant's status under Irish law (e.g. the first applicant's lack of parental rights in regard to her, the impossibility of the third applicant to be jointly adopted by her parents and her limited succession rights in respect of her parents). The Court, unanimously, held that:

As it observed in its above-mentioned *Marckx* judgment, 'respect' for family life, understood as including the ties between near relatives, implies an obligation for the State to act in a manner calculated to allow these ties to develop normally. And in the present case the normal development of the natural family ties between the first and second applicants and their daughter requires, in the Court's opinion, that she should be placed, legally and socially, in a position akin to that of a legitimate child. Examination of the third applicant's present legal situation, seen as a whole, reveals, however, that it differs considerably from that of a legitimate child; in addition, it has not been shown that there are any means available to her or her parents to eliminate or reduce the differences. Having regard to the particular circumstances of this case and notwithstanding the wide margin of appreciation enjoyed by Ireland in this area . . . the absence of an appropriate legal regime reflecting the third applicant's natural family ties amounts to a failure to respect her family life. Moreover, the close and intimate relationship between the third applicant and her parents is such that there is of necessity also a resultant failure to respect the family life of each of the latter.

There is accordingly, as regards all three applicants, a breach of Article 8 . . . (paras 74–6)

However, as we have seen above (p 511) in *Slivenko v Latvia*, judgment of 9 October 2003, a Grand Chamber of the full-time Court took a narrower view of family life. The Grand Chamber refused to accept that the relationship between a daughter/granddaughter and their parents/grandparents amounted to family life as the latter were not dependant upon the former (paragraph 97 of the judgment). Judge Kovler, the Judge of Russian nationality, in his partly concurring and partly dissenting opinion disagreed with the majority's restrictive approach.

In my humble opinion, in paragraph 97 of its judgment the Court has narrowed the concept of 'family life' by taking it to cover ties within the 'core family' only. In other words, the Court has opted for the traditional concept of a family based on the conjugal covenant—that is to say, a conjugal family consisting of a father, a mother and their children below the age of majority, while adult children and grandparents are excluded from the circle. That might be correct within the strict legal meaning of the term as used by European countries in their civil legislation, but the manner in which the Court has construed Article 8 § 1 in its case-law opens up other horizons by placing the emphasis on broader family ties.

In the actual text of the *Marckx* judgment cited in the instant case, the Court observed that ' "family life", within the meaning of Article 8, includes at least the ties between near relatives, for instance those between grandparents and grandchildren, since such relatives may play a considerable part in family life' and concluded that ' "respect" for a family life so understood implies an obligation for the State to act in a manner calculated to allow these ties to develop normally' (see *Marckx v Belgium*, judgment of 13 June 1979, Series A No 31, p. 21, § 45; see also *Scozzari and Giunta v Italy* [GC], Nos 39221/98 and 41963/98, § 221, ECHR 2000-VIII). To put it another way, the Court could at least have made a more careful distinction between the 'family' in the strict legal sense of the term and the broader concept of 'family life' set out in the *Marckx* judgment.

Accordingly, the assertion in the present judgment that 'the existence of "family life" could not be relied on by the applicants in relation to the first applicant's elderly parents, adults who did not belong to the core family' departs from the case-law referred to above and does not take into account the socio-logical and human aspects of contemporary European families (I am deliberately leaving aside Muslim and African families since my reasoning relates solely to the geographical area within the Court's juris-diction). Reference may be made, for example, to the Littré *Dictionnaire de la langue française*, which defines *'famille'* ('family') as *'l'ensemble des individus de même sang qui vivent les uns à côté des autres'* ('a group of persons related by blood who live together'). Even if that concept is not necessarily a legal one, it reflects the perception of those subject to our courts' jurisdiction.

The restrictive concept of a conjugal family (known as a 'nuclear family' in legal anthropology) is becoming obsolete in the light of the obvious changes reflected in family legislation recently enacted in a number of European States. At the same time, the tradition of the 'extended family', so strong in east and southern European countries, is enshrined in those countries' basic laws. For example, the Constitution of the Russian Federation—the State of which the applicants are now nationals—provides: 'Children over eighteen years of age who are able to work shall provide for their parents who are unfit for work' (Article 38 § 3). There are similar provisions in the Constitutions of Ukraine (Article 51 § 2), Moldova (Article 48 § 4) and other countries. This means that in those countries the tradition of helping one's elderly parents is firmly established as a moral imperative written into the Constitution. Those were essentially the considerations guiding the applicants in their ultimately unsuccessful request to the Latvian authorities not to separate them from their elderly, sick ascendants. 'Family life' was plainly inconceivable for them if they were denied the possibility of looking after those relatives. What could be more natural or more humane?

It follows, in my opinion, that the applicants' removal amounted to unjustified interference not only with their 'private life' and 'home' but also, and above all, with their 'family life'.

6   The applicants in *Abdulaziz, Cabales and Balkandali v UK*, A.94 (1985) 7 EHRR 471, claimed that the refusal of the British immigration authorities to allow their foreign husbands to join them in the UK amounted to, *inter alia*, a breach of their right to family life under Article 8. The British Government, as part of its defence, asserted that Mrs Cabales' marriage was void under Philippine law, the State where the marriage ceremony took place, because it had not been solemnised with a licence. Nevertheless, the Court ruled that:

... by guaranteeing the right to respect for family life, Article 8 'presupposes the existence of a family'. However, this does not mean that all intended family life falls entirely outside its ambit. Whatever else the word 'family' may mean, it must at any rate include the relationship that arises from a lawful and genuine marriage, such as that contracted by Mr and Mrs Abdulaziz and Mr and Mrs Balkandali. ....
Mr and Mrs Cabales had gone through a ceremony of marriage and the evidence before the Court

confirms that they believed themselves to be married and that they genuinely wished to cohabit and lead a normal family life. And indeed they subsequently did so. In the circumstances, the committed relationship thus established was sufficient to attract the application of Article 8. (paras 62 and 63)

Hence, the Court was more concerned with the substance of a relationship than its formal status. The Court, unanimously, went on to find that the applicants' rights under Article 8 had not been violated because; 'the duty imposed by Article 8 cannot be considered as extending to a general obligation on the part of a Contracting State to respect the choice by married couples of the country of their matrimonial residence and to accept the non-national spouses for settlement in that country.' (para 68) But the UK was in breach of Article 14 taken together with Article 8 as its immigration rules had unjustifiably discriminated against the applicants on the ground of their gender (males were able to gain entry for their foreign female partners more easily).

7   The nature of the relationship between a divorced parent and his/her child and the concept of 'family life' was examined by the Court in *Berrehab v Netherlands* A.138 (1988) 11 EHRR 322. The applicant was a Moroccan citizen who had married a Dutch national (Mrs Koster) in 1977. After the marriage the Dutch authorities granted him permission to enter, and work, in the Netherlands 'for the sole purpose of enabling him to live with his Dutch wife'. In 1979 they were divorced and soon afterwards she gave birth to their daughter. Despite, the divorce Mr Berrehab had regular contact with his daughter (he saw her four times a week for several hours each time) and he provided financial contributions towards her maintenance and education. In 1983 he was deported from the Netherlands as his reason for being allowed to stay in the country had ended. Two years later he remarried Mrs Koster and was subsequently given permission to reside in the Netherlands in order to live with his wife. Mr Berrehab claimed that his deportation amounted to a violation of his (and his daughter's) right to respect for their family life. In its judgment the Court:

... does not see cohabitation as a *sine qua non* of family life between parents and minor children. It has held that the relationship created between the spouses by a lawful and genuine marriage—such as that contracted by Mr and Mrs Berrehab—has to be regarded as 'family life' (see *Abdulaziz v UK* A.94 (1985)). It follows from the concept of family on which Article 8 is based that a child born of such a union is *ipso jure* part of that relationship: hence, from the moment of the child's birth and by the very fact of it, there exists between him and his parents a bond amounting to 'family life', even if the parents are not then living together. Subsequent events, of course, may break that tie, but this was not so in the instant case.

    ... Mr Berrehab saw his daughter four times a week ... the frequency and regularity of his meetings with her prove that he valued them very greatly. It cannot therefore be maintained that the ties of 'family life' between them had been broken. (para 21)

A majority of the Court (six to one) concluded that given the close ties between Mr Berrehab and his daughter, the deportation was not a proportionate response by the Dutch authorities and their actions could not be justified as necessary to preserve the economic well-being of the Netherlands under Article 8(2).

8   The Court has also been faced with a number of cases where aliens have been convicted of criminal behaviour, and ordered to be deported, and the aliens claim that their removal has (or will) infringe their right to respect for their family (and private) lives. For example in *Moustaquim v Belgium* (1991) 13 EHRR 802, A.193, the applicant was a Moroccan national who arrived in Belgium (with his mother) when he was nearly two years old to live with his father, who had emigrated to that country where he ran a butcher's shop. Three of his seven siblings were born in Belgium and one of his elder brothers had acquired Belgian nationality. The applicant had a residence permit, until he was deported. While the applicant was still a minor (up until September 1981) the Liege Juvenile Court dealt with 147 charges against him (including eighty-two of aggravated theft) for which he was given various custodial orders. In 1982 the Liege Court of Appeal found Moustaquim guilty of twenty-two charges (including four offences of aggravated theft and twelve offences of attempted aggravated theft) and sentenced him to over two years' imprisonment. During 1983 the Ministry of Justice referred the applicant's case to the Advisory Board on Aliens. The Board concluded that the deportation of the applicant would be justified in law but 'inappropriate' because of his youth and the fact that his whole family (father, mother and siblings) lived in Belgium. However a royal order was made in 1984 requiring Moustaquim to leave Belgium and not return for ten years. Eventually, the *Conseil d'Etat* confirmed the order as being necessary for public safety. The applicant left Belgium in June 1984 and was allowed to return in January 1990, when the order was suspended for a trial period of two years provided he did not prejudice public order. The applicant complained to the Commission that his deportation from Belgium had, *inter alia*, infringed his right to respect for his family and private life under Article 8. The Commission, by ten votes to three, expressed the opinion that there had been a breach of that Article. The Court found that:

Mr Moustaquim lived in Belgium, where his parents and his seven brothers and sisters also resided. He had never broken off relations with them. The measure complained of resulted in his being separated from them for more than five years, although he tried to remain in touch by correspondence. There was accordingly interference by a public authority with the right to respect for family life guaranteed in paragraph 1 of Article 8. (para 36)

The deportation order was 'in accordance with the law' and made for a legitimate aim, preventing disorder. However, a majority of the Court, seven votes to two, found that it was not 'necessary in a democratic society'.

The Court does not in any way underestimate the Contracting States' concern to maintain public order, in particular in exercising their right, as a matter of well-established international law and subject to their treaty obligations, to control the entry, residence and expulsion of Aliens ... Mr Moustaquim's alleged offences in Belgium have a number of special features. They all go back to when the applicant was an adolescent ... Moreover, at the time the deportation order was made, all the applicant's close relatives ... had been living in Liege for a long while ... Mr Moustaquim himself was less than two years old when he arrived in Belgium. From that time on he had lived there for about twenty years with his family or not far away from them. He had returned to Morocco only twice, for holidays. He had received all his schooling in French. His family life was thus seriously disrupted by the measure taken against him, which the Advisory Board on Aliens had judged to be 'inappropriate'. Having regard to these various circumstances, it appears that, as far as respect for the applicant's family life is concerned, a proper balance was not achieved between the interests involved, and that the means employed was therefore disproportionate to the legitimate aim pursued. Accordingly, there was a violation of Article 8. (paras 43–6)

By contrast in *El Boujaidi v France* (1997) 30 EHRR 223, 1997-VI 1980, the Court determined that a deportation was not in breach of the applicant's rights under Article 8. The applicant was also born in Morocco (in 1967) and was a national of that state. In 1974 he went, with his mother and four siblings, to join his father in France. During 1987 the Annecy Criminal Court sentenced him to thirty months' imprisonment for dealing in heroin. In 1989 the Lyons Court of Appeal sentenced him to six years' imprisonment for consumption of and trafficking in heroin, additionally the court confirmed a permanent exclusion order on the applicant. The applicant was released from prison in June 1991, but he remained in France unlawfully. During that time he was arrested for an attempted robbery. He was sentenced to one year's imprisonment for this offence. In July 1993 he asked the Lyons Court of Appeal to rescind the exclusion order as he was now living with a Frenchwoman (Mrs M.) and on 6 July 1993 she had given birth to his child. The Court refused the applicant's request and the order was enforced in August 1993. The applicant complained to the Commission arguing that his exclusion from French territory violated Article 8. The Commission, by eleven votes to two, found no breach. As to whether there had been an interference with the applicant's private and family life, the Court held that this question:

... must be determined by the Court in the light of the position when the exclusion order became final ... That means at the beginning of 1989 ... Mr El Boujaidi cannot therefore plead his relationship with Mrs M. and the fact that he is the father of her child, since these circumstances came into being long after that date ... However, the Court observes that he arrived in France in 1974 at the age of seven and lived there until 26 August 1993. He received most of his schooling there and worked there for several years. In addition, his parents, his three sisters and his brother—with whom it was not contested that he remained in contact—live there ... Consequently, the Court is in no doubt that enforcement of the exclusion order amounted to interference with the applicant's right to respect for his private and family life. (para 33)

The Court found the order was in 'accordance with the law' and had the legitimate aim of 'the prevention of disorder or crime'. The Court determined if the order was 'necessary in a democratic society' in the following manner:

... while he asserted that he had no close family in Morocco, he did not claim that he knew no Arabic or that he had never returned to Morocco before the exclusion order was enforced. It also seems that he has never shown any desire to acquire French nationality. Accordingly, even though most of his family and social ties are in France, it has not been established that he has lost all links with his country of origin ... In addition, the applicant had a previous conviction ... for heroin dealing in 1987—when the Lyons Court of Appeal sentenced him to six years' imprisonment and ordered his permanent exclusion from French territory for drug use and drug trafficking. Once he was released, and at a time when he was unlawfully present in France, he continued to lead a life of crime and committed an attempted robbery. The seriousness of the offence on account of which the measure in issue was imposed on the applicant and his subsequent conduct count heavily against him. (para 40)

Therefore, a majority of the Court, eight votes to one, held that the enforcement of the permanent exclusion order against the applicant was not disproportionate. Foighel J wrote a dissenting opinion in which he expressed an entirely different approach to the legal position of persons like the applicant:

Mr El Boujaidi belongs to the category of 'integrated aliens' or 'second-generation immigrants'. As such he did not choose his country of residence of his own free will and he went through his entire upbringing, schooling etc. under the same conditions as French nationals.

... aliens who have spent all—or practically all—their lives in a State should in principle be treated in the same way as nationals as regards the question of their expulsion. ... An effective consequence of this principle would be that—with the possible exception of absolutely extraordinary cases—integrated aliens would not be subject to expulsion.

... The criminal law of the country of residence should normally be sufficient to punish criminal acts committed by an integrated alien, in the same way as it is deemed sufficient to punish criminal acts committed by a national. (paras 2–4)

Clearly if the Court was to adopt this stance it would potentially have a significant impact on those continental Member states that have large populations of settled alien 'guestworkers'.

The judgments of the Court in these cases reveal the use of a complex matrix of factors to determine the extent of the applicants' 'private and family life' and the proportionality of their deportations. Matters influencing the nature of 'family life' include: where the applicant's parents and siblings live, the degree of contact between them and the applicant, and how long they (and the applicant) have lived in the host state. While the factors considered in deciding the proportionality of deportation encompass: the age of the applicant when he/she committed the crime(s), the numbers and nature of the crime(s), the frequency of the applicant's visits to his/her national state, the applicant's linguistic competence in the language of the national state and the applicant's desire to acquire the nationality of the host state. Sherlock has noted unease because of '... the uncertainty inherent in the case-by-case approach taken by the Court in which it balances all the particular circumstances of the case before it.' (A Sherlock, 'Deportation of Aliens and Article 8 of the ECHR' (1998) 23 *EL Rev* HR62 at p 70).

Nevertheless, the full-time Court has continued to utilise the above methodology. An example of it finding a breach of Article 8 occurred in *Radovanovic v Austria*, judgment of 22 July 2004. The applicant, a national of Serbia and Montenegro, had been born in Vienna (during 1979) to parents lawfully residing in Austria who were nationals of former Yugoslavia. He stayed with his parents in Vienna for seven months and then he went to live with his grandparents in Yugoslavia. He remained in that country until he was 10 years old and then he returned to live with his parents in Austria. He completed his secondary education in Austria. In 1997 he was convicted of aggravated robbery and burglary by the Vienna Juvenile Court, which sentenced him to thirty months' imprisonment (twenty-four months were suspended). Subsequently, the Vienna Federal Police Office issued a statutory residence prohibition order against the applicant which prohibited him from remaining/living in Austria for an unlimited period of time. The domestic courts upheld the legality of the order and in 1998 the applicant was expelled to Serbia and Montenegro. The Chamber was unanimous in concluding that:

33. The Court notes that the applicant, a single young adult at the time of his expulsion, is not a second generation immigrant as, despite his birth in Austria, he did not permanently live there until the age of ten. Given the young age at which he arrived, the Court will nevertheless assess the necessity of the interference by applying the same criteria it usually applies in cases of second generation immigrants who have not yet founded a family of their own in the host country. These criteria, so far as material, are the nature and gravity of the offence committed by the applicant and the length of his stay in the host country. In addition the applicant's family ties and the social ties he established in the host country by receiving his schooling and by spending the decisive years of his youth there are to be taken into account (see *Benhebba v France*, No 53441/99, §§ 32–3, 15 June 2003).

34. The Court considers the present case needs to be distinguished from a number of cases concerning the expulsion of second generation immigrants, in which the Court found no violation of Article 8 of the Convention (see *Boujlifa v France*, judgment of 21 October 1997, *Reports* 1997-VI, p 2264, § 42; *Bouchelkia v France*, judgment of 29 January 1997, *Reports* 1997-I, p 65, §§ 50–1; *El Boujaïdi v France*, judgment of 26 September 1997, *Reports* 1997-I, p 63, §§ 40–1; and *Dalia* [*v France* 1998-I] p 92, §§ 53–4). These cases all involved second generation immigrants who arrived in the host country at an early age and were convicted of serious offences with lengthy terms of unconditional imprisonment. Furthermore, they concerned drug offences, the kind of offence, for which the Court has shown understanding of domestic authorities' firmness with regard to those who actively contribute to its spread (see *C. v Belgium*, 7 August 1996, *Reports* 1996-III, p 924, § 35; *Dalia*, cited above, p 92, § 54, *Baghli v France*, No 34374/97, 30 November 1999, § 48 *in fine*, ECHR 1999-VIII; and *Yilmaz v Germany*, No 52853/99, § 46, 17 April 2003). In the present case, despite the shorter duration of the applicant's stay in Austria the Court attaches considerable weight to the fact that although the applicant was convicted

of aggravated robbery, he was only sentenced to a six-month unconditional term of imprisonment, whereas twenty-four months were suspended on probation.

35. In the applicant's case the Austrian authorities balanced his right to respect for private and family life against the public interest and gave priority to the latter interest in order to prevent disorder and crime. Without disregarding the serious nature of the offences, the Court notes, however, that the applicant committed them as a juvenile, that he had no previous criminal record and that the major part of the relatively high sentence was suspended on probation by the Juvenile Court. Therefore the Court is not convinced by the Government's argument and the administrative authorities' assessment that the applicant constituted such a serious danger to public order which necessitated the imposition of the measure concerned (see *mutatis mutandis*, *Ezzouhdi v France*, No 47160/99, § 34, 13 February 2001).

36. Given the applicant's birth in Austria, where he later also completed his secondary education and vocational training while living with his family, and also taking into account that his family had already lawfully stayed in Austria for a long time and that the applicant himself had an unlimited residence permit when he committed the offence, and considering that, after the death of his grandparents in Serbia and Montenegro, he no longer has any relatives there, the Court finds that his family and social ties with Austria were much stronger than with Serbia and Montenegro.

37. The Court therefore considers that, in the circumstances of the present case, the imposition of a residence prohibition of unlimited duration was an overly rigorous measure. A less intrusive measure, such as a residence prohibition of a limited duration would have sufficed. The Court thus concludes that the Austrian authorities, by imposing a residence prohibtion of unlimited duration against the applicant, have not struck a fair balance between the interests involved and that the means employed were disproportionate to the aim pursued in the circumstances of the case (see *mutatis mutandis*, *Ezzouhdi*, cited above, § 35; and *Yilmaz*, cited above, §§ 48–9).

38. Accordingly, there has been a violation of Article 8 of the Convention.

Whilst, the Court found a breach, because of the unlimited length of the order, the judgment suggests that an exclusion for a shorter period of time might not have violated Article 8, even though the applicant (by the time of his exclusion a young adult) had no family living in Serbia.

9   A number of applicants have challenged various aspects of State authorities' decisions regarding the assumption of public care over their children. In *W v UK*, A.121-A (1987) 10 EHRR 29, the applicant challenged the decision-making process followed by a local authority to assume the parental rights of the applicant and his wife in respect of their youngest child (S) and subsequently to place S with long-term foster parents while denying W (and his wife) access to S. The applicant and his wife had a history of serious marital and financial difficulties. S was born in October 1978 and his parents placed him in the voluntary care of the local authority in March 1979 (as his mother was suffering from post-natal depression and alcoholism). In August 1979 the local authority passed resolutions assuming parental rights over S, but the applicant and his wife were not informed that such resolutions were being considered. Early in 1980 an unidentified official in the authority's Social Services Department determined that S should be placed with foster parents on a long-term basis with a view to adoption. In March 1980 the authority's Adoption and Foster Care Committee, without consulting the applicant (or his wife), approved the proposal to place S with long-term foster parents and restrict access to him by his natural parents. During the next month the Area Director of Social Services decided that W (and his wife) should not be allowed to visit S (in order to avoid jeopardising S developing a good relationship with his foster parents). W and his wife

began legal proceedings to challenge the local authority's actions, but in June 1981 the High Court held that it would not be in S's best interests to be returned to their care. The Court of Appeal confirmed that decision in October 1981. Subsequently, the Local Ombudsman upheld the applicant's complaint of maladministration in respect of the decision-making procedure followed by the local authority. In 1984 the High Court approved an application by the foster parents to adopt S. W complained to the Commission alleging, *inter alia*, that the procedures followed by the local authority had violated his right to respect for his family life. By thirteen votes to one the Commission found a breach of Article 8. The plenary Court began its judgment by observing that:

The mutual enjoyment by parent and child of each other's company constitutes a fundamental element of family life. Furthermore, the natural family relationship is not terminated by reason of the fact that the child is taken into public care. It follows—and this was not contested by the Government—that the Authority's decisions resulting from the procedures at issue amounted to interferences with the applicant's right to respect for his family life. (para 59)

The Court found that the interferences were 'in accordance with the law' and had the legitimate aim of protecting the health or rights and freedoms of others (i.e. S). Therefore, the contentious issue was whether the authority's conduct was 'necessary in a democratic society'.

The Court recognises that, in reaching decisions in so sensitive an area, local authorities are faced with a task that is extremely difficult. To require them to follow on each occasion an inflexible procedure would only add to their problems. They must therefore be allowed a measure of discretion in this respect.

On the other hand, predominant in any consideration of this aspect of the present case must be the fact that the decisions may well prove to be irreversible: thus, where a child has been taken away from his parents and placed with alternative carers, he may in the course of time establish with them new bonds which it might not be in his interests to disturb or interrupt by reversing a previous decision to restrict or terminate parental access to him. This is accordingly a domain in which there is an even greater call than usual for protection against arbitrary interferences.

It is true that Article 8 contains no explicit procedural requirements, but this is not conclusive of the matter. The local authority's decision-making process clearly cannot be devoid of influence on the substance of the decision, notably by ensuring that it is based on the relevant considerations and is not one-sided and, hence, neither is nor appears to be arbitrary. Accordingly, the Court is entitled to have regard to that process to determine whether it has been conducted in a manner that, in all the circumstances, is fair and affords due respect to the interests protected by Article 8. . . .

The relevant considerations to be weighed by a local authority in reaching decisions on children in its care must perforce include the views and interests of the natural parents. The decision-making process must therefore, in the Court's view, be such as to secure that their views and interests are made known to and duly taken into account by the local authority and that they are able to exercise in due time any remedies available to them. . . .

There are three factors which have a bearing on the practicalities of the matter. Firstly, as the Commission pointed out, there will clearly be instances where the participation of the natural parents in the decision-making process either will not be possible or will not be meaningful—as, for example, where they cannot be traced or are under a physical or mental disability or where an emergency arises. Secondly, decisions in this area, while frequently taken in the light of case reviews or case conferences, may equally well evolve from a continuous process of monitoring on the part of the local authority's officials. Thirdly, regular contacts between the social workers responsible and the parents often provide an appropriate channel for the communication of the latter's views to the authority.

In the Court's view, what therefore has to be determined is whether, having regard to the particular circumstances of the case and notably the serious nature of the decisions to be taken, the parents have been involved in the decision-making process, seen as a whole, to a degree sufficient to provide them with the requisite protection of their interests. If they have not, there will have been a failure to respect their family life and the interference resulting from the decision will not be capable of being regarded as 'necessary' within the meaning of Article 8. . . . the Court considers that in conducting its review in the context of Article 8 it may also have regard to the length of the local authority's decision-making process and of any related judicial proceedings. As the Commission has rightly pointed out, in cases of this kind there is always the danger that any procedural delay will result in the de facto determination of the issue submitted to the court before it has held its hearing. And an effective respect for family life requires that future relations between parent and child be determined solely in the light of all relevant considerations and not by the mere effluxion of time. (paras 62–5)

These principles were applied by the Court and led it to conclude that the local authority had not involved the applicant sufficiently in the decisions it had taken, early in 1980, regarding S. The length of the domestic court proceedings was also a subsidiary factor in the Court's application of Article 8. Consequently, a unanimous Court found a violation of that provision. The judgment of the Court was highly significant in requiring public authorities to follow fair procedures that ensured that parents were properly involved in decision-making regarding the care of their children. However, having regard to the diverse range of situations in which public authorities have to reach decisions regarding the care of children, the Court did not mandate a specific form of procedure, but instead focussed upon the duty on the relevant state agencies to ensure that the parents' opinions were adequately considered. The Court found breaches of this requirement in the similar cases of *B v UK* A.121-B (1987) and *R v UK*, A.121-C (1987) 10 EHRR 74. The law in England and Wales was subject to major reforms by the Children Act 1989 which provided, *inter alia*, local authorities would have to apply to the courts for care orders, such orders would automatically include provisions allowing reasonable contact with parents and disputes about contact and its termination would be resolved by the courts. Procedural aspects of the Scottish system of child welfare protection were considered in *McMichael v UK*, A.307-B (1995) 20 EHRR 205. The first and second applicants were married in 1990 and both had a history of mental illness. In November 1987 the second applicant gave birth to a son (A.) whom she denied was the son of the first applicant (although both applicants were living together at the time). The Reporter to the local Children's Panel arranged for a children's hearing to be convened (this was before a tribunal of independent members drawn from the Panel) to consider the need for compulsory care of A., because the second applicant's doctors had found that she was suffering from a recurrence of her mental illness. In December the children's hearing granted a warrant for A to be kept in a place of safety by the local authority. In February 1988 the children's hearing held a session at which the second applicant attended, and the first applicant was also present as her representative. The children's hearing had a report on A, compiled by the local social work department. In accordance with the Children's Hearings (Scotland) Rules 1986, the applicants were not given copies of the report (or other documents before the hearing), but the chairman informed them of the substance of the relevant documents. The children's hearing decided that A was in need of compulsory care. In 1993 the Sheriff granted an application by A's foster parents to adopt him. The applicants complained to the Commission alleging, *inter alia*, that they had not had a fair hearing before the children's hearing in breach of Article 8. A unanimous Commission upheld that claim. After citing its decision in *W v UK*, the Court sought to elaborate the different procedural rights granted by Articles 6(1) and 8.

Thus, Article 6(1) affords a procedural safeguard, namely the 'right to a court' in the determination of one's 'civil rights and obligations' (see *Golder v UK* A.18); whereas not only does the procedural requirement inherent in Article 8 cover administrative procedures as well as judicial proceedings, but it is ancillary to the wider purpose of ensuring proper respect for, inter alia, family life ... The difference between the purpose pursued by the respective safeguards afforded by Articles 6(1) and 8 may, in the light of the particular circumstances, justify the examination of the same set of facts under both Articles ...' (para 91)

Because of the applicants' inability to have access to some of the documents before the children's hearing the Court found a breach of their right to respect for their family life (unanimously in the case of the second applicant and by six votes to three in the case of the first applicant).

The greater the restrictions placed upon the legal rights of natural parents *vis a vis* their children by public authorities, the more the Court will require of the State in terms of justification. In *Johansen v Norway* (1996) 23 EHRR 33, 1996-III, the applicant left home when she was 16 and gave birth to her first child when she was 17 (in 1977). She was dependent on assistance from the welfare authorities. In 1989 she gave birth to a daughter (S) and the local Client and Patient Committee decided to take S into care because the applicant was considered to be physically and mentally unable to care for S. In May 1990 the Committee examined the applicant's case (the applicant and her lawyer were present) and decided, by four votes to two, to deprive the applicant of her parental responsibilities in respect of S, to place S in a foster home with a view to adoption and to deny the applicant access to S. Subsequently, the applicant moved to Denmark and S remained with her foster parents. The applicant alleged that, *inter alia*, depriving her of her parental rights over S amounted to a violation of Article 8. The Commission agreed, by eleven votes to two. The Court explained its approach in the following terms:

... the authorities enjoy a wide margin of appreciation in assessing the necessity of taking a child into care. However, a stricter scrutiny is called for both of any further limitations, such as restrictions placed by those authorities on parental rights and access, and of any legal safeguards designed to secure an effective protection of the right of parents and children to respect for their family life. Such further limitations entail the danger that the family relations between the parents and a young child are effectively curtailed. (para 64)

In respect of the authorities' decisions in this case:

These measures were particularly far-reaching in that they totally deprived the applicant of her family life with the child and were inconsistent with the aim of reuniting them. Such measures should only be applied in exceptional circumstances and could only be justified if they were motivated by an overriding requirement pertaining to the child's best interests ... (para 78)

A majority of the Court, eight votes to one, did not consider that the child's best interests required such draconian state intervention and, therefore, the Norwegian authorities had exceeded their margin of appreciation, thereby violating the applicant's rights under Article 8.

A unanimous Grand Chamber of the full-time Court has held that governmental authorities in possession of relevant information concerning a child subject to public care measures must generally make that material available to the parent(s) without the latter having to formally seek its disclosure. In *T.P. and K.M.* v *UK*, judgment of 10 May 2001 the first applicant was a young single mother with a daughter (the second applicant) nearly 5 years old. The local authority became concerned that the daughter was the victim of sexual abuse. An interview, recorded on video, was conducted with the daughter (in the absence of the first applicant) by a consultant child psychiatrist (employed by the local health authority) and a social worker (employed by the local social services) in November 1987. The child revealed that she had been abused by a man named X. The first applicant's current boyfriend shared the same fore-name (X.Y.). Later that day, the local authority applied to the magistrates court for a place of safety order in respect of the daughter on the basis that she was being abused at home by X.Y. The court granted that order and she was taken into public care. During the following year the first applicant was only allowed very limited access to her daughter. In subsequent judicial proceedings the consultant and the health authority objected to the video of the second appli-cant's interview being disclosed to the first applicant. In November 1988 the first applicant's solicitors were given a transcript of the daughter's interview and it became apparent that the person she had identified as her abuser was not X.Y. Subsequently, the High Court granted leave for the second applicant to be returned to live with the first applicant. The applicants complained to Strasbourg that, *inter alia*, the unjustifiable taking into care of the second appli-cant had violated their right to respect for their family life. Before the Court, the Government contended that the first applicant could have applied to the High Court for an order obliging the local authority to disclose the video tape of the interview at any time after the second appli-cant had been taken into public care. However, the Court considered that this possibility did not satisfy the duties incumbent upon domestic authorities.

82. .... The positive obligation on the Contracting State to protect the interests of the family requires that this material be made available to the parent concerned, even in the absence of any request by the parent. If there were doubts as to whether this posed a risk to the welfare of the child, the matter should have been submitted to the court by the local authority at the earliest stage in the proceedings possible for it to resolve the issue involved.

Hence there had been a breach of Article 8. The decision in *T.P.* is a further important strengthening of parental rights under Article 8, as it places the primary responsibility for dis-closure upon those public authorities that possess the relevant materials. Given that many parents experiencing the compulsory taking of their children into care are likely to be in a dis-tressed state, at that time, requiring the public authorities to take the initiative in disclosing relevant information will reduce the burden upon the parents and, perhaps, enable them to gain a better understanding of the situation.

Judicial authorities of Member states are also required to disclose relevant evidence to par-ents. For example, in *Buchberger v Austria*, judgment of 20 December 2001, the applicant was a single mother who had two young children. Her job was delivering papers in the morning. One day she was forty-five minutes late returning from work (because she claimed she had been unwell) and a neighbour had contacted the local authority as she had seen the applicant's 2-year-old son wandering around in his garden wearing only pyjamas despite the freezing temperature. The local Youth Welfare Office took the applicant's two young sons into provi-sional care and applied to the District Court for the transfer of custody of the boys to the Office. After a hearing, at which the applicant was assisted by counsel, the District Court ordered the prompt return of the boys to the applicant. In subsequent appellate proceedings the Office submitted a report to the Regional Court. The Regional Court also obtained several court files concerning other civil and criminal proceedings against the applicant. She was not informed of this further evidence. Custody of the boys was transferred to the Office by the Regional Court as it found that their living conditions with the applicant were desolate and chaotic. The European Court was unanimous in determining that the procedure followed by the Regional Court violated the applicant's right to respect for her family life.

43. .... It is not in dispute that this additional evidence has not been brought to the applicant's atten-tion. However, in the circumstances of the case the Regional Court should not have decided without

having given the applicant an opportunity to react thereto. The additional evidence was of particular importance to the proceedings as the Regional Court considered it sufficiently strong to overturn the first instance decision. The Regional Court did not merely rely on the outcome of previous court proceedings but considered the further contents of the case-file. Moreover, it relied on a recent report by the Youth Welfare Office, a document which the applicant had never seen.

44. In the Court's opinion, the failure of the Regional Court to inform the applicant of the additional evidence obtained during the appeal proceedings which deprived her of the possibility to react thereto reveals an insufficient involvement of her in the decision-making process.

A Grand Chamber of the full-time Court elaborated limitations on the rights of parents to participate in official decision-making procedures concerning the custody and care of their children in *K. and T. v Finland*, judgment of 12 July 2001. This was also the first occasion on which a Grand Chamber gave a re-hearing judgment (under Article 43) following an earlier Chamber judgment on the same facts. K. was the mother of two children (P., born in 1986, and M., born in 1988) by diferent fathers. From the summer of 1991 she had been cohabiting with T. K. had a history of serious mental illness involving periods of compulsory and voluntary hospitalisation. During March 1993, when K. was pregnant with T.'s child, her mother informed the social welfare authorities that K.'s mental health was bad (K. had allegedly destroyed family photographs by piercing the eyes of the persons appearing in them). K. was subsequently placed in voluntary psychiatric care for several weeks. M. was showing signs of behavioural problems and the social welfare authorities decided to place him in a children's home for three months (K. and T. did not object to this placement). On 18 June 1993 K. went into hospital where she gave birth to a daughter (J.). The local Social Director, exercising statutory powers, issued an emergency care order taking J. into public care. The order was served on the hospital and immediately after J.'s birth she was taken from K. to the children's ward. Three days later the Social Director issued another emergency order placing M. in public care. In July 1993 the local Social Welfare Board made 'normal' public care orders in respect of M. and J.. K. was only allowed to see the children when she was accompanied by her personal nurse. Both K. and T. had been able to express their opposition to the making of these orders before the Board reached its decisions. During the summer of 1993 T. spent much time with J. caring for her in the hospital and later in a family centre. In the autumn of 1993 the County Administrative Court confirmed the care orders in respect of J. and M.. At the start of 1994 J. and M. were placed, by the Board, with a foster family in a city 120 km from the applicant's home. The applicants were restricted, by the authorities, to visiting their children once a month. From January 2001 M. and J. have been allowed unsupervised visits to and by the applicants once a month.

The applicants complained to the former Commission in 1994 and their case was referred to the new Court in 1998. The Chamber, in a Judgment given on 27 April 2000, unanimously found, *inter alia*, a breach of the applicants' right to respect for their family life under Article 8 in respect of the Finnish authorities' decisions to take M. and J. into care and the failure to take appropriate measures to reunite the family. Just a few days before the expiry of the three months deadline for seeking a referral to the Grand Chamber under Article 43, the respondent State sought a re-examination of those matters where the Chamber had found a violation of the Convention. The applicants did not contest the request. In October 2000 the five member Grand Chamber Panel accepted the Finnish request and the Grand Chamber held a hearing in the spring of 2001.

The Grand Chamber adopted a more precise framework of analysis when applying Article 8 than that utilized by the Chamber. The latter examined the taking of M. and J. into care as a whole. Whereas:

160. The Grand Chamber, for its part, considers it appropriate to examine the emergency care order and the normal care order for each child separately as they were different kinds of decision, which had different consequences—an emergency care order being of short, limited duration and a normal care order being of a more permanent nature—and which were the product of separate decision-making processes, even though one measure followed immediately after the other. In the Grand Chamber's view there are substantive and procedural differences to be taken into account which warrant examining the two sets of decisions separately.

A large majority of the Grand Chamber (fourteen votes to three) determined that the emergency order taking J. into care as soon as she had been born was not necessary in a democratic society and therefore in breach of Article 8.

168. .... the taking of a new-born baby into public care at the moment of its birth is an extremely harsh measure. There must be extraordinarily compelling reasons before a baby can be physically removed from the care of its mother, against her will, immediately after birth as a consequence of a procedure in which neither she nor her partner has been involved. The shock and disarray felt by even a perfectly healthy mother are easy to imagine. .... The reasons relied on by the national authorities were relevant but, in the Court's view, not sufficient to justify the serious intervention in the family life of the applicants. Even having regard to the national authorities' margin of appreciation, the Court considers that the making of the emergency care order in respect of J. and the methods used in implementing that decision were disproportionate in their effects on the applicants' potential for enjoying a family life with their new-born child as from her birth.. This being so, whilst there may have been a "necessity" to take some precautionary measures to protect the child J., the interference in the applicants' family life entailed in the emergency care order made in respect of J. cannot be regarded as having been 'necessary' in a democratic society.

Judge Palm, joined by Judge Gaukur Jorundsson, dissented as they considered that the Finnish authorities had acted within the margin of appreciation accorded to domestic authorities when exercising child protection responsibilities.

In fact the Court has, in all earlier judgments concerning the taking of children into public care, accepted the national authorities' assessments of the necessity of the care order. In the present judgment the Court rejects for the first time the competent national authorities' understanding of the necessity of the measure they took at the time. ....
    Even if, with the benefit of hindsight, it may seem harsh to separate a new-born baby from its mother, the authorities were at that time forced to take an immediate decision whether it was a risk for the child to stay with a mother who was mentally ill and totally unpredictable and who remained free to leave the hospital with the child if no decision was taken.
    Under these circumstances and having regard to their margin of appreciation, I find that the Finnish authorities were reasonably entitled to think that it was necessary to take J. into emergency care.

Judge Bonello was even more outspoken in his support for the domestic action:

The Finnish authorities were confronted with a situation in which a vulnerable new-born would be at the mercy of someone in relentless captivity to recurrent psychosis, a person about whom the only thing predictable was her unpredictability. A person from whom uncontrollable reactions were as inseparable as was the resort to destructive violence. The infant's best interests, if that article of faith were to retain any meaning, would have been poorly served by making her the responsibility of the irresponsible. Perfectly 'normal' mothers, in the embrace of post-natal trauma, have turned the best-honed maternal instincts to the destruction of their offspring. Why that possibility is factored in when dealing with normal mothers, but discounted when dealing with guaranteed psychopaths, still, I believe, calls for explanation.

Regarding the emergency care order in respect of M. the Grand Chamber, by thirteen votes to four, decided that there had not been a breach of Article 8. The majority considered that this order did not have the same impact on the applicants' family life as J.'s order. M. was already separated from his family, due to his voluntary placement in the children's home, but without the order he could have been removed from that safe environment by the applicants. The dissentients (Judges: Ress, Fuhrmann, Pantiru, and Kovler) considered that:

Before public authorities have recourse to emergency measures in such delicate issues as care orders the imminent danger should be really established. An imminent danger is the precondition for an emergency care order. If it is still possible to hear the parents of the child and to discuss with them the necessity of the measure, there should be no room for an emergency action.

M. was in no imminent danger since he had already been placed in a children's home. The whole procedure gives the impression of a *coup de force*. A procedure to have normal care orders prepared with the involvement of the parents would have been under the circumstances a reasonable and fully satisfactory way.

The Grand Chamber was united in determining that the normal care orders in respect of both J. and M. did not violate Article 8.

173. In a situation in which, as detailed in the medical and social reports, the mother of the children was seriously mentally ill, there were social problems in the family and the prospects for the healthy development of the children in foster care appeared far more positive than the expected development in the care of their biological parents, the authorities could reasonably base the contested decisions on the assessment that was made of what was in the best interests of the children. As to the procedural guarantee inherent in Article 8, the evidence shows that the applicants were properly involved in the decision-making process leading to the making of the normal care orders and that they were provided with the requisite protection of their interests . . .

The judgment of the majority in *K. and T.* discloses a fair balance between the interests of parents and their children. Where leaving children with their parents creates an immediate serious risk to the children's welfare, the authorities are empowered to take unilateral emergency care measures to protect the children. But, the authorities will be obliged to demonstrate that such a severe decision, and the procedures by which it was reached, were compatible with parental rights under Article 8.

10   The nature and extent of the positive obligation upon States to enable contact between a divorced parent and his/her children was outlined in *Glaser v UK* [2000] 3 FCR 193.

65. The Court's case-law has consistently held that Article 8 includes a right for a parent to have measures taken with a view to his or her being reunited with the child, and an obligation for the national authorities to take such measures. This applies not only to cases dealing with the compulsory taking of children into public care and the implementation of care measures (see, inter alia, the *Olsson v Sweden (No 2)* judgment of 27 November 1992, Series A No 250, pp 35–6, § 90), but also to cases where contact and residence disputes concerning children arise between parents and/or other members of the children's family (eg the *Hokkanen v Finland* judgment of 23 September 1994, Series A No 299, p 20, § 55).

66. The obligation of the national authorities to take measures to facilitate contact by a non-custodial parent with children after divorce is not, however, absolute (*mutatis mutandis*, Hokkanen judgment cited above, p 22, § 58). The establishment of contact may not be able to take place immediately and

may require preparatory or phased measures. The co-operation and understanding of all concerned will always be an important ingredient. While national authorities must do their utmost to facilitate such co-operation, any obligation to apply coercion in this area must be limited since the interests as well as the rights and freedoms of all concerned must be taken into account, and more particularly the best interests of the child and his or her rights under Article 8 of the Convention. Where contacts with the parent might appear to threaten those interests or interfere with those rights, it is for the national authorities to strike a fair balance between them (see *Hokkanen v Finland* cited above, § 58; *Olsson v Sweden (No 2)*, cited above, pp 35–6, § 90). The key consideration is whether those authorities have taken all necessary steps to facilitate contact as can reasonably be demanded in the special circumstances of each case (*mutatis mutandis, Hokkanen v Finland*, cited above, § 58). Other important factors in proceedings concerning children are that time takes on a particular significance as there is always a danger that any procedural delay will result in the de facto determination of the issue before the court (*H. v UK* judgment of 8 July 1987, Series A No 120, pp 63–4, §§ 89–90), and that the decision-making procedure provides requisite protection of parental interests. [*W v UK* judgment of 8 July 1987, Series A n° 121, pp 28–9, §§ 62–4.]

The Court was unanimous in concluding that the English and Scottish authorities had, in respect of a very difficult post-divorce situation, achieved a fair balance between the competing interests of the applicant, his ex-wife and their children. The judgment also makes clear the limitations of the Court's role in scrutinising the actions (or inaction) of the national authorities.

64. Where the measures in issue concern parental disputes over their children, however, it is not for the Court to substitute itself for the competent domestic authorities in regulating contact questions, but rather to review under the Convention the decisions that those authorities have taken in the exercise of their power of appreciation. In so doing, it must determine whether the reasons purporting to justify any measures taken with regard to an applicant's enjoyment of his right to respect for family life are relevant and sufficient ... '

An example of the Court finding a State in breach of the re-unification obligation occurred in *Ignaccolo-Zenide v Romania*, judgment of 25 January 2000. The applicant was a French national who married a Romanian national (D.Z.) in 1980. They had two daughters (born in 1981 and 1984). A divorce was granted to the applicant and D.Z. by a French court in 1989. The court approved an agreement between the former spouses that parental responsibility was given to D.Z. and the applicant received access and staying rights. During the next year D.Z. moved to the United States and the applicant complained to the French courts that D.Z. was denying her access to her daughters. In May 1991 the Metz Court of Appeal gave parental responsibility to both parents and ordered that the children should live with the applicant. She subsequently brought a number of actions in different courts in the United States, but D.Z. did not comply with those judgments requiring him to return his daughters to the applicant. In 1994 D.Z. and his daughters went to live in Romania. Both the United States and French governments requested the Romanian government to return the children to the applicant in accordance with the 1980 Hague Convention on the Civil Aspects of International Child Abduction. The applicant also made an urgent application under Article 2 of the Hague Convention to the Romanian courts for an order requiring D.Z. to comply with the 1991 judgment of the Metz Court of Appeal. In December 1994 the Bucharest Court of First Instance issued such an order. The applicant subsequently visited Romania eight times for the purpose of meeting her daughters but, despite several attempts by the Romanian authorities to enforce the Bucharest Court order, the applicant was only able to see her daughters once for a few minutes in 1997. The meeting did not go well and the daughters' expressed the wish never to see the applicant again. Before the Court the applicant claimed that the Romanian authorities had not taken sufficient steps to facilitate the return of her daughters. In the judgment of the Chamber:

94. ... As to the State's obligation to take positive measures, the Court has repeatedly held that Article 8 includes a parent's right to the taking of measures with a view to his or her being reunited with his or her child and an obligation on the national authorities to take such action (see, for example, the follow-ing judgments: *Eriksson v Sweden*, 22 June 1989, Series A No 156, pp 26–7, ...).However, the national authorities' obligation to take measures to facilitate reunion is not absolute, since the reunion of a par-ent with children who have lived for some time with the other parent may not be able to take place immediately and may require preparatory measures to be taken. The nature and extent of such prep-aration will depend on the circumstances of each case, but the understanding and cooperation of all concerned are always an important ingredient. Whilst national authorities must do their utmost to facili-tate such cooperation, any obligation to apply coercion in this area must be limited since the interests as well as the rights and freedoms of all concerned must be taken into account, and more particularly the best interests of the child and his or her rights under Article 8 of the Convention. Where contacts with the parent might appear to threaten those interests or interfere with those rights, it is for the national authorities to strike a fair balance between them ...

95. Lastly, the Court considers that the positive obligations that Article 8 of the Convention lays on the Contracting States in the matter of reuniting a parent with his or her children must be interpreted in the light of the Hague Convention of 25 October 1980 on the Civil Aspects of International Child Abduction ('the Hague Convention'). This is all the more so in the instant case as the respondent State is also a party to that instrument, Article 7 of which contains a list of measures to be taken by States to secure the prompt return of children.

96. What is decisive in the present case is therefore whether the national authorities did take all steps to facilitate execution of the order of 14 December 1994 that could reasonably be demanded ...

An overwhelming majority of the Court, six votes to one, concluded that the Romanian authorities had failed to make 'adequate and effective' efforts to enforce the applicant's right to the return of her daughters. The Court emphasized that in abduction cases '102 ... the adequacy of a measure is to be judged by the swiftness of its implementation', because of the danger that the passage of time will undermine the relationship between the abducted children and the parent lawfully entitled to their custody. Here there had been several delays in bailiffs visiting D.Z.'s home to look for the children in 1995 and total inaction by the authorities between December 1995–January 1997. Consequently, these deficiencies meant that there had been a breach of Article 8.

The judgment in *Ignaccolo-Zenide* demonstrated a sensitive awareness of the potentially destructive effect of the elapse of time upon the durability of the relationship between a separated child and his/her parent(s).

12   State regulation of the adoption of children was examined by the Court in *Keegan v Ireland*, A.290 (1994) 18 EHRR 342. The applicant met his former girlfriend (Miss V) in May 1986 and they started living together in February 1987. Around Christmas 1987 they decided to have a child. On the 14 February 1988 they became engaged. A week later it was confirmed that V was pregnant. However, soon afterwards the relationship between the applicant and V broke down and they ceased living together. In September 1988 V gave birth to a daughter (S) of whom the applicant was the father. The applicant saw S when she was one day old, but he was prevented from seeing her again by V (and her parents). In November 1988 V wrote to the applicant informing him that she had made arrangements for S to be adopted. Under

Irish law the applicant had no right to be heard by the statutory Adoption Board, which approved applications from persons to adopt children placed for adoption. The applicant sought to be appointed as S's guardian by the courts in order to challenge her adoption, but he was unsuccessful. S was, subsequently, adopted. The applicant complained to the Commission alleging, *inter alia*, that Irish law failed to respect his right to respect for family life by allowing the adoption of his daughter without his knowledge or consent. A unanimous Commission considered that there had been a breach of Article 8. After citing its previous rulings in *Johnston v Ireland* and *Berrehab v Netherlands* (considered above), the Court stated that:

In the present case, the relationship between the applicant and the child's mother lasted for two years during one of which they co-habited. Moreover, the conception of their child was the result of a deliberate decision and they had also planned to get married. Their relationship at this time had thus the hallmark of family life for the purposes of Article 8. The fact that it subsequently broke down does not alter this conclusion any more than it would for a couple who were lawfully married and in a similar situation. It follows that from the moment of the child's birth there existed between the applicant and his daughter a bond amounting to family life. (para 45)

All the judges went on to find that the interference with the applicant's right to respect for his family life was not 'necessary in a democratic society' as the Irish Government had provided no justification based upon the needs of S. Therefore, it is clear that the Court requires weighty reasons, derived from the needs of the particular child, to justify an adoption as being compatible with Article 8. The Court did not elaborate the procedure to be followed by the adoption process under Article 8, as it went on to find that the applicant's lack of standing in S's adoption and his inability to challenge the decision in the Irish courts violated Article 6(1).

In the later case of *Söderbäck v Sweden* (1998) 29 EHRR 95, 1998-VII, the Court, unanimously, found the child's relationship with the adoptive father (which had lasted for over six years) to be sufficiently weighty to justify the adoption despite the objection of her natural father. The applicant had been a friend of K. W. from 1980, although they did not have a steady relationship. In 1982 K. W. gave birth to a daughter (M.) of whom the applicant was the father. The applicant only saw M. on an occasional basis, due to an alcohol problem that he was experiencing. In 1983 K. W. met M. W. and they began to co-habit later that year. During 1989 they married. A few months earlier M. W. had applied to the District Court for permission to adopt M. The District Court heard the applicant's objections to the adoption request, but decided to approve the adoption as the court found that M. W. had taken part in the care of M since she was eight months old and she saw him as her father. The applicant's complaint alleging a breach of Article 8 was rejected by the European Court of Human Rights:

... having regard to the assessment of the child's best interests made by the domestic court, as well as to the limited relations that the applicant had with M during the relevant period, the Court is satisfied that the decision fell within the margin of appreciation. Given the aims sought to be achieved by allowing the adoption to go ahead, it cannot be said that the adverse effects it had on the applicant's relations with the child were disproportionate. (para 34)

Therefore, the Court was recognizing that the ties between a child and the proposed adoptive parent may be of sufficient duration and quality to outweigh those between the child and her/ his natural parent.

Home

Gillow v UK A.109 (1986) 11 EHRR 335
European Court of Human Rights

The applicants, Mr and Mrs Gillow, moved from England to Guernsey in 1956 so that Mr Gillow could take up employment on the island. In 1957, Mr Gillow bought a plot of land on the island and, after obtaining permission, he built a house called 'Whiteknights' on the site. The Gillows occupied the house as their family residence until 1960 when the family left Guernsey, as Mr Gillow had accepted employment overseas. During the ensuing years the house was let to persons who had licences to occupy it granted by the States of Guernsey Housing Authority. By 1979 the house was unoccupied and the Gillows applied for a licence to enable them to occupy Whiteknights as their retirement home. The authorities refused the applicants permission to occupy Whiteknights and successfully prosecuted them when they lived in the property without a licence. The applicants sold Whiteknights in 1980. Subsequently, they complained to the Commission that, *inter alia*, their right to respect for their home under Article 8 had been violated by the Housing Authority's conduct. The Commission was unanimous in finding a breach of that right.

. . .

A. WAS WHITEKNIGHTS MR AND MRS GILLOW'S HOME WITHIN THE MEANING OF THE CONVENTION?

46. According to the applicants, they had established Whiteknights as their home in 1958. Although they had subsequently left Guernsey, they had retained ownership of the house, to which they always intended to return, and had kept their furniture in it. On their return in 1979, they lived in the property with a view to taking up permanent residence once the negotiations with the Housing Authority about their residential status had been concluded and the necessary repairs had been carried out.

These statements, the accuracy of which the Court has no cause to doubt, are supported by the fact that in 1956 the applicants had sold their former home in Lancashire and moved with their family and furniture to Guernsey. Furthermore, the Court is satisfied that they had not established any other home elsewhere in the United Kingdom. Although the applicants had been absent from Guernsey for almost nineteen years, they had in the circumstances retained sufficient continuing links with Whiteknights for it to be considered their home, for the purposes of Article 8 of the Convention, at the time of the disputed measures.

B. WAS THERE ANY INTERFERENCE BY A PUBLIC AUTHORITY WITH THE EXERCISE OF THE APPLICANTS' RIGHT TO RESPECT FOR THEIR HOME?

47. Following the enactment of the Housing Law 1969—which was not amended on this point by the Housing Law 1975—, the applicants were obliged to seek a licence to occupy Whiteknights because, as a consequence of the change in the law, they had lost their residence qualifications. In the Court's opinion, the fact that, on pain of prosecution, they were obliged to obtain a licence to live in their own house on their return to Guernsey in 1979, the refusal of the licences applied for, the institution of criminal proceedings against them for unlawful occupation of the property and, in Mr Gillow's case, his conviction and the imposition of a fine constituted interferences with the exercise of the applicants' right to respect for their home.

C. WERE THE INTERFERENCES JUSTIFIED?

48. In order to determine whether these interferences were justified under the terms of paragraph 2 of Article 8, the Court must examine in turn whether they were in accordance with the law, whether they had an aim that was legitimate under that paragraph and whether they were necessary in a democratic society for the aforesaid aim.

. . .

2. LEGITIMATE AIM

54. The Court refers to the statistics supplied both by the Government and by the applicants concerning the population of Guernsey and the number of empty houses. Although the situation could be said to have improved in some respects in the period between 1976 and 1981, this does not alter the fact that the island is very limited in area. It is therefore legitimate for the authorities to try to maintain the population within limits that permit the balanced economic development of the island. It is also legitimate, in this connection, to show a certain preference for persons who have strong attachments to the island or are engaged in an employment essential to the community when considering whether to grant licences to occupy premises let at a modest rent. The relevant legislation was thus designed to promote the economic well-being of the island. The Court does not find it to be established that the legislation pursued any other purpose.

. . .

3. NECESSARY IN A DEMOCRATIC SOCIETY

56. . . . Whilst recognising the relevance of the facts relied on by the applicants, the Court considers that the Guernsey legislature is better placed than the international judge to assess the effects of any relaxation of the housing controls. Furthermore, when considering whether to grant a licence, the Housing Authority could exercise its discretion so as to avoid any disproportionality in a particular case. It follows that the statutory obligation imposed on the applicants to seek a licence to live in their home cannot be regarded as disproportionate to the legitimate aim pursued.

There has accordingly been no breach of Article 8 as far as the terms of the contested legislation are concerned.

57. There remains, however, the question whether the manner in which the Housing Authority exercised its discretion in the applicants' case—refusal of permanent and temporary licences, and referral of the matter to the Law Officers with a view to prosecution—corresponded to a pressing social need and, in particular, was proportionate to the legitimate aim pursued.

The statistics submitted to the Court show that, during the relevant period—1979 and 1980—the population of the island had been kept within the levels of recent years, having even marginally declined, and the availability of houses for occupation had not suffered any significant deterioration. Against this background, whilst not overlooking the fact that the average population per square mile of the island was still high in comparison with other countries, the Court considers that insufficient weight was given to the applicants' particular circumstances. They had built Whiteknights as a residence for themselves, and their family. At that time, they possessed residence qualifications and continued to do so until the entry into force of the Housing Law 1969, so that during that period they were entitled to occupy the house without a licence. The property was Mr and Mrs Gillow's place of residence for two years before they left Guernsey in 1960. Thereafter, they had retained ownership of the house and left furniture there. By letting it over a period of eighteen years to persons approved by the Housing Authority, they contributed to the Guernsey housing stock. On their return in 1979, they had no other home in the United Kingdom or elsewhere; Whiteknights was vacant and there were no prospective tenants.

As for the refusals of the temporary licences, the decisions of the Housing Authority were, despite the granting of certain periods of grace, even more striking. Whiteknights needed repairs after eighteen years of rented use, with the result that it could not be occupied in the meantime by anyone other than the applicants.

Finally, as regards the referral of the case to the Law Officers with a view to prosecution, the Government stated that the Housing Authority deferred taking this course on several occasions. This, however, in the Court's view did not materially alleviate Mr and Mrs Gillow's already precarious situation.

58. The Court therefore concludes that the decisions by the Housing Authority to refuse the applicants permanent and temporary licences to occupy Whiteknights, as well as the conviction and fining of Mr Gillow, constituted interferences with the exercise of their right to respect for their home which were disproportionate to the legitimate aim pursued.

There has accordingly been a breach of Article 8 of the Convention as far as the application of the legislation in the particular circumstances of the applicants' case was concerned.

...

NOTES

1 The Court was unanimous in finding a breach of Article 8 in the way in which the licensing laws had been applied to the Gillows; however their complaints under Articles 6, 14, Protocol 1 and Protocol 4 were rejected. The Court was comprised of President Wiarda and Judges: Ryssdal, Vilhjalmsson, Lagergren, Pettiti, Evans, and Macdonald.

2 The British Government sought to argue that the term 'home' only applied to a residence legally established in accordance with national law (*Buckley v UK* (1996) 23 EHRR 101, 1996-II 483). The applicant was a gypsy who had bought land and then moved three caravans onto the property and lived there with her family for a number of years. The local planning authority refused her permission to use her land for residential purposes and when she refused to remove her caravans she was subject to criminal proceedings for failing to comply with an enforcement notice. She claimed that the authority's actions infringed her right to respect for her home. The Court, unanimously, rejected the Government's narrow interpretation of 'home'.

Although in the *Gillow* case the applicants' home had initially been established legally, similar considerations apply in the present case. The Court is satisfied that the applicant bought the land to establish her residence there. She has lived there almost continuously since 1988 ... and it has not been suggested that she has established, or intends to establish, another residence elsewhere. The case therefore concerns the applicant's right to respect for her 'home'. (para 54)

Hence, the Court was focusing on the factual realities of the situation, rather than the domestic legal status of the applicant's residence, when determining whether the applicant could assert the existence of a home commanding respect by the national authorities under Article 8(1). But, a majority of the Court (6 to 3) went on to hold that the authorities' treatment of the applicant could be justified under Article 8(2) as being necessary for the economic well-being of the country and for the protection of the health and rights of other (local) persons.

3 In *Niemietz v Germany* A 251B (above p 485), the Court interpreted 'home' broadly to include professional/business premises such as a lawyer's office. This was because the equivalent term in the French text of the Convention ('*domicile*') had a wider meaning than the English term. Furthermore, an expansive definition was consistent with Article 8's underlying aim of protecting persons against arbitrary interferences by public authorities. However, the Court expressed the view that States might have a greater right to interfere with professional/business premises, compared with domestic dwellings, provided they could justify their actions under Article 8(2).

A Chamber was unanimous in finding breaches of companies' right to respect for their homes in *Societe Colas Est and Others v France*, judgment of 16 April 2002. The three applicants were major construction companies. Complaints were made, by a trade association, to the French competition authorities that the applicants were engaging in illegal practices concerning the tendering for roadwork projects. The head of the National Investigation Office, exercising powers granted by a 1945 ordinance, authorised coordinated raids by inspectors on the offices of fifty-six companies, including the applicants, to seize documents concerning the alleged illegal practices. Subsequently, the domestic courts rejected the applicants' challenges to the lawfulness of the inspections and seizure of the documents. The companies were fined between 3 and 6 million Francs each in respect of unlawful practices. Before the Court the applicants contended that there had been a violation of the right to respect for their homes by the inspectors raiding their offices to seize incriminating documents. The Chamber held that:

41. The Court reiterates that the Convention is a living instrument which must be interpreted in the light of present-day conditions (see, *mutatis mutandis*, *Cossey v the United Kingdom*, judgment of 27 September 1990, Series A No 184, p 14, § 35 *in fine*). As regards the rights secured to companies by the Convention, it should be pointed out that the Court has already recognised a company's right under Article 41 to compensation for non-pecuniary damage sustained as a result of a violation of Article 6 § 1 of the Convention (see *Comingersoll v Portugal* [GC], No 35382/97, §§ 33–5, ECHR 2000-IV). Building on its dynamic interpretation of the Convention, the Court considers that the time has come to hold that in certain circumstances the rights guaranteed by Article 8 of the Convention may be construed as including the right to respect for a company's registered office, branches or other business premises (see, *mutatis mutandis*, *Niemietz*, cited above, p 34, § 30).

...

49. ... At the material time—and the Court does not have to express an opinion on the legislative reforms of 1986, whereby inspectors' investigative powers became subject to prior authorisation by a judge—the relevant authorities had very wide powers which, pursuant to the 1945 ordinance, gave them exclusive competence to determine the expediency, number, length and scale of inspections. Moreover, the inspections in issue took place without any prior warrant being issued by a judge and without a senior police officer being present. That being so, even supposing that the entitlement to interfere may be more far-reaching where the business premises of a juristic person are concerned (see, *mutatis mutandis*, *Niemietz*, cited above, p 34, § 31), the Court considers, having regard to the manner of proceeding outlined above, that the impugned operations in the competition field cannot be regarded as strictly proportionate to the legitimate aims pursued ...

50. In conclusion, there has been a violation of Article 8 of the Convention.

So the business premises of companies can fall within Article 8's concept of a home. However, the judgment in *Colas* indicated that the Court may be more protective of business premises occupied by non-corporate persons (such as the lawyer in *Niemietz*) than those of legal persons. Is this a sensible distinction- what level of protection should small companies, with only a few shareholders, enjoy?

4 Some of the limits on the Court's wide interpretation of 'home' were revealed in *Loizidou v Turkey* (1996) 23 EHRR 513, 1996-VI 2216. The applicant grew up in northern Cyprus and owned several plots of land in that part of the island. During 1972 she moved to another part of the island with her husband. Before the Turkish occupation of northern Cyprus, in 1974, she claimed that work had begun on one of her plots to build a block of flats and that her family intended to live in one of the flats as their home. Mrs Loizidou alleged that since the military occupation the Turkish forces in northern Cyprus had prevented her gaining access

to her property in breach of her rights to respect for her home under Article 8 and peaceful enjoyment of her property under Article 1 of Protocol 1. The Court, unanimously, rejected her alleged breach of Article 8 because:

… the applicant did not have her home on the land in question. In its opinion it would strain the meaning of the notion 'home' in Article 8 to extend it to comprise property on which it is planned to build a house for residential purposes. Nor can that term be interpreted to cover an area of a State where one has grown up and where the family has its roots but where one no longer lives. (para 66)

However, a majority (11 to 6) found that there had been a breach of the applicant's proprietary rights under Protocol 1 (see below p 922). Again, the Court was concentrating on the factual aspects of the applicant's residential circumstances in determining whether her 'home' had been subject to interference by state authorities. At what stage of construction should a property be deemed to constitute a person's home?

5   The full-time Court found a second property could be classified as a person's home in *Demades v Turkey*, judgment of 31 July 2003. The applicant contended that he owned a house in Kyrenia (together with his principal home in Nicosia) and that since 1974 he had been denied access to the property by Turkish armed forces.

31. The Court notes that the applicant's house in Kyrenia was a fully furnished and completely equipped house, which he and his family made regular use of and in which they lived for substantial periods of time over the year. The house was treated by the applicant and his family as a home. It served inter alia as a holiday home and for providing hospitality and entertainment to relatives, friends and persons associated with the applicant's business activities.

32. The Court notes in this context that it may not always be possible to draw precise distinctions, since a person may divide his time between two houses or form strong emotional ties with a second house, treating it as his home. Therefore, a narrow interpretation of the word 'home' could give rise to the same risk of inequality of treatment as a narrow interpretation of the notion of 'private life', by excluding persons who find themselves in the above situations.

33. The Court recalls that the Convention is a living instrument to be interpreted in the light of societal changes and in line with present-day conditions (see *Cossey v the United Kingdom*, judgment of 27 September 1990, Series A No 184, p. 14, § 35). Furthermore, it notes that in its relevant case-law it has adopted an extensive interpretation of the notion of 'home' (see, inter alia, *Société Colas Est and Others v France* No 37971/97, §§ 40–2, ECHR 2002-II; and *Niemietz v Germany*, judgment of 16 December 1992, Series A No 251-B, §§ 29–30).

34. Accordingly, the Court considers that in the circumstances of the present case, the house of the applicant qualified as 'home' within the meaning of Article 8 of the Convention at the time when the acts complained of took place.

35. The Court observes that the present case differs from the *Loizidou* case since, unlike Mrs Loizidou, the applicant actually had a home in Kyrenia, albeit a secondary one.

36. The Court notes that since 1974 the applicant has been unable to gain access to and to use that home. In connection with this the Court recalls that, in its judgment in the case of *Cyprus v Turkey* ([ECHR 2001-IV] §§ 172–5), it concluded that the complete denial of the right of Greek-Cypriot displaced persons to respect for their homes in northern Cyprus since 1974 constituted a continuing violation of Article 8 of the Convention. The Court reasoned as follows:

'172. The Court observes that the official policy of the "TRNC" authorities to deny the right of the displaced persons to return to their homes is reinforced by the very tight restrictions operated by the same authorities on visits to the north by Greek Cypriots living in the south. Accordingly, not only are displaced persons unable to apply to the authorities to reoccupy the homes which they left behind, they are physically prevented from even visiting them.

'173. The Court further notes that the situation impugned by the applicant Government has obtained since the events of 1974 in northern Cyprus. It would appear that it has never been reflected in 'legislation' and is enforced as a matter of policy in furtherance of a bi-zonal arrangement designed, it is claimed, to minimise the risk of conflict which the intermingling of the Greek and Turkish-Cypriot communities in the north might engender. That bi-zonal arrangement is being pursued within the framework of the inter-communal talks sponsored by the United Nations Secretary-General (see paragraph 16 above).

'174. The Court would make the following observations in this connection: firstly, the complete denial of the right of displaced persons to respect for their homes has no basis in law within the meaning of Article 8 § 2 of the Convention (see paragraph 173 above); secondly, the inter-communal talks cannot be invoked in order to legitimate a violation of the Convention; thirdly, the violation at issue has endured as a matter of policy since 1974 and must be considered continuing.

'175. In view of these considerations, the Court concludes that there has been a continuing violation of Article 8 of the Convention by reason of the refusal to allow the return of any Greek-Cypriot displaced persons to their homes in northern Cyprus.'

37. The Court sees no reason in the instant case to depart from the above reasoning and findings in the case of *Cyprus v Turkey* (op. cit.). Accordingly, it concludes that there has been a continuing violation of Article 8 of the Convention by reason of the complete denial of the right of the applicant to respect for his home.

Judge Golcuklu, the Judge of Turkish nationality, dissented as he believed the status of northern Cyprus should be resolved through international negotiations and bi-lateral talks between the two communities on Cyprus. The judgment of the Chamber suggests that the more time spent in, and use made of, a second property the stronger the claim will be for it to be classified as a home under Article 8. Given the popularity of second homes (both within national territories and, increasingly, in other Member States) the judgment in *Demades* offers the potential for such properties to be brought within the protection of Article 8 with consequent enhanced legal rights for owners (which may be especially reassuring to foreign nationals).

6   States can be held liable under Article 8 for causing, or allowing others to create, severe environmental pollution which interferes with persons' right to respect for their homes. In *Lopez Ostra v Spain*, A.303C (1994) 20 EHRR 277, the applicant claimed that her family home had been subject to serious pollution (including gas fumes and pestilent smells) from a private sector tannery reprocessing plant, which had been built with a state subsidy on municipal land only twelve metres from the applicant's flat. The pollution persisted for several years and the applicant's family eventually had to move to accommodation provided by the local authority because their health was being adversely affected by the pollution. The Court held that severe environmental pollution could interfere with the right to respect for a person's home even where it did not seriously endanger the health of the residents. The Spanish authorities sought to justify the operation of the reprocessing plant as being necessary for the economic well-being of the town, however the Court held that '... the State did not succeed in striking a fair balance between the interest of the town's economic well-being -that of having a waste-treatment plant- and the applicant's effective enjoyment of her right to respect for her home and her private and family life.' (para 58) Therefore, the Court unanimously found a breach of the applicant's rights under Article 8 and awarded her 4 million pesetas' compensation for pecuniary and non-pecuniary damage. This was the first occasion where the Court

had upheld an environmental pollution claim brought under Article 8. However, in the earlier case of *Powell and Rayner v UK*, A.172 (1990) 12 EHRR 355, the Court implicitly acknowledged that environmental claims could, in appropriate circumstances, be brought within the ambit of Article 8. There two persons living underneath the flight paths of aircraft using Heathrow airport claimed that the noise generated by the jet engines interfered with their rights to respect for their homes. However, the Commission and the Court concluded that the airport was necessary for the economic well-being of the UK and the relevant authorities had taken sufficient steps (such as providing noise insulation for the worst affected homes) to respect the applicants' rights under Article 8. See below (p 568) for a discussion of the positive obligations on States to 'respect' persons' rights under Article 8(1).

A Grand Chamber of the Court has developed the principles in *Lopez Ostra* to find a State liable under Article 8 where it failed to warn local residents of the risks they faced from a nearby private chemical factory and the safety procedures that they should observe if there was an accident at the plant: *Guerra v Italy* (1998) 26 EHRR 357, 1998-I 210. The forty female applicants lived in the town of Manfredonia about one kilometre from a chemical factory. They alleged, and it was not disputed by the Government, that the plant had released large quantities of pollutants over many years (including: inflammable gases, sulphur dioxide and nitric oxide). In 1976 there had been an explosion at the factory which released arsenic compounds which resulted in 150 people being admitted to hospital with acute poisoning. The release of other highly toxic chemicals from the separate factory disaster in Seveso prompted the (former) EEC to issue a Directive regarding safety matters at dangerous industrial sites. This Directive was incorporated into Italian law during 1988 and local mayors were, *inter alia*, obliged to inform their residents of hazardous industrial activities in the locality together with the procedures to be followed in an emergency. In 1989 an official panel of experts had made recommendations to the central government about the factory at Manfredonia, however, no safety information had been provided to the local population by the end of 1995. The applicants, therefore, brought a complaint under the ECHR. The Court, unanimously, concluded that there had been a breach of their rights to respect for their private and family lives; because they had waited many years '... for essential information that would have enabled them to assess the risks they and their families might run if they continued to live at Manfredonia, a town particularly exposed to danger in the event of an accident at the factory.' (para 60) The Court awarded each applicant nonpecuniary damages of 10 million lire. We can presume that the long history of pollution from this particular factory was a decisive factor in the Court's willingness to find the authorities liable for failing to provide advice to the local population.

There was profound disagreement between a Chamber and a Grand Chamber in respect of the approach to applying Article 8 to the regulation of night flights using Heathrow airport. The eight applicants in *Hatton and Others v UK*, judgment of 2 October 2001, lived near the airport or under flight paths of aircraft using the airport. They complained that the Department of Transport's system of regulating night flights, using noise quotas and numbers of flights, had not been preceded by rigorous investigations into the incidents of sleep disturbance of affected residents or the economic benefits of night flights. A majority of the Chamber, five votes to two, held that:

97. The Court would, however, underline that in striking the required balance, States must have regard to the whole range of material considerations. Further, in the particularly sensitive field of environmental protection, mere reference to the economic well-being of the country is not sufficient to outweigh the rights of others. The Court recalls that in the above-mentioned *Lopez Ostra v Spain* case, and notwithstanding the undoubted economic interest for the national economy of the tanneries

concerned, the Court looked in considerable detail at 'whether the national authorities took the measures necessary for protecting the applicant's right to respect for her home and for her private and family life . . . ' (judgment of 9 December 1994, p 55, § 55). It considers that States are required to minimise, as far as possible, the interference with these rights, by trying to find alternative solutions and by generally seeking to achieve their aims in the least onerous way as regards human rights. In order to do that, a proper and complete investigation and study with the aim of finding the best possible solution which will, in reality, strike the right balance should precede the relevant project.

The majority went on to conclude that the Government had not undertaken adequate inquiries into the costs and benefits of the night flights regime there had been a breach of Article 8. The Government responded by seeking a referral of the case to a Grand Chamber, under Article 43, arguing that the test applied by the Chamber had been inconsistent with the established jurisprudence that accorded States a wide margin of appreciation in environmental/planning decisions which involved complex balancing of competing interests.

In its judgment, *Hatton and Others v* UK, judgment of 8 July 2003, the Grand Chamber began by acknowledging that whilst there was no express right to a clean and quiet environment guaranteed by the Convention previous jurisprudence, including *Powell and Rayner v United Kingdom* and *Lopez Ostra v Spain*, established that:

98. Article 8 may apply in environmental cases whether the pollution is directly caused by the State or whether State responsibility arises from the failure properly to regulate private industry. Whether the case is analysed in terms of a positive duty on the State to take reasonable and appropriate measures to secure the applicants' rights under paragraph 1 of Article 8 or in terms of an interference by a public authority to be justified in accordance with paragraph 2, the applicable principles are broadly similar. In both contexts regard must be had to the fair balance that has to be struck between the competing interests of the individual and of the community as a whole; and in both contexts the State enjoys a certain margin of appreciation in determining the steps to be taken to ensure compliance with the Convention. Furthermore, even in relation to the positive obligations flowing from the first paragraph of Article 8, in striking the required balance the aims mentioned in the second paragraph may be of a certain relevance (see the above-mentioned *Powell and Rayner* judgment, § 41 and the above-mentioned *López Ostra* judgment, § 51).

But the Grand Chamber acknowledged the democratic legitimation of national authorities and their primary role in evaluating local needs and determining matters of general policy. Therefore, the Court's scrutiny of domestic decisions concerning environmental issues should examine their substantive merits to ensure that they were compatible with Article 8 subject to a 'wide margin of appreciation' being accorded to governments. Additionally, the Court should examine the national decision-making process to ensure that sufficient attention had been given to the interests of the applicant.

In respect of the substantive merits of the Heathrow night flights scheme the Government asserted that hundreds of thousands of London residents were in a similar situation to the applicants, the property market in the region was thriving and none of the applicants had claimed that they were unable to sell their homes because of noise pollution. Other European hub airports (including Paris Charles de Gaulle, Amsterdam Schipol, and Frankfurt) had less severe restrictions on night flights and if further restrictions were placed on Heathrow night flights it would be placed at a major competitive disadvantage. Also, the night flights using Heathrow were integral parts of the airlines networks. The Government contended that it had undertaken detailed studies of the effects of aircraft noise disturbance on residents and public consultations prior to introducing the 1993 night flights regulations.

The applicants supported the judgment of the Chamber and emphasized that even a few aircraft flying at night can cause serious sleep disturbance to individuals. British Airways, reflecting the views of airline trade associations, claimed that night flights at Heathrow play a major role in the transport infrastructure of the UK and contribute significantly to the UK economy and living standards of UK citizens.

The Grand Chamber distinguished the situation in this application from the previous environmental cases of *Lopez Ostra* and *Guerra v Italy*, where the Court had found breaches of Article 8, as the Spanish and Italian authorities had failed to comply with national law whereas the Heathrow night flights scheme was in conformity with British law. A large majority of the Grand Chamber, twelve votes to five, rejected the Chamber's approach to environmental cases:

122. The Court must consider whether the Government can be said to have struck a fair balance between [the economic] interests [of the UK] and the conflicting interests of the persons affected by noise disturbances, including the applicants. Environmental protection should be taken into consideration by Governments in acting within their margin of appreciation and by the Court in its review of that margin, but it would not be appropriate for the Court to adopt a special approach in this respect by reference to a special status of environmental human rights. In this context the Court must revert to the question of the scope of the margin of appreciation available to the State when taking policy decisions of the kind at issue.

123. The Court notes that the introduction of the 1993 Scheme for night flights was a general measure not specifically addressed to the applicants in this case, although it had obvious consequences for them and other persons in a similar situation. However, the sleep disturbances relied on by the applicants did not intrude into an aspect of private life in a manner comparable to that of the criminal measures considered in the case of *Dudgeon* to call for an especially narrow scope for the State's margin of appreciation (see *Dudgeon v the United Kingdom*, [A.45] p 21, § 52 [(1981)]). Rather, the normal rule applicable to general policy decisions would seem to be pertinent here, the more so as this rule can be invoked even in relation to individually addressed measures taken in the framework of a general policy, such as in the above-mentioned *Buckley* [v *United Kingdom* 1996-IV 74] case. Whilst the State is required to give due consideration to the particular interests the respect for which it is obliged to secure by virtue of Article 8, it must in principle be left a choice between different ways and means of meeting this obligation. The Court's supervisory function being of a subsidiary nature, it is limited to reviewing whether or not the particular solution adopted can be regarded as striking a fair balance.

The majority considered that the Government's decision to adopt a quota based system (reflecting the noise levels of different types of aircraft) to regulate night flights was not incompatible with Article 8 and it was reasonable to assume that such flights 'contribute at least to a certain extent to the general economy'. Also the majority felt that it was significant that the limited number of persons (2–3 per cent according to the Government's 1992 sleep study) particularly affected by night flights could move elsewhere without financial loss as the housing market in the applicants' area was thriving. Therefore the Grand Chamber did not find that the Government had overstepped their margin of appreciation in making the policy decision concerning the 1993 night flights scheme at Heathrow.

Regarding the procedural aspect of the domestic decision-making process the Grand Chamber held that determinations:

128. .... concerning complex issues of environmental and economic policy such as in the present case must necessarily involve appropriate investigations and studies in order to allow them to strike a fair balance between the various conflicting interests at stake. However, this does not mean that decisions can only be taken if comprehensive and measurable data are available in relation to each and every aspect of the matter to be decided.

The Government had regularly monitored night flights at Heathrow and restrictions, beginning in 1962, were reviewed every five years. Prior to the introduction of the 1993 scheme there had been a number of studies and investigations carried out over many years. The applicants had opportunities to make representations concerning the consultation paper that preceded the 1993 scheme and could have sought judicial review if their views had been ignored. Consequently, the majority did not consider that there had been any fundamental flaws in the procedural aspects of the creation of the 1993 scheme. Therefore, the applicants had not suffered a breach of Article 8.

Five judges (Costa—the President of the Chamber which had originally determined the case, Ress, Turmen, Zupancic, and Steiner) issued a joint dissenting opinion which advocated a much stronger role for the Court in responding to complaints concerning environmental pollution. They began by emphasizing the close connection between human rights protection, health being the most basic human need, and the 'urgent need for decontamination of the environment'. Whilst they acknowledged that the Convention text does not contain a provision on pollution ('yet') the dissenters noted that recent times had witnessed emerging provisions concerning pollution including the European Union's Charter of Fundamental Rights and the Kyoto Protocol. Consequently, they considered that environmental pollution was a matter for international law/jurisdiction. In their opinion the earlier case law reflected an evolutive interpretation of the Convention such that:

2. ... In the field of environmental human rights, which was practically unknown in 1950, the Commission and the Court have increasingly taken the view that Article 8 embraces the right to a health environment, and therefore to protection against pollution and nuisances caused by harmful chemicals, offensive smells, agents which precipitate respiratory ailments, noise and so on.

From this perspective the Grand Chamber's determination that there had been no breach of Article 8:

5. ... seems to us to deviate from the above developments in the case-law and even to take a step backwards. It gives precedence to economic considerations over basic health conditions ...

The dissenters considered that in the context of constant disturbance of persons' sleep at night by aircraft noise there was a positive obligation upon States to 'ensure as far as possible that ordinary people enjoy normal sleeping conditions'. Consequently:

17. ... The margin of appreciation of the State is narrowed down because of the fundamental nature of the right to sleep, which may be outweighed only by the real, pressing (if not urgent needs) of the State. Incidentally, the Court's own subsidiary role, reflected in the use of the 'margin of appreciation', is itself becoming more and more marginal when it comes to such constellations as the relationship between the protection of the right to sleep as an aspect of privacy and health on the one hand and the very general economic interest on the other hand.

In their assessment the Government's claims regarding the economic need for night flights were based upon reports produced by the aviation industry and the Government had not made serious attempts to asses the impact of aircraft noise on the applicants' sleep prior to the introduction of the 1993 scheme. Hence the Government had failed to reach a fair balance between the economic well-being of the UK and the protection of the applicants' sleep from the effects of nocturnal aircraft noise.

The Grand Chamber's judgment is significant for establishing the authoritative approach of the full-time Court to cases involving environmental complaints under Article 8. Whilst the majority endorsed the original Court's recognition that serious forms of environmental pollution could result in infringement of persons' rights to respect for their private/family lives and homes, and that States were under both negative duties not to cause such pollution themselves and positive obligations to provide effective regulation of private sector pollution; the

Grand Chamber was not willing to apply the Chamber's enhanced level of scrutiny of domestic policy decisions concerning pollution control measures. Although the Grand Chamber judgment referred to 'environmental human rights' for the first time in the Court's jurisprudence, the majority applied the established wide margin of appreciation doctrine to governmental policy decisions concerning environmental protection. The Grand Chamber affirmed the primary role of domestic authorities in determining the fair balance between the interests of local residents affected by a particular source of environmental pollution and the needs of the nation. Environmentalists maybe unhappy that the Grand Chamber emphasized its supervisory role, but previous case law demonstrates that it is not without substance. For example, in *Lopez Ostra* and *Guerra* the original Court found breaches of Article 8 where domestic authorities failed to deal with industrial facilities producing serious forms of environmental pollution. Furthermore, the Grand Chamber's judgment in *Hatton* reveals that the contemporary Court will examine both the substance of the domestic policy decision to assess its compatibility with Article 8 and the procedure followed by the domestic authorities in reaching that decision to ensure that the individual complainants have been afforded an adequate opportunity to participate in the decision-making process.

The Court's methodology of examining both the substantive and procedural aspects of environmental decision-making was applied by a unanimous Chamber in the later case of *Taskin and Others v Turkey*, judgment of 10 November 2004. The ten applicants lived near a site where, in 1992, the Ministry of the Environment granted permission for a company to operate a goldmine. The permit authorized the use of cyanide to extract the gold. The applicants challenged the granting of the permit in the courts, arguing that the cyanidation process created a danger of pollution to the underlying aquifers. In May 1997 the Supreme Administrative Court upheld their challenge finding that the mining permit was not in the general interest due to the risks for the environment and human health. The local Governor ordered the closure of the mine in February 1998. During 1999 the Prime Minister sought a report, from the Turkish Institute of Scientific and Technical Research, on the environmental impact of the use of cyanide at the mine. That report indicated that risks noted in the Supreme Court's judgment had now been eliminated or reduced. Consequently, ministers authorized the resumption of mining. The applicants, again, challenged those decisions in the domestic courts. In 2002 the Turkish Cabinet decided that the mining company should be allowed to continue its extraction of gold. That decision was not made public. Before the European Court the applicants submitted, *inter alia*, that the granting of the permit for extracting gold by the use of cyanide violated their rights under Article 8. The Chamber ruled that in respect of the substantive decision to grant the permit the Supreme Court had found that it was contrary to the public interest, therefore the Chamber did not need to further examine that issue. Regarding the decision-making processes concerning the authorisation of mining the Chamber found that the administrative authorities had failed to comply with domestic legislation or court decisions thereby depriving the applicants of effective procedural protection. Consequently, there had been a breach of Article 8. Similar conclusions were reached in *Ockan and Others v Turkey*, judgment of 28 March 2006, where another 315 local residents successfully challenged the authorities actions regarding the mine.

Another Spanish local authority failed to protect a person's home from severe noise pollution in *Moreno Gomez v Spain*, judgment of 16 November 2004. The applicant began living in a flat located in a residential part of Valencia during 1970. From 1974 the local council licensed over 120 bars, pubs and discotheques to operate in the vicinity of her home. Despite repeated complaints by the applicant, and other local residents, the local authority failed to reduce the level of noise caused by the licensed establishments (an expert report commissioned by the

Council in 1993 stated that the night time noise levels were unacceptable and exceeded permitted limits and in 1995 the police told the council that the nightclubs did not close on time). A unanimous Chamber found a breach of Article 8.

61. Although the Valencia City Council has used its powers in this sphere to adopt measures (such as the bylaw concerning noise and vibrations) which should in principle have been adequate to secure respect for the guaranteed rights, it tolerated, and thus contributed to, the repeated flouting of the rules which it itself had established during the period concerned. Regulations to protect guaranteed rights serve little purpose if they are not duly enforced and the Court must reiterate that the Convention is intended to protect effective rights, not illusory ones. The facts show that the applicant suffered a serious infringement of her right to respect for her home as a result of the authorities' failure to take action to deal with the night-time disturbances.

62. In these circumstances, the Court finds that the respondent State has failed to discharge its positive obligation to guarantee the applicant's right to respect for her home and her private life, in breach of Article 8 of the Convention.

Accordingly, the Chamber ordered Spain to pay the applicant 3,884 euros just satisfaction to cover the cost of double glazing her bedroom (879 euros) and to compensate her for non-pecuniary damage suffered.

A unanimous Chamber found that the domestic authorities had failed to adequately respect the home and private life of a woman who lived in a council flat located within the 'sanitary security zone' designated around Russia's largest iron smelter. The Severstal steel plant at Cherepovets had been built in Soviet times and in 1965 the Government established a 5 km wide zone around the plant to separate it from residential areas. However, thousands of persons lived within that zone (the plant employs approximately 60,000 workers). The applicant in *Fadeyeva v Russia*, judgment of 9 June 2005, has lived in the zone since 1982. The Severstal plan was privatised in 1993. The applicant brought proceedings against the steelworks and the local authority complaining that the pollution from the plant was very severe (dust levels were 1.6–1.9 times higher than the maximum permitted level and there were excessive concentrations of hazardous chemicals discharged into the atmosphere including hydrogen sulphide and ammonia). The outcome of those proceedings resulted in the applicant being placed on the council's waiting list for new housing (she was person number 6,820 on the list, the applicant claimed that the first person on the list had been waiting since 1968 for a new council home). The Government's current programme for reducing the pollution from the Severstal plant aims to achieve safe levels of emissions by 2010–15. The Court found that:

88. In the instant case, however, the very strong combination of indirect evidence and presumptions makes it possible to conclude that the applicant's health deteriorated as a result of her prolonged exposure to the industrial emissions from the Steverstal steel-plant. Even assuming that the pollution did not cause any quantifiable harm to her health, it inevitably made the applicant more vulnerable to various diseases. Moreover, there can be no doubt that it adversely affected the quality of life at her home. Therefore, the Court accepts that the actual detriment to the applicant's health and well-being reached a level sufficient to bring it within the scope of Article 8 of the Convention.

...

132. In sum, the Court finds the following. The State authorised the operation of a polluting enterprise in the middle of a densely populated town. Since the toxic emissions from this enterprise exceeded the safe limits established by the domestic legislation and might endanger the health of those living nearby, the State established that a certain territory around the plant should be free of any dwelling. However, these legislative measures were not implemented in practice.

133. It would be going too far to state that the State or the polluting enterprise were under an obligation to provide the applicant with free housing, and, in any event, it is not the Court's role to dictate precise measures which should be adopted by the States in order to comply with their positive duties
under Article 8 of the Convention. In the present case, however, although the situation around the
plant called for a special treatment of those living within the zone, the State did not offer the applicant
any effective solution to help her move from the dangerous area. Furthermore, although the polluting
enterprise at issue operated in breach of domestic environmental standards, there is no information
that the State designed or applied effective measures which would take into account the interests of
the local population, affected by the pollution, and which would be capable of reducing the industrial
pollution to acceptable levels.

134. The Court concludes that, despite the wide margin of appreciation left to the respondent State, it
has failed to strike a fair balance between the interests of the community and the applicant's effective
enjoyment of her right to respect for her home and her private life. There has accordingly been a violation of Article 8.

The Chamber considered that as the applicant's lengthy exposure to the plant's industrial pollution had caused her 'much inconvenience, mental distress and even a degree of physical suffering' she should be awarded 6,000 euros compensation for non-pecuniary damage (this sum
took into account the fact that the Court could not award compensation for damage suffered
prior to 1998, the date when Russia became bound by the Convention).

For an examination of the obligations upon States, under Article 2, to protect persons from
lethal pollution disasters see *Oneryildiz v Turkey*, above p 120.

7   An extreme example of an interference with peoples' homes was found to have occurred
in *Akdivar v Turkey* (1996) 1 BHRC 137, 1996-IV 1193, where a Grand Chamber of the Court
(by nineteen votes to two) determined that the security forces' deliberate burning of the applicants' homes and contents amounted to a serious interference with their rights to respect for
their family lives and homes. The destruction of the homes followed a terrorist attack, by the
PKK (Workers' Party of Kurdistan), on a nearby gendarme station in which a soldier was
killed. Subsequently, in *Mentes v Turkey* (1997) 26 EHRR 595, 1997-VIII 2689, another Grand
Chamber (by sixteen votes to five) accepted the Commission's finding of fact that gendarmes
had required residents, including the applicants, to leave their homes in the lower neighbourhood of Saggoze village and the soldiers had then set fire to those properties with all the residents' belongings inside (including the clothing and footwear of the residents' children). This
action, again, took place in the context of the security forces campaign in South East Turkey
against the rebel PKK. However, in neither case did the Court consider that the evidence was
sufficient to establish the existence of an administrative practice regarding the destruction of
villagers' homes by security forces. In *Selcuk and Asker v Turkey* (1998) 26 EHRR 477, 1998-II,
a Chamber of the Court found, by eight votes to one, that the burning of the homes of the
applicants (a 54-year-old woman and a man of 60) by the security forces amounted, *inter
alia*, to 'grave and unjustified' interferences with the applicants' right to respect for their
homes.

8   Another tactic of the Turkish security forces in combating the PKK was found to violate
persons' right to respect for their homes in *Dogan and Others v Turkey*, judgment of 29 June
2004. The authorities prevented the fifteen applicants from returning to their homes, located
in a village in south-east Turkey where widespread terrorist activities were taking place, for
nine years. A unanimous Chamber determined that the authorities refusal to allow the applicants access to their village constituted '159. . . . a serious and unjustified interference with the
right to respect for family lives and homes.' The scale of the security forces' strategy was

revealed by the fact that approximately 1,500 applications similar to *Dogan* had been registered with the Court by the time of the above judgment (Registrar's press release 29 June 2004). Subsequently, the Turkish Parliament enacted the Law on Compensation for Losses resulting from Terrorism and the Fight against Terrorism (2004); this statute established Compensation Commissions in seventy-six provinces to which persons who had suffered damage through acts of terrorism or anti-terrorism measures taken by the authorities could apply for compensation. By early 2006 over 170,000 persons had applied to the Commissions. In *Icyer v Turkey*, decision of 9 February 2006, the applicant complained to the Court regarding his alleged eviction and subsequent exclusion from his home/village in 1994. The Government responded that there was currently no prohibition on his return to the village and as he had not applied for compensation under the 2004 Law he had failed to exhaust domestic remedies. The Court found that the Law provided a practical remedy for the applicant and that as he had failed to utilise that domestic remedy his application should be declared inadmissible. More generally, the Court observed that the 2004 Law demonstrated Turkey had addressed the systemic problem identified in *Dogan*. Subsequently, nearly 1,500 similar applications were rejected by the Court for non-exhaustion of domestic remedies.

9   A Grand Chamber majority, of ten, in *Chapman v UK*, judgment of 18 January 2001, stated that:

99. It is important to recall that Article 8 does not in terms give a right to be provided with a home. Nor does any of the jurisprudence of the Court acknowledge such a right. While it is clearly desirable that every human being has a place where he or she can live in dignity and which he or she can call home, there are unfortunately in the Contracting States many persons who have no home. Whether the State provides funds to enable everyone to have a home is a matter for political not judicial decision.

However, the minority, of seven, issued a joint dissenting opinion in which they expressed the view that:

7. We would also take issue with the relevance or validity of the statement in paragraph 99 of the judgment to the effect that Article 8 does not give a right to be provided with a home. . . . Furthermore, it is not the Court's case-law that a right to be provided with a home is totally outside the ambit of Article 8. The Court has accepted that there may be circumstances where the authorities' refusal to take steps to assist in housing problems could disclose a problem under Article 8—see for example the case of *Marzari v Italy*, where the Court held a refusal of the authorities to provide housing assistance to an individual suffering from a severe disease might in certain circumstances raise an issue because of the impact of such refusal on the private life of the individual (No 3644/97, decision of 4 May 1999) . . .

The Court was clearly very divided on the issue of whether Article 8 obliges States to provide assistance to persons to establish a home. *Chapman* is examined further below at p 583.

10   A unanimous Chamber found the summary powers of a local authority to evict a gypsy family from a council owned caravan site violated Article 8 in *Connors v UK*, judgment of 27 May 2004. The applicant and his family led a traditional travelling lifestyle for a number of years. However, they suffered harassment and consequently settled on a gypsy site run by Leeds City Council in 1984. Thirteen years later the applicant and his family moved off the site as they were adversely affected by anti-social behaviour of others. They were not able to adjust to living in a house and returned to the site in October 1998. The Council provided them with a licence to occupy a specified plot. Clause 18 of the licence provided that, 'no nuisance is to be caused by the occupier, his guests, nor any member of his family to any other person . . . ' In December 1998 the Council gave the applicant a written warning that continued incidents of anti-social behaviour by his adult sons at the site (they did not live on the site but frequently visited the applicant) could jeopardize his occupation of the site. In January 2000 the Council served a notice to quit on the applicant and his family requiring them to leave the site. No reasons were given for the notice. In subsequent summary legal proceedings the Council made reference to the requirements of clause 18 in the applicant's licence. The County Court granted the Council a possession order in June 2000. The Council undertook not to enforce the order for one month. The applicant did not leave the site voluntarily and in August 2000 he and his family were forcibly evicted. Before the Court the applicant contended that the eviction had interfered with his right to respect for his private life, family life and home. The Government accepted that contention and the parties agreed that the interference had been in accordance with the law and for a legitimate aim, namely protecting the rights of other occupants of the site and the Council. The issue of dispute between the parties was the necessity of the interference. The applicant complained that the summary possession proceedings did not enable him to challenge the allegations made against his family. The Government contended that judicial review proceedings were available to ensure that local authorities acted in accordance with the principles of reasonableness and procedural propriety.

93. The Court would not under-estimate the difficulties of the task facing the authorities in finding workable accommodation solutions for the gypsy and traveller population and accepts that this is an area in which national authorities enjoy a margin of appreciation in adopting and pursuing their social and housing policies. The complexity of the situation has, if anything, been enhanced by the apparent shift in habit in the gypsy population which remains nomadic in spirit if not in actual or constant practice. The authorities are being required to give special consideration to a sector of the population which is no longer easy to define in terms of the nomadism which is the *raison d'être* of that special treatment.

94. However, even allowing for the margin of appreciation which is to be afforded to the State in such circumstances, the Court is not persuaded that the necessity for a statutory scheme which permitted the summary eviction of the applicant and his family has been sufficiently demonstrated by the Government. The power to evict without the burden of giving reasons liable to be examined as to their merits by an independent tribunal has not been convincingly shown to respond to any specific goal or to provide any specific benefit to members of the gypsy community. … It would rather appear that the situation in England as it has developed, for which the authorities must take some responsibility, places considerable obstacles in the way of gypsies pursuing an actively nomadic lifestyle while at the same time excluding from procedural protection those who decide to take up a more settled lifestyle.

95. In conclusion, the Court finds that the eviction of the applicant and his family from the local authority site was not attended by the requisite procedural safeguards, namely the requirement to establish proper justification for the serious interference with his rights and consequently cannot be regarded as justified by a 'pressing social need' or proportionate to the legitimate aim being pursued. There has, accordingly, been a violation of Article 8 of the Convention.

Hence, domestic law provided inadequate protection for gypsies living on public authority camp sites. Subsequently, the enactment of section 209 of the Housing Act 2004 extended statutory protection to local authority sites occupied by gypsies.

11   The full-time Court affirmed that the term 'home' in Article 8 was an autonomous concept in *Prokopovich v Russia*, judgment of 18 November 2004.

36. The Court recalls the Convention organs' case-law that the concept of 'home' within the meaning of Article 8 is not limited to those which are lawfully occupied or which have been lawfully established. 'Home' is an autonomous concept which does not depend on classification under domestic law. Whether or not a particular habitation constitutes a 'home' which attracts the protection of Article 8 § 1

will depend on the factual circumstances, namely, the existence of sufficient and continuous links with a specific place (see the following authorities: *Buckley v the United Kingdom*, judgment of 25 September 1996, *Reports of Judgments and Decisions* 1996-IV, §§ 52–4, and Commission's report of 11 January 1995, § 63; *Gillow v the United Kingdom*, judgment of 24 November 1986, Series A No 109, § 46; *Wiggins v the United Kingdom*, No 7456/76, Commission decision of 8 February 1978, Decisions and Reports (DR) 13, p 40).

Accordingly, the Chamber was united in determining that the flat of her deceased male partner, which she had lived in for ten years, was her home. The eviction of the applicant, a few days after the sudden death of her partner, by police officers (one of whom had acquired the tenancy of the flat) breached Article 8 as it was not in conformity with Russian law (evictions had to be ordered by a court).

12 A unanimous Chamber held that the right to respect for a person's home extended to an obligation upon States to undertake effective investigations into complaints regarding alleged unlawful searches of homes by State agents. The applicant in *H.M. v Turkey*, judgement of 8 August 2006, was a teacher and union official who had complained about alleged police violence and had been acquitted of participating in unlawful protests. He subsequently lodged a complaint with the public prosecutor that his home had been searched by plain clothed persons, who claimed to be police officers, without a search warrant. The prosecutor ended his investigation, after five days, when the police denied any involvement in the alleged search. Having regard to the prosecutor's failure to take statements from the applicant's family members, who asserted that they had witnessed the unlawful search, the Chamber concluded that there had not been an effective investigation and therefore a breach of Article 8 had occurred.

Correspondence

Halford v UK 1997-III 1004 (1997) 24 EHRR 523
European Court of Human Rights

In 1983 Alison Halford was appointed to the post of Assistant Chief Constable with the Merseyside police force. By this appointment she became the most senior ranking female police officer in the UK. During the following seven years she applied, unsuccessfully, eight times for appointment to the post of Deputy Chief Constable with the Merseyside and other forces. She believed that her Chief Constable had recommended against her promotion because he objected to her commitment towards equal treatment for men and women. In 1990 she began proceedings, before an Industrial Tribunal, against the Chief Constable and the Home Secretary (who had to approve appointments of Deputy Chief Constables) alleging that they had subjected her to unlawful sex discrimination. Subsequently, she believed, that certain members of the Merseyside Police Authority had conducted a campaign against her involving leaks to the press, interception of her telephone calls and the bringing of disciplinary proceedings against her. In 1991 she was suspended from duty and the Police Authority resolved to bring disciplinary charges against her. She challenged the disciplinary action in the High Court and the latter held that the Chairman and Deputy Chairman of the Police Authority had acted unfairly. Her sex discrimination claim was settled in 1992 with the Chief Constable making an *ex gratia* payment of £10,000 to her and the Home Secretary contributing £5,000 towards her personal expenses. It was also agreed that she would retire from the police on medical grounds (due to an old knee injury). The Home Office reviewed its selection procedures for senior police officers in the light of proposals from the Equal Opportunities Commission. Ms Halford alleged that calls from her office telephones, one of which had been provided for her private use and for which she had approval to use in respect of her sex discrimination claim, had been intercepted for the purpose of obtaining information to use against her in the discrimination proceedings. She also believed that calls from her home telephone had been intercepted for a similar purpose. She complained to the Commission that the above allegations amounted to, *inter alia*, an interference with her right to respect for her correspondence under Article 8. The Commission (by twenty-six to one) found a violation of Article 8 in respect of the reasonable likelihood of interception of calls from her office telephone, but (unanimously) there had been no breach of Article 8 with regard to her home telephone.

...

43. The Government submitted that telephone calls made by Ms Halford from her workplace fell outside the protection of Article 8, because she could have had no reasonable expectation of privacy in relation to them. At the hearing before the Court, counsel for the Government expressed the view that an employer should in principle, without the prior knowledge of the employee, be able to monitor calls made by the latter on telephones provided by the employer.

44. In the Court's view, it is clear from its case-law that telephone calls made from business premises as well as from the home may be covered by the notions of 'private life' and 'correspondence' within the meaning of Article 8 § 1 (see the above-mentioned *Klass and Others* judgment [A.28 (1978)]; the *Malone v UK* judgment of 2 August 1984, Series A No 82, p 30, § 64; the above-mentioned *Huvig* judgment, [A176-B (1990)]; and, *mutatis mutandis*, the above-mentioned *Niemietz* judgment, [A.251-B (1992)], pp 33–5, §§ 29–33).

45. There is no evidence of any warning having been given to Ms Halford, as a user of the internal telecommunications system operated at the Merseyside police headquarters, that calls made on that system would be liable to interception. She would, the Court considers, have had a reasonable expectation of privacy for such calls, which expectation was moreover reinforced by a number of factors. As Assistant Chief Constable she had sole use of her office where there were two telephones, one of which was specifically designated for her private use. Furthermore, she had been given the assurance, in response to a memorandum, that she could use her office telephones for the purposes of her sex-discrimination case ...

46. For all of the above reasons, the Court concludes that the conversations held by Ms Halford on her office telephones fell within the scope of the notions of 'private life' and 'correspondence' and that Article 8 is therefore applicable to this part of the complaint.

2. EXISTENCE OF AN INTERFERENCE

47. The Government conceded that the applicant had adduced sufficient material to establish a reasonable likelihood that calls made from her office telephones had been intercepted. The Commission also considered that an examination of the application revealed such a reasonable likelihood.

48. The Court agrees. The evidence justifies the conclusion that there was a reasonable likelihood that calls made by Ms Halford from her office were intercepted by the Merseyside police with the primary aim of gathering material to assist in the defence of the sex-discrimination proceedings brought against them. ... This interception constituted an 'interference by a public authority', within the meaning of Article 8 § 2, with the exercise of Ms Halford's right to respect for her private life and correspondence.

49. Article 8 § 2 further provides that any interference by a public authority with an individual's right to respect for private life and correspondence must be 'in accordance with the law'.

According to the Court's well-established case-law, this expression does not only necessitate compliance with domestic law, but also relates to the quality of that law, requiring it to be compatible with the rule of law. In the context of secret measures of surveillance or interception of communications by public authorities, because of the lack of public scrutiny and the risk of misuse of power, the domestic law must provide some protection to the individual against arbitrary interference with Article 8 rights. Thus, the domestic law must be sufficiently clear in its terms to give citizens an adequate indication as to the circumstances in and conditions on which public authorities are empowered to resort to any such secret measures (see the above-mentioned Malone judgment, p 32 § 67; and, *mutatis mutandis*, the *Leander v Sweden* judgment of 26 March 1987, Series A No 116, p 23, §§ 50–1).

50. In the present case, the Government accepted that if, contrary to their submission, the Court were to conclude that there had been an interference with the applicant's rights under Article 8 in relation to her office telephones, such interference was not 'in accordance with the law' since domestic law did not provide any regulation of interceptions of calls made on telecommunications systems outside the public network.

51. The Court notes that the 1985 Act does not apply to internal communications systems operated by public authorities, such as that at Merseyside police headquarters, and that there is no other provision in domestic law to regulate interceptions of telephone calls made on such systems. ... It cannot therefore be said that the interference was 'in accordance with the law' for the purposes of Article 8 § 2 of the Convention, since the domestic law did not provide adequate protection to Ms Halford against the interferences by the police with her right to respect for her private life and correspondence.

It follows that there has been a violation of Article 8 in relation to the interception of calls made on Ms Halford's office telephones.

B. THE HOME TELEPHONE

1. APPLICABILITY OF ARTICLE 8 TO THE COMPLAINT RELATING TO THE HOME TELEPHONE

52. It is clear from the Court's case-law (see the citations at paragraph 44 above) that telephone conversations made from the home are covered by the notions of 'private life' and 'correspondence' under Article 8 of the Convention. Indeed, this was not disputed by the Government.

Article 8 is, therefore, applicable to this part of Ms Halford's complaint.

2. EXISTENCE OF AN INTERFERENCE

53. The applicant alleged that calls made from her telephone at home also were intercepted by the Merseyside police for the purposes of defending the sex discrimination proceedings. She referred to the evidence of interception which she had adduced before the Commission, and to the further specification made to the Court ...

In addition she submitted that, contrary to the Commission's approach, she should not be required to establish that there was a 'reasonable likelihood' that calls made on her home telephone were intercepted. Such a requirement would be inconsistent with the Court's pronouncement in the above-mentioned *Klass and Others* case that the menace of surveillance could in itself constitute an interference with Article 8 rights. In the alternative, she contended that if the Court did require her to show some indication that she had been affected, the evidence brought by her was satisfactory; given the secrecy of the alleged measures it would undermine the effectiveness of the protection afforded by the Convention if the threshold of proof were set too high.

54. The Government explained that they could not disclose whether or not there had been any interception of calls made from the telephone in Ms Halford's home, since the finding which the Interception of Communications Tribunal was empowered to make under the 1985 Act was deliberately required to be couched in terms which did not reveal whether there had been an interception on a public telecommunications system properly authorised under the Act or whether there had in fact been no interception. They could, however, confirm that the Tribunal was satisfied that there had been no contravention of sections 2 to 5 of the 1985 Act in Ms Halford's case . . .

55. The Commission, applying its case-law, required the applicant to establish that there was a 'reasonable likelihood' that calls made on her home telephone had been intercepted (see, for example, the report of the Commission on application No 12175/ 86, *Hewitt and Harman v UK*, 9 May 1989, Decisions and Reports 67, pp 98–9, §§ 29–32). Having reviewed all the evidence, it did not find such a likelihood established.

56. The Court recalls that in the above-mentioned *Klass* case it was called upon to decide, inter alia, whether legislation which empowered the authorities secretly to monitor the correspondence and telephone conversations of the applicants, who were unable to establish whether such measures had in fact been applied to them, amounted to an interference with their Article 8 rights. The Court held in that case that 'in the mere existence of the legislation itself there is involved, for all those to whom the legislation could be applied, a menace of surveillance; this menace necessarily strikes at freedom of communication between users of the postal and telecommunication services and thereby constitutes an "interference by a public authority" with the exercise of the applicants' right to respect for private and family life and for correspondence' (p 21, § 41).

The Court further recalls that in its above-mentioned Malone judgment, in addition to finding that one telephone conversation to which the applicant had been a party had been intercepted at the request of the police under a warrant issued by the Home Secretary, it observed that 'the existence in England and Wales of laws and practices which permit and establish a system for effecting secret surveillance of communications amounted in itself to an 'interference' (pp 30–1, § 64).

57. However, the essence of Ms Halford's complaint, unlike that of the applicants in the *Klass* case (cited above, p 20, § 38), was not that her Article 8 rights were menaced by the very existence of admitted law and practice permitting secret surveillance, but instead that measures of surveillance were actually applied to her. Furthermore, she alleged that the Merseyside police intercepted her calls unlawfully, for a purpose unauthorised by the 1985 Act . . .

In these circumstances, since the applicant's complaint concerns specific measures of telephone interception which fell outside the law, the Court must be satisfied that there was a reasonable likelihood that some such measure was applied to her.

58. In this respect the Court notes, first, that the Commission, which under the Convention system is the organ primarily charged with the establishment and verification of the facts (see, for example, the *Aksoy v Turkey* judgment of 18 December 1996, *Reports of Judgments and Decisions* 1996-VI, p 2272, § 38), considered that the evidence presented to it did not indicate a reasonable likelihood that calls made on the applicant's home telephone were being intercepted (see the report of the Commission, paragraph 65).

59. The Court observes that the only item of evidence which tends to suggest that calls made from Ms Halford's home telephone, in addition to those made from her office, were being intercepted, is the information concerning the discovery of the Merseyside police checking transcripts of conversations. Before the Court, the applicant provided more specific details regarding this discovery, namely that it was made on a date after she had been suspended from duty. . . . However, the Court notes that this information might be unreliable since its source has not been named. Furthermore, even if it is assumed to be true, the fact that the police were discovered checking transcripts of the applicant's

telephone conversations on a date after she had been suspended does not necessarily lead to the conclusion that these were transcripts of conversations made from her home.

60. The Court, having considered all the evidence, does not find it established that there was an interference with Ms Halford's rights to respect for her private life and correspondence in relation to her home telephone.

In view of this conclusion, the Court does not find a violation of Article 8 of the Convention with regard to telephone calls made from Ms Halford's home.

....

FOR THESE REASONS, THE COURT

1. Holds unanimously that Article 8 of the Convention is applicable to the complaints concerning both the office and home telephones;

2. Holds unanimously that there has been a violation of Article 8 in relation to calls made on the applicant's office telephones;

3. Holds unanimously that there was no violation of Article 8 in relation to calls made on the applicant's home telephone;

...

Unanimously, that the respondent State is to pay the applicant, within three months, in respect of pecuniary and non-pecuniary damage £10,600. ....

NOTES

1 The Chamber was composed of President Bernhardt and Judges: Pettiti, Russo, Spielmann, Foighel, Morenilla, Freeland, Lopes Rocha, and Kuris.

2 Where complainants allege that they have been subject to unlawful interferences with their correspondence by public authorities it is now clear that the Court will require them to adduce sufficient evidence for the Court to be satisfied that 'there was a reasonable likelihood' of such interference. An alternative ground of challenge, as in the *Klass* case discussed below, is for complainants to allege that the domestic legal regime governing the interception of correspondence when applied to their circumstances amounts to a violation of Article 8, because, for example, it does not provide adequate procedural safeguards.

3 The legality of the interception of postal communications and telephone tapping under the Convention had first been addressed by the Court in *Klass v Germany*, A.28 (1978) 2 EHRR 214. There the Court held that the West German law permitting the interception of postal and telephonic communications in national security cases was consistent with Article 8; although an 'interference by a public authority' with the 'right to respect' for a person's 'private and family life … and his correspondence', it was justified as being necessary in the 'interests of national security' and/or for 'the prevention of disorder or crime'. The Court accepted that some power of interception was permissible to prevent espionage and terrorism and, bearing in mind the 'margin of appreciation' doctrine, concluded that the controls built into the West German system to prevent abuse were sufficient. Under that system, permission to intercept communications was given by a government minister applying certain criteria as to 'reasonable suspicion', etc. An independent Commission, chaired by a person qualified for judicial office, reviewed and could reverse the Minister's decisions. A Board composed of government and opposition members of parliament kept a more general watch on the system. Where national security allowed, a person whose communications had been intercepted must have been informed of this occurrence after the event. Such a person could challenge the legality of the interception in the German courts. Although the Court stated that it was 'in principle desirable to entrust supervisory control to a judge', the above safeguards were sufficient, at least in a national security context.

4   In *Malone v UK*, A.82 (1984) 7 EHRR 14, the applicant had been prosecuted for allegedly handling stolen property (eventually he was acquitted on certain counts and the jury disagreed on others), during his trial the prosecution acknowledged that his telephone had been tapped. He challenged the legality of the tapping before the High Court, but it held that the tapping did not violate any of his legal rights recognised by English law (see, *Malone v Metropolitan Police Comr (No 2)* [1979] Ch 344). Subsequently, Malone complained to the Commission that the tapping (and the alleged metering of the telephone numbers he called from his telephone) violated his rights under Article 8. The Court ruled that the English practice of the Home Secretary issuing warrants authorising the police to tap a person's telephones was not 'in accordance with the law', as required by Article 8(2), because:

... on the evidence before the Court, it cannot be said with any reasonable certainty what elements of the powers to intercept are incorporated in legal rules and what elements remain within the discretion of the executive. In view of the attendant obscurity and uncertainty as to the state of the law in this essential respect, the Court cannot but reach a similar conclusion to that of the Commission. In the opinion of the Court, the law of England and Wales does not indicate with reasonable clarity the scope and manner of exercise of the relevant discretion conferred on the public authorities. To that extent, the minimum degree of legal protection to which citizens are entitled under the rule of law in a democratic society is lacking ... '. (para 79)

Regarding the alleged metering of Malone's calls, the Court held that:

As the Government rightly suggested, a meter check printer registers information that a supplier of a telephone service may in principle legitimately obtain, notably in order to ensure that the subscriber is correctly charged or to investigate complaints or possible abuses of the service. By its very nature, metering is therefore to be distinguished from interception of communications, which is undesirable and illegitimate in a democratic society unless justified. The Court does not accept, however, that the use of data obtained from metering, whatever the circumstances and purposes, cannot give rise to an issue under Article 8. The records of metering contain information, in particular the numbers dialled, which is an integral element in the communications made by telephone. Consequently, release of the information to the police without the consent of the subscriber also amounts, in the opinion of the Court, to an interference with a right guaranteed by Article 8. .... apart from the simple absence of prohibition, there would appear to be no legal rules concerning the scope and manner of exercise of the discretion enjoyed by the public authorities. Consequently, although lawful in terms of domestic law, the interference resulting from the existence of the practice in question was not 'in accordance with the law', within the meaning of paragraph 2 of Article 8 ... '. (paras 84, 87)

Therefore, the Court, unanimously, found a breach of Article 8.

The full-time Court considered the modern form of telephone metering by the police, whereby they secretly seek access to the itemised calls/billing records of suspects/subscribers held by their telecoms suppliers, in *P.G. and J.H. v UK*, judgment of 25 September 2001 (and see above p 505). The police suspected the applicants were involved in a planned robbery and, *inter alia*, obtained the calls/billing records of a fellow suspect (B.) in order to try and link the applicants to the conspiracy. The Court held that:

42. It is not in dispute that the obtaining by the police of information relating to the numbers called on the telephone in B.'s flat interfered with the private lives or correspondence (in the sense of telephone

communications) of the applicants who made use of the telephone in the flat or were telephoned from the flat. The Court notes, however, that metering, which does not *per se* offend against Article 8 if, for example, done by the telephone company for billing purposes, is by its very nature to be distinguished from the interception of communications which may be undesirable and illegitimate in a democratic society unless justified (see *Malone*, cited above, pp. 37–8, §§ 83–4).

Furthermore, the Court found that the obtaining of the call/billing information by the police was based upon section 45 of the Telecommunications Act 1984 and section 28(3) of the Data Protection Act 1984 and was a proportional response to an investigation concerning serious crime. Therefore, the actions of the police fell within Article 8(2) and no breach of Article 8 had occurred in regard to the telephone metering.

The enactment and use of the 1984 legislation distinguished the metering in *P.G. and J.H.* from the administrative practice in *Malone*.

5   The British Parliament enacted the Interception of Communications Act 1985, referred to in the above extracts from *Halford*, so as to comply with the Court's judgment in *Malone*. The Act, *inter alia*, made it a criminal offence to intentionally intercept a postal communication or a communication transmitted by a public telecommunications system. The Home Secretary was given a statutory discretion to issue warrants for the lawful interception of communications in defined circumstances (eg for the purpose of detecting serious crime). A Tribunal was also created to determine complaints that communications had been unlawfully intercepted. In *Christie v UK* 78A DR E Com HR 119 (1994), see above p 502, the Commission expressed the view that in respect of communications by a trade unionist with links to communist Eastern Europe the 1985 Act satisfied Article 8's procedural and legality requirements. However, the Court's judgment in *Halford* identified a lacuna in the Act's failure to regulate the interception of communications made on internal networks operated by public authorities. Ms Halford also sought to argue that she did not have an effective domestic remedy, as required by Article 13, in respect of the alleged interception of her home telephone. The Government responded, in part, that the 1985 Act provided her with such redress (e.g. via the Tribunal). The Court did not evaluate whether the safeguards created under the Act met the requirements of Article 13, because it held that Ms Halford had not established that she had 'an arguable claim' (that her home calls had been intercepted in breach of Article 8) that merited a remedy under Article 13. In the summer of 1999 the Home Office issued a consultation paper (*Interception of Communications in UK*, Cm 4368) proposing changes to the 1985 Act in order to comply with the Convention and to update the law in the light of subsequent technological developments (e.g. the growth of the internet). The Government suggested a new system of warrants that would be targeted at specific persons (and allow interception of all forms of communication used by the named person). In the light of the Court's ruling in *Halford* the paper recommended widening the scope of the 1985 Act to also cover non-public telecommunications networks. However, employers would be able to record employees communications 'in the course of lawful business practice'. These proposals were generally enacted in the Regulation of Investigatory Powers Act 2000. Section 1 makes it a criminal offence for any person intentionally and without lawful authority to intercept, at any place in the UK, any communication in the course of transmission by means of public or private telecommunications systems. However, persons with a right to control the use or operation of a private telecommunications system, such as the owners of the system, are authorised to intercept communications on their systems. Furthermore, under section 4, the Home Secretary is empowered to issue regulations authorising conduct which appears to him to be 'legitimate practice' for the monitoring of communications by businesses during the course of their activities. The Secretary's

power to issue warrants authorising the interception of all forms of communications made or received by a named person, made under sections 5 and 8, replace the former powers contained in the 1985 Act. Also the previous system of supervision and complaints handling is updated with a Commissioner, appointed by the Prime Minister (s. 57), reviewing the exercise and performance of the Secretary's powers to issue warrants. A Tribunal, whose members must hold/have held high judicial office and are appointed by the Sovereign, will determine all complaints against the security and intelligence services, together with those involving other law enforcement bodies (e.g. the police) in respect of their actions concerning the interception of communications.

6   The regulation of telephone tapping in France was found not to be 'in accordance with the law', because of uncertainty regarding the scope of the power to order intercepts and the lack of adequate safeguards in *Kruslin v France*, A.176-A (1990) 12 EHRR 547. An investigating judge had issued a warrant for the police to tap the home telephone of a suspect. Subsequently, Kruslin used that phone and made statements which implicated himself in serious crimes for which he was eventually sentenced to fifteen years' imprisonment. Kruslin claimed that the interception violated Article 8. The Court, unanimously, acknowledged that case law of the French Court of Cassation had interpreted specific articles of the Code of Criminal Procedure as empowering the issuing of warrants to tap telephones. Very significantly, the Court treated this case law as satisfying the domestic legal basis requirement of 'in accordance with the law' (see below, p 585):

In relation to paragraph 2 of Article 8 of the Convention and other similar clauses, the Court has always understood the term 'law' in its 'substantive' sense, not its 'formal' one; it has included both enactments of lower rank than statutes ... and unwritten law. The *Sunday Times, Dudgeon* and *Chappell* judgments admittedly concerned the United Kingdom, but it would be wrong to exaggerate the distinction between common-law countries and Continental countries as the Government rightly pointed out. Statute law is, of course, also of importance in common-law countries. Conversely, case-law has traditionally played a major role in Continental countries, to such an extent that whole branches of positive law are largely the outcome of decisions by the courts. ... Were it to overlook case-law, the Court would undermine the legal system of the Continental States almost as much as the *Sunday Times* judgment would have 'struck at the very roots' of the United Kingdom's legal system if it had excluded the common law from the concept of 'law'. In a sphere covered by the written law, the 'law' is the enactment in force as the competent courts have interpreted it in the light, if necessary, of any new practical developments.' (para 29)

But the Court did not consider that French law satisfied the Convention requirement of 'sufficient precision':

Tapping and other forms of interception of telephone conversations represent a serious interference with private life and correspondence and must accordingly be based on a 'law' that is particularly precise. It is essential to have clear, detailed rules on the subject, especially as the technology available for use is continually becoming more sophisticated.

    ... Above all, the system does not for the time being afford adequate safeguards against various possible abuses. For example, the categories of people liable to have their telephones tapped by judicial order and the nature of the offences which may give rise to such an order are nowhere defined. Nothing obliges a judge to set a limit on the duration of telephone tapping. Similarly unspecified are the procedures for drawing up the summary reports containing intercepted conversations ... the circumstances in which recordings may or must be erased or the tapes be destroyed, in particular where an accused has been discharged by an investigating judge or acquitted by a court. (paras 33 and 35)

Therefore, Kruslin's application was successful. The Court's elaboration of some of the factors that domestic law must address in regulating the interception of telecommunications provides a helpful check-list that can be used to evaluate the compatibility of other legal systems' provisions on tapping with Article 8. Note, the same judges gave an identical judgment against the tapping of a suspected tax evader's telephone in *Huvig v France*, A.176-B (1990) 12 EHRR 528.

7   The Swiss law and practice of telephone tapping was also found not to be 'in accordance with the law' in *Kopp v Switzerland*, 1998-III 524. The applicant was a lawyer whose wife had been a member of the Swiss Federal Government (she had served as Head of the Federal Department of Justice and Police). Accusations had been made that while in office she had provided confidential official information to the applicant for the benefit of one of his clients. The wife resigned and an official inquiry was launched (it eventually reported that the allegations were unfounded). During the course of the inquiry the Federal Court granted an application by the Federal Attorney-General for an order that all the applicant's telephone lines be tapped (this was on the basis that the applicant was a 'third party' who might be in communication with an offender). Swiss law provided for the protection of clients' communications with their lawyers to be legally privileged. The tapping was ended after three weeks and the applicant was subsequently informed that it had occurred and the recordings had been destroyed. He challenged the legality of the interception in the Swiss courts but they upheld the lawfulness of the tapping. The Commission, unanimously, found a violation of Article 8. The Court (also unanimously) applied *Halford* to rule that the applicant's professional telephone conversations fell within the ambit of this Article:

In the Court's view, it is clear from its case-law that telephone calls made from or to business premises, such as those of a law firm, may be covered by the notions of 'private life' and 'correspondence' within the meaning of Article 8(1). . . . (para 50)

The main issue for the Court was whether Swiss law provided sufficient foreseeability regarding which of the applicant's intercepted calls were legally privileged and which were not. In the judgment of the Court the domestic law was not sufficiently precise on this matter. Furthermore, the Court found it an 'astonishing' practice that an official within the legal department of the Post Office determined which intercepted calls were legally privileged. The Court favoured an independent judge, not a member of the executive, determining the status of intercepted conversations where questions of legal privilege between lawyers and their clients arose. Consequently, the interference with the applicant's telephone calls did not satisfy the requirements of Article 8(2). As in *Niemietz* (above p 485) the Court was maintaining a vigorous attitude towards the sanctity of lawyer/client communications.

The secret interception by the Swiss Federal Public Prosecutor's Office of a telephone call from a woman in the former Soviet embassy in Berne to a businessman (the caller was seeking to buy a beauty product) was also found to be in breach of Article 8 in *Amann v Switzerland* (see above, p 502).

8   The Dutch scheme regulating the recording of prisoners' telephone conversations was found to violate Article 8 in *Doerga v The Netherlands*, judgment of 27 April 2004. In early January 1995 the applicant was serving a sentence of imprisonment in Marwei penitentiary. The authorities suspected that he had given the police, via a telephone call, a false tip-off regarding an alleged escape plan by fellow inmates. Therefore, the prison authorities decided to intercept, record and retain copies of the applicant's telephone conversations made from

the prison. In October 1995 an explosive device was detonated in the car of the applicant's ex-girlfriend which seriously injured her son. Subsequently the applicant was convicted of, *inter alia*, causing an explosion and sentenced to a further nine years' imprisonment. Part of the evidence against the applicant was based upon an intercepted telephone conversation in which he warned his sister never to approach the ex-girlfriend's car. The applicant submitted that the interception of his telephone conversations violated Article 8 as it was not based upon clear statutory provisions. The Government contended that the domestic scheme satisfied Article 8(2) as being in accordance with the law as the interception arrangements were based upon a published circular issued by the Deputy Minister of Justice and internal regulations of Marwei penitentiary. The Chamber, unanimously, determined that:

52. The Court finds that the rules at issue in the present case are lacking both in clarity and detail in that neither circular No 1183/379 nor the internal regulations of the Marwei penitentiary give any precise indication as to the circumstances in which prisoners' telephone conversations may be monitored, recorded and retained by penitentiary authorities or the procedures to be observed. . . .

53. Although the Court accepts, having regard to the ordinary and reasonable requirements of imprisonment, that it may be necessary to monitor detainees' contacts with the outside world, including contacts by telephone, it does not find that the rules at issue can be regarded as being sufficiently clear and detailed to afford appropriate protection against arbitrary interference by the authorities with the applicant's right to respect for his private life and correspondence.

54. The interference complained of was not therefore 'in accordance with the law' as required by the second paragraph of Article 8 and there has been a violation of this provision. In these circumstances, an examination of the necessity of the interference is not required.

9   The interception of written correspondence has mainly been challenged in the context of communications with and from prisoners. In *Golder v UK*, A.18 (1975) 1 EHRR 524, the Court found that the refusal to allow a prisoner to write to his solicitor for legal advice, concerning the possibility of suing a prison officer, was an interference with the right to respect for correspondence which could not be said to be 'necessary in a democratic society' (regarding this concept see below p 589). A number of prisoners complained about the stopping, by prison authorities, of letters that they had tried to send to family members, lawyers and the media in *Silver v UK*, A.61 (1983) 5 EHRR 347. The Court held that many of the administrative restrictions on prisoners' correspondence developed and applied by the Home Office did not meet the criteria of being 'in accordance with the law' (on this concept see below p 586). By way of contrast in *Schönenberger and Durmaz v Switzerland*, A.137 (1988) 11 EHRR 202, a lawyer's letter to a potential client being held in custody was retained by the public prosecutor. The Court held that this interference with the lawyer's right to respect for his correspondence was not a proportionate response to the State's legitimate aim of preventing crime and therefore a breach of Article 8 had occurred. In *Campbell v UK*, A.233 (1992) 15 EHRR 137, the Government admitted that letters from the Commission to prisoners were opened, but not read, to ensure that they genuinely originated from the Strasbourg authorities. The Court, by eight votes to one, did not consider that this practice was 'necessary in a democratic society' and therefore amounted to a breach of Article 8.

For its part, the Court considers that it is of importance to respect the confidentiality of mail from the Commission since it may concern allegations against the prison authorities or prison officials. . . . The opening of letters from the Commission undoubtedly gives rise to the possibility that they will be read and may also conceivably, on occasions, create the risk of reprisals by the prison staff against the prisoner concerned.

Moreover, there is no compelling reason why such letters from the Commission should be opened. The risk, adverted to by the Government, of Commission stationery being forged in order to smuggle prohibited material or messages into prison, is so negligible that it must be discounted. (para 62)

In *Petra v Romania*, 1998-VIII, the applicant (prisoner) complained that he had been obliged to hand over letters he had written to the Commission to the governor of his prison, who sent them to the authorities in Bucharest for eventual forwarding to Strasbourg, and that letters from the Commission to him arrived open and after lengthy delays. The Government accepted that the applicant had experienced an 'interference by a public authority' with his right to respect for his correspondence. The Court, unanimously, found that these interferences were not 'in accordance with the law' as the relevant legal provisions were too vague and some were not publicly available.

... the domestic provisions applicable to the monitoring of prisoners' correspondence ... leave the national authorities too much latitude. In particular, they go no further than indicating in a very general way the right of convicted prisoners to receive and send mail and they give prison governors the power to keep any letter or any newspaper, book or magazine 'unsuited to the process of rehabilitating a prisoner'. Monitoring of correspondence therefore seems to be automatic, independent of any decision by a judicial authority and unappealable.

The implementing regulations have not been published, so that the applicant was unable to acquaint himself with them.' (para 37)

The censorship of a prisoner's mail, to the Court, in breach of domestic legislation was found to have violated Article 8 in *Pisk-Piskowski v Poland*, judgment of 14 June 2005. When the Court received the applicant's letter it had been stamped 'District Court in Legnica censored on 22.11.02'. Therefore, the Court considered that there was a reasonable likelihood that the letter had been opened by the authorities. Legislation passed in 1997 clearly prohibited censorship of the correspondence between convicted prisoners and 'institutions set up by international treaties ratified by the Republic of Poland concerning the protection of human rights'.

10 The Court was unanimous in concluding that a Trustee in Bankruptcy's reading and copying of legal correspondence sent to a bankrupt person was not 'necessary in a democratic society' and, therefore, in breach of Article 8. In *Foxley v UK* (2000) The Times, 4 July, the applicant had been a former ammunition procurement officer at the Ministry of Defence who was convicted of corruption in 1993. He was sentenced to four years' imprisonment. The court also found that he had benefited from the crimes to the extent of £2 million. Consequently, the court made a confiscation order against Foxley (under the Criminal Justice Act 1988) for £1.5 million, being his total realisable assests. In 1995 enforcement proceedings were begun against him and Ms S D was appointed as Receiver to realise his property. In 1996 Foxley was declared bankrupt, in proceedings begun by the Ministry of Defence, and Ms S D was appointed as his Trustee in Bankruptcy. In September of that year she obtained, *ex parte*, an Order from Reading County Court (made under the Insolvency Act 1986) for the Post Office to redirect Foxley's mail to her for three months. The purpose of the interception of his mail was to enable the Trustee to try and track down Foxley's assets. During that time 71 letters were redirected to the Trustee. This correspondence included two letters from Foxley's legal advisers relating to his application under the Convention, letters from the Legal Aid Board involving civil proceedings to which he was a party and a letter from the police. Each of these letters was copied by the Trustee and then forwarded to Foxley. After the Order expired the Post Office continued to redirect his mail for a further three weeks and the Trustee copied those items. The applicant complained to Strasbourg that the interception of his correspondence violated Article 8. The Court found a breach in respect of the interference with Foxley's correspondence after the Order expired because:

35. .... The Government do not dispute the fact that two mail deliveries were re-directed by the Post Office to the Trustee in Bankruptcy after the expiry date. It is to be noted that, regardless of the alleged breakdown in the administrative arrangements for redirecting the applicant's correspondence relied on by the Government, it nevertheless remains the case that the Trustee in Bankruptcy exercised her discretion to open letters and to retain copies of some of them. In the view of the Court, the Trustee in Bankruptcy must be taken to have known that the re-direction Order which she herself applied for and obtained no longer provided her with a legal basis to interfere with the applicant's correspondence. On that account, the actions of the Trustee in Bankruptcy after 27 December 1996 were not in accordance with the law....

As for the interception of Foxley's legal correspondence during the period of the Order:

43. The Court recalls that the notion of necessity implies that the interference corresponds to a pressing social need and, in particular, that it is proportionate to the legitimate aim pursued. In determining whether an interference is 'necessary in a democratic society' regard may be had to the State's margin of appreciation (see the Campbell v UK judgment of 25 March 1992, Series A No 233, p 18, § 44). It further observes that in the field under consideration—the concealment of a bankrupt's assets to the detriment of his creditors—the authorities may consider it necessary to have recourse to the interception of a bankrupt's correspondence in order to identify and trace the sources of his income. Nevertheless, the implementation of the measures must be accompanied by adequate and effective safeguards which ensure minimum impairment of the right to respect for his correspondence. This is particularly so where, as in the case at issue, correspondence with the bankrupt's legal advisers may be intercepted. The Court notes in this connection that the lawyer-client relationship is, in principle, privileged and correspondence in that context, whatever its purpose, concerns matters of a private and confidential nature (the above-mentioned Campbell judgment, pp 18–19, §§ 46 and 48).

44. Admittedly, as the Government have pointed out, it may be difficult to identify from the envelope whether its contents attract legal professional privilege. However, the Government have not challenged the accuracy of the applicant's allegations that letters from his legal advisers, once opened, were read, photocopied and a copy committed to file before being forwarded to him. The Court can see no justification for this procedure and considers that the action taken was not in keeping with the principles of confidentiality and professional privilege attaching to relations between a lawyer and his client. It notes in this connection that the Government have not sought to argue that the privileged channel of communication was being abused; nor have they invoked any other exceptional circumstances which would serve to justify the interference with reference to their margin of appreciation.

45. The Court would further observe that the fact that the Trustee in Bankruptcy was also the court-appointed Receiver made it even more compelling to forward, unread, the applicant's correspondence from his legal adviser in connection with the receivership proceedings. However, and the Government have not contradicted the applicant's declaration, the Trustee in Bankruptcy retained copies of the relevant letters before transmitting them to the applicant.

46. For the above reasons, the Court finds that there was no pressing social need for the opening, reading and copying to file of the applicant's correspondence with his legal advisers and that, accordingly, the interference was not 'necessary in a democratic society' within the meaning of Article 8 § 2. Accordingly, there has been a breach of Article 8 in that respect. ....

The judgment is significant for the Court's protection of legal correspondence beyond the context of interferences with mail to and from prisoners. In this case the breach of Article 8 took place in the realm of civil proceedings.

Respect for the rights protected under Article 8(1)

X and Y v Netherlands A.91 (1985) 8 EHRR 235
European Court of Human Rights

Y was a 16-year-old mentally handicapped girl who had been living in a privately run home for disabled children. One night, the son-in-law of the directress forced Y to have sexual intercourse with him. This action caused Y to experience major mental disturbance. X, who was Y's father, notified the police of the matter. Later the public prosecutor's office decided not to initiate a prosecution against the son-in-law. X appealed against that decision to the Court of Appeal, but that court upheld the prosecutor's decision as complaints by persons over 16 had to be made by them (even thought Y was incapable of making such a complaint because of her disabilities). Mr X complained to the Commission on behalf of Y and himself arguing that the Netherlands had failed, *inter alia*, to respect their rights to respect for their private and family life. The Commission, unanimously, found a breach of Article 8, but concluded that as regards Mr X no separate issue arose concerning his right to respect for family life.

...

22. There was no dispute as to the applicability of Article 8: the facts underlying the application to the Commission concern a matter of 'private life', a concept which covers the physical and moral integrity of the person, including his or her sexual life.

23. The Court recalls that although the object of Article 8 is essentially that of protecting the individual against arbitrary interference by the public authorities, it does not merely compel the State to abstain from such interference: in addition to this primarily negative undertaking, there may be positive obligations inherent in an effective respect for private or family life. These obligations may involve the adoption of measures designed to secure respect for private life even in the sphere of the relations of individuals between themselves.

1. NECESSITY FOR CRIMINAL-LAW PROVISIONS

24. The applicants argued that, for a young girl like Miss Y, the requisite degree of protection against the wrongdoing in question would have been provided only by means of the criminal law. In the Government's view, the Convention left it to each State to decide upon the means to be utilised and did not prevent it from opting for civil-law provisions.

The Court, which on this point agrees in substance with the opinion of the Commission, observes that the choice of the means calculated to secure compliance with Article 8 in the sphere of the relations of individuals between themselves is in principle a matter that falls within the Contracting States' margin of appreciation. In this connection, there are different ways of ensuring 'respect for private life', and the nature of the State's obligation will depend on the particular aspect of private life that is at issue. Recourse to the criminal law is not necessarily the only answer.

25. The Government cited the difficulty encountered by the legislature in laying down criminal-law provisions calculated to afford the best possible protection of the physical integrity of the mentally

handicapped: to go too far in this direction might lead to unacceptable paternalism and occasion an inadmissible interference by the State with the individual's right to respect for his or her sexual life.

The Government stated that under Article 1401 of the Civil Code, taken together with Article 1407, it would have been possible to bring before or file with the Netherlands courts, on behalf of Miss Y:

— an action for damages against Mr B, for pecuniary or non-pecuniary damage;
— an application for an injunction against Mr B, to prevent repetition of the offence;
— a similar action or application against the directress of the children's home.

The applicants considered that these civil-law remedies were unsuitable. They submitted that, amongst other things, the absence of any criminal investigation made it harder to furnish evidence on the four matters that had to be established under Article 1401, namely a wrongful act, fault, damage and a causal link between the act and the damage. Furthermore, such proceedings were lengthy and involved difficulties of an emotional nature for the victim, since he or she had to play an active part therein.

26. At the hearings, the Commission's Delegate adopted the applicants' submissions in their essentials; he also doubted whether Article 1401 could provide a proper basis for an award of compensation for non-pecuniary damage. He added that the need for protection existed *erga omnes*, whilst an injunction could only be directed to a limited circle of persons. Finally, the civil law lacked the deterrent effect that was inherent in the criminal law.

27. The Court finds that the protection afforded by the civil law in the case of wrongdoing of the kind inflicted on Miss Y is insufficient. This is a case where fundamental values and essential aspects of private life are at stake. Effective deterrence is indispensable in this area and it can be achieved only by criminal-law provisions; indeed, it is by such provisions that the matter is normally regulated.

Moreover, as was pointed out by the Commission, this is in fact an area in which the Netherlands has generally opted for a system of protection based on the criminal law. The only gap, so far as the Commission and the Court have been made aware, is as regards persons in the situation of Miss Y; in such cases, this system meets a procedural obstacle which the Dutch legislature had apparently not foreseen.

28. According to the Government, it was the exceptional nature of the facts of the case which disclosed the gap in the law and it could not be said that there had been any failure on the part of the legislature. The Criminal Code admittedly contained no specific provision to the effect that it was an offence to make sexual advances to the mentally handicapped. However, criminal proceedings could in certain circumstances be instituted on the basis of Article 239(2) of the Criminal Code, with or without a complaint by the victim, against anyone who violated the sexual integrity of a mentally handicapped person. Under this Article, it was an offence to commit an act of indecency 'while another person is present against his will', a phrase which the Supreme Court had interpreted as also covering a person who was the actual victim of an indecent act.

According to the applicants, on the other hand, the current Criminal Code offered insufficient protection.

29. Two provisions of the Criminal Code are relevant to the present case, namely Article 248*ter* and Article 239(2).

Article 248*ter* requires a complaint by the actual victim before criminal proceedings can be instituted against someone who has contravened this provision. [This Article penalises a person who abuses a dominant position in order to deliberately cause a minor to commit indecent acts.] The Arnhem Court of Appeal held that, in the case of an individual like Miss Y, the legal representative could not act on the victim's behalf for this purpose. The Court of Appeal did not feel able to fill this gap in the law by means of a broad interpretation to the detriment of Mr B. It is in no way the task of the European Court of Human Rights to take the place of the competent national courts in the interpretation of domestic law, it regards it as established that in the case in question criminal proceedings could not be instituted on the basis of Article 248*ter*.

As for Article 239(2), this is apparently designed to penalise indecent exposure and not indecent assault, and was not clearly applicable to the present case. Indeed, no one, even the public prosecutor's office, seems to have considered utilising this provision at the time, or even referring to it at the outset of the Strasbourg proceedings.

30. Thus, neither Article 248*ter* nor Article 139(2) of the Criminal Code provided Miss Y with practical and effective protection. It must therefore be concluded, taking account of the nature of the wrong-doing in question, that she was the victim of a violation of Article 8 of the Convention.

...

For these reasons, THE COURT unanimously

1. Holds that there has been a violation of Article 8 as regards Miss Y:

...

3. Holds that the respondent State is to pay to Miss Y three thousand (3,000) Dutch guilders under Article 50.

NOTES

1   The Court was composed of President Ryssdal and Judges: Wiarda, Walsh, Evans, Russo, Bernhardt and Gersing.

2   The first case in which the Court stated that Article 8 involved positive obligations on states to 'respect' people's Article 8(1) rights was *Marckx v Belgium* (1979) A.31 (above p 523).

3   Another early case involving the positive aspect of respect was *Airey v Ireland*, A.32 (1979) 2 EHRR 305. The applicant was a woman from a poor background who had been assaulted by her alcoholic husband. At first she tried to obtain his approval to conclude a separation agreement with her, but after seven years' of failure she sought to obtain a decree of judicial separation. However, the legal costs of such an application to the High Court were up to £1,200 and she could not afford them (her weekly wage was £40) and no legal aid was available. She complained to Strasbourg alleging, *inter alia*, a breach of her right to respect for her family life caused by the lack of an accessible legal procedure in family law matters. A majority, four votes to three, of the Court found a violation of Article 8.

The Court does not consider that Ireland can be said to have 'interfered' with Mrs Airey's private or family life: the substance of her complaint is not that the State has acted but that it has failed to act. However, although the object of Article 8 is essentially that of protecting the individual against arbitrary interference by the public authorities, it does not merely compel the State to abstain from such interference: in addition to this primarily negative undertaking, there may be positive obligations inherent in an effective respect for private or family life ...

In Ireland, many aspects of private or family life are regulated by law. As regards marriage, husband and wife are in principle under a duty to cohabit but are entitled, in certain cases, to petition for a decree of judicial separation; this amounts to recognition of the fact that the protection of their private or family life may sometimes necessitate their being relieved from the duty to live together.

Effective respect for private or family life obliges Ireland to make this means of protection effectively accessible, when appropriate, to anyone who may wish to have recourse thereto. However, it was not effectively accessible to the applicant: not having been put in a position in which she could apply to the High Court, she was unable to seek recognition in law of her de facto separation from her husband. She has therefore been the victim of a violation of Article 8. (paras 32–3)

This ruling does not create a general right to legal aid in domestic disputes, but obliges States to either simplify judicial proceedings, thereby allowing applications in person, or provide expert legal help for lay persons. The Court later refused to develop the above reasoning to impose an obligation on States to create a right of divorce in domestic family law. Mr Johnston and his long term partner (Janice Williams-Johnston) sought to argue that their right to respect for their family life created such an obligation for Ireland in *Johnston v Ireland*, A.112 (1986) 9 EHRR 203 (and see above, p 524). However, an overwhelming majority of the Court, sixteen votes to one, held that:

It is true that, on this question, Article 8, with its reference to the somewhat vague notion of 'respect' for family life, might appear to lend itself more readily to an evolutive interpretation than does Article 12. Nevertheless, the Convention must be read as a whole and the Court does not consider that a right to divorce, which it has found to be excluded from Article 12 can, with consistency, be derived from Article 8, a provision of more general purpose and scope. The Court is not oblivious to the plight of the first and second applicants. However, it is of the opinion that, although the protection of private or family life may sometimes necessitate means whereby spouses can be relieved from the duty to live together (see the *Airey* judgment, A.32), the engagements undertaken by Ireland under Article 8 cannot be regarded as extending to an obligation on its part to introduce measures permitting the divorce and the re-marriage which the applicants seek. On this point, there is therefore no failure to respect the family life of the first and second applicants. (paras 57–8).

Hence, the scope of other Articles of the Convention can have a direct impact on the meaning of 'respect' in Article 8. In 1995, by a margin of 0.6 per cent of the vote, the Irish electorate voted to remove the constitutional ban on divorce in that country.

4   Other cases that we have examined above involving arguments that a State should undertake positive acts in order to respect the rights of individuals include *X, Y and Z v UK* (above, p 519), where it was unsuccessfully contended that the UK was under a duty to register X as the father of Z, and *Lopez Ostra v Spain* (above, p 546), where the applicant successfully asserted that the Spanish authorities had failed to protect her from the effects of serious industrial pollution. Applicants have not always found it easy to establish a breach of this positive duty of respect as the Court has tended to accord States a wide 'margin of appreciation' (for a consideration of this concept see below, p 629) in such cases.

5   Transsexuals are a group who only recently found it possible to overcome the broad margin of appreciation historically given to States, in respect of their legal and administrative recognition of such persons, by the Court. In *Rees v UK* (1986) 9 EHRR 56, A.106, a majority of twelve to three judges found that the UK was not failing to respect the right to private life of a post-operative transsexual by refusing to amend its birth registration system to alter the recorded sex of the applicant. A similar decision was reached, by ten votes to eight, in *Cossey v UK* (1990) 13 EHRR 622, A.184. However, in *B v France* (1992) 16 EHRR 1, A.232-C, the applicant won her case as a majority of the Court (15 votes to 6) held that the refusal of the French authorities to allow the applicant to change her forename to a feminine one, coupled with their refusal to amend the contemporary civil status register, created such difficulties for the applicant in her daily life that the state had not done enough to respect her private life under Article 8 (see further, A Mowbray, 'Transsexuals and Human Rights' (1992) *Journal of Forensic Psychiatry* 531). *Sheffield and Horsham v UK* (1998) 27 EHRR 163, 1998-V, renewed transsexuals' challenges to their treatment under English law. Kristina Sheffield was a 52-year-old post-operative transsexual who had been registered as a male at birth. After completion of her medical treatment she was given a new passport and driving licence which reflected her new name (which she had changed by deed poll). But, her birth certificate, social security and police records continued to record her original name and gender. Also when she entered into a motor insurance contract she had to give her sex as male. Rachel Horsham, a British citizen,

was also a 52-year-old post-operative transsexual. She had been living in the Netherlands since 1974 and had acquired Dutch citizenship in 1993. After completing gender re-assignment surgery in 1992 she requested a new passport from the British authorities. This was granted after an order from the Dutch courts recognised her new status. Nevertheless, the British authorities would not amend her British birth certificate and they informed her that if she were to marry a man, even abroad, that marriage would not be recognised if she were to become domiciled in the UK. Both applicants claimed, *inter alia*, that the British authorities had failed to respect their right to private lives under Article 8. The Commission found a breach of that right (by fifteen votes to one). Subsequently, Liberty (the human rights NGO) was given permission to submit a written brief on the comparative treatment of transsexuals in Member states, to the Court. The majority of the Court, 11 votes to 9, began by reiterating that

... the notion of 'respect' is not clear-cut, especially as far as the positive obligations inherent in that concept are concerned: having regard to the diversity of the practices followed and the situations obtaining in the Contracting States, the notion's requirements will vary considerably from case to case. In determining whether or not a positive obligation exists, regard must be had to the fair balance that has to be struck between the general interest of the community and the interests of the individual, the search for which balance is inherent in the whole of the Convention (see the ... *Rees* judgment, p.15:37; and the ... *Cossey* judgment, p.15:37). (para 52)

In its view:

... the applicants have not shown that since the date of adoption of its *Cossey* judgment in 1990 there have been any findings in the area of medical science which settle conclusively the doubts concerning the causes of the condition of transsexualism. ... As to legal developments in this area, the Court has examined the comparative study which has been submitted by Liberty. However, the Court is not fully satisfied that the legislative trends outlined by *amicus* suffice to establish the existence of any common European approach to the problems created by the recognition in law of post-operative gender status. In particular, the survey does not indicate that there is as yet any common approach as to how to address the repercussions which the legal recognition of a change of sex may entail for other areas of law such as marriage, filiation, privacy or data protection, or the circumstances in which a transsexual may be compelled by law to reveal his or her pre-operative gender.

The Court is accordingly not persuaded that it should depart from its *Rees* and *Cossey* decisions and conclude that on the basis of scientific and legal developments alone the respondent State can no longer rely on a margin of appreciation to defend its continuing refusal to recognise in law a transsexual's post-operative gender. For the Court, it continues to be the case that transsexualism raises complex scientific, legal, moral and social issues, in respect of which there is no generally shared approach among the Contracting States (see the *X Y and Z v UK* judgment ...).

Nor is the Court persuaded that the applicants' case histories demonstrate that the failure of the authorities to recognise their new gender gives rise to detriment of sufficient seriousness as to override the respondent State's margin of appreciation in this area (cf *B v France*). (paras 56–9)

Accordingly, the majority found no breach of Article 8. But, the Court was unimpressed with the British Government's inertia over the legal position of transsexuals.

... the Court cannot but note that despite its statements in the *Rees* and *Cossey* cases on the importance of keeping the need for appropriate legal measures in this area under review having regard in particular to scientific and societal developments, it would appear that the respondent State has not taken any steps to do so. (para 60)

However, in 2002 a Grand Chamber of the full-time Court was united in finding that the partial recognition by British administrative authorities of post-operative transsexuals' new identities did not satisfy the requirements of Article 8. In *Christine Goodwin* v *UK*, judgment of 11 July 2002, the applicant had been born a man but underwent gender re-assignment surgery provided by the National Health Service. She had to, *inter alia*, enter into a special arrangement with the Department of Social Security (involving her paying national insurance contributions directly to the Department after her sixtieth birthday) in order to prevent her employer from discovering her original gender, due to the fact that the Department continued to classify her as a male in respect of contributions and pension entitlements. Before the Court she alleged that the British Government, despite warnings from the original Court, had failed to take any further measures to reduce the suffering experienced by her, and other post-operative transsexuals, in their daily lives. The Court endorsed the well-established fair balance test to determine the existence of positive obligations under this Article. Whilst noting the earlier British transsexuals judgments the Grand Chamber emphasized the importance of interpreting Convention rights in a practical and dynamic manner. Furthermore:

78. ... The Court is struck by the fact that nonetheless the gender re-assignment which is lawfully provided is not met with full recognition in law, which might be regarded as the final and culminating step in the long and difficult process of transformation which the transsexual has undergone. The coherence of the administrative and legal practices within the domestic system must be regarded as an important factor in the assessment carried out under Article 8 of the Convention. Where a State has authorised the treatment and surgery alleviating the condition of a transsexual, financed or assisted in financing the operations and indeed permits the artificial insemination of a woman living with a female-to-male transsexual (as demonstrated in the case of *X., Y. and Z.* v *the United Kingdom* [1997-II 619]), it appears illogical to refuse to recognise the legal implications of the result to which the treatment leads.

The Grand Chamber did not consider that the contemporary state of medical science provided any conclusive argument as to the question of the extent of legal recognition of post-operative transsexuals required by the Convention. Regarding the consensus amongst Member states and in the wider international community the results of a survey, submitted by Liberty, demonstrated a continuing trend towards the legal recognition of the new identities of such persons. Very significantly the Grand Chamber observed that:

85. ... In the later case of *Sheffield and Horsham*, the Court's judgment laid emphasis on the lack of a common European approach as to how to address the repercussions which the legal recognition of a change of sex may entail for other areas of law such as marriage, filiation, privacy or data protection. While this would appear to remain the case, the lack of such a common approach among forty-three Contracting States with widely diverse legal systems and traditions is hardly surprising. In accordance with the principle of subsidiarity, it is indeed primarily for the Contracting States to decide on the measures necessary to secure Convention rights within their jurisdiction and, in resolving within their domestic legal systems the practical problems created by the legal recognition of post-operative gender status, the Contracting States must enjoy a wide margin of appreciation. The Court accordingly attaches less importance to the lack of evidence of a common European approach to the resolution of the legal and practical problems posed, than to the clear and uncontested evidence of a continuing international trend in favour not only of increased social acceptance of transsexuals but of legal recognition of the new sexual identity of post-operative transsexuals.

At the domestic level the Grand Chamber noted that an Interdepartmental Working Group had produced a report in the spring of 2000 examining options for resolving the difficulties faced by post-operative transsexuals and in *Bellinger v Bellinger* [2001] 3 FCR 1, the Court of Appeal had expressed 'dismay' that no official action had been taken to implement the report. The Grand Chamber held that:

90. ... In the twenty first century the right of transsexuals to personal development and to physical and moral security in the full sense enjoyed by others in society cannot be regarded as a matter of

controversy requiring the lapse of time to cast clearer light on the issues involved. In short, the unsatisfactory situation in which post-operative transsexuals live in an intermediate zone as not quite one gender or the other is no longer sustainable.

93. ... Having regard to the above considerations, the Court finds that the respondent Government can no longer claim that the matter falls within their margin of appreciation, save as regards the appropriate means of achieving recognition of the right protected under the Convention. Since there are no significant factors of public interest to weigh against the interest of this individual applicant in obtaining legal recognition of her gender re-assignment, it reaches the conclusion that the fair balance that is inherent in the Convention now tilts decisively in favour of the applicant. There has, accordingly, been a failure to respect her right to private life in breach of Article 8 of the Convention.

So, the continuing reluctance of the British authorities to accord full legal recognition to the new personalities of post-operative transsexuals was finally found not to be justifiable in the light of the general international treatment of such persons. The British Government responded, constructively, by securing the enactment of the Gender Recognition Act 2004. The Act entitled transsexual persons who (a) have/had gender dysphoria, (b) have lived in the acquired gender for the preceding two years and (c) who intend to live in the acquired gender until death, to apply to Gender Recognition Panels (comprising at least one lawyer and one registered medical practitioner/chartered psychologist) for a certificate, which will entitle them to a new birth certificate (reflecting their acquired gender) and to marry someone of the opposite gender to their acquired gender. Under this statutory scheme transsexuals will not be obliged to have undergone surgery in order to be entitled to a certificate. The Act did not apply retrospectively, consequently a male to female transsexual who was denied a pension (after the Court's judgment in *Christine Goodwin* and before the Act came into effect in 2005) until she reached the male retirement age was found to have suffered a breach of Article 8 by a unanimous Chamber in *Grant v United Kingdom*, judgment of 23 May 2006. However, the Chamber observed that the Government had acted with 'laudable expedition' in securing the passage of the Act.

6 While the Court has been cautious not to create a general right of access for individuals to personal data held on them by State authorities, it has recognised that in certain circumstances individuals can legitimately claim that in order to respect their private and family lives the State must facilitate such access. One such situation is where the state has assumed responsibility for the upbringing of a young person. In *Gaskin v UK* (1989) 12 EHRR 36, A.160, the applicant was a man who had been brought up in the voluntary care of a local authority. After he had reached adulthood he sought access to the case records regarding his childhood kept on him by the authority. These records comprised files written by persons such as foster parents, social workers and medical practitioners. The applicant wished to gain access to his records in order to learn about his past and because he wished to sue the authority for alleged negligence in performing its child-care duties to him. In accordance with the existing national administrative policy the local authority would only allow Gaskin access to those files which the authors were willing to permit him to see (sixty-five documents out of a total of 352). He asserted that the refusal to allow him access to all the files was a breach of his right to respect for his private and family life under Article 8(1). The Commission, on the casting vote of the acting President, found a breach of that right. The Court, by eleven votes to six, held that:

In the Court's opinion, persons in the situation of the applicant have a vital interest, protected by the Convention, in receiving the information necessary to know and to understand their childhood and early development. On the other hand, it must be borne in mind that confidentiality of public records is of importance for receiving objective and reliable information, and that such confidentiality can also be necessary for the protection of third persons. Under the latter aspect, a system like the British one, which makes access to records dependent on the consent of the contributor, can in principle be considered to be compatible with the obligations under Article 8, taking into account the State's margin of appreciation. The Court considers, however, that under such a system the interests of the individual seeking access to records relating to his private and family life must be secured when a contributor to the records either is not available or improperly refuses consent. Such a system is only in conformity with the principle of proportionality if it provides that an independent authority finally decides whether access has to be granted in cases where a contributor fails to answer or withholds consent. No such procedure was available to the applicant in the present case.

Accordingly, the procedures followed failed to secure respect for Mr Gaskin's private and family life as required by Article 8 of the Convention. There has therefore been a breach of that provision. (para 49)

The full-time Court reached a similar conclusion in the later case of *M.G. v UK*, judgment of 24 September 2002. The applicant had been in the voluntary care of his local authority during various periods of his childhood in the 1960s. In 1995 he requested access to his social service records. The authority provided him with summaries of that information but would not give him full access. The authority informed him that the Access to Personal Files Act 1987 did not apply to records, like his, created prior to 1989. The Court, unanimously, held that:

30. . . . Most importantly, and as in Mr Gaskin's case, he had no appeal against a refusal of access to any independent body. . . .

31. In such circumstances, the Court concludes that there has been a failure to fulfil the positive obligation to protect the applicant's private and family life in respect of his access to his social service records from April 1995 when the applicant first requested them.

Significantly, the Court noted that the Data Protection Act 1998 had, since March 2000, given the applicant a statutory right of access to his care/personal files (held in both manual and electronic form) irrespective of the date of their creation. Furthermore, the Act granted him enforcement rights before the Data Protection Commissioner and the domestic courts.

Developing the above reasoning in *Gaskin* the Court has also ruled that where a State engages in dangerous actions, which expose persons to special health risks, then the authorities must facilitate access for the affected persons to relevant information concerning those actions. In *McGinley and Egan v UK* (1998) 27 EHRR 1, 1998-III, the applicants were former servicemen who had been on official duties at the sites of British atmospheric nuclear weapons tests held in the Pacific Ocean during the late 1950s. Many years after they had left the services they claimed war pensions in respect of illnesses which they asserted had been caused by their exposure to the nuclear tests. The Ministry of Defence disputed their claims arguing that the applicants' medical records did not disclose any links between the tests and their current illnesses. The independent Pensions Appeal Tribunal rejected the applicants' claims. The applicants complained to the Commission that, *inter alia*, they had been denied access to official records of the radiation levels at the test sites in breach of Article 8. A majority of the Commission (twenty-three votes to three) found a violation of this Article. The Court stated that:

Where a Government engages in hazardous activities, such as those in issue in the present case, which might have hidden adverse consequences on the health of those involved in such activities, respect for private and family life under Article 8 requires that an effective and accessible procedure be established which enables such persons to seek all relevant and appropriate information. (para 101)

A majority of the Court (five votes to four) concluded that the statutory disclosure of documents procedure available to appellants before the Pensions Appeal Tribunal satisfied the above Convention requirement, therefore no breach of Article 8 had occurred.

However, in the later case of *Roche v United Kingdom*, judgment of 19 October 2005, a unanimous Grand Chamber held that:

165. The Court's *McGinley and Egan* judgment did not imply that a disclosure procedure linked to litigation could, as a matter of principle, fulfil the positive obligation of disclosure to an individual, such as the present applicant, who has consistently pursued such disclosure independently of any litigation.

The Grand Chamber concluded that the Government's protracted and limited disclosure of information to the applicant, regarding the poison gas tests that he was subject to at Porton Down in the early 1960s, did not satisfy the requirements of Article 8. Hence, the above cases demonstrate that where public authorities are in a close relationship with vulnerable persons (such as children in care or personnel subject to military discipline) the right to respect under Article 8 can encompass informational rights.

A Grand Chamber was divided in respect of the extent of the authorities' obligation to provide information on her natural parents to a person who had been deliberately abandoned by them in *Odievre v France*, judgment of 13 February 2003. The applicant's natural mother had formally abandoned her daughter to the local Health and Social Services Department, in 1965, with a request that the birth be kept secret. This process of abandonment had a long history in France going back to 1638 and was designed to provide an alternative to illegal abortions or infanticide. The applicant was adopted in 1969. In 1990 the applicant was able to obtain non-identifying information about her natural parents (including their nationality, health and occupations) from the authorities. However, she was unable to gain information about her two siblings from the authorities due to secrecy surrounding her birth and abandonment. Before the Court she argued that that the authorities failure to disclose to her information in their files about her birth and natural family violated her right to respect for her private life. The Government responded that it was seeking to protect the identity of the applicant's mother and the circumstances of the applicant's birth in accordance with the express request of the mother. The authorities considered that it was a legitimate aim to have a system which alleviated the distress of mothers who did not have the capacity/will to bring up their children and that the process of formal abandonment was used by about 600 mothers *per* year in present times. The Court held that:

28. ... Birth, and in particular the circumstances in which a child is born, forms part of a child's, and subsequently the adult's, private life guaranteed by Article 8 of the Convention. That provision is therefore applicable in the instant case.

But the judges were split on the issue of whether the French authorities had complied with their duties under this Article. A majority, of ten, concluded that:

47. The Court reiterates that the choice of the means calculated to secure compliance with Article 8 in the sphere of the relations of individuals between themselves is in principle a matter that falls within the Contracting States' margin of appreciation. In this connection, there are different ways of ensuring 'respect for private life', and the nature of the State's obligation will depend on the particular aspect of private life that is at issue ...

48. The Court observes that most of the Contracting States do not have legislation that is comparable to that applicable in France, at least as regards the child's permanent inability to establish parental ties with the natural mother if she continues to keep her identity secret from the child she has brought into the world. However, it notes that some countries do not impose a duty on natural parents to declare their identities on the birth of their children and that there have been cases of child abandonment in various other countries that have given rise to renewed debate about the right to give birth

anonymously. In the light not only of the diversity of practice to be found among the legal systems and traditions but also of the fact that various means are being resorted to for abandoning children, the Court concludes that States must be afforded a margin of appreciation to decide which measures are apt to ensure that the rights guaranteed by the Convention are secured to everyone within their jurisdiction.

48. The Court observes that in the present case the applicant was given access to non-identifying information about her mother and natural family that enabled her to trace some of her roots, while ensuring the protection of third-party interests.

49. In addition, while preserving the principle that mothers may give birth anonymously, the system recently set up in France improves the prospect of their agreeing to waive confidentiality, something which, it will be noted in passing, they have always been able to do even before the adoption of the law of 22 January 2002. The new legislation will facilitate searches for information about a person's biological origins, as a National Council on Access to Information about Personal Origins has been set up. The Council is an independent body composed of members of the national legal service, representatives of associations having an interest in the subject-matter of the law and professional people with good practical knowledge of the issues. The legislation is already in force and the applicant may use it to request disclosure of her mother's identity, subject to the latter's consent being obtained to ensure that her need for protection and the applicant's legitimate request are fairly reconciled. Indeed, though unlikely, the possibility that the applicant will be able to obtain the information she is seeking through the new Council that has been set up by the legislature cannot be excluded.

The French legislation thus seeks to strike a balance and to ensure sufficient proportion between the competing interests. The Court observes in that connection that the States must be allowed to determine the means which they consider to be best suited to achieve the aim of reconciling those interests. Overall, the Court considers that France has not overstepped the margin of appreciation which it must be afforded in view of the complex and sensitive nature of the issue of access to information about one's origins, an issue that concerns the right to know one's personal history, the choices of the natural parents, the existing family ties and the adoptive parents.

Consequently, there has been no violation of Article 8 of the Convention.

Whereas, a sizeable minority, of seven judges, believed that:

12. ... the suggestion that the States had to be afforded a margin of appreciation owing to the absence of a *common denominator* between their domestic laws simply does not tally with the extracts of comparative law on which the Court itself relies. Thus, as the Court notes: 'It is relatively rare for mothers to be entitled to give birth anonymously under European domestic legislation.' ...

13. In fact, no other legislative system is so weighted in favour of the protection of maternal anonymity—a birth in secret followed by the abandonment of the child in secret—as that formalised and institutionalised in France ...

21. Unlike the majority, we therefore consider that in the instant case the French legislation has not struck a fair balance between the interests concerned (see paragraph 49, *in fine*) and that there has been a violation of Article 8 of the Convention.

Do you consider the Court was unduly deferential to the French system, which prioritized the preservation of maternal identity as a means of securing the welfare of unwanted children through the formal abandonment process, over the wishes of such a child (now an adult) to discover her natural mother/family?

7   In *Botta v Italy* (1998) 26 EHRR 241, 1998-I 412, the applicant was a disabled person who claimed that the Italian authorities had not taken sufficient action to enforce domestic legal

provisions requiring private businesses to provide facilities for disabled persons. During 1991 Mr Botta complained to the mayor of a beach resort that none of the private beach contractors had installed facilities for disabled people (such as access ramps and specially equipped lavatories) that were required under Italian law. His complaints were rejected and by 1997 some of the relevant private beaches had built access ramps. The council had adopted a plan that all the appropriate facilities were to be constructed by the summer of 1999. The applicant complained to the Commission that the Italian public authorities had failed to 'respect' his 'private life' by their failure to enforce the provision of necessary facilities for disabled people on the private beaches. The Commission (by twenty-four votes to six) found no violation of his rights under Article 8. The Court, unanimously, also held that his complaint fell outside the scope of this Article.

... the right asserted by Mr Botta, namely the right to gain access to the beach and the sea at a place distant from his normal place of residence during the holidays, concerns interpersonal relations of such broad and indeterminate scope that there can be no conceivable direct link between the measures the State was urged to take in order to make good the omissions of the private bathing establishments and the applicant's private life. (para 35)

Interestingly, the Commission had expressed the view, before the Court, that the social nature of Mr Botta's claim was more appropriate for resolution under the 'flexible protection machinery' of the European Social Charter (see DJ Harris, *The European Social Charter*, 2nd edn (2001) Transnational Publishers Inc: Ardsley NY). The Court's judgment may enable disabled persons to make successful applications under Article 8 if they can show that the action required of the State is of direct importance to the very essence of their 'physical and psychological integrity'; this might include the provision of essential medical or social welfare support.

8   The Court has also expressed the opinion that States are not obliged to make social welfare payments in order comply with their Convention duty to respect a person's family life. In *Petrovic v Austria*, 1998-II 579, the applicant was the father of a young child who applied to the Austrian authorities for a parental leave allowance so that he could look after his child, while his wife continued to work. The Austrian administration, and later the domestic courts, ruled that only women were eligible for this type of allowance. Petrovic then complained to the Commission alleging a breach of Article 14 (right to non-discriminatory treatment) taken together with Article 8 (right to respect for family life). The Commission (by twenty-five votes to five) found a violation. Before the Court, the Government argued that such an allowance did not come within the scope of Article 8 as that provision did not obliged States to provide financial assistance to families. The Court held that:

In this connection the Court, like the Commission, considers that the refusal to grant Mr Petrovic a parental leave allowance cannot amount to a failure to respect family life, since Article 8 does not impose any positive obligation on States to provide the financial assistance in question. (para 26)

However, if States decided to make available such a payment, as Austria had done for mothers, then it fell within the ambit of Article 8. A majority of the Court (seven votes to two) then held that Austria's refusal to make such an allowance available to fathers did not exceed the State's margin of appreciation when judged by the standards of the time when Petrovic sought an allowance (i.e. the late 1980s). Subsequently, in 1990, the Austrian parliament had amended its legislation to enable fathers to claim the parental leave allowance. Again, we see the Court adopting a very cautious attitude towards the imposition of financial obligations upon States under the terms of Article 8.

9   In *Earl Spencer and Countess Spencer v UK* (January 1998) Applications Nos 28851/95 and 28852/95 [1998] EHRLR 348, the brother of Princess Diana and his ex-wife alleged that the UK was in breach of its positive duty to respect the applicants' private lives by failing to provide a general right to privacy in domestic law. A number of tabloid newspapers had published articles about the Countess' admission to a clinic for treatment regarding an eating disorder and alcoholism. A photograph of her in the grounds of the clinic, which had been taken without her consent, was also published in the media. The applicants had later successfully brought proceedings against two acquaintances for breach of confidence in respect of disclosures concerning the applicants' private lives. The British Government contended that (1) the applicants had a remedy in breach of confidence against the newspapers which they had not pursued and, therefore, they had not exhausted their domestic remedies as required under Article 26 and (2) breach of confidence together with other domestic remedies for violations of privacy satisfied the Government's obligations under Article 8. The plenary Commission declared the applications inadmissible. The British media interpreted this decision as implicit recognition by the European Commission of the protection given to individuals privacy by the self-regulatory system operated by the Press Complaints Commission within the UK.

10   A Chamber of the full-time Court was unanimous in finding that the German courts had failed to adequately protect the private life of Princess Caroline, the eldest daughter of Prince Rainer III of Monaco, from intrusive media reporting in *Von Hannover v Germany*, judgment of 24 June 2004. The applicant did not perform any functions on behalf of the State of Monaco, though she was the president of various cultural foundations and represented the ruling family at some social events. She lived in the Paris area for most of the time. Since the early 1990s she had sought, frequently via the courts, to prevent the tabloid press in several European countries from publishing photos (taken by 'Paparazzi' photographers) of her and her family engaged in everyday activities. In 1993 she sought an injunction from the German courts to prevent the Burda media company further publishing a series of photographs it had printed in its 'Bunte' magazine showing her, *inter alios*, with her daughter canoeing, with a man in a restaurant and shopping with her bodyguard. The Constitutional Court ruled that as she was a figure of contemporary society '*par excellence*' she had to tolerate the publication of photos taken of her in public places as the public had a legitimate interest in knowing how she behaved in public. However, the publication of the photos of her and her children infringed her right to protection of her personality. In a second set of proceedings, begun in 1997, she unsuccessfully sought to persuade the German courts to prevent Burda from republishing further photos showing her skiing, visiting a horse show with her husband (Prince Ernst August von Hannover) and leaving her house.

Before the Court, the applicant contended that German law, in violation of Article 8, provided minimal protection for her private life from the publication by the 'entertainment press' of 'voyeuristic' photos of her engaging in domestic activities. The Government responded that the public had a legitimate interest in knowing how figures of contemporary society behaved in public and the domestic courts had prohibited the publication of photos taken of the applicant in a 'secluded place'. The Association of Editors of German Magazines, in a written submission, submitted that the public had a legitimate interest in being informed about public figures, as well as politicians, and that the boundary between political commentary and entertainment was becoming blurred. The Chamber held that:

50. The Court reiterates that the concept of private life extends to aspects relating to personal identity, such as a person's name (see *Burghartz v Switzerland*, judgment of 22 February 1994, A. 280-B) or a person's picture (see *Schussel v Austria* (dec.) No 42409/98, 21 February 2002).

. . .

53. In the present case there is no doubt that the publication by various German magazines of photos of the applicant in her daily life either on her own or with other people falls within the scope of her private life.

After acknowledging, the well-established, existence of positive obligations upon States to provide effective respect for private and family life the Chamber observed that:

59. Although freedom of expression also extends to the publication of photos, this is an area in which the protection of the rights and reputation of others takes on particular importance. The present case does not concern the dissemination of 'ideas', but of images containing very personal or even intimate 'information' about an individual. Furthermore, photos appearing in the tabloid press are often taken in a climate of continual harassment which induces in the person concerned a very strong sense of intrusion into their private life or even of persecution.

60. In the cases in which the Court has had to balance the protection of private life against the freedom of expression it has always stressed the contribution made by photos or articles in the press to a debate of general interest (see, as a recent authority, *News Verlags GmbH & CoKG v Austria*, No 31457/96, § 52 et seq., ECHR 2000-I, and *Krone Verlag GmbH & Co. KG v Austria*, No 34315/96, § 33 et seq., 26 February 2002). The Court thus found, in one case, that the use of certain terms in relation to an individual's private life was not 'justified by considerations of public concern' and that those terms did not '[bear] on a matter of general importance' (see *Tammer* [v *Estonia*, ECHR 2001-I] § 68) and went on to hold that there had not been a violation of Article 10. In another case, however, the Court attached particular importance to the fact that the subject in question was a news item of 'major public concern' and that the published photographs 'did not disclose any details of [the] private life' of the person in question (see *Krone Verlag*, cited above, § 37) and held that there had been a violation of Article 10. Similarly, in a recent case concerning the publication by President Mitterand's former private doctor of a book containing revelations about the President's state of health, the Court held that 'the more time passed the more the public interest in President Mitterand's two seven-year presidential terms prevailed over the requirements of the protection of his rights with regard to medical confidentiality' (see *Plon (Société) v France*, No 58148/00, 18 May 2004) and held that there had been a breach of Article 10.

. . .

61. The Court points out at the outset that in the present case the photos of the applicant in the various German magazines show her in scenes from her daily life, thus engaged in activities of a purely private nature such as practising sport, out walking, leaving a restaurant or on holiday. The photos, in which the applicant appears sometimes alone and sometimes in company, illustrate a series of articles with such anodyne titles as 'Pure happiness', 'Caroline . . . a woman returning to life', . . .

63. The Court considers that a fundamental distinction needs to be made between reporting facts— even controversial ones—capable of contributing to a debate in a democratic society relating to politicians in the exercise of their functions, for example, and reporting details of the private life of an individual who, moreover, as in this case, does not exercise official functions. While in the former case the press exercises its vital role of 'watchdog' in a democracy by contributing to 'impart[ing] information and ideas on matters of public interest' (*Observer and Guardian* [v *UK*, A.216 (1991)) it does not do so in the latter case.

64. Similarly, although the public has a right to be informed, which is an essential right in a democratic society that, in certain special circumstances, can even extend to aspects of the private life of public figures, particularly where politicians are concerned (see *Plon (Société)*, cited above, ibid), this is not the case here. The situation here does not come within the sphere of any political or public debate because the published photos and accompanying commentaries relate exclusively to details of the applicant's private life.

65. As in other similar cases it has examined, the Court considers that the publication of the photos and articles in question, of which the sole purpose was to satisfy the curiosity of a particular readership regarding the details of the applicant's private life, cannot be deemed to contribute to any debate of general interest to society despite the applicant being known to the public (see, *mutatis mutandis*, *Jaime Campmany y Diez de Revenga and Juan Luís Lopez-Galiacho Perona v Spain* (dec.), No 54224/00, 12 December 2000; *Julio Bou Gibert and El Hogar Y La Moda J.A. v Spain* (dec.), No 14929/02, 13 May 2003; and *Prisma Presse* [v *France* (dec.), Nos 66910/01 and 71612/01, 1 July 2003]).

66. In these conditions freedom of expression calls for a narrower interpretation (see *Prisma Presse*, cited above, and, by converse implication, *Krone Verlag*, cited above, § 37).

67. In that connection the Court also takes account of the resolution of the Parliamentary Assembly of the Council of Europe on the right to privacy, which stresses the 'one-sided interpretation of the right to freedom of expression' by certain media which attempt to justify an infringement of the rights protected by Article 8 of the Convention by claiming that 'their readers are entitled to know everything about public figures'.

68. The Court finds another point to be of importance: even though, strictly speaking, the present application concerns only the publication of the photos and articles by various German magazines, the context in which these photos were taken—without the applicant's knowledge or consent—and the harassment endured by many public figures in their daily lives cannot be fully disregarded (see paragraph 59 above).

In the present case this point is illustrated in particularly striking fashion by the photos taken of the applicant at the Monte Carlo Beach Club tripping over an obstacle and falling down. It appears that these photos were taken secretly at a distance of several hundred metres, probably from a neighbouring house, whereas journalists and photographers' access to the club was strictly regulated.

. . .

72. The Court has difficulty in agreeing with the domestic courts' interpretation of section 23(1) of the Copyright (Arts Domain) Act, which consists in describing a person as such as a figure of contemporary society '*par excellence*'. Since that definition affords the person very limited protection of their private life or the right to control the use of their image, it could conceivably be appropriate for politicians exercising official functions. However, it cannot be justified for a 'private' individual, such as the applicant, in whom the interest of the general public and the press is based solely on her membership of a reigning family whereas she herself does not exercise any official functions.

In any event the Court considers that, in these conditions, the Act has to be interpreted narrowly to ensure that the State complies with its positive obligation under the Convention to protect private life and the right to control the use of one's image.

73. Lastly, the distinction drawn between figures of contemporary society '*par excellence*' and 'relatively' public figures has to be clear and obvious so that, in a state governed by the rule of law, the individual has precise indications as to the behaviour he or she should adopt. Above all, they need to know exactly when and where they are in a protected sphere or, on the contrary, in a sphere in which they must expect interference from others, especially the tabloid press.

74. The Court therefore considers that the criteria on which the domestic courts based their decisions were not sufficient to protect the applicant's private life effectively. As a figure of contemporary society '*par excellence*' she cannot—in the name of freedom of the press and the public interest—rely on protection of her private life unless she is in a secluded place out of the public eye and, moreover, succeeds in proving it (which can be difficult). Where that is not the case, she has to accept that she might be photographed at almost any time, systematically, and that the photos are then very widely disseminated even if, as was the case here, the photos and accompanying articles relate exclusively to details of her private life.

75. In the Court's view, the criterion of spatial isolation, although apposite in theory, is in reality too vague and difficult for the person concerned to determine in advance. In the present case merely classifying the applicant as a figure of contemporary society '*par excellence*' does not suffice to justify such an intrusion into her private life.

d. Conclusion

76. As the Court has stated above, it considers that the decisive factor in balancing the protection of private life against freedom of expression should lie in the contribution that the published photos and articles make to a debate of general interest. It is clear in the instant case that they made no such contribution since the applicant exercises no official function and the photos and articles related exclusively to details of her private life.

77. Furthermore, the Court considers that the public does not have a legitimate interest in knowing where the applicant is and how she behaves generally in her private life even if she appears in places that cannot always be described as secluded and despite the fact that she is well known to the public.

Even if such a public interest exists, as does a commercial interest of the magazines in publishing these photos and these articles, in the instant case those interests must, in the Court's view, yield to the applicant's right to the effective protection of her private life.

78. Lastly, in the Court's opinion the criteria established by the domestic courts were not sufficient to ensure the effective protection of the applicant's private life and she should, in the circumstances of the case, have had a 'legitimate expectation' of protection of her private life.

79. Having regard to all the foregoing factors, and despite the margin of appreciation afforded to the State in this area, the Court considers that the German courts did not strike a fair balance between the competing interests.

80. There has therefore been a breach of Article 8 of the Convention.

81. Having regard to that finding, the Court does not consider it necessary to rule on the applicant's complaint relating to her right to respect for her family life.

In his concurring opinion Judge Zupancic stated:

... He who willingly steps upon the public stage cannot claim to be a private person entitled to anonymity. Royalty, actors, academics, politicians etc. perform whatever they perform publicly. They may not seek publicity, yet, by definition, their image is to some extent public property.

...

Moreover, I believe that the courts have to some extent and under American influence made a fetish of the freedom of the press. The *Persönlichkeitsrecht* (German civil law concept of personality rights) doctrine imparts a higher level of civilized interpersonal deportment.

It is time that the pendulum swung back to a different kind of balance between what is private and secluded and what is public and unshielded.

The question here is how to ascertain and assess this balance. I agree with the outcome of this case. However, I would suggest a different determinative test: the one we have used in *Halford v United Kingdom*, judgment of 25 June 1997, Reports 1997-III, which speaks of 'reasonable expectation of privacy'.

The judgment of the Court determined that a person's picture falls within the Article 8(1) concept of private life and that States are under a positive obligation to protect such pictures from abuse by others. The media will only be able to justify the publication of a person's photo if it makes a contribution to an issue of general interest. The Court did not accept that pictures of the domestic life of a member of a royal family fell into that category. Serious investigative journalism (e.g. exposing political or financial corruption) should not fear the implications of this judgment. However, Member states may have to reconsider their domestic arrangements to ensure that the publishers of 'Paparazzi' type photographs can justify their continued publication (e.g. to expose the hypocrisy of public figures caught cheating on their spouses?).

11   The Grand Chamber in *Chapman v UK*, judgment of 18 January 2001, identified an inchoate obligation upon States to facilitate the traditional lifestyles of minorities. The applicant was born a gypsy and travelled constantly in caravans with her family in search of work. She and her husband, together with their children, stopped in various temporary and unofficial camp sites whilst they were on a waiting list for a permanent site. The police and local authority officials repeatedly moved them from their unofficial camps. This disrupted the education of her children. Consequently, in 1985, the applicant bought a piece of land, in Hertfordshire, with the intention of residing in a mobile home on the plot. She applied for planning permission to use her land for residential purposes but this was refused by the local authority, as the land was within the Green Belt (an area protected from residential development). Subsequently, she was fined several hundreds of pounds by the magistrates' court for continuing to live on her land without planning permission. The applicant complained to the Commission alleging that the enforcement actions interfered with her rights to respect for her home, private and family life as a gypsy with a traditional lifestyle of living in mobile homes, which allowed for travelling, as protected by Article 8. The Commission, by eighteen votes to nine, found no breach of that Article.

The majority of the Grand Chamber, ten judges, considered that:

93. . . . there may be said to be an emerging international consensus amongst the Contracting States of the Council of Europe recognising the special needs of minorities and an obligation to protect their security, identity and lifestyle . . . not only for the purpose of safeguarding the interests of the minorities themselves but to preserve a cultural diversity of value to the whole community.

94. However, the Court is not persuaded that the consensus is sufficiently concrete for it to derive any guidance as to the conduct or standards which Contracting States consider desirable in any particular situation. The Framework Convention [for the Protection of National Minorities (1995)], for example, sets out general principles and goals but signatory states were unable to agree on means or implementation. This reinforces the Court's view that the complexity and sensitivity of the issues involved in policies balancing the interests of the general population, in particular with regard to environmental protection and the interests of a minority with possibly conflicting requirements, renders the Court's role a strictly supervisory one.

. . .

95. Nonetheless, although the fact of being a member of a minority with a traditional lifestyle different from that of the majority of a society does not confer an immunity from general laws intended to safeguard assets common to the whole society such as the environment, it may have an incidence on the manner in which such laws are to be implemented. As intimated in the *Buckley* [*v UK*] judgment, the vulnerable position of gypsies as a minority means that some special consideration should be given to their needs and their different lifestyle both in the relevant regulatory planning framework and in arriving at the decisions in particular cases (loc cit, paras 76, 80, 84). To this extent there is thus a positive obligation imposed on the Contracting States by virtue of Article 8 to facilitate the gypsy way of life . . .

However, the majority were not willing to accept the applicant's contention that because the number of gypsies in the UK was greater than the number of spaces available in authorised gypsy sites the actions taken against her were automatically a breach of Article 8. According to the Court:

98. . . . This would be tantamount to imposing on the United Kingdom, as on all the other Contracting States, an obligation by virtue of Article 8 to make available to the gypsy community an adequate

number of suitably equipped sites. The Court is not convinced, despite the undoubted evolution that has taken place in both international law, as evidenced by the Framework Convention, and domestic legislations in regard to protection of minorities, that Article 8 can be interpreted to involve such a far-reaching positive obligation of general social policy being imposed on States (see paragraphs 93–4 above).

Hence the Court's task was to determine whether the respondent State had 'relevant and sufficient' reasons for the measures taken against the applicant. The majority found that test was satisfied having regard to, *inter alia*, the Planning Inspectors' hearing the applicant's submissions and visiting the site, the extension of time given to the applicant to comply with planning requirements and the applicant's freedom to seek lawful places for her mobile home on authorized sites outside Hertfordshire. Consequently no violation of Article 8 had occurred.

The seven dissentients issued a joint opinion in which they disagreed with the majority's assessment that the planning proceedings taken against the applicant were necessary in a democratic society. In the belief of the dissentients, the developing European consensus 'recognizing the special needs of minorities and an obligation to protect their security, identity and lifestyle', demanded a greater degree of protection for the applicant than that accorded to her by the majority.

3. . . . This consensus includes a recognition that the protection of the rights of minorities, such as gypsies, requires not only that Contracting States refrain from policies or practices which discriminate against them but that also, where necessary, they should take positive steps to improve their situation through, for example, legislation or specific programmes. We cannot therefore agree with the majority's assertion that the consensus is not sufficiently concrete or with their conclusion that the complexity of the competing interests renders the Court's role a strictly supervisory one (see paragraphs 93–4). This does not reflect in our view the clearly recognised need of gypsies to protection of their effective enjoyment of their rights and perpetuates their vulnerability as a minority with differing needs and values from the general community. The impact of planning and enforcement measures on the enjoyment by a gypsy of the right to respect for home, private and family life therefore has a dimension beyond environmental concerns. Having regard to the potential seriousness of an interference which prohibits a gypsy from pursuing his or her lifestyle at a particular location, we consider that, where the planning authorities have not made any finding that there is available to the gypsy any alternative, lawful site to which he or she can reasonably be expected to move, there must exist compelling reasons for the measures concerned.

Hence the dissentients believed that the European consensus required more practical measures of support for persons like the applicant from States than the majority were willing to require under the Convention. The relatively large size of the group of dissentients in *Chapman* suggests that the Court may in the future demand even greater practical measures of support for minorities from States.

12 A unanimous Chamber has held that inherent in the right to respect for correspondence is a positive obligation upon States to provide writing materials and stamped envelopes to allow a prisoner to correspond with the Court. In *Cotlet v Romania*, judgment of 3 June 2003, the Chamber found that there were no stamped envelopes for overseas correspondence available in the prison where the applicant was being detained and he had not received the two free envelopes a month he was entitled to. Consequently, there had been breach of Article 8.

13 An early explanation of the positive duty of 'respect' was that:

this approach to the interpretation of Article 8 reflects a social view of human rights according to which it is the obligation of the State to take whatever action is needed to promote human dignity and worth. It attributes a much greater role to the State in the promotion of human welfare than does the liberal view. In the latter, the individual is to be protected from the State; in the social view, the individual achieves freedom and dignity through the State. The positive approach clearly bears the imprint of socialist philosophy, and, in the West, is associated with the development of the welfare state. (A M Connelly, 'Problems of Interpretation of Article 8 of the ECHR' (1986) 35 *International and Comparative Law Quarterly*, 567 at pp 574–5.)

14   More generally the author has concluded that:

We have seen that the textual basis for the positive obligations enforced by the Court under Article 8 is the duty upon states to 'respect' the rights elaborated in paragraph one of that provision. Whilst the Court's justification for developing these obligations has been to seek to ensure that the guaranteed rights are effectively safeguarded by states. In the early jurisprudence the Court declared that the notion of respect was ill-defined in the context of positive obligations and therefore states would be accorded a wide margin of appreciation when determining if they had complied with their Convention responsibilities. However, over time the Court limited the use of the margin of appreciation in deciding whether a specific positive obligation existed. The fair balance test emerged as the common judicial method for determining both the existence of individual positive obligations and compliance with the requirements of an established positive obligation. A. R. Mowbray, *The Devlopment of Positive Obligations under the ECHR by the European Court of Human Rights* (Oxford: Hart Publishing, 2004), at p 186.

Article 8(2)

Interference by public authorities with the rights protected by Article 8

Generally, applicants must prove that the respondent State has in some way acted in a manner which causes an interference with protected rights (e.g. by a public official withholding the lawyer's letter in *Schonenberger and Durmaz v Switzerland* (above p 565)). However, in certain cases involving Article 8 rights the Court has been willing to find that the applicant has been a victim of an interference with protected rights through the existence of a particular statutory regime. In *Norris v Ireland* (above p 487), the criminal prohibitions on private consensual homosexual acts were held to amount to an 'interference' with the applicant's right to respect for his private life even though he had never been subject to police questioning or prosecution. The Court held that:

It is true that, unlike Mr Dudgeon, Mr Norris was not the subject of any police investigation. However, the Court's finding in the *Dudgeon* case (above p 487) that there was an interference with the applicant's right to respect for his private life was not dependent upon this additional factor. As was held in that case, 'the maintenance in force of the impugned legislation constitutes a continuing interference with the applicant's right to respect for his private life ... within the meaning of Article 8(1). In the personal circumstances of the applicant, the very existence of this legislation continuously and directly affects his private life ... (para 41). (para 38)

Therefore, where applicants can establish that the existence of legislation infringes important rights under Article 8 and has a deleterious effect on their lives they may be able to bring a successful case under this Article. Also where legislation permits secret measures, such as the interception of telephone calls, applications can successfully argue that the existence of these laws amounts to an interference with their protected rights. In *Klass v Germany* (above p 560), the Court held that:

> ... in the mere existence of the legislation itself, there is involved, for all those to whom the legislation could be applied, a menace of surveillance; this menace necessarily strikes at freedom of communication between users of the postal and telecommunications services and thereby constitutes an 'interference by a public authority' with the applicants' right to respect for private and family life and correspondence. (para 41)

This is a helpful broadening, by the Court, of the notion of an 'interference', because if these secret measures are effectively implemented individuals will not normally know, or be able to prove, that they have in fact been subject to them. See also the judgment of the Court in *Halford v UK* (above p 556).

In accordance with the law

Silver v UK A.61 (1983) 5 EHRR 347
European Court of Human Rights

The seven applicants (six of whom were prisoners) complained that the stopping and delaying of their mail by the prison authorities amounted, *inter alia*, to a breach of Article 8. The detailed rules governing correspondence to and from prisoners were contained in confidential Standing Orders and Circular Instructions, types of internal administrative guidance, issued by the Home Secretary to prison governors. Members of Parliament had access to these provisions and prisoners were given information about some of the rules via cell cards. The Commission (with one dissentient) found the censorship of most of the applicants' correspondence to be in breach of Article 8.

...

A. WERE THE INTERFERENCES 'IN ACCORDANCE WITH THE LAW'?

1. GENERAL PRINCIPLES

85. In its SUNDAY TIMES judgment [*Sunday Times v UK* A.30 (1979)], the Court examined the meaning of the expression 'prescribed by law', noting in this connection certain differences which exist between the French and English versions of Articles 8, 9, 10 and 11 of the Convention, Article 1 of Protocol No 1 and Article 2 of Protocol No 4.

The Government accepted that the principles enounced in the said judgment concerning the expressing 'prescribed by law/*prévues par la loi*' in Article 10 were also applicable to the expression 'in accordance with the law/*prévue par la loi*' in Article 8. Indeed, this must be so, particularly because the two provisions overlap as regards freedom of expression through correspondence and not to give them an identical interpretation could lead to different conclusions in respect of the same interference.

86. A first principle that emerges from the SUNDAY TIMES judgment is that the interference in question must have some basis in domestic law. in the present case, it was common ground between Government, Commission and applicants that a basis for the interferences was to be found in the Prison Act and the Rules, but not in the Orders and Instructions which lacked the force of law ...

There was also no dispute that the measures complained of were in conformity with English law.

87. A second principle is that 'the law must be adequately accessible: the citizen must be able to have an indication that is adequate, in the circumstances, of the legal rules applicable to a given case'. Clearly, the Prison Act and the Rules met this criterion, but the Orders and Instructions were not published.

88. A third principle is that 'a norm cannot be regarded as a 'law' unless it is formulated with sufficient precision to enable the citizen to regulate his conduct: he must be able—if need be with appropriate advice—to foresee, to a degree that is reasonable in the circumstances, the consequences which a given action may entail' (ibid).

A law which confers a discretion must indicate the scope of that discretion. However, the Court has already recognised the impossibility of attaining absolute certainty in the framing of laws and the risk that the search for certainty may entail excessive rigidity (ibid). These observations are of particular weight in the 'circumstances' of the present case, involving as it does, in the special context of imprisonment, the screening of approximately 10 million items of correspondence in a year .... It would scarcely be possible to formulate a law to cover every eventuality. Indeed, the applicants themselves did not deny that some discretion should be left to the authorities.

In view of these considerations, the Court points out once more that 'many laws are inevitably couched in terms which, to a greater or lesser extent, are vague and whose interpretation and application are questions of practice' (ibid). And in the present case the operation of the correspondence control system was not merely a question of practice that varied in each individual instance: the Orders and Instructions established a practice which had to be followed save in exceptional circumstances. ... In these conditions, the Court considers that although those directives did not themselves have the force of law, they may—to the admittedly limited extent to which those concerned were made sufficiently aware of their contents—be taken into account in assessing whether the criterion of foreseeability was satisfied in the application of the Rules.

89. For this reason, the Court cannot accept the applicant's additional contention that the conditions and procedures governing interferences with correspondence—and in particular the directives set out in the Order and Instructions—should be contained in the substantive law itself.

90. The applicants further contended that the law itself must provide safeguards against abuse.

The Government recognised that the correspondence control system must itself be subject to control and the Court finds it evident that some form of safeguards must exist. One of the principles underlying the Convention is the rule of law, which implies that an interference by the authorities with an individual's rights should be subject to effective control. (See inter alia *Klass v Germany* A.28 (1978).) This is especially so where, as in the present case, the law bestows on the executive wide discretionary powers, the application whereof is a matter of practice which is susceptible to modification but not to any Parliamentary scrutiny (see paragraph 26 above).

However, the Court does not interpret the expression 'in accordance with the law' as meaning that the safeguards must be enshrined in the very text which authorises the imposition of restrictions ...

[The Court then examined the circumstances surrounding the censorship and delaying of the applicants' mail. The Court concluded that most of the interferences with the applicants' right to respect for their correspondence were not foreseeable and, therefore, were not 'in accordance with the law'.]

For these reasons, THE COURT unanimously

...

Holds that, with the exception of Mr Silver's letter no 7, Mr Noe's letters nos 10 and 12 and Mr Cooper's letters nos 28 to 31, the stopping or delaying of all the letters written by or addressed to each applicant which are at issue in the present case constituted a violation of Article 8; ...

NOTES

1   The Court was composed of President Wiarda, and Judges: Thor Vilhjalmsson, Gölcüklü, Matscher, Pettiti, Evans and Russo.

2 The *Sunday Times* case is examined below at p 633.

3 The Court elaborated upon the requirements of 'in accordance with the law' when examining the interception of telephone calls in *Halford v UK* (above p 556).

4 The need for a reasonably precise domestic legal framework regulating the use of hi-tech surveillance devices, such as concealed transmitters, by law enforcement agencies was confirmed by a unanimous Court in *Khan v UK* (2000) The Times, 23 May. The applicant arrived at Manchester airport, from Pakistan, in September 1992. He was searched by customs officers, but no drugs were found on him. In January 1993, the Chief Constable of South Yorkshire authorised, in accordance with administrative Guidelines issued by the Home Office in 1984, the installation of a listening device on B.'s premises (the Chief Constable believed that conventional methods of surveillance were unlikely to provide evidence that B was dealing in drugs). The aural surveillance device recorded a conversation in B's house during which Khan admitted involvement in the illegal importation of drugs. Subsequently, the trial judge ruled that the tape recording of Khan's conversation obtained by the use of the surveillance device was admissible. Thereupon Khan pleaded guilty to a charge of being knowingly concerned in the fraudulent evasion of the prohibition on the importation of heroin. He was sentenced to three years' imprisonment. Khan eventually appealed to the House of Lords (*R v Khan (Sultan)* [1996] 3 All ER 289), where Lord Nolan, on behalf of his brethren, gave a speech in which he held that there was no right to privacy in English law and the admission of the recording was not unlawful or unfair. The Court ruled that:

26. ... In the context of covert surveillance by public authorities, in this instance the police, domestic law must provide protection against arbitrary interference with an individual's right under Article 8. Moreover, the law must be sufficiently clear in its terms to give individuals an adequate indication as to the circumstances in which and the conditions on which public authorities are entitled to resort to such covert measures (*Malone v UK* ...).

27. At the time of the events in the present case, there existed no statutory system to regulate the use of covert listening devices, although the Police Act 1997 now provides such a statutory framework. The Home Office Guidelines at the relevant time were neither legally binding nor were they directly publicly accessible. The Court also notes that Lord Nolan in the House of Lords commented that under English law there is, in general, nothing unlawful about a breach of privacy. There was, therefore, no domestic law regulating the use of covert listening devices at the relevant time.

Consequently, the Court found a breach of Article 8. The judgment is to be welcomed as demonstrating the Court applying its well established jurisprudence regarding the rule of law requirements of Article 8 to new technological methods of State surveillance. The Police Act 1997, implemented in 1999, defined the range of circumstances in which senior police officers or specially appointed Commissioners could approve the use of intrusive surveillance devices. Individuals could complain to the Commissioners if they believed the use of such devices was *ultra vires* the statutory framework.

In 2005, the Committee of Ministers issued Recommendation (2005)10 on 'special investigation techniques' in relation to serious crimes including acts of terrorism. The Recommended observed that whilst such techniques are 'numerous, varied and constantly evolving' their common characteristics were their secret nature and the fact that they could interfere with fundamental rights. However, the Committee recognised that these techniques were 'vital tools' in the fight against serious crime. The Recommendation expressed the view that Member states should, *inter alia*, 'take appropriate legislative measures to ensure adequate control of the implementation of special investigation techniques by judicial authorities or other independent bodies through prior authorisation, supervision during the investigation or ex post facto review'. This Recommendation therefore builds upon the judgment in *Khan*.

5   For the application of this concept to a continental civil law jurisdiction see *Kruslin v France* (above, p 563).

Necessary in a democratic society

1   In *Silver v UK* (above) it was noted that:

On a number of occasions, the Court had stated its understanding of the phrase 'necessary in a democratic society', the nature of its functions in the examination of issues turning on that phrase and the manner in which it will perform those functions. It suffices here to summarise certain principles:

(a)   the adjective 'necessary' is not synonymous with 'indispensable', neither has it the flexibility of such expressions as 'admissible', 'ordinary', 'useful', 'reasonable', or 'desirable'. (see *Handyside v UK* A.24 (1976))

(b)   the Contracting States enjoy a certain but not unlimited margin of appreciation in the matter of the imposition of restrictions, but it is for the Court to give the final ruling on whether they are compatible with the Convention.

(c)   the phrase 'necessary in a democratic society' means that, to be compatible with the Convention, the interference must, inter alia, correspond to a 'pressing social need' and be 'proportionate to the legitimate aim pursued'.

(d)   those paragraphs of Articles of the Convention which provide for an exception to a right guaranteed are to be narrowly interpreted (see *Klass v Germany* A.28 (1978). (para 97)

2   *Handyside* is examined below at p 623.

3   Examples of where the Court has found state action to be 'necessary' include: the maintenance of a secret register of persons considered to be a threat to national security, see *Leander v Sweden* (above p 501) and to allow officials to intercept communications in order to combat espionage and terrorism, see *Klass v Germany* (above, p 560). The regulation of housing (in *Gillow v UK*, above p 541 and *Buckley v UK*, above p 543) was considered to be 'necessary' for the economic well-being of the country.

4   A wide 'margin of appreciation' has been accorded by the court to national authorities in a number of circumstances including: (a) technically complex regulatory processes (e.g. the control of noise pollution in *Powell and Rayner v UK* (above p 547); (b) matters of social policy where there are no common European standards (e.g. regulating the use of *in vitro* fertilisation treatment, see *Evans v UK*, above p 518) and (c) where issues of national security are involved (e.g. *Leander v Sweden*, above p 501). Ovey considers that the case law does not reveal any clear distinction in the breadth of the margin of appreciation according to whether the respondent State is under positive or negative obligations: see, C Ovey, 'The Margin of Appreciation and Article 8 of the Convention (1998) 19 *Human Rights Law Journal* 10. More generally on this doctrine see below p 629.

5   The Court found that there was no 'pressing social need' for the maintenance of criminal sanctions against private consensual homosexual activity by adults in *Dudgeon v UK* and *Norris v Ireland* (above, p 487). In both cases the Court was heavily influenced by the fact that the great majority of Council of Europe Member States did not consider it necessary or appropriate to criminalise such behaviour. Also, the British armed forces' investigations into the private lives

and subsequent discharge of homosexual personnel were not justifiable under Article 8(2) in *Smith and Grady v UK* (1999), above p 489.

6 The issuing and execution of the search warrant against the applicant's law offices in *Niemietz v Germany* (above, p 485) was held, by the Court, not to be a proportionate interference with the applicant's right to respect for his private life. Although the public prosecutor was concerned with a substantial crime, the warrant issued was drafted in very wide terms and impinged upon professional secrecy. The ability of the French customs service to conduct searches of homes without the need for a judge to issue a search warrant led the Court to find a breach of Article 8 in *Funke v France* A.256-A (1993) 16 EHRR 297. Three customs officers and a senior police officer searched the applicant's home for evidence of alleged offences involving foreign financial transactions. The Court held that:

Above all, in the absence of any requirement of a judicial warrant the restrictions and conditions provided for in law, which were emphasised by the Government . . . , appear too lax and full of loopholes for the interferences with the applicant's rights to have been strictly proportionate to the legitimate aim pursued. (para 57)

Again, in *Camenzind v Switzerland* (1997) 28 EHRR 458, 1997-VIII 2880, the Court reiterated that where domestic law authorized a search without the need for a judicial warrant, the Court would be particularly vigilant in ensuring that the requirements of Article 8 had been complied with. There the telecommunication authorities had evidence that Mr Camenzind had been using an unauthorised cordless telephone. The director of the Berne telecommunications authority issued a warrant, under the Federal Administrative Criminal Law Act 1974, for the search of the applicant's house with a view to finding and seizing the telephone. A single official executed the warrant, with the applicant's permission, by checking the conformity of every telephone and television set in each room of the applicant's house; no unauthorised equipment was found, but the applicant admitted that he had previously tested such a telephone. No furniture was searched nor were any documents examined. The Court, with one dissent, concluded that the limited scope of the search meant that it was a proportionate response by the authorities towards the legitimate aim of preventing disorder or crime. In *Chappell v UK*, A.152 (1989) 12 EHRR 1, the Court upheld the concurrent execution of a judicial warrant to search for obscene videos by eleven police officers and an Anton Piller order (issued by the civil courts authorising plaintiff film companies to enter Chappell's video rental premises with the objective of seizing allegedly illegal copies of their films) by five employees of the film companies and their solicitors. Although the Court was critical of the concurrent nature of the searches and the aggregate number of persons involved in searching Chappell's premises, the Court ruled that they were a proportionate response to the legitimate aims of preventing crime and protecting the rights of the film companies. Marc-Andre Eissen, a former Registrar of the Court, has observed that while the term proportionality is not found in the text of the Convention, the Court has discovered its essence contained in the express language of various Articles. In regard to the phrase 'necessary in a democratic society' embodied in paragraph 2 of Articles 8–11, he states that: 'from "necessity" to proportionality is but a small step, since for a measure to be necessary it must surely correspond to a "pressing social need" both as a matter of principle and regarding its impact, its scale and its compass.' (at p 126) More generally, he concludes:

Over the years proportionality has put down solid and lasting roots in the case-law of the European Court of Human Rights, and these roots will in all likelihood go even deeper, continuing to broaden the scope of the principle so as to embrace even more aspects of the Convention. Indeed the extent to which this has already occurred suggests that it has even now acquired the status of a general principle in the Convention system, a status which it already has in numerous legal systems and in community law. (at p 146). ['The Principle of Proportionality in the Case-Law of the European Court of Human Rights' in Macdonald, Matscher and Petzold (eds) *The European System for the Protection of Human Rights* (Dordrecht: Martinus Nijhoff, 1993).]

In a later study Dr Yutaka Arai-Takahashi concluded:

It must be recalled that under the Convention, there exist two types of proportionality evaluation emphasised by the Strasbourg organs. Firstly, they have asserted that a 'fair balance' must be struck between the right of individual applicants and the general interests of the public. A search for such balance is considered as 'inherent' in the whole of the Convention. The second meaning of proportionality is a modified and more specific version of the first and defined as a reasonable relationship between the means employed, including their severity and duration, and the public objective to be sought. This corresponds to the third element of the proportionality test developed by the European Community law and German administrative law. [Y Arai-Takahashi, *The Margin of Appreciation Doctrine and the Principle of Proportionality in the Jurisprudence of the ECHR* (Antwerp: Intersentia, 2002), p 193.]

Legitimate aim of interference

1 The final requirement, under Article 8(2), for States which seek to justify an interference with protected Article 8(1) rights is to show that their actions were taken for a legitimate purpose. Only those aims listed in Article 8(2) can be invoked by States, but the aims are couched in broad terms.

2 National security' has been successfully invoked in a number of cases including *Leander v Sweden* (above, p 501) and *Klass v Germany* (above, p 560). However, the Court did not uphold the British armed forces treatment of homosexual personnel in *Smith and Grady v UK* (above, p 489).

3 'Public safety' was accepted by the Court as one of the justifications for the British planning authorities refusal to allow Buckley to live in her caravans on her land in the countryside. The authorities had determined that there was a danger to road traffic safety if she were allowed to live on her land and thereby seek access to and from the public highway. See *Buckley v UK* (above, p 543).

4 The 'economic well-being of the country' was accepted by the Court as the justification for Guernsey's housing control laws in *Gillow v UK* (above, p 541).

5 In *Malone v UK* (above, p 561) the Court recognized that a legal regime authorizing the interception of communications, with appropriate safeguards to meet the requirements of Article 8(2), may be justified as being necessary 'for the prevention of disorder or crime'. Also in *McLeod v UK* (1998) 27 EHRR 493, 1998-VII, the Court held that the power of the police to enter private premises to prevent a breach of the peace had this legitimate aim. The applicant was involved in lengthy and acrimonious legal proceedings with her ex-husband concerning the former matrimonial home, which she occupied with her frail mother who was in her seventies, and its contents. She had failed to comply with a court order to deliver specified property to her ex-husband and the court granted her seven days to comply or face imprisonment for contempt of court. Her ex-husband offered to collect the listed items from the former matrimonial home at a specified time. His solicitors arranged for two police officers to be present at the house when the ex-husband (together with his brother, sister and a solicitor's clerk) arrived to collect the specified items. One of the police officers knocked at the door and the applicant's mother informed him that her daughter was not at home. The mother stated that the police officer told her that they had a court order to execute. She, thereupon, let all of them into the house. The police officers did not remove any property, but checked that only the listed items were taken. For most of the time the officers were located on the driveway of the house. During the course of the removal operation the applicant returned to the house and became angry. The police only allowed her to inspect the contents of the removal van, rather than unload its contents, as they feared there was likely to be a breach of the peace. Subsequently, the applicant successfully sued her ex-husband for trespass, but her similar claim against the police was rejected by the Court of Appeal (see, *McLeod v Metropolitan Police Comr* [1994] 4 All ER 553). That court held that the police officers' actions could be justified under the common law preventive power recognized in *Thomas v Sawkins* [1935] 2 KB 249 and preserved by section 17(6) of the Police and Criminal Evidence Act 1984. The applicant complained to the Commission alleging, *inter alia*, that the entry of the police into her home and the failure of the English courts to grant her protection amounted to a violation of her right to respect for her private life and home under Article 8. By a majority, of fourteen to two, the Commission found no breach of that Article. The Court concluded that the police officers' power of entry to private premises to deal with or prevent a breach of the peace was defined with sufficient clarity for it to be 'in accordance with the law'. However, a majority of the Court, seven votes to two, decided that the entry of the officers into the applicant's home was a disproportionate response to the legitimate aim pursued:

... upon being informed that the applicant was not present, the police officers should not have entered her house, as it should have been clear to them that there was little or no risk of disorder or crime occurring. ... The fact that an altercation did occur upon her return is, in its opinion, immaterial in ascertaining whether the police officers were justified in entering the property initially. (para 57)

Judges Freeland and Mifsud Bonnici wrote a partly dissenting opinion in which they concluded that the police had acted in a proportionate manner. They noted:

... as a matter of common knowledge, the intensity and bitterness of domestic disputes tend all too often to escalate into disorder or violence, particularly where the division of property is involved; and it is by no means unusual for British police to be called on to intervene to prevent such escalation. (para 4)

While the judgment of the Court holds that this controversial power of entry is compatible with Article 8, it reinforces domestic *dicta* that the police must be cautious in their utilisation of such an intrusive power.

A unanimous Chamber followed the approach of *McLeod* in a later case where the police mistakenly obtained and executed a search warrant on the wrong premises. In *Keegan v United Kingdom*, judgment of 18 July 2006, the complainants were an innocent family whose home was forcibly entered and searched by the police in the erroneous belief that an armed robber was living in the house.

33. ... although the police did not act with malice and indeed with the best of intentions, there was no reasonable basis for their action in breaking down the applicants' door early one morning while they were in bed. Put in Convention terms, there might have been relevant reasons, but, as in the circumstances they were based on a misconception which could, and should, have been avoided with proper precautions, they cannot be regarded as sufficient (see *mutatis mutandis, McLeod* ...).

Consequently, although the police had been acting in pursuit of the legitimate aim of preventing disorder and crime the Chamber found a breach of Article 8.

6 The Court upheld the prosecution and conviction of the applicants in *Laskey, Jaggard and Brown v UK* (above, p 495) as being in pursuit of the legitimate aim of the 'protection of health'.

7 The criminal prohibitions on consensual homosexual conduct successfully challenged in *Dudgeon v UK* (above, p 487), were accepted by the Court as being for the legitimate aim of the 'protection of ... morals'. The Court elaborated upon the scope of this justification by noting that it:

... may imply safeguarding the moral ethos or moral standards of a society as a whole, but may also, as the Government pointed out, cover protection of the moral interests and welfare of a particular section of society, for example schoolchildren. (para 47)

8 The justification of interferences taken for 'the protection of the rights and freedoms of others was successfully invoked in *Chappell v UK* (above, p 590), where it was acknowledged that the search of Chappell's business premises under the authority of the Anton Piller order was aimed at protecting the intellectual property rights of the film companies against illegal copying/distribution of their films.

9 McHarg has expressed the view that:

The relationship between human rights and public interest exceptions is one of the most important issues in contemporary human rights jurisprudence. Not only is the interpretation given to exceptions a key determinant of the utility of rights in practice, but this is also the area in which the political or value-laden nature of the choices facing the court is most obvious, raising questions as to the legitimacy of judicial rather than democratic decision-making. ... the European Court and Commission of Human Rights have found the relationship problematic, failing to develop a coherent set of tests for determining when rights prevail over the public interest or *vice versa*.' [A McHarg, 'Reconciling Human Rights and the Public Interest: Conceptual Problems and Doctrinal Uncertainty in the Jurisprudence of the European Court of Human Rights' (1999) Modern Law Review 671 at 695.]

Does this criticism accord with your understanding of the above cases?

11 ARTICLE 9 FREEDOM OF THOUGHT, CONSCIENCE AND RELIGION

The Court's general approach

Kokkinakis v Greece A.260-A (1993) 17 EHRR 397
European Court of Human Rights

Mr Kokkinakis was born in 1909 and had converted from the Christian Eastern Orthodox Church to the Jehovah's Witnesses in 1936. Since that time he had been arrested by the Greek authorities more than 60 times for proselytism. This had resulted in him being interned and imprisoned on several occasions. In 1986 Mr Kokkinakis and his wife called at the home of a Mrs Kyriakaki and engaged in a discussion with her. Mr Kyriakaki, who was the cantor at a local Orthodox church, called the police and Mr and Mrs Kokkinakis were arrested. They were charged under Law 1363/1938 which stated that: 'Anyone engaging in proselytism shall be liable to imprisonment and a fine . . . By proselytism is meant, in particular, any direct or indirect attempt to intrude on the religious beliefs of a person of a different religious persuasion, with the aim of undermining those beliefs, either by any kind of inducement or promise of an inducement or moral support or material assistance, or by fraudulent means or by taking advantage of his inexperience, trust, need, low intellect or naivety.' The criminal court convicted Mr and Mrs Kokkinakis of proselytism on the basis that they took advantage of Orthodox Christians' inexperience, low intellect and naivety. The court emphasised that the defendants went to Mrs Kyriakaki's house and '. . . told her that they brought good news; by insisting in a pressing manner, they gained admittance to the house and began to read from a book on the Scriptures which they interpreted with reference to a king of heaven . . . encouraging [Mrs Kyriakaki] by means of their judicious, skilful explanations . . . to change her Orthodox Christian beliefs.' The defendants were each sentenced to four months' imprisonment. They appealed to the Crete Court of Appeal which quashed Mrs Kokkinakis's conviction and upheld Mr Kokkinakis's conviction, but reduced his sentence to three months' imprisonment. He then challenged the constitutionality of Law 1363/1938 before the Court of Cassation, but it rejected his contention. Subsequently Mr Kokkinakis applied to the Commission claiming a violation of, *inter alia*, Article 9. The Commission unanimously found a violation of this Article.

. . .

A. GENERAL PRINCIPLES

31. As enshrined in Article 9, freedom of thought, conscience and religion is one of the foundations of a 'democratic society' within the meaning of the Convention. It is, in its religious dimension, one of the most vital elements that go to make up the identity of believers and their conception of life, but it is also a precious asset for atheists, agnostics, sceptics and the unconcerned. The pluralism indissociable from a democratic society, which has been dearly won over the centuries, depends on it.

While religious freedom is primarily a matter of individual conscience, it also implies, inter alia, freedom to 'manifest [one's] religion'. Bearing witness in words and deeds is bound up with the existence of religious convictions.

According to Article 9, freedom to manifest one's religion is not only exercisable in community with others, 'in public' and within the circle of those whose faith one shares, but can also be asserted 'alone' and in private'; furthermore, it includes in principle the right to try to convince one's neighbour, for example through 'teaching', failing which, moreover, 'freedom to change [one's] religion or belief', enshrined in Article 9, would be likely to remain a dead letter.

. . .

33. The fundamental nature of the rights guaranteed in Article 9 § 1 is also reflected in the wording of the paragraph providing for limitations on them. Unlike the second paragraphs of Articles 8, 10 and 11, which cover all the rights mentioned in the first paragraphs of those articles, that of Article 9 refers only to 'freedom to manifest one's religion or belief'. In so doing, it recognises that in democratic societies, in which several religions coexist within one and the same population, it may be necessary to place restrictions on this freedom in order to reconcile the interests of the various groups and ensure that everyone's beliefs are respected.

. . .

B. APPLICATION OF THE PRINCIPLES

36. The sentence passed by the Lasithi Criminal Court and subsequently reduced by the Crete Court of Appeal . . . amounts to an interference with the exercise of Mr Kokkinakis's right to 'freedom to manifest [his] religion or belief'. Such an interference is contrary to Article 9 unless it is 'prescribed by law', directed at one or more of the legitimate aims in paragraph 2 and 'necessary in a democratic society' for achieving them.

1. 'PRESCRIBED BY LAW'

. . .

40. The Court has already noted that the wording of many statutes is not absolutely precise. The need to avoid excessive rigidity and to keep pace with changing circumstances means that many laws are inevitably couched in terms which, to a greater or lesser extent, are vague (see, for example and *mutatis mutandis*, the *Müller v Switzerland* judgment of 24 May 1988, Series A No 133, p 20, § 29). Criminal-law provisions on proselytism fall within this category. The interpretation and application of such enactments depend on practice.

In this instance there existed a body of settled national case-law. . . . This case-law, which had been published and was accessible, supplemented the letter of section 4 and was such as to enable Mr Kokkinakis to regulate his conduct in the matter.

As to the constitutionality of section 4 of Law no 1363/1938, the Court reiterates that it is, in the first instance, for the national authorities and in particular the courts, to interpret and apply domestic law (see, as the most recent authority, the *Hadjianastassiou v Greece* judgment of 16 December 1992, Series A No 252, p 18, § 42). And the Greek courts that have had to deal with the issue have ruled that there is no incompatibility . . .

41. The measure complained of was therefore 'prescribed by law' within the meaning of Article 9 § 2 of the Convention.

2. LEGITIMATE AIM

42. The Government contended that a democratic State had to ensure the peaceful enjoyment of the personal freedoms of all those living on its territory. If, in particular, it was not vigilant to protect a person's religious beliefs and dignity from attempts to influence them by immoral and deceitful means, Article 9 § 2 would in practice be rendered wholly nugatory.

43. In the applicant's submission, religion was part of the 'constantly renewable flow of human thought' and it was impossible to conceive of its being excluded from public debate. A fair balance of personal rights made it necessary to accept that others' thought should be subject to a minimum of influence, otherwise the result would be a 'strange society of silent animals that [would] think but . . . not express themselves, that [would] talk but . . . not communicate, and that [would] exist but . . . not coexist'.

44. Having regard to the circumstances of the case and the actual terms of the relevant courts' decisions, the Court considers that the impugned measure was in pursuit of a legitimate aim under Article 9 § 2, namely the protection of the rights and freedoms of others, relied on by the Government.

3. 'NECESSARY IN A DEMOCRATIC SOCIETY'

45. Mr Kokkinakis did not consider it necessary in a democratic society to prohibit a fellow citizen's right to speak when he came to discuss religion with his neighbour. He was curious to know how a discourse delivered with conviction and based on holy books common to all Christians could infringe the rights of others. Mrs Kyriakaki was an experienced adult woman with intellectual abilities; it was not possible, without flouting fundamental human rights, to make it a criminal offence for a Jehovah's Witness to have a conversation with a cantor's wife. Moreover, the Crete Court of Appeal, although the facts before it were precise and absolutely clear, had not managed to determine the direct or indirect nature of the applicant's attempt to intrude on the complainant's religious beliefs; its reasoning showed that it had convicted the applicant 'not for something he had done but for what he was'.
   The Commission accepted this argument in substance.

46. The Government maintained on the contrary, that the Greek courts had based themselves on plain facts which amounted to the offence of proselytism: Mr Kokkinakis's insistence on entering Mrs Kyriakaki's home on a false pretext; the way in which he had approached her in order to gain her trust; and his 'skilful' analysis of the Holy Scriptures calculated to 'delude' the complainant, who did not possess any 'adequate grounding in doctrine' (see paragraphs 9–10 above). They pointed out that if the State remained indifferent to attacks on freedom of religious belief, major unrest would be caused that would probably disturb the social peace.

47. The Court has consistently held that a certain margin of appreciation is to be left to the Contracting States in assessing the existence and extent of the necessity of an interference, but this margin is subject to European supervision, embracing both the legislation and the decisions applying it, even those given by an independent court. The Court's task is to determine whether the measures taken at national level were justified in principle and proportionate.
   In order to rule on this latter point, the Court must weigh the requirements of the protection of the rights and liberties of others against the conduct of which the applicant stood accused. In exercising its supervisory jurisdiction, the Court must look at the impugned judicial decisions against the background of the case as a whole (see, inter alia and *mutatis mutandis*, the *Barfod v Denmark* judgment of 22 February 1989, Series A No 149, p 12, § 28).

48. First of all, a distinction has to be made between bearing Christian witness and improper proselytism. The former corresponds to true evangelism, which a report drawn up in 1956 under the auspices of the World Council of Churches describes as an essential mission and a responsibility of every Christian and every Church. The latter represents a corruption or deformation of it. It may, according to the same report, take the form of activities offering material or social advantages with a view to gaining new members for a Church or exerting improper pressure on people in distress or in need; it may

even entail the use of violence or brainwashing; more generally, it is not compatible with respect for the freedom of thought, conscience and religion of others.

Scrutiny of section 4 of Law no 1363/1938 shows that the relevant criteria adopted by the Greek legislature are reconcilable with the foregoing if and in so far as they are designed only to punish improper proselytism, which the Court does not have to define in the abstract in the present case.

49. The Court notes, however, that in their reasoning the Greek courts established the applicant's liability by merely reproducing the wording of section 4 and did not sufficiently specify in what way the accused had attempted to convince his neighbour by improper means. None of the facts they set out warrants that finding.

That being so, it has not been shown that the applicant's conviction was justified in the circumstances of the case by a pressing social need. The contested measure therefore does not appear to have been proportionate to the legitimate aim pursued or, consequently, 'necessary in a democratic society . . . for the protection of the rights and freedoms of others'.

50. In conclusion, there has been a breach of Article 9 of the Convention.

. . .

FOR THESE REASONS, THE COURT

1. Holds by six votes to three that there has been a breach of Article 9;
. . .

NOTES

1   The majority were comprised of President Ryssdal and Judges: Bernhardt, Pettiti, De Meyer, Martens, and Lopes Rocha.

In his partly concurring judgment Pettiti J emphasised the importance of this case as

. . . the first real case concerning freedom of religion to have come before the European Court . . . ' (p 25) Therefore, he considered that the majority's reasoning: ' . . . could also have better reflected the fact that Article 9 applies also to non-religious philosophical beliefs and that the application of it must protect people from abuse by certain sects; but here it is for the States to legislate so that any deviation leading to attempts at brainwashing are regulated by the ordinary law. Non-criminal proselytism remains the main expression of freedom of religion. Attempting to make converts is not in itself an attack on the freedom and beliefs of others or an infringement of their rights. (p 27)

He concluded that the Greek law on proselytism was in breach of the Convention because; 'the expression 'proselytism that is not respectable', which is a criterion used by the Greek courts when applying the Law, is sufficient for the enactment and the case-law applying it to be regarded as contrary to Article 9.' (p 25) This was due to the vagueness of the charge and the lack of a clear definition of proselytism in Greek law. For academic support of his view see, TJ Gunn, 'Adjudicating Rights of Conscience Under the ECHR' in JD van der Vyver and J Witte (ed), *Religious Human Rights in Global Perspective* (The Hague: Martinus Nijhoff, 1996).

De Meyer J cited the dictionary definition (from *Le Petit Robert*) of proselytism as 'zeal in spreading the faith'. He determined that Mr Kokkinakis had shown such zeal but had not acted improperly (Mrs Kyriakaki had let him into her house and she had not asked him to leave). Similarly Martens J observed that:

. . . what occasioned this debate was a normal and perfectly inoffensive call by two elderly Jehovah's Witnesses (the applicant was 77 at the time) trying to sell some of the sect's booklets to a lady who, instead of closing the door, allowed the old couple entry, either because she was no match for their insistence or because she believed them to be bringing tidings from relatives on the mainland. There is no trace of violence or of anything that could properly be styled coercion; at the worst there was a trivial lie. If resort to criminal proceedings was at all warranted, a prosecution for disturbance of domestic peace would seem the severest possible response. (p 33)

As a matter of principle he also considered that it was contrary to Article 9 for States to make it a criminal offence for persons to attempt to induce others to change their religion. His research indicated that Greece was the only party to the Convention which made proselytism a criminal offence per se.

Valticos J (the elected judge of Greek nationality) dissented from the majority with regard to both the scope of Article 9 and the assessment of the facts. In his conception Article 9:

... is designed to ensure religious peace and tolerance, not to permit religious clashes and even wars, particularly at a time when many sects manage to entice simple, naive souls by doubtful means. ... I may add that the term 'teaching' in Article 9 undoubtedly refers to religious teaching in school curricular or in religious institutions, and not to personal door-to-door canvassing as in the present case. (p 30)

As for the Greek definition of criminal proselytism he considered that:

this definition of, if one may so term it, rape of the belief of others cannot in any way be regarded as contrary to Article 9 of the Convention. On the contrary, it is such as to protect individuals' freedom of religious belief. (p 31)

His evaluation of the facts was that:

... we have a militant Jehovah's Witness, a hard-bitten adept of proselytism, a specialist in conversion, a martyr of the criminal courts whose earlier convictions have served only to harden him in his militancy, and, on the other hand, the ideal victim, a naive woman, the wife of a cantor in the Orthodox Church (if he manages to convert her, what a triumph!). He swoops on her, trumpets that he has good news for her (the play on words is obvious, but no doubt not to her), manages to get himself let in and, as an experienced commercial traveller and cunning purveyor of a faith he wants to spread, expounds to her his intellectual wares cunningly wrapped up in a mantle of universal peace and radiant happiness. Who, indeed, would not like peace and happiness? But is this the mere exposition of Mr Kokkinakis's beliefs or is it not rather an attempt to beguile the simple soul of the cantor's wife? Does the Convention afford its protection to such undertakings? Certainly not. (p 31)

Contrast this portrayal of the facts with that of Martens J above. Foighel and Loizou JJ also dissented. Like Valticos J, they held that the Greek definition of unlawful proselytism was in conformity with Article 9. Furthermore:

the term 'teach' entails openness and uprightness and the avoidance of the use of devious or improper means or false pretexts as in this case in order to gain access to a person's home and, once there, by abusing the courtesy and hospitality extended, take advantage of the ignorance or inexperience in theological doctrine of someone who has no specialist training and try to get that person to change his or her religion. ... The persistent efforts of some fanatics to convert others to their own beliefs by using unacceptable psychological techniques on people, which amount in effect to coercion, cannot in our view come within the ambit of the natural meaning of the term 'teach' to be found in paragraph 1 of this Article. (pp 40–1)

2   PW Edge has observed that:

The majority are compounding two distinct justifications for freedom of religion here-social justifications that religious freedom helps to produce a functioning pluralist society where individuals all feel a part of the State's society; and the personal development argument which sees religious freedom, in a way similar to the right to privacy, as providing scope for personal development and self-definition. ['Current Problems in Article 9 of the ECHR') [1996] *Juridical Review* 42 at p 47.]

3 The Court has subsequently applied its approach in *Kokkinakis* to acts of proselytism carried out by Greek military officers of another sect in *Larissis v Greece*, 1998-I 362. The three applicants were Air Force officers in the same unit who were members of the Pentecostal Church (which held that all members were under a duty to engage in proselytism). Airman A. claimed that two of the applicants had engaged him in religious discussions on seven occasions (during which they had claimed that some of their members had the divine power to speak in foreign languages) and they repeatedly asked him if he had visited a Pentecostal church when he returned from various periods of leave. Airman K. asserted that the applicants had engaged him in theological discussions on about eighty occasions. Airman N.K., who had converted to the Pentecostal church, stated that he had voluntarily sought the religious help of the applicants, but his father claimed that N.K. was a highly susceptible young person. One of the applicants had been summoned to a fellow believer's house where he had preached a sermon calling upon all the family and their neighbours to join the Pentecostal church. Mrs Z., whose husband had joined the Pentecostal church, visited the applicants' homes where they urged her to convert (she also alleged that the applicants informed her that she and her children were possessed by the devil). She developed mental problems and decided to sever all links with the applicants and their church. The Greek military courts convicted the applicants of proselytism (under the same law as in *Kokkinakis*) in respect of these activities and sentenced each of them to approximately one year's imprisonment (convertible into financial penalties), but suspended the penalties provided the applicants did not commit new offences within three years. The applicants complained to the Commission alleging, *inter alia*, a breach of their rights under Article 9. The Commission found a violation of Article 9 in respect of the convictions involving the civilians (twenty-four votes to five), but no breach in respect of the convictions involving the junior military personnel. The Court restated the distinction between 'proper' and 'improper' proselytism articulated in *Kokkinakis*. However, different factors applied to the applicants' behaviour towards their subordinates and ordinary civilians. Regarding the former:

> ...the Court notes that the hierarchical structures which are a feature of life in the armed forces may colour every aspect of the relations between military personnel, making it difficult for a subordinate to rebuff the approaches of an individual of superior rank or to withdraw from a conversation initiated by him. Thus, what would in the civilian world be seen as an innocuous exchange of ideas which the recipient is free to accept or reject, may, within the confines of military life, be viewed as a form of harassment or the application of undue pressure in abuse of power. It must be emphasised that not every discussion about religion or other sensitive matters between individuals of unequal rank will fall within this category. Nonetheless, where the circumstances so require, States may be justified in taking special measures to protect the rights and freedoms of subordinate members of the armed forces. (para 51)

A majority of the Court (eight to one and seven to two) found that the convictions of the applicants in respect of their proselytism towards the junior personnel were not in breach of Article 9. However, by seven votes to two the Court concluded that the convictions involving the civilians were in breach of Article 9, as the applicants had not behaved improperly and the civilians were not subject to the same pressures and constraints in responding to the applicants as the junior airmen had been. In his dissent Valticos J (joined by Morenilla J) considered that, '... the prestige of the officers' uniform may have had an effect even on civilians...' Counsel for the applicants has criticised the decision, in his view '... the Court is often far too conservative and deferential to the existing legislation of the Member states.' (J. W. Montgomery, 'When is Evangelism Illegal?' (1998) *New Law Journal* 524 at p 525.) Would the Court's reasoning be applicable to other hierarchical state organisations such as the police service? What about proselytism in the context of unequal professional relationships, e.g. between medical doctors and their patients or teachers and their pupils?

The limitations that a military career may place on the exercise of Article 9 rights are considered further in the *Kalac* judgment, below p 607.

4 The extent to which States and their national legal systems should protect persons' religious beliefs from denigration and ridicule by others has caused difficulties for the Commission and the Court in the field of artistic expression; especially as artists will be trying to argue their right to freedom of expression under Article 10 (see further below, p 661). In *Choudhury v UK* (1991) 12 HRLJ 172, the applicant complained that English law had failed to protect his right to freedom of religion under Article 9. Mr Choudhury was a Muslim who had been refused permission by the High Court to bring a private prosecution against Salman Rushdie, and his publishers, in respect of his novel *The Satanic Verses*, which the applicant contended was blasphemous in its treatment of leading figures in Islam. The High Court ruled that under English law the offence of blasphemy only applied to publications directed against the Christian religion (see: *R v Chief Metropolitan Stipendiary Magistrate, ex p Choudhury* [1991] 1 All ER 306). The Commission unanimously declared the application inadmissible because:

[Mr Choudhury] does not claim, and it clearly is not the case, that any State authority, or any body for which the United Kingdom Government may be responsible under the Convention, directly interfered in the applicant's freedom to manifest his religion or belief.

The question in the present case is therefore whether the freedom of Article 9 of the Convention may extend to guarantee a right to bring any specific form of proceedings against those who, by authorship or publication, offend the sensitivities of an individual or a group of individuals. The Commission finds no indication in the present case of a link between freedom from interference with the freedoms of Article 9(1) of the Convention and the applicant's complaints.

Accordingly, this part of the application must be declared incompatible *ratione materiae* with the provisions of the Convention within the meaning of Article 27(2). (pp 172–3)

Likewise, the Commission declared the applicant's complaint under Article 14, of discriminatory treatment of Islam compared to Christianity in the English law on blasphemy, inadmissible because his substantive complaint had been held to fall outside the protection of Article 9. Hence the Commission was not willing to interpret Article 9(1) as providing religious believers with a right to prosecute those who allegedly insulted their beliefs.

However, the Court, in the context of applying Article 10, has stated that in certain circumstances States may be under a Convention obligation to protect believers from extreme attacks upon their beliefs. In *Otto-Preminger Institute v Austria* (1994) 19 EHRR 34, A.295-A, the applicant organisation ran an 'art-house' cinema in Innsbruck. During May 1985 they planned to show a film called *Das Liebeskonzil* (Council in Heaven) which contained a production of the nineteenth-century play, of the same title, written by Oskar Panizza (who had been imprisoned for blasphemy in 1895 by the German courts for publishing his play). According to the Court the film: '... portrays the God of the Jewish religion, the Christian religion and the Islamic religion as an apparently senile old man prostrating himself before the devil with whom he exchanges a deep kiss and calling the devil his friend. ... Other scenes show the Virgin Mary permitting an obscene story to be read to her and the manifestation of a degree of erotic tension between the Virgin Mary and the devil. The adult Jesus Christ is portrayed as a low grade mental defective...' (para 22) The applicant informed its 2,700 members of the showings and it also advertised the events to the general public (only persons over 17 years of age would be admitted) via window displays throughout Innsbruck and in a brief announcement in a regional newspaper. The Innsbruck diocese of the Roman Catholic church (87 per cent of Tyrolleans are

Roman Catholic believers) requested the Public Prosecutor to bring criminal charges against the applicant in respect of its proposed film performances. The Prosecutor instituted proceedings against the applicant's manager and applied for the seizure of the film under the Media Act. The Regional Court ordered the immediate seizure of the film. Subsequently, the Regional Court approved the forfeiture of the film. The applicant contended that these orders amounted to a violation of its right to freedom of expression under Article 10. The Commission concluded (by nine votes to five) that the seizure of the film violated Article 10 and that the forfeiture was a similar violation (by thirteen votes to one). Before the Court, the Austrian Government argued that the court orders were necessary to 'protect the rights of others' in the form of the right to respect for their religious beliefs held by the Tyrolleans and, therefore, could be justified under Article 10(2) (for further elaboration of this provision see below, p 712). The majority of the Court agreed with this argument:

Those who choose to exercise the freedom to manifest their religion, irrespective of whether they do so as members of a religious majority or a minority, cannot reasonably expect to be exempt from all criticism. They must tolerate and accept the denial by others of their religious beliefs and even the propagation by others of doctrines hostile to their faith. However, the manner in which religious beliefs and doctrines are opposed or denied is a matter which may engage the responsibility of the State, notably its responsibility to ensure the peaceful enjoyment of the right guaranteed under Article 9 to the holders of those beliefs and doctrines. Indeed, in extreme cases the effect of particular methods of opposing or denying religious beliefs can be such as to inhibit those who hold such beliefs from exercising their freedom to hold and express them.

In the *Kokkinakis* judgment the Court held, in the context of Article 9, that a State may legitimately consider it necessary to take measures aimed at repressing certain forms of conduct, including the imparting of information and ideas, judged incompatible with the respect for the freedom of thought, conscience and religion of others. The respect for the religious feelings of believers as guaranteed in Article 9 can legitimately thought to have been violated by provocative portrayals of objects of religious veneration; and such portrayals can be regarded as malicious violation of the spirit of tolerance, which must also be a feature of democratic society. (para 47)

The majority (President Ryssdal and Judges; Gölcüklü, Matscher, Walsh, Macdonald and Gotchev) then invoked the controversial margin of appreciation doctrine (see below, p 629) to determine that the seizure/forfeiture of the film 'was necessary in a democratic society' and that no breach of Article 10 had occurred:

... it is not possible to discern throughout Europe a uniform conception of the significance of religion in society, even within a single country such conceptions may vary. For that reason it is not possible to arrive at a comprehensive definition of what constitutes a permissible interference with the exercise of the right to freedom of expression where such expression is directed against the religious feelings of others. A certain margin of appreciation is therefore to be left to the national authorities in assessing the existence and extent of the necessity of such interference. (para 50)

The three dissentients (Judges; Palm, Pekkanen, and Makarczyk) considered that:

The Convention does not, in terms, guarantee a right to protection of religious feelings. More particularly, such a right cannot be derived from the right to freedom of religion, which in effect includes a right to express views critical of the religious opinions of others.

Nevertheless, it must be accepted that it may be 'legitimate' for the purpose of Article 10 to protect the religious feelings of certain members of society against criticism and abuse to some extent; tolerance works both ways and the democratic character of a society will be affected if violent and abusive attacks on the reputation of a religious group are allowed. Consequently, it must also be accepted that it may be 'necessary in a democratic society' to set limits to the public expression of such criticism or abuse. To this extent, but no further, we can agree with the majority. (para 6)

However, the dissentients did not consider that the seizure/forfeiture of the film was a proportionate response by the Austrian authorities when considered in the light of the applicant's warnings to prospective viewers of the nature of the film, and the fact that only paying adults would be able to see the film.

In the later case of *Wingrove v UK* (1996) 24 EHRR 1, 1996-V 1937, a majority of the Court upheld the lawfulness of the British Board of Film Classification's refusal to grant a classification certificate (thereby preventing its lawful distribution within the UK) to the applicant's eighteen-minute long video work entitled *Visions of Ecstasy*. The video, which had no dialogue, was claimed by the applicant film director to be based upon the life of St Teresa of Avila, a sixteenth-century Carmelite nun, who experienced ecstatic visions of Jesus Christ. The Court described the work as portraying, '... *inter alia*, a female character astride the recumbent body of the crucified Christ engaged in an act of an overtly sexual nature.' (para 61) The Board, and later the statutory Video Appeals Committee, concluded that the video was blasphemous and should not therefore be given a certificate. The applicant claimed that these decisions violated his right to freedom of expression under Article 10. The Commission (by fourteen votes to two) found there had been a violation of this Article. The Government relied upon the Court's decision in *Otto-Preminger Institute* to contend that States may restrict the publication of provocative depictions of objects of religious veneration in order to ensure respect for the religious beliefs of followers of the religion concerned. The Court's majority (President Bernhardt and Judges; Thor Vilhjalmsson, Pettiti, Morenilla, Freeland, Mifsud Bonnici and Gotchev) agreed that States might restrict video works under Article 10(2) in order to protect the right of other citizens not to be offended in their religious feelings.

It is true that the English law of blasphemy only extends to the Christian faith. Indeed the anomaly of this state of affairs in a multi-denominational society was recognised by the Divisional Court in *R v Chief Magistrate, ex p Choudhury* [above]. However, it is not for the European Court to rule *in abstracto* as to the compatibility of domestic law with the Convention. The extent to which English law protects other beliefs is not in issue before the Court which must confine its attention to the case before it. The uncontested fact that the law of blasphemy does not treat on an equal footing the different religions practised in the United Kingdom does not detract from the legitimacy of the aim pursued in the present context. (para 50)

Following the approach in *Otto-Preminger Institute*, the Court then upheld the authorities' refusal to classify the video as being within the State's broad margin of appreciation concerning expression directed at religious beliefs.

Whereas there is little scope under Article 10(2) of the Convention for restrictions on political speech or on debate of questions of public interest, a wider margin of appreciation is generally available to the Contracting States when regulating freedom of expression in relation to matters liable to offend intimate personal convictions within the sphere of morals or, especially, religion. Moreover, as in the field of morals, and perhaps to an even greater degree, there is no uniform European conception of the requirements of 'the protection of the rights of others' in relation to attacks on their religious convictions. What is likely to cause substantial offence to persons of a particular religious persuasion will vary significantly from time to time and from place to place, especially in an era characterised by an ever growing array of faiths and denominations. By reason of their direct and continuous contact with the vital forces of their countries, State authorities are in principle in a better position than the international judge to give an opinion on the exact content of these requirements with regard to the rights of others as well as on the 'necessity' of a 'restriction' intended to protect from such material those whose deepest feelings and convictions would be seriously offended. (para 58)

Judge De Meyer in his dissent expressed the view that in respect of the criminal law of blasphemy: '... the necessity of such laws is very much open to question. I would rather join in Mr Patten's [a former Home Office Minister] remark that for the faithful "the strength of their own belief is the best armour against mockers and blasphemers."' (para 4) The other dissentient, Lohmus J was concerned that:

In cases of prior restraint (censorship) there is interference by the authorities with freedom of expression even though the members of the society whose feelings they seek to protect have not called for such interference. The interference is based on the opinion of the authorities that they understand correctly the feelings they claim to protect. The actual opinion of believers remains unknown. I think that is why we cannot conclude that the interference corresponded to a 'pressing social need'.

The law of blasphemy only protects the Christian religion and, more specifically, the established Church of England. The aim of the interference was therefore to protect the Christian faith alone and not other beliefs. This in itself raises the question whether the interference was 'necessary in a democratic society'. (paras 3–4)

Lord Lester has criticized the majority's judgment in *Wingrove* as a 'timorous ruling'. In his opinion: 'I do not discern a satisfactory logical, philosophical or jurisprudential basis for protecting political expression and media freedom more strongly than artistic and cultural expression. The distinction sought to be made between them seems arbitrary and unworkable. Many famous works of art, literature and music have been censored because they shock or offend against the political, religious, sexual or aesthetic mores of the prevailing orthodoxy.' ('Universality versus Subsidiarity: A Reply' [1998] EHRLR 73 at 77.)

5   MD Evans has expressed the view that:

... the Strasbourg organs have themselves blurred the freedom of religion into a general melange of mutual respect not only between religions but between the freedom of religion and other human rights. This suggests that while international law might provide a degree of protection for religious liberty, it may not go as far as some religious believers consider necessary ... (*Religious Liberty and International Law in Europe* (Cambridge: Cambridge University Press, 1997), at 365).

Article 9(1)

Freedom of thought, conscience and religion: protected beliefs

1   Pacifism has been recognised as a belief falling within the protection of Article 9(1). In *Arrowsmith v UK* (1978) 3 EHRR 218, the applicant had been sentenced to 18 months' imprisonment under the Incitement to Disaffection Act 1934 for distributing leaflets, calling upon military personnel to refuse to serve in Northern Ireland, outside an army base in England. She claimed that her conviction and sentence violated her right to manifest her pacifist belief under Article 9(1). The Government accepted her definition of pacifism as being, 'the commitment, in both theory and practice, to the philosophy of securing one's political or other objectives without resort to the threat or use of force against another human being under any

circumstances, even in response to the threat or use of force.' The Commission expressed the opinion that:

... pacifism as a philosophy and, in particular, as defined above, falls within the ambit of the right to freedom of thought and conscience. The attitude of pacifism may therefore be seen as a belief ('conviction') protected by Article 9(1). (para 69)

Then the Commission considered whether Ms Arrowsmith had been manifesting her belief (for a general examination of this topic see below p 431) by distributing the leaflets:

... the term 'practice' as employed in Article 9(1) does not cover each act which is motivated or influenced by a religion or a belief. It is true that public declarations proclaiming generally the idea of pacifism and urging the acceptance of a commitment to non-violence may be considered as a normal and recognised manifestation of pacifist belief. However, when the actions of individuals do not actually express the belief concerned they cannot be considered to be as such protected by Article 9(1) even when they are motivated or influenced by it. (para 71)

After examining the contents of Arrowsmith's leaflets the Commission concluded that they did not reflect pacifist views, but a policy opposed to British military involvement in Northern Ireland. Consequently, distributing the leaflets was not a manifestation of a protected belief and Arrowsmith's conviction/imprisonment did not violate Article 9. Subsequently, the Committee of Ministers agreed with the Commission's Opinion: Res. DH(79)4.

2   In *C v UK* (1983) 37 D & R 142, the applicant was a Quaker, a fundamental aspect of whose beliefs involves pacifism, who refused to pay that proportion of his income tax (40%) which was said to be allocated to defence expenditure. The Inland Revenue obtained a court judgment against C for the amount of his full tax liability. He complained, to the Commission, that the British authorities actions to compel him to pay taxes for defence expenditure was contrary to Article 9(1) as an outrage to his conscience and violated his right to manifest his belief through practice. Following *Arrowsmith* the Commission stated that:

Article 9 primarily protects the sphere of personal beliefs and religious creeds, ie the area which is sometimes called the *forum internum*. In addition, it protects acts which are intimately linked to these attitudes, such as acts of worship or devotion which are aspects of the practice of a religion or belief in a generally recognised form. However, in protecting this personal sphere, Article 9 of the Convention does not always guarantee the right to behave in the public sphere in a way which is dictated by such a belief:- for instance by refusing to pay certain taxes because part of the revenue so raised may be applied for military expenditure. ...

It follows that Article 9 does not confer on the applicant the right to refuse, on the basis of his convictions, to abide by legislation, the operation of which is provided for by the Convention, and which applies neutrally and generally in the public sphere, without impinging on the freedoms guaranteed by Article 9. (p 147)

Therefore, the Commission declared the application manifestly ill-founded.

3   A Christian objected to participation in compulsory civil defence courses organised by his canton and was fined and imprisoned for his refusal to attend the designated courses. He believed that the courses sought to instil into the minds of participants the idea that chemical and nuclear warfare was a normal occurrence and not a violation of basic human rights: *Fadini v Switzerland* (1993) 16 EHRR CD13. The Commission held that as States were not obliged to exempt persons from military or civilian service under Article 4(3)(b) it was not possible to interpret Article 9 as providing such a right. Therefore, the application was manifestly ill-founded.

4 *Valsamis v Greece* and *Efstratiou v Greece* (1996) 24 EHRR 294, 1996-VI 2312 and 2347, involved parents requesting that their children be exempted from participating in school parades on the National Day of Greece. The parents' objection was based upon their membership of the Jehovah's Witnesses, whose beliefs forbid any conduct or practice associated with war or violence. In a small number of municipalities the school parades were accompanied by military parades, therefore the applicants asked that their children be exempted from their respective parades (even though there was no military presence at these celebrations). The children's headteachers refused the requests in accordance with a circular issued by the Ministry of Education and Religious Affairs stating that no children should be exempted from national celebrations. The children did not attend the school parades and each child was punished by suspension from school for one day by their headteachers. The parents complained to the Commission alleging, *inter alia*, a breach of their rights under Article 2 of Protocol 1 (States shall respect parents religious and philosophical convictions in matters of education and teaching) and Article 9. The Commission concluded (by nineteen votes to ten) that there had been no breach of Protocol 1, as the relevant parades did not have a military character, and (by seventeen votes to twelve) there had been no breach of Article 9. A majority of the Court (seven judges) concluded that:

While it is not for the Court to rule on the Greek State's decisions as regards the setting and planning of the school curriculum, it is surprised that pupils can be required on pain of suspension from school—even if only for a day—to parade outside the school precincts on a holiday. Nevertheless, it can discern nothing, either in the purpose of the parade or in the arrangements for it, which could offend the applicants' pacifist convictions to an extent prohibited by the second sentence of Article 2 of Protocol No 1. Such commemorations of national events serve, in their way, both pacifist objectives and the public interest. The presence of military representatives at some of the parades which take place in Greece on the day in question does not in itself alter the nature of the parades. (para 31)

Consequently, there was no breach of the Protocol or Article 9. Judges Thor Vilhjalmsson and Jambrek dissented. In their opinion:

Victoria Valsamis stated that the parade she did not participate in had a character and symbolism that were clearly contrary to her neutralist, pacifist and thus religious, beliefs. We are of the opinion that the Court has to accept that and we find no basis for seeing Victoria's participation in this parade as necessary in a democratic society; even if this public event clearly was for most people an expression of national values and unity. (p 32)

For the dissenters the Greek authorities' actions amounted to a violation of the parents' rights under Protocol 1 and the children's rights under Article 9.

5 The pacifist beliefs of Jehovah's Witnesses were also at issue in the case of *Tsirlis and Kouloumpas v Greece* (1997) 25 EHRR 198, 1997-III 909. There two ministers of the Jehovah's Witnesses refused to perform military service because of their religious beliefs. Despite the fact that the Supreme Administrative Court of Greece had recognised the Jehovah's Witnesses as a 'known religion' from the 1970s and a Law passed in 1988 exempted all ministers of 'known religions' from military service, the military courts convicted the applicants of insubordination and sentenced them to four years' imprisonment. The Court unanimously held that the military authorities' treatment of the applicants was in breach of Article 5(1), right to liberty, as Greek law exempted ministers like themselves from military service. In the light of this finding the Court did not examine the applicants' alleged breach of Article 9.

6 Other non-religious beliefs, such as veganism, have been accepted by the Commission as falling within the protection of Article 9(1). For example, in *H v UK* (1993) 16 EHRR CD 44, the applicant was a convicted prisoner who refused to work in the prison print shop because he contended that some of the dyes were derived from animal products and as a vegan he objected to working with animal products. The prison authorities found him guilty of a disciplinary offence and he lost two days' remission from his sentence and was fined. The Commission expressed the view that, '... vegan convictions with regard to animal products fall within the scope of Article 9(1)...' (p 45) However, the Commission found that the government could justify their actions under Article 9(2) as a proportionate interference with H's rights taken in the interests of preserving good order in the prison system; therefore, his complaint was found to be manifestly ill-founded.

7   In *Buscarini v San Marino* (1999) 30 EHRR 208, the Court expressly stated that Article 9 covers the freedom not to hold religious beliefs or to practise a religion. The applicants had been elected to the parliament of the Republic of San Marino in 1993. However, they were not allowed to take their seats until they swore an oath which included the words 'I ... swear on the Holy Gospels ever to be faithful to and obey the Constitution of the Republic ...'. The applicants objected to the wording of the oath as they considered that it infringed their freedom of religion and conscience under Article 9. The Commission, unanimously, upheld their complaint. The Court was also unanimous in its interpretation and application of Article 9 to the applicants' case. 'That freedom entails, *inter alia*, freedom to hold or not to hold religious beliefs and to practise or not to practise a religion.' (para 34) The Government sought to argue that having regard to the history, traditions and social fabric of San Marino, requiring parliamentarians to take the oath was necessary to maintain public order. But, the Court did not consider that such an obligation was necessary in a democratic society.

It is not in doubt that, in general, San Marinese law guarantees freedom of conscience and religion. In the instant case, however, requiring the applicants to take the oath on the Gospels was tantamount to requiring two elected representatives of the people to swear allegiance to a particular religion, a requirement which is not compatible with Article 9. As the Commission rightly stated in its report, it would be contradictory to make the exercise of a mandate intended to represent different views of society within Parliament subject to a prior declaration of commitment to a particular set of beliefs. (para 39)

Therefore, the Court found a violation of Article 9.

The right to manifest a person's religion or belief

Kalac v Turkey 1997-IV 1199, (1997) 27 EHRR 552
European Court of Human Rights

The applicant had pursued a career as a judge advocate in the Turkish Air Force. In 1990 he held the rank of Group Captain and was serving as the High Command's Director of Legal Affairs. During August 1990 the Supreme Military Council, composed of the Prime Minister, Minister of Defence, Chief of Staff and eleven generals, ordered the compulsory retirement of three officers (including the applicant) and twenty-eight non-commissioned officers for breaches of discipline and scandalous conduct. The applicant was alleged to have 'adopted unlawful fundamentalist opinions'. Subsequently, the President of the Republic approved the order. The applicant sought to challenge the order before the Supreme Administrative Court of the Armed Forces, but that body ruled that it did not have jurisdiction over the order. Before the Commission the applicant alleged that he had been removed from his post on account of his religious convictions in breach of Article 9. The Commission, unanimously, found a breach of that Article.

...

25. The Government argued that the question whether Mr Kalaç should be allowed to remain a member of the armed forces lay at the heart of the problem submitted to the Court. His compulsory retirement was not an interference with his freedom of conscience, religion or belief but was intended to remove from the military legal service a person who had manifested his lack of loyalty to the foundation of the Turkish nation, namely secularism, which it was the task of the armed forces to guarantee. The applicant belonged to the Süleyman sect, as a matter of fact, if not formally, and participated in the activities of the Süleyman community, which was known to have unlawful fundamentalist tendencies. Various documents annexed to the memorial to the Court showed that the applicant had given it legal assistance, had taken part in training sessions and had intervened on a number of occasions in the appointment of servicemen who were members of the sect. On the basis of those documents, a committee of five officers drawn from the highest echelons of the military had concluded that by taking and carrying out instructions from the leaders of the sect Group Captain Kalaç had breached military discipline and should accordingly be compulsorily retired pursuant to section 50(c) of the Military Personnel Act. The Supreme Military Council had based its decision on this opinion, which had been approved by the high command and the air force chief of staff.

Lastly, facilities to practise one's religion within the armed forces were provided in Turkey for both Muslims and the adherents of other faiths. However, the protection of Article 9 could not extend, in the case of a serviceman, to membership of a fundamentalist movement, in so far as its members' activities were likely to upset the army's hierarchical equilibrium.

26. The Commission, basing its opinion on the documents submitted to it by the Government, took the view that the applicant's compulsory retirement constituted interference with the right guaranteed by Article 9 § 1 and concluded that there had been a breach of that provision on the ground that the interference in question was not prescribed by law within the meaning of the second paragraph, finding that the relevant provisions did not afford adequate protection against arbitrary decisions. The Delegate observed that, in support of their memorial to the Court, the Government had produced documents which, during the proceedings before the Commission, had been said to be 'secret in the interests of national security'. In any event, these documents did not support the argument that Mr Kalaç had any links with a sect.

27. The Court reiterates that while religious freedom is primarily a matter of individual conscience, it also implies, inter alia, freedom to manifest one's religion not only in community with others, in public and within the circle of those whose faith one shares, but also alone and in private (see the *Kokkinakis v Greece* judgment of 25 May 1993, Series A No 260-A, p 17, § 31). Article 9 lists a number of forms which manifestation of one's religion or belief may take, namely worship, teaching, practice and observance. Nevertheless, Article 9 does not protect every act motivated or inspired by a religion or belief. Moreover, in exercising his freedom to manifest his religion, an individual may need to take his specific situation into account.

28. In choosing to pursue a military career Mr Kalaç was accepting of his own accord a system of military discipline that by its very nature implied the possibility of placing on certain of the rights and freedoms of members of the armed forces limitations incapable of being imposed on civilians (see the *Engel and Others v Netherlands* judgment of 8 June 1976, Series A No 22, p 24, § 57). States may adopt for their armies disciplinary regulations forbidding this or that type of conduct, in particular an attitude inimical to an established order reflecting the requirements of military service.

29. It is not contested that the applicant, within the limits imposed by the requirements of military life, was able to fulfil the obligations which constitute the normal forms through which a Muslim practises his

religion. For example, he was in particular permitted to pray five times a day and to perform his other religious duties, such as keeping the fast of Ramadan and attending Friday prayers at the mosque.

30. The Supreme Military Council's order was, moreover, not based on Group Captain Kalaç's religious opinions and beliefs or the way he had performed his religious duties but on his conduct and attitude. According to the Turkish authorities, this conduct breached military discipline and infringed the principle of secularism.

31. The Court accordingly concludes that the applicant's compulsory retirement did not amount to an interference with the right guaranteed by Article 9 since it was not prompted by the way the applicant manifested his religion.

There has therefore been no breach of Article 9.

FOR THESE REASONS, THE COURT UNANIMOUSLY

...

Holds that there has been no breach of Article 9 of the Convention.

NOTES

1   The Court was comprised of President Ryssdal and Judges: Gölcüklü, Pettiti, Russo, Spielmann, Foighel, Freeland, Baka, and Gotchev.

2   The Court's judgment indicates that the right to manifest one's religion or belief is more circumscribed than the right to freedom of thought, conscience and religion. By voluntarily pursuing a chosen career the applicant was held to have accepted the consequent necessary limitations on the right to manifest his religious belief.

3   A similar approach to this right had been articulated by the Commission in the earlier case of *Ahmad v UK* (1981) 4 EHRR 126. Mr Ahmad was a devout Muslim who was under a religious duty to attend Friday prayers at a mosque if he was within travelling distance of such an establishment. From 1968 until 1972 he was employed as a full time teacher by the Inner London Education Authority. During that time Ahmad did not seek permission to attend a mosque for Friday prayers. In 1974 he was moved to another teaching area in London and he chose a school near a mosque. He then asserted the right to attend the mosque for prayers even if this conflicted with his teaching duties on Fridays. His employers refused him permission to attend prayers on Friday afternoons and stated that if he wished to be absent from work at that time he must switch to a part-time contract of employment. He then resigned from his position and claimed constructive dismissal. Eventually the Court of Appeal, by a majority of two to one, rejected his claim: see *Ahmad v ILEA* [1978] 1 All ER 574. The Commission expressed the view that a person, '... may, in the exercise of his freedom to manifest his religion, have to take into account his particular professional or contractual position.' (p 133) Relevant factors in Mr Ahmad's case were his voluntary acceptance of his full-time teaching contract in 1968 and his failure to inform his employers for six years that he might need time off on Fridays to attend a mosque. Consequently, the Commission declared his application to be manifestly ill-founded.

4   Likewise, in *Stedman v UK* (1997) 23 EHRR CD 168, the Commission found the applicant's complaints to be inadmissible because of her contractual obligations. She argued that her dismissal from employment by a private sector company for refusing to agree to work on Sundays (on a rota basis) was a violation of, *inter alia*, her freedom to manifest her Christian religion

in worship, practice and observance as guaranteed by Article 9. However the Commission stated that:

...the applicant was dismissed for failing to agree to work certain hours rather than for her religious belief as such and was free to resign and did in effect resign from her employment.

The Commission thus considers that, had the applicant been employed by the State and dismissed in similar circumstances, such dismissal would not have amounted to an interference with her rights under Article 9(1). A fortiori the United Kingdom cannot be expected to have legislation that would protect employees against such dismissals by private employers. (para 1)

5 For an example of a non-contractual limitation of the right to manifest one's protected beliefs see *C v UK* (above, p 605).

6 The Court found a breach of this right in *Serif v Greece* (14 December 1999). The applicant was a Greek citizen who was elected by fellow Moslems in Thrace to be their Mufti (religious leader). However, the President of Greece had appointed another person to that position. Subsequently the applicant was convicted of 'usurping the functions of a minister of a known religion' and fined. The Court was unanimous in holding that:

The facts underlying the applicant's conviction, as they transpire from the relevant domestic court decisions, were issuing a message about the religious significance of a feast, delivering a speech at a religious gathering, issuing another message on the occasion of a religious holiday and appearing in the clothes of a religious leader. In these circumstances, the Court considers that the applicant's conviction amounts to an interference with his right under Article 9(1) of the Convention, 'in community with others and in public, to manifest his religion in worship and teaching'.

...in the Court's view, punishing a person for the mere fact that he acted as the religious leader of a group that willingly followed him can hardly be considered compatible with the demands of religious pluralism in a democratic society.

...Although the Court recognises that it is possible that tension is created in situations where a religious or any other community becomes divided, it considers that this is one of the unavoidable consequences of pluralism. The role of the authorities in such circumstances is not to remove the cause of tension by eliminating pluralism, but to ensure that the competing groups tolerate each other... (paras 39, 51, and 53)

Consequently, States must be careful about when and how they intervene in the domestic struggles within particular religious groups.

An analogous breach was found by a unanimous Chamber in the later case of *Agga v Greece*, judgment of 17 October 2002 [note, the same applicant successfully invoked this right in two similar applications: judgments of 13 July 2006].

The full-time Court has on two occasions found that the Bulgarian government unlawfully interfered in the organisational arrangements of Bulgarian Muslims. A Grand Chamber, unanimously, found a breach of Article 9 in *Hasan and Chaush v Bulgaria*, 2000-XI. Following the emergence of democracy in Bulgaria some Muslim believers and activists sought to replace the establish leadership of their religion in the country, as they believed the leadership had collaborated with the former communist regime. In 1991 a new government (Union of Democratic Forces) was formed after a general election. Early in 1992 the Directorate of Religious Denominations, a governmental body attached to the Council of Ministers, declared the election, in 1988, of the Chief Mufti of Bulgarian Muslims (Mr Gendzhev) null and void and proclaimed his removal from that position. In September 1992 the National Conference of Muslims elected the first applicant as Chief Mufti and approved a new statute to govern their organization. The Directorate of Religious Denominations registered the statute and new leadership in the following month. Mr Gendzhev's supporters elected him the

President of the Supreme Holy Council and proclaimed themselves the legitimate representatives of Muslim believers. At the end of 1994 a new government, formed by the Bulgarian Socialist Party, was elected. In February 1995 the Deputy Prime Minister issued a Decree approving the statute of Mr Gendzhev's organisation. Later that month the Directorate of Religious Denominations issued a decision registering Mr Gendzhev as the leader of the Bulgarian Muslim community. Thereupon, the new leadership, accompanied by private security guards, entered the premises of the Chief Mufti's Office in Sofia and forcibly evicted the staff. The applicant contended the police protected the new occupants. Subsequently, the new leader took control of all the assets of Bulgarian Muslim religious organizations. The first applicant challenged the lawfulness of the actions of the Council of Ministers before the Supreme Court, but his appeal was dismissed in July 1995. Mr Hasan was re-elected Chief Mufti by a conference of his supporters, however, the Council of Ministers did not reply to his request to be registered as the leader. In 1996 the Supreme Court ruled that the Council of Ministers had acted unlawfully by tacitly refusing to register him as Chief Mufti. The Council of Ministers did not grant registration to the applicant. Subsequently, the Union of Democratic Forces formed a new government in 1997 and it encouraged the applicant and his supporters to negotiate an agreement with Mr Gendzhev and his organisation. A unification conference was held in October 1997 and it elected a new leadership composed of the first applicant's supporters and others. Later that month the Deputy Prime Minister registered the newly elected leadership. Mr Gendzhev continued to claim he was the Chief Mufti but his position was not recognised by the Bulgarian courts. The applicants asserted that the forced replacement of their leadership in 1995, endorsed by the government, amounted to a violation of their right to manifest their religion. The Grand Chamber held that:

62. The Court recalls that religious communities traditionally and universally exist in the form of organised structures. They abide by rules which are often seen by followers as being of a divine origin. Religious ceremonies have their meaning and sacred value for the believers if they have been conducted by ministers empowered for that purpose in compliance with these rules. The personality of the religious ministers is undoubtedly of importance to every member of the community. Participation in the life of the community is thus a manifestation of one's religion, protected by Article 9 of the Convention.

Where the organisation of the religious community is at issue, Article 9 of the Convention must be interpreted in the light of Article 11, which safeguards associative life against unjustified State interference. Seen in this perspective, the believers' right to freedom of religion encompasses the expectation that the community will be allowed to function peacefully, free from arbitrary State intervention. Indeed, the autonomous existence of religious communities is indispensable for pluralism in a democratic society and is thus an issue at the very heart of the protection which Article 9 affords. It directly concerns not only the organisation of the community as such but also the effective enjoyment of the right to freedom of religion by all its active members. Were the organisational life of the community not protected by Article 9 of the Convention, all other aspects of the individual's freedom of religion would become vulnerable.

...

78. Nevertheless, the Court considers, like the Commission, that facts demonstrating a failure by the authorities to remain neutral in the exercise of their powers in this domain must lead to the conclusion that the State interfered with the believers' freedom to manifest their religion within the meaning of Article 9 of the Convention. It recalls that, but for very exceptional cases, the right to freedom of religion as guaranteed under the Convention excludes any discretion on the part of the State to determine whether religious beliefs or the means used to express such beliefs are legitimate. State action favouring one leader of a divided religious community or undertaken with the purpose of forcing the community to come together under a single leadership against its own wishes would likewise constitute an

interference with freedom of religion. In democratic societies the State does not need to take measures to ensure that religious communities are brought under a unified leadership (see *Serif*, cited
above, § 52).

82. The Court therefore finds, like the Commission, that Decree R-12, the decision of the Directorate of
Religious Denominations of 23 February 1995, and the subsequent refusal of the Council of Ministers
to recognise the existence of the organisation led by Mr Hasan were more than acts of routine registration or of correcting past irregularities. Their effect was to favour one faction of the Muslim community, granting it the status of the single official leadership, to the complete exclusion of the hitherto
recognised leadership. The acts of the authorities operated, in law and in practice, to deprive the
excluded leadership of any possibility of continuing to represent at least part of the Muslim community
and of managing its affairs according to the will of that part of the community.

   There was therefore an interference with the internal organisation of the Muslim religious community and with the applicants' right to freedom of religion as protected by Article 9 of the Convention.

The Grand Chamber went on to find that the interference was not 'prescribed by law' as it was
arbitrary and the repeated failures by the Council of Ministers to comply with the judgments
of the Supreme Court concerning the applicants constituted a breach of the rule of law.

   Subsequently, the organization headed by Mr Gendzhev challenged the government's activities in organizing the 1997 unification conference in *Supreme Holy Council of the Muslim
Community v Bulgaria*, judgment of 16 December 2004. The applicant organization asserted
that the authorities had manipulated that conference with the aim of favouring one leadership
faction over the other. A united Chamber observed that:

83. The Court considers that the applicant organisation's allegation that the mayors of a number of
localities and political figures participated too closely in the selection of delegates to the October 1997
assembly does not appear implausible.

The Chamber went on to hold that:

80. . . . Neutral mediation between groups of believers would not in principle amount to State interference with the believers' rights under Article 9 of the Convention, although the State authorities must
be cautious in this particularly delicate area.

. . .

94. In the present case, the relevant law and practice and the authorities' actions in October 1997 had
the effect of compelling the divided community to have a single leadership against the will of one of the
two rival leaderships.

95. As a result, one of the groups of leaders was favoured and the other excluded and deprived of the
possibility of continuing to manage autonomously the affairs and assets of that part of the community
which supported it.

. . .

98. In sum, the Court considers that the Bulgarian authorities went beyond the limits of their margin of
appreciation under Article 9(2) of the Convention.

99. It follows that the interference with the applicant organisation's rights under Article 9 of the
Convention in 1997 was not necessary in a democratic society for the protection of public order or the
rights and freedoms of others and was therefore contrary to that provision.

These two cases disclose strong suggestions of political considerations influencing governmental decisions concerning the recognition of religious leaders and their organisations. Two

governments, composed of different political parties, were responsible for the unlawful inter-ferences with Muslim organizations in Bulgaria.

The refusal of the Moldovan government and courts to grant legal recognition to a new religious organisation (the first applicant) which had split from the recognized, Orthodox Christian, Metropolitan Church of Moldova was determined to be an unjustifiable interfer-ence by a unanimous Chamber in *Metropolitan Church of Bessarabia and Others v Moldova*, 2001-XII. Under Moldovan law an unrecognized religious organization was not able to oper-ate, e.g. its clergy could not perform religious services and the organization was not entitled to judicial protection of its assets. Consequently, the Court concluded that the authorities' refusal was not a proportionate response to the legitimate aim of protecting public order and safety. Hence, States may be liable for interfering with the organisation of religious groups by either withdrawing official recognition (as in *Hasan and Chaush*) or refusing recognition (as in *Metropolitan Church*).

7   The Court has ruled that the ritual slaughter of animals in accordance with religious requirements falls within this aspect of Article 9: *The Jewish Liturgical Association Cha'are Shalom Ve Tsedek v France* (27 June 2000). The applicant Association had its origins in the 1980s as an orthodox group which split from the main Central Consistory (Union of Jewish Congregations of France). The Government had authorised the Central Consistory to designate persons who would conduct the ritual slaughter (involving in part the cutting of the throat of animals which had not been stunned) and certification of meat in conformity with the 'Shulchan Aruch' (prescriptions governing kosher meat). The applicant Association wished the animals to be slaughtered in accordance with even stricter religious requirements than those observed by the Central Consistory's designated slaughterers. Consequently, the Association applied to the authorities for permission to appoint its own certified slaughterers. The Minister of the Interior refused the Association's request because, *inter alia*, the Association was not suf-ficiently representative within the French Jewish community. The Association brought a com-plaint at Strasbourg alleging a breach of its right under Article 9 to manifest its religion through observance of the rites of the Jewish religion. The Court held that:

73. The Court next reiterates that Article 9 lists a number of forms which manifestation of one's reli-gion or belief may take, namely worship, teaching, practice and observance (see the *Kalaç v Turkey* judgment of 1 July 1997, *Reports* 1997-IV, p 1209, § 27). It is not contested that ritual slaughter, as indeed its name indicates, constitutes a rite or '*rite*' (the word in the French text of the Convention corresponding to 'observance' in the English), whose purpose is to provide Jews with meat from animals slaughtered in accordance with religious prescriptions, which is an essential aspect of practice of the Jewish religion. The applicant association employs ritual slaughterers and *kashrut* inspectors [person's who ensure the observance of Jewish food law] who slaughter animals in accordance with its prescriptions on the question, and it is likewise the applicant association which, by certifying as '*glatt*' [the strictest form of] kosher the meat sold in its members' butcher's shops, exercises religious super-vision of ritual slaughter.

74. It follows that the applicant association can rely on Article 9 of the Convention with regard to the French authorities' refusal to approve it, since ritual slaughter must be considered to be covered by a right guaranteed by the Convention, namely the right to manifest one's religion in observance, within the meaning of Article 9.

A majority of the Court, twelve votes to five, went on to conclude that there had not been a breach of the Association's right as the organization, and its members, could easily obtain sup-plies of 'glatt' meat from Belgium or they could seek to reach an agreement with the Central Con-sistory for the latter body to designate members of the Association as approved slaughterers.

Significantly, the Court stated that, '... the right to freedom of religion guaranteed by Article 9 of the Convention cannot extend to the right to take part in person in the performance of ritual slaughter ...' (para 81). Furthermore, States can also seek to justify restrictions on the religious slaughter of animals under the exceptions contained in Article 9(2), such as public safety or health.

8 The prohibition of female students wearing the Islamic headscarf, covering their hair and throat, whilst attending classes and examinations at Istanbul University was found not to violate Article 9 by a Chamber and Grand Chamber in *Leyla Sahin v Turkey*, judgment of 10 November 2005. In 1997 the applicant, who had completed four years of medical study at another Turkish medical school, enrolled at the Faculty of Medicine at Istanbul University. During February 1998 the Vice Chancellor of Istanbul University issued a circular, based upon the Constitution and his legal powers, providing that students wearing the Islamic headscarf (or with beards) must not be admitted to classes etc. Consequently, the applicant, who wore such a scarf out of religious conviction, was denied access to lectures and examinations. She challenged the legality of the circular before the administrative courts, but her complaints were rejected. She was subject to a formal disciplinary warning by the Dean of the Faculty of Medicine, in May 1998, for failing to comply with the University rules on dress. In April 1999, after a disciplinary hearing, she was suspended from the University, for one semester, in respect of her participation in an unauthorised demonstration at the University (against the dress rules). Her challenge to that decision was dismissed by the administrative court. Later in 1999 she abandoned her studies in Turkey and registered at Vienna University. She complained to Strasbourg alleging, *inter alia*, a breach of her right to manifest her religion. The Chamber was unanimous in finding no breach of the Convention. She then sought a re-hearing before the Grand Chamber. The latter found that the applicant's decision to wear the headscarf was motivated by a religion or belief (the Court did not decide whether the wearing of the scarf was a religious duty) and the University's decision to place restrictions on the wearing of the scarf was an interference with her right to manifest her religion. However, the restrictions were prescribed by law and for the legitimate aims of protecting the rights and freedoms of others and of protecting public order. The Grand Chamber found that the well established Turkish constitutional principle of secularism was the:

116. ... paramount consideration underlying the ban on the wearing of religious symbols in universities. In such a context, where the values of pluralism, respect for the rights of others and, in particular, equality before the law of men and women are being taught and applied in practice, it is understandable that the relevant authorities should wish to preserve the secular nature of the institution concerned and so consider it contrary to such values to allow religious attire, including, as in the present case, the Islamic headscarf, to be worn.

117. The Court must now determine whether in the instant case there was a reasonable relationship of proportionality between the means employed and the legitimate objectives pursued by the interference.

118. Like the Chamber (see paragraph 111 of its judgment), the Grand Chamber notes at the outset that it is common ground that practising Muslim students in Turkish universities are free, within the limits imposed by educational organisational constraints, to manifest their religion in accordance with habitual forms of Muslim observance. In addition, the resolution adopted by Istanbul University on 9 July 1998 shows that various other forms of religious attire are also forbidden on the university premises [prohibiting students from wearing clothes manifesting any religion, faith, race or political/ideological persuasion].

119. It should also be noted that when the issue of whether students should be allowed to wear the Islamic headscarf surfaced at Istanbul University in 1994 in relation to the medical courses, the Vice

Chancellor reminded them of the reasons for the rules on dress. Arguing that calls for permission to wear the Islamic headscarf in all parts of the university premises were misconceived and pointing to the public-order constraints applicable to medical courses, he asked the students to abide by the rules, which were consistent with both the legislation and the case-law of the higher courts.

120. Furthermore, the process whereby the regulations that led to the decision of 9 July 1998 were implemented took several years and was accompanied by a wide debate within Turkish society and the teaching profession. The two highest courts, the Supreme Administrative Court and the Constitutional Court, have managed to establish settled case-law on this issue. It is quite clear that throughout that decision-making process the university authorities sought to adapt to the evolving situation in a way that would not bar access to the university to students wearing the veil, through continued dialogue with those concerned, while at the same time ensuring that order was maintained and in particular that the requirements imposed by the nature of the course in question were complied with.

121. In that connection, the Court does not accept the applicant's submission that the fact that there were no disciplinary penalties for failing to comply with the dress code effectively meant that no rules existed. As to how compliance with the internal rules should have been secured, it is not for the Court to substitute its view for that of the university authorities. By reason of their direct and continuous contact with the education community, the university authorities are in principle better placed than an international court to evaluate local needs and conditions or the requirements of a particular course (see, *mutatis mutandis*, *Valsamis v Greece*, judgment of 18 December 1996, *Reports* 1996-VI, p 2325, § 32). Besides, having found that the regulations pursued a legitimate aim, it is not open to the Court to apply the criterion of proportionality in a way that would make the notion of an institution's 'internal rules' devoid of purpose. Article 9 does not always guarantee the right to behave in a manner governed by a religious belief (*Pichon and Sajous v France* (dec.), No 49853/99, ECHR 2001-X) and does not confer on people who do so the right to disregard rules that have proved to be justified (see the opinion of the Commission, § 51, contained in its report of 6 July 1995 appended to the *Valsamis* judgment cited above, p 2337).

122. In the light of the foregoing and having regard to the Contracting States' margin of appreciation in this sphere, the Court finds that the interference in issue was justified in principle and proportionate to the aim pursued.

123. Consequently, there has been no breach of Article 9 of the Convention.

Judge Tulkens dissented. She did not believe that the reasons underlying the restriction on the applicant's freedom to wear the Islamic headscarf at the University were relevant and sufficient.

10. . . . While everyone agrees on the need to prevent radical Islamism, a serious objection may nevertheless be made to such reasoning. Merely wearing the headscarf cannot be associated with fundamentalism and it is vital to distinguish between those who wear the headscarf and 'extremists' who seek to impose the headscarf as they do other religious symbols. Not all women who wear the headscarf are fundamentalists and there is nothing to suggest that the applicant held fundamentalist views. She is a young adult woman and a university student and might reasonably be expected to have a heightened capacity to resist pressure, it being noted in this connection that the judgment fails to provide any concrete example of the type of pressure concerned. The applicant's personal interest in exercising the right to freedom of religion and to manifest her religion by an external symbol cannot be wholly absorbed by the public interest in fighting extremism.

. . .

12. . . . The applicant, a young adult university student, said—and there is nothing to suggest that she was not telling the truth—that she wore the headscarf of her own free will. In this connection, I fail to see how the principle of sexual equality can justify prohibiting a woman from following a practice which, in the absence of proof to the contrary, she must be taken to have freely adopted. Equality and non-discrimination are subjective rights which must remain under the control of those who are entitled

to benefit from them. 'Paternalism' of this sort runs counter to the case-law of the Court, which has developed a real right to personal autonomy on the basis of Article 8 (*Keenan v the United Kingdom*, judgment 3 April 2001, § 92; *Pretty v the United Kingdom*, judgment of 29 April 2002, §§ 65–7; *Christine Goodwin v the United Kingdom*, judgment of 11 July 2002, § 90). Finally, if wearing the headscarf really was contrary to the principle of the equality of men and women in any event, the State would have a positive obligation to prohibit it in all places, whether public or private.

We have also seen the successful invocation of the need to protect the constitutional principle of secularism by Turkey in *Kalac*, above, and the principle was also central to the dissolution of the party in *Refah Partisi*, below p 732.

Article 9(2)

Express limitations on the right to manifest a person's religion or belief

....

Manoussakis v Greece 1996-IV 1346 (1996) 23 EHRR 387
European Court of Human Rights

The applicants were Jehovah's Witnesses living in Crete who rented a private room in a building for the purpose of holding religious and other meetings. In June 1983 they lodged, with the Minister of Education and Religious Affairs, an application for permission to use the room as a place of worship. Law No 1363/1938 provided that the construction and operation of temples (defined as any type of building open to the public for the purpose of divine worship) required the authorisation of the recognised ecclesiastical authorities and the Ministry of Education and Religious Affairs. Failure to obtain authorisation was made a criminal offence punishable with closure of the place of worship and imprisonment for persons operating the temple. A Royal Decree in 1939 provided that it was for the Minister of Education and Religious Affairs to determine whether there were essential reasons for granting an application. In July 1983 a local Orthodox parish church notified the police that the applicants' room was being used as an unauthorised place of worship and requested the taking of punitive action against those persons responsible for the room. During the subsequent two years the Ministry informed the applicants that it was not in a position to make a determination of their application. In 1986 the public prosecutor began criminal proceedings against the applicants under the 1938 Law. The first instance criminal court acquitted the applicants, but on appeal they were convicted and sentenced to three months' imprisonment (convertible to a fine). The applicants complained to the Commission that, *inter alia*, their rights under Article 9 had been violated. A unanimous Commission subsequently upheld the applicants' claim under this Article.

...

II. ALLEGED VIOLATION OF ARTICLE 9 OF THE CONVENTION

A. WHETHER THERE WAS AN INTERFERENCE

36. The validity of the private agreement concluded by the applicants on 30 March 1983 is not in dispute.

The applicants' conviction by the Heraklion Criminal Court sitting on appeal for having used the premises in question without the prior authorisation required under Law No 1363/1938 was therefore an interference with the exercise of their 'freedom . . . to manifest [their] religion . . ., in worship . . . and observance'. Such interference breaches Article 9 unless it was 'prescribed by law', pursued one or more of the legitimate aims referred to in paragraph 2 and was 'necessary in a democratic society' to attain such aim or aims.

B. JUSTIFICATION OF THE INTERFERENCE

1. 'Prescribed by law'

37. In the applicants' submission, Law No 1363/1938 and its implementing Decree of 20 May/2 June 1939 lay down a general and permanent prohibition on the establishment of a church or a place of worship of any religion—the law uses the term 'faith'—other than the orthodox religion. They maintained that this prohibition could only be lifted by a formal decision or a specific discretionary measure.

This discretionary power was, in their view, clearly derived from section 1 of Law No 1363/1938, which empowers the Government to grant or to refuse the authorisation, or to remain silent in response to an application duly submitted, without setting any limit as to time or establishing any substantive condition.

They argued that a law which made the practice of a religion subject to the prior grant of an authorisation, whose absence incurred liability to a criminal sanction, constituted an 'impediment' to that religion and could not be regarded as a law designed to protect freedom of religion within the meaning of Article 13 of the Constitution. As regards freedom of religion and worship, the Constitution purported to be more, or at least not less, protective than the Convention because the only grounds on which it permitted restrictions to be placed on the practice of any 'known religion' were 'public order' and 'public morals'.

In addition, the applicants pointed to the unusual character, as regards Greek public and administrative law, of the procedure established by Law No 1363/1938 for the construction or the operation of a place of worship. It was the only procedure in respect of which provision was made for the intervention of two authorities, administrative and religious. They criticised the manner in which the Supreme Administrative Court interpreted this Law, namely in the context of the restrictions, suggestions and directives of the Constitution, and the importance attached by that court to compliance with the conditions laid down by Royal Decree of 20 May/2 June 1939 for submitting in due form applications for authorisation together with all that those conditions entailed in terms of inquisitorial process and the difficulty in obtaining such authorisation. The wording of this decree conferred a number of different discretionary powers, each of which was sufficient basis for a negative response to the application.

38. The Court notes that the applicants' complaint is directed less against the treatment of which they themselves had been the victims than the general policy of obstruction pursued in relation to Jehovah's Witnesses when they wished to set up a church or a place of worship. They are therefore in substance challenging the provisions of the relevant domestic law.

However, the Court does not consider it necessary to rule on the question whether the interference in issue was 'prescribed by law' in this instance because, in any event, it was incompatible with Article 9 of the Convention on other grounds.

2. Legitimate aim

39. According to the Government, the penalty imposed on the applicants served to protect public order and the rights and freedoms of others. In the first place, although the notion of public order had features that were common to the democratic societies in Europe, its substance varied on account of national characteristics. In Greece virtually the entire population was of the Christian Orthodox faith, which was closely associated with important moments in the history of the Greek nation. The Orthodox Church had kept alive the national conscience and Greek patriotism during the periods of foreign

occupation. Secondly, various sects sought to manifest their ideas and doctrines using all sorts of 'unlawful and dishonest' means. The intervention of the State to regulate this area with a view to protecting those whose rights and freedoms were affected by the activities of socially dangerous sects was indispensable to maintain public order on Greek territory.

40. Like the applicants, the Court recognises that the States are entitled to verify whether a movement or association carries on, ostensibly in pursuit of religious aims, the activities which are harmful to the population. Nevertheless, it recalls that Jehovah's Witnesses come within the definition of 'known religion' as provided for under Greek law. (See *Kokkinakis v Greece*.) This was moreover conceded by the Government.

However, having regard to the circumstances of the case and taking the same view as the Commission, the Court considers that the impugned measure pursued a legitimate aim for the purposes of Article 9(2) of the Convention, namely the protection of public order.

3. 'Necessary in a democratic society'

41. The main thrust of the applicants' complaint is that the restrictions imposed on Jehovah's Witnesses by the Greek Government effectively prevent them from exercising their right to freedom of religion. In terms of the legislation and administrative practice, their religion did not, so they claimed, enjoy in Greece the safeguards guaranteed to it in all the other Member States of the Council of Europe. The 'pluralism, tolerance and broadmindedness without which there is no democratic society' was therefore seriously jeopardised in Greece.

They contended that the Jehovah's Witnesses' movement should be presumed—even if the presumption was a rebuttable one—to respect certain moral rules and not in itself to prejudice public order. Its doctrines and its rites abided by and extolled social order and individual morality. Accordingly, the political authorities should intervene only in the event of abuse or perversion of such doctrines and rites, and should do so punitively rather than preventively.

More particularly, their conviction had been persecutory, unjustified and not necessary in a democratic society as it had been 'manufactured' by the State. The State had compelled the applicants to commit an offence and to bear the consequences solely because of their religious beliefs. The apparently innocent requirement of an authorisation to operate a place of worship had been transformed from a mere formality into a lethal weapon against the right to freedom of religion. The term 'dilatory' used by the Commission to describe the conduct of the Minister of Education and Religious Affairs in relation to their application for an authorisation was euphemistic.

The struggle for survival by certain religious communities outside the Eastern Orthodox Church, and specifically by Jehovah's Witnesses, was carried on in a climate of interference and oppression by the State and the dominant church as a result of which Article 9 of the Convention had become a dead letter. The Article was the object of frequent and blatant violations aimed at eliminating freedom of religion. The applicants cited current practice in Greece in support of their contentions, giving numerous examples. They requested the Court to examine their complaints in the context of these other cases.

42. According to the Government, in order to resolve the question of the necessity of the applicants' conviction, the Court should first examine the necessity of the requirement of prior authorisation, which owed its existence to historical considerations. In their view, the former presupposed the latter. The applicants' true aim was not to complain about their conviction but to fight for the abolition of that requirement.

There were essential public order grounds to justify making the setting up of a place of worship subject to approval by the State. In Greece this control applied to all faiths; otherwise it would be both unconstitutional and contrary to the Convention. Jehovah's Witnesses were not exempt from the requirements of legislation which concerned the whole population. The setting up of a church or a place of worship in Greece was, so the Government affirmed, often used as a means of proselytism, in particular by Jehovah's Witnesses who engaged in intensive proselytism, thereby infringing the law that the Court had itself found to be in conformity with the Convention. (See *Kokkinakis v Greece*.)

The sanction imposed on the applicants had been light and had been motivated not by the manifestation by them of their religion but by their disobedience to the law and their failure to comply with an administrative procedure. It was the result of the applicants' culpable neglect to have recourse to the remedy available under the Greek legal system.

Finally, the Government referred to the fact that various States parties to the Convention had legislation containing restrictions similar to those enacted in Greece in this field.

43. The Commission considered that the authorisation requirement introduced by Law No 1363/1938 might appear open to criticism. In the first place, the intervention of the Greek Orthodox Church in the procedure raised a complex question under paragraph 2 of Article 9. Secondly, classifying as a criminal offence the operation of a place of worship without the authorities' prior authorisation was disproportionate to the legitimate aim pursued, especially when, as in this case, the underlying cause of the applicants' conviction lay in the dilatory attitude of the relevant authorities.

44. As a matter of case law, the Court has consistently left the Contracting States a certain margin of appreciation in assessing the existence and extent of the necessity of an interference, but this margin is subject to European supervision, embracing both the legislation and the decisions applying it. The Court's task is to determine whether the measures taken at national level were justified in principle and proportionate.

In delimiting the extent of the margin of appreciation in the present case the Court must have regard to what is at stake, namely the need to secure true religious pluralism, an inherent feature of the notion of a democratic society. Further, considerable weight has to be attached to that need when it comes to determining, pursuant to paragraph 2 of Article 9, whether the restriction was proportionate to the legitimate aim pursued. The restrictions imposed on the freedom to manifest religion by the provisions of Law No 1363/1938 and of the Decree of 20 May/2 June 1939 call for very strict scrutiny by the Court.

45. The Court notes in the first place that Law No 1363/1938 and the Decree of 20 May/2 June 1939—which concerns churches and places of worship that are not part of the Greek Orthordox Church—allow far-reaching interferences by the political, administrative and ecclesiastical authorities with the exercise of religious freedom. In addition to the numerous formal conditions prescribed in section 1(1) and (3) of the decree, some of which confer a very wide discretion on the police, mayor or chairman of the district council, there exists in practice the possibility for the Minister of Education and Religious Affairs to defer his reply indefinitely—the decree does not lay down any time-limit—or to refuse his authorisation without explanation or without giving a valid reason. In this respect, the Court observes that the decree empowers the Minister—in particular when determining whether the number of those requesting an authorisation corresponds to that mentioned in the decree—to assess whether there is a 'real need' for the religious community in question to set up a church. This criterion may in itself constitute grounds for refusal, without reference to the conditions laid down in Article 13(2) of the Constitution.

46. The Government maintained that the power of the Minister of Education and Religious Affairs to grant or refuse the authorisation requested was not discretionary. He was under a duty to grant the authorisation if he found that the three conditions set down in Article 13(2) of the Constitution were satisfied, namely that it must be in respect of a known religion, that there must be no risk of prejudicing public order or public morals and that there is no danger of proselytism.

47. The Court observes that, in reviewing the lawfulness of refusals to grant the authorisation, the Supreme Administrative Court has developed case law limiting the Minister's power in this matter and according the local ecclesiastical authority a purely consultative role.

The right to freedom of religion as guaranteed under the Convention excludes any discretion on the part of the State to determine whether religious beliefs or the means used to express such beliefs are legitimate. Accordingly, the Court takes the view that the authorisation requirement under Law No 1363/1938 and the Decree of 20 May/2 June 1939 is consistent with Article 9 of the Convention only in so far as it is intended to allow the Minister to verify whether the formal conditions laid down in those enactments are satisfied.

48. It appears from the evidence and from the numerous other cases cited by the applicants and not contested by the Government that the State has tended to use the possibilities afforded by the above-mentioned provisions to impose rigid, or indeed prohibitive, conditions on practice of religious beliefs by certain non-orthodox movements, in particular Jehovah's Witnesses. Admittedly the Supreme Administrative Court quashes for lack of reasons any unjustified refusal to grant an authorisation, but the extensive case law in this field seems to show a clear tendency on the part of the administrative and ecclesiastical authorities to use these provisions to restrict the activities of faiths outside the Orthodox church.

49. In the instant case the applicants were prosecuted and convicted for having operated a place of worship without first obtaining the authorisations required by law.

50. In their memorial the Government maintained that under section 1(1) of the Decree of 20 May/2 June 1939 an authorisation from the local bishop was necessary only for the construction and opera-tion of a church and not for a place of worship as in the present case. An application to the Minister of Education and Religious Affairs, indeed one such as that submitted by the applicants, was sufficient.

51. The Court notes, nevertheless, that both the Heraklion public prosecutor's office, when it was bringing proceedings against the applicants, and the Heraklion Criminal Court sitting on appeal, in its judgment of 15 February 1990, relied expressly on the lack of the bishop's authorisation as well as the lack of an authorisation from the Minister of Education and Religious Affairs. The latter, in response to five requests made by the applicants between 25 October 1983 and 10 December 1984, replied that he was examining their file. To date, as far as the Court is aware, the applicants have not received an express decision. Moreover, at the hearing a representative of the Government himself described the Minister's conduct as unfair and attributed it to the difficulty that the latter might have had in giving legally valid reasons for an express decision refusing the authorisation or to his fear that he might pro-vide the applicants with grounds for appealing to the Supreme Administrative Court to challenge an express administrative decision.

52. In these circumstances the Court considers that the Government cannot rely on the applicants' fail-ure to comply with a legal formality to justify their conviction. The degree of severity of the sanction is immaterial.

53. Like the Commission, the Court is of the opinion that the impugned conviction had such a direct effect on the applicants' freedom of religion that it cannot be regarded as proportionate to the legit-imate aim pursued, nor, accordingly, as necessary in a democratic society.

In conclusion, there has been a violation of Article 9.

. . .

For these reasons, THE COURT unanimously

. . .

Holds that there has been a breach of Article 9 of the Convention;

. . .

NOTES

1   The Court was composed of President Bernhardt and Judges: Macdonald, Valticos, Martens, Loizou, Freeland, Wildhaber, Gotchev, and Kuris. Martens J issued a separate concurring opin-ion in which he expressed the view that Law No 1363/1938 was in breach of Article 9 for con-taining too many discretionary elements (such as the 'advisory' role of the established clerical

authorities) to satisfy the Convention's 'prescribed by law' requirements (for an examination of these in the context of Article 8 see above p 586).

2   The above judgment makes clear that States may operate a prior registration/approval scheme for places of worship. However, the Court will closely examine whether the application of a national scheme to a particular group of worshippers complies with the conditions laid down in Article 9(2).

3   In *Pentidis v Greece*, 1997-III 983, the applicants, who were Jehovah's Witnesses, had been convicted under Law No 1363/1938 for establishing a place of worship (a rented room) without authorization by the competent authorities. The Commission found a breach of Article 9. Before the Court, the applicants stated that they had applied, in February 1997, to the Minister for permission to operate their place of worship. By early May 1997 the Minister had granted them permission and they requested the Court to strike out their case. The Court agreed to their request.

4   In *Martins Casimiro and Cerveira Ferreira v Luxembourg* (decision of 27 April 1999), the applicants and their son, F, were Seventh-day Adventists (this religious group believed Saturday should be a day of total rest). They sought permission from the domestic courts for their son to be exempted from the legal duty of attending school on Saturdays. When their request was refused the applicants complained to the Court alleging a breach of their right to freely manifest their religion. The Court declared their application inadmissible because:

The dispensation requested by the applicants would have had the effect of excluding the child from the normal school timetable as Saturday was one of the days of the school week. The court of first instance had stated that dispensation of that sort would have infringed the rights of the other pupils, too, as it was potentially disruptive of the school system. States had a duty to ensure that children were able to exercise their right to education. Furthermore, where the parents' right to respect for their religious convictions, rather than enhancing the child's right to education, came into conflict with it, the interests of the child prevailed. Under the circumstances, the Court held that the statutory provision that precluded the applicants from being granted general dispensation from the obligation to ensure that their son, a minor, attended school on Saturdays was justified for the protection of the rights and freedoms of others, notably the right to education . . .

12 ARTICLE 10 FREEDOM OF EXPRESSION

The Court's general approach

Handyside v United Kingdom A.24 (1976) 1 EHRR 737
European Court of Human Rights

The applicant was a publisher who secured the British rights to a book called *The Little Red Schoolbook* which was originally written and published in Denmark. After translations it had also been published by others in a number of Member states; including, Belgium, France, Germany, Greece, Italy and Sweden. The applicant arranged an English translation and then prepared an edition for the UK with the help of various children and teachers. This was to be a reference book of 208 pages and costing 30p. It included chapters on, *inter alia*, 'Education', 'Teachers' and 'Pupils'; the latter chapter contained 26 pages of information on matters concerning sex (topics included, abortion, homosexuality, intercourse and masturbation). After printing, the applicant sent out several hundred review copies and placed a number of advertisements in the specialist educational/publishing press. Subsequently, the book was subject to widespread comment, both favourable and critical, in popular newspapers. A number of complaints were made to the Director of Public Prosecutions about the book and he asked the Metropolitan Police to investigate the matter. They obtained a search warrant, granted by the judicial authorities under the Obscene Publications Act 1959, authorising a search of the applicant's business premises. A number of copies of the book were seized during the search. Soon afterwards the applicant was charged with having in his possession several hundred copies of an obscene publication (*The Schoolbook*) for gain; contrary to the 1959 Act. The Magistrates' Court found him guilty and fined him £50 and made a forfeiture order for the destruction of the books that had been seized. The applicant appealed to the Inner London Quarter Sessions, but that court upheld the Magistrates' decisions and the books were destroyed. Several thousand copies of the book had been sold throughout the UK before the applicant had been prosecuted. No proceedings were brought in Northern Ireland, the Channel Islands or the Isle of Man, but unsuccessful prosecutions were brought in Scotland. Later the applicant published a revised edition of the book taking account of the prosecution's criticisms of the original text, no legal action was taken against the amended version. The applicant complained to the Commission alleging a breach of a number of his Convention rights, including his right to freedom of expression under Article 10. By a majority (of eight votes to five, with one abstention) the Commission found no violation of Article 10.

I. ON THE ALLEGED VIOLATION OF ARTICLE 10 OF THE CONVENTION
...

43. The various measures challenged—the applicant's criminal conviction, the seizure and subsequent forfeiture and destruction of the matrix and of hundreds of copies of the Schoolbook—were without any doubt, and the Government did not deny it, 'interferences by public authority' in the exercise of his freedom of expression which is guaranteed by paragraph I of the text cited above. Such interferences entail a 'violation' of Article 10 if they do not fall within one of the exceptions provided for in paragraph 2, which is accordingly of decisive importance in this case.

44. If the 'restrictions' and 'penalties' complained of by Mr Handyside are not to infringe Article 10, they must, according to paragraph 2, in the first place have been 'prescribed by law'. The Court finds that this was the case. In the United Kingdom legal system, the basis in law for the measures in question was the 1959/1964 Acts . . . Besides, this was not contested by the applicant who further admitted that the competent authorities had correctly applied those Acts.

45. Having thus ascertained that the interferences complained of satisfied the first of the conditions in paragraph 2 of Article 10, the Court then investigated whether they also complied with the others. According to the Government and the majority of the Commission, the interferences were 'necessary in a democratic society', 'for the protection of . . . morals'.

46. Sharing the view of the Government and the unanimous opinion of the Commission, the Court first finds that the 1959/1964 Acts have an aim that is legitimate under Article 10 § 2, namely, the protection of morals in a democratic society . . .

47. The Court must also investigate whether the protection of morals in a democratic society necessitated the various measures taken against the applicant and the Schoolbook under the 1959/1964 Acts. . . .

The Commission's report and the subsequent hearings before the Court in June 1976 brought to light clear-cut differences of opinion on a crucial problem, namely, how to determine whether the actual 'restrictions' and 'penalties' complained of by the applicant were 'necessary in a democratic society', 'for the protection of morals'. According to the Government and the majority of the Commission, the Court has only to ensure that the English courts acted reasonably, in good faith and within the limits of the margin of appreciation left to the Contracting States by Article 10 § 2. On the other hand the minority of the Commission sees the Court's task as being not to review the Inner London Quarter Sessions judgment but to examine the Schoolbook directly in the light of the Convention and of nothing but the Convention.

48. The Court points out that the machinery of protection established by the Convention is subsidiary to the national systems safeguarding human rights (judgment of 23 July 1968 on the merits of the 'Belgian Linguistic' case, Series A No 6, p 35, § 10 *in fine*). The Convention leaves to each Contracting State, in the first place, the task of securing the rights and freedoms it enshrines. The institutions created by it make 'their own contribution to this task but they become involved only through contentious proceedings and once all domestic remedies have been exhausted' (Article 26).

These observations apply, notably, to Article 10 § 2. In particular, it is not possible to find in the domestic law of the various Contracting States a uniform European conception of morals. The view taken by their respective laws of the requirements of morals varies from time to time and from place to place, especially in our era which is characterised by a rapid and far-reaching evolution of opinions on the subject. By reason of their direct and continuous contact with the vital forces of their countries, State authorities are in principle in a better position than the international judge to give an opinion on the exact content of these requirements as well as on the 'necessity' of a 'restriction' or 'penalty' intended to meet them. The Court notes at this juncture that, whilst the adjective 'necessary', within the meaning of Article 10 § 2, is not synonymous with 'indispensable' (cf, in Articles 2 § 2 and 6 § 1, the words 'absolutely necessary' and 'strictly necessary' and, in Article 15 § 1, the phrase 'to the extent strictly required by the exigencies of the situation'), neither has it the flexibility of such expressions as 'admissible', 'ordinary' (cf Article 4 § 3), 'useful' (cf the French text of the first paragraph of Article 1 of Protocol No 1), 'reasonable' (cf Articles 5 § 3 and 6 § 1) or 'desirable'. Nevertheless, it is for the national authorities to make the initial assessment of the reality of the pressing social need implied by the notion of 'necessity' in this context.

Consequently, Article 10 § 2 leaves to the Contracting States a margin of appreciation. This margin is given both to the domestic legislator ('prescribed by law') and to the bodies, judicial amongst others, that are called upon to interpret and apply the laws in force (*Engel and Others* judgment of 8 June 1976, Series A No 22, pp 41–2, § 100; cf, for Article 8 § 2, *De Wilde, Ooms and Versyp* judgment of 18 June 1971, Series A No 12, pp 45–6, § 93, and the *Golder* judgment of 21 February 1975, Series A No 18, pp 21–2, § 45).

49. Nevertheless, Article 10 § 2 does not give the Contracting States an unlimited power of appreciation. The Court, which, with the Commission, is responsible for ensuring the observance of those States engagements (Article 19), is empowered to give the final ruling on whether a 'restriction' or 'penalty' is reconcilable with freedom of expression as protected by Article 10. The domestic margin of appreciation thus goes hand in hand with a European supervision. Such supervision concerns both the aim of the measure challenged and its 'necessity'; it covers not only the basic legislation but also the decision applying it, even one given by an independent court. In this respect, the Court refers to Article 50 of the Convention ('decision or . . . measure taken by a legal authority or any other authority') as well as to its own case-law (*Engel and Others* judgment of 8 June 1976, Series A No 22, pp 41–2, § 100).

The Court's supervisory functions oblige it to pay the utmost attention to the principles characterising a 'democratic society'. Freedom of expression constitutes one of the essential foundations of such a society, one of the basic conditions for its progress and for the development of every man. Subject to paragraph 2 of Article 10, it is applicable not only to 'information' or 'ideas' that are favourably received or regarded as inoffensive or as a matter of indifference, but also to those that offend, shock or disturb the State or any sector of the population. Such are the demands of that pluralism, tolerance and broadmindedness without which there is no 'democratic society'. This means, amongst other things, that every 'formality', 'condition', 'restriction' or 'penalty' imposed in this sphere must be proportionate to the legitimate aim pursued.

From another standpoint, whoever exercises his freedom of expression undertakes 'duties and responsibilities' the scope of which depends on his situation and the technical means he uses. The Court cannot overlook such a person's 'duties' and 'responsibilities' when it enquires, as in this case, whether 'restrictions' or 'penalties' were conducive to the 'protection of morals' which made them 'necessary' in a 'democratic society'.

50. It follows from this that it is in no way the Court's task to take the place of the competent national courts but rather to review under Article 10 the decisions they delivered in the exercise of their power of appreciation.

However, the Court's supervision would generally prove illusory if it did no more than examine these decisions in isolation; it must view them in the light of the case as a whole, including the publication in question and the arguments and evidence adduced by the applicant in the domestic legal system and then at the international level. The Court must decide, on the basis of the different data available to it, whether the reasons given by the national authorities to justify the actual measures of 'interference' they take are relevant and sufficient under Article 10 § 2 (cf, for Article 5 § 3, the *Wemhoff* judgment of 27 June 1968, Series A No 7, pp 24–5, § 12, the *Neumeister* judgment of 27 June 1968, Series A No 8, p 37, § 5, the *Stögmüller* judgment of 10 November 1969, Series A No; 9, p 39, § 3, the *Mattznetter* judgment of 10 November 1969, Series A No 10, p 31, § 3, and the *Ringeisen* judgment of 16 July 1971, Series A No 13, p 42, § 104.

51. Following the method set out above, the Court scrutinized under Article 10 § 2 the individual decisions complained of, in particular, the judgment of the Inner London Quarter Sessions. . . .

52. The Court attaches particular importance to a factor to which the judgment of 29 October 1971 did not fail to draw attention, that is, the intended readership of the Schoolbook. It was aimed above all at children and adolescents aged from twelve to eighteen. Being direct, factual and reduced to essentials

in style, it was easily within the comprehension of even the youngest of such readers. The applicant had made it clear that he planned a wide-spread circulation. . . .

Basically the book contained purely factual information that was generally correct and often useful, as the Quarter Sessions recognised. However, it also included, above all in the section on sex and in the passage headed 'Be yourself' in the chapter on pupils . . . sentences or paragraphs that young people at a critical stage of their development could have interpreted as an encouragement to indulge in precocious activities harmful for them or even to commit certain criminal offences. In these circumstances, despite the variety and the constant evolution in the United Kingdom of views on ethics and education, the competent English judges were entitled, in the exercise of their discretion, to think at the relevant time that the Schoolbook would have pernicious effects on the morals of many of the children and adolescents who would read it.

However, the applicant maintained, in substance, that the demands of the 'protection of morals' or, to use the wording of the 1959/1964 Acts, of the war against publications likely to 'deprave and corrupt', were but a pretext in his case. The truth of the matter, he alleged, was that an attempt had been made to muzzle a small-scale publisher whose political leanings met with the disapproval of a fragment of public opinion. Proceedings were set in motion, said he, in an atmosphere little short of 'hysteria', stirred up and kept alive by ultra-conservative elements. . . .

For its part the Court finds that the anti-authoritarian aspects of the Schoolbook as such were not held in the judgment of 29 October 1971 to fall foul of the 1959/1964 Acts. Those aspects were taken into account only insofar as the appeal court considered that, by undermining the moderating influence of parents, teachers, the Churches and youth organisations, they aggravated the tendency to 'deprave and corrupt' which in its opinion resulted from other parts of the work. It should be added that the revised edition was allowed to circulate freely by the British authorities despite the fact that the anti-authoritarian passages again appeared there in full and even, in some cases, in stronger terms.

As the Government noted, this is hard to reconcile with the theory of a political intrigue.

The Court thus allows that the fundamental aim of the judgment of 29 October 1971, applying the 1959/1964 Acts, was the protection of the morals of the young, a legitimate purpose under Article 10 § 2. Consequently the seizures effected on 31 March and 1 April 1971, pending the outcome of the proceedings that were about to open, also had this aim.

53. It remains to examine the 'necessity' of the measures in dispute, beginning with the said seizures. . . .

54. A series of arguments which merit reflection was advanced by the applicant and the minority of the Commission concerning the 'necessity' of the sentence and the forfeiture at issue.

Firstly, they drew attention to the fact that the original edition of the Schoolbook was the object of no proceedings in Northern Ireland, the Isle of Man and the Channel Islands and of no conviction in Scotland and that, even in England and Wales, thousands of copies circulated without impediment despite the judgment of 29 October 1971. . . . The competent authorities in Northern Ireland, the Isle of Man and the Channel Islands may, in the light of local conditions, have had plausible reasons for not taking action against the book and its publisher. . . . Their failure to act—into which the Court does not have to enquire and which did not prevent the measures taken in England from leading to revision of the Schoolbook—does not prove that the judgment of 29 October 1971 was not a response to a real necessity, bearing in mind the national authorities' margin of appreciation.

These remarks also apply, *mutatis mutandis*, to the circulation of many copies in England and Wales.

. . .

57. The applicant and the minority of the Commission laid stress on the further point that, in addition to the original Danish edition, translations of the 'Little Book' appeared and circulated freely in the majority of the member States of the Council of Europe.

Here again, the national margin of appreciation and the optional nature of the 'restrictions' and 'penalties' referred to in Article 10 § 2 prevent the Court from accepting the argument. The Contracting States have each fashioned their approach in the light of the situation obtaining in their respective territories;

they have had regard, inter alia, to the different views prevailing there about the demands of the protection of morals in a democratic society. The fact that most of them decided to allow the work to be distributed does not mean that the contrary decision of the Inner London Quarter Sessions was a breach of Article 10. Besides, some of the editions published outside the United Kingdom do not include the passages, or at least not all the passages, cited in the judgment of 29 October 1971 as striking examples of a tendency to 'deprave and corrupt'.

...

59. On the strength of the data before it, the Court thus reaches the conclusion that no breach of the requirements of Article 10 has been established in the circumstances of the present case.

...

FOR THESE REASONS, THE COURT

Holds by thirteen votes to one that there has been no breach of Article 10 of the Convention;

...

NOTES

1   The Court was composed of; President Balladore Pallieri and Judges: Zekia, Wiarda, Pedersen, Thor Vilhjalmsson, Petren, Ryssdal, Bozer, Ganshof van der Meersch, Fitzmaurice, Bindschedler-Robert, Evrignis, and Delvaux. Judge Mosler dissented on the ground that he had a different conception of the meaning to be given to the term 'necessary' in Article 10(2). For him this expression meant that the measures taken by the national authorities had to be 'appropriate for achieving the [legitimate] aim' under Article 10(2). He did not believe that the English measures were appropriate to achieve their aim of protecting schoolchildren from gaining access to the book as (1) many copies had already been distributed before the prosecution of Handyside and (2) he could not understand why legal action against the publication of the book had not been taken in other parts of the UK if the authorities considered that it presented such a danger to the moral welfare of youngsters.

2   The majority's elaboration of the concept of 'necessary in a democratic society' as involving the existence of a 'pressing social need' has been accepted in subsequent cases as the authoritative interpretation.

3   When studying the cases involving Article 10 do you think that the Court's judgments exhibit the values of 'pluralism, tolerance and broadmindedness' when confronted with those who express views that 'offend, shock or disturb the State or any sector of the population'?

4   The Court has ruled that in certain circumstances Article 10, as with a number of other substantive rights enshrined in the Convention, imposes positive obligations upon Member states. In *Ozgur Gundem v Turkey* (16 March 2000), the applicant newspaper was represented by its editor and owners. The paper had been published between 1992 and 1994. During that time the paper alleged that it had been subject to serious attacks and harassment, for which the Turkish authorities were directly or indirectly responsible, and that despite repeated requests the government had done little to protect the paper and its staff. It was not disputed that seven persons connected with the paper (including journalists) had been killed by 'unknown perpetrators', armed attacks on newsagents selling the paper had occurred and two bombs had exploded at offices of the paper. The paper argued, *inter alia*, that the State's failure to protect the paper and its personnel violated Article 10. In a unanimous judgment:

The Court recalls the key importance of freedom of expression as one of the preconditions for a functioning democracy. Genuine, effective exercise of this freedom does not depend merely on the State's duty not to interfere, but may require positive measures of protection, even in the sphere of relations between individuals (*mutatis mutandis*, the *X and Y v The Netherlands*, A.91 (1985)). In determining whether or not a positive obligation exists, regard must be had to the fair balance that has to be struck between the general interest of the community and the interests of the individual, the search for which is called for throughout the Convention. The scope of this obligation will inevitably vary, having regard to the diversity of situations obtaining in Contracting States, the difficulties involved in policing modern societies and the choices which must be made in terms of priorities and resources. Nor must such an obligation be interpreted in such a way as to impose an impossible or disproportionate burden on the authorities (see, *Rees v UK*, A.106 (1986) and *Osman v UK*, Reports 1998-VIII).

In the present case, the authorities were aware that *Ozgur Gundem*, and persons associated with it, had been subject to a series of violent acts and that the applicants feared that they were being targeted deliberately in efforts to prevent publication and distribution of the newspaper. No response however was given to almost all petitions and requests for protection submitted by the newspaper or its staff. The Government have only been able to identify one protective measure concerning the distribution of the newspaper which was taken while the newspaper was still in existence. . . .

The Court has noted the Government's submissions concerning its strongly-held conviction that *Ozgur Gundem* and its staff supported the PKK and acted as its propaganda tool. This does not, even if true, provide a justification for failing to take steps effectively to investigate and, where necessary, provide protection against unlawful acts involving violence.

The Court concludes that the Government have failed, in the circumstances, to comply with their positive obligation to protect *Ozgur Gundem* in the exercise of its freedom of expression. (paras 43–6)

Where the interferences with persons' freedom of expression are less extreme than in the above case the corresponding positive obligations upon States will also be of reduced magnitude.

For example, in *Appleby and Others v UK*, judgment of 6 May 2003, a Chamber refused to hold that States were under a positive obligation to secure a general right of access to private property for persons wishing to engage in political expression. The applicants sought to gain access to the privately owned town centre, the 'Galleries' shopping and office complex, in Washington (Tyne and Wear), to publicize their opposition to the proposed development of a public park in another part of the town. The company that owned the Galleries refused the applicants access to its property, as it stated that it had a policy of strict neutrality concerning all political and religious issues. Before the Court the applicants contended that Article 10 obliged the government to secure their right to freedom of expression within the Galleries. By a large majority, six votes to one, the Court held that:

47. [Article 10] notwithstanding the acknowledged importance of freedom of expression, does not bestow any freedom of forum for the exercise of that right. While it is true that demographic, social, economic and technological developments are changing the ways in which people move around and come into contact with each other, the Court is not persuaded that this requires the automatic creation of rights of entry to private property, or even, necessarily, to all publicly owned property (government offices and ministries, for instance). Where, however, the bar on access to property has the effect of preventing any effective exercise of freedom of expression or it can be said that the essence of the right has been destroyed, the Court would not exclude that a positive obligation could arise for the State to protect the enjoyment of the Convention rights by regulating property rights. A corporate town where the entire municipality is controlled by a private body might be an example . . .

48. In the present case, the restriction on the applicants' ability to communicate their views was limited to the entrance areas and passageways of the Galleries. It did not prevent them from obtaining individual permission from businesses within the Galleries (the manager of a hypermarket granted permission for a stand within his store on one occasion) or from distributing their leaflets on the public access paths into the area. It also remained open to them to campaign in the old town centre and to employ

alternative means, such as calling door-to-door or seeking exposure in the local press, radio and television. The applicants did not deny that these other methods were available to them. Their argument, essentially, was that the easiest and most effective method of reaching people was to use the Galleries ... The Court does not consider, however, that the applicants can claim that they were, as a result of the refusal of the private company, Postel, effectively prevented from communicating their views to their fellow citizens. Some 3,200 people submitted letters in support [of the applicants' petition to oppose the proposed development]. Whether more would have done so if the stand had remained in the Galleries is speculation which is insufficient to support an argument that the applicants were unable otherwise to exercise their freedom of expression in a meaningful manner.

49. Balancing the rights in issue and having regard to the nature and scope of the restriction in this case, the Court does not find that the respondent State failed in any positive obligation to protect the applicants' freedom of expression.

50. Consequently, there has been no violation of Article 10 of the Convention.

Judge Maruste issued a dissenting opinion in which he expressed the view that:

... the property rights of the owners of the shopping mall were unnecessarily given priority over the applicants' freedom of expression and assembly.

The case raises the important issue of the State's positive obligations in a modern liberal society where many traditionally State-owned services like post, transport, energy, health and community services and others have been or could be privatised. In this situation, should private owners' property rights prevail over other rights or does the State still have some responsibility to secure the proper balance between private and public interests?

... It cannot be the case that through privatisation the public authorities can divest themselves of all responsibility to protect rights and freedoms other than property rights. They still bear responsibility for deciding how the forum created by them is to be used and for ensuring that public interests and individuals' rights are respected. It is in the public interest to permit reasonable exercise of individual rights and freedoms, including the freedoms of speech and assembly on the property of a privately owned shopping centre, and not to make some public services and institutions inaccessible to the public and participants in demonstrations. The Court has consistently held that, if there is a conflict between rights and freedoms, the freedom of expression takes precedence. But in this case it appears to be the other way round—property rights prevailed over freedom of speech.

Of course, it would clearly be too far-reaching to say that no limitations can be put on the exercise of rights and freedoms on private land or premises. They should be exercised in a manner consistent with respect for owners' rights too. And that is exactly what the Chamber did not take into account in this case. The public authorities did not carry out a balancing exercise and did not regulate how the privately owned *forum publicum* was to be used in the public interest. The old traditional rule that the private owner has an unfettered right to eject people from his land and premises without giving any justification and without any test of reasonableness being applied is no longer fully adapted to contemporary conditions and society. Consequently, the State failed to discharge its positive obligations under Articles 10 and 11.

Do you think the applicants suffered a significant restriction on their freedom of expression through being denied access to the Galleries?

The margin of appreciation

Another important aspect of the Court's judgment in *Handyside* is its articulation of the idea of the 'margin of appreciation'. This variable discretion is granted to national authorities by the Court when it examines whether a State has violated an applicant's Convention rights under Articles 8–11. It has also been applied, less frequently, in cases involving other rights including, Article 5 (*Winterwerp v Netherlands*, A.33 (1979) 2 EHRR 387), Article 14 (*Rasmussen v Denmark*, A.87 (1984) 7 EHRR 371) and Article 1 of the First Protocol (*James v UK*, A.98 (1986) 8 EHRR 123). The creation and use of this concept by the Court has been controversial with different judges taking opposing stances on the concept (e.g. see below the majority and dissenting judgments in *The Sunday Times v UK*) and academic writers supporting or criticizing the doctrine.

1   In a major study examining the Court's utilization of the concept across the range of Convention rights Howard Yourow describes the construct in the following terms:

... the margin doctrine is a technique for weighing and balancing claims and state defenses, especially in the determination of necessity for state action under the Article 8–11 limitation clauses. It is a method of determining aberrant state action, in conjunction with the consensus standard. It is also a more formal standard for the determination of deference to state discretion in several different but interrelated categories within the vertical division of power between Strasbourg and the State Parties: deference to the will of the democratic legislature, to state executive and judicial fact-finding in the individual cases, to state interpretation of the Convention, and to choice of means in carrying out responsibility for enforcement under the subsidiarity principle. [H. C. Yourow, *The Margin of Appreciation Doctrine in the Dynamics of European Human Rights Jurisprudence* (Dordrecht: Martinus Nijhoff, 1996), pp 195–6.]

2   During an early analysis of the case law Thomas O'Donnell explained that the phrase 'the margin of appreciation' was a translation of the French concept of *marge d'appreciation*, which was a method of judicial review devised by the *Conseil d'Etat*. He deduced three standards used by the European Court of Human Rights when applying the doctrine to Convention rights. First, the consensus standard where the existence of a common practice among Member states (e.g. regarding the legal status of illegitimate children as in the *Marckx* case (above, p 523)) led the Court to adopt a narrow margin of appreciation when judging the legality of respondent States' conduct. Secondly, the protection of fundamental rights whereby the Court categorized specific rights as essential for the maintenance of a democratic political system (e.g. freedom of the press in *The Sunday Times* case (below)) with the consequence that the Court accorded states a narrow margin of appreciation to interfere with these basic liberties. Thirdly, the use of textual analysis of the relevant Convention provisions to determine the breadth of the margin in different cases (e.g. the terms of Article 10(2) encouraged a wide discretion being accorded to the British authorities in *Handyside* (above)). He was generally supportive of the device:

The margin of appreciation doctrine is an important and probably enduring concept in the jurisprudence of the Court. . . . The margin of appreciation continues to allow governments some flexibility in meeting their obligations. But it also allows the Court some flexibility. Subject to the Court's establishment of clear and principled standards for its use, the doctrine of margin of appreciation can become the necessary jurisprudential grease in the enforcement mechanisms provided by the Convention. [TA O'Donnell, 'The Margin of Appreciation Doctrine: Standards in the Jurisprudence of the European Court of Human Rights' (1982) 4 *Human Rights Quarterly* 474 at 496.]

3   A similar view of the significance of the doctrine as a mechanism for demarcating the roles of national governments and the Strasbourg institutions regarding the protection of fundamental liberties was expounded by a former President of the Commission and the Court.

... many of the rights and freedoms are defined in the Convention in too general terms to be fully 'self-executing', while the evolution of social and moral concepts may add a further element of uncertainty as to the scope or implications of those rights and freedoms. The so-called 'supervisory function', therefore, has in it a creative, legislative element comparable to that of the judiciary in common law countries; so that in certain cases its exercise might strain the enthusiasm of the Member States for the Convention. The doctrine of the 'margin of appreciation', as I see it, is one of the more important safeguards developed by the Commission and the Court to reconcile the effective operation of the Convention with the sovereign powers and responsibilities of governments in a democracy. With the doctrine, moreover, goes the principle applied by the Commission and the Court in certain cases that a balance must be sought between the exercise by the individual of the right guaranteed to him and the protection of the public interest. A striking example is the *Klass* case where, in appreciating whether the surveillance of certain individuals was a legitimate interference with their freedom of correspondence under Article 8, the Court took judicial notice of the evolution in democratic societies of concepts regarding the treatment of terrorism in Europe. [Sir Humphrey Waldock, 'The Effectiveness of the System set up by the European Convention on Human Rights' (1980) 1 *Human Rights Law Journal* 1 at 9).]

Professor J G Merrills also echoes this positive view of the concept:

... the margin of appreciation is a way of recognising that the international protection of human rights and sovereign freedom of action are not contradictory but complementary. Where the one ends, the other begins. In helping the international judge to decide how and where the boundary is to be located, the concept of the margin of appreciation has a vital part to play. [*The Development of International Law by the European Court of Human Rights*, 2nd edn (Manchester: Manchester University Press, 1993), pp 174–5.]

4 Timothy Jones, however, is critical of the Court's use of this 'imprecise legal doctrine'. He considers that:

Although the Court has often repeated that the limitations to Convention rights must be narrowly interpreted, the general effect of permitting national authorities a margin of appreciation can only be to devalue Convention rights and freedoms at the expense of the limitations. [Timothy H Jones, 'The Devaluation of Human Rights Under the European Convention' (1995) *Public Law* 430 at p 449.]

5 Judge Macdonald has expressed scepticism regarding the pragmatic justification that the doctrine is necessary to avoid damaging conflicts between States and the Court in the era leading up to a truly uniform system of European human rights protection.

The argument assumes that there is still a need for some pragmatic device which can accommodate the sovereignty concerns of the Contracting States. But perhaps the Convention system is now sufficiently mature to be able to move beyond the margin of appreciation and grapple more openly with the questions of appropriateness which that device obscures.... The margin of appreciation should not permit the Court's evasion of its responsibility to articulate the reasons why its intervention in particular cases may or may not be appropriate. Until this responsibility is taken more seriously, the principled reasons which both justify and limit the Court's role will remain buried beneath the pragmatism of the margin of appreciation, and the emergence of a theoretical vision of its role in the European legal order will continue to be limited. [R St J Macdonald, 'The Margin of Appreciation' in *The European System for the Protection of Human Rights*, eds Macdonald, Matscher and Petzold (Dordrecht: Martinus Nijhoff, 1993), at 124.]

6 Paul Mahoney, subsequently Registrar of the Court, believes that the doctrine is a 'legitimate principle of interpretation of the Convention'. In his opinion the origins of the concept are found in the basic philosophical values embodied in the Convention system. Such values include, (1) evolutive interpretation, as the Court is required to interpret the general textual language of the Convention, (2) subsidiarity, as Article 1 locates primary responsibility for safeguarding Convention rights with the Member states, (3) democracy, as the Convention system recognises that Member states' parliaments have the major responsibility for regulating changes in matters of social, economic and political controversy and (4) cultural diversity, due to the fact that Member states reflect a great variety of cultural and ideological beliefs. Consequently:

...the international enforcement bodies which operate under the Convention must in their turn pay a degree of deference, through the doctrine of the margin of appreciation, to the sovereignty of the Contracting States. 'Sovereignty' not so much in the sense of the exercise of *imperium*, that is the State being supreme or not being accountable; but rather in the sense of the freedom of different societies to disagree, to choose different solutions according to their own notions and needs (perhaps even from one region of the country to another), in relation to the regulation of the vast range of human activity covered by the Convention. (p 3)

Factors which he identifies as influencing the scope of the margin of appreciation are, (1) the existence of common ground among member states regarding a right under the Convention will generally result in the Court granting a narrow margin to deviant states, (2) the nature of the right (e.g. a wide margin is accorded in respect of state actions interfering with the right to property), (3) the nature of the duty incumbent on the state (is it a positive or negative one), (4) the nature of the legitimate aim pursued by the state when interfering with the right (e.g. the protection of morals enables states to claim a wider margin because of cultural diversity), (5) the nature of the activity being regulated (e.g. the importance for the individual and the implications for society as a whole), (6) the circumstances surrounding the case (e.g. if the state is experiencing a state of emergency a greater margin will be allowed) and (7) the actual wording of the Convention (e.g. the limitations on the right to liberty in Article 5 are exhaustively defined, therefore there is little discretion for states). In conclusion he does not feel that the doctrine deserves some of the criticisms that it has been subject to. 'Marvellous Richness of Diversity or Invidious Cultural Relativism?' (1998) 19. *Human Rights Law Journal* 1.

Applying the above analysis Mahoney has argued that the principle of subsidiarity requires the Court to apply differing margins of appreciation to the various types of expression falling within Article 10.

...that logic gives priority to the *universality* of the standard of freedom of expression laid down in Article 10 in regard to political and public-concern speech, but much more scope for *subsidiarity*—that is the exercise of democratic discretion at local level—in regard to cultural or artistic speech....Between those two clear poles exists a vast territory of human expression-public, private, collective, professional, commercial, social, scientific, etc—blending a multitude of interests. Whether the pull is in the direction of universality or the direction of subsidiarity will depend on the context and on the mix of interests at stake. The tension between universality and subsidiarity will always be present, to a varying degree, in all free speech cases. ('Universality versus Subsidiarity in the Strasbourg Case Law on Free Speech: Explaining Some Recent Judgments' [1997] *European Human Rights Law Review* 364, 379).

Lord Lester has criticized this differential application of the margin doctrine to various forms of expression (see above p 604).

7   Jeroen Schokkenbroek has identified three categories of cases where the Court utilises the margin doctrine. First, where the relevant Convention provision involves a balancing of interests (e.g. paragraph 2 of Articles 8–11). Secondly, where the Article in question contains vague expressions (e.g. the phrase 'public emergency threatening the life of the nation' in Article 15(1)). Thirdly, where the Court has to determine whether a state has failed to comply with a positive obligation to protect a Convention right (e.g. the right of access to a court under Article 6(1)).

His main criticism of the Court's application of the doctrine is that the concept has not always been applied consistently. This may be due to the different composition of Chambers of the Court. Therefore, '... it would be highly desirable if the Court were to adopt a more coherent approach, stating clearly in its judgments the principles which govern the decision to have recourse to the margin of appreciation and the width of the margin.' ('The Basis, Nature and Application of the Margin of Appreciation Doctrine in the Case-Law of the European Court of Human Rights' (1998) 19 *Human Rights Law Journal* 30 at p 36).

8 After a detailed analysis of the case law Dr Yutaka Arai-Takahashi has concluded that:

Even in the increasingly harmonised constitutional dimension, however, the diversity of values embraced by Member states makes it hardly conceivable for the Strasbourg organs to establish an 'autonomous' meaning for such elusive notions as 'morals' or 'public interest'. Nor is it desirable to enforce uniform standards of the Convention at the expense of regional legitimacy and of richness in cultural values and traditions amongst Member States. The margin of appreciation must be understood as an essential constitutional device designed to preserve the fundamental prerequisite and virtue of a liberal democratic society: value pluralism. The doctrine's only defensible rationale during *and after* the process of integration is to enable the Strasbourg Court to provide endorsement of the maintenance of cultural diversity, ensuring to the citizens of Europe the means to articulate and practice their preferred values within a multi-cultural democracy. [Y. Arai-Takahashi, *The Margin of Appreciation Doctrine and the Principle of Proportionality in the Jurisprudence of the ECHR* (Antwerp: Intersentia, 2002), p 249.

....

Sunday Times v UK A.30 (1979) 2 EHRR 245
European Court of Human Rights

During the late 1950s the Distillers drugs company began selling a sedative which contained the drug thalidomide. By the early 1960s it was discovered that the taking of thalidomide by women during certain stages of pregnancy could cause severe deformities in their babies. The company then withdrew the drug. Subsequently, civil actions for alleged negligence were brought against the company on behalf of the disabled children. A settlement, involving seventy cases, was reached in 1968. Several hundred other actions were subject to continuing negotiations between the plaintiffs' lawyers and the company. In 1972 the Sunday Times newspaper published an article criticizing the law relating to the liability of drug companies and calling upon Distillers to 'think again' about the level of their current offer of compensation to the thalidomide victims. Distillers asked the Attorney-General to bring proceedings for contempt of court against the newspaper, but he declined to do so. The editor then sent the Attorney-General a draft of another article which he proposed to publish. This piece contained evidence and argument to suggest that Distillers had not exercised due care in testing the safety of thalidomide before marketing it. Thereupon, the Attorney-General sought an injunction, under the law of contempt of court, to prevent the newspaper publishing the article. The Divisional Court ([1972] 3 All ER 1136) granted the injunction, but the Court of Appeal ([1973] 1 All ER 815) discharged it. On appeal, the House of Lords ([1973] 3 All ER 54) renewed the injunction. The publisher, editor and a group of journalists then complained to the Commission of, *inter alia*, a breach of their rights under Article 10. The Commission (by eight votes to five) found that the injunction was a violation of the applicants' rights to freedom of expression.

...

I. ON ARTICLE 10

...

44. Originally, the injunction in question was granted by the Divisional Court and concerned only the draft *Sunday Times* article... It was discharged by the Court of Appeal... but the House of Lords restored it and considerably *widened* its scope by directing the Divisional Court to order

> 'That... Times Newspapers Ltd, by themselves, their servants, agents or otherwise, be restrained from publishing, or causing or authorising or procuring to be published or printed, any article or matter which prejudges the issues of negligence, breach of contract or breach of duty, or deals with the evidence relating to any of the said issues arising on any actions pending or imminent against Distillers... in respect of the development, distribution or use of the drug "thalidomide".'

45. It is clear that there was an 'interference by public authority' in the exercise of the applicants' freedom of expression which is guaranteed by paragraph 1 of Article 10. Such an interference entails a 'violation' of Article 10 if it does not fall within one of the exceptions provided for in paragraph 2 (*Handyside* judgment of 7 December 1976, Series A No 24, p 21, § 43). The Court therefore has to examine in turn whether the interference in the present case was 'prescribed by law', whether it had an aim or aims that is or are legitimate under Article 10 § 2 and whether it was 'necessary in a democratic society' for the aforesaid aim or aims.

A. WAS THE INTERFERENCE 'PRESCRIBED BY LAW'?

...

47. The Court observes that the word 'law' in the expression 'prescribed by law' covers not only statute but also unwritten law. Accordingly, the Court does not attach importance here to the fact that contempt of court is a creature of the common law and not of legislation. It would clearly be contrary to the intention of the drafters of the Convention to hold that a restriction imposed by virtue of the common law is not 'prescribed by law' on the sole ground that it is not enunciated in legislation: this would deprive a common-law State which is Party to the Convention of the protection of Article 10 § 2 and strike at the very roots of that State's legal system.

...

48. The expression 'prescribed by law' appears in paragraph 2 of Articles 9, 10 and 11 of the Convention, the equivalent in the French text being in each case 'prévues par la loi'. However, when the same French expression appears in Article 8 § 2 of the Convention, in article 1 of Protocol No 1 and in Article 2 of Protocol No 4, it is rendered in the English text as 'in accordance with the law', 'provided for by law' and 'in accordance with law', respectively. Thus confronted with versions of a law-making treaty which are equally authentic but not exactly the same, the Court must interpret them in a way that reconciles them as far as possible and is most appropriate in order to realise the aim and achieve the object of the treaty (see the *Wemhoff* judgment of 27 June 1968, Series A No 7, p 23, § 8, and Article 33 § 4 of the Vienna Convention of 23 May 1969 on the Law of Treaties).

49. In the Court's opinion, the following are two of the requirements that flow from the expression 'prescribed by law'. Firstly, the law must be adequately accessible: the citizen must be able to have an indication that is adequate in the circumstances of the legal rules applicable to a given case. Secondly, a norm cannot be regarded as a 'law' unless it is formulated with sufficient precision to enable the citizen to regulate his conduct: he must be able—if need be with appropriate advice—to foresee, to a degree that is reasonable in the circumstances, the consequences which a given action may entail. Those consequences need not be foreseeable with absolute certainty: experience shows this to be unattainable. Again, whilst certainty is highly desirable, it may bring in its train excessive rigidity and the law must be able to keep pace with changing circumstances. Accordingly, many laws are inevitably

couched in terms which, to a greater or lesser extent, are vague and whose interpretation and application are questions of practice.

50. In the present case, the question whether these requirements of accessibility and foreseeability were satisfied is complicated by the fact that different principles were relied on by the various Law Lords concerned. The Divisional Court had applied the principle that a deliberate attempt to influence the settlement of pending proceedings by bringing public pressure to bear on a party constitutes contempt of court (the 'pressure principle' . . .). Certain members of the House of Lords also alluded to this principle whereas others preferred the principle that it is contempt of court to publish material which prejudges, or is likely to cause public prejudgment of, the issues raised in pending litigation (the 'prejudgment principle' . . .).

51. The applicants do not claim to have been without an indication that was adequate in the circumstances of the 'pressure principle'. . . .

The Court also considers that there can be no doubt that the 'pressure principle' was formulated with sufficient precision to enable the applicants to foresee to the appropriate degree the consequences which publication of the draft article might entail. . . .

52. The applicants contend, on the other hand, that the prejudgment principle was novel and that they therefore could not have had an adequate indication of its existence. . . .

As regards the formulation of the 'prejudgment principle', the Court notes that reference was made in the House of Lords to various authorities . . .

To sum up, the Court does not consider that the applicants were without an indication that was adequate in the circumstances of the existence of the 'prejudgment principle'. Even if the Court does have certain doubts concerning the precision with which that principle was formulated at the relevant time, it considers that the applicants were able to foresee, to a degree that was reasonable in the circumstances, a risk that publication of the draft article might fall foul of the principle.

53. The interference with the applicants' freedom of expression was thus 'prescribed by law' within the meaning of Article 10 § 2.

B. DID THE INTERFERENCE HAVE AIMS THAT ARE LEGITIMATE UNDER ARTICLE 10 § 2?

54. In the view of the applicants, the Government and the minority of the Commission, the law of contempt of court serves the purpose of safeguarding not only the impartiality and authority of the judiciary but also the rights and interests of litigants.

The majority of the Commission, on the other hand, whilst accepting that the law of contempt has the general aim of securing the fair administration of justice and that it thereby seeks to achieve purposes similar to those envisaged in Article 10 § 2 where it speaks of maintaining the authority and impartiality of the judiciary, considered that it was not called upon to examine separately whether that law has the further purpose of protecting the rights of others.

55. The Court first emphasises that the expression 'authority and impartiality of the judiciary' has to be understood 'within the meaning of the Convention' (see, *mutatis mutandis*, the *König* judgment of 28 June 1978, Series A No 27, pp 29–30, § 88). For this purpose, account must be taken of the central position occupied in this context by Article 6 which reflects the fundamental principle of the rule of law (see, for example, the *Golder* judgment of 21 February 1975, Series A No 18, p 17, § 34).

The term 'judiciary' ('*pouvoir judiciaire*') comprises the machinery of justice or the judicial branch of government as well as the judges in their official capacity. The phrase 'authority of the judiciary' includes, in particular, the notion that the courts are, and are accepted by the public at large as being, the proper forum for the ascertainment of legal rights and obligations and the settlement of disputes relative thereto; further, that the public at large have respect for and confidence in the courts' capacity to fulfil that function.

56. In the present case, the Court shares the view of the majority of the Commission that, insofar as the law of contempt may serve to protect the rights of litigants, this purpose is already included in the phrase 'maintaining the authority and impartiality of the judiciary': the rights so protected are the rights of individuals in their capacity as litigants, that is as persons involved in the machinery of justice, and the authority of that machinery will not be maintained unless protection is afforded to all those involved in or having recourse to it. It is therefore not necessary to consider as a separate issue whether the law of contempt has the further purpose of safeguarding 'the rights of others'.

57. It remains to be examined whether the aim of the interference with the applicants' freedom of expression was the maintenance of the authority and impartiality of the judiciary.

The reasons why the draft article was regarded as objectionable by the House of Lords ... may be briefly summarised as follows:

— by 'prejudging' the issue of negligence, it would have led to disrespect for the processes of the law or interfered with the administration of justice;

— it was of a kind that would expose Distillers to public and prejudicial discussion of the merits of their case, such exposure being objectionable as it inhibits suitors generally from having recourse to the courts;

— it would subject Distillers to pressure and to the prejudices of prejudgment of the issues in the litigation and the law of contempt was designed to prevent interference with recourse to the courts;

— prejudgment by the press would have led inevitably in this case to replies by the parties, thereby creating the danger of a 'trial by newspaper' incompatible with the proper administration of justice;

— the courts owe it to the parties to protect them from the prejudices of prejudgment which involves their having to participate in the flurries of pre-trial publicity.

The Court regards all these various reasons as falling within the aim of maintaining the 'authority ... of the judiciary' as interpreted by the Court in the second sub-paragraph of paragraph 55 above.

Accordingly, the interference with the applicants' freedom of expression had an aim that is legitimate under Article 10 § 2.

C. WAS THE INTERFERENCE 'NECESSARY IN A DEMOCRATIC SOCIETY' FORMAINTAINING THE AUTHORITY OF THE JUDICIARY?

...

59. The Court has already had the occasion in its above-mentioned *Handyside* judgement to state its understanding of the phrase 'necessary in a democratic society', the nature of its functions in the examination of issues turning on that phrase and the manner in which it will perform those functions. ...

This does not mean that the Court's supervision is limited to ascertaining whether a respondent State exercised its discretion reasonably, carefully and in good faith. Even a Contracting State so acting remains subject to the Court's control as regards the compatibility of its conduct with the engagements it has undertaken under the Convention ...

Again, the scope of the domestic power of appreciation is not identical as regards each of the aims listed in Article 10 § 2. The *Handyside* case concerned the 'protection of morals'. The view taken by the Contracting States of the 'requirements of morals', observed the Court, 'varies from time to time and from place to place, especially in our era', and 'State authorities are in principle in a better position than the international judge to give an opinion on the exact content of these requirements' (p 22, § 48).

Precisely the same cannot be said of the far more objective notion of the 'authority' of the judiciary. The domestic law and practice of the Contracting States reveal a fairly substantial measure of common ground in this area. This is reflected in a number of provisions of the Convention, including Article 6, which have no equivalent as far as 'morals' are concerned. Accordingly, here a more extensive European supervision corresponds to a less discretionary power of appreciation. . . .

60. Both the minority of the Commission and the Government attach importance to the fact that the institution of contempt of court is peculiar to common-law countries and suggest that the concluding words of Article 10 § 2 were designed to cover this institution which has no equivalent in many other member States of the Council of Europe.

However, even if this were so, the Court considers that the reason for the insertion of those words would have been to ensure that the general aims of the law of contempt of court should be considered legitimate aims under Article 10 § 2 but not to make that law the standard by which to assess whether a given measure was 'necessary'. If and to the extent that Article 10 § 2 was prompted by the notions underlying either the English law of contempt of court or any other similar domestic institution, it cannot have adopted them as they stood: it transposed them into an autonomous context. It is 'necessity' in terms of the Convention which the Court has to assess, its role being to review the conformity of national acts with the standards of that instrument. . . .

61. Again, the Court cannot hold that the injunction was not 'necessary' simply because it could or would not have been granted under a different legal system. As noted in the judgment of 9 February 1967 in the 'Belgian Linguistic' case, the main purpose of the Convention is 'to lay down certain international standards to be observed by the Contracting States in their relations with persons under their jurisdiction' (Series A No 5, p 19). This does not mean that absolute uniformity is required and, indeed, since the Contracting States remain free to choose the measures which they consider appropriate, the Court cannot be oblivious of the substantive or procedural features of their respective domestic laws (see, *mutatis mutandis*, judgment of 23 July 1968 in the *'Belgian Linguistic'* case, Series A No 6, pp 34–5).

62. It must now be decided whether the 'interference' complained of corresponded to a 'pressing social need', whether it was 'proportionate to the legitimate aim pursued' whether the reasons given by the national authorities to justify it are 'relevant and sufficient under Article 10 § 2' (above-mentioned *Handyside* judgment, pp 22–4, §§ 48–50).

. . .

Nevertheless, the proposed *Sunday Times* article was couched in moderate terms and did not present just one side of the evidence or claim that there was only one possible result at which a court could arrive; although it analysed in detail evidence against Distillers, it also summarised arguments in their favour and closed with the words 'There appears to be no neat set of answers . . .'. In the Court's opinion, the effect of the article, if published, would therefore have varied from reader to reader. Accordingly, even to the extent that the article might have led some readers to form an opinion on the negligence issue, this would not have had adverse consequences for the 'authority of the judiciary', especially since, as noted above, there had been a nationwide campaign in the meantime.

. . .

As the Court remarked in its *Handyside* judgment, freedom of expression constitutes one of the essential foundations of a democratic society; subject to paragraph 2 of Article 10, it is applicable not only to information or ideas that are favourably received or regarded as inoffensive or as a matter of indifference, but also to those that offend, shock or disturb the State or any sector of the population (p 23, § 49).

These principles are of particular importance as far as the press is concerned. They are equally applicable to the field of the administration of justice, which serves the interests of the community at large and requires the co-operation of an enlightened public. There is general recognition of the fact that the courts cannot operate in a vacuum. Whilst they are the forum for the settlement of disputes, this does not mean that there can be no prior discussion of disputes elsewhere, be it in specialised journals, in the general press or amongst the public at large. Furthermore, whilst the mass media must not overstep the bounds imposed in the interests of the proper administration of justice, it is incumbent on them to impart information and ideas concerning matters that come before the courts just as in other areas of public interest. Not only do the media have the task of imparting such information and ideas: the public also has a right to receive them (see, *mutatis mutandis*, the *Kjeldsen, Busk Madsen and Pedersen* judgment of 7 December 1976, Series A No 23, p 26, § 52).

To assess whether the interference complained of was based on 'sufficient' reasons which rendered it 'necessary in a democratic society', account must thus be taken of any public interest aspect of the case. The Court observes in this connection that, following a balancing of the conflicting interests involved, an absolute rule was formulated by certain of the Law Lords to the effect that it was not permissible to prejudge issues in pending cases:... the Court points out that it has to take a different approach. The Court is faced not with a choice between two conflicting principles but with a principle of freedom of expression that is subject to a number of exceptions which must be narrowly interpreted (see, *mutatis mutandis*, the *Klass* judgment of 6 September 1978, Series A No 28, p 21, § 42).... It is not sufficient that the interference involved belongs to that class of the exceptions listed in article 10 § 2 which has been invoked; neither is it sufficient that the interference was imposed because its subject-matter fell within a particular category or was caught by a legal rule formulated in general or absolute terms: the Court has to be satisfied that the interference was necessary having regard to the facts and circumstances prevailing in the specific case before it.

66. The thalidomide disaster was a matter of undisputed public concern. It posed the question whether the powerful company which had marketed the drug bore legal or moral responsibility towards hundreds of individuals experiencing an appalling personal tragedy or whether the victims could demand or hope for indemnification only from the community as a whole; fundamental issues concerning protection against the compensation for injuries resulting from scientific developments were raised and many facets of the existing law on these subjects were called in question.

As the Court has already observed, Article 10 guarantees not only the freedom of the press to inform the public but also the right of the public to be properly informed.

In the present case, the families of numerous victims of the tragedy, who were unaware of the legal difficulties involved, had a vital interest in knowing all the underlying facts and the various possible solutions. They could be deprived of this information, which was crucially important for them, only if it appeared absolutely certain that its diffusion would have presented a threat to the 'authority of the judiciary'.

...

It is true that, if the *Sunday Times*/ article had appeared at the intended time, Distillers might have felt obliged to develop in public, and in advance of any trial, their arguments on the facts of the case...; however, those facts did not cease to be a matter of public interest merely because they formed the background to pending litigation. By bringing to light certain facts, the article might have served as a brake on speculative and unenlightened discussion.

67. Having regard to all the circumstances of the case and on the basis of the approach described... above, the Court concludes that the interference complained of did not correspond to a social need sufficiently pressing to outweigh the public interest in freedom of expressing within the meaning of the Convention. The Court therefore finds the reasons for the restraint imposed on the applicants not to be sufficient under Article 10 § 2. That restraint proves not to be proportionate to the legitimate aim pursued; it was not necessary in a democratic society for maintaining the authority of the judiciary.

68. There has accordingly been a violation of Article 10.

FOR THESE REASONS, THE COURT

Holds by eleven votes to nine that there has been a breach of Article 10 of the Convention: . . .

NOTES

1   The majority was comprised of, President Balladore Pallieri and Judges: Mosler, Zekia, O'Donoghue, Pedersen, Evrigenis, Teitgen, Lagergren, Gölcüklü, Pinheiro Farinha, and Garcia De Enterria. The dissentients were Judges: Wiarda, Cremona, Thor Vilhjalmsson, Ryssdal, Ganshof Van Der Meersch, Fitzmaurice, Bindschedler-Robert, Liesch, and Matscher. In their joint dissent the minority disagreed with the majority regarding (a) the extent of the margin of appreciation to be given to the UK in respect of the law of contempt of court and (b) the necessity of the interference with the applicants' freedom of expression. The dissentients did not believe that the national margin of appreciation was narrower in cases involving the maintenance of the authority of the judiciary than in disputes concerning the protection of morals.

Even though there might exist a fairly broad measure of common ground between the Contracting States as to the substance of Article 6, it nevertheless remains the fact that the judicial institutions and the procedures can vary considerably from one country to another. Thus, contrary to what the majority of the Court holds, the notion of the authority of the judiciary is by no means divorced from national circumstances and cannot be determined in a uniform way. (pp 51–2)

The dissentients were also satisfied that the House of Lords was entitled to consider that it was necessary to restore the injunction, in order to prevent the applicants prejudicing the administration of justice in the civil action against Distillers.

2   The Court's judgment contains several very important rulings. These include the relationship between the rights granted by Article 10(1) and the limitations permitted under Article 10(2). According to the Court, the former have precedence and the latter must be interpreted narrowly. Also, the Court was willing to accept that common law jurisprudence could, if it was sufficiently accessible and precise, satisfy the requirements of Article 10(2) as being 'prescribed by law'. For the Court's acceptance of case law in civil law States as meeting the analogous requirements of being 'in accordance with the law' under Article 8(2) see, *Kruslin v France* (1990) above p 563.

3   The *Sunday Times* case was a significant factor in the British government's decision to seek statutory reform of parts of the common law in the Contempt of Court Act 1981. Aspects of that legislation have been considered by the Court in *Goodwin v UK, Reports of Judgments and Decisions* (1996) 22 EHRR 123, 1996-II 483, below p 717.

Article 10(1)

The scope of freedom of expression

POLITICAL EXPRESSION

Lingens v Austria A.103 (1986) 8 EHRR 407
European Court of Human Rights

The applicant was the editor of a magazine (*Profil*) published in Austria. Shortly after the Austrian general election in 1975, Simon Wiesenthal (President of the Jewish Documentation Centre) accused the leader of the Austrian Liberal Party (Friedrich Peter) of having served in the SS infantry during the Second World War. Mr Peter admitted that fact but denied any personal involvement in the massacre of civilians by his brigade. The next day Mr Peter had a meeting with the Austrian Chancellor (Bruno Kreisky) about the formation of a new government. Subsequently, Mr Kreisky gave a television interview during which he supported Mr Peter and criticised Mr Wiesenthal's organisation as a 'political mafia'. Soon afterwards the applicant published two articles that contained strong criticism of Mr Kreisky, including the terms 'basest opportunism', 'immoral' and 'undignified'. Mr Kreisky then brought a private prosecution against Lingens for alleged criminal defamation. The Vienna Regional Court accepted that Lingens had published his articles in good faith, but as he had not been able to prove the truth of his statements (as required by the Austrian Criminal Code) he was found guilty. The court fined Lingens 20,000 schillings and ordered the confiscation of copies of the offending articles. The Vienna Court of Appeal upheld the conviction, but reduced the fine to 15,000 schillings. Lingens complained to the Commission that his conviction violated his rights under Article 10. The Commission unanimously found a violation of that Article.

I. ALLEGED VIOLATION OF ARTICLE 10

. . .

36. . . . the Court agrees with the Commission and the Government that the conviction in question was indisputably based on Article 111 of the Austrian Criminal Code (see paragraph 21 above); it was moreover designed to protect 'the reputation or rights of others' and there is no reason to suppose that it had any other purpose (see Article 18 of the Convention). The conviction was accordingly 'prescribed by law' and had a legitimate aim under Article 10 § 2 of the Convention.

37. In their respective submissions the Commission, the Government and the applicant concentrated on the question whether the interference was 'necessary in a democratic society' for achieving the above-mentioned aim. . . .

41. In this connection, the Court has to recall that freedom of expression, as secured in paragraph 1 of Article 10, constitutes one of the essential foundations of a democratic society and one of the basic conditions for its progress and for each individual's self-fulfilment. Subject to paragraph 2, it is applicable not only to 'information' or 'ideas' that are favourably received or regarded as inoffensive or as a matter of indifference, but also to those that offend, shock or disturb. Such as the demands of that pluralism, tolerance and broadmindedness without which there is no 'democratic society' (see the above-mentioned *Handyside* judgment, Series A No 24, p 23, § 49).

These principles are of particular importance as far as the press is concerned. Whilst the press must not overstep the bounds set, inter alia, for the 'protection of the reputation of others', it is nevertheless incumbent on it to impart information and ideas on political issues just as on those in other areas of public interest. Not only does the press have the task of imparting such information and ideas: the public also has a right to receive them (see, *mutatis mutandis*, the above-mentioned *Sunday Times* judgment, Series A No 30, p 40, § 65). In this connection, the Court cannot accept the opinion, expressed in the judgment of the Vienna Court of Appeal, to the effect that the task of the press was to impart information, the interpretation of which had to be left primarily to the reader.

42. Freedom of the press furthermore affords the public one of the best means of discovering and forming an opinion of the ideas and attitudes of political leaders. More generally, freedom of political debate is at the very core of the concept of a democratic society which prevails throughout the Convention.

The limits of acceptable criticism are accordingly wider as regards a politician as such than as regards a private individual. Unlike the latter, the former inevitably and knowingly lays himself open to close scrutiny of his every word and deed by both journalists and the public at large, and he must consequently display a greater degree of tolerance. No doubt Article 10 § 2 enables the reputation of others—that is to say, of all individuals—to be protected, and this protection extends to politicians too, even when they are not acting in their private capacity; but in such cases the requirements of such protection have to be weighed in relation to the interests of open discussion of political issues.

43. The applicant was convicted because he had used certain expressions ('basest opportunism', 'immoral' and 'undignified') apropos of Mr Kreisky, who was Federal Chancellor at the time, in two articles published in the Viennese magazine *Profil* on 14 and 21 October 1975. The articles dealt with political issues of public interest in Austria which had given rise to many heated discussions concerning the attitude of Austrians in general—and the Chancellor in particular—to National Socialism and to the participation of former Nazis in the governance of the country. The content and tone of the articles were on the whole fairly balanced but the use of the aforementioned expressions in particular appeared likely to harm Mr Kreisky's reputation.

However, since the case concerned Mr Kreisky in his capacity as a politician, regard must be had to the background against which these articles were written. They had appeared shortly after the general election of October 1975. Many Austrians had thought beforehand that Mr Kreisky's party would lose its absolute majority and, in order to be able to govern, would have to form a coalition with Mr Peter's party. When, after the elections, Mr Wiesenthal made a number of revelations about Mr Peter's Nazi past, the Chancellor defended Mr Peter and attacked his detractor, whose activities he described as 'mafia methods'; hence Mr Lingens' sharp reaction...

What was at issue was not his right to disseminate information but his freedom of opinion and his right to impart ideas; the restrictions authorised in paragraph 2 of Article 10 nevertheless remained applicable. ...

In the Court's view, a careful distinction needs to be made between facts and value-judgments. The existence of facts can be demonstrated, whereas the truth of value-judgments is not susceptible of proof. The Court notes in this connection that the facts on which Mr Lingens founded his value-judgment were undisputed, as was also his good faith.

Under paragraph 3 of Article 111 of the Criminal Code, read in conjunction with paragraph 2, journalists in a case such as this cannot escape conviction for the matters specified in paragraph 1 unless they can prove the truth of their statements.

As regards value-judgments this requirement is impossible of fulfilment and it infringes freedom of opinion itself, which is a fundamental part of the right secured by Article 10 of the Convention. ...

47. From the various foregoing considerations it appears that the interference with Mr Lingens' exercise of the freedom of expression was not 'necessary in a democratic society . . . for the protection of the reputation . . . of others'; it was disproportionate to the legitimate aim pursued. There was accordingly a breach of Article 10 of the Convention.

. . .

FOR THESE REASONS, THE COURT UNANIMOUSLY

Holds that there has been a breach of Article 10 of the Convention;

. . .

NOTES

1   The Court was composed of; President Ryssdal and Judges: Ganshof Van Der Meersch, Cremona, Wiarda, Thor Vilhjalmsson, Bindschedler-Robert, Lagergren, Gölcüklü, Matscher, Pinheiro Farina, Pettiti, Walsh, Evans, Macdonald, Russo, Bernhardt, Gersing, and Spielmann.

2   The above judgment is notable for the vigorous protection given to media comment on political ideas and politicians by the Court. It is especially important in preventing states from requiring the media to prove the truthfulness of their good faith value-judgments regarding political figures.

3 The same principles were applied by the Court in *Oberschlick v Austria*, A.204 (1991) 19 EHRR 389, where another magazine editor published the details of a criminal information, which he had lodged with the authorities, alleging that the secretary general of the Austrian Liberal Party had unlawfully espoused views similar to Nazi policy. Furthermore, the magazine article elaborated upon the nature of the criminal charges. Oberschlick was convicted by the Austrian courts under the same defamation law as Lingens. A majority of the Court (sixteen votes to three) concluded that there had been a violation of the applicant's rights under Article 10, because the Austrian courts had required him to prove the truth of parts of the article which were value-judgments. In a more recent case he also successfully challenged an Austrian conviction for publishing an article in which he called a leading politician an 'idiot': *Oberschlick v Austria (No 2), Reports of Judgments and Decisions* (1997) 25 EHRR 357, 1997-IV 1266. Jorg Haider, the leader of the Austrian Freedom Party and Governor of Carinthia, had given a speech in which he claimed that all soldiers who served in the Second World War (irrespective of which side they were on) had fought for peace and freedom and that they were the only people entitled to freedom of expression in modern times. Oberschlick published the speech together with his criticisms under the title 'P S: Idiot instead of Nazi'. The Austrian courts upheld Haider's claim of defamation against the applicant. The Commission (by fourteen votes to one) found a breach of Article 10. A majority of the Court (seven votes to two) also held that the applicant's conviction violated his rights under that provision.

In the Court's view, the applicant's article, and in particular the word 'Idiot', may certainly be considered polemical, but they did not on that account constitute a gratuitous personal attack, as the author provided an objectively understandable explanation for them derived from Mr Haider's speech-which was itself provocative. As such, they were part of the political discussion provoked by Mr Haider's speech and amounted to an opinion, whose truth is not susceptible of proof. Such an opinion may, however, be excessive, in particular in the absence of any factual basis, but ... that was not so in this instance. It is true that calling a politician [an Idiot] in public may offend him. In the instant case, however, the word does not seem disproportionate to the indignation knowingly aroused by Mr Haider. (paras 33–4)

Therefore, the Court did not consider that it was necessary for the Austrian courts to have convicted the applicant of defamation in order to protect the reputation or rights of Haider. Matscher and Thor Vilhjalmsson JJ dissented on the basis that they considered 'an insult can never be a value judgment' deserving protection under Article 10. However, it is clear that the majority of the Court was willing to safeguard political commentators' use of highly pejorative language where it was part of a reasoned critique. J McBride has observed that: 'the recognition that insults can be protected is undoubtedly important but determining whether the use of one was justified is often likely to be problematic.' [Judges, Politicians and the Limits to Critical Comment' (1998) 23 E L Rev HR 77 88.]

On the latter point see *Wabl*, below note 10.

In the later case of *Wirtschafts-Trend Zeitschriften-Verlags GMBH v Austria*, judgment of 27 October 2005, the publishers of 'Profil' (see above *Lingens*) successful claimed a breach of Article 10 in respect of their civil liability for a book review which criticized Jorg Haider's reference to (Nazi) concentration camps as 'punishment camps'. The unanimous Chamber found the fact that Haider had used that description was a sufficient basis for the magazine's value judgments.

4 A large majority (six votes to one) of a Chamber found that a journalist's reference to a right-wing politician as a 'closet Nazi' was a value judgment which could be justified in *Scharsach and News Verlagsgesellschaft mbH v Austria*, judgment of 13 November 2003. The named politician had, *inter alia*, publicly criticized legislation which banned National Socialist activities. Therefore, the Chamber did not think that the journalist's article on a matter of public interest exceeded fair comment and his conviction for defamation (accompanied by a fine of 4,360 euros) constituted a breach of Article 10.

5   The acceptable limits of media commentary on a political figure were found to have been breached in *Tammer v Estonia*, judgment of 6 February 2001. The applicant was a journalist who published an article in which he described the lover of a former Prime Minister (she had given birth to the latter's child whilst he was married to another person) and who had then served as one of his officials whilst being active in his political party, as being a person who broke up another's marriage and an unfit and careless mother (using offensive Estonian words). The woman brought a private prosecution against the applicant for having insulted her. The domestic courts found him guilty and fined him. The Court was unanimous in rejecting the applicant's claim that he had suffered a violation of Article 10.

68. ... it observes that Ms Laanaru resigned from her governmental position in October 1995 ... Despite her continued involvement in the political party the Court does not find it established that the use of the impugned terms in relation to Ms Laanaru's private life was justified by considerations of public concern or that they bore on a matter of general importance. In particular, it has not been substantiated that her private life was among the issues that affected the public in April 1996 [when the article was published]. The applicant's remarks could therefore scarcely be regarded as serving the public interest.

Hence, the use of insulting terminology to describe aspects of the private life of a political figure did not come within the boundaries of protected political expression. In contrast the conviction of a newspaper editor and the publisher for infringing the privacy of a senior parliamentarian, by reporting the conviction of her husband for drunkenness and assaulting a police officer, was found to have breached Article 10 in *Karhuvaara and Iltalehti v Finland*, judgment of 16 November 2004. The Court acknowledged that the applicants' factual references to the parliamentarian in the coverage of the husband's conviction had a degree of legitimate public interest.

45. On the other hand, it is to be noted that the subject matter of the contested reporting did not have any express bearing on political issues or any direct links with the person of Mrs A. as a politician. Consequently, the articles in question did not pertain to any matter of great public interest as far as Mrs A.'s involvement was concerned. However, the public has the right to be informed, which is an essential right in a democratic society that, in certain special circumstances, may even extend to aspects of the private life of public figures, particularly where politicians are concerned (see *Von Hannover v Germany*, [ECHR 2004] § 64). In this connection the Court notes the District Court's opinion, according to which the conviction of the spouse of a politician could affect people's voting decisions. In the Court's opinion this indicates that, at least to some degree, a matter of public interest was involved in the reporting.

It is significant that the newspaper articles in this case did not contain any criticism of the politician.

6   The Court has ruled that the freedom of political expression is even wider when it is directed at the institutions of government, rather than against specific politicians. In *Castells v Spain*, A.236 (1992) 14 EHRR 445, the applicant was a Spanish Senator representing a party which supported independence for the Basque Country. He wrote an article in 1979 for a magazine, circulating in the Basque region, which accused the state of a number of murders. In his words: 'Behind these acts there can only be the Government ... We know that they are

increasingly going to use as a political instrument the ruthless hunting down of Basque dissi-
dents and their political elimination.' Subsequently, Castells was convicted of insulting the
Government after the Supreme Court held that defence of truth was not available in respect
of this offence. Castells then complained to the Strasbourg authorities. The Court, unanimously, stated that:

While freedom of expression is important for everybody, it is especially so for an elected representative
of the people. He represents his electorate, draws attention to their preoccupations and defends their
interests. Accordingly, interferences with the freedom of expression of an opposition Member of
Parliament, like the applicant call for the closest scrutiny on the part of the Court... The limits of permissible criticism are wider with regard to the Government than in relation to a private citizen, or even
a politician. In the democratic system the actions or omissions of the Government must be subject to
the close scrutiny not only of the legislative and judicial authorities but also of the press and public
opinion. Furthermore, the dominant position which the Government occupies makes it necessary for it
to display restraint in resorting to criminal proceedings, particularly where other means are available
for replying to the unjustified attacks and criticisms of its adversaries or the media. (paras 42–6)

The Court concluded that as the Spanish courts had prevented Castells from pleading the
truthfulness of his statements, as he had wished to do, there had been a violation of his rights
under Article 10(1).

The combined effects of the judgments in *Lingens* and *Castells* has been the creation by the
Court of complimentary European defences, under Article 10, of fair comment for good
faith media commentaries upon politicians and the truthfulness of factual statements about
public bodies.

Subsequently, the full-time Court criticized Ukrainian deformation law for failing to distinguish between value judgments and statements of fact in *Ukrainian Media Group v Ukraine*,
judgment of 29 March 2005.

7   A Grand Chamber of the Court has applied *Castells* to protect vitriolic criticism of government policy by an opposition politician in *Incal v Turkey, Reports of Judgments and Decisions*
(1998) 29 EHRR 449, 1998-IV 1569. The applicant, a lawyer by profession, was a member of
the executive committee of the Izmir section of the People's Labour Party ('the HEP'). That
committee decided to distribute a leaflet which was highly critical of the measures being taken
by local authorities against illegal traders and squatters (most of whom were Kurds). The committee sent a copy of the leaflet to the Izmir prefecture and asked for permission to distribute
it. The leaflet was referred to the security police who considered that it contained illegal separatist propaganda and, therefore, they sent it to the public prosecutor. At the request of the
public prosecutor the National Security Court issued an injunction ordering the seizure of the
leaflet. Subsequently, all 10,000 copies of the leaflet were seized and the applicant was convicted
of non-public incitement to commit an offence for which he was sentenced to six months'
imprisonment and banned from driving for fifteen days (also conviction of this offence meant
that the applicant was debarred from the civil service and forbidden to take part in a number of
activities within political organisations and trade unions). The applicant complained to the
Commission alleging a breach of, *inter alia*, Article 10. A unanimous Commission upheld that
claim. The Court accepted that the applicant's conviction had the legitimate aim of preventing
disorder. In the Court's opinion:

The leaflet began by complaining of an atmosphere of hostility towards citizens of Kurdish origin in
Izmir and suggested that the measures concerned were directed against them in particular, to force
them to leave the city. The text contained a number of virulent remarks about the policy of the Turkish

Government and made serious accusations, holding them responsible for the situation. Appealing to 'all democratic patriots', it described the authorities' actions as 'terror and as part of a 'special war' being conducted 'in the country' against 'the Kurdish people'. It called on citizens to 'oppose' this situation, in particular by means of 'neighbourhood committees'. The Court certainly sees in these phrases appeals to, among others, the population of Kurdish origin, urging them to band together to raise certain political demands. Although the reference to 'neighbourhood committees' appears unclear, those appeals cannot, however, if read in context, be taken as incitement to the use of violence, hostility or hatred between citizens. (para 50)

While the Court was willing to take into account the problems of preventing terrorism when evaluating the leaflet it did, '... not discern anything which would warrant the conclusion that Mr Incal was in any way responsible for the problems of terrorism in Turkey, and more specifically in Izmir' (para 58). Therefore, the Court, unanimously, held that the applicant's conviction was disproportionate to the aim pursued and consequently in breach of Article 10.

Hence the Court is willing to safeguard the outspoken criticisms voiced by opposition politicians provided they respect the democratic process by refraining from inciting violence against the state or other citizens: see further, A Mowbray, 'The Role of the European Court of Human Rights in the Promotion of Democracy' (1999) *Public Law* 703.

A similar approach was followed by a Grand Chamber of the full-time Court in respect of a Marxist critique of the Turkish Government's actions towards the Kurds made by a trade union leader. The applicant in *Ceylan v Turkey* (1999) 30 EHRR 73 was the president of the petroleum workers' union and during 1991 he wrote an article, entitled 'The time has come for the workers to speak out—tomorrow it will be too late', which was published by a weekly newspaper in Istanbul. The piece included the following statements: 'The steadily intensifying State terrorism in Eastern and South-Eastern Anatolia is nothing other than a perfect reflection of the imperialist-controlled policies being applied to the Kurdish people on the international plane... genocide [was] being carried out against the Kurds in Turkey... and that an attempt [was] being made to... gag and suffocate the Kurdish people'. Subsequently the Istanbul National Security Court convicted the applicant of non-public incitement to hatred and hostility, he was sentenced to one year and eight months' imprisonment, plus a fine of 100,000 Turkish liras. He complained to the Commission alleging, *inter alia*, a breach of Article 10. By thirty votes to two, the Commission found a violation of that provision. Before the Court it was not disputed that the applicant's conviction interfered with his freedom of expression and was 'prescribed by law'. The Court also found that the interference furthered the legitimate aims of maintaining 'national security', 'preventing disorder' and preserving 'territorial integrity' in the context of separatist violence in south-east Turkey. But the Court, sixteen votes to one, did not consider that the applicant's conviction was 'necessary in a democratic society'.

The Court observes, however, that the applicant was writing in his capacity as a trade-union leader, a player on the Turkish political scene, and that the article in question, despite its virulence, does not encourage the use of violence or armed resistance or insurrection. In the Court's view, this is a factor which it is essential to take into consideration. (para 36)

Should the advocacy of violence be accorded protection under Article 10? Is it relevant that a number of European States have experienced terrorist campaigns by various groups claiming political (and recently religious) motivation? What if a State is responding to a perceived terrorist campaign by the use of military and security forces in ways which violate Convention rights—does this justify critics' encouragement of violent opposition? A majority of the Court was not willing to find a breach of Article 10 where an opposition politician was punished for appearing to express support for a 'terrorist organization'. In *Zana v Turkey* (1997)

27 EHRR 667, 1997-VII 2539, the applicant (a former mayor of Diyarbakir) while serving a prison sentence during 1987 gave an interview to journalists in which he said that: 'I support the PKK [Workers' Party of Kurdistan] national liberation movement; on the other hand, I am not in favour of massacres. Anyone can make mistakes, and the PKK kill women and children by mistake . . . ' The interview was subsequently published in a national newspaper. Later, the Diyarbakir National Security Court convicted the applicant of 'defending an act punishable by law as a serious crime' and sentenced him to twelve months' imprisonment for his statement. The Commission, with the President's casting vote, rejected the applicant's complaint under Article 10. The Court found that the interference with the applicant's freedom of expression was 'prescribed by law' and for the legitimate aims of maintaining national security and public safety, preventing crime and preserving territorial integrity (according to the Government, since 1985, the confrontation between the PKK and security forces had resulted in 4,036 civilian and 3,884 security forces deaths). Furthermore, the Court (by twelve votes to eight) held that the applicant's conviction was 'necessary in a democratic society' because:

Those words [he spoke in his interview] could be interpreted in several ways but, at all events, they are both contradictory and ambiguous. They are contradictory because it would seem difficult simultaneously to support the PKK, a terrorist organisation which resorts to violence to achieve its ends, and to declare oneself opposed to massacres; they are ambiguous because Mr Zana disapproves of the massacres of women and children, he at the same time describes them as 'mistakes' that anybody could make. The statement cannot, however, be looked at in isolation. It had a special significance in the circumstances of the case, as the applicant must have realised. . . . the interview coincided with murderous attacks carried out by the PKK on civilians in south-east Turkey, where there was extreme tension at the material time. In those circumstances the support given to the PKK—described as a 'national liberation movement'—by the former mayor of Diyarbakir, the most important city in south-east Turkey, in an interview published in a major national daily newspaper, had to be regarded as likely to exacerbate an already explosive situation in that region. (paras 58–60)

The dissentients did not consider that the interference with the applicant's freedom of expression was proportionate because, *inter alia*:

The mere fact that in his statement the applicant indicated support for a political organisation whose aims and means the Government reject and combat cannot, therefore, be a sufficient reason for prosecuting and sentencing him. . . . According to the applicant, he was misinterpreted by the Government and had in reality told the journalists that he was opposed to violence. He claimed that, as an activist in the Kurdish cause since the 1960s, he had always spoken out against violence and referred to having been imprisoned for belonging to the 'Path of Freedom' organisation, which had always advocated non-violent action. This claim by the applicant as to the content of his statement and the personal background against which it had to be interpreted, was not dealt with by the Government or discussed by the majority in the judgment.

For a further consideration of expression involving the alleged endorsement of violence see: *Karata v Turkey* (below p 666) and *Erdogdu and Ince v Turkey* (below p 688).

8　A unanimous Chamber doubted whether a speech by an opposition politician in which he described the country's President as a liar and slanderer could be classified as the expression of an opinion in a political debate. The Chamber in *Pakdemirli v Turkey*, judgment of 22 February 2005, considered that the comments amounted to a hail of insults, albeit in the context of a lengthy relationship of political antagonism between the two politicians. Therefore, the domestic courts' determination that the applicant's comments amounted to defamation could be justified under Article 10(2) as being for the protection of the reputation/rights of the President. However, the Chamber concluded that the amount of damages that the applicant had been ordered to pay (approximately 60,000 euros, the highest amount ever awarded by a Turkish court) was not a proportionate sum and resulted in the applicant having suffered a breach of Article 10.

9 The Court has stated that special protection should be afforded to political expression taking place within public representative democratic institutions. The applicant in *Jerusalem v Austria*, judgment of 27 February 2001, was a member of the Vienna Municipal Council (which also acted as the Regional Parliament). During a debate on sects she expressed the view that a specified organisation was a sect. Later, that organisation obtained an injunction preventing her from repeating the statement. When examining her complaint that the injunction violated her freedom of expression under Article 8 the Court, unanimously, held that:

40. As regards the impugned statements of the applicant, the Court observes that they were made in the course of a political debate within the Vienna Municipal Council. It is not decisive that this debate occurred before the Vienna Municipal Council sitting as the local council and not as the *Land* Parliament. Irrespective of whether the applicant's statements were covered by parliamentary immunity, the Court finds that they were made in a forum which was at least comparable to Parliament as concerns the public interest in protecting the participants' freedom of public expression. In a democracy, Parliament or such comparable bodies are the essential fora for political debate. Very weighty reasons must be advanced to justify interfering with the freedom of expression exercised therein.

The Court went on to find that as the Austrian courts had required the applicant to prove the truth of her statements and, at the same time, denied her the opportunity to produce evidence to support her words she had suffered a breach of Article 10. How far down the domestic hierarchy of representative bodies (national and regional parliaments, city councils etc.) should this principle be applied? For the Court's evaluation of the compatibility of parliamentary immunity with a member of the public's right to defend her reputation via defamation proceedings see *A. v UK*, above p 395. [Art 6]

10 The limits of a politician's ability to counter-attack defamatory media comments about him/herself were revealed in *Wabl v Austria* (21 March 2000). The applicant was a Green member of the Austrian Parliament who had participated in a protest campaign against the stationing of fighter planes near Graz airport. During the protests a police officer accused the applicant of scratching his arm (proceedings were later dropped against the applicant). A local newspaper published an article with the headline 'Police Officer claims: AIDS test for Wabl!' in the text the officer argued that the applicant should have an 'AIDS-test' in order to discover if he had the disease (and might thereby have passed it on to the officer). The applicant asked the newspaper to publish a rectification and it did so a few days later stating '... we wish to apologise for any gross claims which were not appropriate to our standards of fairness...' The same edition of the paper also included a report from the local public health expert who reassured the public that 'AIDS' could not be caught from scratches. On the same day as the paper published its rectification the applicant gave a press conference in which he stated that the newspaper's coverage was 'Nazi-journalism'. The newspaper publishers sought an injunction to prevent the applicant repeating his comment that they were responsible for Nazi journalism. Eventually, the Supreme Court granted the injunction because the applicant's right to freedom of expression could not justify such a serious attack on the paper's reputation. The applicant also successfully sued the publishers for defamation in respect of their original article. He then complained to the Commission alleging that the Supreme Court's injunction violated his rights under Article 10. The Commission found no breach. A majority of the Court (six votes to one) concluded that, ... the Supreme Court was entitled to consider that the injunction was 'necessary in a democratic society' for the protection of the reputation and rights of others' (para 45). In finding no violation the majority was particularly influenced by the 'not only polemical but particularly offensive' nature of the applicant's remark.

In her dissent Judge Greve expressed the belief that, 'a democratic political debate requires that where a politician is attacked, not for his political views but on a purely personal level, he should not be in a more disadvantageous position than the press, and that he should be allowed sufficient latitude to reply to press attacks'.

The Court's repugnance towards Nazi ideology is examined below in *Lehideux*. The judgment in *Wabl* cautions politicians to exercise restraint in attacking the media and not to allow themselves to be provoked into making hasty counter-blasts to scurrilous journalism.

11 The Court has not allowed the same wide limits of acceptable criticism in respect of civil servants, acting in their official capacity, as it has of politicians. In *Janowski v Poland* (1999) 29 EHRR 705, the applicant was a journalist who encountered two municipal guards ordering street vendors to leave a square in a Polish town. He formed the view that the guards were acting unlawfully, because the council had not passed a resolution to clear the square. A verbal exchange ensued between him and the guards in which he called the them 'oafs' and 'dumb'. Janowski was subsequently convicted of 'insulting a civil servant . . . during and in connection with carrying out his official duties' and fined 1,500,000 zlotys. He complained to the Commission which, by eight votes to seven, found a breach of Article 10. The Court held that:

. . . those limits may in some circumstances be wider with regard to civil servants exercising their powers than in relation to private individuals. However, it cannot be said that civil servants knowingly lay themselves open to close scrutiny of their every word and deed to the extent to which politicians do and should therefore be treated on an equal footing with the latter when it comes to the criticism of their actions (cf *Oberschlick v Austria (No 2)* 1997, para 29).

What is more, civil servants must enjoy public confidence in conditions free of undue perturbation if they are to be successful in performing their tasks and it may therefore prove necessary to protect them from offensive and abusive verbal attacks when on duty. (para 33).

A majority of the Court, twelve votes to five, went on to find that that the applicant's conviction was a proportionate response to the legitimate aim of preventing disorder and did not breach Article 10. Significantly, a number of senior members of the Court, including the President, a Vice-President and a Chamber President, dissented. President Wildhaber found no 'pressing need' for the applicant's conviction; 'since the applicant used only two moderately insulting words, in a spontaneous and lively discussion, to defend a position which was legally correct and in which he had no immediate personal interest.' Judges Bratza and Rozakis considered that the applicant's comments fell within the protected category of matters of public concern as he perceived the officials to be acting in excess of their authority. Likewise Judge Bonello concluded that: 'I fail to discern any urgent social exigency in condemning those who attempt to prevent abuses, even through immoderate disapproval. The state has a greater necessity to silence those who usurp power than those who raise their voices when power is usurped.' The majority's decision on the facts of this case certainly seems unduly protective of officials in the light of these powerful dissents.

In the later case of *Yankov v Bulgaria* (2003), see above p 210 [Art 3], a unanimous Chamber, presided over by Judge Rozakis, distinguished *Janowski* in respect of the applicant's criticism of officials in a manuscript.

136. The applicant also made remarks such as 'well-fed idlers' and 'simple villagers' (about the prison warders), 'a provincial parvenu' (about a police officer whose name was also stated) and 'powerful unscrupulous people' (apparently about prosecutors and investigators generally).

137. While the above statements were undoubtedly insulting, they were far from being grossly offensive. The Court also notes that they were made in a manuscript in which the applicant, in a language and style characteristic of personal memoirs or a similar literary form, recounted his arrest and detention. It was a narrative in which the applicant described moments of his life as a detainee and explained his opinion about the criminal proceedings against him, taking a critical stand as regards allegedly unlawful acts by State officials (distinguish, *Janowski v Poland*, § 32).

138. The Court considers that since the offensive remarks were written in the context of substantive criticism of the administration of justice and officials involved in it, made in a literary form, the State authorities should have shown restraint in their reaction.

139. What is more, the Court is struck by the fact that the applicant was punished for having written down his own thoughts in a private manuscript which, apparently, he had not shown to anyone at the time it was seized. He had neither 'uttered' nor 'disseminated' any offensive or defamatory statements. In particular, there was no allegation that the applicant had circulated the text among the other detainees.

140. To that extent, the case may raise issues relating to the applicant's freedom of thought under Article 9 of the Convention or his right to respect for his private life under Article 8. However, in so far as the manuscript was seized when the applicant was about to hand it over to his lawyer and thus to 'impart' its content and make it available to others, the Court does not need to decide whether it would be more appropriate to consider the case from the standpoint of those provisions.

141. Nonetheless, the fact that the applicant's remarks were never made public is relevant to the assessment of the proportionality of the interference under Article 10 of the Convention. The Court notes in this respect, in addition, that the manuscript was not in a form ready for publication and that there was no immediate danger of its dissemination, even if it had been taken out of the prison.

142. While the members of the prison administration who saw the applicant's manuscript after its seizure must have felt personally insulted by certain remarks which concerned them, it is difficult to accept that that was a sufficient reason to punish the applicant in response. Civil servants have a duty to exercise their powers by reference to professional considerations only, without being unduly influenced by personal feelings. The need to ensure that civil servants enjoy public confidence in conditions free of undue perturbation can justify an interference with the freedom of expression only where there is a real threat in this respect. The applicant's manuscript obviously did not pose such a threat.

143. Having regard to all the relevant circumstances, it cannot be accepted that a fair balance was struck between the competing rights and interests: the applicant's right to freedom of expression on the one hand and the need to maintain the authority of the judiciary and to protect the reputation of civil servants. By punishing the applicant, a prisoner, with seven days' confinement in a disciplinary cell for having included moderately offensive remarks in a private manuscript critical of the justice system, which had not been circulated among the detainees, the authorities overstepped their margin of appreciation.

144. The Court finds, therefore, that the interference with the applicant's freedom of expression was not necessary in a democratic society within the meaning of Article 10 § 2 of the Convention.

145. There has therefore been a violation of Article 10 of the Convention.

The Chamber's requirement that insulting comments must create a 'real threat' (paragraph 142) to public confidence in civil servants if they are to be lawfully punished under Article 10 is a welcome strengthening of the protection of freedom of expression concerning public officials.

12 In *Thorgeirson v Iceland* A.239 (1992) 14 EHRR 843, the respondent Government sought to draw a distinction between political expression and the discussion of other matters of public

interest. In the Government's opinion Article 10 did not accord the second category of expression the same breadth of protection as the former. The applicant was a journalist who wrote two articles in a daily newspaper about allegations of police brutality. Describing the 'Reykjavik night-life jungle' he wrote that 'the beasts in uniform in the aforementioned jungle attacked [a named fellow journalist]' and of 'those wild beasts in uniform that creep around'. At the instigation of the Reykjavik Police Association, the public prosecutor charged Thorgeirson with criminal defamation of unspecified members of the Reykjavik police force. He was convicted and fined 10,000 crowns. The European Court, by eight votes to one, rejected the Government's purported distinction: '. . . there is no warrant in [the Court's] case-law for distinguishing, in the manner suggested by the Government, between political discussion and discussion of other matters of public concern. (para 64)

The Court concluded that the applicant's articles were directed at a matter of serious public interest and that placed in their context the language used was not excessive. Therefore, his conviction was not a proportionate response and violated Article 10. This judgment reinforces the protection given to the media by the Court when journalists are seeking to draw popular attention to matters of legitimate public concern. The Court, applied this reasoning to a satirical newspaper's publication of the tax affairs of a senior businessman in *Fressoz and Roire v France*, 1999-I. The applicants were the publishing director and a journalist on the French weekly *Le Canard enchaine*. During 1989 there was industrial unrest over pay levels in the Peugeot motor company and the chairman/ managing director of the company, Mr Jacques Calvert, refused to award the increase being sought by the workers. The applicants then published an article which disclosed that Mr Calvert had received pay increases totalling 46% in recent years. The article also contained extracts derived from Mr Calvert's tax forms which had been sent anonymously to the newspaper. Eventually, the applicants were convicted of handling photocopies of the tax returns obtained through a breach of professional confidence by an unidentified tax official and fined 15,000 francs. The applicants complained to the Commission alleging, *inter alia*, a breach of Article 10. The Commission, by twenty-one votes to eleven, upheld that complaint. A unanimous Court held that the newspaper article dealt with a matter of general interest.

The article was published during an industrial dispute—widely reported in the press—at one of the major French car manufacturers. The workers were seeking a pay rise which the management were refusing. The article showed that the company chairman had received large pay increases during the period under consideration while at the same time opposing his employees' claims for a rise. By making such a comparison against that background, the article contributed to a public debate on a matter of general interest. It was not intended to damage Mr Calvert's reputation but to contribute to the more general debate on a topic that interested the public . . . (para 50)

As local taxpayers had access to official lists of the taxable income of fellow residents in France, financial reviews frequently published the remuneration of senior business executives and the applicants had published the article in good faith, the Court concluded that the conviction of the applicants was a disproportionate interference with their freedom of expression which violated Article 10. This ruling further expands the scope of protected expression involving matters of general interest to cover not only comments upon the behaviour of state officials but also the financial rewards received by the senior personnel of major (private sector) companies. Because of the economic and social power exercised by such persons their remuneration can be seen as being of legitimate concern to the public (whether as employees, shareholders or consumers); compare the public debate about 'fat cat' salaries for senior British company directors during the late 1990s.

13 A majority of a Grand Chamber of the Court has also accorded Article 10 protection to a television journalist who produced a programme in which other persons expressed unlawful racist views: *Jersild v Denmark*, A.298 (1994) 19 EHRR 1. The applicant worked for the Danish Broadcasting Company on its Sunday News Magazine (a serious programme dealing with a wide range of social and political issues aimed at a well-informed audience). The programme editors decided to produce a segment on a group of young people, called 'the Greenjackets', who had been featured in the newspapers because of their racist comments. The applicant recorded several hours of interviews with members of the Greenjackets and then edited these recordings to produce a programme segment lasting a few minutes. This piece was then broadcast as part of one edition of the programme. The segment contained a number of racist comments made by members of the Greenjackets, including the statement by one interviewee that 'a nigger is not a human being, it's an animal, that goes for all the other foreign workers as well, Turks, Yugoslavs and whatever they are called'. Subsequently, the public prosecutor brought criminal proceedings against the Greenjacket members for making unlawful racist comments and against the applicant for aiding and abetting the expression of such unlawful speech. The applicant was convicted and fined 1,000 kroner (the Greenjackets were also found guilty). The Commission (by twelve votes to four) considered that the applicant's conviction violated Article 10. The Court emphasized '. . . the vital importance of combating racial discrimination in all its forms and manifestations.' (para 30). Indeed, it felt that, 'there can be no doubt that the remarks in respect of which the Greenjackets were convicted were more than insulting to members of the targeted groups and did not enjoy the protection of Article 10.' (para 35) However:

News reporting based on interviews, whether edited or not, constitutes one of the most important means whereby the press is able to play its vital role of 'public watchdog' . . . The punishment of a journalist for assisting in the dissemination of statements made by another person in an interview would seriously hamper the contribution of the press to discussion of matters of public interest and should not be envisaged unless there are particularly strong reasons for doing so. (para 35)

As the applicant did not have a racist purpose when compiling his report and taken as a whole his segment could not objectively be viewed as having such a purpose, his conviction was not necessary in a democratic society. The dissentients considered that (a) the majority did not accord sufficient protection to those persons who have to suffer from racist hatred and (b) they did not believe that the applicant had done enough to counterbalance/challenge the racist views expressed in his broadcast. The common ground between all members of the Court was that the intentional promotion of racist opinions would not be granted the protection of Article 10. In the later case of *Lehideux and Isorni v France*, 1998-VII, the Court developed this approach by stating that support for a pro-Nazi policy would not enjoy the protection of this Article. The two applicants, who died before the Court pronounced its judgment, published an advertisement in the French newspaper *Le Monde* during 1984 which was headed 'People Of France, You Have Short Memories'. The advertisement went on to defend the actions of Marshall Philippe Petain (the leader of the Vichy government in France during the Second World War who was subsequently sentenced to death by the French courts for collaboration with the Nazis). The text claimed, *inter alia*: 'That in the thick of difficulties which no French Head of State had ever known, Nazi atrocities and persecutions, he protected them against German omnipotence and barbarism, thus ensuring that two million prisoners of war were saved.' An association of former resistance members filed a criminal complaint and civil suit against the applicants for publicly defending the crimes of collaboration with the enemy. Eventually, the Paris Court of Appeal found the applicants guilty and awarded civil damages of one franc against them. They then complained to the Commission alleging a breach of, *inter alia*, Article 10. By twenty-three votes to eight the Commission expressed the opinion that there had been a breach of that Article. The Court found that there had been an interference with the applicants' right to freedom of expression and that it had the legitimate aims of protecting the reputations of others and preventing disorder or crime. However, the Court was divided on whether the interference was 'necessary in a democratic society'. A majority of fifteen considered that it was not. The majority distinguished debate over the aims and policies of Petain from, '... the category of clearly established historical facts—such as the Holocaust— whose negation or revision would be removed from the protection of Article 10 by Article 17.' (para 47) Furthermore:

There is no doubt that, like any other remark directed against the Convention's underlying values (see, *mutatis mutandis*, the *Jersild v Denmark* judgment . . .), the justification of a pro-Nazi policy could not be allowed to enjoy the protection afforded by Article 10. In the present case, however, the applicants explicitly stated their disapproval of 'Nazi atrocities and persecution' and of 'German omnipotence and barbarism'. Thus they were not so much praising a policy as a man, and doing so for a purpose-namely securing revision of Philippe Petain's conviction- whose pertinence and legitimacy at least, if not the means employed to achieve it, were recognised by the Court of Appeal. (para 53)

Therefore, having regard to the fact that the events referred to in the advertisement had occurred more than forty years ago, the majority held that the applicants' conviction violated their rights under Article 10. The six dissenters emphasised that the French authorities should have been accorded a wider margin of appreciation in this case. In the opinion of Judges Foighel, Loizou and Freeland:

In cases involving the right to freedom of expression the Court has generally been particularly restrictive in its approach to the margin of appreciation, although it has been prepared to accept a wider margin in relation to issues likely to offend personal convictions in the religious or moral domain. The latter category, based as it is on the principle that the margin of appreciation is wider where the aim pursued cannot be objectively defined on the European scale, is in our view not to be regarded as confined to those particular issues. It may include an issue such as that in question in the present case, where the aim pursued arose out of historical circumstances peculiar to France and where the French authorities were uniquely well placed, by virtue of their direct and continuous contact with the vital forces of their country, to assess the consequences for the protection of the rights of other groups, such as the associations of former resistance fighters and of deportees who were civil parties to the domestic proceedings, and more generally for the process of healing the wounds and divisions in French society resulting from the events of the 1940s. (para 4)

This case reinforces the judgment in *Jersild* by elaborating upon the types of expression that will be denied protection under Article 10. These now include: intentionally racist statements, expression supporting Nazi ideology and revisionist views seeking to deny historical facts concerning major human rights abuses such as the Holocaust (defamatory statements are similarly excluded, see *Tolstoy Miloslavsky v UK*, below p 694).

14 British restrictions on the ability of a pressure group to inform electors of the beliefs of Parliamentary candidates were found to be in breach of Article 10 by a majority of a Grand Chamber, in *Bowman v UK* (1998) 26 EHRR 1, 1998-I 175. The applicant was the executive director of the 'Society for the Protection of the Unborn Child', an organisation of 50,000 persons which is opposed to, *inter alia*, abortion and campaigns for a change in the current law regarding abortion in the UK. The major political parties in the UK do not have official policies regarding abortion, but leave it to the conscience of their individual Members of Parliament. The Society, therefore, took the view that if electors were to be able to change the law governing abortion by their choice of MPs they needed to know the local candidates' views on abortion. Consequently, just before the general election in 1992, the applicant arranged the distribution of 1.5 million leaflets containing this information on individual candidates. 25,000 of these leaflets were distributed in Halifax. In 1993, the applicant was charged with contravening section 75 of the Representation of the People Act 1983, which prohibits, during the election period, unauthorised persons expending more than £5 in publishing materials with the view to promoting (or preventing) the election of a candidate. Conviction may be punished with imprisonment for up to one year and/or a fine of up to £5,000 and/or disqualification from voting/election for up to five years. The court directed the acquittal of the applicant because the summons against her had been issued out of time. However, she had been convicted of a similar offence in 1979. She complained to the Commission of an alleged violation of her right to freedom of expression under Article 10 and a majority (twenty-eight votes to one) found a breach. The Court determined that section 75 amounted to a restriction on her freedom of expression by limiting the amount of money she could spend on promotional leaflets for the Society during election campaigns. All the parties accepted that this restriction was 'prescribed by law' and the Court concluded that it was for the legitimate aim of 'protecting the rights of others' (ie those of the candidates and electors in Halifax). Therefore, the main issue for the Court was whether section 75 was 'necessary in a democratic society'. The majority (fourteen judges) noted that under Article 3 of the First Protocol to the Convention, States had undertaken to hold 'free elections'.

Free elections and freedom of expression, particularly freedom of political debate, together form the bedrock of any democratic system... The two rights are inter-related and operate to reinforce each other... For this reason, it is particularly important in the period preceding an election that opinions and information of all kinds are permitted to circulate freely. Nevertheless, in certain circumstances the two rights may come into conflict and it may be considered necessary, in the period preceding or during an election, to place certain restrictions, of a type which would not usually be acceptable, on freedom of expression, in order to secure the 'free expression of the opinion of the people in the choice of the legislature'. [note, this is the wording of Article 3 of the First Protocol] The Court recognises that, in striking the balance between these two rights, the Contracting States have a margin of appreciation... (paras 42–3).

The Court then examined the proportionality of the restrictions imposed on the applicant's dissemination of promotional materials:

...s.75 of the 1983 Act operated, for all practical purposes, as a total barrier to Mrs Bowman's publishing information with a view to influencing the voters of Halifax in favour of an anti-abortion candidate. It is not satisfied that it was necessary thus to limit her expenditure to £5 in order to achieve the legitimate aim of securing equality between candidates, particularly in view of the fact that there were no restrictions placed upon the freedom of the press to support or oppose the election of any particular candidate or upon political parties and their supporters to advertise at national or regional level, provided that such advertisements were not intended to promote or prejudice the electoral prospects of any particular candidate in any particular constituency. It accordingly concludes that the restriction in question was disproportionate to the aim pursued. (para 47)

The six dissentients did not consider that the restrictions imposed on election publications by the 1983 Act were in breach of Article 10. Valticos J thought that, 'there is something slightly ridiculous in seeking to give the British Government lessons in how to hold elections and run a democracy...' Loizou, Baka and Jambrek JJ believed that the restrictions fell within the UK's margin of appreciation and that they were part of a 'balanced democratic electoral system'. Freeland and Levits JJ perceived section 75 as promoting fairness between candidates.

The low level of permitted expenditure (£5 or less) under s 75 seems to have been a decisive factor in the Court's assessment of the proportionality of the restrictions governing the applicant (and other campaigners/pressure groups). Section 131 of the Political Parties, Elections and Referendums Act 2000, increased the permitted level of expenditure to £500 in respect of each parliamentary candidate.

15   The prohibition on certain groups of local government officers from engaging in party political activities was upheld by a majority of the Court in *Ahmed v UK*, 1998-VI. The former (Conservative) Government had established a Committee, chaired by Sir David Widdicombe an eminent QC, to examine the roles of councillors and officers in local government. In its report the Committee noted that the tradition of local government service in the UK had been one of politically neutral officers serving whichever party was in control. To maintain that impartiality the Committee recommended that either the terms and conditions of officers or legislation should prohibit senior officers from engaging in defined party political activities. This proposal was accepted by the Government which secured the passage of the Local Government and Housing Act 1989. Under the Act, the Secretary of State for the Environment was empowered to make Regulations limiting the political activities of local government officers. Regulations were issued in 1990 which applied to three groups of officers: (a) the most senior officers in local government (e.g. chief executives and heads of departments; totalling about 12,000 officers), (b) officers whose salary exceeds approximately £26,000 per annum and whose posts have not been exempted by their local authorities (about 28,000 officers in total) and (c) officers on lower salaries whose duties involve them in, *inter alia*, giving regular advice to local authority committees or speaking on behalf of their authorities to the media on a regular basis (approximately 7,000 officers in total). Officers falling within these groups were prohibited from, *inter alia*, (i) standing as a candidate or canvassing in elections for the House of Commons, European Parliament or any local authority, (ii) holding an office within any political party and (iii) publishing any written or artistic work with the intention of affecting public support for a political party. However, officers holding such 'politically restricted posts' were not prevented from being members of political parties. Politically restricted officers could apply for exemption from the Regulations to an independent Adjudicator. The applicants were four local government officers who held politically restricted posts which prevented them from engaging in party political activities. They, together with their trade union, challenged the Regulations by way of judicial review proceedings. The High Court and the Court of Appeal dismissed the challenges. Thereupon, the applicants applied to the Commission arguing that the Regulations violated their rights under several Articles including freedom of expression. The Commission, by thirteen votes to four, expressed the opinion that there had been a breach of Article 10. Before the Court, the (new Labour) Government did not deny that the Regulations interfered with the applicants' freedom of expression under Article 10(1), but it sought to claim that the interference was justified under Article 10(2). The Court found the Regulations were 'prescribed by law' and had the legitimate aim of protecting the rights of others, both councillors and the electorate, to effective democracy at the local level. According to the Court the aim of protecting effective political democracy was not restricted to situations where the constitutional order was threatened by a political party (e.g. as in *Vogt v Germany*, below p 677).

To limit this notion to that context would be to overlook both the interests served by democratic institutions such as local authorities and the need to make provision to secure their proper functioning where this is considered necessary to safeguard those interests. The Court recalls in this respect that democracy is a fundamental feature of the European public order. . . . For the Court this notion of effective political democracy is just as applicable to the local level as it is to the national level bearing in mind the extent of decision-making entrusted to local authorities and the proximity of the local elect-orate to the policies which their local politicians adopt. (para 52)

A majority of the Court, six votes to three, held that the Regulations (as applied to the applicants) were 'necessary in a democratic society'. In its view the Widdicombe Report had identified the 'pressing social need' for action to preserve the political impartiality of relevant local government officers. Furthermore, the Regulations were a proportionate response as they only applied to approximately 2 per cent of local government officers and the holders of politically restricted posts were able to join political parties and make political comments, provided the latter were not partisan. Therefore, the Court found no breach of the applicants' rights under Article 10 (or other provisions in the Convention). The dissentients did not consider the restrictions placed on the applicants were either required by a pressing social need ('other democratic societies appear to function without such general and far-reaching restrictions' para 5) or proportional (e.g. restricted officers had to resign before they were able to stand for election to Parliament or the European Parliament ('This particular interference can hardly be deemed instrumental in strengthening democracy, since a healthy democracy has need of the best and most experienced parliamentarians.' para 6). Professor Morris has also expressed criticism of the Court's judgment:

Its broad-brush approach towards the question of proportionality stood in marked contrast to that of the Commission, which had emphasised, inter alia, the large class of employees embraced by the Regulations and the limited possibilities of exemption. The Court did not address points raised by the applicants relating to the discretion accorded to employers in defining employees' duties; the potential gap between contractual duties and the frequency with which they were performed in practice; and the application of the restrictions to those whose duties were purely of a professional or technical nature. [Gillian S Morris, 'The political activities of local government workers and the ECHR' (1999) PL 211 at 216.]

16 The Court adopted a similar stance in respect of restrictions on the political activities of police officers in *Rekvényi v Hungary* (20 May 1999). The Hungarian Constitution was amended in 1993 to prohibit career members of the police (and members of the armed forces and civil national security services) from engaging 'in any political activity' or joining any political party. Regulations elaborated what forms of political conduct were permitted, e.g. officers could stand for election to Parliament if their membership of the police service was suspended for the sixty days preceding the election. The applicant, a police officer and the Secretary General of the Police Independent Trade Union, complained that these restrictions violated, *inter alia*, his right to freedom of expression. The Commission, by twenty-one votes to nine, found a violation of Article 10. The Court, unanimously, found that there had been an interference with the applicant's freedom of political expression, but that it could be justified under Article 10(2). The historical situation during the Communist period in Hungary, when the police force was a 'tool' of the ruling political party, was invoked by the Government to explain the Constitutional ban.

The Court notes that Hungary is not alone, in that a number of Contracting States restrict certain political activities on the part of their police. . . . Ultimately the police force is at the service of the State. Members of the public are therefore entitled to expect that in their dealings with the police they are confronted with politically-neutral officers who are detached from the political fray . . . In the Court's view, the desire to ensure that the crucial role of the police in society is not compromised through the corrosion of the political neutrality of its officers is one that is compatible with democratic principles.

This objective takes on a special historical significance in Hungary because of that country's experience of a totalitarian regime which relied to a great extent on its police's direct commitment to the ruling party.

Accordingly, the Court concludes that the restriction in question pursued legitimate aims within the meaning of paragraph 2 of Article 10, namely the protection of national security and public safety and the prevention of disorder. (para 41)

As the Regulations allowed the police to engage in a number of forms of political expression the Court held that the restrictions were a proportionate response to a pressing social need. Would the Court have reached the same conclusion if the Constitutional ban on political activity had not been subject to limitations and exceptions?

The Court has also considered restrictions on the freedom of expression of civil servants (teachers) in *Vogt v Germany* (below p 677) and military personnel (below p 703).

17 The academic views, on a contentious issue of constitutional law, of a senior judge expressed in a public lecture were infringed under Article 10 by the adverse reactions of a Head of State in *Wille v Liechtenstein* (28 October 1999). The applicant had been a member of the Government of Liechtenstein in 1992 when there had been conflict between Prince Hans-Adam II, the Head of State, and the Government over a matter of political competence concerning a plebiscite. The applicant did not stand for re-election to parliament and in 1993 the Diet nominated him to be President of the Liechtenstein Administrative Court. The Prince formally appointed the applicant to that position for a fixed term. During February 1995 the applicant gave a lecture at the Liechtenstein-Institut, a research body, on the 'Nature and Functions of the Liechtenstein Constitutional Court'. In the course of that lecture the applicant expressed his belief that the Constitutional Court was competent to rule on the interpretation of the constitution in cases of disagreement between the Prince and the Diet. The applicant's lecture was reported in the national newspaper. Ten days later the Prince wrote (on heraldic notepaper) to the applicant at his home address stating '....in my eyes your attitude, Dr Wille, makes you unsuitable for public office. I do not intend to get involved in a long public or private debate with you, but I should like to inform you in good time that I shall not appoint you again to a public office should you be proposed by the Diet or any other body....' Subsequently the Diet, unanimously, concluded that the applicant's lecture had not called into question his judicial office. There was also a public exchange of correspondence between the applicant and the Prince. In 1997 the Diet proposed the applicant's re-appointment to the Presidency of the Administrative Court, as his original term of office had expired. The Prince refused to accept the proposed appointment. Later the applicant complained to the Commission alleging, *inter alia*, a breach of Article 10. By 15 votes to 4 the Commission upheld the complaint. The Court rejected the Government's argument that the Prince's letter was merely an item of private correspondence. Furthermore:

46. The Court reiterates in this connection that the responsibility of a State under the Convention may arise for acts of all its organs, agents and servants. As is the case in international law generally, their rank is immaterial since the acts by persons accomplished in an official capacity are imputed to the State in any case. In particular, the obligations of a Contracting Party under the Convention can be violated by any person exercising an official function vested in him (see *Ireland v UK*, Comm Report 25.1.76, Yearbook 19, p 512, at p 758). ....

50. Considering the contents of this letter the Court finds that there has been an interference by a State authority with the applicant's freedom of expression. The measure complained of occurred in the middle of the applicant's term of office as President of the Administrative Court; it was unconnected with any concrete recruitment procedures involving an appraisal of personal qualifications. From the terms

of the letter of 27 February 1995 it appears that the Prince had come to a resolution regarding his future conduct towards the applicant, which related to the exercise of one of his sovereign powers, ie his power to appoint State officials. Moreover, the said letter was expressly addressed to the applicant as the President of the Administrative Court, though sent to his place of residence. Thus, the measure complained of was taken by an organ which was competent to act in the manner it did and whose acts engage the responsibility of Liechtenstein as a State under the Convention. The right of the applicant to exercise his freedom of expression was interfered with once the Prince, criticising the contents of the applicant's speech, announced the intention to sanction the applicant because he had freely expressed his opinion. The announcement by the Prince of his intention not to reappoint the applicant to a public post constituted a reprimand for the previous exercise by the applicant of his right to freedom of expression and, moreover, had a chilling effect on the exercise by the applicant of his freedom of expression, as it was likely to discourage him from making statements of that kind in the future.

51. It follows that there was an interference with the exercise of the applicant's right to freedom of expression, as secured in Article 10 § 1.

The Court then examined whether the Prince's interference was 'necessary in a democratic society'. A majority, 16 votes to 1, concluded that it was not.

64. ... Since the applicant was a high-ranking judge at that time, the Court must bear in mind that, whenever the right of freedom of expression of persons in such a position is at issue, the 'duties and responsibilities' referred to in Article 10 § 2 assume a special significance since it can be expected of public officials serving in the judiciary that they should show restraint in exercising their freedom of expression in all cases where the authority and impartiality of judiciary are likely to be called in question. Nevertheless the Court finds that an interference with the freedom of expression of a judge in a position such as the applicant's calls for close scrutiny on the part of the Court.

65. As regards the applicant's lecture on 16 February 1995, the Court observes that this lecture formed part of a series of academic lectures at a Liechtenstein research institute on questions of constitutional jurisdiction and fundamental rights . . . The applicant's discourse included a statement on the competences of the Constitutional Court under Article 112 of the Liechtenstein Constitution. It was the applicant's view that the term 'Government' used in this provision included the Prince, an opinion allegedly in conflict with the principle of the Prince's immunity from the jurisdiction of the Liechtenstein judiciary . . . .

66. In the applicant's view this statement was an academic comment on the interpretation of Article 112 of the Constitution. The Government, on the other hand, maintained that although it was being made in the guise of a legally aseptic statement, it constituted, in essence, a highly political statement involving an attack on the existing constitutional order and not reconcilable with the public office held by the applicant at the time.

67. The Court accepts that the applicant's lecture, since it dealt with matters of constitutional law and more specifically with the issue of whether one of the sovereigns of the State was subject to the jurisdiction of a constitutional court, inevitably had political implications. It holds that questions of constitutional law, by their very nature, have political implications. It cannot find, however, that this element alone should have prevented the applicant from making any statement on this matter. The Court further observes that in the context of introducing a bill amending the Constitutional Court Act in 1991, the Liechtenstein Government had, in its accompanying comments, held a similar view, which had been opposed by the Prince but had found agreement in the Liechtenstein Diet, albeit only by a majority . . . The opinion expressed by the applicant cannot be regarded as an untenable proposition since it was shared by a considerable number of persons in Liechtenstein. Moreover, there is no evidence to conclude that the applicant's lecture contained any remarks on pending cases, severe criticism of persons or public institutions or insults of high officials or the Prince.

68. Turning to the Prince's reaction, the Court observes that he announced his intention not to appoint the applicant to public office again, should the applicant be proposed by the Diet or any other body. The Prince considered that the above-mentioned statement by the applicant clearly infringed the Liechtenstein Constitution. In this context, he also made reference to a political controversy with the Liechtenstein Government in October 1992 and, in conclusion, he reproached the applicant, who had been a member of Government at that time and President of the Liechtenstein Administrative Court since 1993, with regarding himself as not being bound by the Constitution. In the Prince's view, the applicant's attitude towards the Constitution made him unsuitable for public office.

69. The Prince's reaction was based on general inferences drawn from the applicant's previous conduct in his position as a member of Government, in particular on the occasion of the political controversy in 1992, and his brief statement, as reported in the press, on a particular, though controversial, constitutional issue of judicial competence. No reference was made to any incident suggesting that the applicant's view, as expressed at the lecture in question, had a bearing on his performance as President of the Administrative Court or on any other pending or imminent proceedings. Also the Government did not refer to any instance where the applicant, in the pursuit of his judicial duties or otherwise, had acted in an objectionable way.

70. On the facts of the present case, the Court finds that, while relevant, the reasons relied on by the Government in order to justify the interference with the applicant's right to freedom of expression are not sufficient to show that the interference complained of was 'necessary in a democratic society'. Even allowing for a certain margin of appreciation, the Prince's action appears disproportionate to the aim pursued. Accordingly the Court holds that there has been a violation of Article 10 of the Convention.

The Court awarded the applicant 10,000 Swiss Francs non-pecuniary damage for the distress that he had suffered. The Court's judgment emphasises the close connection between matters of constitutional law and political discourse. It is also significant for the Court's ruling that States are potentially liable under the Convention for the actions of all their organs, including those of the Head of State when acting in an official capacity. This European legal accountability is of value to individuals as under domestic law such office-holders may not be amenable to normal legal actions (e.g. the personal prerogative immunity of the British Sovereign from criminal or civil proceedings in domestic courts).

18   The Court addressed the issue of political advertising in *VGT Verein Gegen Tierfabriken v Switzerland*, judgment of 28 June 2001. The applicant association had the aim of protecting animals. In response to television commercials broadcast on Swiss television by the meat industry, the applicant produced a commercial of just under one minute in length. The applicant's commercial showed a sow building a nest in the forest for her piglets and then inside a large building with pigs kept in small pens. The commercial ended with the words, 'eat less meat, for the sake of your health, the animals and the environment!' The company responsible for advertisements on Swiss national television refused to accept the applicant's commercial as it considered the advertisement to be of a political character. Subsequently, the Federal Court upheld the decision not to broadcast the commercial as Swiss legislation prohibited political advertising. The applicant contended that the refusal to broadcast the advertisement violated its freedom of expression. A unanimous Chamber endorsed the domestic courts' view that the commercial had a political character.

57. In the Court's opinion the commercial indubitably fell outside the regular commercial context in the sense of inciting the public to purchase a particular product. Rather, with its concern for the protection of animals, expressed partly in drastic pictures, and its exhortation to reduce meat consumption, the commercial reflected controversial opinions pertaining to modern society in general and also lying at the heart of various political debates.

The Court found that the ban on political advertisements had a basis in Swiss law and was for the legitimate aim, under Article 10(2), of preventing wealthy groups from obtaining a competitive advantage in politics. As to whether the ban on the applicant's advertisement was 'necessary in a democratic society' the Chamber held that:

69. It follows that the Swiss authorities had a certain margin of appreciation to decide whether there was a 'pressing social need' to refuse the broadcasting of the commercial. Such a margin of appreciation is particularly essential in commercial matters, especially in an area as complex and fluctuating as that of advertising (see *markt intern Verlag GmbH and Klaus Beermann v Germany*, judgment of 20 November 1989, Series A No 165, pp 19–20, § 33, and *Jacubowski v Germany*, judgment of 23 June 1994, Series A No 291-A, p 14, § 26).

70. However, the Court has found above that the applicant association's film fell outside the regular commercial context inciting the public to purchase a particular product. Rather, it reflected controversial opinions pertaining to modern society in general (see paragraph 57 above). The Swiss authorities themselves regarded the content of the applicant association's commercial as being 'political' within the meaning of section 18(5) of the Federal Radio and Television Act. Indeed, it cannot be denied that in many European societies there was, and is, an ongoing general debate on the protection of animals and the manner in which they are reared.

71. As a result, in the present case the extent of the margin of appreciation is reduced, since what is at stake is not a given individual's purely 'commercial' interests, but his participation in a debate affecting the general interest (see *Hertel* [*v Switzerland* 1998-VI]).

72. The Court will consequently examine carefully whether the measure in issue was proportionate to the aim pursued. In that regard, it must balance the applicant association's freedom of expression, on the one hand, with the reasons adduced by the Swiss authorities for the prohibition of political advertising, on the other, namely to protect public opinion from the pressures of powerful financial groups and from undue commercial influence; to provide for a certain equality of opportunity among the different forces of society; to ensure the independence of broadcasters in editorial matters from powerful sponsors; and to support the press.

73. It is true that powerful financial groups can obtain competitive advantages in the area of commercial advertising and may thereby exercise pressure on, and eventually curtail the freedom of, the radio and television stations broadcasting the commercials. Such situations undermine the fundamental role of freedom of expression in a democratic society as enshrined in Article 10 of the Convention, in particular where it serves to impart information and ideas of general interest, which the public is moreover entitled to receive. Such an undertaking cannot be successfully accomplished unless it is grounded in the principle of pluralism of which the State is the ultimate guarantor. This observation is especially valid in relation to audio-visual media, whose programmes are often broadcast very widely (see *Informationsverein Lentia and Others v Austria (no. 1)*, judgment of 24 November 1993, Series A No 276, p 16, § 38).

74. In the present case, the contested measure, namely the prohibition of political advertising as provided in section 18(5) of the Federal Radio and Television Act, was applied only to radio and television broadcasts, and not to other media such as the press. The Federal Court explained in this respect in its judgment of 20 August 1997 that television had a stronger effect on the public on account of its dissemination and immediacy. In the Court's opinion, however, while the domestic authorities may have had valid reasons for this differential treatment, a prohibition of political advertising which applies only to certain media, and not to others, does not appear to be of a particularly pressing nature.

75. Moreover, it has not been argued that the applicant association itself constituted a powerful financial group which, with its proposed commercial, aimed at endangering the independence of the broadcaster; at unduly influencing public opinion or at endangering equality of opportunity among

the different forces of society. Indeed, rather than abusing a competitive advantage, all the applicant association intended to do with its commercial was to participate in an ongoing general debate on animal protection and the rearing of animals. The Court cannot exclude that a prohibition of 'political advertising' may be compatible with the requirements of Article 10 of the Convention in certain situations. Nevertheless, the reasons must be 'relevant' and 'sufficient' in respect of the particular interference with the rights under Article 10. In the present case, the Federal Court, in its judgment of 20 August 1997, discussed at length the general reasons which justified a prohibition of 'political advertising'. In the Court's opinion, however, the domestic authorities have not demonstrated in a 'relevant and sufficient' manner why the grounds generally advanced in support of the prohibition of political advertising also served to justify the interference in the particular circumstances of the applicant association's case.

76. The domestic authorities did not adduce the disturbing nature of any particular sequence, or of any particular words, of the commercial as a ground for refusing to broadcast it. It therefore mattered little that the pictures and words employed in the commercial at issue may have appeared provocative or even disagreeable.

77. In so far as the Government pointed out that there were various other possibilities to broadcast the information at issue, the Court observes that the applicant association, aiming at reaching the entire Swiss public, had no other means than the national television programmes of the Swiss Radio and Television Company at its disposal, since these programmes were the only ones broadcast throughout Switzerland. The Commercial Television Company was the sole instance responsible for the broadcasting of commercials within these national programmes. Private regional television channels and foreign television stations cannot be received throughout Switzerland.

78. The Government have also submitted that admitting the applicant association's claim would be to accept a 'right to broadcast' which in turn would substantially interfere with the rights of the Commercial Television Company to communicate information. Reference was further made to the danger of untimely interruptions in television programmes by means of commercials. The Court recalls that its judgment is essentially declaratory. Its task is to determine whether the Contracting States have achieved the result called for by the Convention. Various possibilities are conceivable as regards the organisation of broadcasting television commercials; the Swiss authorities have entrusted the responsibility in respect of national programmes to one sole private company. It is not the Court's task to indicate which means a State should utilise in order to perform its obligations under the Convention (see *De Cubber v Belgium*, judgment of 26 October 1984, Series A No 86, p 20, § 35).

79. In the light of the foregoing, the measure in issue cannot be considered as 'necessary in a democratic society'. Consequently, there has been a violation of Article 10 of the Convention.

The above judgment reveals that the Court will accord States a narrower margin of appreciation to restrict advertisements of a political nature compared to those concerned with purely business/commercial interests (on the latter see *Krone Verlag*, below p 674). Paragraph 75 also left open the possibility that in, unspecified, circumstances States might be able to justify a ban on political advertising under Article 10(2). However, the Court's rigorous protection of political expression means that States will require powerful reasons to justify such bans. We may speculate that political advertising that expressed views contrary to the values of the Convention (e.g. pro-Nazi) could legitimately be prohibited by States.

In the subsequent case of *Murphy v Ireland*, judgment of 10 July 2003, another Chamber ruled that States should be granted a wider margin of appreciation when regulating advertisements of a religious nature. The applicant, a pastor, had sought to have a radio advertisement, inviting listeners to attend a video presentation about Christ at his faith centre, broadcast on a local commercial radio station. The station was willing to broadcast the advertisement, but the Independent Radio and Television Commission prevented the broadcast as legislation prohibited advertisements 'directed towards any religious . . . end . . .' on Irish radio and television stations. The Government sought to justify the ban, before the Court, on the ground, *inter alia*, of religious sensitivities in Ireland as there had been a long history of religious division. The Court, unanimously, held that:

67. In this latter respect, there is little scope under Article 10 § 2 of the Convention for restrictions on political speech or on debate of questions of public interest (see, *mutatis mutandis*, among many other authorities, *Lingens v Austria*, judgment of 8 July 1986, Series A No 103, § 42; *Castells v Spain*, judgment of 23 April 1992, Series A No 236, § 43; and *Thorgeir Thorgeirson v Iceland*, judgment of 25 June 1992, Series A No 239, § 63). However, a wider margin of appreciation is generally available to the Contracting States when regulating freedom of expression in relation to matters liable to offend intimate personal convictions within the sphere of morals or, especially, religion. Moreover, as in the field of morals, and perhaps to an even greater degree, there is no uniform European conception of the requirements of 'the protection of the rights of others' in relation to attacks on their religious convictions. What is likely to cause substantial offence to persons of a particular religious persuasion will vary significantly from time to time and from place to place, especially in an era characterised by an ever growing array of faiths and denominations. By reason of their direct and continuous contact with the vital forces of their countries, State authorities are in principle in a better position than the international judge to give an opinion on the exact content of these requirements with regard to the rights of others as well as on the 'necessity' of a 'restriction' intended to protect from such material those whose deepest feelings and convictions would be seriously offended (the *Wingrove* [v UK 1996-V] judgment, at § 58).

The Court therefore observes that it is this margin of appreciation which distinguishes the present case from the above-cited case of *Vgt Verein gegen Tierfabriken v Switzerland*. In the latter case, the Court considered that the advertisement prohibited concerned a matter of public interest to which a reduced margin of appreciation applied.

. . .

81. . . . the Court observes that there appears to be no clear consensus between the Contracting States as to the manner in which to legislate for the broadcasting of religious advertisements. Certain States have similar prohibitions (for example, Greece, Switzerland and Portugal), certain prohibit religious advertisements considered offensive (for example, Spain and see also Council Directive 89/552/EEC) and certain have no legislative restriction (the Netherlands). There appears to be no 'uniform conception of the requirements of the protection of the rights of others' in the context of the legislative regulation of the broadcasting of religious advertising (see paragraph 67 above).

82. In the circumstances, and given the margin of appreciation accorded to the State in such matters, the Court considers that the State has demonstrated that there were 'relevant and sufficient' reasons justifying the interference with the applicant's freedom of expression within the meaning of Article 10 of the Convention.

In consequence, it concludes that there has been no violation of the Convention.

More generally on the topic of freedom of expression concerning religious beliefs see above p 601 [Art 9 *Choudhury*]

Artistic expression

....

Müller v Switzerland A.133 (1988) 13 EHRR 212
European Court of Human Rights

Josef Muller is a painter who has exhibited his works on many occasions in private galleries and museums in Switzerland and other countries. In 1981 he was invited by the organisers (who subsequently became his fellow applicants in this case) of a contemporary art exhibition,

'Fri-Art 81' marking the 500th anniversary of the Canton of Fribourg's entry into the Swiss Confederation, to produce and exhibit works in their event. He produced three large paintings which were on show when the exhibition began. The exhibition had been advertised in the press and on posters, and free access was available to everyone. A juvenile reacted violently to Muller's paintings and her father complained to the local public prosecutor. The prosecutor informed an investigating judge that the paintings appeared to fall within the scope of Article 204 of the Criminal Code, which prohibited obscene publications. The judge went to the exhibition and then had the pictures removed and seized by the police. In 1982 the Sarine District Criminal Court convicted the applicants of publishing obscene material, each of them was fined 300 Swiss francs and the confiscated paintings were ordered to be deposited with the cantonal art museum for safekeeping. The Cantonal Court dismissed the applicants' appeals noting that: 'these are not works which, in treating a particular subject or scene, allude to sexual activity more or less discreetly. They place it in the foreground, depicting it not in the embrace of man and woman but in vulgar images of sodomy, fellatio between males, bestiality, erect penises and masturbation.' The Federal Court also dismissed their further appeals. In 1988 the Sarine District Criminal Court granted Muller's application to have the paintings returned to him. The applicants complained of a violation of their rights under Article 10. The Commission expressed the opinion that there had been a violation of this Article in respect of the confiscation of the paintings (eleven votes to three) but there had been no breach of the Convention in respect of the convictions (unanimously).

AS TO THE LAW

27. The applicants indisputably exercised their right to freedom of expression—the first applicant by painting and then exhibiting the works in question, and the nine others by giving him the opportunity to show them in public at the 'Fri-Art 81' exhibition they had mounted.

Admittedly, Article 10 does not specify that freedom of artistic expression, in issue here, comes within its ambit; but neither, on the other hand, does it distinguish between the various forms of expression. As those appearing before the Court all acknowledged, it includes freedom of artistic expression—notably within freedom to receive and impart information and ideas—which affords the opportunity to take part in the public exchange of cultural, political and social information and ideas of all kinds. Confirmation, if any were needed, that this interpretation is correct, is provided by the second sentence of paragraph 1 of Article 10, which refers to 'broadcasting, television or cinema enterprises', media whose activities extend to the field of art. Confirmation that the concept of freedom of expression is such as to include artistic expression is also to be found in article 19 § 2 of the International Covenant on Civil and Political Rights, which specifically includes within the right of freedom of expression information and ideas 'in the form of art'.

28. The applicants clearly suffered 'interference by public authority' with the exercise of their freedom of expression—firstly, by reason of their conviction by the Sarine District Criminal Court on 24 February 1982, which was confirmed by the Fribourg Cantonal Court on 26 April 1982 and then by the Federal Court on 26 January 1983 . . . and secondly on account of the confiscation of the paintings, which was ordered at the same time but subsequently lifted . . .

I. THE APPLICANTS' CONVICTION

1. 'PRESCRIBED BY LAW'

29. In the applicants' view, the terms of Article 204 § 1 of the Swiss Criminal Code, in particular the word 'obscene', were too vague to enable the individual to regulate his conduct and consequently neither

the artist nor the organisers of the exhibition could foresee that they would be committing an offence. This view was not shared by the Government and the Commission.

According to the Court's case-law, 'foreseeability' is one of the requirements inherent in the phrase 'prescribed by law' in Article 10 § 2 of the Convention. A norm cannot be regarded as a 'law' unless it is formulated with sufficient precision to enable the citizen—if need be, with appropriate advice—to foresee, to a degree that is reasonable in the circumstances, the consequences which a given action may entail . . .

In the present instance, it is also relevant to note that there were a number of consistent decisions by the Federal Court on the 'publication' of 'obscene' items. . . . These decisions, which were accessible because they had been published and which were followed by the lower courts, supplemented the letter of Article 204 § 1 of the Criminal Code. The applicants' conviction was therefore 'prescribed by law' within the meaning of Article 10 § 2 of the Convention.

2. THE LEGITIMACY OF THE AIM PURSUED

30. The Government contended that the aim of the interference complained of was to protect morals and the rights of others. On the latter point, they relied above all on the reaction of a man and his daughter who visited the 'Fri-Art 81' exhibition . . .

The applicants' conviction consequently had a legitimate aim under Article 10 § 2.

3. 'NECESSARY IN A DEMOCRATIC SOCIETY'

31. The submissions of those appearing before the Court focused on the question whether the disputed interference was 'necessary in a democratic society' for achieving the aforementioned aim.

In the applicants' view, freedom of artistic expression was of such fundamental importance that banning a work or convicting the artist of an offence struck at the very essence of the right guaranteed in Article 10 and had damaging consequences for a democratic society. No doubt the impugned paintings reflected a conception of sexuality that was at odds with the currently prevailing social morality, but, the applicants argued, their symbolical meaning had to be considered, since these were works of art. Freedom of artistic expression would become devoid of substance if paintings like those of Josef Felix Müller could not be shown to people interested in the arts as part of an exhibition of experimental contemporary art.

In the Government's submission, on the other hand, the interference was necessary, having regard in particular to the subject-matter of the paintings and to the particular circumstances in which they were exhibited.

For similar reasons and irrespective of any assessment of artistic or symbolical merit, the Commission considered that the Swiss courts could reasonably hold that the paintings were obscene and were entitled to find the applicants guilty of an offence under Article 204 of the Criminal Code.

32. The Court has consistently held that in Article 10 § 2 the adjective 'necessary' implies the existence of a 'pressing social need' (see, as the most recent authority, the *Lingens* judgment of 8 July 1986, Series A No 103, p 25, § 39). The Contracting States have a certain margin of appreciation in assessing whether such a need exists, but this goes hand in hand with a European supervision, embracing both the legislation and the decisions applying it . . .

In exercising its supervisory jurisdiction, the Court cannot confine itself to considering the impugned court decisions in isolation; it must look at them in the light of the case as a whole, including the paintings in question and the context in which they were exhibited. The Court must determine whether the interference at issue was 'proportionate to the legitimate aim pursued' and whether the reasons adduced by the Swiss courts to justify it are 'relevant and sufficient' (see the same judgment, p 26, § 40).

. . . Those who create, perform, distribute or exhibit works of art contribute to the exchange of ideas and opinions which is essential for a democratic society. Hence the obligation on the State not to encroach unduly on their freedom of expression.

34. Artists and those who promote their work are certainly not immune from the possibility of limitations as provided for in paragraph 2 of Article 10. Whoever exercises his freedom of expression undertakes, in accordance with the express terms of the paragraph, 'duties and responsibilities'; their scope will depend on his situation and the means he uses (see, *mutatis mutandis*, the *Handyside* judgment previously cited, p 23, § 49). In considering whether the penalty was 'necessary in a democratic society', the Court cannot overlook this aspect of the matter.

33. The applicants' conviction on the basis of Article 204 of the Swiss Criminal Code was intended to protect morals. Today, as at the time of the *Handyside* judgment (previously, cited, p 22, § 48), it is not possible to find in the legal and social orders of the Contracting States a uniform European conception of morals. The view taken of the requirements of morals varies from time to time and from place to place, especially in our era, characterised as it is by a far-reaching evolution of opinions on the subject. By reason of their direct and continuous contact with the vital forces of their countries, State authorities are in principle in a better position than the international judge to give an opinion on the exact content of these requirements as well as on the 'necessity' of a 'restriction' or 'penalty' intended to meet them.

36. In the instant case, it must be emphasised that—as the Swiss courts found both at the cantonal level at first instance and on appeal and at the federal level—the paintings in question depict in a crude manner sexual relations, particularly between men and animals . . . They were painted on the spot—in accordance with the aims of the exhibition, which was meant to be spontaneous—and the general public had free access to them, as the organisers had not imposed any admission charge or any age-limit. Indeed, the paintings were displayed in an exhibition which was unrestrictedly open to—and sought to attract—the public at large.

The Court recognises, as did the Swiss courts, that conceptions of sexual morality have changed in recent years. Nevertheless, having inspected the original paintings, the Court does not find unreasonable the view taken by the Swiss courts that those paintings, with their emphasis on sexuality in some of its crudest forms, were 'liable grossly to offend the sense of sexual propriety of persons of ordinary sensitivity'. Note, this is the Swiss definition of obscenity. . . . In the circumstances, having regard to the margin of appreciation left to them under Article 10 § 2, the Swiss courts were entitled to consider it 'necessary' for the protection of morals to impose a fine on the applicants for publishing obscene material.

The applicants claimed that the exhibition of the pictures had not given rise to any public outcry and indeed that the press on the whole was on their side. It may also be true that Josef Felix Müller has been able to exhibit works in a similar vein in other parts of Switzerland and abroad, both before and after the 'Fri-Art 81' exhibition. It does not, however, follow that the applicants' conviction in Fribourg did not, in all the circumstances of the case, respond to a genuine social need, as was affirmed in substance by all three of the Swiss courts which dealt with the case.

37. In conclusion, the disputed measure did not infringe Article 10 of the Convention.

II. THE CONFISCATION OF THE PAINTINGS

. . .

3. 'NECESSARY IN A DEMOCRATIC SOCIETY'

40. Here again, those appearing before the Court concentrated their submissions on the 'necessity' of the interference.

The applicants considered the confiscation to be disproportionate in relation to the aim pursued. In their view, the relevant courts could have chosen a less Draconian measure or, in the interests of protecting human rights, could have decided to take no action at all. They claimed that by confiscating the paintings the Fribourg authorities in reality imposed their view of morals on the country as a whole and that this was unacceptable, contradictory and contrary to the Convention, having regard to the well-known diversity of opinions on the subject.

The Government rejected these contentions. In declining to take the drastic measure of destroying the paintings, the Swiss courts took the minimum action necessary. The discharge of the confiscation order on 20 January 1988, which the first applicant could have applied for earlier, clearly showed that the confiscation had not offended the proportionality principle; indeed, it represented an application of it.

The Commission considered the confiscation of the paintings to be disproportionate to the legitimate aim pursued. In its view, the judicial authorities had no power to weigh the conflicting interests involved and order measures less severe than confiscation for an indefinite period.

...

42. A principle of law which is common to the Contracting States allows confiscation of 'items whose use has been lawfully adjudged illicit and dangerous to the general interest' (see, *mutatis mutandis*, the *Handyside* judgment previously cited, Series A No 24, p 30, § 63). In the instant case, the purpose was to protect the public from any repetition of the offence.

43. The applicants' conviction responded to a genuine social need under Article 10 § 2 of the Convention (see paragraph 36 above). The same reasons which justified that measure also apply in the view of the Court to the confiscation order made at the same time.

Undoubtedly, as the applicants and the Commission rightly emphasised, a special problem arises where, as in the instant case, the item confiscated is an original painting: on account of the measure taken, the artist can no longer make use of his work in whatever way he might wish.

Thus Josef Felix Müller lost, in particular, the opportunity of showing his paintings in places where the demands made by the protection of morals are considered to be less strict than in Fribourg.

It must be pointed out, however . . . it is open to the owner of a confiscated work to apply to the relevant cantonal court to have the confiscation order discharged or varied if the item in question no longer presents any danger or if some other, more lenient, measure would suffice to protect the interests of public morals. In its decision of 20 January 1988, the Sarine District Criminal Court stated that the original confiscation 'was not absolute but merely of indeterminate duration, which left room to apply for a reconsideration' . . . It granted Mr Müller's application because 'the preventive measure [had] fullfilled its function, namely to ensure that such paintings [were] not exhibited in public again without any precautions' (ibid).

Admittedly, the first applicant was deprived of his works for nearly eight years, but there was nothing to prevent him from applying earlier to have them returned; the relevant case-law of the Basle Court of Appeal was public and accessible, and, what is more, the Agent of the Government himself drew his attention to it during the Commission's hearing on 6 December 1985; there is no evidence before the Court to show that such an application would have failed.

That being so, and having regard to their margin of appreciation, the Swiss courts were entitled to hold that confiscation of the paintings in issue was 'necessary' for the protection of morals.

44. In conclusion, the disputed measure did not infringe Article 10 of the Convention.

FOR THESE REASONS, THE COURT

Holds by six votes to one that the applicants' conviction did not infringe Article 10 of the Convention;

Holds by five votes to two that the confiscation of the paintings did not infringe Article 10 of the Convention.

NOTES

1 The majority was comprised of President Ryssdal and Judges: Cremona, Bindschedler-Robert, Evans, and Bernhardt. Spielmann J dissented as he believed that the applicants' convictions and the confiscation of Muller's paintings should be considered together. In his opinion

'freedom of expression is the rule and interferences by the State, properly justified, must remain the exception'. As the paintings had been returned to Muller in 1988, he did not consider that it was 'necessary' to seize them in 1981 or convict the applicants. De Meyer J partly dissented on the ground that in the context of the exhibition of the paintings in 1981 he did not consider that it was necessary for them to be confiscated.

2   Restricting access to works of art, so that only certain sections of the public can view them, may not of itself prevent States successfully invoking Article 10(2) as a justification for convicting the artists/organisers or confiscating the works of art For example, in *Otto Preminger Institute v Austria* (1994) 19 EHRR 34, A.295-A (discussed above, p 601) only paying viewers over 17 years of age would have been admitted to the cinema, but the majority of the Court still found the Austrian authorities' actions (including the seizure/forfeiture of the film) to be lawful under Article 10(2) as being 'necessary' to protect the religious feelings of the local Catholic population.

3   See also *Wingrove v UK, Reports of Decisions and Judgments* (1996) 24 EHRR 1, 1996-V 1937 (above, p 603), for another unsuccessful claim that distribution of a video work had been prevented in breach of Article 10.

4   Artistic expression may contain a significant political statement or message and the application of Article 10 to this hybrid form of expression was examined by the Court in *Karata v Turkey* (8 July 1999). The applicant, a Turk of Kurdish origin, published a collection of his own poems (entitled 'The song of a rebellion—Dersim'—the latter being the name of a former region where there had been many riots between Kurdish clans and government forces between 1847 and 1938) in 1991. The poems contained verses which included;

> ...thousands of years
> of disasters have not altered our lives
> for our Kurdistan
> for our Dersim
> we will sacrifice our heads, drunk on the fire of rebellion
>
> ...
>
> the whelps of the Ottoman whore
> repeatedly pound our mountains
> the waters that run
> our springtime
>
> ...
>
> they are preparing genocide
> like those who know no bounds.

Subsequently, the Istanbul National Security Court convicted the applicant of disseminating propaganda against the 'indivisible unity of the State' and sentenced him to one year, eight months' imprisonment and a fine of 41 million Turkish Lira. The Commission, by twenty-six votes to six, rejected the applicant's complaint under Article 10. The Court found that the interference with the applicant's freedom of expression was 'prescribed by law' and had legitimate aims (protection of national security and territorial integrity and the prevention of disorder and crime). However, a majority of the Court (twelve votes to five) did not consider that his conviction and sentence was a proportionate response.

The work in issue contained poems which, through the frequent use of pathos and metaphors, called for self-sacrifice for 'Kurdistan' and included some particularly aggressive passages directed at the Turkish authorities. Taken literally, the poems may be construed as inciting readers to hatred, revolt and the use of violence. In deciding whether they in fact did so, it must nevertheless be borne in mind that the medium used by the applicant was poetry, a form of artistic expression that appeals to only a minority of readers. . . .

In the instant case, the poems had an obvious political dimension. Using colourful imagery, they expressed deep-rooted discontent with the lot of the population of Kurdish origin in Turkey. In that connection, the Court recalls that there is little scope under Article 10(2) of the Convention for restrictions on political speech or on debate on matters of public interest . . .

The Court observes, however, that the applicant is a private individual who expressed his views through poetry—which by definition is addressed to a very small audience-rather than through the mass media, a fact which limited their potential impact on 'national security', '[public] order' and 'territorial integrity' to a substantial degree. Thus, even though some of the passages from the poems seem very aggressive in tone and to call for the use of violence, the Court considers that the fact that they were artistic in nature and of limited impact made them less a call to an uprising than an expression of deep distress in the face of a difficult political situation. (paras 49–52)

Hence the Court was according greater latitude to political expression by artists working in minority (elite?) forms of art. But four dissentients, led by the President of the Court, considered that the crucial factor was the content of the work-not its form.

Where there are competing Convention interests the Court will have to engage in a weighing exercise to establish the priority of one interest over the other. Where the opposing interest is the right to life or physical integrity, the scales will tilt away from freedom of expression (e.g. *Zana v Turkey* (1997)).

It will therefore normally be relatively easy to establish that it is necessary in a democratic society to restrict speech which constitutes incitement to violence. Violence as a means of political expression being the antithesis of democracy, irrespective of the ends to which it is directed, incitement to it will tend to undermine democracy. . . . Violence is intrinsically inimical to the Convention. Unlike the advocacy of opinions on the free marketplace of ideas, incitement to violence is the denial of a dialogue, the rejection of the testing of different thoughts and theories in favour of a clash of might and power. It should not fall within the ambit of Article 10. . . .

The majority of the Court says that poetry is a form of artistic expression that 'appeals only to a minority of readers' and is 'of limited impact'. We disagree with this assessment. It seems to us that the Court saw the poetic form as being more important than the substance, that is to say the tone and content. We consider that the Court should be wary of adopting an ivory tower approach. One only has to think of words of the 'Marseillaise' as an example of a poetic call to arms. (Joint Partly Dissenting Opinion of Judges Wildhaber, Pastor Ridruejo, Costa and Baka).

Yet, in the later case of *Alinak v Turkey*, judgment of 29 March 2005, a unanimous Chamber (Presided over by Judge Costa) took account of the fact that the form of publication was a novel, when assessing whether it was necessary in a democratic society for the author's words to be censored. The applicant, a former MP, wrote a novel, using fictional characters, based on real events concerning the ill-treatment of residents of an actual village by members of the Turkish security forces. Passages in the book were very emotive and critical of the authorities. For example:

You cannot terminate it by killing them. There are too many to kill. Whomsoever you want to kill is only the cog of the machine. Even if you break the cog of the machine there are too many degenerated people out there waiting to become the cog! When you are struggling with the first ones, the same old tyrannising machinery continues to function, and this goes on forever. We have to stop this machinery!

A few weeks after the novel was published the State Security Court ordered the seizure of copies of the book. The Chamber determined that:

41. The Court notes that the book contains passages in which graphic details are given of fictional ill-treatment and atrocities committed against villagers, which no doubt creates in the mind of the reader

a powerful hostility towards the injustice to which the villagers were subjected in the tale. Taken literally, certain passages might be construed as inciting readers to hatred, revolt and the use of violence. In deciding whether they in fact did so, it must nevertheless be borne in mind that the medium used by the applicant was a novel, a form of artistic expression that appeals to a relatively narrow public compared to, for example, the mass media.

...

45. ... Thus, even though some of the passages from the book seem very hostile in tone, the Court considers that their artistic nature and limited impact reduce them to an expression of deep distress in the face of tragic events, rather than a call to violence.

The Chamber went on to conclude that the seizure of the book was a disproportionate response and amounted to a violation of Article 10.

Commercial expression

markt intern Verlag GmbH and Klaus Beermann v Germany
A.164 (1989) 12 EHRR 161
European Court of Human Rights

The applicant publishing company was founded to defend the interests of small and medium-sized retail companies against the competition of large supermarkets and mail-order enterprises. Mr Beermann was the editor-in-chief. The company published a weekly bulletin which provided information on the commercial activities of the large firms in the beauty products industry and this was sold to subscribers. In 1975 Beermann published an article in the bulletin about an English mail-order company ('Cosmetic Club International') which retold the allegations of a German chemist about her claimed failure to obtain a refund from the English company. The article noted that the mail-order company denied any knowledge of the complaint and promised a swift investigation of the matter. The bulletin had published previous articles on the mail-order company advising retailers to be cautious in their dealings with the firm. The mail-order company instituted proceedings in the Hamburg Regional Court against the applicants and the court granted an injunction preventing the bulletin repeating the 1975 statements. The applicants appealed and the Hanseatic Court of Appeal found in their favour. The company appealed to the Federal Court of Justice which ordered the applicants to refrain from republishing the 1975 statements (with a fine of up to 500,000 DM or imprisonment for up to six months for breach of the order) under the terms of the Unfair Competition Act 1909 (this stated that 'Any person who in the course of business commits, for purposes of competition, acts contrary to honest practices may be enjoined from further engaging in those acts and held liable in damages.'). The Federal Constitutional Court declined to review the judgment. The applicants petitioned the Commission which (by twelve votes to one) found a violation of Article 10.

AS TO THE LAW

24. The applicants claimed that the prohibition imposed on them by the German courts under section 1 of the 1909 Act and the broad interpretation which those courts gave to that provision had infringed Article 10 of the Convention ...

A. APPLICABILITY OF ARTICLE 10

25. The Government primarily disputed the applicability of Article 10. Before the Court they argued that if the case were examined under that provision, it would fall, by reason of the contents of the publication of 20 November 1975 and the nature of *markt intern's* activities, at the extreme limit of Article 10s field of application. The wording and the aims of the information bulletin in question showed that it was not intended to influence or mobilise public opinion, but to promote the economic interests of a given group of undertakings. In the Government's view, such action fell within the scope of the freedom to conduct business and engage in competition, which is not protected by the Convention.

The applicants did not deny that they defended the interests of the specialised retail trade. However, they asserted that *markt intern* did not intervene directly in the process of supply and demand. The undertaking depended exclusively on its subscribers and made every effort, as was proper, to satisfy the requirements of its readers, whose preoccupations the mainstream press neglected. To restrict the freedom of expression to news items of a political or cultural nature would result in depriving a large proportion of the press of any protection. ...

It is clear that the contested article was addressed to a limited circle of tradespeople and did not directly concern the public as a whole; however, it conveyed information of a commercial nature. Such information cannot be excluded from the scope of Article 10 § 1 which does not apply solely to certain types of information or ideas or forms of expression (see, *mutatis mutandis*, the *Müller* judgment of 24 May 1988, Series A No 133, p 19, § 27).

B. COMPLIANCE WITH ARTICLE 10

27. In the Court's view, the applicants clearly suffered an 'interference by public authority' in the exercise of the right protected under Article 10, in the form of the injunction issued by the Federal Court of Justice restraining them from repeating the statements appearing in the information bulletin of 20 November 1975. ...

1. 'PRESCRIBED BY LAW'

...

29. The applicants argued that the disputed interference was not 'prescribed by law', because it was not foreseeable. The relevant German legislation did not indicate the dividing line between freedom of the press and unfair competition. ...

The Government maintained, on the other hand, that, because of their considerable experience of litigation, the applicants had been familiar with the text and the interpretation of the 1909 Act long before the contested article was published. On this question the Commission shared the Government's view. ...

30. The Court has already acknowledged the fact that frequently laws are framed in a manner that is not absolutely precise. This is so in spheres such as that of competition, in which the situation is constantly changing in accordance with developments in the market and in the field of communication ...

In this instance, there was consistent case-law on the matter from the Federal Court of Justice ...

This case-law which was clear and abundant and had been the subject of extensive commentary, was such as to enable commercial operators and their advisers to regulate their conduct in the relevant sphere.

2. LEGITIMATE AIM

...

According to the actual wording of the judgment of 16 January 1980, the contested article was liable to raise unjustified suspicions concerning the commercial policy of the Club and thus damage its business.

The Court finds that the interference was intended to protect the reputation and the rights of others, legitimate aims under paragraph 2 of Article 10.

3. 'NECESSARY IN A DEMOCRATIC SOCIETY'

32. The applicants argued that the injunction in question could not be regarded as 'necessary in a democratic society'. The Commission agreed with this view.

The Government, however, disputed it. In their view, the article published on 20 November 1975 did not contribute to a debate of interest to the general public, but was part of an unlawful competitive strategy aimed at ridding the beauty products market of an awkward competitor for specialist retailers. . . .

33. The Court has consistently held that the Contracting States have a certain margin of appreciation in assessing the existence and extent of the necessity of an interference, but this margin is subject to a European supervision as regards both the legislation and the decisions applying it, even those given by an independent court . . . .

Such a margin of appreciation is essential in commercial matters and, in particular, in an area as complex and fluctuating as that of unfair competition. Otherwise, the European Court of Human Rights would have to undertake a re-examination of the facts and all the circumstances of each case. The Court must confine its review to the question whether the measures taken on the national level are justifiable in principle and proportionate . . .

34. In this case, in order to establish whether the interference was proportionate it is necessary to weigh the requirements of the protection of the reputation and the rights of others against the publication of the information in question. In exercising its power of review, the Court must look at the impugned court decision in the light of the case as a whole . . .

Markt intern published several articles on the Club criticising its business practices and these articles, including that of 20 November 1975, were not without a certain effect . . . On the other hand, the Club honoured its promises to reimburse dissatisfied customers and, in 1975, 11,870 of them were reimbursed . . .

The national courts did weigh the competing interests at stake . . .

The Federal Court of Justice based its judgment of 16 January 1980 on the premature nature of the disputed publication and on the lack of sufficient grounds for publicising in the information bulletin an isolated incident and, in doing so, took into consideration the rights and legal interests meriting protection . . .

35. In a market economy an undertaking which seeks to set up a business inevitably exposes itself to close scrutiny of its practices by its competitors. Its commercial strategy and the manner in which it honours its commitments may give rise to criticism on the part of consumers and the specialised press. In order to carry out this task, the specialised press must be able to disclose facts which could be of interest to its readers and thereby contribute to the openness of business activities.

However, even the publication of items which are true and describe real events may under certain circumstances be prohibited: the obligation to respect the privacy of others or the duty to respect the confidentiality of certain commercial information are examples. In addition, a correct statement can be and often is qualified by additional remarks, by value judgments, by suppositions or even insinuations. It must also be recognised that an isolated incident may deserve closer scrutiny before being made public; otherwise an accurate description of one such incident can give the false impression that the incident is evidence of a general practice. All these factors can legitimately contribute to the assessment of statements made in a commercial context, and it is primarily for the national courts to decide which statements are permissible and which are not.

36. In the present case, the article was written in a commercial context; *markt intern* was not itself a competitor in relation to the Club but it intended—legitimately—to protect the interests of chemists

and beauty product retailers. The article itself undoubtedly contained some true statements, but it also expressed doubts about the reliability of the Club, and it asked the readers to report 'similar experiences' at a moment when the Club had promised to carry out a prompt investigation of the one reported case.

According to the Federal Court of Justice . . . there was not sufficient cause to report the incident at the time of the publication. The Club had agreed to undertake an immediate investigation in order to clarify the position. Furthermore, the applicants had been aware that criticisms of the Club could not be fully justified before further clarification had been sought, as they themselves had described the reply of the Club as a provisional answer. In the opinion of the Federal Court they should therefore have taken into consideration that any such premature publication of the incident was bound to have adverse effects on the Club's business because it gave the specialised retailers an effective argument capable of being used against the Club with their customers, and one which could be used even if the incident should turn out to be an isolated mishap from which no conclusion could be drawn as to the Club's business policy.

37. In the light of these findings and having regard to the duties and responsibilities attaching to the freedoms guaranteed by Article 10, it cannot be said that the final decision of the Federal Court of Justice—confirmed from the constitutional point of view by the Federal Constitution Court—went beyond the margin of appreciation left to the national authorities. It is obvious that opinions may differ as to whether the Federal Court's reaction was appropriate or whether the statements made in the specific case by *markt intern* should be permitted or tolerated. However, the European Court of Human Rights should not substitute its own evaluation for that of the national courts in the instant case, where those courts, on reasonable grounds, had considered the restrictions to be necessary.

38. Having regard to the foregoing, the Court reaches the conclusion that no breach of Article 10 has been established in the circumstances of the present case.

FOR THESE REASONS, THE COURT

Holds, by nine votes to nine, with the casting vote of the President (Rule 20 § 3 of the Rules of Court), that there has been no violation of Article 10 of the Convention.

JOINT DISSENTING OPINION OF JUDGES GÖLCÜKLU, PETTITI, RUSSO, SPIELMANN, DE MEYER, CARRILLO, SALCEDO AND VALTICOS

It is just as important to guarantee the freedom of expression in relation to the practices of a commercial undertaking as it is in relation to the conduct of a head of government, which was at issue in the Lingens case. . . .

The fact that a person defends a given interest, whether it is an economic interest or any other interest, does not, moreover, deprive him of the benefit of freedom of expression.

In order to ensure the openness of business activities, it must be possible to disseminate freely information and ideas concerning the products and services proposed to consumers. Consumers, who are exposed to highly effective distribution techniques and to advertising which is frequently less than objective, deserve, for their part too, to be protected, as indeed do retailers.

In this case, the applicants had related an incident which in fact occurred, as has not been contested, and requested retailers to supply them with additional information.

They had exercised in an entirely normal manner their basic right to freedom of expression.

This right was, therefore, violated in their regard by the contested measures.

Having said this, we consider it necessary to make three further observations in relation to the present judgment.

We find the reasoning set out therein with regard to the 'margin of appreciation' of States a cause for serious concern. As is shown by the result to which it leads in this case, it has the effect in practice of considerably restricting the freedom of expression in commercial matters.

By claiming that it does not wish to undertake a re-examination of the facts and all the circumstances of the case, the Court is in fact eschewing the task, which falls to it under the Convention, of carrying out 'European supervision' as to the conformity of the contested 'measures' 'with the requirements' of that instrument.

On the question of the need to 'weigh the competing interests at stake', it is sufficient to note that in this case the interests which the applicants sought 'legitimately' to protect were not taken into consideration at all.

NOTES

1   The majority was comprised of President Ryssdal and Judges: Cremona, Thor Vilhjalmsson, Matscher, Walsh, Evans, Bernhardt, Palm, and Foighel. Martens J (with the approval of Macdonald J) issued a separate dissenting opinion. They expressed the view that, 'the socio-economic press is just as important as the political and cultural press for the progress of our modern societies and for the development of every man.' They were also critical of the German legal regime because, '... a rule extending the scope of the law on unfair competition to the detriment of freedom of the press is unknown in the other Member states of the Council of Europe, and rightly so because, in certain respects, all newspapers may be regarded as partisan, having espoused the cause of certain specific interests'.

2   The majority was not willing to accord the same degree of protection under Article 10 to publications concerned with commercial/business matters, even when they contained true statements of fact, that they were to political and artistic expression. Of course, much of the contemporary media is owned by private sector companies which have as one of their dominant aims the creations of profits for their owners. Therefore, the expression of matters of political or public interest and the creation of artistic works may be underpinned by commercial factors.

3   The Hanseatic Court of Appeal had previously granted an injunction, under the 1909 Act, preventing a vet from giving further statements to the general press criticising his fellow vets for failing to provide adequate emergency care during the night time. In *Barthold v Germany*, A.90 (1985) 7 EHRR 383, the Court (by five votes to two) held that ruling violated the applicant's rights under Article 10. The Court felt that the approach of the Court of Appeal, '... risks discouraging members of the liberal professions from contributing to public debate on topics affecting the life of the community if ever there is the slightest likelihood of their utterances being treated as entailing, to some degree, an advertising effect.' (para 58) Such a response was not a proportionate response and consequently not 'necessary in a democratic society'. This case can, therefore, be distinguished from *markt intern* as (a) the publication was in an ordinary newspaper and (b) the article was concerned with a matter of general public interest. In the later case of *Hertel v Switzerland* (1998) 28 EHRR 534, 1998-VI, a majority of the Court (six votes to three) held that a State's margin of appreciation should be reduced when commercial speech also encompassed matters of public interest.

Such a margin of appreciation is particularly essential in commercial matters, especially in an area as complex and fluctuating as that of unfair competition ... It is however necessary to reduce the extent of the margin of appreciation when what is at stake is not a given individual's purely 'commercial' statements, but his participation in a debate affecting the general interest, for example, over public health; in the instant case, it cannot be denied that such a debate existed. It concerned the effects of microwaves on human health ... In that respect, the present case is substantially different from the *markt intern* and *Jacubowski* cases ... (para 47)

Therefore, the majority found that the injunction granted by the Swiss courts against the applicant (an independent researcher), at the request of an association representing electrical manufacturers, which prohibited him from restating his view that food prepared in a microwave oven is a danger to health was not 'necessary in a democratic society'. In the opinion of the Court:

The effect of the injunction was thus partly to censor the applicant's work and substantially to reduce his ability to put forward in public views which have their place in a public debate whose existence cannot be denied. It matters little that his opinion is a minority one and may appear to be devoid of merit since, in a sphere in which it is unlikely that any certainty exists, it would be particularly unreasonable to restrict freedom of expression only to generally accepted ideas. (para 50)

Hence the Court was seeking to protect the ability of controversial, but *bona fide*, contributors to participate in public debates about matters of general interest.

4   The 1909 Act was also central to the case of *Jacubowski v Germany*, A.291-A (1994) 19 EHRR 64. The applicant was a journalist who had been the editor-in-chief of a news agency run by a commercial company. The owners of the agency dismissed him in July 1984. Within a few weeks the agency issued a press release explaining its own reorganisation and criticising the applicant's management (in October 1984 the applicant secured a court order requiring the agency to publish another press release in which he was able to state his response to the criticisms). In September 1984 the applicant sent a collection of newspaper articles critical of the news agency together with a circular letter stating his wish to discuss future developments to forty clients of the news agency. Several months later the applicant established his own public-relations agency. Jacubowski's former employers initiated proceedings under the 1909 Act against him. The Dusseldorf Court of Appeal granted an injunction against Jacubowski preventing him from issuing further similar mailings. The Federal Constitutional Court declined to intervene. The applicant then complained to Strasbourg alleging a violation of Article 10. The Commission unanimously found a breach, but the Court (by six votes to three) dismissed his claims. The Court held that the German courts had not exceeded the national margin of appreciation in commercial matters. In particular the Court gave emphasis to the fact that all the German courts had concluded that Jacubowski's actions, in publishing his own circular to former clients, had been unfair competition in breach of 'accepted moral standards' designed to attract them to his new business. Also, he was able to voice his opinions and defend himself by other means. Therefore, the Court decided that the injunction was not a disproportionate interference with the applicant's freedom of expression.

5   The Court has unanimously held that advertising by a lawyer falls within the scope of Article 10: in *Casado Coca v Spain* (1994) 18 EHRR 1, A.285. The applicant was a lawyer practising in Barcelona who published advertisements, in a local property owners' newsletter which gave his name, his status as a lawyer and his office address/telephone number. The Barcelona Bar Council brought disciplinary proceedings against him, at that time advertising by members of the Bar was prohibited unless it related to changes in the details of a practice, and he received a written warning for disregarding the ban on professional advertising. He challenged this penalty before the domestic courts, but the Constitutional Court found no breach of his fundamental rights. The Commission (on the casting vote of the President) found a breach of Article 10. Before the Court, the Spanish Government argued that advertising did not fall within the ambit of Article 10. This bold contention was rejected:

The Court would first point out that Article 10 guarantees freedom of expression to 'everyone'. No distinction is made in it according to whether the type of aim pursued is profit-making or not... In its *Barthold v Germany* judgment (above) the Court left open the question whether commercial advertising as such came within the scope of the guarantees under Article 10, but its later case-law provides guidance on this matter. Article 10 does not apply solely to certain types of information or ideas or forms of expression (see the *markt intern Verlag GmbH and Klaus Beermann v Germany* judgment (above)), in particular those of a political nature; it also encompasses artistic expression (see the *Muller v Switzerland* judgment (above)), information of a commercial nature (see *markt intern Verlag*)—as the Commission rightly pointed out—and even light music and commercials transmitted by cables (see the *Groppera Radio AG v Switzerland* judgment (1990) A.173). In the instant case the impugned notices merely gave the applicant's name, profession, address and telephone number. They were clearly published with the aim of advertising, but they provided persons requiring legal assistance with information that was of definite use and likely to facilitate their access to justice. Article 10 is therefore applicable. (paras 35–7)

The Court found that the restrictions on Bar advertisements were 'prescribed by law' and had the legitimate aim of protecting the interests of the public and ensuring respect for members of the Bar. 'In this connection, the special nature of the profession practised by members of the Bar must be considered; in their capacity as officers of the court they benefit from an exclusive right of audience and immunity from legal process in respect of their oral presentation of cases in court, but their conduct must be discreet, honest and dignified.' (para 46) Furthermore, a majority of the judges (seven votes to two) considered that the limitations placed upon the applicant's freedom to advertise his services were 'necessary in a democratic society'. The majority emphasised that the margin of appreciation to be given to States' regulation of advertising was 'particularly essential' and:

The wide range of regulations and the different rates of change in the Council of Europe's member States indicate the complexity of the issue. Because of their direct, continuous contact with their members, the Bar authorities and the country's courts are in a better position than an international court to determine how, at a given time, the right balance can be struck between the various interests involved, namely the requirements of the proper administration of justice, the dignity of the profession, the right of everyone to receive information about legal assistance and affording members of the Bar the possibility of advertising their practices. (para 55)

The majority noted that the penalty imposed on the applicant was 'almost a token one in nature', therefore the authorities' actions had been a proportionate interference which could be justified under Article 10(2).

A unanimous Chamber of the full-time Court refused to grant a State a 'wide' margin of appreciation to regulate newspaper advertising in *Krone Verlag GmbH & Co KG (No 3) v Austria*, judgment of 11 December 2003. The applicant company was the publisher of a daily newspaper. In December 1994 the Salzburg edition of its paper published several advertisements comparing its subscription price to that of another (identified) local paper. The other paper responded by applying to the courts, under the Unfair Competition Act, for an injunction to prevent the applicant from re-printing its advertisement. Eventually the Austrian courts granted an injunction preventing the applicant from publishing advertisements comparing its price with that of the other paper unless the advertisements detailed, *inter alia*, the different coverage of foreign/domestic politics, economic and cultural issues in the two newspapers. The applicant complained that the injunction violated its freedom of expression guaranteed by Article 10. The Strasbourg judgment held that:

30. The Court reiterates that under its case-law the States parties to the Convention have a certain margin of appreciation in assessing the necessity of an interference, but this margin is subject to European supervision as regards both the relevant rules and the decisions applying them (see *markt intern Verlag GmbH and Klaus Beermann*, § 33). Such a margin of appreciation is particularly essential in the

complex and fluctuating area of unfair competition. The same applies to advertising. The Court's task is therefore confined to ascertaining whether the measures taken at national level are justifiable in principle and proportionate (see *Casado Coca v Spain*, judgment of 24 February 1994, Series A No 285-A, p 28, § 50; and *Jacubowski v Germany*, judgment of 26 May 1994, No 15088/89, § 26).

31. For the public, advertising is a means of discovering the characteristics of services and goods offered to them. Nevertheless, it may sometimes be restricted, especially to prevent unfair competition and untruthful or misleading advertising. In some contexts, the publication of even objective, truthful advertisements might be restricted in order to ensure respect for the rights of others or owing to the special circumstances of particular business activities and professions. Any such restrictions must, however, be closely scrutinised by the Court, which must weigh the requirements of those particular features against the advertising in question; to this end, the Court must look at the impugned penalty in the light of the case as a whole (see *Casado Coca*, cited above, § 51).

32. Turning to the circumstances of the present case, the Court considers that the domestic courts based their decision first and foremost on the assumption that the two newspapers were not of comparable quality and that a comparison of their prices would therefore be misleading. On the other hand, the courts also stated that the two newspapers were competitors in the same market and for the same circle of readers. The Court finds these two statements rather inconsistent.

33. In looking further at the impact of the impugned injunction on the applicant company, the Court observes that no penalty was imposed. However, the measure at issue has quite far-reaching consequences as regards future advertising involving price comparison: the applicant company will also need to provide information on how its reporting style differs on matters of foreign or domestic politics, economy, culture, science, health, environmental issues and law. The Court considers the injunction to be far too broad, impairing the very essence of price comparison. Moreover, its practical implementation—though not impossible in general—appears to be highly difficult for the applicant company. Furthermore, the applicant company risks the imposition of fines for non-compliance with this order.

34. The Court notes that the domestic courts have given priority to the protection of the reputation of the other competitor and the rights of the consumers against misleading advertising in the instant case. However, when balancing the conflicting interests involved and taking account of the impact of the injunction on the applicant company's possibilities in future for advertising involving price comparison, the Court considers that the Austrian courts have overstepped their margin of appreciation in the present case, and that the measure at issue is disproportionate, and therefore not 'necessary in a democratic society' within the meaning of Article 10 § 2 of the Convention.

35. Accordingly, there has been a violation of Article 10 of the Convention.

Here, the Court considered that the extent of the restrictions placed on the applicant's freedom to advertise the comparative price of its newspaper were too onerous even though the domestic authorities were accorded a 'certain' margin of appreciation.

6   The full-time Court has held that States may be required to provide legal aid to impecunious defendants subject to defamation actions brought against them by economically powerful companies. In *Steel and Morris v UK*, see above p 407 the Chamber held that:

94. The Court further does not consider that the fact that the plaintiff in the present case was a large multinational company should in principle deprive it of a right to defend itself against defamatory allegations or entail that the applicants should not have been required to prove the truth of the statements made. It is true that large public companies inevitably and knowingly lay themselves open to close scrutiny of their acts and, as in the case of the businessmen and women who manage them, the limits of acceptable criticism are wider in the case of such companies (see *Fayed v the United Kingdom*,

judgment of 21 September 1994, Series A No 294-B, § 75). However, in addition to the public interest in open debate about business practices, there is a competing interest in protecting the commercial success and viability of companies, for the benefit of shareholders and employees, but also for the wider economic good. The State therefore enjoys a margin of appreciation as to the means it provides under domestic law to enable a company to challenge the truth, and limit the damage, of allegations which risk harming its reputation (see *Markt Intern Verlag GmbH and Beerman v Germany*, judgment of 20 November 1989, Series A No 165, §§ 33–38).

95. If, however, a State decides to provide such a remedy to a corporate body, it is essential, in order to safeguard the countervailing interests in free expression and open debate, that a measure of procedural fairness and equality of arms is provided for. The Court has already found that the lack of legal aid rendered the defamation proceedings unfair, in breach of Article 6 § 1. The inequality of arms and the difficulties under which the applicants laboured are also significant in assessing the proportionality of the interference under Article 10. As a result of the law as it stood in England and Wales, the applicants had the choice either to withdraw the leaflet and apologise to McDonald's, or bear the burden of proving, without legal aid, the truth of the allegations contained in it. Given the enormity and complexity of that undertaking, the Court does not consider that the correct balance was struck between the need to protect the applicants' rights to freedom of expression and the need to protect McDonald's rights and reputation. The more general interest in promoting the free circulation of information and ideas about the activities of powerful commercial entities, and the possible 'chilling' effect on others are also important factors to be considered in this context, bearing in mind the legitimate and important role that campaign groups can play in stimulating public discussion (see, for example, *Lingens v Austria*, judgment of 8 July 1986, Series A No 103, § 44, *Bladet Tromsø* § 64, *Thorgeir Thorgeirson* § 68). The lack of procedural fairness and equality therefore gave rise to a breach of Article 10 in the present case.

7 Professor Munro has commented:

The recognition of a category of commercial speech may be traced back earlier than the European Convention, to First Amendment case law in the United States. Indeed, it may not go too far to say that the categorisation approach to issues of freedom of expression may itself be attributed broadly to American origins. . . .

Granting acceptance of a market economy, there is a general acceptance that advertising necessarily has a place in it. More positively, it is reasonable to contend that advertising performs useful social and educational functions. Speaking for the majority of the United States Supreme Court in *Virginia State Board of Pharmacy v Virginia Citizens Consumer Council*, Blackmun J. said:

> 'So long as we preserve a predominantly free enterprise economy, the allocation of our resources in large measure will be made through numerous private economic decisions. It is a matter of public interest that those decisions, in the aggregate, be intelligent and well informed. To this end the free flow of commercial information is indispensable . . .
>
> 'As to the particular consumer's interest in the free flow of commercial information, that interest may be as keen, if not keener by far, than his interest in the day's most urgent political debate. [425 U.S. 748, 763 (1976)] . . .'

When advertising represents the artistic creations of individuals, there is also justification by the same arguments for self-expression as apply to other artistic works. There could even be constructed an argument that businesses have rights to self-expression, given that expression has economic as well as personal and political applications.

If advertising may be justified on the basis of its social utility, there should be no difficulty in defending other types of commercial speech such as corporate communications. The activities of business and commerce are, in general, in the public interest, so commercial speech scarcely deserves to be treated as 'low value' speech as if it involved criminality. . . . Colin R Munro, 'The Value of Commercial Speech' 62(1) [2003] *Cambridge Law Journal* 134, at pp 135 and 156–7.

8 Utilizing the economic analysis of public choice theory Maya Hertig Randall has proposed that:

Instead of apprehending speech in terms of 'high' or 'low' value, it would be more beneficial to think not in terms of hierarchy but in terms of difference. We should ask ourselves whether the speech characteristics are relevant in the light of the purpose of the regulation invoked to justify the restriction of freedom of expression. 'Commercial Speech under the European Convention on Human Rights: Subordinate or Equal?' *Human Rights Law Review* (2006) 6(1) 53, at p 85.

Freedom to hold opinions

The dismissal of a state employee because of her political opinions and activities has been adjudged to amount to an interference with her rights under Article 10(1). In *Vogt v Germany* (1995) 21 EHRR 205, A.323, the applicant had been a secondary-school language teacher employed by the government of Lower Saxony. During her time as a student in the early 1970s she had joined the German Communist Party and she continued her membership throughout her training as a probationary teacher. In 1979, before the end of her probationary period, she was appointed a permanent civil servant (the formal status of teachers in state schools in Germany). Her assessment report for 1981 described her work as entirely satisfactory and stated that she was held in high regard by her pupils and their parents and by colleagues. However, in 1982 the regional council began disciplinary proceedings against her for allegedly failing to comply with the duty of loyalty to the constitution which all German civil servants were under a statutory duty to respect. The basis of the case against her was that she had engaged in political activities on behalf of the Communist Party, such as distributing its literature and standing as a candidate for the party in federal elections (in a series of cases the Federal Administrative Court had ruled that civil servants who played an active role in the Communist Party were in breach of their duty of loyalty, because they were necessarily identifying with the party's anti-constitutional aims). In 1987 the local Administrative Court found that she had breached her duty of loyalty and ordered her dismissal. Despite her claims that in her opinion membership of the Communist Party was not in breach of her duty of loyalty, the German appellate courts upheld her dismissal. The Commission (by thirteen votes to one) considered that there had been a breach of, *inter alia*, Article 10. The Court (by seventeen votes to two) held that the applicant fell within Article 10:

The Court reiterates that the right of recruitment to the civil service was deliberately omitted from the Convention. Consequently, the refusal to appoint a person as a civil servant cannot as such provide the basis for a complaint under the Convention. This does not mean, however, that a person who has been appointed as a civil servant cannot complain on being dismissed if that dismissal violates one of his or her rights under the Convention. Civil servants do not fall outside the scope of the Convention. . . . According to the authorities, she had by her activities on behalf of the [German Communist Party] and by her refusal to dissociate herself from that party expressed views inimical to the above-mentioned system. It follows that there was indeed an interference with the exercise of the right protected by Article 10 of the Convention. (paras 43–4)

The Court found that the authorities' actions were 'prescribed by law' and had the legitimate aims of protecting national security, preventing disorder and protecting the rights of others.

The Court notes that a number of Contracting States impose a duty of discretion on their civil servants. . . . This notion has a special importance in Germany because of that country's experience under the Weimar Republic, which, when the Federal Republic was founded after the nightmare of Nazism, led to its constitution being based on the principle of a 'democracy capable of defending itself'. (para 50)

However, a bare majority of the Court (ten votes to nine) considered that it was not 'necessary in a democratic society' for Mrs Vogt to have been dismissed. The majority felt that the punishment was disproportionate having regard to : (1) the virtual impossibility of such persons finding employment as teachers elsewhere in Germany, (2) that her position did not involve security risks, (3) that her work at school had been wholly satisfactory, (4) '... not even the prolonged investigations lasting several years were apparently capable of yielding any instance where Mrs Vogt had actually made specific pronouncements belying her emphatic assertion that she upheld the values of the German constitutional order' (para 60) and (5) the Communist Party had not been banned in Germany and, therefore, the applicant's activities on its behalf were lawful.

The dissentients believed that the dismissal of the applicant was a proportionate response in the light of: (1) the fact that her activities on behalf of the Communist Party had intensified after she had been appointed as a civil servant, (2) the 'special history' of Germany's constitutional order and (3) '... at the relevant time the East-West confrontation and the antagonism between the communist regime on the one side and the West German democratic order on the other made it necessary to strengthen the democratic order and not to allow it to be undermined.'

The judgments in this case provide a fascinating illustration of the breadth of factors, including constitutional history and geo-political relationships, that the Court is willing to examine when applying Article 10.

Right to receive and impart information and ideas

Autronic AG v Switzerland A.178 (1990) 12 EHRR 485
European Court of Human Rights

The applicant was a limited company incorporated in Switzerland which specialised in electronics. During the early 1980s it sold 90 cm dish aerials for the domestic reception of television programmes broadcast by satellites. At that time the only programmes capable of being received by persons using the aerial in Switzerland were programmes broadcast by a Soviet Union telecommunications satellite (G-Horizont). The applicant applied to the Head Office of the Swiss national Post and Telecommunications Authority (PTT) in the spring of 1982 for permission to give a showing, at the Basle Trade Fair, of the Soviet television programmes which could be received by its aerial. The PTT wrote to the Soviet Union's embassy in Berne which granted permission for the duration of fair. In the summer of 1982 the applicant made a similar application to the PTT in respect of another trade exhibition. The request was passed on to the Soviet Union's embassy, but they did not reply. Therefore, the PTT informed the applicant that it could not grant permission and that an unauthorized reception of the Soviet broadcasts would be contrary to the Swiss Radio Regulations. Some months later the applicant applied to the PTT for a declaratory ruling that the reception for private use of uncoded television programmes broadcast by foreign satellites did not require the consent of the broadcasting state's authorities. In 1983 the PTT ruled that it could only grant a receiving licence with the consent of the broadcasting state's authorities. The applicant sought to challenge that ruling in the Swiss court, but the Federal Court decided that the applicant did not have an interest worthy of protection as only 'eccentrics' would be inclined to buy its equipment.

The applicant complained to the Commission of an alleged interference with its right to receive information, namely foreign satellite television programmes, contained in Article 10. A majority (eleven votes to two, with one abstention) found a violation.

...

A. APPLICABILITY OF ARTICLE 10

44. In the Government's submission, the right to freedom of expression was not relevant to the applicant company's complaint in the present case.... Freedom of expression that was exercised as in the present case, exclusively for pecuniary gain came under the head of economic freedom, which was outside the scope of the Convention. The 'information' in question was therefore not protected by Article 10.

...

47. In the Court's view, neither Autronic AG's legal status as a limited company nor the fact that its activities were commercial nor the intrinsic nature of freedom of expression can deprive Autronic AG of the protection of Article 10. The Article applies to 'everyone', whether natural or legal persons. The Court has, moreover, already held on three occasions that it is applicable to profit-making corporate bodies (see the *Sunday Times* judgment of 26 April 1979, Series A No 30, the *Markt Intern Verlag GmbH and Klaus Beermann* judgment of 20 November 1989, Series A No 165, and the *Groppera Radio AG* judgment of 28 March 1990, Series A No 173). Furthermore, Article 10 applies not only to the content of information but also to the means of transmission or reception since any restriction imposed on the means necessarily interferes with the right to receive and impart information. Indeed the Article expressly mentions in the last sentence of its first paragraph certain enterprises essentially concerned with the means of transmission.

Before the Convention institutions the applicant company complained of an interference with its freedom to receive information and ideas regardless of frontiers, and not with its freedom to impart them. Like the Commission, the Court is of the view that the reception of television programmes by means of a dish or other aerial comes within the right laid down in the first two sentences of Article 10 § 1, without it being necessary to ascertain the reason and purpose for which the right is to be exercised. As the administrative and judicial decisions complained of... prevented Autronic AG from lawfully receiving G-Horizont's transmissions, they therefore amounted to 'interference by public authority' with the exercise of freedom of expression.

...

B. COMPLIANCE WITH ARTICLE 10

...

2. PARAGRAPH 2 OF ARTICLE 10

53. It must be determined whether the interference complained of was 'prescribed by law', was in pursuance of one or more of the legitimate aims listed in paragraph 2 and was 'necessary in a democratic society' in order to achieve them.

(a) 'Prescribed by law'

It does not appear necessary to decide the question, since even supposing that the 'prescribed by law' condition is satisfied, the court comes to the conclusion that the interference was not justified (see paragraphs 60–3 below).

(b) Legitimate aim

58. The Government contended that the impugned interference was in pursuance of two aims recognised in the Convention.

The first of these was the 'prevention of disorder' in telecommunications. It was important to have regard to the limited number of frequencies available, to prevent the anarchy that might be caused by unlimited international circulation of information and to ensure cultural and political pluralism.

Secondly, the interference was, the Government maintained, aimed at 'preventing the disclosure of information received in confidence': the secrecy of telecommunications, which covered the television transmissions in question and was guaranteed in Article 22 of the International Telecommunications Convention, had to be protected. . . .

59. The Court finds that the interference was in pursuance of the two aims cited by the Government, which were fully compatible with the Convention—the prevention of disorder in telecommunications and the need to prevent the disclosure of confidential information.

(c) 'Necessary in a democratic society'

60. The applicant company submitted that the refusal to give it permission did not correspond to any pressing social need; it was not necessary in order to prevent the disclosure of confidential information, since broadcasters anxious to restrict their broadcasts to a particular audience would encode them. . . .

61. The Court has consistently held that the Contracting States enjoy a certain margin of appreciation in assessing the need for an interference, but this margin goes hand in hand with European supervision, whose extent will vary according to the case. Where, as in the instant case, there has been an interference with the exercise of the rights and freedoms guaranteed in paragraph 1 of Article 10, the supervision must be strict, because of the importance of the rights in question; the importance of these rights has been stressed by the Court many times. . . .

62. The Government maintained that the Court, in carrying out its review, should look at matters as they stood at the material time and, in particular, should ignore the legal and technical developments that had taken place since. . . .

The Court observes that later developments can be taken into account in so far as they contribute to a proper understanding and interpretation of the relevant rules.

In the technical field, several other telecommunications satellites broadcasting television programmes have come into service. In the legal field, developments have included, at international level, the signature within the Council of Europe on 5 May 1989 of the European Convention on Transfrontier Television and, at national level, the fact that several member States allow reception of uncoded television broadcasts from telecommunications satellites without requiring the consent of the authorities of the country in which the station transmitting to the satellite is situated.

The latter circumstance is not without relevance, since the other States signatories to the International Telecommunications Convention and the international authorities do not appear to have protested at the interpretation of Article 22 of this Convention and the provisions of the Radio Regulations that it implies. The contrary interpretation of these provisions, which was relied on by the Swiss Government in support of the interference, is consequently not convincing. . . .

63. That being so, the Government's submission based on the special characteristics of telecommunications satellites cannot justify the interference. The nature of the broadcasts in issue, that is to say uncoded broadcasts intended for television views in the Soviet Union, in itself precludes describing them as 'not intended for the general use of the public' within the meaning of numbers 1992–1994 of the Radio Regulations. Leaving aside the international rules discussed above, there was therefore no need to prohibit reception of these broadcasts.

Before the Court the Swiss Government also argued that a total ban on unauthorised reception of transmissions from telecommunications satellites was the only way of ensuring 'the secrecy of international correspondence', because there was no means of distinguishing signals conveying such correspondence from signals intended for the general use of the public. That submission is unpersuasive, since the Government had already conceded before the Commission that there was no risk of obtaining secret information by means of dish aerials receiving broadcasts from telecommunications satellites.

The Court concludes that the interference in question was not 'necessary in a democratic society' and that there has accordingly been a breach of Article 10.

...

FOR THESE REASONS, THE COURT

Holds by sixteen votes to two that Article 10 applied and that there has been a breach of it;

NOTES

1 The majority was comprised of President Ryssdal and Judges: Cremona, Thor Vilhjalmsson, Gölcüklü, Pettiti, Walsh, Evans, Macdonald, Russo, Bernhardt, Spielmann, De Meyer, Carrillo Salcedo, Martens, Palm, and Foighel. Bindschedler-Robert and Matscher JJ issued a dissenting opinion in which they expressed the view that:

... Article 10 presupposes a minimum of identification between the person claiming to rely on the right protected by that Article and the 'information' transmitted or received. In the instant case, however, the content of the information-by pure chance Soviet programmes in Russian-was a matter of complete indifference to the company and to the visitors to the trade fair who were likely to see the programmes; the sole purpose was to give a demonstration of the technical characteristics of the dish aerial in order to promote sales of it. That being so, we consider it an abuse of process on the part of the company to invoke freedom of information, and Article 10 is accordingly not, in our opinion, applicable in the instant case. (para 1)

They also considered that the Swiss response was reasonable in the light of the conventions governing international broadcasting and the practice of the majority of States regarding the receipt of foreign satellite broadcasts.

2 During the 1990s the use of satellites to broadcast television, and radio, programmes directly to people's homes became a major commercial activity with large media companies investing billions of pounds in the hardware (and software) to broadcast encrypted programmes to subscribers.

3 The Court has interpreted the right to impart information and ideas as encompassing the retransmission of commercial radio programmes, including light music, by a local cable operator. In *Groppera Radio AG v Switzerland* (1990) 12 EHRR 321, A.173, extracts below p 682, the judgment stated that:

... the Court does not consider it necessary to give on this occasion a precise definition of what is meant by 'information' and 'ideas'. 'Broadcasting' is mentioned in the Convention precisely in relation to freedom of expression. Like the Commission, the Court considers that both broadcasting of programmes over the air and cable retransmission of such programmes are covered by the right enshrined in the first two sentences of Article 10(1), without there being any need to make distinctions according to the content of the programmes. (para 55)

Obviously, the substance of broadcasts may be highly significant in determining whether a State can justify interfering with them lawfully under Article 10(2).

4 The Grand Chamber has been unwilling to construe the right to receive information in Article 10(1) as creating any general positive duties on governmental bodies in Member states to foster public awareness of important matters, such as local environmental hazards. In

Guerra v Italy, Reports of Judgments and Decisions (1998) 26 EHRR 357, 1998-I 210, discussed above p 547:

The Court reiterates that freedom to receive information, referred to in paragraph [1] of Article 10 of the Convention, 'basically prohibits a government from restricting a person from receiving information that others wish or may be willing to impart to him' (see the *Leander v Sweden* judgment (1987) A.116). That freedom cannot be construed as imposing on a State, in circumstances such as those of the present case, positive obligations to collect and disseminate information of its own motion. (para 53)

This ruling makes it very difficult for applicants to assert any general right to freedom of information against state bodies under the terms of Article 10(1).

Another Grand Chamber, unanimously, adopted the above approach in *Roche v United Kingdom*, judgment of 19 October 2005.

The licensing of broadcasting, television, or cinema

....

Groppera Radio AG v Switzerland A.173 (1990) 12 EHRR 321
European Court of Human Rights

The applicants were a company incorporated under Swiss law which produced radio programmes, the owner of that company and two journalists who worked for the company. In 1979 a private Italian company built a radio station on the Pizzo Groppera, an Italian mountain six kilometres from the Swiss border. The station had the most powerful FM radio transmitter in Europe and was, therefore, able to broadcast over a distance of 200km to the north-west thereby reaching nearly one third of the Swiss population (especially in the Zurich area). The owner of the radio station was a man who used the transmitter as a means of evading the state broadcasting monopoly in Switzerland. Throughout the early 1980s the station broadcast programmes which were wholly financed by Swiss advertisers. In 1982 the Swiss federal government altered the law to allow local radio stations to be established within the country, thereby ending the monopoly of the Swiss Radio Broadcasting Company. The owner of the Groppera station was granted one of the new Swiss local licences on condition that his company ceased broadcasting from the Italian mountain. He then sold the Groppera station to the applicant company and its current owner. The applicant company continued broadcasting to the Zurich area from the Groppera station using the name 'Sound Radio'; its programmes contained, light music, information bulletins and commercials. In 1983 the Swiss federal government issued an Ordinance which allowed the licensing of community-antenna installations. Such licence holders were able to operate a local distribution network through which they could rebroadcast radio programmes to their subscribers provided that the programmes originated from transmitters which complied with the International Telecommunications Convention. Several of the licensed local community networks in Switzerland rebroadcast the programmes transmitted by the applicant company. However, in 1984 they were warned by the Swiss Post and Telecommunications Authority that as the applicant company's broadcasts did not comply with the international rules (e.g. the Groppera station had never been granted a broadcasting licence by the Italian authorities) they were acting contrary to their community licences (and committing a criminal offence) by rebroadcasting the applicant's programmes. One licence holder, the Maur cooperative, challenged the PTT's decision in an administrative law appeal. However, before the appeal was heard the Groppera transmitter was damaged by lightning (and never resumed transmitting), therefore the Swiss Federal Court ruled that it was not necessary to examine the merits of the appeal. The applicants complained to the Commission that the Swiss authorities' ban on the retransmission of their broadcasts by local cable operators infringed their right to impart information and ideas regardless of frontiers under Article 10(1). The Commission (by seven votes to six) found a violation of Article 10.

II. ALLEGED VIOLATION OF ARTICLE 10

A. WHETHER THERE WAS AN INTERFERENCE

... the Court does not consider it necessary to give on this occasion a precise definition of what is meant by 'information' and 'ideas'. 'Broadcasting' is mentioned in the Convention precisely in relation to freedom of expression. Like the Commission, the Court considers that both broadcasting of programmes over the air and cable retransmission of such programmes are covered by the right enshrined in the first two sentences of Article 10 § 1, without there being any need to make distinctions according to the content of the programmes. The disputed administrative decisions certainly interfered with the cable retransmission of Sound Radio's programmes and prevented the subscribers in the Maur area from receiving them by that means; they therefore amounted to 'interference by public authority' with the exercise of the aforesaid freedom.

B. WHETHER THE INTERFERENCE WAS JUSTIFIED

56. The Government submitted, in the alternative, that the interference was in keeping with paragraph 1 in fine, according to which Article 10 'shall not prevent States from requiring the licensing of broadcasting ... enterprises'; in the further alternative, they argued that it was justified under paragraph 2.

1. Paragraph I, third sentence, of Article 10

59. The Court agrees with the Government that the third sentence of Article 10 § 1 is applicable in the present case. What has to be determined is the scope of its application.

60. The insertion of the sentence in issue, at the advanced stage of the preparatory work on the Convention, was clearly due to technical or practical considerations such as the limited number of available frequencies and the major capital investment required for building transmitters. It also reflected a political concern on the part of several States, namely that broadcasting should be the preserve of the State. Since then, changed views and technical progress, particularly the appearance of cable transmission, have resulted in the abolition of State monopolies in many European countries and the establishment of private radio stations—often local ones—in addition to the public services. Furthermore, national licensing systems are required not only for the orderly regulation of broadcasting enterprises at the national level but also in large part to give effect to international rules. ...

61. The object and purpose of the third sentence of Article 10 § 1 and the scope of its application must however be considered in the context of the Article as a whole and in particular in relation to the requirements of paragraph 2.

There is no equivalent of the sentence under consideration in the first paragraph of Articles 8, 9 and 11, although their structure is in general very similar to that of Article 10. Its wording is not unlike that of the last sentence of Article 11 § 2. In this respect, however, the two Articles differ in their structure. Article 10 sets out some of the permitted restrictions even in paragraph 1. Article 11, on the other hand, provides only in paragraph 2 for the possibility of special restrictions on the exercise of the freedom of association by members of the armed forces, the police and the administration of the State, and it could be inferred from this that those restrictions are not covered by the requirements in the first sentence of paragraph 2, except for that of lawfulness ('lawful'/'*légitimes*'). A comparison of the two Articles thus indicates that the third sentence of Article 10 § 1, in so far as it amounts to an exception to the principle set forth in the first and second sentences, is of limited scope. ...

This supports the conclusion that the purpose of the third sentence of Article 10 § 1 of the Convention is to make it clear that States are permitted to control by a licensing system the way in which broadcasting is organised in their territories, particularly in its technical aspects. It does not, however, provide that licensing measures shall not otherwise be subject to the requirements of paragraph 2, for that would lead to a result contrary to the object and purpose of Article 10 taken as a whole.

62. The sentence in question accordingly applies in the instant case inasmuch as it permits the orderly control of broadcasting in Switzerland.

...

64. In sum, the interference was in accordance with the third sentence of paragraph 1; it remains to be determined whether it also satisfied the conditions in paragraph 2, that is to say whether it was 'prescribed by law' had a legitimate aim or aims and was 'necessary in a democratic society' in order to achieve them.

2. Paragraph 2 of Article 10

(A) 'Prescribed by law'

... In short, the rules in issue were such as to enable the applicants and their advisers to regulate their conduct in the matter.

(B) Legitimate aim

69. The Government contended that the impugned interference pursued two aims recognised by the Convention.

The first of these was the 'prevention of disorder' in telecommunications, the order in question being laid down in the International Telecommunication Convention and the Radio Regulations and being universally binding. Sound Radio had disregarded three basic principles of the international frequency order:

(a) the licensing principle, whereby the establishment or operation of a broadcasting station by a private person or by an enterprise was subject to the issue of a licence (number 2020 of the Radio Regulations), as Sound Radio had never received a licence from the Italian authorities;

(b) the co-ordination principle, which required special agreements to be concluded between States where the frequency used was between 100 and 108 MHz (number 584 of the Radio Regulations), because there was no such agreement between Switzerland and Italy;

(c) the principle of economic use of the frequency spectrum (Article 33 of the International Telecommunication Convention and number 2666 of the Radio Regulations), because the Pizzo Groppera had the most powerful VHF transmitter in Europe.

The Government submitted, secondly, that the interference complained of was for the 'protection of the ... rights of others', as it was designed to ensure pluralism, in particular of information, by allowing a fair allocation of frequencies internationally and nationally.

...

70. The Court finds that the interference in issue pursued both the aims relied on, which were fully compatible with the Convention, namely the protection of the international telecommunications order and the protection of the rights of others.

(C) 'Necessary in a democratic society'

71. The applicants submitted that the ban affecting them did not answer a pressing social need; in particular, it went beyond the requirements of the aims being pursued. It was tantamount to censorship or jamming.

The Government stated that they had had no other recourse seeing that their representations to the Italian authorities continued to be fruitless. . . .

72. According to the Court's settled case-law, the Contracting States enjoy a certain margin of appreciation in assessing whether and to what extent an interference is necessary, but this margin goes hand in hand with European supervision covering both the legislation and the decisions applying it; when carrying out that supervision, the Court must ascertain whether the measures taken at national level are justifiable in principle and proportionate (see, as the most recent authority, the *Markt Intern Verlag GmbH and Klaus Beermann* judgment of 20 November 1989, Series A No 165, pp 19–20, § 33).

73. In order to verify that the interference was not excessive in the instant case, the requirements of protecting the international telecommunications order as well as the rights of others must be weighed against the interest of the applicants and others in the retransmission of Sound Radio's programmes by cable.

The Court reiterates, firstly, that once the 1983 Ordinance had come into force, most Swiss cable companies ceased retransmitting the programmes in question. . . . Moreover, the Swiss authorities never jammed the broadcasts from the Pizzo Groppera, although they made approaches to Italy and the International Telecommunication Union. . . . Thirdly, the impugned ban was imposed on a company incorporated under Swiss law—the Maur co-operative—whose subscribers all lived on Swiss territory and continued to receive the programmes of several other stations. Lastly and above all, the procedure chosen could well appear necessary in order to prevent evasion of the law; it was not a form of censorship directed against the content or tendencies of the programmes concerned, but a measure taken against a station which the authorities of the respondent State could reasonably hold to be in reality a Swiss station operating from the other side of the border in order to circumvent the statutory telecommunications system in force in Switzerland.

The national authorities accordingly did not in the instant case overstep the margin of appreciation left to them under the Convention.

C. CONCLUSION

74. In conclusion, no breach of Article 10 is made out, as the disputed measure was in accordance with paragraph 1 in fine and satisfied the requirements of paragraph 2.

. . .

FOR THESE REASONS, THE COURT

. . .

Holds by sixteen votes to three that there has been no breach of Article 10;

NOTES

1 The plenary court was composed of President Ryssdal and Judges: Cremona, Thor Vilhjalmsson, Bindschedler-Robert, Gölcüklü, Matscher, Pinheiro Farina, Walsh, Evans, Macdonald, Russo, Spielmann, Valticos, Martens, Palm, and Foighel. In his dissent Pettiti J observed that: 'freedom of expression, which is a fundamental right including the right to receive a communication, is even more necessary in the field of telecommunications. The countries of Eastern Europe have been encouraged on the path to democracy thanks to broadcasts across frontiers . . .'. Likewise, Bernhardt J in his dissent expressed the view that: 'this freedom of cross-boundary communication is an essential element of present-day democracy and must be taken into account when interpreting the other provisions in Article 10.' De Meyer J did not consider that the Swiss authorities were justified in banning the retransmission of the applicants' broadcasts as it was not certain that they were unlawful under international law.

2 The Court's interpretation in *Groppera* of the licensing power enshrined in Article 10(1) is very important as it makes clear that while States can avail themselves of this power to regulate broadcasting within their territories, these regulatory systems must comply with the conditions laid out in Article 10(2). Consequently, States cannot simply justify their interference with broadcasters by reference to the licensing power under Article 10(1), they must also show that the particular interference was lawful under Article 10(2). Furthermore, broadcasting technology is having a profound effect upon national and international systems of regulation. As we have already noted, above p 681, by the 1990s extra-territorial broadcasts were being beamed down from satellites with large reception areas, rather than from land based transmitters with limited foreign coverage. Additionally, the newly emerging digital broadcast technology is rapidly expanding the numbers of television and radio channels that can be broadcast on the available frequencies; therefore, States will find it increasingly difficult to argue that a scarcity of broadcasting capacity entitles them to a dominant occupancy of the available channels (see below the *Lentia* judgment).

3 A Chamber of the Court subsequently refined the plenary Court's above interpretation of the licensing power in *Informationsverein Lentia v Austria* (1993) 17 EHRR 93, A.276. There a number of persons, organisations and a private company sought unsuccessfully to establish radio and television stations in Austria. However, they were unable to do so because Austrian constitutional and federal legislation provided that broadcasting was a public service monopoly through the radio and television programmes produced by the Austrian Broadcasting Corporation. The applicants complained to the Commission that the impossibility of obtaining operating licences infringed their right to communicate information under Article 10(1). The Commission (unanimously in respect of one applicant and by fourteen votes to one in respect of the other applicants) found a breach of Article 10. The Court (unanimously) accepted the Government's contention that the licensing power, contained in Article 10(1), enabled national authorities to take account of matters going beyond purely technical considerations when exercising that prerogative.

Technical aspects are undeniably important, but the grant or refusal of a licence may also be made conditional on other considerations, including such matters as the nature and objectives of a proposed station, its potential audience at national, regional or local level, the rights and needs of a specific audience and the obligations deriving from international legal instruments.

This may lead to interferences whose aims will be legitimate under the third sentence of paragraph 1, even though they do not correspond to any of the aims set out in paragraph 2. The compatibility of such interferences with the Convention must nevertheless be assessed in the light of the other requirements of paragraph 2. (para 32)

As the public monopoly of broadcasting in Austria was capable of contributing to the quality and balance of programmes the Court held that such a licensing system was consistent with the state's licensing power. However, it was then necessary to examine whether it satisfied the conditions of Article 10(2). The Government emphasised the political dimension of the audiovisual media and the importance of ensuring that programmes were objective, impartial, diverse and balanced in their coverage.

The Court has frequently stressed the fundamental role of freedom of expression in a democratic society.... Such an undertaking cannot be successfully accomplished unless it is grounded in the principle of pluralism, of which the State is the ultimate guarantor. This observation is especially valid in relation to audio-visual media, whose programmes are often broadcast very widely.

Of all the means of ensuring that these values are respected, a public monopoly is the one which imposes the greatest restrictions on the freedom of expression.... The far-reaching character of such restrictions means that they can only be justified where they correspond to a pressing social need.

As a result of the technical progress made over the last decades, justification for these restrictions can no longer today be found in considerations relating to the number of frequencies and channels available; the Government accepted this. Secondly, for the purposes of the present case they have lost much of their *raison d'être* in view of the multiplication of foreign programmes aimed at Austrian audiences. . . . Finally and above all, it cannot be argued that there are no equivalent less restrictive solutions; it is sufficient by way of example to cite the practice of certain countries which either issue licences subject to specified conditions of variable content or make provision for forms of private participation in the activities of the national corporation. (paras 38–9)

Also, the Government's argument that the small size of the Austrian broadcasting market meant that it could not sustain a number of private broadcasters and economic forces would lead to the creation of private monopolies was rejected by the Court.

Their assertions are contradicted by the experience of several European States, of a comparable size to Austria, in which the coexistence of private and public stations, according to rules which vary from country to country and accompanied by measures preventing the development of private monopolies, shows the fears expressed to be groundless. (para 42)

Therefore, the Court ruled that the interferences with the applicants' rights were disproportionate to the aim pursued and accordingly were not necessary in a democratic society. Hence there had been a violation of Article 10. This was a highly significant judgment which may have pleased States in clarifying the breadth of their licensing power, but balanced that authority by continuing to emphasise the need for licensing decisions to be compatible with the requirements of Article 10(2). Furthermore, the Court's analysis, especially its emphasis on pluralism in the media, makes it virtually impossible for States to defend a state monopoly of audio-visual broadcasting as being compatible with Article 10 in contemporary times.

Austria's subsequent attempt to liberalise the holding of broadcasting licences by non-state groups was held by a unanimous Court to have violated Article 10 in the case of *Radio ABC v Austria*, 1997-VI 2188. The applicant non-profit making association had applied unsuccessfully for a licence to operate a radio station in the Vienna area on several occasions since 1989. However, the Court noted with satisfaction that in 1997 Austria had introduced new legislation designed to satisfy its broadcasting obligations under the Convention. The Court refused to examine the compatibility of the 1997 Act with Article 10 in *Tele 1 Privatfernsehgesellschaft MHB v Austria* (21 October 2000), as the applicant company had neither applied for a satellite broadcasting licence nor notified the Broadcasting Authority of any cable broadcasting activities. Therefore, the Court would not consider *in abstracto* if the Act met the requirements of the Convention.

Article 10(2)

Duties and responsibilities

1   The subject matter of a piece of 'expression' falling within Article 10(1) will have a direct effect upon the nature of the author/publisher's duties and responsibilities under Article 10(2). In *Otto-Preminger Institute v Austria* (1994) 19 EHRR 34, A.295-A (discussed above, p 601), the Court stated that:

However, as is borne out by the wording itself of Article 10(2), whoever exercises the rights and freedoms enshrined in the first paragraph of that Article undertakes 'duties and responsibilities'. Among them- in the context of religious opinions and beliefs-may legitimately be included an obligation to avoid as far as possible expressions that are gratuitously offensive to others and thus an infringement of their rights, and which therefore do not contribute to any form of public debate capable of furthering progress in human affairs. (para 49)

2   The broader political and social context in which a publication takes place is also relevant when assessing the nature of these obligations. In *Erdogdu and Ince v Turkey* (8 July 1999), the applicants were the editor and a journalist of a monthly review (*Democratic Opposition*) published in Istanbul. During 1992 the review published an interview, conducted by Mr Ince, with a Turkish sociologist regarding the Kurdish issue. In the interview the sociologist expressed his analysis of Kurdish society and expressed the view that in some regions the formation of a Kurdish State could be detected. Subsequently, the Istanbul National Security Court found the applicants guilty of disseminating propaganda against the indivisibility of the State. The Commission, by thirty one votes to one, found a breach of Article 10. A unanimous Court upheld that opinion. It found that the published interview did not incite violence. However, the Court stressed that:

. . . the 'duties and responsibilities' which accompany the exercise of the right to freedom of expression by media professionals assume special significance in situations of conflict and tension. Particular caution is called for when consideration is being given to the publication of the views of representatives of organisations which resort to violence against the State lest the media become a vehicle for the dissemination of hate speech and the promotion of violence. At the same time, where such views cannot be categorised as such, Contracting States cannot with reference to the protection of territorial integrity or national security or the prevention of crime or disorder restrict the right of the public to be informed of them by bringing the weight of the criminal law to bear on the media. (para 54)

Consequently, where there is civil strife in a society the media must be careful not to encourage further acts of violence.

3   The Court has also interpreted this phrase as imposing obligations upon the manner in which journalists research their articles. In *Bladet Tromso and Stensaas v Norway* (20 May 1999), the applicant local newspaper and its editor had been found liable, and ordered to pay damages, for publishing defamatory statements in respect of the crew of a seal hunting vessel. The applicants had published a number of articles concerning the behaviour of seal hunters. The major source of these articles was a Mr Lindberg who was a freelance journalist. In March of 1988 he was appointed as an unpaid seal hunting inspector by the Ministry of Fisheries. After serving on board a seal hunting ship, for one month, he gave an interview to the applicants in which he alleged that some hunters were killing seals unlawfully. The applicants then published those allegations and denials of them by some crew members from the ship on which Lindberg had served. Two months later Lindberg sent his official report on the expedition to the Ministry. In it he alleged a series of breaches of the regulations governing seal hunting and he identified five named crew members as responsible for this alleged misconduct. The government decided to withhold publication of the report as it contained allegations of criminal behaviour. However, the applicants had received a copy of the report and they published extracts from it and then a few days later they published the whole report, but they deleted the names of the crew members identified by Lindberg. Further denials by the crew of the ship were also published. In February 1989 Lindberg produced a film, containing footage shot during his service as an inspector, which showed breaches of the regulations by seal hunters. The film gained coverage on national and international television programmes and the Norwegian Government responded by establishing a Commission of Inquiry. The latter body reported in 1990 and found that most of Lindberg's allegations against named hunters

were not proven, but that several breaches of hunting regulations had occurred. Subsequently, the crew successfully sued Lindberg and the applicants for defamation. The Commission found, by twenty-four votes to seven, that the Norwegian courts had violated the applicants' rights under Article 10. Before the Court it was accepted that there had been an infringement of the applicants' freedom of expression and that it had been 'prescribed by law' and was for the legitimate aim of protecting the 'reputation or rights' of the seal hunters. The contentious issue was whether the other conditions in Article 10(2) had been satisfied. The Court held that:

By reason of the 'duties and responsibilities' inherent in the exercise of the freedom of expression, the safeguard afforded by Article 10 to journalists in relation to reporting on issues of general interest is subject to the proviso that they are acting in good faith in order to provide accurate and reliable information in accordance with the ethics of journalism...

The Court notes that the expressions in question consisted of factual statements, not value-judgments (cf *Lingens v Austria* A.103 (1986)). They did not emanate from the newspaper itself but were based on or were directly quoting from the Lindberg report, which the newspaper had not verified by independent research...It must therefore be examined whether there were any special grounds in the present case for dispensing the newspaper from its ordinary obligation to verify factual statements that were defamatory of private individuals. In the Court's view, this depends in particular on the nature and degree of the defamation at hand and the extent to which the newspaper could reasonably regard the Lindberg report as reliable with respect to the allegations in question.' (paras 65–6)

The majority of the Court, thirteen votes, considered that while some of the accusations were relatively serious their adverse effects were reduced as the applicants had not named individual seal hunters.

As regards the second issue, the trustworthiness of the Lindberg report, it should be observed that the report had been drawn up by Mr Lindberg in an official capacity as an inspector appointed by the Ministry of Fisheries to monitor the seal hunt....In the view of the Court, the press should normally be entitled, when contributing to public debate on matters of legitimate concern, to rely on the contents of official reports without having to undertake independent research. Otherwise, the vital public-watchdog role of the press may be undermined...(para 68)

Consequently, the applicants were entitled to have relied upon the accuracy of the contents of the Lindberg report and the domestic judgment of defamation against them was a disproportionate action which violated Article 10. Whereas according to the dissentients:

Few stories can be so important in a democratic society or deserving of protection under Article 10 of the Convention, that the basic ethics of journalism— which require inter alia journalists to check their facts before going to press with a story in circumstances such as the present- can be sacrificed for the commercial gratification of an immediate scoop.

Hence the Court generally requires journalists to check the accuracy of their factual assertions before publication, if the journalists are to satisfy this element of Article 10(2). However, a large majority of the judges is willing to allow journalists to rely on the content of official reports, even unpublished ones, as the factual basis for their articles. To what extent do you think the Court's decision in the above case was influenced by the applicants' publication of the whole of the Lindberg report and their reporting of individual hunters' denials of unlawful behaviour?

In the later case of *Selisto v Finland*, judgment of 16 November 2004, the Chamber, six votes to one, found that the criminal conviction of the applicant journalist for defamation in writing a series of articles dealing with surgery undertaken by an unnamed doctor, who allegedly had an alcohol abuse problem, violated Article 10. The Chamber noted that the factual basis of the applicant's articles had not been disputed.

60. ... It is also of importance that the depicted events and quotations in the article of 27 February 1996 were derived from the police's pre-trial record, which was a public document. In the Court's opinion no general duty to verify the veracity of statements contained in such documents can be imposed on reporters and other members of the media, who must be free to report on events based on information gathered from official sources. If this were not the case the efficacy of Article 10 of the Convention would to a large degree be lost.

4   The Court has accorded protection, under Article 10, to journalists who quote from the work of other media persons. In *Thoma v Luxembourg*, judgment of 29 March 2001, the applicant was a radio broadcaster who presented a weekly programme dealing with environmental issues. In one broadcast he quoted extensively from a newspaper article written by another journalist (Josy Braun) in which the latter accused many forestry officials of corruption. Subsequently, sixty-three officials successfully sued the applicant for damaging their reputations. The Court held that:

64. ... A general requirement for journalists systematically and formally to distance themselves from the content of a quotation that might insult or provoke others or damage their reputation is not reconcilable with the press's role of providing information on current events, opinions and ideas. In the instant case, the résumé of the programme shows that in any event the applicant consistently took the precaution of mentioning that he was beginning a quotation and of citing the author, and that, in addition, he described the entire article by his fellow journalist as 'strongly worded' when commenting on it. He had also asked a third party, a woodlands owner, whether he thought that what Josy Braun had written in his article was true.

Therefore, the Court found that the civil judgments against the applicant were not 'necessary in a democratic society' and had violated his right to freedom of expression.

5   Another factor influencing the scope of the author/publisher's duties and responsibilities is the type of media involved. In *Jersild v Denmark* (1994) 19 EHRR 1, A.298 (discussed above, p 651), the Court observed that:

In considering the 'duties and responsibilities' of a journalist, the potential impact of the medium concerned is an important factor and it is commonly acknowledged that the audio-visual media often have a much more immediate and powerful effect than the print media ... (para 31)

6   The occupation of a person may also affect the extent of such duties and responsibilities. A majority of the Court in *Ahmed v UK* (above p 654) adopted a more tolerant attitude towards restrictions on the freedom of expression of local government officers because:

... whenever the right to freedom of expression of public servants such as the applicants is in issue the 'duties and responsibilities' referred to in Article 10(2) assume a special significance, which justifies leaving to the authorities of the respondent State a certain margin of appreciation in determining whether the impugned interference is proportionate to the aim as stated. (para 61)

Similarly the Court has required 'restraint' in the exercise of freedom of expression of serving judges when making extra-judicial public comments: see *Wille v Liechtenstein* (above, p 656).

Formalities, conditions, restrictions or penalties

1   The majority of a Grand Chamber of the original Court stated that the prevention of the media from publishing a contentious article (often termed prior restraint) by State authorities can be justified as being in accordance with the Convention depending upon the circumstances of the case. In *Observer and Guardian v UK* (1991) 14 EHRR 153, A.216 (see, below p 700):

For the avoidance of doubt...the Court would only add to the foregoing that Article 10 of the Convention does not in terms prohibit the imposition of prior restraints on publication, as such. This is evidenced not only by the words 'conditions', 'restrictions', 'preventing' and 'prevention' which appear in that provision, but also by the Court's *Sunday Times* judgment (1979) and its *markt intern Verlag GmbH and Klaus Beermann* judgment (1989). On the other hand, the dangers inherent in prior restraints are such that they call for the most careful scrutiny on the part of the Court. This is especially so as far as the press is concerned, for news is a perishable commodity and to delay its publication, even for a short period, may well deprive it of all its value and interest. (para 60)

De Meyer J (joined by Pettiti, Russo, Foighel and Bigi JJ) wrote a dissenting opinion in which he argued that prior restraint was generally prohibited by the Convention.

I firmly believe that 'the press must be left free to publish news, whatever the source, without censorship, injunctions, or prior restraint' [Black J in *New York Times v United States* (1971) 403 US 713 at 717 (the Pentagon papers case)]: in a free and democratic society there can be no room, in time of peace, for restrictions of that kind, and particularly not if these are resorted to, as they were in the present case, for 'governmental suppression of embarrassing information' [Douglas J *ibid* 723] or ideas. Of course, those who publish any material which a pressing social need required should remain unpublished may subsequently be held liable in court, as may those acting in breach of a duty of confidentiality. They may be prosecuted if and in so far as this is prescribed by penal law, and they may in any case be sued for compensation if damage has been caused. They may also be subject to other sanctions provided for by law, including, as the case may be, confiscation and destruction of the material in question and forfeiture of the profit obtained.

Under no circumstances, however, can prior restraint, even in the form of judicial injunctions, either temporary or permanent, be accepted, except in what the Convention describes as a 'time of war or other public emergency threatening the life of the nation' and, even then, only 'to the extent strictly required by the exigencies of the situation'. [Article 15].

2   The full-time Court has held that domestic law authorizing prior restraints on publications must be sufficiently precise to enable the media to know when they may be prevented from exercising freedom of expression. In *Gaweda v Poland*, judgment of 14 March 2002, the applicant had applied to the Polish courts, in 1993 and 1994, for the registration of the titles of two periodicals that he wished to publish. The proposed titles were 'The Social and Political Monthly—A European Moral Tribunal' and 'Germany—a Thousand year-old Enemy of Poland'. The domestic courts refused to register the titles as the courts considered that they were untruthful and so contrary to the Press Act 1984. A united Chamber of the European Court stated that:

40. The Court considers that, although Article 10 of the Convention does not in terms prohibit the imposition of prior restraints on publications...the relevant law must provide a clear indication of the circumstances when such restraints are permissible and, *a fortiori*, when the consequences of the restraint are to block publication of a periodical completely, as in the present case. This is so because of the potential threat that such prior restraints, by their very nature, pose to the freedom of expression guaranteed by Article 10.

41. In the present case, the system for the registration of periodicals is governed by the Press Act of 1984. Under section 20 of that Act, a court can refuse registration only if it establishes that the request for registration does not contain various information concerning the prospective periodical or if it finds that it would infringe the right to protection of the titles of any existing periodicals. Section 5

of the Ordinance on the registration of periodicals, as applicable at the material time, provided that registration was not permissible if it would be inconsistent with the regulations in force or 'with the real state of affairs'.

42. The courts, when refusing the applicant's request to have the two periodicals registered, relied essentially on section 5 of the ordinance in so far as it required that the registration be refused if it would be 'inconsistent with the real state of affairs'. In its decision of 9 September 1993 the Bielsko-Biała Regional Court refused registration considering that the proposed title would suggest that a European institution had been established in Kęty, which was clearly not true. On 17 February 1994, in its further decision under scrutiny in the present case, the court considered that the registration of a periodical entitled *Germany—A thousand-year-old enemy of Poland* would be inconsistent with the real state of affairs in that it unduly concentrated on negative aspects of Polish-German relations and thus gave an unbalanced picture of the facts.

43. As is clear from the above, the courts in the present case inferred from the notion 'inconsistent with the real state of affairs' contained in section 5 of the ordinance a power to refuse registration where they considered that a title did not satisfy the test of truth, i.e. that the proposed titles of the periodicals conveyed an essentially false picture. While the terms used in this limb were ambiguous and lacked the clarity that one would expect in a legal provision of this nature, they suggested at most that registration could be refused where the request for registration did not conform to the technical details specified by section 20 of the Press Act. To go further, as the courts did in the present case, and require of the title of a magazine that it embody truthful information, is, firstly, inappropriate from the standpoint of freedom of the press. The title of a periodical is not a statement as such, since its function is essentially to identify the given periodical on the press market for its actual and prospective readers. Secondly, such interpretation would require a legislative provision which clearly authorised it. In short, the interpretation given by the courts introduced new criteria, which could not be foreseen on the basis of the text specifying situations in which the registration of a title could be refused.

...

47. The Court acknowledges that the judicial character of the system of registration is a valuable safeguard of freedom of the press. However, the decisions given by the national courts in this area must also conform to the principles of Article 10. The Court observes that in the present case this in itself did not prevent the courts from imposing a prior restraint on the printed media which entailed a ban on publication of entire periodicals on the basis of their titles.

48. The Court concludes that the law applicable in the present case was not formulated with sufficient precision to enable the applicant to regulate his conduct. Therefore, the manner in which restrictions were imposed on the applicant's exercise of his freedom of expression was not 'prescribed by law' within the meaning of Article 10 § 2 of the Convention.

49. In the light of the above considerations the Court does not consider it necessary to examine whether the other requirements laid down by paragraph 2 of Article 10 of the Convention were satisfied. The Court also notes in this respect that, in any event, the Government did not develop their arguments in support of their conclusion that in the present case these requirements had been met.

50. Accordingly, the Court concludes that there has been a violation of Article 10 of the Convention.

3 In the later case of *Cumpana and Mazare v Romania*, judgment of 17 December 2004, a united Grand Chamber treated a judicial order banning two journalists from working in that profession for one year, as a penalty for defamation of two public officials, fell within the concept of prior restraints.

118. As regards the order prohibiting the applicants from working as journalists for one year, which, moreover, was not remitted, the Court reiterates that prior restraints on the activities of journalists call

for the most careful scrutiny on its part and are justified only in exceptional circumstances . . . The Court considers that, although it would not appear from the circumstances of the case that the sanction in question had any significant practical consequences for the applicants, it was particularly severe and could not in any circumstances have been justified by the mere risk of the applicants' reoffending.

119. The Court considers that by prohibiting the applicants from working as journalists as a preventive measure of general scope, albeit subject to a time-limit, the domestic courts contravened the principle that the press must be able to perform the role of a public watchdog in a democratic society.

The Court went on to find a breach of Article 10 (see below p 699)

Prescribed by law

The Court's elaboration of the meaning to be given to this phrase has been examined above in the *Sunday Times* case (p 633). As the judgment in *Tolstoy Miloslavsky* (below) reveals in particular contexts, such as the calculation of the quantum of damages to be awarded by a jury, the domestic legal provisions may be very generalized and yet satisfy this provision of the Convention. In *Rekvényi v Hungary* (above, p 655) the Court stated that:

The level of precision required of domestic legislation- which cannot in any case provide for every eventuality- depends to a considerable degree on the content of the instrument in question, the field it is designed to cover and the number and status of those to whom it is addressed . . . Because of the general nature of constitutional provisions, the level of precision required of them may be lower than for other legislation. (para 34)

In the context of judicial orders backed by penal sanctions the Court, by sixteen votes to one, found that magistrates' orders binding over two hunt saboteurs to keep the peace and not to behave *contra bonos mores* did not comply with the level of precision required by this element of Article 10(2): *Hashman and Harrup v UK* [2000] Crim LR 185. The two applicants had blown a hunting horn and shouted ('hallooing') while driving in a car on a road near a fox hunt. Their purpose was to distract the hounds and prevent the killing of foxes. On the relevant day one hound left the pack and was run over and killed by a lorry, however the applicants stated that they were nowhere near the location where the hound was killed. A complaint was made to the local magistrates and they bound over the applicants to keep the peace and be of good behaviour in the sum of £100 for twelve months. The applicants appealed to the Crown Court. The court found, *inter alia*, that the applicants' actions were unlawful, but as no violence had been involved it could not be said that they had committed a breach of the peace. However, their conduct was *contra bonos mores* (defined as behaviour which is 'wrong rather than right in the judgment of the majority of contemporary fellow citizens') and their appeal should be rejected. The applicants complained to the Commission alleging, *inter alia*, a breach of Article 10. By twenty-five votes to four the Commission found a breach of that provision. The Court noted that the applicants had not been found to have committed a breach of the peace and therefore the binding over order had prospective effect (unlike the order in *Steel*, below). Furthermore, 'with specific reference to the facts of the present case, the Court does not accept that it must have been evident to the applicants what they were being ordered not [to] do for the period of their binding over' (para 40). Therefore, the order did not comply with Article 10(2). It is highly desirable for the Court to demand greater precision in domestic penal provisions and orders, compared with civil law obligations, under this element of Article 10(2). Indeed in 1994 the English Law Commission had recommended abolition of the power to bind over; 'because an order binding someone to be of good behaviour is made in such wide terms, it fails to give sufficient indication to the person bound over of the conduct which he or she must avoid in order to be safe from coercive sanctions ... ' ('Binding Over', para 4.34).

If the actions of public officials, such as police officers, were not in conformity with national law then the Court will hold that those actions were not 'prescribed by law'; see the Court's judgment regarding Needham, Polden and Cole in *Steel v UK* (below, p 705).

Necessary in a democratic society

The Court's interpretation of this provision as involving the obligation on a respondent State to show that its actions were motivated by the existence of 'a pressing social need' has been noted above in the *Handyside* case (p 623). In addition, the Court also considers whether the respondent State's conduct was a proportional response in respect of the legitimate aim being pursued.

....

Tolstoy Miloslavsky v UK A.316 (1995) 20 EHRR 442
European Court of Human Rights

The applicant, Count Nikolai Tolstoy Miloslavsky (a descendant of the famous Russian author), is a British citizen and historian. He wrote a pamphlet entitled 'War Crimes and the Wardenship of Winchester College', in which he claimed that the Warden of the College (Lord Aldington) was a '...major war criminal, whose activities merit comparison with those of the worst butchers of Nazi Germany or Soviet Russia...'. The allegations concerned Lord Aldington's alleged role as a senior military officer in Austria during the summer of 1945 when many thousands of Cossack and Yugoslav prisoners-of-war and refugees were handed over to Soviet and Titoist communist forces. Another person who bore a grievance against Lord Aldington circulated the pamphlet to parents, boys, staff and former members of Winchester College (a well known public school), parliamentarians and the press in 1987. Lord Aldington began proceedings against that person for libel and the applicant joined those proceedings at his own request. The defendants pleaded the defences of 'justification' (i.e. the substantial truth of their publication) and 'fair comment'. Lord Aldington asked for trial by a single judge, but the applicant exercised his right to trial by jury. The trial lasted for nearly two months during which both Lord Aldington and the applicant gave evidence and were cross-examined. In his summing-up the trial judge informed the jury that if they found for Lord Aldington they should award a sum of damages which would compensate him for the wrong that had been done to him by the applicant's publication. The jury, unanimously, found in favour of Lord Aldington (and rejected the defences raised by the applicant), and awarded him £1,500,000 damages (an amount three times larger than the previous highest English libel jury award). The trial judge, at the request of Lord Aldington, also granted an injunction restraining the defendants from publishing the words contained in the pamphlet or allegations to a similar effect. Lord Aldington offered not to enforce £1,200,000 of the damages awarded, but the applicant declined the offer claiming that the trial had been a travesty of justice. The Court of Appeal refused to grant the applicant leave to appeal unless he provided £125,000 security for Lord Aldington's costs in respect of the appeal. The applicant was unable to provide such a sum and his appeal was dismissed. Neither did he pay any part of the damages or costs awarded to Lord Aldington.

At the time of the applicant's trial the Court of Appeal could only set aside a jury's award of damages where it was capricious, unconscionable or irrational. However, in the later case of *Rantzen v Mirror Group Newspapers (1986) Ltd* [1993] 4 All ER 975, the Court of Appeal had regard to Article 10 of the Convention and ruled that a libel jury's almost limitless power to award damages was not compatible with 10(2). Therefore, trial judges should guide such juries by referring them to awards made by the Court of Appeal. Also, the Court of Appeal should subject jury awards of large sums to a more searching scrutiny to ensure that they were necessary to compensate the plaintiff.

Subsequently the applicant complained to the Commission alleging a violation of several Convention rights. However, the Commission only upheld his claim under Article 10 (unanimously).

I. ALLEGED VIOLATION OF ARTICLE 10 OF THE CONVENTION

33. The applicant alleged a violation of Article 10 of the Convention . . .

He maintained that the quantum of the damages awarded against him could not be considered to have been 'prescribed by law'. In addition, the size of the award and the breadth of the injunction had been disproportionate to the aim of protecting Lord Aldington's 'reputation or rights' and had thus not been 'necessary in a democratic society'.

34. The Government disputed these contentions. The Commission shared the applicant's view that the award was disproportionate but did not state any opinion on his other complaints.

35. The Court observes in the first place that the case before it is limited solely to a complaint concerning the amount of damages awarded and the court injunction. In this regard it is unlike the defamation cases it has examined hitherto (see, for instance, the *Lingens v Austria* judgment of 8 July 1986, Series A No 103, pp 24–8, §§34–47; the *Castells v Spain* judgment of 23 April 1992, Series A No 236, pp 20–4, §§ 33–50; and the *Thorgeir Thorgeirson v Iceland* judgment of 25 June 1992, Series A No 239, pp 24–8, §§ 55–70), which have concerned either the decision determining liability alone or both that and the sanction.

Both the award of damages and the injunction clearly constituted an interference with the exercise by the applicant of his right to freedom of expression, as guaranteed by paragraph 1 of Article 10 and this was not disputed before the Court. Such an interference entails a violation of Article 10 unless it was 'prescribed by law', pursued an aim or aims that is or are legitimate under Article 10 § 2 and was 'necessary in a democratic society' to attain the aforesaid aim or aims.

A. WAS THE AWARD 'PRESCRIBED BY LAW'?

36. As regards the amount of damages awarded, the applicant complained that it was not 'prescribed by law'.

I. General principles

37. The expression 'prescribed by law' in Article 10 § 2 must be interpreted in the light of the general principles concerning the corresponding words 'in accordance with the law' in Article 8 § 2 (see the *Sunday Times v UK (No 1)* judgment of 26 April 1979, Series A No 30, pp 30–1, §§ 48–9; cf the *Malone v UK* judgment of 2 August 1984, Series A No 82, p 31, § 66), which have been summarised in the *Margareta and Roger Andersson v Sweden* judgment of 25 February 1992 (Series A No 226-A, p 25, § 75), as follows:

'. . . the expression . . . requires first that the impugned measures should have a basis in domestic law. It also refers to the quality of the law in question, requiring that it be accessible to the persons concerned and formulated with sufficient precision to enable them—if need be, with appropriate legal advice—to foresee, to a degree that is reasonable in the circumstances, the consequences which a given action may entail. A law which confers a discretion is not in itself inconsistent with this requirement, provided that the scope of the discretion and the manner of its exercise are indicated with sufficient clarity, having regard to the legitimate aim in question, to give the individual adequate protection against arbitrary interference'.

The Court further reiterates that the word 'law' covers not only statute but also common law (see the above-mentioned *Sunday Times* judgment, p 30, § 47).

2. Application of the above principles

38. The applicant did not deny that the award had a basis in domestic law. However, he complained that the law in question did not enable him to foresee to a reasonable degree that the amount would be as high as £1.5 million.

At English common law there was no upper or lower limit on the amount of damages. The extent to which a judge could give guidance was strictly circumscribed. No specific figures could be suggested and awards of damages in other libel cases or even in personal injury cases had to be disregarded for the purposes of comparison. Guidance could only be given to help the jury to appreciate the real value of large sums of money, for instance by inviting them to reflect on the value of a house . . . At the material time, there had been no principle recognised in English law that required the award to be proportionate to the aim of repairing the damage to the plaintiff's reputation. The jury gave no reasons for its decision and the award could be overturned by the Court of Appeal only if it was so unreasonable that it could not have been made by sensible people but must have been arrived at capriciously, unconscionably or irrationally . . .

The applicant pointed out that, as a result of the above, in his case the trial judge had not directed the jury to ensure that the award was proportionate to the damage that Lord Aldington had suffered. The jury had, on the contrary, been encouraged to consider 'enormous damages' and had been informed by the judge that 'there is no league of damages in defamation cases'. The award made, although it had supposedly not included any punitive damages, had been three times the largest amount previously awarded by an English libel jury and had been substantially greater than the sum that would be awarded to a plaintiff suffering permanent and extremely severe physical or mental disablement in a personal injury action. It would have been impossible for the applicant's legal advisers to predict that an award of the magnitude in question would be made.

39. The Government argued that a remedy such as the libel award made in the applicant's case needed to be flexible to accommodate the facts of each individual case, especially the facts of so exceptional a case as the present one. Only by maintaining such flexibility could the law achieve the purpose of compensation under the law of libel, namely to empower the jury to award, in the light of the relevant criteria at common law . . . , the sum that it considered to be appropriate in the circumstances. In any event, it was not for the Court to assess English libel law in the abstract.

40. The Court notes in the first place that the libel as found by the jury was of an exceptionally serious nature. Indeed, during the hearing at the High Court, counsel for the applicant and the applicant himself had accepted that, if libel were to be established, the jury would have to award a very substantial sum in damages (see paragraph 11 above).

41. The Court accepts that national laws concerning the calculation of damages for injury to reputation must make allowance for an open-ended variety of factual situations. A considerable degree of flexibility may be called for to enable juries to assess damages tailored to the facts of the particular case. Indeed, this is reflected in the trial judge's summing-up to the jury in the present case. . . . It follows that the absence of specific guidelines in the legal rules governing the assessment of damages must be seen as an inherent feature of the law of damages in this area.

Accordingly, it cannot be a requirement of the notion of 'prescribed by law' in Article 10 of the Convention that the applicant, even with appropriate legal advice, could anticipate with any degree of certainty the quantum of damages that could be awarded in his particular case.

42. It is further observed that the discretion enjoyed by the jury in the assessment of damages was not unfettered. A jury was bound to take into account such factors as injury to feelings, the anxiety and uncertainty undergone in the litigation, the absence of apology, the reaffirmation of the truth of the matters complained of, vindication of the plaintiff's reputation. . . . It was for the trial judge to direct the jury on the law. In addition, the Court of Appeal had power to set aside an award, inter alia on the ground of irrationality and to order a new trial. It therefore appears that, although the principle of proportionality as such may not have been recognised under the relevant national law, decisions on awards were subject to a number of limitations and safeguards.

43. In jury trials, the lack of reasoning for awards of damages is the norm and is to a large extent unavoidable. The applicant's submission to the effect that the absence of reasons affected the foreseeability of a particularly high award being made in his case is thus not persuasive. Moreover, the argument could apply to any award whatever the magnitude and concerns less the size of the award than the very nature of the jury system itself.

44. Having regard to the fact that a high degree of flexibility may be justified in this area . . . , the various criteria to be taken into account by juries in the assessment of damages as well as the review exercised by the Court of Appeal, the Court reaches the conclusion that the relevant legal rules concerning damages for libel were formulated with sufficient precision. In short, the award was 'prescribed by law'.

B. DID THE AWARD AND THE INJUNCTION PURSUE A LEGITIMATE AIM?

45. The award and the injunction clearly pursued the legitimate aim of protecting the 'reputation or rights of others'. This was not disputed.

C. WERE THE AWARD AND THE INJUNCTION 'NECESSARY IN A DEMOCRATIC SOCIETY'?

1. The award

46. The applicant and the Commission were of the view that the amount of damages awarded—£1.5 million—was disproportionate to the legitimate aim of protecting Lord Aldington's reputation or rights . . .

47. The Government maintained that there was a reasonable relationship of proportionality between the amount of the award and the aim of compensating the damage done to Lord Aldington and restoring his reputation. They pointed out that Article 10 imposed 'duties and responsibilities'. The applicant's pamphlet had been false and unfair and had been expressly designed to provoke a libel action. . . .

48. The Court recalls at the outset that its review is confined to the award as it was assessed by the jury, in the circumstances of judicial control existing at the time, and does not extend to the jury's finding of libel. It follows that its assessment of the facts is even more circumscribed than would have been the case had the complaint also concerned the latter.

In this connection, it should also be observed that perceptions as to what would be an appropriate response by society to speech which does not or is not claimed to enjoy the protection of Article 10 of the Convention may differ greatly from one Contracting State to another. The competent national authorities are better placed than the European Court to assess the matter and should therefore enjoy a wide margin of appreciation in this respect.

49. . . . However, the Court takes note of the fact that the applicant himself and his counsel accepted that if the jury were to find libel, it would have to make a very substantial award of damages . . . While this is an important element to be borne in mind it does not mean that the jury was free to make any award it saw fit since, under the Convention, an award of damages for defamation must bear a reasonable relationship of proportionality to the injury to reputation suffered.

The jury had been directed not to punish the applicant but only to award an amount that would compensate the non-pecuniary damage to Lord Aldington. . . . The sum awarded was three times the size of the highest libel award previously made in England . . . and no comparable award has been made since. An award of the present size must be particularly open to question where the substantive national law applicable at the time fails itself to provide a requirement of proportionality.

50. In this regard it should be noted that, at the material time, the national law allowed a great latitude to the jury. The Court of Appeal could not set aside an award simply on the grounds that it was excessive but only if the award was so unreasonable that it could not have been made by sensible people and must have been arrived at capriciously, unconscionably or irrationally. . . . In a more recent case, *Rantzen v Mirror Group Newspapers Ltd*, the Court of Appeal itself observed that to grant an almost limitless discretion to a jury failed to provide a satisfactory measurement for deciding what was 'necessary in a democratic society' for the purposes of Article 10 of the Convention. It noted that the common law—if properly understood—required the courts to subject large awards of damages to a more searching scrutiny than had been customary.

As to what guidance the judge could give to the jury, the Court of Appeal stated that it was to be hoped that in the course of time a series of decisions of the Court of Appeal . . . would establish some standards as to what would be 'proper' awards. In the meantime the jury should be invited to consider the purchasing power of any award which they might make and to ensure that any award they made was proportionate to the damage which the plaintiff had suffered and was a sum which it was necessary to award him to provide adequate compensation and to re-establish his reputation . . .

The Court cannot but endorse the above observations by the Court of Appeal to the effect that the scope of judicial control, at the trial and on appeal, at the time of the applicant's case did not offer adequate and effective safeguards against a disproportionately large award.

51. Accordingly, having regard to the size of the award in the applicant's case in conjunction with the lack of adequate and effective safeguards at the relevant time against a disproportionately large award, the Court finds that there has been a violation of the applicant's rights under Article 10 of the Convention.

2. The injunction

52. The applicant further alleged that the injunction . . . was disproportionate to the aim of protecting Lord Aldington's reputation or rights. It was sweepingly broad and was ordered as a consequence of a verdict of the jury for which no reasons were given and which the judge had interpreted in the widest possible way. It prevented any comment on the role of Lord Aldington in relation to the handover of Cossacks and Yugoslavs . . .

At any rate, the injunction was disproportionate if considered together with the award, as the measures served in part the same function. The jury was not aware when it made the award that the judge would order an injunction. It was thus very likely that the award was intended not only to compensate Lord Aldington but also to deter the applicant from publishing in the future.

53. The Government contested these allegations. They maintained that in the light of the jury's verdict the judge had been entitled to prevent future repetition of the libel by the applicant and this had been the purpose of the injunction . . .

D. RECAPITULATION

55. In sum, the Court concludes that the award was 'prescribed by law' but was not 'necessary in a democratic society' as there was not, having regard to its size in conjunction with the state of national law at the relevant time, the assurance of a reasonable relationship of proportionality to the legitimate aim pursued. Accordingly, on the latter point, there has been a violation of Article 10. On the other hand, the injunction, either taken alone or together with the award, did not give rise to any breach of that Article.

. . .

FOR THESE REASONS, THE COURT

Holds unanimously that the award was 'prescribed by law' within the meaning of Article 10 of the Convention;

Holds unanimously that the award, having regard to its size taken in conjunction with the state of national law at the relevant time was not 'necessary in a democratic society' and thus constituted a violation of the applicant's rights under Article 10;

Holds unanimously that the injunction, either taken alone or together with the award, did not give rise to a breach of Article 10;

NOTES

1 The Court was composed of President Ryssdal and Judges: Walsh, Russo, Palm, Foighel, Pekkanen, Freeland, Repik, and Jambrek.

2 Dicta in paragraph 48 of the judgment above indicates that the Court does not consider that defamatory statements fall within the protection of Article 10. Hence their status under the Convention is analogous to that of intentionally racist expression: see, *Jersild* (above, p 651).

3 The Irish Government argued that the standard proportionality test applied by the Court was not appropriate where the rights of the unborn were at issue. The Court rejected this contention and followed its established practice of having regard to whether the restriction complained of was 'proportionate to the legitimate aim pursued': *Open Door and Dublin Well Woman v Ireland* (below, p 707).

4 A unanimous Grand Chamber of the full-time Court considered the imposition of sentences of seven months' imprisonment on two journalists for defaming a deputy mayor and judge in *Cumpana and Mazare v Romania*, judgment of 17 December 2004. The Grand Chamber held that:

115. Although sentencing is in principle a matter for the national courts, the Court considers that the imposition of a prison sentence for a press offence will be compatible with journalists' freedom of expression as guaranteed by Article 10 of the Convention only in exceptional circumstances, notably where other fundamental rights have been seriously impaired, as, for example, in the case of hate speech or incitement to violence (see, *mutatis mutandis*, *Feridun Yazar v Turkey*, No 42713/98, § 27, 23 September 2004, and *Sürek and Özdemir v Turkey* [GC], Nos 23927/94 and 24277/94, § 63, 8 July 1999). In this connection, the Court notes the recent legislative initiatives by the Romanian authorities, leading to the removal of the offence of insult from the Criminal Code and the abolition of prison sentences for defamation.

116. The circumstances of the present case—a classic case of defamation of an individual in the context of a debate on a matter of legitimate public interest—present no justification whatsoever for the imposition of a prison sentence. Such a sanction, by its very nature, will inevitably have a chilling effect, and the fact that the applicants did not serve their prison sentence does not alter that conclusion, seeing that the individual pardons they received are measures subject to the discretionary power of the President of Romania; furthermore, while such an act of clemency dispenses convicted persons from having to serve their sentence, it does not expunge their conviction.

Therefore, the prison sentences combined with the added penalties of disqualification from exercising their civil rights for the period of imprisonment and prohibition from working as journalists for one year were 'manifestly disproportionate' in the judgment of the Court and constituted a breach of Article 10. This approach by the Court to the imprisonment of journalists for defamatory comments is a welcome enhancement of the protection of media persons seeking to expose alleged corruption by public officials.

Legitimate aims of interferences with freedom of expression

NATIONAL SECURITY

1   In *Observer and Guardian v UK* (1991) 14 EHRR 153, A.216, the publishers, editors and journalists of two newspapers complained about injunctions issued by the English courts preventing them publishing claims of official misconduct made by Peter Wright in his infamous book *Spycatcher*. Wright had been employed by the British Security Service (on the legality of this organization's activities under the Convention see *Hewitt and Harman* above, p 502) for many years until he retired to Australia in 1976. Then he wrote the book containing his memoirs, which, *inter alia*, alleged that the Security Service had conducted illegal activities to try and undermine the 1974–9 British Labour Government and that a former head of the Service had been a Soviet agent. In 1985, the UK Government began proceedings in the Australian courts to restrain the publication of *Spycatcher* claiming that the disclosure of information gained by Wright during his employment by the Service would be a breach of his duty of confidence derived from his former position. While the Australian proceedings were still pending, the applicants published articles based on the manuscript of the book. Thereupon, the Attorney General began proceedings against the applicant newspaper publishers in the English courts, relying on the breach of confidence principle, for injunctions to prevent them publishing any further articles based on *Spycatcher* material. The evidential basis of the Attorney General's claim was two affidavits sworn by the Cabinet Secretary (Sir Robert Armstrong) in which he asserted that any publication of information coming from Wright would cause unquantifiable damage to the Service and undermine the confidence of friendly countries in the Service. The High Court granted interim injunctions (pending the full hearing of the action) against the applicants in June 1986. Those injunctions were subsequently upheld by the Court of Appeal (July 1986) and by a majority of the House of Lords (30 July 1987). However, on 14 July 1987, *Spycatcher* was published in the USA and became a best-seller. The British Government did not prevent personal imports of the book into the UK, but did take steps to prevent the book being available in public libraries and British booksellers. In June 1988, the High Court of Australia refused to prevent publication of the book in Australia, on the ground that under international law the British Government's interests in its security services was unenforceable in the Australian courts. In October 1988, the House of Lords held, in the substantive proceedings against the applicants, that no injunction should be granted against the applicants as the worldwide publication of *Spycatcher* had destroyed any secrecy as to its contents. However, members and former members of the Security Service owed a lifelong duty of confidence to the Crown: see, *A-G v Guardian Newspapers Ltd (No 2)* [1988] 3 All ER 545.

The Commission found a violation, by six votes to five, of Article 10 in respect of interim injunctions issued against the applicants between July 1986 and 30 July 1987. A unanimous Commission also found a breach of Article 10 in respect of the injunctions between 30 July 1987 and October 1988. Before the Court, the Government argued that all the injunctions were, *inter alia*, necessary for the protection of national security. The Court accepted that the injunctions had aims that were legitimate under Article 10(2). However, the Court was divided on the issue whether the injunctions were necessary between July 1986–July 1987. A majority (fourteen votes to ten) held that they were necessary, because, having regard to the margin of appreciation to be accorded to national courts in this context; ... 'it was not unreasonable to suppose that where a former senior employee of a security service—an 'insider', such as Mr Wright—proposed to publish, without authorisation, his memoirs, there was at least a risk they would comprise material the disclosure of which might be detrimental to that service...' (para 61). As for the injunctions between 30 July 1987 and October 1988, the Court was unanimously of the view that they were not necessary in a democratic society.

As regards the interests of national security relied on, the Court observes that in this respect the Attorney General's case underwent, to adopt the words of Scott J, 'a curious metamorphosis'... As emerges from Sir Robert Armstrong's evidence... injunctions were sought at the outset, inter alia, to preserve the secret character of information that ought to be kept secret. By 30 July 1987, however, the information had lost that character... By then, the purpose of the injunctions had thus become confined to the promotion of the efficiency and reputation of the Security Service, notably by: preserving confidence in that Service on the part of third parties; making it clear that the unauthorised publication of memoirs by its former members would not be countenanced; and deterring others who might be tempted to follow in Mr Wright's footsteps.

The Court does not regard these objectives as sufficient to justify the continuation of the interference complained of. It is, in the first place, open to question whether the actions against Observer and Guardian could have served to advance the attainment of these objectives any further than had already been achieved by the steps taken against Mr Wright himself.... Above all, continuation of the restrictions after July 1987 prevented newspapers from exercising their right and duty to purvey information, already available, on a matter of legitimate public concern. (para 69)

The Court's judgment is significant in that it demonstrates the exercise of the Strasbourg 'European supervision' to rule that a government's claim of national security interests was not fully justified under Article 10(2). The domestic proceedings are commented upon by E Barendt in 'Spycatcher and Freedom of Speech' (1989) Public Law 204 and the European dimension by I Leigh in 'Spycatcher in Strasbourg' (1992) Public Law 200.

2   The Court applied a similar analysis in *Sunday Times v UK (No 2)* (1991) 14 EHRR 229, A.217, holding (unanimously) that it was not necessary for the English courts to grant injunctions preventing this newspaper publishing serial extracts from *Spycatcher* once the book had been published in the USA.

3   The Government responded to the *Spycatcher* saga by securing the passage of the Official Secrets Act 1989. Under section 1 it is now a criminal offence for a current or former member of the Security or Intelligence Services to disclose any information relating to security or intelligence matters which he has acquired through his membership of those organisations, unless the disclosure is made in accordance with his official duty. In 1997 Richard Tomlinson, a former member of the Intelligence Service (MI6), was convicted of breaching this provision in regard to plans to publish his memoirs outside the UK (he served nine months' imprisonment).

4   The Court has also rejected another Government's claim that national security interests should prevail over freedom of expression in the analogous case of *Vereniging Weekblad Bluf! v Netherlands* (1995) 20 EHRR 189, A.306-A. The applicant was a left-wing association which published a weekly journal called *Bluf!*. In the spring of 1987 the staff of *Bluf!* gained possession of a 1981 quarterly report produced, for internal readership, by the Dutch internal security service (the BVD). The report showed that the BVD was interested in the activities of the Dutch Communist Party and the anti-nuclear movement. The editor of *Bluf!* decided to publish the report as a supplement to an issue of the journal. However, before the issue was distributed an investigating judge ordered the seizure of the entire print run. Nevertheless, the applicant was able to reprint the issue and sell 2,500 copies on the streets of Amsterdam the next day. To

prevent public disorder the authorities did not seek to stop the sale of the issue on the streets. Subsequently, the public prosecutor secured an order from the courts requiring the withdrawal of the issue from circulation. The applicant complained to the Commission that the seizure and withdrawal orders violated Article 10. By 16 votes to 2 the Commission found a violation. Before the Court, the applicant contended that it was contrary to the concept of the rule of law, embodied in the 'prescribed by law' element of Article 10(2), for States to seize/withdraw publications unless those orders were made in the context of criminal proceedings. The judges, unanimously, rejected that contention:

The Court cannot accept the argument that Article 10 precludes ordering the seizure and withdrawal from circulation of printed matter other than in criminal proceedings. National authorities must be able to take such measures solely in order to prevent punishable disclosure of a secret without taking criminal proceedings against the party concerned, provided that national law affords that party sufficient procedural safeguards. Netherlands law satisfies that condition.... (para 32)

Hence, the orders were 'prescribed by law' and they had the legitimate aim of protecting national security because:

The Court recognises that the proper functioning of a democratic society based on the rule of law may call for institutions like the BVD which, in order to be effective, must operate in secret and be afforded the necessary protection. In this way a State may protect itself against the activities of individuals and groups attempting to undermine the basic values of a democratic society. In view of the particular circumstances of the case...the interferences were unquestionably designed to protect national security...(paras 35–6)

However, the Court doubted whether the information contained in the six-year-old BVD report was sufficiently sensitive to justify the Dutch authorities prohibiting its distribution. In the light of the earlier judgments in *The Guardian and Observer* and *The Sunday Times (No 2)*, the Court also noted that it had ruled that it was not necessary to prevent the disclosure of information that had already been made public.

Admittedly, in the instant case the extent of publicity was different. However, the information in question was made accessible to a large number of people, who were able in their turn to communicate it to others. Furthermore, the events were commented on by the media. That being so, the protection of the information as a State secret was no longer justified and the withdrawal of issue No 267 of *Bluf!* no longer appeared necessary to achieve the legitimate aim pursued. It would have been quite possible, however, to prosecute the offenders. (para 45)

Therefore, the Court found the Dutch authorities' actions had violated the applicant's freedom of expression under Article 10.

The judgment reveals the Court again making its own assessment of whether national security interests, even in the sensitive field of security service operations, require the limitation of freedom of expression concerning such activities. Clearly, the more historic that information is and/or the wider the existing dissemination of that information, the less likely the Court will be to uphold the necessity of further restrictions on publication.

Territorial integrity or public safety

The aim of preserving territorial integrity was recognised by the Court in *Ceylan v Turkey*, (above, p 645) and the objective of protecting public safety was upheld by the Court in *Grigoriades v Greece* (below, p 704).

For the prevention of disorder or crime

1   This phrase encompasses two separate aims and the notion of 'disorder' is sufficiently flexible to include the prevention of disorder within discrete groups in society (such as the military): see, *Engel v Netherlands* (1976) 1 EHRR 647, A.22 (other aspects of this case are examined above, p 365). Two of the applicants, Dona and Schul (who were military conscripts) had been sentenced to three and four months' detention in a disciplinary unit for having published and distributed an edition of a journal, entitled *Alarm*, to other soldiers. The specific edition contained the statement:

...in addition to ordinary punishments, the army bosses have at their disposal a complete series of other measures-of which transfer is only one-to suppress the soldiers....That only comes to an end when these people, who can only prove their authority by punishment and intimidation, have to look for a normal job.

The military disciplinary authorities found the applicants guilty of publishing a writing tending to undermine discipline. Before the Court, the Government argued that the interference with the applicants' freedom of expression was justified to prevent disorder within the army. The Court, unanimously, held that:

...the concept of 'order' as envisaged by this provision, refers not only to public order or '*ordre public*' within the meaning of Articles 6(1) and 9(2) of the Convention and Article 2(3) of Protocol No 4: it also covers the order that must prevail within the confines of a specific social group. This is so, for example, when, as in the case of the armed forces, disorder in that group can have repercussions on order in society as a whole. It follows that the disputed penalties met this condition if and to the extent that their purpose was the prevention of disorder within the Netherlands armed forces.

Mr Dona and Mr Schul admittedly maintain that Article 10(2) takes account of the 'prevention of disorder' only in combination with the 'prevention of crime'. The Court does not share this view. While the French version uses the conjunctive '*et*', the English employs the disjunctive 'or'. Having regard to the context and the general system of Article 10, the English version provides a surer guide on this point. (para 98)

The Court went on to find that the Dutch military authorities had well-founded reasons for finding that the applicants had attempted to undermine military disciple by publishing the edition of *Alarm* and that the punishments were necessary to prevent disorder. Indeed, the Court ruled that, 'there was thus no question of depriving them of their freedom of expression but only of punishing the abusive exercise of that freedom on their part' (para 101). Therefore, the applicants' claims under Article 10 were rejected.

2   In the later case of *Vereinigung Demokratischer Soldaten Osterreichs and Gubi v Austria* (1994) 20 EHRR 55, A.302, the Court adopted a more tolerant and protective attitude towards the distribution of critical publications to military personnel. The applicant association published a monthly magazine ('*The Hedgehog*') aimed at soldiers in the Austrian army. However, the Federal Minister of Defence refused to allow the magazine to be distributed at the barracks in the same way (at public expense) as the other two military magazines published in Austria. Gubi was a conscript soldier who was caught distributing an issue of *The Hedgehog* in his barracks. He was sentenced to three days' custody, by his commanding officer, for distributing the magazine. The applicants complained that the authorities' decisions violated Article 10. The Commission (by twelve votes to nine) found a breach of that Article. The Court accepted that the authorities had acted for the legitimate purpose of preventing disorder in the military. But

the majority (six votes to three) did not consider that the government had acted proportionately in refusing to distribute the magazine.

None of the issues of The Hedgehog submitted in evidence recommended disobedience or violence, or even questioned the usefulness of the army. Admittedly, most of the issues set out complaints, put forward proposals for reforms or encourage the readers to institute legal complaints or appeals proceedings. However, despite their often polemical tenor, it does not appear that they overstepped the bounds of what is permissible in the context of a mere discussion of ideas, which must be tolerated in the army of a democratic State just as it must be in the society that such an army serves. (para 38)

Likewise a larger majority of the Court (eight votes to one) held that the action against Gubi was a disproportionate response having regard to the contents of the magazine he was caught distributing.

Hence, it now seems that the Court will safeguard the distribution of critical publications within the armed forces of Member states provided such journals do not seek to undermine the existence or operational effectiveness of the military services. Such an approach is to be welcomed as a safeguard against the dangers of insularity, complacency and authoritarianism occurring within these powerful organizations. Indeed in *Grigoriades v Greece* (1997) 27 EHRR 464, 1997-VII 2575, the majority of a Grand Chamber found a breach where a conscript officer had been punished for sending a letter criticising the army to his commanding officer. In his letter the applicant wrote that, 'the army remains a criminal and terrorist apparatus which, by creating an atmosphere of intimidation and reducing to tatters the spiritual welfare of the radical youth, clearly aims at transforming people to mere parts of an apparatus of domination which ruins human nature and transforms human relations from relations of friendship and love to relations of dependence . . .'. The military courts found the applicant guilty of insulting the army and sentenced him to three months' imprisonment. He complained to the Commission which expressed the opinion that there had been a breach of Article 10 (by twenty-eight votes to one). The Court accepted that the applicant's conviction had the objective of seeking to maintain an effective military defence (which on this occasion was classified as falling within the legitimate aim of 'protecting national security and public safety'). In considering if the conviction was 'necessary in a democratic society' the Court held:

Article 10 does not stop at the gates of army barracks. It applies to military personnel as to all other persons within the jurisdiction of the Contracting States. . . . It is true that the contents of the letter included certain strong and intemperate remarks concerning the armed forces in Greece. However, the Court notes that those remarks were made in the context of a general and lengthy discourse critical of army life and the army as an institution. The letter was not published by the applicant or disseminated by him to a wider audience. . . . Nor did it contain any insults directed against either the recipient of the letter or any other person. Against such a background the Court considers the objective impact on military discipline to have been insignificant. (paras 45–7)

Consequently, by 12 votes to 8, the Court determined that the applicant's conviction was a breach of Article 10.

3 The Court applied the prevention of disorder aim to a public protest situation in *Chorherr v Austria* (1993) 17 EHRR 358, A.266-B. During October 1985 a military ceremony was held in Vienna's Rathausplatz to celebrate the thirtieth anniversary of Austrian neutrality and the fortieth anniversary of the end of the Second World War. About 50,000 people attended. While the ceremony was being held the applicant, and a friend, walked among the spectators distributing copies of a leaflet which called for a referendum on the purchase of fighter aircraft by the Austrian armed forces. The applicant wore a rucksack with an enlargement of the leaflet on the back which projected about 50 cm above his head (this contained the slogan 'Austria does not need any interceptor fighter planes'). The applicant's actions caused a commotion among some of the spectators whose views were blocked and two police officers informed him that he was disturbing public order and that he should cease his demonstration. The applicant refused, asserting his right to freedom of expression, and he was arrested. At the police station administrative criminal proceedings were instituted against him and he was released later that day (one and a half hours after the military ceremony had ended). Chorherr challenged the conduct of the police before the Constitutional Court, but it dismissed his claim. Eventually he was fined 700 schillings for breach of the peace. The applicant complained to the Commission alleging, *inter alia*, a breach of his rights under Article 10. The Commission, on the casting vote of the acting president, found a violation of that provision. All the participants to the proceedings before the Court accepted that the measures taken against Chorherr interfered with his right to freedom of expression under Article 10(1). However, a majority of the Court, six votes to three, found the interference to be justified under Article 10(2). The majority considered the measures were 'prescribed by law' and had the legitimate aim of preventing disorder at the military ceremony. In its opinion the police response to Chorherr's behaviour was within the State's margin of appreciation and proportionate because:

... when he chose this event for his demonstration against the Austrian armed forces, Mr Chorherr must have realised that it might lead to a disturbance requiring measures of restraint, which in this instance, moreover, were not excessive. (para 33)

Hence, the venue of a public protest is a major factor in determining the lawfulness of State restrictions on the conduct of the protestors under Article 10(2).

4 The reasoning in *Chorherr* was developed by the Court in *Steel v UK* (1998) 28 EHRR 603, 1998-VII. The case was brought by a number of persons who had engaged in various forms of public protest. Ms Steel, together with sixty others, had attempted to obstruct and disrupt a grouse shoot in Yorkshire. She walked in front of a member of the shoot as he lifted his shotgun to fire, thereby preventing the shooting of grouse. The police warned the protesters to stop their protest and when the warning was ignored the police arrested thirteen demonstrators (including the applicant). She was detained for 44 hours by the police and subsequently the Crown Court upheld a complaint of breach of the peace against her. The court ordered that she agree to be bound over to keep the peace for twelve months in the sum of £100 (if a person breaches such an order they are liable to forfeit the specified sum of money). Steel refused to be bound over and was committed to prison for twenty-eight days. Ms Lush, the second applicant, (together with about twenty-five other protesters) broke into a construction site that was part of the M11 motorway extension in East London. The protesters climbed up trees that were to be felled and climbed onto machinery. The protesters were removed on several occasions by security guards and the former did not use any violence nor did they damage any machinery. Finally the applicant was arrested, while standing under the bucket of a mechanical digger, for conduct likely to provoke a disturbance of the peace. She was detained by the police for seventeen hours and later the magistrates' court found the complaint against her made out. The Court ordered her to agree to be bound over for twelve months to keep the peace in the sum of £100. When Lush refused she was committed to prison for seven days. The remaining applicants, Ms Needham, Mr Polden and Mr Cole, held a protest outside a London conference centre where the 'Fighter Helicopter II' conference was being held. The applicants distributed leaflets and held up banners saying 'Work for Peace not War'. They were arrested by the police for alleged breach of the peace. After seven hours detention they were released.

In subsequent proceedings the prosecution decided not to call any evidence and the magistrates dismissed the case against the applicants. All the various applicants complained to the Commission alleging, *inter alia*, a breach of their right to freedom of expression under Article 10. A unanimous Commission found that there had been no breach of this Article in respect of Steel and Lush, but there had been a violation in regard to the other applicants. Before the Court, the British Government sought to argue that Article 10 was not applicable to Steel and Lush as their protests had not been peaceful. This argument was rejected:

The Court recalls that the first and second applicants were arrested while protesting against a grouse shoot and the extension of a motorway respectively. It is true that these protests took the form of physically impeding the activities of which the applicants disapproved, but the Court considers nonetheless that they constituted expressions of opinion within the meaning of Article 10 (see, for example, *Chorherr v Austria*...). The measures taken against the applicants were, therefore, interferences with their right to freedom of expression. (para 92)

The Court went on to find that the arrests and detention of Steel and Lush were 'prescribed by law' and for the legitimate aims of preventing disorder and protecting the rights of others. However, the judges were divided on the question of whether the authorities' actions were 'necessary in a democratic society'. The Court stated that:

It is true that States enjoy a certain margin of appreciation in assessing whether and to what extent any interference with the exercise of freedom of expression is necessary, particularly as regards the choice of reasonable and appropriate means to be used to ensure that lawful activities can take place peacefully (see the above mentioned *Chorherr* judgment...). (para 101)

In respect of Ms Steel a bare majority of the Court (five votes to four) decided that there was no breach of Article 10:

Forty-four hours is undoubtedly a long period of detention in such a case. However, the Court recalls that Ms Steel's behaviour prior to her arrest had created a danger of serious physical injury to herself and others and had formed part of a protest against grouse shooting which risked culminating in disorder and violence. Particularly given the risk of an early resumption by her, if released, of her protest activities against field sports, and the possible consequences of this eventuality, both of which the police were best placed to assess, the Court does not consider that this detention was disproportionate. (para 105)

However, in their joint partly dissenting opinion Judges Valticos and Makarczyk wrote that:

What is not in any event debatable is that to detain for 44 hours and then sentence to twenty-eight days' imprisonment a person who, albeit in an extreme manner, jumped up and down in front of a member of the shoot to prevent him from killing a feathered friend is so manifestly extreme, particularly in a country known for its fondness for animals, that it amounted, in our view, to a violation of the Convention.

Although the Court recognised that Ms Lush's conduct was arguably less serious than Steel's, all the judges agreed that her arrest and detention was not a disproportionate response by the state. As for the other three applicants the Court, unanimously, ruled that:

... the measures taken against Ms Needham, Mr Polden and Mr Cole were not 'lawful' or 'prescribed by law', since it is not satisfied that the police had grounds reasonably to apprehend that the applicants' peaceful protest would cause a breach of the peace. For similar reasons... it considers that the interference with the exercise by the applicants of their right to freedom of expression was also disproportionate to the aims of preventing disorder and protecting the rights of others, and was not, therefore, 'necessary in a democratic society. (para 110)

Therefore, the Court found a breach of Article 10 in respect of these applicants. One positive aspect of this decision was the Court's willingness to treat physical behaviour, especially that of a symbolic nature, as a form of expression falling within Article 10(1). Nevertheless, where such conduct creates a threat to public order the Court allows the national authorities considerable latitude in restricting or terminating the exercise of this type of expression.

5   The British Government sought to justify the disclosure order and contempt of court proceedings brought against the applicant journalist in *Goodwin v UK* (below, p 717) as being necessary 'for the prevention of crime'. However, the Court ruled that it did not have to decide if this aim was relevant in that case as the interferences had the undisputed aim of protecting the rights of others.

For the protection of health or morals

Open Door and Dublin Well Woman v Ireland A.246 (1992) 15 EHRR 244
European Court of Human Rights

The applicants were; (1) Open Door Counselling, a non-profit-making company engaged in counselling pregnant women in Ireland, (2) Dublin Well Woman Centre, a non-profit-making company providing medical and counselling services to women in Dublin, (3) two individual counsellors working for Dublin Well Woman and (4) two Irish women of child-bearing age. In 1983, after a referendum, the Irish Constitution was amended to include Article 40.3.3 which read: 'The State acknowledges the right to life of the unborn and, with due regard to the equal right to life of the mother, guarantees in its laws to respect, and, as far as practicable, by its laws to defend and vindicate that right.' In 1985 the Society for the Protection of Unborn Children (Ireland) brought a private action against the applicant companies claiming that they were acting unlawfully in respect of Article 40.3.3 by counselling women to seek abortions outside Ireland. It was accepted by the applicant companies that they, *inter alia*, discussed abortion as one option with pregnant women and made arrangements (if such a woman so requested) for her to be referred to a clinic in Great Britain. The High Court found that the applicant companies' activities violated Article 40.3.3 and granted an injunction perpetually restraining them from undertaking such conduct. On appeal, the Supreme Court rejected the applicants' arguments but amended the injunction to require, '... the defendants and each of them, their servants or agents be perpetually restrained from assisting pregnant women within the jurisdiction to travel abroad to obtain abortions by referral to a clinic, by the making for them of travel arrangements, or by informing them of the identity and location of and the method of communicating with a specified clinic...'. Costs were awarded against the applicant companies as a result of which Open Door had no assets and ceased its activities. The applicants complained to the Commission that the injunction violated, *inter alia*, their rights to impart or receive information contrary to Article 10 of the Convention. The Commission found a breach in respect of the applicant companies and their counsellors, by eight votes to five, and in regard to the women applicants, by seven votes to six.

In separate proceedings the European Court of Justice held that the medical termination of pregnancy, performed in accordance with the law of the State in which it was carried out, was a service within the meaning of Article 60 of the Treaty of Rome. However, the provision of information by Irish student associations to their members, about abortion facilities in other

Member states of the European Community, was too remote from the performance of medical terminations for Irish judicial restrictions on the distribution of such information to be in breach of the Treaty: *Society for the Protection of Unborn Children (Ireland) Ltd v Stephen Grogan* [1991] ECR I–4685. Also, the Irish courts gave judgement in the notorious case of *A-G v X* [1992] 1 IR 1, where the Attorney General had sought an injunction to prevent a 14-year-old girl (who claimed that she had been raped) from leaving Ireland to have an abortion. The Supreme Court ruled that the termination of pregnancy was lawful under Article 40.3.3 where there was a substantial risk to the life of the mother if the pregnancy was not ended. In the circumstances, the girl had expressed the desire to commit suicide, the Supreme Court discharged the injunction preventing her leaving the country. As a result of these legal developments the Irish Government made the following statement,during the oral hearing before the European Court of Human Rights: '. . . persons who are deemed to be entitled under Irish law to avail themselves of termination of pregnancy in these circumstances must be regarded as being entitled to have appropriate access to information in relation to the facilities for such operations, either in Ireland or abroad.'

. . .

ALLEGED VIOLATION OF ARTICLE 10

53. The applicants alleged that the Supreme Court injunction, restraining them from assisting pregnant women to travel abroad to obtain abortions, infringed the rights of the corporate applicants and the two counsellors to impart information, as well as the rights of Mrs X and Ms Geraghty to receive information. They confined their complaint to that part of the injunction which concerned the provision of information to pregnant women as opposed to the making of travel arrangements or referral to clinics (see paragraph 20 above) . . .

A. WAS THERE AN INTERFERENCE WITH THE APPLICANTS' RIGHTS?

55. The Court notes that the Government accepted that the injunction interfered with the freedom of the corporate applicants to impart information. Having regard to the scope of the injunction which also restrains the 'servants or agents' of the corporate applicants from assisting 'pregnant women' . . . there can be no doubt that there was also an interference with the rights of the applicant counsellors to impart information and with the rights of Mrs X and Ms Geraghty to receive information in the event of being pregnant. . . .

B. WAS THE RESTRICTION 'PRESCRIBED BY LAW'?

60. Taking into consideration the high threshold of protection of the unborn provided under Irish law generally and the manner in which the courts have interpreted their role as the guarantors of constitutional rights, the possibility that action might be taken against the corporate applicants must have been, with appropriate legal advice, reasonably foreseeable (See the *Sunday Times v UK* judgment of 26 April 1979, Series A No 30, p 31, § 49). This conclusion is reinforced by the legal advice that was actually given to Dublin Well Woman that, in the light of Article 40.3.3˚, an injunction could be sought against its counselling activities . . .

The restriction was accordingly 'prescribed by law'.

C. DID THE RESTRICTION HAVE AIMS THAT WERE LEGITIMATE UNDER ARTICLE 10 § 2?

61. The Government submitted that the relevant provisions of Irish law are intended for the protection of the rights of others—in this instance the unborn—, for the protection of morals and, where appropriate, for the prevention of crime.

62. The applicants disagreed, contending inter alia that, in view of the use of the term 'everyone' in Article 10 § 1 and throughout the Convention, it would be illogical to interpret the 'rights of others' in Article 10 § 2 as encompassing the unborn.

63. The Court cannot accept that the restrictions at issue pursued the aim of the prevention of crime since, as noted above neither the provision of the information in question nor the obtaining of an abortion outside the jurisdiction involved any criminal offence. However, it is evident that the protection afforded under Irish law to the right to life of the unborn is based on profound moral values concerning the nature of life which were reflected in the stance of the majority of the Irish people against abortion as expressed in the 1983 referendum. . . . The restriction thus pursued the legitimate aim of the protection of morals of which the protection in Ireland of the right to life of the unborn is one aspect. It is not necessary in the light of this conclusion to decide whether the term 'others' under Article 10 § 2 extends to the unborn.

D. WAS THE RESTRICTION NECESSARY IN A DEMOCRATIC SOCIETY?

64. The Government submitted that the Court's approach to the assessment of the 'necessity' of the restraint should be guided by the fact that the protection of the rights of the unborn in Ireland could be derived from Articles 2, 17 and 60 of the Convention. They further contended that the 'proportionality' test was inadequate where the rights of the unborn were at issue. The Court will examine these issues in turn.

1. Article 2

65. The Government maintained that the injunction was necessary in a democratic society for the protection of the right to life of the unborn and that Article 10 should be interpreted inter alia against the background of Article 2 of the Convention which, they argued, also protected unborn life. The view that abortion was morally wrong was the deeply held view of the majority of the people in Ireland and it was not the proper function of the Court to seek to impose a different viewpoint.

66. The Court observes at the outset that in the present case it is not called upon to examine whether a right to abortion is guaranteed under the Convention or whether the foetus is encompassed by the right to life as contained in Article 2. The applicants have not claimed that the Convention contains a right to abortion, as such, their complaint being limited to that part of the injunction which restricts their freedom to impart and receive information concerning abortion abroad.

Thus the only issue to be addressed is whether the restrictions on the freedom to impart and receive information contained in the relevant part of the injunction are necessary in a democratic society for the legitimate aim of the protection of morals as explained above (see paragraph 63). It follows from this approach that the Government's argument based on Article 2 of the Convention does not fall to be examined in the present case. On the other hand, the arguments based on Articles 17 and 60 fall to be considered below (see paragraphs 78 and 79).

2. Proportionality

67. The Government stressed the limited nature of the Supreme Court's injunction which only restrained the provision of certain information. . . . There was no limitation on discussion in Ireland about abortion generally or the right of women to travel abroad to obtain one. They further contended that the Convention test as regards the proportionality of the restriction was inadequate where a question concerning the extinction of life was at stake. The right to life could not, like other rights, be measured according to a graduated scale. It was either respected or it was not. Accordingly, the traditional approach of weighing competing rights and interests in the balance was inappropriate where the destruction of unborn life was concerned. Since life was a primary value which was antecedent to and a prerequisite for the enjoyment of every other right, its protection might involve the infringement of other rights such as freedom of expression in a manner which might not be acceptable in the defence of rights of a lesser nature.

The Government also emphasised that, in granting the injunction, the Supreme Court was merely sustaining the logic of Article 40.3.3° of the Constitution. The determination by the Irish courts that the provision of information by the relevant applicants assisted in the destruction of unborn life was not open to review by the Convention institutions.

68. The Court cannot agree that the State's discretion in the field of the protection of morals is unfettered and unreviewable (see, *mutatis mutandis*, for a similar argument, the *Norris v Ireland* judgment of 26 October 1988, Series A No 142, p 20, § 45).

It acknowledges that the national authorities enjoy a wide margin of appreciation in matters of morals, particularly in an area such as the present which touches on matters of belief concerning the nature of human life. . . .

However this power of appreciation is not unlimited. It is for the Court, in this field also, to supervise whether a restriction is compatible with the Convention.

69. As regards the application of the 'proportionality' test, the logical consequence of the Government's argument is that measures taken by the national authorities to protect the right to life of the unborn or to uphold the constitutional guarantee on the subject would be automatically justified under the Convention where infringement of a right of a lesser stature was alleged. It is, in principle, open to the national authorities to take such action as they consider necessary to respect the rule of law or to give effect to constitutional rights. However, they must do so in a manner which is compatible with their obligations under the Convention and subject to review by the Convention institutions. To accept the Government's pleading on this point would amount to an abdication of the Court's responsibility under Article 19 'to ensure the observance of the engagements undertaken by the High Contracting Parties . . .'.

70. Accordingly, the Court must examine the question of 'necessity' in the light of the principles developed in its case-law (see, inter alia, the *Observer* and *Guardian v UK* judgment of 26 November 1991, Series A No 216, pp 29–30, § 59). It must determine whether there existed a pressing social need for the measures in question and, in particular, whether the restriction complained of was 'proportionate to the legitimate aim pursued' (ibid). . . .

72. While the relevant restriction, as observed by the Government, is limited to the provision of information, it is recalled that it is not a criminal offence under Irish law for a pregnant woman to travel abroad in order to have an abortion. Furthermore, the injunction limited the freedom to receive and impart information with respect to services which are lawful in other Convention countries and may be crucial to a woman's health and well-being. Limitations on information concerning activities which, notwithstanding their moral implications, have been and continue to be tolerated by national authorities, call for careful scrutiny by the Convention institutions as to their conformity with the tenets of a democratic society.

73. The Court is first struck by the absolute nature of the Supreme Court injunction which imposed a 'perpetual' restraint on the provision of information to pregnant women concerning abortion facilities abroad, regardless of age or state of health or their reasons for seeking counselling on the termination of pregnancy. The sweeping nature of this restriction has since been highlighted by the case of *A-G v X* and by the concession made by the Government at the oral hearing that the injunction no longer applied to women who, in the circumstances as defined in the Supreme Court's judgment in that case, were not free to have an abortion in Ireland or abroad . . .

74. On that ground alone the restriction appears over broad and disproportionate. Moreover, this assessment is confirmed by other factors.

75. In the first place, it is to be noted that the corporate applicants were engaged in the counselling of pregnant women in the course of which counsellors neither advocated nor encouraged abortion, but confined themselves to an explanation of the available options. . . . The decision as to whether or not to

act on the information so provided was that of the woman concerned. There can be little doubt that following such counselling there were women who decided against a termination of pregnancy. Accordingly, the link between the provision of information and the destruction of unborn life is not as definite as contended. Such counselling had in fact been tolerated by the State authorities even after the passing of the Eighth Amendment in 1983 until the Supreme Court's judgment in the present case. Furthermore, the information that was provided by the relevant applicants concerning abortion facilities abroad was not made available to the public at large.

76. It has not been seriously contested by the Government that information concerning abortion facilities abroad can be obtained from other sources in Ireland such as magazines and telephone directories . . . or by persons with contacts in Great Britain. Accordingly, information that the injunction sought to restrict was already available elsewhere although in a manner which was not supervised by qualified personnel and thus less protective of women's health. Furthermore, the injunction appears to have been largely ineffective in protecting the right to life of the unborn since it did not prevent large numbers of Irish women from continuing to obtain abortions in Great Britain.

77. In addition, the available evidence, which has not been disputed by the Government, suggests that the injunction has created a risk to the health of those women who are now seeking abortions at a later stage in their pregnancy, due to lack of proper counselling, and who are not availing themselves of customary medical supervision after the abortion has taken place. . . . Moreover, the injunction may have had more adverse effects on women who were not sufficiently resourceful or had not the necessary level of education to have access to alternative sources of information. . . . These are certainly legitimate factors to take into consideration in assessing the proportionality of the restriction.

3. Articles 17 and 60

78. The Government, invoking Articles 17 and 60 of the Convention, have submitted that Article 10 should not be interpreted in such a manner as to limit, destroy or derogate from the right to life of the unborn which enjoys special protection under Irish law.

79. Without calling into question under the Convention the regime of protection of unborn life that exists under Irish law, the Court recalls that the injunction did not prevent Irish women from having abortions abroad and that the information it sought to restrain was available from other sources (see paragraph 76 above). Accordingly, it is not the interpretation of Article 10 but the position in Ireland as regards the implementation of the law that makes possible the continuance of the current level of abortions obtained by Irish women abroad.

4. Conclusion

80. In the light of the above, the Court concludes that the restraint imposed on the applicants from receiving or imparting information was disproportionate to the aims pursued. Accordingly there has been a breach of Article 10.

. . .

FOR THESE REASONS, THE COURT

. . .

Holds by fifteen votes to eight that there has been a violation of Article 10; . . .

NOTES

1 The majority of the plenary Court was comprised of: President Ryssdal and Judges; Thor Viljhalmsson, Gölcüklü, Macdonald, Bernhardt, Spielmann, De Meyer, Valticos, Martens, Palm, Foighel, Pekkanen, Loizou, Morenilla, and Freeland. Cremona J emphasized the paramount place accorded to the protection of unborn life in the fabric of Irish public policy (endorsed by the electorate in the constitutional referendum which preceded Article 40.3.3) as the basis for his dissent. A similar view was expressed by Matscher J In their combined dissenting opinion Pettiti, Russo, Lopes Rocha, and Bigi JJ wrote:

In our view, the restrictions were justified and, in any event, did not overstep the bounds of what was permissible. It was by any standards a minimal interference with the right to freedom of expression—concerning the aspect of that freedom relating to the communication and receipt of information—aimed at securing the primacy of values such as the right to life of the unborn child in accordance with the principle of the Irish legal system, which cannot be criticised on the basis of different principles applied in other legal systems.'

De Meyer J agreed with the decision of the majority, but on the separate reasoning that he did not believe that prior restraints, such as the Supreme Court's injunction, were permissible under Article 10 (see his dissent in *The Observer and Guardian* above, p 693). Baka J considered the injunction to be a proportionate response having regard to the constitutional rights of the unborn in Ireland. Likewise, Blayney J (the ad hoc Irish judge appointed because Walsh J had been a member of the Supreme Court which issued the injunction) considered that the injunction was the only measure possible to uphold Article 40.3.3.

2   The Court made clear that it was not going to express a view on the controversial question of whether the Convention provides a right to abortion in the above judgment, even though that issue was highly pertinent to the constitutional provisions in Ireland.

3   After the above ruling the Irish Government proposed three constitutional amendments. Sixty percent of the voters in a referendum approved an amendment to Article 40 which provides: 'Subsection 3 of this section shall not limit freedom to obtain or make available, in the State, subject to such conditions as may be laid down by law, information relating to services lawfully available in another State.' Article 40.3.5. See, L Flynn, 'Ireland' (ch 5) in C A Gearty (ed) *European Civil Liberties and the ECHR* (1997) Martinus Nijhoff: The Hague. For a consideration of the EC dimension to the saga see, B Wilkinson, 'Abortion, the Irish Constitution and the EEC' (1992) *Public Law* 20.

4   The British Government successfully invoked the aim of protecting morals to justify the conviction of the publisher and destruction of copies of his book in *Handyside v UK* (above, p 623).

For the protection of the reputation or rights of others

1   This aim has commonly been invoked by States when they seek to defend national court judgments in defamation cases before the Court, e.g. *Tolstoy Miloslavsky* (above, p 694).

2   The Court has determined a series of cases where the media published criticisms of domestic judges and were then subject to legal sanctions. In *Barfod v Denmark* (1989) 13 EHRR 493, A.149, the Greenland Local Government had introduced a controversial new tax which had been challenged by a number of persons. The Greenland High Court, composed of a professional judge and two lay judges (both of whom were local government employees) upheld the legality of the tax. Subsequently, the applicant, who was not a journalist, wrote a critical article for a magazine in which he stated that the lay judges 'did their duty'. The professional judge considered that this comment might damage the lay judges' reputations in the eyes of the public and impair confidence in the legal system; therefore he asked for a criminal investigation to be commenced. Later, the applicant was charged with defamation of character. The District Court found him guilty and fined him 2,000 Danish Crowns. On appeal the High Court agreed

with the applicant that the two lay judges should have refrained from participating in the case because of their employment, but it upheld the applicant's conviction as he had made serious accusations against them without adducing any proof. The Commission, by 14 votes to 1, found a violation of Article 10. Before the Court, the applicant accepted the Government's argument that his conviction had the aims of protecting the reputation of others (the lay judges) and, indirectly, maintaining the authority of the judiciary. The Court's judgment concentrated upon whether the interference with the applicant's freedom of expression was necessary in a democratic society.

The Court noted that the Greenland High Court had affirmed the applicant's right to criticize the composition of the court which determined the tax case. However:

The High Court's finding that there was no proof of the accusations against the lay judges remains unchallenged; the applicant must accordingly be considered to have based his accusations on the mere fact that the lay judges were employed by the Local Government ... it was certainly not proof of actual bias and the applicant cannot reasonably have been unaware of that.

The State's legitimate interest in protecting the reputation of the two lay judges was accordingly not in conflict with the applicant's interest in being able to participate in free public debate on the question of the structural impartiality of the High Court. (paras 33–34)

Therefore, a majority of the Court, six votes to one, concluded that the applicant's conviction had not violated Article 10.

In *Prager and Oberschlick v Austria* (1995) 21 EHRR 1, A.313, the first applicant was a journalist and the second applicant a publisher of the Austrian journal *Forum* (for other cases brought by this applicant see above, p 642). During 1987 the journal published a 13-page article entitled 'Danger! Harsh Judges!' written by Prager. After a short summary of the main conclusions the article described in detail the attitudes of nine members of the Vienna Regional Criminal Court. Passages of the article included the following: 'They treat each accused at the outset as if he had already been convicted.' 'Some Austrian criminal court judges are capable of anything.' 'Nothing was comparable to ... Judge [J]'s arrogant bullying.' 'Type: rabid ... [J].' Judge J brought a prosecution against the applicants for defamation. The Eisenstadt Regional Court found Prager guilty and sentenced him to 120-day fines at the rate of 30 ATS per day. Oberschlick was ordered to pay Judge J damages of 30,000 ATS and the remaining stocks of the relevant issue of the journal were confiscated. The Vienna Court of Appeal upheld the judgment, but reduced the damages to 20,000 ATS. The Commission, by 15 votes to 12, rejected the applicants' contention that there had been a breach of Article 10. The Court accepted that the aim of the interferences was to protect the Viennese judges' reputations and to maintain the authority of the judiciary. After restating its established view that the media has the role of informing the people about matters of public interest, the Court held that:

This undoubtedly includes questions concerning the functioning of the system of justice, an institution that is essential for any democratic society. The press is one of the means by which politicians and public opinion can verify that judges are discharging their heavy responsibilities in a manner that is in conformity with the aim which is the basis of the task entrusted to them.

Regard must, however, be had to the special role of the judiciary in society. As the guarantor of justice, a fundamental value in a law-governed State, it must enjoy public confidence if it is to be successful in carrying out its duties. It may therefore prove necessary to protect such confidence against destructive attacks that are essentially unfounded, especially in view of the fact that judges who have been criticised are subject to a duty of discretion that precludes them from replying. (para 34)

Even allowing that '... journalistic freedom also covers possible recourse to a degree of exaggeration, or even provocation' (para 37) a bare majority of the Court (five votes to four) concluded that the interferences with the applicants' freedom of expression were proportionate responses. This was because the majority considered that the applicants had not established a sufficient factual basis for their excessively wide accusations against the Viennese judges.

Nor, in the Court's view, could Mr Prager invoke his good faith or compliance with the ethics of journalism. The research that he had undertaken does not appear adequate to substantiate such serious allegations. In this connection it suffices to note that, on his own admission, the applicant had not attended a single criminal trial before Judge J. Furthermore he had not given the judge any opportunity to comment on the accusations leveled against him. (para 37)

The four dissenting judges took an entirely opposing view of the research undertaken by the author:

... Mr Prager after his curiosity had been aroused by academic literature, not only spent a lot of time [six months, during which he visited the court on a daily basis for three and a half months] and energy in verifying on the spot the reasons for the phenomena described by sociologists, but was honestly shocked by what he found. (para 2)

Also, they felt that the Austrian courts had only taken into account the specified isolated passages and not the context of the whole article. For the dissentients, the applicants' conviction was not necessary in a democratic society.

In *De Haes and Gijsels v Belgium* (1997) 25 EHRR 1, 1997-I 198, the first applicant was a journalist and the second applicant a publisher of the weekly magazine *Humo*. The applicants published five lengthy articles, over a period of several months during 1986, criticising the judges of the Antwerp Court of Appeal for their determination of a controversial divorce and child custody case. The case concerned a Belgian notary who was granted custody of his children despite unproven allegations of child abuse having been made against him by his ex-wife/parents-in-law. The applicants claimed that the notary had received favourable treatment in the courts because of his family and political connections. In one article they stated: 'Most of the judges of the Third Division of the Court of Appeal, who awarded custody to the notary, also belong to extreme-right-wing circles. Judge [YB] is the son of a bigwig in the gendarmerie who was convicted in 1948 of collaboration ...' Subsequently, that judge, together with two fellow judges and an advocate-general (who had all been criticized by name in *Humo*), began proceedings against the applicants seeking damages for the allegedly defamatory criticisms published in the magazine. The Brussels *tribunal de premiere instance* upheld the action and ordered the applicants to pay each of the plaintiffs one franc in respect of non-pecuniary damage and publish the whole of its judgment in the magazine (and in six daily newspapers at the applicants' expense). The Brussels Court of Appeal and the Court of Cassation rejected the applicants' appeals. The applicants petitioned the Commission and that body found, *inter alia*, a breach of Article 10 (by six votes to three). Before the Court it was accepted that the interferences with the applicants' freedom of expression had the legitimate aim of protecting the reputation or rights of the named judges/advocate-general. The Court, therefore, concentrated upon the issue of whether the defamation judgments were 'necessary in a democratic society'. It was noted that the applicants' articles: '... contain a mass of detailed information about the circumstances in which the decisions on the custody of Mr X's children were taken. That information was based on thorough research into the allegations against Mr X and on the opinions of several experts who were said to have advised the applicants to disclose them in the interests of the children' (para 39). However, the Court was unwilling to afford Article 10 protection to a part of the applicants' criticisms:

One of the allusions to the alleged political sympathies was inadmissible-the one concerning the past history of the father of one of the judges criticised. It is unacceptable that someone should be exposed to opprobrium because of matters concerning a member of his family. A penalty was justifiable on account of that allusion by itself. (para 45)

But, as for the other parts, the majority of the Court (seven votes to two) considered that:

Looked at against the background of the case, the accusations in question amount to an opinion, whose truth, by definition, is not susceptible of proof. Such an opinion may, however, be excessive, in particular in the absence of any factual basis, but it was not so in this instance; in that respect the present case differs from the *Prager and Oberschlick* case.

Although Mr De Haes and Mr Gijsels' comments were without doubt severely critical, they nevertheless appear proportionate to the stir and indignation caused by the matters alleged in their articles. As to the journalists' polemical and even aggressive tone, which the Court should not be taken to approve, it must be remembered that Article 10 protects not only the substance of the ideas and information expressed but also the form in which they are conveyed.

In conclusion, the Court considers that, regard being had to the seriousness of the circumstances of the case and of the issues at stake, the necessity of the interference with the exercise of the applicants' freedom of expression has not been shown, except as regards the allusion to the past history of the father of one of the judges in question. (paras 47–9)

From the above judgments it is clear that the Court will only accord the protection of Article 10 to media criticisms of domestic judges where the commentators can establish a factual basis for their accusations. The more vitriolic the criticism the greater the need to show an evidential basis for the views expressed. Critical commentary on institutional factors affecting the judiciary, rather than personal attacks on named judges, and on judicial decisions which have general social/political implications appear easier to justify before the Court. However, the majority's approach in *Prager and Oberschlick* places an excessively high evidential/ research burden upon journalists.

Where a judge is also a political figure then the Court is willing to accord the media wider freedom to make critical value-judgments about such a person. In *Hirco v Slovakia*, judgment of 20 July 2004, the applicant was the publisher of a weekly journal. In 1994 he published several articles expressing criticism of the domestic courts' rulings in a civil case between a Minister and a poet [these proceedings were later found to have infringed Article 10 by the Court in *Feldek v Slovakia*, judgment of 12 July 2001]. One of the articles included an interview with the poet's lawyer in which the latter noted that a, named, Supreme Court judge who had participated in the proceedings was an election candidate for a political party which had strong views on the topic of the proceedings. The lawyer expressed the view that the judge's political links had influenced his decision in the proceedings. Subsequently, the judge won damages against the applicant for interfering with his civil and professional honour. The Court held that, '46. . . . the limits of acceptable criticism are wider in respect of a judge who enters political life.' Taking account of the facts that the critical articles were not published in bad faith and the domestic proceedings were related to an important issue subject to political debate the Court, unanimously, found a breach of Article 10. For an examination of the lawfulness under Article 6(1) of a politician sitting as a judge see *Pabla Ky v Finland*, above p 431.

3   The Court has accorded States a narrower margin of appreciation to restrict and punish lawyers' criticisms of the administration of justice. In *Nikula v Finland*, judgment of 21 March 2002, the Court was faced with the unusual situation where a defence lawyer had been convicted of defamation in respect of her criticisms, during court proceedings, of the conduct of the prosecutor. The applicant had represented a businessman charged with fraud. The prosecutor decided not to bring charges against the defendant's brother, who had been involved in the same business, but to summon him as a prosecution witness. The applicant objected to the brother being called as a witness and she read out in court a memorandum entitled 'Role

manipulation and unlawful presentation of evidence'. In the document she accused the prosecutor of '... procedural tactics, to make a witness out of a co-accused so as to support the indictment... deliberate abuse of discretion... committing role manipulation, thereby breaching his official duties and jeopardising legal security...' After the conclusion of the trial, the defendant having been convicted, the prosecutor initiated a private prosecution against the applicant. Subsequently, the Court of Appeal convicted her of negligent defamation and fined her 716 euros together with 505 euros damages to be paid to the prosecutor. On appeal the Supreme Court upheld her conviction, but waived the fine due to the minor nature of the offence. Before the Strasbourg Court, the applicant complained that her right to express herself freely as a defence lawyer had been violated, in breach of Article 10, by the defamation conviction. Applying Article 10(2) the Court found that her conviction was 'prescribed by law' and served the legitimate aim of protecting the prosecutor's reputation and rights. Therefore, the contentious issue was whether the conviction was 'necessary in a democratic society'. The Court observed that lawyers play a central role in the administration of justice, as intermediaries between the public and the courts, consequently they must contribute to the maintenance of public confidence in that system.

46. ... While lawyers too are certainly entitled to comment in public on the administration of justice, their criticism must not overstep certain bounds. In that connection, account must be taken of the need to strike the right balance between the various interests involved, which include the public's right to receive information about questions arising from judicial decisions, the requirements of the proper administration of justice and the dignity of the legal profession. The national authorities have a certain margin of appreciation in assessing the necessity of an interference, but this margin is subject to European supervision as regards both the relevant rules and the decisions applying them ... However, in the field under consideration in the present case there are no particular circumstances—such as a clear lack of common ground among, member states regarding the principles at issue or a need to make allowance for the diversity of moral conceptions—which would justify granting the national authorities a wide margin of appreciation (cf, for example, the *Sunday Times v the United Kingdom* judgment of 26 April 1979, Series A No 30, pp 35–7, § 59, with further reference to the *Handyside v the United Kingdom* judgment of 7 December 1976, Series A No 24).

The Court considered that although some of the applicant's comments were 'inappropriate', they were made in the courtroom and related to the prosecutor's conduct of the case. According to the Court, '51. ... in that procedural context [the prosecutor] had to tolerate very considerable criticism by the applicant in her capacity as defence counsel.' In the view of the Court:

55. It is therefore only in exceptional cases that restriction—even by way of a lenient criminal sanction—of defence counsel's freedom of expression can be accepted as necessary in a democratic society.

Consequently, a large majority of the Court, five votes to two, concluded that the conviction of the applicant was not 'necessary in a democratic society'.

Judges Caflisch and Pastor Ridruejo issued a Dissenting Opinion in which they expressed the belief that:

56. Clearly the accusations made by the applicant in open court were of some gravity. They amounted to stating, not only that prosecutor T. had acted wrongly—which, in and of itself, was legitimate—, but also that he had abused his functions and acted dishonestly. This is one of the worst things to say about a public official, magistrate or not. Not only does it mean that the magistrate is unfit to discharge his/her duties and, possibly, to fill other posts; it also taints the reputation of the judiciary. In other words, the interests protected by the measure are of considerable importance.

Taking account of the waiving of the applicant's fine by the Supreme Court and the absence of a criminal record in respect of her conviction, they considered that the measures taken against her were proportional and fell within Article 10(2).

The judgment of the Court is to be strongly endorsed compared to that of the dissentients. The latter minority appear to have conflated the separate positions of prosecutors and judges. As the Court correctly explained these are different functions and defence counsel should have greater freedom to criticise prosecutors, *qua* their institutional opponents, compared to their latitude to censure judges (who must be independent and impartial in order to satisfy the demands of Article 6). The refusal of the Court to accord national authorities a wide margin of appreciation in restricting the freedom of expression of defence counsel is also very important in safeguarding the ability of such lawyers to properly represent their clients' interests.

4 The 'rights of others' includes legal rights, such as proprietary and contractual rights. In *Goodwin v UK* (1996) 22 EHRR 123, 1996-II 483, the applicant had been employed as a trainee journalist by the publisher of a specialist journal (*The Engineer*). A few months after he began working for the journal a source rang him to provide information, on an unattributable basis, regarding the financial problems of a company (Tetra Ltd). Goodwin telephoned Tetra to confirm the information and obtain their comments. The information derived from a draft of Tetra's confidential business plan and, therefore, the next day Tetra applied (ex parte) to the High Court for an injunction to prevent the publishers of *The Engineer* from publishing any information derived from the plan. The court granted the injunction and Tetra notified all the national newspapers and relevant journals of the order (thereby preventing them from disclosing details of the plan). Subsequently, the High Court ordered Goodwin and his employer/publisher to disclose his notes of the telephone conversation with his source (which identified that person) so that Tetra could take further action against that person. The order was made under section 10 of the Contempt of Court Act 1981 which states that, 'No court may require a person to disclose . . . the source of information contained in a publication for which he is responsible, unless it be established to the satisfaction of the court that disclosure is necessary in the interests of justice . . .'. Goodwin and his employer/publisher refused to comply and appealed. Both the Court of Appeal and the House of Lords confirmed the disclosure order (*X Ltd v Morgan-Grampian (Publishers) Ltd* [1990] 2 All ER 1). Goodwin continued to refuse to disclose his notes and was found guilty of contempt of court and fined £5,000. He complained to the Commission that the disclosure order and fine constituted a violation of his rights under Article 10. By eleven votes to six the Commission found a breach. It was not disputed before the Court that these measures had the aim of protecting Tetra's rights. The Court held, however, that the:

Protection of journalistic sources is one of the basic conditions for press freedom, as is reflected in the laws and the professional codes of conduct in a number of Contracting States and is affirmed in several international instruments on journalistic freedoms . . . Without such protection, sources may be deterred from assisting the press in informing the public on matters of public interest. As a result the vital public-watchdog role of the press may be undermined and the ability of the press to provide accurate and reliable information may be adversely affected. Having regard to the importance of the protection of journalistic sources for press freedom in a democratic society and the potentially chilling effect an order of source disclosure has on the exercise of that freedom, such a measure cannot be compatible with Article 10 of the Convention unless it is justified by an overriding requirement in the public interest. (para 39)

The majority of the Court (eleven votes to seven) felt that the High Court injunction protected Tetra from having its confidential financial information published by the media. Therefore, the issue was whether it was also necessary to require the applicant to disclose his source. The majority acknowledged that the company had legitimate reasons in unmasking a disloyal employee and seeking to prevent future unauthorised disclosures, but these were not sufficient to amount to an overriding public interest. Consequently, the disclosure order and fine imposed on the applicant were in breach of Article 10. The dissentients felt that the majority accorded insufficient weight to the interests of Tetra and the domestic courts were in a better position to balance those interests against the rights of the applicant and the public.

This is a very important judgment for the media as it demonstrates the Court protecting one of the basic means by which they obtain their information. Hence, Article 10 encompasses news gathering techniques as well as the distribution of acquired information. For a discussion of this case see: S Tierney, 'Press Freedom and Public Interest: The Developing Jurisprudence of the European Court of Human Rights' [1998] EHRLR 419.

In *Roemen and Schmit v Luxembourg*, judgment of 25 February 2003, a unanimous Chamber of the full-time Court rigorously applied *Goodwin* to the searches of a journalist's home and office, ordered by an investigating judge, seeking to discover who had supplied him with information. The first applicant had published an article in a daily newspaper disclosing that a Minister had been given a fiscal fine for value-added tax fraud. The Chamber stated:

57. ... The Court considers that, even if unproductive, a search conducted with a view to uncover a journalist's source is a more drastic measure than an order to divulge the source's identity. This is because investigators who raid a journalist's workplace unannounced and armed with search warrants have very wide investigative powers, as, by definition, they have access to all the documentation held by the journalist. The Court reiterates that 'limitations on the confidentiality of journalistic sources call for the most careful scrutiny by the Court' (see *Goodwin*, cited above, pp 500–1, § 40). It thus considers that the searches of the first applicant's home and workplace undermined the protection of sources to an even greater extent than the measures in issue in *Goodwin*.

The Chamber concluded that the searches were a disproportionate interference with the applicant's freedom of expression and breached Article 10.

5 A person's right to respect for his/her religious beliefs and feelings, as guaranteed by Article 9, also falls within the aim of protecting the 'rights of others'; see, *Otto-Preminger-Institute v Austria* (above, p 601).

6 The dissentients (Judges Spielmann, Pekkanen and Van Dijk) in *Ahmed v the UK* (above p 654) warned of the dangers of the Court accepting an ever widening spectrum of 'rights'. '... [W]e would highlight the risk of that notion being stretched so far as to lose almost all distinct meaning if it is held to cover 'rights' such as that to effective political democracy at the local level' (para 1). However, the Court in determining the inadmissibility of the application brought by *McGuinness v UK* (8/6/1999), continued to interpret the phrase broadly to encompass key constitutional principles. The applicant had been elected as a Member of Parliament in respect of a constituency in Northern Ireland. However, in accordance with his party's policy (Sinn Fein, an Irish republican party), he refused to take the oath of allegiance to the monarch, required of MPs before taking their seats. Consequently, he was prevented from taking his seat and barred from using the services and facilities available to MPs. He complained that his treatment amounted to a breach of Article 10. In declaring his complaint manifestly ill-founded the Court observed that:

Freedom of expression is of paramount importance for the elected representatives of the people, whose role is to represent their electorate, draw attention to their constituents' concerns and defend their interests. On the other hand, the expression 'the protection of the rights of others' should be interpreted as extending to the protection of the constitutional principles forming the basis of democracy. In the present case, the requirement that elected representatives of the House of Commons take an oath of allegiance to the monarch could be viewed as an affirmation of loyalty to the constitutional principles which support the UK constitutional system—a constitutional monarchy—and as such could be construed as a reasonable condition.

7 The Court was not willing to decide whether 'others' included unborn children in *Open Door and Dublin Well Woman v Ireland* (above, p 707).

For maintaining the authority and impartiality of the judiciary

1 The Court has interpreted this aim broadly to encompass the protection of individual judges from unjustified criticism by the media (see above, p 712 Note 2) and more generally the maintenance of public confidence in the machinery of justice (see *The Sunday Times*, above p 633).

2 A unanimous Court found a breach of Article 10 in *Weber v Switzerland* (1990) 12 EHRR 508, A.177. The applicant was a well-known Swiss ecologist and journalist. During 1980 a newspaper published a vitriolic letter attacking the applicant's integrity. Weber responded by lodging a complaint of defamation against the author of the letter. The investigating judge ordered the disclosure of the accounts of the applicant's environmental association. Weber became dissatisfied with the conduct of the investigating judge and on 1 March 1982 he lodged a criminal complaint alleging misuse of judicial authority and coercion against the judge. The next day Weber held a press conference at which he stated, *inter alia*, that he had lodged the criminal complaint against the judge. Subsequently, Weber was fined 300 Swiss francs for breaching the confidentiality of a judicial investigation by holding his press conference. The Commission, unanimously, found that the fine violated Weber's rights under Article 10. Before the Court it was accepted that the fine infringed Weber's right to freedom of expression and that the interference was prescribed by law. The Court found that the interference had the legitimate aim of seeking to ensure the proper conduct of the judicial investigation and therefore it fell within Article 10(2) as being designed to protect the 'authority and impartiality of the judiciary'. However, the Court did not accept that the interference was 'necessary in a democratic society'.

As to the submission that the impugned statements by Mr Weber on 2 March 1982 could be interpreted as an attempt to bring pressure to bear on the investigating judge and could therefore have been prejudicial to the proper conduct of the investigation, the Court notes that by that time the investigation was practically complete, because on the previous day the judge had committed [the letter writer] for trial, and that from then on any attempt of that kind would have been belated and thus devoid of effect. . . . It was accordingly not necessary to impose a penalty on the applicant from this point of view . . . (para 51)

While the applicant succeeded on the facts of his case, it is clear that the Court interprets this legitimate aim as encompassing the prohibition on parties to legal proceedings bringing improper media pressure on judges hearing their cases.

3 In *Worm v Austria* (1997) 25 EHRR 454, 1997-V 1534, the applicant was a journalist who had an article published in the Austrian magazine *Profil* (this journal also published the article that was the basis of the *Lingens* judgment, above p 639). The article was concerned with the ongoing criminal trial of a former Minister of Finance (Androsch) for alleged tax evasion. In the piece Worm wrote that the defendant's activities 'permits no other interpretation than that

Androsch was evading taxes'. A few months later the court (composed of two professional judges and two lay judges) convicted Androsch of tax evasion and fined him 1.8 million ATS. Thereupon Worm was charged with the offence of having exercised prohibited influence on criminal proceedings. The Vienna Regional Criminal Court acquitted him, but the public prosecutor appealed and the Vienna Court of Appeal found Worm guilty and fined him 48,000ATS (and made the magazine's publisher jointly liable for the fine). The applicant complained to the Commission which, by eighteen votes to eleven, expressed the opinion that there had been a breach of Article 10. The Court found that the applicant's conviction pursued the aim of 'maintaining the authority and impartiality of the judiciary'.

The phrase 'authority of the judiciary' includes, in particular, the notion that the courts are, and are accepted by the public at large as being, the proper forum for the settlement of legal disputes and for the determination of a person's guilt or innocence on a criminal charge; further, that the public at large have respect for and confidence in the court's capacity to fulfil that function . . .

'Impartiality' normally denotes lack of prejudice or bias (see the *Piersack v Belgium* judgment (1982) A.53). However, the Court has repeatedly held that what is at stake in maintaining the impartiality of the judiciary is the confidence which the courts in a democratic society must inspire in the accused, as far as criminal proceedings are concerned, and also in the public at large . . .

It follows that, in seeking to maintain the 'authority and impartiality of the judiciary', the Contracting States are entitled to take account of considerations going—beyond the concrete case—to the protection of the fundamental role of courts in a democratic society. (para 40)

In considering whether the applicant's conviction was 'necessary in a democratic society' the Court stated:

Restrictions on freedom of expression permitted by the second paragraph of Article 10 'for maintaining the authority and impartiality of the judiciary' do not entitle States to restrict all forms of public discussion on matters pending before the courts. There is general recognition of the fact that the courts cannot operate in a vacuum. While the courts are the forum for the determination of a person's guilt or innocence on a criminal charge, this does not mean that there can be no prior or contemporaneous discussion of the subject matter of criminal trials elsewhere, be it in specialised journals, in the general press or among the public at large (see *The Sunday Times (No 1)* judgment). Provided that it does not overstep the bounds imposed in the interests of the proper administration of justice, reporting, including comment, on court proceedings contributes to their publicity and is thus perfectly consonant with the requirement under Article 6(1) of the Convention that hearings be public. Not only do the media have the task of imparting such information and ideas: the public also has a right to receive them. This is all the more so where a public figure is involved, such as, in the present case, a former member of the Government. . . .

However, public figures are entitled to the enjoyment of the guarantees of a fair trial set out in Article 6, which in criminal proceedings include the right to an impartial tribunal, on the same basis as every other person. This must be borne in mind by journalists when commenting on pending criminal proceedings since the limits of permissible comment may not extend to statements which are likely to prejudice, whether intentionally or not, the chances of a person receiving a fair trial or to undermine the confidence of the public in the role of the courts in the administration of criminal justice. (para 50)

A majority of the Court (seven votes to two) concluded that the Vienna Court of Appeal's conviction of the applicant had not exceeded the national margin of appreciation and, therefore, Article 10 had not been breached.

This case complements the *Sunday Times (No 1)* judgment (where there were press comments on a pending civil action) by demonstrating how the Court applies Article 10 to media discussion of a continuing criminal trial. The Court's analysis in *Worm* indicates that journalists must be very cautious in their commentary, as compared with their objective factual reporting, on such proceedings. Significantly, the Court considered that it was permissible under Article 10 for the Vienna Court of Appeal to have regard to the susceptibility of the lay judges in the Androsch trial to media comments upon the case. Therefore, the media may have to be even more circumspect in its comments on trials being determined by lay persons.

4 A unanimous Grand Chamber of the full-time Court concluded that the imprisonment, for five days, of a defence lawyer for his 'discourteous' comments to the judges presiding over the criminal trial was a disproportionate sentence which failed to achieve the right balance between the need to protect the authority of the judiciary and the applicant's right to freedom of expression in *Kyprianou v Cyprus*, judgment of 15 December 2005 (see above, p 439). This finding of a breach of Article 10 reflects the contemporary Court's recognition of the importance, for the proper administration of justice, of safeguarding the freedom of expression of lawyers to defend their clients (see also *Nikula* above, p 715).

13

ARTICLE 11 FREEDOM OF ASSEMBLY AND ASSOCIATION

The Court's general approach

United Communist Party of Turkey v Turkey 1998-I, (1998) 26 EHRR 121
European Court of Human Rights

The first applicant ('the *TBKP*') was a (dissolved) political party and the other applicants were Mr Sargin, Chairman of the party, and Mr Yagci, General Secretary of the party. The party was formed in June 1990 and on the day of its formation the constitution and programme of the party were sent to the Principal State Counsel at the Court of Cassation for assessment of their compatibility with the Constitution and Law No 2820 on the regulation of political parties. A few days later, while the party was preparing to participate in a general election, the Counsel applied to the Constitutional Court for an order dissolving the *TBKP*. The Counsel specified a number of grounds for the order (based particularly on the party's programme towards a peaceful and democratic solution of the 'Kurdish problem'). In July 1991 the Constitutional Court made an order dissolving the party. The effect of this order was the liquidation of the party and the transfer of its assets to the Treasury. Also the individual applicants, together with other founders and managers of the party, were banned from holding similar office in any other political body. The Constitutional Court based its order on the fact that the *TBKP* used the word 'communist' in its name contrary to Law No 2820, and that the party's constitution and programme contained statements likely to undermine the territorial integrity of the State and the unity of the nation in violation of the national Constitution. The applicants complained to the Commission alleging, *inter alia*, that the dissolution of the *TBKP* amounted to a breach of Article 11. The Commission, unanimously, found a violation of that Article.

...

AS TO THE LAW

I. ALLEGED VIOLATION OF ARTICLE 11 OF THE CONVENTION

18. The applicants maintained that the fact that the United Communist Party of Turkey ('the *TBKP*') had been dissolved and its leaders—including Mr Sargin and Mr Yagci—banned from holding similar office in any other political party had infringed their right to freedom of association, as guaranteed by Article 11 of the Convention . . .

A. APPLICABILITY OF ARTICLE 11

1. Submissions of those appearing before the Court

(A) The Government

19. The Government submitted that Article 11 did not in any event apply to political parties. Where in its constitution or programme a party attacked a State's constitutional order, the Court should declare the Convention to be inapplicable *ratione materiae* or apply Article 17, rather than apply Article 11.

Even a cursory examination of the Convention showed that neither Article 11 nor any other Article made any mention of political parties or referred to the States' constitutional structures. It was significant that the only Article containing a reference to political institutions was in Protocol No 1 (Article 3) and did not confer any right on individuals as it was worded so as to create an obligation on the States . . .

20. The constitution and programme of the *TBKP* were clearly incompatible with Turkey's fundamental constitutional principles. By choosing to call itself 'communist', the *TBKP* perforce referred to a subversive doctrine and a totalitarian political goal that undermined Turkey's political and territorial unity and jeopardised the fundamental principles of its public law, such as secularism. 'Communism' invariably presupposed seizing power and aimed to establish a political order that would be unacceptable, not just in Turkey but also in the other member States of the Council of Europe. Further, the use of certain names was also proscribed in other legal systems in the West. In that respect, the Government referred to the German, Polish and Portuguese constitutions. In any event, whatever the intentions of the *TBKP* and its leaders in choosing the name 'communist' in 1990 (after the fall of the Berlin Wall) may have been, that name could not, in the Government's view, be considered devoid of political meaning.

. . . In the Government's submission, the States Parties to the Convention had at no stage intended to submit their constitutional institutions, and in particular the principles they considered to be the essential conditions of their existence, to review by the Strasbourg institutions. For that reason, where a political party such as the *TBKP* had called those institutions or principles into question, it could not seek application of the Convention or its Protocols.

At the very least, Article 17 of the Convention should be applied in respect of the *TBKP* since the party had called into question both the bases of the Convention and the freedoms it secured. In that connection, the Government cited the Commission's decisions in the cases of *Glimmerveen and Hagenbeek v Netherlands* (application Nos 8348/78 and 8406/78, Decisions and Reports ('DR') 18, p 187); *Kühnen v Germany* (application No 12194/86, DR 56, p 205); *H W P and K v Austria* (application No 12774/87, DR 62, p 216) and *Remer v Germany* (application No 25096/94, DR 82-B, p 117). In a context of vicious terrorism such as Turkey was experiencing, the need to preclude improper use of the Convention by applying Article 17 was even more obvious, as the Turkish authorities had to prohibit the use of 'expressions' and the formation of 'associations' that would inevitably incite violence and enmity between the various sections of Turkish society.

(B) The applicants

22. The applicants maintained that there was no doubt that political parties came within the ambit of Article 11. They pointed out that the scope of the Convention could not be restricted by relying on the Turkish Constitution. Domestic law had to be construed in the light of the Convention, not the other way round.

(C) The Commission

23. The Commission expressed the opinion that there was nothing in the wording of Article 11 to limit its scope to a particular form of association or group or suggest that it did not apply to political parties. On the contrary, if Article 11 was considered to be a legal safeguard that ensured the proper functioning of democracy, political parties were one of the most important forms of association it protected. In that connection, the Commission referred to a number of decisions in which it had examined, under Article 11, various restrictions on the activities of political parties and even the dissolution of such parties, thereby implicitly accepting that Article 11 applied to that type of association (see the *German*

Communist Party case, application no 250/57, *Yearbook* 1, P 225; the *Greek* case, *Yearbook*, 1969, p 170 § 392; the *France, Norway, Denmark, Sweden and the Netherlands v Turkey* case, applications Nos 9940–9944/82, DR 35, p 143).

At the hearing before the Court the Delegate of the Commission also said that it was unnecessary to apply Article 17 of the Convention since the present case was clearly distinguishable from the rare cases in which the Commission had had recourse to that provision. In such cases the aim of the offending actions of the applicants concerned had been to spread violence (see the *German Communist Party* case cited above) or hatred (see the *Remer* case cited above). Conversely, there was nothing in the *TBKP*'s constitution or programme to suggest that it was not a democratic party, or that it resorted to illegal or undemocratic methods, encouraged the use of violence, aimed to undermine Turkey's democratic and pluralist political system or pursued objectives that were racist or likely to destroy the rights and freedoms of others.

2. The Court's assessment

24. The Court considers that the wording of Article 11 provides an initial indication as to whether political parties may rely on that provision. It notes that although Article 11 refers to 'freedom of association with others, including the right to form . . . trade unions . . . ;' the conjunction 'including' clearly shows that trade unions are but one example among others of the form in which the right to freedom of association may be exercised. It is therefore not possible to conclude, as the Government did, that by referring to trade unions—for reasons related mainly to issues that were current at the time—those who drafted the Convention intended to exclude political parties from the scope of Article 11.

25. However, even more persuasive than the wording of Article 11, in the Court's view, is the fact that political parties are a form of association essential to the proper functioning of democracy. In view of the importance of democracy in the Convention system (see paragraph 45 below), there can be no doubt that political parties come within the scope of Article 11.

27. The Court notes on the other hand that an association, including a political party, is not excluded from the protection afforded by the Convention simply because its activities are regarded by the national authorities as undermining the constitutional structures of the State and calling for the imposition of restrictions. As the Court has said in the past, while it is in principle open to the national authorities to take such action as they consider necessary to respect the rule of law or to give effect to constitutional rights, they must do so in a manner which is compatible with their obligations under the Convention and subject to review by the Convention institutions (see the *Open Door and Dublin Well Woman v Ireland* judgment of 29 October 1992, Series A No 246-A, p 29, § 69).

28. The Preamble to the Convention refers to the 'common heritage of political traditions, ideals, freedom and the rule of law' (see paragraph 45 below), of which national constitutions are in fact often the first embodiment. Through its system of collective enforcement of the rights it establishes (see the *Loizidou v Turkey (Preliminary Objections)* judgment of 23 March 1995, Series A No 310, p 26, § 70), the Convention reinforces, in accordance with the principle of subsidiarity, the protection afforded at national level, but never limits it (Article 60 of the Convention).

29. The Court points out, moreover, that Article 1 requires the States Parties to 'secure to everyone within their jurisdiction the rights and freedoms defined in Section 1 of th[e] Convention'. That provision, together with Articles 14, 2 to 13 and 63, demarcates the scope of the Convention *ratione personae, materiae* and *loci* (see the *Ireland v UK* judgment of 18 January 1978, Series A No 25, p 90, § 238). It makes no distinction as to the type of rule or measure concerned and does not exclude any part of the member States' jurisdiction from scrutiny under the Convention. It is, therefore, with respect to their jurisdiction as a whole—which is often exercised in the first place through the Constitution—that the States Parties are called on to show compliance with the Convention.

30. The political and institutional organisation of the member States must accordingly respect the rights and principles enshrined in the Convention. It matters little in this context whether the provisions

in issue are constitutional (see, for example, the *Gitonas v Greece* judgment of 1 July 1997, *Reports of Judgments and Decisions* 1997-V) or merely legislative (see, for example, the *Mattieu-Mohin and Clerfayt v Belgium* judgment of 2 March 1987, Series A No 113). From the moment that such provisions are the means by which the State concerned exercises its jurisdiction, they are subject to review under the Convention.

31. Moreover, it may on occasion prove difficult, even artificial, in proceedings before the Court, to attempt to distinguish between what forms part of a State's institutional structures and what relates to fundamental rights in the strict sense. That is particularly true of an order for dissolution of the kind in issue in the present case. In view of the role played by political parties (see paragraph 25 above), such measures affect both freedom of association and, consequently, democracy in the State concerned.

32. It does not, however, follow that the authorities of a State in which an association, through its activities, jeopardises that State's institutions are deprived of the right to protect those institutions. In this connection, the Court points out that it has previously held that some compromise between the requirements of defending democratic society and individual rights is inherent in the system of the Convention (see, *mutatis mutandis*, the *Klass v Germany* of 6 September 1978, Series A No 28, p 28, § 59). For there to be a compromise of that sort any intervention by the authorities must be in accordance with paragraph 2 of Article 11, which the Court considers below (see paragraphs 37 et seq). Only when that review is complete will the Court be in a position to decide, in the light of all the circumstances of the case, whether Article 17 of the Convention should be applied.

33. Before the Commission the Government also submitted, in the alternative, that while Article 11 guaranteed freedom to form an association, it did not on that account prevent one from being dissolved.

The Commission took the view that freedom of association not only concerned the right to form a political party but also guaranteed the right of such a party, once formed, to carry on its political activities freely.

The Court reiterates that the Convention is intended to guarantee rights that are not theoretical or illusory, but practical and effective (see, among other authorities, the *Artico v Italy* judgment of 13 May 1980, Series A No 37, p 16, § 33, and the *Loizidou* judgment cited above, p 27, § 72). The right guaranteed by Article 11 would be largely theoretical and illusory if it were limited to the founding of an association, since the national authorities could immediately disband the association without having to comply with the Convention. It follows that the protection afforded by article 11 lasts for an association's entire life and that dissolution of an association by a country's authorities must accordingly satisfy the requirements of paragraph 2 of that provision (see paragraphs 35–47 below).

34. In conclusion Article 11 is applicable to the facts of the case.

B. COMPLIANCE WITH ARTICLE 11

1. Whether there has been an interference

. . .

35. Before the Commission, the Government submitted that the dissolution of the *TBKP* had not constituted an interference with Mr Sargin and Mr Yagci's right to freedom of association. However, it did not reiterate that argument before the Court.

36. Like the Commission, the Court concludes that there has been an interference with that right in respect of all three applicants, having regard (in the case of Mr Sargin and Mr Yagci) to their role as founders and leaders of the party and to the ban which prevented them from discharging similar responsibilities in any other political grouping . . .

2. Whether the interference was justified

37. Such an interference will constitute a breach of Article 11 unless it was 'prescribed by law', pursued one or more legitimate aims under paragraph 2 and was 'necessary in a democratic society' for the achievement of those aims.

(A) 'Prescribed by law'

38. It was common ground that the interference was 'prescribed by law', as the measures ordered by the Constitutional Court were based on Articles 2, 3 § 1, 6, 10 § 1 and 14 § 1, and former Article 68 of the Constitution and sections 78, 81 and 96(3) of Law No 2820 on the regulation of political parties . . .

(B) Legitimate aim

39. The Government maintained that the interference pursued a number of legitimate aims: ensuring national security, public safety and territorial integrity and protecting the rights and freedom of others . . .

40. The Commission distinguished between the different grounds relied on by the Constitutional Court for dissolving the *TBKP*. Inasmuch as the interference was based on the use of the word 'communist' in the party's name, it could not, in the Commission's view, be said to be justified by any of the legitimate aims referred to in Article 11. Indeed, the Constitutional Court had recognised that there was nothing to suggest that the *TBKP* would not respect democratic institutions or that it intended to establish a dictatorship . . .

On the other hand, inasmuch as the dissolution was based on a distinction drawn in the *TBKP's* programme between Turks and Kurds, it could, in the Commission's view, be said to have been ordered with the aim of protecting territorial integrity and thus 'national security'. It was not that the *TBKP* was a terrorist organisation or one sponsoring terrorism, but it could be regarded as openly pursuing the creating of a separate Kurdish nation and consequently a redistribution of the territory of the Turkish State.

41. Like the Commission, the Court considers that the dissolution of the *TBKP* pursued at least one of the 'legitimate aims' set out in Article 11: the protection of 'national security'.

(C) 'Necessary in a democratic society'

(i) General principles

42. The Court reiterates that notwithstanding its autonomous role and particular sphere of application, Article 11 must, in the present case, also be considered in the light of Article 10. The protection of opinions and the freedom to express them is one of the objectives of the freedoms of assembly and association as enshrined in Article 11 (see, among other authorities, the *Young, James and Webster v UK* judgment of 13 August 1981, Series A, No 44, p 23, § 57, and the *Vogt v Germany* judgment of 26 September 1995, Series A No 323, p 30, § 64).

43. That applies all the more in relation to political parties in view of their essential role in ensuring pluralism and the proper functioning of democracy (see paragraph 25 above).

As the Court has said many times, there can be no democracy without pluralism. It is for that reason that freedom of expression as enshrined in Article 10 is applicable, subject to paragraph 2, not only to 'information' or 'ideas' that are favourably received or regarded as inoffensive or as a matter of indifference, but also to those that offend, shock or disturb (see, among many other authorities, the *Vogt* judgment cited above, p 25, § 52). The fact that their activities form part of a collective exercise of freedom of expression in itself entitles political parties to seek the protection of Articles 10 and 11 of the Convention.

44. In the *Informationsverein Lentia v Austria* judgment the Court described the State as the ultimate guarantor of the principle of pluralism (see the judgment of 24 November 1993, Series A No 276, p 16,

§ 38). In the political sphere that responsibility means that the State is under the obligation, among others, to hold, in accordance with Article 3 of Protocol No 1, free elections at reasonable intervals by secret ballot under conditions which will ensure the free expression of the opinion of the people in the choice of the legislature. Such expression is inconceivable without the participation of a plurality of political parties representing the different shades of opinion to be found within a country's population. By relaying this range of opinion, not only within political institutions but also—with the help of the media—at all levels of social life, political parties make an irreplaceable contribution to political debate, which is at the very core of the concept of a democratic society (see the *Lingens v Austria* judgment of 8 July 1986, Series A No 103, p 26, § 42, and the *Castells v Spain* judgment of 23 April 1992, Series A No 236, p 23, § 43).

45. Democracy is without doubt a fundamental feature of the European public order (see the *Loizidou* judgment cited above, p 27, § 75).

That is apparent, firstly, from the Preamble to the Convention, which establishes a very clear connection between the Convention and democracy by stating that the maintenance and further realisation of human rights and fundamental freedoms are best ensured on the one hand by an effective political democracy and on the other by a common understanding and observance of human rights (see the *Klass* judgment cited above, p 28, § 59). The Preamble goes on to affirm that European countries have a common heritage of political tradition, ideals, freedom and the rule of law. The Court has observed that in that common heritage are to be found the underlying values of the Convention (see the *Soering v UK* judgment of 7 July 1989, Series A No 161, p 35, § 88); it has pointed out several times that the Convention was designed to maintain and promote the ideals and values of a democratic society (see the *Kjeldsen, Busk Madsen and Pedersen v Denmark* judgment of 7 December 1976, Series A No 23, p 27, § 53, and the *Soering* judgment cited above, p 34, § 87).

In addition, Articles 8, 9, 10 and 11 of the Convention require that interference with the exercise of the rights they enshrine must be assessed by the yardstick of what is 'necessary in a democratic society'. The only type of necessity capable of justifying an interference with any of those rights is, therefore, one which may claim to spring from 'democratic society'. Democracy thus appears to be the only political model contemplated by the Convention and, accordingly, the only one compatible with it.

The Court has identified certain provisions of the Convention as being characteristic of democratic society. Thus in its very first judgment it held that in a 'democratic society within the meaning of the Preamble and the other clauses of the Convention', proceedings before the judiciary should be conducted in the presence of the parties and in public and that that fundamental principle was upheld in Article 6 of the Convention (see the *Lawless v Ireland* judgment of 14 November 1960 (preliminary objections and questions of procedure), Series A No 1, p 13). In a field closer to the one concerned in the instant case, the Court has on many occasions stated, for example, that freedom of expression constitutes one of the essential foundations of a democratic society and one of the basic conditions for its progress and each individual's self-fulfilment (see, among other authorities, the *Vogt* judgment cited above, p 25, § 52), whereas in the *Mattieu-Mohin and Clerfayt* judgment cited above, it noted the prime importance of Article 3 of Protocol No 1, which enshrines a characteristic principle of an effective political democracy (p 22, § 47).

46. Consequently, the exceptions set out in Article 11 are, where political parties are concerned, to be construed strictly; only convincing and compelling reasons can justify restrictions on such parties' freedom of association. In determining whether a necessity within the meaning of Article 11 § 2 exists, the Contracting States possess only a limited margin of appreciation, which goes hand in hand with rigorous European supervision embracing both the law and the decisions applying it, including those given by independent courts. The Court has already held that such scrutiny was necessary in a case concerning a Member of Parliament who had been convicted of proferring insults (see the *Castells* judgment cited above, pp 22–3, § 42); such scrutiny is all the more necessary where an entire political party is dissolved and its leaders banned from carrying on any similar activity in the future.

47. When the Court carries out its scrutiny, its task is not to substitute its own view for that of the relevant national authorities but rather to review under Article 11 the decisions they delivered in the exercise of their discretion. This does not mean that it has to confine itself to ascertaining whether the respondent State exercised its discretion reasonably, carefully and in good faith; it must look at the interference complained of in the light of the case as a whole and determine whether it was 'proportionate to the legitimate aim pursued' and whether the reasons adduced by the national authorities to justify it are 'relevant and sufficient'. In so doing, the Court has to satisfy itself that the national authorities applied standards which were in confirmity with the principles embodied in Article 11 and, moreover, that they based their decisions on an acceptable assessment of the relevant facts (see, *mutatis mutandis*, the *Jersild v Denmark* judgment of 23 Spetember 1994, Series A No 298, p 26, § 31).

(ii) Application of the principles to the present case

...

(B) The Court's assessment

51. The Court notes at the outset that the *TBKP* was dissolved even before it had been able to start its activities and that the dissolution was therefore ordered solely on the basis of the *TBKP*'s constitution and programme, which however—as is for that matter apparent from the Constitutional Court's decision—contain nothing to suggest that they did not reflect the party's true objectives and its leaders' true intentions (see paragraph 58 below). ...

The Court can therefore confine its review to the other two grounds, which were upheld by the Constitutional Court.

53. In the first of these it was alleged that the *TBKP* had included the word 'communist' in its name, contrary to section 96(3) of Law no 2820. ... The Constitutional Court held, in particular, that that provision prohibited the formation of political parties on a purely formal ground: the mere fact of using a name proscribed in that section sufficed to trigger its application and consequently to entail the dissolution of any political party that, like the *TBKP*, had contravened it. ...

54. The Court considers that a political party's choice of name cannot in principle justify a measure as drastic as dissolution, in the absence of other relevant and sufficient circumstances. ... The Court also attaches much weight to the Constitutional Court's finding that the *TBKP* was not seeking, in spite of its name, to establish the domination of one social class over the others, and that, on the contrary, it satisfied the requirements of democracy, including political pluralism, universal suffrage and freedom to take part in politics. ...

Accordingly, in the absence of any concrete evidence to show that in choosing to call itself 'communist', the *TBKP* had opted for a policy that represented a real threat to Turkish society or the Turkish State, the Court cannot accept that the submission based on the party's name may, by itself, entail the party's dissolution.

55. The second submission accepted by the Constitutional Court was that the *TBKP* sought to promote separatism and the division of the Turkish nation. ...

56. The Court notes that although the *TBKP* refers in its programme ... to the Kurdish 'people' and 'nation' and Kurdish 'citizens', it neither describes them as a 'minority' nor makes any claim—other than for recognition of their existence—for them to enjoy special treatment or rights, still less a right to secede from the rest of the Turkish population. On the contrary, the programme states: 'The TBKP will strive for a peaceful, democratic and fair solution of the Kurdish problem, so that the Kurdish and Turkish peoples may live together of their free will within the borders of the Turkish Republic, on the basis of equal rights and with a view to democratic restructuring founded on their common interests. ...

The *TBKP* also said in its programme: 'A solution to the Kurdish problem will only be found if the parties concerned are able to express their opinions freely, if they agree not to resort to violence in any form in order to resolve the problem and if they are able to take part in politics with their own national identity.'

57. The Court considers one of the principal characteristics of democracy to be the possibility it offers of resolving a country's problems through dialogue, without recourse to violence, even when they are irksome. Democracy thrives on freedom of expression. From that point of view, there can be no justification for hindering a political group solely because it seeks to debate in public the situation of part of the State's population and to take part in the nation's political life in order to find, according to democratic rules, solutions capable of satisfying everyone concerned. To judge by its programme, that was indeed the *TBKP*'s objective in this area. That distinguishes the present case from those referred to by the Government. . . .

58. Admittedly, it cannot be ruled out that a party's political programme may conceal objectives and intentions different from the ones it proclaims. To verify that it does not, the content of the programme must be compared with the party's actions and the positions it defends. In the present case, the *TBKP*'s programme could hardly have been belied by any practical action it took since it was dissolved immediately after being formed and accordingly did not even have time to take any action. It was thus penalised for conduct relating solely to the exercise of freedom of expression.

59. The Court is also prepared to take into account the background of cases before it, in particular the difficulties associated with the fight against terrorism (see, among other authorities, the *Ireland v UK* judgment cited above, pp 9 et seq, §§ 11 et seq, and the *Aksoy v Turkey* judgment of 18 December 1996, *Reports* 1996-VI, p . . . , §§ 70 and 84). In the present case, however, it finds no evidence to enable it to conclude, in the absence of any activity by the *TBKP*, that the party bore any responsibility for the problems which terrorism poses in Turkey.

60. Nor is there any need to bring Article 17 into play as nothing in the constitution and programme of the *TBKP* warrants the conclusion that it relied on the Convention to engage in activity or perform acts aimed at the destruction of any of the rights and freedoms set forth in it (see, *mutatis mutandis*, the *Lawless v Ireland* judgment of 1 July 1961 (merits) Series A No 3, pp 45–46, § 7).

61. Regard being had to all the above, a measure as drastic as the immediate and permanent dissolution of the *TBKP*, ordered before its activities had even started and coupled with a ban barring its leaders from discharging any other political responsibility, is disproportionate to the aim infringed Article 11 of the Convention.

. . .

FOR THESE REASONS, THE COURT UNANIMOUSLY

Holds that there has been a violation of Article 11 of the Convention;

. . .

NOTES

1 The Grand Chamber was composed of President Bernhardt and Judges: Gölcüklü, Matscher, Macdonald, Russo, Valticos, Palm, Foighel, Pekkanen, Loizou, Morenilla, Freeland, Baka, Lopes Rocha, Wildhaber, Makarczyk, Kuris, Lohmus, and Van Dijk.

2 The judgment clearly demonstrates that the Court follows the same analytical framework in applying Article 11 as it does in cases invoking Articles 8, 9, and 10 (see previous chapters). This method involves examining whether there has been an 'interference' with the applicant's rights granted by paragraph one of the Article and, if that is so, then considering whether the interference was 'justified' under paragraph two of the Article (i.e. was it 'prescribed by law', did it have a 'legitimate aim' and was it 'necessary in a democratic society'): see paragraphs 35 and 37 in the judgment above.

3   The Court was also willing to interpret the right to freedom of association broadly so as to include political parties (even where the State fears that a specific party may undermine the prevailing constitutional arrangements, although the State can take action to protect its institutions from that party provided its actions satisfy the conditions of Article 11(2)). However, the limitations contained within Article 11 are construed strictly when applied to political parties, because of the latter's fundamental role in the maintenance of democratic societies. Hence, the Court will only allow States a limited margin of appreciation when determining if an interference with a political party's Article 11(1) rights was necessary under Article 11(2).

4   In its judgment the Court held that the right to freedom of association is not restricted to the initial right to form an association but also continues throughout the lifetime of the organisation. If state authorities wish to dissolve a particular association they must comply with the conditions laid down in Article 11(2).

5   Earlier the two individual applicants in the above case had succeeded in another action they had brought under the Convention against Turkey. In *Yagci and Sargin v Turkey* (1995) 20 EHRR 505, A.319, they challenged the authorities' conduct leading up to the establishment of the United Communist Party of Turkey. During 1987 the applicants held a press conference in Brussels at which they announced their intention of returning to Turkey in order to form the party. As soon as they alighted from the plane in Ankara (on 16 November 1987) the police arrested them. They were charged with leading an organisation which, *inter alia*, had the unlawful aim of establishing the domination of one social class. The National Security Court ordered that they be held in custody pending trial. Eventually the applicants were released from custody in May 1990 (and, as we know from the above case, they established the Party the following month). The Turkish courts finally acquitted the applicants in January 1992. Subsequently, the European Court of Human Rights held, by eight votes to one, that the above treatment violated the applicants' rights under Article 5(3) and Article 6(1).

6   Another Grand Chamber applied the principles articulated in the *United Communist Party* judgment in the later case of *Socialist Party v Turkey* (1998) 27 EHRR 51, 1998-III. The applicants in this case were another Turkish political party and two Chairmen of the Party. In 1988, when the Socialist Party was preparing to take part in a general election, State Counsel applied to the Constitutional Court for an order dissolving the Party. The Constitutional Court dismissed the application as unfounded. However, criminal proceedings were then brought against the leaders of the Party (including one of the applicants) in the National Security Courts for allegedly disseminating harmful propaganda. All the accused were acquitted following a repeal of the relevant legislation. In 1991 the Party was formally allowed by the authorities to participate in the general election. However, a few months later State Counsel made a second application for the Party to be dissolved on the grounds that it had engaged in activities likely to undermine the territorial integrity and unity of the nation contrary to the Constitution. Counsel particularly relied upon election publications from the Party and speeches made by the Chairman. In July 1992 the Constitutional Court ordered the dissolution of the Party as it had argued for the creation of an independent federated State (comprising separate States for Turks and Kurds). The applicants complained to the Commission which, unanimously, found a breach of Article 11. Before the Court, the Turkish Government sought to distinguish the *United Communist Party* case on the basis that in the present action the dissolution of the Party was based upon its activities after its formation (and not simply on its constitution and programme). The Court, unanimously, found that there had been an interference with the applicants' right to freedom of association and that it was 'prescribed by law' and had the 'legitimate aim' of protecting national security (on the same basis as in the *United Communist Party*). Therefore, the major question was whether the dissolution was 'necessary in a democratic society'. The Court noted:

Having analysed [the Chairman's] statements, the Court finds nothing in them that can be considered a call for the use of violence, an uprising or any other form of rejection of democratic principles. On the contrary, he stressed on a number of occasions the need to achieve the proposed political reform in accordance with democratic rules, through the ballot box and by holding referenda. At the same time, he spoke out against 'the former culture idolising violence . . .'.

At the hearing the Agent for the Government stated that [the Chairman] had 'justified the use of violent and terrorist methods' by saying in particular 'The Kurd has proved himself through the fight of impoverished peasants by linking its destiny [to theirs]' . . . Furthermore, by calling on those present to 'sow courage, rather than watermelons', [the Chairman] had, in the Government's submission, 'exhorted them to stop all activities other than the destruction of order'. Lastly, by using the phrase 'The Kurdish people are standing up' he had called upon them to revolt.

While the Court accepts that these phrases were directed at citizens of Kurdish origin and constituted an invitation to them to rally together and assert certain political claims, it finds no trace of any incitement to use violence or infringe the rules of democracy. In that regard, the relevant statements were scarcely any different from those made by other political groups that were active in other countries of the Council of Europe. . . .

In the Court's view, the fact that such a political programme is considered incompatible with the current principles and structures of the Turkish State does not make it incompatible with the rules of democracy. It is of the essence of democracy to allow diverse political programmes to be proposed and debated, even those that call into question the way a State is currently organised, provided that they do not harm democracy itself. (paras. 46–7)

Therefore, the Court held that the dissolution of the Party had been a disproportionate action that was in breach of Article 11. The effect of this judgment is to safeguard the right of political parties to continue non-violent campaigns for political manifestos which challenge the basic ideologies and constitutional structures of their States, so long as the parties adhere to the Convention's idea of political democracy. In *United Communist Party* the Court identified a number of the elements which constitute this form of society including: the free expression of the people (by secret ballot) in the choice of the legislature, the plurality of political parties contesting such elections, respect for human rights (especially freedom of expression) and the rule of law: see further A. Mowbray, 'The Role of the European Court of Human Rights in the Promotion of Democracy' (1999) *Public Law* 703.

7   A unanimous Grand Chamber found no breach of Article 11 in respect of the dissolution of a political party supporting fundamentalist Islamic views in *Refah Partisi (The Welfare Party) and Others v Turkey*, judgment of 13 February 2003. The applicant political party and three of its leading members alleged a breach of their right to freedom of association. After the Turkish general election of 1995, Refah was the largest political party in the national parliament (with 158 members out of a total of 450). Refah formed a coalition government with another party. In May 1997, Principal State Counsel applied to the Constitutional Court seeking the dissolution of Refah on the ground that it had become a centre of activities contrary to the principles of secularism. State counsel relied on a number of statements made by leading figures in Refah advocating, *inter alia*, the abolition of secularism in Turkey, establishing the supremacy of the Koran through holy war (jihad) and the introduction of Islamic law (sharia)

in Turkey. In January 1998, the Constitutional Court dissolved Refah, ordered the transfer of the party's assets to the Treasury and terminated the applicants' office as MPs/ banned them from becoming members or leaders of any other political party for five years. A Chamber of the European Court, by five votes to four, found no breach of the applicants' rights under Article 11. Thereupon, the applicants obtained the permission of the Grand Chamber for a re-hearing under Article 43. The Grand Chamber found that the domestic judgment against the applicants was 'prescribed by law' and had the legitimate aims, under Article 11(2), of protecting national security and public safety, preventing disorder or crime and protecting the rights and freedoms of others. As to whether it was 'necessary in a democratic society' the Grand Chamber held that:

98. On that point, the Court considers that a political party may promote a change in the law or the legal and constitutional structures of the State on two conditions: firstly, the means used to that end must be legal and democratic; secondly, the change proposed must itself be compatible with fundamental democratic principles. It necessarily follows that a political party whose leaders incite to violence or put forward a policy which fails to respect democracy or which is aimed at the destruction of democracy and the flouting of the rights and freedoms recognised in a democracy cannot lay claim to the Convention's protection against penalties imposed on those grounds (see *Yazar and Others v Turkey*, Nos 22723/93, 22724/93, and 22725/93, § 49, ECHR 2002-II, and, *mutatis mutandis*, the following judgments: *Stankov and the United Macedonian Organisation Ilinden v Bulgaria*, Nos 29221/95 and 29225/95, § 97, ECHR 2001-IX, and *Socialist Party and Others v Turkey*, judgment of 25 May 1998, *Reports* 1998-III, pp 1256–7, §§ 46–7).

99. The possibility cannot be excluded that a political party, in pleading the rights enshrined in Article 11 and also in Articles 9 and 10 of the Convention, might attempt to derive therefrom the right to conduct what amounts in practice to activities intended to destroy the rights or freedoms set forth in the Convention and thus bring about the destruction of democracy (see *Communist Party (KPD) v Germany*, No 250/57, Commission decision of 20 July 1957, Yearbook 1, p 222). In view of the very clear link between the Convention and democracy (see paragraphs 86–9 above), no one must be authorised to rely on the Convention's provisions in order to weaken or destroy the ideals and values of a democratic society. Pluralism and democracy are based on a compromise that requires various concessions by individuals or groups of individuals, who must sometimes agree to limit some of the freedoms they enjoy in order to guarantee greater stability of the country as a whole (see, *mutatis mutandis*, *Petersen v Germany* (dec.), No 39793/98, ECHR 2001-XII).

In that context, the Court considers that it is not at all improbable that totalitarian movements, organised in the form of political parties, might do away with democracy, after prospering under the democratic regime, there being examples of this in modern European history.

100. The Court reiterates, however, that the exceptions set out in Article 11 are, where political parties are concerned, to be construed strictly; only convincing and compelling reasons can justify restrictions on such parties' freedom of association. In determining whether a necessity within the meaning of Article 11 § 2 exists, the Contracting States have only a limited margin of appreciation. Although it is not for the Court to take the place of the national authorities, which are better placed than an international court to decide, for example, the appropriate timing for interference, it must exercise rigorous supervision embracing both the law and the decisions applying it, including those given by independent courts. Drastic measures, such as the dissolution of an entire political party and a disability barring its leaders from carrying on any similar activity for a specified period, may be taken only in the most serious cases (see the following judgments: *United Communist Party of Turkey and Others*, cited above, p 22, § 46; *Socialist Party and Others*, cited above, p 1258, § 50; and *Freedom and Democracy Party (ÖZDEP) v Turkey* [GC], No 23885/94, § 45, ECHR 1999-VIII). Provided that it satisfies the conditions set out in paragraph 98 above, a political party animated by the moral values imposed by a religion cannot

be regarded as intrinsically inimical to the fundamental principles of democracy, as set forth in the Convention.

(δ) Imputability to a political party of the acts and speeches of its members

101. The Court further considers that the constitution and programme of a political party cannot be taken into account as the sole criterion for determining its objectives and intentions. The political experience of the Contracting States has shown that in the past political parties with aims contrary to the fundamental principles of democracy have not revealed such aims in their official publications until after taking power. That is why the Court has always pointed out that a party's political programme may conceal objectives and intentions different from the ones it proclaims. To verify that it does not, the content of the programme must be compared with the actions of the party's leaders and the positions they defend. Taken together, these acts and stances may be relevant in proceedings for the dissolution of a political party, provided that as a whole they disclose its aims and intentions (see *United Communist Party of Turkey and Others*, cited above, p 27, § 58, and *Socialist Party and Others*, cited above, pp 1257–8, § 48).

(ε) The appropriate timing for dissolution

102. In addition, the Court considers that a State cannot be required to wait, before intervening, until a political party has seized power and begun to take concrete steps to implement a policy incompatible with the standards of the Convention and democracy, even though the danger of that policy for democracy is sufficiently established and imminent. The Court accepts that where the presence of such a danger has been established by the national courts, after detailed scrutiny subjected to rigorous European supervision, a State may 'reasonably forestall the execution of such a policy, which is incompatible with the Convention's provisions, before an attempt is made to implement it through concrete steps that might prejudice civil peace and the country's democratic regime' (see the Chamber's judgment, § 81).

103. The Court takes the view that such a power of preventive intervention on the State's part is also consistent with Contracting Parties' positive obligations under Article 1 of the Convention to secure the rights and freedoms of persons within their jurisdiction. Those obligations relate not only to any interference that may result from acts or omissions imputable to agents of the State or occurring in public establishments but also to interference imputable to private individuals within non-State entities (see, for example, with regard to the State's obligation to make private hospitals adopt appropriate measures to protect life, *Calvelli and Ciglio v Italy* [GC], No 32967/96, § 49, ECHR 2002-I). A Contracting State may be justified under its positive obligations in imposing on political parties, which are bodies whose *raison d'être* is to accede to power and direct the work of a considerable portion of the State apparatus, the duty to respect and safeguard the rights and freedoms guaranteed by the Convention and the obligation not to put forward a political programme in contradiction with the fundamental principles of democracy.

....

110. While it can be considered, in the present case, that Refah's policies were dangerous for the rights and freedoms guaranteed by the Convention, the real chances that Refah would implement its programme after gaining power made that danger more tangible and more immediate. That being the case, the Court cannot criticise the national courts for not acting earlier, at the risk of intervening prematurely and before the danger concerned had taken shape and become real. Nor can it criticise them for not waiting, at the risk of putting the political regime and civil peace in jeopardy, for Refah to seize power and swing into action, for example by tabling bills in Parliament, in order to implement its plans.

In short, the Court considers that in electing to intervene at the time when they did in the present case the national authorities did not go beyond the margin of appreciation left to them under the Convention.

The Grand Chamber found that the statements of the individual applicants, and other identified members of Refah, could be imputed to the Party as it had not taken any disciplinary action against them.

119. The Court sees no reason to depart from the Chamber's conclusion that a plurality of legal systems, as proposed by Refah, cannot be considered to be compatible with the Convention system. In its judgment, the Chamber gave the following reasoning:

'70. ... the Court considers that Refah's proposal that there should be a plurality of legal systems would introduce into all legal relationships a distinction between individuals grounded on religion, would categorise everyone according to his religious beliefs and would allow him rights and freedoms not as an individual but according to his allegiance to a religious movement.

'The Court takes the view that such a societal model cannot be considered compatible with the Convention system, for two reasons.

'Firstly, it would do away with the State's role as the guarantor of individual rights and freedoms and the impartial organiser of the practice of the various beliefs and religions in a democratic society, since it would oblige individuals to obey, not rules laid down by the State in the exercise of its above-mentioned functions, but static rules of law imposed by the religion concerned. But the State has a positive obligation to ensure that everyone within its jurisdiction enjoys in full, and without being able to waive them, the rights and freedoms guaranteed by the Convention (see, *mutatis mutandis*, *Airey v Ireland*, judgment of 9 October 1979, Series A No 32, p. 14, § 25).

'Secondly, such a system would undeniably infringe the principle of non-discrimination between individuals as regards their enjoyment of public freedoms, which is one of the fundamental principles of democracy. A difference in treatment between individuals in all fields of public and private law according to their religion or beliefs manifestly cannot be justified under the Convention, and more particularly Article 14 thereof, which prohibits discrimination. Such a difference in treatment cannot maintain a fair balance between, on the one hand, the claims of certain religious groups who wish to be governed by their own rules and on the other the interest of society as a whole, which must be based on peace and on tolerance between the various religions and beliefs (see, *mutatis mutandis*, the judgment of 23 July 1968 in the "Belgian linguistic" case, Series A No 6, pp. 33–5, §§ 9 and 10, and *Abdulaziz, Cabales and Balkandali v the United Kingdom*, judgment of 28 May 1985, Series A No 94, pp. 35–6, § 72).'

....

123. The Court concurs in the Chamber's view that sharia is incompatible with the fundamental principles of democracy, as set forth in the Convention:

'72. Like the Constitutional Court, the Court considers that sharia, which faithfully reflects the dogmas and divine rules laid down by religion, is stable and invariable. Principles such as pluralism in the political sphere or the constant evolution of public freedoms have no place in it. The Court notes that, when read together, the offending statements, which contain explicit references to the introduction of sharia, are difficult to reconcile with the fundamental principles of democracy, as conceived in the Convention taken as a whole. It is difficult to declare one's respect for democracy and human rights while at the same time supporting a regime based on sharia, which clearly diverges from Convention values, particularly with regard to its criminal law and criminal procedure, its rules on the legal status of women and the way it intervenes in all spheres of private and public life in accordance with religious precepts. ... In the Court's view, a political party whose actions seem to be aimed at introducing sharia in a State party to the Convention can hardly be regarded as an association complying with the democratic ideal that underlies the whole of the Convention.'

124. The Court must not lose sight of the fact that in the past political movements based on religious fundamentalism have been able to seize political power in certain States and have had the opportunity to set up the model of society which they had in mind. It considers that, in accordance with the Convention's provisions, each Contracting State may oppose such political movements in the light of its historical experience.

125. The Court further observes that there was already an Islamic theocratic regime under Ottoman law. When the former theocratic regime was dismantled and the republican regime was being set up, Turkey opted for a form of secularism which confined Islam and other religions to the sphere of private religious practice. Mindful of the importance for survival of the democratic regime of ensuring respect for the principle of secularism in Turkey, the Court considers that the Constitutional Court was justified in holding that Refah's policy of establishing sharia was incompatible with democracy . . .

. . .

130. The Court considers that, whatever meaning is ascribed to the term 'jihad' used in most of the speeches mentioned above (whose primary meaning is holy war and the struggle to be waged until the total domination of Islam in society is achieved), there was ambiguity in the terminology used to refer to the method to be employed to gain political power. In all of these speeches the possibility was mentioned of resorting 'legitimately' to force in order to overcome various obstacles Refah expected to meet in the political route by which it intended to gain and retain power.

131. Furthermore, the Court endorses the following finding of the Chamber:

'74. . . .

'While it is true that [Refah's] leaders did not, in government documents, call for the use of force and violence as a political weapon, they did not take prompt practical steps to distance themselves from those members of [Refah] who had publicly referred with approval to the possibility of using force against politicians who opposed them. Consequently, Refah's leaders did not dispel the ambiguity of these statements about the possibility of having recourse to violent methods in order to gain power and retain it (see, *mutatis mutandis*, *Zana v. Turkey*, judgment of 25 November 1997, *Reports* 1997-VII, p. 2549, § 58).'

(α) Overall examination of 'pressing social need'

132. In making an overall assessment of the points it has just listed above in connection with its examination of the question whether there was a pressing social need for the interference in issue in the present case, the Court finds that the acts and speeches of Refah's members and leaders cited by the Constitutional Court were imputable to the whole of the party, that those acts and speeches revealed Refah's long-term policy of setting up a regime based on sharia within the framework of a plurality of legal systems and that Refah did not exclude recourse to force in order to implement its policy and keep the system it envisaged in place. In view of the fact that these plans were incompatible with the concept of a 'democratic society' and that the real opportunities Refah had to put them into practice made the danger to democracy more tangible and more immediate, the penalty imposed on the applicants by the Constitutional Court, even in the context of the restricted margin of appreciation left to Contracting States, may reasonably be considered to have met a 'pressing social need'.

(β) Proportionality of the measure complained of

133. After considering the parties' arguments, the Court sees no good reason to depart from the following considerations in the Chamber's judgment:

'82. . . . The Court has previously held that the dissolution of a political party accompanied by a temporary ban prohibiting its leaders from exercising political responsibilities was a drastic measure and that measures of such severity might be applied only in the most serious cases (see the previously cited *Socialist Party and Others v Turkey* judgment, p 1258, § 51). In the present case it has just found that the interference in question met a 'pressing social need'. It should also be noted that after [Refah's] dissolution only five of its MPs (including the applicants) temporarily forfeited their parliamentary office and their role as leaders of a political party. The 152 remaining MPs continued to sit in Parliament and pursued their political careers normally. . . . The Court considers in that connection that the nature and severity of the interference are also factors to be taken into account when assessing its proportionality (see, for example, *Sürek v Turkey (No 1)* [GC], No 26682/95, § 64, ECHR 1999-IV).'

134. The Court also notes that the pecuniary damage alleged by the applicants was made up largely of a loss of earnings and is speculative in nature. In view of the low value of Refah's assets, their transfer to the Treasury can have no bearing on the proportionality of the interference in issue. Moreover, the Court observes that the prohibition barring three of the applicants, Mr Necmettin Erbakan, Mr Şevket Kazan and Mr Ahmet Tekdal, from engaging in certain types of political activity for a period of five years was temporary, and that, through their speeches and the stances they adopted in their capacity as the chairman and vice-chairmen of the party, they bear the main responsibility for Refah's dissolution.

It follows that the interference in issue in the present case cannot be regarded as disproportionate in relation to the aims pursued.

4. The Court's conclusion regarding Article 11 of the Convention

135. Consequently, following a rigorous review to verify that there were convincing and compelling reasons justifying Refah's dissolution and the temporary forfeiture of certain political rights imposed on the other applicants, the Court considers that those interferences met a 'pressing social need' and were 'proportionate to the aims pursued'. It follows that Refah's dissolution may be regarded as 'necessary in a democratic society' within the meaning of Article 11 § 2.

136. Accordingly, there has been no violation of Article 11 of the Convention.

Clearly, the frequent expression of extreme views contrary to recognized Convention values, including religious and political pluralism and the prohibition on the use of violence to effect political change, by leading members of Refah led the Grand Chamber to conclude that the dissolution of the party was compatible with Article 11(2). On the importance of the principle of secularism for Turkey see *Leyla Sahin* above p 614. Commenting on *Refah*, D. McGoldrick has observed that, '...it must be admitted that there can be some severe tensions between Islamic beliefs and the organisation of modern democratic states.' ('Multiculturalism and its Discontents' (2005) 5(1) *Human Rights Law Review* 27, at p 48)

Article 11(1)

The right to freedom of peaceful assembly

Ezelin v France A.202 (1991) 14 EHRR 362
European Court of Human Rights

The applicant was a lawyer (*avocat*) who practised in Basse-Terre (Guadeloupe). In 1983 he was the Vice-Chairman of the Trade Union of the Guadeloupe Bar. During February of that year a number of Guadeloupe independence movements and trade unions held a public demonstration in Basse-Terre to protest against the conviction of three militants for criminal damage to public buildings. Prior notice of the demonstration had been given and the authorities had not prohibited it. According to the police about 1,000 demonstrators took part in the march and during its course the crowd chanted abuse against a named police officer (saying 'one day you will pay'), outside the law courts the demonstrators also shouted abuse at the judges and unknown persons painted graffiti on the walls of the administrative building (calling the judges 'pimps'). The applicant carried a placard during the demonstration which read 'Trade Union of the Guadeloupe Bar against the Security and Freedom Act'. A subsequent judicial investigation was unable to identify which of the demonstrators had been responsible for uttering the insulting/threatening words or painting the graffiti. However, the Principal Public Prosecutor asked the Chairman of the Guadeloupe Bar to bring disciplinary proceedings against the applicant for allegedly having infringed Article 106 of the Decree regulating the profession of *avocat* (which, *inter alia*, made such persons liable to disciplinary sanction for 'breach of integrity honour or discretion, even relating to non-professional matters'). The Bar Council decided not to impose any disciplinary sanction on the applicant as the earlier judicial investigation had not revealed any evidence that he had committed acts in breach of Article 106. The Prosecutor appealed against that ruling to the Basse-Terre Court of Appeal which found the applicant guilty and sentenced him to a formal reprimand. The Court of Appeal's judgment stated that: '... it is not alleged that Mr Ezelin took part in this demonstration any more actively than by his constant presence and by carrying a placard.... He was there in his capacity as an *avocat*, since he carried a placard announcing his profession, and at no time did he dissociate himself from the demonstrators' offensive and insulting acts or leave the procession. Such misconduct on the part of a member of the Bar publicly proclaiming his profession cannot be justified...'. The Court of Cassation dismissed the applicant's appeal and he then complained to the Commission. The latter body, by 15 votes to 6, found a breach of Article 11.

...

ALLEGED VIOLATION OF ARTICLE 11

...

37. Notwithstanding its autonomous role and particular sphere of application, Article 11 must, in the present case, also be considered in the light of Article 10 (see the *Young, James and Webster* judgment of 13 August 1981, Series A No 44, p 23, § 57). The protection of personal opinions, secured by Article 10, is one of the objectives of freedom of peaceful assembly as enshrined in Article 11.

A. WHETHER THERE WAS AN INTERFERENCE WITH THE EXERCISE OF THE FREEDOM OF PEACEFUL ASSEMBLY

38. In the Government's submission, Mr Ezelin had not suffered any interference with the exercise of his freedom of peaceful assembly and freedom of expression: he had been able to take part in the procession of 12 February 1983 unhindered and to express his convictions publicly, in his professional capacity and as he wished; he was reprimanded only after the event and on account of personal conduct deemed to be inconsistent with the obligations of his profession.

39. The Court does not accept this submission. The term 'restrictions' in paragraph 2 of Article 11—and of Article 10—cannot be interpreted as not including measures—such as punitive measures—taken not before or during but after a meeting (cf in particular, as regards Article 10, the *Handyside* judgment of 7 December 1976, Series A No 24, p 21, § 43, and the *Müller* judgment of 24 May 1988, Series A No 133, p 19, § 28).

40. In the second place, the Government maintained that despite the peaceful nature of Mr Ezelin's own intentions and behaviour, the sanction of which he complained had in no way infringed his freedom of peaceful assembly seeing that the demonstration had got out of hand.

In the Commission's opinion, no intentions that were not peaceful could be imputed to the applicant.

41. The Court points out that prior notice had been given of the demonstration in question and that it was not prohibited. In joining it, the applicant availed himself of his freedom of peaceful assembly. Moreover, neither the report made by the Chief Superintendent of the Basse-Terre police nor any other evidence shows that Mr Ezelin himself made threats or daubed graffiti.

The Court of Appeal found the charge of not having 'dissociate[d] himself from the demonstrators' offensive and insulting acts or [left] the procession' . . . proven. The Court of Cassation noted that at no time did he 'express his disapproval of these excesses or leave the procession in order to dissociate himself from these criminal acts' . . .

The Court accordingly finds that there was in this instance an interference with the exercise of the applicant's freedom of peaceful assembly.

B. WHETHER THE INTERFERENCE WAS JUSTIFIED

42. It must therefore be determined whether the sanction complained of was 'prescribed by law', prompted by one or more of the legitimate aims set out in paragraph 2 and 'necessary in a democratic society' for achieving them.

1. 'Prescribed by law'

. . .

In the instant case the legal basis of the sanction complained of lay solely in the special rules governing the profession of *avocat*. Article 106 of the relevant Decree of 9 June 1972 provides unequivocally that any *avocat*, even in his non-professional activities, has special obligations . . . ; and the Court of Cassation has held that these include the respect due to the judicial authorities . . .

That being so, the interference was 'prescribed by law'.

2. Legitimate aim

. . .

47. It is apparent from the evidence that Mr Ezelin incurred the punishment because he had not dissociated himself from the unruly incidents which occurred during the demonstration. As the Commission noted, the authorities took the view that such an attitude was a reflection of the fact that the applicant, as an *avocat*, endorsed and actively supported such excesses. The interference was therefore in pursuit of a legitimate aim, the 'prevention of disorder'.

3. Necessity in a democratic society

48. In the applicant's submission, the interference of which he was complaining was not 'necessary in a democratic society'. To claim that he should have left the procession in order to express his disapproval of acts committed by other demonstrators was, he said, to deny his right to freedom of peaceful assembly.

49. The Government, on the other hand, submitted that the disputed measure did indeed answer a 'pressing social need', having regard in particular to Mr Ezelin's position as an *avocat* and to the local background. By not disavowing the unruly incidents that had occurred during the demonstration, the applicant had *ipso facto* approved them. . . .

50. The Commission contended that a disciplinary penalty based on an impression to which Mr Ezelin's behaviour might give rise was not compatible with the strict requirement of a 'pressing social need' and therefore could not be regarded as 'necessary in a democratic society'.

51. The Court has examined the disciplinary sanction in question in the light of the case as a whole in order to determine in particular whether it was proportionate to the legitimate aim pursued, having

regard to the special importance of freedom of peaceful assembly and freedom of expression, which are closely linked in this instance.

52. The proportionality principle demands that a balance be struck between the requirements of the purposes listed in Article 11 § 2 and those of the free expression of opinions by word, gesture or even silence by persons assembled on the streets or in other public places. The pursuit of a just balance must not result in *avocats* being discouraged, for fear of disciplinary sanctions, from making clear their beliefs on such occasions.

53. Admittedly, the penalty imposed on Mr Ezelin was at the lower end of the scale of disciplinary penalties given in Article 107 of the Degree of 9 June 1972 . . . ; it had mainly moral force, since it did not entail any ban, even a temporary one, on practising the profession or on sitting as a member of the Bar Council. The Court considers, however, that the freedom to take part in a peaceful assembly—in this instance a demonstration that had not been prohibited—is of such importance that it cannot be restricted in any way, even for an *avocat*, so long as the person concerned does not himself commit any reprehensible act on such an occasion.

In short, the sanction complained of, however, minimal, does not appear to have been 'necessary in a democratic society'. It accordingly contravened Article 11.

. . .

FOR THESE REASONS, THE COURT

. . .

Holds by six votes to three that there has been a violation of Article 11; . . .

NOTES

1   The Court was comprised of Judges: Cremona, Gölcüklü, Walsh, Spielmann, De Meyer, and Pekkanen. President Ryssdal dissented as he believed that the authorities' punishment of Ezelin did not exceed the margin of appreciation to be accorded to national regulation of professional (ie lawyers') behaviour. Similarly, Matscher J thought that there was 'not the slightest doubt' that Ezelin was in serious breach of his ethical duty of 'discretion' and, therefore, the minimal punishment imposed on him was proportionate. Pettiti J also felt the punishment was within France's margin of appreciation. He also observed that 'the Court, in its majority, like the Commission, showed the importance which it attached to the right to demonstrate, but did the case under examination provide an appropriate occasion for expressing this principle?'

2   This was the first case in which the Court found a breach of the right of peaceful assembly. The judgment does not distinguish between the freedom to peacefully assemble for static meetings or moving processions. The Court also accorded a broad scope to the right by interpreting it as being infringed through the imposition of subsequent punishments. Individuals seeking to assert the right must, however, ensure that they do not commit any 'reprehensible' acts on the occasion of the assembly. Although the Court did not elaborate upon the meaning of that term it will presumably include actions which are not compatible with peaceful forms of protest (e.g. acts of violence directed at opponents or police officers seeking to lawfully control assemblies in accordance with Article 11(2)).

3   The Court had provided an insight into its approach to this right in the earlier case of *Plattform 'Artze fur das Leben' v Austria* (1988) 13 EHRR 204, A.139, which directly concerned Article 13 (the right to an effective domestic remedy for violation of Convention rights). The applicant association was a group of doctors who campaigned against abortion. In 1980 they notified the police that they intended to hold a religious service at Stadl-Paura Church, in

Upper Austria, and then march to the surgery of a doctor who performed abortions. The police did not object and gave permission for the use of the highway. Subsequently, two counter-demonstrations were banned by the police. Shortly before the march began the organisers feared that incidents might occur so they changed the route to process to an alter on a nearby hillside (rather than march to the doctor's surgery). The police did not object, but warned that it would be impossible to prevent counter-demonstrators throwing objects at the marchers. About 500 counter-demonstrators tried to disrupt the association's service and march by shouting at them and throwing eggs and clumps of grass at the participants. Eventually, when physical violence was about to occur, special riot-control police formed a cordon between the protestors and the counter-demonstrators. Later the association made a disciplinary complaint against the police alleging that they had failed to provide sufficient protection for its members. The Upper Austrian Safety Authority rejected the complaint. The association lodged an appeal with the Constitutional Court but it ruled that the Court had no jurisdiction. In 1982 the association obtained permission for a second demonstration against abortion to be held in the cathedral square in Salzburg. About 350 counter-demonstrators gathered in the square and the police formed a cordon between them and the association's members. Eventually, the police cleared the square. The association complained to the Commission about the alleged failings of the Austrian police and other State authorities to protect the Convention rights of the association and its members. The Commission unanimously found a breach of Article 13. Before the Court, the Government argued that Article 11 did not impose any positive obligations on States to protect demonstrations, therefore it was not possible for the association to argue that any of its substantive Convention rights had been violated. The Court, unanimously, stated:

A demonstration may annoy or give offence to persons opposed to the ideas or claims that it is seeking to promote. The participants must, however, be able to hold the demonstration without having to fear that they will be subjected to physical violence by their opponents; such a fear would be liable to deter associations or other groups supporting common ideas or interests from openly expressing their opinions on highly controversial issues affecting the community. In a democracy the right to counter-demonstrate cannot extend to inhibiting the exercise of the right to demonstrate.

Genuine, effective freedom of peaceful assembly cannot, therefore, be reduced to a mere duty on the part of the State not to interfere: a purely negative conception would not be compatible with the object and purpose of Article 11. Like Article 8, Article 11 sometimes requires positive measures to be taken, even in the sphere of relations between individuals, if need be (see, *mutatais mutandis, X and Y v Netherlands* (1985) A.91).

While it is the duty of Contracting States to take reasonable and appropriate measures to enable lawful demonstrations to proceed peacefully, they cannot guarantee this absolutely and they have a wide discretion in the choice of the means to be used . . . In this area the obligation they enter into under Article 11 of the Convention is an obligation as to measures to be taken and not as to results to be achieved. (paras 32 and 34)

Having regard to the fact that large numbers of police, including riot-control units, were deployed at the 1980 demonstration and one hundred officers separated the association's members from the counter-demonstrators in Salzburg, the Court concluded 'it thus clearly appears that the Austrian authorities did not fail to take reasonable and appropriate measures' (para 39). Hence, as the association had no arguable claim that Article 11 had been violated, Article 13 did not apply in the present case. While the applicant association lost their action, the judgment of the Court revealed an interpretation of Article 11 which was favourable to the rights of peaceful protestors by subjecting States to both negative and positive duties in regard to such persons. However, as we have seen in relation to the positive duty of respect under

Article 8, the Court accords States a broad latitude in fulfilling such positive obligations. Clearly, applicants cannot expect the Court to reject contemporaneous police decisions which involve 'reasonable and appropriate measures' to safeguard the Article 11 rights of peaceful protestors.

4 The Commission has expressed the view that the right applies to both private and public meetings, prior authorisation procedures for meetings in public locations do not interfere with the right and complete bans on demonstrations can be lawful under Article 11(2). In *Rassemblement Jurassien and Unité Jurassienne v Switzerland* (1979) 17 DR 93 the applicants were associations whose objectives included 'freeing the people of the Jura from domination by Bern' and securing 'the independence of the whole Jura territory'. In 1977 the Canton Bern Executive had decided to remove the reference to the People of the Jura from the canton constitution. In response the applicants organised a demonstration to take place at a hotel in the town of Moutier. An anti-separatist group organised a meeting in a restaurant in Moutier on the same day. Thereupon, the Executive Council banned all political meetings within the boundaries of Moutier for two days (including the day of the applicants' planned demonstration). The applicants unsuccessfully challenged the ban before the Swiss courts. They then petitioned the Commission alleging, *inter alia*, a breach of Article 11. The Commission stated that the right of peaceful assembly was a fundamental right and:

As such this right covers both private meetings and meetings in public thoroughfares. Where the latter are concerned, their subjection to an authorisation procedure does not normally encroach upon the essence of the right. Such a procedure is in keeping with the requirements of Article 11(1), if only in order that the authorities may be in a position to ensure the peaceful nature of a meeting, and accordingly does not as such constitute interference with the exercise of the right.' (p 119)

Furthermore, the Commission considered that having regard to the political tensions existing in Moutier, the limited geographical coverage of the ban and its short duration, the authorities' response had not been disproportionate. Therefore, the application was declared inadmissible. In the later case of *Christians Against Racism and Fascism v UK* (1980) 21 DR 138, the Commission elaborated upon its approach to orders banning all demonstrations. The applicant association had been created at the initiative of several denominations 'to act as a broad ecumenical voice from the Christian Church on issues of racism and fascism'. As part of its activities the association planned to hold a procession from St Paul's Cathedral to Westminster Cathedral on 22 April 1978. However, in February 1978 the Metropolitan Police Commissioner, with the consent of the Home Secretary, made an order banning all public processions in London for two months (ie until 24 April 1978). One consequence of the order was to prevent the applicant association holding its procession on the 22 April. The association therefore petitioned the Commission alleging a breach of its rights under Article 11. The Commission stated, 'a general ban of demonstrations can only be justified if there is a real danger of their resulting in disorder which cannot be prevented by other less stringent measures' (p 150). The background to this ban was a tense atmosphere in England resulting from several public processions by the National Front and counter-demonstrations which, despite large police deployments, had resulted in riots and disturbances. Before the ban had been imposed there were several other imminent demonstrations planned by the National Front in London. Therefore, the Commission concluded that it was not unreasonable for the authorities to issue the ban, especially as the applicant association could either have held its procession outside the London area or hold a different form of protest (eg such as a meeting). Consequently, the application was declared inadmissible. Hence governments have the burden of establishing the impracticality of less restrictive measures than complete bans on all demonstrations. Presumably the longer the duration of the ban, the wider its geographical scope and the more comprehensive the forms of assembly banned, the more difficult that task would be.

5   A Chamber of the full-time Court found a breach of the right to peaceful assembly in *Djavit An v Turkey*, judgment of 20 February 2003. The applicant was a Cypriot national of Turkish origin living in the northern part of Cyprus. He was an opponent of the Turkish-Cypriot authorities and the Turkish military presence in northern Cyprus. The applicant held the position of Turkish-Cypriot coordinator of the 'Movement for an Independent and Federal Cyprus', an unregistered association of Turkish and Greek Cypriots founded to develop close relations between the two communities. Between 1992 and 1998 the Turkish-Cypriot authorities refused the applicant permission to cross the 'green line', separating the Turkish and Greek communities, forty-six times (and granted him permission on six occasions) when he wished to attend bi-communal events and meetings in the Greek-Cypriot community. The Chamber, subject to the dissent of the Turkish *ad-hoc* Judge, found that there were no laws in the 'Turkish Republic of Northern Cyprus' regulating the issuing of permits to person wishing to cross the green line. Consequently, the interferences with the applicant's freedom of peaceful assembly were not "prescribed by law" as required by Article 11(2). More generally, the Court affirmed the views of the Commission in *Rassemblement Jurassien* and *Christians Against Racism and Fascism* that:

56. ... this right covers both private meetings and meetings in public thoroughfares as well as static meetings and public processions; in addition it can be exercised by individuals and those organising the assembly ... the Court considers that, although the essential object of Article 11 is to protect the individual against arbitrary interference by public authorities with the exercise of the rights protected, there may in addition be positive obligations to secure the effective enjoyment of these rights.

6   The full-time Court has found Bulgaria to be in breach of this provision in two cases involving the same organization representing minority Macedonian interests. In *Stankov and the United Macedonian Organisation Ilinden v Bulgaria*, judgment of 2 October 2001, a Chamber, by six votes to one, determined that the authorities repeated prohibition of commemorative meetings arranged by the applicant organisation between 1994 and 1997 could not be justified as being necessary in a democratic society. The Chamber found that no public disorder had occurred at previous meetings held by the applicant organisation and it advocated non-violent political change on behalf of a small minority of people. Four years later in *United Macedonian Organisation Ilinden and Ivanov v Bulgaria*, judgment of 20 October 2005, a unanimous Chamber concluded that the applicants' right to freedom of assembly had been violated in respect of twelve events between 1998 and 2003. The Chamber also found that on one occasion where the applicant organization was able to hold a meeting the authorities did not do all they reasonably could to protect its members from physical violence by counter-demonstrators. The Chamber delivered a separate judgment in *United Macedonian Organisation-PIRIN and Others v Bulgaria*, judgment of 20 October 2005, which concluded that the Bulgarian Constitutional Court's dissolution of the applicant political party in 2000 breached Article 11. In the unanimous judgment of the Chamber, the party's peaceful advocacy of autonomy or secession for the region of Pirin Macedonia was not sufficient to justify the dissolving of the organisation. Later, the Court, by five votes to two, found another breach of the right to peaceful assembly in respect of bans imposed on two public rallies which PIRIN sought to hold during 1998 in Sofia. The Court concluded that the authorities belief that separatist views would be expressed at the rallies did not justify the imposition of bans: *Ivanov and Others v Bulgaria*, judgment of 24 November 2005

(note, this was a different Mr Ivanov from the applicant in the earlier case). Another complaint brought by the *United Macedonian Organisation Ilinden v Bulgaria*, judgment of 19 January 2006, involving the refusal of the authorities to register the association during the late 1990s was found, by six votes to one, to amount to a breach of the right to freedom of association. The Chamber considered that as the organization only had about 3000 supporters and its public influence was minimal the State's argument that it had been necessary to refuse to register the association in order to protect the majority of the population in the Pirin region was not a proportionate justification. These cases disclose serious and repeated failings in the Bulgarian authorities conduct towards this section of its population.

7   The domestic authorities' banning of a silent protest, organised by a Green MP, at a cemetery where SS veterans were gathering to mark the deaths of SS soldiers in the Second World War was found to breach the MP's right to freedom of assembly by a large majority (six votes to one) of the Chamber in *Ollinger v Austria*, judgment of 29 June 2006. The Austrian Constitutional Court had concluded that the ban on the applicant's protest was justified in order to protect members of the public who would be visiting the graves of their relatives. However, the Chamber determined that the ban was a disproportionate measure as the applicant's assembly had been planned as a silent protest and was not directed at the beliefs of the cemetery users. The judgment reveals that domestic authorities may have to engage in a tripartite balancing of interests involving protestors, counter-protestors and affected members of the public when evaluating how to regulate peaceful assemblies.

The right to freedom of association with others

1   The plenary Court has ruled that public law associations fall outside the scope of Article 11. In *Le Compte, Van Leuven and De Meyere v Belgium* (1981) 4 EHRR 1, A.43, the applicants were medical doctors who had been subject to disciplinary proceedings and punishments by the Belgian *Ordre des medecins*. The *Ordre* had been established by an Act of the Belgian Parliament and its disciplinary functions were defined in a Royal Decree. The latter instrument required all doctors practising in Belgium to be registered with the *Ordre*. Other private associations of doctors also existed in Belgium to protect their professional interests. The applicants complained to the Commission that, *inter alia*, the obligation to join the *Ordre* inhibited their freedom of association and the mere existence of the *Ordre* had the effect of eliminating freedom of association. The Commission, unanimously, found no breach of Article 11(1) as the *Ordre* did not constitute an association within the meaning of that provision. The Court likewise, unanimously, found no breach of that Article.

The Court notes firstly that the Belgian *Ordre des medecins* is a public-law institution. It was founded not by individuals but by the legislature; it remains integrated within the structures of the State and judges are appointed to most of its organs by the Crown. It pursues an aim which is in the general interest, namely the protection of health, by exercising under the relevant legislation a form of control over the practice of medicine. Within the context of this latter function, the *Ordre* is required in particular to keep the register of medical practitioners. For the performance of the tasks conferred on it by the Belgian State, it is legally invested with administrative as well as rule-making and disciplinary prerogatives out of the orbit of the ordinary law . . . and, in this capacity, employs processes of a public authority . . .

Having regard to these various factors taken together, the *Ordre* cannot be considered as an association within the meaning of Article 11. However, there is a further requirement: if there is not to be a violation, the setting up of the *Ordre* by the Belgian State must not prevent practitioners from forming together or joining professional associations. Totalitarian regimes have resorted-and resort- to the compulsory-regimentation of the professions by means of closed and exclusive organisations taking the place of the professional associations and the traditional trade unions. The authors of the Convention intended to prevent such abuses ...

The Court notes that in Belgium there are several associations formed to protect the professional interests of medical practitioners and which they are completely free to join or not ... In these circumstances the existence of the *Ordre* and its attendant consequence- that is to say, the obligation on practitioners to be entered on the register of the *Ordre* and to be subject to the authority of its organs- clearly have neither the object nor the effect of limiting, even less suppressing, the right guaranteed by Article 11(1). (paras 64–5)

Hence the Court wished to uphold the legitimacy of state supported regulatory organizations for the liberal professions, such as medicine. However, it imposed the correlative duty on States to ensure that such public law associations are not monopolistic and that practitioners can create and join their own supplementary professional associations if they so desire.

In the later case of *Sigurdur A Sigurjonsson v Iceland* (1993) 16 EHRR 462, A.264, (examined below p 763), the Government argued that the *Frami* association of taxicab drivers was a professional organization of a public law character that fell outside the scope of Article 11. Although the association had been formed by taxicab drivers to protect their professional interests it also performed functions which served the public interest, such as approving the suitability of vehicles for use as taxicabs and fixing the rates for taxicabs. This submission was rejected:

The Court agrees with the applicant and the Commission that the above-mentioned elements are not sufficient for *Frami* to be regarded as a public-law association outside the ambit of Article 11. Admittedly, *Frami* performed certain functions which were to some extent provided for in the applicable legislation and which served not only its members but also the public at large. However, the role of supervision of the implementation of the relevant rules was entrusted primarily to another institution ... *Frami* was established under private law and enjoyed full autonomy in determining its own aims, organisation and procedure. ... *Frami* was therefore predominantly a private law–organisation and must thus be considered an 'association' for the purposes of Article 11. (para 31)

The key criteria adopted by the Court to distinguish public law associations are: (a) the form of law under which the organisations are constituted (b) the degree of State control and influence over the organizations and (c) the extent to which the organizations perform public functions, as opposed to the private aims of their members.

In *Chassagnou v France* (1999) 29 EHRR 615 (examined below p 766), the Court stated that:

If Contracting States were able, at their discretion, by classifying an association as 'public' or 'para-administrative', to remove it from the scope of Article 11, that would give them such latitude that it might lead to results incompatible with the object and purpose of the Convention ... The term 'association' therefore possesses an autonomous meaning; the classification in national law has only relative value and constitutes no more than a starting-point. (para 100)

Having regard to the facts that the statutory hunting associations were composed of private individuals, were not integrated within the structures of the State and did not enjoy prerogatives outside the scope of the ordinary law, the Court concluded that they were 'associations' which fell within the ambit of Article 11.

2   For the application of this right to political parties see the *United Communist Party of Turkey* and *The Socialist Party* cases, above p 723. In *Ahmed v UK* (above p 654), the applicants also alleged that the Regulations prevented them being active in an organisational/administrative capacity and holding offices within political parties were contrary to Article 11. The Court did not directly rule on whether Article 11(1) provides these specific rights.

The Court notes that it has found the interferences with the applicants' rights under Article 10 to be justified from the standpoint of the requirements of the second paragraph of that Article. Notwithstanding its autonomous role and particular sphere of application, Article 11 must in the present case also be considered in the light of Article 10 having regard to the fact that the freedom to hold opinions and to receive and impart information and ideas is one of the objectives of freedom of assembly and association as enshrined in Article 11 . . . In the Court's view, the conclusions which it reached regarding the foreseeability of the impugned measures, the legitimacy of the aim pursued by them and their necessity hold true for the purposes of the requirements of the second paragraph of Article 11. It would also reiterate that [the relevant part of the Regulations] is limited to restricting the extent of the applicants' participation in an administrative and representative capacity in a political party of which they are members. The Regulations do not restrict the applicants' rights to join any political party of their choosing.

The Court finds accordingly that there has been no violation of the applicants' rights under Article 11 of the Convention. (paras 70–1)

3   The Court has stated that:

. . . the right to form an association is an inherent part of the right set forth in Article 11, even if that Article only makes express reference to the right to form trade unions. That citizens should be able to form a legal entity in order to act collectively in a field of mutual interest is one of the most important aspects of the right to freedom of association, without which that right would be deprived of any meaning. The way in which national legislation enshrines this freedom and its practical application by the authorities reveal the state of democracy in the country concerned. Certainly States have a right to satisfy themselves that an association's aim and activities are in conformity with the rules laid down in legislation, but they must do so in a manner compatible with their obligations under the Convention and subject to review by the Convention institutions. (*Sidiropoulos v Greece*, 1998-IV, at para 40).

In a unanimous judgment the Court went on to find a breach of Article 11, as the Greek courts' refusal to register the applicants' proposed cultural association ('Home of Macedonian Civilisation') was a disproportionate response to the legitimate aims of protecting national security and preventing disorder. Although some Greek newspapers had accused the applicants of seeking to undermine the territorial integrity of Greece in favour of the neighbouring 'Former Yugoslav Republic of Macedonia', the Court concluded that there was nothing illegitimate in the aims of the proposed association. However, if the association were to engage in other, unlawful, activities at a later time then the Greek authorities had powers to dissolve the association.

4   Later examples of States violating Article 11 through their refusals to register political parties include: *Presidential Party of Mordovia v Russia*, judgment of 5 October 2004, where the authorities' refusal to re-register the applicant political association was contrary to domestic law and therefore not 'prescribed by law' and *Partidul Comunistilor (Nepeceristi) and Ungureanu v Romania*, judgment of 3 February 2005. In the latter case the Court found that the refusal of the Romanian courts to register the applicant communist political party was a disproportionate measure having regard to the fact that the applicant's constitution and political programme did not contain anything contrary to democratic principles. Furthermore, whilst the Court was sensitive to the history of totalitarian communism in Romania prior to 1989, it noted that political parties advocating Marxist ideology were present in a number of Member States.

5   The Court has upheld the discretion of national authorities to refuse to register associations which have adopted misleading (and potentially defamatory) names. In *APEH Uldozotteinek Szovetsege, Ivanyi, Roth and Szerdahelyi v Hungary* (No 32367/96), decision of 31 August 1999, the first applicant was an unregistered association formed with the name 'Alliance of APEH's persecutees' by the other applicants. APEH is the abbreviated name of the Hungarian national tax authority. The Supreme Court refused to register the association because, *inter alia*, its name was misleading in that it suggested the association was linked to the tax authority and the name was defamatory. The Court found that the applicants could have founded and registered an association to promote the interests of taxpayers if they had chosen another name. Therefore, the interference with their right to freedom of association was not severe and it was legitimate for the authorities to refuse to register an association with a misleading nomenclature. Consequently, the application was declared manifestly ill-founded. Hence Article 11 does not give persons an unqualified right to form associations under any name of their own choice.

6 A unanimous Grand Chamber found no breach of Article 11 in respect of the authorities' refusal to register an association called the 'Union of People of Silesian Nationality' in *Gorzelik and Others v Poland*, judgment of 17 February 2004. The domestic refusal was based on the name of the association and provisions within the organisation's memorandum of association which characterized Silesians as a 'national minority'. If the association had been registered the effect would have been to confer electoral privileges on the organization as a representative of a 'national minority'. The Grand Chamber accepted that there was a 'pressing social need' for the Polish authorities to regulate the ability of associations to describe themselves as organisations of a 'national minority' and thereby claim electoral privileges. Furthermore, the authorities' refusal of registration under the chosen name was a proportional response as the applicants could have established a registered association to carry out their cultural activities under another name which did not assert that the members were a national minority.

7 A unanimous Chamber of the full-time Court determined that a regional law prohibiting Freemasons from being nominated/appointed to specified public offices (including universities, leisure and cultural organisations) violated the right to freedom of association of a Masonic association in *Grande Oriente D'Italia Di Palazzo Giustiniani v Italy*, judgment of 2 August 2001. The applicant association had been created in 1805 and was, under Italian law, an unrecognized private-law association which grouped together several Masonic Lodges (having approximately 12,500 members). In 1996 the Marches Region passed a Regional Law requiring applicants for specified public offices to declare, *inter alia*, that they were not members of a Masonic Lodge. The applicant contended that such a restriction interfered with its freedom of association under Article 11 by depriving its members of access to numerous regional public offices and that the Regional Law also created a negative image of the association. The Chamber considered that the applicant fell within the scope of Article 11 because it was:

15. ... not suspected of undermining the constitutional structures. Additionally, and above all, the Court accepts that the measure in question may cause the applicant association-as it submits-damage in terms of loss of members and prestige.

In the view of the Chamber, the interference was 'prescribed by law' and, given the recent controversy about the activities of certain Freemasons in Italian public life, the Regional Law fell within the legitimate aims of protecting national security and preventing disorder under Article 11(2). As to whether the restriction was 'necessary in a democratic society':

24. The Court has examined the impugned measure in the light of the case as a whole in order to determine, in particular, whether it was proportionate to the legitimate aim pursued.

25. The proportionality principle demands that a balance be struck between the requirements of the purposes listed in Article 11 § 2 of the Convention and those of the free exercise of freedom of

association. The pursuit of a just balance must not result in individuals being discouraged, for fear of having their applications for office rejected, from exercising their right of association on such occasions.

26. Compared with the total number of members of the applicant association, the number of actual or potential members of the association who may be confronted with the dilemma of choosing between being Freemasons and competing for the public offices referred to in section 5 of the 1996 Law cannot be said to be large. Consequently, the damage which the applicant association may suffer is likewise limited. The Court considers, however, that freedom of association is of such importance that it cannot be restricted in any way, even in respect of a candidate for public office, so long as the person concerned does not himself commit any reprehensible act by reason of his membership of the association. It is also clear that the association will suffer the consequences of its members' decisions. In short, the prohibition complained of, however minimal it might be for the applicant association, does not appear 'necessary in a democratic society'.

Therefore, the Chamber found a breach of Article 11. Paragraph 26 of the judgment is a very robust application of the right to freedom of association by the Court. In assessing the proportionality of the Marches' restriction on Freemasons it is relevant to note that it was the most severe response of a regional legislature in Italy (others had required applicants/nominees for public offices to declare any associations to which they belonged or prohibited such persons from being members of secret associations).

8   On the same day as the judgment in *Grande Oriente*, another Chamber found a violation of the right to freedom of association of a judge who was disciplined for having been a member of a Masonic Lodge forming part of the Grande Oriente D'Italia di Palazzo Giustiniani in *N.F. v Italy*, judgment of 2 August 2001. In 1990 guidelines passed by the National Council of the Judiciary stated that a judge's membership of lawful associations, which were governed by specific rules of conduct (e.g. the Freemasons), could be problematic. Nevertheless, in 1991 the applicant became a member of the Adriano Lemmi Lodge in Milan. During the summer of 1992 the applicant became aware, via press reports, that prosecutors had begun investigations into some of the Lodges associated with the Grande Oriente. Therefore, in October 1992 the applicant asked to distance himself from the association and in the following month he was made a 'dormant member'. In 1994 he was summoned before a disciplinary section of the National Council of the Judiciary and accused of having undermined the prestige of the judiciary by committing a serious breach of his duties through his membership of the Freemasons. Despite the applicant's contention that the National Council of the Judiciary had only issued revised guidelines stating that judicial office was incompatible with membership of the Freemasons in 1993, the disciplinary section found he had breached Article 18 of the Royal Legislative Decree No 511 of 1946 (which provided that a disciplinary sanction would be imposed on any judge who 'fails to fulfil his duties or behaves, in or outside the office, in a manner unworthy of the trust and consideration which he must enjoy'). The disciplinary section issued a warning to the applicant. Subsequently, the National Council of the Judiciary opposed the promotion of the applicant on two occasions in the light of the disciplinary warning that had been issued to him. The major issue for the Court was whether the disciplinary sanction imposed on the applicant had been 'prescribed by law'. He contended that at the time he joined the Freemasons it was not foreseeable that membership would be deemed to be contrary to judicial duties under the 1946 Decree.

29. With regard to the requirement of foreseeability, the Court reiterates that a law is 'foreseeable' if it is formulated with sufficient precision to enable the individual—if need be with appropriate advice—to regulate his conduct (see *Hasan and Chaush v Bulgaria* [GC], No 30985/96, § 84, ECHR 2000-XI).

30. It therefore needs to be determined in particular whether domestic law laid down with sufficient precision the conditions in which a judge should refrain from joining the Freemasons.

31. The Court notes first that Article 18 of the 1946 decree does not define whether and how a judge can exercise his or her right of association. Furthermore, the Constitutional Court noted that this provision was of a general nature. That said, the guidelines passed by the National Council of the Judiciary in 1990 had stated that a judge's membership of lawful associations which, like the Freemasons, were governed by specific rules of conduct could be problematical for him or her. The Court must therefore determine whether Article 18, combined with the above-mentioned guidelines support the proposition that the sanction in question was foreseeable. In that connection the Court notes that these guidelines had been passed in the context of an examination of the specific question of judges' membership of the Freemasons and that the National Council of the Judiciary, the body responsible for supervising the discipline and independence of judges, had the power to enact such provisions. However, even if the guidelines had primarily been concerned with membership of the Freemasons, the wording used to refer to it ('membership . . . raises delicate problems') was ambiguous and could give the impression that not all Masonic lodges were being taken into consideration, especially as these guidelines were passed after the big debate in Italy on the illegality of the secret lodge, P2; indeed, the guidelines merely stated that 'naturally, members of the judiciary are prohibited by law from joining the associations proscribed by Law No 17 of 1982'. With regard to other associations, they contained the following passage: 'the [National] Council [of the Judiciary] considers it necessary to suggest to the Minister of Pardons and Justice that it might be advisable to consider including among the restrictions on judges' rights of association reference to all associations which—for their organisation and purposes—impose particularly strong bonds of hierarchy and solidarity on their members.'

Accordingly, the wording of the guidelines of 22 March 1990 was not sufficiently clear to enable the users, who, being judges, were nonetheless informed and well-versed in the law, to realise—even in the light of the preceding debate—that their membership of an official Masonic lodge could lead to sanctions being imposed on them.

The Court's assessment is confirmed by the fact that the National Council of the Judiciary itself felt the need to come back to the issue on 14 July 1993 and state in clear terms that the exercise of judicial functions was incompatible with membership of the Freemasons.

32. In these conditions the Court concludes that the condition of foreseeability was not satisfied and that, accordingly, the interference was not prescribed by law.

33. Having reached that conclusion, the Court does not need to satisfy itself that the other requirements (legitimate aim, necessity of the interference and special limits for certain categories) required by the first and second sentences of paragraph 2 of Article 11 have been complied with.

34. Accordingly, there has been a violation of Article 11 of the Convention.

Three members of the Court dissented as they considered that a 'highly trained' judge knowing the legal background to the statutory dissolution of the P2 Lodge in the early 1980s should have foreseen that membership of the Freemason was incompatible with judicial office in Italy. According to Judge Bonello; '20. . . . . It is risible, in my view, to hold that he could have believed in good faith that an Italian judge could embrace Freemasonry with the blessing of the law.'

9 A Grand Chamber reached a similar conclusion to that in *N.F.* during the later case of *Maestri v Italy*, judgment of 17 February 2004. The applicant was a judge who had been a member of a Masonic Lodge affiliated to the Grande Oriente D'Italia di Palazzo Giustiniani from 1981 until March 1993. In 1995, the National Council of the Judiciary found that his former membership of the Freemasons breached Article 18 of the 1946 Royal Legislative Decree and he was given a reprimand. The applicant contended that this sanction had resulted in his career being stalled. Once again the basic issue for the Court was the question whether the prohibition on membership of the Freemasons by Italian judges was sufficiently foreseeable at the time of the applicant's membership. The Grand Chamber held that:

40. Lastly, the Court considers it important to emphasise that the debate of 22 March 1990 did not take place in the context of disciplinary supervision of judges, as was the case for the directive of 14 July 1993, but in the context of their career progression. It is therefore clear from an overall examination of the debate that the National Council of the Judiciary was questioning whether it was advisable for a judge to be a Freemason, but there was no indication in the debate that membership of the Freemasons could constitute a disciplinary offence in every case.

41. Accordingly, the wording of the directive of 22 March 1990 was not sufficiently clear to enable the applicant, who, being a judge, was nonetheless informed and well-versed in the law, to realise—even in the light of the preceding debate and of developments since 1982—that his membership of a Masonic lodge could lead to sanctions being imposed on him.

The Court's assessment is confirmed by the fact that the National Council of the Judiciary itself felt the need to come back to the issue on 14 July 1993 and state in clear terms that the exercise of judicial functions was incompatible with membership of the Freemasons.

42. That being so, the Court concludes that the condition of foreseeability was not satisfied in respect of the period after March 1990 either and that, accordingly, the interference was not prescribed by law. There has therefore been a violation of Article 11 of the Convention.

Six judges dissented and in a Joint Dissenting Opinion Judges Bonello, Straznicka, Birsan, Jungwiert, and Del Tufo stated:

10. In our view it is important from the outset to recall very briefly some facts that deeply affected Italian Freemasonry from the 1970s onwards: the detection of P2, a secret and deviant Masonic lodge ... the suspicion that some Masonic lodges were implicated in subversive plots to overthrow Italian democracy ... and indications that part of Italian Freemasonry had close links with the Mafia, terrorism and organised crime. The report by the Parliamentary Commission of Inquiry on the P2 lodge, transmitted by President Tina Anselmi in 1984, should be kept in mind, too, as should, *inter alia*, the fact that a Grand Master of the Grande Oriente of Italy left the association and founded a new observance in consequence of the disreputable situation Italian Freemasonry was in, and the fact that, for the same reasons, British Freemasonry formally decided to withhold recognition of the Grande Oriente (the official Masonic association) of Italy and banned its affiliates from having connections with their Italian brothers.

It is against this social and historical background that the events at issue took place, and that the applicant remained affiliated to the Freemasons.

The dissentients considered that it was 'bewildering' that the 'emphatic, public and reiterated proscription of Freemasonry for Italian judges' was not considered to be sufficiently foreseeable by the majority.

It is important to appreciate that both N.F. and Maestri won their cases on the ground that domestic law governing judicial membership of the Freemasons was imprecise. These judgments are not authority for a general principle that prohibitions on judicial membership of the Freemasons are always incompatible with Article 11.

10 A Chamber has held that Member States are under a positive obligation to effectively investigate interferences by individuals with the freedom of association of others. In *Ouranio Toxo and Others v Greece*, judgment of 20 October 2005, the applicant organisation was a political party founded to defend the interests of the Macedonian minority living in Greece. It hung a sign outside its headquarters with its name in Greek and Macedonian. The local priests called on their followers to protest against the 'enemies of Greece' and the town council passed a resolution to organise protests against the applicant party. After the police removed the sign it was replaced and protestors, including the mayor and councillors, gather outside the headquarters. A number of people attacked the headquarters and the staff inside. Despite telephone calls to the local police station (500 metres away) no police were deployed to protect the applicant's staff. Subsequently, the public prosecutor charged the individual applicants (members of the party's secretariat) with inciting discord, but none of the protestors who attacked the headquarters/staff were charged. The Chamber found that the Government had not provided any explanation as to why no police were available to protect the applicants from foreseeable harm. Consequently, the acts and omissions of the authorities amounted to a breach of the applicants' freedom of association.

11 A unanimous Chamber held that the dissolution of a public-sector trade union (having 40,000 members working in the post office and telecommunications service) constituted a breach of Article 11 in *Tum Haber Sen and Cinar v Turkey*, judgment of 21 February 2006. The Chamber found that the dissolution of the trade union had occurred simply because its members were civil servants. However, the Government had provided no explanation why such a measure was required in order to satisfy a 'pressing social need'.

12 Professor Alkema has noted that the inclination to associate is inherent in human nature, and that association is fundamental for the development of the personalities of individual human beings and for society as a whole. In terms of the legal right he believes that:

It is desirable to extend the general notion of the freedom of association laid down in Article 11 of the ECHR into two directions. It should be broad and comprise all organisational and legal forms of co-operation between individuals irrespective of a profit motive. It should also go in depth and deal with the legal details of the organisations and cover the diverse aspects of membership, structure and formalities. Article 11 thus offers a comprehensive framework within which any interference can be tested on legality and necessity. [E Alkema, 'Freedom of association and civil society' 34A Yearbook of the European Convention on Human Rights (Dordrecht: Martinus Nijhoff, 1994), 52 at 82.]

How far does this conception of Article 11 exceed the current jurisprudence?

The right to form and to join trade unions for the protection of his interests

....

National Union of Belgian Police v Belgium A.19 (1975) 1 EHRR 578
European Court of Human Rights

The applicant trade union was founded in 1922 and was open to all members of the municipal police. In 1961 it had approximately 7,200 members but this had fallen to roughly 5,700 in 1974 (in the latter year there were about 12,000 municipal police officers in Belgium). The applicant claimed that this reduction in membership was the result of government policy to reduce the number of unions, representing public employees, that would be consulted about trade union matters by the Government. An Act of 1961 provided for the King (i.e. the Government) to determine the forms of consultation with trade unions representing public sector workers. A later Royal Decree (of 2 August 1966) provided that the Government would only be consulting with those unions that were the 'most representative' of public employees and to satisfy this criterion unions had, *inter alia*, to be open to all staff working for the provinces and municipalities.

Subsequently, the Minister of the Interior refused to accept that the applicant union satisfied the above criterion as it was not open to membership by all local government workers. Consultation by the Government was valuable to trade unions as it enabled them to be informed of the Government's proposals as they developed and allowed the unions to make their views known before any final decision was reached by the Government. Although unions not recognised as representative were barred from the consultation process they could, *inter alia*, submit claims to the relevant supervisory authority, ask to be heard by it and make representations on behalf of their members. The applicant union sought to challenge the Minister's refusal to consult with it by bringing an action in the Belgian courts, however the *Conseil d'Etat* dismissed the application. Thereupon, the applicant complained to the Commission alleging that the Government's refusal to consult with it amounted to a breach of the union's rights under Article 11 (and also of discriminatory treatment under Articles 11 and 14). The Commission, unanimously, found no breach of the Convention.

AS TO THE LAW

34. The applicant's complaints may be summarised as follows: The National Union of Belgian Police complains of the Government not recognising it as one of the most representative organisations that the Ministry of the Interior is required to consult under the Act of 27 July 1961, which relates to such matters as staff structures, conditions of recruitment and promotion, pecuniary status and salary scales of provincial and municipal staff. The applicant union, which is excluded from this consultation as regards both questions of interest to all such staff and questions peculiar to the municipal police, considers that it is put at a disadvantage compared with the three trade unions open to that staff as a whole, as defined in Article 2 § 2 of the Royal Decree of 2 August 1966. The applicant submits that this provision greatly restricts its field of action, thereby tending to oblige the members of the municipal police to join the organisations considered to be 'representative' but having a 'political' character incompatible with the 'special vocation' of the police . . . .

I. ON THE ALLEGED VIOLATION OF ARTICLE II

37. Article II § I of the Convention reads: 'Everyone has the right to freedom of peaceful assembly and to freedom of association with others, including the right to form and to join trade unions for the protection of his interests'.

38. The majority of the Commission has expressed the opinion that the essential components of trade union activity, which in its view include the right to be consulted, come within the scope of the provision cited above.

The Court notes that while Article II § I presents trade union freedom as one form or a special aspect of freedom of association, the Article does not guarantee any particular treatment of trade unions, or their members, by the State, such as the right to be consulted by it. Not only is this latter right not mentioned in Article II § I, but neither can it be said that all the Contracting States in general incorporate it in their national law or practice, or that it is indispensable for the effective enjoyment of trade union freedom. It is thus not an element necessarily inherent in a right guaranteed by the Convention, which distinguishes it from the 'right to a court' embodied in Article 6 (*Golder* judgment of 21 February 1975, Series A No 18, p 18, § 36).

In addition, trade union matters are dealt with in detail in another convention, also drawn up within the framework of the Council of Europe, namely the Social Charter of 18 October 1961. Article 6 § I of the Charter binds the Contracting States 'to promote joint consultation between workers and employers'. The prudence of the terms used shows that the Charter does not provide for a real right to consultation. Besides, Article 20 permits a ratifying State not to accept the undertaking in Article 6 § I. Thus it cannot be supposed that such a right derives by implication from Article II § I of the 1950 Convention, which incidentally would amount to admitting that the 1961 Charter took a retrograde step in this domain.

39. The Court does not, however, share the view expressed by the minority in the Commission who describe the phrase 'for the protection of his interests' as redundant. These words, clearly denoting purpose, show that the Convention safeguards freedom to protect the occupational interests of trade union members by trade union action, the conduct and development of which the Contracting States must both permit and make possible. In the opinion of the Court, it follows that the members of a trade union have a right, in order to protect their interests, that the trade union should be heard. Article II § I certainly leaves each State a free choice of the means to be used towards this end. While consultation is one of these means, there are others. What the Convention requires is that under national law trade unions should be enabled, in conditions not at variance with Article II, to strive for the protection of their members' interests.

40. No-one disputes the fact that the applicant union can engage in various kinds of activity vis-à-vis the Government. It is open to it, for instance, to present claims and to make representations for the protection of the interests of its members or certain of them. Nor does the applicant union in any way allege that the steps it takes are ignored by the Government. In these circumstances, the fact alone that the Minister of the Interior does not consult the applicant under the Act of 27 July 1961 does not constitute a breach of Article II § I considered on its own.

41. As regards the alleged infringement of personal freedom to join or remain a member of the applicant union, the Court stresses the fact that every member of the municipal police retains this freedom as of a right, notwithstanding the Royal Decree of 2 August 1966. It may be the fact that the steady and appreciable decline in the membership of the National Union of Belgian Police is to be explained at least in part, as the applicant maintains, by the disadvantage the applicant is placed at compared with trade unions enjoying a more favourable position. It may be the fact too that this state of affairs is capable of diminishing the usefulness and practical value of belonging to the applicant union. However, it is brought about by Belgium's general policy of restricting the number of organisations to be consulted. This policy is not on its own incompatible with trade union freedom; the steps taken to implement it escape supervision by the Court provided that they do not contravene Articles II and 14 read in conjunction.

42. Having thus found that there is no violation of paragraph 1 of Article II, the Court is not called upon to have regard to paragraph 2, on which in any case both the Commission and the Government stated they did not rely.

. . .

FOR THESE REASONS, THE COURT,

Holds unanimously that there has been no breach of Article II; . . .

NOTES

1   The plenary Court was composed of President Balladore Pallieri and Judges; Mosler, Verdross, Rodenbourg, Zekia, Cremona, Wiarda, O'Donoghue, Pedersen, Vilhjalmsson, Ryssdal, Ganshof Van Der Meersch, Fitzmaurice, and Bindschedler-Robert. Judge Zekia issued a separate opinion in which he expressed the view that:

Time may however come, although I am not sure that it has not come, when the right of consultation, like the right of collective bargaining, will be taken for granted and considered predominant within the scope of the normal activities of a trade union. In such an eventuality the right to be consulted will have to be recognised as inherently included in Article 11(1). (p 24)

The Court, by ten votes to four, also rejected the applicant union's claim of discriminatory treatment (under Articles 11 and 14) as the legitimate aim of the Government's policy on consultation was to avoid 'trade union anarchy.'

2   The above judgment makes clear that the right to form and join trade unions is not a separate right but a part of the general right of freedom of association guaranteed by Article 11(1). Professor Hepple considers that the specific reference to trade unions in this Article was designed to ensure that they were treated as 'associations' under the Convention, irrespective of their categorization and status under the domestic law of member States: B Hepple, 'Freedom to form and join or not to join trade unions' 34A *Yearbook of the European Convention on Human Rights* (Dordrecht: Martinus Nijhoff, 1994), 162 at 168.

3   A unanimous Court expressly held that this right applies to States in their capacity as employers in *Swedish Engine Drivers' Union v Sweden* (1976) 1 EHRR 617, A.20. The applicant union represented about 25 per cent of the drivers employed by the Swedish State Railways, with the majority of drivers belonging to a section of one of the three principal federations of Swedish state employees. From 1969 the Swedish National Collective Bargaining Office, which represented the state as employer, declared that it would not conclude collective agreements (regarding the terms of employment and conditions of work of engine drivers) with the applicant union. Such collective agreements would only be agreed with the major federations of state employees. However, the Office was willing to continue discussing engine drivers' terms of employment with the applicant. The union was unsuccessful in challenging the Office's decision before the Swedish Labour Court. Later the union complained to the Commission alleging, *inter alia*, a breach of its rights under Article 11. The Commission, unanimously, found no breach of the Convention. Before the Court, the Swedish Government argued that the Convention applied to the state as holder of public power, not as employer. This contention was rejected by the Court:

The Convention nowhere makes an express distinction between the functions of a Contracting State as holder of public power and its responsibilities as employer. In this respect, Article 11 is no exception. What is more, paragraph 2 *in fine* of this provision clearly indicates that the State is bound to respect the freedom of assembly and association of its employees, subject to the possible imposition of 'lawful restrictions' in the case of members of its armed forces, police or administration.

  Article 11 is accordingly binding upon the 'State as employer', whether the latter's relations with its employees are governed by public or private law. . . . Neither does the Court consider that it has to rule on the applicability, whether direct or indirect, of Article 11 to relations between individuals *stricto sensu*. (para 37)

The Court then applied identical reasoning to that used in the *National Union of Belgian Police* judgment to determine that:

. . . the Article does not secure any particular treatment of trade unions, or their members, by the State, such as the right that the State should conclude any given collective agreement with them. Not only is this latter right not mentioned in Article 11(1), but neither can it be said that all the Contracting States incorporate it in their national law or practice, or that it is indispensable for the effective enjoyment of trade union freedom. It is thus not an element necessarily inherent in a right guaranteed by the Convention. (para 39)

Consequently, a united Court concluded that there had been no breach of the applicant union's rights under the Convention.

4   The same Chamber of judges who determined the *Swedish Engine Drivers' Union* action also heard the case of *Schmidt and Dahlström v Sweden* (1976) 1 EHRR 632, A.21. The applicants were members of trade unions affiliated to two of the major federations representing public sector workers in Sweden. Mr Schmidt was a university law professor and Mr Dahlstrom an officer in the Swedish army. In early 1971 protracted negotiations between the applicants' federations and the National Collective Bargaining Office (the same body as in the *Swedish Engine Drivers' Union* case) regarding a new collective agreement collapsed. The federations called strikes by some of their members, neither of the applicants were called out or went on strike. The Office responded by locking-out certain public sector workers, including Professor Schmidt. After several weeks of industrial action, the Office and the federations reached a new collective agreement. However, the Office refused to give retrospective pay increases to employees who belonged to unions that had called their members out on strike. The applicants, who had not been on strike, were nevertheless refused such pay increases as they belonged to unions which had called strikes. The applicants challenged the Office's decision before the Swedish Labour Court, but it ruled against them. They then complained to the Commission alleging that the Office's refusal to award them retrospective pay increases violated their rights under Article 11. The Commission, by nine votes to one with one abstention, found no violation of the Convention. Applying its, by now, standard approach to Article 11(1) the Court, unanimously, held that this provision does not secure any particular treatment of trade union members by contracting States. Therefore, the applicants did not have a right to retroactivity of benefits. As for the applicants' contention that the Office's decision had the effect of discouraging them from exercising their 'organic right' to strike found in Article 11, the Court held:

> . . . the Convention safeguards freedom to protect the occupational interests of trade union members by trade union action, the conduct and development of which the Contracting States must both permit and make possible (*National Union of Belgian Police*). Article 11(1) nevertheless leaves each State a free choice of the means to be used towards this end. The grant of a right to strike represents without any doubt one of the most important of these means, but there are others. Such a right, which is not expressly enshrined in Article 11, may be subject under national law to regulation of a kind that limits its exercise in certain instances. The Social Charter of 1961 only guarantees the right to strike subject to such regulation . . . For its part, the 1950 Convention requires that under national law trade unionists should be enabled, in conditions not at variance with Article 11, to strive through the medium of their organisations for the protection of their occupational interests. Examination of the file in this case does not disclose that the applicants have been deprived of this capacity. (para 36)

Consequently, there had been no breach of the applicants' Convention rights.

The Court's reluctance to recognise the existence of unqualified substantive trade union rights, such as the right to strike or to be consulted by public sector employers, under Article 11(1) is undoubtedly influenced by the Court's desire not to encroach upon the regime of economic and social rights created by the European Social Charter. Furthermore, the above cases suggest that the Court was unwilling to adopt the role of a supra-national arbiter of public sector employment disputes.

5   A unanimous Chamber of the full-time Court found that Britain had failed to adequately safeguard the Article 11 rights of trade unions and their members in the joined cases of *Wilson and The National Union of Journalist, Palmer, Wyeth and The National Union of Rail, Maritime and Transport Workers, Doolan and Others v United Kingdom*, Judgment of 2 July 2002. During the early 1990s two employers, the publisher of the *Daily Mail* newspaper and a dock company, sought to terminate collective bargaining arrangements with the applicant trade unions. The employers offered financial incentives, including higher rates of pay, to their employees who signed new personal contracts of employment relinquishing trade union rights. The individual applicants refused the new contracts and sought to challenge the legality of the employers' actions. Ultimately, the House of Lords found in favour of the employers. In addition the (Conservative) Government sought changes to employment law which prevented employees from challenging action taken by employers to alter their relationship with all/any

class of their employees unless the employer had acted in a manner which no reasonable employer would take. Parliament approved that amendment in section 13 of the Trade Union Reform and Employment Rights Act 1993. The applicants contended, before the Court, that the domestic law at the relevant time failed to protect their rights under Article 11. The incumbent (Labour) Government sought to defend the case by emphasising the voluntary nature of the system of collective bargaining and recognition operating in the United Kingdom. The Court held that:

46. ... Furthermore, it is of the essence of the right to join a trade union for the protection of their interests that employees should be free to instruct or permit the union to make representations to their employer or to take action in support of their interests on their behalf. If workers are prevented from so doing, their freedom to belong to a trade union, for the protection of their interests, becomes illusory. It is the role of the State to ensure that trade union members are not prevented or restrained from using their union to represent them in attempts to regulate their relations with their employers.

....

48. Under United Kingdom law at the relevant time it was, therefore, possible for an employer effectively to undermine or frustrate a trade union's ability to strive for the protection of its members' interests. The Court notes that this aspect of domestic law has been the subject of criticism by [the] Social Charter's Committee of Independent Experts and the ILO's Committee on Freedom of Association. It considers that, by permitting employers to use financial incentives to induce employees to surrender important union rights, the respondent State failed in its positive obligation to secure the enjoyment of the rights under Article 11 of the Convention. This failure amounted to a violation of Article 11, as regards both the applicant unions and the individual applicants.

Whilst the above judgment did not accord the trade unions all the protection that they sought, for example the Court declined to find a duty upon employers to recognise particular trade unions within Article 11, it demonstrated that the full-time Court was responsive to the needs of a healthy trade union system within a free-market economy. Significantly, even allowing for the 'wide' margin of appreciation accorded to States in securing the Article 11 rights of trade unions, the Court was united in determining that the Government had failed to comply with its positive obligations under that Article. Indeed, by securing the passage of legislation undermining the ability of trade unions to represent their members the previous Government could be viewed as having unduly favoured one side in the delicate balance of collective bargaining within the United Kingdom. The Court's willingness to find in favour of the applicants may also have been bolstered by the condemnation of the relevant domestic legal provisions by other international bodies. For a commentary on this judgment by an academic expert on trade union law see K.D. Ewing, 'The Implications of Wilson and Palmer' (2003) 32 *Industrial Law Journal* 1.

The negative right to freedom of association

Young, James and Webster v UK A.44 (1981) 4 EHRR 38
European Court of Human Rights

The existence of closed shops (defined by the Court as 'an undertaking or workplace in which, as a result of an agreement or arrangement between one or more trade unions and one or more employers or employers' associations, employees of a certain class are in practice required to be or become members of a specified union' (para 13) have a long history in the UK. There have been both 'pre-entry' closed shops, where an employee must join the union before being engaged, and 'post-entry' closed shops, where an employee must join the union after being engaged. In 1968 a majority of the Royal Commission on Trade Unions and Employer' Associations rec- ommended greater legal protection should be given to existing employees who were dismissed for refusing to join a union following the introduction of a closed shop. The Industrial Relations Act 1971, introduced by Mr Heath's Conservative government, gave workers the right to be a member of no union or to refuse to be a member of a particular union. When the Labour Party returned to power in 1974 it secured the passage of the Trade Union and Labour Relations Act 1974, which repealed the 1971 legislation and stated that it was only 'unfair' to dismiss an employee for refusing to join a union in a closed shop workplace where; (a) the employee objected to being a member of any union on religious grounds or (b) the employee on any reasonable ground objected to being a member of a particular union. Subsequently an amending Act removed the latter ground in 1976. In 1975 British Rail (BR) concluded an agreement with three trade unions, the National Union of Railwaymen (NUR), the Transport Salaried Staffs' Association (TSSA) and the Associated Society of Locomotive Engineers and Firemen (ASLEF), providing that membership of one of those unions was a condition of employment for designated categories of staff. Prior to the agreement about 7,000 employees (out of 250,000) were not members of the specified unions. Eventually fifty-four employees were dismissed for refusing to join one of the unions. The three applicants were among that group. Mr Young, a clerical officer, had been employed by BR since 1972. He refused to join either of the unions that he was eligible for membership, as he objected to their political views (the NUR had as one of its aims 'to work for the supersession of the capitalist system by a Socialist order of society' and the TSSA only gave political donations to the Labour Party). Mr James, a shunter, had been employed by BR since 1974 (although he had also worked for BR during an earlier time in his life). He refused to join the NUR (the only union he was eli- gible for) as he did not believe that it properly looked after its members' interests. Mr Webster, a clerical officer, had been employed by BR since 1958. He refused to join either the NUR or TSSA as he was opposed to the trade union movement as it then operated. The applicants complained to the Commission alleging that their lawful dismissals, under the prevailing leg- islation, for refusing to join a designated union amounted to, *inter alia*, a breach of their rights to freedom of thought, conscience, expression and association under Articles 9, 10 and 11. The Commission, by fourteen votes to three, expressed the opinion that there had been a vio- lation of Article 11, and that it was not necessary to examine the complaints under Articles 9 and 10.

As to the law

I. PRELIMINARY: RESPONSIBILITY OF THE RESPONDENT STATE

. . . Before the substance of the matter is examined, it must be considered whether responsibility can be attributed to the respondent State, the United Kingdom.

The Government conceded that, should the Court find that the termination of the applicants' con- tracts of employment constituted a relevant interference with their rights under Article II and that that interference could properly be regarded as a direct consequence of TULRA and the Amendment Act, the responsibility of the respondent State would be engaged by virtue of the enactment of that legislation.

A similar approach was adopted by the Commission in its report.

49. Under Article I of the Convention, each Contracting State 'shall secure to everyone within [its] juris- diction the rights and freedoms defined in . . . [the] Convention'; hence, if a violation of one of those

rights and freedoms is the result of non-observance of that obligation in the enactment of domestic legislation, the responsibility of the State for that violation is engaged. Although the proximate cause of the events giving rise to this case was the 1975 agreement between British Rail and the railway unions, it was the domestic law in force at the relevant time that made lawful the treatment of which the applicants complained. The responsibility of the respondent State for any resultant breach of the Convention is thus engaged on this basis. Accordingly, there is no call to examine whether, as the applicants argued, the State might also be responsible on the ground that it should be regarded as employer or that British Rail was under its control.

II. THE ALLEGED VIOLATION OF ARTICLE II

I. THE EXISTENCE OF AN INTERFERENCE WITH AN ARTICLE II RIGHT

51. A substantial part of the pleadings before the Court was devoted to the question whether Article II guarantees not only freedom of association, including the right to form and to join trade unions, in the positive sense, but also, by implication, a 'negative right' not to be compelled to join an association or a union.

Whilst the majority of the Commission stated that it was not necessary to determine this issue, the applicants maintained that a 'negative right' was clearly implied in the text. The Government, which saw the Commission's conclusion also as in fact recognising at least a limited negative right, submitted that Article II did not confer or guarantee any right not to be compelled to join an association. They contended that this right had been deliberately excluded from the Convention and that this was demonstrated by the following passage in the *travaux préparatoires*:

'On account of the difficulties raised by the "closed-shop system" in certain countries, the Conference in this connection considered that it was undesirable to introduce into the Convention a rule under which "no one may be compelled to belong to an association" which features in [Article 20 § 2 of] the United Nations Universal Declaration' (Report of 19 June 1950 of the Conference of Senior Officials, Collected Edition of the *'Travaux Préparatoires'*, vol IV, p 262).

52. The Court does not consider it necessary to answer this question on this occasion.

The Court recalls, however, that the right to form and to join trade unions is a special aspect of freedom of association (see the *National Union of Belgian Police* judgment of 27 October 1975, Series A No 19, p 17, § 38); it adds that the notion of a freedom implies some measure of freedom of choice as to its exercise.

Assuming for the sake of argument that, for the reasons given in the above-cited passage from the *travaux préparatoires*, a general rule such as that in Article 20 § 2 of the Universal Declaration of Human Rights was deliberately omitted from, and so cannot be regarded as itself enshrined in, the Convention, it does not follow that the negative aspect of a person's freedom of association falls completely outside the ambit of Article II and that each and every compulsion to join a particular trade union is compatible with the intention of that provision. To construe Article II as permitting every kind of compulsion in the field of trade union membership would strike at the very substance of the freedom it is designed to guarantee . . .

53. The Court emphasises once again that, in proceedings originating in an individual application, it has, without losing sight of the general context, to confine its attention as far as possible to the issues raised by the concrete case before it (see, inter alia, the *Guzzardi* judgment of 6 November 1980, Series A No 39, pp 31–2, § 88). Accordingly, in the present case, it is not called upon to review the closed shop system as such in relation to the Convention or to express an opinion on every consequence or form of compulsion which it may engender; it will limit its examination to the effects of that system on the applicants.

54. As a consequence of the agreement concluded in 1975 ... the applicants were faced with the dilemma either of joining NUR (in the case of Mr James) or TSSA or NUR (in the cases of Mr Young and Mr Webster) or of losing jobs for which union membership had not been a requirement when they were first engaged and which two of them had held for several years. Each applicant regarded the membership condition introduced by that agreement as an interference with the freedom of association to which he considered that he was entitled; in addition, Mr Young and Mr Webster had objections to trade union policies and activities coupled, in the case of Mr Young, with objections to the political affiliations of the specified unions ...

As a result of their refusal to yield to what they considered to be unjustified pressure, they received notices terminating their employment. Under the legislation in force at the time ... their dismissal was 'fair' and, hence, could not found a claim for compensation, let alone reinstatement or re-engagement.

55. The situation facing the applicants clearly runs counter to the concept of freedom of association in its negative sense.

Assuming that Article II does not guarantee the negative aspect of that freedom on the same footing as the positive aspect, compulsion to join a particular trade union may not always be contrary to the Convention.

However, a threat of dismissal involving loss of livelihood is a most serious form of compulsion and, in the present instance, it was directed against persons engaged by British Rail before the introduction of any obligation to join a particular trade union.

In the Court's opinion, such a form of compulsion, in the circumstances of the case, strikes at the very substance of the freedom guaranteed by Article II. For this reason alone, there has been an interference with that freedom as regards each of the three applicants.

56. Another facet of this case concerns the restriction of the applicants' choice as regards the trade unions which they could join of their own volition. An individual does not enjoy the right to freedom of association if in reality the freedom of action or choice which remains available to him is either non-existent or so reduced as to be of no practical value ... such freedom of action or choice as might have been left to the applicants in this respect would not in any way have altered the compulsion to which they were subjected since the would in any event have been dismissed if they had not become members of one of the specified unions.

57. Moreover, notwithstanding its autonomous role and particular sphere of application, Article II must, in the present case, also be considered in the light of Articles 9 and 10 (see, *mutatis mutandis*, the *Kjeldsen, Busk Madsen and Pedersen* judgment of 7 December 1976, Series A No 23, p 26, § 52).

Mr Young and Mr Webster had objections to trade union policies and activities, coupled, in the case of Mr Young, with objections to the political affiliations of TSSA and NUR ... Mr James' objections were of a different nature, but he too attached importance to freedom of choice and he had reached the conclusion that membership of NUR would be of no advantage to him ...

The protection of personal opinion afforded by Articles 9 and 10 in the shape of freedom of thought, conscience and religion and of freedom of expression is also one of the purposes of freedom of association as guaranteed by Article II. Accordingly, it strikes at the very substance of this Article to exert pressure, of the kind applied to the applicants, in order to compel someone to join an association contrary to his convictions.

In this further respect, the treatment complained of—in any event as regards Mr Young and Mr Webster—constituted an interference with their Article II rights.

2. THE EXISTENCE OF A JUSTIFICATION FOR THE INTERFERENCE FOUND BY THE COURT

58. The Government expressly stated that, should the Court find an interference with a right guaranteed by paragraph 1 of Articles 9, 10 or II, they would not seek to argue that such interference was justified under paragraph 2.

The Court has nevertheless decided that it should examine this issue of its own motion, certain considerations of relevance in this area being contained in the documents and information with which it has been furnished.

59. An interference with the exercise of an Article II right will not be compatible with paragraph 2 unless it was 'prescribed by law', had an aim or aims that is or are legitimate under that paragraph and was 'necessary in a democratic society' for the aforesaid aim or aims (see, *mutatis mutandis*, the *Sunday Times* judgment of 26 April 1979, Series A No 30, p 29, § 45).

60. The applicants argued that the restrictions of which they complained met none of these three conditions.

The Court does not find it indispensable to determine whether the first two conditions were satisfied, these being issues which were not fully argued before it. It will assume that the interference was 'prescribed by law', within the meaning of the Convention (see the above-mentioned *Sunday Times* judgment, pp 30–1, §§46–9), and had the aim, amongst other things, of protecting the 'rights and freedoms of others', this being the only one of the aims listed in paragraph 2 that might be relevant.

61. In connection with the last point, the Court's attention has been drawn to a number of advantages said to flow from the closed shop system in general, such as the fostering of orderly collective bargaining, leading to greater stability in industrial relations; the avoidance of a proliferation of unions and the resultant trade union anarchy; the counteracting of inequality of bargaining power; meeting the need of some employers to negotiate with a body fully representative of the workforce; satisfying the wish of some trade unionists not to work alongside non-union employees; ensuring that trade union activities do not enure to the benefit of those who make no financial contribution thereto.

Any comment on these arguments would be out of place in the present case since the closed shop system as such is not under review (see paragraph 53 above).

62. On the other hand, what has to be determined is the 'necessity' for the interference complained of: in order to achieve the aims of the unions party to the 1975 agreement with British Rail, was it 'necessary in a democratic society' to make lawful the dismissal of the applicants, who were engaged at a time when union membership was not a condition of employment?

63. A number of principles relevant to the assessment of the 'necessity' of a given measure have been stated by the Court in its *Handyside* judgment of 7 December 1976 (Series A No 24).

Firstly, 'necessary' in this context does not have the flexibility of such expressions as 'useful' or 'desirable' (p 22, § 48). The fact that British Rail's closed shop agreement may in a general way have produced certain advantages is therefore not of itself conclusive as to the necessity of the interference complained of.

Secondly, pluralism, tolerance and broadmindedness are hall-marks of a 'democratic society' (p 23, § 49). Although individual interests must on occasion be subordinated to those of a group, democracy does not simply mean that the views of a majority must always prevail: a balance must be achieved which ensures the fair and proper treatment of minorities and avoids any abuse of a dominant position. Accordingly, the mere fact that the applicants' standpoint was adopted by very few of their colleagues is again not conclusive of the issue now before the Court.

Thirdly, any restriction imposed on a Convention right must be proportionate to the legitimate aim pursued (p 23, § 49).

64. The Court has noted in this connection that a majority of the Royal Commission on Trade Unions and Employers' Associations, which reported in 1968, considered that the position of existing employees in a newly-introduced closed shop was one area in which special safeguards were desirable . . . Again, recent surveys suggest that, even prior to the entry into force of the Employment Act 1980 . . . many closed shop arrangements did not require existing non-union employees to join a specified union (see paragraph 13 above); the Court has not been informed of any special reasons

justifying the imposition of such a requirement in the case of British Rail. Besides, according to statistics furnished by the applicants, which were not contested, a substantial majority even of union members themselves disagreed with the proposition that persons refusing to join a union for strong reasons should be dismissed from employment. Finally, in 1975 more than 95 per cent of British Rail employees were already members of NUR, TSSA or ASLEF . . .

All these factors suggest that the railway unions would in no way have been prevented from striving for the protection of their members' interests (see the above-mentioned *National Union of Belgian Police* judgment, p 18, § 39) through the operation of the agreement with British Rail even if the legislation in force had not made it permissible to compel non-union employees having objections like the applicants to join a specified union.

65. Having regard to all the circumstances of the case, the detriment suffered by Mr Young, Mr James and Mr Webster went further than was required to achieve a proper balance between the conflicting interests of those involved and cannot be regarded as proportionate to the aims being pursued. Even making due allowance for a State's 'margin of appreciation' (see, *inter alia*, the above-mentioned *Sunday Times* judgment, p 36, § 59), the Court thus finds that the restrictions complained of were not 'necessary in a democratic society', as required by paragraph 2 of Article II.

There has accordingly been a violation of Article II.

...

FOR THESE REASONS, THE COURT

Holds by eighteen votes to three that there has been a breach of Article II of the Convention; . . .

NOTES

1   The plenary Court was composed of President Wiarda and Judges; Ryssdal, Zekia, Cremona, Ganshof Van Der Meersch, Bindschedler-Robert, Evrigenis, Liesch, Gölcüklü, Matscher, Pinheiro Farinha, Garcia De Enterria, Pettiti, Walsh, Evans Macdonald, Russo, and Bernhardt. The Court ruled, unanimously, that it was not necessary to examine Articles 9 and 10 separately, as they had been taken account of in the application of Article 11. Judges Ganshof Van Der Meersch, Bindschedler-Robert, Liesch, Gölcüklü, Matscher, Pinheiro Farinha, and Pettiti issued a concurring opinion in which they strongly supported the negative aspect of the right.

. . . Protection of freedom of association would be incomplete if it extended to no more than the positive aspect. It is one and the same right that is involved. The '*travaux preparatoires*' of the Convention—which anyway are not conclusive—speak only of 'undesirability' and so do not enable one to conclude that the negative aspect of trade union freedom was intended to be excluded from the ambit of Article 11. . . .

We should like to point out that it is not necessary, for there to be a violation of Article 11, that the refusal to join an association was justified by considerations connected with freedom of thought, of conscience or of religion, or with freedom of expression. In our view, the mere fact of being obliged to give the reasons for one's refusal constitutes a violation of freedom of association.

Trade union freedom, a form of freedom of association, involves freedom of choice: it implies that a person has a choice as to whether he will belong to an association or not and that, in the former case, he is able to choose the association. However, the possibility of choice, an indispensable component of freedom of association, is in reality non-existent where there is a trade union monopoly of the kind encountered in the present case. (p 28)

In direct contrast, Judge Sorensen (joined by Thor Vilhjalmsson and Lagergren JJ) produced a dissenting opinion which articulated an entirely different conception of the negative freedom of association.

...It clearly emerges from...the drafting history that the State Parties to the Convention could not agree to assume any international obligation in the matter, but found that it should be subject to national regulation only....

no cannon of interpretation can be adduced in support of extending the scope of the Article to a matter which deliberately has been left out and reserved for regulation according to national law and traditions of each State Party to the Convention....

The so-called positive and negative freedom of association are not simply two sides of the same coin or, as the Court puts it, two aspects of the same freedom. There is no logical link between the two.

The positive freedom of association safeguards the possibility of individuals, if they so wish, to associate with each other for the purpose of protecting common interests and pursuing common goals, whether of an economic, professional, political, cultural, recreational or other character, and the protection consists in preventing public authorities from intervening to frustrate such common action. It concerns the individual as an active participant in social activities, and it is in a sense a collective right in so far as it can only be exercised jointly by a plurality of individuals. The negative freedom of association, by contrast, aims at protecting the individual against being grouped together with other individuals with whom he does not agree or for purposes which he does not approve....However strongly such protection of the individual may sometimes be needed, it is neither in logic nor by necessary implication part of the positive freedom of association. (paras 2, 5 and 6)

Which view do you think reflects the proper interpretation of Article 11? Was the majority in effect creating a new right?

2 Ironically it was the incoming Conservative government, led by Mrs Thatcher, that had to represent the British state interests before the Court. Her government's ideological sympathy with the applicants no doubt explains why it did not seek to try and justify their dismissals under Article 11(2). Indeed, a year before the Court gave judgment, the Conservative government secured a change in legislation (the Employment Act 1980) which provided that, *inter alia*, henceforth in a closed shop situation it was 'unfair' to dismiss an employee where he/she objected on grounds of conscience or other deeply-held personal conviction to being a member of any or a particular trade union.

3 The factual context of the above case was distinguished in *Sibson v UK* (1993) 17 EHRR 193, A.258-A. The applicant had been employed by a major company (Courtaulds) as a heavy goods vehicle driver based at one of its depots in Lancashire since 1973. His work had been entirely satisfactory. Up until 1985 he had been a member of the Transport and General Workers Union (he held the post of branch secretary from 1981–84). In July 1985 he resigned from that union because of the way in which it dealt with a complaint he had made against a fellow member. Sibson then joined another union. However, his fellow workers immediately ostracised him and obstructed his work. There was no formal closed shop at the depot, but virtually all the other workers belonged to the TGWU. In October 1985 a large majority of the TGWU members at the depot voted (i) in favour of a closed shop agreement and (ii) industrial action if Sibson continued to work at the depot. The company then asked Sibson to either rejoin the TGWU and continue working from his existing depot or move to another depot nearby (where his earnings would be the same). Sibson resigned claiming constructive dismissal. Eventually, the Court of Appeal determined that the company had a contractual right to require Sibson to move to the other depot and therefore he had not been constructively dismissed. He complained to the Commission that the compulsion to either rejoin the TGWU or move to another depot amounted to a violation of his rights under Article 11. By eight votes to six, the Commission found no breach of the Convention. The Court held that the applicant's position was different from that in *Young, James and Webster* because: (a) Sibson did not have any objections in principle to trade union membership (therefore Articles 9 and 10 were

not relevant in his case), (b) there was no closed shop agreement in force and (c) Sibson was not faced with the choice of joining the TGWU or dismissal (he had the offer to work at the company's other depot). Consequently the Court, by seven votes to two, found no violation of the Convention as, '... Mr Sibson was not subject to a form of treatment striking at the very substance of the freedom of association guaranteed by Article 11' (para 29). This decision shows the qualified nature of the negative aspect of the right of association recognized by the Court. The range of factors evaluated by the Court suggests that the greater the degree of conscientious objection to trade union membership and the more severe the employment consequences for the individual concerned, the more likely the Court is to find a breach of Article 11.

4　In *Sigurdur A Sigurjonsson v Iceland* (1993) 16 EHRR 462, A.264, the Court strengthened the jurisprudential basis of the negative element of freedom of association. Under Regulations passed in 1983 taxi drivers working in Reykjavik had to be members of the Frami Automobile Association. This professional association had been formed in 1936 by taxi drivers to protect their interests by, *inter alia*, negotiating their working hours and wage rates, promoting solidarity among taxi drivers and seeking to maintain limitations on the numbers of taxicabs. The applicant was granted a taxicab licence by the relevant state committee in 1984 and at the same time he joined Frami. In 1985 he stopped paying his Frami membership fees and informed them that he no longer wished to be a member. Frami requested the committee to revoke the applicant's licence which it did. Sigurjonsson then challenged that decision in the Icelandic courts. The Supreme Court eventually ruled that the Regulation imposing an obligation to join Frami lacked a statutory basis. Thereupon, the Government secured a new Act (the Motor Vehicles for Public Hire Law 1989) which made taxicab licences conditional on trade union membership. New Regulations (no 308/1989) were issued under the 1989 Act which gave Frami various public interest powers, such as approving the suitability of vehicles for use as taxicabs. The applicant rejoined Frami but expressed the view that membership was contrary to his own wishes and interests. He also complained to the Commission alleging a violation of his rights under, *inter alia*, Articles 11, 9 and 10. The Commission, by seventeen votes to one, found a violation of Article 11 (and unanimously considered that it was not necessary to examine Articles 9 and 10). Before the Court, the Government argued that the negative aspect of Article 11 should be construed restrictively, having regard to the *travaux preparatoires*. In response the Court observed that the earlier judgment in *Young, James and Webster* 'did not attach decisive importance to them' (para 35). Furthermore, the Court considered that since that decision a new common ground was emerging at the international level. Eleven members of the EC had adopted the Community Charter of the Fundamental Social Rights of Workers in 1989 (which provided workers/employers shall have the freedom to join/not join trade unions/professional organisations), the Committee of Independent Experts under the European Social Charter (1961) considered that the Charter contained an implicit negative right and the International Labour Organisation believed that compulsory union membership violated their Conventions nos. 87 and 98. Therefore a majority of the Court, eight votes to one, held that:

> ... it should be recalled that the Convention is a living instrument which must be interpreted in the light of present-day conditions (see, *Soering v UK* (1989) A.161). Accordingly, Article 11 must be viewed as encompassing a negative right of association. It is not necessary for the Court to determine in this instance whether this right is to be considered on an equal footing with the positive right. (para 35)

The Court ruled that the compulsion (by the 1989 Act) for the applicant to join Frami, against his wishes, violated his right to freedom of Association under Article 11(1). Consequently it was necessary to examine whether the interference was justified under Article 11(2). The 1989

Act provided the basis for the interference being 'prescribed by law' and it had the legitimate aim of protecting the 'rights and freedoms of others'. The contentious issue, therefore, was whether the interference was 'necessary in a democratic society'. While the Court acknowledged that Frami had a public service role, it did not consider that compulsory membership of the association was required in order to perform those functions. This was because the major responsibility for supervising the law on taxicabs fell to the state licensing committee. Overall:

> ... the reasons adduced by the Government, although they can be considered relevant, are not sufficient to show that it was 'necessary' to compel the applicant to be a member of Frami, on pain of losing his licence and contrary to his own opinions. In particular, notwithstanding Iceland's margin of appreciation, the measures complained of were disproportionate to the legitimate aim pursued. Consequently, there has been a violation of Article 11. (para 41)

Additionally the Court, unanimously, determined that it was not necessary to examine the applicant's complaints under Articles 9 and 10. Thor Vilhjalmsson J dissented on the ground, which he had expressed in the minority opinion in *Young, James and Webster*, that the drafters had never intended to include a negative right within Article 11(1). 'I think that the negative freedom is so special and so clearly distinguishable from the positive freedom of association, that a legal interpretation of the Article cannot result in the inclusion of the negative freedom within its sphere of application.' The judgment of the majority in this case recognizes a maturation of the 'negative aspect' of freedom of association, as it was described in *Young, James and Webster*, into a 'negative right', primarily because of the emergence of a similar right in various parallel international agreements. It may also be pertinent to note that the 1980s witnessed a shift towards an individualistic perspective on political, economic and social issues by many European societies. However, the Court was cautious not to rule on the status of this right *vis-a-vis* the positive right which is expressly incorporated in Article 11.

5   The Court has been willing to hold that States may in principle be under a positive duty to intervene in economic relationships between private persons and associations in order to safeguard the formers' negative right to freedom of association. In *Gustafsson v Sweden* (1996) 22 EHRR 409, 1996-II 637, the applicant was a businessman who owned a summer restaurant and youth hostel on the island of Gotland. He did not belong to either of the restaurant employers' associations, which meant that he was not a party to the collective labour agreement between those associations and the Hotel and Restaurant Workers' Union (HRF), nor would he sign an agreement with that union. Gustafsson objected in principle to collective bargaining and claimed that he paid his workers more than the collective agreement rate. In 1987, because of his refusal to sign an agreement with the HRF it placed his restaurant under a 'blockade' and declared a boycott against it. During the next summer other unions introduced sympathy action against Gustafsson with the consequence that deliveries to the restaurant were stopped. He requested the government to intervene, to prevent the unions' blockade and sympathy action, but the authorities refused stating that it was a dispute between private subjects. The Supreme Administrative Court dismissed Gustafsson's challenge of the government's decision. In 1991, the applicant sold the restaurant due to the difficulties he had in running it with the unions' continuing industrial action. He complained to the Commission that the lack of state protection against the unions' actions amounted to a violation of, *inter alia*, his negative right to freedom of association. By a majority, of thirteen to four, the Commission concluded that there had been a violation of Article 11. The Court began by considering the principles of State liability under Article 11.

The matters complained of by the applicant, although they were made possible by national law, did not involve a direct intervention by the State. The responsibility of Sweden would nevertheless be engaged if those matters resulted from a failure on its part to secure to him under domestic law the rights set forth in Article 11 of the Convention (*Sibson v UK* (1994) A.258-A). Although the essential object of Article 11 is to protect the individual against arbitrary interferences by the public authorities with his or her exercise of the rights protected, there may in addition be positive obligations to secure the effective enjoyment of these rights. . . . It follows that the national authorities may, in certain circumstances, be obliged to intervene in the relationships between private individuals by taking reasonable and appropriate measures to secure the effective enjoyment of the negative right to freedom of association (see, *mutatis mutandis, Plattform 'Artzte Fur Das Leben' v Austria* (1991) A.139). (para 45)

However, the Court recognised that Article 11(1) also safeguards the freedom of trade union members to protect their occupational interests by means of trade union action. Therefore:

In view of the sensitive character of the social and political issues involved in achieving a proper balance between the competing interests and, in particular, in assessing the appropriateness of State intervention to restrict union action aimed at extending a system of collective bargaining, and the wide degree of divergence between the domestic systems in the particular area under consideration, the Contracting States should enjoy a wide margin of appreciation in their choice of the means to be employed. (para 46)

The government, relying on information provided by the HRF, sought to dispute whether the applicant provided better terms and conditions of employment for his workers than those laid down in the applicable collective agreements. Furthermore the applicant was in effect challenging the essential basis of the Swedish industrial relations system which had been in existence for sixty years. A majority of the Court, twelve votes to seven, concluded that the applicant's principal objection was:

. . . of a political nature, namely his disagreement with the collective bargaining system in Sweden. However, Article 11 of the Convention does not as such guarantee a right not to enter into a collective agreement (cf *Swedish Engine Drivers' Union v Sweden* (1976) A.20). The positive obligation incumbent on the State under Article 11, including the aspect of protection of personal opinion, may well extend to treatment connected with the operation of a collective bargaining system, but only where such treatment impinges on freedom of association. Compulsion which, as here, does not significantly affect the enjoyment of that freedom, even if it causes economic damage, cannot give rise to any positive obligation under Article 11.

Furthermore, the applicant has not substantiated his submission to the effect that the terms of employment which he offered were more favourable than those required under a collective agreement. Bearing in mind the special role and importance of collective agreements in the regulation of labour relations in Sweden, the Court sees no reason to doubt that the union action pursued legitimate interests consistent with Article 11 of the Convention. . . .

In the light of the foregoing, having regard to the margin of appreciation to be accorded to the respondent State in the area under consideration, the Court does not find that Sweden failed to secure the applicant's rights under Article 11 of the Convention. (paras 52–4)

The combination of the uncertain status of the negative right of freedom of association, the ambiguous nature of States' positive duties under Article 11 and the countervailing legitimate interests of trade unions may explain the Court's unwillingness to find a breach of the Convention in this case. In a partly dissenting opinion President Ryssdal and Judges; Spielmann, Palm, Foighel, Pekkanen, Loizou, Makarczyk, and Repik expressed the view: 'It is apparent, however, from the Court's case law that Article 11 is not a vehicle for regulating industrial relations in general or for generally protecting against prejudice suffered as a result of industrial action taken by one of the actors in the labour market against another.' During July 1998 the Court, by 16 votes to 1, dismissed Gustafsson's request for a revision of the judgment (based in part on further evidence regarding the terms on which he had employed his restaurant workers). The Court stated that this further evidence would not have had a decisive influence on the original determination, because that was based upon the 'special role and importance of collective agreements in the regulation of labour relations in Sweden' (para 32).

6   The full-time Court has recognized that Article 11 contains a 'negative' freedom of association in *Chassagnou v France* (1999) 29 EHRR 615. There the applicants were landowners who owned small plots of land that were subject to the 'Loi Verdeille' of 1964. This law required them to become members of municipal hunters' associations and allow members of those associations to hunt on their land. Despite the applicants' ethical objections to hunting, the French courts held that they were subject to the requirements of the 1964 law. The applicants then complained to the Commission alleging, *inter alia*, a breach of their freedom under Article 11 not to be forced to join an association against their wishes (the applicants' complaint under Article 1 of Protocol No 1 is examined below, p 682). The Commission upheld the claim by twenty-four votes to eight. Before the Court it was accepted that the statutory obligation requiring the applicants to join a hunting association violated their negative freedom of association. However, the Government sought to justify the obligation under Article 11(2) as being for the legitimate aim of protecting the rights and freedoms of others; ie to secure democratic participation in the leisure activity of hunting for as many people as possible. A large majority of the Court, twelve votes to five, held that the statutory obligations were not 'necessary in a democratic society' and consequently there had been a breach of Article 11.

To compel a person by law to join an association such that it is fundamentally contrary to his own convictions to be a member of it, and to oblige him, on account of his membership of that association, to transfer his rights over the land he owns so that the association in question can attain objectives of which he disapproves, goes beyond what is necessary to ensure that a fair balance is struck between conflicting interests and cannot be considered proportionate to the aim pursued. (para 117)

7   A Grand Chamber found Danish pre-entry closed shop arrangements to be in breach of 'the negative right to trade union freedom' in the cases of *Sorensen v Denmark* and *Rasmussen v Denmark*, judgment of 11 January 2006. The first applicant was offered a temporary job, prior to going to university, by a company (part of the Danish consumer COOP) to work between May and August 1996. The offer of employment was subject to an obligation to become a member of a designated trade union (the company had a collective agreement with that union governing the terms of employment of the company's employees). When he received his initial payslip he discovered that he had been registered as a member of that union and a subscription had been deducted. He objected to his employer, as he had applied for membership of another trade union. The company then dismissed him. His legal challenges were rejected by the Danish courts as they ruled that the Act on Protection against Dismissal due to Association Membership 1982 (passed as a result of the Court's judgment in *Young, James and Webster*) permitted dismissal of employees where the latter knew, prior to their employment, that membership of a specified association was a condition of employment (i.e. a pre-entry closed shop scheme). The second applicant, a gardener, became a member of a specific union in the 1980s. But, he became unable to support its political affiliations and he joined another union. After a period of unemployment he was offered a job as a gardener by a company on condition that he join the first trade union. He joined that union, despite his opposition to its political views, in order to secure the job. Before the Court both applicants

contended, *inter alia*, that the negative right to freedom of association was of equal status to the positive right and that closed shop agreements could no longer be justified in democratic societies. The Government disputed that the negative element was on an equal footing to the positive right and that, given the sensitive social/ political issues involved, a wide margin of appreciation should be left to States to regulate closed shop arrangements. In third-party written comments the Danish Confederation of Trade Unions contended that closed shop arrangements were of crucial importance in securing fair competition and combating illegal work. The Confederation feared that a judgment in favour of the applicants might result in the destruction of the Danish model of employment relations which had wide political support for over a century.

55. The parties have discussed at length whether in the area of trade-union membership the negative aspect of the freedom of association should be considered on an equal footing with the positive right. The Court notes that hitherto it has not taken any definite stand on that point (see *Young, James and Webster, Sigurdur Sigurjónsson*, and (in a different context) *Chassagnou and Others*, all cited above).

56. The Court does not in principle exclude that the negative and the positive aspects of the Article 11 right should be afforded the same level of protection in the area under consideration. However, it is difficult to decide this issue in the abstract since it is a matter that can only be properly addressed in the circumstances of a given case. At the same time, an individual cannot be considered to have renounced his negative right to freedom of association in situations where, in the knowledge that trade-union membership is a pre-condition of securing a job, he accepts an offer of employment notwithstanding his opposition to the condition imposed. Accordingly, the distinction made between pre-entry closed-shop agreements and post-entry closed-shop agreements in terms of the scope of the protection guaranteed by Article 11 is not tenable. At most this distinction is to be seen as a consideration which will form part of the Court's assessment of the surrounding circumstances and the issue of their Convention-compatibility.

57. It is further to be observed that by virtue of Article 1 of the Convention, each Contracting Party 'shall secure to everyone within [its] jurisdiction the rights and freedoms defined in . . . [the] Convention'. The discharge of this general duty may entail positive obligations inherent in ensuring the effective exercise of the rights guaranteed by the Convention. Thus, in the context of Article 11, although the essential object is to protect the individual against arbitrary interference by public authorities with the exercise of the rights protected, the national authorities may in certain circumstances be obliged to intervene in the relationship between private individuals by taking reasonable and appropriate measures to secure the effective enjoyment of those rights (see, *mutatis mutandis, Young, James and Webster*, § 49 and *Gustafsson* § 45, both cited above, and *Wilson & the National Union of Journalists and Others v the United Kingdom*, Nos 30668/96, 30671/96, and 30678/96, § 41, ECHR 2002-V).

In the present case, the matters about which the applicants complain did not involve direct intervention by the State. However, Denmark's responsibility would be engaged if these matters resulted from a failure on its part to secure to the applicants under domestic law their negative right to freedom of association.

58. The boundaries between the State's positive and negative obligations under Article 11 of the Convention do not lend themselves to precise definition. The applicable principles are nonetheless similar. Whether the case is analysed in terms of a positive duty on the State or in terms of interference by a public authority which requires to be justified, the criteria to be applied do not differ in substance. In both contexts regard must be had to the fair balance to be struck between the competing interests of the individual and of the community as a whole (see, *mutatis mutandis, Broniowski v Poland* [GC], No 31443/96, § 144, ECHR 2004-, and *Hatton and Others v the United Kingdom* [GC], No 36022/97, §§ 98 et seq., ECHR 2003-VIII).

In the area of trade-union freedom and in view of the sensitive character of the social and political issues involved in achieving a proper balance between the respective interests of labour and management, and given the wide degree of divergence between the domestic systems in this field, the Contracting States enjoy a wide margin of appreciation as to how the freedom of trade unions to protect the occupational interests of their members may be secured (see *Swedish Engine Drivers' Union v Sweden*, judgment of 6 February 1976, Series A No 20, pp 14–15, § 39; *Gustafsson*, cited above, pp 652–3, § 45; and *Schettini and Others v Italy* (dec.), No 29529/95, 9 November 2000; *Wilson & the National Union of Journalists and Others*, cited above, § 44). Thus, the Court has so far not found fault with a Contracting State's failure to impose on an employer an obligation to recognise a trade union or to provide for a system of compulsory collective bargaining (see *Wilson & the National Union of Journalists and Others*, § 44 and cases cited therein).

However, where the domestic law of a Contracting State permits the conclusion of closed-shop agreements between unions and employers which run counter to the freedom of choice of the individual inherent in Article 11, the margin of appreciation must be considered reduced. The Court recalls in this connection that although individual interests must on occasion be subordinated to those of a group, democracy does not simply mean that the views of a majority must always prevail: a balance must be achieved which ensures the fair and proper treatment of minorities and avoids any abuse of a dominant position (see *Young, James and Webster*, cited above, § 63, and *Chassagnou and Others*, cited above, §§ 112 and 113). In assessing whether a Contracting State has remained within its margin of appreciation in tolerating the existence of closed-shop agreements, particular weight must be attached to the justifications advanced by the authorities for them and, in any given case, the extent to which they impinge on the rights and interests protected by Article 11. Account must also be taken of changing perceptions of the relevance of closed-shop agreements for securing the effective enjoyment of trade-union freedom.

The Court sees no reason not to extend these considerations to both pre- and post-entry closed-shop agreements.

....

63. As to whether the applicants' personal views and opinions were compromised, it is to be noted that both applicants objected to membership of SID [the trade union they were required to join] because they could not subscribe to the political views of that trade union (and those of the other trade unions affiliated to the Danish Confederation of Trade Unions (LO). Instead, the applicant Sørensen joined the Danish Free Trade Union, and the applicant Rasmussen wishes to re-join the Christian Trade Union. The Government have pointed out that the applicants had the possibility of subscribing to a form of 'non-political membership' of SID or of any other trade union pursuant to the Act on Private Contributions to Political Parties and Disclosure of the Accounts of Political Parties. However, it is to be observed that such 'non-political membership' does not entail any reduction in the payment of the membership fee to the specific trade union. In any event, there is no guarantee that 'non-political membership' will not give rise to some form of indirect support for the political parties to which the specific trade union contributes financially.

64. In these circumstances the court concludes that both applicants were compelled to join SID and that this compulsion struck at the very substance of the freedom of association guaranteed by Article 11.

65. It remains to be determined whether the respondent Government, in authorising the use of the closed-shop agreements at issue, failed in the circumstances to secure the applicants' effective enjoyment of their negative right to freedom of association and thereby violated Article 11 of the Convention. The Court's assessment must be focused on whether a fair balance has been struck between the applicants' interests and the need to ensure that trade unions are enabled to strive for the protection of their members' interest (see paragraph 58 above).

66. The Court notes the special features of the Danish labour market, in particular the fact that the relationship between employers and employees is governed by a combination of agreements (collective and individual), labour-law principles, general statutes and statutory rules. Moreover, the institution of closed-shop agreements is a long-standing practice in Denmark, although they are unlawful in the public-sector labour market and are not concluded in the part of the private-sector labour market covered by the general agreement between DA [Confederation of Danish Employers] and LO. Closed-shop agreements thus presently affect only approximately 220,000 wage-earners, which is equivalent to less than 10 per cent of all Danish employees on the labour market.

....

68. In January 2003 and again in January 2005 the Minister of Employment presented a Bill to Parliament to amend the Danish Act on Protection against Dismissal due to Association Membership, which aimed at ensuring, among other things, that in the future no agreements could be lawfully concluded which imposed a duty on an employer to employ exclusively or to give preference to persons who were members of an association or a specific association. In the Explanatory Memorandum to the Bill the Government stated among other things that they 'consider that there should be freedom for an employee to decide whether to become a member of an association—just as there should be freedom to choose not to become a member of an association—without this leading to a risk of not being recruited or of being dismissed' and that they 'find it unreasonable that a clause in a collective agreement may prevent an employee who does not wish to be a member of an association or a specific association from obtaining or keeping employment with an employer or may prevent an employer from considering the candidate's qualifications alone'.

69. In the beginning of May 2003 it became clear that the Bill had failed to secure the necessary majority in Parliament and was withdrawn. Nevertheless, it was tabled anew in December 2004 and discussed by Parliament in January 2005. However, once again a majority in favour of changing the law could not be secured.

70. It is to be observed that these legislative attempts to eliminate entirely the use of closed-shop agreements in Denmark would appear to reflect the trend which has emerged in the Contracting Parties, namely that such agreements are not an essential means for securing the interests of trade unions and their members and that due weight must be given to the right of individuals to join a union of their own choosing without fear of prejudice to their livelihood. In fact, only a very limited number of Contracting States including Denmark and Iceland continue to permit the conclusion of closed-shop agreements.

71. It is true that in the context of the Danish debate on this topic LO has voiced its opposition to the attempts to eliminate the remaining areas where pre-entry closed-shop agreements continue to be applied. LO has pointed to the severe consequences which the prohibition of closed-shop clauses would entail, and in particular its view that it would become difficult or impossible to enforce collective agreements *vis-à-vis* small non-affiliated employers. However, the Court considers that these concerns have been adequately addressed by the Minister for Employment in his reply to question no. 7 put by the Parliamentary Committee, namely that an annulment of a closed-shop provision in a collective-bargaining agreement with a non-organised employer would not change the fact that the collective-bargaining agreement is still valid and must be complied with. Furthermore, the Court has not been informed that the concerns expressed by LO have materialised in any of the very many Contracting Parties which have abolished closed-shop agreements entirely.

72. The Court also observes that the wish of the Danish legislature to bring an end to the use of closed-shop agreements in the private sector is consistent with the manner in which the 1961 Social Charter has been applied to the issue of pre-entry closed-shop agreements. In its Conclusions XIV-1, XV-1 and XVI-1 the European Committee of Social Rights found that the Danish Act on Protection against

Dismissal due to Association Membership infringed Article 5 of the Social Charter and accordingly the Governmental Committee proposed that a recommendation be addressed to Denmark. Admittedly, at the 740th meeting of the Ministers' Deputies in February 2001 the required majority was not obtained. However, shortly thereafter, in September 2002, the Danish Government informed the Governmental Committee of the European Social Charter of their intention to introduce a bill prohibiting closed-shop agreements and the latter therefore decided to await the next assessment by the European Committee of Social Rights. Subsequently, when it had become clear that the bill had failed to secure the necessary majority in Parliament and was withdrawn, in its Conclusions XVII-1 of March 2004 the European Committee of Social Rights maintained that the Danish Act on Protection against Dismissal due to Association Membership infringed Article 5 of the Social Charter, in response to which the Government stated that once the parliamentary situation was more favourable they would resubmit the draft legislation.

73. Reference should also be made to the Community Charter of the Fundamental Social Rights of Workers, adopted by the Heads of State or Government of eleven member States of the European Communities on 9 December 1989. This text provides that every employer and every worker shall have the freedom to join or not to join professional organisations or trade unions without any personal or occupational damage being thereby suffered by them.

74. Article 12 of the Charter of Fundamental Rights of the European Union, proclaimed in Nice on 7 December 2000 (2000/C 364/01), is devoted to freedom of assembly and association. The above-mentioned provisions of the Community Charter of the Fundamental Social Rights of Workers are of obvious relevance for the interpretation of the scope of Article 12. It will be recalled in this connection that Article 53 of the Nice Charter states that nothing therein shall be interpreted as restricting or adversely affecting human rights and fundamental freedoms as recognised, in their respective fields of application, by Union law and international law and by international agreements to which the Union, the Community or all the Member States are party, including the European Convention for the Protection of Human Rights and Fundamental Freedoms, and by the Member States' constitutions.

75. In view of the above it appears that there is little support in the Contracting States for the maintenance of closed-shop agreements and that the European instruments referred to above clearly indicate that their use in the labour market is not an indispensable tool for the effective enjoyment of trade-union freedoms.

76. In conclusion, taking all the circumstances of the case into account and balancing the competing interests at issue, the Court finds that the respondent State has failed to protect the applicants' negative right to trade union freedom.

77. Accordingly, there has been a violation of Article 11 of the Convention in respect of both applicants.

Judges Rozakis, Bratza and Vajic issued a joint partly dissenting opinion in which they expressed the view that there was 'a very clear distinction in the degree of compulsion' to which the two applicants had been subject. Whilst they agreed with the majority that the threat of dismissal and the potential loss of livelihood was a serious form of compulsion regarding Mr Rasmussen, there was much less compulsion in the case of Mr Sorensen (his employment would have lasted only for ten weeks and he faced no difficulties in obtaining other short-term employment). Therefore, they did not consider that the latter had suffered a breach of Article 11.

Judge Lorenzen, the Judge of Danish nationality, with the agreement of Judge Zupancic, dissented as he considered that neither applicant had been 'substantially' affected by the closed shop agreements (in his opinion Mr Rasmussen had not established that the closed shop arrangements had limited his employment opportunities).

It is significant that the Grand Chamber was still not prepared to state unequivocally that the negative aspect/right of freedom of association had the same status as the positive aspect/right. However, the judgment makes it clear that the Court will not accord a wide margin of appreciation to those States (very few) that authorise the creation of closed shops. Do you think it would have made any difference to the Grand Chamber's conclusions if Danish law had given greater protection to workers' political beliefs?

Article 11(2)

The restrictions contained in the first sentence

1 Many of the elements in this sentence are similar to those found in Article 10(2). The Court has stated that an interference with the rights guaranteed by Article 11(1), '... constitutes a breach of Article 11 unless it satisfies the requirements of paragraph 2 which are identical to those laid down in paragraph 2 of Article 10, the only exception being where the last sentence of paragraph 2 of Article 11 is applicable.: *Vogt v Germany* (1995) 21 EHRR 205, A.323, para 66.

2 The term 'restrictions' has been interpreted by the Commission as being capable of encompassing a complete prohibition of the exercise of the rights enshrined in Article 11(1): *Rassemblement Jurassien and Unité Jurassienne v Switzerland* (1979) 17 DR 93 (above, p 742).

3 The Court has given a broad scope to the legitimate aim of protecting 'national security' by recognizing its applicability to governmental measures designed to maintain the territorial integrity of a State: *United Communist Party of Turkey v Turkey* (1998), (above, p 723).

4 The Commission applied the legitimate aim of preventing 'disorder or crime' in *G v Germany* (1989) 60 DR 256. There the applicant was an anti-nuclear protestor who participated in a sit-down protest outside a US military barracks in Germany. The effect of the blockade was to stop traffic on the road outside the barracks for a few minutes. The police ordered the applicant, and his fellow protestors, to leave the road and when he refused he was carried away. Subsequently G was convicted of unlawful coercion and fined 100 DM. He complained to the Commission alleging, *inter alia*, that the authorities' actions violated his right to freedom of peaceful assembly under Article 11. The Commission found that:

... in the circumstances of the present case, the applicant's conviction for having participated in a sit-in can reasonably be considered as necessary in a democratic society for the prevention of disorder and crime. In this respect, the Commission considers especially that the applicant had not been punished for his participation in the demonstration ... as such, but for particular behaviour in the course of the demonstration, namely the blocking of a public road, thereby causing more obstruction than would normally arise from the exercise of the right of peaceful assembly ... balancing the public interest in the prevention of disorder and the interest of the applicant and the other demonstrators in choosing the particular form of a sit-in, the applicant's conviction for the criminal offence of unlawful coercion does not appear disproportionate to the aims pursued.' (p 263)

Therefore, the Commission declared the application manifestly ill-founded.

5 The Court has explained its approach to applying the legitimate aim of the 'protection of the rights and freedoms of others' in *Chassagnou v France* (1999) (above, p 766).

Where these 'rights and freedoms' are themselves among those guaranteed by the Convention or its Protocols, it must be accepted that the need to protect them may lead States to restrict other rights or freedoms likewise set forth in the Convention. It is precisely this constant search for a balance between the fundamental rights of each individual which constitutes the foundation of a 'democratic society'. The balancing of individual interests that may well be contradictory is a difficult matter, and Contracting States must have a broad margin of appreciation in this respect, since the national authorities are in principle better placed than the European Court to assess whether or not there is a 'pressing social need' capable of justifying interference with one of the rights guaranteed by the Convention.

It is a different matter where restrictions are imposed on a right or freedom guaranteed by the Convention in order to protect 'rights and freedoms' not, as such, enunciated therein. In such a case only indisputable imperatives can justify interference with enjoyment of a Convention right. (para 113)

Hence the legal source and nature of the particular 'rights and freedoms of others' at issue will determine the extent of the Court's deference towards the State authorities' balancing of conflicting rights and the Court's willingness to uphold restrictions on applicants' Article 11(1) rights.

The restrictions contained in the second sentence

Council of Civil Service Unions v UK 50 DR 228 (1987)
European Commission of Human Rights

The applicants were a trade union (which coordinated the activities of nine individual trade unions with members working for the civil service) and six current and former civil servants who worked (or had worked) at Government Communications Headquarters (GCHQ). The latter organization was formed in 1947, as a civilian staffed branch of government, to ensure the security of the UK's military and official communications and to provide signals intelligence for the government. At the time of this complaint GGHQ employed about 7,000 civil servants at Cheltenham and elsewhere.

From 1947 until 1984 the staff at GCHQ were allowed to be members of trade unions and in 1982 4,454 of those employees were paid up trade union members. Between 1979 and 1981 various forms of industrial action, such as one-day strikes and overtime bans, were taken on seven occasions by union members at GCHQ. These actions were generally part of national campaigns over pay and conditions being mounted by the civil service unions. Under Article 4 of the Civil Service Order 1982, the Minister for the Civil Service (who at that time was the Prime Minister, Mrs Thatcher) had the power to '... make regulations or give instructions ... for controlling the conduct of the Service and providing for ... the conditions of service of all such persons...'. On 22 December 1983 the Prime Minister gave an oral direction, under Article 4, that the conditions of service applicable to civil servants working at GCHQ should be revised to prohibit membership of any trade union other than a departmental staff association approved by the Director of GCHQ. On 25 January 1984 the Foreign Secretary, who had departmental responsibility for GCHQ, issued two certificates under the Employment Protection Act 1975 and the Employment Protection (Consolidation) Act 1978 stating that the employees at GCHQ were to be excepted from those Acts for the purpose of safeguarding national security (thereby preventing such employees from bringing complaints before Industrial Tribunals). On the same day he informed the House of Commons of the trade union ban at GCHQ. The next day GCHQ staff were sent a letter informing them that they were no longer permitted to be members of any existing trade unions. Furthermore disciplinary action might be taken against anyone engaging in new industrial action. Staff not wishing to remain at GCHQ were to be given the possibility of a transfer to another part of the civil service (if another post could not be found the employee would be eligible for premature retirement on redundancy terms). Staff remaining at GCHQ would receive an ex gratia payment of £1,000 in recognition of the loss of trade union membership rights.

In February 1984, the House of Commons Employment Committee recommended that the Government and the civil service unions hold discussions with a view to preserving trade union membership rights at GCHQ while meeting the Government's concerns about the harmful effects of industrial action at GCHQ. The Government refused to change its policy and in 1985 an approved staff association was formed at GCHQ. By 1987 all the staff at GCHQ had accepted the new conditions of service except for 35 persons (including some of the applicants) and 49 per cent of the employees had joined the staff association. The applicants sought to challenge the Government's decision, to ban trade union membership at GCHQ, in the courts but the House of Lords ruled against them on the ground that the Minister had acted in the interests of national security (in the famous case of *Council of Civil Service Unions v Minister for the Civil Service* [1984] 3 All ER 935). Subsequently, the applicants complained to the Commission that the Government's actions removed the individual applicants' right to belong to a trade union and deprived the unions of any role in industrial relations at GCHQ contrary to Article 11.

THE LAW

1. The applicants complain under Article 11 of the Convention that the respondent Government have removed the right of individual employees at CGHQ to belong to a trade union.

...

The Commission finds—in agreement with the parties—that there has been an interference by a public authority with the exercise of the applicants' right, under Article 11 para 1, to form and to join trade unions, namely in that on 25 January 1984, upon instructions of the Prime Minister as Minister for the Civil Service, the Secretary of State for Foreign and Commonwealth Affairs issued two certificates with the result that GCHQ staff were thenceforth no longer permitted to be members of any existing trade union.

The Commission's next task is to examine whether such interference was justified under Article 11 para 2 of the Convention. First it must consider whether the interference falls to be considered under the first or the second sentence of Article 11 para 2.

...

The Commission observes that the first sentence of Article 11 para 2 provides criteria for justifying an interference with the rights under Article 11 para 1. The second sentence specifically envisages restrictions on the exercise of these rights by various categories of persons employed by the State. The Commission finds that the restrictions at issue fall to be examined primarily under the second sentence, if the staff serving at GCHQ can be considered as members . . . of the administration of the State. The Commission must therefore turn its attention to the meaning and scope of these terms.

In this respect, the Commission notes that the applicants have placed much reliance on various other international instruments as a background to their interpretation in particular in the second sentence of Article 11 para 2 of the terms members . . . of the administration of the State.

It is true that the Commission has occasionally had recourse to other international instruments under international law (see *Swedish Engine Drivers Union v Sweden*, Comm Report 27.5.74, paras 65 ff, Eur Court HR, Series B no 18, p 42). In the present case, it notes that for instance Article 22 para 1 of the International Covenant on Civil and Political Rights of 1966 ensures the right to form and join trade unions. The second sentence of Article 22 para 2 is similar to the second sentence of Article 11 para 2 of the Convention, while only mentioning 'the armed forces and . . . the police' but not the administration of the State. Again, Article 8 para 1(a) of the International Covenant on Economic, Social and Cultural Rights of 1966 also guarantees the right to form and join trade unions. Nevertheless, Article 8 para 2 which resembles the second sentence in Article 11 para 2 of the Convention now expressly includes the 'members . . . of the administration of the State'.

In the Commission's opinion these differences sufficiently demonstrate that there can be no settled view under international law as to the position of members of the 'administration of the State' in respect of trade union rights, and that these instruments cannot therefore be of assistance to the Commission in the present case.

In interpreting the term 'members . . . of the administration of the State' the applicants point out that the second sentence covers police and army personnel and those who have a specific connection with the exercise of official authority or who administer the basic functions of the State, eg high-ranking civil servants. It should not be construed to cover all persons working at GCHQ simply because their work is directly or indirectly associated with national security. Otherwise there would be no need for the phrase 'in the interests of national security' in the first sentence of Article 11 para 2.

In the Government's submissions, the words 'members . . . of the administration of the State' are not limited to high-ranking civil servants. This would be inconsistent with the practice in a number of States of imposing restrictions on persons in the public service by reference not only to their level of responsibility but also to the nature of the services they perform. The function of CGHQ can be defeated just as effectively by the radio officer or the teleprinter operator. GCHQ can only operate as an integral whole. The phrase thus also covers employees whose duties are necessary for the proper performance of vital Government functions.

The Commission has examined whether the staff serving at GCHQ fall under the terms 'members . . . of the administration of the State'. To a certain extent, the meaning and scope of these terms is uncertain and the Commission will not attempt to define them in detail. Nevertheless, the Commission notes that the terms are mentioned, in the same sentence in Article 11 para 2, together with 'members of the armed forces (and) of the police'. In the present case, the Commission is confronted with a special institution, namely GCHQ, whose purpose resembles to a large extent that of the armed forces and the police insofar as GCHQ staff directly or indirectly, by ensuring the security of the respondent Government's military and official communications, fulfil vital functions in protecting national security.

The Commission is therefore satisfied that the staff serving at GCHQ can be considered as 'members . . . of the administration of the State' within the meaning of the second sentence of Article 11 para 2 of the Convention. It must therefore examine whether the further conditions of the second sentence of Article 11 para 2 have been met, in particular whether the restrictions at issue were 'lawful' within the meaning of that provision.

The applicants have pointed out that this must mean lawful under the Convention, having regard to the aim of the latter to prevent the interference with fundamental rights other than by means which are prescribed by law and which are necessary in a democratic society. They submit that the term 'prescribed by law' in the first sentence of Article 11 para 2 is not met in that Section 121(4) of the 1975 Act and Section 138(4) of the 1978 Act grant to the State discretionary powers without any adequate indication how these powers should be exercised. Moreover, the powers conferred by Article 4 of the Order in Council of 1982 do not adequately indicate the conditions on which contractual terms and conditions may be regulated. Further, no provisions are made for judicial control of the State assertion that national security is at stake.

The Government submit that the measures imposed on GCHQ staff were lawful restrictions within the meaning of the second sentence of Article 11 para 2. Under the first sentence of Article 11 para 2 the Government contend that Article 4 of the 1982 Civil Service Order in Council expressly confers powers upon the Minister for the Civil Service. The power of the Secretary of State to issue certificates is expressly conferred by Section 121(4) of the 1975 Act and Section 138(4) of the 1978 Act. These provisions are all sufficiently clear and precise in their terms to give those affected an adequate indication as to the conditions in which certificates may be issued, namely where the exception of civil servants from the protection of the Acts is required for purposes of national security.

The Commission recalls that it has so far not expressed an opinion in its case-law on the meaning of the term 'lawful' in this particular context. In the Commission's view, however, 'lawful' within the meaning of the second sentence of Article 11 para 2 means in the first place that the measures at issue must at least have been in accordance with national law.

In the present case the Commission observes that, according to Article 4 of the 1982 Civil Service Order in Council, the Minister for the Civil Service may regulate the conditions of service of civil servants. It is true that this order is rather broad in that it does not specifically refer to the regulation of trade union membership. However, these powers of the Minister must be seen in connection with the two Employment Protection Acts of 1975 and 1978 which restrict the exercise of the powers under the Civil Service Order in Council and on the basis of which provisions the Foreign Secretary, on 25 February 1984, signed and issued certificates. In particular, Section 138(4) of the 1978 Act and the corresponding Section 121(4) of the 1975 Act expressly refer to the issuing of such certificates for the purpose of safeguarding national security. The Commission finds that the measures at issue met this condition in that the staff at GCHQ were concerned with vital functions of national security.

Against this legislative background the Commission considers that the relevant legal provisions provided an adequate and sufficient indication to those employed at CGHQ as to the possibility of steps being taken to regulate trade union membership. In this respect the Commission notes, in addition, that the measures at issue were subject to judicial control by the domestic courts. In the Commission's opinion, the measures were, therefore, taken in accordance with national law.

The applicants have also submitted that the 'lawful restrictions' of a right cannot imply its destruction. Furthermore, the second sentence is also subject to the principle of proportionality and, as an exception clause, should be narrowly construed since a broad interpretation would remove millions of public sector employees throughout Europe from the protection of Article 11. In the context of the terms 'necessary in a democratic society' in the first sentence of Article 11 para 2, the applicants contend that the measures were disproportionate in that there was no 'pressing social need' for the Government to deny trade union rights after 37 years, and to deny them only 2 1/2 years after the industrial action occurred. The Government failed to consult the trade unions before issuing the certificates, and failed to act on the recommendations of the House of Commons Employment Committee, even though the trade unions were willing to offer guarantees.

The Government submit that the term 'lawful' in the second sentence of Article 11 para 2 cannot be interpreted as requiring that restrictions should also be 'necessary in a democratic society'. In the context of the first sentence of Article 11 para 2 the Government submit that undoubtedly the industrial action at CGHQ was intended to harm the Government who alone can appreciate the effects of the action. The lapse of time until the certificates were issued can be explained by the fact that the Government undertook a full reappraisal of the measures required to prevent a recurrence of the threat to national security. The Government also found that the guarantees offered by the trade unions were not adequate. A fair balance has now been secured between the interests of national security and the rights under Article 11 by creating a departmental staff association at GCHQ.

The Commission has examined first the applicants' submission that the term 'restrictions' in the second sentence of Article 11 para 2 cannot imply complete suppression of the exercise of the right in Article 11. However, the Commission recalls that the same term is also employed in the first sentence of Article 11 para 2. This provision has been interpreted by the Commission as also covering a complete prohibition of the exercise of the rights in Article 11 (see eg No 8191/78, *Rassemblement jurassien and Unité jurassienne v Switzerland*, Dec 10.10.79, DR 197 p 93). Accordingly, the term 'restrictions' in the second sentence of Article 11 para 2 is sufficiently broad also to cover the measures at issue.

Second, the Commission notes the applicants' submissions that the term 'lawful' in the second sentence of Article 11 para 2 includes the principle of proportionality. In this respect, the Commission finds that, even if the term 'lawful' ('légitime') should require something more than a basis in national law, in particular a prohibition of arbitrariness, there can be no doubt that this condition was in any event also observed in the present case.

The Commission recalls its case-law according to which States must be given a wide discretion when ensuring the protection of their national security (see *Leander v Sweden*, Comm Report 17.5.85, para 68, Eur Court HR, Series A No 116, p 43).

In the present case, the Commission has considered the Government's position when issuing the certificates. In particular, the Government had to ensure that the functioning of CGHQ would no longer be vulnerable to disruption by industrial action. After industrial action had occurred in 1981 and once the Government had acknowledged the functions of GCHQ in May 1983, the time and means were lacking for the Government to conduct substantial negotiations with the trade unions. The guarantees offered by the latter were in the Government's assessment not adequate. The Government were aware that trade union officials outside GCHQ could organise industrial action within GCHQ in which GCHQ staff would participate as loyal trade union members. Thus, it could not be excluded that industrial action could again occur at GCHQ at any moment. In this respect the Commission notes in particular that the House of Lords, in its judgment of 2 November 1984, unanimously accepted that the basis of the Government's actions related to the interests of national security.

The Commission considers that in this light and against the whole background of industrial action and the vital functions of GCHQ the action taken, although drastic, was in no way arbitrary. The measures would therefore also be 'lawful' within a wider meaning of that term in the second sentence of Article 11 para 2.

The Commission is thus satisfied that the measures at issue, while interfering with the applicants' rights under Article 11 para 1, were justified under the second sentence of Article 11 para 2 as being 'lawful restrictions (imposed) on the exercise of these rights by members... of the administration of the State'. Therefore, there is no further need to examine the measures in relation to the conditions of the first sentence of Article 11 para 2. It follows that this part of the application is manifestly ill-founded within the meaning of Article 27 para 2 of the Convention.

...

For these reasons, the Commission

DECLARES THE APPLICATION INADMISSIBLE.

NOTES

1 G. S. Morris has commented that, 'the declaration by the European Commission that the unions' case was inadmissible under the Convention fatally weakened their chances of securing a modification of the Government's position.' ('Freedom of Association and the Interests of the State', p 49 in K. D. Ewing, C. A. Gearty, and B. A. Hepple (eds), *Human Rights and Labour Law: Essays for Paul O'Higgins* (London: Mansell, 1994).

2 Within a few days of returning to power the new Labour Government announced (on 15 May 1997) that it was rescinding the ban on trade union membership at GCHQ. Employees would be free to belong to a trade union or staff association of their choice. In September 1997, the Director of GCHQ, the Chairman of the Government Communications Staff Federation and the General Secretaries of the Civil Service Unions signed a legally binding agreement which provided: (a) the GCSF was recognized for consultation and negotiation on matters exclusive to GCHQ, (b) the other civil service unions were recognized for service wide matters and for representation of individual members, (c) the unions agreed not to take any industrial action that would disrupt GCHQ operations (the Foreign Secretary has the right to make the final decision on whether any threatened action would be disruptive) and (d) the unions have a unilateral right of access to binding arbitration if a dispute is unresolved. As a

consequence of this agreement the Foreign Secretary revoked the certificate restricting GCHQ employees' access to Industrial (now Employment) Tribunals. While the ban was in operation fourteen employees were dismissed for refusing to relinquish their trade union rights. Eight of these persons were below the age of retirement in September 1997 and therefore eligible to reapply for employment at GCHQ under the new employment conditions. One of them resumed working at GCHQ later that month. (Foreign and Commonwealth Office, Press Release 3 September 1997)

3 Subsequently the Commission and the Court have continued to refrain from providing a clear definition of the phrase 'members ... of the administration of the State'. In *Vogt v Germany* (examined above, p 677), the Commission expressed the opinion that a state employed school teacher did not fall into this category.

It considers that the applicant, as a secondary-school teacher, was not a member of 'the administration of the State' within the meaning of this provision. The functions of the teaching profession do not resemble those of the armed forces and the police (as to this criterion, see *Council of Civil Service Unions v the UK* (1987) DR 50) and in particular do not by definition involve the exercise of State authority. (A.323, p 52)

In the judgment in *Vogt* it was held:

... the Court agrees with the Commission that the notion of 'administration of the State' should be interpreted narrowly, in the light of the post held by the official concerned. However, even if teachers are to be regarded as being part of the 'administration of the State' for the purposes of Article 11(2), a question which the Court does not consider it necessary to determine in the instant case, Mrs Vogt's dismissal was, for the reasons previously given in relation to Article 10, disproportionate to the legitimate aim pursued. There has accordingly also been a breach of Article 11. (paras 67–8)

The Court's stated willingness to construe this phrase narrowly is to be welcomed, but it is significant that the Court did not rule that state employed teachers fall outside the ambit of the phrase (as the Commission had done). Nevertheless, the above dicta appears to suggest that the Court applied a proportionality test, as was argued by the applicants in *Council of Civil Service Unions*, even when an applicant comes within the second sentence of Article 11(2). However, the full-time Court has not yet provided a definitive interpretation of this sentence. In *Rekvenyi v Hungary* (above, p 655) the Court stated that:

... the term 'lawful' in this sentence alludes to the very same concept of lawfulness as that to which the Convention refers elsewhere when using the same or similar expressions, notably the expressions 'in accordance with the law' and 'prescribed by law' found in the second paragraph of Articles 9 to 11. As recalled above in relation to Article 10, the concept of lawfulness in the Convention, apart from positing conformity with domestic law, also implies, qualitative requirements in the domestic law such as foreseeability and, generally, an absence of arbitrariness.

... it is not necessary in the present case to settle the disputed issue of the extent to which the interference in question is, by virtue of the second sentence of Article 11(2), excluded from being subject to the conditions other than lawfulness enumerated in the first sentence of that paragraph ... the Court considers that, in any event, the interference with the applicant's freedom of association satisfied those conditions ... (paras 59 and 61)

In *Ahmed v UK* (above, p 654) the Court did not examine whether local government officers came within the second sentence.

In *Grand Oriente D'Italia Di Palazzo Giustiniani* (above p 747) the Chamber implicitly considered that the specified public offices did not fall within this sentence.

31. As to whether the offices covered by section 5 of the 1996 Law fall within the scope of 'the administration of the State', the Court notes that the offices listed in Schedules A and B to the 1996 Law were not part of the organisational structure of the Region, but fell into two other categories: regional organisations and nominations and appointments for which the Regional Council was responsible. According to the Court's case-law, 'the notion of "administration of the State" should be interpreted narrowly, in the light of the post held by the official concerned' (see *Vogt v Germany*, judgment of 26 September 1995, Series A No 323, p 31, § 67). The Court reiterates that in *Vogt* it did not consider it necessary to determine the issue whether a teacher—a permanent civil servant—was part of the administration of the State (ibid, p 31, § 68). In the present case it notes on the basis of the evidence before it that the link between the offices referred to in Schedules A and B to the 1996 Law and the Marches Region is undoubtedly looser than the link which existed between Mrs Vogt, a permanent teacher, and her employer.

32. Accordingly, the interference in question cannot be justified under the second sentence of Article 11 § 2 either.

14

ARTICLE 12 RIGHT TO MARRY

F v Switzerland A.128 (1987) 10 EHRR 411
European Court of Human Rights

The applicant was a Swiss national born in 1943. In 1963 he married Miss G. and then divorced her in 1964. In 1966 he married a divorcee. During 1978 he began cohabiting with another woman and in 1981 his wife obtained a divorce. The court issued an order prohibiting F. from remarrying within one year (under Article 150 of the Swiss Civil Code a court granting a divorce shall fix a period of between one to three years during which the party at fault shall not be entitled to remarry). In January 1983 Miss N. responded to the applicant's advertisement for a secretary. Within four days they were cohabiting and in February 1983 the couple married. Two weeks later F. began divorce proceedings. At the beginning of April his wife left the matrimonial home after F. renewed a relationship with a former mistress. In October of that year the Civil Court gave judgment in favour of the wife, approved a payment of compensation by F., of 17,000 Swiss francs, to his (former) wife for non-pecuniary damage and imposed a three year prohibition on F. remarrying (because his unacceptable attitude made him solely responsible for the breakdown of the marriage). F.'s domestic appeals were dismissed. In March 1986, F. and his cohabitee stated that they wished to marry; however, the authorities refused to permit the marriage as F.'s ban was still in force. The couple married in January 1987, when the ban had expired, and their child was born in February 1987. F. complained to the Commission alleging that the three year prohibition on remarriage was incompatible with his right to marry guaranteed by Article 12. By ten votes to seven, the Commission found a breach of that Article.

32. Article 12 (art 12) secures the fundamental right of a man and a woman to marry and to found a family. The exercise of this right gives rise to personal, social and legal consequences. It is 'subject to the national laws of the Contracting States', but 'the limitations thereby introduced must not restrict or reduce the right in such a way or to such an extent that the very essence of the right is impaired' (see the *Rees* judgment of 17 October 1986, Series A No 106, p 19, para 50).

   In all the Council of Europe's member States, these 'limitations' appear as conditions and are embodied in procedural or substantive rules. The former relate mainly to publicity and the solemnisation of marriage, while the latter relate primarily to capacity, consent and certain impediments.

33. The prohibition imposed on F was applied under rules governing the exercise of the right to marry, as Article 12 (art 12) does not distinguish between marriage and remarriage.

   The Court notes that a waiting period no longer exists under the laws of other Contracting States, the Federal Republic of Germany having abolished it in 1976, and Austria in 1983. In this connection, it recalls its case-law according to which the Convention must be interpreted in the light of present-day conditions (see the *Airey* judgment of 9 October 1979, Series A No 32, para 26). However, the fact that, at the end of a gradual evolution, a country finds itself in an isolated position as regards one aspect of its legislation does not necessarily imply that that aspect offends the Convention, particularly in a field—matrimony—which is so closely bound up with the cultural and historical traditions of each society and its deep-rooted ideas about the family unit.

34. The measure complained of ultimately amounts to a civil sanction. According to the Federal Court's case-law, it is an order consequent upon a fault of exceptional gravity that has played a decisive role in the breakdown of a marriage...

Although automatically applicable because mandatory as a matter of public policy, Article 150 of the Civil Code nonetheless allows the courts some degree of discretion: the prohibition period to be imposed on the party at fault in the event of divorce granted on the ground of adultery may range from one to three years... In the instant case the Lausanne District Civil Court chose the maximum period, holding that F's unacceptable attitude rendered him solely responsible for the breakdown of the marriage...

The divorce court therefore did not confine itself to appraising the consequences of the breakdown of marriage, by approving the agreement made between the couple on 16 May 1983, which provided for payment of compensation for non-pecuniary damage... it also assessed the applicant's past conduct in order to draw conclusions about his right to remarry.

35. The Government contended firstly that the application of Article 150 in the instant case was neither unreasonable nor arbitrary nor disproportionate. The sanction complained of undoubtedly did amount to an interference with the exercise of the right to marry, but it did not impair that right's very essence. As part of the Swiss conception of divorce based on matrimonial fault, the system of temporarily prohibiting remarriage was explained by the legislature's determination to protect not only the institution of marriage but also the rights of others and even the person affected by the prohibition.

36. The Court recognises that the stability of marriage is a legitimate aim which is in the public interest. It doubts, however, whether the particular means used were appropriate for achieving that aim. In Switzerland itself, the Study Group on the partial reform of family law and subsequently the Committee of Experts on Family Law Reform would seem to have had similar doubts, since they recommended the repeal of Article 150 of the Civil Code...

In any event, the Court cannot accept the argument that the temporary prohibition of remarriage is designed to preserve the rights of others, namely those of the future spouse of the divorced person.

On 22 May 1986, the woman with whom F was cohabiting obtained a reduction of the waiting time following her own divorce, which had become absolute a month earlier... The prohibition on F expired on 21 December 1986, after which the registrar was able to carry out the necessary formalities... The marriage accordingly took place on 23 January 1987. During the intervening period—of some seven or eight months—the applicant's future wife could consider that she was personally and directly wronged by the measure affecting F. Given that she was neither under age nor insane, her rights were in no way protected by the measure in question.

An unborn child may also be adversely affected by such a prohibition. Admittedly the concept of an 'illegitimate child' no longer exists in Swiss law, under which children born out of wedlock now have almost the same status and the same rights as children born in wedlock. Children born out of wedlock may nonetheless suffer on account of certain prejudices and thus be socially handicapped. While in the instant case the applicant's child was born one month after his parents' marriage... the death of one of the parents or even a delay in completing the legal formalities would have been enough to cause the child to be born out of wedlock.

37. The Government further considered that compelling the person concerned to take time for reflection also helped to protect him from himself. In the Court's view, this argument is not of sufficient weight to justify the impugned interference in the case of a person of full age in possession of his mental faculties.

38. The Government relied in addition on the *Johnston* judgment of 18 December 1986, according to which 'the prohibition on divorce [cannot], in a society adhering to the principle of monogamy, ... be

regarded as injuring the substance of the right guaranteed by Article 12 (art 12)' (Series A No 112, p 24, para 52). In the Government's submission, the same applied a fortiori to a mere temporary prohibition on remarriage. No right to remarry could be recognised given that the exercise of it necessarily depended on another right—the right to divorce—which did not flow from the Convention; in short, remarriage subsequent to a divorce could not be equated with a first marriage.

... F's situation is quite distinct from Mr Johnston's, since what was at issue in the case of the latter was the right of a man who was still married to have his marriage dissolved. If national legislation allows divorce, which is not a requirement of the Convention, Article 12 (art 12) secures for divorced persons the right to remarry without unreasonable restrictions.

39. There remains the Government's argument that judicial separation, the waiting period required before divorce can be granted or an innocent spouse's right to oppose divorce have consequences for those concerned which are identical with those of a temporary prohibition on remarriage. The Court considers that such situations are different and that in any case they occur prior to any decree of divorce.

40. In conclusion, the disputed measure, which affected the very essence of the right to marry, was disproportionate to the legitimate aim pursued. There was, therefore, a violation of Article 12 (art 12).

... FOR THESE REASONS, THE COURT

1. Holds by nine votes to eight that there has been a breach of Article 12...'

NOTES

1   The Court was composed of President Ryssdal and Judges: Lagergren, Pettiti, Evans, Macdonald, Russo, Bernhardt, Spielmann, and Carrillo Salcedo.

2   Judges Thor Vilhjalmsson, Bindschedler-Robert, Gölcüklü, Matscher, Pinheiro Farina, Walsh, De Meyer, and Valticos issued a joint dissenting opinion in which they expressed the view that:

In our opinion, the facts of the case disclose no violation of the applicant's fundamental rights.

The circumstances in which, after two previous divorces, the third marriage of the person concerned was dissolved were such that the Lausanne Civil Court was entitled to impose on him, when it granted the third divorce, the waiting period of three years provided for in Article 150 of the Swiss Civil Code.

The restriction thus placed on the exercise by the applicant of his right to marry and found a family did not affect the substance of that right. It was merely temporary. It was neither arbitrary nor unreasonable. It was based on legitimate reasons and could be considered to be commensurate with their gravity. It did not go beyond the powers of the competent national authorities.

Those authorities—both the judiciary and the legislature—were entitled to consider, in the exercise of their discretion in the matter, that the restriction in question was justified in order to protect not only the institution of marriage but also the future spouses of a person who, as the Swiss courts had established, had grossly violated fundamental conjugal rights.

With regard to marriage, the State has more extensive powers than in some other fields. This is particularly apparent when one compares the very brief and non-exhaustive reference to 'national laws' in Article 12 (art 12) of the Convention with the more circumscribed and restrictive wording of the second paragraph of each of Articles 8, 9, 10 and 11 (art 8-2, art 9-2, art 10-2, art 11-2).

In this context, such doubts as may be felt as to whether a certain legal rule is appropriate or opportune or should be applied in a given case do not suffice to found a breach of the right secured by Article 12 (art 12) of the Convention. In order for it to be concluded that there has been a breach of this right, it must be shown that the State has impaired the essence of the right or that it has restricted the exercise thereof in an arbitrary or unreasonable manner. That has not been shown in this case.

The dissentients emphasised the wide discretion accorded to States, by the distinct language of Article 12, to regulate the institution marriage in their own domestic legal and social environments. We have already seen in previous chapters how the common language of the second paragraphs to Articles 8–11 has been interpreted much more restrictively by the Court. Key elements in the Court's judgment were the application of a proportionality test to evaluate whether specific restrictions on a person's right to marry were compatible with the right enshrined in Article 12 and the recognition that where national law allows divorce Article 12 guarantees divorced persons the right to remarry, subject to reasonable restrictions.

3 A unanimous Grand Chamber of the full-time Court found a violation of the right to marry of a post-operative transsexual in *Christine Goodwin v United Kingdom*, judgment of 11 July 2002 (see above p 572).

97. The Court recalls that in the cases of *Rees* [v UK A.106 (1986)], *Cossey* [v UK A.184 (1990)] and *Sheffield and Horsham* [v UK 1998-V] the inability of the transsexuals in those cases to marry a person of the sex opposite to their re-assigned gender was not found in breach of Article 12 of the Convention. These findings were based variously on the reasoning that the right to marry referred to traditional marriage between persons of opposite biological sex (the *Rees* judgment, p 19, § 49), the view that continued adoption of biological criteria in domestic law for determining a person's sex for the purpose of marriage was encompassed within the power of Contracting States to regulate by national law the exercise of the right to marry and the conclusion that national laws in that respect could not be regarded as restricting or reducing the right of a transsexual to marry in such a way or to such an extent that the very essence of the right was impaired (the *Cossey* judgment, p 18, §§ 44–6, the *Sheffield and Horsham* judgment, p 2030, §§ 66–7). Reference was also made to the wording of Article 12 as protecting marriage as the basis of the family (*Rees*, loc cit).

98. Reviewing the situation in 2002, the Court observes that Article 12 secures the fundamental right of a man and woman to marry and to found a family. The second aspect is not however a condition of the first and the inability of any couple to conceive or parent a child cannot be regarded as *per se* removing their right to enjoy the first limb of this provision.

99. The exercise of the right to marry gives rise to social, personal and legal consequences. It is subject to the national laws of the Contracting States but the limitations thereby introduced must not restrict or reduce the right in such a way or to such an extent that the very essence of the right is impaired (see the *Rees* judgment, p 19, § 50; the *F. v Switzerland* judgment of 18 December 1987, Series A No 128, § 32).

100. It is true that the first sentence refers in express terms to the right of a man and woman to marry. The Court is not persuaded that at the date of this case it can still be assumed that these terms must refer to a determination of gender by purely biological criteria (as held by Ormrod J. in the case of *Corbett v Corbett* [1971] PR 83). There have been major social changes in the institution of marriage since the adoption of the Convention as well as dramatic changes brought about by developments in medicine and science in the field of transsexuality. The Court has found above, under Article 8 of the Convention, that a test of congruent biological factors can no longer be decisive in denying legal recognition to the change of gender of a post-operative transsexual. There are other important factors—the acceptance of the condition of gender identity disorder by the medical professions and health authorities within Contracting States, the provision of treatment including surgery to assimilate the individual as closely as possible to the gender in which they perceive that they properly belong and the assumption by the transsexual of the social role of the assigned gender. The Court would also note that Article 9 of the recently adopted Charter of Fundamental Rights of the European Union departs, no doubt deliberately, from the wording of Article 12 of the Convention in removing the reference to men and women.

101. The right under Article 8 to respect for private life does not however subsume all the issues under Article 12, where conditions imposed by national laws are accorded a specific mention. The Court has therefore considered whether the allocation of sex in national law to that registered at birth is a limitation impairing the very essence of the right to marry in this case. In that regard, it finds that it is artificial to assert that post-operative transsexuals have not been deprived of the right to marry as, according to law, they remain able to marry a person of their former opposite sex. The applicant in this case lives as a woman, is in a relationship with a man and would only wish to marry a man. She has no possibility of doing so. In the Court's view, she may therefore claim that the very essence of her right to marry has been infringed.

102. The Court has not identified any other reason which would prevent it from reaching this conclusion. The Government have argued that in this sensitive area eligibility for marriage under national law should be left to the domestic courts within the State's margin of appreciation, adverting to the potential impact on already existing marriages in which a transsexual is a partner. It appears however from the opinions of the majority of the Court of Appeal judgment in *Bellinger v Bellinger* ([2001] 3 FCR 1) that the domestic courts tend to the view that the matter is best handled by the legislature, while the Government have no present intention to introduce legislation.

103. It may be noted from the materials submitted by Liberty that though there is widespread acceptance of the marriage of transsexuals, fewer countries permit the marriage of transsexuals in their assigned gender than recognise the change of gender itself. The Court is not persuaded however that this supports an argument for leaving the matter entirely to the Contracting States as being within their margin of appreciation. This would be tantamount to finding that the range of options open to a Contracting State included an effective bar on any exercise of the right to marry. The margin of appreciation cannot extend so far. While it is for the Contracting State to determine *inter alia* the conditions under which a person claiming legal recognition as a transsexual establishes that gender re-assignment has been properly effected or under which past marriages cease to be valid and the formalities applicable to future marriages (including, for example, the information to be furnished to intended spouses), the Court finds no justification for barring the transsexual from enjoying the right to marry under any circumstances.

104. The Court concludes that there has been a breach of Article 12 of the Convention in the present case.

The above judgment accords States much less freedom to restrict the right to marry of transsexuals than the previous rulings of the original Court. Article 9 of the Charter of Fundamental Rights of the European Union, signed on 7 December 2000, referred to in paragraph 100 above, stipulates: 'The right to marry and the right to found a family shall be guaranteed in accordance with the national laws governing the exercise of these rights.'

4 The Court refused to interpret Article 12 as embodying a right to divorce in *Johnston v Ireland*, A.112 (1986) 9 EHRR 203. The background to this case has already been explained (above, p 524).

51. In order to determine whether the applicants can derive a right to divorce from Article 12 (art 12), the Court will seek to ascertain the ordinary meaning to be given to the terms of this provision in their context and in the light of its object and purpose (see the *Golder* judgment of 21 February 1975, Series A No 18, p 14, § 29, and Article 31 § 1 of the Vienna Convention of 23 May 1969 on the Law of Treaties).

52. The Court agrees with the Commission that the ordinary meaning of the words 'right to marry' is clear, in the sense that they cover the formation of marital relationships but not their dissolution. Furthermore, these words are found in a context that includes an express reference to 'national laws'; even if, as the applicants would have it, the prohibition on divorce is to be seen as a restriction on

capacity to marry, the Court does not consider that, in a society adhering to the principle of mono-gamy, such a restriction can be regarded as injuring the substance of the right guaranteed by Article 12 (art 12).

Moreover, the foregoing interpretation of Article 12 (art 12) is consistent with its object and purpose as revealed by the travaux préparatoires. The text of Article 12 (art 12) was based on that of Article 16 of the Universal Declaration of Human Rights, paragraph 1 of which reads:

> 'Men and women of full age, without any limitation due to race, nationality or religion, have the right to marry and to found a family. They are entitled to equal rights as to marriage, during marriage and at its dissolution.'

In explaining to the Consultative Assembly why the draft of the future Article 12 (art 12) did not include the words found in the last sentence of the above-cited paragraph, Mr Teitgen, Rapporteur of the Committee on Legal and Administrative Questions, said:

> 'In mentioning the particular Article of the Universal Declaration, we have used only that part of the paragraph of the Article which affirms the right to marry and to found a family, but not the subse-quent provisions of the Article concerning equal rights after marriage, since we only guarantee the right to marry.' (Collected Edition of the Travaux préparatoires, vol 1, p 268)

In the Court's view, the travaux préparatoires disclose no intention to include in Article 12 (art 12) any guarantee of a right to have the ties of marriage dissolved by divorce.

53. The applicants set considerable store on the social developments that have occurred since the Convention was drafted, notably an alleged substantial increase in marriage breakdown.

It is true that the Convention and its Protocols must be interpreted in the light of present-day con-ditions (see, among several authorities, the above-mentioned *Marckx* judgment, Series A No 31, p 26, § 58). However, the Court cannot, by means of an evolutive interpretation, derive from these instru-ments a right that was not included therein at the outset. This is particularly so here, where the omis-sion was deliberate. . . .

54. The Court thus concludes that the applicants cannot derive a right to divorce from Article 12 (art 12).

The Court's reasoning is also of general significance as it reveals (in paragraph 53) some of the limitations on the Court's dynamic approach to the interpretation of Convention rights.

5 The applicants in *X and Y v Switzerland*, 13 DR 241 (1978), were a married couple who had been held separately on remand in the same prison. The authorities refused to allow the appli-cants to have sexual relations while in prison. The applicants alleged a violation of Articles 8 and 12. The Commission dismissed their application as manifestly ill-founded. In respect of Article 8 the Commission stated that:

> . . . it is generally considered to be justified for the prevention of disorder in prison not to allow sexual relations of married couples in prison. The Commission accepts that in fact the security and good order in prison would be seriously endangered if all married prisoners were allowed to keep up their conjugal life in prison. In this case the respect for privacy would require that the prison authorities renounce their right of constant supervision. Uncontrolled visits or contacts could, inter alia, facilitate the exchange of secret messages, the smuggling in of goods such as drugs or even arms. Especially with regard to prisoners on remand, who may be detained if there is danger that they might abscond and/or destroy evidence if they were released, the purpose of their detention requires strict supervision of their contacts with visitors or co-accused. (p 243)

Therefore, the prohibition on the applicant's sexual relations fell within Article 8(2). The Commission went on to rule that, 'an interference with family life which is justified under Article 8(2) cannot at the same time constitute a violation of Article 12' (p 244).

A similar approach was adopted by a unanimous Chamber in *Aliev v Ukraine*, Judgment of 29 April 2003. The Chamber held that:

188. Whilst noting with approval the reform movements in several European countries to improve prison conditions by facilitating conjugal visits, the Court considers that the refusal of such visits may for the present time be regarded as justified for the prevention of disorder and crime within the meaning of the second paragraph of Article 8 of the Convention . . .

The reference to 'for the present time' suggests that this is an issue which the Court may be willing to revisit in the future. Regarding the authorities prevention of a prisoner conceiving a child with his wife via artificial insemination see *Dickson v UK*, judgment of 18 April 2006, above p 518.

6 Prisoners have been more successful in challenging the authorities' refusals to allow them to marry. For example, in *Hamer v UK*, 24 DR 5 (1979), the applicant was a prisoner serving a sentence of five years' imprisonment for property offences. Soon after he began his sentence the applicant applied for permission (from the Governor of his prison and then from the Home Secretary) to marry his girlfriend (whom he had been living with for about ten weeks prior to his arrest). Under the Marriage Act 1949, marriages could only take place in designated buildings (such as parish churches). The Home Secretary refused the applicant's request stating that it was official policy only to allow prisoners temporary release to attend weddings, in designated buildings, where there was a child to legitimate. The applicant complained of a breach of Article 12. The Commission was unanimous in its Opinion that there had been a violation of that Article. It distinguished the applicant's case from those (like *X and Y v Switzerland*, above note 5) where prisoners had been denied conjugal relations with their spouses in prisons:

58. . . . different considerations apply in the case of the right to marry. This is, essentially, a right to form a legal relationship, to acquire a status. Its exercise by prisoners involves no general threat to prison security or good order . . . In particular a marriage ceremony can take place under the supervision of the prison authorities.

72. In the Commission's opinion the imposition by the State of any substantial period of delay on the exercise of this right must in general be seen as an injury to its substance. . . . Further, no general consideration of public interest arising from the fact of imprisonment itself can justify such interference in the case of a prisoner. As the Commission has already pointed out, no particular difficulties are involved in allowing the marriage of prisoners. In addition there is no evidence before the Commission to suggest that, as a general proposition, it is in any way harmful to the public interest to allow the marriage of prisoners. Marriage may, on the contrary, be a stabilising and rehabilitative influence.

The Committee of Minister's agreed with the Commission's Opinion and found a breach of the applicant's right to marry (Resolution DH(81)5).

A similar breach of Article 12 was found in respect of the British authorities' refusal to allow a prisoner serving a life sentence, for murder committed during a robbery, to marry: *Draper v UK*, 24 DR 73 (1980). The Government sought to argue that as the applicant had no prospect of an early release and he could not live with his intended wife before release, there had been no unlawful interference with his right to marry. This argument was rejected because:

60. . . . the Commission does not regard it as relevant that the applicant could not cohabit with his wife or consummate his marriage while serving his sentence. The essence of the right to marry, in the Commission's opinion, is the formation of a legally binding association between a man and a woman. It is for them to decide whether or not they wish to enter such an association in circumstances where they cannot cohabit.

62. .... It is conceivable that in cases involving certain types of offence, [such as murder of a spouse] a restriction on the right to marry could be justified on the basis of considerations of public interest, regardless of the type or length of sentence imposed on the perpetrator. However in the Commission's opinion a general restriction on all life sentence prisoners cannot be so justified ...

The Committee of Ministers also found a violation of Article 12 (Resolution DH(81)4). The Government responded to these adverse decisions by securing the passage of the Marriage Act 1983, which, *inter alia*, authorised marriage ceremonies to take place inside prisons.

7   The general legislative ban on a father-in-law marrying his daughter-in-law was found to violate Article 12 by a unanimous Chamber in *B. and L. v United Kingdom*, judgment of 13 September 2005. B.'s marriage to A. ended in divorce in 1987. They had a son C. L. married C. and they had a son W. B. and L. developed a relationship in 1995 (after C. had left the matrimonial home). B. and L. have been cohabiting since 1996. L. and C. divorced in 1997. W. lives with B. and L. and calls the former 'Dad'. In 2002 B. enquired as to whether he and L. Could marry. The local Superintendent Registrar of Deaths and marriages informed B. that, under the Marriage Act 1946 as amended, B. and L. could only marry if A. and C. were deceased. The applicants complained to the Court alleging a breach of Article 12. In response the Government submitted that, *inter alia*, the ban on B. and L. marrying was not absolute as they could marry if their former spouses were dead or by obtaining permission through a personal Act of Parliament. Furthermore, the Government observed that twenty-one Member states imposed an absolute or conditional ban on such marriages and the national authorities were in the best position to determine whether such marriages should be permitted.

37. The Court must however examine the facts of the case in the context pertaining in the United Kingdom. It observes that this bar on marriage is aimed at protecting the integrity of the family (preventing sexual rivalry between parents and children) and preventing harm to children who may be affected by the changing relationships of the adults around them. These are, without doubt, legitimate aims.

38. Nonetheless, the bar on marriage does not prevent the relationships occurring. This case shows that. There are no incest, or other criminal law, provisions to prevent extra-marital relationships between parents-in-law and children-in-law being established notwithstanding that children may live in these homes. It cannot therefore be said that in the present case the ban on the applicants' marriage prevents any alleged confusion or emotional insecurity to the second applicant's son.

39. As regards the need to protect the family from deleterious influences, the Court notes that the majority of the Group in the House of Lords reporting on the possible amendments to the law had taken the view that the bar should be lifted as it was based on tradition and no justification had been shown to exist. That the view of the minority, who considered that the bar remained necessary to prevent unhealthy internal family dynamics, prevailed shows that opinions in this area are divided. Further, the significance that the Court would otherwise attach to the legislature's consideration of the matter is outweighed by one important factor.

40. Under United Kingdom law the bar on a marriage of this degree of affinity is not subject to an absolute prohibition. Marriages can take place, pursuant to a personal Act of Parliament. From the information before the Court, it transpires that individuals in a similar situation to these applicants have been permitted to marry: in the *Monk* case [*Valerie Mary Hill and Alan Monk (Marriage Enabling) Act 1985*, a personal Act permitting the marriage of a mother-in-law and her son-in-law], where there were also children in the household, it was declared that the impediment placed on the marriage served no useful purpose of public policy. The inconsistency between the stated aims of the incapacity and the waiver applied in some cases undermines the rationality and logic of the measure. The Government

have argued that the general rule remains valid as the Parliamentary procedure provides a means of ensuring that exceptions are only made where no harm will ensue. The Court would only comment that there is no indication of any detailed investigation into family circumstances in the Parliamentary procedure and that in any event a cumbersome and expensive vetting process of this kind would not appear to offer a practically accessible or effective mechanism for individuals to vindicate their rights. It would also view with reservation a system that would require a person of full age in possession of his or her mental faculties to submit to a potentially intrusive investigation to ascertain whether it is suitable for them to marry (see, *mutatis mutandis, F. v Switzerland,* §§ 35–7).

41. The Court concludes that there has been, in the circumstances of this case, a violation of Article 12 of the Convention.

So, the key to the Chamber's unwillingness to defer to the national legislature's view of permissible marital relationships was that exceptions could be secured by an expensive *ad hoc* personal Act procedure.

15 ARTICLE 13   RIGHT TO AN EFFECTIVE REMEDY

Silver v UK A.61 (1983) 5 EHRR 347
European Court of Human Rights

The background to this case has already been outlined (above, p 586).

B. ARTICLE 13 TAKEN IN CONJUNCTION WITH ARTICLE 8 (ART 13+8)

111. . . . The Commission, having examined various possible channels of complaint, came to the conclusion that there was no effective domestic remedy and, hence, a violation of Article 13 (art 13). The Government requested the Court to hold that the facts of the case disclosed no breach of that provision or, alternatively, that they would disclose no such breach after the coming into effect of the revised Orders [regulating correspondence to and from prisoners].

I12. Having held that the scope of the present case does not extend to the correspondence control system in force since December 1981 . . . the Court is unable to examine the Government's alternative plea.

113. The principles that emerge from the Court's jurisprudence on the interpretation of Article 13 (art 13) include the following:

(a)   where an individual has an arguable claim to be the victim of a violation of the rights set forth in the Convention, he should have a remedy before a national authority in order both to have his claim decided and, if appropriate, to obtain redress (see the above-mentioned *Klass* judgment, Series A No 28, p 29, § 64);

(b)   the authority referred to in Article 13 (art 13) may not necessarily be a judicial authority but, if it is not, its powers and the guarantees which it affords are relevant in determining whether the remedy before it is effective (ibid, p 30, § 67);

(c)   although no single remedy may itself entirely satisfy the requirements of Article 13 (art 13), the aggregate of remedies provided for under domestic law may do so (see, mutatis mutandis, the above-mentioned *X v UK* judgment, Series A No 46, p 26, § 60, and the *Van Droogenbroeck* judgment of 24 June 1982, Series A No 50, p 32, § 56);

(d)   neither Article 13 (art 13) nor the Convention in general lays down for the Contracting States any given manner for ensuring within their internal law the effective implementation of any of the provisions of the Convention—for example, by incorporating the Convention into domestic law (see the *Swedish Engine Drivers' Union* judgment of 6 February 1976, Series A No 20, p 18, § 50).

It follows from the last-mentioned principle that the application of Article 13 (art 13) in a given case will depend upon the manner in which the Contracting State concerned has chosen to discharge its obligation under Article 1 (art 1) directly to secure to anyone within its jurisdiction the rights and freedoms set out in section I (see the above-mentioned *Ireland v UK* judgment, Series A No 25, p 91, § 239).

114. In the present case, it was not suggested that any remedies were available to the applicants other than the four channels of complaint examined by the Commission, namely an application to the Board of Visitors, an application to the Parliamentary Commissioner for Administration [the Parliamentary Ombudsman], a petition to the Home Secretary and the institution of proceedings before the English courts.

115. As regards the first two channels, the Court, like the Commission, considers that they do not constitute an 'effective remedy' for the present purposes.

The Board of Visitors cannot enforce its conclusions...nor can it entertain applications from individuals like Mrs. Colne who are not in prison.

As regards the Parliamentary Commissioner, it suffices to note that he has himself no power to render a binding decision granting redress...

116. As for the Home Secretary, if there were a complaint to him as to the validity of an Order or Instruction under which a measure of control over correspondence had been carried out, he could not be considered to have a sufficiently independent standpoint to satisfy the requirements of Article 13 (art 13) (see, mutatis mutandis, the above-mentioned *Klass* judgment, Series A No 28, p 26, § 56): as the author of the directives in question, he would in reality be judge in his own cause. The position, however, would be otherwise if the complainant alleged that a measure of control resulted from a mis-application of one of those directives. The Court is satisfied that in such cases a petition to the Home Secretary would in general be effective to secure compliance with the directive, if the complaint was well-founded. The Court notes, however, that even in these cases, at least prior to 1 December 1981, the conditions for the submission of such petitions imposed limitations on the availability of this remedy in some circumstances...

117. The English courts, for their part, are endowed with a certain supervisory jurisdiction over the exercise of the powers conferred on the Home Secretary and the prison authorities by the Prison Act and the Rules...However, their jurisdiction is limited to determining whether or not those powers have been exercised arbitrarily, in bad faith, for an improper motive or in an ultra vires manner.

In this connection, the applicants stressed that the Convention, not being incorporated into domestic law, could not be directly invoked before the English courts; however, they acknowledged that it was relevant for the interpretation of ambiguous legislation, according to the presumption of the latter's conformity with the treaty obligations of the UK.

118. The applicants made no allegation that the interferences with their correspondence were contrary to English law...Like the Commission, the Court has found that the majority of the measures complained of in the present proceedings were incompatible with the Convention...In most of the cases, the Government did not contest the Commission's findings. Neither did they maintain that the English courts could have found the measures to have been taken arbitrarily, in bad faith, for an improper motive or in an ultra vires manner.

In the Court's view, to the extent that the applicable norms, whether contained in the Rules or in the relevant Orders or Instructions, were incompatible with the Convention there could be no effective remedy as required by Article 13 (art 13) and consequently there has been a violation of that Article (art 13).

To the extent, however, that the said norms were compatible with Article 8 (art 8), the aggregate of the remedies available satisfied the requirements of Article 13 (art 13), at least in those cases in which it was possible for a petition to be submitted to the Home Secretary...a petition to the Home Secretary was available to secure compliance with the directives issued by him and, as regards compliance with the Rules, the English courts had the supervisory jurisdiction described in paragraph 117 above.

119. To sum up, in those instances where the norms in question were incompatible with the Convention and where the Court has found a violation of Article 8 (art 8) to have occurred there was no effective remedy and Article 13 (art 13) has therefore also been violated. In the remaining cases, there is no reason to assume that the applicants' complaints could not have been duly examined by the Home Secretary and/or the English courts and Article 13 (art 13) has therefore not been violated...

FOR THESE REASONS, THE COURT UNANIMOUSLY

. . .

Holds that there has been a violation of Article 13 to the extent specified in paragraph 119 of the judgment;

. . .

NOTES

1   The Court was composed of President Wiarda and Judges: Thor Vilhjalmsson, Gölcüklü, Matscher, Pettiti, Evans, and Russo.

2   Even where the Court has found no breach of a substantive Convention right applicants may be able to establish that they had/have an 'arguable claim' of a violation which necessitated States providing them with an 'effective remedy' that satisfied the requirements of Article 13. For example, in *Leander v Sweden*, A.116 (1987) 9 EHRR 433, as we have already noted (above, p 501) the respondent State had been able to justify, under Article 8(2), the secret files kept on the applicant. However, the Court went on to consider if there had been a breach of Article 13.

78. . . . For the purposes of the present proceedings, an 'effective remedy' under Article 13 (art 13) must mean a remedy that is as effective as can be having regard to the restricted scope for recourse inherent in any system of secret checks on candidates for employment in posts of importance from a national security point of view. It therefore remains to examine the various remedies available to the applicant under Swedish law in order to see whether they were 'effective' in this limited sense (ibid, p 31, § 69).

79. There can be no doubt that the applicant's complaints have raised arguable claims under the Convention at least in so far as Article 8 (art 8) is concerned and that, accordingly, he was entitled to an effective remedy in order to enforce his rights under that Article as they were protected under Swedish law . . .

The Court has found the Swedish personnel control system as such to be compatible with Article 8 (art 8). In such a situation, the requirements of Article 13 (art 13) will be satisfied if there exists domestic machinery whereby, subject to the inherent limitations of the context, the individual can secure compliance with the relevant laws . . .

80. The Government argued that Swedish law offered sufficient remedies for the purposes of Article 13 (art 13), namely
  (i)   a formal application for the post, and, if unsuccessful, an appeal to the Government;
  (ii)   a request to the National Police Board for access to the secret police-register on the basis of the Freedom of the Press Act, and, if refused, an appeal to the administrative courts;
  (iii) a complaint to the Chancellor of Justice [an office established under the constitution responsible for supervising public authorities];
  (iv)   a complaint to the Parliamentary Ombudsman.

The majority of the Commission found that these four remedies, taken in the aggregate, met the requirements of Article 13 (art 13), although none of them did so taken alone.

81. The Court notes first that both the Chancellor of Justice and the Parliamentary Ombudsman have the competence to receive individual complaints and that they have the duty to investigate such complaints in order to ensure that the relevant laws have been properly applied by the National Police Board . . . In the performance of these duties, both officials have access to all the information contained in the secret police-register . . . Several decisions from the Parliamentary Ombudsman evidence that these powers are also used in relation to complaints regarding the operation of the personnel control

system . . . Furthermore, both officials must, in the present context, be considered independent of the Government. This is quite clear in respect of the Parliamentary Ombudsman. As far as the Chancellor of Justice is concerned, he may likewise be regarded as being, at least in practice, independent of the Government when performing his supervisory functions in relation to the working of the personnel control system . . .

82. The main weakness in the control afforded by the Ombudsman and the Chancellor of Justice is that both officials, apart from their competence to institute criminal and disciplinary proceedings . . . lack the power to render a legally binding decision. On this point, the Court, however, recalls the necessarily limited effectiveness that can be required of any remedy available to the individual concerned in a system of secret security checks. The opinions of the Parliamentary Ombudsman and the Chancellor of Justice command by tradition great respect in Swedish society and in practice are usually followed . . . It is also material—although this does not constitute a remedy that the individual can exercise of his own accord—that a special feature of the Swedish personnel control system is the substantial parliamentary supervision to which it is subject, in particular through the parliamentarians on the National Police Board who consider each case where release of information is requested . . .

83. To these remedies, which were never exercised by Mr Leander, must be added the remedy to which he actually had recourse when he complained, in a letter of 5 February 1980 to the Government, that the National Police Board, contrary to the provisions of section 13 of the Personnel Control Ordinance, had omitted to invite him to comment, in writing or orally, on the information contained in the register . . . The Government requested the opinion of the Board in this connection; whereupon Mr Leander was given the opportunity to reply, which he did in a letter of 11 March 1980. In its decision of 14 May 1980, which covered also Mr Leander's complaints of 22 October and 4 December 1979, the Government, that is the entire Cabinet, dismissed Mr Leander's various complaints . . .

The Court recalls that the authority referred to in Article 13 (art 13) need not necessarily be a judicial authority in the strict sense, but that the powers and procedural guarantees an authority possesses are relevant in determining whether the remedy is effective. There can be no question about the power of the Government to deliver a decision binding on the Board . . .

84. It should also be borne in mind that for the purposes of the present proceedings, an effective remedy under Article 13 (art 13) must mean a remedy that is as effective as can be, having regard to the restricted scope for recourse inherent in any system of secret surveillance for the protection of national security (see paragraphs 78–9 above).

Even if, taken on its own, the complaint to the Government were not considered sufficient to ensure compliance with Article 13 (art 13), the Court finds that the aggregate of the remedies set out above (see paragraphs 81–3) satisfies the conditions of Article 13 (art 13) in the particular circumstances of the instant case (see, *mutatis mutandis*, the above-mentioned *Klass* judgment, Series A No 28, p 32, § 72).

Accordingly, the Court concludes that there was no violation of Article 13 (art 13).

Three judges dissented as they did not consider that Sweden had provided the applicant with an effective remedy, the dissenters were particularly concerned that neither the Chancellor of Justice or the Parliamentary Ombudsman issued legally binding decisions. In subsequent cases, see Note 3 below, the Court has become more rigorous in assessing whether domestic remedies applying to decisions involving issues of national security met the demands of Article 13.

3   A number of cases have involved the question whether the process of judicial review in English law amounts to an 'effective remedy' for the purposes of Article 13. In *Soering v UK* (see above, p 192), the Court was unanimous in concluding that it did.

116. . . . In [the applicant's] submission, he had no effective remedy in the United Kingdom in respect of his complaint under Article 3 (art 3). The majority of the Commission arrived at the same conclusion.

The United Kingdom Government however disagreed, arguing that Article 13 (art 13) had no application in the circumstances of the present case or, in the alternative, that the aggregate of remedies provided for under domestic law was adequate.

117. In view of the Court's finding regarding Article 3 (art 3) ... the applicant's claim under that Article (art 3) cannot be regarded either as incompatible with the provisions of the Convention or as not 'arguable' on its merits ...

118. The United Kingdom Government relied on the aggregate of remedies provided by the Magistrates' Court proceedings, an application for habeas corpus and an application for judicial review ...

119. The Court will commence its examination with judicial review proceedings since they constitute the principal means for challenging a decision to extradite once it has been taken.

Both the applicant and the Commission were of the opinion that the scope of judicial review was too narrow to allow the courts to consider the subject matter of the complaint which the applicant has made in the context of Article 3 (art 3). The applicant further contended that the courts' lack of jurisdiction to issue interim injunctions against the Crown was an additional reason rendering judicial review an ineffective remedy.

120. Article 13 (art 13) guarantees the availability of a remedy at national level to enforce the substance of the Convention rights and freedoms in whatever form they may happen to be secured in the domestic legal order ... The effect of Article 13 (art 13) is thus to require the provision of a domestic remedy allowing the competent 'national authority' both to deal with the substance of the relevant Convention complaint and to grant appropriate relief (see, inter alia, the *Silver* judgment of 25 March 1983, Series A No 61, p 42, § 113 (a)).

121. In judicial review proceedings the court may rule the exercise of executive discretion unlawful on the ground that it is tainted with illegality, irrationality or procedural impropriety ... In an extradition case the test of 'irrationality', on the basis of the so-called '*Wednesbury* principles', would be that no reasonable Secretary of State could have made an order for surrender in the circumstances (ibid). According to the United Kingdom Government, a court would have jurisdiction to quash a challenged decision to send a fugitive to a country where it was established that there was a serious risk of inhuman or degrading treatment, on the ground that in all the circumstances of the case the decision was one that no reasonable Secretary of State could take. Although the Convention is not considered to be part of United Kingdom law (ibid), the Court is satisfied that the English courts can review the 'reasonableness' of an extradition decision in the light of the kind of factors relied on by Mr Soering before the Convention institutions in the context of Article 3 (art 3).

122. Mr Soering did admittedly make an application for judicial review together with his application for habeas corpus and was met with an unfavourable response from Lord Justice Lloyd on the issue of 'irrationality' ... However, as Lord Justice Lloyd explained, the claim failed because it was premature, the courts only having jurisdiction once the Minister has actually taken his decision (ibid). Furthermore, the arguments adduced by Mr Soering were by no means the same as those relied on when justifying his complaint under Article 3 (art 3) before the Convention institutions. His counsel before the Divisional Court limited himself to submitting that the assurance by the United States authorities was so worthless that no reasonable Secretary of State could regard it as satisfactory under the Treaty. This is an argument going to the likelihood of the death penalty being imposed but says nothing about the quality of the treatment awaiting Mr Soering after sentence to death, this being the substance of his allegation of inhuman and degrading treatment.

There was nothing to have stopped Mr Soering bringing an application for judicial review at the appropriate moment and arguing '*Wednesbury* unreasonableness' on the basis of much the same material that he adduced before the Convention institutions in relation to the 'death row phenomenon'. Such a claim would have been given 'the most anxious scrutiny' in view of the fundamental nature of the human right at stake … The effectiveness of the remedy, for the purposes of Article 13 (art 13), does not depend on the certainty of a favourable outcome for Mr Soering (see the *Swedish Engine Drivers' Union* judgment of 6 February 1976, Series A No 20, p 18, § 50), and in any event it is not for this Court to speculate as to what would have been the decision of the English courts.

123. The English courts' lack of jurisdiction to grant interim injunctions against the Crown … does not, in the Court's opinion, detract from the effectiveness of judicial review in the present connection, since there is no suggestion that in practice a fugitive would ever be surrendered before his application to the Divisional Court and any eventual appeal therefrom had been determined.

124. The Court concludes that Mr Soering did have available to him under English law an effective remedy in relation to his complaint under Article 3 (art 3). This being so, there is no need to inquire into the other two remedies referred to by the United Kingdom Government.

There is accordingly no breach of Article 13 (art 13).

The ability of domestic courts to grant injunctions (including interim ones) against the Crown, when applying English law, was greatly extended by the House of Lords' landmark ruling in *M v Home Office* [1993] 3 All ER 537.

However, in the later case of *Chahal v UK* (see above, p 203) the Court was united in finding a breach of Article 13.

141. The applicants maintained that the only remedy available to them in respect of their claims under Articles 3, 5 and 8 of the Convention (art 3, art 5, art 8) was judicial review, the advisory panel procedure … being neither a 'remedy' nor 'effective'.

They submitted, first, that the powers of the English courts to put aside an executive decision were inadequate in all Article 3 (art 3) asylum cases, since the courts could not scrutinise the facts to determine whether substantial grounds had been shown for belief in the existence of a real risk of ill-treatment in the receiving State, but could only determine whether the Secretary of State's decision as to the existence of such a risk was reasonable according to the '*Wednesbury*' principles …

This contention had particular weight in cases where the executive relied upon arguments of national security. In the instant case, the assertion that Mr Chahal's deportation was necessary in the interests of national security entailed that there could be no effective judicial evaluation of the risk to him of ill-treatment in India or of the issues under Article 8 (art 8). That assertion likewise prevented any effective judicial control on the question whether the applicant's continued detention was justified.

142. The Government accepted that the scope of judicial review was more limited where deportation was ordered on national security grounds. However, the Court had held in the past that, where questions of national security were in issue, an 'effective remedy' under Article 13 (art 13) must mean 'a remedy that is effective as can be', given the necessity of relying upon secret sources of information (see the *Klass v Germany* judgment of 6 September 1978, Series A No 28, p 31, para 69, and the *Leander v Sweden* judgment of 26 March 1987, Series A No 116, p 32, para 84).

Furthermore, it had to be borne in mind that all the relevant material, including the sensitive material, was examined by the advisory panel whose members included two senior judicial figures—a Court of Appeal judge and a former president of the Immigration Appeal Tribunal … The procedure before the panel was designed, on the one hand, to satisfy the need for an independent review of the totality of the material on which the perceived threat to national security was based and, on the other hand, to ensure that secret information would not be publicly disclosed. It thus provided a form of independent, quasi-judicial scrutiny.

143. For the Commission, the present case could be distinguished from that of *Vilvarajah* [A.215 (1991)] … where the Court held that judicial review in the English courts amounted to an effective remedy in respect of the applicants' Article 3 (art 3) claims. Because the Secretary of State invoked national security considerations as grounds for his decisions to deport Mr Chahal and to detain him pending

deportation, the English courts' powers of review were limited. They could not themselves consider the evidence on which the Secretary of State had based his decision that the applicant constituted a danger to national security or undertake any evaluation of the Article 3 (art 3) risks. Instead, they had to confine themselves to examining whether the evidence showed that the Secretary of State had carried out the balancing exercise required by the domestic law . . .

144. The intervenors [including Amnesty International and Liberty] were all of the view that judicial review did not constitute an effective remedy in cases involving national security. Article 13 (art 13) required at least that some independent body should be appraised of all the facts and evidence and entitled to reach a decision which would be binding on the Secretary of State. . . .

145. The Court observes that Article 13 (art 13) guarantees the availability at national level of a remedy to enforce the substance of the Convention rights and freedoms in whatever form they might happen to be secured in the domestic legal order. The effect of this Article (art 13) is thus to require the provision of a domestic remedy allowing the competent national authority both to deal with the substance of the relevant Convention complaint and to grant appropriate relief, although Contracting States are afforded some discretion as to the manner in which they conform to their obligations under this provision (art 13) (see the *Vilvarajah* judgment cited at paragraph 73 above, p 39, para 122).

Moreover, it is recalled that in certain circumstances the aggregate of remedies provided by national law may satisfy the requirements of Article 13 (art 13) (see, inter alia, the above-mentioned *Leander* judgment, p 30, para 77).

146. The Court does not have to examine the allegation of a breach of Article 13 taken in conjunction with Article 5 para 1 (art 13+5-1), in view of its finding of a violation of Article 5 para 4 (art 5-4) . . . Nor is it necessary for it to examine the complaint under Article 13 in conjunction with Article 8 (art 13+8), in view of its finding concerning the hypothetical nature of the complaint under the latter provision (art 8) . . .

147. This leaves only the first applicant's claim under Article 3 combined with Article 13 (art 13+3). It was not disputed that the Article 3 (art 3) complaint was arguable on the merits and the Court accordingly finds that Article 13 (art 13) is applicable (see the above-mentioned *Vilvarajah* judgment, p 38, para 121).

148. The Court recalls that in its *Vilvarajah* judgment (ibid, p 39, paras 122–6), it found judicial review proceedings to be an effective remedy in relation to the applicants' complaints under Article 3 (art 3). It was satisfied that the English courts could review a decision by the Secretary of State to refuse asylum and could rule it unlawful on the grounds that it was tainted with illegality irrationality or procedural impropriety . . . In particular, it was accepted that a court would have jurisdiction to quash a challenged decision to send a fugitive to a country where it was established that there was a serious risk of inhuman or degrading treatment, on the ground that in all the circumstances of the case the decision was one that no reasonable Secretary of State could take . . .

149. The Court further recalls that in assessing whether there exists a real risk of treatment in breach of Article 3 (art 3) in expulsion cases such as the present, the fact that the person is perceived as a danger to the national security of the respondent State is not a material consideration . . .

150. It is true, as the Government have pointed out, that in the cases of *Klass* and *Leander* . . . the Court held that Article 13 (art 13) only required a remedy that was 'as effective as can be' in circumstances where national security considerations did not permit the divulging of certain sensitive information. However, it must be borne in mind that these cases concerned complaints under Articles 8 and 10 of the Convention (art 8, art 10) and that their examination required the Court to have regard to the national security claims which had been advanced by the Government. The requirement of a remedy which is 'as effective as can be' is not appropriate in respect of a complaint that a person's deportation will expose him or her to a real risk of treatment in breach of Article 3 (art 3), where the issues concerning national security are immaterial.

151. In such cases, given the irreversible nature of the harm that might occur if the risk of ill-treatment materialised and the importance the Court attaches to Article 3 (art 3), the notion of an effective remedy under Article 13 (art 13) requires independent scrutiny of the claim that there exist substantial grounds for fearing a real risk of treatment contrary to Article 3 (art 3). This scrutiny must be carried out without regard to what the person may have done to warrant expulsion or to any perceived threat to the national security of the expelling State.

152. Such scrutiny need not be provided by a judicial authority but, if it is not, the powers and guarantees which it affords are relevant in determining whether the remedy before it is effective (see the above-mentioned *Leander* judgment, p 29, para 77).

153. In the present case, neither the advisory panel nor the courts could review the decision of the Home Secretary to deport Mr Chahal to India with reference solely to the question of risk, leaving aside national security considerations. On the contrary, the courts' approach was one of satisfying themselves that the Home Secretary had balanced the risk to Mr Chahal against the danger to national security . . . It follows from the above considerations that these cannot be considered effective remedies in respect of Mr Chahal's Article 3 (art 3) complaint for the purposes of Article 13 of the Convention (art 13).

154. Moreover, the Court notes that in the proceedings before the advisory panel the applicant was not entitled, inter alia, to legal representation, that he was only given an outline of the grounds for the notice of intention to deport, that the panel had no power of decision and that its advice to the Home Secretary was not binding and was not disclosed . . . In these circumstances, the advisory panel could not be considered to offer sufficient procedural safeguards for the purposes of Article 13 (art 13).

155. Having regard to the extent of the deficiencies of both the judicial review proceedings and the advisory panel, the Court cannot consider that the remedies taken together satisfy the requirements of Article 13 in conjunction with Article 3 (art 13+3).

Accordingly, there has been a violation of Article 13 (art 13).

The decisive factor in *Chahal* was the limited powers of review possessed by English courts when confronted with a Government assertion that the decision being challenged had been taken in the interests of national security. Significantly, the Court also held that its less onerous *Leander* standard of a remedy that was 'as effective as can be', having regard to national security considerations, did not apply to Article 13 cases based upon an arguable violation of Article 3 as the latter provision did not permit States to invoke issues of national security as a relevant factor. In *Smith and Grady v UK*, (see above, p 489), a unanimous Court also found a breach of Article 13 in respect of claims under Article 8.

131. The applicants submitted that Article 13 contained two minimum requirements. First, the relevant national authority had to have jurisdiction to examine the substance of an individual's complaint by reference to the Convention or other corresponding provisions of national law and, secondly, that authority had to have jurisdiction to grant remedy if it accepted that the individual's complaint was well-founded. Moreover, the precise scope of the obligations under Article 13 would depend on the nature of the individual's complaint. The context of the present case was the application of a blanket policy which interfered with the Article 8 rights of a minority group and not an assessment of an individual extradition or expulsion in the context of Article 3 as in the *Soering* and *Vilvarajah* cases . . .

132. In the applicants' view, the judicial review remedy did not meet the first of these requirements of Article 13 for two connected reasons. Since the Ministry of Defence policy was a blanket policy admitting of no exceptions, it was impossible for the domestic courts to consider the merits of the applicants' individual complaints. However, the impact of the policy on them varied from case to case. In contrast, the domestic courts could and indeed were bound to apply the 'most anxious scrutiny' to the individual facts in the above-mentioned extradition and expulsion cases of *Soering* and *Vilvarajah*. Secondly, the domestic courts could not ask themselves whether a fair balance had been struck

between the general interest and the applicants' rights. The domestic courts were confined to asking themselves whether it had been shown that the policy as a whole was irrational or perverse and the burden of proving irrationality was on the applicants. They were required to show that the policy-maker had 'taken leave of his senses' and the applicants had to show that this high threshold had been crossed before the domestic courts could intervene. Moreover, the applicants pointed to the comments of the High Court and of the Court of Appeal as the best evidence that those courts lacked jurisdiction to deal with the substance of the applicants' Convention complaints. In this context, the *Soering* and *Vilvarajah* cases cited above could be distinguished because the test applied in judicial review proceedings concerning proposed extraditions and expulsions happened to coincide with the Convention test.

133. The applicants further contended that their judicial review proceedings did not comply with the second requirement of Article 13 because the domestic courts were not able to grant a remedy even though four out of the five judges who examined the applicants' case considered that the policy was not justified.

134. Although the applicants invoked Article 13 of the Convention in relation to all of their complaints, the Court recalls that it is the applicants' right to respect for their private lives which is principally at issue in the present case...In such circumstances, it is of the view that the applicants' complaints under Article 13 of the Convention are more appropriately considered in conjunction with Article 8.

135. The Court recalls that Article 13 guarantees the availability of a remedy at national level to enforce the substance of Convention rights and freedoms in whatever form they may happen to be secured in the domestic legal order. Thus, its effect is to require the provision of a domestic remedy allowing the competent national authority both to deal with the substance of the relevant Convention complaint and to grant appropriate relief. However, Article 13 does not go so far as to require incorporation of the Convention or a particular form of remedy, Contracting States being afforded a margin of appreciation in conforming with their obligations under this provision. Nor does the effectiveness of a remedy for the purposes of Article 13 depend on the certainty of a favourable outcome for the applicant (see the *Vilvarajah* judgment...p 39, § 122).

136. The Court has found that the applicants' right to respect for their private lives...was violated by the investigations conducted and by the discharge of the applicants pursuant to the policy of the Ministry of Defence against homosexuals in the armed forces. As was made clear by the High Court and the Court of Appeal in the judicial review proceedings, since the Convention did not form part of English law, questions as to whether the application of the policy violated the applicants' rights under Article 8 and, in particular, as to whether the policy had been shown by the authorities to respond to a pressing social need or to be proportionate to any legitimate aim served, were not questions to which answers could properly be offered. The sole issue before the domestic courts was whether the policy could be said to be 'irrational'.

137. The test of 'irrationality' applied in the present case was that explained in the judgment of Sir Thomas Bingham MR: a court was not entitled to interfere with the exercise of an administrative discretion on substantive grounds save where the court was satisfied that the decision was unreasonable in the sense that it was beyond the range of responses open to a reasonable decision-maker. In judging whether the decision-maker had exceeded this margin of appreciation, the human rights context was important, so that the more substantial the interference with human rights, the more the court would require by way of justification before it was satisfied that the decision was reasonable. It was, however, further emphasised that, notwithstanding any human rights context, the threshold of irrationality which an applicant was required to surmount was a high one. This is, in the view of the Court, confirmed by the judgments of the High Court and the Court of Appeal themselves. The Court notes that the main judgments in both courts commented favourably on the applicants' submissions challenging the reasons advanced by the Government in justification of the policy. Simon Brown LJ considered that the balance of argument lay with the applicants and that their arguments in favour of a conduct-based code were

powerful . . . Sir Thomas Bingham MR found that those submissions of the applicants were of 'very considerable cogency' and that they fell to be considered in depth with particular reference to the potential effectiveness of a conduct-based code . . . Furthermore, while offering no conclusive views on the Convention issues raised by the case, Simon Brown LJ expressed the opinion that 'the days of the policy were numbered' in light of the United Kingdom's Convention obligations . . . and Sir Thomas Bingham MR observed that the investigations and the discharge of the applicants did not appear to show respect for their private lives. He considered that there might be room for argument as to whether there had been a disproportionate interference with their rights under Article 8 of the Convention . . . Nevertheless, both courts concluded that the policy could not be said to be beyond the range of responses open to a reasonable decision-maker and, accordingly, could not be considered to be 'irrational'.

138. In such circumstances, the Court considers it clear that, even assuming that the essential complaints of the applicants before this Court were before and considered by the domestic courts, the threshold at which the High Court and the Court of Appeal could find the Ministry of Defence policy irrational was placed so high that it effectively excluded any consideration by the domestic courts of the question of whether the interference with the applicants' rights answered a pressing social need or was proportionate to the national security and public order aims pursued, principles which lie at the heart of the Court's analysis of complaints under Article 8 of the Convention. The present applications can be contrasted with the cases of *Soering* and *Vilvarajah* cited above. In those cases, the Court found that the test applied by the domestic courts in applications for judicial review of decisions by the Secretary of State in extradition and expulsion matters coincided with the Court's own approach under Article 3 of the Convention.

139. In such circumstances, the Court finds that the applicants had no effective remedy in relation to the violation of their right to respect for their private lives guaranteed by Article 8 of the Convention. Accordingly, there has been a violation of Article 13 of the Convention.

Thus the answer to the question whether English judicial review satisfies the requirements of Article 13 depends upon the context and substance of the particular application. The traditional deference of the domestic judiciary to the Government in cases involving considerations of national security meant that the process of judicial review did not meet the minimum requirements of Article 13 for such cases in the judgment of the Court (*Chahal* and *Smith and Grady*). Whereas, in respect of other areas of governmental decision-making, such as 'ordinary' extradition and deportation decisions (e.g. *Soering* and *Vilvarajah*), judicial review was capable of fulfilling the demands of Article 13.

4   The Court elaborated upon the procedural requirements of an effective domestic remedy concerning the lawfulness of decisions to deport foreigners on national security grounds in *Al-Nashif v Bulgaria*, judgment of 20 June 2002. The applicant was a stateless person of Palestinian origin who had been living lawfully in Bulgaria since 1992. In 1999 the authorities revoked his permanent residence permit and ordered his deportation as he had been teaching religious classes. The applicant sought judicial review of the decision to deport him and the Passport Department responded by certifying that his deportation was ordered because he had undertaken acts contrary to national security. The effect of such certification was to prevent the Sofia District Court from subjecting the deportation decision to judicial review. Thereupon, the applicant was deported to Syria. The Chamber held that:

137. . . . Even where an allegation of a threat to national security is made, the guarantee of an effective remedy requires as a minimum that the competent independent appeals authority must be informed of the reasons grounding the deportation decision, even if such reasons are not publicly available. The authority must be competent to reject the executive's assertion that there is a threat to national

security where it finds it arbitrary or unreasonable. There must be some form of adversarial proceedings, if need be through a special representative after a security clearance. Furthermore, the question whether the impugned measure would interfere with the individual's right to respect for family life and, if so, whether a fair balance is struck between the public interest involved and the individual's rights must be examined.

As such a remedy had not been available to the applicant the Chamber found a violation of Article 13 (three judges dissented as they considered that the applicant had no arguable claim of a violation of Article 8 and therefore Article 13 was not applicable).

5   The full-time Court has also become increasingly stringent in assessing the adequacy of an aggregation of individual domestic remedies in satisfying Article 13. For example, in *Paul and Audrey Edwards v United Kingdom*, judgment of 14 March 2002 and see above p 117, the Government submitted that a inquiry into the killing of the applicant's son and the option for the applicants to sue the prison authorities for alleged negligence in the care of their son cumulatively met the requirements of Article 13. The Chamber, unanimously, found procedural defects in the inquiry (e.g. the applicants were not able to fully participate in its hearings) and the inability of the applicants to obtain compensation for the non-pecuniary damage their son and they had suffered meant that:

101. Notwithstanding the aggregate of remedies referred to by the Government, the Court finds that in this case the applicants did not have available to them an appropriate means of obtaining a determination of their allegations that the authorities failed to protect their son's right to life and the possibility of obtaining an enforceable award of compensation for the damage suffered thereby. In the Court's view, this is an essential element of a remedy under Article 13 for a bereaved parent.

102. Accordingly, there has been a breach of Article 13 of the Convention.

6   The Court has developed an extensive body of jurisprudence interpreting Article 13 as requiring States to undertake effective investigations into arguable claims that substantive Convention rights have been violated. Where relatives/friends alleged that a person has been unlawfully killed by State personnel, contrary to Article 2, the Court has ruled that such an investigation is necessary to satisfy Article 13. For example, in *Kaya v Turkey*, 1998-I, the applicant contended that his brother had been deliberately shot dead by the security forces. The Chamber, by eight votes to one, held that:

107. In the instant case the applicant is complaining that he and the next-of-kin have been denied an 'effective' remedy which would have brought to light the true circumstances surrounding the killing of Abdülmenaf Kaya. In the view of the Court the nature of the right which the authorities are alleged to have violated in the instant case, one of the most fundamental in the scheme of the Convention, must have implications for the nature of the remedies which must be guaranteed for the benefit of the relatives of the victim. In particular, where those relatives have an arguable claim that the victim has been unlawfully killed by agents of the State, the notion of an effective remedy for the purposes of Article 13 entails, in addition to the payment of compensation where appropriate, a thorough and effective investigation capable of leading to the identification and punishment of those responsible and including effective access for the relatives to the investigatory procedure . . . Seen in these terms the requirements of Article 13 are broader than a Contracting State's procedural obligation under Article 2 to conduct an effective investigation.

The Chamber went on to find a breach of Article 13 as the domestic inquiry into the death of the applicant's brother had been seriously deficient (e.g. the authorities had unquestioningly assumed that the deceased was a terrorist killed during a clash with members of the security forces). Similarly, a unanimous Grand Chamber held in *Ilhan v Turkey*, judgment of 27 June

2000 and see above p 106 [Art 2], that '97. [w]here an individual has an arguable claim that he has been tortured or subjected to serious ill-treatment by the State . . . ' an effective investigation was mandated by Article 13. As there had been significant defects in the domestic inquiry, including the prosecutor failing to interview key witnesses:

103. For these reasons, no effective criminal investigation can be considered to have been conducted in accordance with Article 13. The Court finds therefore that no effective remedy has been provided in respect of Abdullatif Ilhan's injuries and thereby access to any other available remedies, including a claim for compensation has also been denied.

Consequently, there has been a violation of Article 13 of the Convention.

The above judgment is also important for linking a failure to provide an effective domestic investigation and the consequent inability of the applicant to secure other forms of domestic redress, such as compensation, as key elements in the Court's finding of a breach of Article 13. The Court has also applied Article 13 to applications concerning alleged forced disappearances of persons by State agents in breach of Article 5. For example, in *Kurt v Turkey*, 1998-III and see above p 252:

140. . . . In the view of the Court, where the relatives of a person have an arguable claim that the latter has disappeared at the hands of the authorities, the notion of an effective remedy for the purposes of Article 13 entails, in addition to the payment of compensation where appropriate, a thorough and effective investigation capable of leading to the identification and punishment of those responsible and including effective access for the relatives to the investigatory procedure (see, *mutatis mutandis*, the . . . *Aksoy, Aydin* and *Kaya* judgments . . .). Seen in these terms, the requirements of Article 13 are broader than a Contracting State's obligation under Article 5 to conduct an effective investigation into the disappearance of a person who has been shown to be under their control and for whose welfare they are accordingly responsible.

A large majority of the Court, seven votes to two, determined that there had been a breach of Article 13 as there had been no genuine investigation by the public prosecutor into the applicant's petitions concerning the whereabouts of her son.

For a detailed analysis of the effective investigation duties under Article 13 see A. Mowbray, *The Development of Positive Obligations under the European Convention on Human Rights by the European Court of Human Rights* (Oxford: Hart Publishing, 2004), pp 211–20.

7   A Grand Chamber of the full-time Court pronounced a major expansion of the scope of Article 13 to encompass an obligation upon the legal systems of Member states to provide an effective remedy in respect of complaints of unreasonable delays in the determination of persons' civil rights or criminal charges against them (contrary to Article 6(1)) in *Kudla v Poland*, judgment of 26 October 2000. The applicant complained that fraud charges against him had not been conclusively determined by the Polish courts after nine years. The Court held that:

146. In many previous cases in which the Court has found a violation of Article 6 § 1 it did not consider it necessary also to rule on an accompanying complaint made under Article 13. More often than not this was because in the circumstances Article 6 § 1 was deemed to constitute a *lex specialis* in relation to Article 13.

Thus, where the Convention right asserted by the individual is a 'civil right' recognised under domestic law—such as the right of property—the protection afforded by Article 6 § 1 will also be available (see, for example, the *Sporrong and Lönnroth v Sweden* judgment of 23 September 1982, Series A No 52, pp 31–2, § 88). In such circumstances the safeguards of Article 6 § 1, implying the full panoply of a judicial procedure, are stricter than, and absorb, those of Article 13 (see, for example, the *Brualla Gómez de la Torre* [*v Spain* 1997-VIII] judgment, p 2957, § 41).

The Court has applied a similar logic in cases where the applicant's grievance has been directed at the adequacy of an existing appellate or cassation procedure coming within the ambit of both Article 6 § 1 under its 'criminal' head and Article 13 (see the *Kamasinski v Austria* judgment of 19 December 1989, Series A No 168, pp. 45–6, § 110—in relation to nullity proceedings before the Supreme Court).

In such cases there is no legal interest in re-examining the same subject-matter of complaint under the less stringent requirements of Article 13.

147. There is, however, no overlap and hence no absorption where, as in the present case, the alleged Convention violation that the individual wishes to bring before a 'national authority' is a violation of the right to trial within a reasonable time, contrary to Article 6 § 1. The question of whether the applicant in a given case did benefit from trial within a reasonable time in the determination of civil rights and obligations or a criminal charge is a separate legal issue from that of whether there was available to the applicant under domestic law an effective remedy to ventilate a complaint on that ground. In the present case the issue to be determined before the Article 6 § 1 'tribunals' was the criminal charges brought against the applicant, whereas the complaint that he wanted to have examined by a 'national authority' for the purposes of Article 13 was the separate one of the unreasonable length of the proceedings.

In comparable cases in the past, the Court has nonetheless declined to rule on an accompanying complaint of the absence of an effective remedy as guaranteed by Article 13, considering it unnecessary in view of its prior finding of a breach of the 'reasonable time' requirement laid down in Article 6 § 1 (see, among other examples, . . . *Pizzetti* [v Italy A.257-C (1993)]).

148. In the Court's view, the time has come to review its case-law in the light of the continuing accumulation of applications before it in which the only, or principal, allegation is that of a failure to ensure a hearing within a reasonable time in breach of Article 6 § 1.

The growing frequency with which violations in this regard are being found has recently led the Court to draw attention to 'the important danger' that exists for the rule of law within national legal orders when 'excessive delays in the administration of justice' occur 'in respect of which litigants have no domestic remedy' (see, for example, *Bottazzi v Italy* [GC], No 34884/97, § 22, ECHR 1999-V; *Di Mauro v Italy* [GC], No 34256/96, § 23, ECHR 1999-V; *A.P. v Italy* [GC], No 35265/97, § 18, 28 July 1999, unreported; and *Ferrari v Italy* [GC], No 33440/96, § 21, 28 July 1999, unreported).

149. Against this background, the Court does now perceive the need to examine the applicant's complaint under Article 13 taken separately, in addition to its earlier finding of a violation of Article 6 § 1 for failure to try him within a reasonable time.

. . . .

152. On the contrary, the place of Article 13 in the scheme of human rights protection set up by the Convention would argue in favour of implied restrictions of Article 13 being kept to a minimum.

By virtue of Article 1 (which provides: 'The High Contracting Parties shall secure to everyone within their jurisdiction the rights and freedoms defined in Section I of this Convention'), the primary responsibility for implementing and enforcing the guaranteed rights and freedoms is laid on the national authorities. The machinery of complaint to the Court is thus subsidiary to national systems safeguarding human rights. This subsidiary character is articulated in Articles 13 and 35 § 1 of the Convention.

The purpose of Article 35 § 1, which sets out the rule on exhaustion of domestic remedies, is to afford the Contracting States the opportunity of preventing or putting right the violations alleged against them before those allegations are submitted to the Court (see, as a recent authority, *Selmouni v France* [GC], No 25803/94, § 74, ECHR 1999-V). The rule in Article 35 § 1 is based on the assumption, reflected in Article 13 (with which it has a close affinity), that there is an effective domestic remedy available in respect of the alleged breach of an individual's Convention rights (ibid).

In that way, Article 13, giving direct expression to the States' obligation to protect human rights first and foremost within their own legal system, establishes an additional guarantee for an individual in order to ensure that he or she effectively enjoys those rights. The object of Article 13, as emerges from the *travaux préparatoires* (see the Collected Edition of the 'Travaux Préparatoires' of the European Convention on Human Rights, vol. II, pp 485 and 490, and vol III, p 651), is to provide a means whereby individuals can obtain relief at national level for violations of their Convention rights before having to set in motion the international machinery of complaint before the Court. From this perspective, the right of an individual to trial within a reasonable time will be less effective if there exists no opportunity to submit the Convention claim first to a national authority; and the requirements of Article 13 are to be seen as reinforcing those of Article 6 § 1, rather than being absorbed by the general obligation imposed by that Article not to subject individuals to inordinate delays in legal proceedings.

153. The Government, however, argued that requiring a remedy for inordinate length of proceedings under Article 13 is tantamount to imposing on States a new obligation to establish a 'right of appeal', in particular a right to appeal on the merits, which, as such, is guaranteed only in criminal matters under Article 2 of Protocol No. 7 to the Convention; and that in practice the exercise of such a remedy could only prolong proceedings in domestic courts . . .

154. The Court does not accept the Government's submissions.

A remedy for complaining about unreasonable length of proceedings does not as such involve an appeal against the 'determination' of any criminal charge or of civil rights and obligations. In any event, subject to compliance with the requirements of the Convention, the Contracting States—as the Court has held on many previous occasions—are afforded some discretion as to the manner in which they provide the relief required by Article 13 and conform to their Convention obligation under that provision (see, for example, the *Kaya v Turkey* judgment of 19 February 1998, *Reports* 1998-I, pp 329–30, § 106).

As to the suggestion that requiring yet a further remedy would result in domestic proceedings' being made even more cumbersome, the Court would observe that even though at present there is no prevailing pattern in the legal orders of the Contracting States in respect of remedies for excessive length of proceedings, there are examples emerging from the Court's own case-law on the rule on exhaustion of domestic remedies which demonstrate that it is not impossible to create such remedies and operate them effectively (see, for instance, *Gonzalez Marin v Spain* (dec), No 39521/98, ECHR 1999-VII, and *Tomé Mota v Portugal* (dec.), No 32082/96, ECHR 1999-IX).

155. If Article 13 is, as the Government argued, to be interpreted as having no application to the right to a hearing within a reasonable time as safeguarded by Article 6 § 1, individuals will systematically be forced to refer to the Court in Strasbourg complaints that would otherwise, and in the Court's opinion more appropriately, have to be addressed in the first place within the national legal system. In the long term the effective functioning, on both the national and international level, of the scheme of human rights protection set up by the Convention is liable to be weakened.

156. In view of the foregoing considerations, the Court considers that the correct interpretation of Article 13 is that that provision guarantees an effective remedy before a national authority for an alleged breach of the requirement under Article 6 § 1 to hear a case within a reasonable time.

As such a remedy was not provided by the Polish courts the applicant had suffered a violation of Article 13 (in addition to the separate breach of his right to the determination of the criminal charges against him within a reasonable time under Article 6(1)). Judge Casadevall dissented because:

3. . . . there have been more and more findings of violations based solely or principally on the excessive length of proceedings in a good many member States. But by the terms of the Convention, the Court has a duty to consider and try applications as submitted to it by litigants. To state, as the Court does in paragraph 149, that the time has now come, on account of the number of applications relating to length of proceedings, to examine the complaint under Article 13 taken separately smacks, in my view, more of expediency than of law.

4. Moreover, it is not certain that the level of judicial protection afforded at European level by the Convention will be strengthened merely because the Court will now be able to find a double violation—firstly on account of the excessive length of the proceedings and secondly on account of the lack of any effective remedy to complain of it. The finding of an additional violation of Article 13 is not in itself such as to overcome the endemic structural problems besetting the judicial systems of certain member States, any more than the finding that there is a practice incompatible with the Convention has been. It will not make it easier to reduce the Court's case-load, at least not in the medium term.

5. The aim of this finding of a violation of Article 13 is to confront the States with their responsibilities, in accordance with the subsidiarity principle, and to encourage them to establish in their domestic legal systems an effective remedy that will enable litigants to complain of excessive length of proceedings. Supposing such a remedy is instituted, I can hardly see how the structural problem of the unreasonable length of proceedings could be remedied by the obligation to first exhaust, as required by Article 35 of the Convention, an additional remedy designed to make it possible to complain of the length of proceedings.

There is nothing to warrant an assumption that such an action would be heard within a more reasonable time than the main proceedings. Nor does anything warrant an assumption that the main proceedings would be speeded up as a result of bringing such an action. Ultimately *only the litigant would suffer the consequences of this situation*.

The judgment in *Kudla* reveals that the large numbers of applications to the Court alleging a breach of the reasonable time guarantee in Article 6(1), see above p 426, was a major factor influencing the Grand Chamber to adopt the new interpretation of Article 13. Subsequently, Chambers applied *Kudla* to find breaches of Article 13 in cases against various States that had failed to provide an effective domestic remedy in respect of unreasonable delay complaints including: *Nuvoli v Italy*, judgment of 16 May 2002 and *Rados and others v Croatia*, judgment of 7 November 2002.

On 17 September 2004, the Polish Parliament enacted legislation in response to *Kudla* enabling persons to complain to the appellate courts about unreasonable delays in the lower courts' determination of their cases, the appellate courts were empowered to instruct the lower courts to accelerate proceedings and award compensation to the complainants. On 30 September 2004, the European Court announced that it was giving priority to the determination of four leading cases concerning complaints about the length of proceedings in Polish trials. At the same time, the Court was adjourning its consideration of approximately 700 similar complaints against Poland. On 9 March 2005, the Court ruled in two of the test cases that the applications were inadmissible as the complainants had failed to exhaust domestic remedies by not making applications to the Polish appellate courts under the terms of the 2004 Act. A few months later the Court, unanimously, found that the ability of litigants to seek damages against the Government, under the 2004 Act, in respect of complaints that their cases had not been determined within a reasonable time by the Polish courts was an effective remedy under Article 13. In *Krasuski v Poland*, judgment of 14 June 2005, the Chamber ruled that:

66. The means available to an applicant in domestic law for raising a complaint about the length of the proceedings are 'effective', within the meaning of Article 13 of the Convention, if they 'prevent the alleged violation or its continuation, or provid[e] adequate redress for any violation that has already occurred'. Article 13 thus offers an alternative: a remedy is 'effective' if it can be used either to expedite a decision by the courts dealing with the case or to provide the litigant with adequate redress for delays that have already occurred. The fact that a given remedy is of a purely compensatory nature is not decisive, regardless of whether the proceedings in question have been terminated or are still pending (see *Kudla*, cited above, §§ 158–9; *Caldas Ramirez de Arrellano v Spain* (dec.), No 68874/01,

ECHR 2003-I; *Mifsud v France* (dec.) [GC], No 57220/00, ECHR 2002-VIII; and *Paulino Tomás v Portugal* (dec.), No 58698/00, ECHR 2003-VIII).

2. Application of the above principles to the present case

(a) Applicability of Article 13

67. There has been no dispute over the applicability of Article 13 in the present case. The parties agreed that the applicant's complaint under Article 6 § 1, declared admissible by the Court, satisfied the test of 'arguability' for the purposes of Article 13.

(b) Compliance with Article 13

68. In previous similar cases before the Court the Polish Government have been unsuccessful in their pleading that a civil action under Article 417 of the Civil Code created an effective remedy in length of proceedings cases. In particular, their arguments were rejected as being unsupported by any documentary evidence but merely based on the Polish Constitutional Court's *obiter dictum* interpretation of that provision in the judgment of 4 December 2001 and not on any relevant judicial practice (see, for instance, *Małasiewicz v Poland*, No 22072/02, § 32).

69. However, in view of the recent developments at domestic level, most notably the entry into force of the 2004 Act, the Court finds good reasons to reconsider its previous position.

To begin with, the Court finds that section 16 of the 2004 Act created a completely new legal situation in comparison to that subsisting previously. In contrast to the past, the possibility of seeking damages under Article 417 of the Civil Code for the protracted length of judicial proceedings which have terminated now has an explicit legal basis. Also, on a plain reading of section 16, it is clear that the hitherto existing ambiguity as to the application of Article 417 to cases involving compensation for a breach of the right to a hearing within a reasonable time has been removed.

70. The Court does not find any *prima facie* evidence in support of the applicant's argument that the remedy in question would be 'unrealistic' in this case. Thus, the applicant has not contested the availability of that remedy but confined himself to a bare statement that the remedy would not be effective, without substantiating his assertion in any way. Given that the 2004 Act entered into force on 17 September 2004, the absence of the established judicial practice in respect of Article 417 is not decisive (see, *mutatis mutandis*, *Charzyński v Poland* (dec.) No 15212/03, § 41, ECHR 2004- . . .). Nor does the fact that he cannot base his action on—in his view—the more favourable, amended provisions of Article 417 make his possible attempt to seek damages futile or purposeless.

71. It is true that the effectiveness of the remedy depends on the Polish civil courts' ability to handle such actions with special diligence and attention, especially in terms of the length of time taken for their determination. It is also true that the level of compensation awarded at domestic level may constitute an important element for the assessment of the adequacy of the remedy (see, *mutatis mutandis*, *Paulino Tomás v Portugal* (dec.) cited above). However, mere doubts as to the effective functioning of a newly created statutory remedy does not absolve the applicant from having recourse to it. It cannot be assumed by the Court that the Polish courts will not give proper effect to the new provision.

72. Having regard to the foregoing, the Court considers that from 17 September 2004, the date on which the 2004 Act entered into force, an action for damages based on Article 417 of the Civil Code acquired a sufficient level of certainty to become an 'effective remedy' within the meaning of Article 13 of the Convention for an applicant alleging a violation of the right to a hearing within a reasonable time in judicial proceedings in Poland.

73. There has accordingly been no violation of Article 13 in the present case.

In *Surmeli v Germany*, judgment of 8 June 2006, a unanimous Grand Chamber found a breach of Article 13 as German law failed to provide an effective remedy to enable the applicant to expedite civil proceedings, in which he was the complainant, or obtain compensation for the delays he had suffered.

8   The full-time Court has interpreted Article 13 as requiring Member states to provide a domestic remedy capable of preventing the execution of measures that are contrary to the Convention and whose effects are potentially irreversible. In *Conka v Belgium*, judgment of 5 February 2002, the applicants were Slovakian nationals who complained that their deportation from Belgium violated, *inter alia*, Article 13 in that they did not have such a remedy available to them. Under Belgian law they could have made an application to the *Conseil d'Etat* using a special extremely urgent procedure to challenge the lawfulness of the deportation orders made against them. However, the applicants contended that this procedure did not meet the requirements of Article 13 as making such an application did not automatically stay the deportation process until the *Conseil d'Etat* had reached a decision. The Chamber held that:

79. The Court considers that the notion of an effective remedy under Article 13 requires that the remedy may prevent the execution of measures that are contrary to the Convention and whose effects are potentially irreversible (see, *mutatis mutandis, Jabari* [v Turkey, 2000-VIII] § 50). Consequently, it is inconsistent with Article 13 for such measures to be executed before the national authorities have examined whether they are compatible with the Convention, although Contracting States are afforded some discretion as to the manner in which they conform to their obligations under this provision (see *Chahal* [v UK, 1996-V] § 145).

. . . .

81. An application for a stay of execution under the extremely urgent procedure is not suspensive either. The Government stressed, however, that the president of the division may at any time—even on bank holidays and on a few hours' notice, as frequently occurred in deportation cases—summon the parties to attend so that the application can be considered and, if appropriate, an order made for a stay of the deportation order before its execution. It will be noted that the authorities are not legally bound to await the *Conseil d'Etat*'s decision before executing a deportation order. It is for that reason that the *Conseil d'Etat* has, for example, issued a practice direction directing that on an application for a stay under the extremely urgent procedure the registrar shall, at the request of the judge, contact the Aliens Office to establish the date scheduled for the repatriation and to make arrangements regarding the procedure to be followed as a consequence. Two remarks need to be made about that system.

82. Firstly, it is not possible to exclude the risk that in a system where stays of execution must be applied for and are discretionary they may be refused wrongly, in particular if it was subsequently to transpire that the court ruling on the merits has nonetheless to quash a deportation order for failure to comply with the Convention, for instance, if the applicant would be subjected to ill-treatment in the country of destination or be part of a collective expulsion. In such cases, the remedy exercised by the applicant would not be sufficiently effective for the purposes of Article 13.

83. Secondly, even if the risk of error is in practice negligible—a point which the Court is unable to verify, in the absence of any reliable evidence—it should be noted that the requirements of Article 13, and of the other provisions of the Convention, take the form of a guarantee and not of a mere statement of intent or a practical arrangement. That is one of the consequences of the rule of law, one of the fundamental principles of a democratic society, which is inherent in all the Articles of the Convention (see, *mutatis mutandis, Iatridis v Greece* [GC], No 31107/96, § 58, ECHR 1999-II).

However, it appears that the authorities are not required to defer execution of the deportation order while an application under the extremely urgent procedure is pending, not even for a minimum reasonable period to enable the *Conseil d'Etat* to decide the application. Furthermore, the onus is in practice on the *Conseil d'Etat* to ascertain the authorities' intentions regarding the proposed expulsions and to act accordingly, but there does not appear to be any obligation on it to do so. Lastly, it is merely on the basis of internal directions that the registrar of the *Conseil d'Etat*, acting on the instructions of a judge, contacts the authorities for that purpose, and there is no indication of what the consequences might be should he omit to do so. Ultimately, the alien has no guarantee that the *Conseil d'Etat* and the authorities will comply in every case with that practice, that the *Conseil d'Etat* will deliver its decision, or even hear the case, before his expulsion, or that the authorities will allow a minimum reasonable period of grace.

Each of those factors makes the implementation of the remedy too uncertain to enable the requirements of Article 13 to be satisfied.

. . . .

85. In conclusion, the applicants did not have a remedy available that satisfied the requirements of Article 13 to air their complaint under Article 4 of Protocol No. 4. Accordingly, there has been a violation of Article 13 of the Convention . . .

Three judges dissented as they considered that applications under the extremely urgent procedure in practice had suspensive effect. The judgment in *Conka* was endorsed by the Grand Chamber in that later case of *Mamatkulov and Askarov v Turkey*, judgment of 4 February 2005.

16 ARTICLE 14 PROHIBITION OF DISCRIMINATION

'Belgian Linguistic' case (No 2) A.6 (1968) 1 EHRR 252
European Court of Human Rights

The factual background to this complaint and the Court's findings are detailed below (at p 957).

8. According to Article 14 (art 14) of the Convention, the enjoyment of the rights and freedoms set forth therein shall be secured without discrimination ('*sans distinction aucune*') on the ground, inter alia, of language; and by the terms of Article 5 of the Protocol (P1-5), this same guarantee applies equally to the rights and freedoms set forth in this instrument. It follows that both Article 2 of the Protocol (P1-2) and Article 8 (art 8) of the Convention must be interpreted and applied by the Court not only in isolation but also having regard to the guarantee laid down in Article 14 (art 14+P1-2, art 14+8).

9. While it is true that this guarantee has no independent existence in the sense that under the terms of Article 14 (art 14) it relates solely to 'rights and freedoms set forth in the Convention', a measure which in itself is in conformity with the requirements of the Article enshrining the right or freedom in question may however infringe this Article when read in conjunction with Article 14 (art 14) for the reason that it is of a discriminatory nature.

Thus, persons subject to the jurisdiction of a Contracting State cannot draw from Article 2 of the Protocol (P1–2) the right to obtain from the public authorities the creation of a particular kind of educational establishment; nevertheless, a State which had set up such an establishment could not, in laying down entrance requirements, take discriminatory measures within the meaning of Article 14 (art 14).

To recall a further example, cited in the course of the proceedings, Article 6 (art 6) of the Convention does not compel States to institute a system of appeal courts. A State which does set up such courts consequently goes beyond its obligations under Article 6 (art 6). However it would violate that Article, read in conjunction with Article 14 (art 14+6), were it to debar certain persons from these remedies without a legitimate reason while making them available to others in respect of the same type of actions.

In such cases there would be a violation of a guaranteed right or freedom as it is proclaimed by the relevant Article read in conjunction with Article 14 (art 14). It is as though the latter formed an integral part of each of the Articles laying down rights and freedoms. No distinctions should be made in this respect according to the nature of these rights and freedoms and of their correlative obligations, and for instance as to whether the respect due to the right concerned implies positive action or mere abstention. This is, moreover, clearly shown by the very general nature of the terms employed in Article 14 (art 14): 'the enjoyment of the rights and freedoms set forth in this Convention shall be secured'.

10. In spite of the very general wording of the French version ('*sans distinction aucune*'), Article 14 (art 14) does not forbid every difference in treatment in the exercise of the rights and freedoms recognised. This version must be read in the light of the more restrictive text of the English version ('without discrimination'). In addition, and in particular, one would reach absurd results were one to give Article 14 (art 14) an interpretation as wide as that which the French version seems to imply. One would, in effect,

be led to judge as contrary to the Convention every one of the many legal or administrative provisions which do not secure to everyone complete equality of treatment in the enjoyment of the rights and freedoms recognised. The competent national authorities are frequently confronted with situations and problems which, on account of differences inherent therein, call for different legal solutions; moreover, certain legal inequalities tend only to correct factual inequalities. The extensive interpretation mentioned above cannot consequently be accepted.

It is important, then, to look for the criteria which enable a determination to be made as to whether or not a given difference in treatment, concerning of course the exercise of one of the rights and freedoms set forth, contravenes Article 14 (art 14). On this question the Court, following the principles which may be extracted from the legal practice of a large number of democratic States, holds that the principle of equality of treatment is violated if the distinction has no objective and reasonable justification. The existence of such a justification must be assessed in relation to the aim and effects of the measure under consideration, regard being had to the principles which normally prevail in democratic societies. A difference of treatment in the exercise of a right laid down in the Convention must not only pursue a legitimate aim: Article 14 (art 14) is likewise violated when it is clearly established that there is no reasonable relationship of proportionality between the means employed and the aim sought to be realised.

In attempting to find out in a given case, whether or not there has been an arbitrary distinction, the Court cannot disregard those legal and factual features which characterise the life of the society in the State which, as a Contracting Party, has to answer for the measure in dispute. In so doing it cannot assume the rôle of the competent national authorities, for it would thereby lose sight of the subsidiary nature of the international machinery of collective enforcement established by the Convention. The national authorities remain free to choose the measures which they consider appropriate in those matters which are governed by the Convention. Review by the Court concerns only the conformity of these measures with the requirements of the Convention.

11. In the present case the Court notes that Article 14, even when read in conjunction with Article 2 of the Protocol (art 14+P1-2), does not have the effect of guaranteeing to a child or to his parent the right to obtain instruction in a language of his choice. The object of these two Articles (art 14+P1-2), read in conjunction, is more limited: it is to ensure that the right to education shall be secured by each Contracting Party to everyone within its jurisdiction without discrimination on the ground, for instance, of language.

This is the natural and ordinary meaning of Article 14 read in conjunction with Article 2 (art 14+P1-2). Furthermore, to interpret the two provisions as conferring on everyone within the jurisdiction of a State a right to obtain education in the language of his own choice would lead to absurd results, for it would be open to anyone to claim any language of instruction in any of the territories of the Contracting Parties.

The Court notes that, where the Contracting Parties intended to confer upon everyone within their jurisdiction specific rights with respect to the use or understanding of a language, as in Article 5 (2) and Article 6 (3) (a) and (e) (art 5-2, art 6-3-a, art 6-3-e) of the Convention, they did so in clear terms. It must be concluded that if they had intended to create for everyone within their jurisdiction a specific right with respect to the language of instruction, they would have done so in express terms in Article 2 of the Protocol (P1-2). For this reason also, the Court cannot attribute to Article 14, when read in conjunction with Article 2 of the Protocol (art 14+P1-2), a meaning which would secure to everyone within the jurisdiction of a Contracting Party a right to education conducted in the language of his own choice.

It remains true that, by virtue of Article 14 (art 14), the enjoyment of the right to education and the right to respect of family life, guaranteed respectively by Article 2 of the Protocol (P1-2) and Article 8 (art 8) of the Convention, are to be secured to everyone without discrimination on the ground, inter alia, of language.

12. In order to determine the questions referred to it, the Court will therefore examine whether or not there exist in the present case unjustified distinctions, that is to say discriminations, which affect the

exercise of the rights enshrined in Article 2 of the Protocol and Article 8 of the Convention, read in conjunction with Article 14 (art 14+P1–2, art 14+8). In this examination, the Court will take into account the factual and legal features that characterise the situation in Belgium, which is a plurilingual State comprising several linguistic areas.

...

NOTES

1   The composition of the Court is elaborated below (at p 961).

2   The judgment reveals the symbiotic nature of the relationship between the prohibition on discrimination contained in Article 14 and the substantive rights/freedoms enshrined in other Articles of the Convention (and its Protocols). In determining if a difference in treatment with respect to Convention rights infringes Article 14 the Court will examine whether the distinction (a) pursues a legitimate aim and (b) if it is a proportionate measure.

3   The Court's interpretation of Article 14 in the above case makes it clear that there can be a breach of the prohibition on discrimination in circumstances where there is no violation of the related substantive Convention right. A dramatic example of this occurred in *Adulaziz, Cabales and Balkandali v UK*, A.94 (1985) 7 EHRR 471. The applicants were aliens lawfully settled in the UK. They complained that under the existing Immigration Rules their (alien) husbands were refused permission to enter and settle in the UK with them. The Court did not find a breach of the applicants' right to respect for their family life under Article 8 (see above, p 525). However, the applicants also contended that there had been discriminatory treatment which violated Article 14.

II. ALLEGED VIOLATION OF ARTICLE 14 TAKEN TOGETHER WITH ARTICLE 8 (ART 14+8)

A. INTRODUCTION

70. The applicants claimed that, as a result of unjustified differences of treatment in securing the right to respect for their family life, based on sex, race and also—in the case of Mrs Balkandali—birth, they had been victims of a violation of Article 14 of the Convention, taken together with Article 8 (art 14+8). The former Article (art 14) reads as follows:

> 'The enjoyment of the rights and freedoms set forth in [the] Convention shall be secured without discrimination on any ground such as sex, race, colour, language, religion, political or other opinion, national or social origin, association with a national minority, property, birth or other status.'

In the event that the Court should find Article 8 (art 8) to be applicable in the present case, the Government denied that there was any difference of treatment on the ground of race and submitted that since the differences of treatment on the ground of sex and of birth had objective and reasonable justifications and were proportionate to the aims pursued, they were compatible with Article 14 (art 14).

71. According to the Court's established case-law, Article 14 (art 14) complements the other substantive provisions of the Convention and the Protocols. It has no independent existence since it has effect solely in relation to 'the enjoyment of the rights and freedoms' safeguarded by those provisions. Although the application of Article 14 (art 14) does not necessarily presuppose a breach of those provisions—and to this extent it is autonomous—there can be no room for its application unless the facts at issue fall within the ambit of one or more of the latter (see ... *Rasmussen* judgment, Series A No 87, p 12, para 29).

   The Court has found Article 8 (art 8) to be applicable ... Although the United Kingdom was not obliged to accept Mr Abdulaziz, Mr Cabales and Mr Balkandali for settlement and the Court therefore did not find a violation of Article 8 (art 8) taken alone . . . the facts at issue nevertheless fall within the ambit of that Article (art 8) . . .

Article 14 (art 14) also is therefore applicable.

72. For the purposes of Article 14 (art 14), a difference of treatment is discriminatory if it 'has no objective and reasonable justification', that is, if it does not pursue a 'legitimate aim' or if there is not a 'reasonable relationship of proportionality between the means employed and the aim sought to be realised' (see, inter alia, the *Belgian Linguistic*' judgment . . .

The Contracting States enjoy a certain margin of appreciation in assessing whether and to what extent differences in otherwise similar situations justify a different treatment in law (see the above-mentioned *Rasmussen* judgment, *ibid*, p 15, para 40), but it is for the Court to give the final ruling in this respect.

73. In the particular circumstances of the case, the Court considers that it must examine in turn the three grounds on which it was alleged that a discriminatory difference of treatment was based.

B. ALLEGED DISCRIMINATION ON THE GROUND OF SEX

74. As regards the alleged discrimination on the ground of sex, it was not disputed that under the 1980 Rules it was easier for a man settled in the United Kingdom than for a woman so settled to obtain permission for his or her non-national spouse to enter or remain in the country for settlement. . . . Argument centred on the question whether this difference had an objective and reasonable justification.

75. According to the Government, the difference of treatment complained of had the aim of limiting 'primary immigration' . . . and was justified by the need to protect the domestic labour market at a time of high unemployment. They placed strong reliance on the margin of appreciation enjoyed by the Contracting States in this area and laid particular stress on what they described as a statistical fact: men were more likely to seek work than women, with the result that male immigrants would have a greater impact than female immigrants on the said market. Furthermore, the reduction, attributed by the Government to the 1980 Rules, of approximately 5,700 per annum in the number of husbands accepted for settlement in the United Kingdom . . . was claimed to be significant. This was said to be so especially when the reduction was viewed in relation to its cumulative effect over the years and to the total number of acceptances for settlement.

This view was contested by the applicants. For them, the Government's plea ignored the modern role of women and the fact that men may be self-employed and also, as was exemplified by the case of Mr Balkandali . . . create rather than seek jobs. Furthermore, the Government's figure of 5,700 was said to be insignificant and, for a number of reasons, in any event unreliable . . .

76. The Government further contended that the measures in question were justified by the need to maintain effective immigration control, which benefited settled immigrants as well as the indigenous population. Immigration caused strains on society; the Government's aim was to advance public tranquillity, and a firm and fair control secured good relations between the different communities living in the United Kingdom.

To this, the applicants replied that the racial prejudice of the United Kingdom population could not be advanced as a justification for the measures.

77. In its report, the Commission considered that, when seen in the context of the immigration of other groups, annual emigration and unemployment and economic activity rates, the impact on the domestic labour market of an annual reduction of 2,000 (as then estimated by the Government) in the number of husbands accepted for settlement in the United Kingdom . . . was not of a size or importance to justify a difference of treatment on the ground of sex and the detrimental consequences thereof on the family life of the women concerned. Furthermore, the long-standing commitment to the reunification of the families of male immigrants, to which the Government had referred as a reason for accepting wives while excluding husbands, no longer corresponded to modern requirements as to the equal

treatment of the sexes. Neither was it established that race relations or immigration controls were enhanced by the rules: they might create resentment in part of the immigrant population and it had not been shown that it was more difficult to limit abuses by non-national husbands than by other immigrant groups. The Commission unanimously concluded that there had been discrimination on the ground of sex, contrary to Article 14 (art 14), in securing the applicants' right to respect for family life, the application of the relevant rules being disproportionate to the purported aims.

At the hearings before the Court, the Commission's Delegate stated that this conclusion was not affected by the Government's revised figure (about 5,700) for the annual reduction in the number of husbands accepted for settlement.

78. The Court accepts that the 1980 Rules had the aim of protecting the domestic labour market. The fact that, as was suggested by the applicants, this aim might have been further advanced by the abolition of the 'United Kingdom ancestry' and the 'working holiday' rules . . . in no way alters this finding. Neither does the Court perceive any conclusive evidence to contradict it in the Parliamentary debates, on which the applicants also relied. It is true, as they pointed out, that unemployment in the United Kingdom in 1980 was lower than in subsequent years, but it had nevertheless already attained a significant level and there was a considerable increase as compared with previous years . . .

While the aforesaid aim was without doubt legitimate, this does not in itself establish the legitimacy of the difference made in the 1980 Rules as to the possibility for male and female immigrants settled in the United Kingdom to obtain permission for, on the one hand, their non-national wives or fiancées and, on the other hand, their non-national husbands or fiancés to enter or remain in the country.

Although the Contracting States enjoy a certain 'margin of appreciation' in assessing whether and to what extent differences in otherwise similar situations justify a different treatment, the scope of this margin will vary according to the circumstances, the subject-matter and its background (see the above-mentioned *Rasmussen* judgment, Series A No 87, p 15, para 40).

As to the present matter, it can be said that the advancement of the equality of the sexes is today a major goal in the member States of the Council of Europe. This means that very weighty reasons would have to be advanced before a difference of treatment on the ground of sex could be regarded as compatible with the Convention.

79. In the Court's opinion, the Government's arguments summarised in paragraph 75 above are not convincing.

It may be correct that on average there is a greater percentage of men of working age than of women of working age who are 'economically active' (for Great Britain 90 per cent of the men and 63 per cent of the women) and that comparable figures hold good for immigrants (according to the statistics, 86 per cent for men and 41 per cent for women for immigrants from the Indian sub-continent and 90 per cent for men and 70 per cent for women for immigrants from the West Indies and Guyana) . . .

Nevertheless, this does not show that similar differences in fact exist—or would but for the effect of the 1980 Rules have existed—as regards the respective impact on the United Kingdom labour market of immigrant wives and of immigrant husbands. In this connection, other factors must also be taken into account. Being 'economically active' does not always mean that one is seeking to be employed by someone else. Moreover, although a greater number of men than of women may be inclined to seek employment, immigrant husbands were already by far outnumbered, before the introduction of the 1980 Rules, by immigrant wives . . . many of whom were also 'economically active'. While a considerable proportion of those wives, in so far as they were 'economically active', were engaged in part-time work, the impact on the domestic labour market of women immigrants as compared with men ought not to be underestimated.

In any event, the Court is not convinced that the difference that may nevertheless exist between the respective impact of men and of women on the domestic labour market is sufficiently important to justify the difference of treatment, complained of by the applicants, as to the possibility for a person settled in the United Kingdom to be joined by, as the case may be, his wife or her husband.

80. In this context the Government stressed the importance of the effect on the immigration of husbands of the restrictions contained in the 1980 Rules, which had led, according to their estimate, to an annual reduction of 5,700 (rather than 2,000, as mentioned in the Commission's report) in the number of husbands accepted for settlement.

Without expressing a conclusion on the correctness of the figure of 5,700, the Court notes that in point of time the claimed reduction coincided with a significant increase in unemployment in the United Kingdom and that the Government accepted that some part of the reduction was due to economic conditions rather than to the 1980 Rules themselves . . .

In any event, for the reasons stated in paragraph 79 above, the reduction achieved does not justify the difference in treatment between men and women.

81. The Court accepts that the 1980 Rules also had, as the Government stated, the aim of advancing public tranquillity. However, it is not persuaded that this aim was served by the distinction drawn in those rules between husbands and wives.

82. There remains a more general argument advanced by the Government, namely that the United Kingdom was not in violation of Article 14 (art 14) by reason of the fact that it acted more generously in some respects—that is, as regards the admission of non-national wives and fiancées of men settled in the country—than the Convention required.

The Court cannot accept this argument. It would point out that Article 14 (art 14) is concerned with the avoidance of discrimination in the enjoyment of the Convention rights in so far as the requirements of the Convention as to those rights can be complied with in different ways. The notion of discrimination within the meaning of Article 14 (art 14) includes in general cases where a person or group is treated, without proper justification, less favourably than another, even though the more favourable treatment is not called for by the Convention.

83. The Court thus concludes that the applicants have been victims of discrimination on the ground of sex, in violation of Article 14 taken together with Article 8 (art 14+8).

C. ALLEGED DISCRIMINATION ON THE GROUND OF RACE

84. As regards the alleged discrimination on the ground of race, the applicants relied on the opinion of a minority of the Commission. They referred, inter alia, to the whole history of and background to the United Kingdom immigration legislation . . . and to the Parliamentary debates on the immigration rules.

In contesting this claim, the Government submitted that the 1980 Rules were not racially motivated, their aim being to limit 'primary immigration' . . .

A majority of the Commission concluded that there had been no violation of Article 14 (art 14) under this head. Most immigration policies—restricting, as they do, free entry—differentiated on the basis of people's nationality, and indirectly their race, ethnic origin and possibly their colour. While a Contracting State could not implement 'policies of a purely racist nature', to give preferential treatment to its nationals or to persons from countries with which it had the closest links did not constitute 'racial discrimination'. The effect in practice of the United Kingdom rules did not mean that they were abhorrent on the grounds of racial discrimination, there being no evidence of an actual difference of treatment on grounds of race.

A minority of the Commission, on the other hand, noted that the main effect of the rules was to prevent immigration from the New Commonwealth and Pakistan. This was not coincidental: the legislative history showed that the intention was to 'lower the number of coloured immigrants'. By their effect and purpose, the rules were indirectly racist and there had thus been a violation of Article 14 (art 14) under this head in the cases of Mrs Abdulaziz and Mrs Cabales.

85. The Court agrees in this respect with the majority of the Commission.

The 1980 Rules, which were applicable in general to all 'non-patrials' wanting to enter and settle in the United Kingdom, did not contain regulations differentiating between persons or groups on the ground of their race or ethnic origin. The rules included in paragraph 2 a specific instruction to immigration officers to carry out their duties without regard to the race, colour or religion of the intending entrant ... and they were applicable across the board to intending immigrants from all parts of the world, irrespective of their race or origin.

As the Court has already accepted, the main and essential purpose of the 1980 Rules was to curtail 'primary immigration' in order to protect the labour market at a time of high unemployment. This means that their reinforcement of the restrictions on immigration was grounded not on objections regarding the origin of the non-nationals wanting to enter the country but on the need to stem the flow of immigrants at the relevant time.

That the mass immigration against which the rules were directed consisted mainly of would-be immigrants from the New Commonwealth and Pakistan, and that as a result they affected at the material time fewer white people than others, is not a sufficient reason to consider them as racist in character: it is an effect which derives not from the content of the 1980 Rules but from the fact that, among those wishing to immigrate, some ethnic groups outnumbered others.

The Court concludes from the foregoing that the 1980 Rules made no distinction on the ground of race and were therefore not discriminatory on that account. . . .

86. The Court accordingly holds that the applicants have not been victims of discrimination on the ground of race.

D. ALLEGED DISCRIMINATION ON THE GROUND OF BIRTH

87. Mrs Balkandali claimed that she had also been the victim of discrimination on the ground of birth, in that, as between women citizens of the United Kingdom and Colonies settled in the United Kingdom, only those born or having a parent born in that country could, under the 1980 Rules, have their non-national husband accepted for settlement there ...

It was not disputed that the 1980 Rules established a difference of treatment on the ground of birth, argument being centred on the question whether it had an objective and reasonable justification.

In addition to relying on the Commission's report, Mrs Balkandali submitted that the elimination of this distinction from subsequent immigration rules ... demonstrated that it was not previously justified.

The Government maintained that the difference in question was justified by the concern to avoid the hardship which women having close ties to the United Kingdom would encounter if, on marriage, they were obliged to move abroad in order to remain with their husbands.

The Commission considered that, notwithstanding the subsequent elimination of this difference, the general interest and the possibly temporary nature of immigration rules required it to express an opinion. It took the view that a difference of treatment based on the mere accident of birth, without regard to the individual's personal circumstances or merits, constituted discrimination in violation of Article 14 (art 14).

88. The Court is unable to share the Commission's opinion. The aim cited by the Government is unquestionably legitimate, for the purposes of Article 14 (art 14). It is true that a person who, like Mrs Balkandali, has been settled in a country for several years may also have formed close ties with it, even if he or she was not born there. Nevertheless, there are in general persuasive social reasons for giving special treatment to those whose link with a country stems from birth within it. The difference of treatment must therefore be regarded as having had an objective and reasonable justification and, in particular, its results have not been shown to transgress the principle of proportionality. This conclusion is not altered by the fact that the immigration rules were subsequently amended on this point.

89. The Court thus holds that Mrs Balkandali was not the victim of discrimination on the ground of birth.

. . .

FOR THESE REASONS, THE COURT UNANIMOUSLY

Holds that Article 8 was applicable in the present case but that, taken alone, it has not been violated;

Holds that Article 14 was applicable in the present case;

Holds that Article 14 taken together with Article 8 has been violated by reason of discrimination against each of the applicants on the ground of sex; . . .

The judgment is very important for its ruling on the Court's attitude towards differences of treatment based solely on the gender of persons. Paragraph 78 of the report indicates that States face a heavy burden in justifying such differences under the requirements of Article 14.

4 In *Schmidt v Germany*, A.291-B (1994) 18 EHRR 513 a man challenged the legal duty imposed on men living in Baden-Wurttemberg to serve in the local fire brigade or pay a financial contribution *in lieu* of service. He claimed that the imposition of such burdens on men (women living in the *Land* were not obliged to serve in the fire brigade or pay the levy) amounted to a violation of his rights under, *inter alia*, Article 14 taken together with Article 4(3)(d) (this provision allows States to require person to undertake 'any work or service which forms part of normal civic obligations'). The Court, by six votes to three, upheld the applicant's assertion of unlawful discrimination.

25. According to the applicant, the Contracting States do not enjoy any margin of appreciation as regards equality of the sexes. He argued that service in the fire brigade was comparable for men and for women and that account could be taken of the biological differences between the two sexes by a sensible division of the various tasks. The concern to protect women could not in itself justify a difference of treatment in this context. As at 31 December 1991, 68,612 women had served in fire brigades in Germany and even in Baden-Württemberg the fire brigades had accepted women since 1978. The financial contribution was of a purely fiscal nature, as in Baden-Württemberg no man had ever been called upon to serve. There was in any case discrimination since women were just as capable as men of paying the levy in question.

26. The Commission in substance accepted the applicant's argument.

27. In the Government's view, on the other hand, the difference of treatment is based on objective and reasonable grounds. Fire brigade duty is a traditional civic obligation in Baden-Württemberg, defined by the Federal Constitutional Court as a 'genuine and potential obligation to perform a public duty'. The Government maintained that, in making this duty compulsory solely for the male sex, the legislature had taken account of the specific requirements of service in the fire brigade and the physical and mental characteristics of women. The sole aim which it had pursued in this respect was the protection of women. The financial contribution was purely compensatory in nature.

28. The Court notes that some German *Länder* do not impose different obligations for the two sexes in this field and that even in Baden-Württemberg women are accepted for voluntary service in the fire brigade.

Irrespective of whether or not there can nowadays exist any justification for treating men and women differently as regards compulsory service in the fire brigade, what is finally decisive in the present case is that the obligation to perform such service is exclusively one of law and theory. In view of the continuing existence of a sufficient number of volunteers, no male person is in practice obliged to serve in a fire brigade. The financial contribution has—not in law but in fact—lost its compensatory character and has become the only effective duty. In the imposition of a financial burden such as this, a difference of treatment on the ground of sex can hardly be justified.

29. There has accordingly been a violation of Article 14 taken in conjunction with Article 4 para 3 (d) (art 14+4(3)(d)) of the Convention. . . .

An example of the full-time Court finding that a man had suffered gender discrimination contrary to Article 14 occurred in *Willis v United Kingdom*, judgment of 11 June 2002. The applicant and his wife had two children and for most of their married life the wife was the major income earner for the family. During her employment she paid full social-security contributions. Sadly, the wife developed cancer and in November 1995 the applicant gave up his work to care for her. In June 1996 the wife died. The applicant then applied to the Benefits Agency for the payment of financial benefits equivalent to those that would have been paid to a widow who had a family to bring up (these included a widow's lump sum payment of £1,000 and a widowed mother's allowance of £72.50 per week plus sums for each child). The Agency informed the applicant that such benefits did not exist for widowers. He complained to the Court alleging a breach of Article 14 in conjunction with Article 1 of Protocol No 1. The Chamber, unanimously, determined that the widow's benefits were pecuniary rights that fell within the ambit of Article 1. As to the application of Article 14:

40. The Court notes that the applicant's wife worked throughout the best part of her marriage to the applicant and during that time paid full social-security contributions as an employed earner in exactly the same way as a man in her position would have done. It notes also that the applicant gave up work to nurse his wife and care for their children on 3 November 1995 and that, being a relatively low earner, it proved uneconomic for him to return to work on a part-time basis following his wife's death. Despite all this, the applicant was entitled to significantly fewer financial benefits upon his wife's death than he would have been if he were a woman and she had been a man.

41. The Court observes also that the authorities' refusal to grant the applicant a widow's payment and a widowed mother's allowance was based exclusively on the fact that he was a man. It has not been argued that the applicant failed to satisfy any of the other statutory conditions for the award of those benefits and he was accordingly in a like situation to women as regards his entitlement to them.

42. The Court considers that the difference in treatment between men and women as regards entitlement to the widow's payment and widowed mother's allowance, of which the applicant was a victim, was not based on any 'objective and reasonable justification'.

43. There has accordingly been a violation of Article 14 of the Convention taken in conjunction with Article 1 of Protocol No 1.

The Welfare Reform and Pensions Act 1999 replaced the widow's payment with a bereavement payment and the widowed mother's allowance with the widowed parent's allowance. Both the new benefits were payable to men and women who met the qualifying conditions.

5   The Court has taken a similar stance in regard to discriminatory treatment based on the legitimacy of a person's birth. For example, in *Inze v Austria*, A.126 (1987) 10 EHRR 394, the applicant had been born out of wedlock and the Carinthian Hereditary Farms Act 1903 provided that precedence should be given to legitimate children over illegitimate ones when determining the order of succession to such properties. Applying the above legislation the Austrian Courts refused to recognise the applicant's claim to his deceased mother's farm (the farm passed to the applicant's legitimate younger half-brother). The applicant complained to the Commission alleging a breach of Article 14 taken in conjunction with Article 1 of Protocol No 1 (the right to property). By a majority, of six votes to four, the Commission found a violation. The Court was unanimous in holding that:

41. . . . the Convention is a living instrument, to be interpreted in the light of present-day conditions (see, among various authorities, the *Johnston* judgment of 18 December 1986, Series A No 112, p 25, § 53). The question of equality between children born in and children born out of wedlock as regards their civil rights is today given importance in the member States of the Council of Europe. This is shown

by the 1975 European Convention on the Legal Status of Children born out of Wedlock, which is presently in force in respect of nine member States of the Council of Europe. It was ratified by the Republic of Austria on 28 May 1980, with a reservation . . . which is not relevant to the facts of the present case. Very weighty reasons would accordingly have to be advanced before a difference of treatment on the ground of birth out of wedlock could be regarded as compatible with the Convention (see, *mutatis mutandis*, the *Abdulaziz, Cabales and Balkandali* judgment, Series A n° 94, p 38, § 78).

42. The Government advanced the following arguments. The criteria for selecting the principal heir were a consequence of the fact that only one heir was entitled to take over a hereditary farm. Furthermore, those criteria were based on objective reasons; in particular, the precedence given to legitimate children corresponded to what could be presumed to be the deceased's intentions. In any event, the provisions of section 7(2) of the Provincial Act only applied to intestate succession and an owner who objected thereto could always make a will.

In addition, the birth criterion reflected the convictions of the rural population and the social and economic condition of farmers. Again, illegitimate children, unlike legitimate children, were usually not brought up on their parents' farm and did not have close links with it.

Finally, one had to bear in mind the special treatment reserved to the surviving spouse, who was normally entitled to stay on the farm and to be maintained by the principal heir.

43. Like the Commission, the Court is not persuaded by the Government's arguments. Most of them are based on general and abstract considerations—concerning such matters as the deceased's intentions, the place where illegitimate children are brought up and the surviving spouse's relations with his or her legitimate children -which may sometimes not reflect the real situation. For instance, Mr Inze was brought up and had worked on the farm in question until the age of 23 . . . Those considerations cannot justify a rule of this kind.

While it is true that the applicant's mother could have made a will in his favour, this does not alter the fact that, in the instant case, he was deprived by law of the possibility of taking over the farm on her death intestate.

44. The Court also considers that the argument relating to the convictions of the rural population merely reflects the traditional outlook. The Government themselves have recognised the ongoing developments in rural society and have accordingly prepared a Bill which takes them into account. In future, the attribution of a hereditary farm is to be based on objective circumstances, notably training for running farms and the fact of having been brought up on the particular property . . .

The Court wishes to make it clear that these proposed amendments cannot in themselves be taken as demonstrating that the previous rules were contrary to the Convention. They do however show that the aim of the legislation in question could also have been achieved by applying criteria other than that based on birth in or out of wedlock.

45. The Court therefore concludes that there was a breach of Article 14 of the Convention, taken together with Article 1 of Protocol No 1 (art 14+P1-1). . . .

In the earlier case of *Marckx v Belgium*, A.31 (1979) 2 EHRR 330 (see above, p 523) the Court had observed that:

. . . at the time when the Convention of 4 November 1950 was drafted, it was regarded as permissible and normal in many European countries to draw a distinction in this area between the 'illegitimate' and the 'legitimate' family. However, the Court recalls that this Convention must be interpreted in the light of present-day conditions (*Tyrer* judgment, A.26 (1978), para 31). In the instant case, the Court cannot but be struck by the fact that the domestic law of the great majority of the member States of the Council of Europe has evolved and is continuing to evolve, in company with the relevant international instruments, towards full juridical recognition of the maxim '*mater semper certa est*'. (para 41)

Therefore, in contemporary times the Court is very suspicious of any differential application of Convention rights based upon illegitimacy.

6 The Court has also adopted an identical approach in respect of differential treatment affecting Convention rights based upon a person's nationality. For example, in *Gaygusuz v Austria* (1996) 23 EHRR 365, *Reports* 1996-IV, the applicant was a Turkish national who had worked in Austria between 1973 and 1984. Up until March 1987 he received a number of social security benefits, including unemployment and sickness payments, from the Austrian authorities. He then applied for an advance on his pension in the form of emergency assistance. The authorities refused his request as the legislation required applicants to be Austrian nationals in order to be eligible for such assistance. In September 1987 the applicant returned to live in Turkey. Mr Gaygusuz complained to the Commission alleging, *inter alia*, a violation of Article 1 of Protocol No 1 in combination with Article 14. A unanimous Commission upheld his claim. Likewise the Court was united in finding a violation of these Articles.

The Court considers that the right to emergency assistance—in so far as provided for in the applicable legislation—is a pecuniary right for the purposes of P1-1. That provision (P1-1) is therefore applicable without it being necessary to rely solely on the link between entitlement to emergency assistance and the obligation to pay 'taxes or other contributions'....

Moreover the Contracting States enjoy a certain margin of appreciation in assessing whether and to what extent differences in otherwise similar situations justify a different treatment. However, very weighty reasons would have to be put forward before the Court could regard a difference of treatment based exclusively on the ground of nationality as compatible with the Convention....

It considers, like the Commission, that the difference in treatment between Austrians and non-Austrians as regards entitlement to emergency assistance, of which Mr Gaygusuz was a victim, is not based on any 'objective and reasonable justification. (paras 41, 42 and 50)

7 The Court found discrimination based upon religion to have occurred in *Hoffmann v Austria*, A.255-C (1993) 17 EHRR 293. The applicant had married a fellow Roman Catholic in 1980. Subsequently, they had two children who were baptised as Roman Catholics. The applicant left the Roman Catholic church and became a Jehovah's Witness. In 1983 the applicant began divorce proceedings against her (former) husband. While those proceedings were pending the applicant left her husband and took their children with her. Later the lower courts granted the applicant custody over the children. However, the Supreme Court granted parental rights to the husband as the children were being brought up in accordance with the applicant's new religious principles (governing such matters as opposition to blood transfusions). The applicant complained to the Commission alleging, *inter alia*, a breach of Article 8 in conjunction with Article 14 due to the denial of custody over the children because of her religion. The Commission, by eight votes to six, found a breach of those Articles. A closely divided Court (five votes to four) upheld the applicant's complaint.

The European Court therefore accepts that there has been a difference in treatment and that that difference was on the ground of religion; this conclusion is supported by the tone and phrasing of the Supreme Court's considerations regarding the practical consequences of the applicant's religion....

Notwithstanding any possible arguments to the contrary, a distinction based essentially on a difference in religion alone is not acceptable. (paras 33 and 36)

The dissentients generally considered that the Supreme Court had not discriminated against the applicant on the grounds of her religion, but had attached significance to the effects of the applicant's religious beliefs on the welfare of her children. This disagreement within the Court reveals the potentially narrow boundary between lawful differential treatment and unlawful discrimination under Article 14.

8 A unanimous Grand Chamber found unlawful religious discrimination to have taken place in *Thlimmenos v Greece* (6/4/2000). The applicant was also a Jehovah's Witness. During 1983 he had been convicted, and sentenced to four years' imprisonment, by a military tribunal for refusing to wear a military uniform. His refusal was motivated by the pacifist beliefs of his religion. In 1988 the applicant sat a public examination for entry into the profession of chartered accountancy (he came second out of sixty candidates). However, the Executive Board of the Greek Institute of Chartered Accountants refused to admit him to the profession because of his earlier conviction. Subsequently, the applicant complained to the Commission alleging, *inter alia*, a breach of Article 14 in conjunction with Article 9. By twenty-two votes to six, the Commission upheld the complaint.

41. The Court notes that the applicant was not appointed a chartered accountant as a result of his past conviction for insubordination consisting in his refusal to wear the military uniform. He was thus treated differently from the other persons who had applied for that post on the ground of his status as a convicted person. The Court considers that such difference of treatment does not generally come within the scope of Article 14 in so far as it relates to access to a particular profession, the right to freedom of profession not being guaranteed by the Convention.

42. However, the applicant does not complain of the distinction that the rules governing access to the profession make between convicted persons and others. His complaint rather concerns the fact that in the application of the relevant law no distinction is made between persons convicted of offences committed exclusively because of their religious beliefs and persons convicted of other offences. In this context the Court notes that the applicant is a member of the Jehovah's Witnesses, a religious group committed to pacifism, and that there is nothing in the file to disprove the applicant's claim that he refused to wear the military uniform only because he considered that his religion prevented him from doing so. In essence, the applicant's argument amounts to saying that he is discriminated against in the exercise of his freedom of religion, as guaranteed by Article 9 of the Convention, in that he was treated like any other person convicted of a felony although his own conviction resulted from the very exercise of this freedom. Seen in this perspective, the Court accepts that the 'set of facts' complained of by the applicant—his being treated as a person convicted of a felony for the purposes of an appointment to a chartered accountant's post despite the fact that the offence for which he had been convicted was prompted by his religious beliefs—'falls within the ambit of a Convention provision', namely Article 9.

43. In order to reach this conclusion, the Court, as opposed to the Commission, does not find it necessary to examine whether the applicant's initial conviction and the authorities' subsequent refusal to appoint him amounted to interference with his rights under Article 9 § 1. In particular, the Court does not have to address, in the present case, the question whether, notwithstanding the wording of Article 4 § 3 (b), the imposition of such sanctions on conscientious objectors to compulsory military service may in itself infringe the right to freedom of thought, conscience and religion guaranteed by Article 9 § 1.

44. The Court has so far considered that the right under Article 14 not to be discriminated against in the enjoyment of the rights guaranteed under the Convention is violated when States treat differently persons in analogous situations without providing an objective and reasonable justification (see the Inze judgment . . . § 41). However, the Court considers that this is not the only facet of the prohibition of discrimination in Article 14. The right not to be discriminated against in the enjoyment of the rights guaranteed under the Convention is also violated when States without an objective and reasonable justification fail to treat differently persons whose situations are significantly different.

45. It follows that Article 14 of the Convention is of relevance to the applicant's complaint and applies in the circumstances of this case in conjunction with Article 9 thereof.

46. The next question to be addressed is whether Article 14 of the Convention has been complied with. According to its case-law, the Court will have to examine whether the failure to treat the applicant differently from other persons convicted of a felony pursued a legitimate aim. If it did the Court will have to examine whether there was a reasonable relationship of proportionality between the means employed and the aim sought to be realised (see the *Inze* judgment cited above, ibid).

47. The Court considers that, as a matter of principle, States have a legitimate interest to exclude some offenders from the profession of chartered accountant. However, the Court also considers that, unlike other convictions for serious criminal offences, a conviction for refusing on religious or philosophical grounds to wear the military uniform cannot imply any dishonesty or moral turpitude likely to undermine the offender's ability to exercise this profession. Excluding the applicant on the ground that he was an unfit person was not, therefore, justified. The Court takes note of the Government's argument that persons who refuse to serve their country must be appropriately punished. However, it also notes that the applicant did serve a prison sentence for his refusal to wear the military uniform. In these circumstances, the Court considers that imposing a further sanction on the applicant was disproportionate. It follows that the applicant's exclusion from the profession of chartered accountants did not pursue a legitimate aim. As a result, the Court finds that there existed no objective and reasonable justification for not treating the applicant differently from other persons convicted of a felony.

48. It is true that the authorities had no option under the law but to refuse to appoint the applicant a chartered accountant. However, contrary to what the Government's representative appeared to argue at the hearing, this cannot absolve the respondent State from responsibility under the Convention. The Court has never excluded that legislation may be found to be in direct breach of the Convention (see, inter alia, *Chassagnou v France*, ECHR 1999-III). In the present case the Court considers that it was the State having enacted the relevant legislation which violated the applicant's right not to be discriminated against in the enjoyment of his right under Article 9 of the Convention. That State did so by failing to introduce appropriate exceptions to the rule barring persons convicted of a felony from the profession of chartered accountants.

49. The Court concludes, therefore, that there has been a violation of Article 14 of the Convention taken in conjunction with Article 9.

Apart from the clear finding of religious discrimination, the judgment is highly significant for the expansion of the concept of discrimination under the Convention elaborated in paragraph 44. Now, the failure to treat persons in different situations differently will also potentially be unlawful. This is the inverse aspect of the established form of discrimination under Article 14 (of treating persons in similar situations differently). States will, therefore, have to be more sensitive to the particular circumstances of individuals when legislating or administering programmes which impinge upon Convention rights.

An example of a situation where a State was able to justify refusing to accord different treatment to a person occurred in *Pretty v UK*, above p 110. In respect of her complaint under Article 14 the applicant contended that *Thlimmenos* obliged the domestic authorities to enable Mrs Pretty's husband to lawfully help her commit suicide, because Mrs Pretty's physical disabilities prevented her from undertaking such an act on her own. The Chamber, unanimously, ruled that:

89. Even if the principle derived from the Thlimmenos case is applied to the applicant's situation however, there is, in the Court's view, objective and reasonable justification for not distinguishing in law between those who are and those who are not physically capable of committing suicide. Under Article 8 of the Convention, the Court has found that there are sound reasons for not introducing into the law exceptions to cater for those who are deemed not to be vulnerable. Similar cogent reasons exist under Article 14 for not seeking to distinguish between those who are able and those who are

unable to commit suicide unaided. The borderline between the two categories will often be a very fine one and to seek to build into the law an exemption for those judged to be incapable of committing suicide would seriously undermine the protection of life which the 1961 Act was intended to safeguard and greatly increase the risk of abuse.

90. Consequently, there has been no violation of Article 14 in the present case.

9 The full-time Court has ruled that discriminatory treatment based upon a person's sexual orientation is contrary to Article 14. In *Salgueiro Da Silva Mouta v Portugal*, judgment of 21 December 1999, the applicant separated from his wife in 1990 and began living with a man in a homosexual relationship. During the following year, as part of divorce proceedings, the applicant agreed with his wife that she would have parental responsibility for their daughter but that he was to have contact rights in respect of his daughter. However, his ex-wife did not enable the applicant to have contact with his daughter. He then applied to the Lisbon Family Court for an order assigning parental responsibility to him. The Family Court granted such an order and the daughter lived with the applicant and his male partner for six months, until she was allegedly abducted by her mother. The applicant's ex-wife appealed against the Family Court decision to the Lisbon Court of Appeal which reversed the lower court's judgment because:

The fact that the child's father, who has come to terms with his homosexuality, wishes to live with another man is a reality which has to be accepted. It is well known that society is becoming more and more tolerant of such situations. However, it cannot be argued that an environment of this kind is the healthiest and best suited to a child's psychological, social and mental development, especially given the dominant model in our society, as the appellant rightly points out. The child should live in a family environment, a traditional Portuguese family, which is certainly not the set-up her father has decided to enter into, since he is living with another man as if they were man and wife. It is not our task here to determine whether homosexuality is or is not an illness or whether it is a sexual orientation towards persons of the same sex. In both cases it is an abnormality and children should not grow up in the shadow of abnormal situations; such are the dictates of human nature and let us remember that it is [the applicant] himself who acknowledged this when, in his initial application of 5 July 1990, he stated that he had definitively left the marital home to go and live with a boyfriend, a decision which is not normal according to common criteria.

The applicant complained to the Strasbourg Court that the decision to award parental responsibility to his ex-wife was based upon his sexual orientation and that constituted a violation of Article 14 combined with Article 8. The Chamber, unanimously, held that:

28. ... The Court is accordingly forced to conclude that there was a difference of treatment between the applicant and M.'s mother which was based on the applicant's sexual orientation, a concept which is undoubtedly covered by Article 14 of the Convention. The Court reiterates in that connection that the list set out in that provision is illustrative and not exhaustive, as is shown by the words 'any ground such as' (in French 'notamment') (see the *Engel and Others v the Netherlands* judgment of 8 June 1976, Series A No 22, pp 30–1, § 72).

2. Justification for the difference in treatment

29. In accordance with the case-law of the Convention institutions, a difference of treatment is discriminatory within the meaning of Article 14 if it has no objective and reasonable justification, that is if it does not pursue a legitimate aim or if there is not a reasonable relationship of proportionality between the means employed and the aim sought to be realised (see the *Karlheinz Schmidt v Germany* judgment of 18 July 1994, Series A No 291-B, pp 32–3, § 24).

30. The decision of the Court of Appeal undeniably pursued a legitimate aim, namely the protection of the health and rights of the child; it must now be examined whether the second requirement was also satisfied.

31. In the applicant's submission, the wording of the judgment clearly showed that the decision to award parental responsibility to the mother was based mainly on the father's sexual orientation, which inevitably gave rise to discrimination against him in relation to the other parent.

32. The Government submitted that the decision in question had, on the contrary, merely touched on the applicant's homosexuality. The considerations of the Court of Appeal to which the applicant referred, when viewed in context, were merely sociological, or even statistical, observations. Even if certain passages of the judgment could arguably have been worded differently, clumsy or unfortunate expressions could not in themselves amount to a violation of the Convention.

. . .

35. It is the Court's view that the above passages from the judgment in question, far from being merely clumsy or unfortunate as the Government maintained, or mere *obiter dicta*, suggest, quite to the contrary, that the applicant's homosexuality was a factor which was decisive in the final decision. That conclusion is supported by the fact that the Court of Appeal, when ruling on the applicant's right to contact, warned him not to adopt conduct which might make the child realise that her father was living with another man 'in conditions resembling those of man and wife' (ibid).

36. The Court is therefore forced to find, in the light of the foregoing, that the Court of Appeal made a distinction based on considerations regarding the applicant's sexual orientation, a distinction which is not acceptable under the Convention (see, *mutatis mutandis*, the *Hoffmann* judgment cited above, p 60, § 36).

The Court cannot therefore find that a reasonable relationship of proportionality existed between the means employed and the aim pursued; there has accordingly been a violation of Article 8 taken in conjunction with Article 14.

In the later case of *L. and V. v Austria*, judgment of 9 January 2003, the Court strengthened its protection against discriminatory treatment based upon sexual orientation by requiring 'particularly serious reasons' to justify the use of this criterion. The applicants had whilst in their twenties engaged in consensual homosexual acts with males between the ages of 14 and 18. Under Austrian law, prior to 2002, it was a criminal offence for males of 19 and over to engage in consensual homosexual acts with males aged between 14 and 18. Consensual heterosexual or lesbian acts between adults and persons over the age of 14 were not criminal at that time in Austria. The applicants complained to Strasbourg that their convictions by the Austrian courts, for which they were given suspended prison sentences, violated Article 14 combined with Article 8. The unanimous Chamber determined that:

49. What is decisive is whether there was an objective and reasonable justification why young men in the 14 to 18 age bracket needed protection against sexual relationships with adult men, while young women in the same age bracket did not need such protection against relations with either adult men or women. In this connection the Court reiterates that the scope of the margin of appreciation left to the Contracting State will vary according to the circumstances, the subject matter and the background; in this respect, one of the relevant factors may be the existence or non-existence of common ground between the laws of the Contracting States . . .

50. In the present case the applicants pointed out, and this has not been contested by the Government, that there is an ever growing European consensus to apply equal ages of consent for heterosexual, lesbian and homosexual relations. Similarly, the Commission observed in *Sutherland* [Commission's report of 1 July 1997] that 'equality of treatment in respect of the age of consent is now recognised by the great majority of member States of the Council of Europe' (loc cit, § 59).

51. The Government relied on the Constitutional Court's judgment of 3 October 1989, which had considered Article 209 of the Criminal Code necessary to avoid 'a dangerous strain . . . be[ing] placed by homosexual experiences upon the sexual development of young males'. However, this approach has

been outdated by the 1995 parliamentary debate on a possible repeal of that provision. As was rightly pointed out by the applicants, the vast majority of experts who gave evidence in Parliament clearly expressed themselves in favour of an equal age of consent, finding in particular that sexual orientation was in most cases established before the age of puberty and that the theory that male adolescents were 'recruited' into homosexuality had thus been disproved. Notwithstanding its knowledge of these changes in the scientific approach to the issue, Parliament decided in November 1996, that is, shortly before the applicants' convictions, in January and February 1997 respectively, to keep Article 209 on the statute book.

52. To the extent that Article 209 of the Criminal Code embodied a predisposed bias on the part of a heterosexual majority against a homosexual minority, these negative attitudes cannot of themselves be considered by the Court to amount to sufficient justification for the differential treatment any more than similar negative attitudes towards those of a different race, origin or colour . . .

53. In conclusion, the Court finds that the Government have not offered convincing and weighty reasons justifying the maintenance in force of Article 209 of the Criminal Code and, consequently, the applicants' convictions under this provision.

54. Accordingly, there has been a violation of Article 14 of the Convention taken in conjunction with Article 8.

A similar analysis was applied in *S.L. v Austria*, judgment of 9 January 2003, in respect of a 15-year-old male who complained that the above legislation prohibited him from engaging in consensual homosexual acts. In 2002 the Austrian Parliament amended the Criminal Code to prohibit sexual acts (heterosexual, homosexual or lesbian) with persons under the age of 16 if that person is not mature enough to understand the meaning of the act.

The Commission opinion in *Sutherland* is examined above p 487.

In *Karner v Austria*, judgment of 24 July 2003, the Court treated differences of treatment on the basis of sexual orientation in the same way as differences on the basis of gender with the consequence that the respondent State was accorded a 'narrow' margin of appreciation when the Court examined if Article 14 had been breached. The applicant (who died after he had made his application to Strasbourg) had lived for a number of years with a homosexual partner in a flat rented by the latter. When the latter died the landlord brought proceedings against the applicant to terminate the tenancy. The applicant sought to rely on the statutory right to succeed to a tenancy given to a deceased tenant's 'life companion'. The Supreme Court ruled that phrase did not apply to persons of the same sex. Before the Strasbourg Court the Government accepted that the applicant had been treated differently on the grounds of his sexual orientation, however the Government argued that this had been as a result of the reasonable justification that domestic law aimed to protect the traditional family. The Court (the Austrian *ad hoc* Judge dissented on the ground that as the applicant was deceased the case should have been struck-out) concluded that the applicant's claim fell within the applicant's right to respect for his home (under Article 8). As for the Government's submission in respect of Article 14:

41. The aim of protecting the family in the traditional sense is rather abstract and a broad variety of concrete measures may be used to implement it. In cases in which the margin of appreciation afforded to member States is narrow, as the position where there is a difference in treatment based on sex or sexual orientation, the principle of proportionality does not merely require that the measure chosen is in principle suited for realising the aim sought. It must also be shown that it was necessary to exclude persons living in a homosexual relationship from the scope of application of Section 14 of the Rent Act in order to achieve that aim. The Court cannot see that the Government has advanced any arguments that would allow of such a conclusion.

42. Accordingly, the Court finds that the Government have not offered convincing and weighty reasons justifying the narrow interpretation of Section 14(3) of the Rent Act that prevented a surviving partner of a couple of the same sex from relying on that provision.

43. Thus, there has been a violation of Article 14 of the Convention, taken together with Article 8.

An example where a State was able to justify the difference of treatment of a homosexual occurred in *Frette v France*, judgment of 26 February 2002. The applicant applied to the social services for prior authorization to adopt a child. The authorities refused him permission, because of his 'choice of lifestyle'. He challenged that decision in the courts and eventually the *Conseil d'Etat* confirmed the refusal observing 'having regard to his lifestyle and despite his clear personal qualities and aptitude for bringing up children, did not provide the requisite safeguards—from an educational, psychological and family perspective—for adopting a child'. The Chamber found that although the Convention did not guarantee a right to adopt children as French law authorised any unmarried person to apply for permission to adopt, the applicant's claim fell within the ambit of Article 8. Regarding the difference of treatment accorded to homosexual applicants under French law, the Chamber, by a narrow majority of four to three, held that as there was little consensus in the approaches of Member states to adoption requests by homosexuals the States should be accorded a wide margin of appreciation to determine the interests of adoptable children. Consequently, there had been no breach of Article 14 taken in conjunction with Article 8.

10   A Grand Chamber adopted a more cautious approach than the original Chamber to the examination of whether there had been a racially motivated killing by military personnel in *Nachova and Others v Bulgaria*, judgment of 6 July 2005, see above p 140.

1. Whether the respondent State is liable for deprivation of life on the basis of the victims' race or ethnic origin

144. The Court has established above that agents of the respondent State unlawfully killed Mr Angelov and Mr Petkov in violation of Article 2 of the Convention. The applicants have further alleged that there has been a separate violation of Article 14 of the Convention in that racial prejudice played a role in their deaths.

145. Discrimination is treating differently, without an objective and reasonable justification, persons in relevantly similar situations (see *Willis v the United Kingdom*, No 36042/97, § 48, ECHR 2002-IV). Racial violence is a particular affront to human dignity and, in view of its perilous consequences, requires from the authorities special vigilance and a vigorous reaction. It is for this reason that the authorities must use all available means to combat racism and racist violence, thereby reinforcing democracy's vision of a society in which diversity is not perceived as a threat but as a source of its enrichment. The Court will revert to that issue below.

146. Faced with the applicants' complaint of a violation of Article 14, as formulated, the Court's task is to establish whether or not racism was a causal factor in the shooting that led to the deaths of Mr Angelov and Mr Petkov so as to give rise to a breach of Article 14 of the Convention taken in conjunction with Article 2.

147. It notes in this connection that in assessing evidence, the Court has adopted the standard of proof 'beyond reasonable doubt'. However, it has never been its purpose to borrow the approach of the national legal systems that use that standard. Its role is not to rule on criminal guilt or civil liability but on Contracting States' responsibility under the Convention. The specificity of its task under Article 19 of the Convention—to ensure the observance by the Contracting States of their engagement to secure the fundamental rights enshrined in the Convention—conditions its approach to the issues of evidence

and proof. In the proceedings before the Court, there are no procedural barriers to the admissibility of evidence or pre-determined formulae for its assessment. It adopts the conclusions that are, in its view, supported by the free evaluation of all evidence, including such inferences as may flow from the facts and the parties' submissions. According to its established case-law, proof may follow from the coexistence of sufficiently strong, clear and concordant inferences or of similar unrebutted presumptions of fact. Moreover, the level of persuasion necessary for reaching a particular conclusion and, in this connection, the distribution of the burden of proof are intrinsically linked to the specificity of the facts, the nature of the allegation made and the Convention right at stake. The Court is also attentive to the seriousness that attaches to a ruling that a Contracting State has violated fundamental rights (see, among others, the following judgments: *Ireland v the United Kingdom*, judgment of 18 January 1978, Series A No 25, § 161; *Ribitsch v Austria*, judgment of 4 December 1995, Series A No 336, p 24, § 32; *Akdivar and Others v Turkey*, judgment of 16 September 1996, *Reports* 1996-IV, p 1211, § 68; *Tanli v Turkey*, No 26129/95, § 111, ECHR 2001-III; and *Ilaşcu and Others v Moldova and Russia* [GC], No 48787/99, § 26, 8 July 2004).

148. The applicants have referred to several separate facts and they maintain that sufficient inferences of a racist act can be drawn from them.

149. First, the applicants considered revealing the fact that Major G. had discharged bursts of automatic fire in a populated area, in disregard of the public's safety. Considering that there was no rational explanation for such behaviour, the applicants were of the view that racist hatred on the part of Major G. was the only plausible explanation and that he would not have acted in that manner in a non-Roma neighbourhood.

150. The Court notes, however, that the use of firearms in the circumstances at issue was regrettably not prohibited under the relevant domestic regulations, a flagrant deficiency which it has earlier condemned. The military police officers carried their automatic rifles 'in accordance with the rules' and were instructed to use all necessary means to effect the arrest. The possibility that Major G. was simply adhering strictly to the regulations and would have acted as he did in any similar context, regardless of the ethnicity of the fugitives, cannot therefore be excluded. While the relevant regulations were fundamentally flawed and fell well short of the Convention requirements on the protection of the right to life, there is nothing to suggest that Major G. would not have used his weapon in a non-Roma neighbourhood.

151. It is true, as the Court has found above, that Major G.'s conduct during the arrest operation calls for serious criticism in that he used grossly excessive force. Nonetheless, it cannot be excluded either that his reaction was shaped by the inadequacy of the legal framework governing the use of firearms and by the fact that he was trained to operate within that framework.

152. The applicants also stated that the military police officers' attitude had been strongly influenced by their knowledge of the victims' Roma origin. However, it is not possible to speculate on whether or not Mr Angelov's and Mr Petkov's Roma origin had any bearing on the officers' perception of them. Furthermore, there is evidence that some of the officers knew one or both of the victims personally.

153. The applicants referred to the statement given by Mr M. M., a neighbour of one of the victims, who reported that Major G. had shouted at him 'you damn Gypsies' immediately after the shooting. While such evidence of a racial slur being uttered in connection with a violent act should have led the authorities in this case to verify Mr M.M.'s statement, that statement is of itself an insufficient basis for concluding that the respondent State is liable for a racist killing.

154. Lastly, the applicants relied on information about numerous incidents involving the use of force against Roma by Bulgarian law enforcement officers that had not resulted in the conviction of those responsible.

155. It is true that a number of organisations, including intergovernmental bodies, have expressed concern about the occurrence of such incidents. However, the Court cannot lose sight of the fact that its sole concern is to ascertain whether in the case at hand the killing of Mr Angelov and Mr Petkov was motivated by racism.

156. In its judgment the Chamber decided to shift the burden of proof to the respondent Government on account of the authorities' failure to carry out an effective investigation into the alleged racist motive for the killing. The inability of the Government to satisfy the Chamber that the events complained of were not shaped by racism resulted in its finding a substantive violation of Article 14 of the Convention, taken together with Article 2.

157. The Grand Chamber reiterates that in certain circumstances, where the events lie wholly, or in large part, within the exclusive knowledge of the authorities, as in the case of death of a person within their control in custody, the burden of proof may be regarded as resting on the authorities to provide a satisfactory and convincing explanation of, in particular, the causes of the detained person's death (see *Salman v Turkey* [GC], No 21986/93, § 100, ECHR 2000-VII). The Grand Chamber cannot exclude the possibility that in certain cases of alleged discrimination it may require the respondent Government to disprove an arguable allegation of discrimination and—if they fail to do so—find a violation of Article 14 of the Convention on that basis. However, where it is alleged—as here—that a violent act was motivated by racial prejudice, such an approach would amount to requiring the respondent Government to prove the absence of a particular subjective attitude on the part of the person concerned. While in the legal systems of many countries proof of the discriminatory effect of a policy or decision will dispense with the need to prove intent in respect of alleged discrimination in employment or the provision of services, that approach is difficult to transpose to a case where it is alleged that an act of violence was racially motivated. The Grand Chamber, departing from the Chamber's approach, does not consider that the alleged failure of the authorities to carry out an effective investigation into the alleged racist motive for the killing should shift the burden of proof to the respondent Government with regard to the alleged violation of Article 14 in conjunction with the substantive aspect of Article 2 of the Convention. The question of the authorities' compliance with their procedural obligation is a separate issue, to which the Court will revert below.

158. In sum, having assessed all relevant elements, the Court does not consider that it has been established that racist attitudes played a role in Mr Angelov's and Mr Petkov's deaths.

159. It thus finds that there has been no violation of Article 14 of the Convention taken together with Article 2 in its substantive aspect.

2. PROCEDURAL ASPECT: WHETHER THE RESPONDENT STATE COMPLIED WITH ITS OBLIGATION TO INVESTIGATE POSSIBLE RACIST MOTIVES

(a) General principles

160. The Grand Chamber endorses the Chamber's analysis in the present case of the Contracting States' procedural obligation to investigate possible racist motives for acts of violence. The Chamber stated, in particular (§§ 156–9):

'... States have a general obligation under Article 2 of the Convention to conduct an effective investigation in cases of deprivation of life.

'... That obligation must be discharged without discrimination, as required by Article 14 of the Convention... [W]here there is suspicion that racial attitudes induced a violent act it is particularly important that the official investigation is pursued with vigour and impartiality, having regard to the need to reassert continuously society's condemnation of racism and ethnic hatred and to maintain the confidence of minorities in the ability of the authorities to protect them from the threat of racist violence. Compliance with the State's positive obligations under Article 2 of the Convention requires that the domestic legal system must demonstrate its capacity to enforce criminal law against those who unlawfully took the life of another, irrespective of the victim's racial or ethnic origin (see *Menson and Others v the United Kingdom* (dec.), No 47916/99, ECHR 2003-V) ...

... [W]hen investigating violent incidents and, in particular, deaths at the hands of State agents, State authorities have the additional duty to take all reasonable steps to unmask any racist motive and to establish whether or not ethnic hatred or prejudice may have played a role in the events. Failing to do so and treating racially induced violence and brutality on an equal footing with cases that have no racist overtones would be to turn a blind eye to the specific nature of acts that are particularly destructive of fundamental rights. A failure to make a distinction in the way in which situations that are essentially different are handled may constitute unjustified treatment irreconcilable with Article 14 of the Convention (see, *mutatis mutandis*, *Thlimmenos v Greece* [GC], No 34369/97, § 44, ECHR 2000-IV). In order to maintain public confidence in their law enforcement machinery, Contracting States must ensure that in the investigation of incidents involving the use of force a distinction is made both in their legal systems and in practice between cases of excessive use of force and of racist killing.

'Admittedly, proving racial motivation will often be extremely difficult in practice. The respondent State's obligation to investigate possible racist overtones to a violent act is an obligation to use best endeavours and not absolute (see, *mutatis mutandis*, *Shanaghan v the United Kingdom*, No 37715/97, § 90, ECHR 2001-III, setting out the same standard with regard to the general obligation to investigate). The authorities must do what is reasonable in the circumstances to collect and secure the evidence, explore all practical means of discovering the truth and deliver fully reasoned, impartial and objective decisions, without omitting suspicious facts that may be indicative of a racially induced violence.'

161. The Grand Chamber would add that the authorities' duty to investigate the existence of a possible link between racist attitudes and an act of violence is an aspect of their procedural obligations arising under Article 2 of the Convention, but may also be seen as implicit in their responsibilities under Article 14 of the Convention taken in conjunction with Article 2 to secure the enjoyment of the right to life without discrimination. Owing to the interplay of the two provisions, issues such as those in the present case may fall to be examined under one of the two provisions only, with no separate issue arising under the other, or may require examination under both Articles. This is a question to be decided in each case on its facts and depending on the nature of the allegations made.

(b) Application of these principles in the present case

162. The Court has already found that the Bulgarian authorities violated Article 2 of the Convention in that they failed to conduct a meaningful investigation into the deaths of Mr Angelov and Mr Petkov. It considers that in the present case it must examine separately the complaint that there was also a failure to investigate a possible causal link between alleged racist attitudes and the killing of the two men.

163. The authorities investigating the deaths of Mr Angelov and Mr Petkov had before them the statement of Mr M.M., a neighbour of the victims, who stated that Major G. had shouted: 'You damn Gypsies' while pointing a gun at him immediately after the shooting. That statement, seen against the background of the many published accounts of the existence in Bulgaria of prejudice and hostility against Roma, called for verification.

164. The Grand Chamber considers—as the Chamber did—that any evidence of racist verbal abuse being uttered by law enforcement agents in connection with an operation involving the use of force against persons from an ethnic or other minority is highly relevant to the question whether or not unlawful, hatred-induced violence has taken place. Where such evidence comes to light in the investigation, it must be verified and—if confirmed—a thorough examination of all the facts should be undertaken in order to uncover any possible racist motives.

165. Furthermore, the fact that Major G. used grossly excessive force against two unarmed and non-violent men also called for a careful investigation.

166. In sum, the investigator and the prosecutors involved in the present case had before them plausible information which was sufficient to alert them to the need to carry out an initial verification and, depending on the outcome, an investigation into possible racist overtones in the events that led to the death of the two men.

167. However, the authorities did nothing to verify Mr M.M.'s statement. They omitted to question witnesses about it. Major G. was not asked to explain why he had considered it necessary to use such a degree of force. No attempt was made to verify Major G.'s record and to ascertain, for example, whether he had previously been involved in similar incidents or whether he had ever been accused in the past of displaying anti-Roma sentiment. Those failings were compounded by the behaviour of the investigator and the prosecutors, who, as the Court has found above, disregarded relevant facts and terminated the investigation, thereby shielding Major G. from prosecution.

168. The Court thus finds that the authorities failed in their duty under Article 14 of the Convention taken together with Article 2 to take all possible steps to investigate whether or not discrimination may have played a role in the events. It follows that there has been a violation of Article 14 of the Convention taken together with Article 2 in its procedural aspect.

Judges Casadevell, Hedigan, Mularoni, Fura-Sandstrom, Gyulumyan, and Spielmann issued a partly dissenting opinion in which they expressed the view that:

2. We cannot subscribe to the new approach adopted by the Court which entails linking a possible violation of Article 14 to the substantive and procedural aspects of Article 2 individually. An overall approach would have been preferable, since it would have better reflected the special nature of Article 14, which has no independent existence as it applies solely to the rights and freedoms guaranteed by the Convention. Since Article 14 has no independent existence, we consider it artificial and unhelpful to distinguish between the substantive and procedural aspects, especially as in the instant case the Court found violations of both these aspects of Article 2. An added problem is that it is too early to measure the impact which this new approach will have on the application and interpretation of Protocol No. 12 to the Convention, which has just come into force in respect of the States which have ratified it.

3. By drawing a distinction between the substantive and procedural aspects, the majority found a violation of Article 14 of the Convention taken together with Article 2 solely on the basis of the authorities' failure to examine whether the events that had led to the deaths of Mr Anguelov and Mr Petkov may have been racially motivated.

4. We agree with that finding. However, looking beyond this purely procedural finding, we are of the view that the other factual elements taken as a whole disclose a violation of Article 14 of the Convention taken together with Article 2.

5. Among these elements, we would note: the fact that shots were fired in a populated area—the Roma district of the village—without regard for the safety of the public; the fact that the military police were aware of the Roma origin of the victims, neither of whom was armed or considered dangerous; the published accounts of the existence of prejudice and hostility against Roma in Bulgaria; the fact that this is not the first case against Bulgaria in which the Court has found that representatives of law and order have inflicted fatal injuries on Roma; Mr M.M.'s evidence that Major G. had hurled racial abuse at him immediately after the shooting, shouting: 'You damn Gypsies'; and, lastly, the authorities' failure to take action and the grave procedural shortcomings which prevented the truth from being established.

6. It is true that the procedural shortcomings constitute a specific factor to which considerable weight must be given. They are central to the question of who must bear the burden of proof, since it is for the domestic authorities to take effective action to elucidate the relevant facts and a breakdown in the

procedure will inevitably have a bearing on the conclusion to be drawn with regard to the substance of the problem.

7. However, by restricting the finding of a violation to the procedural aspect, the majority of the Court did not give sufficient weight to the sufficiently strong, clear and concordant unrebutted presumptions which arose out of the factual evidence in the case taken as a whole and which leads us to conclude that there has been a violation of Article 14 taken together with Article 2 of the Convention.

Do you think the majority were unduly timorous in their application of Article 14? In the later case of *Bekos and Koutropoulos v Greece*, judgment of 13 December 2005, a united Chamber followed the analytical approach established by the majority in *Nachova*. The Chamber concluded that the Greek authorities had, *inter alia*, breached Article 14 in conjunction with Article 3 by reason of their failure to effectively investigate possible racist motives behind the beatings of two ethnic Roma by police officers (which of itself amounted to inhuman and degrading treatment in violation of Article 3). Therefore, once again the Court was willing to find a procedural (effective investigation) breach in the context of alleged racist conduct by public officials, rather than a finding of substantive racist misconduct. However, Chamber President Bratza issued a concurring opinion in which he expressed the belief that States should be required to disprove racist motivation in a wider range of cases than envisaged by *Nachova*. Judge Casadevall also issued a separate opinion in which he explained how he voted 'without great conviction' to find no substantive breach of Article 3 in conjunction with Article 14 out of 'the need for solidarity and cohesion after the Grand Chamber's recent decision in the case of *Nachova*'. Clearly, some judges are not fully satisfied with the majority's approach in *Nachova*.

11 The unanimous Chamber in *Timishev v Russia*, judgment of 13 December 2005 (see below, p 994) articulated the Court's rejection of ethnic discrimination.

58. The Government did not offer any justification for the difference in treatment between persons of Chechen and non-Chechen ethnic origin in the enjoyment of their right to liberty of movement. In any event, the Court considers that no difference in treatment which is based exclusively or to a decisive extent on a person's ethnic origin is capable of being objectively justified in a contemporary democratic society built on the principles of pluralism and respect for different cultures.

59. In conclusion, since the applicant's right of liberty of movement was restricted solely on the ground of his ethnic origin, that difference in treatment constituted racial discrimination within the meaning of Article 14 of the Convention.

12 The Court's policy towards examining allegations of unlawful discrimination under Article 14, when it has already found a breach of a substantive Convention right in the same case, was explained in *Dudgeon v UK*, A.45 (1981) 4 EHRR 149, see above p 487.

Where a substantive Article of the Convention has been invoked both on its own and together with Article 14 and a separate breach has been found of the substantive Article, it is not generally necessary for the Court also to examine the case under Article 14, though the position is otherwise if a clear inequality of treatment in the enjoyment of the right in question is a fundamental aspect of the case... (para 67)

An example of the latter situation occurred in *Aziz v Cyprus*, judgment of 22 June 2004. The applicant was a Cypriot national who lived in Nicosia. The authorities refused to register him on the electoral roll because he was a member of the Turkish-Cypriot community. Aziz alleged a breach of his right to vote contrary to Article 3 of Protocol No. 1 and a breach of Article 14 in that he was prevented from exercising his right to vote on the grounds of his national origins or association with a national minority. The Chamber was unanimous in finding a breach of Article 3 of Protocol No 1 and also of Article 14 taken with that right.

36. The Court considers that, in the instant case, the complaint under Article 14 is not a mere restate-ment of the applicant's complaint under Article 3 of Protocol No 1. The Court notes that the applicant was a Cypriot national, resident in the Government-controlled area of Cyprus. It observes that the dif-ference in treatment in the present case resulted from the very fact that the applicant was a Turkish Cypriot. It emanated from the constitutional provisions regulating the voting rights between members of the Greek-Cypriot and Turkish-Cypriot communities that had become impossible to implement in practice.

37. Although the Court takes note of the Government's arguments, it considers that they cannot justify this difference on reasonable and objective grounds, particularly in the light of the fact that Turkish Cypriots in the applicant's situation are prevented from voting at any parliamentary election.

38. Thus, the Court concludes that there is a clear inequality of treatment in the enjoyment of the right in question, which must be considered a fundamental aspect of the case. There has accordingly been a violation of Article 14 of the Convention in conjunction with Article 3 of Protocol No 1.

Alternatively, where the Court has found a violation of Article 14 (in conjunction with a sub-stantive right) it may decline to examine an argument that the substantive right alone has been breached; for example in *Thlimmenos* (above, note 8) the Court refused to consider whether there had been a breach of Article 9.

13   Livingstone concluded that:

Although the limitations of Article 14 as an anti-discrimination provision are clear it is worth observing that the Commission and Court have been prepared to expand it. In some of the Court's early judg-ments on the article there were those who wished to tie it tightly to the other Convention articles invoked and effectively refuse to find a violation of Article 14 unless a right clearly guaranteed by the primary article had been denied. By refusing to take this path the Commission and Court have given Article 14 an autonomous existence and in so doing have extended the impact of certain Convention rights. [S Livingstone, 'Article 14 and the Prevention of Discrimination in the ECHR' (1997) European Human Rights Law Review 25 at p 33.]

The inherent weakness of Article 14, namely that it does not contain an independent pro-hibition of discrimination, has been addressed by the new Protocol 12 (the text of which can be found with the Convention at the end of the book). Two expert groups were the contem-porary forces behind the creation of this Protocol. The Steering Committee for Equality between Women and Men proposed the inclusion of a fundamental right of women and men to equality in the ECHR (the Committee believed that the creation of such a right was one of the prerequisites for achieving *de jure* and *de facto* equality). Also the European Commission against Racism and Intolerance, established as part of the Plan of Action to combat racism, xenophobia, anti-Semitism and intolerance by the Summit of Heads of State and Governments of the Council of Europe at Vienna in 1993, recommended the drafting of an additional Protocol containing a general prohibition against discrimination on the grounds of race, colour, lan-guage, religion or national or ethnic origin. The Committee of Ministers referred both these proposals to the Steering Committee for Human Rights. In October 1997 the Steering Com-mittee recommended the drafting of an additional Protocol as a legal solution to the two expert groups' recommendations. During the spring of 1998 the Ministers' Deputies (of the Committee of Ministers) authorised the Steering Committee to draft an additional Protocol broadening the scope of Article 14 and containing a non-exhaustive list of discrimination grounds. After consultations with, inter alios, the Court and the Parliamentary Assembly, the Steering Com-mittee finalised a draft Protocol in March 2000. The Committee of Ministers adopted the text in June 2000.

The official explanatory report accompanying the text of Protocol 12 explained its aims and terms as being:

PREAMBLE

14. The brief Preamble refers, in the first recital, to the principle of equality before the law and equal protection of the law. This is a fundamental and well-established general principle, and an essential element of the protection of human rights, which has been recognised in constitutions of member states and in international human rights law . . .

15. While the equality principle does not appear explicitly in the text of either Article 14 of the Convention or Article 1 of this Protocol, it should be noted that the non-discrimination and equality principles are closely intertwined. For example, the principle of equality requires that equal situations are treated equally and unequal situations differently. Failure to do so will amount to discrimination unless an objective and reasonable justification exists (see paragraph 18 below). The Court, in its case-law under Article 14, has already made reference to the 'principle of equality of treatment' (see, for example, the Court's judgment of 23 July 1968 in the *Belgian Linguistic'* case, Series A, No 6, paragraph 10) or to 'equality of the sexes' (see, for example, the judgment of 28 May 1985 in the case of *Abdulaziz, Cabales and Balkandali v UK*, Series A, No 94, paragraph 78).

16. The third recital of the preamble refers to measures taken in order to promote full and effective equality and reaffirms that such measures shall not be prohibited by the principle of non-discrimination, provided that there is an objective and reasonable justification for them (this principle already appears in certain existing international provisions: see, for example, Article 1, paragraph 4, of the International Convention on the Elimination of All Forms of Racial Discrimination, Article 4, paragraph 1, of the Convention on the Elimination of All Forms of Discrimination against Women and, at the regional level, Article 4, paragraph 3, of the Framework Convention for the Protection of National Minorities). The fact that there are certain groups or categories of persons who are disadvantaged, or the existence of *de facto* inequalities, may constitute justifications for adopting measures providing for specific advantages in order to promote equality, provided that the proportionality principle is respected. Indeed, there are several international instruments obliging or encouraging states to adopt positive measures (see, for example, Article 2, paragraph 2, of the International Convention on the Elimination of All Forms of Racial Discrimination, Article 4, paragraph 2, of the Framework Convention for the Protection of National Minorities and Recommendation No R (85) 2 of the Committee of Ministers to member states on legal protection against sex discrimination). However, the present Protocol does not impose any obligation to adopt such measures. Such a programmatic obligation would sit ill with the whole nature of the Convention and its control system which are based on the collective guarantee of individual rights which are formulated in terms sufficiently specific to be justiciable.

ARTICLE 1—GENERAL PROHIBITION OF DISCRIMINATION

17. This article contains the main substantive provisions of the Protocol. Its wording is based on the following general considerations.

18. The notion of discrimination has been interpreted consistently by the European Court of Human Rights in its case-law concerning Article 14 of the Convention. In particular, this case-law has made clear that not every distinction or difference of treatment amounts to discrimination. As the Court has stated, for example, in the judgment in the case of *Abdulaziz, Cabales and Balkandali v UK*: 'a difference of treatment is discriminatory if it 'has no objective and reasonable justification', that is, if it does not pursue a 'legitimate aim' or if there is not a 'reasonable relationship of proportionality between the means employed and the aim sought to be realised'' (judgment of 28 May 1985, Series A, No 94, paragraph 72). The meaning of the term 'discrimination' in Article 1 is intended to be identical to that in Article 14 of the Convention. The wording of the French text of Article 1 ('sans discrimination aucune')

differs slightly from that of Article 14 ('sans distinction aucune'). No difference of meaning is intended; on the contrary, this is a terminological adaptation intended to reflect better the concept of discrimination within the meaning of Article 14 by bringing the French text into line with the English (see, on this precise point, the Court's judgment of 23 July 1968 in the *Belgian Linguistic* case, Series A, No 6, paragraph 10).

19. Since not every distinction or difference of treatment amounts to discrimination, and because of the general character of the principle of non-discrimination, it was not considered necessary or appropriate to include a restriction clause in the present Protocol. For example, the law of most if not all member states of the Council of Europe provides for certain distinctions based on nationality concerning certain rights or entitlements to benefits. The situations where such distinctions are acceptable are sufficiently safeguarded by the very meaning of the notion 'discrimination' as described in paragraph 18 above, since distinctions for which an objective and reasonable justification exists do not constitute discrimination. In addition, it should be recalled that under the case-law of the European Court of Human Rights a certain margin of appreciation is allowed to national authorities in assessing whether and to what extent differences in otherwise similar situations justify a different treatment in law. The scope of the margin of appreciation will vary according to the circumstances, the subject-matter and its background (see, for example, the judgment of 28 November 1984 in the case of *Rasmussen v Denmark*, Series A, No 87, paragraph 40). For example, the Court has allowed a wide margin of appreciation as regards the framing and implementation of policies in the area of taxation (see, for example, the judgment of 3 October 1997 in the case of *National and Provincial Building Society and Others v UK*, Reports of Judgments and Decisions 1997-VII, paragraph 80).

20. The list of non-discrimination grounds in Article 1 is identical to that in Article 14 of the Convention. This solution was considered preferable over others, such as expressly including certain additional non-discrimination grounds (for example, physical or mental disability, sexual orientation or age), not because of a lack of awareness that such grounds have become particularly important in today's societies as compared with the time of drafting of Article 14 of the Convention, but because such an inclusion was considered unnecessary from a legal point of view since the list of non-discrimination grounds is not exhaustive, and because inclusion of any particular additional ground might give rise to unwarranted *a contrario* interpretations as regards discrimination based on grounds not so included. It is recalled that the European Court of Human Rights has already applied Article 14 in relation to discrimination grounds not explicitly mentioned in that provision (see, for example, as concerns the ground of sexual orientation, the judgment of 21 December 1999 in the case of *Salgueiro da Silva Mouta v Portugal*).

21. Article 1 provides a general non-discrimination clause and thereby affords a scope of protection which extends beyond the 'enjoyment of the rights and freedoms set forth in [the] Convention'.

22. In particular, the additional scope of protection under Article 1 concerns cases where a person is discriminated against:
i.   in the enjoyment of any right specifically granted to an individual under national law;
ii. in the enjoyment of a right which may be inferred from a clear obligation of a public authority under national law, that is, where a public authority is under an obligation under national law to behave in a particular manner;
iii. by a public authority in the exercise of discretionary power (for example, granting certain subsidies);
iv. by any other act or omission by a public authority (for example, the behaviour of law enforcement officers when controlling a riot).

23. In this respect, it was considered unnecessary to specify which of these four elements are covered by the first paragraph of Article 1 and which by the second. The two paragraphs are complementary and their combined effect is that all four elements are covered by Article 1. It should also be borne in

mind that the distinctions between the respective categories i–iv are not clear-cut and that domestic legal systems may have different approaches as to which case comes under which category.

24. The wording of Article 1 reflects a balanced approach to possible positive obligations of the Parties under this provision. This concerns the question to what extent Article 1 obliges the Parties to take measures to prevent discrimination, even where discrimination occurs in relations between private persons (so-called 'indirect horizontal effects'). The same question arises as regards measures to remedy instances of discrimination. While such positive obligations cannot be excluded altogether, the prime objective of Article 1 is to embody a negative obligation for the Parties: the obligation not to discriminate against individuals.

25. On the one hand, Article 1 protects against discrimination by public authorities. The Article is not intended to impose a general positive obligation on the Parties to take measures to prevent or remedy all instances of discrimination in relations between private persons. An additional protocol to the Convention, which typically contains justiciable individual rights formulated in concise provisions, would not be a suitable instrument for defining the various elements of such a wide-ranging obligation of a programmatic character. Detailed and tailor-made rules have already been laid down in separate conventions exclusively devoted to the elimination of discrimination on the specific grounds covered by them (see, for example, the Convention on Elimination of All Forms of Racial Discrimination and the Convention on the Elimination of All Forms of Discrimination against Women, which were both elaborated within the United Nations). It is clear that the present Protocol may not be construed as limiting or derogating from domestic or treaty provisions which provide further protection from discrimination . . .

26. On the other hand, it cannot be totally excluded that the duty to 'secure' under the first paragraph of Article 1 might entail positive obligations. For example, this question could arise if there is a clear lacuna in domestic law protection from discrimination. Regarding more specifically relations between private persons, a failure to provide protection from discrimination in such relations might be so clear-cut and grave that it might engage clearly the responsibility of the State and then Article 1 of the Protocol could come into play (see, mutatis mutandis, the judgment of the Court of 26 March 1985 in the case of *X and Y v the Netherlands*, Series A, No 91, paragraphs 23–4, 27 and 30).

27. Nonetheless, the extent of any positive obligations flowing from Article 1 is likely to be limited. It should be borne in mind that the first paragraph is circumscribed by the reference to the 'enjoyment of any right set forth by law' and that the second paragraph prohibits discrimination 'by any public authority'. It should be noted that, in addition, Article 1 of the Convention sets a general limit on state responsibility which is particularly relevant in cases of discrimination between private persons.

28. These considerations indicate that any positive obligation in the area of relations between private persons would concern, at the most, relations in the public sphere normally regulated by law, for which the state has a certain responsibility (for example, arbitrary denial of access to work, access to restaurants, or to services which private persons may make available to the public such as medical care or utilities such as water and electricity, etc). The precise form of the response which the state should take will vary according to the circumstances. It is understood that purely private matters would not be affected. Regulation of such matters would also be likely to interfere with the individual's right to respect for his private and family life, his home and his correspondence, as guaranteed by Article 8 of the Convention.

29. The first paragraph of Article 1 refers to 'any right set forth by law'. This expression seeks to define the scope of the guarantee provided for in this paragraph and to limit its possible indirect horizontal effects (see paragraph 27 above). Since there may be some doubt as to whether this sentence on its own covers all four elements which constitute the basic additional scope of the Protocol (the question could arise in particular with respect to elements iii and iv—see paragraph 22 above), it should be recalled that the first and second paragraphs of Article 1 are complementary. The result is that those four elements

are at all events covered by Article 1 as a whole (see paragraph 23 above). The word 'law' may also cover international law, but this does not mean that this provision entails jurisdiction for the European Court of Human Rights to examine compliance with rules of law in other international instruments.

30. The term 'public authority' in paragraph 2 has been borrowed from Article 8, paragraph 2, and Article 10, paragraph 1, of the Convention and is intended to have the same meaning as in those provisions. It covers not only administrative authorities but also the courts and legislative bodies (see paragraph 23 above).

Hence, while States will not generally be under a legal duty (enshrined in Protocol 12) to introduce programmes of affirmative action/positive discrimination to deal with disadvantaged groups or persons, the Preambles reiterates that where such measures exist and have 'an objective and reasonable justification' they will not be unlawful under the Convention. Furthermore, while the Protocol is primarily concerned with prohibiting discrimination by State authorities and officials in exceptional cases States may be obliged to intervene to prevent 'grave' forms of discrimination in relations between private persons. Protocol 12 came into force on 1 April 2005 for those States that had ratified it (Albania, Armenia, Bosnia & Herzegovina, Croatia, Cyprus, Finland, Georgia, Netherlands, San Marino, Serbia & Montenegro, and the former Yugoslav Republic of Macedonia). It will apply to other States as and when they ratify it. Article 14 will continue to apply to all parties to the Convention.

17 ARTICLE 15 DEROGATION IN TIME OF EMERGENCY

Lawless v Ireland (No 3) A.3 (1961) 1 EHRR 15
European Court of Human Rights

On a number of occasions since the establishment of the Irish Free State in 1921 armed groups, calling themselves the 'Irish Republican Army' (IRA), have been formed to use violence to end British sovereignty in Northern Ireland. During 1939 the IRA 'declared war on Great Britain' and the Irish Government responded by securing the passage of the Offences Against the State (Amendment) Act 1940 (No 2 of 1940) which granted powers of extra-judicial detention to Ministers of the State. During 1956 and 1957 there was a renewed outbreak of IRA violence, including the bombing of the Dublin to Belfast railway line and the ambushing of a Northern Irish police patrol near the border which resulted in one officer being killed. Consequently, the Irish Government issued a proclamation, on 5 July 1957, bringing the special powers of arrest and detention under the 1940 Act into force. A few days later the Irish Minister for External Affairs informed the Secretary-General of the Council of Europe that the 1940 Act had been activated and that his letter should be regarded as notification of derogation under Article 15 of the Convention.

In 1956, during his trial in Ireland on charges of unlawful possession of firearms, the applicant admitted that he was a member of the IRA. He was acquitted of those charges, but convicted of possessing incriminating documents (relating to guerrilla warfare) by the Dublin District Court in May 1957 and sentenced to one month's imprisonment. On 13 July 1957, Lawless was detained on the order of the Minister of Justice, issued under the 1940 Act, as the latter considered Lawless to be engaged in activities prejudicial to the security of the State. Lawless was held in the Curragh Internment Camp. He was released from detention on 11 December 1957, after having given a verbal undertaking that he would not engage 'in any illegal activities under the Offences Against the State Acts'. Lawless complained to Strasbourg alleging a violation of a number of his Convention rights including those of liberty and a fair trial under Article 5 and 6. The Irish Government, *inter alia*, sought to rely upon Article 15 to justify its actions.

22. Whereas it follows from these provisions that, without being released from all its undertakings assumed in the Convention, the Government of any High Contracting Party has the right, in case of war or public emergency threatening the life of the nation, to take measures derogating from its obligations under the Convention other than those named in Article 15, paragraph 2 (art 15-2), provided that such measures are strictly limited to what is required by the exigencies of the situation and also that they do not conflict with other obligations under international law; whereas it is for the Court to determine

whether the conditions laid down in Article 15 (art 15) for the exercise of the exceptional right of derogation have been fulfilled in the present case;

(A) AS TO THE EXISTENCE OF A PUBLIC EMERGENCY THREATENING THE LIFE OF THE NATION

23. Whereas the Irish Government, by a Proclamation dated 5 July 1957 and published in the Official Gazette on 8 July 1957, brought into force the extraordinary powers conferred upon it by Part II of the Offences against the State (Amendment) Act, 1940, 'to secure the preservation of public peace and order';

24. Whereas, by letter dated 20 July 1957 addressed to the Secretary-General of the Council of Europe, the Irish Government expressly stated that 'the detention of persons under the Act is considered necessary to prevent the commission of offences against public peace and order and to prevent the maintaining of military or armed forces other than those authorised by the Constitution';

25. Whereas, in reply to the Application introduced by G R Lawless before the Commission, the Irish Government adduced a series of facts from which they inferred the existence, during the period mentioned, of 'a public emergency threatening the life of the nation' within the meaning of Article 15 (art 15);

26. Whereas, before the Commission, G R Lawless submitted in support of his application that the aforesaid facts, even if proved to exist, would not have constituted a 'public emergency threatening the life of the nation' within the meaning of Article 15 (art 15); whereas, moreover, he disputed some of the facts adduced by the Irish Government;

27. Whereas the Commission, following the investigation carried out by it in accordance with Article 28 (art 28) of the Convention, expressed a majority opinion in its Report that in 'July 1957 there existed in Ireland a public emergency threatening the life of the nation within the meaning of Article 15, paragraph 1 (art 15-1), of the Convention';

28. Whereas, in the general context of Article 15 (art 15) of the Convention, the natural and customary meaning of the words 'other public emergency threatening the life of the nation' is sufficiently clear; whereas they refer to an exceptional situation of crisis or emergency which affects the whole population and constitutes a threat to the organised life of the community of which the State is composed; whereas, having thus established the natural and customary meaning of this conception, the Court must determine whether the facts and circumstances which led the Irish Government to make their Proclamation of 5 July 1957 come within this conception; whereas the Court, after an examination, find this to be the case; whereas the existence at the time of a 'public emergency threatening the life of the nation', was reasonably deduced by the Irish Government from a combination of several factors, namely: in the first place, the existence in the territory of the Republic of Ireland of a secret army engaged in unconstitutional activities and using violence to attain its purposes; secondly, the fact that this army was also operating outside the territory of the State, thus seriously jeopardising the relations of the Republic of Ireland with its neighbour; thirdly, the steady and alarming increase in terrorist activities from the autumn of 1956 and throughout the first half of 1957;

29. Whereas, despite the gravity of the situation, the Government had succeeded, by using means available under ordinary legislation, in keeping public institutions functioning more or less normally, but whereas the homicidal ambush on the night 3 to 4 July 1957 in the territory of Northern Ireland near the border had brought to light, just before 12 July—a date, which, for historical reasons is particularly critical for the preservation of public peace and order—the imminent danger to the nation caused by the continuance of unlawful activities in Northern Ireland by the IRA and various associated groups, operating from the territory of the Republic of Ireland;

30. Whereas, in conclusion, the Irish Government were justified in declaring that there was a public emergency in the Republic of Ireland threatening the life of the nation and were hence entitled, applying the provisions of Article 15, paragraph 1 (art 15-1), of Convention for the purposes for which those provisions were made, to take measures derogating from their obligations under the Convention;

(B) AS TO WHETHER THE MEASURES TAKEN IN DEROGATION FROM OBLIGATIONS UNDER THE CONVENTION WERE 'STRICTLY REQUIRED BY THE EXIGENCIES OF THE SITUATION'

31. Whereas Article 15, paragraph 1 (art 15-1), provides that a High Contracting Party may derogate from its obligations under the Convention only 'to the extent strictly required by the exigencies of the situation'; whereas it is therefore necessary, in the present case, to examine whether the bringing into force of Part II of the 1940 Act was a measure strictly required by the emergency existing in 1957;

32. Whereas GR Lawless contended before the Commission that even if the situation in 1957 was such as to justify derogation from obligations under the Convention, the bringing into operation and the enforcement of Part II of the Offences against the State (Amendment) Act 1940 were disproportionate to the strict requirements of the situation;

33. Whereas the Irish Government, before both the Commission and the Court, contended that the measures taken under Part II of the 1940 Act were, in the circumstances, strictly required by the exigencies of the situation in accordance with Article 15, paragraph 1 (art 15-1), of the Convention;

34. Whereas while the majority of the Commission concurred with the Irish Government's submissions on this point, some members of the Commission drew from the facts established different legal conclusions;

35. Whereas it was submitted that in view of the means available to the Irish Government in 1957 for controlling the activities of the IRA and its splinter groups the Irish Government could have taken measures which would have rendered superfluous so grave a measure as detention without trial; whereas, in this connection, mention was made of the application of the ordinary criminal law, the institution of special criminal courts of the type provided for by the Offences against the State Act, 1939, or of military courts; whereas it would have been possible to consider other measures such as the sealing of the border between the Republic of Ireland and Northern Ireland;

36. Whereas, however, considering, in the judgment of the Court, that in 1957 the application of the ordinary law had proved unable to check the growing danger which threatened the Republic of Ireland; whereas the ordinary criminal courts, or even the special criminal courts or military courts, could not suffice to restore peace and order; whereas, in particular, the amassing of the necessary evidence to convict persons involved in activities of the IRA and its splinter groups was meeting with great difficulties caused by the military, secret and terrorist character of those groups and the fear they created among the population; whereas the fact that these groups operated mainly in Northern Ireland, their activities in the Republic of Ireland being virtually limited to the preparation of armed raids across the border was an additional impediment to the gathering of sufficient evidence; whereas the sealing of the border would have had extremely serious repercussions on the population as a whole, beyond the extent required by the exigencies of the emergency;

Whereas it follows from the foregoing that none of the above-mentioned means would have made it possible to deal with the situation existing in Ireland in 1957; whereas, therefore, the administrative detention—as instituted under the Act (Amendment) of 1940—of individuals suspected of intending to take part in terrorist activities, appeared, despite its gravity, to be a measure required by the circumstances;

37. Whereas, moreover, the Offences against the State (Amendment) Act of 1940, was subject to a number of safeguards designed to prevent abuses in the operation of the system of administrative detention; whereas the application of the Act was thus subject to constant supervision by Parliament, which not only received precise details of its enforcement at regular intervals but could also at any time, by a Resolution, annul the Government's Proclamation which had brought the Act into force; whereas the Offences against the State (Amendment) Act 1940, provided for the establishment of a 'Detention Commission' made up of three members, which the Government did in fact set up, the members being an officer of the Defence Forces and two judges; whereas any person detained under this Act could refer his case to that Commission whose opinion, if favourable to the release of the person concerned, was binding upon the Government; whereas, moreover, the ordinary courts could themselves compel the Detention Commission to carry out its functions;

Whereas, in conclusion, immediately after the Proclamation which brought the power of detention into force, the Government publicly announced that it would release any person detained who gave an undertaking to respect the Constitution and the Law and not to engage in any illegal activity, and that the wording of this undertaking was later altered to one which merely required that the person detained would undertake to observe the law and refrain from activities contrary to the 1940 Act; whereas the persons arrested were informed immediately after their arrest that they would be released following the undertaking in question; whereas in a democratic country such as Ireland the existence of this guarantee of release given publicly by the Government constituted a legal obligation on the Government to release all persons who gave the undertaking;

Whereas, therefore, it follows from the foregoing that the detention without trial provided for by the 1940 Act, subject to the above-mentioned safeguards, appears to be a measure strictly required by the exigencies of the situation within the meaning of Article 15 (art 15) of the Convention;

38. Whereas, in the particular case of GR Lawless, there is nothing to show that the powers of detention conferred upon the Irish Government by the Offences against the State (Amendment) Act 1940, were employed against him, either within the meaning of Article 18 (art 18) of the Convention, for a purpose other than that for which they were granted, or within the meaning of Article 15 (art 15) of the Convention, by virtue of a measure going beyond what was strictly required by the situation at that time; whereas on the contrary, the Commission, after finding in its Decision of 30 August 1958 on the admissibility of the Application that the Applicant had in fact submitted his Application to it after having exhausted the domestic remedies, observed in its Report that the general conduct of GR Lawless, 'his association with persons known to be active members of the IRA, his conviction for carrying incriminating documents and other circumstances were such as to draw upon the Applicant the gravest suspicion that, whether or not he was any longer a member, he still was concerned with the activities of the IRA at the time of his arrest in July 1957; whereas the file also shows that, at the beginning of GR Lawless's detention under Act No 2 of 1940, the Irish Government informed him that he would be released if he gave a written undertaking 'to respect the Constitution of Ireland and the Laws' and not to 'be a member of or assist any organisation that is an unlawful organisation under the Offences against the State Act, 1939'; whereas in December 1957 the Government renewed its offer in a different form, which was accepted by GR Lawless, who gave a verbal undertaking before the Detention Commission not to 'take part in any activities that are illegal under the Offences against the State Acts 1939 and 1940' and was accordingly immediately released;

(C) AS TO WHETHER THE MEASURES DEROGATING FROM OBLIGATIONS UNDER THE CONVENTION WERE 'INCONSISTENT WITH . . . OTHER OBLIGATIONS UNDER INTERNATIONAL LAW'

39. Whereas Article 15, paragraph 1 (art 15-1), of the Convention authorises a High Contracting Party to take measures derogating from the Convention only provided that they 'are not inconsistent with . . . other obligations under international law';

40. Whereas, although neither the Commission nor the Irish Government have referred to this provision in the proceedings, the function of the Court, which is to ensure the observance of the engagements undertaken by the Contracting Parties in the Convention (Article 19 of the Convention) (art 19), requires it to determine proprio motu whether this condition has been fulfilled in the present case;

41. Whereas no facts have come to the knowledge of the Court which give it cause hold that the measure taken by the Irish Government derogating from the Convention may have conflicted with the said Government's other obligations under international law;

(D) AS TO WHETHER THE LETTER OF 20TH JULY 1957 FROM THE IRISH GOVERNMENT TO THE SECRETARY-GENERAL OF THE COUNCIL OF EUROPE WAS A SUFFICIENT NOTIFICATION FOR THE PURPOSES OF ARTICLE 15, PARAGRAPH 3 (ART 15-3), OF THE CONVENTION

42. Whereas Article 15, paragraph 3 (art 15-3), of the Convention provides that a Contracting Party availing itself of the right of derogation under paragraph 1 of the same Article (art 15-1) shall keep the Secretary-General of the Council of Europe fully informed of the measures which it has taken and the reasons therefor and shall also inform him when such measures have ceased to operate;

43. Whereas, in the present case, the Irish Government, on 20 July 1957, sent the Secretary-General of the Council of Europe a letter informing him—as is stated therein: 'in compliance with Article 15 (3) (art 15-3) of the Convention'—that Part II of the Offences against the State (Amendment) Act, 1940, had been brought into force on 8th July 1957; whereas copies of the Irish Government's Proclamation on the subject and of the 1940 Act itself were attached to the said letter; whereas the Irish Government explained in the said letter that the measure in question was 'considered necessary to prevent the commission of offences against public peace and order and to prevent the maintaining of military or armed forces other than those authorised by the Constitution';

44. Whereas GR Lawless contested before the Commission the Irish Government's right to rely on the letter of 20 July 1957 as a valid notice of derogation under Article 15, paragraph 3 (art 15-3), of the Convention; whereas, in substance, he contended before the Commission: that the letter had not the character of a notice of derogation, as the Government had not sent it for the purpose of registering a formal notice of derogation; that even if the letter were to be regarded as constituting such a notice, it did not comply with the strict requirements of Article 15, paragraph 3 (art 15-3), in that it neither adduced, as a ground for detention without trial, the existence of a time of war or other public emergency threatening the life of the nation nor properly defined the nature of the measure taken by the Government; whereas the Principal Delegate of the Commission, in the proceedings before the Court, made known a third contention of GR Lawless to the effect that the derogation, even if it had been duly notified to the Secretary-General on 20 July 1957, could not be enforced against persons within the jurisdiction of the Republic of Ireland in respect of the period before 23 October 1957, when it was first made public in Ireland;

45. Whereas the Commission expressed the opinion that the Irish Government had not delayed in bringing the enforcement of the special measures to the attention of the Secretary-General with explicit reference to Article 15, paragraph 3 (art 15-3), of the Convention; whereas the terms of the letter of 20 July 1957, to which were attached copies of the 1940 Act and of the Proclamation bringing it into force, were sufficient to indicate to the Secretary-General the nature of the measures taken and that consequently, while noting that the letter of 20 July did not contain a detailed account of the reasons which had led the Irish Government to take the measures of derogation, it could not say that in the present case there had not been a sufficient compliance with the provisions of Article 15, paragraph 3 (art 15-3); whereas, with regard to GR Lawless' third contention the Delegates of the Commission added, in the proceedings before the Court, that Article 15, paragraph 3 (art 15-3), of the Convention

required only that the Secretary-General of the Council of Europe be informed of the measures of derogation taken, without obliging the State concerned to promulgate the notice of derogation within the framework of its municipal laws;

46. Whereas the Irish Government, in their final submissions, asked the Court to state, in accordance with the Commission's opinion, that the letter of 20 July 1957 constituted a sufficient notification for the purposes of Article 15, paragraph 3 (art 15-3), of the Convention or, alternatively, to declare that there is nothing in the said paragraph 3 (art 15-3) which, in the present case, detracts from the Irish Government's right to rely on paragraph 1 of the said Article 15 (art 15-1);

47. Whereas the Court is called upon in the first instance, to examine whether, in pursuance of paragraph 3 of Article 15 (art 15-3) of the Convention, the Secretary-General of the Council of Europe was duly informed both of the measures taken and of the reason therefor; whereas the Court notes that a copy of the Offences against the State (Amendment) Act, 1940, and a copy of the Proclamation of 5 July, published on 8 July 1957, bringing into force Part II of the aforesaid Act were attached to the letter of 20 July; that it was explained in the letter of 20 July that the measures had been taken in order 'to prevent the commission of offences against public peace and order and to prevent the maintaining of military or armed forces other than those authorised by the Constitution'; that the Irish Government thereby gave the Secretary-General sufficient information of the measures taken and the reasons therefor; that, in the second place, the Irish Government brought this information to the Secretary-General's attention only 12 days after the entry into force of the measures derogating from their obligations under the Convention; and that the notification was therefore made without delay; whereas, in conclusion, the Convention does not contain any special provision to the effect that the Contracting State concerned must promulgate in its territory the notice of derogation addressed to the Secretary-General of the Council of Europe;

Whereas the Court accordingly finds that, in the present case, the Irish Government fulfilled their obligations as Party to the Convention under Article 15, paragraph 3 (art 15-3), of the Convention;

48. For these reasons,

THE COURT

Unanimously, . . .

(iv) States that the detention of GR Lawless from 13 July to 11 December 1957 was founded on the right of derogation duly exercised by the Irish Government in pursuance of Article 15 (art 15) of the Convention in July 1957;

(v) States that the communication addressed by the Irish Government to the Secretary-General of the Council of Europe on 20 July 1957 constituted sufficient notification within the meaning of Article 15, paragraph 3 (art 15-3), of the Convention;

Decides, accordingly, that in the present case the facts found do not disclose a breach by the Irish Government of their obligations under the European Convention for the Protection of Human Rights and Fundamental Freedoms; . . .

NOTES

1   The Court was composed of President Cassin and Judges: Maridakis, Rodenbourg, McGonigal, Balladore Pallieri, Arnalds, and Arik.

2   Judge Maridakis issued a concurring Individual Opinion in which he expressed the view that:

By 'public emergency threatening the life of the nation' it is to be understood a quite exceptional situation which imperils or might imperil the normal operation of public policy established in accordance with the lawfully expressed will of the citizens, in respect alike of the situation inside the country and of relations with foreign Powers.

3 The rather archaic language and style of the Court's judgment can be explained by the fact that this was the first case determined by that institution. Nevertheless, its interpretation of the terms 'other public emergency threatening the life of the nation', given in paragraph 28, has been applied in subsequent cases.

4 Although the Irish Government relied upon Article 15 to justify its extra-judicial measures designed to combat IRA terrorism in *Lawless*, when it brought a later complaint against the United Kingdom's use of extra-judicial powers of arrest and detention in Northern Ireland it sought to argue that the requirements of Article 15 had not been satisfied. The background to the *Ireland v UK* case has already been explained (above, p 145). The Court held that:

B. ON ARTICLE 5 TAKEN TOGETHER WITH ARTICLE 15 (ART 15+5)

202. The applicant Government maintain that the powers relating to extra-judicial deprivation of liberty which were applied in Northern Ireland from 9 August 1971 to March 1975 were not in complete conformity with Article 15 (art 15) and, accordingly, violated Article 5 (art 5).

The Commission is unanimous in not accepting this claim and it is disputed by the respondent Government.

...

204. Article 5 (art 5) does not appear among the entrenched provisions listed in paragraph 2 of Article 15 (art 15-2) and is therefore one of the Articles subject to the 'right of derogation' reserved by the Contracting States, the exercise of which is regulated by paragraphs 1 and 3 (art 15-1, art 15-3).

1. ON THE 'PUBLIC EMERGENCY THREATENING THE LIFE OF THE NATION'

205. Article 15 (art 15) comes into play only 'in time of war or other public emergency threatening the life of the nation'. The existence of such an emergency is perfectly clear from the facts summarised above . . . and was not questioned by anyone before either the Commission or the Court. The crisis experienced at the time by the six counties therefore comes within the ambit of Article 15 (art 15).

2. ON THE 'EXTENT STRICTLY REQUIRED'

206. The Contracting States may make use of their right of derogation only 'to the extent strictly required by the exigencies of the situation'. The Irish Government consider the 'extent strictly required' to have been exceeded, whereas the British Government and the Commission assert the contrary.

(a) The rôle of the Court

207. The limits on the Court's powers of review (see judgment of 23 July 1968 on the merits of the *'Belgian Linguistic'* case, Series A No 6, p 35, para 10 in fine; *Handyside* judgment of 7 December 1976, Series A No 24, p 22, para 48) are particularly apparent where Article 15 (art 15) is concerned.

It falls in the first place to each Contracting State, with its responsibility for 'the life of [its] nation', to determine whether that life is threatened by a 'public emergency' and, if so, how far it is necessary to go in attempting to overcome the emergency. By reason of their direct and continuous contact with the pressing needs of the moment, the national authorities are in principle in a better position than the international judge to decide both on the presence of such an emergency and on the nature and scope of derogations necessary to avert it. In this matter Article 15 para 1 (art 15-1) leaves those authorities a wide margin of appreciation.

Nevertheless, the States do not enjoy an unlimited power in this respect. The Court, which, with the Commission, is responsible for ensuring the observance of the States' engagements (Article 19) (art 19), is empowered to rule on whether the States have gone beyond the 'extent strictly required by the exigencies' of the crisis (*Lawless* judgment of 1 July 1961, Series A No 3, p 55, para 22, and pp 57–59, paras 36–38). The domestic margin of appreciation is thus accompanied by a European supervision.

(b) Questions of evidence

... 209. The Court is not bound, under the Convention or under the general principles applicable to international tribunals, by strict rules of evidence. In order to satisfy itself, the Court is entitled to rely on evidence of every kind, including, insofar as it deems them relevant, documents or statements emanating from governments, be they respondent or applicant, or from their institutions or officials. ...

(c) Questions concerning the merits

211. The Court has to decide whether the United Kingdom went beyond the 'extent strictly required'. For this purpose the Court must, as in the *Lawless* case (judgment of 1 July 1961, Series A No 3, pp 57–9, paras 36–37), enquire into the necessity for, on the one hand, deprivation of liberty contrary to paragraph 1 of Article 5 (art 5-1) and, on the other hand, the failure of guarantees to attain the level fixed by paragraphs 2 to 4 (art 5-2, art 5-3, art 5-4).

(I) On the necessity for derogation from paragraph 1 of Article 5 (art 5-1)
by extra-judicial deprivation of liberty

212. Unquestionably, the exercise of the special powers was mainly, and before 5 February 1973 even exclusively, directed against the IRA as an underground military force. The intention was to combat an organisation which had played a considerable subversive rôle throughout the recent history of Ireland and which was creating, in August 1971 and thereafter, a particularly far-reaching and acute danger for the territorial integrity of the United Kingdom, the institutions of the six counties and the lives of the province's inhabitants ... Being confronted with a massive wave of violence and intimidation, the Northern Ireland Government and then, after the introduction of direct rule (30 March 1972), the British Government were reasonably entitled to consider that normal legislation offered insufficient resources for the campaign against terrorism and that recourse to measures outside the scope of the ordinary law, in the shape of extra-judicial deprivation of liberty, was called for. When the Irish Republic was faced with a serious crisis in 1957, it adopted the same approach and the Court did not conclude that the 'extent strictly required' had been exceeded (*Lawless* judgment of 1 July 1961, Series A No 3, pp 35–36, para 14, and pp 57–58, para 36).

However, under one of the provisions complained of, namely Regulation 10, a person who was in no way suspected of a crime or offence or of activities prejudicial to peace and order could be arrested for the sole purpose of obtaining from him information about others—and this sometimes occurred ... This sort of arrest can be justifiable only in a very exceptional situation, but the circumstances prevailing in Northern Ireland did fall into such a category. Many witnesses could not give evidence freely without running the greatest risks ... the competent authorities were entitled to take the view, without exceeding their margin of appreciation, that it was indispensable to arrest such witnesses so that they could be questioned in conditions of relative security and not be exposed to reprisals. Moreover and above all, Regulation 10 authorised deprivation of liberty only for a maximum of 48 hours.

213. ... it appears to the Court that the extra-judicial measures brought into operation could, in the situation described above, reasonably have been considered strictly required for the protection of public security and that, in the context of Article 15 (art 15), their intrinsic necessity, once recognised, could not be affected by the restriction of their field of application.

214. The Irish Government submit that experience shows extra-judicial deprivation of liberty to have been ineffectual. They contend that the policy introduced on 9 August 1971 not only failed to put a brake on terrorism but also had the result of increasing it ... Consequently, the British Government, after attenuating the policy in varying degrees following the introduction of direct rule ... abandoned it on 5 December 1975: since then, it appears that no one has been detained in the six counties under the

emergency legislation, despite the persistence of an intense campaign of violence and even though the Emergency Provisions Amendment Act has remained in force . . . This, claim the applicant Government, confirms that extra-judicial deprivation of liberty was not an absolute necessity.

The Court cannot accept this argument.

It is certainly not the Court's function to substitute for the British Government's assessment any other assessment of what might be the most prudent or most expedient policy to combat terrorism. The Court must do no more than review the lawfulness, under the Convention, of the measures adopted by that Government from 9 August 1971 onwards. For this purpose the Court must arrive at its decision in the light, not of a purely retrospective examination of the efficacy of those measures, but of the conditions and circumstances reigning when they were originally taken and subsequently applied.

Adopting, as it must, this approach, the Court accepts that the limits of the margin of appreciation left to the Contracting States by Article 15 para 1 (art 15–1) were not overstepped by the United Kingdom when it formed the opinion that extra-judicial deprivation of liberty was necessary from August 1971 to March 1975.

(II) On the necessity for derogation from the guarantees under paragraphs 2 to 4 of Article 5 (art 5-2, art 5-3, art 5-4)

215. The Court must now examine under Article 15 para 1 (art 15-1) the necessity for the far-reaching derogations found by it to have been made from paragraphs 2 to 4 of Article 5 (art 5-2, art 5-3, art 5-4) . . .

216. Neither Regulations 10 and 11 (1) nor section 10 of the Emergency Provisions Act afforded any remedy, judicial or administrative, against arrests effected thereunder. Although persons arrested under Regulation 11 (1) could, before 7 November 1972, apply to the Civil Authority for release on bail, the Terrorists Order deprived them of this right by revoking Regulation 11 (4) under which it arose. However, the duration of such arrests never exceeded 48 hours as regards Regulation 10, seventy-two hours as regards section 10 of the Emergency Provisions Act and, in practice, seventy-two hours as regards Regulation 11 . . .

217. Similarly, Regulation 11 (2), Article 4 of the Terrorists Order and paragraph 11 of Schedule 1 to the Emergency Provisions Act did not provide for any remedy. Detention under Regulation 11 (2) sometimes continued for longer than twenty-eight days, but it was never to be for an indefinite period and the detainee could, if the administrative authority agreed, apply to the courts for release on bail (Regulation 11 (4) and the *McElduff* case, judgment of 12 October 1971). On the other hand, interim custody imposed under Article 4 of the Terrorists Order, or subsequently under paragraph 11 of Schedule 1 to the Emergency Provisions Act, continued until adjudication by the commissioner; the Chief Constable invariably referred the case to him within the initial twenty-eight day time-limit but the commissioner gave his decision after several weeks or even after six months . . .

218. Individuals deprived of their liberty under Regulation 12 (1), Article 5 of the Terrorists Order or paragraph 24 of Schedule 1 to the Emergency Provisions Act were in many cases interned or detained for some years. Nevertheless, the advisory committee set up by Regulation 12 (1) afforded, notwithstanding its non-judicial character, a certain measure of protection that cannot be discounted. By establishing commissioners and an appeal tribunal, the Terrorists Order brought further safeguards which were somewhat strengthened by the Emergency Provisions Act . . .

219. There was in addition the valuable, if limited, review effected by the courts, when the opportunity arose, by virtue of the common law . . .

220. An overall examination of the legislation and practice at issue reveals that they evolved in the direction of increasing respect for individual liberty. The incorporation right from the start of more satisfactory judicial, or at least administrative, guarantees would certainly have been desirable,

especially as Regulations 10 to 12 (1) dated back to 1956–1957 and were made under an Act of 1922, but it would be unrealistic to isolate the first from the later phases. When a State is struggling against a public emergency threatening the life of the nation, it would be rendered defenceless if it were required to accomplish everything at once, to furnish from the outset each of its chosen means of action with each of the safeguards reconcilable with the priority requirements for the proper functioning of the authorities and for restoring peace within the community. The interpretation of Article 15 (art 15) must leave a place for progressive adaptations.

The Northern Ireland Government sought in the first place—unsuccessfully—to meet the most pressing problem, to stem the wave of violence that was sweeping the region. After assuming direct responsibility for the future of the province, the British Government and Parliament lost little time in moderating in certain respects the severity of the laws applied in the early days. The Court asked itself whether those laws should not have been attenuated even more, especially as regards interim custody ... but does not consider that it can give an affirmative answer. It must not be forgotten that the crisis experienced at the time by the six counties was serious and, hence, of a kind that justified far-reaching derogations from paragraphs 2 to 4 of Article 5 (art 5-2, art 5-3, art 5-4). In view of the Contracting States' margin of appreciation, the Court does not find it established that the United Kingdom exceeded in this respect the 'extent strictly required' referred to in Article 15 para 1 (art 15-1).

221. According to the applicant Government, the non-contested violations of Article 3 (art 3) are relevant under Articles 5 and 15 (art 15+5) taken together. They claim that deprivation of liberty was sometimes imposed on the strength of information extracted in conditions contrary to Article 3 (art 3) and was thereby rendered unlawful under Article 15 (art 15). The Irish argument is also said to be confirmed by the existence of those violations since they would probably have been prevented by the impugned legislation if it had afforded genuine guarantees to the persons concerned.

The Court emphasises, as do the respondent Government and the Commission, that Articles 3 and 5 (art 3, art 5) embody quite separate obligations. Moreover, the violations of Article 3 (art 3) found in the present judgment fail to show that it was not necessary to apply the extra-judicial powers in force.

3. ON THE 'OTHER OBLIGATIONS UNDER INTERNATIONAL LAW'

222. Article 15 para 1 (art 15-1) in fine prohibits any derogation inconsistent 'with other obligations under international law'. There is nothing in the data before the Court to suggest that the United Kingdom disregarded such obligations in this case; in particular, the Irish Government never supplied to the Commission or the Court precise details on the claim formulated or outlined on this point in their application of 16 December 1971.

4. ON THE OBSERVANCE OF PARAGRAPH 3 OF ARTICLE 15 (ART 15-3)

223. The Court finds proprio motu, in the light of its *Lawless* judgment of 1 July 1961 (Series A No 3, pp 61–62, para 47), that the British notices of derogation dated 20 August 1971, 23 January 1973 and 16 August 1973 ... fulfilled the requirements of Article 15 para 3 (art 15-3).

5. CONCLUSION

224. The Court has accordingly come to the conclusion that, since the requirements of Article 15 (art 15) were met, the derogations from Article 5 (art 5) were not, in the circumstances of the case, in breach of the Convention.

A significant aspect of the above judgment was the Court's express recognition, in paragraph 207, that States are to be accorded a wide margin of appreciation in determining if the threats encompassed by Article 15 have arisen in their territories and how they should respond to them. For an examination of this concept see above, p 629.

Brannigan and McBride v UK A.258-B (1993) 17 EHRR 539
European Court of Human Rights

Between 1972 and 1992 over three thousand deaths were attributable to terrorism in Northern Ireland. Other parts of the United Kingdom have also been subject to a considerable amount of terrorist violence linked to the situation in Northern Ireland. Under section 12 of the Prevention of Terrorism (Temporary Provisions) Act 1984, police officers were given the power to arrest and detain, for questioning, persons whom officers had reasonable grounds for suspecting to be concerned in the commission, preparation or instigation of acts of terrorism relating to Northern Ireland. Officers could detain such person for up to forty-eight hours. The Secretary of State (for Northern Ireland) could also authorise, under the section, the continued detention of such persons for a maximum of five additional days (hence no person could be detained for more than seven days in total without being charged in respect of a criminal offence). On 29 November 1988, in *Brogan v UK*, (above, p 300), the Court ruled that the detention of persons for a minimum time of four days and six hours under section 12 violated Article 5(3) of the Convention. The Home Secretary made a statement to Parliament, on 22 December 1988 in which he explained the difficulties of introducing judicial controls over the arrest and detention of terrorist suspects.

We must pay proper regard to the tremendous pressures that are already faced by the judiciary, especially in Northern Ireland, where most cases have to be considered. We are also concerned that information about terrorist intentions, which often forms part of the case for an extension of detention, does not find its way back to the terrorists as a consequence of judicial procedures, which at least in the United Kingdom legal tradition generally require someone accused and his legal advisers to know the information alleged against him . . . .

In the meantime, the position cannot be left as it stands. I have already made clear to the House that we shall ensure that the police continue to have the powers they need to counter terrorism, and they continue to need to be able to detain suspects for up to seven days in some cases. To ensure that there can be no doubt about the ability of the police to deal effectively with such cases, the Government are today taking steps to give notice of derogation under Article 15 (art 15) of the European Convention of Human Rights, and Article 4 of the International Covenant on Civil and Political Rights. There is a public emergency within the meaning of these provisions in respect of terrorism connected with the affairs of Northern Ireland in the United Kingdom. . .

On 23 December 1988 the United Kingdom informed the Secretary General of the Council of Europe that the Government had availed itself of the right of derogation conferred by Article 15(1) to the extent that the exercise of powers under section 12 of the 1984 Act might be inconsistent with the obligations imposed by Article 5(3) Convention. The declaration stated:

. . . Following [the *Brogan* judgment], the Secretary of State for the Home Department informed Parliament on 6 December 1988 that, against the background of the terrorist campaign, and the overriding need to bring terrorists to justice, the Government did not believe that the maximum period of detention should be reduced. He informed Parliament that the Government were examining the matter with a view to responding to the judgment. On 22 December 1988, the Secretary of State further informed Parliament that it remained the Government's wish, if it could be achieved, to find a judicial process under which extended detention might be reviewed and where appropriate authorised by a judge or other judicial officer. But a further period of reflection and consultation was necessary before the Government could bring forward a firm and final view. Since the judgment of 29 November 1988 as well as previously, the Government have found it necessary to continue to exercise, in relation to terrorism connected with the affairs of Northern Ireland, the powers described above enabling further detention without charge, for periods of up to five days, on the authority of the Secretary of State, to the extent strictly required by the exigencies of the situation to enable necessary enquiries and investigations properly to be completed in order to decide whether criminal proceedings should be instituted. To the extent that the exercise of these powers may be inconsistent with the obligations imposed by the Convention the Government have availed themselves of the right of derogation conferred by Article 15(1) of the Convention and will continue to do so until further notice . . .

The Government reviewed whether the powers of extended detention could be conferred on the normal courts, but concluded that it would not be appropriate to involve courts in such decisions for the reasons given in a Written Answer in Parliament by the Secretary of State, Mr David Waddington, on 14 November 1989:

Decisions to authorise the detention of terrorist suspects for periods beyond 48 hours may be, and often are, taken on the basis of information, the nature and source of which could not be revealed to a suspect or his legal adviser without serious risk to individuals assisting the police or the prospect of further valuable intelligence being lost. Any new procedure which avoided those dangers by allowing a court to make a decision on information not presented to the detainee or his legal adviser would represent a radical departure from the principles which govern judicial proceedings in this country and could seriously affect public trust and confidence in the independence of the judiciary. The Government would be most reluctant to introduce any new procedure which could have this effect. (Official Report, 14 November 1989, col 210)

In a further notice dated 12 December 1989 the United Kingdom informed the Secretary General that a satisfactory procedure for the review of detention of terrorist suspects involving the judiciary had not been identified and that the derogation would therefore remain in place for as long as circumstances require. The first applicant was arrested by the police on 9 January 1989 and the Secretary of State authorised, under section 12, his continued detention until 15 January. During that time the applicant was interrogated on forty-three occasions. The second applicant was arrested on 5 January 1989 and the Secretary of State authorized his detention until 9 January. The applicants complained to the Commission that their periods of detention violated Article 5(3) as interpreted by the Court in *Brogan*. By eight votes to five, the Commission found no breach of the Convention in the light of the United Kingdom's derogation of 23 December 1988.

37. The Government, noting that both of the applicants were detained for longer periods than the shortest period found by the Court to be in breach of Article 5 para 3 (art 5-3) in the case of *Brogan*, conceded that the requirement of promptness had not been respected in the present cases . . . They further accepted that, in the absence of an enforceable right to compensation in respect of the breach of Article 5 para 3 (art 5-3), Article 5 para 5 (art 5-5) had not been complied with.

Having regard to its judgment in the case of *Brogan*, the Court finds that Article 5 paras 3 and 5 (art 5-3, art 5-5) have not been respected . . .

38. However, the Government further submitted that the failure to observe these requirements of Article 5 (art 5) had been met by their derogation of 23 December 1988 under Article 15 (art 15) of the Convention.

The Court must therefore examine the validity of the Government's derogation in the light of this provision. It recalls at the outset that the question whether any derogation from the United Kingdom's obligations under the Convention might be permissible under Article 15 (art 15) by reason of the terrorist campaign in Northern Ireland was specifically left open by the Court in the *Brogan* case . . .

VALIDITY OF THE UNITED KINGDOM'S DEROGATION UNDER ARTICLE 15 (ART 15)

39. The applicants maintained that the derogation under Article 15 (art 15) was invalid. This was disputed by both the Government and the Commission. . . .

1. THE COURT'S APPROACH TO THE MATTER

41. The applicants argued that it would be inconsistent with Article 15 para 2 (art 15-2) if, in derogating from safeguards recognised as essential for the protection of non-derogable rights such as Articles 2 and 3 (art 2, art 3), the national authorities were to be afforded a wide margin of appreciation. This was especially so where the emergency was of a quasi-permanent nature such as that existing in Northern Ireland. To do so would also be inconsistent with the *Brogan* judgment where the Court had regarded judicial control as one of the fundamental principles of a democratic society and had already—they claimed—extended to the Government a margin of appreciation by taking into account in paragraph 58 (p 32) the context of terrorism in Northern Ireland (loc cit.).

42. In their written submissions, Amnesty International maintained that strict scrutiny was required by the Court when examining derogation from fundamental procedural guarantees which were essential for the protection of detainees at all times, but particularly in times of emergency. Liberty, Interights and the Committee on the Administration of Justice ('Liberty and Others') submitted for their part that, if States are to be allowed a margin of appreciation at all, it should be narrower the more permanent the emergency becomes.

43. The Court recalls that it falls to each Contracting State, with its responsibility for 'the life of [its] nation', to determine whether that life is threatened by a 'public emergency' and, if so, how far it is necessary to go in attempting to overcome the emergency. By reason of their direct and continuous contact with the pressing needs of the moment, the national authorities are in principle in a better position than the international judge to decide both on the presence of such an emergency and on the nature and scope of derogations necessary to avert it. Accordingly, in this matter a wide margin of appreciation should be left to the national authorities (see the *Ireland v UK* judgment of 18 January 1978, Series A No 25, pp 78–79, para 207).

Nevertheless, Contracting Parties do not enjoy an unlimited power of appreciation. It is for the Court to rule on whether inter alia the States have gone beyond the 'extent strictly required by the exigencies' of the crisis. The domestic margin of appreciation is thus accompanied by a European supervision (ibid). At the same time, in exercising its supervision the Court must give appropriate weight to such relevant factors as the nature of the rights affected by the derogation, the circumstances leading to, and the duration of, the emergency situation.

2. EXISTENCE OF A PUBLIC EMERGENCY THREATENING THE LIFE OF THE NATION

44. Although the applicants did not dispute that there existed a public emergency 'threatening the life of the nation', they submitted that the burden rested on the Government to satisfy the Court that such an emergency really existed.

45. It was, however, suggested by Liberty and Others in their written submissions that at the relevant time there was no longer any evidence of an exceptional situation of crisis. They maintained that reconsideration of the position could only properly have led to a further derogation if there was a demonstrable deterioration in the situation since August 1984 when the Government withdrew their previous derogation. For the Standing Advisory Commission on Human Rights, on the other hand, there was a public emergency in Northern Ireland at the relevant time of a sufficient magnitude to entitle the Government to derogate.

46. Both the Government and the Commission, referring to the existence of public disturbance in Northern Ireland, maintained that there was such an emergency.

47. Recalling its case-law in *Lawless v Ireland* (judgment of 1 July 1961, Series A No 3, p 56, para 28) and *Ireland v UK* (loc. cit., Series A No 25, p 78, para 205) and making its own assessment, in the light of all the material before it as to the extent and impact of terrorist violence in Northern Ireland and elsewhere in the United Kingdom...the Court considers there can be no doubt that such a public emergency existed at the relevant time.

It does not judge it necessary to compare the situation which obtained in 1984 with that which prevailed in December 1988 since a decision to withdraw a derogation is, in principle, a matter within the discretion of the State and since it is clear that the Government believed that the legislation in question was in fact compatible with the Convention . . .

3. WERE THE MEASURES STRICTLY REQUIRED BY THE EXIGENCIES OF THE SITUATION?

(a) General considerations

48. The Court recalls that judicial control of interferences by the executive with the individual's right to liberty provided for by Article 5 (art 5) is implied by one of the fundamental principles of a democratic society, namely the rule of law (see the above-mentioned *Brogan* judgment, Series A No 145-B, p 32, para 58). It further observes that the notice of derogation invoked in the present case was lodged by the respondent Government soon after the judgment in the above-mentioned *Brogan* case where the Court had found the Government to be in breach of their obligations under Article 5 para 3 (art 5-3) by not bringing the applicants 'promptly' before a court.

The Court must scrutinise the derogation against this background and taking into account that the power of arrest and detention in question has been in force since 1974. However, it must be observed that the central issue in the present case is not the existence of the power to detain suspected terrorists for up to seven days—indeed a complaint under Article 5 para 1 (art 5-1) was withdrawn by the applicants . . . —but rather the exercise of this power without judicial intervention.

(b) Was the derogation a genuine response to an emergency situation?

49. For the applicants, the purported derogation was not a necessary response to any new or altered state of affairs but was the Government's reaction to the decision in *Brogan* and was lodged merely to circumvent the consequences of this judgment.

50. The Government and the Commission maintained that, while it was true that this judgment triggered off the derogation, the exigencies of the situation have at all times since 1974 required the powers of extended detention conferred by the Prevention of Terrorism legislation. It was the view of successive Governments that these powers were consistent with Article 5 para 3 (art 5-3) and that no derogation was necessary. However, both the measures and the derogation were direct responses to the emergency with which the United Kingdom was and continues to be confronted.

51. The Court first observes that the power of arrest and extended detention has been considered necessary by the Government since 1974 in dealing with the threat of terrorism. Following the *Brogan* judgment the Government were then faced with the option of either introducing judicial control of the decision to detain under section 12 of the 1984 Act or lodging a derogation from their Convention obligations in this respect. The adoption of the view by the Government that judicial control compatible with Article 5 para 3 (art 5-3) was not feasible because of the special difficulties associated with the investigation and prosecution of terrorist crime rendered derogation inevitable. Accordingly, the power of extended detention without such judicial control and the derogation of 23 December 1988 being clearly linked to the persistence of the emergency situation, there is no indication that the derogation was other than a genuine response.

(c) Was the derogation premature?

52. The applicants maintained that derogation was an interim measure which Article 15 (art 15) did not provide for since it appeared from the notice of derogation communicated to the Secretary General of the Council of Europe on 23 December 1988 that the Government had not reached a 'firm or final view' on the need to derogate from Article 5 para 3 (art 5-3) and required a further period of reflection and consultation. Following this period the Secretary of State for the Home Department confirmed the

derogation in a statement to Parliament on 14 November 1989 . . . Prior to this concluded view Article 15 (art 15) did not permit derogation. Furthermore, even at this date the Government had not properly examined whether the obligation in Article 5 para 3 (art 5-3) could be satisfied by an 'officer authorised by law to exercise judicial power'.

53. The Government contended that the validity of the derogation was not affected by their examination of the possibility of judicial control of extended detention since, as the Commission had pointed out, it was consistent with the requirements of Article 15 para 3 (art 15-3) to keep derogation measures under constant review.

54. The Court does not accept the applicants' argument that the derogation was premature.

While it is true that Article 15 (art 15) does not envisage an interim suspension of Convention guarantees pending consideration of the necessity to derogate, it is clear from the notice of derogation that 'against the background of the terrorist campaign, and the over-riding need to bring terrorists to justice, the Government did not believe that the maximum period of detention should be reduced'. However it remained the Government's wish 'to find a judicial process under which extended detention might be reviewed and where appropriate authorised by a judge or other judicial officer' . . .

The validity of the derogation cannot be called into question for the sole reason that the Government had decided to examine whether in the future a way could be found of ensuring greater conformity with Convention obligations. Indeed, such a process of continued reflection is not only in keeping with Article 15 para 3 (art 15-3) which requires permanent review of the need for emergency measures but is also implicit in the very notion of proportionality.

(d) Was the absence of judicial control of extended detention justified?

55. The applicants further considered that there was no basis for the Government's assertion that control of extended detention by a judge or other officer authorised by law to exercise judicial power was not possible or that a period of seven days' detention was necessary. They did not accept that the material required to satisfy a court of the justification for extended detention could be more sensitive than that needed in proceedings for habeas corpus. They and the Standing Advisory Commission on Human Rights also pointed out that the courts in Northern Ireland were frequently called on to deal with submissions based on confidential information—for example, in bail applications—and that there were sufficient procedural and evidential safeguards to protect confidentiality. Procedures also existed where judges were required to act on the basis of material which would not be disclosed either to the legal adviser or to his client. This was the case, for example, with claims by the executive to public interest immunity or application by the police to extend detention under the Police and Criminal Evidence (Northern Ireland) Order 1989 . . .

56. On this point the Government responded that none of the above procedures involved both the non-disclosure of material to the detainee or his legal adviser and an executive act of the court. The only exception appeared in Schedule 7 to the Prevention of Terrorism (Temporary Provisions) Act 1989 where inter alia the court may make an order in relation to the production of, and search for, special material relevant to terrorist investigations. However, paragraph 8 of Schedule 7 provides that, where the disclosure of information to the court would be too sensitive or would prejudice the investigation, the power to make the order is conferred on the Secretary of State and not the court . . .

It was also emphasised that the Government had reluctantly concluded that, within the framework of the common-law system, it was not feasible to introduce a system which would be compatible with Article 5 para 3 (art 5-3) but would not weaken the effectiveness of the response to the terrorist threat. Decisions to prolong detention were taken on the basis of information the nature and source of which could not be revealed to a suspect or his legal adviser without risk to individuals assisting the police or the prospect of further valuable intelligence being lost. Moreover, involving the judiciary in the process of granting or approving extensions of detention created a real risk of undermining their independence as they would inevitably be seen as part of the investigation and prosecution process.

In addition, the Government did not accept that the comparison with habeas corpus was a valid one since judicial involvement in the grant or approval of extension would require the disclosure of a considerable amount of additional sensitive information which it would not be necessary to produce in habeas corpus proceedings. In particular, a court would have to be provided with details of the nature and extent of police inquiries following the arrest, including details of witnesses interviewed and information obtained from other sources as well as information about the future course of the police investigation.

Finally, Lords Shackleton and Jellicoe and Viscount Colville in their reports had concluded that arrest and extended detention were indispensable powers in combating terrorism. These reports also found that the training of terrorists in remaining silent under police questioning hampered and protracted the investigation of terrorist offences. In consequence, the police were required to undertake extensive checks and inquiries and to rely to a greater degree than usual on painstaking detective work and forensic examination...

57. The Commission was of the opinion that the Government had not overstepped their margin of appreciation in this regard.

58. The Court notes the opinions expressed in the various reports reviewing the operation of the Prevention of Terrorism legislation that the difficulties of investigating and prosecuting terrorist crime give rise to the need for an extended period of detention which would not be subject to judicial control... Moreover, these special difficulties were recognised in its above-mentioned *Brogan* judgment (see Series A No 145-B, p 33, para 61).

It further observes that it remains the view of the respondent Government that it is essential to prevent the disclosure to the detainee and his legal adviser of information on the basis of which decisions on the extension of detention are made and that, in the adversarial system of the common law, the independence of the judiciary would be compromised if judges or other judicial officers were to be involved in the granting or approval of extensions.

The Court also notes that the introduction of a 'judge or other officer authorised by law to exercise judicial power' into the process of extension of periods of detention would not of itself necessarily bring about a situation of compliance with Article 5 para 3 (art 5-3). That provision—like Article 5 para 4 (art 5-4)—must be understood to require the necessity of following a procedure that has a judicial character although that procedure need not necessarily be identical in each of the cases where the intervention of a judge is required...

59. It is not the Court's role to substitute its view as to what measures were most appropriate or expedient at the relevant time in dealing with an emergency situation for that of the Government which have direct responsibility for establishing the balance between the taking of effective measures to combat terrorism on the one hand, and respecting individual rights on the other (see the above-mentioned *Ireland v UK* judgment, Series A No 25, p 82, para 214, and the *Klass v Germany* judgment of 6 September 1978, Series A No 28, p 23, para 49). In the context of Northern Ireland, where the judiciary is small and vulnerable to terrorist attacks, public confidence in the independence of the judiciary is understandably a matter to which the Government attach great importance.

60. In the light of these considerations it cannot be said that the Government have exceeded their margin of appreciation in deciding, in the prevailing circumstances, against judicial control.

(e) Safeguards against abuse

61. The applicants, Amnesty International and Liberty and Others maintained that the safeguards against abuse of the detention power were negligible and that during the period of detention the detainee was completely cut off from the outside world and not permitted access to newspapers, radios or his family. Amnesty International, in particular, stressed that international standards such as the 1988 United Nations Body of Principles for the Protection of All Persons under Any Form of Detention or Imprisonment (General Assembly Resolution 43/173 of 9 December 1988) ruled out

incommunicado detention by requiring access to lawyers and members of the family. Amnesty submitted that being brought promptly before a judicial authority was especially important since in Northern Ireland habeas corpus has been shown to be ineffective in practice. In their view Article 5 para 4 (art 5-4) should be considered non-derogable in times of public emergency.

In addition, it was contended that a decision to extend detention cannot in practical terms be challenged by habeas corpus or judicial review since it is taken completely in secret and, in nearly all cases, is granted. This is evident from the fact that, despite the thousands of extended detention orders, a challenge to such a decision has never been attempted.

62. Although submissions have been made by the applicants and the organisations concerning the absence of effective safeguards, the Court is satisfied that such safeguards do in fact exist and provide an important measure of protection against arbitrary behaviour and incommunicado detention.

63. In the first place, the remedy of habeas corpus is available to test the lawfulness of the original arrest and detention. There is no dispute that this remedy was open to the applicants had they or their legal advisers chosen to avail themselves of it and that it provides an important measure of protection against arbitrary detention (see the above-mentioned *Brogan* judgment, Series A No 145-B, pp 34–35, paras 63–65). The Court recalls, in this context, that the applicants withdrew their complaint of a breach of Article 5 para 4 (art 5-4) of the Convention . . . In the second place, detainees have an absolute and legally enforceable right to consult a solicitor after forty-eight hours from the time of arrest. Both of the applicants were, in fact, free to consult a solicitor after this period . . .

Moreover, within this period the exercise of this right can only be delayed where there exists reasonable grounds for doing so. It is clear from judgments of the High Court in Northern Ireland that the decision to delay access to a solicitor is susceptible to judicial review and that in such proceedings the burden of establishing reasonable grounds for doing so rests on the authorities. In these cases judicial review has been shown to be a speedy and effective manner of ensuring that access to a solicitor is not arbitrarily withheld . . .

It is also not disputed that detainees are entitled to inform a relative or friend about their detention and to have access to a doctor.

65. In addition to the above basic safeguards the operation of the legislation in question has been kept under regular independent review and, until 1989, it was subject to regular renewal.

(f) Conclusion

66. Having regard to the nature of the terrorist threat in Northern Ireland, the limited scope of the derogation and the reasons advanced in support of it, as well as the existence of basic safeguards against abuse, the Court takes the view that the Government have not exceeded their margin of appreciation in considering that the derogation was strictly required by the exigencies of the situation.

4. OTHER OBLIGATIONS UNDER INTERNATIONAL LAW

67. The Court recalls that under Article 15 para 1 (art 15-1) measures taken by the State derogating from Convention obligations must not be 'inconsistent with its other obligations under international law' . . .

68. In this respect, before the Court the applicants contended for the first time that it was an essential requirement for a valid derogation under Article 4 of the 1966 United Nations International Covenant on Civil and Political Rights ('the Covenant'), to which the United Kingdom is a Party, that a public emergency must have been 'officially proclaimed'. Since such proclamation had never taken place the derogation was inconsistent with the United Kingdom's other obligations under international law. In their view this requirement involved a formal proclamation and not a mere statement in Parliament.

69. For the Government, it was open to question whether an official proclamation was necessary for the purposes of Article 4 of the Covenant, since the emergency existed prior to the ratification of the

Covenant by the United Kingdom and has continued to the present day. In any event, the existence of the emergency and the fact of derogation were publicly and formally announced by the Secretary of State for the Home Department to the House of Commons on 22 December 1988. Moreover there had been no suggestion by the United Nations Human Rights Committee that the derogation did not satisfy the formal requirements of Article 4.

70. The Delegate of the Commission considered the Government's argument to be tenable.

71. The relevant part of Article 4 of the Covenant states:

In time of public emergency which threatens the life of the nation and the existence of which is officially proclaimed . . . '

72. The Court observes that it is not its role to seek to define authoritatively the meaning of the terms 'officially proclaimed' in Article 4 of the Covenant. Nevertheless it must examine whether there is any plausible basis for the applicant's argument in this respect.

73. In his statement of 22 December 1988 to the House of Commons the Secretary of State for the Home Department explained in detail the reasons underlying the Government's decision to derogate and announced that steps were being taken to give notice of derogation under both Article 15 (art 15) of the European Convention and Article 4 of the Covenant. He added that there was 'a public emergency within the meaning of these provisions in respect of terrorism connected with the affairs of Northern Ireland in the United Kingdom . . . ' . . .

In the Court's view the above statement, which was formal in character and made public the Government's intentions as regards derogation, was well in keeping with the notion of an official proclamation. It therefore considers that there is no basis for the applicants' arguments in this regard.

5. SUMMARY

74. In the light of the above examination, the Court concludes that the derogation lodged by the United Kingdom satisfies the requirements of Article 15 (art 15) and that therefore the applicants cannot validly complain of a violation of Article 5 para 3 (art 5-3). It follows that there was no obligation under Article 5 para 5 (art 5-5) to provide the applicants with an enforceable right to compensation. . . .

FOR THESE REASONS, THE COURT

1. Holds by twenty-two votes to four that the United Kingdom's derogation satisfies the requirements of Article 15 (art 15) and that therefore the applicants cannot validly complain of a violation of Article 5 para 3 (art 5-3); . . . '

NOTES

1   The plenary Court was composed of President Ryssdal and Judges: Bernhardt, Thor Vilhjalmsson, Gölcüklü, Matscher, Macdonald, Russo, Spielmann, Valticos, Martens, Palm, Foighel, Pekkanen, Loizou, Morenilla, Bigi, Freeland, Baka, Lopes Rocha, Wildhaber, Mifsud Bonnici, and Gotchev.

2   Judge Pettiti in his Dissenting Opinion expressed the view that:

. . . The member States of the Council of Europe which went through serious periods of terrorism (for example Italy) confronted such terrorism while retaining judicial involvement in extended police custody. It would be possible to find in comparative law and in criminal procedure examples of judicial mechanisms protecting the use by the police of 'informers' who have to remain anonymous. In camera hearings can be envisaged. The British system too has recourse to the principle of immunity which makes it possible for the public prosecutor not to disclose certain prosecution evidence. It is thus possible to avoid the disadvantages of the ordinary procedural rules applicable at this stage (see the

Edwards v UK judgment of 16 December 1992, Series A No 247-B). Is there not, on the part of the police, a desire to conceal from the courts some of their practices?....

In the *Brannigan and McBride* case, in my opinion, the Government's action fell outside the margin of appreciation which the Court is able to recognise. The fundamental principle which must prevail and which is consistent with British and European tradition is that detention cannot be extended from four days to seven days without the involvement of a judge, who is the guarantor of individual freedoms and fundamental rights.

3   In his dissent Judge Walsh observed:

2. The terms of Article 15 para 1 (art 15-1) of the Convention have been invoked as a justification for this step, namely that there is a 'time of war or other public emergency threatening the life of the nation'. In the present case 'the nation' is presumed to be the entire United Kingdom. While there is ample evidence of political violence in Northern Ireland which could be described as threatening the life of that region of the United Kingdom there is no evidence that the life of the rest of the United Kingdom, viz. the island of Great Britain, is threatened by 'the war or public emergency in Northern Ireland', which is separated by sea from Great Britain and of which it does not form a part.

3. Furthermore there is no evidence that the operation of the courts in either Northern Ireland or Great Britain has been restricted or affected by 'the war or public emergency' in Northern Ireland. It is the United Kingdom Government which wishes to restrict the operation of the courts by being unwilling to allow arrested persons to be brought before a judge as prescribed by Article 5 para 3 (art 5-3) of the Convention. ....

4   Judge De Meyer dissented because:

...The Government of the United Kingdom have tried to escape the consequences of [the *Brogan*] judgment by lodging once again a notice of derogation under Article 15 in order to continue the practice concerned. In my view, this is not permissible: they failed to convince me that such a far-reaching departure from the rule of respect for individual liberty could, either after or before the end of 1988, be 'strictly required by the exigencies of the situation'. ....

5   Judge Makarczyk's dissent considered it to be of vital importance that:

...the United Kingdom Government should attempt to prove before the Court...that extended administrative detention does in fact contribute to eliminate the reasons for which the extraordinary measures needed to be introduced—in other words the prevention and combating of terrorism. But, as far as I can see, no such attempt has been made either in the Government's memorial and the attached documents, or in the pleading before the Court. Instead, the Government's main arguments have centred on the alleged detrimental effects on the judiciary of control by a judge of extended detention without the normal judicial procedure. ....

6   While the Court was not willing to formally reduce the breadth of the margin of appreciation accorded to States under Article 15 when a public emergency was of long duration, the judgment (at paragraph 43) indicates that this is a significant consideration in the Court's assessment of the lawfulness of a particular derogation.

Aksoy v Turkey 1996-VI 2287
European Court of Human Rights

The facts in regard to the applicant's complaint under Article 3 have been described above at p 161. In response to the applicant's allegation that he had suffered a violation of Article 5(3), by being detained for at least fourteen days without judicial supervision (see above p 303), the

Government sought to rely upon its notice of derogation submitted to the Secretary General in 1990 (and subsequently revised) covering specified provinces in South-East Turkey.

68. The Court recalls that it falls to each Contracting State, with its responsibility for 'the life of [its] nation', to determine whether that life is threatened by a 'public emergency' and, if so, how far it is necessary to go in attempting to overcome the emergency. By reason of their direct and continuous contact with the pressing needs of the moment, the national authorities are in principle better placed than the international judge to decide both on the presence of such an emergency and on the nature and scope of the derogations necessary to avert it. Accordingly, in this matter a wide margin of appreciation should be left to the national authorities.

Nonetheless, Contracting Parties do not enjoy an unlimited discretion. It is for the Court to rule whether, *inter alia*, the States have gone beyond the "extent strictly required by the exigencies" of the crisis. The domestic margin of appreciation is thus accompanied by a European supervision. In exercising this supervision, the Court must give appropriate weight to such relevant factors as the nature of the rights affected by the derogation and the circumstances leading to, and the duration of, the emergency situation (see the *Brannigan and McBride v the United Kingdom* judgment of 26 May 1993, Series A No 258-B, pp 49–50, para. 43).

2. EXISTENCE OF A PUBLIC EMERGENCY THREATENING THE LIFE OF THE NATION

69. The Government, with whom the Commission agreed on this point, maintained that there was a public emergency 'threatening the life of the nation' in South-East Turkey. The applicant did not contest the issue, although he submitted that, essentially, it was a matter for the Convention organs to decide.

70. The Court considers, in the light of all the material before it, that the particular extent and impact of PKK terrorist activity in South-East Turkey has undoubtedly created, in the region concerned, a 'public emergency threatening the life of the nation' (see, *mutatis mutandis*, the *Lawless v Ireland* judgment of 1 July 1961, Series A No 3, p 56, para 28, the above-mentioned *Ireland v the United Kingdom* judgment [A. 25 (1978)], p 78, para 205, and the above-mentioned *Brannigan and McBride* judgment, p 50, para. 47).

3. WHETHER THE MEASURES WERE STRICTLY REQUIRED BY THE EXIGENCIES OF THE SITUATION

(a) The length of the unsupervised detention

71. The Government asserted that the applicant had been arrested on 26 November 1992 along with thirteen others on suspicion of aiding and abetting PKK terrorists, being a member of the Kiziltepe branch of the PKK and distributing PKK tracts. He was held in custody for fourteen days, in accordance with Turkish law, which allows a person detained in connection with a collective offence to be held for up to thirty days in the state of emergency region.

72. They explained that the place in which the applicant was arrested and detained fell within the area covered by the Turkish derogation. This derogation was necessary and justified, in view of the extent and gravity of PKK terrorism in Turkey, particularly in the South East. The investigation of terrorist offences presented the authorities with special problems, as the Court had recognised in the past, because the members of terrorist organisations were expert in withstanding interrogation, had secret support networks and access to substantial resources. A great deal of time and effort was required to secure and verify evidence in a large region confronted with a terrorist organisation that had strategic and technical support from neighbouring countries. These difficulties meant that it was impossible to provide judicial supervision during a suspect's detention in police custody.

73. The applicant submitted that he was detained on 24 November 1992 and released on 10 December 1992. He alleged that the post-dating of arrests was a common practice in the state of emergency region.

74. While he did not present detailed arguments against the validity of the Turkish derogation as a whole, he questioned whether the situation in South-East Turkey necessitated the holding of suspects for fourteen days or more without judicial supervision. He submitted that judges in South-East Turkey would not be put at risk if they were permitted and required to review the legality of detention at shorter intervals.

75. The Commission could not establish with any certainty whether the applicant was first detained on 24 November 1992, as he claimed, or on 26 November 1992, as alleged by the Government, and it therefore proceeded on the basis that he was held for at least fourteen days without being brought before a judge or other officer authorised by law to exercise judicial power.

76. The Court would stress the importance of Article 5 in the Convention system: it enshrines a fundamental human right, namely the protection of the individual against arbitrary interference by the State with his or her right to liberty. Judicial control of interferences by the executive with the individual's right to liberty is an essential feature of the guarantee embodied in Article 5 para. 3, which is intended to minimise the risk of arbitrariness and to ensure the rule of law (see the above-mentioned *Brogan and Others* judgment, p 32, para 58). Furthermore, prompt judicial intervention may lead to the detection and prevention of serious ill-treatment, which, as stated above (paragraph 62), is prohibited by the Convention in absolute and non-derogable terms.

77. In the *Brannigan and McBride* judgment (cited at paragraph 68 above), the Court held that the United Kingdom Government had not exceeded their margin of appreciation by derogating from their obligations under Article 5 of the Convention to the extent that individuals suspected of terrorist offences were allowed to be held for up to seven days without judicial control.

In the instant case, the applicant was detained for at least fourteen days without being brought before a judge or other officer. The Government have sought to justify this measure by reference to the particular demands of police investigations in a geographically vast area faced with a terrorist organisation receiving outside support (see paragraph 72 above).

78. Although the Court is of the view—which it has expressed on several occasions in the past (see, for example, the above-mentioned *Brogan and Others* judgment)—that the investigation of terrorist offences undoubtedly presents the authorities with special problems, it cannot accept that it is necessary to hold a suspect for fourteen days without judicial intervention. This period is exceptionally long, and left the applicant vulnerable not only to arbitrary interference with his right to liberty but also to torture. Moreover, the Government have not adduced any detailed reasons before the Court as to why the fight against terrorism in South-East Turkey rendered judicial intervention impracticable.

(b) Safeguards

79. The Government emphasised that both the derogation and the national legal system provided sufficient safeguards to protect human rights. Thus, the derogation itself was limited to the strict minimum required for the fight against terrorism; the permissible length of detention was prescribed by law and the consent of a public prosecutor was necessary if the police wished to remand a suspect in custody beyond these periods. Torture was prohibited by Article 243 of the Criminal Code and Article 135 (a) stipulated that any statement made in consequence of the administration of torture or any other form of ill-treatment would have no evidential weight.

80. The applicant pointed out that long periods of unsupervised detention, together with the lack of safeguards provided for the protection of prisoners, facilitated the practice of torture. Thus, he was

tortured with particular intensity on his third and fourth days in detention, and was held thereafter to allow his injuries to heal; throughout this time he was denied access to either a lawyer or a doctor. Moreover, he was kept blindfolded during interrogation, which meant that he could not identify those who mistreated him. The reports of Amnesty International ('Turkey: a Policy of Denial', February 1995), the European Committee for the Prevention of Torture and the United Nations Committee against Torture showed that the safeguards contained in the Turkish Criminal Code, which were in any case inadequate, were routinely ignored in the state of emergency region.

81. The Commission considered that the Turkish system offered insufficient safeguards to detainees, for example there appeared to be no speedy remedy of habeas corpus and no legally enforceable rights of access to a lawyer, doctor, friend or relative. In these circumstances, despite the serious terrorist threat in South-East Turkey, the measure which allowed the applicant to be detained for at least fourteen days without being brought before a judge or other officer exercising judicial functions exceeded the Government's margin of appreciation and could not be said to be strictly required by the exigencies of the situation.

82. In its above-mentioned *Brannigan and McBride* judgment the Court was satisfied that there were effective safeguards in operation in Northern Ireland which provided an important measure of protection against arbitrary behaviour and incommunicado detention. For example, the remedy of habeas corpus was available to test the lawfulness of the original arrest and detention, there was an absolute and legally enforceable right to consult a solicitor forty-eight hours after the time of arrest and detainees were entitled to inform a relative or friend about their detention and to have access to a doctor (op cit, pp 55–6, paras 62–3).

83. In contrast, however, the Court considers that in this case insufficient safeguards were available to the applicant, who was detained over a long period of time. In particular, the denial of access to a lawyer, doctor, relative or friend and the absence of any realistic possibility of being brought before a court to test the legality of the detention meant that he was left completely at the mercy of those holding him.

84. The Court has taken account of the unquestionably serious problem of terrorism in South-East Turkey and the difficulties faced by the State in taking effective measures against it. However, it is not persuaded that the exigencies of the situation necessitated the holding of the applicant on suspicion of involvement in terrorist offences for fourteen days or more in incommunicado detention without access to a judge or other judicial officer.

4. WHETHER THE TURKISH DEROGATION MET THE FORMAL REQUIREMENTS OF ARTICLE 15 PARA. 3

85. None of those appearing before the Court contested that the Turkish Republic's notice of derogation complied with the formal requirements of Article 15 para. 3, namely to keep the Secretary General of the Council of Europe fully informed of the measures which were taken in derogation from the Convention and the reasons therefor.

86. The Court is competent to examine this issue of its own motion (see the above-mentioned *Lawless* judgment, p 55, para 22, and the above-mentioned *Ireland v the United Kingdom* judgment, p 84, para 223), and in particular whether the Turkish notice of derogation contained sufficient information about the measure in question, which allowed the applicant to be detained for at least fourteen days without judicial control, to satisfy the requirements of Article 15 para 3. However, in view of its finding that the impugned measure was not strictly required by the exigencies of the situation (see paragraph 84 above), the Court finds it unnecessary to rule on this matter.

5. CONCLUSION

87. In conclusion, the Court finds that there has been a violation of Article 5 para. 3 of the Convention.

...

FOR THESE REASONS, THE COURT

3. Holds by eight votes to one that there has been a violation of Article 5(3) of the Convention;

NOTES

1 The composition of the Court has already been elaborated above (at p 163). Judge Golcuklu dissented as he considered that Aksoy had not exhausted domestic remedies.

2 *Aksoy* is a rare example of the Court determining that the conditions of Article 15 had not been satisfied by the respondent State.

3 In the subsequent case of *Sakik and Others v Turkey*, judgment of 26 November 1997, the Court, unanimously, found that the above derogations were not applicable to the applicants' complaints as their detention had taken place outside the geographical areas specified in Turkey's derogations. The six applicants were former members of the Turkish National Assembly who were arrested, on the orders of the public prosecutor, as they left the parliament building in Ankara. They were held in police custody for between twelve and fourteen days before being brought before a judge. The applicants complained, *inter alia*, of a breach of Article 5(3). The Government submitted that as it had exercised the right of derogation under Article 15 no breach of Article 5 had occurred.

35. The applicants submitted that the derogation in question did not apply to the measures imposed on them. The Commission agreed.

36. The Court notes that Legislative Decrees nos. 424, 425 and 430, which are referred to in the derogation of 6 August 1990 and the letter of 3 January 1991, apply, according to the descriptive summary of their content, only to the region where a state of emergency has been proclaimed, which, according to the derogation, does not include the city of Ankara. However, the applicants' arrest and detention took place in Ankara on the orders first of the public prosecutor attached to the Ankara National Security Court and later of the judges of that court.

37. The Government submitted that this was no bar to the derogation's applicability. The facts of the case constituted only the prolongation of a terrorist campaign being conducted from inside the area where the state of emergency had been proclaimed, in south-east Turkey. The terrorist threat was not confined to any particular part of Turkish territory. That had to be taken into account if the Turkish derogation was to be interpreted in the light of its object and purpose, namely to enable 'normality for the purposes of the Convention' to be restored throughout the country as quickly as possible.

38. In its *Aksoy v Turkey* judgment the Court has already noted the unquestionably serious problem of terrorism in south-east Turkey and the difficulties faced by the State in taking effective measures against it. It held in that connection that the particular extent and impact of Kurdish Workers' Party (PKK) activity in south-east Turkey had undoubtedly created, in the region concerned, a 'public emergency threatening the life of the nation' (see the judgment of 18 December 1996, *Reports of Judgments and Decisions* 1996-VI, pp 2281 and 2284, §§ 70 and 84).

39. It should be noted, however, that Article 15 authorises derogations from the obligations arising from the Convention only 'to the extent strictly required by the exigencies of the situation'.

40. In the present case the Court would be working against the object and purpose of that provision if, when assessing the territorial scope of the derogation concerned, it were to extend its effects to a part of Turkish territory not explicitly named in the notice of derogation. It follows that the derogation in question is inapplicable *ratione loci* to the facts of the case.

Consequently, it is not necessary to determine whether it satisfies the requirements of Article 15.

The Court went on to find violations of Article 5 paragraphs (3), (4), and (5). The judgment in *Sakik* reveals the Court interpreting the precise wording of derogations strictly.

Article 16 Restrictions on political activity of aliens

Piermont v France A.314 (1995)
European Court of Human Rights

The applicant, a German national, was at the relevant time a member of the European Parliament (representing the German Green Party). She was an environmentalist and a pacifist. In early 1986 she visited French Polynesia during the election campaign for the territorial assembly, having been invited by the leader of the French Polynesian Liberation Front. As soon as she arrived at Tahiti, the airport police, following orders from the French High Commissioner, asked her to be careful in her comments on French internal matters, otherwise she would be expelled. She subsequently took part in two peaceful public meetings at which she criticised French nuclear testing in the Pacific. Thereupon, the High Commissioner made an order expelling her. She travelled on to another French territory, New Caledonia, where she was refused entry on the order of the High Commissioner. After unsuccessfully challenging the authorities' actions in the French courts the applicant complained to Strasbourg alleging, *inter alia*, a breach of Article 10. The Government sought to invoke Article 16 to rebut the applicant's complaint. The Court determined that:

60. Article 16 of the Convention provides:

'Nothing in Articles 10, 11 and 14 shall be regarded as preventing the High Contracting Parties from imposing restrictions on the political activity of aliens.'

61. According to the Government, Mrs Piermont could not rely on her status either as a member of the European Parliament or as a European citizen and she therefore came within the scope of Article 16. She had, they submitted, been invited less in her capacity as an MEP than as a member of the German 'Greens' party and she had expressed her views at the independence demonstration on issues relating to the territorial integrity of the host country and national defence, fields which lay outside the competence of the Community. Furthermore, the recognition, after the material time, of a 'citizenship of the Union' was irrelevant. Lastly, the member States of the Community had reserved the right to lay down the circumstances in which nationality could be acquired or lost. Accordingly, anyone who did not possess the nationality of the country in which he intended to exercise the freedoms guaranteed in Articles 10, 11 and 14 had to be regarded as an alien.

62. The applicant replied that the restrictions in Article 16 did not apply in her case because of her dual status as a European citizen and an MEP. To object that she was an alien when the nature of her functions entailed taking an interest in the whole of the Community's territory seemed to her to be beside the point.

63. The Commission accepted the applicant's submissions in substance.

64. The Court cannot accept the argument based on European citizenship, since the Community treaties did not at the time recognise any such citizenship. Nevertheless, it considers that Mrs Piermont's possession of the nationality of a member State of the European Union and, in addition to that, her status as a member of the European Parliament do not allow Article 16 of the Convention to be raised against her, especially as the people of the [Overseas Territories] take part in the European Parliament elections.

In conclusion, this provision (art. 16) did not authorise the State to restrict the applicant's exercise of the right guaranteed in Article 10.

....

FOR THESE REASONS, THE COURT

....

3. *Holds* by five votes to four that there has been a breach of Article 10 of the Convention as regards the measure taken in French Polynesia;

....

NOTES

1 The Court was composed of Judges: Pettiti, Palm, Loizou, Morenilla, and Makarczyk. President Ryssdal and Judges: Matscher, Freeland, and Jungwiert issued a Joint Partly Dissenting Opinion in which they expressed the view:

4. The judgment asserts, without supporting reasoning, that Mrs Piermont's 'possession of the nationality of a member State of the European Union and, in addition to that, her status as a member of the European Parliament do not allow Article 16 of the Convention to be raised against her, especially as the people of the OTs take part in the European Parliament elections' (paragraph 64). It thus, in effect, adds by judicial action a new immunity to those which the member States saw fit to provide for members of the European Parliament by the terms of the Protocol of 8 April 1965 on the privileges and immunities of the European Communities. We cannot subscribe to this approach. Mrs Piermont, a German national, was at the relevant time (before, as the judgment acknowledges, a European citizenship was recognised by the Community treaties) indubitably an alien in the eyes of French law, notwithstanding her status as a member of the European Parliament (and the elections for which campaigning was in progress were not elections to the European Parliament). We consider, therefore, that Article 16 has to be regarded as at least of some relevance: its reference to 'aliens' is unambiguous and without express exception; and convincing grounds would be required for an exception to be inferred. We are not satisfied that such grounds exist.

5. It does not, however, follow that, even if Article 16 is relevant, any restriction at all, at the unfettered discretion of the host State, may justifiably be imposed on the political activity of an alien without contravention of Article 10. Account must be taken of the increased internationalisation of politics in modern circumstances, and, so far as the present case in particular is concerned, of the interest which nowadays an MEP may legitimately have in the affairs of a Community territory. In the light of these developments, limits may have to be admitted to the restrictions on the political activity of aliens permissible under Article 16. With this in mind, and having regard to the approach adopted by the Court in its *Groppera Radio AG and Others v Switzerland* judgment of 28 March 1990 (Series A No 173) to the interpretation of the third sentence of paragraph 1 of Article 10, we would accept that the object and purpose of Article 16 should, like that sentence, be examined in the context of paragraph 2 of Article 10. In particular, when the proportionality of the interference with Mrs Piermont's freedom of expression is under consideration, account should be taken of the principle embodied in Article 16.

The dissentients went on to conclude that the action taken against the applicant was a proportionate restriction on her freedom of expression as the expulsion order was not served on her until she was about to leave French Polynesia.

2 Whilst the majority and the minority differed on the applicability of Article 16 to the applicant, even the latter group recognised that the development of the EC/EU was affecting the mechanisms of democratic politics in those States.

3 The Maastricht Treaty (1992) established citizenship of the Union for every person holding nationality of a Member State of the European Union (Articles 17-22 of the EC Treaty). Citizenship of the Union complements national citizenship. Citizens of the Union enjoy rights including freedom of movement within Member States and the right to vote/stand as a candidate at elections for the European Parliament and municipal elections in the State of residence.

4 Since the 1970s the Parliamentary Assembly, of the Council of Europe, has been calling for the repeal of Article 16.

Article 17 Prohibition of abuse of rights

....

Norwood v United Kingdom decision of 16 November 2004
European Court of Human Rights

The applicant was the regional organiser for the British National Party, described as 'an extreme right wing political party' by the Court. Between November 2001 and January 2002 he displayed a large poster, produced by the BNP, in the window of his flat in a village near Oswestry. The poster depicted the terrorist attack on the World Trade Centre twin towers (9/11) accompanied with the words 'Islam out of Britain—Protect the British People' and a symbol of a crescent and star in a prohibition sign. Following a complaint from a member of the public the police removed the poster. Subsequently, the applicant was convicted of an aggravated offence (under section 5 of the Public Order Act 1986) of displaying, with hostility towards a racial or religious group, any writing, sign or other visible representation which is threatening, abusive or insulting, within the sight of a person likely to be caused harassment, alarm, or distress by it. He was fined £300. His appeal to the High Court was rejected. He then complained to Strasbourg alleging a breach of Article 10, in his submission this provision protected unwelcome and provocative views and he lived in a rural area not greatly affected by racial or religious tension.

. . . However, the Court would refer to Article 17 of the Convention which states:

'Nothing in [the] Convention may be interpreted as implying for any State, group or person any right to engage in any activity or perform any act aimed at the destruction of any of the rights and freedoms set forth herein or at their limitation to a greater extent than is provided for in the Convention.'

The general purpose of Article 17 is to prevent individuals or groups with totalitarian aims from exploiting in their own interests the principles enunciated by the Convention. The Court, and previously, the European Commission of Human Rights, has found in particular that the freedom of expression guaranteed under Article 10 of the Convention may not be invoked in a sense contrary to Article 17 (see, *inter alia, W.P. and Others v Poland* (dec.), No 42264/98, 2 September 2004; *Garaudy v France*, (dec.), No 65831/01, 24 June 2003; *Schimanek v Austria*, (dec.) No 32307/96, 1 February 2000; and also *Glimmerveen and Hagenbeek v The Netherlands*, Nos 8348/78 and 8406/78, Commission decision of 11 October 1979, *Decisions and Reports* 18, p 187).

The poster in question in the present case contained a photograph of the Twin Towers in flame, the words 'Islam out of Britain—Protect the British People' and a symbol of a crescent and star in a prohibition sign. The Court notes and agrees with the assessment made by the domestic courts, namely that the words and images on the poster amounted to a public expression of attack on all Muslims in the United Kingdom. Such a general, vehement attack against a religious group, linking the group as a whole with a grave act of terrorism, is incompatible with the values proclaimed and guaranteed by the Convention, notably tolerance, social peace and non-discrimination. The applicant's display of the poster in his window constituted an act within the meaning of Article 17, which did not, therefore, enjoy the protection of Articles 10 or 14 (see the cases cited above, and also *Jersild v Denmark*, judgment of 23 September 1994, Series A No 298, § 35).

It follows that the application must be rejected as being incompatible *ratione materiae* with the provisions of the Convention, pursuant to Article 35 §§ 3 and 4.

FOR THESE REASONS, THE COURT UNANIMOUSLY

Declares the application inadmissible.

NOTES

1   The Court was composed of President Costa and Judges: Bratza, Cabral Barreto, Turmen, Butkevych, Ugrekhelidze, and Fura-Sandstrom.

2   In *W.P. and Others v Poland*, decision of 2 September 2004, the Court, unanimously, found inadmissible the applicants' complaint that the Polish authorities had violated Articles 11 and 14 by prohibiting them from forming an association called The National and Patriotic Association of Polish Victims of Bolshevism and Zionism.

2. ... The Court observes that the general purpose of Article 17 is to prevent totalitarian groups from exploiting in their own interests the principles enunciated by the Convention. To achieve that purpose, it is not necessary to take away every one of the rights and freedoms guaranteed from persons found to be engaged in activities aimed at the destruction of any of those rights and freedoms. Article 17 covers essentially those rights which, if invoked, will facilitate the attempt to derive there from a right to engage personally in activities aimed at the destruction of any of the rights and freedoms set forth in the Convention (see *J. Glimmerveen and J. Hagenbeek v The Netherlands*, Nos 8348/78 and 8406/78, Commission decision of 11 October 1979, *Decisions and Reports* 18, p 187; *Roger Garaudy v France* (dec.), No 65831/01, 24 June 2003).

Turning to the facts of the present case, the Court notes that the memorandum of association of the National and Patriotic Association of Polish Victims of Bolshevism and Zionism included in points 6, 12 and 15 statements alleging the persecution of Poles by the Jewish minority and the existence of inequality between them. The Court agrees with the Government that these ideas can be seen as reviving anti-Semitism. The applicants' racist attitudes also transpire from the anti-Semitic tenor of some of their submissions made before the Court. It is therefore satisfied that the evidence in the present case justifies the need to bring Article 17 into play (cf. *United Communist Party of Turkey and Others v Turkey*, judgment of 30 January 1998, Reports of Judgments and Decisions 1998-I, § 60).

The applicants essentially seek to employ Article 11 as a basis under the Convention for a right to engage in activities which are contrary to the text and spirit of the Convention and which right, if granted, would contribute to the destruction of the rights and freedoms set forth in the Convention.

Consequently, the Court finds that, by reason of the provisions of Article 17 of the Convention, the applicants cannot rely on Article 11 of the Convention to challenge the prohibition of the formation of the National and Patriotic Association of Polish Victims of Bolshevism and Zionism.

3. The applicants further complained under Article 14 of the Convention taken together with Article 11 that 'the judiciary of the so-called Third Republic of Poland controlled by Jewish interests' prohibited the formation of associations by ethnic Poles.

The Government submitted that the facts of the case did not disclose discrimination against the applicants.

The Court again notes that by making the above complaint, whose wording is anti-Semitic and offensive, the applicants essentially seek to use Article 14 taken together with Article 11 to provide a basis under the Convention for a right to engage in activities which are contrary to the text and spirit of the Convention and which right, if granted, would contribute to the destruction of the rights and freedoms set forth in the Convention.

Consequently, the Court finds that, by reason of the provisions of Article 17 of the Convention, the applicants cannot rely on Article 14 taken together with Article 11 of the Convention.

The views of the Court, found in paragraph two of the above decision, on the scope of Article 17 indicate that the Court takes a measured approach to the application of that provision. In the context of persons seeking to promote ideas contrary to the values of the Convention, Article 17 will be particularly applicable to those persons' attempts to invoke Articles 10 and 11.

3   Other examples of Article 17 being applied to determine complaints inadmissible include the conviction of an Islamic convert for writing/publishing a book denying the Holocaust/crimes against humanity committed by the Nazis in *Garaudy v France*, decision of 24 June 2003 and the conviction of persons for possessing, with a view to distribution, leaflets inciting racial discrimination in *Glimmerveen and Hagenbeek v The Netherlands*, 18 DR 196 (1979).

Article 18 Limitations on use of restrictions on rights

Gusinskiy v Russia judgment of 19 May 2004
European Court of Human Rights

The applicant, a Russian and Israeli national was the former Chairman and majority shareholder in Media Most a Russian private media company. In 2000 Media Most was in conflict with Gazprom, a gas monopoly controlled by the State, over the former's debts to the latter. On 13 June 2000 the applicant was arrested and detained in connection with suspected fraud. During Gusinskiy's detention the Acting Minister for Press and Mass Communications offered to drop the criminal charges against him if he sold Media Most to Gazprom, at a price to be determined by the latter. At the same time Gazprom asked Gusinskiy to sign such an agreement. He was released from detention on 16 June in exchange for an undertaking not to leave the country. On 20 July the applicant signed an agreement with Gazprom which provided, *inter alia*, for the termination of criminal proceedings against him. Six days later the special cases investigator stayed the prosecution against Gusinskiy and cancelled the restraint order on his travelling abroad. The applicant immediately left Russia. Following his departure Media Most refused to honour the July agreement claiming it had been obtained by duress. The applicant contended, *inter alia*, that his detention was an abuse of State power and the authorities had sought to force him to sell his company on unfavourable terms to a State enterprise. He invoked Article 18 of the Convention which provides that, 'The restrictions permitted under this Convention to the said rights and freedoms shall not be applied for any purpose other than those for which they have been prescribed.' In response the unanimous Chamber held that:

73. The Court recalls that Article 18 of the Convention does not have an autonomous role. It can only be applied in conjunction with other Articles of the Convention. There may, however, be a violation of Article 18 in connection with another Article, although there is no violation of that Article taken alone. It follows further from the terms of Article 18 that a violation can only arise where the right or freedom concerned is subject to restrictions permitted under the Convention (see *Kamma v The Netherlands*, No 4771/71, Commission's report of 14 July 1974, (DR) 1, p. 4; *Oates v Poland* (dec.), No 35036/97, 11 May 2000).

74. The Court has found above . . . that the applicant's liberty was restricted 'for the purpose of bringing him before the competent legal authority on reasonable suspicion of having committed an offence'. However, when considering the allegation under Article 18 of the Convention the Court must ascertain whether the detention was in addition, and hence contrary to Article 18, applied for any other purpose than that provided for in Article 5 § 1 (c).

75. The Government did not dispute that the 'July Agreement', namely Annex 6 to it, linked the termination of the Russian Video [fraud] investigation with the sale of the applicant's media to Gazprom, a company controlled by the State. The Government did not dispute either that Annex 6 was signed by the Acting Minister for Press and Mass Communications. Lastly, the Government did not deny that one of the reasons for which Mr Nikolayev closed the proceedings against the applicant on 26 July 2000 was that the applicant had made up for the harm caused by the alleged fraud by transferring Media Most shares to a company controlled by the State.

. . .

76. In the Court's opinion, it is not the purpose of such public-law matters as criminal proceedings and detention on remand to be used as part of commercial bargaining strategies. The facts that Gazprom asked the applicant to sign the 'July Agreement' when he was in prison, that a State Minister endorsed such an agreement with his signature, and that a State investigating officer later implemented it by dropping the charges, insistently suggest that the applicant's prosecution was used to intimidate him.

77. In such circumstances the Court cannot but find that the restriction of the applicant's liberty permitted under Article 5 § 1 (c) was applied not only for the purpose of bringing him before the competent legal authority on reasonable suspicion of having committed an offence, but also for alien reasons.

78. There has, accordingly been a violation of Article 18 in conjunction with Article 5 of the Convention.

. . . .

FOR THESE REASONS, THE COURT UNANIMOUSLY

1. *Holds* that there has been a violation of Article 5 of the Convention;

2. *Holds* that there has been a violation of Article 18 of the Convention in conjunction with Article 5;

. . . .

NOTES

1   The Court was composed of President Rozakis and Judges: Lorenzen, Tulkens, Botoucharova, Kovler, Zagrebelsky, and Hajiyev.

2   This was a dramatic, but rare, example of Article 18 being successfully invoked by an applicant. The Court's clear disapproval of the use of criminal proceedings and detention for commercial State interests is to be welcomed. *Gusinskiy* disclosed worrying interferences by a senior minister and a State business enterprise in the operation of the Russian criminal justice system.

ARTICLE 41 (FORMERLY ARTICLE 50) JUST SATISFACTION

The Court's early approach to just satisfaction

De Wilde, Ooms and Versyp v Belgium (No 2) A.14 (1972) 1 EHRR 438
European Court of Human Rights

In a previous decision (see above, p 312) the Court had found that Belgium had violated the applicants', who were self-confessed vagrants, right under Article 5(4) to a review of the lawfulness of their detention by a court. Subsequently, the applicants applied to the Belgian Government for compensation. After this was refused they requested the Commission to refer their claim for compensation to the Court under Article 50. The Commission referred the case, but the Government argued that the applicants' request was inadmissible and ill-founded.

I. THE ADMISSIBILITY OF THE APPLICANTS' CLAIMS

14. In its written observations of October 1971 and January 1972 and also at the oral hearings, the Government requested the Court to rule

'that the applications for compensation lodged with the Commission on behalf of the applicants are not admissible since the domestic remedies have not been exhausted.'

15. In support of this submission, the Government relied, in the first place, on Article 26 of the Convention contending that this provision applied not only to the original petition addressed by an individual to the Commission under Article 25 but also to a claim for compensation made by him after the Court has held that in his case there has been a violation of a right guaranteed by the Convention.

Article 26 reads: 'The Commission may only deal with the matter after all domestic remedies have been exhausted, according to the generally recognised rules of international law . . .'; Article 27(3) then provides that 'the Commission shall reject any petition referred to it which it considers inadmissible under Article 26'. This last provision therefore defines a condition to which the Commission's 'dealing with' the case is subjected; it concerns 'petitions' lodged with that organ. In other words, this provision relates to the institution of the proceedings which fall within Section III of the Convention. The present cases no longer relate to such proceedings but to the final phase of proceedings brought before the Court in accordance with Section IV on the conclusion of those to which the petitions of Jacques De Wilde, Franz Ooms and Edgard Versyp gave rise before the Commission. The claims made by the three applicants for compensation are not new petitions; they relate to the reparation to be decided by the Court in respect of a violation adjudged by the Court and they have nothing to do with the introduction of proceedings before the Commission under Articles 25, 26 and 27 of the Convention; while the Commission transmitted them to the Court, it did so without any accompanying report and solely with a view to giving the Court the assistance which, in a general way, it lends to the Court in accordance with Rule 71 of its Rules of Procedure.

The Court, like the Delegates of the Commission, is therefore of the opinion that Article 26 is not applicable in the present matter.

16. In support of its plea of inadmissibility, the Government put forward a second argument based on Article 50: as they had not exhausted domestic remedies, the applicants had not established, according to the Government, that Belgian internal law 'allows only partial reparation to be made for the consequences' of the violation found by the Judgment of 18 June 1971; it followed that their claims for damages were inadmissible.

In the Court's opinion, the part of the sentence just quoted states merely a rule going to the merits. If the draftsmen of the Convention had meant to make the admissibility of claims for 'just satisfaction' subordinate to the prior exercise of domestic remedies, they would have taken care to specify this in Article 50 as they did in Article 26, combined with Article 27(3), in respect of petitions addressed to the Commission. In the absence of such an explicit indication of their intention, the Court cannot take the view that Article 50 enunciates in substance the same rule as Article 26.

Moreover, Article 50 has its origin in certain clauses which appear in treaties of a classical type—such as Article 10 of the German-Swiss Treaty on Arbitration and Conciliation, 1921, and Article 32 of the Geneva General Act of the Pacific Settlement of International Disputes, 1928—and have no connection with the rule of exhaustion of domestic remedies.

In addition, if the victim, after exhausting in vain the domestic remedies before complaining at Strasbourg of a violation of his rights, were obliged to do so a second time before being able to obtain from the Court just satisfaction, the total length of the procedure instituted by the Convention would scarcely be in keeping with the idea of the effective protection of Human Rights. Such a requirement would lead to a situation incompatible with the aim and object of the Convention.

17. The Court therefore sees no reason to declare the claims in question inadmissible and will proceed to examine into their merits.

II. THE MERITS OF THE APPLICANTS' CLAIMS

18. The present stage of these cases revolves around Article 50 of the Convention, which reads:

> 'If the Court finds that a decision or a measure taken by a legal authority or any other authority of a High Contracting Party is completely or partially in conflict with the obligations arising from the present Convention, and if the internal law of the said Party allows only partial reparation to be made for the consequences of this decision or measure, the decision of the Court shall, if necessary, afford just satisfaction to the injured party.'

19. In its written observations of October 1971 and January 1972 and at the oral hearings, the Government requested the Court to rule:
— that the conditions required for the application of Article 50 of the Convention have not been fulfilled in the present cases;
— that it is not necessary to afford satisfaction to the applicants.

At the hearing in the afternoon of 14 February, the Commission's final submission was as follows:

> 'May it please the Court to grant the applicants appropriate satisfaction, bearing in mind that a new remedy has been introduced in Belgian law following the Judgment given on 18 June 1971 by the European Court of Human Rights, and thus indirectly following the applications lodged by MM. De Wilde, Ooms and Versyp with the Commission.'

20. The Government submitted in particular that Belgian internal law enables the national courts to order the State to make reparation for damage caused by an illegal situation for which it is responsible

whether this situation constitutes a breach of rules of internal law or of rules of international law. It would follow that the applicants have to take proceedings before the national courts; as they have not done so their claims for damages were not only inadmissible (see para 16 above) but also without foundation.

The Court cannot accept this view.

No doubt, the treaties from which the text of Article 50 was borrowed had more particularly in view of cases where the nature of the injury would make it possible to wipe out entirely the consequences of a violation but where the internal law of the State involved precludes this being done. Nevertheless, the provisions of Article 50 which recognise the Court's competence to grant to the injured party a just satisfaction also cover the case where the impossibility of *restitutio in integrum* follows from the very nature of the injury; indeed, common sense suggests that this must be so *a fortiori*. The Court sees no reason why, in the latter case just as in the former, it should not have the right to award to the injured persons the just satisfaction that they had not obtained from the Government of the respondent State.

This is clearly the position in the present cases. Neither the Belgian internal law, nor indeed any other conceivable system of law, can make it possible to wipe out the consequences of the fact that the three applicants did not have available to them the right, guaranteed by Article 5(4), to take proceedings before a court in order to have the lawfulness of their detention decided. Furthermore, the Belgian Government has declined to give De Wilde, Ooms and Versyp the compensation which they claimed.

The mere fact that the applicants could have brought and could still bring their claims for damages before a Belgian court does not therefore require the Court to dismiss those claims as being ill-founded any more than it raises an obstacle to their admissibility (see para 16 above).

21. Where the consequences of a violation are only capable of being wiped out partially, the affording of 'just satisfaction' in application of Article 50 requires that:

  (i)   the Court has found 'a decision or measure taken' by an authority of a Contracting State to be 'in conflict with the obligations arising from the . . . Convention';

  (ii) there is an 'injured party';

  (iii) the Court considers it 'necessary' to afford just satisfaction.

According to the Government, none of these conditions has been fulfilled in the present cases.

22. First, the Court's Judgment of 18 June 1971 was, it is alleged, directed only to a situation created by a 'certain deficiency in legislation in case-law' which did not amount to a 'decision' or 'measure'.

The Court cannot accept this view. In the cases brought before it which had their origin in petitions lodged under Article 25, the Court was not called upon to give a decision on an abstract problem relating to the compatibility of provisions of Belgian law with the Convention but on the specific case of the application of the provisions in law to the applicants. In questions of liability arising from the failure to observe the Convention, there is in any event no room to distinguish between acts and omissions.

23. Nor can the existence of an 'injured party' be denied. In the context of Article 50, these two words must be considered as synonymous with the term 'victim' as used in Article 25; they denote the person directly affected by the act or omission which is in issue. De Wilde, Ooms and Versyp, whom the Commission rightly found to be victims in declaring their petitions admissible, are thus also 'injured parties'.

24. On the other hand, the Government is correct in questioning the existence of damage. Each of the applicants claims, as just satisfaction, the sum of 300 BF per day of detention. For this claim to be successful, it would be necessary that their deprivation of liberty had been caused by the absence—found by the Court to be contrary to Article 5(4) of the Convention—of any right to take proceedings before a court by which the lawfulness of their detention might be decided. But this is not the case here. In its Judgment of 18 June 1971, the Court did not find 'either irregularity or arbitrariness in the placing of the three applicants at the disposal of the Government' and it had 'no reason to find the resulting detention

incompatible with Article 5(1)(e) of the Convention'. The Court therefore does not see how the taking of proceedings to test merely the point of lawfulness dealt with in the requirements of Article 5(4) could have enabled the applicants to obtain their release any sooner.

Moreover, the applicants had the benefit of free legal aid before the Commission, and later with the Commission's Delegates, and they have not made any point concerning costs which they have incurred without reimbursement.

Finally, the Court does not find that in the present cases any moral damage could have been caused by the lack of a remedy which met the requirements of Article 5(4).

25. Although, for the reasons given above, the Court finds it has to refuse to grant the compensation claimed by the applicants, it notes that Belgium has taken, as the Committee of Ministers stated on 18 January 1972 in connection with Article 54 of the Convention, legislative measures with a view to ensuring in matters of vagrancy the application of the Convention in that State.

FOR THESE REASONS, THE COURT, DECLARES:

1. Unanimously, that the applicants' claims for damages are admissible; and

2. By fourteen votes to one, that the applicants' claims for damages are not well-founded.

NOTES

1 The Court was comprised of President Waldock and Judges: Balladore, Palliere, Cassin, Holmback, Verdross, Rolin, Rodenbourg, Ross, Wold, Mosler, Zekia, Favre, Cremona, Wiarda and Sigurjonsson. Judges Holmback, Ross, and Wold issued a concurring opinion in which they advocated a different interpretation of Article 50.

It is a well-known fact that this Article is modelled on clauses found in a number of arbitration treaties, e.g. the German-Swiss Treaty of Arbitration and Conciliation 1921, Article 10, and the Geneva General Act for the Pacific Settlement of International Disputes 1928, Article 32. These clauses were inserted to deal with the situation that a State, although willing enough to fulfil its international obligations, for constitutional reasons is unable to do so without changing its Constitution. They confer on the arbitral tribunal the power to transform this obligation into an obligation to pay to the injured party an equitable satisfaction of another kind.

We assume that Article 50 serves the same purpose as these model clauses and that it should be interpreted accordingly. On this basis, it is obvious that the article according to it wording does not apply to the cases before the Court. . . .

In our opinion, the applicants have afforded no proof that Belgian law does not allow full reparation to be made, whereas the Belgian Agent has convincingly argued that Belgian law provides remedies for the granting of full compensation. It follows that the said condition for the application of Article 50 is not fulfilled. (paras 2, 3 and 5)

Judge Zekia dissented to the extent that he would have allowed the applicants to claim for their costs.

They are surely entitled to be reimbursed for the extra expenses incurred before the Commission and this Court. It is true that we do not exactly know whether they did incur any expense or, if they did, what was the amount incurred, but this, I suggest, could easily be referred to the Registry of this Court to be ascertained and dealt with. In my view the applicants ought not to be deprived of their costs in vindicating their rights in the way they did. (para 10)

2 The above judgment of the Court is important not only for explaining the origins of the obscure language found in Article 50, but also for establishing the Court's approach to the provision of redress under this Article. The Court determined that requests for just satisfaction were not separate applications, subject to the admissibility criteria laid down in Articles 25–27 (now Article 35), but were the final stage in the Court's proceedings in cases where it had already found the particular respondent State to have violated the applicants' Convention rights. Also, the Court's emphasis upon its role as the arbiter of just satisfaction was highly significant.

3   In a study of the early case law one commentator concluded that:

In order to ensure a remedy the Court has largely ignored the actual words and drafting history of Article 50 as imposing inappropriate restrictions on its powers; it has shown a consistently flexible approach to the question of when Article 50 is applicable.' [C D Gray, 'Remedies For Individuals Under The European Convention On Human Rights' (1981) 6 *Human Rights Review* 153 at 171.]

The contemporary categories of just satisfaction

Building upon the foundations laid down in the early cases the Court is now willing to consider awarding just satisfaction in the form of financial compensation to successful applicants for (a) 'pecuniary damage' and (b) 'non-pecuniary damage', sustained as a consequence of the violation of their Convention rights and also (c) for legal costs and expenses incurred in defending those rights. Below are some examples of how the Court has applied Article 50 in each of these categories. With effect from November 1998, Protocol 11 abbreviated the text of Article 50 to provided that:

If the Court finds that there has been a violation of the Convention or the protocols thereto, and if the internal law of the High Contracting Party concerned allows only partial reparation to be made, the Court shall, if necessary, afford just satisfaction to the injured party. (Article 41)

Pecuniary damage

1   A complex and politically sensitive judgment on compensation for the seizure of real and personal property belonging to a former monarch, and other members of the former royal family, was delivered by a Grand Chamber in the *Case of the Former King of Greece and Others v Greece*, judgment of 28 November 2002 (and see below p 941 for an examination of the earlier judgment concerning the substantive merits of the applicants' complaints). In the just satisfaction proceedings the applicants contended that the restoration of their property together with compensation for non-pecuniary damage and their costs/expenses in bringing the proceedings would constitute *restitutio in integrum*. If their property was not returned to them they sought full compensation based upon the current value of the assets. The Government submitted that the finding of a violation by the Court or the award of a symbolic sum could reasonably be considered to provide just satisfaction. For the Government the context of the 'transfer' of the applicants' property was of major significance as it was associated with the constitutional change of Greece from a monarchy to a republic.

44. In that connection, the Government wished to remind the Court of the known European precedents in this field during the 20th century, that is regime changes from monarchies to the republican form of parliamentary government, namely in Portugal (1910), in Germany and Austria (1919), in Greece (1924), in Spain (1931) and in Italy (1946). Although there had been differences between these changes of regime, there was nevertheless a common feature that characterised the fate of the possessions of

the members of the former royal families: with the exception of the private property of King Manuel II of Portugal, the private possessions of all former European monarchs or emperors had in one way or another been expropriated without compensation or without full compensation. Such long established practice, justified not by reasons of political expediency but in view of the privileges afforded in the past to the former royal families and the necessity to ensure the enforcement of radical constitutional changes (the abolition of monarchies), should be taken into account in the award of just satisfaction. The Court should not deny the right of the Greek State "to resolve an issue which it considered to be prejudicial for its status as a republic" (see paragraph 88 of the principal judgment), through the award of excessive compensation, the payment of which was likely to have very serious financial implications for the Hellenic Republic.

If the Court was to award compensation the Government argued, *inter alia*, that not all the Tatoi estate should be included (because the former King had donated part to a foundation in 1992), the market value of the individual properties should not be used (as the estates were so large it was impossible to find similar transactions in Greece which could be used as comparators), the 'objective' value of the properties (based upon a domestic scheme of taxable values for inheritances and expropriations) should be utilised. The privileges and tax exemptions (e.g. from inheritance tax given to the Greek crown) awarded to the former royal family during past times should also be included in the calculation of pecuniary damage according to the Government. The latter also disputed the status of many personal belongings claimed by the applicants, in the view of the Government they were gifts offered to the Head of State. Regarding the award of non-pecuniary damage the Government:

69. ...noted that the applicants' allegations that they were the victims of political persecution had been rejected by the Commission, which had also found that there had been no violation of the applicants' rights under Articles 3, 6 and 8 of the Convention (see the Commission's decision as to the admissibility of the application of 21 April 1998, unpublished), observing, on that point: 'the applicants' claims to the opposite appear most unfortunate taking into consideration the unconstitutional role played by the first applicant in the politics of Greece prior to his departure from the country in 1967: by appointing the colonels' government after the military coup of 21 April 1967, the former king undermined ... the very foundations of parliamentary democracy and of the rule of law, that is the pillars of democratic government, whose protection constitutes the *raison d'être* of the Council of Europe'.

70. In view of the above, the Government submitted that 'not a single Greek drachma could possibly be granted by the Hellenic Republic to the former monarch', in view of the 'highly political character of the applicants' claims'.

Finally, the Government stated that the applicants could visit their ancestors' royal graves provided they complied with domestic legal requirements (including recognising the Greek Republic, waiving any claims to official titles and registering in the Municipal Register under a forename and surname).

The Grand Chamber began by emphasising that if the nature of the breach of the Convention allowed for *restitutio in integrum* then it was for the respondent State to undertake such measures. However, if national law did not permit *restitutio in integrum* then the Court was empowered to grant just satisfaction under Article 41. Furthermore, in cases involving the expropriation of property:

75. The lawfulness of such a dispossession inevitably affects the criteria to be used for determining the reparation owed by the respondent State, since the pecuniary consequences of a lawful taking cannot be assimilated to those of an unlawful dispossession. In this connection, international case-law, of courts or arbitration tribunals, gives the Court valuable guidance; although that case-law concerns more particularly the expropriation of industrial and commercial undertakings, the principles identified

in that field are valid for situations such as the one in the instant case. In the *Amoco International Finance Corporation* case the Iran–United States Claims Tribunal stated, referring to the judgment of the Permanent Court of International Justice in the *Case Concerning the Factory at Chorzów* (judgment of 13 September 1928, *Collection of Judgments*, Series A No 17, p 47) that:

> 'a clear distinction must be made between lawful and unlawful expropriations, since the rules applicable to the compensation to be paid by the expropriating State differ according to the legal characterisation of the taking.' (*Amoco International Finance Corporation v Iran*, Interlocutory Award of 14 July 1987, Iran–U.S. Claims Tribunal Reports (1987–II), § 192)

The Grand Chamber, therefore, considered that where a dispossession had not been *per se* illegal subsequent compensation did not have to seek to erase all the consequences of the interference with the relevant property. In this case:

78. . . . As the lack of any compensation, rather than the inherent illegality of the taking, was the basis of the violation found, the compensation need not necessarily reflect the full value of the properties. In its search for appropriate compensation the Court must seek guidance in the general standards expressed in its case-law on Article 1 of Protocol No 1, according to which a taking of property without payment of an amount reasonably related to its value would normally constitute a disproportionate interference which could not be considered justifiable under Article 1 of Protocol No 1 (see the *James and Others v the United Kingdom* judgment of 21 February 1986, Series A No 98, p 36, § 54). However, while it is true that even in many cases of lawful expropriation, such as a distinct taking of land for road construction or other public purposes, only full compensation may be regarded as reasonably related to the value of the property, this rule is not without exceptions. As stated in the *James v the United Kingdom* case cited above, legitimate objectives of 'public interest', such as pursued in measures of economic reform or measures designed to achieve greater social justice, may call for less than reimbursement of the full market value (ibid). The Court considers that less than full compensation may be equally, if not *a fortiori*, called for where the taking of property is resorted to with a view to completing 'such fundamental changes of a country's constitutional system as the transition from monarchy to republic' (see paragraph 87 of the principal judgment).

79. In conclusion, unless the Government decide on their own initiative to return the properties to the applicants, the Court deems it appropriate to fix a lump sum based, as far as possible, on an amount 'reasonably related' to the value of the property taken, i.e. an amount which the Court would have found acceptable under Article 1 of Protocol No 1, had the Greek State compensated the applicants. In determining this amount the Court will take into account the claims of each applicant, the question of the movable property, the valuations submitted by the parties and the possible options for calculating the pecuniary damage, as well as the lapse of time between the dispossession and the present judgment. The Court considers that in the unique circumstances of the present case resort to equitable considerations is particularly called for.

The Grand Chamber accepted the applicants' request that in assessing their pecuniary damage separate awards should be made for each applicant. It also agreed that the whole of the Tatoi estate should be included in the assessment of just satisfaction as the agreement concerning the foundation had been repealed by a later law. However, the fact that substantial parts of the applicants' estates had been donated or sold for a token sum to their ancestors was also a factor to be taken into account when assessing the level of compensation to be awarded by the Court. The judges held that, 'as a matter of principle, the Court considers that the first applicant should be compensated for his personal belongings that are still in Greece'. (para 84) As the parties were still in disagreement regarding the details of these the Court resolved to include compensation for their pecuniary value in the overall lump sum on an equitable basis.

The Grand Chamber decided not to adopt the market value of the applicants' property when determining the sum of pecuniary damage. This was for two reasons. First the wide disparities in the assessments put forward by experts instructed by the parties (the applicants submitted an expert's total of 472 million euros whereas two experts produced totals of 550 million euros and 346 million euros on behalf of the Government). Secondly, because the nature of the dispossession meant that full compensation was not required. Therefore, the Court adopted the 'objective' value method. The parties agreed on the objective value of the Mons Repos estate (17.5 million euros) but disagreed on the objective values of Polydendri (applicants' 56 million euros and the Government 31 million euros) and Tatoi (applicants' 198 million euros and the Government 21.8 million euros—taking account of the land given to the foundation).

The next major ruling of the Grand Chamber was whether it should reduce the amount of just satisfaction payable in the light of the privileges and benefits received by the royal family in the past.

95. The Court recalls that in paragraph 98 of its principal judgment it held:

'... as regards the Government's argument that the issue of compensation was indirectly covered, the Court notes first that compensation provided for by Legislative Decree No 225/1973 is irrelevant to the instant case, Law No 2215/1994 being the sole legal basis of the interference of which the applicants complain. Nor can the circumstances to which the Government refer be regarded as payment of compensation. In this respect the Court agrees with the applicants when they argue that in the context of the expropriation in question there are no reciprocal or mutual debts to be set off against each other. The privileges afforded in the past to the royal family or the tax exemptions and the writing-off of all the debited taxes owed by the former royal family, have no direct relevance to the issue of proportionality, but could possibly be taken into account in order to make an accurate assessment of the applicants' claims for just satisfaction under Article 41 of the Convention.'

96. In view of that ruling, the Court agrees with the Government when they argue that the pecuniary damage allegedly suffered by the applicants should be adjusted downwards in view of the privileges and other benefits awarded in the past to the properties in question.

97. However, the Court considers that the pecuniary loss cannot be calculated as merely the arithmetical difference between the "objective" value of the properties and the present monetary value of the hypothetical tax burden, since that would be tantamount to the retrospective imposition of taxes on the former royal family by the Court.

Once again there was a significant disparity in the calculations produced by the parties. The applicants' calculated that their ancestors' privileges had been worth 33 million euros whilst the Government presented the figure of 579 million euros. The Grand Chamber agreed with the applicants' valuers that the Government's total was 'grossly exaggerated'.

99. ....To accept these figures would mean that the applicants owe the Greek State a sum ... which is even higher than the market value of the properties ... as calculated by the Government's own valuers ... The Court is not prepared to accept that conclusion.

Therefore, on an equitable basis, the Grand Chamber (unanimously) awarded the first applicant 12 million euros, the second applicant 900,000 euros and the third applicant 300,000 euros compensation for pecuniary damage.

Regarding the matter of non-pecuniary damage the Grand Chamber stated that:

101. The Court wishes to emphasise that it is not its task to examine either the role played by the first applicant in the politics of Greece prior to his departure from the country in 1967 or the reasons that led up to the abolition of the monarchy in 1974. Although the Court cannot ignore the political features

of the case, and has not done so, it is certainly not its role to enter into a discussion with the parties as to who is to be blamed for the dispute between them.

102. That said, the Court considers that, having regard to what is at stake in the case and all its special features, no special issue arises in relation to non-pecuniary damage, including the question of access to the royal graves.

Finally, the applicants claimed nearly £984,000 in costs and expenses. The Government considered the amounts claimed to be exorbitant. The Grand Chamber agreed that the total appeared excessive, particularly as the former Commission had dismissed many of the applicants' complaints. Taking account of fee levels in the United Kingdom and the complex issues dealt with under Article 41 the Court awarded the applicants 500,000 euros in respect of their costs/expenses.

The judgment provides a unique and fascinating study of the financial costs associated with the ending of a monarchy assessed under the provisions of the European Convention on Human Rights. The Grand Chamber ultimately awarded sums of just satisfaction in respect of pecuniary damage and costs/expenses relating to the proceedings far below the claims of the parties; for example the applicants claimed 472 million euros in respect of pecuniary damage and the Government countered this by asserting that the applicants' ancestors had received fiscal and other privileges worth 579 million euros. The total compensation for pecuniary damage suffered by the applicants, 13.2 million euros, was nevertheless a very substantial amount of money for the Court to award. Jurisprudentially the judgment is important for the Grand Chamber's elaboration of the circumstances where full compensation is not required under the Convention (Article 41 and Article 1 of Protocol No 1) in respect of 'public interest' expropriations. The dispossession of property from a former royal family, as part of the constitutional change to a republic, was held to fall within this category alongside measures of economic reform recognised in previous case law (e.g. the nationalization of aircraft and ship manufacturing companies in *Lithgow v United Kingdom*, A.102 (1986)). The Grand Chamber's acceptance that the manner in which a former royal family acquired its property (e.g. through gifts from public authorities) can be included as a factor in the determination of the amount of pecuniary damage will also be likely to reduce the sums payable under the Convention if the property is expropriated by order of a democratic national parliament. These considerations help to explain why the Grand Chamber awarded much less than the applicants claimed.

2 Depreciation in the value of a person's home attributable to State action or inaction, which is in breach of the Convention, has been held to amount to pecuniary damage. In *Lopez Ostra v Spain*, A.303-C (1994) 20 EHRR 279 (above, p 546), the Spanish authorities were found responsible for the serious industrial pollution which constituted a violation of the applicant's right to respect for her home and family life under Article 8. Mrs Lopez Ostra claimed just satisfaction of: 7 million Ptas for the cost of a new home, 2.5 million Ptas for the inconvenience caused by her undesired move, 295,000 Ptas for expenses incurred in settling into the new house, 12 million Ptas for the distress of living in her former home while subject to the pollution and 3 million Ptas for the anxiety caused by her daughter's serious illness (brought on by the pollution). The Commission and the Government contended that these amounts were excessive. The Court ruled that:

... Mrs Lopez Ostra sustained some damage on account of the violation of Article 8. Her old flat must have depreciated and the obligation to move must have entailed expense and inconvenience. On the other hand, there is no reason to award her the cost of her new house since she has kept her former home. Account must be taken of the fact that for a year the municipal authorities paid the rent of the flat occupied by the applicant and her family in the centre of Lorca and that the waste-treatment plant was temporarily closed by the investigating judge on 27 October 1993.

The applicant, moreover, undeniably sustained non-pecuniary damage. In addition to the nuisance caused by the gas fumes, noise and smells from the plant, she felt distress and anxiety as she saw the situation persisting and her daughter's health deteriorating.

The heads of damage accepted do not lend themselves to precise quantification. Making an assessment on an equitable basis in accordance with Article 50, the Court awards Mrs Lopez Ostra 4 million Ptas. (para 65)

3　Where a person has been subject to a criminal fine, in respect of a conviction which the Court has held to be in breach of the Convention, the sum paid can be claimed as pecuniary damage. For example, in *Jersild v Denmark*, A.298 (1994) 19 EHRR 1 (above, p 651), the applicant journalist had been convicted and fined by the Danish courts for aiding and abetting the making of degrading (racist) statements by others. The Court found this conviction to be in breach of the applicant's right to freedom of expression guaranteed by Article 10. The applicant sought reimbursement of the fine (1,000 Dkr) as pecuniary damage under Article 50. In its judgment the Court stated, 'The Government did not object and the Court finds that the amount should be awarded' (para 41). Also in *Oberschlick v Austria*, A.204 (1991) 19 EHRR 389 (above, p 642), another journalist had been convicted, after a private prosecution had been brought against him, of defamation. The Austrian courts had, *inter alia*, fined the applicant. His claim for just satisfaction in respect of this sum was upheld by the Court.

The applicant sought firstly sums corresponding to the fine imposed (4,000 schillings) and the costs awarded to the private prosecutor (14,123.84 schillings) by the Austrian courts. Having regard to the direct link between these items and the violation of Article 10 found by the Court, he is, as the Government agreed, entitled to recover the full amount of 18,123.84 schillings). (para 66)

However, the Court has not always been so willing to award just satisfaction to successful applicants in respect of their criminal fines. In *Schmautzer v Austria*, A.328-A (1995) 21 EHRR 511, the Court found that the imposition of a fine on the applicant, by the administrative authorities, for driving his car without wearing a seat belt violated Article 6(1). The applicant then claimed repayment of a sum equivalent to his fine as pecuniary damage.

The Government contended that the Court had no jurisdiction to quash convictions pronounced by national courts or to order repayment of fines. Moreover, it could not, in awarding reparation, speculate as to what the outcome of the proceedings would have been if the applicant had had access to a tribunal within the meaning of Article 6(1) of the Convention.

The Court agrees. It cannot speculate as to what the outcome of the proceedings in issue might have been if the violation of the Convention had not occurred. It considers that, in the circumstances of the case, the present judgment affords the applicant sufficient reparation. (paras 43–4)

Clearly, the Austrian Government was adopting a different stance to the recoverability of criminal fines under Article 50 in *Schmautzer* compared to its previous view in *Oberschlick*. Also the cases may be distinguished as *Schmautzer* involved the breach of a procedural right and *Oberschlick* a substantive right.

The full-time Court has also been circumspect when deciding whether to award pecuniary damage in respect of criminal fines imposed during domestic proceedings which the Court subsequently determined had violated procedural rights of the defendant. For example, in *Blum v Austria*, judgment of 3 February 2005, the applicant farmer had been convicted of employing a foreign worker who did not have a work permit. The applicant had been fined approximately 1,100 euros. He alleged, *inter alia*, that the domestic proceedings had violated Article 6(1) in that his case had taken over five years to be finally determined. The Chamber, unanimously, found a breach of the reasonable time requirement in that Article. Blum claimed pecuniary damage for the fine he had been required to pay. His claim for such damage was dismissed:

45. The Court does not discern any causal link between the violation found and the pecuniary damage alleged; it therefore rejects this claim.

Do you think that by adopting such an approach the Court is implicitly endorsing the merits of the applicant's conviction?

Non-pecuniary damage

1 Applicants who have been subject to excessive periods of detention in breach of the Convention have claimed compensation for non-pecuniary damage. Two Turkish political activists who were held on remand for two and a half years successfully invoked Article 5(3) in *Yagci and Sargin v Turkey*, A.319 (1995) 20 EHRR 505 (see above, p 731). They also requested unquantified compensation under Article 50. The Court determined that:

. . . having regard to the particular circumstances of the case, that the applicants sustained non-pecuniary damage which the findings of violations in . . . this judgment cannot make good. It awards them each 30,000 (French francs) under this head. (para 75)

Relevant factors were the Turkish authorities' failure to provide convincing reasons for the continued detention of the applicants and the National Security Court's use of stereotyped words in its detention orders.

However, the new full-time Court has been divided in its response to such claims. In *Nikolova v Bulgaria*, (25/3/1999) the Court was unanimous in finding that the respondent State had breached the applicant's rights under Article 5(3) and (4) when she was held for three and a half months on remand, in respect of the charge of misappropriating large amounts of public funds, without adequate judicial examinations of the lawfulness of her detention. She sought just satisfaction in respect of alleged non-pecuniary damage and her claim was supported by the Commission. But, a majority of the Court, eleven votes, rejected her request.

The Court recalls that in certain cases which concerned violations of Article 5(3) and (4) it has granted claims for relatively small amounts in respect of non-pecuniary damage (see *Van Droogenbeck v Belgium* A.63 (1983) . . .). However, in more recent cases concerning violations of either or both paragraphs (3) and (4) of Article 5, the Court has declined to accept such claims (see *Pauwels v Belgium* A.135 (1988) . . .). In some of these judgments the Court noted that just satisfaction can be awarded only in respect of damage resulting from a deprivation of liberty that the applicant would not have suffered if he or she had had the benefit of the guarantees of Article 5(3) and concluded, according to the circumstances, that the finding of a violation constituted sufficient just satisfaction in respect of any non-pecuniary damage suffered.

In the present case the Court sees no reason to depart from the above case-law. The Court cannot speculate as to whether or not the applicant would have been detained if there had been no violation of the Convention. As to the alleged frustration suffered by her on account of the absence of adequate procedural guarantees during her detention, the Court finds that in the particular circumstances of the case the finding of a violation is sufficient. (para 76)

Judge Bonello, joined by Judge Maruste, wrote a partly dissenting opinion in which he stated that:

I consider it wholly inadequate and unacceptable that a court of justice should 'satisfy' the victim of a breach of fundamental rights with a mere handout of legal idiom. . . .

The Convention confers on the Court two separate functions: firstly, to determine whether a violation of a fundamental right has taken place, and secondly, to give 'just satisfaction' should the breach be ascertained. The Court has rolled these two distinct functions into one. Having addressed the first, it feels absolved from discharging the second.

In doing so, the Court fails in both its judicial and its pedagogical functions. The State that has violated the Convention is let off virtually scot-free. The award of just satisfaction, besides reinstating the victim in his fundamental right, serves as a concrete warning to erring governments. The most persuasive tool for implementing the Convention is thus lying unused.

The only 'legal' argument used so far in favour of refusing to award any compensation at all for non-pecuniary damage has been based on the admittedly infelicitous wording of Article 41 . . .

The Court seems to feel authorised to deny just satisfaction to the victim on the strength of the 'if necessary' condition. This, I submit, places an improper construction on Article 41. 'If necessary' is applicable *only* where there is a concurrence of both the conditions posited by Article 41, i.e. the finding of a violation of the Convention *and* the ability of the domestic system to provide for some partial reparation. When these two conditions combine (and only then) may the Court find it unnecessary to award additional just satisfaction. This is what Article 41 clearly states.

In cases like the present one, in which the internal law provides for no satisfaction at all, the 'if necessary' condition becomes irrelevant and the Convention leaves the Court no discretion at all as to whether to award compensation or not. . . .

Of course, the Court is called upon to carry out a careful balancing exercise when assessing the quantum of compensation to be awarded. In certain cases that award could, and should, be nominal or even token. I would not vote for awarding substantial compensation to a convicted serial rapist, should some aspect of his right to family life have been formally breached. Nor would I be excessively generous with awards to a drug trafficker because the interpreter at his trial failed the test of high competence.

What I am disenchanted with is that any court should short-change a victim. I voted against that.

Similarly, Judge Fischbach, joined by Judges Kuris and Casadevall, dissented on the matter of just satisfaction.

We consider that the applicant's detention on remand, which lasted more than three and a half months, without adequate safeguards and therefore in breach of Article 5(3) and (4) of the Convention, must have caused the victim feelings of anxiety and frustration such that a mere finding of a violation cannot in itself suffice to compensate for the non-pecuniary damage she sustained. . . .

Nor do we agree with the majority's reasoning, with reference to the most recent case-law . . .

We take the view that the issue of compensation for non-pecuniary damage is one that has to be determined in the light of the particular facts of each case, whereas the principle adopted by the majority in its reasoning is such as to restrict in advance the scope for awarding compensation for non-pecuniary damage sustained by the victims of breaches of Article 5(3) and (4).

Judge Greve also issued a partly dissenting opinion in which she stated that:

As pointed out by the majority in the present case, the Court's rulings have not, however, followed a consistent pattern in these cases but rather followed a case-by-case approach even when, as in the instant case, violations of Article 5(3) and (4) have been established.

In my view, it would under these circumstances be preferable for the Court normally to use its discretion to award the injured party some equitable satisfaction—be it only token—rather than simply state that the mere finding of a violation/violations constituted sufficient just satisfaction in respect of any non-pecuniary damage suffered. The question in each individual case would then be what amount constituted equitable satisfaction under the circumstances. I cannot identify any reasons for making an exception in the present case.

In the subsequent case of *TW v Malta* (1999) 29 EHRR 185 the Court was again unanimous in finding a breach of Article 5(3) in respect of the nineteen day detention on remand of the applicant in respect of charges of sexual and physical abuse of his daughter. Fourteen judges voted not to award the applicant any just satisfaction in respect of his claim for alleged non-pecuniary damage. Judge Bonello, the Judge of Maltese nationality, issued another partly dissenting opinion which repeated (verbatim) his views expressed above. Judges Tulkens and Casadevall also dissented as they favoured the payment of just satisfaction to the applicant because:

... We cannot of course maintain that the applicant's detention would have ended if he had been able to obtain speedy judicial review of his detention, but on account of the absence of that safeguard the applicant may well have suffered a certain amount of non-pecuniary damage not wholly compensated by the finding of a violation. ... since Article 5(5) of the Convention, in specifying what is required of domestic law, expressly provides: 'Everyone who has been the victim of arrest or detention in contravention of the provisions of this Article shall have an enforceable right to compensation', there is all the more reason in our opinion to consider that the mere fact that the Court has found a violation is not sufficient to make good any damage. In the instant case, therefore, the Court should have awarded some measure of pecuniary satisfaction, especially as the sum claimed by the applicant was reasonable and could on that account constitute satisfaction on an equitable basis.

A Grand Chamber of the Court, unanimously, awarded £1,000 compensation for non-pecuniary damage suffered by a 70-year-old man, suspected of attempted rape, who had been denied bail under section 25 of the Criminal Justice and Public Order Act 1994 (because he had previously been convicted of manslaughter): *Caballero v UK* [2000] Crim LR 587. The Government conceded that there had been a violation of Article 5(3). The Court noted that:

31. In the present case affidavit evidence, which is not disputed by the Government, was submitted by the applicant to the effect that, had it not been for s 25 of the 1994 Act, he would have had a good chance of being released on bail prior to his trial. The applicant further argued that any such release on bail prior to his trial could have been his last days of liberty given his advanced age, his ill-health and the long sentence he was serving [subsequently, he had been convicted of, inter alia, attempted rape and given a life sentence], a submission on which the Government also did not comment. The Court awards the applicant, on an equitable basis, £1,000 compensation for non-pecuniary damage.

A unanimous Chamber distinguished between applicants who had suffered a breach of Article 5(1) and those who had successfully invoked Articles 5(3) and (4) in *Beet and Others v UK*, judgment of 1 March 2005.

46. As concerns the breach of Article 5 found in respect of *Beet*, the Court recalls that it found that the detention was unlawful in that the magistrates did not have jurisdiction to make the order of committal due to a failure properly to inquire into the applicant's means. It is true, as pointed out by the Government, that in cases concerning procedural defects under Article 5, in particular Article 5 §§ 3 and 4, the Court has held that just satisfaction was to be awarded only in respect of damage resulting from a deprivation of liberty that the applicant would not have suffered if he or she had had the benefit of the missing guarantees (e.g. *Nikolova v Bulgaria* [GC], No 31195/96, ECHR 1999-II, § 76). However where there are findings of unlawfulness in the detention itself under the first paragraph of Article 5, it may be noted that generally the Court makes an award which reflects the importance of the right to liberty which should not be removed save under the conditions provided for in domestic law and in conformity with the rule of law. As well as the length of the detention, the degree of arbitrariness disclosed by the circumstances of the case may be a factor influencing the appropriateness of making any award (e.g. *Conka and Others v Belgium*, No 51564/99, ECHR 2002-I; *Assanidzé v Georgia*,

No 71503/01, ECHR 2004-...). Domestic scales of damages are not decisive, or, in all cases, relevant to applications under the Convention.

47. In the present case, making an assessment on an equitable basis, therefore, the Court considers it appropriate to make an award to this applicant. Having regard to the circumstances, including the lack of substantiation or supporting documents, the Court awards EUR 5,000.

Hence, it is now appears very difficult for successful applicants under Articles 5(3) and (4) to obtain compensation for non-pecuniary damage.

2 The victims of physical maltreatment by State officials (such as police officers), which infringes Article 3, can claim for non-pecuniary damage. For example, a suspected drugs dealer (Ribitsch) complained that he had been assaulted by a police officer while being detained for questioning. He obtained medical evidence of bruising to his arm. The Court found a breach of Article 3 as the respondent State had not provided a plausible explanation of how the injuries could have been caused in a legitimate manner. In regard to Article 50

Mr Ribitsch maintained that he had suffered non-pecuniary damage on which he set the figure of 250,000 Sch.

The Government did not make any observation on the question.

The Delegate of the Commission argued that a relatively high sum should be awarded in order to encourage people in the same position as Mr Ribitsch to bring court proceedings. The Court considers that the applicant suffered undeniable non-pecuniary damage. Taking the various relevant factors into account, and making its assessment on an equitable basis, as required by Article 50, it awards him 100,000 Sch. [Ribitsch v Austria, A.336 (1995), paras 43–6, (see above, p 174)]

3 Where applicants have experienced a loss of opportunity to represent their interests fully, because the bodies determining their cases did not comply with the institutional and procedural safeguards required by the Convention, the Court has been willing to consider making an award for non-pecuniary damage. In *McMichael v UK*, A.308 (1995) 20 EHRR 205 (see above, p 532), the applicants successfully argued that the authorities refusal to allow them to see official social welfare reports during a Scottish children's hearing amounted to a breach of their right to respect for their family life (Article 8). In applying Article 50 the Court observed that:

While the present applicants may not have suffered a loss of real opportunities to the same extent as previous applicants who had been denied access to a proper remedy, it cannot be affirmed with certainty that no practical benefit could have accrued to them if the procedural deficiency in question had not existed. More importantly, the Court accepts that some, although not the major part, of the evident trauma, anxiety and feeling of injustice experienced by both applicants in connection with the care proceedings is to be attributed to their inability to see the confidential documents and reports in question. An award of financial compensation is therefore warranted. Making an assessment on an equitable basis, as it is required to do under the terms of Article 50, the Court awards the applicants jointly the sum of £8,000. (para 103)

The final part of the Court's reasoning also demonstrates that where successful applicants can prove that they have suffered distress and anxiety, as a result of officials' failure to comply with the Convention, they can claim this as another form of non-pecuniary damage. The Court applied this latter head of damage in *Lopez Ostra* (above, p 546).

4 The methodology used to calculate the amount of non-pecuniary damage to be awarded to applicants who have suffered unreasonable delays in the length of their proceedings before domestic courts, in breach of Article 6(1), was explained by a unanimous Chamber in *Riccardi Pizzati v Italy*, judgment of 10 November 2004. The Italian courts had taken over twenty-six years to determine the applicant's property dispute with her neighbour. The Court of Appeal found that a breach of the reasonable time guarantee and awarded her 5,000 euros in compensation for non-pecuniary damage sustained as a consequence of the delays (she had claimed 103,000 euros). The Chamber found a breach of Article 6(1) and:

26. As regards an equitable assessment of the non-pecuniary damage sustained as a result of the length of proceedings, the Court considers that a sum varying between EUR 1,000 and 1,500 per year's duration of the proceedings (and not per year's delay) is a base figure for the relevant calculation. The outcome of the domestic proceedings (whether the applicant loses, wins or ultimately reaches a friendly settlement) is immaterial to the non-pecuniary damage sustained on account of the length of the proceedings.

The aggregate amount will be increased by EUR 2,000 if the stakes involved in the dispute are considerable, such as in cases concerning labour law, civil status and capacity, pensions, or particularly serious proceedings relating to a person's health or life.

The basic award will be reduced in accordance with the number of courts dealing with the case throughout the duration of the proceedings, the conduct of the applicant—particularly the number of months or years due to unjustified adjournments for which the applicant is responsible—to the stakes involved in the dispute—for example where the financial stakes are of little importance for the applicant—and on the basis of the standard of living in the country concerned. A reduction may also be envisaged where the applicant has been only briefly involved in the proceedings in his or her capacity as heir.

The amount may also be reduced where the applicant has already obtained a finding of a violation in domestic proceedings and a sum of money by using a domestic remedy. Apart from the fact that the existence of a domestic remedy is in full keeping with the subsidiarity principle embodied in the Convention, such a remedy is closer and more accessible than an application to the Court, is faster, and is processed in the applicant's own language; it thus offers advantages that need to be taken into consideration.

. . . .

30. As regards non-pecuniary damage, however, the Court considers that in respect of proceedings which lasted more than twenty-six years for one level of jurisdiction EUR 46,000 could be regarded as an equitable sum. However, the Court notes that the applicant's conduct did slightly contribute to delaying the proceedings. Accordingly, the Court considers that the applicant should be awarded EUR 36,000 less 30% on account of the finding of a violation by the domestic court (see paragraph 26 above), that is, EUR 25,200.

31. From that sum should also be deducted the amount of compensation awarded to the applicant at domestic level, that is, EUR 5,000. Accordingly, the applicant is entitled to EUR 20,200 in compensation for non-pecuniary damage, plus any tax that may be chargeable.

Do you think it was fair of the Chamber to reduce the applicant's compensation by 10,000 euros because of her 'slight' contribution to delays in the domestic proceedings? In the subsequent Grand Chamber proceedings (see above, p 428) the unanimous Court found that the domestic award of 5,000 euros (14 per cent of what the Court would have awarded) was 'manifestly unreasonable'. However, the Grand Chamber reduced its award of compensation for non-pecuniary damage to 11,200 euros in the light of the existence of a domestic remedy (under the Pinto Act). A further 1,600 euros was added to compensate the applicant for the 'frustration' of having to wait over one year for payment of her Pinto Act compensation by the domestic authorities. Hence, the Grand Chamber was according States a considerable discount in respect of Article 41 compensation where they provided a domestic compensatory remedy (even where that was subsequently found by the Court not to satisfy Convention requirements).

5   The Court has been willing to award compensation in respect of non-pecuniary damage sustained by legal persons/associations. For example, in *Supreme Holy Council of the Muslim Community v Bulgaria*, judgment of 16 December 2004 (see above, p 612), the unanimous Chamber determined that:

116. . . . The unjustified State interference with the organisation of the religious community must have caused non-pecuniary damage to the applicant organisation. Deciding on an equitable basis, the Court awards 5,000 euros in respect of non-pecuniary damage, to be paid to Mr N. Gendzhev as the representative of the applicant organisation.

Costs and expenses

1   The key criteria applied by the Court when determining if, and how much, to award successful applicants under Article 50 in respect of their legal costs and expenses incurred in asserting or defending their Convention rights were stated in the Gibraltar shootings case (*McCann v UK*, A.324 (1995) 21 EHRR 97 (see above, p 77)) as being: '. . . only costs which are actually and necessarily incurred and reasonable as to *quantum* . . . are recoverable under this head' (para 220). The requirement that the costs be 'actually' incurred was invoked to deny the applicants any just satisfaction in respect of their legal costs before the Gibraltar inquest, as their legal representatives had acted free of charge. Consequently the Court ruled that:

In this connection, it has not been claimed that they are under any obligation to pay the solicitor the amounts claimed under this item. In these circumstances, the costs cannot be claimed under Article 50 since they have not been actually incurred. (para 221)

Hence, only those professional costs which applicants are under a legal duty to pay are recoverable under Article 50. Therefore, human rights lawyers must ensure that they bill their clients for ECHR related work, even if they are disposed on ethical/public interest grounds to waive their fees, because unless successful applicants are formally obliged to pay the fees they will not be recoverable under Article 50/41.

2   As to the condition that the costs and expenses must have been 'necessarily' incurred in *Tolstoy Miloslavsky v UK*, A.323 (1995) 20 EHRR 442 (above, p 694), the applicant claimed, *inter alia*, 104,000 Swiss francs in respect of professional fees and expenses charged by his adviser for handling the application to the Commission. The Government asked the Court to take a critical look at the amount of costs claimed. The Court determined that it was 'not satisfied that all the costs and expenses were necessarily incurred' (para 78), therefore it awarded a total of 40,000 SF in respect of that part of the applicant's claim for just satisfaction. Also the Court considered that the total amount claimed should be reduced because, 'the applicant has succeeded only in respect of one of his complaints under the Convention' (ibid). This ruling indicates that legal costs and expenses related to unsuccessful aspects of an applicant's case will potentially be ineligible for reimbursement under Article 50/41.

3   The calculation of the reasonableness of costs was examined by the Court in *Papamichalopoulos v Greece*, A.330-B (1995) 21 EHRR 439. The applicants had successfully argued that the Government's seizure of their land in 1967, and the subsequent failure to make reparation, violate their right to property under Article 1 of Protocol No 1. They then sought just satisfaction for, *inter alia*, their legal costs and expenses which they claimed as being approximately 3 billion dr.

The Court notes that the applicants calculated the above mentioned sums on the basis of the relevant national scales . . . and in proportion to their claims for pecuniary damage.

. . .

It is settled case law that the Court is not bound by the rules of domestic practice in this area . . .

The Court therefore cannot allow in full the applicants' claims, whose quantum is indisputably very large. However, having regard to the circumstances of the case, the multiplicity and length of the national proceedings, both judicial and administrative, the fact that Counsel for the applicants took part in the negotiations with a view to a friendly settlement, and the special complexity of the question of the application of Article 50, the Court considers it reasonable to award them 65 million dr, including value added tax. (para 47)

From this reasoning it is clear that the Court pays close regard to the actual work undertaken (e.g. the amount of time expended) by the applicants' lawyers in assessing the appropriate level of fees. Though national methods of calculating legal costs are not decisive for the Court, it may 'derive some assistance from them.' (*Tolstoy Miloslavsky*, para 77) In the latter case the Delegate of the Commission asked the Court to consider adopting a uniform (ie pan European) standard for the calculation of reasonable fee rates under Article 50. However, the Court declined this invitation because, 'given the great differences at present in rates of fees from one Contracting State to another, a uniform approach to the assessment of fees under Article 50 does not seem appropriate' (ibid). Indeed, with the growing membership of the Council of Europe it is likely that the range of national fee rates is widening, making the attainment of a common standard more remote.

4   The Court has been willing to allow applicants to claim for their legal costs and expenses incurred in seeking to protect or defend their Convention rights before national courts. For example, in *Oberschlick* (above, p 642) the applicant claimed 9,753 schillings in respect of his defence expenditure before the Austrian criminal courts. The Court determined that: 'these items fall to be taken into account, since they were incurred to prevent or redress the breaches found by the Court. The amount, which was accepted by the Government, appears reasonable to the Court and is therefore awarded in full' (para 70).

5   The Court has not been willing to allow States to claim their legal costs and expenses where they have successfully brought an inter-State application or, under the former Strasbourg control system, referred a national's case to the Court (see now Article 36). In *Loizidou v Turkey (Article 50)*, 1998-IV, the judges were unanimous in holding that:

48. The Court recalls the general principle that States must bear their own costs in contentious proceedings before international tribunals (see, for example, Article 64 of the Statute of the International Court of Justice and the Advisory Opinion of that Court in 'Application for Review of Judgement No 158 of the United Nations Administrative Tribunal', ICJ Reports 1993, p 211, § 96). It considers that this rule has even greater application when, in keeping with the special character of the Convention as an instrument of European public order (*ordre public*), High Contracting Parties bring cases before the Convention institutions, whether by virtue of [former] Article 24 or [former] Article 48 (c), as part of the collective enforcement of the rights set out in the Convention or by virtue of [former] Article 48 (b) in order to protect the rights of their nationals. In principle, it is not appropriate, in the Court's view, that States which act, inter alia, in pursuit of the interests of the Convention community as a whole, even where this coincides with their own interests, be reimbursed their costs and expenses for doing so.

Accordingly the Court dismisses the Cypriot Government's claim for costs and expenses.

General issues

In 1996 the original Court adopted the general practice of awarding successful applicants default interest for delayed settlement of just satisfaction awards by respondent States. States were allowed three months from the date of the Court's judgment detailing the sum of just satisfaction to be paid. If payment was not made by the expiry of that period of time then simple interest was also payable on the sum due. The Court set the rate of default interest in accordance with the statutory rate prevailing in the respondent State. This practice was formalized under the Rules of Court adopted by the full-time Court in November 1998. The Grand Chamber in *Christine Goodwin v UK*, judgment of 11 July 2002 (see above p 575) amended this system in the light of the adoption of the euro by a number of Member States.

121. The applicant claims for legal costs and expenses GBP 17,000 for solicitors' fees and GBP 24,550 for the fees of senior and junior counsel. Costs of travel to the Court hearing, together with accommodation and other related expenses were claimed in the sum of GBP 2,822. This made a total of GBP 44,372.

122. The Government submitted that the sum appeared excessive in comparison to other cases from the United Kingdom and in particular as regarded the amount of GBP 39,000 claimed in respect of the relatively recent period during which the applicant's current solicitors have been instructed which would only relate to the consolidated observations and the hearing before the Court.

123. The Court finds that the sums claimed by the applicant for legal costs and expenses, for which no detail has been provided by way of hours of work and fee rates, are high having regard to the level of complexity of, and procedures adopted in, this case. Having regard to the sums granted in other United Kingdom cases and taking into account the sums of legal aid paid by the Council of Europe, the Court awards for this head 39,000 euros (EUR), together with any value-added tax that may be payable. The award is made in euros, to be converted into pounds sterling at the date of settlement, as the Court finds it appropriate that henceforth all just satisfaction awards made under Article 41 of the Convention should in principle be based on the euro as the reference currency.

C. DEFAULT INTEREST

124. As the award is expressed in euros to be converted into the national currency at the date of settlement, the Court considers that the default interest rate should also reflect the choice of the euro as the reference currency. It considers it appropriate to take as the general rule that the rate of the default interest to be paid on outstanding amounts expressed in euro should be based on the marginal lending rate of the European Central Bank to which should be added three percentage points.

Judges Fischbach and Turmen issued opinions favouring the use of fixed rates of default interest. Judge Greve issued a partly dissenting opinion in which she stated:

... There is agreement among the judges that the euro is *a suitable reference currency* for all awards under Article 41. The Court wants such *awards paid promptly*, and the default interest rate is intended to be an incentive for prompt payment *without* it having a *punitive character*. So far I fully agree.

Under the Court's new policy awards are made in the euro to be converted into national currencies at the day of settlement. This means that in the present case the applicant will suffer a loss in the value of her award if her national currency, the pound sterling, continues to gain strength vis-à-vis the euro. Conversion into national currency first at the day of settlement in contradistinction to a conversion at the day of the judgment will favour applicants from the euro countries and applicants that have national currencies on a par with the euro, or weaker. All other applicants will suffer a loss under the changed policy. This, in my opinion, conflicts with the provisions of Article 14 in combination with Article 41. Moreover, it conflicts with the Court's desire that the awards shall to be as fair as possible, that is to maintain the value of the award as accurately as possible.

The latter objective is also the rationale for changing the Court's previous practice of using the default interest rate in each member State as basis for the Court's decision in individual cases.

The majority is attempting to secure that awards become fair by using varying interest rates as they evolve throughout the period of default. The marginal lending rate used by the European Central Bank (ECB) when lending money overnight to commercial banks plus three percentage points will be used. This will in the present case, as in many other cases, give the applicant a lower default interest rate than the rate previously used by the Court, the national default interest rate.

The marginal lending rate is interest paid by banks to the ECB, when they need quick emergency loans. That is, it is a rate which forms the ceiling for the commercial money market; and of little, if any, practical interest to most of the applicants in the Court. The default interest rates provided for in each of the States parties to the Convention for their part do reflect the situation in the national money markets regarding the rates to be paid by applicants who may have to opt for borrowing money while awaiting payment of an award of just satisfaction. For this reason national default interest rates compensate the individuals in a manner not secured by the new default interest rate opted for by the Court's majority.

Furthermore, I believe that an applicant receiving an award ought to be able to know herself the applicable default interest rate. The marginal lending rate used by the ECB when lending money overnight to commercial banks is not easily available to all applicants in Europe. The rate has been stable for quite some time but if need be it could be set on a weekly if not even daily basis. Although it will be for the State to prove that it has actually paid the applicant in compliance with the judgment, and for the Committee of Ministers in the Council of Europe to check that this is correct, I find this to be an added bureaucratic procedure which makes it more difficult for applicants to keep track themselves. At all events the basis on which the Court's majority sets the new default interest rate is removed from the actual rate which an applicant, who needs to borrow money on an interim basis while awaiting payment of the award in a judgement, will have to pay. This is not compensated by the new varying interest rate, and this rather abstract search for fairness does not, in my opinion, merit a potentially bureaucratic new procedure.

Despite the economic cogency of her arguments, the Court has followed the majority's approach in subsequent cases.

Limitations of claims for just satisfaction

1   Successful applicants regularly requested the original Court to make formal declarations or orders against the respondent States. However, the Court constantly repeated that it did not have the power to require States to take (or refrain from) specified conduct. In *Yagci and Sargin* (above, p 877) the applicants invited the Court to request that Turkey comply with the undertakings it made when ratifying the Convention (the applicants also detailed a number of remedies which they believed would overcome defects in Turkish law). The invitation was declined because:

The Court notes that the Convention does not empower it to accede to such a request. It reiterates that it is for the State to choose the means to be used in its domestic legal system in order to comply with the provisions of the Convention or to redress the situation that has given rise to the violation of the Convention. (para 81)

Similarly, in *Tolstoy Miloslavsky* (above, p 882), the applicant asked the Court to make a 'declaratory' judgment that he was only liable, if at all, to pay Lord Aldington such damages as were necessary to provide adequate compensation and that the British government would indemnify him if he were required to pay a larger sum. This request was dismissed as, 'the Court is not empowered under Article 50 of the Convention to make a declaration such as that requested by the applicant' (para 72).

Generally, the full-time court has adopted a similar response. However, in *Assanidze v Georgia*, judgment of 8 April 2004 (and see above p 59), a unanimous Grand Chamber formally directed 'that the respondent State must secure the applicant's release at the earliest possible date'; in addition to paying him 150,000 euros compensation for non-pecuniary and pecuniary damage.

202. As regards the measures which the Georgian State must take, subject to supervision by the Committee of Ministers, in order to put an end to the violation that has been found, the Court reiterates that its judgments are essentially declaratory in nature and that, in general, it is primarily for the State concerned to choose the means to be used in its domestic legal order in order to discharge its legal obligation under Article 46 of the Convention, provided that such means are compatible with the conclusions set out in the Court's judgment (see, among other authorities, *Scozzari and Giunta v Italy* [GC], Nos 39221/98 and 41963/98, § 249, ECHR 2000 VIII; *Brumarescu v Romania* (just satisfaction) [GC], No 28342/95, § 20, ECHR 2001-I; *Akdivar and Others v Turkey*, judgment of 1 April 1998 (Article 50), Reports 1998-II, pp 723–4, § 47; *Marckx v Belgium*, judgment of 13 June 1979, Series A No 31, § 58). This discretion as to the manner of execution of a judgment reflects the freedom of choice attaching to the primary obligation of the Contracting States under the Convention to secure the rights and freedoms guaranteed (Article 1) (*mutatis mutandis, Papamichalopoulos v Greece*, judgment of 31 August 1995 (Article 50), Series A No 330-B, pp. 58–9, § 34).

However, by its very nature, the violation found in the instant case does not leave any real choice as to the measures required to remedy it.

203. In these conditions, having regard to the particular circumstances of the case and the urgent need to put an end to the violation of Article 5 § 1 and Article 6 § 1 of the Convention . . . the Court considers that the respondent State must secure the applicant's release at the earliest possible date.

Judge Costa issued a concurring opinion in which he expressed reservations about this development in the Court's remedial jurisprudence. He considered that:

7. The more specific the wording of the judgment, the easier the Committee of Ministers' task of supervising the execution of measures imposed on the States becomes from the legal perspective. However, that is not necessarily true of the political aspects, since, if it has no choice as to the measures to be implemented, the respondent State will be left with only one alternative: either to comply with the Court's order (in which case all will be well) or to run the risk of blocking the situation.

But, he felt, as a matter of principle, 'it would have been illogical and even immoral to leave Georgia with a choice of (legal) means, when the sole method of bringing arbitrary detention to an end is to release the prisoner'. Clearly, the prolonged unlawful detention of the applicant was the decisive factor motivating the Grand Chamber to issue its direction in *Assanidze*. In his speech marking the opening of the judicial year, given on 21 January 2005, President Wildhaber noted that the day after the judgment in *Assanidze* had been delivered the applicant had been released from prison in Ajaria.

Another Grand Chamber directed the respondent States to 'take all necessary measures to put an end to the arbitrary detention of the applicants still imprisoned and secure their immediate release' in *Ilascu and Others v Moldova and Russia*, judgment of 8 July 2004 (and see above p 61).

In *Broniowski v Poland*, judgment of 22 June 2004 (and see above p 44), given the systemic failures of domestic legislation and administration to safeguard the property rights of the numerous Bug river claimants, the Grand Chamber directed that Poland must 'through appropriate legal measures and administrative practices, secure the implementation of the property right in question in respect of the remaining Bug river claimants or provide them with equivalent redress in lieu'. Hence, the full-time Court is also willing to issue directions, in exceptional cases, where rights other than that of liberty have been infringed.

2   The Court requires applicants to precisely comply with the requirements of the Rules of Court when making claims for just satisfaction. For example, in *Vendittelli v Italy* A.293-A (1994), the applicant's lawyer failed to submit the just satisfaction claim within the specified time period. The Court, after finding a breach of Article 1 of Protocol No 1, rejected the claim for just satisfaction:

44. . . . Even if allowance is made for the difficulty of assembling all the necessary vouchers, it considers that the time allowed in this case for making these claims was sufficient.

   That being so, the claims must be dismissed as being out of time.

This robust approach has been continued by the full-time Court. For example, in *Giniewski v France*, judgment of 31 January 2006, the unanimous Chamber found the applicant had suffered a breach of Article 10. However, as he had not submitted a claim for just satisfaction within the specified time no award was made in his favour.

3   Although the Court disapproves of a State attaching a prior claim to a sum of just satisfaction awarded under Article 41, it has no legal authority under the Convention to prohibit such action. In *Selmouni v France* (1999) 29 EHRR 403 (above, p 166) the Court noted that:

132. The applicant pointed out that he had been ordered to pay, jointly and severally with the other persons convicted in the proceedings against them, a customs fine of twelve million French francs. Accordingly, the applicant asked the Court to specify in its judgment that the sums awarded under Article 41 should be exempt from attachment.

133. The Court considers that the compensation fixed pursuant to Article 41 and due by virtue of a judgment of the Court should be exempt from attachment. It would be incongruous to award the applicant an amount in compensation for, inter alia, ill-treatment constituting a violation of Article 3 of the Convention and costs and expenses incurred in securing that finding if the State itself were then to be both the debtor and creditor in respect of that amount. Although the sums at stake were different in kind, the Court considers that the purpose of compensation for non-pecuniary damage would inevitably be frustrated and the Article 41 system perverted if such a situation were to be deemed satisfactory. However, the Court does not have jurisdiction to accede to such a request . . . It must therefore leave this point to the discretion of the French authorities.

Conclusions

In a study undertaken by the author it was observed that:

The contemporary cases reveal that the Court is willing to accept a wide range of claims within the established categories of pecuniary damage, non-pecuniary damage and costs/expenses. However, in practice the Court is very cautious regarding the actual awarding of just satisfaction for damage claims. As we have discovered, in recent years, applicants have only had a relatively low rate of success in obtaining compensation awards under these headings. Furthermore, even when the Court makes such an award it tends to be a much smaller amount than that claimed by the applicant. Claims for costs/expenses have a far higher success rate, provided that applicants can establish that the costs/expenses have actually been incurred and that they are for a reasonable amount. . . .

   Aspects of the Court's application of Article 50 in recent times raise serious concerns about the consistency of the case law (eg over the treatment of criminal fines as pecuniary damages . . .). Other judgments are extremely opaque regarding the Court's basis for awarding a specified amount of compensation. Also, the Court makes moral judgments about the nature of different types of applicants such as convicted criminals and terrorists, when evaluating their claims for just satisfaction. However, the Court generally fails to make express reference to these considerations or justify their use. These weaknesses in the jurisprudence on Article 50 will need to be addressed by the Court if it is to provide a more coherent system of redress for successful applicants. Furthermore, it is in the interests of both applicants and states that Article 50 should be applied fairly, openly and consistently. [A R Mowbray, 'The European Court of Human Rights' Approach to Just Satisfaction' [1997] *Public Law* 647 at 658–9.]

In the autumn of 2006 the Registry of the Court established a specialist unit to ensure consistency and simplification in the awarding of just satisfaction. It clearly faces a daunting task.

20 ARTICLE 47 ADVISORY OPINIONS

Decision On The Competence Of The Court To Give An Advisory Opinion
European Court of Human Rights
2 June 2004

Following the break-up of the USSR on 8 December 1991 the leaders of the Republic of Belarus, the Russian Federation, and Ukraine signed an Agreement on the creation of the Commonwealth of Independent States (CIS). On 21 December 1991, the heads of eleven States (Azerbaijan, Armenia, Belarus, Kazakstan, Kyrgyz, Moldova, Russian Federation, Tajikistan, Turkmenistan, Uzbekistan, and Ukraine) signed a Protocol to the earlier Agreement in which they established the CIS. Georgia joined the CIS in 1993. The CIS drew up a Convention on Human Rights and Fundamental Freedoms of the Commonwealth of Independent States which was opened for signature by Member states in 1995. This Convention entered into force in 1998, having been ratified by Belarus, the Kyrgyz Republic and the Russian Federation. The CIS Convention contains a number of substantive rights and obligations expressed in similar terms to the ECHR. The CIS Convention provides for the creation of a Human Rights Commission of the CIS to, *inter alia*, examine individual applications by persons concerning alleged violations of the CIS Convention by Member states (the CIS Commission had not been established by June 2004).

Following the drafting of the CIS Convention concerns arose in the Council of Europe about the possibility incompatibility between ratification of the CIS Convention and the ECHR in respect of members of the CIS seeking to join the Council of Europe. Subsequently, when Moldova and the Ukraine applied to join the Council of Europe they agreed not to ratify the CIS Convention. Russia, in its application to the Council of Europe undertook to ensure that the CIS Convention did not interfere with the procedure and guarantees of the ECHR. In May 2001, the Parliamentary Assembly of the Council of Europe adopted Resolution 1249 (2001) in which the Assembly expressed continuing concern about the compatibility of the CIS Convention and the ECHR. The Assembly considered that the CIS Convention offered less protection in both the content of its guarantees and the independence of its enforcement arrangements. At the same time the Assembly adopted Recommendation 1519 (2001):

.... [T]he Assembly, taking into account the weakness of the CIS commission as an institution for the protection of human rights (from the point of view of its control mechanism; its political nature; the legal nature of its decisions; the impartiality, independence and competence of its members), and considering that the CIS commission should not be regarded as 'another procedure of international investigation or settlement' in the sense of Article 35 paragraph 2.b of the European Convention on Human Rights, recommends that the Committee of Ministers request that the Court give an advisory opinion on the interpretation of Article 35 paragraph 2.b of the European Convention on Human Rights with regard to this specific issue.

In June 2001 the Committee of Ministers, at a meeting of the Ministers' Deputies, agreed to accept the advice of the Parliamentary Assembly and in January 2002 the Chairman of the Committee of Ministers requested the Court to give an advisory opinion, under Article 47 of the ECHR, on the issue raised in the above Recommendation.

In accordance with Article 31(b) of the ECHR the request was assigned to the Grand Chamber of the Court and, after discussions, the Court informed all State parties to the ECHR that it was prepared to receive their written comments (which at this stage should be limited to the question whether the request fell within the Court's advisory jurisdiction. Ten States submitted comments.

22. Six of the ten Governments which submitted written comments took the view that the Court did not have jurisdiction to give an advisory opinion on the matter submitted to it. The Governments of the Czech Republic, Germany and Ukraine considered that the issue clearly fell outwith the scope of the Court's advisory jurisdiction because it was covered by the second branch of the exception set out in Article 47 § 2, since it concerned a question 'which the Court or the Committee of Ministers might have to consider in consequence of any such proceedings as could be instituted in accordance with the Convention', namely whether the procedure of the CIS Commission is 'another procedure of international investigation or settlement' for the purposes of Article 35 § 2(b). The Government of the Russian Federation considered that while a positive answer to the Court's second question could serve as an additional argument confirming the lack of jurisdiction, the issue of the co-existence of the two conventions was not in any event a legal question concerning the interpretation of the Convention and Protocols thereto. The Government of Georgia similarly expressed the view that the Court did not have consultative jurisdiction to examine the co-existence of the two conventions, since the Court was not competent 'to determine the legal role of other international instruments'. They also referred to the possibility of the question arising in the context of contentious proceedings. Finally, the Government of Moldova agreed, without specifying any reasons, that the Court did not have jurisdiction.

23. The four other Governments which submitted written comments were of the view that the Court did have jurisdiction to give an advisory opinion on the matter referred to it. The Government of Malta considered that the request did not deal with a question which might have to be considered by the Court or the Committee of Ministers in consequence of proceedings instituted in accordance with the Convention, since the question was not related to any particular case which had already been lodged with the Court or was being dealt with by the Committee of Ministers. They further considered that the matter concerned the interpretation of Article 55 of the Convention. The Government of Turkey also considered that the Court had jurisdiction, as the request was not related to any specific application. The Governments of Poland and Slovakia were generally favourable to the Court giving an advisory opinion, although they expressed certain reservations in the event that any cases raising the issue were actually pending before the Court. In this connection, the Government of Slovakia indicated that the Court's jurisdiction would not be excluded by Article 47 § 2 if the advisory opinion were 'more general than concrete in its substance'.

III. THE ADVISORY JURISDICTION OF THE COURT

24. The Court notes firstly that requests under Article 47 of the Convention may relate only to legal questions concerning the interpretation of the Convention and the Protocols thereto. It considers that although the request of the Committee of Ministers refers in general terms to the co-existence of the Convention on Human Rights and Fundamental Freedoms of the Commonwealth of Independent States and the European Convention on Human Rights, the Court is not called upon to examine in the abstract whether the CIS system or the CIS Commission are compatible with the Convention or how recourse to them might hinder access to the Court. It is clear from the terms of Parliamentary Assembly Recommendation 1519 (2001), to which it makes specific reference, that the request relates

essentially to the concrete question whether the CIS Commission may be regarded as 'another procedure of international investigation or settlement' within the meaning of Article 35 § 2(b) of the Convention. Indeed, the Recommendation proposes that the Committee of Ministers request an advisory opinion 'on the interpretation of Article 35 paragraph 2.b of the European Convention on Human Rights with regard to this specific issue'. The Court is therefore satisfied that the request for an advisory opinion concerns a legal question concerning the interpretation of the Convention.

25. The Court must next ascertain whether its jurisdiction to give an advisory opinion is excluded by Article 47 § 2 of the Convention on the ground that the request raises a question relating to the content or scope of the rights or freedoms defined in Section I of the Convention and the Protocols thereto or any other question which the Court or the Committee of Ministers might have to consider in consequence of any such proceedings as could be instituted in accordance with the Convention. The Court considers it self-evident that the question raised in the request does not relate to the content or scope of the rights or freedoms defined in the Convention and Protocols. However, it finds it necessary to examine whether the question is one which the Court or the Committee of Ministers might have to consider in connection with proceedings instituted under the Convention.

26. The Court recalls that it has been set up to ensure the observance of the engagements undertaken by the High Contracting Parties in the Convention and the Protocols thereto (Article 19 of the Convention) and that, by virtue of Article 32 § 1, its jurisdiction extends to 'all matters concerning the interpretation and application of the Convention and the protocols thereto which are referred to it as provided in Articles 33, 34 and 47.' In the Court's view, it is clear that the 'proceedings' referred to in Article 47 § 2 are those instituted by the introduction of an application under either Article 33 (inter-State cases) or Article 34 (individual applications) of the Convention.

27. The Court further observes that Article 35 of the Convention sets out the conditions for the admissibility of applications lodged under Articles 33 and 34 and that pursuant to paragraph 4 of Article 35 the Court 'shall reject any application which it considers inadmissible under this Article'. Consequently, it is part of the Court's task, in conducting proceedings instituted under the Convention, to examine whether the application falls foul of any of the grounds for inadmissibility and, in particular, with regard to individual applications submitted under Article 34, whether substantially the same matter has already been submitted to another procedure of international investigation or settlement. The Court therefore considers that the phrase 'any other question which the Court or the Committee of Ministers might have to consider in consequence of any such proceedings as could be instituted in accordance with the Convention' includes questions concerning the admissibility of applications lodged under Articles 33 and 34 of the Convention. It observes in this connection that 'any other question' can only refer to questions not relating to the content or scope of the rights or freedoms defined in the Convention and Protocols, since the Court's advisory jurisdiction in that respect is specifically precluded under the first branch of Article 47 § 2.

28. The Court finds support for this approach in the *travaux préparatoires* to Protocol No 2 to the Convention, from which it transpires that the intention in conferring advisory jurisdiction on the Court was to complement the Court's existing judicial jurisdiction under former Article 48 of the Convention, that is its competence to examine individual applications or inter-State complaints (which at that time could only be referred to it by a State Party or by the former European Commission of Human Rights ('the Commission')). Thus, a distinction was drawn between matters which fell within the Court's existing jurisdiction, which by virtue of former Article 45 extended to 'all cases concerning the interpretation and application of the present Convention which the High Contracting Parties or the Commission shall refer to it in accordance with Article 48', and other questions concerning the interpretation of the Convention, which could not arise in connection with the examination of such cases. The aim was to confer on the Court 'a general jurisdiction to interpret the Convention, which would therefore include matters arising out of the application of the Convention but not resulting from "contentious proceedings"' (see

AS/Jur(11)8, AS/Jur(11)25 rev. 2 and Doc. 1061). The examples which were given of issues which might come within this general jurisdiction concerned primarily procedural points such as the election of judges, the duties of the Secretary General of the Council of Europe under the Convention and the procedure of the Committee of Ministers in exercising its role in the execution of judgments. Furthermore, the commentary on the draft Protocol No 2, prepared in June 1962, stated that the object of the limitations on the Court's jurisdiction to give advisory opinions was 'to prevent exercise of the consultative competence of the Court in questions which could come within the Court's primary function, namely, its judicial function' (see CM(62)147 rev.). In that connection, it was added, with specific reference to the reasons for the inclusion of the second branch of the limitations, that 'the Court or the Committee of Ministers might, in consequence of the institution of proceedings, have to consider questions other than those concerning the content or scope of rights and freedoms'. By way of explanation, it was stated that the intention was to exclude, *inter alia*, 'questions of competence or of procedure which might come before one of the bodies provided for by the Convention in consequence of the institution of proceedings'. Thus, 'the consultative competence of the Court does not extend to questions regarding the conditions of admissibility of applications' (ibid). The Court notes in this connection that while at that time the Court had ultimate jurisdiction with regard to the interpretation and application of the Convention, including admissibility criteria, admissibility issues fell primarily within the competence of the Commission, whereas the Convention now confers on the Court itself the responsibility of examining the admissibility of applications.

29. The Court recalls that the question whether a matter raised in an individual application had already been submitted to another procedure of international investigation or settlement has in fact been addressed in the context of individual applications on a number of occasions in the past by the Commission in relation to the similar provision which was contained in former Article 27 § 1(b) of the Convention. In several decisions the Commission concluded that the matter was not 'substantially the same' and consequently did not find it necessary to examine whether the other procedure at issue fell within the terms of former Article 27 § 1(b) (see *Council of Civil Service Unions v the United Kingdom*, No 11603/85, decision of 20 January 1987, Decisions and Reports ('DR') 50, p 228, concerning the Committee on Freedom of Association of the International Labour Organization (applicants not identical); and *Pauger v Austria*, No 16717/90, decision of 9 January 1995, DR 80, p 24 (issue not the same), and *Peltonen v Finland*, No 19583/92, decision of 20 February 1995, DR 80, p 38 (applicant not the same), both concerning the United Nations Human Rights Committee). In other cases, however, it accepted, albeit implicitly, that the other procedure to which the same matter had been submitted was indeed 'another procedure of international investigation or settlement' (see *Calcerrada Fornieles and Cabeza Mato v Spain*, No 17512/90, decision of 6 July 1992, DR 73, p 214, *Pauger v Austria*, No 24872/94, decision of 9 January 1995, DR 80, p 170, and *C.W. v Finland*, No 17230/90, decision of 9 October 1991, unreported, all concerning the UN Human Rights Committee; and *Cereceda Martin v Spain*, No 16358/90, decision of 12 October 1992, DR 73, p 120, concerning the Committee on Freedom of Association of the International Labour Organisation, all of which were declared inadmissible in application of Article 27 § 1(b)).

30. More significantly, in two other cases the Commission made it clear that the mere fact that the matter had been submitted to another procedure of international investigation or settlement did not suffice in itself to exclude the Commission's competence and that a qualitative assessment was also necessary in order to ensure that the procedure fulfilled certain criteria. Thus, in the case of *Lukanov v Bulgaria* (No 21915/93, decision of 12 January 1995, DR 80, p 108), the Commission had to consider whether the procedure for examination of the applicant's situation by the Human Rights Committee of the Inter-Parliamentary Union could be regarded as 'another procedure of international investigation or settlement'. In reaching the conclusion that it could not, the Commission expressed the view that the term 'another procedure' referred to 'judicial or quasi-judicial proceedings similar to those set up by the Convention' and that the term 'international investigation or settlement' referred to institutions

and procedures set up by States, thus excluding non-governmental bodies, which it considered the Inter-Parliamentary Union to be. Similarly, in the case of *Varnava and others v Turkey* (Nos 16064–6/90 and 16068–73/90, decision of 14 April 1998, DR 93, p 5), which concerned the United Nations Committee on Missing Persons in Cyprus, the Commission not only asserted that the procedures envisaged referred to those instituted by way of a 'petition' lodged formally or substantively by the applicant but also took into account the limited nature of the committee's investigative capacity and the fact that the committee could not attribute responsibility for the deaths of any missing persons. In these cases, therefore, the Commission adopted the approach of ascertaining, in the context of its examination of admissibility, whether a particular procedure fell within the scope of former Article 27 § 1(b) of the Convention.

31. The Court itself has been called on to examine questions under Article 35 § 2(b) in only a handful of cases (see *Yagmurdereli v Turkey*, No 29590/96, decision of 13 February 2001, in which the Court noted that since Turkey had not ratified the Optional Protocol to the International Covenant on Civil and Political Rights, the same matter could not have been submitted to the UN Human Rights Committee, and *Smirnova v Russia*, Nos 46133/99 and 48183/99, decision of 3 October 2002, in which the Court found that the matter referred to the UN Human Rights Committee was not 'substantially the same'; see also *Hartman v the Czech Republic*, No 53341/99, decision of 17 December 2002, in which the matter was not addressed, as the complaint was declared inadmissible on another ground, and *Folgerø v Norway*, No 15472/02, communicated to the respondent Government on 4 December 2003, both concerning the UN Human Rights Committee). Nevertheless, the Court endorses the approach of the Commission and considers that the decisions of the Commission—in particular, those in the cases of *Lukanov* and *Varnava*—amply demonstrate that in the context of proceedings instituted under Article 34 of the Convention an examination of the question whether the same matter has already been submitted to another procedure of international investigation or settlement may be required and that this examination is not limited to a formal verification but extends, where appropriate, to ascertaining whether the nature of the supervisory body, the procedure which it follows and the effect of its decisions are such that the Court's jurisdiction is excluded by Article 35 § 2(b). Consequently, the question whether a particular procedure comes within the scope of Article 35 § 2(b) is a question which the Court might have to consider in consequence of proceedings instituted in accordance with the Convention and its advisory jurisdiction is in principle excluded.

32. Turning to the specific procedure established by the CIS Convention, namely the examination of applications by the CIS Commission, the Court notes that one of the States Parties to the Convention, namely the Russian Federation, has also ratified the CIS Convention, while five further States Parties to the Convention are also member States of the Commonwealth of Independent States, namely Armenia, Azerbaijan, Georgia, Moldova and Ukraine. Three of these (Armenia, Georgia and Moldova) have signed the CIS Convention. The CIS Convention has entered into force. Moreover, many substantive provisions of that Convention echo those which the Court has the task of interpreting and applying. In these circumstances, the Court considers that it cannot be excluded that the question whether the procedure before the CIS Commission can be regarded as 'another procedure of international investigation or settlement' within the meaning of Article 35 § 2(b) might have to be considered in the future in the context of the Court's examination of an individual application lodged under Article 34 of the Convention. Moreover, as noted above this would entail an analysis of, *inter alia*, the independence and impartiality of the CIS Commission, the nature of its proceedings and the effect of its decisions.

33. The Court notes finally that certain of the Governments which submitted written comments considered that the Court was not precluded from giving an advisory opinion as long as the request was not related to any specific application pending before it. In the view of the Court, this approach to the interpretation of Article 47 § 2 does not reflect the wording of that provision, which speaks of 'such proceedings as *could* be instituted in accordance with the Convention' [emphasis added] and not to proceedings which have in fact been instituted. Furthermore, the commentary on the draft Protocol No 2

expressly stated that the proceedings referred to were 'past, present, future or merely hypothetical' (see CM(62)147 rev.). The Court considers that the purpose of the provisions excluding its advisory jurisdiction is to avoid the potential situation in which the Court adopts in an advisory opinion a position which might prejudice its later examination of an application brought under Articles 33 or 34 of the Convention and that it is irrelevant that such an application has not and may never be lodged. In this respect, it again refers to the *travaux préparatoires*, in which it was stated that it was necessary 'to ensure that the Court shall never be placed in the difficult position of being required, as the result of a request for its opinion, to make a direct or indirect pronouncement on a legal point with which it might subsequently have to deal as a main consideration in some case brought before it' (see CM(61)91). The Court considers therefore that it suffices to exclude its advisory jurisdiction that the legal question submitted to it is one which it might be called upon to address in the future in the exercise of its primary judicial function, that is in the examination of the admissibility or merits of a concrete case.

34. The Court notes finally the view of the Government of Malta that the Court is in effect being called upon to give an interpretation of Article 55 of the Convention and to determine the relationship of another regional arrangement with the Convention. In that respect, the Court refers to its conclusion above (para 24) that the request submitted to it by the Committee of Ministers is in fact limited to the more specific question whether the CIS system can be regarded as 'another procedure of international investigation or settlement' for the purposes of Article 35 § 2(b). The Court considers, therefore, that the request does not seek to obtain an advisory opinion on the general issue of the co-existence of the two Conventions and that it is consequently not called upon in the context of the present decision to address any issues arising out of Article 55 of the Convention.

35. In conclusion, the Court finds that the request for an advisory opinion relates to a question which the Court might have to consider in consequence of proceedings instituted in accordance with the Convention and that it therefore does not have competence to give an advisory opinion on the matter referred to it.

For these reasons, the Court unanimously

Decides that the request for an advisory opinion is not within its competence as defined in Article 47 of the Convention.

NOTES

1   The Grand Chamber was composed of President Wildhaber and Judges: Rozakis, Costa, Ress, Bratza, Caflisch, Turmen, Birsan, Butkevych, Vajic, Pellonpaa, Baka, Maruste, Kovler, Zagrebelsky, Mularoni, and Fura-Sandstrom.

2   The authority of the Court to give advisory opinions was originally conferred by Protocol 2, which came into effect in 1970. The above request was the first one submitted to the Court. In the light of the Committee of Ministers' restraint in using this mechanism and the Grand Chamber's interpretation of the limits of its jurisdiction (see particularly paragraph 28 of the Decision) do you think this power is of any practical significance?

21 FIRST PROTOCOL ARTICLE 1: PROTECTION OF PROPERTY

The Court's general approach

Sporrong and Lönnroth v Sweden A.52 (1982) 5 EHRR 35
European Court of Human Rights

The Sporrong Estate (which had legal personality) owned a property in a central district of Stockholm. In July 1956, the Government granted the City Council of Stockholm a zonal expropriation permit which covered 164 properties, including the Sporrong property. The Council intended to build a viaduct across the area and one pillar of the viaduct was planned to stand on the Estate's land. Under the applicable legislation the Government specified five years as the time-limit within which the expropriation had to be effected (within that time the Council had to summon the property owner(s) to appear before the Real Estate Court for the fixing of compensation). Subsequently, at the request of the Council, the Government extended the time-limit in respect of the Sporrong property in 1961, 1964, 1968 and 1969. In May 1975 the Council put forward revised plans in which the Sporrong property was not to be developed and the existing building retained. Four years later the Government cancelled the expropriation permit in respect of the Sporrong property. Between 1954–1979 the Sporrong property had also been subject to a prohibition on construction, issued by the Stockholm County Administrative Board. The Estate had never tried to sell its property while these orders were in force. Mrs Lonnroth owned three-quarters of a property in another district of Stockholm. In September 1971, the Government authorized the Council to expropriate 115 properties, including Mrs Lonnroth's, as the Council proposed to build a multi-storey car park on the site. Subsequently, the Council abandoned that proposal and the expropriation permit was cancelled in September 1979. Between 1968 and 1980 Mrs Lonnroth's property was also subject to a prohibition on construction. While the above orders were in force Mrs Lonnroth had tried to sell her property on seven occasions but prospective buyers withdrew after they consulted the Council. The applicants complained to the Commission alleging unjustifiable interferences by the Swedish authorities with their right to peaceful enjoyment of their possessions, as guaranteed by Article 1 of Protocol No 1. The Commission, by ten votes to three, found no breach of that provision.

As to the law

I. THE ALLEGED VIOLATION OF ARTICLE 1 OF PROTOCOL NO 1 (P1-1)

56. The applicants complained of the length of the period during which the expropriation permits, accompanied by prohibitions on construction, affecting their properties had been in force. It amounted, in their view, to an unlawful infringement of their right to the peaceful enjoyment of their possessions, as guaranteed by Article 1 of Protocol No 1 (P1-1), which reads as follows:

'Every natural or legal person is entitled to the peaceful enjoyment of his possessions. No one shall be deprived of his possessions except in the public interest and subject to the conditions provided for by law and by the general principles of international law.

The preceding provisions shall not, however, in any way impair the right of a State to enforce such laws as it deems necessary to control the use of property in accordance with the general interest or to secure the payment of taxes or other contributions or penalties.'

57. In its *Marckx* judgment of 13 June 1979, the Court described as follows the object of this Article (P1-1):

'By recognising that everyone has the right to the peaceful enjoyment of his possessions, Article 1 (P1-1) is in substance guaranteeing the right of property. This is the clear impression left by the words 'possessions' and 'use of property' (in French: *'biens'*, *'propriété'*, *'usage des biens'*); the *'travaux préparatoires'*, for their part, confirm this unequivocally: the drafters continually spoke of 'right of property' or 'right to property' to describe the subject-matter of the successive drafts which were the forerunners of the present Article 1 (P1-1).' (Series A No 31, p 27, par 63)'

It has to be determined whether the applicants can complain of an interference with this right and, if so, whether the interference was justified.

1. THE EXISTENCE OF AN INTERFERENCE WITH THE APPLICANTS' RIGHT OF PROPERTY

58. The applicants did not dispute that the expropriation permits and prohibitions on construction in question were lawful in themselves. On the other hand, they complained of the length of the time-limits granted to the City of Stockholm for the institution of the judicial proceedings for the fixing of compensation for expropriation (five years, extended for three, then for five and finally for ten years, in the case of the Sporrong Estate; ten years in the case of Mrs Lönnroth; . . .). They also complained of the fact that the expropriation permits and the prohibitions on construction had been maintained in force for a lengthy period (twenty-three and eight years for the permits; twenty-five and twelve years for the prohibitions; . . . They pointed to the adverse effects on their right of property allegedly occasioned by these measures when they were combined in such a way. They contended that they had lost the possibility of selling their properties at normal market prices. They added that they would have run too great a risk had they incurred expenditure on their properties, and that if all the same they had had work carried out after obtaining a building permit, they would have been obliged to undertake not to claim—in the event of expropriation—any indemnity for the resultant capital appreciation. They also alleged that they would have encountered difficulties in obtaining mortgages had they sought them. Finally, they recalled that any 'new construction' on their own land was prohibited.

Though not claiming that they had been formally and definitively deprived of their possessions, the Sporrong Estate and Mrs Lönnroth alleged that the permits and prohibitions at issue subjected the enjoyment and power to dispose of their properties to limitations that were excessive and did not give rise to any compensation. Their right of property had accordingly, so they contended, been deprived of its substance while the measures in question were in force.

59. The Government accepted that market forces might render it more difficult to sell or let a property that was subject to an expropriation permit and that the longer the permit remained in force the more serious this problem would become. They also recognised that prohibitions on construction restricted the normal exercise of the right of property. However, they asserted that such permits and prohibitions

were an intrinsic feature of town planning and did not impair the right of owners to 'the peaceful enjoyment of (their) possessions', within the meaning of Article 1 of Protocol No 1 (P1-1).

60. The Court is unable to accept this argument.

Although the expropriation permits left intact in law the owners' right to use and dispose of their possessions, they nevertheless in practice significantly reduced the possibility of its exercise. They also affected the very substance of ownership in that they recognised before the event that any expropriation would be lawful and authorised the City of Stockholm to expropriate whenever it found it expedient to do so. The applicants' right of property thus became precarious and defeasible.

The prohibitions on construction, for their part, undoubtedly restricted the applicants' right to use their possessions.

The Court also considers that the permits and prohibitions should in principle be examined together, except to the extent that analysis of the case may require a distinction to be drawn between them. This is because, even though there was not necessarily a legal connection between the measures . . . and even though they had different periods of validity, they were complementary and had the single objective of facilitating the development of the city in accordance with the successive plans prepared for this purpose.

There was therefore an interference with the applicants' right of property and, as the Commission rightly pointed out, the consequences of that interference were undoubtedly rendered more serious by the combined use, over a long period of time, of expropriation permits and prohibitions on construction.

2. THE JUSTIFICATION FOR THE INTERFERENCE WITH THE APPLICANTS' RIGHT OF PROPERTY

61. It remains to be ascertained whether or not the interference found by the Court violated Article 1 (P1-1).

That Article (P1-1) comprises three distinct rules. The first rule, which is of a general nature, enounces the principle of peaceful enjoyment of property; it is set out in the first sentence of the first paragraph. The second rule covers deprivation of possessions and subjects it to certain conditions; it appears in the second sentence of the same paragraph. The third rule recognises that the States are entitled, among other things, to control the use of property in accordance with the general interest, by enforcing such laws as they deem necessary for the purpose; it is contained in the second paragraph.

The Court must determine, before considering whether the first rule was complied with, whether the last two are applicable.

(a) The applicability of the second sentence of the first paragraph

62. It should be recalled first of all that the Swedish authorities did not proceed to an expropriation of the applicants' properties. The applicants were therefore not formally 'deprived of their possessions' at any time: they were entitled to use, sell, devise, donate or mortgage their properties.

63. In the absence of a formal expropriation, that is to say a transfer of ownership, the Court considers that it must look behind the appearances and investigate the realities of the situation complained of . . . Since the Convention is intended to guarantee rights that are 'practical and effective' (see the *Airey* judgment of 9 October 1979, Series A No 32, p 12, par 24), it has to be ascertained whether that situation amounted to a *de facto* expropriation, as was argued by the applicants.

In the Court's opinion, all the effects complained of (see paragraph 58 above) stemmed from the reduction of the possibility of disposing of the properties concerned. Those effects were occasioned by limitations imposed on the right of property, which right had become precarious, and from the consequences of those limitations on the value of the premises. However, although the right in question lost some of its substance, it did not disappear. The effects of the measures involved are not such that they can be assimilated to a deprivation of possessions. The Court observes in this connection that the applicants could continue to utilise their possessions and that, although it became more difficult to sell properties in Stockholm affected by expropriation permits and prohibitions on construction, the possibility of selling subsisted; according to information supplied by the Government, several dozen sales were effected . . .

There was therefore no room for the application of the second sentence of the first paragraph in the present case.

(b) The applicability of the second paragraph

64. The prohibitions on construction clearly amounted to a control of 'the use of [the applicants'] property', within the meaning of the second paragraph.

65. On the other hand, the expropriation permits were not intended to limit or control such use. Since they were an initial step in a procedure leading to deprivation of possessions, they did not fall within the ambit of the second paragraph. They must be examined under the first sentence of the first paragraph.

(c) Compliance with the first sentence of the first paragraph as regards the expropriation permits

66. The applicants' complaints concerned in the first place the length of the time-limits granted to the City of Stockholm, which they regarded as contrary to both Swedish law and the Convention. . . .

69. The fact that the permits fell within the ambit neither of the second sentence of the first paragraph nor of the second paragraph does not mean that the interference with the said right violated the rule contained in the first sentence of the first paragraph.

For the purposes of the latter provision, the Court must determine whether a fair balance was struck between the demands of the general interest of the community and the requirements of the protection of the individual's fundamental rights (see, *mutatis mutandis*, the judgment of 23 July 1968 in the *'Belgian Linguistic'* case, Series A No 6, p 32, para 5). The search for this balance is inherent in the whole of the Convention and is also reflected in the structure of Article 1 (P1-1).

The Agent of the Government recognised the need for such a balance. At the hearing on the morning of 23 February 1982, he pointed out that, under the Expropriation Act, an expropriation permit must not be issued if the public purpose in question can be achieved in a different way; when this is being assessed, full weight must be given both to the interests of the individual and to the public interest

The Court has not overlooked this concern on the part of the legislature. Moreover, it finds it natural that, in an area as complex and difficult as that of the development of large cities, the Contracting States should enjoy a wide margin of appreciation in order to implement their town-planning policy. Nevertheless, the Court cannot fail to exercise its power of review and must determine whether the requisite balance was maintained in a manner consonant with the applicants' right to 'the peaceful enjoyment of [their] possessions', within the meaning of the first sentence of Article 1 (P1-1).

70. A feature of the law in force at the relevant time was its inflexibility. With the exception of the total withdrawal of the expropriation permits, which required the agreement of the municipality, the law provided no means by which the situation of the property owners involved could be modified at a later date. The Court notes in this connection that the permits granted to the City of Stockholm were granted for five years in the case of the Sporrong Estate—with an extension for three, then for five and finally for ten years—and for ten years in the case of Mrs Lönnroth. In the events that happened, they remained in force for twenty-three years and eight years respectively. During the whole of this period, the applicants were left in complete uncertainty as to the fate of their properties and were not entitled to have any difficulties which they might have encountered taken into account by the Swedish Government. The Commission's report furnishes an example of such difficulties. Mrs Lönnroth had requested the Government to withdraw the expropriation permit. The City Council replied that the existing plans did not authorise any derogation; the Government, for their part, refused the request on the ground that they could not revoke the permit without the Council's express consent . . .

The Courts has not overlooked the interest of the City of Stockholm in having the option of expropriating properties in order to implement its plans. However, it does not see why the Swedish legislation should have excluded the possibility of re-assessing, at reasonable intervals during the lengthy periods for which each of the permits was granted and maintained in force, the interests of the City and the interests of the owners. In the instant case, the absence of such a possibility was all the less satisfactory in that the town-planning schemes underlying the expropriation permits and, at the same time, the intended use prescribed for the applicants' properties were modified on several occasions. . . .

72. The Court also finds that the existence throughout this period of prohibitions on construction accentuated even further the prejudicial effects of the length of the validity of the permits. Full enjoyment of the applicants' right of property was impeded for a total period of twenty-five years in the case of the Sporrong Estate and of twelve years in the case of Mrs Lönnroth. In this connection, the Court notes that in 1967 the Parliamentary Ombudsman considered that the adverse effects on property owners that could result from extended prohibitions were irreconcilable with the position that should obtain in a State governed by the rule of law . . .

73. Being combined in this way, the two series of measures created a situation which upset the fair balance which should be struck between the protection of the right of property and the requirements of the general interest: the Sporrong Estate and Mrs Lönnroth bore an individual and excessive burden which could have been tendered legitimate only if they had had the possibility of seeking a reduction of the time-limits or of claiming compensation. Yet at the relevant time Swedish law excluded these possibilities and it still excludes the second of them.

In the Court's view, it is not appropriate at this stage to determine whether the applicants were in fact prejudiced (see, *mutatis mutandis*, the above-mentioned *Marckx* judgment, Series A No 31, p 13, para 27): it was in their legal situation itself that the requisite balance was no longer to be found.

74. The permits in question, whose consequences were aggravated by the prohibitions on construction, therefore violated Article 1 (P1-1), as regards both applicants.

(d) Compliance with Article 1 (P1-1) as regards the prohibitions on construction

75. In view of the foregoing, the Court does not consider it necessary to determine whether the prohibitions on construction, taken alone, also infringed Article 1 (P1-1).

. . .

FOR THESE REASONS, THE COURT

1. Holds by ten votes to nine that there has been a violation of Article 1 of Protocol No 1, as regards both applicants; . . .

NOTES

1 The majority was comprised of President Wiarda and Judges: Ganshof Van Der Meersch, Bindschedler-Robert, Liesch, Gölcüklü, Matscher, Pinheiro Farina, Garcia De Enterria, Pettiti, and Russo. The Court identified three rules within the text of Article 1. However, it is not a simple task to determine which rule should be applied to a particular factual context. Indeed, in the above case eight judges (Zekia, Cremona, Thor Vilhjalmsson, Lagergren, Evans, Macdonald, Bernhardt and Gersing) considered that the Swedish authorities' actions should be evaluated under the third rule (found in the second paragraph of Article 1).

It is obvious that, for the second paragraph to apply, restrictions on the use of private possessions must leave the owner at least a certain degree of freedom, otherwise the restrictions amount to deprivation; in this case no 'use' is left. But it cannot be decisive against the applicability of the second paragraph that the final outcome of the measures taken may be the expropriation of the properties concerned. Where the use of the properties is still possible although restricted, this provision remains applicable, even if the intention behind the measures is the eventual deprivation of ownership. This is confirmed in the present case by the fact that deprivation in reality never took place. The use of the property by the owner was never terminated by State action. It was temporarily restricted in view of possible expropriations in the future.

In our opinion, therefore, the second paragraph is applicable in regard to the measures complained of in the present case. (Joint Dissenting Opinion: para 3)

The dissentients concluded that the authorities' measures in respect of the applicants' properties did not exceed the legitimate aim permitted by the third rule.

2 In a later judgment (A.88. (1984)) the Court (by twelve votes to five) held that Sweden should pay just satisfaction of 800,000 Swedish Crowns for damage suffered by the Sporrong Estate and 200,000 Swedish Crowns for the damage experienced by Mrs Lonnroth.

3 Subsequently the Court, unanimously, interpreted the three rules identified within Article 1 as being inter-linked: in *James v UK*, A.98 (1986) 8 EHRR 123 (below, p 928).

The three rules are not, however, 'distinct' in the sense of being unconnected. The second and third rules are concerned with particular instances of interference with the right to peaceful enjoyment of property and should therefore be construed in the light of the general principle enunciated in the first rule. (para 37)

4 In contemporary cases the Court tends to apply a general fair balance test to assess the lawfulness of governmental interferences with private property, irrespective of the particular rule that may apply under Article 1. For example, in *Immobiliare Saffi v Italy*, (28 July 1999), the applicant company owned an apartment and during 1983 the company obtained a court order requiring the tenant to vacate the apartment. However, for 11 years the company was unable to obtain the assistance of the police to enforce the possession order, because of a governmental policy of staggering the enforcement of such orders (designed to alleviate a serious housing crisis). The Court characterised the State's behaviour as amounting to a control of the applicant's use of its property, under the second paragraph of Article 1 (third rule).

49. The Court reiterates that an interference, particularly one falling to be considered under the second paragraph of Article 1 of Protocol No 1, must strike a 'fair balance' between the demands of the general interest and the requirements of the protection of the individual's fundamental rights. The concern to achieve this balance is reflected in the structure of Article 1 as a whole, and therefore also in its second paragraph. There must be a reasonable relationship of proportionality between the means employed and the aim pursued. In determining whether this requirement is met, the Court recognises that the State enjoys a wide margin of appreciation with regard both to choosing the means of enforcement and to ascertaining whether the consequences of enforcement are justified in the general interest for the purpose of achieving the object of the law in question. In spheres such as housing, which plays a central role in the welfare and economic policies of modern societies, the Court will respect the legislature's judgment as to what is in the general interest unless that judgment is manifestly without reasonable foundation . . .

The judges were unanimous in concluding that the applicant had been subject to an excessive burden that did not represent a fair balance between its Convention right of property and the requirements of the general interest. This was due to the length of time involved in the wait for the enforcement of the possession order, the applicant's inability to challenge the delay in the enforcement of the possession order before the domestic courts and the absence of compensation for the delay. Therefore, the Court found a breach of Article 1 and ordered Italy to pay the applicant 28 million Lire compensation for pecuniary damage (relating to loss of rent in respect of the apartment).

5 The Court has utilised the fair balance test to imply a general right to compensation under Article 1 where governments take private property in the public interest: see *James* (below, p 928) para 54 and *Lithgow* (below, p 938). In *Holy Monasteries v Greece* A.301-A (1994) 20 EHRR 1, the applicants were a number of ancient ecclesiastical bodies, founded between the ninth and thirteenth centuries, which had been subject to a Law enacted in 1987 that provided the State would become the owner of all monastic property unless the monasteries could provide designated evidence of title to the property (this was problematic because under Greek law real property transactions only had to be registered since 1856 and legacies since 1946). The 1987 Law provided virtually no compensation to the monasteries. The Court stated that:

71. Compensation terms under the relevant legislation are material to the assessment whether the contested measure respects the requisite fair balance and, notably, whether it does not impose a disproportionate burden on the applicants. In this connection, the taking of property without payment of an amount reasonably related to its value will normally constitute a disproportionate interference and a total lack of compensation can be considered justifiable under Article 1 only in exceptional circumstances. Article 1 does not, however, guarantee a right to full compensation in all circumstances, since legitimate objectives of 'public interest' may call for less than reimbursement of the full market value . . .

The judges were unanimous in determining that the State had deprived the monasteries of their possessions within the meaning of the second sentence of Article 1 (the second rule). Furthermore, the 1987 Law imposed a 'considerable burden' on the monasteries deprived of their property, and thereby failed to preserve a fair balance between the interests of the monasteries and the general public. Consequently, there was a breach of Article 1 in respect of those monasteries which had not reached a voluntary agreement with the Government over the ownership of monastic property. Excessive delays in the making of final compensation payments to persons whose property has been expropriated by States will also amount to a breach of Article 1's fair balance requirement. In *Almeida Garrett, Mascarenhas Falcao v Portugal* (11 January 2000), the Court was unanimous in finding a breach of this provision in respect of the applicants who had not received final compensation in respect of the expropriation of their lands some twenty-five years earlier (as part of the agrarian reforms undertaken after the 1974 revolution). The Court held that the failure to provide final compensation to the applicants constituted an interference with their right to the peaceful enjoyment of their possessions. Furthermore, the uncertainty experienced by the applicants as to when they would receive their compensation meant that they had suffered an 'excessive burden' which upset the fair balance required.

A rare example of the Court finding the deprivation of property without the payment of compensation to be lawful under Article 1 occurred in the context of German reunification. In *Jahn and Others v Germany*, judgment of 30 June 2005, the Grand Chamber was confronted with the Federal Republic's legislative response to persons claiming property rights derived from the expropriation of land by the former communist authorities. In 1945 persons who owned over 100 hectares of land had it expropriated and it was added to a pool of State-owned land. Parcels of eight hectares of this state pool were then allocated to 'new farmers'. The latter were able to pass these pieces of land to their heirs provided that certain proportions of it were used for agricultural purposes. In early 1990 the German Democratic Parliament passed a law (known as the Modrow law after the President of the State Council) which lifted all the restrictions on the disposal of this land. In October 1990, when German unification took place, the Modrow law became part of the law of the Federal Republic of Germany. In 1992 the German Parliament passed the second Property Rights Amendment Act which sought to restore the property rights of heirs to the new farmers to that prior to the enactment of the Modrow law. Under the 1992 Act heirs would only be able to inherit such land if they had been carrying out agricultural activities on the relevant land in 1990 (or during the previous ten years). If the heirs had not been engaged in such activities then title to the land reverted to the tax authorities of the *Land* where the property was located (with no compensation being paid to the heirs). The applicants were all heirs of new farmers who had not been engaged in agriculture during the specified time. The tax authorities claims over the land were upheld by the German Courts. Thereupon, the applicants complained to the Court alleging a breach of Article 1. A Chamber, unanimously, found (judgment of 22 January 2004) that the Government had unlawfully deprived the applicants of their property in violation of Article 1. The Government requested a re-hearing before the Grand Chamber. A large majority (eleven votes to six) reversed the judgment of the Chamber.

107. On 14 July 1992, less than two years after German reunification took effect on 3 October 1990, the German legislature sought to correct the effects of the Modrow Law for reasons of fairness and social justice.

108. The main purpose of the second Property Rights Amendment Act of 14 July 1992, which was based on the principles set out in the GDR by the land reform decrees and the change of possession decrees, was to place all heirs of land acquired under the land reform in the position they would have been in if those principles had been properly applied at the time. This was to prevent heirs who did not fulfil the conditions for allocation of land from obtaining an unfair advantage over those who, at the time, had had to return the land to the pool of state-owned land because they were not themselves farming the land and were not members of an agricultural cooperative.

(iv) Conclusion

109. The Court notes that it has in the past already been required to rule on whether an intervention by the legislature with a view to reforming the economic sector for reasons of social justice (see *James and Others*, examined under the second sentence of the first paragraph of Article 1, and concerning the reform of the British system of long leasehold tenure), or to correct the flaws in an earlier law in the public interest (see *National & Provincial Building Society, Leeds Permanent Building Society and Yorkshire Building Society v the United Kingdom*, judgment of 23 October 1997, *Reports of Judgments and Decisions* 1997-VII, examined under the second paragraph of Article 1, and concerning retrospective tax legislation) respected the 'fair balance' between the relevant interests in the light of Article 1 of Protocol No 1.

110. Admittedly, there are certain similarities between the instant case and the aforementioned cases in that in 1992 the German legislature had sought to correct the flaws in the Modrow Law for reasons of social justice. It differs from the case of *James and Others v the United Kingdom*, in particular, however, as the second Property Rights Amendment Act does not provide for any compensation whatsoever for the applicants.

111. As the Court has stated above . . . a total lack of compensation can be considered justifiable under Article 1 of Protocol No. 1 only in exceptional circumstances.

112. It must therefore examine, in the light of the unique context of German reunification, whether the special circumstances of the case can be regarded as exceptional circumstances justifying the lack of any compensation.

113. In that connection the Court reiterates that the State has a wide margin of appreciation when passing laws in the context of a change of political and economic regime (see *inter alia, Kopecký v Slovakia* [GC], No 44912/98, § 35, ECHR 2004-IX, and *Zvolský and Zvolská* [ECHR 2002-XI] §§ 67–8 and 72). It has also reiterated this point regarding the enactment of laws in the unique context of German reunification (see, most recently, *von Maltzan and Others v Germany* (dec.) [GC], Nos 71916/01, 71917/01, and 10260/02, §§ 77 and 111–12, ECHR 2005).

114. In its judgment of 22 January 2004 the Chamber found that, in order to comply with the principle of proportionality, the German legislature 'could not deprive the applicants of their property for the benefit of the State without making provision for them to be adequately compensated' (see § 91). The Chamber concluded that 'even if the circumstances pertaining to German reunification ha[d] to be regarded as exceptional, the lack of any compensation for the State's taking of the applicants' property upset, to the applicants' detriment, the fair balance which ha[d] to be struck between the protection of property and the requirements of the general interest' (see § 93).

115. The Court does not share the Chamber's opinion on that point however.

116. Three factors seem to it to be decisive in that connection:

(i) firstly, the circumstances of the enactment of the Modrow Law, which was passed by a parliament that had not been democratically elected, during a transitional period between two regimes that was inevitably marked by upheavals and uncertainties. In those conditions, even if the applicants had acquired a formal property title, they could not be sure that their legal position would be maintained, particularly as in the absence of any reference to heirs in the Modrow Law, the position of those among them who were not farming the land themselves and were not members of an agricultural cooperative remained precarious even after that Law had come into force;

(ii) secondly, the fairly short period of time that elapsed between German reunification becoming effective and the enactment of the second Property Rights Amendment Act. Having regard to the huge task facing the German legislature when dealing with, among other things, all the complex issues relating to property rights during the transition to a democratic, market-economy regime, including those relating to the liquidation of the land reform, the German legislature can be deemed to have intervened within a reasonable time to correct the—in its view unjust—effects of the Modrow Law. It cannot be criticised for having failed to realise the full effect of this Law on the very day on which German reunification took effect;

(iii) thirdly, the reasons for the second Property Rights Amendment Act. In that connection the FRG parliament cannot be deemed to have been unreasonable in considering that it had a duty to correct the effects of the Modrow Law for reasons of social justice so that the acquisition of full ownership by the heirs of land acquired under the land reform did not depend on the action or non-action of the GDR authorities at the time. Likewise, the balancing exercise between the relevant interests carried out by the Federal Constitutional Court, particularly in its leading decision of 6 October 2000, in examining the compatibility of that amending Law with the Basic Law, does not appear to have been arbitrary. Given the 'windfall' from which the applicants undeniably benefited as a result of the Modrow Law under the rules applicable in the GDR to the heirs to land acquired under the land reform, the fact that this was done without paying any compensation was not disproportionate (see, *mutatis mutandis, National & Provincial Building Society*, cited above, §§ 80–3). It should also be noted in that connection that the second Property Rights Amendment Act did not benefit the State only, but in some cases also provided for the redistribution of land to farmers.

117. Having regard to all the foregoing considerations and taking account, in particular, of the uncertainty of the legal position of heirs and the grounds of social justice relied on by the German authorities, the Court concludes that in the unique context of German reunification, the lack of any compensation does not upset the 'fair balance' which has to be struck between the protection of property and the requirements of the general interest.

There has therefore been no violation of Article 1 of Protocol No 1.

Do you think these circumstances were sufficiently exceptional to justify the absence of compensation under the 1992 Act? Another aspect of the Federal Republic's response to the expropriation of property by the previous communist authorities is considered in *von Maltzan*, see below p 915.

6 The initial fundamental requirement of Article 1 has been declared to be the need for States to act in a 'lawful' manner (for a further discussion of this concept see *Hentrich v France*, below p 939). In *Iatridis v Greece* (1999) 30 EHRR 97, a landowner built an open-air cinema (the 'Ilioupolis' cinema) in 1950, after having obtained the relevant permits. Three years later the Minister of Agriculture refused to recognise the landowner as owning, *inter alia*, the land on which the cinema had been built. The landowner sought to assert his property rights in the courts, but he was unsuccessful. However, when he died (in 1976) his heirs received an inheritance tax demand in respect of the land on which the cinema had been built. They paid this in 1982. In 1978 the heirs leased the cinema to the applicant who refurbished it. During 1985 the Attica prefecture informed the applicant that the land on which the cinema had been built was State property and his retention of it was wrongful. In 1988 the State Lands Authority assigned the cinema to the local town council. During March 1989 the Attica prefecture ordered the applicant to be evicted from the cinema and the order was served by being posted on the door of the cinema. The next day, while the applicant was absent, officials from the local council executed the order by forcible entry into the premises. The applicant challenged the eviction order in the Athens District Court and, in October 1989, that court quashed the order (because the property was not being unjustifiably occupied by a third party). The applicant made numerous approaches to the authorities to be granted possession of the cinema, but the town council continued to occupy and operate the cinema. In 1996 the applicant complained to the Commission alleging, *inter alia*, a breach of Article 1. By fourteen votes to one, the Commission found a violation. The Court, unanimously, found that the State had interfered with the applicant's possessions.

54. ... In this context, the Court observes at the outset that the ownership of the cinema site has been a matter of dispute between the lessors of the cinema and the State since 1953 and that this dispute had still not been resolved by the date of adoption of this judgment. It is not for the Court, in deciding this case, to take the place of the national courts and determine whether the land in question belonged to the State or whether the lease between K.N.'s [the landowner] heirs and the applicant was void under Greek law. It will confine itself to observing that, before the applicant was evicted, he had operated the cinema for eleven years under a formally valid lease without any interference by the authorities, as a result of which he had built up a clientèle that constituted an asset ... in this connection, the Court takes into account the role played in local cultural life by open-air cinemas in Greece and to the fact that the clientèle of such a cinema is made up mainly of local residents.

55. The Court notes that the applicant, who had a specific licence to operate the cinema he had rented, was evicted from it by Ilioupolis Town Council and has not set up his business elsewhere. It also notes that, despite a judicial decision quashing the eviction order, Mr Iatridis cannot regain possession of the cinema because the Minister of Finance refuses to revoke the assignment of it to the Council ... In those circumstances, there has been interference with the applicant's property rights. Since he holds only a lease of his business premises, this interference neither amounts to an expropriation nor is an instance of controlling the use of property but comes under the first sentence of the first paragraph of Article 1.

56. The applicant drew attention to the fact that, ten years after the Court of First Instance quashed the eviction order, the State was still arbitrarily and unlawfully occupying the cinema and refusing to return it to him.

57. The Government disputed that assertion and pointed out that the site of the cinema was part of a much larger area belonging to the State.

58. The Court reiterates that the first and most important requirement of Article 1 of Protocol No 1 is that any interference by a public authority with the peaceful enjoyment of possessions should be lawful: the

second sentence of the first paragraph authorises a deprivation of possessions only 'subject to the conditions provided for by law' and the second paragraph recognises that the States have the right to control the use of property by enforcing 'laws'. Moreover, the rule of law, one of the fundamental principles of a democratic society, is inherent in all the Articles of the Convention . . . and entails a duty on the part of the State or other public authority to comply with judicial orders or decisions against it . . . It follows that the issue of whether a fair balance has been struck between the demands of the general interest of the community and the requirements of the protection of the individual's fundamental rights (see the *Sporrong and Lönnroth v Sweden* judgment of 23 September 1982, Series A No 52, p 26, § 69) becomes relevant only once it has been established that the interference in question satisfied the requirement of lawfulness and was not arbitrary.

61. . . . The applicant's eviction on 17 March 1989 certainly had a legal basis in domestic law, namely the administrative eviction order issued on 9 February 1989 by a State-controlled body, the Lands Department of the Attica prefecture, the cinema having in the meantime been assigned to Ilioupolis Town Council by the State Lands Authority. However, on 23 October 1989 the Athens Court of First Instance heard the case under summary procedure and quashed the eviction order on the grounds that the conditions for issuing it had not been satisfied. No appeal lay against that decision. From that moment on, the applicant's eviction thus ceased to have any legal basis and Ilioupolis Town Council became an unlawful occupier and should have returned the cinema to the applicant, as was indeed recommended by all the bodies from whom the Minister of Finance sought an opinion, namely the Ministry of Finance, the State Legal Council and the State Lands Authority . . . More specifically, the last-named body proposed that the Minister should revoke the assignment of the cinema to the Town Council, restore the use of it to Mr Iatridis and reinstate him in the property he had leased. The Minister, however, refused to approve that proposal as was necessary if the applicant was to be reinstated in his premises.

62. The Court considers, like the Commission, that the interference in question is manifestly in breach of Greek law and accordingly incompatible with the applicant's right to peaceful enjoyment of his possessions. This conclusion makes it unnecessary to ascertain whether a fair balance has been struck between the demands of the general interest of the community and the requirements of the protection of the individual's fundamental rights.

There has therefore been a violation of Article 1 of Protocol No 1.

Consequently, States must ensure that their actions interfering with private property are in compliance with domestic legal requirements (these also have to satisfy the Convention's rule of law obligations, such as foreseeability). Only when the Court is satisfied that this condition has been met will it examine whether the particular interference satisfies the Article's fair balance test.

7 In recent times the Court has stated that interferences by public authorities with private property must be motivated by a legitimate public interest goal irrespective of which Article 1 rule is applicable to the case.

111. Any interference with the enjoyment of a right or freedom recognised by the Convention must, as can be inferred from Article 18 of the Convention . . . pursue a legitimate aim. The principle of a 'fair balance' inherent in Article 1 of Protocol No 1 itself pre-supposes the existence of a general interest of the community. Moreover, it should be reiterated that the various rules incorporated in Article 1 are not distinct in the sense of being unconnected and that the second and third rules are concerned only with particular instances . . . One of the effects of this is that the existence of a 'public interest' required under the second sentence, or the 'general interest' referred to in the second paragraph, are in fact corollaries of the principle set forth in the first sentence, so that an interference with the exercise of the right to the peaceful enjoyment of possessions within the meaning of the first sentence of Article 1 must also pursue an aim in the public interest. (*Beyeler v Italy* (below, p 924))

In that case the Court held that State controls over the market in works of art was a legitimate aim for the purposes of protecting a nation's cultural heritage.

The concept of 'possessions'

1   In *Marckx v Belgium* (above, p 523), the Court observed that: '... this Article (P1-1) does no more than enshrine the right of everyone to the peaceful enjoyment of "his" possessions, that consequently it applies only to a person's existing possessions and that it does not guarantee the right to acquire possessions whether on intestacy or through voluntary dispositions' (para 50). Therefore, the Court did not find a breach of Article 1 when Belgian law accorded illegitimate children lesser patrimonial rights than legitimate children (however, a majority of the Court, ten votes to five, found the domestic law to be in violation of Article 14 taken in conjunction with Article 1). Following the above elaboration applicants can only invoke Article 1 if they have pre-existing possessions which they allege have been adversely interfered with by, or with the approval of, governmental authorities.

2   Apart from traditional real property interests, such as the land and premises owned by the applicants in *Sporrong and Lonnroth* (above), the Court has been willing to recognise a wide variety of other intangible assets as falling within the concept of possessions in Article 1. For instance, in *Tre Traktörer Aktiebolag v Sweden*, A.159 (1989) 13 EHRR 309, the applicant company had owned a restaurant ('Le Cardinal') in Helsingborg. The local County Administrative Board had issued the company with a licence to serve alcoholic beverages at the restaurant from 1980. During 1981 a tax audit of the company's activities by the Board revealed discrepancies in the records concerning sales of alcoholic beverages (estimated to amount to over 10 per cent of the company's total turnover in the relevant period). Subsequently, the Board revoked the company's licence to serve alcoholic drinks. The company claimed that the revocation of the licence forced it to close the restaurant. Some months later the restaurant was sold by the applicant for 1.5 million Swedish Crowns. The applicant argued that the revocation of the licence violated Article 1. The Commission, by ten votes to one, rejected that proposition. Before the Court, the Government contended that the licence could not be regarded as a 'possession'. The Court did not accept the Government's restrictive view of this term:

Like the Commission, however, the Court takes the view that the economic interests connected with the running of Le Cardinal were 'possessions' for the purposes of Article 1 of the Protocol (P1-1). Indeed, the Court has already found that the maintenance of the licence was one of the principal conditions for the carrying on of the applicant company's business, and that its withdrawal had adverse effects on the goodwill and value of the restaurant...

Such withdrawal thus constitutes, in the circumstances of the case, an interference with [the applicant's] right to the 'peaceful enjoyment of [its] possessions'. (para 53)

However, the unanimous Court concluded that the revocation of the licence was lawful under the second paragraph of Article 1 (third rule) as the State did not fail to strike a fair balance between the economic interests of the applicant company and Swedish social policy regarding the consumption of alcohol by its citizens. Paragraph 53 of the judgment reveals the Court's conception of possessions as encompassing non-material commercial interests such as the goodwill (ie the financial value of a company's reputation) of established businesses. By adopting a wide interpretation of this term the Court has sought to extend the ambit of the protection afforded by Article 1.

3   The grant of outline planning permission for development of a designated piece of land, recorded in an official register, was held to be an element of the landowner's possessions in *Pine Valley Developments Ltd v Ireland*, A.222 (1991) 14 EHRR 319. The applicants were developers who had purchased a site outside Dublin in 1978. At the time of the purchase the rural site had been granted outline planning permission for development of industrial warehousing and offices. In 1982 the Supreme Court ruled that the planning permission had been granted *ultra vires* and was therefore a nullity. The Court observed that:

... When Pine Valley purchased the site, it did so in reliance on the permission which had been duly recorded in a public register kept for the purpose and which it was perfectly entitled to assume was valid ... That permission amounted to a favourable decision as to the principle of the proposed development, which could not be reopened by the planning authority ... In these circumstances it would be unduly formalistic to hold that the Supreme Court's decision did not constitute an interference. Until it was rendered, the applicants had at least a legitimate expectation of being able to carry out their proposed development and this has to be regarded, for the purposes of Article 1 of Protocol No 1, as a component part of the property in question ...

The Court thus concludes that there was an interference with the right of Healy Holdings and Mr Healy [applicants/developers who had bought the site from Pine Valley Developments Ltd in 1981] to the peaceful enjoyment of their possessions. (paras 51 and 53)

The Court (unanimously) decided that Healy Holdings and Mr Healy had suffered a violation of Article 14 taken in conjunction with Article 1 of Protocol No 1 as they, unlike other property owners affected by the Supreme Court's ruling, had not had their outline planning permission retrospectively validated. This judgment demonstrates the Court recognising the legal rights contained within a grant of planning permission attached to land as an interest that was capable of falling within the scope of Article 1. Clearly such rights may be worth considerable sums of money to the relevant landowners. Indeed, the Court awarded Healy Holdings and Mr Healy IR£1,200,000 pecuniary damages (the difference in the value of the site in 1982 with outline planning permission compared to its value after the Supreme Court had declared the grant of planning permission to be a nullity, together with interest from that date): Article 50 judgment, A.246-B (1993).

A Grand Chamber of the full-time Court further explained the concept of a 'legitimate expectation' under Article 1 in *Kopecky v Slovakia*, below Note 8.

4   Vendors' contractual retention of the ownership of designated property (until the purchaser has paid all the monies due under the contract) has been treated as a protected possession by the Court in *Gasus Dosier-und Fordertechnik GmbH v Netherlands* A.306-B (1995) 20 EHRR 403. The applicant company was based in Germany and in June 1980 it received an order from a Dutch company ('Atlas') for a concrete mixer. The applicant agreed to supply the equipment subject to its standard terms of sale (which provided that the vendor retained ownership of the goods delivered until all amounts due have been settled in full). In July 1980 the vendor sent Atlas invoices totalling 125,000 DM and the latter paid 21,000 DM. The concrete mixer was installed on Atlas' premises between 28 July–2 August 1980 (the plant weighed five tonnes). However, on 31 July 1980 the Dutch Tax Bailiff (exercising statutory powers) seized all the moveable assets, including the concrete mixer, on Atlas' premises for forced sale in order to discharge Atlas' tax liabilities. Subsequently, the concrete mixer and Atlas' other assets were sold to another company and the monies raised were used to discharge the tax debts and the claims of another creditor. The applicant complained to the Commission alleging, *inter alia*, that the Dutch authorities had deprived it of its possessions in breach of Article 1. On the casting vote of the President, the Commission found no breach. Before the Court, the

Government argued that at the time of the seizure of the concrete mixer it was no longer a possession of the applicant company. The Court did not accept that submission.

53. The Court recalls that the notion 'possessions' (in French: *biens*) in Article 1 of Protocol No 1 (P1-1) has an autonomous meaning which is certainly not limited to ownership of physical goods: certain other rights and interests constituting assets can also be regarded as 'property rights', and thus as 'possessions', for the purposes of this provision (P1-1). In the present context it is therefore immaterial whether Gasus's right to the concrete-mixer is to be considered as a right of ownership or as a security right in *rem*. In any event, the seizure and sale of the concrete-mixer constituted an 'interference' with the applicant company's right 'to the peaceful enjoyment' of a 'possession' within the meaning of Article 1 of Protocol No 1 (P1-1).

However, a majority of the Court, six votes to three, concluded that the Government's actions were justifiable under the second paragraph of Article 1 (third rule).

66. The Court notes at the outset that the grant to the tax authorities of a power to recover tax debts against goods owned by certain third parties—such as a seller of goods who retains his title—does not in itself prompt the conclusion that a fair balance between the general interest and the protection of the individual's fundamental rights has not been achieved. The power of recovery against goods which are in fact in a debtor's possession although nominally owned by a third party is a not uncommon device to strengthen a creditor's position in enforcement proceedings; it cannot be held incompatible *per se* with the requirements of Article 1 of Protocol No 1 (P1-1). Consequently, a legislature may in principle resort to that device to ensure, in the general interest, that taxation yields as much as possible and that tax debts are recovered as expeditiously as possible. Nonetheless, it cannot be overlooked that, quite apart from the dangers of abuse, the character of legislation by which the State creates such powers for itself is not the same as that of legislation granting similar powers to narrowly defined categories of private creditors. Consequently, further examination of the issue of proportionality is necessary in this case.

The majority considered that the seizure and sale was a proportionate act in regard to the applicant, as the latter could have protected its interests by requiring Atlas to pay in full before delivery of the equipment. By contrast the dissentients believed the Government's conduct did not satisfy Article 1's fair balance test.

5   The flexibility of the Court in applying the concept of possessions was vividly illustrated in *National & Provincial Building Society v UK* (1997) 25 EHRR 127, 1997-VII. During 1985 the Government announced a new method of collecting income tax in respect of the savings accounts operated by building societies. In June 1986 the Woolwich Building Society began judicial review proceedings arguing that the Regulations governing the transition period, leading up to the new tax system, were *ultra vires*. Then one year later the Woolwich initiated separate proceedings against the Inland Revenue claiming repayment of the sums that it had paid under the disputed Regulations. In October 1990 the House of Lords upheld the Woolwich's challenge to the legality of the Regulations. Thereupon the applicant societies commenced proceedings against the Revenue for repayment of the sums they had made under the Regulations. The Government secured the passage of legislation in 1991 which (1) retrospectively validated the Regulations and (2) removed the ability of Building Societies to challenge the Regulations unless they had initiated their legal actions before July 1986. In 1992 the House of Lords also upheld the Woolwich's claim for repayment. The House determined that citizens have a right to recover monies paid to a public authority in respect of an *ultra vires* demand. The applicant societies complained to the Commission that the 1991 Act interfered with their rights to restitution of the monies paid under the Regulations and was therefore in breach of Article 1. The Commission, by thirteen votes to three, found no violation. The Court held that:

> 70. While expressing no concluded view as to whether any of the claims asserted by the applicant societies could properly be considered to constitute possessions, the Court, like the Commission . . . is prepared to proceed on the working assumption that in the light of the [House of Lords' 1992 Woolwich] ruling the applicant societies did have possessions in the form of vested rights to restitution which they sought to exercise in direct and indirect ways in the various legal proceedings instituted in 1991 and 1992. In so doing, it notes that the arguments which have been advanced in support of their contention that they had possessions are indissociably bound up with their complaints that they were unjustifiably deprived of those possessions. It will therefore treat Article 1 of Protocol No 1 as applicable for the purposes of examining whether there was an interference with their legal claims and, if so, whether that interference was justified in the circumstances.

The Court then evaluated the State's actions under the second paragraph of Article 1 (third rule). A significant factor was the Court's recognition that:

> There is in fact an obvious and compelling public interest to ensure that private entities do not enjoy the benefit of a windfall in a changeover to a new tax-payment regime and do not deny the Exchequer revenue simply on account of inadvertent defects in the enabling tax legislation, the more so when such entities have followed the debates on the original proposal in Parliament and, while disagreeing with that proposal, have clearly understood that it was Parliament's firm intention to incorporate it in legislation. (para 81)

Consequently, the judges were unanimous in concluding that there had been no violation of Article 1 as the State's conduct ' . . . did not upset the balance which must be struck between the protection of the applicant societies' rights to restitution and the public interest in securing the payment of taxes' (para 83). There is a certain symmetry in the above judgment (and in the previous *Gasus Dosier* case) as the Court was willing to recognise a diffuse spectrum of legal rights and interests as potentially capable of being classified as possession, however, the Court was also tolerant of States' needs to exert substantial control over such possessions in order to maintain the integrity and effectiveness of their domestic tax systems.

6   The boundaries of the expansive concept of 'possessions' were partially revealed in *Cierva Osorio De Moscovo v Spain* (Decision of 28 October 1999), when a Section of the Court declared the application inadmissible *ratione materiae*. The female applicant had sought to complain that in Spain titles of nobility are passed down in the first place to male heirs and this preference violated her Convention rights. However, the Court ruled that a noble title did not fall within the notion of possessions under Article 1. The possibility that such a title could be commercially exploited (e.g. as a brand name) was not enough to make it a possession. Therefore, not all intangible assets will be characterized as possessions by the Court. Perhaps in this application the Court considered that the financial value of the title/asset was too speculative to deserve the protection of Article 1.

7   A unanimous Chamber determined that a patriarchal system in which adult males married, built/lived in houses on their fathers' land and engaged in rural economic activities constituted possessions within Article 1 in *Dogan and Others v Turkey*, see above p 553 for the Article 8 aspect of the judgment. The applicants contended that the authorities' denial of access to their village by the applicants for nine years (on security grounds according to the Government) breached Article 1.

139. The Court notes that it is not required to decide whether or not in the absence of title deeds the applicants have rights of property under domestic law. The question which arises under this head is whether the overall economic activities carried out by the applicants constituted 'possessions' coming within the scope of the protection afforded by Article 1 of Protocol No 1. In this regard, the Court notes that it is undisputed that the applicants all lived in Boydaş village until 1994. Although they did not have registered property, they either had their own houses constructed on the lands of their ascendants or lived in the houses owned by their fathers and cultivated the land belonging to the latter. The Court further notes that the applicants had unchallenged rights over the common lands in the village, such as the pasture, grazing and the forest land, and that they earned their living from stockbreeding and tree-felling. Accordingly, in the Court's opinion, all these economic resources and the revenue that the applicants derived from them may qualify as 'possessions' for the purposes of Article 1.

The Chamber went on to find a breach of the applicants' right to the peaceful enjoyment of their possessions as they had been subject to an excessive burden by the authorities (no alternative accommodation/employment had been given to them). This was a highly significant judgement given the widespread exclusion of residents from villages in those parts of Turkey subject to states of emergency during the 1990s (during *Dogan* the Government stated that approximately 380,000 persons had been displaced).

8 The Court has received a number of complaints regarding restoration of, or compensation for, the confiscation of property by the former communist governments of central and eastern European Member States. A Grand Chamber elaborated the Court's application of Article 1 to such claims in *Kopecky v Slovakia*, judgment of 28 September 2004. The applicant's father had been convicted, in 1959, of keeping 131 gold coins and 2,151 silver coins contrary to the law. He was sentenced to one year's imprisonment, fined and the coins were confiscated. Records showed that the coins had been taken from the applicant's father and inspected by an expert on the premises of the Regional Administration in Bratislava in December 1958. The subsequent whereabouts of the coins could not be traced. In 1992 the applicant claimed the restitution of the coins under the Extra-Judicial Rehabilitations Act 1991 (his late father's conviction had been quashed by the Supreme Court of the Slovak Republic in spring 1992). The Senica District Court ordered the Ministry of the Interior to restore the coins to the applicant as the last evidence of their whereabouts was on the premises of the Regional Administraion. On appeal by the Ministry the Supreme Court ruled that the 1991 Act required applicants to show where the relevant property was on the day the Act entered into force. The applicant had failed to discharge that burden and therefore the authorities were not obliged to restore the coins to the applicant. He complained to the European Court alleging that the rejection of his claim had prevented him from peacefully enjoying his father's property in breach of Article 1. The Court held that:

35. The following relevant principles have been established by the practice of the Convention institutions under Article 1 of Protocol No 1:

(a) Deprivation of ownership or of another right *in rem* is in principle an instantaneous act and does not produce a continuing situation of 'deprivation of a right' (see *Malhous v the Czech Republic* (dec.) [GC], No 33071/96, ECHR 2000-XII, with further references).

(b) Article 1 of Protocol No. 1 does not guarantee the right to acquire property (see *Van der Mussele v Belgium*, judgment of 23 November 1983, Series A No 70, p 23, § 48, and *Slivenko and Others v Latvia* (dec.) [GC], No 48321/99, § 121, ECHR 2002-II).

(c) An applicant can allege a violation of Article 1 of Protocol No 1 only in so far as the impugned decisions related to his 'possessions' within the meaning of this provision. 'Possessions' can be either 'existing possessions' or assets, including claims, in respect of which the applicant can argue that he or she has at least a 'legitimate expectation' of obtaining effective enjoyment of a property right. By way of contrast, the hope of recognition of a property right which it has been impossible to exercise effectively cannot be considered a 'possession' within the meaning of Article 1 of Protocol No 1, nor can a conditional claim which lapses as a result of the non-fulfilment of the condition (see *Prince Hans-Adam II of Liechtenstein v Germany* [GC], No 42527/98, §§ 82 and 83, ECHR 2001-VIII and *Gratzinger and Gratzingerova v the Czech Republic* (dec.) [GC], No 39794/98, § 69, ECHR 2002-VII).

(d) Article 1 of Protocol No 1 cannot be interpreted as imposing any general obligation on the Contracting States to restore property which was transferred to them before they ratified the Convention. Nor does Article 1 of Protocol No 1 impose any restrictions on the Contracting States' freedom to determine the scope of property restitution and to choose the conditions under which they agree to restore property rights of former owners (see *Jantner v Slovakia*, No 39050/97, § 34, 4 March 2003).

In particular, the Contracting States enjoy a wide margin of appreciation with regard to the exclusion of certain categories of former owners from such entitlement. Where categories of owners are excluded in this way, their claims for restitution cannot provide the basis for a 'legitimate expectation' attracting the protection of Article 1 of Protocol No 1 (see, among other authorities, *Gratzinger and Gratzingerova*, cited above, §§ 70–4).

On the other hand, once a Contracting State, having ratified the Convention including Protocol No 1, enacts legislation providing for the full or partial restoration of property confiscated under a previous regime, such legislation may be regarded as generating a new property right protected by Article 1 of Protocol No 1 for persons satisfying the requirements for entitlement. The same may apply in respect of arrangements for restitution or compensation established under pre-ratification legislation, if such legislation remained in force after the Contracting State's ratification of Protocol No. 1 (see *Broniowski v Poland* [GC], 31443/96, § 125, ECHR 2004-...).

2. APPLICATION OF THE RELEVANT PRINCIPLES TO THE PRESENT CASE

(a) General considerations

36. The Court first takes note of the general context in which the relevant legislation was adopted. Like several other States which passed over to a democratic system of government from the late 1980s onwards, the legal predecessor of Slovakia adopted a series of rehabilitation and restitution laws with a view to providing redress for certain wrongs which had been committed under the preceding communist regime and which were incompatible with the principles of a democratic society.

37. The enactment of laws providing for rehabilitation, restitution of confiscated property or compensation for such property obviously involved comprehensive consideration of manifold issues of a moral, legal, political and economic nature. In a different context the Court has held that the national authorities of the Contracting States have a wide margin of appreciation in assessing the existence of a problem of public concern warranting measures and in implementing social and economic policies (see *The Former King of Greece and Others v Greece* [GC], No 25701/94, § 87, ECHR 2000-XII).

38. A similar approach is *a fortiori* relevant as regards rehabilitation and restitution laws adopted in the above context, such as the Extra-Judicial Rehabilitations Act 1991. In particular, the Court reiterates that the Convention imposes no specific obligation on the Contracting States to provide redress for wrongs or damage caused prior to their ratification of the Convention. Similarly, Article 1 of Protocol No 1 cannot be interpreted as restricting the freedom of the Contracting States to choose the conditions under which they agree to return property which had been transferred to them before they ratified the Convention (see paragraph 35 above).

39. The fact that the scope of restitution under the Extra-Judicial Rehabilitations Act 1991 is limited and that restitution of property is subject to a number of conditions does not therefore, as such, infringe the applicant's rights under Article 1 of Protocol No 1.

40. This does not mean that the implementation by the national authorities of the relevant legal provisions in a particular case cannot give rise to an issue under Article 1 of Protocol No 1. However, before considering whether the way in which the relevant law was applied to Mr Kopecký interfered with his rights as guaranteed by Article 1 of Protocol No 1, the Court must determine whether his claim for restitution amounted to a 'possession' within the meaning of that provision.

(b) Whether there were 'existing possessions'

41. The applicant based his restitution claim on the provisions of the Extra-Judicial Rehabilitations Act 1991. It is not suggested that title to the property he sought to recover vested in him without the intervention of the courts. The proprietary interest invoked by the applicant is therefore in the nature of a claim and cannot accordingly be characterised as an 'existing possession' within the meaning of the Court's case-law. This was not disputed before the Court.

(c) Whether the applicant had an 'asset'

42. It therefore remains to determine whether that claim constituted an 'asset', that is whether it was sufficiently established to attract the guarantees of Article 1 of Protocol No 1. In this context it may also be of relevance whether a 'legitimate expectation' of obtaining effective enjoyment of the coins arose for the applicant in the context of the proceedings complained of (see paragraph 35 above).

....

(i) The notion of 'legitimate expectation'

45. The notion of 'legitimate expectation' within the context of Article 1 of Protocol No 1 was first developed by the Court in the case of *Pine Valley Developments Ltd and Others v Ireland* (judgment of 29 November 1991, Series A No 222, p. 23, § 51). In that case the Court found that a 'legitimate expectation' arose when outline planning permission had been granted, in reliance on which the applicant companies had purchased land with a view to its development. The planning permission, which could not be revoked by the planning authority, was 'a component part of the applicant companies' property' (see paragraph 51 of the judgment cited above).

46. In a more recent case, the applicant had leased land from a local authority for a period of 22 years on payment of an annual ground rent with an option to renew the lease for a further period at the expiry of the term and, in accordance with the terms of lease, had erected at his own expense a number of buildings for light industrial use which he had sub-let for rent. The Court found that the applicant had to be regarded as having at least a 'legitimate expectation' of exercising the option to renew and this had to be regarded, for the purposes of Article 1 of Protocol No 1, as 'attached to the property rights granted to him ... under the lease' (see *Stretch v the United Kingdom*, No 44277/98, § 35, 24 June 2003).

47. In the above cases the persons concerned were entitled to rely on the fact that the legal act on the basis of which they had incurred financial obligations would not be retrospectively invalidated to their detriment. In this class of case the 'legitimate expectation' is thus based on a reasonably justified reliance on a legal act which has a sound legal basis and which bears on property rights.

48. Another aspect of the notion of 'legitimate expectation' was illustrated in *Pressos Compania Naviera S.A. and Others v Belgium* (judgment of 20 November 1995, Series A No 332, p 21, § 31). The case concerned claims for damages arising out of accidents to shipping allegedly caused by the negligence of Belgian pilots. Under the domestic rules of tort such claims came into existence as soon as the damage occurred. The Court classified the claims as 'assets' attracting the protection of Article 1 of Protocol No. 1. It then went on to note that, on the basis of a series of decisions of the Court of Cassation, the applicants could argue that they had a 'legitimate expectation' that their claims deriving from the accidents in question would be determined in accordance with the general law of tort.

The Court did not expressly state that the 'legitimate expectation' was a component of, or attached to, a property right as it had done in *Pine Valley Developments Ltd and Others* and was to do in *Stretch* (see references in paragraphs 45 and 46 above). It was however implicit that no such expectation could come into play in the absence of an 'asset' falling within the ambit of Article 1 of Protocol No 1, in this instance the claim in tort. The 'legitimate expectation' identified in *Pressos Compania Naviera S.A. and Others* was not in itself constitutive of a proprietary interest; it related to the way in which the claim qualifying as an 'asset' would be treated under domestic law and in particular to reliance on the fact that the established case-law of the national courts would continue to be applied in respect of damage which had already occurred.

49. In a line of cases the Court has found that the applicants did not have a 'legitimate expectation' where it could not be said that they had a currently enforceable claim that was sufficiently established. In a case against the Czech Republic where the applicants' claim for restitution of their property under the Extra-Judicial Rehabilitations Act 1991 failed because they had not met one of the essential statutory conditions (nationality of the respondent State), the claim was not sufficiently established for the purposes of Article 1 of Protocol No 1. There was a difference, so the Court held, between a mere hope of restitution, however understandable that hope may be, and a 'legitimate expectation', which must be of a nature more concrete than a mere hope and be based on a legal provision or a legal act such as a judicial decision (see *Gratzinger and Gratzingerova*, decision cited above, § 73).

50. Similarly, no legitimate expectation can be said to arise where there is a dispute as to the correct interpretation and application of domestic law and the applicant's submissions are subsequently rejected by the national courts. In the case of *Jantner* (cited above, §§ 29–33) the applicant's restitution claim was dismissed as the national courts found that he had not established his permanent residence in Slovakia within the meaning of the relevant law and practice. That finding was contested by the applicant, who considered that he had met all the statutory requirements for his restitution claim to be granted. The Court held that under the relevant law, as interpreted and applied by the domestic authorities, the applicant had neither a right nor a claim amounting to a 'legitimate expectation' within the meaning of the Court's case-law to obtain restitution of the property in question.

51. In the cases of *Gratzinger and Gratzingerova* and *Jantner*, which concerned claims for restitution of property, it may be considered that what was in fact in issue was not so much a 'legitimate expectation' according to the principles defined in the *Pine Valley Developments Ltd and Others* judgment (see paragraphs 45–7 above), but rather whether or not the applicants had a claim amounting to an 'asset' as defined in the case of *Pressos Compania Naviera S.A. and Others* (see paragraph 48 above). In the two above mentioned restitution cases it could not be said that the applicants had any property rights which had been adversely affected by their reliance on a legal act. Moreover, as they failed to fulfil a statutory condition for the restitution of property, there was, unlike the situation in the case of *Pressos Compania Naviera S.A. and Others*, no sufficiently established proprietary interest to which a 'legitimate expectation' could be attached.

52. In the light of the foregoing it can be concluded that the Court's case-law does not contemplate the existence of a 'genuine dispute' or an 'arguable claim' as a criterion for determining whether there is a 'legitimate expectation' protected by Article 1 of Protocol No 1. . . . the Court takes the view that where the proprietary interest is in the nature of a claim it may be regarded as an 'asset' only where it has a sufficient basis in national law, for example where there is settled case-law of the domestic courts confirming it.

(ii) Position in the present case

53. In the present case no concrete proprietary interest of the applicant has suffered as a result of his reliance on a specific legal act. He cannot therefore be said to have had a 'legitimate expectation' as defined in *Pine Valley Developments Ltd and Others*. In the light of the above analysis of the case-law, the Court has still to consider whether there was nevertheless a sufficient legal basis in support of the applicant's claim to warrant its being regarded as an 'asset' in the *Pressos Compania Naviera S.A. and Others* sense.

54. Accordingly, the principal question for the Court is whether there was a sufficient basis in domestic law, as interpreted by the domestic courts, for the applicant's claim to qualify as an 'asset' for the purposes of Article 1 of Protocol No 1. In this respect the only point in dispute is whether the applicant could be said to have satisfied the requirement that he show 'where the property [was]' as laid down in section 5(1) of the Extra-Judicial Rehabilitations Act 1991. In particular, the applicant considered that, contrary to the findings of the Bratislava Regional Court and of the Supreme Court, he had fulfilled that requirement by showing when and how the property had been transferred to the State since the competent authority was unable to explain what had subsequently happened to the coins.

55. In their respective decisions the Bratislava Regional Court and the Supreme Court held that section 5(1) of the Extra-Judicial Rehabilitations Act 1991 included an obligation to show where the movable property in question had been on 1 April 1991, when the Act had become operative. The Supreme Court further found that a claim for restitution of movable property under section 5(1) of the Extra-Judicial Rehabilitations Act could only concern the very property which had actually been taken over by the State, and not different objects of the same nature. This decision was consistent with its earlier finding on a similar claim. The Regional Court and the Supreme Court held that the evidence submitted by the applicant and the further evidence taken by the Regional Court itself did not constitute sufficient proof that in 1991 the Ministry of the Interior still possessed the coins which had been taken away from his late father in 1958.

56. Having regard to the information before it and considering that it has only limited power to deal with alleged errors of fact or law committed by the national courts, to which it falls in the first place to interpret and apply the domestic law (see *García Ruiz v Spain* [GC], No 30544/96, § 28, ECHR 1999-I, and *Kopp v Switzerland*, judgment of 25 March 1998, *Reports of Judgments and Decisions* 1998-II, p 540, § 59), the Court finds no appearance of arbitrariness in the way in which the Bratislava Regional Court and the Supreme Court determined the applicant's claim. There is therefore no basis on which the Court could reach a different conclusion on the applicant's compliance with the requirement in issue.

. . . .

59. It is true that the Senica District Court, which decided the case at first instance, found that it was practically impossible for the applicant to fulfil the condition concerning the precise location of the property and ordered the coins to be restored to him. The first-instance judgment was subsequently overturned, in the context of the same proceedings and without having acquired final and binding effect, by higher courts at two levels of jurisdiction. Thus, the judgment delivered by the Senica District Court did not invest the applicant with an enforceable right to have the coins restored (see, *mutatis mutandis, Stran Greek Refineries and Stratis Andreadis v Greece*, judgment of 9 December 1994, Series A No 301-B, p 84, § 59). That judgment was therefore not sufficient to generate a proprietary interest amounting to an 'asset'.

60. In these circumstances, the Court finds that in the context of his restitution claim the applicant had no 'possessions' within the meaning of the first sentence of Article 1 of Protocol No 1. The guarantees of that provision do not therefore apply to the present case.

61. Accordingly, there has been no violation of Article 1 of Protocol No 1.

Four judges dissented as they considered that the applicant had established a 'legitimate expectation' that the coins would be returned to him. Judges Ress, Steiner, and Borrego Borrego expressed the view that, '[t]he rules on the manner of redress and the scope of claims must be interpreted in the sense that they should not hinder redress and restitution more than necessary.'

The judgment of the Grand Chamber in *Kopecky* discloses that Article 1 does not oblige Member States to provide for the restitution (or compensation) of property taken by former totalitarian regimes prior to ratification of the Convention. Furthermore, where States introduce restitution/compensation schemes after ratification they will be accorded a wide margin of appreciation by the Court to define the conditions of eligibility. Understandably, the Court recognised that these are highly political decisions being taken by, generally, economically under-developed States facing dramatic social and economic reforms.

In the subsequent case of *von Maltzan and Others v Germany*, decision of 2 March 2005, another Grand Chamber adopted a similar stance towards the German legislative scheme for compensating persons whose property had been expropriated between 1945 and 1949 in the Soviet Occupied Zone of Germany and after 1949 in the German Democratic Republic. The seventy-one applicants complained that the post-reunification compensation scheme gave them far less than the real value of the property that had been expropriated. The Government retorted that the applications were incompatible *ratione materiae* with the Convention as the applicants did not have any property rights when the Convention came into force in respect of the new *Lander* (i.e. the former territory of the German Democratic Republic) during 1990 nor had they acquired any 'legitimate expectation' of compensation other than that provided under the post-reunification legislative scheme. The Grand Chamber determined that:

110. The Court reiterates that in a number of cases brought before it relating to German reunification it has referred to the exceptional context of that reunification and the enormous task faced by the German legislature in dealing with all the complex issues which inevitably arose at the time of transition from a communist regime to a democratic market-economy system (see, among many other authorities, *Kuna v Germany*, (dec.), No 52449/99, ECHR 2001-V).

In the instant case, by choosing to make good injustices or damage resulting from acts committed at the instigation of a foreign occupying force or by another sovereign State, the German legislature had to make certain choices in the light of the public interest. In that connection, by enacting legislation governing issues of property and rehabilitation after German reunification, it had regard, among other things, to the concepts of 'socially acceptable balance between conflicting interests', 'legal certainty and clarity', 'right of ownership' and 'legal peace' contained in the Joint Declaration. Similarly, in examining the compatibility of that legislation with the Basic Law, the Federal Constitutional Court referred to the principles of 'social justice and the rule of law' and that of the 'prohibition of arbitrariness'.

111. As the Court has stated above, where a State elects to redress the consequences of certain acts that are incompatible with the principles of a democratic regime but for which it is not responsible, it has a wide margin of appreciation in the implementation of that policy.

112. In challenging the constitutionality of the statutes enacted after German reunification, the applicants hoped to obtain either restitution of their property or compensation or indemnification commensurate with the real value of their property. However, the belief that the laws then in force would be changed to the applicants' advantage cannot be regarded as a form of legitimate expectation for the purposes of Article 1 of Protocol No 1. As the Court has stated many times, there is a difference between a mere hope, however understandable that hope may be, and a legitimate expectation, which must be of a more concrete nature and be based on a legal provision or have a solid basis in the domestic case-law (see, *inter alia, Gratzinger and Gratzingerova*, cited above, § 73, and *Kopecký*, cited above, § 52). In the instant case neither the Joint Declaration nor the first leading judgment of the Federal Constitutional Court on the land reform gave the applicants rights that exceeded those conferred on them by the statutes in question.

113. The Court concludes that the applicants have not shown that they had claims that were sufficiently established to be enforceable, and they therefore cannot argue that they had 'possessions' within the meaning of Article 1 of Protocol No 1. Consequently, neither the statutes in question nor the judgments or decisions of the Federal Constitutional Court amounted to an interference with the peaceful enjoyment of their possessions, and the facts of the case do not fall within the ambit of Article 1 of Protocol No 1.

114. It follows that the complaints under Article 1 of Protocol No 1 are incompatible *ratione materiae* with the provisions of the Convention, within the meaning of Article 35 § 3, and must be rejected in accordance with Article 35 § 4.

The Grand Chamber reached the above decision by a majority, but as it was an admissibility decision (albeit a very important one determining an issue of national significance for Germany) the size of the majority was not disclosed and no dissenting opinions published.

9 A Grand Chamber adopted a new, and expansive, approach to the classification of welfare benefits as 'possessions' in *Stec and Others v United Kingdom*, decision of 6 July 2005. The applicants alleged that eligibility for Reduced Earnings Allowance (REA) and Retirement Allowance (RA) involved sexual discrimination in breach of Article 14 combined with Article 1 of Protocol No 1. The Government responded that the complaint was incompatible *ratione materiae* as non-contributory benefits did not fall within Article 1 of the Protocol.

42. The Court notes that REA and RA are non-contributory benefits, to the extent that they have, since 1990, been funded by general taxation rather than the National Insurance Scheme. Although only employees or former employees who have suffered impairment in earning capacity due to an accident at work or an occupational disease are eligible for the benefits, entitlement is not conditional on any or a certain number of contributions having been made to the National Insurance Fund.

43. The Commission was the first Convention organ to consider the extent to which entitlement to pensions and other benefits was protected by Article 1 of Protocol No 1. It applied the principle that the Article did not confer any right to receive a social security benefit or pension. The making of compulsory contributions, for example to a pension fund or a social insurance scheme, might however create such a right, where there was a direct link between the level of contributions and the benefits awarded. Otherwise the applicant did not, at any given moment, have an identifiable and claimable share in the fund (see, for example, *Müller v Austria*, No 5849/72, Commission decision of 1 October 1975, DR 3, p 25; *G v Austria*, No 10094/82, Commission decision of 14 May 1984, DR 38, p 84; *De Kleine Staarman v The Netherlands*, No 10503/83, Commission decision of 16 May 1985, DR 42, p 162).

44. The first judgment of the Court on the subject was *Gaygusuz v Austria* [1996-IV]. The applicant, a Turkish citizen, had lived in Austria from 1973 until 1987. He had worked from 1973 until 1984 but from 1984 to 1987 he was either unemployed or was certified unfit. From July 1986 to March 1987 he was paid an advance on his retirement pension by way of unemployment benefit. When this entitlement expired, he applied for another advance on his pension, in the form of 'emergency assistance'. There were several preconditions for such a payment. A claimant had to be unemployed, but fit and available for work; to have exhausted his entitlement to unemployment benefit; to be in urgent need; and to possess Austrian nationality. The applicant satisfied all these criteria except that of Austrian nationality. In particular, as the Court found, he had been entitled to unemployment benefit since he had paid unemployment insurance contributions in the same way as every employee in Austria and his entitlement to the benefit had been exhausted at the time he applied for emergency assistance. In paragraph 21 of the Court's judgment, it was further noted that the amount of unemployment benefit was 'financed partly from the unemployment insurance contributions every employee had to pay and partly from various governmental sources'. The 'fund' from which benefits were drawn was not, therefore, financed wholly from contributions made by employees or employers.

45. The parties in the present case disagree as to whether the fact that Mr Gaygusuz had made unemployment insurance contributions was crucial to the Court's finding that Article 1 of Protocol No. 1 applied. The applicants submit that the central basis of the Court's decision was, as set out in paragraph 41 of the judgment, that:

'The right to emergency assistance—insofar as provided for in the applicable legislation—is a pecuniary right for the purposes of Article 1 Protocol No. 1.'

The Government for their part rely on paragraph 39, in which the Court emphasized that the payment of contributions was a pre-condition for the payment of unemployment benefit and that:

> 'it follows that there is no entitlement to emergency assistance where such contributions have not been made.'

They submit that the Court would not have found emergency assistance to fall within the scope of Article 1 of Protocol No 1 if eligibility for it had not been dependent on the prior payment of contributions.

46. The Grand Chamber accepts that the *Gaygusuz* judgment was ambiguous on this important point. This is reflected in the fact that two distinct lines of authority subsequently emerged in the case-law of the Convention organs. The Commission, and the Court in some cases, continued to find that a welfare benefit or pension fell within the scope of Article 1 of Protocol No 1 only where contributions had been made to the fund that financed it (see, *Szrabjet and Clarke v the United Kingdom*, Nos 27004/95 and 27011/95, Commission decision of 23 October 1997; *Carlin v the United Kingdom*, No 27537/95, Commission decision of. 3 December 1997; *Coke and Others v the United Kingdom*, No 38696/97, Commission Decision of 9 September 1999; *Stawicki v Poland* (dec.), No 47711/99, 10 February 2000; *Jankovic v Croatia* (dec.), No 43440/98, 12 October 2000; *Kohls v Germany* (dec.), No 72719/01, 13 November 2003; *Kjartan Asmundsson v Iceland*, No 60669/00, judgment of 12 October 2004; and the Chamber judgment of 20 June 2002 in *Azinas v Cyprus*, No 56679/00, §§ 32–4, which was however superseded by the Grand Chamber judgment of 28 April 2004, which decided the case on a different ground). In other cases, however, the Court held that even a welfare benefit in a non-contributory scheme could constitute a possession for the purposes of Article 1 of Protocol No 1 (see *Buchen v the Czech Republic*, No 36541/97, § 46, 26 November 2002; *Koua Poirrez v France*, No 40892/98, § 42, ECHR 2003-X; *Wessels-Bergervoet v The Netherlands*, No 34462/97, ECHR 2002-IV; *Van den Bouwhuijsen and Schuring v The Netherlands* (dec.), No 44658/98, 16 December 2003).

ii. The approach to be applied henceforth

47. Against this background, it is necessary to examine afresh the question whether a claim to a non-contributory welfare benefit should attract the protection of Article 1 of Protocol No 1. Since the Convention is first and foremost a system for the protection of human rights, the Court must have regard to the changing conditions within the respondent State and within Contracting States generally, and must interpret and apply the Convention in a manner which renders its rights practical and effective, not theoretical and illusory (see *Christine Goodwin v the United Kingdom* [GC], No 28957/95, § 74, ECHR 2002-VI).

48. The Convention must also be read as a whole, and interpreted in such a way as to promote internal consistency and harmony between its various provisions (*Klass and Others v Germany*, judgment of 6 September 1978, Series A No 28, § 68; and see also *Maaouia v France* [GC], No 39652/ 98, § 36, ECHR 2000-X and *Kudła v Poland* [GC], No 30210/96, § 152, ECHR 2000-XI). It is noteworthy in this respect that, in its case-law on the applicability of Article 6 § 1, the Court originally held that claims regarding only welfare benefits which formed part of contributory schemes were, because of the similarity to private insurance schemes, sufficiently personal and economic to constitute the subject-matter of disputes for 'the determination of civil rights' (see *Feldbrugge v The Netherlands* and *Deumeland v Germany*, both judgments of 29 May 1986, Series A Nos 99 and 100). However, in the *Salesi v Italy* judgment of 23 February 1993 (Series A No 257-A), Article 6 § 1 was held also to apply to a dispute over entitlement to a non-contributory welfare benefit, the Court emphasising that the applicant had an assertable right, of an individual and economic nature, to social benefits. It thus abandoned the comparison with private insurance schemes and the requirement for a form of 'contract' between the individual and the State. In *Schuler-Zgraggen v Switzerland* (judgment of 24 June 1993, Series A No 263, § 46), the Court held that:

> '. . . the development in the law . . . and the principle of equality of treatment warrant taking the view that today the general rule is that Article 6 § 1 does apply in the field of social insurance, including even welfare assistance.'

49. It is in the interests of the coherence of the Convention as a whole that the autonomous concept of 'possessions' in Article 1 of Protocol No. 1 should be interpreted in a way which is consistent with the concept of pecuniary rights under Article 6 § 1. It is moreover important to adopt an interpretation of Article 1 of Protocol No 1 which avoids inequalities of treatment based on distinctions which, at the present day, appear illogical or unsustainable.

50. The Court's approach to Article 1 of Protocol No. 1 should reflect the reality of the way in which welfare provision is currently organised within the Member States of the Council of Europe. It is clear that within those States, and within most individual States, there exists a wide range of social security benefits designed to confer entitlements which arise as of right. Benefits are funded in a large variety of ways: some are paid for by contributions to a specific fund; some depend on a claimant's contribution record; many are paid for out of general taxation on the basis of a statutorily defined status … The REA and RA are good examples of this. Originally funded out of the national insurance fund, since 1990 they have been financed by general taxation. Given the variety of funding methods, and the interlocking nature of benefits under most welfare systems, it appears increasingly artificial to hold that only benefits financed by contributions to a specific fund fall within the scope of Article 1 of Protocol No. 1. Moreover, to exclude benefits paid for out of general taxation would be to disregard the fact that many claimants under this latter type of system also contribute to its financing, through the payment of tax.

51. In the modern, democratic State, many individuals are, for all or part of their lives, completely dependent for survival on social security and welfare benefits. Many domestic legal systems recognise that such individuals require a degree of certainty and security, and provide for benefits to be paid—subject to the fulfilment of the conditions of eligibility—as of right. Where an individual has an assertable right under domestic law to a welfare benefit, the importance of that interest should also be reflected by holding Article 1 of Protocol No 1 to be applicable.

52. Finally, and in response to the Government's contention, the Court considers that to hold that a right to a non-contributory benefit falls within the scope of Article 1 of Protocol No 1 no more renders otiose the provisions of the Social Charter than to reach the same conclusion in respect of a contributory benefit. Whilst the Convention sets forth what are essentially civil and political rights, many of them have implications of a social or economic nature. The mere fact that an interpretation of the Convention may extend into the sphere of social and economic rights should not be a decisive factor against such an interpretation; there is no water-tight division separating that sphere from the field covered by the Convention (see *Airey v Ireland*, judgment of 9 October 1979, Series A No 32, § 26).

53. In conclusion, therefore, if any distinction can still be said to exist in the case-law between contributory and non-contributory benefits for the purposes of the applicability of Article 1 of Protocol No 1, there is no ground to justify the continued drawing of such a distinction.

54. It must, nonetheless, be emphasised that the principles, most recently summarised in *Kopecky v Slovakia* [GC], No 44912/98, § 35, ECHR 2004-IX, which apply generally in cases under Article 1 of Protocol No. 1, are equally relevant when it comes to welfare benefits. In particular, the Article does not create a right to acquire property. It places no restriction on the Contracting State's freedom to decide whether or not to have in place any form of social security scheme, or to choose the type or amount of benefits to provide under any such scheme (see, *mutatis mutandis, Kopecky* [GC], § 35(d)). If, however, a Contracting State has in force legislation providing for the payment as of right of a welfare benefit— whether conditional or not on the prior payment of contributions—that legislation must be regarded as generating a proprietary interest falling within the ambit of Article 1 of Protocol No 1 for persons satisfying its requirements (ibid).

55. In cases, such as the present, concerning a complaint under Article 14 in conjunction with Article 1 of Protocol No 1 that the applicant has been denied all or part of a particular benefit on a discriminatory

ground covered by Article 14, the relevant test is whether, but for the condition of entitlement about which the applicant complains, he or she would have had a right, enforceable under domestic law, to receive the benefit in question (see *Gaygusuz* . . . cited above). Although Protocol No 1 does not include the right to receive a social security payment of any kind, if a State does decide to create a benefits scheme, it must do so in a manner which is compatible with Article 14.

56. It follows that the applicants' interests fall within the scope of Article 1 of Protocol No 1, and of the right to property which it guarantees. This is sufficient to render Article 14 applicable.

Consequently, the Grand Chamber, by an unspecified majority, declared several of the applications to be admissible. Hence, now the decisive factor in determining if a particular welfare benefit is a 'possession' is whether the applicant has a right to it in domestic law.

In a later judgment (12 April 2006) the Grand Chamber, by sixteen votes to one, found no breach of Article 14 in conjunction with Article 1 of Protocol No 1 as the different age limits for claiming the allowances were based upon pension ages (that were designed to compensate women for their historic reduced earnings capacity when compared to men).

10   A trade mark that has been finally registered by the relevant authority in accordance with national law is a 'possession': *Anheuser-Busch Inc. v Portugal*, judgment of 11 October 2005. In that case the applicant, American, company applied to the Portuguese National Institute for Industrial Property to register 'Budweiser' as a trade mark for its beer. The Institute did not grant the registration immediately as a Czechoslovak company, Budejovicky Budvar, had already registered 'Budweiser Bier' as a designation of origin for its beer. The applicant company obtained a court order setting aside the Czech designation and the Institute registered the 'Budweiser' trade mark. The Czech company challenged that decision and eventually the Portuguese Supreme Court set aside the registration of the applicant's trade mark. The European Court (by five votes to two) found that prior to the final registration of the trade mark the applicant did not have a legally protected legitimate expectation that came within Article 1 of Protocol No 1.

The First Rule: The principle of peaceful enjoyment of property

Papamichalopoulos v Greece A.260-B (1993) 16 EHRR 440
European Court of Human Rights

The applicants were the owners or co-owners of agricultural land in the area of Agia Marina Loimikou (near Marathon, Attica). In 1963 they were given permission, by the Greek Office of Tourism, for the construction of a hotel complex on their land. However, in August 1967 the military dictatorship (see above p 164, the *Greek case*) secured the passage of Law No 109/1967 which transferred an area of 1,165,000 sq m near Agia Marina to the Navy Fund. Ten of the applicants, who owned part of the designated land, applied to State Counsel at the Athens Court of First Instance requesting interim measures and restoration of the original position. In July 1968 State Counsel made orders granting the applications. But, the Navy proceeded to build a naval base and holiday resort for officers on the designated land. During November 1969 a Royal Decree declared the entire Marina Loimikou region a 'naval fortress'. After the restoration of democracy in 1974, the father of two of the applicants commenced proceedings in the Athens Court of First Instance to establish his title to parts of the relevant land. In a judgment given in 1976 the Court upheld the applicant's title and stated that the Navy was obliged to return the land. When the applicant and a bailiff went to the entrance of the military base to serve the judgment on the Navy Fund the commander refused to admit them. Subsequently, the Minister of Defence informed the applicants that the construction of the naval base prevented the return of their land, but the Government would seek to provide them with alternative land. No land was found for the applicants. In 1988 the applicants complained to the Commission alleging a breach of Article 1 as they had been prevented from enjoying their possessions and had received no compensation. The Commission was unanimous in finding a violation. The Court determined that:

41. The occupation of the land in issue by the Navy Fund represented a clear interference with the applicants' exercise of their right to the peaceful enjoyment of their possessions. The interference was not for the purpose of controlling the use of property within the meaning of the second paragraph of Article 1 of Protocol No 1 (P1-1). Moreover, the applicants were never formally expropriated: Law No 109/1967 did not transfer ownership of the land in question to the Navy Fund.

42. Since the Convention is intended to safeguard rights that are 'practical and effective', it has to be ascertained whether the situation complained of amounted nevertheless to a de facto expropriation, as was argued by the applicants (see, among other authorities, the Sporrong and Lönnroth v Sweden judgment of 23 September 1982, Series A No 52, p 24, para 63).

43. It must be remembered that in 1967, under a Law enacted by the military government of the time, the Navy Fund took possession of a large area of land which included the applicants' land; it established a naval base there and a holiday resort for officers and their families.

From that date the applicants were unable either to make use of their property or to sell, bequeath, mortgage or make a gift of it; Mr Petros Papamichalopoulos, the only one who obtained a final court decision ordering the Navy to return his property to him, was even refused access to it . . .

44. The Court notes, however, that as early as 1969 the authorities had drawn the Navy's attention to the fact that part of the land was not available for disposal . . . After democracy had been restored, they sought means of making good the damage caused to the applicants. Thus in 1980 they recommended, if not returning the land, at least exchanging it for other land of equal value . . . This initiative led to the enacting of Law No 1341/1983, which was designed to settle as quickly as possible—in the very terms of the Court of Cassation's judgment of 8 January 1988—the problem created in 1967 . . . The Athens second Expropriation Board having recognised them all in 1983 as having title . . . the applicants thereafter awaited allocation of the promised land. However, neither the land in Attica nor the land in Pieria was able to be used for the proposed scheme . . . in 1992 the applicants attempted to secure part of the 'Semeli estate' but again without success . . .

45. The Court considers that the loss of all ability to dispose of the land in issue, taken together with the failure of the attempts made so far to remedy the situation complained of, entailed sufficiently serious consequences for the applicants de facto to have been expropriated in a manner incompatible with their right to the peaceful enjoyment of their possessions.

46. In conclusion, there has been and there continues to be a breach of Article 1 of Protocol No 1 (P1-1). . . .

FOR THESE REASONS, THE COURT UNANIMOUSLY

. . . 2. Holds that there has been and there continues to be a breach of Article 1 of Protocol No 1 . . .

NOTES

1 The Court was composed of President Bernhardt and Judges: Gölcüklü, Spielmann, Valticos, Pekkanen, Morenilla, Bigi, Wildhaber, and Makarczyk.

2 The Court's invocation of the notion of a '*de facto*' expropriation to characterize State action which in reality, if not in formal legal terms, removes an owner's ability to use or dispose of his/her property was originally developed in *Sporrong and Lonnroth* (above). The application of the first rule of Article 1 to such situations prevents States from seeking to raise the technical defence, under the second rule, that the disputed actions did not deprive the owners of their legal titles to the relevant possessions.

3 Other conduct of the Greek dictatorship provided the starting point for *Stran Greek Refineries and Stratis Andreadis v Greece* A.301-B (1994) 19 EHRR 293. In July 1972 the military junta concluded a contract with the second applicant for the first applicant (of which he was the sole owner) to construct an oil refinery, estimated to cost $76 million, near Athens. The contract obliged the State to provide a site for the refinery by the end of the year. A Royal Decree authorized the second applicant to import $58 million to finance the project. The State failed to provide the land and, after the restoration of democracy, in 1977 a ministerial committee terminated the contract. In November 1978 the first applicant began an action against the State, in the Athens Court of First Instance, for compensation in respect of expenditure incurred under the contract. Two years later the Government sought to invoke a term in the contract for the establishment of an arbitration court to resolve disputes arising under the agreement. The arbitration court made its award in 1984, when it found the State liable for 70 per cent of the losses sustained by the company (amounting to over $16 million). Subsequently, the Government asked the ordinary courts to set aside the arbitration award. Both the Court of First Instance and the Court of Appeal upheld the award. While the matter was before the Court of Cassation, Parliament enacted Law No 1701/1987 which provided that in respect of contracts entered into by the dictatorship between 1967 and 1974 all their terms (including arbitration clauses) were thereby repealed. In 1990 the Greek courts declared the 1984 arbitration award void. The applicants complained to the Commission alleging, *inter alia*, that the enactment and application of Law No 1701 deprived them of their property rights (including the arbitration award of 1984) in breach of Article 1. The Commission, unanimously, found a violation of that provision. The Court first examined whether the applicants had any 'possessions' for the purposes of Article 1. This involved determining whether 'the arbitration award had given rise to a debt that was sufficiently established to be enforceable' (para 59). The judges concluded that the 1984 award met this criterion because: 'According to its wording, the award was final and binding; it did not require any further enforcement measure and no ordinary or special appeal lay against it.... Under Greek legislation arbitration awards have the force of final decisions and are deemed to be enforceable' (para 61). The Court also found that Law No 1701 interfered with the applicants' possessions by preventing them from enforcing the 1984 award. It was then necessary to consider whether the interference could be justified under the first rule of Article 1. The Government contended that the legislative measures were necessary to 'cleanse public life of the disrepute attaching to the military regime and to proclaim the power and the will of the Greek people to defend the democratic institutions' (para 70). The applicants argued that it was unjust to treat every legal relationship with a dictatorial regime as invalid when democracy was restored.

72. The Court does not doubt that it was necessary for the democratic Greek State to terminate a contract which it considered to be prejudicial to its economic interests. Indeed according to the case-law

of international courts and of arbitration tribunals any State has a sovereign power to amend or even terminate a contract concluded with private individuals, provided it pays compensation (*Shufeldt* arbitration award of 24 July 1930, Reports of International Arbitral Awards, League of Nations, vol. II, p 1095). This both reflects recognition that the superior interests of the State take precedence over contractual obligations and takes account of the need to preserve a fair balance in a contractual relationship. However, the unilateral termination of a contract does not take effect in relation to certain essential clauses of the contract, such as the arbitration clause. To alter the machinery set up by enacting an authoritative amendment to such a clause would make it possible for one of the parties to evade jurisdiction in a dispute in respect of which specific provision was made for arbitration (*Losinger* decision of 11 October 1935, Permanent Court of International Justice, Series C No 78, p 110, and arbitral awards in *Lena Goldfields Co Ltd v Soviet Government*, Annual Digest and Reports of Public International Law Cases, vol. 5 (1929–1930) (case No 258), and *Texaco Overseas Petroleum Company and California Asiatic Oil Company v Government of the Arab Republic of Libya*, preliminary decision of 27 November 1975, International Law Reports, vol. 53 1979, p 393).

73. In this connection, the Court notes that the Greek legal system recognises the principle that arbitration clauses are autonomous . . . and that the Athens Court of First Instance . . . the Athens Court of Appeal . . . and, it would appear, the judge-rapporteur of the Court of Cassation . . . applied this principle in the present case. Moreover the two courts found that the applicants' claims originating before the termination of the contract were not invalidated thereby.

  The State was therefore under a duty to pay the applicants the sums awarded against it at the conclusion of the arbitration procedure, a procedure for which it had itself opted and the validity of which had been accepted until the day of the hearing in the Court of Cassation.

74. By choosing to intervene at that stage of the proceedings in the Court of Cassation by a law which invoked the termination of the contract in question in order to declare void the arbitration clause and to annul the arbitration award of 27 February 1984, the legislature upset, to the detriment of the applicants, the balance that must be struck between the protection of the right of property and the requirements of public interest.

75. There has accordingly been a violation of Article 1 of Protocol No 1 (P1-1).

The judgment demonstrates, once again, the Court's expansive attitude towards the concept of possessions, in this case to embrace a binding arbitration award. Furthermore, while the Court was willing to recognize (guided by the general principles of international law articulated by other international courts) the sovereign powers of States over contractual arrangements with private persons and companies, it still required member-States to comply with the fair balance obligation embodied in Article 1. Therefore, the Court ordered the Government to pay the applicants pecuniary damage amounting to the exact totals of the 1984 arbitration award plus simple interest at 6 per cent from the date of the arbitration decision.

4   The Court, by eleven votes six, held that the denial of access of a landowner to her property located in northern Cyprus by Turkish military personnel amounted to a violation of the first rule in *Loizidou v Turkey* (above, p 544).

63. However, as a consequence of the fact that the applicant has been refused access to the land since 1974, she has effectively lost all control over, as well as all possibilities to use and enjoy, her property. The continuous denial of access must therefore be regarded as an interference with her rights under Article 1 of Protocol No 1 (P1-1). Such an interference cannot, in the exceptional circumstances of the present case to which the applicant and the Cypriot Government have referred [ie the military occupation of northern Cyprus by Turkey], be regarded as either a deprivation of property or a control of use within the meaning of the first and second paragraphs of Article 1 of Protocol No 1 (P1-1-1, P1-1-2). However, it clearly falls within the meaning of the first sentence of that provision

(P1-1) as an interference with the peaceful enjoyment of possessions. In this respect the Court observes that hindrance can amount to a violation of the Convention just like a legal impediment (see, mutatis mutandis, the *Airey v Ireland* judgment of 9 October 1979, Series A No 32, p 14, para 25).

64. Apart from a passing reference to the doctrine of necessity as a justification for the acts of the 'TRNC' ['Turkish Republic of Northern Cyprus': an entity not generally recognised by the international community] and to the fact that property rights were the subject of intercommunal talks, the Turkish Government have not sought to make submissions justifying the above interference with the applicant's property rights which is imputable to Turkey.

It has not, however, been explained how the need to rehouse displaced Turkish Cypriot refugees in the years following the Turkish intervention in the island in 1974 could justify the complete negation of the applicant's property rights in the form of a total and continuous denial of access and a purported expropriation without compensation.

Nor can the fact that property rights were the subject of intercommunal talks involving both communities in Cyprus provide a justification for this situation under the Convention.

In such circumstances, the Court concludes that there has been and continues to be a breach of Article 1 of Protocol No 1 (P1-1).

In subsequent just satisfaction proceedings the Court, by fourteen votes to three, held that Turkey was to pay the applicant 300,000 Cypriot pounds for pecuniary damage. This sum was based on the applicant's loss of the use of her land (calculated by reference to the annual ground rent that the applicant would have been able to secure if she had access and control over her property located in northern Cyprus). Additionally, by fifteen votes to two, the Court awarded Mrs Loizidou 20,000 Cypriot pounds for non-pecuniary damage.

The Court is of the opinion that an award should be made under this head in respect of the anguish and feelings of helplessness and frustration which the applicant must have experienced over the years in not being able to use her property as she saw fit. However, like the Delegate of the Commission, the Court would stress that the present case concerns an individual complaint related to the applicant's personal circumstances and not the general situation of the property rights of Greek Cypriots in northern Cyprus . . . (*Loizidou v Turkey (Article 50)*, 1998-IV, paras 39–40).

The Court's caution in emphasising that it was focusing upon the particular circumstances of the applicant's case should be understood in the wider context of the continuing major legal (and political) difficulties that the Turkish occupation of northern Cyprus has created for the Council of Europe.

5   A Grand Chamber of the full-time Court dealt with the general denial, by the authorities in northern Cyprus/Turkish forces, to displaced Greek Cypriots (and their families) of access to their properties located in the north, together with the transfer of ownership (without compensation) from such persons to 'TRNC' authorities/Turkish Cypriots and Turkish settlers in *Cyprus v Turkey* (see above p 125). The Cypriot Government contended that approximately 211,000 Greek Cypriots had been displaced and their property rights interfered with in breach of Article 1.

184. The Court agrees with the Commission's analysis. It observes that the Commission found it established on the evidence that at least since June 1989 the 'TRNC' authorities no longer recognised any ownership rights of Greek Cypriots in respect of their properties in northern Cyprus. This purported deprivation of the property at issue was embodied in a constitutional provision, 'Article 159 of the TRNC Constitution', and given practical effect in 'Law No 52/1995'. It would appear that the legality of the interference with the displaced persons' property is unassailable before the 'TRNC' courts. Accordingly, there is no requirement for the persons concerned to use domestic remedies to secure redress for their complaints.

185. The Court would further observe that the essence of the applicant Government's complaints is not that there has been a formal and unlawful expropriation of the property of the displaced persons but that these persons, because of the continuing denial of access to their property, have lost all control over, as well as possibilities to enjoy, their land. As the Court has noted previously . . . the physical exclusion of Greek-Cypriot persons from the territory of northern Cyprus is enforced as a matter of 'TRNC' policy or practice. The exhaustion requirement does not accordingly apply in these circumstances.

186. The Court recalls its finding in the Loizidou judgment (merits) that that particular applicant could not be deemed to have lost title to her property by operation of 'Article 159 of the TRNC Constitution', a provision which it held to be invalid for the purposes of the Convention (p 2231, § 44). This conclusion is unaffected by the operation of 'Law No 52/1995'. It adds that, although the latter was not invoked before the Court in the Loizidou case, it cannot be attributed any more legal validity than its parent 'Article 159' which it purports to implement.

187. The Court is persuaded that both its reasoning and its conclusion in the Loizidou judgment (merits) apply with equal force to displaced Greek Cypriots who, like Mrs Loizidou, are unable to have access to their property in northern Cyprus by reason of the restrictions placed by the 'TRNC' authorities on their physical access to that property. The continuing and total denial of access to their property is a clear interference with the right of the displaced Greek Cypriots to the peaceful enjoyment of possessions within the meaning of the first sentence of Article 1 of Protocol No 1. It further notes that, as regards the purported expropriation, no compensation has been paid to the displaced persons in respect of the interferences which they have suffered and continue to suffer in respect of their property rights.

188. The Court notes that the respondent Government, in the proceedings before the Commission, sought to justify the interference with reference to the inter-communal talks and to the need to rehouse displaced Turkish-Cypriot refugees. However, similar pleas were advanced by the respondent Government in the Loizidou case and were rejected in the judgment on the merits (pp 2237–8, § 64). The Court sees no reason in the instant case to reconsider those justifications.

189. For the above reasons the Court concludes that there has been a continuing violation of Article 1 of Protocol No 1 by virtue of the fact that Greek-Cypriot owners of property in northern Cyprus are being denied access to and control, use and enjoyment of their property as well as any compensation for the interference with their property rights.

Judge Fuad, the Turkish *ad-hoc* Judge, dissented as he considered that the majority had not given sufficient weight to the 'catastrophic events' between 1963 and 1974 which had 'literally torn the island apart' or to the subsequent involvement of the United Nations in seeking to achieve a solution to the problems of Cyprus.

6   The Court has applied the first rule where the factual and legal complexity of a case 'prevents its being classified in a precise category' (para 106). In *Beyeler v Italy* (5 January 2000), the applicant was a Swiss art dealer/collector/patron who had used an Italian agent to purchase a painting by Van Gogh from its Italian owner in 1977 (at a price of 600 million lire). The Italian authorities were not informed that Mr Beyeler was the actual owner of the painting until 1983. Subsequently, there were numerous exchanges between the applicant and the authorities regarding the ownership and display of the painting. In 1988 the Ministry of Cultural Heritage indicated that it was interested in buying the painting, but public funds were limited. The applicant offered to sell it to the State for $11 million. Three months later he sold the painting to the Peggy Guggenheim collection in Venice for $8.5 million. Thereupon, the authorities purported to exercise their statutory right of pre-emption to purchase the painting at the 1977 sale price. The applicant challenged the authorities' action in the Italian

courts; however, the latter held that as there had not been an accurate disclosure of the parties to the 1977 sale the authorities were entitled to exercise the power of pre-emption in 1988. The applicant complained to the Commission, but a majority (twenty votes to ten) was of the opinion that he had never become the lawful owner of the painting and no breach of Article 1 had occurred. Having regard to the Italian law on agency and the exchanges between the authorities and the applicant, the Court concluded the latter had a 'proprietary interest recognized under Italian law' in the painting since its sale in 1977. Furthermore, that interest constituted a 'possession' for the purposes of Article 1. A majority, sixteen votes to one, determined that the State's actions did not satisfy the fair balance test because:

120. . . . taking punitive action in 1988 on the ground that the applicant had made an incomplete declaration, a fact of which the authorities had become aware almost five years earlier, hardly seems justified. In that connection it should be stressed that where an issue in the general interest is at stake it is incumbent on the public authorities to act in good time, in an appropriate manner and with utmost consistency.

121. That state of affairs allowed the Ministry of Cultural Heritage to acquire the painting in 1988 at well below its market value. Having regard to the conduct of the authorities between 1983 and November 1988, the Court considers that they derived an unjust enrichment from the uncertainty that existed during that period and to which they had largely contributed. Irrespective of the applicant's nationality, such enrichment is incompatible with the requirement of a 'fair balance'.

122. Having regard to all the foregoing factors and to the conditions in which the right of pre-emption was exercised in 1988, the Court concludes that the applicant had to bear a disproportionate and excessive burden. There has therefore been a violation of Article 1 of Protocol No 1.

Do you have any sympathy with Judge Ferrari Bravo's dissenting assessment that '. . . I have very serious doubts as to the moral basis for the arguments advanced by both parties to the dispute'?

7   A united Grand Chamber followed the approach in *Beyeler* and utilized the first rule when faced with an enormously complicated case involving the continuing aftermath of the re-drawing of Poland's borders following the defeat of the Nazis in the Second World War. *Broniowski v Poland*, judgment of 22 June 2004, was the lead case (167 similar applications were pending before the Court and the Polish Government acknowledged that up to 80,000 persons were affected) concerning the systemic failure of the Polish authorities to compensate all their citizens who were repatriated from the former Polish territories beyond the Bug river and consequently had to abandon their properties in those areas. Poland's pre-Second World War territories included significant areas east of the Bug river (in present-day Belarus, Ukraine and Lithuania). In 1939 the USSR invaded those provinces. During 1944 the Polish Committee of National Liberation signed the 'Republican Agreements' with the Soviet Socialist Republics of Ukraine, Belarus and Lithuania agreeing the repatriation of Polish citizens from the territories east of the Bug river (the new eastern border of Poland) and accepting the obligation to compensate such persons for their loss of property in the abandoned territories. Between 1944 and 1953 over 1.2 million persons were repatriated to Poland under these agreements. Polish law provided that such persons could purchase land and properties owned by the State with allowance being given for the value of the property they had been forced to abandon in the territories beyond the Bug river. However, as time progressed the Polish authorities reduced the amount of State property available to compensate the claimants. The applicant, whose grandmother had owned a house and land in what is now Lviv, Ukraine, claimed that his family had received only 2 per cent of the value of that property in compensation from the

Polish authorities and that failure amounted to an interference with his property rights protected by Article 1. As the domestic courts had recognised that the applicant had 'a right to credit' against the Government in respect of his grandmother's property, the Grand Chamber determined that this constituted a 'possession' within the meaning of Article 1. On the question whether the Government had secured a fair balance between the applicant's interests and those of Polish society as a whole:

182. The Court accepts that in situations such as the one in the present case, involving a wide-reaching but controversial legislative scheme with significant economic impact for the country as a whole, the national authorities must have considerable discretion in selecting not only the measures to secure respect for property rights or to regulate ownership relations within the country, but also the appropriate time for their implementation. The choice of measures may necessarily involve decisions restricting compensation for the taking or restitution of property to a level below its market value. Thus, Article 1 of Protocol No 1 does not guarantee a right to full compensation in all circumstances (see *James and Others* [*v UK*, A. 98 (1986)]§ 54).

Balancing the rights at stake, as well as the gains and losses of the different persons affected by the process of transforming the State's economy and legal system, is an exceptionally difficult exercise. In such circumstances, in the nature of things, a wide margin of appreciation should be accorded to the respondent State.

Nevertheless, the Court would reiterate that that margin, however considerable, is not unlimited and that the exercise of the State's discretion, even in the context of the most complex reform of the State, cannot entail consequences at variance with Convention standards.

183. Whilst the Court accepts that the radical reform of the country's political and economic system, as well as the state of the country's finances, may justify stringent limitations on compensation for the Bug River claimants, the Polish State has not been able to adduce satisfactory grounds justifying, in terms of Article 1 of Protocol No 1, the extent to which it has continuously failed over many years to implement an entitlement conferred on the applicant, as on thousands of other Bug River claimants, by Polish legislation.

184. The rule of law underlying the Convention, and the principle of lawfulness in Article 1 of Protocol No 1, require States not only to respect and apply, in a foreseeable and consistent manner, the laws they have enacted, but also, as a corollary of this duty, to ensure the legal and practical conditions for their implementation. In the context of the present case, it was incumbent on the Polish authorities to remove the existing incompatibility between the letter of the law and the State-operated practice which hindered the effective exercise of the applicant's right of property. Those principles also required the Polish State to fulfil in good time, in an appropriate and consistent manner, the legislative promises it had made in respect of the settlement of the Bug River claims. This was a matter of important public and general interest. As rightly pointed out by the Polish Constitutional Court, the imperative of maintaining citizens' legitimate confidence in the State and the law made by it, inherent in the rule of law, required the authorities to eliminate the dysfunctional provisions from the legal system and to rectify the extra-legal practices.

185. In the present case, as ascertained by the Polish courts and confirmed by the Court's analysis of the respondent State's conduct, the authorities, by imposing successive limitations on the exercise of the applicant's right to credit, and by applying the practices that made it unenforceable and unusable in practice, rendered that right illusory and destroyed its very essence.

The state of uncertainty in which the applicant found himself as a result of the repeated delays and obstruction continuing over a period of many years, for which the national authorities were responsible, was in itself incompatible with the obligation arising under Article 1 of Protocol No 1 to secure the peaceful enjoyment of possessions, notably with the duty to act in good time, in an appropriate and consistent manner where an issue of general interest is at stake.

186. Furthermore, the applicant's situation was compounded by the fact that what had become a practically unenforceable entitlement was legally extinguished by the December 2003 legislation, pursuant to which the applicant lost his hitherto existing entitlement to compensation. Moreover, this legislation operated a difference of treatment as between Bug River claimants in so far as those who had never received any compensation were awarded an amount which, although subject to a ceiling of 50,000 PLN, was a specified proportion (15%) of their entitlement, whereas claimants in the applicant's position, who had already been awarded a much lower percentage, received no additional amount.

As stated above (see paragraphs 134 and 182), under Article 1 of Protocol No. 1 the State is entitled to expropriate property—including any compensatory entitlement granted by legislation—and to reduce, even substantially, levels of compensation under legislative schemes. This applies, particularly, to situations in which the compensatory entitlement does not arise from any previous taking of individual property by the respondent State, but is designed to mitigate the effects of a taking or loss of property not attributable to that State. What Article 1 of Protocol No 1 requires is that the amount of compensation granted for property taken by the State be 'reasonably related' to its value (see paragraph 176 above). It is not for the Court to say in the abstract what would be a 'reasonable' level of compensation in the present case. However, given that—as acknowledged by the Government—the applicant's family had received merely 2% of the compensation due under the legislation as applicable before the entry into force of the Protocol in respect of Poland, the Court finds no cogent reason why such an insignificant amount should *per se* deprive him of the possibility of obtaining at least a proportion of his entitlement on an equal basis with other Bug River claimants.

(d) General conclusion

187. Having regard to all the foregoing factors and in particular to the impact on the applicant over many years of the Bug River legislative scheme as operated in practice, the Court concludes that, as an individual, he had to bear a disproportionate and excessive burden which cannot be justified in terms of the legitimate general community interest pursued by the authorities.

There has therefore been a violation of Article 1 of Protocol No 1 in the applicant's case.

Given the systemic problem in the treatment of the Bug river claimants by the Polish Government, found by the Grand Chamber, the latter held that: '... the respondent State must through appropriate legal measures and administrative practices, secure the implementation of the property right in question in respect of the remaining Bug river claimants or provide them with equivalent redress in lieu, in accordance with the principles of protection of property rights under Article 1 of Protocol No 1'. Against this background the Grand Chamber considered that the question of compensation for pecuniary/non-pecuniary damage suffered by the applicant was not ready for determination and should be reserved having regard to any agreement that might be reached between the applicant and the Government, together with any measures taken by the Government in response to the Court's judgment. Whilst general measures were being implemented by the Government, the Court would adjourn examination of other cases lodged by Bug river claimants. A friendly settlement was agreed between the applicant and the Government in September 2005 (see above, p 39). *Broniowski* vividly discloses how the continuing problems caused by historical territorial disputes (the contentious use of the Bug river as the eastern border of Poland can be traced back to at least 1919) affecting Member states may be raised via individual applications under the Convention. The Grand Chamber's strategy of seeking to encourage the agreement of a general solution, compatible with Article 1, for all the remaining Bug river claimants is highly desirable in terms of both justice and its own workload crisis.

8 A unanimous Grand Chamber found that legislation severely curtailing the damages parents could claim against health authorities in respect of their children born with serious

disabilities which had, negligently, not been detected during pregnancy violated this provision in *Draon v France and Maurice v France* judgments of 6 October 2005. The applicants were parents whose children were born with such disabilities. Mistakes by the public medical authorities resulted in the applicants not being alerted to those disabilities before the children were born. The parents sued the hospitals. Whilst their cases were before the courts the French parliament passed legislation, the 'Kouchner' Law of 4 March 2002, which provided that such parents would no longer be able to claim damages in respect of the special burdens arising throughout the child's life caused by their disabilities. This Law was applied to the applicants' claims with the consequence that they were awarded much lower sums of compensation than they would have received under the previously established case law. The applicants contended that the enactment of the Law violated their right to the peaceful enjoyment of their possessions. The Grand Chamber determined that the applicants had a possession in the form of the established right to claim full compensation in respect of their children's disabilities. The Law had abolished a valuable head of damages. In the judgment of the Grand Chamber the application of the Law to the applicants' proceedings had upset the fair balance between the public interest and the applicants' right to the peaceful enjoyment of their property. Consequently, there had been a breach of Article 1. Do you think there would have been a different outcome if the Law had only had prospective effect? Subsequently, the Draon family and the Maurice family each received 2.4 million euros just satisfaction.

The Second Rule: The deprivation of possessions

James v UK A.98 (1986) 8 EHRR 123
European Court of Human Rights

The applicants (including Gerald Cavendish, the Sixth Duke of Westminster) were trustees acting under the will of the Second Duke of Westminster. The Westminster family and its trustees have developed the Belgravia estate, comprising about 2000 houses, in central London which has become one of the most desirable (and expensive) residential areas in the capital. Virtually all the properties in the Belgravia estate were held on long leases (a real-property interest of two types: (i) a building lease, typically for 99 years, under which the tenant pays a ground rent fixed by reference to the value of the bare site and undertakes to build a house on the site and deliver the house up to the landlord at the expiry of the lease and (ii) a premium lease where the tenant pays a capital sum to the landlord for the provision of a house and thereafter a rent). From the perspective of tenants leases are wasting assets because at the end of the lease the tenant's interest terminates and the landlord acquires the premises on the site at no cost. Long leases were widely used in nineteenth century urban development throughout England and Wales. However, from the 1880s onwards, tenants began to demand 'leasehold enfranchisement', that is the right to purchase compulsorily the freehold of their homes. During the 1960s the Labour Party adopted such enfranchisement as part of its policy. When in government the Party secured the passage of the Leasehold Reform Act 1967, subsequently amended by other legislation in 1974. The 1967 Act granted long leasehold tenants the right to buy compulsorily their freehold at approximately site value. The 1974 legislation extended the right to buy to long leasehold tenants of more expensive properties subject to them paying a higher price (based on approximate value of the site and house). The statutory scheme provided that if tenants and landlords could not agree the sums of compensation due for the freeholds then independent tribunals would determine the prices to be paid. Between 1979 and 1983 some eighty tenants of the applicants exercised their rights under the legislation to acquire the freeholds of their homes. In each of these cases the price paid was agreed by negotiation. At least 25 of these persons sold their freeholds within one year of acquiring them under the legislative scheme (the applicants alleged that the former tenants made profits of between £32,000 and £182,000). Consequently, the applicants complained to the Commission contending that the compulsory transfer of their freehold rights under the above legislation breached Article 1. The Commission was unanimous in finding no violation.

B. SECOND SENTENCE OF THE FIRST PARAGRAPH ('THE DEPRIVATION RULE')

1. APPLICABILITY

38. The Court considers that the applicants were 'deprived of [their] possessions', within the meaning of the second sentence of Article 1 (P1-1), by virtue of the contested legislation. This point was not disputed before the Court.

2. 'IN THE PUBLIC INTEREST': PRIVATE INDIVIDUALS AS BENEFICIARIES

39. The applicants' first contention was that the 'public interest' test in the deprivation rule is satisfied only if the property is taken for a public purpose of benefit to the community generally and that, as a corollary, the transfer of property from one person to another for the latter's private benefit alone can never be 'in the public interest'. In their submission, the contested legislation does not satisfy this condition.

The Commission and the Government, on the other hand, were agreed in thinking that a compulsory transfer of property from one individual to another may in principle be considered to be 'in the public interest' if the taking is effected in pursuance of legitimate social policies.

40. The Court agrees with the applicants that a deprivation of property effected for no reason other than to confer a private benefit on a private party cannot be 'in the public interest'. Nonetheless, the compulsory transfer of property from one individual to another may, depending upon the circumstances, constitute a legitimate means for promoting the public interest. In this connection, even where the texts in force employ expressions like 'for the public use', no common principle can be identified in the constitutions, legislation and case-law of the Contracting States that would warrant understanding the notion of public interest as outlawing compulsory transfer between private parties. The same may be said of certain other democratic countries; thus, the applicants and the Government cited in argument a judgment of the Supreme Court of the United States of America, which concerned State legislation in Hawaii compulsorily transferring title in real property from lessors to lessees in order to reduce the concentration of land ownership (*Hawaii Housing Authority v Midkiff* 104 S Ct 2321 [1984]).

41. Neither can it be read into the English expression 'in the public interest' that the transferred property should be put into use for the general public or that the community generally, or even a substantial proportion of it, should directly benefit from the taking. The taking of property in pursuance of a policy calculated to enhance social justice within the community can properly be described as being 'in the public interest'. In particular, the fairness of a system of law governing the contractual or property rights of private parties is a matter of public concern and therefore legislative measures intended to bring about such fairness are capable of being 'in the public interest', even if they involve the compulsory transfer of property from one individual to another.

42. The expression '*pour cause d'utilité publique*' used in the French text of Article 1 (P1-1) may indeed be read as having the narrow sense argued by the applicants, as is shown by the domestic law of some,

but not all, of the Contracting States where the expression or its equivalent is found in the context of expropriation of property. That, however, is not decisive, as many Convention concepts have been recognised in the Court's case-law as having an 'autonomous' meaning. Moreover, the words 'utilité publique' are also capable of bearing a wider meaning, covering expropriation measures taken in implementation of policies calculated to enhance social justice.

The Court, like the Commission, considers that such an interpretation best reconciles the language of the English and French texts, having regard to the object and purpose of Article 1 (P1-1) (see Article 33 of the 1969 Vienna Convention on the Law of Treaties and the *Sunday Times* judgment of 26 April 1979, Series A No 30, p 30, para 48), which is primarily to guard against the arbitrary confiscation of property.

43. The applicants submitted that the use in the same context of different phrases—'public interest' in the first paragraph of Article 1 (P1-1) and 'general interest' in the second paragraph—should, according to a generally recognised principle of treaty interpretation, be assumed to indicate an intention to refer to different concepts. They construed Article 1 (P1-1) as granting the State more latitude to control the use of someone's property than to take it away from him.

In the Court's opinion, even if there could be differences between the concepts of 'public interest' and 'general interest' in Article 1 (P1-1), on the point under consideration no fundamental distinction of the kind contended for by the applicants can be drawn between them.

44. The applicants accepted that measures designed to ensure equitable distribution of economic advantages, for example by way of taxation, are licensed by Article 1 (P1-1), but, so they argued, solely by the second paragraph and not by the first paragraph. The Court, however, sees no cogent reason why a State should be prohibited under Article 1 (P1-1) from implementing such a policy by resort to deprivation of property.

45. For these reasons, the Court comes to the same conclusion as the Commission: a taking of property effected in pursuance of legitimate social, economic or other policies may be 'in the public interest', even if the community at large has no direct use or enjoyment of the property taken. The leasehold reform legislation is not therefore *ipso facto* an infringement of Article 1 (P1-1) on this ground. Accordingly, it is necessary to inquire whether in other respects the legislation satisfied the 'public interest' test and the remaining requirements laid down in the second sentence of Article 1 (P1-1).

3. WHETHER THE LEASEHOLD REFORM LEGISLATION COMPLIED WITH THE 'PUBLIC INTEREST' TEST AND THE REMAINING REQUIREMENTS OF THE DEPRIVATION RULE

(a) Margin of appreciation

46. Because of their direct knowledge of their society and its needs, the national authorities are in principle better placed than the international judge to appreciate what is 'in the public interest'. Under the system of protection established by the Convention, it is thus for the national authorities to make the initial assessment both of the existence of a problem of public concern warranting measures of deprivation of property and of the remedial action to be taken (see, *mutatis mutandis*, the *Handyside* judgment of 7 December 1976, Series A No 24, p 22, para 48). Here, as in other fields to which the safeguards of the Convention extend, the national authorities accordingly enjoy a certain margin of appreciation.

Furthermore, the notion of 'public interest' is necessarily extensive. In particular, as the Commission noted, the decision to enact laws expropriating property will commonly involve consideration of political, economic and social issues on which opinions within a democratic society may reasonably differ widely. The Court, finding it natural that the margin of appreciation available to the legislature in implementing social and economic policies should be a wide one, will respect the legislature's judgment as to what is 'in the public interest' unless that judgment be manifestly without reasonable foundation. In other words, although the Court cannot substitute its own assessment for that of the national authorities, it is bound to review the contested measures under Article 1 of Protocol No 1 (P1-1) and, in so doing, to make an inquiry into the facts with reference to which the national authorities acted.

(b) Whether the aim of the contested legislation was a legitimate one, in principle and on the facts

47. The aim of the 1967 Act . . . was to right the injustice which was felt to be caused to occupying tenants by the operation of the long leasehold system of tenure . . . The Act was designed to reform the existing law, said to be 'inequitable to the leaseholder', and to give effect to what was described as the occupying tenant's 'moral entitlement' to ownership of the house . . .

Eliminating what are judged to be social injustices is an example of the functions of a democratic legislature. More especially, modern societies consider housing of the population to be a prime social need, the regulation of which cannot entirely be left to the play of market forces. The margin of appreciation is wide enough to cover legislation aimed at securing greater social justice in the sphere of people's homes, even where such legislation interferes with existing contractual relations between private parties and confers no direct benefit on the State or the community at large. In principle, therefore, the aim pursued by the leasehold reform legislation is a legitimate one.

48. The applicants suggested that the 1967 Act was not enacted for purposes of public benefit but was in reality motivated by purely political considerations as a vote-seeking measure by the Labour Government then in office.

The Court notes, however, that leasehold reform in England and Wales had been a matter of public concern for almost a century and that, when the 1967 Act was passed, enfranchisement was accepted as a principle by all the major political parties . . . The Court does not find that such political considerations as may have influenced the legislative process, socio-economic legislation being bound to reflect political attitudes to a greater or lesser degree, precluded the objective pursued by the 1967 Act from being a legitimate one 'in the public interest'. . . . The Court therefore agrees with the Commission's conclusion : the United Kingdom Parliament's belief in the existence of a social injustice was not such as could be characterised as manifestly unreasonable.

(c) Means chosen to achieve the aim

50. This, however, does not settle the issue. Not only must a measure depriving a person of his property pursue, on the facts as well as in principle, a legitimate aim 'in the public interest', but there must also be a reasonable relationship of proportionality between the means employed and the aim sought to be realised . . . This latter requirement was expressed in other terms in the *Sporrong and Lönnroth* judgment by the notion of the 'fair balance' that must be struck between the demands of the general interest of the community and the requirements of the protection of the individual's fundamental rights (Series A No 52, p 26, para 69). The requisite balance will not be found if the person concerned has had to bear 'an individual and excessive burden' (ibid, p 28, para 73). Although the Court was speaking in that judgment in the context of the general rule of peaceful enjoyment of property enunciated in the first sentence of the first paragraph, it pointed out that 'the search for this balance is . . . reflected in the structure of Article 1 (P1-1)' as a whole (ibid, p 26, para 69). . . . The Court considers that a measure must be both appropriate for achieving its aim and not disproportionate thereto. Whether this was so on the facts will be examined below when dealing with the applicants' various arguments.

(I) The principle of enfranchisement

51. According to the applicants, the security of tenure that tenants already had under the law in force . . . provided an adequate response and the draconian nature of the means devised to give effect to the alleged moral entitlement, namely deprivation of property, went too far . . . The occupying leaseholder was considered by Parliament to have a 'moral entitlement' to ownership of the house, of which inadequate account was taken under the existing law . . . The concern of the legislature was not simply to regulate more fairly the relationship of landlord and tenant but to right a perceived injustice that went to the very issue of ownership. Allowing a mechanism for the compulsory transfer of the freehold

interest in the house and the land to the tenant, with financial compensation to the landlord, cannot in itself be qualified in the circumstances as an inappropriate or disproportionate method for readjusting the law so as to meet that concern.

(II) Rateable-value limits

52. As to the conditions laid down for enfranchisement, the applicants contended that the restriction of the scope of the legislation to houses below a certain rateable value . . . introduces an arbitrary element . . . The Court notes that, on the Government's undisputed estimate, all but one or two per cent of dwellinghouses held on long leases in England and Wales were within the 1967 Act . . . The explanations given on behalf of the Government during the debates on the Bill for inserting the rateable-value limits . . . cannot be dismissed as irrational . . . Neither can the Court find that the amendment in the 1974 Act, whereby a more valuable class of property was rendered liable to enfranchisement . . . fell outside the State's margin of appreciation.

(III) Compensation

53. The applicants also objected to the compensation terms under the legislation.

54. *(a) Entitlement* The first question that arises is whether the availability and amount of compensation are material considerations under the second sentence of the first paragraph of Article 1 (P1-1), the text of the provision being silent on the point. The Commission, with whom both the Government and the applicants agreed, read Article 1 (P1-1) as in general impliedly requiring the payment of compensation as a necessary condition for the taking of property of anyone within the jurisdiction of a Contracting State.

Like the Commission, the Court observes that under the legal systems of the Contracting States, the taking of property in the public interest without payment of compensation is treated as justifiable only in exceptional circumstances not relevant for present purposes. As far as Article 1 (P1-1) is concerned, the protection of the right of property it affords would be largely illusory and ineffective in the absence of any equivalent principle. Clearly, compensation terms are material to the assessment whether the contested legislation respects a fair balance between the various interests at stake and, notably, whether it does not impose a disproportionate burden on the applicants (see the above-mentioned *Sporrong and Lönnroth* judgment, Series A No 52, pp 26 and 28, paras 69 and 73).

The Court further accepts the Commission's conclusion as to the standard of compensation: the taking of property without payment of an amount reasonably related to its value would normally constitute a disproportionate interference which could not be considered justifiable under Article 1 (P1-1). Article 1 (P1-1) does not, however, guarantee a right to full compensation in all circumstances. Legitimate objectives of 'public interest', such as pursued in measures of economic reform or measures designed to achieve greater social justice, may call for less than reimbursement of the full market value. Furthermore, the Court's power of review is limited to ascertaining whether the choice of compensation terms falls outside the State's wide margin of appreciation in this domain . . .

55. *(b) Applicants' grievances on the facts* The applicants' grievances as to compensation fall under two heads. Firstly, the 1967 basis of valuation does not accord the applicants the full market value of the properties enfranchised . . . Secondly, under both the 1967 and the 1974 bases the property is valued as at the date of the tenant's notice of his desire to acquire . . . the complaint being that the landlord suffers loss as a result of the delay between the date of valuation and payment on completion of the transaction.

56. As to the first head of complaint, the 1967 basis of valuation, the effect of which is that the tenant pays approximately the site value but nothing for the buildings on the site, clearly and deliberately favours the tenant. It was designed to give effect to the view underlying the whole of the contested legislation, namely that 'in equity the bricks and mortar belong to the qualified leaseholder' because of the money he (or his predecessor in title) paid out initially as a capital sum and has then spent over

the years on repairs, maintenance and improvements to the house ... The objective pursued by the leasehold reform legislation is to prevent a perceived unjust enrichment accruing to the landlord on the reversion of the property. In the light of that objective, judged by the Court to be legitimate for the purposes of Article 1 (P1-1), it has not been established, having regard to the respondent State's wide margin of appreciation, that the 1967 basis of valuation is not such as to afford a fair balance between the interests of the private parties concerned and thereby between the general interest of society and the landlord's right of property.

57. As to the second head of complaint, it is possible, as is shown by the circumstances of the enfranchisements affecting the applicants (see paragraph 29 (v) above), for delays, sometimes long, to occur between valuation date and payment of the price. On the other hand, it is open to a landlord who believes that the process of enfranchisement is being deliberately or unnecessarily delayed to refer the matter to the competent tribunal ... The Court accordingly concludes that the compensation procedures laid down in the contested legislation do not inherently lead to delays of such a degree as to involve a violation of Article 1 (P1-1).

58. *(c) General principles of international law* The applicants argued in the alternative that the reference in the second sentence of Article 1 (P1-1) to 'the general principles of international law' meant that the international law requirement of, so they asserted, prompt, adequate and effective compensation for the expropriation of property of foreigners also applied to nationals.

59. The Commission has consistently held that the principles in question are not applicable to a taking by a State of the property of its own nationals. The Government supported this opinion. The Court likewise agrees with it for the following reasons.

60. In the first place, purely as a matter of general international law, the principles in question apply solely to non-nationals. They were specifically developed for the benefit of non-nationals. As such, these principles did not relate to the treatment accorded by States to their own nationals.

61. In support of their argument, the applicants relied first on the actual text of Article 1 (P1-1). In their submission, since the second sentence opened with the words 'No one', it was impossible to construe that sentence as meaning that whereas everyone was entitled to the safeguards afforded by the phrases 'in the public interest' and 'subject to the conditions provided for by law', only non-nationals were entitled to the safeguards afforded by the phrase 'subject to the conditions provided for ... by the general principles of international law'. They further pointed out that where the authors of the Convention intended to differentiate between nationals and non-nationals, they did so expressly, as was exemplified by Article 16 (art 16).

While there is some force in the applicants' argument as a matter of grammatical construction, there are convincing reasons for a different interpretation. Textually the Court finds it more natural to take the reference to the general principles of international law in Article 1 of Protocol No 1 (P1-1) to mean that those principles are incorporated into that Article (P1-1), but only as regards those acts to which they are normally applicable, that is to say acts of a State in relation to non-nationals. Moreover, the words of a treaty should be understood to have their ordinary meaning (see Article 31 of the 1969 Vienna Convention on the Law of Treaties), and to interpret the phrase in question as extending the general principles of international law beyond their normal sphere of applicability is less consistent with the ordinary meaning of the terms used, notwithstanding their context.

62. The applicants further argued that, on the Commission's interpretation, the reference in Article 1 (P1-1) to the general principles of international law would be redundant since non-nationals already enjoyed the protection thereof.

The Court does not share this view. The inclusion of the reference can be seen to serve at least two purposes. Firstly, it enables non-nationals to resort directly to the machinery of the Convention to enforce their rights on the basis of the relevant principles of international law, whereas otherwise they would have to seek recourse to diplomatic channels or to other available means of dispute settlement to do so. Secondly, the reference ensures that the position of non-nationals is safeguarded, in that it excludes any possible argument that the entry into force of Protocol No 1 (P1) has led to a diminution of their rights. In this connection, it is also noteworthy that Article 1 (P1-1) expressly provides that deprivation of property must be effected 'in the public interest': since such a requirement has always been included among the general principles of international law, this express provision would itself have been superfluous if Article 1 (P1-1) had had the effect of rendering those principles applicable to nationals as well as to non-nationals.

63. Finally, the applicants pointed out that to treat the general principles of international law as inapplicable to a taking by a State of the property of its own nationals would permit differentiation on the ground of nationality. This, they said, would be incompatible with two provisions that are incorporated in Protocol No 1 by virtue of Article 5 thereof (P1-5): Article 1 (art 1) of the Convention which obliges the Contracting States to secure to everyone within their jurisdiction the rights and freedoms guaranteed and Article 14 (art 14) of the Convention which enshrines the principle of non-discrimination.

As to Article 1 (art 1) of the Convention, it is true that under most provisions of the Convention and its Protocols nationals and non-nationals enjoy the same protection but this does not exclude exceptions as far as this may be indicated in a particular text (see, for example, Articles 4 para 3 (b), 5 para 1 (f) and 16 of the Convention, Articles 3 and 4 of Protocol No 4) (art 4-3-b, art 5-1-f, art 16, P4-3, P4-4).

As to Article 14 (art 14) of the Convention, the Court has consistently held that differences of treatment do not constitute discrimination if they have an 'objective and reasonable justification' (see, as the most recent authority, the *Abdulaziz, Cabales and Balkandali* judgment of 28 May 1985, Series A No 94, pp 35–36, para 72).

Especially as regards a taking of property effected in the context of a social reform, there may well be good grounds for drawing a distinction between nationals and non-nationals as far as compensation is concerned. To begin with, non-nationals are more vulnerable to domestic legislation: unlike nationals, they will generally have played no part in the election or designation of its authors nor have been consulted on its adoption. Secondly, although a taking of property must always be effected in the public interest, different considerations may apply to nationals and non-nationals and there may well be legitimate reason for requiring nationals to bear a greater burden in the public interest than non-nationals.

64. Confronted with a text whose interpretation has given rise to such disagreement, the Court considers it proper to have recourse to the *travaux préparatoires* as a supplementary means of interpretation (see Article 32 of the Vienna Convention on the Law of Treaties).

Examination of the *travaux préparatoires* reveals that the express reference to a right to compensation contained in earlier drafts of Article 1 (P1-1) was excluded, notably in the face of opposition on the part of the United Kingdom and other States. The mention of the general principles of international law was subsequently included and was the subject of several statements to the effect that they protected only foreigners. Thus, when the German Government stated that they could accept the text provided that it was explicitly recognised that those principles involved the obligation to pay compensation in the event of expropriation, the Swedish delegation pointed out that those principles only applied to relations between a State and non-nationals. And it was then agreed, at the request of the German and Belgian delegations, that 'the general principles of international law, in their present connotation, entailed the obligation to pay compensation to non-nationals in cases of expropriation'.

Above all, in their Resolution (52) 1 of 19 March 1952 approving the text of the Protocol and opening it for signature, the Committee of Ministers expressly stated that, 'as regards Article 1 (P1-1), the general principles of international law in their present connotation entail the obligation to pay compensation to non-nationals in cases of expropriation'. Having regard to the negotiating history as a whole, the Court considers that this Resolution must be taken as a clear indication that the reference to the general principles of international law was not intended to extend to nationals.

The *travaux préparatoires* accordingly do not support the interpretation for which the applicants contended.

65. Finally, it has not been demonstrated that, since the entry into force of Protocol No 1 (P1), State practice has developed to the point where it can be said that the parties to that instrument regard the reference therein to the general principles of international law as being applicable to the treatment accorded by them to their own nationals. The evidence adduced points distinctly in the opposite direction.

66. For all these reasons, the Court concludes that the general principles of international law are not applicable to a taking by a State of the property of its own nationals.

67. *(d) 'Conditions provided for by law'* In the further alternative, the applicants argued that deprivation of property without payment of compensation, or with compensation which is unfair or unjust, does not fulfil the requirement in Article 1 (P1-1) that the deprivation should be 'subject to the conditions provided for by law', interpreting that phrase as adverting not merely to municipal law but to the fundamental principles of law common to all the Contracting States. In their submission, a taking of property will be arbitrary and hence not in accordance with 'the conditions provided for by law' in this sense if, as occurred in their case, the amount paid as compensation for the taking bears no reasonable relation to the value of the property taken.

The Court has consistently held that the terms 'law' or 'lawful' in the Convention '[do] not merely refer back to domestic law but also [relate] to the quality of the law, requiring it to be compatible with the rule of law' (see, as the most recent authority, the *Malone* judgment of 2 August 1984, Series A No 82, p 32, para 67). However on the facts . . . there are no grounds for finding that the enfranchisement of the applicants' properties was arbitrary because of the terms of compensation provided for under the leasehold reform legislation. For the rest, in the Court's opinion, such other requirements as may be included in the phrase 'subject to the conditions provided for by law' were satisfied in the circumstances of the taking of the applicants' properties . . .

(IV) Absence of independent consideration of the reasonableness of each proposed enfranchisement

68. The applicants contended that the operation of the leasehold reform legislation is indiscriminate since it does not provide any machinery whereby the landlord can seek an independent consideration, in any particular case, of either the justification for enfranchisement or the principles on which the compensation is to be calculated, once only it is established that the tenancy is within the ambit of the legislation. . . . It is in the first place for Parliament to assess the advantages and disadvantages involved in the various legislative alternatives available . . . In view of the fact that the legislation was estimated to be likely to affect 98 to 99 per cent of the one and a quarter million dwellinghouses held on long leases in England and Wales . . . the system chosen by Parliament cannot in itself be dismissed as irrational or inappropriate.

(V) Individual transactions

69. The applicants finally submitted that even if enfranchisement is capable in principle of being 'in the public interest', the 80 individual transactions complained of . . . were not justified . . . Parliament decided that landlords affected by the legislation should be deprived of the enrichment, considered unjust, that would otherwise come to them on reversion of the property, at the risk of a number of 'undeserving' tenants being able to make 'windfall profits'. That was a policy decision by Parliament, which the Court cannot find to be so unreasonable as to be outside the State's margin of appreciation. Neither does the operation of the legislation in practice, notably as illustrated by the 80 transactions concerning the applicants, show the scale of anomalies to be such as to render the legislation unacceptable under Article 1 (P1-1). Furthermore, in all the specific transactions complained of, even those where 'windfall profits' were made by tenants in onward sales, the applicants received the prescribed compensation for what Parliament considered to be their entitlement in equity as landlords . . . Any

hardship as a result of the making of a 'windfall profit' was suffered not by the applicants, whose loss and compensation were unaffected, but rather by the predecessor(s) in title of the enfranchising tenant. . . . Accordingly, the requisite balance under Article 1 (P1-1) was not destroyed.

4. RECAPITULATION

70. To sum up, each of the requirements of the second sentence was therefore satisfied in relation to the contested deprivation of possessions suffered by the applicants.

C. First sentence of the first paragraph ('the peaceful enjoyment rule')

71. Alternatively and additionally, the applicants asserted a violation of their rights of peaceful enjoyment of property as guaranteed by the first sentence of Article 1 (P1-1).

The rule (in the second sentence) subjecting deprivation of possessions to certain conditions concerns a particular category, indeed the most radical kind, of interference with the right to peaceful enjoyment of property . . . the second sentence supplements and qualifies the general principle enunciated in the first sentence. This being so, it is inconceivable that application of that general principle to the present case should lead to any conclusion different from that already arrived at by the Court in application of the second sentence.

D. CONCLUSION

72. Neither by reason of the terms and conditions of the Leasehold Reform Act 1967 as amended nor by reason of the particular circumstances of the enfranchisement transactions concerning the applicants' properties has there been a breach of Article 1 of Protocol No 1 (P1-1).
. . .

FOR THESE REASONS, THE COURT UNANIMOUSLY

Holds that there has been no breach . . . of Article 1 of Protocol No 1 . . .

NOTES

1   The Court was composed of President Ryssdal and Judges: Ganshof van der Meersch, Cremona, Wiarda, Thor Vilhjalmsson, Bindschedler-Robert, Evrigenis, Lagergren, Gölcüklü, Matscher, Pinheiro Farinha, Pettiti, Walsh, Evans, Russo, Bernhardt, Gersing, and Spielmann.

2   Judge Thor Vilhjalmsson issued a Concurring Opinion in which he expressed the view that Article 1 did not contain a right to compensation where a person's property was expropriated.

The text of the Article (P1-1) makes no mention of compensation. In my opinion, that should have been done if part of its purpose had been to guarantee a right to compensation. The ordinary meaning of the text as it stands is therefore that it is not concerned with compensation.

Should it nevertheless be felt necessary to confirm this meaning by recourse to supplementary means of interpretation, the *travaux préparatoires* point to the very same conclusion, namely that Article 1 (P1-1) does not confer a right to compensation. The relevant points are the following.

The Committee of Ministers examined in November 1950 various amendments proposed by the Parliamentary Consultative Assembly to the draft Convention on Human Rights. When it became clear that immediate agreement could not be reached with regard to certain matters, it was decided that they should be removed from the draft and submitted to a committee of experts for further study. One of these matters was the right to property. The amendment proposed by the Assembly did not speak of compensation. In spite of that, the majority of the member States considered that compensation should be guaranteed and accordingly the text of the expert committee contained words to that effect (see the Collected Edition of the '*Travaux préparatoires*', volume VII, pp 208 and 223–4). A number of

Governments, however, could not agree to the inclusion in the Convention of the principle of compensation and reference to it was thereafter deleted from the text. A short account of how the text changed during the drafting period is given in the commentary of 18 September 1951 by the Secretary General (loc. cit., volume VIII, pp 4–10).

In view of all this, I am bound to draw the conclusion that the object and purpose of Article 1 of the Protocol (P1-1) did not go so far as to include a guarantee of a right to compensation. Even if the Convention is to be interpreted in the light of present-day conditions, I fail to see any development which could justify now another interpretation of the Article (P1-1).

Do you think the Court was correct in finding an implied right to compensation under Article 1?

3 Judges Bindschedler-Robert, Gölcüklü, Matscher, Pettiti, Russo, and Spielmann issued a Concurring Opinion in which they stated that:

In paragraph 66, the judgment affirms that the general principles of international law are not applicable to a taking by a State of the property of its own nationals.

It must, however, be acknowledged that the reasoning set out in paragraphs 60 to 65 is, taken globally, far from convincing, even though it does contain some not insignificant arguments (for example, the reference to the drafting history in paragraph 64. Nevertheless it should be remembered that it is often dangerous to place too much reliance on such history).

Be this as it may, the thesis accepted by the judgment leads to a difference in the treatment of nationals and aliens under the Convention, which plainly conflicts with both the underlying spirit and the general scheme of the Convention (see Article 1) (art 1). The rare exceptions to this principle are always either expressly stated (cf. for example, Article 16 of the Convention and Articles 3 and 4 of Protocol No 4) (art 16, P4-3, P4-4), or dealt with in a way which leaves no room for doubt (for example, Article 5 para 1 (f) of the Convention) (art 5-1-f).

The judgment does not give a satisfactory answer to this question, which we think is of fundamental importance for the interpretation of the Convention. We are even of the opinion that the arguments developed in paragraphs 61 and 63 are weak and that, generally speaking, the principles of interpretation on which the judgment is based deal merely with points of detail.

Moreover, it must not be forgotten that in the various Contracting States, legal opinion is extremely divided on the issue in question and that, at present, there is growing support for those who consider that the general principles of international law are applicable to nationals under Article 1 of Protocol No 1 (P1-1).

The elasticity of the general principles of international law in this area can also be seen from a number of international arbitration awards which apply them in a flexible manner to nationalisations by third-world developing States.

In these circumstances, we would have preferred it if the issue had not been settled in this judgment, especially as it is not decisive for the final conclusion arrived at in the judgment . . .

However, in the later case of *Lithgow* (below, Note 5), the Court restated its ruling in *James* that 'the general principles of international law' are not applicable to a taking by a State of the property of its own nationals.

4 The above judgment of the Court is very important for elaborating the component elements of the second rule. It is now clear that States' programmes of social (redistributive) justice fall within the legitimate objectives of the rule. Furthermore, the Court invoked its concept of the margin of appreciation (see above, p 629) to accord considerable discretion to States in determining what sorts of social and economic programmes are 'in the public interest'. Only where a national parliament adopts such a programme 'manifestly without reasonable foundation' will the Court consider it not to be 'in the public interest'. The Court also explained that the application of these programmes to particular individuals must satisfy a test of proportionality. Indeed, the fair balance test (articulated in *Sporrong and Lönnroth*) was synonymous with this requirement. Finally, the Court interpreted the phrase 'conditions provided for by law' as meaning that national laws, detailing these programmes, must comply with the Convention's well established 'rule of law' qualities (such as accessibility, foreseeability and non-arbitrariness'): for further elaboration see *Hentrich v France*, below Note 6.

5   A different form of deprivation of possessions, that of nationalisation, was examined by the Court in *Lithgow v UK*, A.102 (1986) 8 EHRR 329. In a significant judgment the Court extended the wide margin of appreciation given to States under the second rule to encompass the setting of compensation terms, as well as determining when deprivation of possessions should occur (see above *James*). The applicants, consisting of companies and individuals, had certain of their interests nationalised under the Aircraft and Shipbuilding Industries Act 1977. The Labour Party had promised to nationalise these industries in its February 1974 election manifesto. After gaining office the Labour Government announced, in July 1974, that the designated industries would be taken into public ownership. That Government won an overall majority in the October 1974 general election and in March 1975 the Secretary of State for Industry announced, in the House of Commons, the introduction of a Bill to give effect to the nationalisation of these industries. The Secretary also explained the method of compensating the owners of the two industries (generally they would receive the average value of their quoted share price during the six months preceding the election of the Labour Government in February 1974). After lengthy parliamentary proceedings (involving serious disagreements between the House of Commons and the House of Lords) the nationalisation Bill received the Royal Assent in March 1977. The applicants complained to the Commission alleging that the compensation they had received for the nationalisation of their proprietary interests in the two industries was grossly inadequate and therefore in breach of Article 1. By thirteen votes to three the Commission rejected that contention. The Court refined the nature of the duty upon States to pay compensation in respect of the deprivation of property by holding that:

109. ... The obligation to pay compensation derives from an implicit condition in Article 1 of Protocol No 1 (P1-1) read as a whole ... rather than from the 'public interest' requirement itself. The latter requirement relates to the justification and the motives for the actual taking, issues which were not contested by the applicants.

...

E. STANDARD OF COMPENSATION

121. The Court further accepts the Commission's conclusion as to the standard of compensation: the taking of property without payment of an amount reasonably related to its value would normally constitute a disproportionate interference which could not be considered justifiable under Article 1 (P1-1). Article 1 (P1-1) does not, however, guarantee a right to full compensation in all circumstances, since legitimate objectives of 'public interest', such as pursued in measures of economic reform or measures designed to achieve greater social justice, may call for less than reimbursement of the full market value (see the above-mentioned *James* judgment, Series A No 98, p 36, para 54).

In this connection, the applicants contended that, as regards the standard of compensation, no distinction could be drawn between nationalisation and other takings of property by the State, such as the compulsory acquisition of land for public purposes.

The Court is unable to agree. Both the nature of the property taken and the circumstances of the taking in these two categories of cases give rise to different considerations which may legitimately be taken into account in determining a fair balance between the public interest and the private interests concerned. The valuation of major industrial enterprises for the purpose of nationalising a whole industry is in itself a far more complex operation than, for instance, the valuation of land compulsorily acquired and normally calls for specific legislation which can be applied across the board to all the undertakings involved. Accordingly, provided always that the aforesaid fair balance is preserved, the standard of compensation required in a nationalisation case may be different from that required in regard to other takings of property.

122. While not disputing that the State enjoyed a margin of appreciation in deciding whether to deprive an owner of his property, the applicants submitted that the Commission had wrongly concluded from this premise that the State also had a wide discretion in laying down the terms and conditions on which property was to be taken.

The Court is unable to accept this submission. A decision to enact nationalisation legislation will commonly involve consideration of various issues on which opinions within a democratic society may reasonably differ widely. Because of their direct knowledge of their society and its needs and resources, the national authorities are in principle better placed than the international judge to appreciate what measures are appropriate in this area and consequently the margin of appreciation available to them should be a wide one. It would, in the Court's view, be artificial in this respect to divorce the decision as to the compensation terms from the actual decision to nationalise, since the factors influencing the latter will of necessity also influence the former. Accordingly, the Court's power of review in the present case is limited to ascertaining whether the decisions regarding compensation fell outside the United Kingdom's wide margin of appreciation; it will respect the legislature's judgment in this connection unless that judgment was manifestly without reasonable foundation.

The Court then concluded by varying majorities (seventeen votes to one and thirteen votes to five) that the method of calculating compensation provided under the 1977 Act was within the State's margin of appreciation and the delay between the time when compensation values were determined (1973–4) and the vesting days (29 April 1977 for the aerospace companies and 1 July 1977 for the shipbuilding companies) when the State took over the industries did not infringe Article 1. Hence the Court was deferring to the political judgment of Member states democratic institutions regarding decisions (i) to nationalise specific industries and (ii) as to how compensation should be calculated in respect of nationalised possessions. Only if such decisions were 'manifestly without reasonable foundation(s)' would the Court find a violation of Article 1. In contemporary times most Western governments have abandoned the ideology of governmental ownership of industries in favour of market forces subject to governmental (and supra-national e.g. via the European Union) regulation.

6   In *Hentrich v France* A.296-A (1994) 18 EHRR 440, the Court developed the meaning of the phrase 'conditions provided for by law' and the proportionality requirement found in Article 1 to impose procedural obligations upon States which seek to deprive persons of their possessions. The applicant, and her husband, purchased approximately 7,000 square metres of land in Strasbourg for 150,000 French francs. The purchase was registered, on payment of duties, by the local tax office during August 1979. In February 1980 a bailiff informed the applicant that the Commissioner of Revenue considered that the purchase price of her land was too low and, therefore, the Treasury was exercising its statutory power of pre-emption to buy the land for the contract price plus a ten per cent premium. The applicant sought to challenge the pre-emption decision in the national courts, but she was unsuccessful. She then complained to the Commission alleging a breach of Article 1. That body, by twelve votes to one, found a breach of Article 1. The Court noted that the French authorities had only exercised their power of pre-emption eighty-eight times between 1980 and 1986 and that since the Court of Cassation's judgment in the applicant's case (1987) the power had not been invoked. The Government did not dispute that the applicant had been deprived of her property by the exercise of its power of pre-emption. Therefore, the Court focused on whether the conditions laid down in rule two had been complied with.

A. PURPOSE OF THE INTERFERENCE

...

39. ...The Court reiterates that the notion of 'public interest' is necessarily extensive and that the States have a certain margin of appreciation to frame and organise their fiscal policies and make arrangements—such as the right of pre-emption—to ensure that taxes are paid. It recognises that the prevention of tax evasion is a legitimate objective which is in the public interest. It does not have to decide in the instant case whether the right of pre-emption could legitimately be designed also to regulate the property market.

B. LAWFULNESS OF THE INTERFERENCE

40. In Mrs Hentrich's submission, the pre-emption procedure was arbitrary as the Revenue had not given reasons for its decision and the taxpayer had not been able to know or criticise the reasons for it subsequently.... While the system of the right of pre-emption does not lend itself to criticism as an attribute of the State's sovereignty, the same is not true where the exercise of it is discretionary and at the same time the procedure is not fair.

In the instant case the pre-emption operated arbitrarily and selectively and was scarcely foreseeable, and it was not attended by the basic procedural safeguards. In particular, Article 668 of the General Tax Code, as interpreted up to that time by the Court of Cassation and as applied to the applicant, did not sufficiently satisfy the requirements of precision and foreseeability implied by the concept of law within the meaning of the Convention.

A pre-emption decision cannot be legitimate in the absence of adversarial proceedings that comply with the principle of equality of arms, enabling argument to be presented on the issue of the underestimation of the price and, consequently, on the Revenue's position—all elements which were lacking in the present case.

The Court notes that the French legal system has in fact been modified in this respect, it now being mandatory for the reasons for administrative pre-emption decisions to be subject to the adversarial principle. It must, however, observe that this development did not avail the applicant, although it could have done.

C. PROPORTIONALITY OF THE INTERFERENCE

43. According to Mrs Hentrich, the fact that it was impossible to defend herself against the effect of the pre-emption—which she described as dishonouring—made the measure a disproportionate one, as did the inadequacy of the compensation paid for the expropriation....

45. In order to assess the proportionality of the interference, the Court looks at the degree of protection from arbitrariness that is afforded by the proceedings in this case.

46. In this instance the trial and appeal courts interpreted the domestic law as allowing the State to avail itself of its right of pre-emption without having to indicate the reasons of fact and law for its decision.

47. The Court notes, firstly, that the Revenue may, through the exercise of its right of pre-emption, substitute itself for any purchaser, even one acting in perfectly good faith, for the sole purpose of warning others against any temptation to evade taxes. This right of pre-emption, which does not seem to have any equivalent in the tax systems of the other States parties to the Convention, does not apply systematically—in other words, every time the price has been more or less clearly underestimated—but only rarely and scarcely foreseeably. Furthermore, the State has other suitable methods at its disposal for discouraging tax evasion where it has serious grounds for suspecting that this is taking place; it can, for instance, take legal proceedings to recover unpaid tax and, if necessary, impose tax fines. Systematic use of these procedures, combined with the threat of criminal proceedings, should be an adequate weapon.

48. The Court considers that the question of proportionality must also be looked at from the point of view of the risk run by any purchaser that he will be subject to pre-emption and therefore penalised by the loss of his property solely in the interests of deterring possible underestimations of price. The exercise of the right of pre-emption entails sufficiently serious consequences for the measure to attain a definite level of severity. Merely reimbursing the price paid—increased by 10%—and the costs and fair expenses of the contract cannot suffice to compensate for the loss of a property acquired without any fraudulent intent.

49. Having regard to all these factors, the Court considers that, as a selected victim of the exercise of the right of pre-emption, Mrs Hentrich 'bore an individual and excessive burden' which could have been rendered legitimate only if she had had the possibility—which was refused her—of effectively challenging the measure taken against her; the 'fair balance which should be struck between the protection of the right of property and the requirements of the general interest' was therefore upset (see, *mutatis mutandis*, the *Sporrong and Lönnroth v Sweden* judgment of 23 September 1982, Series A No 52, p 28, para 73 . . .

D. CONCLUSION

50. Accordingly, there has been a breach of Article 1 of Protocol No 1 (P1-1)[by fivevotes to four] . . .

The judgment clearly strengthens the position of property owners by enabling them to assert procedural rights derived from Article 1 (in addition to their institutional rights under Article 6). Do you think it was significant for the Court's decision that no other Member State exercised a similar power of pre-emption over sales of real property (for a power of pre-emption over sales of artistic works: see *Beyeler v Italy* (above, p 924).

7   A highly political deprivation of possessions was found to have breached Article 1 by a Grand Chamber in *The Former King of Greece and Others v Greece*, judgment of 23 November 2000. The applicants were the former King Constantinos of Greece (a cousin of the Duke of Edinburgh), his sister and his aunt. The former King ascended the throne in 1964, when he was 24 years old. In April 1967 a military coup occurred and in December of that year the King left Greece. The military dictatorship maintained the crowned democracy until 1973, despite the King's self-imposed exile. In June 1973 the dictatorship purported to declare the former King and his heirs deposed and established a Presidential Parliamentary Republic. A few months later the dictatorship issued a legislative decree (No 225/1973) whereby all the moveable and immovable property of the former King and Royal family was confiscated. 120 million drachmas were provided in compensation and had to be claimed by the end of 1975 (the former King and his family never made a claim). In 1974 a civilian government replaced the military dictatorship and in December of that year the electorate voted in favour of a Parliamentary Republic. Between 1974 and 1979 the former King's property was managed by a legislative committee. During the 1980s negotiations took place between the socialist Government and the former King regarding his property and related tax liabilities. In 1992 the conservative Government and the former King reached an agreement whereby he sold certain lands to the State in return for a specified sum and he agreed to pay a defined amount in respect of his (and his family's) tax liabilities. During 1993 the socialists returned to power and in the following year they secured the passage of Law No 2215/1994 which, *inter alia*, rescinded the 1992 agreement and provided that the State was to become the owner of all the property belonging to the applicants. The latter sought to challenge the Law in the Greek courts, but the Special Supreme Court upheld the constitutionality of the measure. The applicants then complained to the Commission alleging a breach of, *inter alia*, their right to property guaranteed by Article 1 of Protocol 1. The Commission (unanimously) upheld their complaint and the case was referred to the Court.

The Government sought to argue that the estates allegedly owned by the applicants were connected with the position of Head of State and therefore fell outside the concept of 'possessions' protected by Article 1. The Court noted its established jurisprudence that the concept of 'possessions' had an autonomous meaning. Having regard to the applicants' evidence that their ancestors had purchased parts of the estates out of their private funds, had on numerous occasions transferred titles to areas of the estates between members of their family and third parties, and from 1974 to 1996 filed tax returns and paid tax in respect of these properties, the Grand Chamber held that:

65. . . . although the Court accepts that the royal property in many ways enjoyed a special status, the fact that the Greek State itself had repeatedly treated it as private property and had not produced a general set of rules governing its status prevents the Court from concluding that it had a *sui generis* and quasi-public character to the effect that it never belonged to the former royal family.

66. Therefore, the Court is of the opinion that the relevant properties were owned by the applicants as private persons rather than in their capacity as members of the royal family; accordingly the contested estates constituted a 'possession' for the purposes of Article 1 of Protocol No 1, which is applicable to the instant case.

The Court also considered that Law No 2215/1994 resulted in a 'deprivation' of the applicants' possessions falling within the second rule of Article 1. Despite the applicants' submission that Law No 2215 was an arbitrary and discriminatory measure the Grand Chamber, acknowledging the Greek Special Supreme Court's judgment upholding the constitutionality of this measure, found that the Law satisfied the condition in Article 1 that the deprivation of possessions was 'provided for by law'.

The next issue for the Court was whether the deprivation of the applicants' possessions pursued a legitimate aim 'in the public interest'. Two major goals were invoked by the Government. First, ecological and archaeological considerations in respect of the protection of special sites within the estates. Secondly, the public interest in preserving the constitutional status of Greece as a republic. Again, following its previous case law, the Court stated that:

87. . . . because of their direct knowledge of their society and its needs, the national authorities are in principle better placed than the international judge to appreciate what is 'in the public interest'. Under the system of protection established by the Convention, it is thus for the national authorities to make the initial assessment as to the existence of a problem of public concern warranting measures of deprivation of property. Here, as in other fields to which the safeguards of the Convention extend, the national authorities accordingly enjoy a certain margin of appreciation. Furthermore, the notion of 'public interest' is necessarily extensive. In particular, the decision to enact laws expropriating property will commonly involve consideration of political, economic and social issues. The Court, finding it natural that the margin of appreciation available to the legislature in implementing social and economic policies should be a wide one, will respect the legislature's judgment as to what is 'in the public interest' unless that judgment is manifestly without reasonable foundation (see the *James and Others v the United Kingdom* judgment of 21 February 1986, Series A No 98, p. 32, § 46). The same applies necessarily, if not *a fortiori*, to such fundamental changes of a country's constitutional system as the transition from monarchy to republic.

The Grand Chamber did not find any evidence to support the Government's asserted first aim of ecological/archaeological preservation. However, the Court upheld the second aim, '88. . . . it does not doubt that it was necessary for the Greek State to resolve an issue which it considered to be prejudicial for its status as a republic'.

The final element of Article 1 to be evaluated was whether the deprivation of the applicants' possessions struck a fair balance between the general interests of the community and the protection of the applicants' fundamental rights. The determination of this issue centred upon the applicants' complaint that Law No 2215/1994 did not provide for any compensation to be paid to them. The Court held that:

89. . . . Compensation terms under the relevant legislation are material to the assessment whether the contested measure respects the requisite fair balance and, notably, whether it imposes a disproportionate burden on the applicants. In this connection, the Court has already found that the taking of property without payment of an amount reasonably related to its value will normally constitute a disproportionate interference and a total lack of compensation can be considered justifiable under Article 1 of Protocol No 1 only in exceptional circumstances (see the *Holy Monasteries v Greece* judgment of 9 December 1994, Series A No 301-A, p 35, § 71).

90. In the present case there is no provision for compensation in Law No 2215/1994. Having regard to the fact that it has already been established that the interference in question satisfied the requirement of lawfulness and was not arbitrary, the lack of compensation does not make the taking of the applicants' property *eo ipso* wrongful (see *a contrario* the *Papamichalopoulos and Others v Greece (Article 50)* judgment of 31 October 1995, Series A No 330-B, pp 59–60, § 36). It remains therefore to be examined whether in the context of a lawful expropriation the applicants had to bear a disproportionate and excessive burden.

The Government argued that the deprivation of the applicants' property without compensation fell into the 'exceptional circumstances' category, because the applicants (and their ancestors) had acquired the properties as aspects of their royal duties and they had been granted privileges (including tax exemptions) for the former royal estates. However, the Court did not accept this submission:

98. The Court considers that the Government have failed to give a convincing explanation as to why the Greek authorities have not awarded any compensation to the applicants for the taking of their property. It accepts that the Greek State could have considered in good faith that exceptional circumstances justified the absence of compensation, but this assessment is not objectively substantiated.

In the first place, the Court points out that at least part of the expropriated property was purchased by the applicants' predecessors in title and paid out of their private funds. Moreover, compensation was provided for the last time the property was expropriated, in 1973. Therefore, the Court considers that the applicants had a legitimate expectation to be compensated by the Greek legislature for the taking of their estates.

Furthermore, as regards the Government's argument that the issue of compensation was indirectly covered, the Court notes first that compensation provided for by Legislative Decree No 225/1973 is irrelevant to the instant case, Law No 2215/1994 being the sole legal basis for the interference of which the applicants complain. Nor can the circumstances to which the Government refer be regarded as payment of compensation. In this respect the Court agrees with the applicants when they argue that in the context of the expropriation in question there are no reciprocal or mutual debts to be set off against each other. The privileges afforded in the past to the royal family or the tax exemptions and the writing off of all the taxes owed by the former royal family have no direct relevance to the issue of proportionality, but could possibly be taken into account in order to make an accurate assessment of the applicants' claims for just satisfaction under Article 41 of the Convention.

99. Therefore the Court is of the opinion that the lack of any compensation for the deprivation of the applicants' property upsets, to the detriment of the applicants, the fair balance between the protection of property and the requirements of public interest.

There has accordingly been a violation of Article 1 of Protocol No 1.

Although fifteen judges found a breach of Article 1, two (Judges Koumantos and Zupancic) dissented. They considered that Article 1 applied to private property and not to 'property assigned to certain persons in connection with their public duties, even where such property also retains some features governed by private law'. In their opinion the facts that (1) a large proportion of the applicants' estates had been given to their ancestors by state bodies, (2) these properties had been subject to favourable legal regimes of taxation and succession and (3) during times of political favour the royal family's rights over these properties were confirmed by special laws, meant that these estates fell outside the protection of P1-1.

Jurisprudentially the above judgment is significant for confirming the broad scope of the autonomous concept of possessions under Article 1. The Grand Chamber was willing to accept that real property fell within this concept even where it had been acquired/retained by a royal family in legally privileged circumstances. Although the Court, following established case law, granted the Greek legislature a wide margin of appreciation in assessing whether there was a 'public interest' justifying depriving the applicants' of their estates, the Court rejected one of the Government's purported legitimate aims. The inability of the Government to produce supporting evidence that the deprivation was directed at preserving ecological/archaeological sites within the estates undermined the credibility of this asserted public interest goal. Hence, even where States have considerable freedom of action under the Convention, the Court will ensure that its European supervision is not merely a theoretical role but a practical safeguard against arbitrary behaviour by national authorities. The underlying political context of the taking of the applicants' estates was revealed by *The Times* newspaper. According to Alan Hamilton: 'King Constantine's lands were seized in 1994 by the Government of Costas Mitsotakis, enraged that the former monarch and his family had set foot in the country at Salonika airport on their way to a cruise round the Greek islands' (24 November 2000). In a separate judgment, given on 28 November 2002, the Grand Chamber awarded the applicants' 13.2 million euros compensation for pecuniary damage (see above p 871[Art 41]).

8   A Chamber was very divided over the question whether a property development company had suffered a deprivation of its possessions through the operation of the English law of adverse possession in *J.A. Pye (Oxford) Ltd v United Kingdom*, judgment of 15 November 2005. The applicant company was the registered owner of twenty-three hectares of agricultural land in Berkshire. Until December 1983 the applicant authorised a neighbouring farmer to occupy the land for grazing. In that month a surveyor, acting for the applicant, wrote to the farmer informing him that he must vacate the land. In January 1984 the applicant refused the farmer's request for a further grazing agreement, as the applicant wished to apply for planning permission to develop the land. Nevertheless, the farmer remained in occupation of the land (in June 1984 the applicant agreed to allow the farmer to cut and use the grass on the land for a payment). The applicant did not respond to the farmer's requests for an extension of the grazing agreement. From September 1984 the farmer continued to occupy and use the applicant's land without the latter's permission. In 1997 the farmer registered cautions in the Land Registry against the applicant's title on the ground that he had acquired to the land by adverse possession (the Limitation Act 1980 and the Land Registration Act 1925 provided that after twelve years of adverse possession the registered owner of land was deemed to hold the land in trust for the squatter). The applicant company challenged the farmer's claim (the former contended the land was worth at least £10 million) through the domestic courts. Eventually, the House of Lords ruled in favour of the farmer. Lord Bingham was highly critical of the operation of the law of adverse possession as it applied to the applicant company (the Land Registration Act 2002 increased the procedural and substantive protection to registered landowners against squatters, but the Act was not retrospective in effect). The applicant could not rely on the Human Rights Act 1998 as it too was not retrospective. The applicant complained to Strasbourg alleging a breach of Article 1 of Protocol No 1. A bare majority of the

Chamber (four votes to three) considered that the respondent State was responsible for the deprivation of the applicant's property because it was the legislation which entitled the squatter to obtain ownership of the land. Furthermore, the majority considered that when the lack of procedural protection (i.e. statutory notification to registered landowners that a squatter was seeking to assert a claim of adverse possession) was combined with the absence of any legal duty on squatters to pay compensation to the registered owner in respect of the value of the land acquired via adverse possession the consequent excessive burden placed on the applicant by the legislation was an unfair balance between the demands of the public interest and the applicant's right to the peaceful enjoyment of its possessions. Therefore, the State had violated Article 1.

Judges Maruste, Garlicki, and Borrego Borrego issued a Joint Dissention Opinion in which they expressed the view that:

2. The real 'fault' in this case, if there has been any, lies with the applicant companies, rather than with the Government. It has to be born in mind that the applicant company was not a private individual or an ordinary company with, one could assume, limited knowledge on relevant real estate legislation. They were a specialised professional real estate developers and such a company had or should have had full knowledge about relevant legislation and the duties involved. . . . The Government have done no more than continue to operate a mechanism which, at the end of a relatively long limitation period, adjusts land ownership to reflect the fact that an action for adverse possession is time barred.

Possession (ownership) carries not only rights but also and always some duties. The purpose of the relevant legislation was to behove a landowner to be vigilant, to protect the possession and not to 'sleep on his or her rights'. . . . The duty in this particular case—to do no more than begin an action for repossession within 12 years—cannot be regarded as excessive or unreasonable.

Whilst the majority were clearly influenced by criticism of the former legal regime by some domestic judges and the Law Commission do you think the applicant company had suffered a disproportionate loss of their property rights? In April 2006 the Grand Chamber accepted the case for a re-hearing under Article 43.

The Third Rule: The right of States to control the use of property

....

Chassagnou v France (1999) 29 EHRR 615
European Court of Human Rights

Prior to the French revolution of 1789 only the nobility possessed the right to hunt. Subsequently the right was accorded to landowners. However, case-law established the notion of tacit consent which enabled hunters to hunt on the land of others provided the latter had not expressly manifested their opposition (e.g. by placing 'private hunting' notices on their lands). In the south of France, where landholdings tended to be small, the theory of tacit consent led to an almost unlimited freedom to hunt (known as *chasse banale*—public hunting). The result was virtually unregulated hunting and the decimation of various game species in different regions. Consequently, the *Loi Verdeille* (Law No 64–696) was enacted in 1964. This provided for the establishment of approved municipal hunters' associations (*associations communales de chasse agreees*—ACCAs), to improve the technical organization of hunting, the preservation of game stocks and the destruction of vermin. Under the Law the owners of landholdings below a specified size, which varied from one *departement* to another, were obliged to become members of any ACCA created in their municipality and to transfer to it the hunting rights over their land in order to create municipal hunting grounds. By 1996 ACCAs had been established in 851 municipalities in thirty-nine *departements*. The applicants were small landowners in areas subject to ACCAs who objected on ethical grounds to hunting. The domestic courts refused to allow them to prevent ACCAs hunting on their land. They complained to the Commission alleging, *inter alia*, a breach of Article 1 (their complaints under Article 11 have already been examined above, p 765). The Commission found a breach of that provision by twenty-seven votes to five.

A. APPLICABILITY OF ARTICLE 1 OF PROTOCOL NO 1

71. Those appearing before the Court agreed that the compulsory transfer of hunting rights over land to an ACCA pursuant to the Loi Verdeille was to be analysed in the light of the second paragraph of Article 1 of Protocol No 1, which reserved to States the right to enact such laws as they deemed necessary to control the use of property in accordance with the general interest. They disagreed on the other hand as to whether there had actually been an interference with the applicants' right to use their property.

72. The applicants submitted that the obligation for them to transfer hunting rights over their land to an ACCA, against their will and without compensation or consideration, constituted an abnormal deprivation of their right to use their property, firstly in that they were obliged to tolerate the presence of hunters on their land, whereas they were opposed to hunting for ethical reasons, and secondly in that they could not use the land they owned for the creation of nature reserves where hunting was prohibited.

73. The Government, on the other hand, submitted that the interference with the applicants' right of property was minor since they had not really been deprived of their right to use their property. The Loi Verdeille had not abolished the right to hunt, which was one attribute of the right of property, but was only intended to attenuate the exclusive exercise of that right by landowners. The only thing the applicants had lost was their right to prevent other people from hunting on their land. But hunting was only practised for six months of the year and Article L. 222-10 of the Countryside Code expressly provided that land within a 150 metre radius of any dwelling (a total area of seven hectares) was not to be hunted over by ACCA members.

74. The Court notes that, although the applicants have not been deprived of their right to use their property, to lease it or to sell it, the compulsory transfer of the hunting rights over their land to an ACCA prevents them from making use of the right to hunt, which is directly linked to the right of property, as they see fit. In the present case the applicants do not wish to hunt on their land and object to the fact that others may come onto their land to hunt. However, although opposed to hunting on ethical grounds, they are obliged to tolerate the presence of armed men and gun dogs on their land every year. This restriction on the free exercise of the right of use undoubtedly constitutes an interference with the applicants' enjoyment of their rights as the owners of property. Accordingly, the second paragraph of Article 1 is applicable in the case.

B. COMPLIANCE WITH THE CONDITIONS LAID DOWN IN THE SECOND PARAGRAPH

75. It is well-established case-law that the second paragraph of Article 1 of Protocol No 1 must be construed in the light of the principle laid down in the first sentence of the Article. Consequently, an interference must achieve a 'fair balance' between the demands of the general interest of the community and the requirements of the protection of the individual's fundamental rights. The search for this balance is reflected in the structure of Article 1 as a whole, and therefore also in the second paragraph thereof: there must be a reasonable relationship of proportionality between the means employed and

the aim pursued. In determining whether this requirement is met, the Court recognises that the State enjoys a wide margin of appreciation with regard both to choosing the means of enforcement and to ascertaining whether the consequences of enforcement are justified in the general interest for the purpose of achieving the object of the law in question . . .

1. AIM OF THE INTERFERENCE

76. The applicants disputed the legitimacy of the aim of the Loi Verdeille. They submitted that it had not been enacted in the general interest but only for the benefit of a specific category of people, namely hunters, since the law itself stated that the aim of the ACCAs was 'to improve the technical organisation of hunting so that the sport [could] be practised in a more satisfactory manner'. The law contemplated wild fauna only in the form of 'game', in other words those species which were traditionally hunted. As for the destruction of vermin, which the creation of the ACCAs was also supposed to promote, the applicants submitted that, even where an ACCA had been set up, the right to destroy vermin was the exclusive prerogative of landowners, persons in possession or tenant farmers (Article L.227-8 of the Countryside Code) and could only be delegated, if necessary, to an ACCA.

77. The applicants further submitted that the detailed rules for implementation of the Loi Verdeille revealed the lack of any justificatory general interest. The compulsory transfer of hunting rights over land to ACCAs was an exception in French law from the principle that no one had the right to hunt on another's land without his consent, a right which also implied, in the applicants' submission, the right not to hunt. But the Loi Verdeille flouted individual beliefs since it did not even contemplate the possibility that there could be landowners who did not wish to hunt. Lastly, for the efficient exploitation of game stocks, there was no need whatsoever for a pre-emption mechanism like the one introduced by the Loi Verdeille. They asserted that, more than thirty years after its enactment, out of 36,200 municipalities in metropolitan France only about 9,200 had ACCAs, roughly 8,700 of which had come into being through application of the compulsory scheme, as against only about 500 formed voluntarily with the agreement of a majority of landowners. The Loi Verdeille was not applicable in the three *départements* of Bas-Rhin, Haut-Rhin and Moselle or on public property belonging to the State or the local and regional authorities. According to the applicants, the fact that the scheme was not generally applicable proved that there was no general interest, the ACCAs existing merely to manage hunting as a leisure activity. They submitted that in France the hunters' lobby, even though it represented only 3% of the population, imposed its policies and forced through rules in breach of European Community law and international law, which afforded better protection to nature. They cited, as evidence of this, the fact that France was the only European country which permitted the shooting of migratory birds during the month of February, in spite of a judgment of the Court of Justice of the European Communities, a judgment of the *Conseil d'Etat* of 10 March 1995 and more than a hundred judgments from all the administrative courts in the country applying an EEC directive.

78. The Government argued that it would be simplistic to assess the general-interest aspect of the Loi Verdeille only by the yardstick of improvements to hunting for the sole benefit of hunters. Stocks of wild fauna and respect for property and crops all benefited from the proper organisation of hunting. The Government pointed out that hunting was an activity with very firm roots in French rural tradition. However, the rule that no one had the right to hunt on land he did not own had been disregarded for many years in an area covering well over half of France. One of the main objectives of the Loi Verdeille, therefore, had been the establishment of a unit of management, without which any rational organisation of hunting, consistent with respect for the environment, had become impossible. In addition, the ACCAs played an educational role, thanks to hunters' participation in the running of the association and the formulation of hunting policy and to the self-policing discipline imposed on all members, whether hunters or not, by the rules of the association and the hunting regulations, with penalties to back them up. The Government likewise rejected the applicants' argument that because the

Loi Verdeille was not applied throughout French territory it did not serve any general interest. They maintained that it could be generally applied throughout the country under democratic conditions, namely the compulsory creation of an ACCA only after consultation of the *département* council, the Chamber of Agriculture and the Hunters' Federation in the *département* concerned, and voluntary creation in other cases. Lastly, the law could not be applied in every part of France because the need to pool hunting grounds depended on the geography of individual *départements*. For example, there could be no question of setting up ACCAs in mountainous or very built-up regions or in *départements* where hunting was already organised.

79. The Court considers that in view of the aims which the Loi Verdeille assigns to the ACCAs, as listed in section 1 thereof, and the explanations provided on this subject, it is undoubtedly in the general interest to avoid unregulated hunting and encourage the rational management of game stocks.

2. PROPORTIONALITY OF THE INTERFERENCE

80. The applicants asserted that the compulsory transfer of hunting rights over their land to an ACCA was a disproportionate interference with the right to the peaceful enjoyment of their possessions. They submitted that they had no means of avoiding this transfer, in spite of the applications they had made to the ACCAs or the prefects to obtain the removal of their properties from the hunting grounds of the ACCAs concerned. They maintained that there was no need to pre-empt small landholdings for the benefit of hunters' associations in order to rationalise game stocks. In those *départements* or municipalities where there were no ACCAs the fact that some landowners did not wish to hunt themselves and prohibited hunting on their land did not cause any problems, either with regard to the proliferation of certain species or with regard to species designated as vermin, which only the owners of the land had the right to destroy.

81. The Government rejected this argument. They submitted that the Loi Verdeille provided a broad range of means whereby landowners who wished to avoid its application could do so. They referred in that connection to the fact that it was open to the applicants to enclose their properties (Articles L. 222-10 and L. 224-3 of the Countryside Code, see paragraph 46 above), to acquire, in accordance with Article R. 222-54 of the Code, additional land contiguous with their own forming a single block exceeding the minimum area laid down in Article L. 222-13 of the Code ... or to ask the ACCAs to include their land in the game reserve that each ACCA was required to set up pursuant to Article L. 222-21 of the Code ...

In addition, the applicants could have asked the Minister or the prefect to include their land in a game reserve or a game and wildlife reserve (Articles L. 222-25 and R. 222-83 of the Code ... Similarly, they could have asked for their land to be decreed a nature reserve or applied for it to be designated as a voluntary nature reserve (Articles L. 242-1 and L. 242-11 of the Countryside Code ...

The Government further emphasised that owners were not compelled to transfer their hunting rights to an ACCA without receiving any consideration; they admittedly lost their exclusive right to hunt but this loss was made good by the fact that for their part they could hunt throughout the ACCA's hunting grounds.

Moreover, compulsory transfer entitled landowners to compensation where on that account they had lost profits through deprivation of a previous source of income (Article L. 222-16 of the Countryside Code ...)

82. The Court considers that none of the options mentioned by the Government would in practice have been capable of absolving the applicants from the statutory obligation to transfer hunting rights over their land to ACCAs. It notes in particular that the fence referred to in Article 224-3 must be continuous, unbroken and incapable of being breached by game animals or human beings, which presupposes that it must be of a certain height and strength. The applicants could not be required to incur considerable expense in order to avoid the obligation to transfer the hunting rights over their land to

the ACCAs. Such a requirement seems all the more unreasonable because the financial viability of using the land in question, apart from Mrs Montion's property, for agricultural purposes would to a large extent be jeopardised by the erection of such a fence.

As to the assertion that it was open to the applicants to ask for their land to be included in a game reserve or nature reserve, the Court notes that neither the ACCAs, nor the Minister nor the prefect are required to grant such requests from private individuals, as shown by the refusals of the applicants' requests in the present case . . . Lastly, it can be seen from the provisions relating to nature reserves . . . that the applicants could not claim to satisfy the specific conditions for designation.

With regard to the various forms of statutory consideration mentioned by the Government, the Court takes the view that these cannot be considered to represent fair compensation for loss of the right of use. It is clear that it was intended in the Loi Verdeille of 1964 for each landowner subject to compulsory transfer to be compensated for deprivation of the exclusive right to hunt on his land by the concomitant right to hunt throughout those parts of the municipality's territory under ACCA control. However, that compensation is valuable only in so far as all the landowners concerned are hunters or accept hunting. But the 1964 Act does not contemplate any measure of compensation for landowners opposed to hunting, who, by definition, do not wish to derive any advantage or profit from a right to hunt which they refuse to exercise. Similarly, compensation for the loss of profits caused by deprivation of a previous source of income concerns only landowners who, before the creation of an ACCA in their municipality, derived income from exercise of their hunting rights, by renting them out for example; this did not apply to the applicants in the present case.

As they are all owners of properties smaller than the minimum areas required for a valid objection . . . the applicants could not therefore avoid the compulsory transfer of the hunting rights over their land to the ACCAs of their municipalities.

83. However, such compulsory transfer is an exception to the general principle laid down by Article 544 of the Civil Code, which provides that ownership means the right to enjoy and dispose of things in the most absolute manner, provided that one does not use them in a way prohibited by law. The compulsory transfer of the right to hunt, which in French law is one of the attributes of the right of property, also derogates from the principle laid down by Article L. 222-1 of the Countryside Code, according to which no one may hunt on land belonging to another without the owner's consent. The Court further notes that under Article R. 228-1 breaches of that rule are punishable by the penalties laid down for Class 5 offences. Lastly, it should be noted that in French law (Article R. 227-7) landowners bear personal responsibility for the destruction of vermin, and that this responsibility, if necessary, may only be delegated in writing to an ACCA, or to any other person of the owner's choice.

84. The Court further observes that, following the adoption in 1964 of the Loi Verdeille, which excluded from the outset the *départements* of Bas-Rhin, Haut-Rhin and Moselle, only 29 of the 93 *départements* concerned in metropolitan France have been made subject to the regime of compulsory creation of ACCAs, that ACCAs have been voluntarily set up in only 851 municipalities and that the Law applies only to landholdings less than 20 hectares in area, to the exclusion of both large private estates and State land . . .

85. In conclusion, notwithstanding the legitimate aims of the Loi Verdeille when it was adopted, the Court considers that the result of the compulsory-transfer system which it lays down has been to place the applicants in a situation which upsets the fair balance to be struck between protection of the right of property and the requirements of the general interest. Compelling small landowners to transfer hunting rights over their land so that others can make use of them in a way which is totally incompatible with their beliefs imposes a disproportionate burden which is not justified under the second paragraph of Article 1 of Protocol No 1. There has therefore been a violation of that provision.

. . .

FOR THESE REASONS THE COURT

Holds by twelve votes to five that there has been a breach of Article 1 of Protocol No 1 . . .

Holds unanimously that the respondent State is to pay each of the nine applicants . . . the sum of 30,000 French francs for non-pecuniary damage . . .

NOTES

1 The Court was composed of President Wildhaber and Judges: Palm, Makarczyk, Kuris, Fuhrmann, Jungwiert, Fischbach, Vaji, Thomassen, Tsatsa-Nikolovska, Baka, and Levits.

2 Judge Caflisch, joined by Judge Pantiru, issued a Partly Dissenting Opinion in which he expressed the view that:

. . . In the present case the legislation complained of has three objectives, namely, to regulate a leisure activity which, if left unregulated, would present a real danger, to democratise hunting and to set up a system for the rational and effective management of game stocks, thus also ensuring the protection of the environment. . . .

  Thus one may take the view, unlike the majority of the Court, that there has been no breach of the Article in question, taken separately, because of the importance of the objective pursued by the *Loi Verdeille*, which goes beyond the mere regulation of a leisure activity, having economic and ecological aspects, because of the margin of appreciation left to the Government in the choice of means to attain that objective and because of the absence of any obvious disproportion between the objective concerned and the means adopted to attain it.

3 In his Dissenting Opinion Judge Costa stated:

3. Above all, it must be pointed out that the object and result of the Loi Verdeille, which has been applied for some thirty-five years, has been to regulate hunting in France, especially in the south of France where, on account of the subdivision of rural landholdings and a very great freedom to hunt, hunting (known as 'public hunting') had become almost a free-for-all. This had a bad effect on game, crops and, in the final analysis, the whole ecosystem. Far from being confined to securing the selfish interests of hunters, the Loi Verdeille pursues a real general-interest objective, namely mitigating the effects of the subdivision of landholdings and preventing poaching, while encouraging the destruction of vermin and making possible the establishment of game reserves. . . .

10. While a balance has to be struck between the general interest and this limited interference with the use of property, I do not find the second pan of the scales to be any heavier than the first, unless one gives way to the temptation to make a god of the right of property, which to my mind would be wrong. We should not render any town planning, regional development, public works, consolidation of land-holdings and the like impossible. One can be wholly in favour of freedom and the rule of law—as the framers of the Convention were—without necessarily making individual freedom an absolute or excluding the general interest from the rule of law—which was manifestly not the intention of those who drafted the Convention. With regard to hunting, an area where each State should have a wide margin of appreciation, and where many European States have laws which restrict the right of private property in order to implement a hunting policy, it seems to me that the Court's judgment goes in an very individualist direction, which will make this type of policy very difficult to conduct. In any event, I have great difficulty in finding in the present case a violation of Article 1 of Protocol No 1. . . .

4 For other cases where the Court has considered opposition to hunting under different Convention provisions see: *Steel v UK* (1998), above p 705 and *Hashman and Harrup v UK* (1999), above p 693.

5 The judgment in *Chassagnou* reveals that the Court follows the common approach to the interpretation of Article 1 when applying the third rule. This involves the application of the 'fair balance' test and its constituent element the requirement of proportionality.

6 The powers of customs authorities were evaluated under the third rule in *Air Canada v UK*, A.316-A (1995) 20 EHRR 150. Between 1983 and 1987 there had been a number of incidents which had raised concerns in the British Customs and Excise regarding the adequacy of the applicant company's security procedures at Heathrow airport. During 1983–4 a series of consignments, believed by Customs to have contained illicit drugs, disappeared from the applicant's transit shed. In March 1986, 809 kilograms of cannabis resin were discovered in a consignment from India. Two months later 300 kilograms of cannabis resin were also intercepted in a consignment from Thailand (two of the company's staff were subsequently convicted in connection with this importation). Customs wrote to the company expressing concern about the large amounts of drugs being smuggled into the country with the assistance of Air Canada employees. In December 1986, Customs wrote to all the airline operators at Heathrow warning them of possible penalties (including the seizure and forfeiture of aircraft) if illegal drugs were found aboard their planes. On 27 April 1987 a Tristar aircraft (worth £60 million) owned by the applicant landed at Heathrow. It was found to contain 331 kilograms of cannabis resin (with a street value of £800,000). On the morning of 1 May 1987, while passengers were waiting to board the plane, Customs officers exercised their statutory powers to seize the aircraft as liable to forfeiture. Later that day the Commissioners of Customs delivered the aircraft back to the applicant on payment of a penalty (£50,000). The applicant unsuccessfully sought to challenge the Commissioners' actions in the English courts. The company then complained to the Commission. The latter found no violation of Article 1 (nine votes to five). The Court held that:

33. . . . the seizure of the aircraft amounted to a temporary restriction on its use and did not involve a transfer of ownership, and, in the second place, that the decision of the Court of Appeal to condemn the property as forfeited did not have the effect of depriving Air Canada of ownership since the sum required for the release of the aircraft had been paid . . .

34. In addition, it is clear from the scheme of the legislation that the release of the aircraft subject to the payment of a sum of money was, in effect, a measure taken in furtherance of a policy of seeking to prevent carriers from bringing, inter alia, prohibited drugs into the United Kingdom. As such, it amounted to a control of the use of property. It is therefore the second paragraph of Article 1 (P1-1) which is applicable in the present case . . .

B. COMPLIANCE WITH THE REQUIREMENTS OF THE SECOND PARAGRAPH

35. It remains to be decided whether the interference with the applicant's property rights was in conformity with the State's right under the second paragraph of Article 1 of Protocol No 1 (P1-1) 'to enforce such laws as it deems necessary to control the use of property in accordance with the general interest'.

36. According to the Court's well-established case-law, the second paragraph of Article 1 (P1-1) must be construed in the light of the principle laid down in the Article's (P1-1) first sentence . . .

41. While the width of the powers of forfeiture conferred on the Commissioners . . . is striking, the seizure of the applicant's aircraft and its release subject to payment were undoubtedly exceptional measures which were resorted to in order to bring about an improvement in the company's security procedures. These measures were taken following the discovery of a container, the shipment of which involved various transport irregularities, holding 331 kilograms of cannabis resin . . . Moreover, this incident was the latest in a long series of alleged security lapses which had been brought to Air Canada's attention involving the illegal importation of drugs into the United Kingdom during the period 1983–87 . . . In particular, Air Canada—along with other operators—had been warned in a letter dated 15 December 1986 from the Commissioners that, where prohibited goods have been carried, they would consider exercising their powers under the 1979 Act including the seizure and forfeiture of aircraft.

42. Against this background there can be no doubt that the measures taken conformed to the general interest in combating international drug trafficking. . . .

47. Finally, taking into account the large quantity of cannabis that was found in the container, its street value as well as the value of the aircraft that had been seized, the Court does not consider the requirement to pay £50,000 to be disproportionate to the aim pursued, namely the prevention of the importation of prohibited drugs into the United Kingdom.

48. Bearing in mind the above, as well as the State's margin of appreciation in this area, it considers that, in the circumstances of the present case, a fair balance was achieved. There has thus been no violation of Article 1 of Protocol No 1 (P1-1). (by five votes to four)

Hence, the Court is willing to find the use of draconian powers of control over private property, by customs authorities, to be compatible with the third rule where the relevant property has been involved in a serious infringement of customs rules. The proportionality element of the third rule indicates that the more serious the breach of national customs prohibitions (e.g. the greater the value of the illicit products involved) the more extensive the customs authorities powers of control over property can be. Persistent breaches of customs regulations by a person will be another factor justifying the exercise of significant powers of control over that person's property by custom authorities. For an analysis of the British authorities powers see: A. R. Mowbray, 'The Compounding of Proceedings by the Customs and Excise: Calculating the Legal Implications' (1988) *British Tax Review* 290.

7   The ability of States to control the use of property in order to 'secure the payment of taxes' was examined in *Gasus Dosier-und Fordertechnik Gmb v The Netherlands* (examined above, p 907). The Court elaborated the background and application of that aspect of the third rule in the following terms:

59. . . . the most natural approach, in the Court's opinion, is to examine Gasus's complaints under the head of 'securing the payment of taxes', which comes under the rule in the second paragraph of Article 1 (P1-1). That paragraph explicitly reserves the right of Contracting States to pass such laws as they may deem necessary to secure the payment of taxes. The importance which the drafters of the Convention attached to this aspect of the second paragraph of Article 1 (P1-1) may be gauged from the fact that at a stage when the proposed text did not contain such explicit reference to taxes, it was already understood to reserve the States' power to pass whatever fiscal laws they considered desirable, provided always that measures in this field did not amount to arbitrary confiscation (see Sir David Maxwell-Fyfe, Rapporteur of the Committee on Legal and Administrative Questions, Second Session of the Consultative Assembly, Sixteenth Sitting (25 August 1950), Collected Edition of the Travaux préparatoires, vol VI, p 140, commenting on the text of the proposed Article 10A, ibid, p 68).

The fact that current tax legislation makes it possible for the tax authorities, on certain conditions, to recover tax debts against a third party's assets does not warrant any different conclusion as to the applicable rule. Neither does it suffice in itself to describe section 16(3) of the 1845 Act as granting powers of arbitrary confiscation.

Conferring upon a particular creditor the power to recover against goods which, although in fact in the debtor's possession, are legally owned by third parties is, in several legal systems, an accepted method of strengthening that creditor's position in enforcement proceedings. Under Netherlands law as it stood at the material time, landlords had a comparable power with respect to unpaid rent, as they did also under French and Belgian law; the Government have also cited several provisions in the tax laws of other member States that give similar powers to the tax authorities in special cases. Consequently, the fact that the Netherlands legislature has seen fit to strengthen the tax authorities' position in enforcement proceedings against tax debtors does not justify the conclusion that the 1845

Act, or section 16(3) of it, is not aimed at 'securing the payment of taxes', or that using the power conferred by that section constitutes a 'confiscation', whether 'arbitrary' or not, rather than a method of recovering a tax debt.

C. COMPLIANCE WITH THE CONDITIONS LAID DOWN IN THE SECOND PARAGRAPH

60. As follows from the previous paragraph, the present case concerns the right of States to enact such laws as they deem necessary for the purpose of 'securing the payment of taxes'.

In the present case the Court is not called upon to ascertain whether this right, as the wording of the provision may suggest, is limited to procedural tax laws (that is to say: laws which regulate the formalities of taxation, including the enforcement of tax debts) or whether it also covers substantive tax laws (that is to say: laws which lay down the circumstances under which tax is due and the amounts payable); the 1845 Act, which is at issue in the present case, was plainly a procedural tax law.

In passing such laws the legislature must be allowed a wide margin of appreciation, especially with regard to the question whether—and if so, to what extent—the tax authorities should be put in a better position to enforce tax debts than ordinary creditors are in to enforce commercial debts. The Court will respect the legislature's assessment in such matters unless it is devoid of reasonable foundation.

The tax power was also applied in the *National & Provincial Building Society* case, above p 908.

9 A unanimous Chamber found a systemic breach of this rule in respect of Polish legislation governing the rents chargeable by private landlords and restrictions on their ability to terminate leases in *Hutten-Czapska v Poland*, judgment of 22 February 2005. The applicant owned a house and plot of land in Gdynia, which had previously belonged to her parents. The house had been subject to state management throughout the period of communist government and had been occupied by various persons designated by the authorities. After the restoration of democracy in Poland the applicant obtained a court order, in 1990, registering her title to the property. The next year she took over management of the property. However, during the subsequent years various statutes placed severe limits on her ability to increase the level of rent chargeable to the established tenants and prevented her from terminating their leases. The Polish Constitutional Court found several of these statutory provisions to be unconstitutional because, *inter alia*, the low levels of rent chargeable only enabled landlords to recover about 60 per cent of the maintenance costs of their properties. In her complaint to the European Court the applicant contended that these restrictions impaired the essence of her right of property. The Chamber concluded that:

185. As the Court has already stated on many occasions, in spheres such as housing of the population, States necessarily enjoy a wide margin of appreciation not only in regard to the existence of the problem of general concern warranting measures for control of individual property but also to the choice of the measures and their implementation. The State control over levels of rent is one of such measures and its application may often cause significant reductions in the amount of rent chargeable (see, in particular, *Mellacher and Others* [v Austria, A. 169 (1989)] § 45).

Also, in situations where, as in the present case, the operation of the rent-control legislation involves wide-reaching consequences for numerous individuals and has significant economic and social consequences for the country as a whole, the authorities must have considerable discretion not only in choosing the form and deciding on the extent of control over the use of property but also in deciding on the appropriate timing for the enforcement of the relevant laws. Nevertheless, that discretion, however considerable, is not unlimited and its exercise, even in the context of the most complex reform of the State, cannot entail consequences at variance with the Convention standards (see *Broniowski*, § 182).

186. The Court once again acknowledges that the difficult housing situation in Poland, in particular an acute shortage of dwellings and the high cost of acquiring flats on the market, and the need to transform the extremely rigid system of distribution of dwellings inherited from the communist regime, justified not only the introduction of remedial legislation protecting tenants during the period of the fundamental reform of the country's political, economic and legal system but also the setting of a low rent, at a level beneath the market value. Yet it finds no justification for the State's continued failure to secure to the applicant and other landlords throughout the entire period under consideration the sums necessary to cover maintenance costs, not to mention even a minimum profit from the lease of flats.

187. Some five years ago the Polish Constitutional Court found that the operation of the rent-control scheme based on the provisions necessarily and unavoidably entailing losses for landlords had resulted in a disproportionate, unjustified and arbitrary distribution of the social burden involved in the housing reform and that the reform had been effected mainly at the expense of landlords. It reiterated that statement in its subsequent judgments, clearly indicating that the failure to abolish the rent-control system by 31 December 2004 might result in a breach of the constitutional principle of the rule of law and undermine citizens' confidence in the State. It repeatedly held that the adopted measures amounted to a continuing violation of the property rights of landlords. It stressed that the manner in which the authorities calculated increases in rent made it impossible, for purely mathematical reasons, for landlords to receive an income from rent or at least recover their maintenance costs.

In the circumstances, it was incumbent on the Polish authorities to eliminate, or at least to remedy with the requisite promptness, the situation found to have been incompatible with the requirements of the applicant's fundamental right of property in line with the Constitutional Court's judgments. Furthermore, the principle of lawfulness in Article 1 of Protocol No 1 and of the foreseeability of the law ensuing from that rule required the State to fulfil its legislative promise to repeal the rent-control scheme—which by no means excluded the adoption of procedures protecting the rights of tenants in a different manner.

188. Having regard to all the foregoing circumstances and, more particularly, to the consequences which the operation of the rent-control scheme entailed for the exercise of the applicant's right to the peaceful enjoyment of her possessions, the Court holds that the authorities imposed a disproportionate and excessive burden on her, which cannot be justified by any legitimate interest of the community pursued by them.

There has accordingly been a violation of Article 1 of Protocol No 1.

As the Chamber recognized that its judgment would affect 100,000 Polish landlords and between 600,000 and 900,000 tenants it stated, under Article 46, that the respondent Government must, '192. ... through appropriate legal and/or other measures, secure a reasonable level of rent to the applicant and those similarly situated, or provide them with a mechanism mitigating the above-mentioned consequences of the State control of rent increases for their right of property.' However, it was for the State to determine what was a reasonable rent or a suitable mitigation scheme. The long-term draconian restrictions placed upon the applicant's control of her property, involving both a significant financial loss in respect of the permitted rent and her inability to gain occupation of the property, meant that even allowing the State a 'wide margin of appreciation' a fair balanced had not been achieved between her rights and the interests of society as a whole. Do you think it was significant that the Polish Constitutional Court had found the relevant domestic legislation to be unconstitutional on several occasions?

Subsequently, the Government successfully petitioned the Grand Chamber to re-hear the case under Article 43. However, the Grand Chamber, unanimously, found a breach of Article 1 of Protocol No 1. The Grand Chamber (Judgment of 19 June 2006) agreed with the Chamber's analysis observing that:

224. ... the violation of the right of property in the present case is not exclusively linked to the question of the levels of rent chargeable but, rather, consists in the combined effect of defective provisions on the determination of rent and various restrictions on landlords' rights in respect of termination of leases, the statutory financial burdens imposed on them and the absence of any legal ways and means making it possible for them either to offset or mitigate the losses incurred in connection with the maintenance of property or to have the necessary repairs subsidised by the State in justified cases.

22 FIRST PROTOCOL ARTICLE 2: RIGHT TO EDUCATION

The Court's general approach

'Belgian Linguistic' case (No 2) A.6 (1968) 1 EHRR 252
European Court of Human Rights

When Belgium gained independence in 1830 it was in practice composed of two areas, the Flemish (where the inhabitants generally spoke Dutch) and the Walloon (where the population generally spoke French). Many of the activities of government were conducted in French (e.g. judicial proceedings). Education was also dominated by the French language. Between 1900 and 1930 a Flemish separatist movement gained popularity and as a result legislation was passed, in 1932, to place the Dutch and French languages on an equal footing. During 1963 new legislation was enacted which divided the national territory into four linguistic regions: the Flemish, French, German and the Brussels conurbation. In the first three regions the legislation required the exclusive use of the Flemish, French and German languages in each of those regions for official purposes. Special arrangements were made for the bilingual communes on the edges of Brussels. The legislation provided that generally state funded schools would only teach in the designated official language of their region and public funds would not be provided to private schools which did not also teach in the relevant official language. Six applications were made to the Commission challenging different aspects of the above legislation by French speaking parents (of over 800 children) residing in Dutch speaking areas of Belgium. The applicants alleged breaches of Article 2 of the First Protocol (P1-2), Article 14 and Article 8. The Commission reported that the legislation was not in breach of the first sentence of P1-2 (nine votes to three) or the second sentence of that Article (unanimously). But, *inter alia*, parts of the legislation applying to Louvain and communes on the periphery of Brussels which prevented certain children from attending French language schools, purely on the basis of their parents' place of residence, breached the first sentence of P1-2 read with Article 14.

1. THE MEANING AND SCOPE OF ARTICLE 2 OF THE PROTOCOL

. . .

3. By the terms of the first sentence of this Article (P1-2), 'no person shall be denied the right to education'.

In spite of its negative formulation, this provision uses the term 'right' and speaks of a 'right to education'. Likewise the preamble to the Protocol specifies that the object of the Protocol lies in the collective enforcement of 'rights and freedoms'. There is therefore no doubt that Article 2 (P1-2) does enshrine a right.

It remains however to determine the content of this right and the scope of the obligation which is thereby placed upon States.

The negative formulation indicates, as is confirmed by the 'preparatory work' (especially Docs. CM/WP VI (51) 7, page 4, and AS/JA (3) 13, page 4), that the Contracting Parties do not recognise such a right to education as would require them to establish at their own expense, or to subsidise, education of any particular type or at any particular level. However, it cannot be concluded from this that the State has no positive obligation to ensure respect for such a right as is protected by Article 2 of the Protocol (P1-2). As a 'right' does exist, it is secured, by virtue of Article 1 (art 1) of the Convention, to everyone within the jurisdiction of a Contracting State.

To determine the scope of the 'right to education', within the meaning of the first sentence of Article 2 of the Protocol (P1-2), the Court must bear in mind the aim of this provision. It notes in this context that all member States of the Council of Europe possessed, at the time of the opening of the Protocol to their signature, and still do possess, a general and official educational system. There neither was, nor is now, therefore, any question of requiring each State to establish such a system, but merely of guaranteeing to persons subject to the jurisdiction of the Contracting Parties the right, in principle, to avail themselves of the means of instruction existing at a given time.

The Convention lays down no specific obligations concerning the extent of these means and the manner of their organisation or subsidisation. In particular the first sentence of Article 2 (P1-2) does not specify the language in which education must be conducted in order that the right to education should be respected. It does not contain precise provisions similar to those which appear in Articles 5 (2) and 6 (3) (a) and (e) (art 5-2, art 6-3-a, art 6-3-e). However the right to education would be meaningless if it did not imply in favour of its beneficiaries, the right to be educated in the national language or in one of the national languages, as the case may be.

4. The first sentence of Article 2 of the Protocol (P1-2) consequently guarantees, in the first place, a right of access to educational institutions existing at a given time, but such access constitutes only a part of the right to education. For the 'right to education' to be effective, it is further necessary that, inter alia, the individual who is the beneficiary should have the possibility of drawing profit from the education received, that is to say, the right to obtain, in conformity with the rules in force in each State, and in one form or another, official recognition of the studies which he has completed . . .

5. The right to education guaranteed by the first sentence of Article 2 of the Protocol (P1-2) by its very nature calls for regulation by the State, regulation which may vary in time and place according to the needs and resources of the community and of individuals. It goes without saying that such regulation must never injure the substance of the right to education nor conflict with other rights enshrined in the Convention.

The Court considers that the general aim set for themselves by the Contracting Parties through the medium of the European Convention on Human Rights, was to provide effective protection of fundamental human rights, and this, without doubt not only because of the historical context in which the Convention was concluded, but also of the social and technical developments in our age which offer to States considerable possibilities for regulating the exercise of these rights. The Convention therefore implies a just balance between the protection of the general interest of the Community and the respect due to fundamental human rights while attaching particular importance to the latter.

6. The second sentence of Article 2 of the Protocol (P1-2) does not guarantee a right to education; this is clearly shown by its wording:

> '. . . In the exercise of any functions which it assumes in relation to education and to teaching, the State shall respect the right of parents to ensure such education and teaching in conformity with their own religious and philosophical convictions.'

This provision does not require of States that they should, in the sphere of education or teaching, respect parents' linguistic preferences, but only their religious and philosophical convictions. To interpret the terms 'religious' and 'philosophical' as covering linguistic preferences would amount to a distortion of their ordinary and usual meaning and to read into the Convention something which is not there. Moreover the 'preparatory work' confirms that the object of the second sentence of Article 2 (P1-2) was in no way to secure respect by the State of a right for parents to have education conducted in a language other than that of the country in question; indeed in June 1951 the Committee of Experts which had the task of drafting the Protocol set aside a proposal put forward in this sense. Several members of the Committee believed that it concerned an aspect of the problem of ethnic minorities and that it consequently fell outside the scope of the Convention (see Doc CM (51) 33 final, page 3). The second sentence of Article 2 (P1-2) is therefore irrelevant to the problems raised in the present case.

...

7. The first question concerns exclusively those provisions of the Acts of 1932 and 1963 which prevented, or prevent, in the regions which are by law deemed unilingual, the establishment or subsidisation by the State of schools not in conformity with the general linguistic requirements.

In the present case, this question principally concerns the State's refusal to establish or subsidise, in the Dutch unilingual region, primary school education (which is compulsory in Belgium) in which French is employed as the language of instruction.

Such a refusal is not incompatible with the requirements of the first sentence of Article 2 of the Protocol (P1-2). In interpreting this provision, the Court has already held that it does not enshrine the right to the establishment or subsidising of schools in which education is provided in a given language. The first sentence of Article 2 (P1-2) contains in itself no linguistic requirement. It guarantees the right of access to educational establishments existing at a given time and the right to obtain, in conformity with the rules in force in each State and in one form or another, the official recognition of studies which have been completed, this last right not being relevant to the point which is being dealt with here. In the unilingual regions, both French-speaking and Dutch-speaking children have access to public or subsidised education, that is to say to education conducted in the language of the region.

...

13. The situation with which the second question is concerned is bound up with that dealt with in the first. The legal provisions mentioned in the first render impossible, in the Dutch unilingual region, the establishment or subsidising by the State of schools which conduct education in French. The legal and administrative measures to which the second question relates, merely supplement them: they tend to prevent the operating of 'mixed language' schools which, in a unilingual region—in this case, the Dutch unilingual region—provide, in the form of non-subsidised classes and in addition to instruction given in the language of the region, full or partial instruction in another language. What is in issue, therefore, is a whole series of provisions with a common aim, namely, the protection of the linguistic homogeneity of the region.

The Court's reply to the second question is the same as that already given to the first.

Neither Article 2 of the Protocol (P1-2), nor Article 8 (art 8) of the Convention are violated by the provisions in dispute.

As the first sentence of Article 2 of the Protocol (P1-2) taken by itself leaves intact the freedom of States to subsidise private schools or to refrain from so doing, the withdrawal of subsidies from schools which do not satisfy the requirements to which the State subjects the grant of such subsidies—in this case the condition that teaching should be conducted exclusively in accordance with the linguistic legislation—does not come within the scope of this Article (P1-2).

...

32. The Court will examine in turn the legal and administrative measures governing access to French-language education at, on the one hand, Louvain and Heverlee, and, on the other, the six communes with special facilities.

Louvain and Heverlee belong to the Dutch-unilingual region. Although the legislature has authorised the maintenance of French-language education there, it has done so, above all, in consideration of the needs arising from the bilingual nature of the University of Louvain. The principles which govern the functioning of education in French in the two communes likewise determine the entrance requirements to this education. The benefits conferred by the provisions in dispute (Section 7 in fine of the Act of 30th July 1963 and the Royal Decrees of 8th August 1963 and 30th November 1966) therefore depend upon their purpose. Essentially, they are accorded to the French-speaking teaching staff, employees and students of the University of Louvain in whose absence the establishment could no longer retain its bilingual character. Likewise, if the French classes at Louvain and Heverlee are still open to children of French-speaking families living outside the Dutch-unilingual region, it is because they serve as teacher training classes for the bilingual University of Louvain. As for the privilege granted to certain children of foreign nationality, this is justified by the customs of international courtesy. Consequently, the exclusion of French-speaking children living in the Dutch unilingual region whose parents are not members of the teaching staff, students or employees of the University, does not amount to a discriminatory measure in view of the legitimacy of the specific objective of the legislature.

The situation is completely different in the case of the six communes 'with special facilities', which belong to the agglomeration surrounding Brussels, the capital of a bilingual State and an international centre. According to the information supplied to the Court, the number of French-speaking families in these communes is high; they constitute, up to a certain point, a zone of a 'mixed' character.

It is in recognition of this fact that Section 7 of the Act of 2nd August 1963 departed from the territorial principle, as the Court noted when dealing with the third question. It appears, indeed, from its first paragraph that the six communes no longer form part of the Dutch unilingual region, but constitute a 'distinct administrative district' invested with its own 'special status'. From this the second paragraph draws a first set of consequences: it provides in substance that the six communes concerned enjoy a bilingual system 'in administrative matters'. As to the third paragraph, the compatibility of which with Articles 8 and 14 (art 8, art 14) of the Convention and with Article 2 of the Protocol (P1-2) is contested by the Applicants, it applies to 'educational matters'. It provides that the language of instruction is Dutch in the six communes; it requires nevertheless, the organisation, for the benefit of children whose maternal or usual language is French, of official or subsidised education in French at the nursery and primary levels, on condition that it is asked for by sixteen heads of family. However, this education is not available to children whose parents live outside the communes under consideration. The Dutch classes in the same communes, on the other hand, in principle accept all children, whatever their maternal or usual language and place of residence of their parents. The residence condition affecting therefore only one of the two linguistic groups, the Court is called upon to examine whether there results therefrom a discrimination contrary to Article 14 of the Convention, read in conjunction with the first sentence of Article 2 of the Protocol (art 14+P1-2) or with Article 8 (art 14+8) of the Convention.

Such a measure is not justified in the light of the requirements of the Convention in that it involves elements of discriminatory treatment of certain individuals, founded even more on language than on residence.

First, this measure is not applied uniformly to families speaking one or the other national language. The Dutch-speaking children resident in the French unilingual region, which incidentally is very near, have access to Dutch-language schools in the six communes, whereas French-speaking children living in the Dutch unilingual region are refused access to French-language schools in those same communes. Likewise, the Dutch classes in the six communes are open to Dutch-speaking children of the Dutch unilingual region whereas the French classes in those communes are closed to the French-speaking children of that region.

Such a situation, moreover, contrasts with that which arises from the possibility of access to French-language schools in the Greater Brussels District, which are open to French-speaking children irrespective of their parents' place of residence (Sections 5 and 19 of the Act of 30th July 1963).

It consequently appears that the residence condition is not imposed in the interest of schools, for administrative or financial reasons: it proceeds solely, in the case of the Applicants, from considerations relating to language. Furthermore the measure in issue does not fully respect, in the case of the majority of the Applicants and their children, the relationship of proportionality between the means employed and the aim sought. In this regard the Court, in particular, points out that the impossibility of entering official or subsidised French-language schools in the six communes 'with special facilities' affects the children of the Applicants in the exercise of their right to education, all the more in that there exist no such schools in the communes in which they live.

The enjoyment of the right to education as the Court conceives it, and more precisely that of the right of access to existing schools, is not therefore on the point under consideration secured to everyone without discrimination on the ground, in particular, of language. In other words, the measure in question is, in this respect, incompatible with the first sentence of Article 2 of the Protocol, read in conjunction with Article 14 (art 14+P1-2) of the Convention. . . .

FOR THESE REASONS, THE COURT,

1. Holds, by eight votes to seven, that Section 7 (3) of the Act of 2nd August 1963 does not comply with the requirements of Article 14 of the Convention read in conjunction with the first sentence of Article 2 of the Protocol (art 14+P1-2), in so far as it prevents certain children, solely on the basis of the residence of their parents, from having access to the French-language schools existing in the six communes on the periphery of Brussels invested with a special status, of which Kraainem is one;

Reserves for the Applicants concerned the right, should the occasion arise, to apply for just satisfaction in regard to this particular point;

2. Holds, unanimously, with regard to the other points at issue, that there has been and there is no breach of any of the Articles of the Convention (art 8, art 14) and the Protocol (P1-2) invoked by the Applicants.

NOTES

1   The Court was composed of President Cassin and Judges: Verdross, Balladore Pallieri, Mosler, Zekia, Favre, Cremona, and Waldock. Judges Holmback, Maridakis, Rodenbourg, Ross, Wold, Wiarda, and Mast issued dissenting opinions in which they expressed the view that, *inter alia*, the special educational arrangements for the communes around Brussels did not place a disproportionate burden on the applicants and were not therefore in breach of the Convention.

2   The above judgment was the first elaboration of the content of Article 2 by the Court. The negative formulation of the first sentence of the Article, combined with the contentious background to the drafting of the Article, limited the ability of the Court to adopt an expansive interpretation of the ambit of the rights contained within the provision. Nevertheless, the Court determined that there was a right of access for individuals to existing educational institutions and for individuals to receive official recognition of the studies they have undertaken. However, States were not obliged to establish or fund any particular type of educational institution. Indeed, the Court expressly observed that the first sentence of Article 2 left States with the discretion to decide whether or not to subsidise private schools. The Court also acknowledged States' authority to regulate the right to education.

3   In the later case of *Kjeldsen, Busk Madsen and Pedersen v Denmark*, (examined below p 965) the Court stated that; 'as is shown by its very structure, Article 2 constitutes a whole that is dominated by its first sentence.' (para 52) Hence the right contained in the second sentence is 'an adjunct' of the basic right to education enshrined in the first sentence.

4   A Grand Chamber of the full-time Court found a breach of this Article in *Cyprus v Turkey*, see above p 119. The applicant Government asserted that the denial of secondary school facilities to Greek-Cypriot children in the north (the secondary schools in that area either taught in Turkish or English) violated the children's right to education and their parents' right for

them to be taught in accordance with their religious and philosophical convictions. The Grand chamber determined, sixteen votes to one, that:

277. The Court notes that children of Greek-Cypriot parents in northern Cyprus wishing to pursue a secondary education through the medium of the Greek language are obliged to transfer to schools in the south, this facility being unavailable in the 'TRNC' ever since the decision of the Turkish-Cypriot authorities to abolish it. Admittedly, it is open to children, on reaching the age of 12, to continue their education at a Turkish or English-language school in the north. In the strict sense, accordingly, there is no denial of the right to education, which is the primary obligation devolving on a Contracting Party under the first sentence of Article 2 of Protocol No. 1 (see the *Kjeldsen, Busk Madsen and Pedersen v Denmark* judgment of 7 December 1976, Series A No 23, pp 25–6 § 52). Moreover, this provision does not specify the language in which education must be conducted in order that the right to education be respected (see the above-mentioned *Belgian linguistic* judgment, pp 30–1, § 3).

278. However, in the Court's opinion, the option available to Greek-Cypriot parents to continue their children's education in the north is unrealistic in view of the fact that the children in question have already received their primary education in a Greek-Cypriot school there. The authorities must no doubt be aware that it is the wish of Greek-Cypriot parents that the schooling of their children be completed through the medium of the Greek language. Having assumed responsibility for the provision of Greek-language primary schooling, the failure of the 'TRNC' authorities to make continuing provision for it at the secondary-school level must be considered in effect to be a denial of the substance of the right at issue. It cannot be maintained that the provision of secondary education in the south in keeping with the linguistic tradition of the enclaved Greek Cypriots suffices to fulfil the obligation laid down in Article 2 of Protocol No 1, having regard to the impact of that option on family life [the authorities in the north prevented males over 16 and females over 18 who had received their education in the south from permanently returning to the north)].

279. The Court notes that the applicant Government raise a further complaint in respect of primary-school education and the attitude of the 'TRNC' authorities towards the filling of teaching posts. Like the Commission, it considers that, taken as a whole, the evidence does not disclose the existence of an administrative practice of denying the right to education at primary-school level.

280. Having regard to the above considerations, the Court concludes that there has been a violation of Article 2 of Protocol No. 1 in respect of Greek Cypriots living in northern Cyprus in so far as no appropriate secondary-school facilities were available to them.

The judgment of the Grand Chamber implicitly found that both the Greek-Cypriot secondary school pupils and their parents' rights under Article 2 had been breached.

5   In *Leyla Sahin v Turkey*, judgment of 10 November 2005 (and see above, p 614), the Grand Chamber held that institutions of higher education fall within the scope of the provision.

136. The Court does not lose sight of the fact that the development of the right to education, whose content varies from one time or place to another, according to economic and social circumstances, mainly depends on the needs and resources of the community. However, it is of crucial importance that the Convention is interpreted and applied in a manner which renders its rights practical and effective, not theoretical and illusory. Moreover, the Convention is a living instrument which must be interpreted in the light of present-day conditions (*Marckx v Belgium*, judgment of 13 June 1979, Series A No 31, p 19, § 41; *Airey v Ireland*, judgment of 9 October 1979, Series A No 32, pp 14–15, § 26; and, as the most recent authority, *Mamatkulov and Askarov v Turkey* [GC], Nos 46827/99 and 46951/99, § 121, 4 February 2005). While the first sentence of Article 2 essentially establishes access to primary and secondary education, there is no watertight division separating higher education from other forms of education. In a number of recently adopted instruments, the Council of Europe has stressed the key role

and importance of higher education in the promotion of human rights and fundamental freedoms and the strengthening of democracy (see, *inter alia*, Recommendation No R (98) 3 and Recommendation No 1353 (1998)). As the Convention on the Recognition of Qualifications concerning Higher Education in the European Region states, higher education 'is instrumental in the pursuit and advancement of knowledge' and 'constitutes an exceptionally rich cultural and scientific asset for both individuals and society'.

137. Consequently, it would be hard to imagine that institutions of higher education existing at a given time do not come within the scope of the first sentence of Article 2 of Protocol No 1. Although that Article does not impose a duty on the Contracting States to set up institutions of higher education, any State so doing will be under an obligation to afford an effective right of access to them. In a democratic society, the right to education, which is indispensable to the furtherance of human rights, plays such a fundamental role that a restrictive interpretation of the first sentence of Article 2 of Protocol No 1 would not be consistent with the aim or purpose of that provision (see, *mutatis mutandis*, the '*Belgian Linguistic case*', cited above, p 33, § 9; and *Delcourt v Belgium*, judgment of 17 January 1970, Series A No 11, p 14, § 25).

. . . .

141. In the light of all the foregoing considerations, it is clear that any institutions of higher education existing at a given time come within the scope of the first sentence of Article 2 of Protocol No 1, since the right of access to such institutions is an inherent part of the right set out in that provision. This is not an extensive interpretation forcing new obligations on the Contracting States: it is based on the very terms of the first sentence of Article 2 of Protocol No 1 read in its context and having regard to the object and purpose of the Convention, a lawmaking treaty (see, *mutatis mutandis*, *Golder v the United Kingdom*, judgment of 21 February 1975, Series A No 18, p 18, § 36).

However, the overwhelming majority of the Grand Chamber (sixteen votes to one) found that the university ban on the wearing of the Islamic headscarf did not constitute an infringement of the applicant's right to education. Following the reasoning applied to the applicant's complaint under Article 9 the Grand Chamber concluded that the restriction was foreseeable, pursued legitimate aims and was proportionate.

6 A unanimous Chamber determined that the refusal to permit the children of a Chechen migrant to continue their education in a school located in a neighbouring Republic, where they had re-located, breached Article 2 in *Timishev v Russia*, judgment of 13 December 2005.

The first sentence of Article 2

....

Campbell and Cosans v UK A.48 (1982) 4 EHRR 293
European Court of Human Rights

The background to this case has been elaborated above at p 224.

III. THE ALLEGED VIOLATION OF THE FIRST SENTENCE OF ARTICLE 2 OF PROTOCOL NO 1 (P1-2).

39. Mrs Cosans alleged that, by reason of his suspension from school . . . her son Jeffrey had been denied the right to education contrary to the first sentence of Article 2 (P1-2).

The Commission found it unnecessary to examine the issue, considering it to be absorbed by the finding of a violation of the second sentence. The government, in an alternative plea, accepted this view but their principal submission was that the right of access to educational facilities which is guaranteed by the first sentence may be made subject to reasonable requirements and that, since Jeffrey's suspension was due to his and his parents' refusal to accept such a requirement, there had been no breach.

40. The Court considers that it is necessary to determine this issue. Of course, the existence of corporal punishment as a disciplinary measure in the school attended by her son Jeffrey underlay both of Mrs Cosans' allegations concerning Article 2 (P1-2), but there is a substantial difference between the factual basis of her two claims. In the case of the second sentence, the situation complained of was attendance at a school where recourse was had to a certain practice, whereas, in the case of the first sentence, [it] was the fact of being forbidden to attend; the consequences of the latter situation are more far-reaching than those of the former. Accordingly, a separate complaint, and not merely a further legal submission or argument, was involved . . .

Again, Article 2 (P1-2) constitutes a whole that is dominated by its first sentence, the right set out in the second sentence being an adjunct of the fundamental right to education (see the . . . *Kjeldsen, Busk Madsen and Pedersen* judgment, pp 25–6, par 52).

Finally, there is also a substantial difference between the legal basis of the two claims, for one concerns a right of a parent and the other a right of a child.

The issue arising under the first sentence is therefore not absorbed by the finding of a violation of the second.

41. The right to education guaranteed by the first sentence of Article 2 (P1-2) by its very nature calls for regulation by the State, but such regulation must never injure the substance of the right nor conflict with other rights enshrined in the Convention or its Protocols (see the judgment of 23 July 1968 on the merits of the '*Belgian Linguistic*' case, Series A No 6, p 32, par 5).

The suspension of Jeffrey Cosans—which remained in force for nearly a whole school year—was motivated by his and his parents' refusal to accept that he receive or be liable to corporal chastisement . . . His return to school could have been secured only if his parents had acted contrary to their convictions, convictions which the United Kingdom is obliged to respect under the second sentence of Article 2 (P1-2) . . . A condition of access to an educational establishment that conflicts in this way with another right enshrined in Protocol No 1 cannot be described as reasonable and in any event falls outside the State's power of regulation under Article 2 (P1-2).

There has accordingly also been, as regards Jeffrey Cosans, breach of the first sentence of that Article (P1-2).

. . .

FOR THESE REASONS, THE COURT

. . .

Holds by six votes to one that there has been, as regards Jeffrey Cosans, breach of the first sentence of the last-mentioned Article (P1-2); . . .

NOTES

1 The Court was composed of President Ryssdal and Judges: Cremona, Thor Vilhjalmsson, Liesch, Pettiti, and Macdonald. Judge Evans, the Judge of British nationality, dissented as he considered that the applicants' beliefs regarding the use of corporal punishment in schools was not a protected conviction within the second sentence of Article 2; therefore, in his opinion, the school's refusal to re-admit Jeffrey until he accepted the school's policy on discipline was a reasonable requirement that did not breach the first sentence of Article 2.

2 The above judgment demonstrates the limits on States' powers to suspend pupils from publicly funded schools.

The second sentence of Article 2

Kjeldsen, Busk Madsen and Pedersen v Denmark A.23 (1976) 1 EHRR 711
European Court of Human Rights

The Danish Government became concerned about the increasing numbers of unwanted pregnancies that were occurring in the early 1960s and, therefore, it established a committee of experts to examine the topic of sex education in state schools. The committee reported in 1968 and proposed that matters of sex education should be integrated into compulsory subjects on the curriculum of state schools (as had happened in Sweden a few years earlier). In 1970 the Danish Parliament, unanimously, passed an Act which added sex education to the topics included in the compulsory curriculum of state schools. Subsequent Circulars and Executive Orders issued by the Minister of Education detailed the content and format of sex education in state schools. In the first year of schooling (for pupils aged 6) instruction began with the concept of family and between the fifth and seventh years of schooling the subjects covered included sexual organs, puberty and sexual activities (e.g. sexual intercourse). The applicants were three sets of parents, their professions encompassed the clergy and teaching, who had children of school age. The applicants objected to compulsory sex education in state schools and after the authorities refused to exempt their children from such classes they complained to the Commission alleging that their Christian beliefs had been violated in breach of P1-2. The Commission expressed the opinion that, *inter alia*, the Danish system of sex education did not violate P1-2 (by seven votes to seven with the casting vote of the President in favour of the State).

I. ON THE ALLEGED VIOLATION OF ARTICLE 2 OF PROTOCOL NO 1 (P1-2)

49. The applicants invoke Article 2 of Protocol No 1 (P1-2) which provides:

'No person shall be denied the right to education. In the exercise of any functions which it assumes in relation to education and to teaching, the State shall respect the right of parents to ensure such education and teaching in conformity with their own religious and philosophical convictions.'

50. In their main submission before the Commission, the Government maintained that the second sentence of Article 2 (P1-2) does not apply to State schools . . . but their arguments have since evolved slightly. In their memorial of 8 March 1976 and at the hearings on 1 and 2 June 1976, they conceded that the existence of private schools perhaps does not necessarily imply in all cases that there is no breach of the said sentence. The Government nevertheless emphasised that Denmark does not force parents to entrust their children to the State schools; it allows parents to educate their children, or to have them educated, at home and, above all, to send them to private institutions to which the State pays very substantial subsidies, thereby assuming a 'function in relation to education and to teaching', within the meaning of Article 2 (P1-2). Denmark, it was submitted, thereby discharged the obligations resulting from the second sentence of this provision.

The Court notes that in Denmark private schools co-exist with a system of public education. The second sentence of Article 2 (P1-2) is binding upon the Contracting States in the exercise of each and every function—it speaks of 'any functions'—that they undertake in the sphere of education and teaching, including that consisting of the organisation and financing of public education.

Furthermore, the second sentence of Article 2 (P1-2) must be read together with the first which enshrines the right of everyone to education. It is on to this fundamental right that is grafted the right of parents to respect for their religious and philosophical convictions, and the first sentence does not distinguish, any more than the second, between State and private teaching.

The 'travaux préparatoires', which are without doubt of particular consequence in the case of a clause that gave rise to such lengthy and impassioned discussions, confirm the interpretation appearing from a first reading of Article 2 (P1-2). While they indisputably demonstrate, as the Government recalled, the importance attached by many members of the Consultative Assembly and a number of governments to freedom of teaching, that is to say, freedom to establish private schools, the 'travaux préparatoires' do not for all that reveal the intention to go no further than a guarantee of that freedom. Unlike some earlier versions, the text finally adopted does not expressly enounce that freedom; and numerous interventions and proposals, cited by the delegates of the Commission, show that sight was not lost of the need to ensure, in State teaching, respect for parents' religious and philosophical convictions.

The second sentence of Article 2 (P1-2) aims in short at safeguarding the possibility of pluralism in education which possibility is essential for the preservation of the 'democratic society' as conceived by the Convention. In view of the power of the modern State, it is above all through State teaching that this aim must be realised.

The Court thus concludes, as the Commission did unanimously, that the Danish State schools do not fall outside the province of Protocol No 1 (P1). In its investigation as to whether Article 2 (P1-2) has been violated, the Court cannot forget, however, that the functions assumed by Denmark in relation to education and to teaching include the grant of substantial assistance to private schools. Although recourse to these schools involves parents in sacrifices which were justifiably mentioned by the applicants, the alternative solution it provides constitutes a factor that should not be disregarded in this case. The delegate speaking on behalf of the majority of the Commission recognised that it had not taken sufficient heed of this factor in paragraphs 152 and 153 of the report.

51. The Government pleaded in the alternative that the second sentence of Article 2(P1-2), assuming that it governed even the State schools where attendance is not obligatory, implies solely the right for parents to have their children exempted from classes offering 'religious instruction of a denominational character'.

The Court does not share this view. Article 2 (P1-2), which applies to each of the State's functions in relation to education and to teaching, does not permit a distinction to be drawn between religious instruction and other subjects. It enjoins the State to respect parents' convictions, be they religious or philosophical, throughout the entire State education programme.

52. As is shown by its very structure, Article 2 (P1-2) constitutes a whole that is dominated by its first sentence. By binding themselves not to 'deny the right to education', the Contracting States guarantee to anyone within their jurisdiction 'a right of access to educational institutions existing at a given time' and 'the possibility of drawing', by 'official recognition of the studies which he has completed', 'profit from the education received' (judgment of 23 July 1968 on the merits of the 'Belgian Linguistic' case, Series A No 6, pp 30–2, paras 3–5).

The right set out in the second sentence of Article 2 (P1-2) is an adjunct of this fundamental right to education (paragraph 50 above). It is in the discharge of a natural duty towards their children—parents being primarily responsible for the 'education and teaching' of their children—that parents may require the State to respect their religious and philosophical convictions. Their right thus corresponds to a responsibility closely linked to the enjoyment and the exercise of the right to education.

On the other hand, 'the provisions of the Convention and Protocol must be read as a whole' (abovementioned judgment of 23 July 1968, ibid, p 30, para 1). Accordingly, the two sentences of Article 2 (P1-2) must be read not only in the light of each other but also, in particular, of Articles 8, 9 and 10 (art 8, art 9, art 10) of the Convention which proclaim the right of everyone, including parents and children, 'to respect for his private and family life', to 'freedom of thought, conscience and religion', and to 'freedom . . . to receive and impart information and ideas'.

53. It follows in the first place from the preceding paragraph that the setting and planning of the curriculum fall in principle within the competence of the Contracting States. This mainly involves questions

of expediency on which it is not for the Court to rule and whose solution may legitimately vary according to the country and the era. In particular, the second sentence of Article 2 of the Protocol (P1-2) does not prevent States from imparting through teaching or education information or knowledge of a directly or indirectly religious or philosophical kind. It does not even permit parents to object to the integration of such teaching or education in the school curriculum, for otherwise all institutionalised teaching would run the risk of proving impracticable. In fact, it seems very difficult for many subjects taught at school not to have, to a greater or lesser extent, some philosophical complexion or implications. The same is true of religious affinities if one remembers the existence of religions forming a very broad dogmatic and moral entity which has or may have answers to every question of a philosophical, cosmological or moral nature.

The second sentence of Article 2 (P1-2) implies on the other hand that the State, in fulfilling the functions assumed by it in regard to education and teaching, must take care that information or knowledge included in the curriculum is conveyed in an objective, critical and pluralistic manner. The State is forbidden to pursue an aim of indoctrination that might be considered as not respecting parents' religious and philosophical convictions. That is the limit that must not be exceeded.

Such an interpretation is consistent at one and the same time with the first sentence of Article 2 of the Protocol (P1-2), with Articles 8 to 10 (art 8, art 9, art 10) of the Convention and with the general spirit of the Convention itself, an instrument designed to maintain and promote the ideals and values of a democratic society.

54. In order to examine the disputed legislation under Article 2 of the Protocol (P1-2),interpreted as above, one must, while avoiding any evaluation of the legislation's expediency, have regard to the material situation that it sought and still seeks to meet.

The Danish legislator, who did not neglect to obtain beforehand the advice of qualified experts, clearly took as his starting point the known fact that in Denmark children nowadays discover without difficulty and from several quarters the information that interests them on sexual life. The instruction on the subject given in State schools is aimed less at instilling knowledge they do not have or cannot acquire by other means than at giving them such knowledge more correctly, precisely, objectively and scientifically. The instruction, as provided for and organised by the contested legislation, is principally intended to give pupils better information; this emerges from, inter alia, the preface to the 'Guide' of April 1971.

Even when circumscribed in this way, such instruction clearly cannot exclude on the part of teachers certain assessments capable of encroaching on the religious or philosophical sphere; for what are involved are matters where appraisals of fact easily lead on to value-judgments. The minority of the Commission rightly emphasised this. The Executive Orders and Circulars of 8 June 1971 and 15 June 1972, the 'Guide' of April 1971 and the other material before the Court . . . plainly show that the Danish State, by providing children in good time with explanations it considers useful, is attempting to warn them against phenomena it views as disturbing, for example, the excessive frequency of births out of wedlock, induced abortions and venereal diseases. The public authorities wish to enable pupils, when the time comes, 'to take care of themselves and show consideration for others in that respect', 'not . . . [to] land themselves or others in difficulties solely on account of lack of knowledge' (section 1 of the Executive Order of 15 June 1972).

These considerations are indeed of a moral order, but they are very general in character and do not entail overstepping the bounds of what a democratic State may regard as the public interest. Examination of the legislation in dispute establishes in fact that it in no way amounts to an attempt at indoctrination aimed at advocating a specific kind of sexual behaviour. It does not make a point of exalting sex or inciting pupils to indulge precociously in practices that are dangerous for their stability, health or future or that many parents consider reprehensible. Further, it does not affect the right of parents to enlighten and advise their children, to exercise with regard to their children natural parental functions as educators, or to guide their children on a path in line with the parents' own religious or philosophical convictions.

Certainly, abuses can occur as to the manner in which the provisions in force are applied by a given school or teacher and the competent authorities have a duty to take the utmost care to see to it that parents' religious and philosophical convictions are not disregarded at this level by carelessness, lack of judgment or misplaced proselytism.... The Court consequently reaches the conclusion that the disputed legislation in itself in no way offends the applicants' religious and philosophical convictions to the extent forbidden by the second sentence of Article 2 of the Protocol (P1-2), interpreted in the light of its first sentence and of the whole of the Convention.

Besides, the Danish State preserves an important expedient for parents who, in the name of their creed or opinions, wish to dissociate their children from integrated sex education; it allows parents either to entrust their children to private schools, which are bound by less strict obligations and moreover heavily subsidised by the State ... or to educate them or have them educated at home, subject to suffering the undeniable sacrifices and inconveniences caused by recourse to one of those alternative solutions.

...

FOR THESE REASONS, THE COURT

Holds by six votes to one that there has been no breach of Article 2 of Protocol No 1

...

NOTES

1   The Court was composed of President Pallieri and Judges: Zekia, Pedersen, Petren, Ryssdal, and Evrigenis. Judge Verdross issued a dissenting opinion in which he expressed the view that:

The Danish Act on state schools does not in any way exempt the children of parents having religious convictions at variance with those of the legislature from attending the whole range of classes on sex education. The conclusion must therefore be that the Danish Act, within the limits indicated above, is not in harmony with the second sentence of P1-2.

2   The judgment of the Court reveals that the basic purpose of the second sentence of Article 2 is to protect pupils from methods and forms of teaching in state schools which amount to indoctrination. States are obliged by this provision to ensure that education and teaching in such schools is undertaken in an objective and pluralistic manner. Consequently, state education is not to be used as an instrument of propaganda by governments.

3   The Commission determined that the refusals by a British local education authority to allow two children to attend single-sex grammar schools, because the schools had no spare places available, did not result in indoctrination at comprehensive schools in violation of their parents' protected beliefs under Article 2: in *W & D M and M & HI v UK* 37 DR 96 (1984).

...there is no evidence in this case that the applicants' children are being indoctrinated in the respective comprehensive schools which they are attending or that the teaching of the children is not conveyed in an objective, critical or pluralistic manner. Moreover, there is no allegation that the comprehensive system denies the applicants their major role in the education of their children, in particular the transmission of their values or philosophical convictions. In the light of the above considerations, the Commission concludes that the respondent Government cannot be said to have overstepped the limits of the obligations it has accepted under P1-2.

It follows that this aspect of the case is manifestly ill-founded ... (p 100)

4   The Commission developed the Court's dicta in *Kjeldsen et al* to create a right for persons to establish private schools: in *Ingrid Jordebo Foundation of Christian Schools and Ingrid Jordebo v Sweden* 51 DR 125 (1987). Mrs Jordebo was the headmistress of a private school (run by the

Foundation) which started in 1976. For several years the school ran classes for the first stage of school education with the approval of the local government School Board. In 1983 the applicants applied for permission from the School Board to run classes for the middle and upper stages of school education. The School Board turned down the applicants' request, because it was not satisfied that the applicants' teachers had the necessary qualifications or skills to provide more advanced teaching. The applicants complained of a breach of P1-2.

The Commission considers that it follows from the judgment of the European Court of Human Rights in the case of *Kjeldsen, Busk Madsen and Pedersen* (A.23, para 50) that Article 2 of Protocol No 1 guarantees the right to start and run a private school. However, such a right cannot be a right without conditions. It must be subject to regulation by the State in order to ensure a proper education system as a whole. . . . Having examined the present case, in particular the reasons for refusing the Foundation permission to run the upper stage of the compulsory school, the Commission finds the refusal compatible with P1-2. . . . It follows that, in this respect, the application is manifestly ill-founded . . . (pp 128–9)

Was the Commission correct to find this right implied in P1-2?

5 The Court provided further guidance on the interpretation of key elements of the second sentence, including the range of educational functions encompassed by the provision and the meaning of 'philosophical convictions', in *Campbell and Cosans*.

II. THE ALLEGED VIOLATION OF THE SECOND SENTENCE OF ARTICLE 2 OF PROTOCOL NO 1 (P1-2).

32. Mrs Campbell and Mrs Cosans alleged that their rights under the second sentence of this Article (P1-2) were violated on account of the existence of corporal punishment as a disciplinary measure in the schools attended by their children.

The Government contested, on various grounds, the conclusion of the majority of the Commission that there had been such a violation.

33. The Government maintained in the first place that functions relating to the internal administration of a school, such as discipline, were ancillary and were not functions in relation to 'education' and to 'teaching', within the meaning of Article 2 (P1-2), these terms denoting the provision of facilities and the imparting of information, respectively.

The Court would point out that the education of children is the whole process whereby, in any society, adults endeavour to transmit their beliefs, culture and other values to the young, whereas teaching or instruction refers in particular to the transmission of knowledge and to intellectual development.

It appears to the Court somewhat artificial to attempt to separate off matters relating to internal administration as if all such matters fell outside the scope of Article 2 (P1-2). The use of corporal punishment may, in a sense, be said to belong to the internal administration of a school, but at the same time it is, when used, an integral part of the process whereby a school seeks to achieve the object for which it was established, including the development and moulding of the character and mental powers of its pupils. Moreover, as the Court pointed out in its *Kjeldsen, Busk Madsen and Pedersen* judgment of 7 December 1976 (Series A No 23, p 24, par 50), the second sentence of Article 2 (P1-2) is binding upon the Contracting States in the exercise of 'each and every' function that they undertake in the sphere of education and teaching, so that the fact that a given function may be considered to be ancillary is of no moment in this context.

34. The Government further argued that in Scotland the 'functions' assumed by central or local government in the educational field did not extend to matters of discipline.

It may be true that the day-to-day maintenance of discipline in the schools in question is left to the individual teacher; when he administers corporal punishment he is exercising not a power delegated to him by the State but a power vested in him by the common law by virtue of his status as a teacher, and the law in this respect can be changed only by Act of Parliament . . . Nevertheless, in regard to education in Scotland, the State has assumed responsibility for formulating general policy . . . and the schools attended by the applicants' children were State schools. Discipline is an integral, even indispensable, part of any educational system, with the result that the functions assumed by the State in Scotland must be taken to extend to question of discipline in general, even if not to its everyday maintenance. Indeed, this is confirmed by the fact that central and local authorities participated in the preparation of the Code of Practice and that the Government themselves are committed to a policy aimed at abolishing corporal punishment . . .

35. Thirdly, in the submission of the Government, the obligation to respect philosophical convictions arises only in the relation to the content of, and mode of conveying, information and knowledge and not in relation to all aspects of school administration.

As the Government pointed out, the *Kjeldsen, Busk Madsen and Pedersen* judgment states (p 26, par 53):

> 'The second sentence of Article 2 (P1-2) implies . . . that the State, in fulfilling the functions assumed by it in regard to education and teaching, must take care that information or knowledge included in the curriculum is conveyed in an objective, critical and pluralistic manner. The State is forbidden to pursue an aim of indoctrination that might be considered as not respecting parents' religious and philosophical convictions. That is the limit that must not be exceeded.'

However, that case concerned the content of instruction, whereas the second sentence of Article 2 (P1-2) has a broader scope, as is shown by the generality of its wording. This was confirmed by the Court in the same judgment when it held that the said sentence is binding upon the Contracting States in the exercise, inter alia, of the function 'consisting of the organisation and financing of public education' (p 24, par 50). And in the present case the functions assumed by the respondent State in this area extend to the supervision of the Scottish educational system in general, which must include questions of discipline (see paragraph 34 above).

36. The Government also contested the conclusion of the majority of the Commission that the applicants' views on the use of corporal punishment amounted to 'philosophical convictions', arguing, inter alia, that the expression did not extend to opinions on internal school administration, such as discipline, and that, if the majority were correct, there was no reason why objections to other methods of discipline, or simply to discipline in general, should not also amount to 'philosophical convictions'.

In its ordinary meaning the word 'convictions', taken on its own, is not synonymous with the words 'opinions' and 'ideas', such as are utilised in Article 10 (art 10) of the Convention, which guarantees freedom of expression; it is more akin to the term 'beliefs' (in the French text: 'convictions') appearing in Article 9 (art 9)—which guarantees freedom of thought, conscience and religion—and denotes views that attain a certain level of cogency, seriousness, cohesion and importance.

As regards the adjective 'philosophical', it is not capable of exhaustive definition and little assistance as to its precise significance is to be gleaned from the *travaux préparatoires*. The Commission pointed out that the word 'philosophy' bears numerous meanings: it is used to allude to a fully-fledged system of thought or, rather loosely, to views on more or less trivial matters. The Courts agrees with the Commission that neither of these two extremes can be adopted for the purposes of interpreting Article 2 (P1-2): the former would too narrowly restrict the scope of a right that is guaranteed to all parents and the latter might result in the inclusion of matters of insufficient weight or substance.

Having regard to the Convention as a whole, including Article 17 (art 17), the expression 'philosophical convictions' in the present context denotes, in the Court's opinion, such convictions as are worthy of respect in a 'democratic society' (see, most recently, the *Young, James and Webster* judgment of 13 August 1981, Series A No 44, p 25, par 63) and are not incompatible with human dignity; in addition, they must not conflict with the fundamental right of the child to education, the whole of Article 2 (P1-2) being dominated by its first sentence (see the above-mentioned *Kjeldsen, Busk Madsen and Pedersen* judgment, pp 25–6, par 52).

The applicants' views relate to a weighty and substantial aspect of human life and behaviour, namely the integrity of the person, the propriety or otherwise of the infliction of corporal punishment and the exclusion of the distress which the risk of such punishment entails. They are views which satisfy each of the various criteria listed above; it is this that distinguishes them from opinions that might be held on other methods of discipline or on discipline in general.

37. The Government pleaded, in the alternative, that the obligation to respect the applicants' convictions had been satisfied by the adoption of a policy of gradually eliminating corporal chastisement. They added that any other solution would be incompatible with the necessity of striking a balance between the opinions of supporters and opponents of this method of discipline and with the terms of the reservation to Article 2 (P1-2) made by the United Kingdom at the time of signing the Protocol, which reads:

'... in view of certain provisions of the Education Acts in force in the United Kingdom, the principle affirmed in the second sentence of Article 2 (P1-2) is accepted by the United Kingdom only so far as it is compatible with the provision of efficient instruction and training, and the avoidance of unreasonable public expenditure.'

The Court is unable to accept the submissions.

(a) While the adoption of the policy referred to clearly foreshadows a move in the direction of the position taken by the applicants, is does not amount to 'respect' for their convictions. As is confirmed by the fact that, in the course of the drafting of Article 2 (P1-2), the words 'have regard to' were replaced by the word 'respect' (see documents CDH (67) 2 p 163) the latter word means more than 'acknowledge' or 'taken into account'; in addition to a primarily negative undertaking, it implies some positive obligation on the part of the State (see *mutatis mutandis*, the *Marckx* judgment of 13 June 1979, series A No 31, p 15, par 31). This being so, the duty to respect parental convictions in this sphere cannot be overridden by the alleged necessity of striking a balance between the conflicting views involved, nor is the Government's policy to move gradually towards the abolition of corporal punishment in itself sufficient to comply with this duty.

The Court accepts that certain solutions canvassed—such as the establishment of a dual system whereby in each sector there would be separate schools for the children of parents objecting to corporal punishment—would be incompatible, especially in the present economic situation, with the avoidance of unreasonable public expenditure. However, the Court does not regard it as established that other means of respecting the applicants' convictions, such as a system of exemption for individual pupils in a particular school, would necessarily be incompatible with 'the provision of efficient instruction and training, and the avoidance of unreasonable public expenditure'.

38. Mrs Campbell and Mrs Cosans have accordingly been victims of a violation of the second sentence of Article 2 of Protocol No 1 (P1-2).

The above judgment makes it clear that issues of discipline in state schools must comply with the requirements of both sentences in P1-2. For the application of Article 3 to disciplinary punishments in private schools see *Costello-Roberts v UK* (above, p 226).

6   We have already seen in the *Belgian Linguistic* judgment (above) that parents' linguistic preferences have not been classified as 'religious' or 'philosophical' convictions.

7   An example of religious convictions was the beliefs of Jehovah's Witnesses in *Valsamis v Greece* (1996) 24 EHRR 294, 1996-VI 2312 (for the background see above, p 606). The Court, by seven votes to two, concluded that the Government had not failed to respect the applicants' pacifist beliefs when it refused to exempt their daughter from attending a compulsory school parade on the National Day of Greece.

8 The Commission also emphasised the limitations on States' duty of respect in *X v UK* 14 DR 179 (1978). The applicant parent wished to see the establishment of nondenominational schools in Northern Ireland (he claimed that state schools in the Province were influenced by the Protestant religion and private schools were under the influence of the Catholic religion). Private persons seeking to create new non-denominational schools had to fund 15 per cent of the capital costs, with the State paying the remainder. The applicant complained that the refusal of the local education authority to fund all the costs of a new integrated school for his (and similar parents) children resulted in his religious and philosophical convictions not being respected. After citing the Court's judgments in *Kjeldsen* and *Belgian Linguistic*, the Commission stated:

Accordingly, interpreting the Article as a whole, there is no positive obligation on the State, in relation to the second sentence of Article 2, to subsidise any particular form of education in order to respect the religious and philosophical beliefs of parents. It is sufficient for the State in order to comply with its obligations under Article 2 to evidence respect for the religious and philosophical beliefs of parents within the existing and developing system of education. (p 180)

Therefore, the Commission declared the application inadmissible.

23 FIRST PROTOCOL ARTICLE 3: RIGHT TO FREE ELECTIONS

Matthews v UK (1999) The Times, 3 March
European Court of Human Rights

Gibraltar is a dependent territory of the UK, but it is not part of the UK. The UK Parliament has the ultimate authority to legislate for Gibraltar, however most legislation for the territory is enacted by the domestic legislature (the House of Assembly). Gibraltar is excluded from a number of parts of the EC Treaty (such as free movement of goods and the common market in agriculture) by virtue of the Treaty of Accession. EC law applies to Gibraltar in respect of, *inter alia*, free movement of persons and consumer protection. An Act, signed by foreign ministers of the (then) European Communities in 1976, provided that elections to the European Parliament would not apply to the UK's dependent territories. In 1994 Ms Matthews applied to the Electoral Registration Officer for Gibraltar to be registered as a voter in the forthcoming elections to the European Parliament. He refused her request because the 1976 Act excluded Gibraltar from the franchise for the European Parliament elections. She then complained to the Commission alleging a breach of her rights under Article 3 of Protocol No 1. The Commission, by eleven votes to six, found no violation of that provision.

AS TO THE LAW

I. ALLEGED VIOLATION OF ARTICLE 3 OF PROTOCOL NO 1 24.

The applicant alleged a breach of Article 3 of Protocol No 1, which provides:

'The High Contracting Parties undertake to hold free elections at reasonable intervals by secret ballot, under conditions which will ensure the free expression of the opinion of the people in the choice of the legislature.'

25. The Government maintained that, for three main reasons, Article 3 of Protocol No 1 was not applicable to the facts of the present case or, in the alternative, that there had been no violation of that provision.

A. WHETHER THE UNITED KINGDOM CAN BE HELD RESPONSIBLE UNDER THE CONVENTION FOR THE LACK OF ELECTIONS TO THE EUROPEAN PARLIAMENT IN GIBRALTAR

26. According to the Government, the applicant's real objection was to Council Decision 76/787 and to the 1976 Act concerning elections to the European Parliament . . . That Act, which had the status of a treaty, was adopted in the Community framework and could not be revoked or varied unilaterally by the United Kingdom. The Government underlined that the European Commission of Human Rights had refused on a number of occasions to subject measures falling within the Community legal order to

scrutiny under the Convention. While they accepted that there might be circumstances in which a Contracting Party might infringe its obligations under the Convention by entering into treaty obligations which were incompatible with the Convention, they considered that in the present case, which concerned texts adopted in the framework of the European Community, the position was not the same. Thus, acts adopted by the Community or consequent to its requirements could not be imputed to the member States, together or individually, particularly when those acts concerned elections to a constitutional organ of the Community itself. At the hearing, the Government suggested that to engage the responsibility of any State under the Convention, that State must have a power of effective control over the act complained of. In the case of the provisions relating to the elections to the European Parliament, the United Kingdom Government had no such control.

27. The applicant disagreed. For her, the Council Decision and 1976 Act constituted an international treaty, rather than an act of an institution whose decisions were not subject to Convention review. She thus considered that the Government remained responsible under the Convention for the effects of the Council Decision and 1976 Act. In the alternative—that is, if the Council Decision and 1976 Act were to be interpreted as involving a transfer of powers to the Community organs—the applicant argued, by reference to Commission case-law, that in the absence of any equivalent protection of her rights under Article 3 of Protocol No 1, the Government in any event retained responsibility under the Convention.

28. The majority of the Commission took no stand on the point, although it was referred to in concurring and dissenting opinions.

29. Article 1 of the Convention requires the High Contracting Parties to 'secure to everyone within their jurisdiction the rights and freedoms defined in . . . [the] Convention'. Article 1 makes no distinction as to the type of rule or measure concerned, and does not exclude any part of the member States' 'jurisdiction' from scrutiny under the Convention (see the *United Communist Party of Turkey v Turkey* judgment of 30 January 1998, *Reports of Judgments and Decisions* 1998-I, pp 17–18, § 29).

30. The Court notes that the parties do not dispute that Article 3 of Protocol No 1 applies in Gibraltar. It recalls that the Convention was extended to the territory of Gibraltar by the United Kingdom's declaration of 23 October 1953 . . . and Protocol No 1 has been applicable in Gibraltar since 25 February 1988. There is therefore clearly territorial 'jurisdiction' within the meaning of Article 1 of the Convention.

31. The Court must nevertheless consider whether, notwithstanding the nature of the elections to the European Parliament as an organ of the EC, the United Kingdom can be held responsible under Article 1 of the Convention for the absence of elections to the European Parliament in Gibraltar, that is, whether the United Kingdom is required to 'secure' elections to the European Parliament notwithstanding the Community character of those elections.

32. The Court observes that acts of the EC as such cannot be challenged before the Court because the EC is not a Contracting Party. The Convention does not exclude the transfer of competences to international organisations provided that Convention rights continue to be 'secured'. Member States' responsibility therefore continues even after such a transfer.

33. In the present case, the alleged violation of the Convention flows from an annex to the 1976 Act, entered into by the United Kingdom, together with the extension to the European Parliament's competences brought about by the Maastricht Treaty. The Council Decision and the 1976 Act . . . and the Maastricht Treaty, with its changes to the EEC Treaty, all constituted international instruments which were freely entered into by the United Kingdom. Indeed, the 1976 Act cannot be challenged before the European Court of Justice for the very reason that it is not a 'normal' act of the Community, but is a treaty within the Community legal order. The Maastricht Treaty, too, is not an act of the Community, but a treaty by which a revision of the EEC Treaty was brought about. The United Kingdom, together with all the other parties to the Maastricht Treaty, is responsible *ratione materiae* under Article 1 of the Convention and, in particular, under Article 3 of Protocol No 1, for the consequences of that Treaty.

34. In determining to what extent the United Kingdom is responsible for 'securing' the rights in Article 3 of Protocol No 1 in respect of elections to the European Parliament in Gibraltar, the Court recalls that the Convention is intended to guarantee rights that are not theoretical or illusory, but practical and effective (see, for example, the above-mentioned *United Communist Party of Turkey* judgment, pp 18–19, § 33). It is uncontested that legislation emanating from the legislative process of the European Community affects the population of Gibraltar in the same way as legislation which enters the domestic legal order exclusively via the House of Assembly. To this extent, there is no difference between European and domestic legislation, and no reason why the United Kingdom should not be required to 'secure' the rights in Article 3 of Protocol No 1 in respect of European legislation, in the same way as those rights are required to be 'secured' in respect of purely domestic legislation. In particular, the suggestion that the United Kingdom may not have effective control over the state of affairs complained of cannot affect the position, as the United Kingdom's responsibility derives from its having entered into treaty commitments subsequent to the applicability of Article 3 of Protocol No 1 to Gibraltar, namely the Maastricht Treaty taken together with its obligations under the Council Decision and the 1976 Act. Further, the Court notes that on acceding to the EC Treaty, the United Kingdom chose, by virtue of Article 227(4) of the Treaty, to have substantial areas of EC legislation applied to Gibraltar . . .

35. It follows that the United Kingdom is responsible under Article 1 of the Convention for securing the rights guaranteed by Article 3 of Protocol No 1 in Gibraltar regardless of whether the elections were purely domestic or European.

B. WHETHER ARTICLE 3 OF PROTOCOL NO 1 IS APPLICABLE TO AN ORGAN SUCH AS THE EUROPEAN PARLIAMENT

36. The Government claimed that the undertaking in Article 3 of Protocol No 1 was necessarily limited to matters falling within the power of the parties to the Convention, that is, sovereign States. They submitted that the 'legislature' in Gibraltar was the House of Assembly, and that it was to that body that Article 3 of Protocol No 1 applied in the context of Gibraltar. For the Government, there was no basis upon which the Convention could place obligations on Contracting Parties in relation to elections for the parliament of a distinct, supranational organisation, and they contended that this was particularly so when the member States of the European Community had limited their own sovereignty in respect of it and when both the European Parliament itself and its basic electoral procedures were provided for under its own legal system, rather than the legal systems of its member States.

37. The applicant referred to previous decisions of the European Commission of Human Rights in which complaints concerning the European Parliament were dealt with on the merits, so that the Commission in effect assumed that Article 3 of Protocol No 1 applied to elections to the European Parliament (see, for example, *Lindsay v UK*, application No 8364/78, decision of 8 March 1978, Decisions and Reports (DR) 15, p 247, and *Tête v France*, application No 11123/84, decision of 9 December 1987, DR 54, p 52). She agreed with the dissenting members of the Commission who did not accept that because the European Parliament did not exist when Protocol No 1 was drafted, it necessarily fell outside the ambit of Article 3 of that Protocol.

38. The majority of the Commission based its reasoning on this jurisdictional point. It considered that 'to hold Article 3 of Protocol No 1 to be applicable to supranational representative organs would be to extend the scope of Article 3 beyond what was intended by the drafters of the Convention and beyond the object and purpose of the provision. . . . [T]he role of Article 3 is to ensure that elections take place at regular intervals to the national or local legislative assembly, that is, in the case of Gibraltar, to the House of Assembly' (see paragraph 63 of the Commission's report).

39. That the Convention is a living instrument which must be interpreted in the light of present-day conditions is firmly rooted in the Court's case-law (see, inter alia, the *Loizidou v Turkey* judgment of

23 March 1995 (*preliminary objections*), Series A No 310, pp 26–27, § 71, with further reference). The mere fact that a body was not envisaged by the drafters of the Convention cannot prevent that body from falling within the scope of the Convention. To the extent that Contracting States organise common constitutional or parliamentary structures by international treaties, the Court must take these mutually agreed structural changes into account in interpreting the Convention and its Protocols. The question remains whether an organ such as the European Parliament nevertheless falls outside the ambit of Article 3 of Protocol No 1.

40. The Court recalls that the word 'legislature' in Article 3 of Protocol No 1 does not necessarily mean the national parliament: the word has to be interpreted in the light of the constitutional structure of the State in question. In the case of Mathieu-*Mohin and Clerfayt v Belgium*, the 1980 constitutional reform had vested in the Flemish Council sufficient competence and powers to make it, alongside the French Community Council and the Walloon Regional Council, a constituent part of the Belgian 'legislature', in addition to the House of Representatives and the Senate (see the *Mathieu-Mohin and Clerfayt v Belgium* judgment of 2 March 1987, Series A No 113, p 23, § 53; see also the Commission's decisions on the application of Article 3 of Protocol No 1 to regional parliaments in Austria (application No 7008/75, decision of 12 July 1976, DR 6, p 120) and in Germany (application No 27311/95, decision of 11 September 1995, DR 82-A, p 158)).

41. According to the case-law of the European Court of Justice, it is an inherent aspect of EC law that such law sits alongside, and indeed has precedence over, domestic law (see, for example, *Costa v ENEL*, 6/64 [1964] ECR 585, and *Amministrazione delle Finanze dello Stato v Simmenthal SpA*, 106/77 [1978] ECR 629). In this regard, Gibraltar is in the same position as other parts of the European Union.

42. The Court reiterates that Article 3 of Protocol No 1 enshrines a characteristic of an effective political democracy (see the above-mentioned *Mathieu-Mohin and Clerfayt* judgment, p 22, § 47, and the above-mentioned *United Communist Party of Turkey* judgment, pp 21–22, § 45). In the present case, there has been no submission that there exist alternative means of providing for electoral representation of the population of Gibraltar in the European Parliament, and the Court finds no indication of any.

43. The Court thus considers that to accept the Government's contention that the sphere of activities of the European Parliament falls outside the scope of Article 3 of Protocol No 1 would risk undermining one of the fundamental tools by which 'effective political democracy' can be maintained.

44. It follows that no reason has been made out which could justify excluding the European Parliament from the ambit of the elections referred to in Article 3 of Protocol No 1 on the ground that it is a supranational, rather than a purely domestic, representative organ.

C. WHETHER THE EUROPEAN PARLIAMENT, AT THE RELEVANT TIME, HAD THE CHARACTERISTICS OF A 'LEGISLATURE' IN GIBRALTAR

45. The Government contended that the European Parliament continued to lack both of the most fundamental attributes of a legislature: the power to initiate legislation and the power to adopt it. They were of the opinion that the only change to the powers and functions of the European Parliament since the Commission last considered the issue in the above-mentioned *Tête* decision (see paragraph 37 above)—the procedure under Article 189b of the EC Treaty—offered less than even a power of co-decision with the Council, and in any event applied only to a tiny proportion of the Community's legislative output.

46. The applicant took as her starting-point in this respect that the European Commission of Human Rights had found that the entry into force of the Single European Act in 1986 did not furnish the European Parliament with the necessary powers and functions for it to be considered as a 'legislature' (see the above-mentioned *Tête* decision). She contended that the Maastricht Treaty increased those powers to such an extent that the European Parliament was now transformed from a mere advisory

and supervisory organ to a body which assumed, or assumed at least in part, the powers and functions of legislative bodies within the meaning of Article 3 of Protocol No 1. The High Contracting Parties had undertaken to hold free elections at reasonable intervals by secret ballot, under conditions which would ensure the free expression of the opinion of the people in the choice of the legislature. She described the powers of the European Parliament not solely in terms of the new matters added by the Maastricht Treaty, but also by reference to its pre-existing powers, in particular those which were added by the Single European Act in 1986.

47. The Commission did not examine this point, as it found Article 3 not to be applicable to supra-national representative organs.

48. In determining whether the European Parliament falls to be considered as the 'legislature', or part of it, in Gibraltar for the purposes of Article 3 of Protocol No 1, the Court must bear in mind the *sui generis* nature of the European Community, which does not follow in every respect the pattern common in many States of a more or less strict division of powers between the executive and the legislature. Rather, the legislative process in the EC involves the participation of the European Parliament, the Council and the European Commission.

49. The Court must ensure that 'effective political democracy' is properly served in the territories to which the Convention applies, and in this context, it must have regard not solely to the strictly legislative powers which a body has, but also to that body's role in the overall legislative process.

50. Since the Maastricht Treaty, the European Parliament's powers are no longer expressed to be 'advisory and supervisory'. The removal of these words must be taken as an indication that the European Parliament has moved away from being a purely consultative body, and has moved towards being a body with a decisive role to play in the legislative process of the European Community. The amendment to Article 137 of the EC Treaty cannot, however, be taken as any more than an indication as to the intentions of the drafters of the Maastricht Treaty. Only on examination of the European Parliament's actual powers in the context of the European Community legislative process as a whole can the Court determine whether the European Parliament acts as the 'legislature', or part of it, in Gibraltar.

51. The European Parliament's role in the Community legislative process depends on the issues concerned...Where a regulation or directive is adopted by means of the consultation procedure (for example under Articles 99 or 100 of the EC Treaty) the European Parliament may, depending on the specific provision, have to be consulted. In such cases, the European Parliament's role is limited. Where the EC Treaty requires the procedure set out in Article 189c to be used, the European Parliament's position on a matter can be overruled by a unanimous Council. Where the EC Treaty requires the Article 189b procedure to be followed, however, it is not open to the Council to pass measures against the will of the European Parliament. Finally, where the so-called 'assent procedure' is used (as referred to in the first paragraph of Article 138b of the EC Treaty), in relation to matters such as the accession of new member States and the conclusion of certain types of international agreements, the consent of the European Parliament is needed before a measure can be passed. In addition to this involvement in the passage of legislation, the European Parliament also has functions in relation to the appointment and removal of the European Commission. Thus, it has a power of censure over the European Commission, which can ultimately lead to the European Commission having to resign as a body (Article 144); its consent is necessary for the appointment of the European Commission (Article 158); its consent is necessary before the budget can be adopted (Article 203); and it gives a discharge to the European Commission in the implementation of the budget, and here has supervisory powers over the European Commission (Article 206). Further, while the European Parliament has no formal right to initiate legislation, it has the right to request the European Commission to submit proposals on matters on which it considers that a Community act is required (Article 138b).

52. As to the context in which the European Parliament operates, the Court is of the view that the European Parliament represents the principal form of democratic, political accountability in the

Community system. The Court considers that whatever its limitations, the European Parliament, which derives democratic legitimation from the direct elections by universal suffrage, must be seen as that part of the European Community structure which best reflects concerns as to 'effective political democracy'.

53. Even when due allowance is made for the fact that Gibraltar is excluded from certain areas of Community activity . . . there remain significant areas where Community activity has a direct impact in Gibraltar. Further, as the applicant points out, measures taken under Article 189b of the EC Treaty and which affect Gibraltar relate to important matters such as road safety, unfair contract terms and air pollution by emissions from motor vehicles and to all measures in relation to the completion of the internal market.

54. The Court thus finds that the European Parliament is sufficiently involved in the specific legislative processes leading to the passage of legislation under Articles 189b and 189c of the EC Treaty, and is sufficiently involved in the general democratic supervision of the activities of the European Community, to constitute part of the 'legislature' of Gibraltar for the purposes of Article 3 of Protocol No 1.

. . .

E. WHETHER THE ABSENCE OF ELECTIONS TO THE EUROPEAN PARLIAMENT IN GIBRALTAR IN 1994 WAS COMPATIBLE WITH ARTICLE 3 OF PROTOCOL NO 1

60. The Government submitted that, even if Article 3 of Protocol No 1 could be said to apply to the European Parliament, the absence of elections in Gibraltar in 1994 did not give rise to a violation of that provision but instead fell within the State's margin of appreciation. They pointed out that in the 1994 elections the United Kingdom had used a single-member constituency, 'first-past-the-post' system. It would have distorted the electoral process to constitute Gibraltar as a separate constituency, since its population of approximately 30,000 was less than 5% of the average population per European Parliament seat in the United Kingdom. The alternative of redrawing constituency boundaries so as to include Gibraltar within a new or existing constituency was no more feasible, as Gibraltar did not form part of the United Kingdom and had no strong historical or other link with any particular United Kingdom constituency.

61. The applicant submitted that she had been completely deprived of the right to vote in the 1994 elections. She stated that the protection of fundamental rights could not depend on whether or not there were attractive alternatives to the current system.

62. The Commission, since it did not find Article 3 of Protocol No 1 to be applicable, did not examine whether or not the absence of elections in Gibraltar was compatible with that provision.

63. The Court recalls that the rights set out in Article 3 of Protocol No 1 are not absolute, but may be subject to limitations. The Contracting States enjoy a wide margin of appreciation in imposing conditions on the right to vote, but it is for the Court to determine in the last resort whether the requirements of Protocol No 1 have been complied with. It has to satisfy itself that the conditions do not curtail the right to vote to such an extent as to impair its very essence and deprive it of effectiveness; that they are imposed in pursuit of a legitimate aim; and that the means employed are not disproportionate. In particular, such conditions must not thwart 'the free expression of the people in the choice of the legislature' (see the above-mentioned *Mathieu-Mohin and Clerfayt* judgment, p 23, § 52).

64. The Court makes it clear at the outset that the choice of electoral system by which the free expression of the opinion of the people in the choice of the legislature is ensured—whether it be based on proportional representation, the 'first-past-the-post' system or some other arrangement—is a matter in which the State enjoys a wide margin of appreciation. However, in the present case the applicant, as a resident of Gibraltar, was completely denied any opportunity to express her opinion in the choice of

the members of the European Parliament. The position is not analogous to that of persons who are unable to take part in elections because they live outside the jurisdiction, as such individuals have weakened the link between themselves and the jurisdiction. In the present case, as the Court has found (see paragraph 34 above), the legislation which emanates from the European Community forms part of the legislation in Gibraltar, and the applicant is directly affected by it.

65. In the circumstances of the present case, the very essence of the applicant's right to vote, as guaranteed by Article 3 of Protocol No 1, was denied. It follows that there has been a violation of that provision.

...

FOR THESE REASONS THE COURT

Holds by fifteen votes to two that there has been a breach of Article 3 of Protocol No 1; ...

NOTES

1   The Court was composed of President Wildhaber and Judges: Palm, Ferrari Bravo, Gaukur Jorundsson, Ress, Cabral Barreto, Costa, Fuhrmann, Fischbach, Vaji, Hedigan, Thomassen, Tsatsa-Nikolovska, Pantiru, and Traja.

2   Judges Freeland and Jungwiert issued a Joint Dissenting Opinion in which they, *inter alia*, supported the Commission's majority view that Article 3 of Protocol No 1 (P1-3) applied to national or local legislative assemblies and not to international legislative bodies.

'Further, by confining the ambit of the provision to bodies within the domestic area and excluding any supranational representative organ, it avoids the uncertainty and invidiousness involved in analysis by an outside body of the characteristics of such an organ, which as experience has shown are likely to be neither straightforward nor static.' (para 3)

They also doubted whether the European Parliament had yet matured into a 'legislature' as it did not have the power to initiate and adopt legislation.

3   The Court's judgment demonstrated a dynamic interpretation of P1-3 that was not limited to the domestic legislative bodies existing when the framers drafted the Convention. By extending the ambit of the Article to the European Parliament the Court was seeking to redress the democratic deficit existing within the structures of the European Union by helping to ensure that all those persons significantly affected by EC laws at least have the opportunity to elect members of the European Parliament. The legal (and political) difficulty for the UK in gaining an expansion of the franchise for such elections to include the residents of Gibraltar is that Spain, a fellow member of the European Union, claims sovereignty over the territory.

The solution that was adopted for the European Parliament election in 2004 was to annex Gibraltar to the constituency of South-West England. The 20,000 voters in Gibraltar were added to the 3.8 million in the South-West. A number of the candidates went to Gibraltar to campaign for votes during the pre-election period.

4   The Court found two implied rights which were enforceable by individuals (to vote and to stand for election to the legislature) in P1-3 when it first interpreted the Article in the case of *Mathieu-Mohin and Clerfayt v Belgium*, A.113 (1987) 10 EHRR 1. The two applicants were French speaking Belgian parliamentarians who lived in a Flemish district of Brussels. Under the devolved-linguistic constitutional arrangements in Belgium the applicants were unable to participate in the decision-making of the Flemish Council which exercised powers over their district. Therefore, the applicants complained that their exclusion from the Flemish Council violated P1-3. The Commission, by ten votes to one, found a breach of that provision. In the Court's view:

47. According to the Preamble to the Convention, fundamental human rights and freedoms are best maintained by 'an effective political democracy'. Since it enshrines a characteristic principle of democracy, Article 3 of Protocol No 1 (P1-3) is accordingly of prime importance in the Convention system.

48. Where nearly all the other substantive clauses in the Convention and in Protocols Nos. 1, 4, 6 and 7 (P1, P4, P6, P7) use the words 'Everyone has the right' or 'No one shall', Article 3 (P1-3) uses the phrase 'The High Contracting Parties undertake'. It has sometimes been inferred from this that the Article (P1-3) does not give rise to individual rights and freedoms 'directly secured to anyone' within the jurisdiction of these Parties (see the *Ireland v UK* judgment of 18 January 1978, Series A No 25, p 91, § 239), but solely to obligations between States.

If that were so, Mrs. Mathieu-Mohin and Mr Clerfayt's application to the Commission would not have been admissible, since—under Article 25 (art 25) of the Convention—only a person claiming to be the victim of a violation of one of his own rights and freedoms has standing to petition the Commission.

49. Such a restrictive interpretation does not stand up to scrutiny. According to its Preamble, Protocol No 1 (P1) ensures 'the collective enforcement of certain rights and freedoms other than those already included in Section I of the Convention'; furthermore, Article 5 of the Protocol (P1-5) provides: 'as between the High Contracting Parties the provisions of Articles 1, 2, 3 and 4 (P1-1, P1-2, P1-3, P1-4) ... shall be regarded as additional Articles to the Convention', all of whose provisions—including Article 25 (art 25)—'shall apply accordingly'. Moreover, the Preamble to Protocol No 4 (P4) refers, inter alia, to the 'rights and freedoms' protected in 'Articles 1 to 3' of Protocol No 1 (P1-1, P1-2, P1-3).

Nor do the *travaux préparatoires* of Protocol No 1 (P1) disclose any intention of excluding the operation of the right of individual petition as regards Article 3 (P1-3), whereas for a long time the idea was canvassed—only to be finally abandoned—of withholding the subject from the Court's jurisdiction. The *travaux préparatoires* also frequently refer to 'political freedom', 'political rights', 'the political rights and liberties of the individual', 'the right to free elections' and 'the right of election'.

50. Accordingly—and those appearing before the Court were agreed on this point—the inter-State colouring of the wording of Article 3 (P1-3) does not reflect any difference of substance from the other substantive clauses in the Convention and Protocols. The reason for it would seem to lie rather in the desire to give greater solemnity to the commitment undertaken and in the fact that the primary obligation in the field concerned is not one of abstention or non-interference, as with the majority of the civil and political rights, but one of adoption by the State of positive measures to 'hold' democratic elections.

51. As to the nature of the rights thus enshrined in Article 3 (P1-3), the view taken by the Commission has evolved. From the idea of an 'institutional' right to the holding of free elections (decision of 18 September 1961 on the admissibility of application No 1028/61, *X v Belgium*, Yearbook of the Convention, vol 4, p 338) the Commission has moved to the concept of 'universal suffrage' (see particularly the decision of 6 October 1967 on the admissibility of application No 2728/66, *X v the Federal Republic of Germany*, op cit, vol 10, p 338) and then, as a consequence, to the concept of subjective rights of participation—the 'right to vote' and the 'right to stand for election to the legislature' (see in particular the decision of 30 May 1975 on the admissibility of applications nos. 6745-6746/76, *W, X, Y and Z v Belgium*, op cit, vol 18, p 244). The Court approves this latter concept.

52. The rights in question are not absolute. Since Article 3 (P1-3) recognises them without setting them forth in express terms, let alone defining them, there is room for implied limitations (see, *mutatis mutandis*, the *Golder* judgment of 21 February 1975, Series A No 18, pp 18–19, § 38). In their internal legal orders the Contracting States make the rights to vote and to stand for election subject to conditions which are not in principle precluded under Article 3 (P1-3) (Collected Edition of the '*Travaux*

Préparatoires', vol III, p 264, and vol IV, p 24). They have a wide margin of appreciation in this sphere, but it is for the Court to determine in the last resort whether the requirements of Protocol No 1 (P1) have been complied with; it has to satisfy itself that the conditions do not curtail the rights in question to such an extent as to impair their very essence and deprive them of their effectiveness; that they are imposed in pursuit of a legitimate aim; and that the means employed are not disproportionate (see, among other authorities and *mutatis mutandis*, the *Lithgow* judgment of 8 July 1986, Series A No 102, p 71, § 194). In particular, such conditions must not thwart 'the free expression of the opinion of the people in the choice of the legislature'.

53. Article 3 (P1-3) applies only to the election of the 'legislature', or at least of one of its chambers if it has two or more ('*Travaux Préparatoires*', vol VIII, pp 46, 50 and 52). The word 'legislature' does not necessarily mean only the national parliament, however; it has to be interpreted in the light of the constitutional structure of the State in question.

   The Court notes at the outset that the 1980 reform vested the Flemish Council with competence and powers wide enough to make it, alongside the French Community Council and the Walloon Regional Council, a constituent part of the Belgian 'legislature' in addition to the House of Representatives and the Senate . . . those appearing before the Court were agreed on this point.

54. As regards the method of appointing the 'legislature', Article 3 (P1-3) provides only for 'free' elections 'at reasonable intervals', 'by secret ballot' and 'under conditions which will ensure the free expression of the opinion of the people'. Subject to that, it does not create any 'obligation to introduce a specific system' ('*Travaux Préparatoires*', vol VII, pp 130, 202 and 210, and vol VIII, p 14) such as proportional representation or majority voting with one or two ballots.

   Here too the Court recognises that the Contracting States have a wide margin of appreciation, given that their legislation on the matter varies from place to place and from time to time.

   Electoral systems seek to fulfil objectives which are sometimes scarcely compatible with each other: on the one hand, to reflect fairly faithfully the opinions of the people, and on the other, to channel currents of thought so as to promote the emergence of a sufficiently clear and coherent political will. In these circumstances the phrase 'conditions which will ensure the free expression of the opinion of the people in the choice of the legislature' implies essentially—apart from freedom of expression (already protected under Article 10 of the Convention) (art 10)—the principle of equality of treatment of all citizens in the exercise of their right to vote and their right to stand for election.

   It does not follow, however, that all votes must necessarily have equal weight as regards the outcome of the election or that all candidates must have equal chances of victory. Thus no electoral system can eliminate 'wasted votes'.

   For the purposes of Article 3 of Protocol No 1 (P1-3), any electoral system must be assessed in the light of the political evolution of the country concerned; features that would be unacceptable in the context of one system may accordingly be justified in the context of another, at least so long as the chosen system provides for conditions which will ensure the 'free expression of the opinion of the people in the choice of the legislature'.

A majority of the Court, thirteen votes to five, went on to conclude that in the context of the linguistic composition of Belgium and its constitutional history the restrictions upon membership of the Flemish Council did not violate P1-3. The judgment reveals that the implied rights found within the Article are far from absolute and the Court will accord States a considerable margin of appreciation in which to create electoral systems and legislative bodies tailored to their particular national requirements

5   The Court's deference to national electoral arrangements was further illustrated in *Gitonas v Greece* (1997) 26 EHRR 691, *Reports* 1997-IV, where the Court was unanimous in finding no violation of P1-3 in respect of the applicants' disqualification from election to the Greek Parliament. Under the Greek constitution defined groups of former public servants

were disqualified from standing for election to the Parliament for a period of three years after they left public service. The applicants who had held senior positions in the public sector, such as Directors of public television channels, complained that their disqualification from election to the Parliament breached their implied rights to stand and be elected to the legislature enshrined in P1-3. The Commission, by varying majorities, found a breach of the applicants' rights under the Article. The Court held that:

> ... States enjoy considerable latitude to establish in their constitutional order rules governing the status of parliamentarians, including criteria for disqualification. Though originating from a common concern—ensuring the independence of members of parliament, but also the electorate's freedom of choice—the criteria vary according to the historical and political factors peculiar to each state. The number of situations provided for in the Constitutions and the legislation on elections in many member States of the Council of Europe shows the diversity of possible choice on the subject. None of these criteria should, however, be considered more valid than any other provided that it guarantees the expression of the will of the people through free, fair and regular elections. (para 39)

The Court concluded that the disqualification of the applicants from being elected to the Greek Parliament was not arbitrary or disproportionate. The Court's endorsement of national restrictions on the eligibility of former senior public servants to stand for parliament seeks to promote fairness in elections by preventing such persons from abusing the prestige and powers of their previous public offices. Subsequently, the Court has also upheld restrictions on the ability of designated classes of local government officers to stand for election to local councils, the United Kingdom Parliament and the European Parliament in *Ahmed v UK* (above, p 654) and limitations on police officers standing for the Hungarian Parliament in *Rekvenyi v Hungary* (above, p 655).

6   Unfortunately in *Ahmed v UK* (above, p 654) the Court did not rule on whether local authority elections are covered by P1-3. This was regrettable as those local authorities which exercise significant governmental powers (including the enacting of bylaws) ought, as a matter of principle, to have their elections subject to the requirements of this Article. Such a development of the jurisprudence would be in conformity with the above judgments in *Mathieu-Mohin* and *Matthews*.

7   The relationship between P1-3 and Article 10 was examined by the Court in *Bowman v UK* (above, p 652).

8   A Grand Chamber unanimously found a violation of the implied right to vote when a person acquitted on a criminal charge of being a member of a mafia-type organisation was subsequently stuck off the electoral register: *Labita v Italy* (6 April 2000). The applicant had been arrested in April 1992 on suspicion of being a member of such an organization. He was then held in prison awaiting trial. In September of 1992 the District Court imposed preventive measures on the applicant. Later these measures were suspended until the end of the applicant's trial. In November 1994 he was acquitted and subsequently released from custody. Later that month the preventive measures were reapplied to the applicant. Under a Presidential Decree of 1967, persons subject to these measures were also to be disenfranchised. Consequently, in January 1995 the local Electoral Committee struck the applicant off the electoral register. When the preventive measures ceased to apply to Labita, in November 1997, he was reinstated on the electoral roll. The applicant alleged, *inter alia*, a breach of P1-3 and the Commission found a violation of that provision (twenty-three votes to five). Before the Court, the Government contended that the disenfranchisement rules were designed to prevent the Mafia exercising influence over elected bodies.

The Court has no doubt that temporarily suspending the voting rights of persons against whom there is evidence of Mafia membership pursues a legitimate aim. It observes, however, that although the special police supervision measure against the applicant was in the instant case imposed during the course of the trial, it was not applied until the trial was over, once the applicant had been acquitted on the ground that 'he had not committed the offence'. The Court does not accept the view expressed by the Government that the serious evidence of the applicant's guilt was not rebutted during the trial. That affirmation is in contradiction with the tenor of the judgments of the Trapani District Court... and the Palermo Court of Appeal... When his name was removed from the electoral register, therefore, there was no concrete evidence on which a 'suspicion' that the applicant belonged to the Mafia could be based...

In the circumstances, the Court cannot regard the measure in question as proportionate.

There has therefore been a violation of Article 3 of Protocol No 1. (para 203)

Hence, once a person has been acquitted on charges of membership of an antidemocratic criminal organisation States will not generally be able to deprive such persons of their political rights embodied in P1-3.

9 A united Chamber ruled in *Podkolzina v Latvia*, judgment of 9 April 2002, that States have the authority to determine the official language to be used in a national parliament; however, any related linguistic requirements for candidates seeking election to a parliament must be applied in a fair and proportional manner. The applicant was a member of the Russian-speaking minority (40 per cent of the total) of the population. Latvian electoral law required candidates for the Parliament to have a certificate attesting that the candidate was competent to the 'third level' in Latvian, the official language. The applicant's name and language certificate (issued by an official committee) was submitted to Central Electoral Commission by the National Harmony Party which sought to register her as one of its candidates for the 1998 general election. A few days later an examiner, employed by the State Language Inspectorate, visited the applicant at her place of work (no prior warning had been given to the applicant). The inspector engaged the applicant in conversation using the Latvian language and asked her why she supported the National Harmony Party. The next day the inspector returned, with three invigilators, and required the applicant to write an essay in Latvian. The applicant became upset and tore up her essay. Subsequently, the State Language Centre, informed the Central Electoral Commission that the applicant did not have a command of Latvian at the 'third level' and the latter body struck the applicant off the list of candidates. The Latvian courts rejected the applicant's legal challenges to the decision of the Central Electoral Commission. She then complained to the Court alleging a breach of her right to stand as a candidate guaranteed by Article 3. The Court held:

33. ... States have broad latitude to establish constitutional rules on the status of members of parliament, including criteria for declaring them ineligible. Although they have a common origin in the need to ensure both the independence of elected representatives and the freedom of electors, these criteria vary in accordance with the historical and political factors specific to each State; the multiplicity of situations provided for in the constitutions and electoral legislation of numerous member States of the Council of Europe shows the diversity of possible approaches in this area. For the purposes of applying Article 3, any electoral legislation must be assessed in the light of the political evolution of the country concerned, so that features that would be unacceptable in the context of one system may be justified in the context of another. However, the State's margin of appreciation in this regard is limited by the obligation to respect the fundamental principle of Article 3, namely 'the free expression of the opinion of the people in the choice of the legislature' (see *Mathieu-Mohin and Clerfayt*, pp 23–4, § 54).

34. In the present case the Court notes that the applicant was struck out of the list of candidates in accordance with section 5, point 7, of the Parliamentary Elections Act, which makes ineligible persons who do not have a command of Latvian at the 'upper' level. In the Government's submission, the obligation for a candidate to understand and speak Latvian is warranted by the need to ensure the proper functioning of Parliament, in which Latvian is the sole working language. They emphasised in particular that the aim of this requirement was to enable MPs to take an active part in the work of the House and effectively defend their electors' interests.

The Court cannot contest that argument. It considers that the interest of each State in ensuring that its own institutional system functions normally is incontestably legitimate. That applies all the more to the national parliament, which is vested with legislative power and plays a primordial role in a democratic State. Similarly, regard being had to the principle of respect for national characteristics enunciated above, the Court is not required to adopt a position on the choice of a national parliament's working language. That decision, which is determined by historical and political considerations specific to each country, is in principle one which the State alone has the power to make. Accordingly, regard being had to the respondent State's margin of appreciation, the Court concludes that requiring a candidate for election to the national parliament to have sufficient knowledge of the official language pursues a legitimate aim.

Nevertheless, when the Court examined the proportionality of the decision to strike the applicant from the list of registered candidates the Chamber expressed 'surprise' that she had been questioned about her political orientation and the Court found that she had been subjected to a process that was not compatible with the 'requirements of procedural fairness'. Therefore, the Chamber, unanimously, concluded that there had been a breach of Article 3.

The judgement in *Podkolzina*, again, shows the Court's sensitivity to the constitutional and political history of Member states. But, it also protects potential candidates from being subject to unfair registration procedures.

10   A unanimous Chamber of the full-time Court found that Cyprus had violated the right to vote in general elections of a member of the minority Turkish-Cypriot community living in the south of the island in *Aziz v Cyprus*, judgment of 22 June 2004. The applicant lives in Nicosia and opposed the Turkish military invasion of the north. The Cypriot constitution entered into force in 1960 and provided for two separate electoral lists, one for the Greek-Cypriot community and one for the Turkish-Cypriot community. In 1963 the participation of Turkish-Cypriot Members of Parliament was suspended and the applicant was not able to participate in any subsequent general elections for the Parliament. The Government submitted that it was the absence of the majority of the Turkish-Cypriot community (only 1,089 Turkish-Cypriots currently lived in the south) that prevented the applicant from electing members of the Turkish-Cypriot designated seats (30 per cent) in Parliament. The Chamber held that:

29. Although the Court notes that States enjoy considerable latitude to establish rules within their constitutional order governing parliamentary elections and the composition of the Parliament, and that the relevant criteria may vary according to the historical and political factors peculiar to each State, these rules should not be such as to exclude some persons or groups of persons from participating in the political life of the country and, in particular, in the choice of the legislature, a right guaranteed by both the Convention and the Constitutions of all Contracting States.

30. In the present case the Court notes that the irregular situation in Cyprus deteriorated following the occupation of northern Cyprus by Turkish troops and has continued for the last thirty years. It further observes that, despite the fact that the relevant constitutional provisions have been rendered ineffective, there is a manifest lack of legislation resolving the ensuing problems. Consequently, the applicant,

as a member of the Turkish-Cypriot community living in the Government-controlled area of Cyprus, was completely deprived of any opportunity to express his opinion in the choice of the members of the House of Representatives of the country of which he is a national and where he has always lived.

31. The Court considers that, in the light of the above circumstances, the very essence of the applicant's right to vote, as guaranteed by Article 3 of Protocol No 1, was impaired. It follows that there has been a violation of that provision.

The Chamber also found that the denial of the applicant's right to vote breached Article 14 in combination with Article 3 of Protocol No 1. In the judgment of the Court the Cypriot authorities had not been able to justify the difference of treatment of the applicant (as a Turkish-Cypriot) from that of Greek-Cypriots on reasonable and objective grounds. Hence, there had been '38. ... a clear inequality of treatment in the enjoyment of the right in question, which must be considered a fundamental aspect of the case.' The many decades during which the applicant had been disenfranchised appears to have been a key element in the Chamber's application of Article 3.

11 A Chamber adopted a deferential attitude towards the authority of States to prescribe residency requirements for parliamentary candidates in *Melnychenko v Ukraine*, judgment of 19 October 2004.

56. As to the condition of residence in relation to the right to stand for elections, as such, the Court has never expressed its opinion on this point. However, in relation to the separate right to vote, the Court has held that it was not *per se* an unreasonable or arbitrary requirement (see *Hilbe v Liechtenstein* (dec.), No 31981/96, ECHR 1999-VI). The Court considers that a residence requirement for voting may be justified on the grounds of (1) the assumption that a non-resident citizen is less directly or continuously concerned with, and has less knowledge of, a country's day-to-day problems; (2) the impracticability for and sometimes undesirability (in some cases impossibility) of parliamentary candidates presenting the different electoral issues to citizens living abroad so as to secure the free expression of opinion; (3) the influence of resident citizens on the selection of candidates and on the formulation of their electoral programmes, and (4) the correlation between one's right to vote in parliamentary elections and being directly affected by the acts of the political bodies so elected (*Polacco and Garofalo v Italy*, No 23450/94, Commission decision of 15 September 1997, referring to previous Commission case-law).

57. However, the Court accepts that stricter requirements may be imposed on the eligibility to stand for election to parliament, as distinguished from voting eligibility ... Hence the Court would not preclude outright a five-year continuous residency requirement for potential parliamentary candidates. Arguably, this requirement may be deemed appropriate to enable such persons to acquire sufficient knowledge of the issues associated with the national parliament's tasks.

But, the Chamber also held that:

59. ... The right to stand as a candidate in an election, which is guaranteed by Article 3 of Protocol No. 1 and is inherent in the concept of a truly democratic regime, would be illusory if one could be arbitrarily deprived of it at any moment. Consequently, while it is true that States have a wide margin of appreciation when establishing eligibility conditions in the abstract, the principle that rights must be effective requires that the eligibility procedure contains sufficient safeguards to prevent arbitrary decisions.

A large majority, six votes to one, went on to find that there had been a breach of this Article as the Ukrainian authorities had refused to register the applicant (a Ukrainian national living as a political refugee in the USA) as a parliamentary candidate when he still held a valid registered place of residence in the Ukraine.

12 The majority (twelve votes to five) of a Grand Chamber determined that the automatic disqualification of the right to vote (in both parliamentary and local authority elections) in respect of all convicted persons whilst detained in prison violated Article 3 in *Hirst v United Kingdom (No 2)*, judgment of 6 October 2005. The applicant had been convicted of manslaughter in 1980 and given a discretionary life sentence. He was released from prison, on licence, in 2004. Under section 3 of the Representation of the People Act 1983, he was disenfranchised throughout the period of his imprisonment. The Government sought to justify the disenfranchisement of all convicted prisoners as being for the twin aims of preventing crime/punishing offenders and enhancing civic responsibility. The majority accepted that these were legitimate aims under Article 3. However, they did not believe that the UK's general ban was a proportional restriction:

82. ... section 3 of the 1983 Act remains a blunt instrument. It strips of their Convention right to vote a significant category of persons and it does so in a way which is indiscriminate. The provision imposes a blanket restriction on all convicted prisoners in prison. It applies automatically to such prisoners, irrespective of the length of their sentence and irrespective of the nature or gravity of their offence and their individual circumstances. Such a general, automatic and indiscriminate restriction on a vitally important Convention right must be seen as falling outside any acceptable margin of appreciation, however wide, that margin might be, and as being incompatible with Article 3 of Protocol No 1.

The dissentients, led by President Wildhaber, believed that:

9. Our own opinion whether persons serving a prison sentence should be allowed to vote in general or other elections matters little. Taking into account the sensitive political character of this issue, the diversity of the legal systems within the Contracting States and the lack of a sufficiently clear basis for such a right in Article 3 of Protocol No 1, we are not able to accept that it is for the Court to impose on national legal systems an obligation either to abolish disenfranchisement for prisoners or to allow it only to a very limited extent.

Clearly, the majority did not like the general nature of the prisoners' disenfranchisement provided for by the British legislation. The decision in *Hirst* demonstrates that, despite the wide margin of appreciation formally accorded to States to determine their own electoral arrangements under Article 3, the full-time Court is increasingly willing to find that significant limitations on democratic rights violate this provision.

13 A Grand Chamber, by thirteen votes to four, determined that there had been no breach of Article 3 regarding a ban imposed on a former senior member of a communist party, who had been involved in unsuccessful coups during the re-emergence of an independent and democratic State, to stand as a candidate in national elections in *Zdanoka v Latvia*, judgment of 16 March 2006. The Court held that:

133. Whilst such a measure may scarcely be considered acceptable in the context of one political system, for example in a country which has an established framework of democratic institutions going back many decades or centuries, it may nonetheless be considered acceptable in Latvia in view of the historico-political context which led to its adoption and given the threat to the new democratic order posed by the resurgence of ideas, which if allowed to gain ground, might appear capable of restoring the former regime.

However, the majority indicated its support for a time-limit to be imposed on the ban. In his Dissenting Opinion Judge Zupancic stated:

... I do not believe for a moment that the Latvian authorities would have prevented Mrs Zdanoka from standing in national elections in Latvia were it only for her Communist *past*. Neither is the true reason her *present* unwillingness to recant and repudiate her Communist views. The domestic Latvian point of view concerns no more (and no less) than Mrs Zdanoka's *future* political dangerousness. This has to do with the demographic *fact* that thirty percent of the existing Latvian population speaks Russian. Presumably, this puts in jeopardy the pro-autonomy rule of the autochthonous majority in whose name the separation of Latvia (and the two other Baltic states) from the Soviet Union was carried out in the first place.

The successful applicant in *Podkolzina*, above Note 9, was from the Russian speaking minority.

14 A general analysis of the Court's case-law by the author resulted in the following conclusions:

The cases that we have analysed certainly reveal the Court's continuing support for representative democracy across a widening group of member-States with diverse constitutional heritages. The current model of European democracy has then been used by the Court in recent times to guide its interpretation and application of a number of Convention rights, including freedom of religion, freedom of expression, freedom of association and the rights to vote and stand in free elections. Furthermore, the factual contexts in which the Court has had to apply the Convention have encompassed many facets of the democratic political process, such as the creation and dissolution of political parties, the criticism of governmental policy by opposition politicians, the eligibility of candidates to stand for elected office, the ability of citizens to vote in elections, the capacity of pressure-groups to seek to influence voters' choices of candidates and the freedom of conscience and religion of elected politicians. The Court has utilised its conception of European democracy for two major purposes. First, as an aid in determining the scope of particular Convention rights. As we have seen, the Court adopted an expansive interpretation of the ambit of P1-3 in *Matthews*, to encompass the European Parliament, relying heavily upon the belief that it was appropriate to subject European parliamentary elections to the demands of this provision because it 'enshrines a characteristic of an effective political democracy'. Similarly the Court unequivocally declared that political parties came within the protection of Article 11 in *United Communist Party of Turkey*, due to the judicial opinion that they 'are a form of association essential to the proper functioning of democracy'. Secondly, the Court has invoked the concept as a guiding factor in determining the intensity of its review of state action under different Convention provisions. For example, the Court noted in *Incal* that it would subject state interference with an opposition politician's freedom of expression to 'the closest scrutiny' due to the importance of this form of political speech for the operation of the democratic process. Likewise, state action to dissolve a political party will be subject to a 'rigorous European supervision' according to the Court in *United Communist Party of Turkey*.

Overall States will be reassured that the Court generally accords them a wide margin of appreciation to prescribe the details of their domestic electoral law in accordance with the demands of their national political histories and current constitutional arrangements, as in *Gitonas* and *Ahmed*. However, this margin is not unlimited, as we have discovered in our earlier examination of *Bowman* and *Matthews*. The judgment in *Gitonas* also indicates that the Court will not assume the general role of a pan-European electoral court reviewing the domestic eligibility of individual candidates for elected office. Furthermore, States can invoke the need to protect the practical requirements of democracy as a legitimate justification for limiting the Convention rights of individuals under Articles 8–11, even when there is no serious threat to the national constitutional order, as in *Ahmed*. Naturally, the Court will evaluate whether the contested limitation meets the well-established 'pressing social need' and proportionality requirements embodied in the Convention condition that state action must be 'necessary in a democratic society'.

Individuals have benefited from the Court's utilisation of the model of European democracy as it has facilitated judgments which have accorded them the rights to, inter alia, form political parties, to vote in European elections and to protect their freedom of conscience and religion when they are elected to national parliaments. Indeed, the judgments in *Matthews* and *Buscarini* indicate that the new full-time

Court is adopting a robust application of the model, which protects individuals *qua* voters and politicians. Therefore, we may conclude that in contemporary times the Court has generally developed and applied its concept of democracy in a progressive manner which has sought to enhance and safeguard the vitality of the political processes operating in member-States.' [A Mowbray, 'The Role of The European Court of Human Rights in the Promotion of Democracy' [1999] *Public Law* 703 at pp 723–5.]

Article 1 Prohibition of imprisonment for debt

In *Goktan v France*, judgment of 2 July 2002 and see below p 1007, a unanimous Chamber observed that Article 1 did not apply to the French system of imprisonment in default of monies owed to the Treasury in respect of fines imposed for criminal offences as Article 1 concerns debts arising under a contractual obligation. Nevertheless, '51. [t]he Court has to express reservations about the imprisonment in default system as such: it constitutes an archaic custodial measure available only to the Treasury...'

Article 2 Freedom of movement

Napijalo v Croatia 13 November 2003
European Court of Human Rights

The applicant, a Croatian national, was driving from Bosnia and Herzegovina on 6 February 1999. At the border he was stopped by a Croatian customs officer who considered that the applicant had committed a customs offence, by failing to declare goods (four cartons of cigarettes and two litres of cooking oil lying on the backseat of the car). The officer imposed a fine, of approximately 30 euros, but as the applicant did not have enough money on him to pay the fine the officer retained the applicant's passport. The applicant wrote, on 10 February 1999, to the Customs Administration requesting the return of his passport. The latter replied that the seizure of his passport was in accordance with the law. The Customs Administration did not return the passport, even though no proceedings were brought against the applicant, but sent it to the police. The applicant initiated civil proceedings, in March 1999, against the Ministry of Finance seeking, *inter alia*, the return of his passport. The courts did not order its return. In April 2001 the applicant was able to collect his passport from the police. He complained to the Court alleging, *inter alia*, that his freedom of movement to leave Croatia, guaranteed under Article 2(2) of Protocol No. 4, had been infringed by the seizure of his passport.

68. The Court reiterates that the right of freedom of movement as guaranteed by paragraphs 1 and 2 of Article 2 of Protocol No. 4 is intended to secure to any person a right to liberty of movement within a territory and to leave that territory, which implies a right to leave for such country of the person's choice to which he may be admitted (see, *mutatis mutandis, Peltonen v Finland*, Commission decision of 20 February 1995, Decisions and Reports (DR) 80-A, p 43, § 31 and *Baumann v France*, judgment of 22 May 2001, *Reports of Judgments and Decisions* 2001-V, p 217, § 61). It follows that liberty of movement prohibits any measure liable to infringe that right or to restrict the exercise thereof which does

not satisfy the requirement of a measure which can be considered as 'necessary in a democratic society' in the pursuit of the legitimate aims referred to in the third paragraph of the above-mentioned Article.

69. Accordingly, the Court considers that a measure by means of which an individual is dispossessed of an identity document such as, for example, a passport, undoubtedly amounts to an interference with the exercise of liberty of movement (see, *mutatis mutandis*, M. v Germany, application No 10307/83, Commission decision of 6 March 1984, DR 37, p 113 and *Baumann v France*, cited above, p 217, § 62).

. . . .

73. The Court finds that as a result of the seizure of the applicant's passport he could not, at the very least from the date of his application for its return on 10 February 1999, retrieve it. Accordingly, it observes that he was denied the use of that identity document, which, had he wished, would have permitted him to leave the country. It therefore finds that the applicant's right to liberty of movement was restricted in a manner amounting to an interference within the meaning of Article 2 of Protocol No 4 to the Convention (see, *mutatis mutandis*, *Guzzardi v Italy*, judgment of 6 November 1980, Series A No 39, p 33, § 92; *Raimondo v Italy*, judgment of 22 February 1994, Series A No 281–1, p 19, § 39; and *Labita v Italy* [GC], *Reports* 2000-IV, pp 38–39, § 193 and *Baumann v France*, cited above, p 217, § 63 and *a contrario, Piermont v France*, judgment of 27 April 1995, Series A No 314, p 20, § 44).

74. It remains to be determined whether that restriction was 'in accordance with the law' and was a 'necessary measure in a democratic society'.

2. REQUIREMENT OF A MEASURE 'IN ACCORDANCE WITH THE LAW'

75. The Government argued that the seizure of the applicant's passport was in accordance with law, namely Section 34 and 35 of the Act on Travel Documents.

76. The applicant did not address this issue.

77. Having regard to the conclusion reached (see § 82 below) the Court does not find it necessary to examine the question.

3. NECESSITY OF THE MEASURE 'IN A DEMOCRATIC SOCIETY' IN THE PURSUIT OF LEGITIMATE AIMS

78. The Court must examine the question whether the seizure and keeping of the passport could be considered a measure which was 'necessary in a democratic society' within the meaning of the third paragraph.

79. The Court notes firstly that although the applicant had refused to pay the fine imposed, no proceedings were ever instituted against him for any customs offence that he had allegedly committed. By not pursuing their initial motivation for the seizure of the applicant's passport the authorities lost any further ground for keeping the passport. Therefore, the applicant was unable to ascertain the grounds justifying the continuing deprivation of his passport.

80. The Court also notes that although the Police showed initiative in order to return the passport, the Zagreb Municipal Court rejected the applicant's request for an interim measure that the passport be returned to him. Thus, it appears that there was no co-operation or co-ordination both within the police and between the police and the judicial authorities. This lack of appropriate administrative procedures resulted, *inter alia*, in the applicant being unable to travel abroad for a prolonged period of time.

81. Having regard to the development of the case and the outcome of the civil proceedings for the return of the passport, the Court notes that the applicant was never charged with any customs offence

and that this aspect of the civil proceedings ended when the police returned the passport. In that connection, the Court does not find any justification for the Customs Administration's refusal to return the applicant's passport or for the Zagreb Municipal Court's rejection of the applicant's request for the interim measure, which both resulted in the continuing seizure of the applicant's passport and the continuing interference with his right to liberty of movement.

82. Having regard to the above, the Court finds that the interference with the applicants liberty of movement was not a measure 'necessary in a democratic society' proportionate to the aims pursued (see, *Labita v Italy*, cited above, p 147, § 197 and *Baumann v France*, cited above, p 219, § 67).

Accordingly, there has been a violation of Article 2 of Protocol No. 4.

....

FOR THESE REASONS, THE COURT UNANIMOUSLY

....

3. *Holds* that there has been a violation of Article 2(2) of Protocol No 4;

....

NOTES

1   The Court was composed of President Rozakis and Judges: Tulkens, Vajic, Levits, Botoucharova, Kovler, and Zagrebelsky.

2   The key to the conclusion in *Napijalo* was the failure of the authorities to provide any acceptable justification, given that no prosecution was brought against the applicant for an alleged customs offence, for the retention of his passport for over two years.

3   In the earlier case of *Baumann v France*, 2001-V, the Court had been deeply divided on whether the confiscation of the applicant's German passport by the French police during a criminal investigation involving his girlfriend amounted to a breach of Article 2. The majority (by four votes to three) concluded that it was not necessary in a democratic society for the French authorities to have retained the applicant's passport once the initial investigation had been completed and he was not considered to be a witness nor was he prosecuted. By contrast the dissenters did not believe that the applicant's freedom of movement in France had been interfered with as he had returned to Germany before the police had seized his passport.

4   Both the original and full-time Court have found special supervision measures imposed by the Italian courts on suspected members of the Mafia to be in breach of Article 2. In *Raimondo v Italy*, A.281-A (1994), the applicant was arrested in 1984 on suspicion of being a member of a Mafia-type organization. In 1985, at the request of the prosecutor, the relevant District Court made an order placing the applicant under special police supervision (this required him to, *inter alia*, inform the police when he left his home, to return to his home by 9 pm and not to leave his home before 7 am). The supervision measures became effective when the applicant was acquitted of the criminal charges in January 1986. The applicant appealed against the special supervision measures and in July 1986, at a private hearing, the Court of Appeal annulled the measures. The Court of Appeal's decision was filed with the registry on 2 December 1986 and the registry informed the police. The local carabinieri notified the applicant of the ending of the measures on 20 December 1986. The applicant complained to Strasbourg alleging the measures amounted to an infringement of his freedom of movement. The unanimous Chamber found that the threat posed by the Mafia to democratic society and the authorities' aim to prevent crime justified the imposition of such measures. Furthermore, the

measures imposed on the applicant were proportionate until the Court of Appeal revoked the order in July 1986.

39. ... It remains to consider the period between 4 July and 20 December, when the decision was notified to the applicant. Even if it is accepted that this decision, taken in private session, could not acquire legal force until it was filed with the registry, the Court finds it hard to understand why there should have been a delay of nearly five months in drafting the grounds for a decision which was immediately enforceable and concerned a fundamental right, namely the applicant's freedom to come and go as he pleased; the latter was moreover not informed of the revocation for eighteen days.

40. The Court concludes that at least from 2 to 20 December 1986 the interference in issue was neither provided for by law nor necessary. There has accordingly been a violation of Article 2 of Protocol No 4.

So, it was the delays in the process of revoking the orders in *Raimondo* that caused the Court to find a breach of Article 2. We have already noted the systematic delays in the Italian legal system under Article 6 (above p 427).

In *Labita v Italy*, (above p 982), the preventive measures imposed on the applicant, which took effect after his acquittal, included informing the authorities when he left his home, returning home by 8 pm, not leaving home before 6am and not going to bars or public meetings. The measures lasted three years. The unanimous Grand Chamber followed *Raimondo* in concluding that the special supervision measures were for a legitimate purpose and in accordance with the law.

195. However, the measures also had to be 'necessary in a democratic society' for those legitimate aims to be achieved.

In this connection, the Court considers that it is legitimate for preventive measures, including special supervision, to be taken against persons suspected of being members of the Mafia, even prior to conviction, as they are intended to prevent crimes being committed. Furthermore, an acquittal does not necessarily deprive such measures of all foundation, as concrete evidence gathered at trial, though insufficient to secure a conviction, may nonetheless justify reasonable fears that the person concerned may in the future commit criminal offences.

196. In the instant case, the decision to put the applicant under special supervision was taken on 10 May 1993 at a time when there effectively existed some evidence that he was a member of the Mafia, but the measure was not put into effect until 19 November 1994 after his acquittal by the Trapani District Court.

The Court has examined the grounds relied on by the Italian courts for refusing to rescind the measure after the applicant's acquittal, namely B.F.'s [a 'pentito'—former Mafioso who later co-operated with the authorities] assertion that the applicant had contacts in the Mafia clan as was proved by the fact that his deceased brother-in-law had been the head of the main clan (decision of the Trapani District Court of 11 June 1996) and the fact that 'the applicant had not shown any real change in his life-style or that he was genuinely repentant' (decision of the Trapani District Court of 21 October 1997).

The Court fails to see how the mere fact that the applicant's wife was the sister of a Mafia boss, since deceased, could justify such severe measures being taken against him in the absence of any other concrete evidence to show that there was a real risk that he would offend. As regards changing his life-style and repenting, the Court is mindful of the fact that the applicant, who has no criminal antecedents, was acquitted of the charge that he was a member of the Mafia on the ground that no concrete evidence in support of that allegation could be found during the preliminary investigation and trial.

197. In conclusion, and without underestimating the threat posed by the Mafia, the Court concludes that the restrictions on the applicant's freedom of movement cannot be regarded as having been 'necessary in a democratic society'.

There has therefore been a violation of Article 2 of Protocol No 4.

Hence, whilst the Grand Chamber was willing to contemplate the lawfulness of preventive measures restricting a person's freedom of movement being imposed on a former defendant who had been acquitted the Court, understandably, required the State to demonstrate the existence of evidence justifying such measures.

5 Another type of Italian order restricting a bankrupt's freedom of movement was found to be in breach of Article 2 in *Luordo v Italy*, judgment of 17 July 2003. The applicant was declared bankrupt by the District Court in November 1984 and that Court terminated his bankruptcy in July 1999. During the period of his bankruptcy Italian law provided that the applicant could not move away from his place of residence without the approval of the bankruptcy judge. The applicant claimed, *inter alia*, that this restriction violated his freedom of movement. A unanimous Chamber ruled that the restriction was in accordance with the law and for a legitimate purpose (to protect the rights of the applicant's creditors).

96. The Court notes at the outset that the restriction placed on the applicant's freedom of movement is not in itself open to criticism. However, the risk with such a system is that it may unreasonably restrict the applicant's freedom to move freely, particularly if the proceedings are protracted, as they were in the instant case in which they lasted fourteen years and eight months. . . .

Consequently, it finds that there was no justification for restricting the applicant's freedom of movement for the full duration of the proceedings, since, while in principle a restriction on the right to move away from the place of residence is necessary to achieve the aim pursued, the necessity will diminish with the passage of time. Even though there is nothing in the case file to indicate that the applicant wished to move away from his place of residence or was refused permission to do so, in the Court's view, the length of the proceedings upset the balance that had to be struck between the general interest in securing the payment of the bankrupt's creditors and the applicant's personal interest in having freedom of movement. The interference with the applicant's freedom was accordingly disproportionate to the aim pursued.

97. Having regard to the foregoing, the Court concludes that there has been an infringement of the applicant's freedom of movement as guaranteed by Article 2 of Protocol No 4.

As in *Raimondo*, the lengthy period of the restrictions, caused by delays in the Italian legal system, was the reason why the Court found a breach in *Luordo*.

6 A unanimous Chamber found Cyprus to have breached Article 2 by virtue of extensive restrictions imposed by police officers (including members of the Central Intelligence Service) on the movements of the applicants in *Denizci and Others v Cyprus*, judgment of 23 May 2001. The nine applicants were Cypriot nationals who had been living in the northern part of Cyprus. When they entered the south, police officers told the applicants which towns they could live in (some of the applicants were provided with houses by the officers). The officers required the applicants to notify them when they moved to other accommodation and also when they wished to go to the north to visit their families. The applicants contended, *inter alia*, that the restrictions placed on their movements and the close monitoring of them by the police violated Article 2.

405. . . . The Court notes that no lawful basis for the applicants' restrictions of movements was advanced by the respondent Government. Moreover, the respondent Government did not claim that the measure was necessary in a democratic society to achieve one of the legitimate aims set forth in paragraphs 3 and 4 of Article 2 of Protocol No 4.

406. The Court concludes that the restrictions on the applicants' freedom of movement were neither provided for by law nor necessary. There has accordingly been a violation of Article 2 of Protocol No 4.

So the police officers' actions had no basis in domestic law!

7 In *Timishev v Russia*, judgment of 13 December 2005, a united Chamber found that an oral instruction given by a senior police officer to subordinates, not to allow 'Chechens' into the Republic of Kabardino-Balkaria, violated this provision on its own and in conjunction with Article 14 (see above, p 828 for this aspect of the case). The applicant, a Russian national, was born and lived in the Chechen Republic. He had to leave that Republic, with his family, when his property in Grozny was destroyed during 1994. Since 1996 they had been living as migrants in the Republic of Kabardino-Balkaria. In June 1999 the applicant was being driven from the Ingushetia Republic to his home in the Republic of Kabardino-Balkaria when police officers refused him entry to the latter Republic at the Urukh checkpoint on the administrative border between the two Republics. He was obliged to make a detour of 300 km to gain entry to the Republic of Kabardino-Balkaria via another checkpoint.

The Chamber detrmined that:

45. The Court notes that the structure of Article 2 of Protocol No 4 is similar to that of Articles 8–11 of the Convention. In order to be compatible with the guarantees of Article 2 of Protocol No 4 the impugned restriction should be 'in accordance with the law', pursue one or more of the legitimate aims contemplated in paragraph 3 and be 'necessary in a democratic society' (see *Raimondo v Italy*, judgment of 22 February 1994, Series A No 281-A, p 19, § 39) or, where the restriction applies to particular areas only, be 'justified by the public interest in a democratic society' as established in paragraph 4.

46. The Government argued that the restriction was imposed in accordance with section 11(22) of the Police Act with a view to deterring criminal offences and guaranteeing public safety. The applicant retorted that the restriction had been unnecessarily broad and the aim thereby pursued too abstract.

47. The Court is not required to rule on the general question whether the political and social situation in Ingushetia or the Kabardino-Balkaria Republic at the material time called for the introduction of checkpoints on a federal motorway and thorough identity checks. The issue for the Court to determine is limited to the specific circumstances of the present case, namely whether the refusal to let the applicant cross the administrative border into Kabardino-Balkaria had a lawful basis.

48. The inquiries carried out by the prosecutor's office and by the Kabardino-Balkaria Ministry of the Interior established that the restriction at issue had been imposed by an oral order given by the deputy head of the public safety police of the Kabardino-Balkaria Ministry of the Interior, Colonel Efendiyev. It appears that the order was not properly formalised or recorded in some other traceable way, enabling the Court to carry out an assessment of its contents, scope and legal basis. Indeed, the reference to section 11(22) of the Police Act appeared for the first time in the Government's submissions in the proceedings before the Court. In any event, in the opinion of the prosecutor's office, the order amounted to a violation of the constitutional right to liberty of movement enshrined in Article 27 of the Russian Constitution.

49. Accordingly, the Court finds that the restriction on the applicant's liberty of movement was not in accordance with the law. This finding makes it unnecessary to examine whether it was necessary in a democratic society.

There has therefore been a violation of Article 2 of Protocol No 4.

However, it appears that the above breach was not an isolated incident as in *Gartukayev v Russia*, judgment of 13 December 2005, the Court found a separate breach of Article 2 in respect of another former Chechen resident who had been denied access to the Republic of Kabardino-Balkaria at a different checkpoint later in 2000. In this case the police had applied an unpublished regulation requiring former Chechen residents to produce a migrant's card before being admitted to the Republic of Kabardino-Balkaria. The Court concluded that as the regulation had not been published, as required by Russian law, the restriction on the applicant's liberty of movement was not 'in accordance with the law' under Article 2. So, once again (see above, p 97 for Article 2 breaches) the Russian authorities responses to the conflict in the Chechen Republic were not in conformity with their Convention obligations.

8 A unanimous Chamber held that a travel ban prohibiting leaving the country, imposed on a dual national who owed at least 150,000 euros in taxes, fell within the legitimate aims of the maintenance of *ordre public* and protection of the rights of others in *Riener v Bulgaria*, judgment of 23 May 2006. However, the Chamber went on to find that the continuance of the ban for nine years without adequate reviews of its necessity amounted to a disproportionate interference with the applicant's right and violated Article 2.

124. In the Court's view, the authorities are not entitled to maintain over lengthy periods restrictions on the individual's freedom of movement without periodic reassessment of their justification in the light of factors such as whether or not the fiscal authorities had made reasonable efforts to collect the debt through other means and the likelihood that the debtor's leaving the country might undermine the chances to collect the money.

This judgment achieves a sensible balance between the rights of the individual and the community interest in ensuring the collection of taxation.

Article 3 Prohibition of expulsion of nationals

In *Denizci* (above) the applicants also alleged that their forcible expulsion from the south to the northern part of Cyprus violated Article 3 of Protocol No 4. The Government did not respond to this allegation, apart from denying the applicants' account of the facts. The Chamber, unanimously, noted that the applicants had not claimed that they were expelled to the territory of another State. Furthermore, the Republic of Cyprus is the only legitimate Government of Cyprus. Therefore, taking account of its finding in respect of Article 2 of Protocol No 4, the Chamber determined that it was not necessary for it to consider whether Article 3 applied in the present case. This outcome enabled the Court to avoid having to rule on the applicability of Article 3 in the context of a national being expelled to a part of a State's formal territory which is not *de facto* controlled by the government.

Article 4 Prohibition of collective expulsion of aliens

Conka v Belgium 5 February 2002
European Court of Human Rights

The applicants were a family of four Slovakian nationals of Roma origin. They arrived in Belgium at the end of 1998 claiming to have suffered persecution by skinheads in Slovakia with the police refusing to protect them. In March 1999 the Minister of the Interior refused their requests for political asylum on the ground that they had not provided adequate evidence of persecution in Slovakia. The Minister ordered that they leave Belgium within five days. The applicants lodged appeals with the Commissioner-General for Refugees. Subsequently, Mr Conka did not attend his scheduled interview at the Commissioner-General's office. Mrs Conka was heard by representatives of the Commissioner-General, in a Belgian prison where she was awaiting trial for alleged theft. In June 1999 the Commissioner-General rejected the applicants' appeals (Mr Conka's due to his failure to attend the interview without good cause and Mrs Conka because the Commissioner-General expressed serious doubts about her credibility and the account she provided). The applicants were ordered to leave Belgium by the end of June (Mrs Conka had by then served her period of imprisonment). The applicants lodged judicial review challenges to the Commissioner-General's decisions with the *Conseil d'Etat*. Their applications were struck out in October 1999 as they had not paid the required court fees.

At the end of September 1999 the applicants and a number of other Slovak Roma families living in Ghent were sent a letter, written in Dutch and Slovak, by the police requiring them to attend the police station on 1 October in order to enable the files concerning their applications for asylum to be completed. When they arrived at the police station, where there was a Slovak interpreter, they were served with new orders to leave Belgium, dated 29 September, and they were detained pending removal. Some of the Roma were allowed to leave the police station for humanitarian reasons, but the applicants were taken to a closed transit centre. While at the centre the Slovakian families received visits from the Slovakian Consul, a delegation of Belgian MPs and representatives of various non-governmental organizations. The applicants' lawyer requested the authorities not to deport his clients on humanitarian grounds. Seventy Slovakian nationals, including the applicants, were flown back to Slovakia on 5 October 1999. In December 1999 the Belgian Minister of the Interior reported to parliament that: 'Owing to the large concentration of asylum-seekers of Slovakian nationality in Ghent, arrangements have been made for their collective repatriation to Slovakia . . . the operation was properly prepared, even if the unfortunate wording of the letter sent by the Ghent police to some of the Slovaks may have been misleading.'

The applicants complained to the Court alleging, *inter alia*, that their removal to Slovakia amounted to a collective expulsion prohibited by Article 4 of Protocol No 4.

59. The Court reiterates its case-law whereby collective expulsion, within the meaning of Article 4 of Protocol No 4, is to be understood as any measure compelling aliens, as a group, to leave a country, except where such a measure is taken on the basis of a reasonable and objective examination of the particular case of each individual alien of the group (see *Andric* [v Sweden (dec.) No 45917/99, 23 February 1999]). That does not mean, however, that where the latter condition is satisfied the background to the execution of the expulsion orders plays no further role in determining whether there has been compliance with Article 4 of Protocol No 4.

60. In the instant case, the applications for asylum made by the applicants were rejected in decisions of 3 March 1999 that were upheld on 18 June 1999. The decisions of 3 March 1999 contained reasons and were accompanied by an order made on the same day requiring the applicants to leave the territory. They were reached after an examination of each applicant's personal circumstances on the basis of their depositions. The decisions of 18 June 1999 were also based on reasons related to the personal circumstances of the applicants and referred to the order of 3 March 1999 to leave the territory, which had been stayed by the appeals under the urgent procedure.

61. The Court notes, however, that the detention and deportation orders in issue were made to enforce an order to leave the territory dated 29 September 1999; that order was made solely on the basis of section 7, first paragraph, point (2), of the Aliens Act, and the only reference to the personal

circumstances of the applicants was to the fact that their stay in Belgium had exceeded three months. In particular, the document made no reference to their application for asylum or to the decisions of 3 March and 18 June 1999. Admittedly, those decisions had also been accompanied by an order to leave the territory, but by itself, that order did not permit the applicants' arrest. The applicants' arrest was therefore ordered for the first time in a decision of 29 September 1999 on a legal basis unrelated to their requests for asylum, but nonetheless sufficient to entail the implementation of the impugned measures. In those circumstances and in view of the large number of persons of the same origin who suffered the same fate as the applicants, the Court considers that the procedure followed does not enable it to eliminate all doubt that the expulsion might have been collective.

62. That doubt is reinforced by a series of factors: firstly, prior to the applicants' deportation, the political authorities concerned had announced that there would be operations of that kind and given instructions to the relevant authority for their implementation; secondly, all the aliens concerned had been required to attend the police station at the same time; thirdly, the orders served on them requiring them to leave the territory and for their arrest were couched in identical terms; fourthly, it was very difficult for the aliens to contact a lawyer; lastly, the asylum procedure had not been completed.

63. In short, at no stage in the period between the service of the notice on the aliens to attend the police station and their expulsion did the procedure afford sufficient guarantees demonstrating that the personal circumstances of each of those concerned had been genuinely and individually taken into account.

In conclusion, there has been a violation of Article 4 of Protocol No 4.

....

FOR THESE REASONS, THE COURT

....

5. *Holds* by four votes to three that there has been a violation of Article 4 of Protocol No 4 to the Convention;

....

NOTES

1 The Court was composed of President Costa and Judges: Fuhrmann, Kuris, Jungwiert, Bratza, Traja, and Velaers.

2 Judge Jungwiert, joined by Judge Kuris, issued a partly dissenting opinion. He believed that the applicants' individual circumstances had been considered by the Belgian authorities prior to their expulsion.

Each decision was accompanied by an order to leave the territory. As the applicants did not comply, measures were taken for them to be forcibly expelled. The applicants were served with a notice requiring them to attend Ghent police station where a final examination of their files was carried out. The Ghent police contacted the Aliens Office. The aliens whose requests for asylum had been turned down and who were not entitled to remain in Belgium on any other grounds were deprived of their liberty and repatriated as part of a group. The fact that some of them were allowed to return home after their individual circumstances had been checked and their immigration status found to be in order shows that, even at that late stage in the deportation process, a final individual examination was carried out.

The fact that the expulsion orders were executed in respect of a group and that some seventy aliens of Slovakian nationality were repatriated together by air does not imply that there was a 'collective expulsion' within the meaning of Article 4 of Protocol No 4, since the personal circumstances of each expelled alien were examined on three occasions. That the last decisions of 29 September 1999 contain no reference to the reasons for the decisions of 3 March 1999 and 18 June 1999, but merely refer to the unlawful situation of those concerned (see section 7, first paragraph, point (2), of the Aliens Act), does not alter the fact that the aliens' individual circumstances were examined and provides sufficient justification for the expulsions in issue. In that connection, I agree with the opinion expressed in the decision in *Andric v Sweden*): 'the fact that a number of aliens receive similar decisions does not lead to the conclusion that there is a collective expulsion when each person has been given the opportunity to put arguments against his expulsion to the competent authorities on an individual basis'.

Furthermore, this provision does not, in my opinion, prevent States from grouping together, for reasons of economy or efficiency, people who, at the end of similar proceedings, are to be expelled to the same country.

These considerations lead me to conclude that there has been no violation of Article 4 of Protocol No 4.

3 Judge Velaers, the *ad hoc* Belgian Judge, in his partly concurring and partly dissenting opinion also found that there had been an examination of the applicants' personal circumstances on the day they were detained at Ghent police station. Do you think the Belgian authorities planned and undertook a collective expulsion?

4 The Article 13 aspects of *Conka* have been examined above at p 805.

5 In the earlier admissibility decision of *Andric v Sweden*, 23 February 1999, cited in *Conka*, the applicant was a Croatian national who had sought political asylum in Sweden during 1994. After a number of appeals his application was rejected in 1998 (in 1999 the authorities suspended his deportation on the basis of the applicant's ill-health). The Government of Sweden announced, in 1996, that it considered that generally Croatian citizens were now afforded protection in Croatia. The applicant complained to the Court that his deportation to Croatia would violate Article 4. A united Chamber declared his application inadmissible because:

The Court finds that collective expulsion is to be understood as any measure compelling aliens, as a group, to leave a country, except where such a measure is taken on the basis of a reasonable and object-ive examination of the particular case of each individual alien of the group. Moreover, the fact that a number of aliens receive similar decisions does not lead to the conclusion that there is a collective expulsion when each person concerned has been given the opportunity to put arguments against his expulsion to the competent authorities on an individual basis (see application no. 14209/88, decision of 16 December 1988, DR 59, p 274).

In the present case, the Court notes that the Swedish Government, in their decisions of 26 May 1994 and 28 November 1996, issued guidelines for the assessment of asylum applications submitted by persons holding both Bosnian and Croatian citizenship. The Government found that, due to the situation in Bosnia-Hercegovina, these persons could not be sent back to that country. The crucial question was thus whether they could be afforded protection in Croatia. Furthermore, in examining the applicant's case, the National Immigration Board and the Aliens Appeals Board had regard to the general situation for persons with double nationality in Croatia.

However, the applicant submitted individual applications to the immigration authorities and was able to present any arguments he wished to make against his possible deportation to Croatia. The authorities took into account not only the general situation in Croatia but also the applicant's state-ments concerning his own background and the risks allegedly facing him upon return. In rejecting his applications, the authorities issued individual decisions concerning the applicant's situation. Moreover, by the decision of 9 December 1998 the Aliens Appeals Board suspended the enforcement of the applicant's deportation on account of his mental health.

In these circumstances, the Court considers that the applicant's possible deportation does not reveal any appearance of a collective expulsion within the meaning of Article 4 of Protocol No 4 to the Convention.

25 SEVENTH PROTOCOL

Article 1 Procedural safeguards relating to expulsion of aliens

....

Lupsa v Romania 8 June 2006
European Court of Human Rights

The applicant was a national of Serbia who had legally lived and worked in Romania between 1989 and 2003. He had co-habited with a Romanian since 1994 and they had a child in 2002. In August 2003, Romanian border police came to his home and deported him. His lawyer sought judicial review of that decision and at the hearing the public prosecutor supplied a copy of the deportation order which stated that the applicant was an 'undesirable person' and there was 'sufficient and serious intelligence that he was engaged in activities capable of endangering national security'. The applicant's lawyer sought an adjournment to enable her to send a copy of the order to the applicant and receive his response. The prosecutor supported her request, but the Bucharest Court of Appeal refused the request and dismissed the applicant's judicial review action. Before the Strasbourg Court the applicant contended, *inter alia*, that the Romanian authorities had infringed the procedural guarantees contained in Article 1.

52. The Court notes further that the above-mentioned guarantees apply only to aliens lawfully resident on the territory of a State that has ratified this Protocol (see *Sejdovic and Sulejmanovic v Italy* (dec.), No 57575/00, 14 March 2002, and *Sulejmanovic and Sultanovic v Italy* (dec.), No 57574/00, 14 March 2002).

53. In the present case the Court notes that it is not disputed that the applicant was lawfully resident on Romanian territory at the time of the deportation. Accordingly, although he was deported urgently for reasons of national security, which is a case authorised by paragraph 2 of Article 1, he was entitled, after being deported, to rely on the guarantees contained in paragraph 1 (see the explanatory report to Protocol No 7).

54. The Court notes that the first guarantee afforded to persons referred to in this Article is that they shall not be expelled except 'in pursuance of a decision reached in accordance with law'.

55. Since the word 'law' refers to the domestic law, the reference to it, like all the provisions of the Convention, concerns not only the existence of a legal basis in domestic law, but also the quality of the law in question: it must be accessible and foreseeable and also afford a measure of protection against arbitrary interferences by the public authorities with the rights secured in the Convention . . .

56. The Court reiterates its finding in respect of its examination of the complaint under Article 8 of the Convention, namely, that Emergency Ordinance No 194/2002, which formed the legal basis for the applicant's deportation, did not afford him the minimum guarantees against arbitrary action by the authorities.

57. Consequently, although the applicant was deported in pursuance of a decision reached in accordance with law, there has been a violation of Article 1 of Protocol No 7 in that the law did not satisfy the requirements of the Convention.

58. In any event the Court considers that the domestic authorities also infringed the guarantees to which the applicant should have been entitled under paragraph 1 a) and b) of that Article.

59. In that connection the Court notes that the authorities failed to provide the applicant with the slightest indication of the offence of which he was suspected and that the public prosecutor's office did not send him the order issued against him until the day of the one hearing before the Court of Appeal. Further, the Court observes that the Court of Appeal dismissed all requests for an adjournment, thus preventing the applicant's lawyer from studying the aforementioned order and producing evidence in support of her application for judicial review of it.

60. Reiterating that any provision of the Convention or its Protocols must be interpreted in such a way as to guarantee rights which are practical and effective as opposed to theoretical and illusory, the Court considers, in the light of the purely formal review by the Court of Appeal in this case, that the applicant was not genuinely able to have his case examined in the light of reasons militating against his deportation.

61. There has therefore been a violation of Article 1 of Protocol No 7.
. . . .

FOR THESE REASONS, THE COURT UNANIMOUSLY
. . .

3. *Holds* that there has been a breach of Article 1 of Protocol No 7;
. . .

NOTES

1   The Court was composed of President Zupancic and Judges: Hedigan, Caflisch, Birsan, Gyulumyan, Myjer, and Thor Bjorgvinsson.

2   The judgment in *Lupsa* reveals that the Court is willing to robustly scrutinise both the characteristics of the domestic substantive law and the procedural remedies available to lawfully resident aliens even in cases where the State asserts that deportation is based upon national security grounds.

Article 2 Right of appeal in criminal matters

Krombach v France 13 February 2001
European Court of Human Rights

The applicant was a German national. In 1977, as a widower with two children, he married a French divorcee with two children. During July 1982 the applicant's wife's son and daughter, who was a French national aged fourteen, were on school holidays at the applicant's home in Germany. The daughter returned home one evening, after having spent the day wind surfing, complaining that she was tired and not sufficiently tanned. The applicant, as he had done several times in the past, gave her an injection of a ferric compound (sold as a treatment for anaemia). The next morning, at about 9.30 am, the applicant found his stepdaughter dead in her bedroom. He tried to revive her by injecting her with various substances and the emergency services were called. A doctor examined her body at about 10.20 am and found no traces of violence, apart from injection marks on her thorax and arm. The doctor estimated that she had died at about 3 am. The German authorities conducted a number of investigations into the death and in 1987 the Munich Court of Appeal confirmed the public prosecutor's decision not to charge the applicant with any offence.

In 1984 the daughter's natural father, a French national, lodged a criminal complaint for involuntary homicide, of his daughter, against a person(s) unknown, with the Paris investigating judge. A French investigation was launched and in February 1991 the Paris investigating judge charged the applicant with assault resulting in unintentional death (under the French Code of Criminal Procedure an alien who commits a serious crime against a French national outside of French territory may be tried under French law). By a judgment in April 1993 the Indictments Division of the Paris Court of Appeal committed the applicant to stand trial in the Paris Assize Court on a charge of involuntary homicide. In February 1995 the applicant informed the President of the Assize Court that he intended to be represented by a lawyer. On 1 March 1995 the applicant's French lawyer, assisted by a German lawyer, lodged submissions with the Assize Court based upon, *inter alia*, Article 6 of the Convention. On 9 March the Assize Court found the applicant guilty of voluntary assault on his stepdaughter unintentionally causing her death and sentenced him to fifteen years' imprisonment. The Assize Court also informed the applicant's lawyers that under the Code of Criminal Procedure absent defendants were prohibited representation and therefore their submissions were inadmissible. In June 1995 the Court of Cassation ruled the applicant's appeal against the Assize Court's judgment inadmissible, under the Code of Criminal Procedure, as he was in contempt of court for not having attended his trial.

The applicant complained to the Court contending, *inter alia*, that the prohibition on appeals to the Court of Cassation where a defendant has been convicted *in absentia* violated Article 2 of Protocol No 7.

96. The Court reiterates that the Contracting States dispose in principle of a wide margin of appreciation to determine how the right secured by Article 2 of Protocol No 7 to the Convention is to be exercised. Thus, the review by a higher court of a conviction or sentence may concern both points of fact and points of law or be confined solely to points of law. Furthermore, in certain countries, a defendant wishing to appeal may sometimes be required to seek permission to do so. However, any restrictions contained in domestic legislation on the right to a review mentioned in that provision must, by analogy with the right of access to a court embodied in Article 6 § 1 of the Convention, pursue a legitimate aim and not infringe the very essence of that right (see *Haser v Switzerland* (dec.), No 33050/96, 27 April 2000, unreported). This rule is in itself consistent with the exception authorised by paragraph 2 of Article 2 and is backed up by the French declaration regarding the interpretation of the Article, which reads: '. . . in accordance with the meaning of Article 2, paragraph 1, the review by a higher court may be limited to a control of the application of the law, such as an appeal to the Supreme Court'.

97. There was no possibility under French law at the material time of lodging an ordinary appeal against a judgment of an assize court, as the only available appeal was an appeal on points of law. At first sight, the French rules of criminal procedure therefore appear to comply with Article 2 of Protocol No 7 (see *Loewenguth v France* (dec.), No 53183/99, ECHR 2000-VI, and *Deperrois v France* (dec.), No 48203/99, 22 June 2000, unreported).

98. However, the Court notes that the French declaration regarding the interpretation of the Protocol does not relate to Article 636 of the Code of Criminal Procedure, which expressly provides that persons convicted after trial *in absentia* have no right of appeal to the Court of Cassation. Consequently, the

applicant had no 'remedy' before a tribunal, within the ordinary meaning of that word, against his conviction, *in absentia*, by a single level of jurisdiction.

99. The applicant's complaint in the instant case was that he had no right of appeal to the Court of Cassation against defects in the trial *in absentia* procedure itself. The Court considers that the fact that the accused may purge his or her contempt is not decisive in that connection, as although purging the contempt may enable the accused to obtain a full retrial of his case in his presence, the positive obligation thus imposed on the State in the event of an arrest is intended essentially to guarantee adversarial process and compliance with the defence rights of a person accused of a criminal offence.

100. In the present case the applicant wished both to defend the charges on the merits and to raise a preliminary procedural objection. The Court attaches weight to the fact that the applicant was unable to obtain a review, at least by the Court of Cassation, of the lawfulness of the Assize Court's refusal to allow the defence lawyers to plead (see, *mutatis mutandis*, *Poitrimol* [v France A. 277-A (1993)] § 38 *in fine*; *Van Geyseghem* [v Belgium ECHR 1999-I] § 35; and, *a contrario*, *Haser*, cited above).

By virtue of Articles 630 and 639 of the Code of Criminal Procedure taken together the applicant, on the one hand, could not be and was not represented in the Assize Court by a lawyer, and, on the other, was unable to appeal to the Court of Cassation as he was a defendant *in absentia*. He therefore had no real possibility of being defended at first instance or of having his conviction reviewed by a higher court.

Consequently, there has also been a violation of Article 2 of Protocol No. 7 to the Convention.

....

FOR THESE REASONS, THE COURT UNANIMOUSLY

....

3. *Holds* that there has been a violation of Article 2 of Protocol No 7 to the Convention;

....

NOTES

1 The Court was composed of President Fuhrmann and Judges: Costa, Loucaides, Kuris, Tulkens, Jungwiert, and Bratza.

2 The judgement in *Krombach*, at paragraph 96, makes clear that whilst States have a broad discretion to regulate the scope and availability of Article 2 reviews, domestic legislation must not undermine this right and any restrictions imposed must be for a legitimate aim.

3 In *Papon v France*, judgment of 25 July 2002, the applicant claimed that the forfeiting of his right of appeal, under the Code of Criminal Procedure, because he had not surrendered to custody breached, *inter alia*, Article 2. Papon had been the secretary-general of the Gironde prefecture between 1942 and 1944. After the liberation of France, the Ministry of the Interior had determined that he should be allowed to continue in public service as he had shown a favourable attitude towards the Resistance during the period of occupation. Subsequently, he held a number of important positions including Paris Police Commissioner and being a town mayor. In 1981, whilst he was Minister of the Budget, the media began to report critical accounts of his activities during the occupation. In 1983 he was charged with crimes against humanity. His trial, before the Gironde Assize Court began in October 1997. In April 1998 the Assize Court convicted him of crimes against humanity (namely, aiding and abetting the unlawful arrest and false imprisonment of Jews, who were subsequently deported to concentration camps, in 1942 and 1944). He was sentenced to ten years' imprisonment. He appealed, on points of law, against his conviction and requested exemption from the obligation to surrender to custody. The Court of Cassation refused his request for exemption. However, the applicant fled to Switzerland (later the Swiss authorities ordered him to leave Switzerland and by the time of his application to the Court he was imprisoned in France). During October 1999, after hearing submissions by the applicant's lawyers, the Court of Cassation held that the applicant had forfeited his right of appeal due to his failure to surrender to custody. A united Chamber of the European Court very briefly rejected his claim of a violation of Article 2.

106. The Court has already had occasion to hold that the French system in force at the material time was in principle compatible with Article 2 of Protocol No. 7 (see, in particular, *Krombach*, para 97, and the decisions cited there).

This seemed a highly partial view of the judgment in *Krombach*. However, the Chamber in *Papon*, unanimously, found that the forfeiture of the applicant's right to appeal on points of law, because of his non-surrender to custody, amounted to a disproportionate interference with his right of access to a court and breached Article 6(1). Judge Costa, the Judge of French nationality, issued an unusual 'declaration' in which he stated:

The applicant maintained that the European Convention on Human Rights had been breached in eleven respects in the proceedings connected with his conviction for aiding and abetting crimes against humanity. His case has been upheld in only one respect; this was inevitable in view of the case-law, which is the same for everyone. I therefore voted accordingly.

This violation occurred because the Court of Cassation applied a provision of the Code of Criminal Procedure which was repealed a few months later by the Law of 15 June 2000. Another few months and France would not have been found to have committed the breach. This observation serves, I think, to put the significance and impact of this judgment into perspective, as does the fact that the applicant's claims for just satisfaction under the heads of pecuniary and non-pecuniary damage have been dismissed.

4 An appeal procedure must be directly available to the defendant if it to be capable of satisfying Article 2. In *Gurepka v Ukraine*, judgment of 6 September 2005, the applicant was a public prosecutor who had been sued for defamation. The applicant did not attend several court hearings in the defamation proceedings (he claimed, *inter alia*, to have been ill). The District Court began 'administrative proceedings' against him in respect of his non-attendance. On 1 December, the applicant attended a hearing at which the District Court imposed a sentence of seven days' administrative imprisonment on him for his repeated failures to attend earlier hearings. He was detained and place in a cell. The next day his employer, the Prosecutors' Office of the Autonomous Republic of Crimea, lodged an extraordinary appeal with the Highest Court of the Autonomous Republic of Crimea contending that the applicant had to be sanctioned under the Disciplinary Statute of the Prosecutors' Office and not by administrative proceedings. The effect of the Prosecutors' Office lodging the appeal was to suspend the enforcement of the applicant's administrative imprisonment. He was released. On the following day the President of the Highest Court rejected the appeal and the applicant was subsequently required to serve the remainder of his period of imprisonment. The applicant complained to Strasbourg that, *inter alia*, he had suffered a breach of Article 2. A, unanimous, Chamber determined that, given the severity of the sanction of imprisonment, the 'administrative proceedings' against the applicant should be classified as being 'criminal' for the purposes of the Convention.

60. The Court has examined the extraordinary review procedure prescribed by the Code of Administrative Offences. It could only be initiated by a prosecutor or by a motion of the president of the higher court. Given that this procedure was not directly accessible to a party to the proceedings and did not depend on his or her motion and arguments, the Court considers that it was not a sufficiently effective remedy for Convention purposes.

Therefore, the Chamber found a violation of Article 2 of Protocol No. 7.

Article 4 Right not to be tried or punished twice

Gradinger v Austria A.328-C (1995)
European Court of Human Rights

In the early hours of 1 January 1987 the applicant, whilst driving his car, caused an accident which resulted in the death of a cyclist. The applicant was found to have a blood alcohol level of 0.8 grams per litre according to a specimen taken at the hospital where he was treated after the accident. On 15 May 1987, the St Polten Regional Court convicted the applicant of causing death by negligence contrary to Article 80 of the Criminal Code. The judgment found that the applicant had been drinking before the accident, but not to the extent that he should be convicted of the more serious offence, under Article 81(2) of the Criminal Code, of causing death by negligence whilst under the influence of drink. The applicant was sentenced to 200 day fines of 160 schillings with 100 days' imprisonment in default of payment. On 16 July 1987, the St Polten district authority issued a sentence order imposing a 12,000 schillings fine, with two weeks' imprisonment in default, for driving under the influence of drink contrary to the Road Traffic Act 1960. The authority had obtained a different medical report on the applicant which concluded, given the time between the accident and the taking of the blood sample at the hospital, that the applicant's blood alcohol level must have been at least 0.95 grams per litre when the accident occurred. The applicant unsuccessfully appealed to the Lower Austria regional government and the Constitutional Court. He then complained to Strasbourg alleging, *inter alia*, that by fining him the district authority had violated Article 4 of Protocol No. 7 as he had been punished twice in respect of the facts that had resulted in his initial conviction by the Regional Court.

53. Like the Commission, the Court observes that the aim of Article 4 of Protocol No 7 is to prohibit the repetition of criminal proceedings that have been concluded by a final decision. That provision (P7-4) does not therefore apply before new proceedings have been opened. In the present case, inasmuch as the new proceedings reached their conclusion in a decision later in date than the entry into force of Protocol No. 7 . . . the conditions for applicability ratione temporis are satisfied.

C. COMPLIANCE WITH ARTICLE 4 (P7-4)

54. In reply to Mr Gradinger's arguments . . . which the Commission endorsed in substance, the Government affirmed that Article 4 of Protocol No 7 did not preclude applying the two provisions in issue consecutively. The latter were different in nature and pursued different aims: whereas Article 81 para. 2 of the Criminal Code punished homicide committed while under the influence of drink, section 5 of the Road Traffic Act punished the mere fact of driving a vehicle while intoxicated. The former was designed to penalise acts that cause death and threaten public safety, the latter to ensure a smooth flow of traffic.

55. The Court notes that, according to the St Pölten Regional Court, the aggravating circumstance referred to in Article 81 para. 2 of the Criminal Code, namely a blood alcohol level of 0.8 grams per litre or higher, was not made out with regard to the applicant. On the other hand, the administrative authorities found, in order to bring the applicant's case within the ambit of section 5 of the Road Traffic Act, that that alcohol level had been attained. The Court is fully aware that the provisions in question differ not only as regards the designation of the offences but also, more importantly, as regards their nature and purpose. It further observes that the offence provided for in section 5 of the Road Traffic Act

represents only one aspect of the offence punished under Article 81 para. 2 of the Criminal Code. Nevertheless, both impugned decisions were based on the same conduct. Accordingly, there has been a breach of Article 4 of Protocol No. 7 (P7-4).

....

FOR THESE REASONS, THE COURT UNANIMOUSLY

....

5. *Holds* that there has been a violation of Article 4 of Protocol No. 7;

.....

NOTES

1   The Court was composed of President Ryssdal and Judges: Matscher, Pettiti, Macdonald, Martens, Foighel, Morenilla, Freeland, and Makarczyk.

2   In the subsequent case of *Oliveira v Switzerland*, judgment of 30 July 1998, a large majority (eight votes to one) of the original Court distinguished *Gradinger* by emphasising that a single act could amount to more than one criminal offence. Whilst driving on an icy road in Zurich, during December 1990, Mrs Oliveira's car veered onto the opposite side of the road causing serious injuries to another driver. In August 1991, the Zurich police magistrate convicted her, under the Federal Road Traffic Act, of failing to control her vehicle. She was fined 200 Swiss francs. In January 1993 the district attorney's office issued her with a penal order fining her 2,000 Swiss francs for negligently causing physical injury contrary to Article 125 of the Swiss Criminal Code. She challenged the order in the Zurich District Court which reduced the fine to 1,500 Swiss francs and quashed the 200 Swiss francs fine imposed earlier by the police magistrate. The Federal Court dismissed her further appeal noting that the District Court had avoided the effects of punishing her twice by quashing the original fine. Nevertheless, she complained to Strasbourg alleging a breach of Article 4.

26. That is a typical example of a single act constituting various offences (*concours idéal d'infractions*). The characteristic feature of this notion is that a single criminal act is split up into two separate offences, in this case the failure to control the vehicle and the negligent causing of physical injury. In such cases, the greater penalty will usually absorb the lesser one.

There is nothing in that situation which infringes Article 4 of Protocol No. 7 since that provision prohibits people being tried twice for the same offence whereas in cases concerning a single act constituting various offences (*concours idéal d'infractions*) one criminal act constitutes two separate offences.

27. It would admittedly have been more consistent with the principles governing the proper administration of justice for sentence in respect of both offences, which resulted from the same criminal act, to have been passed by the same court in a single set of proceedings. Indeed, it appears that that is what ought to have occurred in the instant case as the police magistrate should, in view of the fact that the serious injuries sustained by the injured party were outside his jurisdiction, have sent the case file to the district attorney for him to rule on both offences together. The fact that that procedure was not followed in Mrs Oliveira's case is, however, irrelevant as regards compliance with Article 4 of Protocol No 7 since that provision does not preclude separate offences, even if they are all part of a single criminal act, being tried by different courts, especially where, as in the present case, the penalties were not cumulative, the lesser being absorbed by the greater.

28. The instant case is therefore distinguishable from the case of *Gradinger* cited above, in which two different courts came to inconsistent findings on the applicant's blood alcohol level.

29. In conclusion, there has been no violation of Article 4 of Protocol No 7.

In his dissenting opinion Judge Repik stated in regard to *Gradinger*:

... It is therefore undoubtedly the identity of the *actus reus* and, in particular, of the conduct that the Court held to be the criterion for identifying the 'offence' within the meaning of Article 4 of Protocol No 7. I fully approve the Court's decision in that case. It prevents a single, well-defined *actus reus* being broken down by changing some of its specific aspects and the same individual being prosecuted more than once in respect of the same incident as a result of different legal qualifications.

However, the Court chose exactly the opposite solution in the present case, in that it took the legal qualification as the criterion for identifying the 'offence'. A different legal qualification for 'a single criminal act' sufficed to oust the *non bis in idem* guarantee contained in Article 4 of Protocol No 7.

Yet no difference can be seen between the *Gradinger* case and the Oliveira case that can justify these two wholly conflicting decisions. In both cases, the conduct that led to the prosecution was identical. In both cases, owing to a mistake by the court that first convicted the accused, one aspect of the *actus* was not taken into account in the conviction. Lastly, in both cases, the same conduct, aggravated by the aspect that the first court had omitted to take into account, led to a second conviction under a different legal qualification.

....

3   The full-time Court acknowledged in *Franz Fischer v Austria*, judgment of 29 May 2001, that its predecessor's approaches in *Gradinger* and *Oliveira* appeared 'somewhat contradictory'. Fischer, whilst driving under the influence of alcohol, knocked down a cyclist who was fatally injured. In December 1996 the St Polten district authority, the same body as in *Gradinger*, found him guilty of a number of road traffic offences. These included driving under the influence of drink contrary to the Road Traffic Act. He was sentenced to a fine of 22,010 schillings (with nine days' imprisonment in default). In March 1997 the St Polten Regional Court, (also the same court as in *Gradinger*) convicted Fischer, under Article 81 of the Criminal Code, of causing death by negligence after allowing himself to become intoxicated. He was sentenced to six months' imprisonment. Subsequently, he complained to Strasbourg alleging a breach of Article 4. The unanimous Chamber held that:

25. The Court observes that the wording of Article 4 of Protocol No 7 does not refer to 'the same offence' but rather to trial and punishment 'again' for an offence for which the applicant has already been finally acquitted or convicted. Thus, while it is true that the mere fact that a single act constitutes more than one offence is not contrary to this Article, the Court must not limit itself to finding that an applicant was, on the basis of one act, tried or punished for nominally different offences. The Court, like the Austrian Constitutional Court, notes that there are cases where one act, at first sight, appears to constitute more than one offence, whereas a closer examination shows that only one offence should be prosecuted because it encompasses all the wrongs contained in the others. An obvious example would be an act which constitutes two offences, one of which contains precisely the same elements as the other plus an additional one. There may be other cases where the offences only slightly overlap. Thus, where different offences based on one act are prosecuted consecutively, one after the final decision of the other, the Court has to examine whether or not such offences have the same essential elements.

....

27. It can also be argued that this is what distinguishes the Gradinger case from the Oliveira case. In the Gradinger case the essential elements of the administrative offence of drunken driving did not differ from those constituting the special circumstances of Article 81 § 2 of the Criminal Code, namely driving a vehicle while having a blood alcohol level of 0.8 grams per litre or more. However, there was no such obvious overlap of the essential elements of the offences at issue in the Oliveira case.

28. In the present case, the applicant was first convicted by the administrative authority for drunken driving under sections 5(1) and 99(1)(a) of the Road Traffic Act. In subsequent criminal proceedings he was convicted of causing death by negligence with the special element under Article 81 § 2 of the Criminal Code of 'allowing himself to become intoxicated'. The Court notes that there are two differences between the Gradinger case and the present: the proceedings were conducted in reverse order and there was no inconsistency between the factual assessment of the administrative authority and the criminal courts, as both found that the applicant had a blood alcohol level above 0.8 grams per litre.

29. However, the Court considers that these differences are not decisive. As said above, the question whether or not the *non bis in idem* principle is violated concerns the relationship between the two offences at issue and can, therefore, not depend on the order in which the respective proceedings are conducted. As regards the fact that Mr Gradinger was acquitted of the special element under Article 81 § 2 of the Criminal Code but convicted of drunken driving, whereas the present applicant was convicted of both offences, the Court repeats that Article 4 of Protocol No. 7 is not confined to the right not to be punished twice but extends to the right not to be tried twice. What is decisive in the present case is that, on the basis of one act, the applicant was tried and punished twice, since the administrative offence of drunken driving under sections 5(1) and 99(1)(a) of the Road Traffic Act, and the special circumstances under Article 81 § 2 of the Criminal Code, as interpreted by the courts, do not differ in their essential elements.

. . . .

31. Finally, the Court observes that, in a case like the present, the Contracting State remains free to regulate which of the two offences shall be prosecuted. It further notes that the legal situation in Austria has changed following the Constitutional Court's judgment of 5 December 1996, so that nowadays the administrative offence of drunken driving under sections 5(1) and 99(1)(a) of the Road Traffic Act will not be pursued if the facts also reveal the special elements of the offence under Article 81 § 2 of the Criminal Code.

However, at the material time, the applicant was tried and punished for both offences containing the same essential elements.

32. There has, thus, been a violation of Article 4 of Protocol No 7.

Thus, the Court focuses upon whether the applicant has been tried or punished for two or more similar offences arising out of the same factual circumstances. This approach has been applied in similar later cases including *W.F. v Austria*, judgment of 30 May 2002 and *Sailer v Austria*, judgment of 25 July 2002.

4 In *Goktan v France*, judgment of 2 July 2002, a united Chamber rejected the applicant's complaint that he had been punished twice for the same offence. The applicant was convicted, in 1991, by the Strasbourg Criminal Court for criminal offences involving the importation of drugs and for a customs offence of illegally importing goods. The Criminal Court sentenced him to five years' imprisonment in respect of the criminal offences and imposed a customs fine of 400,000 French francs regarding the customs offence. Subsequently, the public prosecutor secured an order against the applicant for two year's further imprisonment in default of payment of the customs fine. The applicant contended that the latter order violated Article 4 as it amounted to him being sentenced to two consecutive periods of imprisonment for the same offence. The Chamber dismissed this argument:

50. In fact, the Court considers that in the instant case a single criminal court tried the same person for the same criminal conduct, namely dealing in illegally imported drugs. In other words, as in *Oliveira*, cited above, a single criminal act constituted two separate offences: an offence under the general criminal law and a customs offence. As in *Oliveira*, this might also be seen as an example of the same

act being caught by various statutory definitions (*concours idéal de qualifications*), and there is all the more reason to transpose that precedent to the present case (since in *Oliveira* the defendant was convicted by two courts; although the Court found that to be regrettable since it was inconsistent with the proper administration of justice, it nevertheless went on to hold that there had been no violation).

5   A Chamber upheld the lawfulness of supervisory review proceedings undertaken by the Presidium of the Supreme Court in *Nikitin v Russia*, judgment of 20 July 2004. The applicant, a former naval officer, began working for a Norwegian non-governmental organisation in 1995. The Russian Federal Security Service searched the Murmansk office of the organisation and subsequently the applicant was charged with a number of serious offences including treason. Soon after his trial began the St Petersburg City Court adjourned proceedings for further investigations, because, *inter alia*, the indictment was vague and it was unclear whether the applicant's work for the organisation involved the use of official secrets. The prosecution challenged the City Court's decision but it was upheld by the Supreme Court. One year later the City Court acquitted the applicant of all charges. The prosecution unsuccessfully appealed to the Supreme Court. A few weeks later the Procurator-General requested the Presidium of the Supreme Court to review the case in supervisory proceedings, contending, *inter alia*, the judgment had wrongfully applied the law and the indictment had been vague. The Presidium dismissed the request four months later, noting that defects in the proceedings were the responsibility of the prosecution. In 2002 the Constitutional Court ruled that aspects of the supervisory review proceedings, including the quashing of an acquittal on the grounds of an incomplete investigation, were incompatible with the constitution. The applicant alleged before the European Court that the supervisory review proceedings that took place after his final acquittal violated Article 4.

35. The Court notes that the protection against duplication of criminal proceedings is one of the specific safeguards associated with the general guarantee of a fair hearing in criminal proceedings. It reiterates that the aim of Article 4 of Protocol No 7 is to prohibit the repetition of criminal proceedings that have been concluded by a final decision (see, among other authorities, *Gradinger v Austria*, judgment of 23 October 1995, Series A No 328-C, p 65, § 53). The Court further notes that the repetitive aspect of trial or punishment is central to the legal problem addressed by Article 4 of Protocol No 7. In *Oliveira v Switzerland* (judgment of 30 July 1998, *Reports of Judgments and Decisions* 1998-V), the fact that the penalties in the two sets of proceedings were not cumulative was relevant to the finding that there was no violation of the provision where two sets of proceedings were brought in respect of a single act (p 1998, § 27).

36. Turning to the supervisory review of an acquittal conducted in circumstances such as the present case, the Court will first determine what elements, if any, of Article 4 of Protocol No 7 are to be found in such proceedings. For this purpose, it will have regard to the following aspects:

—   whether there had been a 'final' decision before the supervisory instance intervened, or whether the supervisory review was an integral part of the ordinary procedure and itself provided a final decision;

—   whether the applicant was 'tried again' in the proceedings before the Presidium; and

—   whether the applicant became 'liable to be tried again' by virtue of the Procurator-General's request.

Finally, the Court will consider whether, on the basis of this case, the supervisory review could in principle have given rise to any form of duplication of the criminal proceedings, contrary to the protection afforded by Article 4 of Protocol No 7.

1. Whether the applicant had been 'finally acquitted' prior to the supervisory review

37. According to the Explanatory Report to Protocol No 7 to the Convention, which itself refers back to the European Convention on the International Validity of Criminal Judgments, a 'decision is final "if, according to the traditional expression, it has acquired the force of *res judicata*. This is the case when it is irrevocable, that is to say when no further ordinary remedies are available or when the parties have exhausted such remedies or have permitted the time-limit to expire without availing themselves of them" '.

38. The Court notes that the procedural law at the time allowed certain officials to challenge a judgment which had taken effect. The grounds for supervisory review were the same as for bringing an ordinary appeal. With regard to acquittals, the request for supervisory review could be brought within one year of the judgment's taking effect. Assuming that the Presidium granted the Procurator-General's request and that the proceedings were re-launched, the ensuing ruling would still constitute the only decision in the applicant's criminal case, with no other decision remaining concurrently in force, and that decision would be 'final'. Thus, it appears that the domestic legal system in Russia at the time did not regard decisions such as the acquittal in the present case as 'final' until the time-limit for making an application for supervisory review had expired. On that basis, the decision by the Presidium of the Supreme Court on 30 May 2000 not to accept the case for supervisory review would be the 'final' decision in the case. On such an interpretation, Article 4 of Protocol No 7 would have no application whatsoever in the present case, as all the decisions before the Court related to the same single set of proceedings.

38. However, the Court reiterates that a supervisory request for annulment of a final judgment is a form of extraordinary appeal in that it is not directly accessible to the defendant in a criminal case, and its application depends on the discretion of authorised officials. The Court has, for example, not accepted that supervisory review is an effective domestic remedy in either the civil or the criminal contexts (see *Tumilovich v Russia* (dec.), No 47033/99, 22 June 1999; *Berdzenishvili v Russia* (dec.), No 31697/03, 29 January 2004), and it has found that the quashing of a judgment on supervisory review can create problems as to the legal certainty to be afforded to the initial judgment (see *Brumărescu v Romania* [GC], No 28342/95, § 62, ECHR 1999-VII; and *Ryabykh v Russia*, No 52854/99, §§ 56–8, 24 July 2003). The Court will therefore assume in the following paragraphs that the appeal judgment of 17 April 2000, by which the applicant's acquittal acquired final force on that same date, was the 'final decision' for the purposes of Article 4 of Protocol No 7.

2. Whether the applicant was 'tried again' in the proceedings before the Presidium

40. The Court observes that the Procurator-General's request for supervisory review of the acquittal was examined by the Presidium. Its determination was limited, at that stage, to the question whether to grant the request for supervisory review. In the circumstances of the present case, the Presidium did not accept the application for review, and the final decision remained that of 17 April 2000.

41. It follows that the applicant was not 'tried again' within the meaning of Article 4 § 1 of Protocol No 7 to the Convention in the proceedings by which the Presidium of the Supreme Court rejected the Procurator-General's request for supervisory review of the applicant's acquittal.

3. Whether the applicant was 'liable to be tried again'

42. The Court has further considered whether the applicant was 'liable to be tried again', as he alleged. The Court notes that, had the request been upheld, the Presidium would have been required, by the then Article 380 of the Code of Criminal Procedure, to choose one of the options [including quashing the judgment and terminating the prosecution or to order a fresh court examination of the charges at any instance]. Importantly, the Presidium was not empowered to make a new determination on the merits in the same proceedings, but merely to decide whether or not to grant the Procurator-General's request.

43. It appears therefore that the potential for resumption of proceedings in this case would have been too remote or indirect to constitute 'liability' for the purposes of Article 4 § 1 of Protocol No 7.

44. Although the elements discussed in the preceding paragraphs 40–3 are in themselves sufficient to demonstrate that supervisory review in this case did not lead to a violation of Article 4 of Protocol No 7, the Court notes that there exists a substantive, and thus more important, reason to reach the same conclusion. It considers that the crucial point in this case is that supervisory review could not in any event have given rise to a duplication of criminal proceedings, within the meaning of Article 4 § 1 of Protocol No 7, for the following reasons.

45. The Court observes that Article 4 of Protocol No 7 draws a clear distinction between a second prosecution or trial, which is prohibited by the first paragraph of this Article, and the resumption of a trial in exceptional circumstances, which is provided for in its second paragraph. Article 4 § 2 of Protocol No 7 expressly envisages the possibility that an individual may have to accept prosecution on the same charges, in accordance with domestic law, where a case is reopened following the emergence of new evidence or the discovery of a fundamental defect in the previous proceedings.

46. The Court notes that the Russian legislation in force at the material time permitted a criminal case in which a final decision had been given to be reopened on the grounds of new or newly discovered evidence or a fundamental defect (Articles 384–90 of the Code of Criminal Procedure). This procedure obviously falls within the scope of Article 4 § 2 of Protocol No 7. However, the Court notes that, in addition, a system also existed which allowed the review of a case on the grounds of a judicial error concerning points of law and procedure (supervisory review, Articles 371–83 of the Code of Criminal Procedure). The subject matter of such proceedings remained the same criminal charge and the validity of its previous determination. If the request was granted and the proceedings were resumed for further consideration, the ultimate effect of supervisory review would be to annul all decisions previously taken by courts and to determine the criminal charge in a new decision. To this extent, the effect of supervisory review is the same as reopening, because both constitute a form of continuation of the previous proceedings. The Court therefore concludes that for the purposes of the *ne bis in idem* principle supervisory review may be regarded as a special type of reopening falling within the scope of Article 4 § 2 of Protocol No 7.

47. The applicant's argument that the supervisory review was unnecessary and amounted to an abuse of process is not relevant to the question of compliance with Article 4 of Protocol No 7: the manner in which the power was exercised is relative to the overall fairness of criminal proceedings, but cannot be decisive for the purpose of identifying the procedure as a 'reopening' as opposed to a 'second trial'. On the facts of the present case, the proceedings aimed at securing a supervisory review were an attempt to have the proceedings reopened rather than an attempted 'second trial'.

48. Finally, the Court notes that the conformity with the requirement of lawfulness under Article 4 § 2 of Protocol No 7 is undisputed in the present case.

49. The Court concludes that the applicant was not liable to be tried or punished again within the meaning of Article 4 § 1 of Protocol No 7 to the Convention, and that accordingly there has been no violation of that provision.

This is an important judgment which provides valuable insights into how the Court interprets Article 4(2). Do you think the Court was overly generous to Russia in categorising the supervisory review process as a reopening falling within Article 4(2)?

APPENDIX

COUNCIL OF EUROPE

CONVENTION FOR THE PROTECTION OF HUMAN RIGHTS AND FUNDAMENTAL FREEDOMS AS AMENDED BY PROTOCOL NO. 11

WITH PROTOCOL NOS. 1, 4, 6, 7,12 AND 13

The text of the Convention had been amended according to the provisions of Protocol No. 3 (ETS No. 45), which entered into force on 21 September 1970, of Protocol No. 5 (ETS No. 55), which entered into force on 20 December 1971 and of Protocol No. 8 (ETS No. 118), which entered into force on 1 January 1990, and comprised also the text of Protocol No. 2 (ETS No. 44) which, in accordance with Article 5, paragraph 3 thereof, had been an integral part of the Convention since its entry into force on 21 September 1970. All provisions which had been amended or added by these Protocols are replaced by Protocol No. 11 (ETS No. 155), as from the date of its entry into force on 1 November 1998. As from that date, Protocol No. 9 (ETS No. 140), which entered into force on 1 October 1994, is repealed.

Registry of the European Court of Human Rights
September 2003

CONVENTION FOR THE PROTECTION OF HUMAN RIGHTS AND FUNDAMENTAL FREEDOMS

Rome, 4.XI.1950

The governments signatory hereto, being members of the Council of Europe,

Considering the Universal Declaration of Human Rights proclaimed by the General Assembly of the United Nations on 10th December 1948;

Considering that this Declaration aims at securing the universal and effective recognition and observance of the Rights therein declared;

Considering that the aim of the Council of Europe is the achievement of greater unity between its members and that one of the methods by which that aim is to be pursued is the maintenance and further realisation of human rights and fundamental freedoms;

Reaffirming their profound belief in those fundamental freedoms which are the foundation of justice and peace in the world and are best maintained on the one hand by an effective political democracy and on the other by a common understanding and observance of the human rights upon which they depend;

Being resolved, as the governments of European countries which are like-minded and have a common heritage of political traditions, ideals, freedom and the rule of law, to take the first steps for the collective enforcement of certain of the rights stated in the Universal Declaration,

Have agreed as follows:

Article 1—Obligation to respect human rights

The High Contracting Parties shall secure to everyone within their jurisdiction the rights and freedoms defined in Section I of this Convention.

SECTION I—RIGHTS AND FREEDOMS

Article 2—Right to life

1   Everyone's right to life shall be protected by law. No one shall be deprived of his life intentionally save in the execution of a sentence of a court following his conviction of a crime for which this penalty is provided by law.

2   Deprivation of life shall not be regarded as inflicted in contravention of this article when it results from the use of force which is no more than absolutely necessary:

   a   in defence of any person from unlawful violence;

   b   in order to effect a lawful arrest or to prevent the escape of a person lawfully detained;

   c   in action lawfully taken for the purpose of quelling a riot or insurrection.

Article 3—Prohibition of torture

No one shall be subjected to torture or to inhuman or degrading treatment or punishment.

Article 4—Prohibition of slavery and forced labour

1   No one shall be held in slavery or servitude.

2   No one shall be required to perform forced or compulsory labour.

3   For the purpose of this article the term 'forced or compulsory labour' shall not include:

   a   any work required to be done in the ordinary course of detention imposed according to the provisions of Article 5 of this Convention or during conditional release from such detention;

   b   any service of a military character or, in case of conscientious objectors in countries where they are recognised, service exacted instead of compulsory military service;

   c   any service exacted in case of an emergency or calamity threatening the life or well-being of the community;

   d   any work or service which forms part of normal civic obligations.

Article 5—Right to liberty and security

1   Everyone has the right to liberty and security of person. No one shall be deprived of his liberty save in the following cases and in accordance with a procedure prescribed by law:

   a   the lawful detention of a person after conviction by a competent court;

   b   the lawful arrest or detention of a person for non-compliance with the lawful order of a court or in order to secure the fulfilment of any obligation prescribed by law;

   c   the lawful arrest or detention of a person effected for the purpose of bringing him before the competent legal authority on reasonable suspicion of having committed an offence or when it is reasonably considered necessary to prevent his committing an offence or fleeing after having done so;

   d   the detention of a minor by lawful order for the purpose of educational supervision or his lawful detention for the purpose of bringing him before the competent legal authority;

   e   the lawful detention of persons for the prevention of the spreading of infectious diseases, of persons of unsound mind, alcoholics or drug addicts or vagrants;

   f   the lawful arrest or detention of a person to prevent his effecting an unauthorised entry into the country or of a person against whom action is being taken with a view to deportation or extradition.

2   Everyone who is arrested shall be informed promptly, in a language which he understands, of the reasons for his arrest and of any charge against him.

3   Everyone arrested or detained in accordance with the provisions of paragraph 1.c of this article shall be brought promptly before a judge or other officer authorised by law to exercise judicial power and shall be entitled to trial within a reasonable time or to release pending trial. Release may be conditioned by guarantees to appear for trial.

4   Everyone who is deprived of his liberty by arrest or detention shall be entitled to take proceedings by which the lawfulness of his detention shall be decided speedily by a court and his release ordered if the detention is not lawful.

5   Everyone who has been the victim of arrest or detention in contravention of the provisions of this article shall have an enforceable right to compensation.

Article 6—Right to a fair trial

1   In the determination of his civil rights and obligations or of any criminal charge against him, everyone is entitled to a fair and public hearing within a reasonable time by an independent and impartial tribunal established by law. Judgment shall be pronounced publicly but the press and public may be excluded from all or part of the trial in the interests of morals, public order or national security in a democratic society, where the interests of juveniles or the protection of the private life of the parties so require, or to the extent strictly necessary in the opinion of the court in special circumstances where publicity would prejudice the interests of justice.

2   Everyone charged with a criminal offence shall be presumed innocent until proved guilty according to law.

3   Everyone charged with a criminal offence has the following minimum rights:

   a   to be informed promptly, in a language which he understands and in detail, of the nature and cause of the accusation against him;

   b   to have adequate time and facilities for the preparation of his defence;

   c   to defend himself in person or through legal assistance of his own choosing or, if he has not sufficient means to pay for legal assistance, to be given it free when the interests of justice so require;

   d   to examine or have examined witnesses against him and to obtain the attendance and examination of witnesses on his behalf under the same conditions as witnesses against him;

   e   to have the free assistance of an interpreter if he cannot understand or speak the language used in court.

Article 7—No punishment without law

1   No one shall be held guilty of any criminal offence on account of any act or omission which did not constitute a criminal offence under national or international law at the time when it was committed. Nor shall a heavier penalty be imposed than the one that was applicable at the time the criminal offence was committed.

2   This article shall not prejudice the trial and punishment of any person for any act or omission which, at the time when it was committed, was criminal according to the general principles of law recognised by civilised nations.

Article 8—Right to respect for private and family life

1   Everyone has the right to respect for his private and family life, his home and his correspondence.

2   There shall be no interference by a public authority with the exercise of this right except such as is in accordance with the law and is necessary in a democratic society in the interests of national security, public safety or the economic well-being of the country, for the prevention of disorder or crime, for the protection of health or morals, or for the protection of the rights and freedoms of others.

Article 9—Freedom of thought, conscience and religion

1   Everyone has the right to freedom of thought, conscience and religion; this right includes freedom to change his religion or belief and freedom, either alone or in community with others and in public or private, to manifest his religion or belief, in worship, teaching, practice and observance.

2   Freedom to manifest one's religion or beliefs shall be subject only to such limitations as are prescribed by law and are necessary in a democratic society in the interests of public safety, for the protection of public order, health or morals, or for the protection of the rights and freedoms of others.

Article 10—Freedom of expression

1   Everyone has the right to freedom of expression. This right shall include freedom to hold opinions and to receive and impart information and ideas without interference by public authority and regardless of frontiers. This article shall not prevent States from requiring the licensing of broadcasting, television or cinema enterprises.

2   The exercise of these freedoms, since it carries with it duties and responsibilities, may be subject to such formalities, conditions, restrictions or penalties as are prescribed by law and are necessary in a democratic society, in the interests of national security, territorial integrity or public safety, for the prevention of disorder or crime, for the protection of health or morals, for the protection of the reputation or rights of others, for preventing the disclosure of information received in confidence, or for maintaining the authority and impartiality of the judiciary.

Article 11—Freedom of assembly and association

1   Everyone has the right to freedom of peaceful assembly and to freedom of association with others, including the right to form and to join trade unions for the protection of his interests.

2   No restrictions shall be placed on the exercise of these rights other than such as are prescribed by law and are necessary in a democratic society in the interests of national security or public safety, for the prevention of disorder or crime, for the protection of health or morals or for the protection of the rights and freedoms of others. This article shall not prevent the imposition of lawful restrictions on the exercise of these rights by members of the armed forces, of the police or of the administration of the State.

Article 12—Right to marry

Men and women of marriageable age have the right to marry and to found a family, according to the national laws governing the exercise of this right.

Article 13—Right to an effective remedy

Everyone whose rights and freedoms as set forth in this Convention are violated shall have an effective remedy before a national authority notwithstanding that the violation has been committed by persons acting in an official capacity.

Article 14—Prohibition of discrimination

The enjoyment of the rights and freedoms set forth in this Convention shall be secured without discrimination on any ground such as sex, race, colour, language, religion, political or other opinion, national or social origin, association with a national minority, property, birth or other status.

Article 15—Derogation in time of emergency

1 In time of war or other public emergency threatening the life of the nation any High Contracting Party may take measures derogating from its obligations under this Convention to the extent strictly required by the exigencies of the situation, provided that such measures are not inconsistent with its other obligations under international law.

2 No derogation from Article 2, except in respect of deaths resulting from lawful acts of war, or from Articles 3, 4 (paragraph 1) and 7 shall be made under this provision.

3 Any High Contracting Party availing itself of this right of derogation shall keep the Secretary General of the Council of Europe fully informed of the measures which it has taken and the reasons therefor. It shall also inform the Secretary General of the Council of Europe when such measures have ceased to operate and the provisions of the Convention are again being fully executed.

Article 16—Restrictions on political activity of aliens

Nothing in Articles 10, 11 and 14 shall be regarded as preventing the High Contracting Parties from imposing restrictions on the political activity of aliens.

Article 17—Prohibition of abuse of rights

Nothing in this Convention may be interpreted as implying for any State, group or person any right to engage in any activity or perform any act aimed at the destruction of any of the rights and freedoms set forth herein or at their limitation to a greater extent than is provided for in the Convention.

Article 18—Limitation on use of restrictions on rights

The restrictions permitted under this Convention to the said rights and freedoms shall not be applied for any purpose other than those for which they have been prescribed.

SECTION II—EUROPEAN COURT OF HUMAN RIGHTS

Article 19—Establishment of the Court

To ensure the observance of the engagements undertaken by the High Contracting Parties in the Convention and the Protocols thereto, there shall be set up a European Court of Human Rights, hereinafter referred to as «the Court». It shall function on a permanent basis.

Article 20—Number of judges

The Court shall consist of a number of judges equal to that of the High Contracting Parties.

Article 21—Criteria for office

1 The judges shall be of high moral character and must either possess the qualifications required for appointment to high judicial office or be jurisconsults of recognised competence.

2 The judges shall sit on the Court in their individual capacity.

3 During their term of office the judges shall not engage in any activity which is incompatible with their independence, impartiality or with the demands of a full-time office; all questions arising from the application of this paragraph shall be decided by the Court.

Article 22—Election of judges

1 The judges shall be elected by the Parliamentary Assembly with respect to each High Contracting Party by a majority of votes cast from a list of three candidates nominated by the High Contracting Party.

2 The same procedure shall be followed to complete the Court in the event of the accession of new High Contracting Parties and in filling casual vacancies.

Article 23—Terms of office

1   The judges shall be elected for a period of six years. They may be re-elected. However, the terms of office of one-half of the judges elected at the first election shall expire at the end of three years.

2   The judges whose terms of office are to expire at the end of the initial period of three years shall be chosen by lot by the Secretary General of the Council of Europe immediately after their election.

3   In order to ensure that, as far as possible, the terms of office of one-half of the judges are renewed every three years, the Parliamentary Assembly may decide, before proceeding to any subsequent election, that the term or terms of office of one or more judges to be elected shall be for a period other than six years but not more than nine and not less than three years.

4   In cases where more than one term of office is involved and where the Parliamentary Assembly applies the preceding paragraph, the allocation of the terms of office shall be effected by a drawing of lots by the Secretary General of the Council of Europe immediately after the election.

5   A judge elected to replace a judge whose term of office has not expired shall hold office for the remainder of his predecessor's term.

6   The terms of office of judges shall expire when they reach the age of 70.

7   The judges shall hold office until replaced. They shall, however, continue to deal with such cases as they already have under consideration.

Article 24—Dismissal

No judge may be dismissed from his office unless the other judges decide by a majority of two-thirds that he has ceased to fulfil the required conditions.

Article 25—Registry and legal secretaries

The Court shall have a registry, the functions and organisation of which shall be laid down in the rules of the Court. The Court shall be assisted by legal secretaries.

Article 26—Plenary Court

The plenary Court shall

a   elect its President and one or two Vice-Presidents for a period of three years; they may be re-elected;

b   set up Chambers, constituted for a fixed period of time;

c   elect the Presidents of the Chambers of the Court; they may be re-elected;

d   adopt the rules of the Court, and

e   elect the Registrar and one or more Deputy Registrars.

Article 27—Committees, Chambers and Grand Chamber

1   To consider cases brought before it, the Court shall sit in committees of three judges, in Chambers of seven judges and in a Grand Chamber of seventeen judges. The Court's Chambers shall set up committees for a fixed period of time.

2   There shall sit as an ex officio member of the Chamber and the Grand Chamber the judge elected in respect of the State Party concerned or, if there is none or if he is unable to sit, a person of its choice who shall sit in the capacity of judge.

3   The Grand Chamber shall also include the President of the Court, the Vice-Presidents, the Presidents of the Chambers and other judges chosen in accordance with the rules of the Court. When a case is referred to the Grand Chamber under Article 43, no judge from the Chamber which rendered the

judgment shall sit in the Grand Chamber, with the exception of the President of the Chamber and the judge who sat in respect of the State Party concerned.

Article 28—Declarations of inadmissibility by committees

A committee may, by a unanimous vote, declare inadmissible or strike out of its list of cases an application submitted under Article 34 where such a decision can be taken without further examination. The decision shall be final.

Article 29—Decisions by Chambers on admissibility and merits

1   If no decision is taken under Article 28, a Chamber shall decide on the admissibility and merits of individual applications submitted under Article 34.

2   A Chamber shall decide on the admissibility and merits of inter-State applications submitted under Article 33.

3   The decision on admissibility shall be taken separately unless the Court, in exceptional cases, decides otherwise.

Article 30—Relinquishment of jurisdiction to the Grand Chamber

Where a case pending before a Chamber raises a serious question affecting the interpretation of the Convention or the protocols thereto, or where the resolution of a question before the Chamber might have a result inconsistent with a judgment previously delivered by the Court, the Chamber may, at any time before it has rendered its judgment, relinquish jurisdiction in favour of the Grand Chamber, unless one of the parties to the case objects.

Article 31—Powers of the Grand Chamber

The Grand Chamber shall

a   determine applications submitted either under Article 33 or Article 34 when a Chamber has relinquished jurisdiction under Article 30 or when the case has been referred to it under Article 43; and

b   consider requests for advisory opinions submitted under Article 47.

Article 32—Jurisdiction of the Court

1   The jurisdiction of the Court shall extend to all matters concerning the interpretation and application of the Convention and the protocols thereto which are referred to it as provided in Articles 33, 34 and 47.

2   In the event of dispute as to whether the Court has jurisdiction, the Court shall decide.

Article 33—Inter-State cases

Any High Contracting Party may refer to the Court any alleged breach of the provisions of the Convention and the protocols thereto by another High Contracting Party.

Article 34—Individual applications

The Court may receive applications from any person, non-governmental organisation or group of individuals claiming to be the victim of a violation by one of the High Contracting Parties of the rights set forth in the Convention or the protocols thereto. The High Contracting Parties undertake not to hinder in any way the effective exercise of this right.

Article 35—Admissibility criteria

1   The Court may only deal with the matter after all domestic remedies have been exhausted, according to the generally recognised rules of international law, and within a period of six months from the date on which the final decision was taken.

2 The Court shall not deal with any application submitted under Article 34 that

  a is anonymous; or

  b is substantially the same as a matter that has already been examined by the Court or has already been submitted to another procedure of international investigation or settlement and contains no relevant new information.

3 The Court shall declare inadmissible any individual application submitted under Article 34 which it considers incompatible with the provisions of the Convention or the protocols thereto, manifestly ill-founded, or an abuse of the right of application.

4 The Court shall reject any application which it considers inadmissible under this Article. It may do so at any stage of the proceedings.

Article 36—Third party intervention

1 In all cases before a Chamber or the Grand Chamber, a High Contracting Party one of whose nationals is an applicant shall have the right to submit written comments and to take part in hearings.

2 The President of the Court may, in the interest of the proper administration of justice, invite any High Contracting Party which is not a party to the proceedings or any person concerned who is not the applicant to submit written comments or take part in hearings.

Article 37—Striking out applications

1 The Court may at any stage of the proceedings decide to strike an application out of its list of cases where the circumstances lead to the conclusion that

  a the applicant does not intend to pursue his application; or

  b the matter has been resolved; or

  c for any other reason established by the Court, it is no longer justified to continue the examination of the application.

However, the Court shall continue the examination of the application if respect for human rights as defined in the Convention and the protocols thereto so requires.

2 The Court may decide to restore an application to its list of cases if it considers that the circumstances justify such a course.

Article 38—Examination of the case and friendly settlement proceedings

1 If the Court declares the application admissible, it shall

  a pursue the examination of the case, together with the representatives of the parties, and if need be, undertake an investigation, for the effective conduct of which the States concerned shall furnish all necessary facilities;

  b place itself at the disposal of the parties concerned with a view to securing a friendly settlement of the matter on the basis of respect for human rights as defined in the Convention and the protocols thereto.

2 Proceedings conducted under paragraph 1.b shall be confidential.

Article 39—Finding of a friendly settlement

If a friendly settlement is effected, the Court shall strike the case out of its list by means of a decision which shall be confined to a brief statement of the facts and of the solution reached.

Article 40—Public hearings and access to documents

1 Hearings shall be in public unless the Court in exceptional circumstances decides otherwise.

2   Documents deposited with the Registrar shall be accessible to the public unless the President of the Court decides otherwise.

Article 41—Just satisfaction

If the Court finds that there has been a violation of the Convention or the protocols thereto, and if the internal law of the High Contracting Party concerned allows only partial reparation to be made, the Court shall, if necessary, afford just satisfaction to the injured party.

Article 42—Judgments of Chambers

Judgments of Chambers shall become final in accordance with the provisions of Article 44, paragraph 2.

Article 43—Referral to the Grand Chamber

1   Within a period of three months from the date of the judgment of the Chamber, any party to the case may, in exceptional cases, request that the case be referred to the Grand Chamber.

2   A panel of five judges of the Grand Chamber shall accept the request if the case raises a serious question affecting the interpretation or application of the Convention or the protocols thereto, or a serious issue of general importance.

3   If the panel accepts the request, the Grand Chamber shall decide the case by means of a judgment.

Article 44—Final judgments

1   The judgment of the Grand Chamber shall be final.

2   The judgment of a Chamber shall become final

   a   when the parties declare that they will not request that the case be referred to the Grand Chamber; or

   b   three months after the date of the judgment, if reference of the case to the Grand Chamber has not been requested; or

   c   when the panel of the Grand Chamber rejects the request to refer under Article 43.

3   The final judgment shall be published.

Article 45—Reasons for judgments and decisions

1   Reasons shall be given for judgments as well as for decisions declaring applications admissible or inadmissible.

2   If a judgment does not represent, in whole or in part, the unanimous opinion of the judges, any judge shall be entitled to deliver a separate opinion.

Article 46—Binding force and execution of judgments

1   The High Contracting Parties undertake to abide by the final judgment of the Court in any case to which they are parties.

2   The final judgment of the Court shall be transmitted to the Committee of Ministers, which shall supervise its execution.

Article 47—Advisory opinions

1   The Court may, at the request of the Committee of Ministers, give advisory opinions on legal questions concerning the interpretation of the Convention and the protocols thereto.

2   Such opinions shall not deal with any question relating to the content or scope of the rights or freedoms defined in Section I of the Convention and the protocols thereto, or with any other question which the Court or the Committee of Ministers might have to consider in consequence of any such proceedings as could be instituted in accordance with the Convention.

3   Decisions of the Committee of Ministers to request an advisory opinion of the Court shall require a majority vote of the representatives entitled to sit on the Committee.

Article 48—Advisory jurisdiction of the Court

The Court shall decide whether a request for an advisory opinion submitted by the Committee of Ministers is within its competence as defined in Article 47.

Article 49—Reasons for advisory opinions

1   Reasons shall be given for advisory opinions of the Court.

2   If the advisory opinion does not represent, in whole or in part, the unanimous opinion of the judges, any judge shall be entitled to deliver a separate opinion.

3   Advisory opinions of the Court shall be communicated to the Committee of Ministers.

Article 50—Expenditure on the Court

The expenditure on the Court shall be borne by the Council of Europe.

Article 51—Privileges and immunities of judges

The judges shall be entitled, during the exercise of their functions, to the privileges and immunities provided for in Article 40 of the Statute of the Council of Europe and in the agreements made thereunder.

SECTION III—MISCELLANEOUS PROVISIONS

Article 52—Inquiries by the Secretary General

On receipt of a request from the Secretary General of the Council of Europe any High Contracting Party shall furnish an explanation of the manner in which its internal law ensures the effective implementation of any of the provisions of the Convention.

Article 53—Safeguard for existing human rights

Nothing in this Convention shall be construed as limiting or derogating from any of the human rights and fundamental freedoms which may be ensured under the laws of any High Contracting Party or under any other agreement to which it is a Party.

Article 54—Powers of the Committee of Ministers

Nothing in this Convention shall prejudice the powers conferred on the Committee of Ministers by the Statute of the Council of Europe.

Article 55—Exclusion of other means of dispute settlement

The High Contracting Parties agree that, except by special agreement, they will not avail themselves of treaties, conventions or declarations in force between them for the purpose of submitting, by way of petition, a dispute arising out of the interpretation or application of this Convention to a means of settlement other than those provided for in this Convention.

Article 56—Territorial application

1   Any State may at the time of its ratification or at any time thereafter declare by notification addressed to the Secretary General of the Council of Europe that the present Convention shall, subject to paragraph 4 of this Article, extend to all or any of the territories for whose international relations it is responsible.

2   The Convention shall extend to the territory or territories named in the notification as from the thirtieth day after the receipt of this notification by the Secretary General of the Council of Europe.

3   The provisions of this Convention shall be applied in such territories with due regard, however, to local requirements.

4   Any State which has made a declaration in accordance with paragraph 1 of this article may at any time thereafter declare on behalf of one or more of the territories to which the declaration relates that it accepts the competence of the Court to receive applications from individuals, non-governmental organisations or groups of individuals as provided by Article 34 of the Convention.

Article 57—Reservations

1   Any State may, when signing this Convention or when depositing its instrument of ratification, make a reservation in respect of any particular provision of the Convention to the extent that any law then in force in its territory is not in conformity with the provision. Reservations of a general character shall not be permitted under this article.

2   Any reservation made under this article shall contain a brief statement of the law concerned.

Article 58—Denunciation

1   A High Contracting Party may denounce the present Convention only after the expiry of five years from the date on which it became a party to it and after six months' notice contained in a notification addressed to the Secretary General of the Council of Europe, who shall inform the other High Contracting Parties.

2   Such a denunciation shall not have the effect of releasing the High Contracting Party concerned from its obligations under this Convention in respect of any act which, being capable of constituting a violation of such obligations, may have been performed by it before the date at which the denunciation became effective.

3   Any High Contracting Party which shall cease to be a member of the Council of Europe shall cease to be a Party to this Convention under the same conditions.

4   The Convention may be denounced in accordance with the provisions of the preceding paragraphs in respect of any territory to which it has been declared to extend under the terms of Article 56.

Article 59—Signature and ratification

1   This Convention shall be open to the signature of the members of the Council of Europe. It shall be ratified. Ratifications shall be deposited with the Secretary General of the Council of Europe.

2   The present Convention shall come into force after the deposit of ten instruments of ratification.

3   As regards any signatory ratifying subsequently, the Convention shall come into force at the date of the deposit of its instrument of ratification.

4   The Secretary General of the Council of Europe shall notify all the members of the Council of Europe of the entry into force of the Convention, the names of the High Contracting Parties who have ratified it, and the deposit of all instruments of ratification which may be effected subsequently.

Done at Rome this 4th day of November 1950, in English and French, both texts being equally authentic, in a single copy which shall remain deposited in the archives of the Council of Europe. The Secretary General shall transmit certified copies to each of the signatories.

PROTOCOL TO THE CONVENTION FOR THE PROTECTION OF HUMAN RIGHTS AND FUNDAMENTAL FREEDOMS

Paris, 20.III.1952

The governments signatory hereto, being members of the Council of Europe,

Being resolved to take steps to ensure the collective enforcement of certain rights and freedoms other than those already included in Section I of the Convention for the Protection of Human Rights and

Fundamental Freedoms signed at Rome on 4 November 1950 (hereinafter referred to as 'the Convention'),

Have agreed as follows:

Article 1—Protection of property

Every natural or legal person is entitled to the peaceful enjoyment of his possessions. No one shall be deprived of his possessions except in the public interest and subject to the conditions provided for by law and by the general principles of international law.

The preceding provisions shall not, however, in any way impair the right of a State to enforce such laws as it deems necessary to control the use of property in accordance with the general interest or to secure the payment of taxes or other contributions or penalties.

Article 2—Right to education

No person shall be denied the right to education. In the exercise of any functions which it assumes in relation to education and to teaching, the State shall respect the right of parents to ensure such education and teaching in conformity with their own religious and philosophical convictions.

Article 3—Right to free elections

The High Contracting Parties undertake to hold free elections at reasonable intervals by secret ballot, under conditions which will ensure the free expression of the opinion of the people in the choice of the legislature.

Article 4—Territorial application

Any High Contracting Party may at the time of signature or ratification or at any time thereafter communicate to the Secretary General of the Council of Europe a declaration stating the extent to which it undertakes that the provisions of the present Protocol shall apply to such of the territories for the international relations of which it is responsible as are named therein.

Any High Contracting Party which has communicated a declaration in virtue of the preceding paragraph may from time to time communicate a further declaration modifying the terms of any former declaration or terminating the application of the provisions of this Protocol in respect of any territory.

A declaration made in accordance with this article shall be deemed to have been made in accordance with paragraph 1 of Article 56 of the Convention.

Article 5—Relationship to the Convention

As between the High Contracting Parties the provisions of Articles 1, 2, 3 and 4 of this Protocol shall be regarded as additional articles to the Convention and all the provisions of the Convention shall apply accordingly.

Article 6—Signature and ratification

This Protocol shall be open for signature by the members of the Council of Europe, who are the signatories of the Convention; it shall be ratified at the same time as or after the ratification of the Convention. It shall enter into force after the deposit of ten instruments of ratification. As regards any signatory ratifying subsequently, the Protocol shall enter into force at the date of the deposit of its instrument of ratification.

The instruments of ratification shall be deposited with the Secretary General of the Council of Europe, who will notify all members of the names of those who have ratified.

Done at Paris on the 20th day of March 1952, in English and French, both texts being equally authentic, in a single copy which shall remain deposited in the archives of the Council of Europe. The Secretary General shall transmit certified copies to each of the signatory governments.

PROTOCOL NO. 4 TO THE CONVENTION FOR THE PROTECTION OF HUMAN RIGHTS AND FUNDAMENTAL FREEDOMS SECURING CERTAIN RIGHTS AND FREEDOMS OTHER THAN THOSE ALREADY INCLUDED IN THE CONVENTION AND IN THE FIRST PROTOCOL THERETO

Strasbourg, 16.IX.1963

The governments signatory hereto, being members of the Council of Europe,

Being resolved to take steps to ensure the collective enforcement of certain rights and freedoms other than those already included in Section I of the Convention for the Protection of Human Rights and Fundamental Freedoms signed at Rome on 4th November 1950 (hereinafter referred to as the 'Convention') and in Articles 1 to 3 of the First Protocol to the Convention, signed at Paris on 20th March 1952,

Have agreed as follows:

Article 1—Prohibition of imprisonment for debt

No one shall be deprived of his liberty merely on the ground of inability to fulfil a contractual obligation.

Article 2—Freedom of movement

1   Everyone lawfully within the territory of a State shall, within that territory, have the right to liberty of movement and freedom to choose his residence.

2   Everyone shall be free to leave any country, including his own.

3   No restrictions shall be placed on the exercise of these rights other than such as are in accordance with law and are necessary in a democratic society in the interests of national security or public safety, for the maintenance of ordre public, for the prevention of crime, for the protection of health or morals, or for the protection of the rights and freedoms of others.

4   The rights set forth in paragraph 1 may also be subject, in particular areas, to restrictions imposed in accordance with law and justified by the public interest in a democratic society.

Article 3—Prohibition of expulsion of nationals

1   No one shall be expelled, by means either of an individual or of a collective measure, from the territory of the State of which he is a national.

2   No one shall be deprived of the right to enter the territory of the state of which he is a national.

Article 4—Prohibition of collective expulsion of aliens

Collective expulsion of aliens is prohibited.

Article 5—Territorial application

1   Any High Contracting Party may, at the time of signature or ratification of this Protocol, or at any time thereafter, communicate to the Secretary General of the Council of Europe a declaration stating the extent to which it undertakes that the provisions of this Protocol shall apply to such of the territories for the international relations of which it is responsible as are named therein.

2   Any High Contracting Party which has communicated a declaration in virtue of the preceding paragraph may, from time to time, communicate a further declaration modifying the terms of any former declaration or terminating the application of the provisions of this Protocol in respect of any territory.

3   A declaration made in accordance with this article shall be deemed to have been made in accordance with paragraph 1 of Article 56 of the Convention.

4   The territory of any State to which this Protocol applies by virtue of ratification or acceptance by that State, and each territory to which this Protocol is applied by virtue of a declaration by that State under this article, shall be treated as separate territories for the purpose of the references in Articles 2 and 3 to the territory of a State.

5   Any State which has made a declaration in accordance with paragraph 1 or 2 of this Article may at any time thereafter declare on behalf of one or more of the territories to which the declaration relates that it accepts the competence of the Court to receive applications from individuals, non-governmental organisations or groups of individuals as provided in Article 34 of the Convention in respect of all or any of Articles 1 to 4 of this Protocol.'

Article 6—Relationship to the Convention

As between the High Contracting Parties the provisions of Articles 1 to 5 of this Protocol shall be regarded as additional Articles to the Convention, and all the provisions of the Convention shall apply accordingly.

Article 7—Signature and ratification

1   This Protocol shall be open for signature by the members of the Council of Europe who are the signatories of the Convention; it shall be ratified at the same time as or after the ratification of the Convention. It shall enter into force after the deposit of five instruments of ratification. As regards any signatory ratifying subsequently, the Protocol shall enter into force at the date of the deposit of its instrument of ratification.

2   The instruments of ratification shall be deposited with the Secretary General of the Council of Europe, who will notify all members of the names of those who have ratified.

In witness whereof the undersigned, being duly authorised thereto, have signed this Protocol.

Done at Strasbourg, this 16th day of September 1963, in English and in French, both texts being equally authoritative, in a single copy which shall remain deposited in the archives of the Council of Europe. The Secretary General shall transmit certified copies to each of the signatory states.

PROTOCOL NO. 6 TO THE CONVENTION FOR THE PROTECTION OF HUMAN RIGHTS AND FUNDAMENTAL FREEDOMS CONCERNING THE ABOLITION OF THE DEATH PENALTY

Strasbourg, 28.IV.1983

The member States of the Council of Europe, signatory to this Protocol to the Convention for the Protection of Human Rights and Fundamental Freedoms, signed at Rome on 4 November 1950 (hereinafter referred to as 'the Convention'),

Considering that the evolution that has occurred in several member States of the Council of Europe expresses a general tendency in favour of abolition of the death penalty;

Have agreed as follows:

Article 1—Abolition of the death penalty

The death penalty shall be abolished. No-one shall be condemned to such penalty or executed.

Article 2—Death penalty in time of war

A State may make provision in its law for the death penalty in respect of acts committed in time of war or of imminent threat of war; such penalty shall be applied only in the instances laid down in the law and in accordance with its provisions. The State shall communicate to the Secretary General of the Council of Europe the relevant provisions of that law.

Article 3—Prohibition of derogations

No derogation from the provisions of this Protocol shall be made under Article 15 of the Convention.

Article 4—Prohibition of reservations

No reservation may be made under Article 57 of the Convention in respect of the provisions of this Protocol.

Article 5—Territorial application

1 Any State may at the time of signature or when depositing its instrument of ratification, acceptance or approval, specify the territory or territories to which this Protocol shall apply.

2 Any State may at any later date, by a declaration addressed to the Secretary General of the Council of Europe, extend the application of this Protocol to any other territory specified in the declaration. In respect of such territory the Protocol shall enter into force on the first day of the month following the date of receipt of such declaration by the Secretary General.

3 Any declaration made under the two preceding paragraphs may, in respect of any territory specified in such declaration, be withdrawn by a notification addressed to the Secretary General. The withdrawal shall become effective on the first day of the month following the date of receipt of such notification by the Secretary General.

Article 6—Relationship to the Convention

As between the States Parties the provisions of Articles 1 and 5 of this Protocol shall be regarded as additional articles to the Convention and all the provisions of the Convention shall apply accordingly.

Article 7—Signature and ratification

The Protocol shall be open for signature by the member States of the Council of Europe, signatories to the Convention. It shall be subject to ratification, acceptance or approval. A member State of the Council of Europe may not ratify, accept or approve this Protocol unless it has, simultaneously or previously, ratified the Convention. Instruments of ratification, acceptance or approval shall be deposited with the Secretary General of the Council of Europe.

Article 8—Entry into force

1 This Protocol shall enter into force on the first day of the month following the date on which five member States of the Council of Europe have expressed their consent to be bound by the Protocol in accordance with the provisions of Article 7.

2 In respect of any member State which subsequently expresses its consent to be bound by it, the Protocol shall enter into force on the first day of the month following the date of the deposit of the instrument of ratification, acceptance or approval.

Article 9—Depositary functions

The Secretary General of the Council of Europe shall notify the member States of the Council of:

a   any signature;

b   the deposit of any instrument of ratification, acceptance or approval;

c   any date of entry into force of this Protocol in accordance with articles 5 and 8;

d   any other act, notification or communication relating to this Protocol.

In witness whereof the undersigned, being duly authorised thereto, have signed this Protocol.

Done at Strasbourg, this 28th day of April 1983, in English and in French, both texts being equally authentic, in a single copy which shall be deposited in the archives of the Council of Europe. The Secretary General of the Council of Europe shall transmit certified copies to each member State of the Council of Europe.

PROTOCOL NO. 7 TO THE CONVENTION FOR THE PROTECTION OF HUMAN RIGHTS AND FUNDAMENTAL FREEDOMS

Strasbourg, 22.XI.1984

The member States of the Council of Europe signatory hereto,

Being resolved to take further steps to ensure the collective enforcement of certain rights and freedoms by means of the Convention for the Protection of Human Rights and Fundamental Freedoms signed at Rome on 4 November 1950 (hereinafter referred to as 'the Convention'),

Have agreed as follows:

Article 1—Procedural safeguards relating to expulsion of aliens

1   An alien lawfully resident in the territory of a State shall not be expelled therefrom except in pursuance of a decision reached in accordance with law and shall be allowed:

   a   to submit reasons against his expulsion,

   b   to have his case reviewed, and

   c   to be represented for these purposes before the competent authority or a person or persons designated by that authority.

2   An alien may be expelled before the exercise of his rights under paragraph 1.a, b and c of this Article, when such expulsion is necessary in the interests of public order or is grounded on reasons of national security.

Article 2—Right of appeal in criminal matters

1   Everyone convicted of a criminal offence by a tribunal shall have the right to have his conviction or sentence reviewed by a higher tribunal. The exercise of this right, including the grounds on which it may be exercised, shall be governed by law.

2   This right may be subject to exceptions in regard to offences of a minor character, as prescribed by law, or in cases in which the person concerned was tried in the first instance by the highest tribunal or was convicted following an appeal against acquittal.

Article 3—Compensation for wrongful conviction

When a person has by a final decision been convicted of a criminal offence and when subsequently his conviction has been reversed, or he has been pardoned, on the ground that a new or newly discovered fact shows conclusively that there has been a miscarriage of justice, the person who has suffered punishment as a result of such conviction shall be compensated according to the law or the practice of the State concerned, unless it is proved that the non-disclosure of the unknown fact in time is wholly or partly attributable to him.

Article 4—Right not to be tried or punished twice

1   No one shall be liable to be tried or punished again in criminal proceedings under the jurisdiction of the same State for an offence for which he has already been finally acquitted or convicted in accordance with the law and penal procedure of that State.

2   The provisions of the preceding paragraph shall not prevent the reopening of the case in accordance with the law and penal procedure of the State concerned, if there is evidence of new or newly discovered facts, or if there has been a fundamental defect in the previous proceedings, which could affect the outcome of the case.

3   No derogation from this Article shall be made under Article 15 of the Convention.

Article 5—Equality between spouses

Spouses shall enjoy equality of rights and responsibilities of a private law character between them, and in their relations with their children, as to marriage, during marriage and in the event of its dissolution. This Article shall not prevent States from taking such measures as are necessary in the interests of the children.

Article 6—Territorial application

1   Any State may at the time of signature or when depositing its instrument of ratification, acceptance or approval, specify the territory or territories to which the Protocol shall apply and state the extent to which it undertakes that the provisions of this Protocol shall apply to such territory or territories.

2   Any State may at any later date, by a declaration addressed to the Secretary General of the Council of Europe, extend the application of this Protocol to any other territory specified in the declaration. In respect of such territory the Protocol shall enter into force on the first day of the month following the expiration of a period of two months after the date of receipt by the Secretary General of such declaration.

3   Any declaration made under the two preceding paragraphs may, in respect of any territory specified in such declaration, be withdrawn or modified by a notification addressed to the Secretary General. The withdrawal or modification shall become effective on the first day of the month following the expiration of a period of two months after the date of receipt of such notification by the Secretary General.

4   A declaration made in accordance with this Article shall be deemed to have been made in accordance with paragraph 1 of Article 56 of the Convention.

5   The territory of any State to which this Protocol applies by virtue of ratification, acceptance or approval by that State, and each territory to which this Protocol is applied by virtue of a declaration by that State under this Article, may be treated as separate territories for the purpose of the reference in Article 1 to the territory of a State.

6   Any State which has made a declaration in accordance with paragraph 1 or 2 of this Article may at any time thereafter declare on behalf of one or more of the territories to which the declaration relates that it accepts the competence of the Court to receive applications from individuals, non-governmental organisations or groups of individuals as provided in Article 34 of the Convention in respect of Articles 1 to 5 of this Protocol.

Article 7—Relationship to the Convention

As between the States Parties, the provisions of Article 1 to 6 of this Protocol shall be regarded as additional Articles to the Convention, and all the provisions of the Convention shall apply accordingly.

Article 8—Signature and ratification

This Protocol shall be open for signature by member States of the Council of Europe which have signed the Convention. It is subject to ratification, acceptance or approval. A member State of the Council of Europe may not ratify, accept or approve this Protocol without previously or simultaneously ratifying the Convention. Instruments of ratification, acceptance or approval shall be deposited with the Secretary General of the Council of Europe.

Article 9—Entry into force

1   This Protocol shall enter into force on the first day of the month following the expiration of a period of two months after the date on which seven member States of the Council of Europe have expressed their consent to be bound by the Protocol in accordance with the provisions of Article 8.

2   In respect of any member State which subsequently expresses its consent to be bound by it, the Protocol shall enter into force on the first day of the month following the expiration of a period of two months after the date of the deposit of the instrument of ratification, acceptance or approval.

Article 10—Depositary functions

The Secretary General of the Council of Europe shall notify all the member States of the Council of Europe of:

a   any signature;

b   the deposit of any instrument of ratification, acceptance or approval;

c   any date of entry into force of this Protocol in accordance with Articles 6 and 9;

d   any other act, notification or declaration relating to this Protocol.

In witness whereof the undersigned, being duly authorised thereto, have signed this Protocol.

Done at Strasbourg, this 22nd day of November 1984, in English and French, both texts being equally authentic, in a single copy which shall be deposited in the archives of the Council of Europe. The Secretary General of the Council of Europe shall transmit certified copies to each member State of the Council of Europe.

PROTOCOL NO. 12 TO THE CONVENTION FOR THE PROTECTION OF HUMAN RIGHTS AND FUNDAMENTAL FREEDOMS

Rome, 4.XI.2000

The member States of the Council of Europe signatory hereto,

Having regard to the fundamental principle according to which all persons are equal before the law and are entitled to the equal protection of the law;

Being resolved to take further steps to promote the equality of all persons through the collective enforcement of a general prohibition of discrimination by means of the Convention for the Protection of Human Rights and Fundamental Freedoms signed at Rome on 4 November 1950 (hereinafter referred to as 'the Convention');

Reaffirming that the principle of non-discrimination does not prevent States Parties from taking measures in order to promote full and effective equality, provided that there is an objective and reasonable justification for those measures,

Have agreed as follows:

Article 1—General prohibition of discrimination

1   The enjoyment of any right set forth by law shall be secured without discrimination on any ground such as sex, race, colour, language, religion, political or other opinion, national or social origin, association with a national minority, property, birth or other status.

2   No one shall be discriminated against by any public authority on any ground such as those mentioned in paragraph 1.

Article 2—Territorial application

1   Any State may, at the time of signature or when depositing its instrument of ratification, acceptance or approval, specify the territory or territories to which this Protocol shall apply.

2   Any State may at any later date, by a declaration addressed to the Secretary General of the Council of Europe, extend the application of this Protocol to any other territory specified in the declaration.

In respect of such territory the Protocol shall enter into force on the first day of the month following the expiration of a period of three months after the date of receipt by the Secretary General of such declaration.

3   Any declaration made under the two preceding paragraphs may, in respect of any territory specified in such declaration, be withdrawn or modified by a notification addressed to the Secretary General of the Council of Europe. The withdrawal or modification shall become effective on the first day of the month following the expiration of a period of three months after the date of receipt of such notification by the Secretary General.

4   A declaration made in accordance with this article shall be deemed to have been made in accordance with paragraph 1 of Article 56 of the Convention.

5   Any State which has made a declaration in accordance with paragraph 1 or 2 of this article may at any time thereafter declare on behalf of one or more of the territories to which the declaration relates that it accepts the competence of the Court to receive applications from individuals, nongovernmental organisations or groups of individuals as provided by Article 34 of the Convention in respect of Article 1 of this Protocol.

Article 3—Relationship to the Convention

As between the States Parties, the provisions of Articles 1 and 2 of this Protocol shall be regarded as additional articles to the Convention, and all the provisions of the Convention shall apply accordingly.

Article 4—Signature and ratification

This Protocol shall be open for signature by member States of the Council of Europe which have signed the Convention. It is subject to ratification, acceptance or approval. A member State of the Council of Europe may not ratify, accept or approve this Protocol without previously or simultaneously ratifying the Convention. Instruments of ratification, acceptance or approval shall be deposited with the Secretary General of the Council of Europe.

Article 5—Entry into force

1   This Protocol shall enter into force on the first day of the month following the expiration of a period of three months after the date on which ten member States of the Council of Europe have expressed their consent to be bound by the Protocol in accordance with the provisions of Article 4.

2   In respect of any member State which subsequently expresses its consent to be bound by it, the Protocol shall enter into force on the first day of the month following the expiration of a period of three months after the date of the deposit of the instrument of ratification, acceptance or approval.

Article 6—Depositary functions

The Secretary General of the Council of Europe shall notify all the member States of the Council of Europe of:

a   any signature;

b   the deposit of any instrument of ratification, acceptance or approval;

c   any date of entry into force of this Protocol in accordance with Articles 2 and 5;

d   any other act, notification or communication relating to this Protocol.

In witness whereof the undersigned, being duly authorised thereto, have signed this Protocol.

Done at Rome, this 4th day of November 2000, in English and in French, both texts being equally authentic, in a single copy which shall be deposited in the archives of the Council of Europe. The Secretary General of the Council of Europe shall transmit certified copies to each member State of the Council of Europe.

PROTOCOL NO. 13 TO THE CONVENTION FOR THE PROTECTION OF HUMAN RIGHTS AND FUNDAMENTAL FREEDOMS CONCERNING THE ABOLITION OF THE DEATH PENALTY IN ALL CIRCUMSTANCES

Vilnius, 3.V.2002

The member States of the Council of Europe signatory hereto,

Convinced that everyone's right to life is a basic value in a democratic society and that the abolition of the death penalty is essential for the protection of this right and for the full recognition of the inherent dignity of all human beings;

Wishing to strengthen the protection of the right to life guaranteed by the Convention for the Protection of Human Rights and Fundamental Freedoms signed at Rome on 4 November 1950 (hereinafter referred to as 'the Convention');

Noting that Protocol No. 6 to the Convention, concerning the Abolition of the Death Penalty, signed at Strasbourg on 28 April 1983, does not exclude the death penalty in respect of acts committed in time of war or of imminent threat of war;

Being resolved to take the final step in order to abolish the death penalty in all circumstances,

Have agreed as follows:

Article 1—Abolition of the death penalty

The death penalty shall be abolished. No one shall be condemned to such penalty or executed.

Article 2—Prohibitions of derogations

No derogation from the provisions of this Protocol shall be made under Article 15 of the Convention.

Article 3—Prohibitions of reservations

No reservation may be made under Article 57 of the Convention in respect of the provisions of this Protocol.

Article 4—Territorial application

1   Any state may, at the time of signature or when depositing its instrument of ratification, acceptance or approval, specify the territory or territories to which this Protocol shall apply.

2   Any state may at any later date, by a declaration addressed to the Secretary General of the Council of Europe, extend the application of this Protocol to any other territory specified in the declaration. In respect of such territory the Protocol shall enter into force on the first day of the month following the expiration of a period of three months after the date of receipt by the Secretary General of such declaration.

3   Any declaration made under the two preceding paragraphs may, in respect of any territory specified in such declaration, be withdrawn or modified by a notification addressed to the Secretary General. The withdrawal or modification shall become effective on the first day of the month following the expiration of a period of three months after the date of receipt of such notification by the Secretary General.

Article 5—Relationship to the Convention

As between the states Parties the provisions of Articles 1 to 4 of this Protocol shall be regarded as additional articles to the Convention, and all the provisions of the Convention shall apply accordingly.

Article 6—Signature and ratification

This Protocol shall be open for signature by member states of the Council of Europe which have signed the Convention. It is subject to ratification, acceptance or approval. A member state of the Council of Europe may not ratify, accept or approve this Protocol without previously or simultaneously ratifying the Convention. Instruments of ratification, acceptance or approval shall be deposited with the Secretary General of the Council of Europe.

Article 7—Entry into force

1   This Protocol shall enter into force on the first day of the month following the expiration of a period of three months after the date on which ten member states of the Council of Europe have expressed their consent to be bound by the Protocol in accordance with the provisions of Article 6.

2   In respect of any member state which subsequently expresses its consent to be bound by it, the Protocol shall enter into force on the first day of the month following the expiration of a period of three months after the date of the deposit of the instrument of ratification, acceptance or approval.

Article 8—Depositary functions

The Secretary General of the Council of Europe shall notify all the member states of the Council of Europe of:

a   any signature;

b   the deposit of any instrument of ratification, acceptance or approval;

c   any date of entry into force of this Protocol in accordance with Articles 4 and 7;

d   any other act, notification or communication relating to this Protocol;

In witness whereof the undersigned, being duly authorised thereto, have signed this Protocol.

Done at Vilnius, this 3rd day of May 2002, in English and in French, both texts being equally authentic, in a single copy which shall be deposited in the archives of the Council of Europe. The Secretary General of the Council of Europe shall transmit certified copies to each member state of the Council of Europe.

PROTOCOL NO. 14 TO THE CONVENTION FOR THE PROTECTION OF HUMAN RIGHTS AND FUNDAMENTAL FREEDOMS, AMENDING THE CONTROL SYSTEM OF THE CONVENTION

STRAS BOURG, 13. V. 2004

Preamble

The member States of the Council of Europe, signatories to this Protocol to the Convention for the Protection of Human Rights and Fundamental Freedoms, signed at Rome on 4 November 1950 (hereinafter referred to as 'the Convention'),

Having regard to Resolution No. 1 and the Declaration adopted at the European Ministerial Conference on Human Rights, held in Rome on 3 and 4 November 2000;

Having regard to the Declarations adopted by the Committee of Ministers on 8 November 2001, 7 November 2002 and 15 May 2003, at their 109th, 111th and 112th Sessions, respectively;

Having regard to Opinion No. 251 (2004) adopted by the Parliamentary Assembly of the Council of Europe on 28 April 2004;

Considering the urgent need to amend certain provisions of the Convention in order to maintain and improve the efficiency of the control system for the long term, mainly in the light of the continuing increase in the workload of the European Court of Human Rights and the Committee of Ministers of the Council of Europe;

Considering, in particular, the need to ensure that the Court can continue to play its preeminent role in protecting human rights in Europe,

Have agreed as follows:

Article 1

Paragraph 2 of Article 22 of the Convention shall be deleted.

Article 2

Article 23 of the Convention shall be amended to read as follows:

'Article 23—Terms of office and dismissal

1   The judges shall be elected for a period of nine years. They may not be re-elected.

2   The terms of office of judges shall expire when they reach the age of 70.

3   The judges shall hold office until replaced. They shall, however, continue to deal with such cases as they already have under consideration.

4   No judge may be dismissed from office unless the other judges decide by a majority of twothirds that that judge has ceased to fulfil the required conditions.'

Article 3

Article 24 of the Convention shall be deleted.

Article 4

Article 25 of the Convention shall become Article 24 and its text shall be amended to read as follows:

'Article 24—Registry and rapporteurs

1   The Court shall have a registry, the functions and organisation of which shall be laid down in the rules of the Court.

2   When sitting in a single-judge formation, the Court shall be assisted by rapporteurs who shall function under the authority of the President of the Court. They shall form part of the Court's registry.'

Article 5

Article 26 of the Convention shall become Article 25 ('Plenary Court') and its text shall be amended as follows:

1   At the end of paragraph d, the comma shall be replaced by a semi-colon and the word 'and' shall be deleted.

2   At the end of paragraph e, the full stop shall be replaced by a semi-colon.

3   A new paragraph f shall be added which shall read as follows:

   'f   make any request under Article 26, paragraph 2.'

Article 6

Article 27 of the Convention shall become Article 26 and its text shall be amended to read as follows:

'Article 26—Single-judge formation, committees, Chambers and Grand Chamber

1   To consider cases brought before it, the Court shall sit in a single-judge formation, in committees of three judges, in Chambers of seven judges and in a Grand Chamber of seventeen judges. The Court's Chambers shall set up committees for a fixed period of time.

2   At the request of the plenary Court, the Committee of Ministers may, by a unanimous decision and for a fixed period, reduce to five the number of judges of the Chambers.

3   When sitting as a single judge, a judge shall not examine any application against the High Contracting Party in respect of which that judge has been elected.

4   There shall sit as an *ex officio* member of the Chamber and the Grand Chamber the judge elected in respect of the High Contracting Party concerned. If there is none or if that judge is unable to sit, a person chosen by the President of the Court from a list submitted in advance by that Party shall sit in the capacity of judge.

5   The Grand Chamber shall also include the President of the Court, the Vice-Presidents, the Presidents of the Chambers and other judges chosen in accordance with the rules of the Court. When a case is referred to the Grand Chamber under Article 43, no judge from the Chamber which rendered the judgment shall sit in the Grand Chamber, with the exception of the President of the Chamber and the judge who sat in respect of the High Contracting Party concerned.'

Article 7

After the new Article 26, a new Article 27 shall be inserted into the Convention, which shall read as follows:

'Article 27—Competence of single judges

1   A single judge may declare inadmissible or strike out of the Court's list of cases an application submitted under Article 34, where such a decision can be taken without further examination.

2   The decision shall be final.

3   If the single judge does not declare an application inadmissible or strike it out, that judge shall forward it to a committee or to a Chamber for further examination.'

Article 8

Article 28 of the Convention shall be amended to read as follows:

'Article 28—Competence of committees

1   In respect of an application submitted under Article 34, a committee may, by a unanimous vote,

  a   declare it inadmissible or strike it out of its list of cases, where such decision can be taken without further examination; or

  b   declare it admissible and render at the same time a judgment on the merits, if the underlying question in the case, concerning the interpretation or the application of the Convention or the Protocols thereto, is already the subject of well-established case-law of the Court.

2   Decisions and judgments under paragraph 1 shall be final.

3   If the judge elected in respect of the High Contracting Party concerned is not a member of the committee, the committee may at any stage of the proceedings invite that judge to take the place of one of the members of the committee, having regard to all relevant factors, including whether that Party has contested the application of the procedure under paragraph 1.b.'

Article 9

Article 29 of the Convention shall be amended as follows:

1   Paragraph 1 shall be amended to read as follows: 'If no decision is taken under Article 27 or 28, or no judgment rendered under Article 28, a Chamber shall decide on the admissibility and merits of

individual applications submitted under Article 34. The decision on admissibility may be taken separately.'

2 At the end of paragraph 2 a new sentence shall be added which shall read as follows: 'The decision on admissibility shall be taken separately unless the Court, in exceptional cases, decides otherwise.'

3 Paragraph 3 shall be deleted.

Article 10

Article 31 of the Convention shall be amended as follows:

1 At the end of paragraph a, the word 'and' shall be deleted.

2 Paragraph b shall become paragraph c and a new paragraph b shall be inserted and shall read as follows:

'b decide on issues referred to the Court by the Committee of Ministers in accordance with Article 46, paragraph 4; and'.

Article 11

Article 32 of the Convention shall be amended as follows:

At the end of paragraph 1, a comma and the number 46 shall be inserted after the number 34.

Article 12

Paragraph 3 of Article 35 of the Convention shall be amended to read as follows:

'3 The Court shall declare inadmissible any individual application submitted under Article 34 if it considers that :

a the application is incompatible with the provisions of the Convention or the Protocols thereto, manifestly ill-founded, or an abuse of the right of individual application; or

b the applicant has not suffered a significant disadvantage, unless respect for human rights as defined in the Convention and the Protocols thereto requires an examination of the application on the merits and provided that no case may be rejected on this ground which has not been duly considered by a domestic tribunal.'

Article 13

A new paragraph 3 shall be added at the end of Article 36 of the Convention, which shall read as follows:

'3 In all cases before a Chamber or the Grand Chamber, the Council of Europe Commissioner for Human Rights may submit written comments and take part in hearings.'

Article 14

Article 38 of the Convention shall be amended to read as follows:

'Article 38—Examination of the case

The Court shall examine the case together with the representatives of the parties and, if need be, undertake an investigation, for the effective conduct of which the High Contracting Parties concerned shall furnish all necessary facilities.'

Article 15

Article 39 of the Convention shall be amended to read as follows:

'Article 39—Friendly settlements

1 At any stage of the proceedings, the Court may place itself at the disposal of the parties concerned with a view to securing a friendly settlement of the matter on the basis of respect for human rights as defined in the Convention and the Protocols thereto.

2   Proceedings conducted under paragraph 1 shall be confidential.

3   If a friendly settlement is effected, the Court shall strike the case out of its list by means of a decision which shall be confined to a brief statement of the facts and of the solution reached.

4   This decision shall be transmitted to the Committee of Ministers, which shall supervise the execution of the terms of the friendly settlement as set out in the decision.'

Article 16

Article 46 of the Convention shall be amended to read as follows:

'Article 46—Binding force and execution of judgments

1   The High Contracting Parties undertake to abide by the final judgment of the Court in any case to which they are parties.

2   The final judgment of the Court shall be transmitted to the Committee of Ministers, which shall supervise its execution.

3   If the Committee of Ministers considers that the supervision of the execution of a final judgment is hindered by a problem of interpretation of the judgment, it may refer the matter to the Court for a ruling on the question of interpretation. A referral decision shall require a majority vote of two thirds of the representatives entitled to sit on the Committee.

4   If the Committee of Ministers considers that a High Contracting Party refuses to abide by a final judgment in a case to which it is a party, it may, after serving formal notice on that Party and by decision adopted by a majority vote of two thirds of the representatives entitled to sit on the Committee, refer to the Court the question whether that Party has failed to fulfil its obligation under paragraph 1.

5   If the Court finds a violation of paragraph 1, it shall refer the case to the Committee of Ministers for consideration of the measures to be taken. If the Court finds no violation of paragraph 1, it shall refer the case to the Committee of Ministers, which shall close its examination of the case.'

Article 17

Article 59 of the Convention shall be amended as follows:

1   A new paragraph 2 shall be inserted which shall read as follows:

'2   The European Union may accede to this Convention.'

2   Paragraphs 2, 3 and 4 shall become paragraphs 3, 4 and 5 respectively.

Final and transitional provisions

Article 18

1   This Protocol shall be open for signature by member States of the Council of Europe signatories to the Convention, which may express their consent to be bound by

a   signature without reservation as to ratification, acceptance or approval; or

b   signature subject to ratification, acceptance or approval, followed by ratification, acceptance or approval.

2   The instruments of ratification, acceptance or approval shall be deposited with the Secretary General of the Council of Europe.

Article 19

This Protocol shall enter into force on the first day of the month following the expiration of a period of three months after the date on which all Parties to the Convention have expressed their consent to be bound by the Protocol, in accordance with the provisions of Article 18.

Article 20

1 From the date of the entry into force of this Protocol, its provisions shall apply to all applications pending before the Court as well as to all judgments whose execution is under supervision by the Committee of Ministers.

2 The new admissibility criterion inserted by Article 12 of this Protocol in Article 35, paragraph 3.b of the Convention, shall not apply to applications declared admissible before the entry into force of the Protocol. In the two years following the entry into force of this Protocol, the new admissibility criterion may only be applied by Chambers and the Grand Chamber of the Court.

Article 21

The term of office of judges serving their first term of office on the date of entry into force of this Protocol shall be extended ipso jure so as to amount to a total period of nine years. The other judges shall complete their term of office, which shall be extended *ipso jure* by two years.

Article 22

The Secretary General of the Council of Europe shall notify the member States of the Council of Europe of:

a any signature;

b the deposit of any instrument of ratification, acceptance or approval;

c the date of entry into force of this Protocol in accordance with Article 19; and

d any other act, notification or communication relating to this Protocol.

In witness whereof, the undersigned, being duly authorised thereto, have signed this Protocol.

Done at Strasbourg, this 13th day of May 2004, in English and in French, both texts being equally authentic, in a single copy which shall be deposited in the archives of the Council of Europe. The Secretary General of the Council of Europe shall transmit certified copies to each member State of the Council of Europe.

INDEX